THE SPORT AMERICANA®

Basketball
Card

PRICE GUIDE
and
Alphabetical Checklist

By

DR. JAMES BECKETT

EDGEWATER BOOK COMPANY • CLEVELAND

SPORT AMERICANA is a registered trademark of

EDGEWATER BOOK COMPANY
P.O. BOX 40238
CLEVELAND, OHIO 44140

Manufactured in the United States of America.

First Printing

ISBN 0-937424-55-2

About the Author

Jim Beckett, the leading authority on sport card values in the United States, maintains a wide range of activities in the world of sports. He possesses one of the finest collections of sports cards and autographs in the world, has made numerous appearances on radio and television, and has been frequently cited and quoted in many national publications. He was awarded the first "Special Achievement Award" for Contributions to the Hobby by the National Sports Collectors Convention in 1980 and the "Jock-Jasperson Award" for Hobby Dedication in 1983.

Dr. Beckett is the author of *The Sport Americana Baseball Card Price Guide*, *The Official Price Guide to Baseball Cards*, *The Sport Americana Price Guide to Baseball Collectibles*, *The Sport Americana Baseball Memorabilia and Autograph Price Guide*, *The Sport Americana Football, Hockey, Basketball and Boxing Price Guide*, *The Official Price Guide to Football Cards*, *The Official Price Guide to Hockey and Basketball Football Cards*, and *The Sport Americana Alphabetical Baseball Card Checklist*. In addition, he is the founder, publisher and editor of *Beckett Baseball Card Monthly*, *Beckett Football Card Monlthly*, *Beckett Basketball Monthly*, *Beckett Hockey Monthly* and *Beckett Focus on Future Stars*, publications dedicated to advancing the card collecting hobby.

Jim Beckett received his Ph.D. in Statistics from Southern Methodist University in 1975. He resides in Dallas with his wife, Patti, and their daughters, Christina, Rebecca, and Melissa.

Acknowledgments

This edition is dedicated to the memory of Dennis W. Eckes, Mr. Sport Americana, who passed away tragically and unexpectedly earlier this year. Denny and I started all this back in 1978 as we began working on our first Price Guide book. He will be missed by all who knew him. For those who didn't know him, you should know that he left a wonderful legacy of a thriving hobby that he was instrumental in helping build. Denny's vision is still being realized. We hope to carry on with the same high ideals Denny always exemplified.

This edition of the Price Guide contains several new sets and, of course, completely revised prices on all the cards listed. A great deal of hard work went into this volume, and it could not have been done without a considerable amount of help from many people. Our thanks are extended to each and every one of you.

The success of the Beckett Price Guides has always been the result of a team effort. This *Basketball Card Price Guide* is our best yet, thanks to our numerous contributors and full-time staff members. As the hobby continues to grow, we have grown right along by adding a Technical Services group. Those who didn't handle the technical details or assist in pricing for this edition of the annual basketball guide contributed by picking up the slack for those who did.

The Technical Services group includes Manager Jay Johnson, Senior Analyst B.A. Murry, and Price Guide Analysts Theo Chen (all sports), Mike Hersh (hockey), Dan Hitt (football), Mary Huston (minor leagues), Rich Klein (all sports), and Grant Sandground (baseball/basketball). Technical Services staffers Wendy Bird, Jana Threatt and Scott Layton capably assisted their efforts. The price gathering and analytical talents of this fine group of hobbyists has helped make our Beckett team stronger, while making this guide and its companion *Beckett Basketball Monthly* Price Guide even more widely recognized as the hobby's most reliable and relied upon sources of pricing information.

It is very difficult to be "accurate" — one can only do one's best. Our particular job is especially difficult since we're shooting at moving targets as prices fluctuate all the time. Combining the efforts of many full-time pricing experts has definitely proven better than relying upon the labors of just one person, and I thank all of them for working together to provide you, our readers, the most accurate prices possible.

Those who have worked closely with us on this and many other books, have again proven themselves invaluable in every aspect of producing this book: Mike Aronstein, *Baseball Hobby News* (Frank and Vivian Barning), Jerry Bell, Chris Benjamin, Sy Berger (Topps Chewing Gum), Mike Blaisdell, Bill Bossert (Mid-Atlantic Coin Exchange), Mike Cramer (Pacific Trading Cards), Bill and Diane Dodge, Gervise Ford, Steve Freedman, Larry and Jeff Fritsch, Steve Galletta, Tony Galovich, Jim Galusha, Dick Gariepy, Dick Gilkeson, Mike and Howard Gordon, George Grauer, John Greenwald, Wayne Grove, Bill Haber, Michael Hartney, Bill Henderson, George Henn, Jerry Hersh, Steve Johnson, Judy and Norman Kay, Alan Kaye (*Sports Card News*), Lesnik Public Relations (Timm Boyle and Bob Ibach), Robert Levin (The Star Company), Lew Lipset, Jim Macie, Paul Marchant, Dr. John McCue, Michael Moretto, Brian Morris, Jack Pollard, Tom Reid,

Table Of Contents

Gavin Riley, Alan Rosen (Mr. Mint), John Rumierz, San Diego Sport Collectibles (Bill Goepner and Nacho Arredondo), Kevin Savage (Sports Gallery), Mike Schechter (MSA), Bill Shonscheck, John Spalding, Nigel Spill (Oldies and Goodies), Sports Collectors Store (Pat Quinn and Don Steinbach), Frank Steele, Murvin Sterling, Dan Stickney, Steve Taft, Paul S. Taylor, Lee Temanson, Bill Wesslund, Kit Young, Robert Zanze, and Bill Zimpleman.

Many other individuals have provided price input, illustrative material, checklist verifications, errata, and/or background information. At the risk of inadvertently overlooking or omitting these many contributors, we should like to personally thank Ajay Acharya, Jerry Adamic, Tom Akins, Travis Albrecht, Rich Altman, Dennis Anderson, Ellis Anmuth, Arkansas Sports Distributing, Toni Axtell, Baseball Cards Plus, Josh Baver, Bay State Cards (Lenny DeAngelico), Chris Becirel, Carl Bergstrom, Beulah Sports, Brian Bigelow (Candl), Walter Bird, Fritz Brogan, Karen Sue Brown, Dan Bruner (The Card King), Buckhead Baseball Cards (Marc Spector), Shawn Burke, Zac Burke, California Card Co., Danny Cariseo, Phil Carpenter, Cee Tim's Cards, Dwight Chapin, Rich Chavez, Jaworski Cherry, Mark Clenemos, Shane Cohen (Grand Slam), Barry Colla, Matt Collett, Danny Collins, Ben Coulter, Robert Curtis, Herb Dallas Jr., David Diehl, Cliff Dolgins, Discount Dorothy, Ed Emmitt, Mark Enger, David Erickson, James Fendley, Terry Fennell, Steve Foster, Doug French, Donny Frost, Steve Gerber, Michael R. Gionet, Steve Gold (AU Sports), Jeff Goldstein, Darin Goodwin, Gary W. Graber, David Grauf (Cards for the Connoisseur), Nick Grier, Don Guilbert, Hall's Nostalgia, Chad Harris, Jacob Harrison, Lenny Helicher, Vaughn Hickman, Clay Hill, Alisa Hills, H.L.T. and T. Sports (Harold and Todd Nelkin), Will Ho, Verdeen Hogan, Home Plate of Provo (Ken Edick), Keith Hora, Gene Horvath, Thomas James, Andy Jenkins, Kevin Jeu, Richard Johnson, Darryl Jordan, Tom Judd, Bruce Kangas, Jay Kasper, Kim Kellogg, Joe Kelly, Dan Kent, Jeff Kluger, Paul Krasinkewicz Jr., Mayank Keshaviah, Nicholas Krupke, Thomas Kunnecke, Dan Lavin, Weldon Nathan Leon, Irv Lerner, Howie Levy of Blue Chip, W. Freeman Ligon III, R.J. Lyons, Jack Maiden, Larry Marks, Maurice Massey, Robert Matonis, Gary O. May, Jack Mayes, Anthony McCoy, Mike McDonald (Sports Page), Timothy McElroy, Erik McKenzie, Dale C. Meek, Steve Melnick, Blake Meyer, Darren Milbrandt, Alan Miller, William Moorhead, Joe Morano, Paul Morrison, David Mowett, Fred Muollo, Funz Napolitano, No Gum Just Cards, Brad Norwood, John O'Hara, Trace Ono, Paul Orlick, Ricky Parker, Clay Pasternack, Earl Petersen, Tom Pfirrmann, John Pollack, Darren Porter, Jonathan Ramos, Phil Regli, David Renshaw, Louis Rene Reyes, Mark Risk, Juan Rivera, Chuck Roethel, Aaron Rosenberg, Allen Rosenblatt, Marty Rothlisberger, Terry Sack, Joe Sak, Garret Salomon, Arnold Sanchez, Bob Santos, Nathan Schank, Kenneth Seiple, Steven Senft, Steve Shaffar, Mike Shanholtz, Mark Shields, Terry C. Shook, Paul Siebert, Glen Sidler, Darrin Silverman, Gail Smith, Raymond Smith, Doug Stauduhar, Allen Stengel, Cary Stephenson, Michael Stuy, Doug Such, Mark Tanaka (Front Row), Chris Tateosian, Steve Taylor, Craig Thomas, Peter Tsang, Warren Utsunomiya, David Volk, Billy Wagner, J. Walden, David Weber, Richard West, Bob Wilke (The Shoe Box), Brian Wilkie, Mark Williams, World Series Cards (Neil Armstrong), Alex Yang, Mike Yost, and Zards Cards.

Every year we make active solicitations for input to that year's edition, and we are particularly appreciative of help (large and small) provided for this volume. While we receive many inquiries, comments, and questions regarding material within this book — and, in fact, each and every one is read and digested — time constraints prevent us from personally replying. We hope that the letters will continue and that, even though no reply is received, you will feel that you are making significant contributions to the hobby through your interest and comments.

In the years since this guide debuted, Beckett Publications has grown beyond any rational expectation. A great many talented and hard working individuals have been instrumental in this growth and success. Our whole team is to be congratulated for what we together have accomplished.

Our Beckett Publications team is led by Vice Presidents Joe Galindo and Fred Reed, Associate Publisher Claire Backus, and Director of Marketing Jeff Amano. Providing able assistance are:

Editorial — Pepper Hastings, Susan K. Elliott, Rudy J. Klancnik, Theo Chen, Jeff Cohen, Randy Cummings, E.J. Hradek, Matt Keifer, Mike Payne, Gary Santaniello, Louis Marroquin, Steve Wilson, Catherine Button Colbert, George Watson.

Advertising — Frances Knight, Rebecca Reed. Administration — Lori Lindsey, Teri McGahey, Angela Hogans.

Production — Reed Poole, Theresa Anderson, Omar Mediano, Sara Jenks, Kaki Matheson,

Lisa O'Neill, Valerie Wegener, Robert Yearby, Airey Baringer, Barbara Barry, Maria L. Gonzalez-Davis, Renata Campos, Carmen Hand.

Design — Lynne Chinn, Therese Bellar, Wendy Tripp. Computer Services — Rich Olivieri, Kirk McKinney.

Dealer Services — Cindy Struble, Louise Bird, Cathryn Black, Kim Ford, Anita Gonzalez, Gayle Jeffcoat, Fran Keng, Sheryl McCain, Mike Moss, LaQuita Norton, Linda Rainwater, Carol Slawson, Lisa Spaight, Jim Tereschuk.

Dealer Operations — Tom Collins, Lisa Borden, Gena Andrews, Nancy Bassi, Deana Chapman, Belinda Cross, Louise Ebaugh, Jeany Finch, Julie Grove, Ronda Pearson, Maggie Seward.

Marketing — Beth Harwell, Jeff Greer, Joanna K. Guajardo, Karen Penhollow, Ruth Price, Mark Stokes.

Beckett Sports Products — Chris Calandro, Amy Kirk, Patrick Richard, Kim Whitesell.

Company Services — Mary Campana, Leslie Brown, Joanna Hayden, Marion Jarrell, Lynn Nelson, Sabrina Polley, Christiann Thomas.

Information Services — Sammy Cantrell, Mark Harwell.

Circulation — Debra S. Kingsbury, Suzee Payton, Barbara Hinkle, Jenny Harwell, Lori Harmeyer.

Fulfillment Services — Monte King, Fernando Albieri, Roy Bond, Billy Culbert, Patrick Cunningham, Andrew Drago, Danny Evans, Bruce Felps, George Field, Sara Field, Gean Paul Figari, Mark Goeglein, Marcio Guimaraes, Charles Hodges, Rex Hudson, Don James, Chris Longeway, Robson Magno, Glen Morante, Mila Morante, Daniel Moscoso, Daniel Moscoso Jr., Abraham Pacheco, Guillermo Pacheco, Roberto Ramirez, Gabriel Santos, Steve Slawson, Mark Whitesell.

In addition, our consultants James and Sandi Beane and Dan Swanson performed several major system programming jobs for us again this year to help us accomplish our work faster and more accurately. The whole Beckett Publications team has my thanks for jobs well done. Thank you, everyone.

I also would like to thank my family, especially my wife, Patti, and daughters, Christina, Rebecca, and Melissa, for putting up with me again.

Preface

Isn't it great? Finally we have a book just for basketball card collectors. Everyone knows about the tremendous growth in interest in baseball cards, but basketball cards are quite popular as well. In fact, interest in basketball cards is currently at an all-time high. They are becoming increasingly visible at the nation's card shows and stores.

The reason for the emergence of these cards in particular is due in large part to the continuing and increasing popularity of the sport itself. This increased popularity has made basketball superstars well known to millions of fans who watch them during the winter and spring and read about them all year. Megastars such as Michael Jordan, Larry Bird and Magic Johnson are among the most famous and recognizeable athletes in the world. Finally, the comparatively high cost of premium baseball cards has persuaded many collectors to pursue cards of other sports as a more affordable means of pursuing the sports collectibles hobby. Nevertheless, as you can see from the prices in this book, basketball cards are valuable — and they are perceived by a growing number of collectors as being good values for their hobby dollar.

Many of the features contained in the other Beckett Price Guides have been incorporated into this volume since condition grading, nomenclature, and many other aspects of collecting are common to the card hobby in general. We hope you find the book both interesting and useful in your collecting pursuits.

Basketball cards are also typically produced in smaller sets than baseball, football and hockey sets, making it easier for collectors to complete them. In fact, the 1990-91 NBA Hoops set — including Series I and II — was the most comprehensive basketball set ever, with 440 cards (a little more than half as many cards as recent 792-card Topps baseball sets). Also, the small size of all except the most recent basketball card sets has another positive aspect: There are more star cards and fewer commons.

The Beckett guide has been successful where others have failed because it is complete, current and valid. This Price Guide contains not just one, but three prices by condition for all the cards listed. These account for almost all the basketball cards in existence. The prices were added to the card lists just prior to printing and reflect not the author's opinions or desires, but the current retail prices for each card, based on extensive input from every significant source

(including sports memorabilia conventions/ shows, ads in various hobby publications, current mail order catalogs, local club meetings, auction results and other first-hand reportings of actually realized prices).

What is the BEST price guide available today? Of course, card sellers will prefer the price guide with the highest prices as the best, while card buyers will naturally prefer the one with the lowest prices. Accuracy, however, is the true test. Use the Price Guide used by more collectors and dealers than all of the others combined. Look for the Beckett name. I won't put my name on anything I won't stake my reputation on. Our Price Guides aren't the lowest or the highest — but the most accurate and reliable.

To facilitate your use of this book, read the complete introductory section in the pages following before going to the price listings. Every collectibles field has its own terminology; we've tried to capture most of the terms and definitions specific to sports cards in our glossary. Carefully read the section on grading (evaluating the condition) of your cards, as you will not be able to determine which price column is appropriate for a given card without first knowing its condition.

Welcome to the world of collecting cards.

Sincerely, Dr. James Beckett

Introduction

Welcome to the exciting world of sports card collecting, America's fastest growing avocation. You have made a good choice in buying this book, since it will open up to you the entire panorama of this field in the simplest, most concise way.

Hundreds of thousands of different sports cards have been issued during the past century. And the number of total cards put out by all manufacturers last year has been estimated in the billions with a retail value of several hundred million dollars. Sales of older (non-current year) cards by dealers may account for an even greater amount. With all that collectible cardboard available in the marketplace, it should be no surprise that several million sports fans like you collect sports cards today, and that number is growing each year.

The growth of *Beckett Baseball Card Monthly, Beckett Basketball Monthly, Beckett Football Card Monthly, Beckett Hockey Monthly* and *Beckett Focus on Future Stars* is another indication of this rising crescendo of popularity for sports cards. Founded less than six years ago by Dr. James Beckett, the author of this Price Guide, *BBCM* has reached the pinnacle of the sports card hobby with approximately one million readers anxiously awaiting each enjoyable and informative issue. The other four magazines have met similar success, with hundreds of thousands of readers devoted to each.

So collecting sports cards — while still pursued as a hobby with youthful exuberance by kids in your neighborhood — has also taken on the trappings of an industry, with thousands of full- and part-time card dealers, as well as vendors of supplies, clubs and conventions. Each year since 1980, in fact, thousands of hobbyists have assembled for a National Sports Collectors Convention, at which hundreds of dealers have displayed their wares, seminars have been conducted, autographs penned by sports notables, and millions of cards changed hands. These colossal affairs have been staged in Los Angeles, Detroit, St. Louis, Chicago, New York, Anaheim, Arlington (TX), San Francisco, Atlantic City, Chicago, Arlington again, Anaheim again and next year in Atlanta. So sports card collecting really is national in scope!

This increasing interest has been reflected in card values. As more collectors compete for available supplies, card prices (especially for premium-grade cards) rise. A national publication indicated a "very strong advance" in sports

card prices during the past decade, and a quick perusal of the prices in this book compared to the figures in earlier editions of this Price Guide will confirms this. Which brings us back to the book you have in your hands. It is the best guide available to the exciting world of your favorite sport's cards. Read it and use it. May your enjoyment and your card collection increase in the coming months and years.

How to Collect

Each collection is personal and reflects the individuality of its owner. There are no set rules on how to collect cards. Since card collecting is a hobby or leisure pastime, what you collect, how much you collect, and how much time and money you spend collecting are entirely up to you. The funds you have available for collecting and your own personal taste should determine how you collect. Information and ideas presented here are intended to help you get maximum enjoyment from this hobby.

It is impossible to collect every card ever produced. Therefore, beginners as well as intermediate and advanced collectors usually specialize in some way. One of the reasons why this hobby is so popular is that individual collectors can define and tailor their collecting methods to match their own tastes. To give you some ideas of the various approaches to collecting, we will list some of the more popular areas of specialization.

Many collectors specialize in the cards of a specific sport or sports that they personally follow. Many collect complete sets from particular years. For example, their goal may be to assemble complete sets from all the years since their birth or since they became avid sports fans. Or they may try to collect a card for every player during that specified period of time.

Many others wish to acquire only cards of certain players. Usually such players are the superstars of their respective sports, but occasionally collectors will specialize in all the cards of players who attended certain colleges or who came from certain towns. Some collectors are only interested in the first cards or Rookie Cards of particular players.

Another fun way to collect cards (for team sports) is by team. Most fans have a favorite team or two, and it is natural for that loyalty to be translated into a desire for cards of the players on particular teams. This concept can also be applied to your favorite college's products. For instance, Georgia Tech collectors would pursue cards of Mark Price, John Salley, Tom Hammonds, Dennis Scott, Kenny Anderson, etc.

Obtaining Cards

Several avenues are open to sports card collectors. Cards can be purchased in the traditional way at the local candy, grocery, or drug stores, with bubble gum, freebies or special bonus set cards. In recent years, it has also become possible to purchase complete sets of the various sorts cards through mail order advertisers found in traditional sports media publications, such as *The Sporting News*, *Sport*, *Basketball Digest*, *Street & Smith* yearbooks and others. These sets are also advertised in the ever-increasing number of card collecting periodicals. Many collectors will begin by subscribing to at least one of the hobby publications, which can provide solid, up-to-date information.

Most serious card collectors obtain old (and new) cards from one or more of several main sources: (1) trading with or buying from other collectors or dealers; (2) responding to sale or auction ads in hobby publications; (3) attending sports collectibles shows or conventions; and/or (4) shopping at local hobby stores. We advise that you try all three methods since each has its own distinct advantages: (1) trading is a great way to make new friends and obtain cards you want without spending cash; (2) hobby periodicals help you keep up with what's going on in the hobby (including when and where the conventions are happening and when new products will be available); (3) shows provide the opportunity to view thousands or even millions of collectibles under one roof (usually with competitive prices), and you also have the chance to meet many other collectors who may have interests similar to yours; and (4) stores provide a relaxed atmosphere, personal service, a diversity of material and the opportunity to develop a rapport with the owner or employees.

Preserving Your Cards

Cards are fragile. They must be handled properly in order to retain their value. Careless handling can easily result in creased or bent cards. It is, however, not recommended that tweezers or tongs be used to pick up your cards, since such utensils could mar or indent card surfaces and thus reduce those cards' conditions and values. In general, your cards should be handled as little as possible. This is easier to say than to do. Among the storage formats available are individual card holders, custom boxes, storage trays, and display sheets. Card holders are good for displaying prize cards. Boxes allow

you to store hundreds of cards while taking up very little room. Storing cards in display pages in a three-ring album allows you to view your collection at any time without the need to touch the cards themselves. For large collections, collectors generally use a combination of the above methods: perhaps individual storage for cards of a certain value, display sheets for those of a lesser value, and finally storage boxes for complete sets, commons or minor stars.

Individual card holders come in many forms, from card sleeves to hard plastic shields. Sleeves are like miniature plastic bags that should hold your card(s) firmly, but not tightly. They offer protection against accidental spillage but not against more serious physical damage. Sleeves made from polypropylene or polyethylene are the cheapest, most common — and the safest for long-term storage. Sleeves made from Mylar (a form of polyester) are clearer, stiffer, just as safe, but less common and much more expensive. More solid individual card storage is available in various materials such as hard acrylic, Lucite or even Plexiglas. These card protectors are good for display and offer protection against almost every physical harm imaginable. However, they are relatively expensive and the materials used have not been around long enough to ensure long term safety. The best way to store valuable individual cards is to insert them into polypropylene, polyethylene or Mylar sleeves and then into a card protector of your choice.

Since modern cards are issued in sets of several hundred cards, it is obviously not feasible to store each card in an individual holder. For years now there have been cardboard boxes made specifically for the storage of sports cards. They are made to hold various quantities of cards. Look for boxes with completely flat bottoms because those with flaps protruding can cause serious damage to cards. Because the cardboard used to make all card storage boxes is acidic to some degree, some precautions should be taken to minimize possible chemical damage to your cards. When storing sets in boxes, you should consider first putting the "key" cards in the set into "safe" sleeves within the box. This allows you to find them more easily, anyway. Finally, it should be noted that acid-free cardboard boxes are available, but not yet in sizes made to fit sports cards, and at prices that are several times more expensive than regular boxes.

Display sheets are an inexpensive, flexible and popular way to store and show off sports cards. When purchasing sheets for your cards, be sure you find the pocket size that fits the cards snugly. Don't put your oversized 1969-70 Topps basketball cards in a sheet designed to fit standard 2-1/2 by 3-1/2 inch cards. Most hobby and collectibles shops and virtually all collectors' conventions will have these pages available in quantity for various sizes, or you can purchase them directly from the advertisers in this book. If you intend to store your cards for a long time, try to buy sheets made of polypropylene or polyethylene as opposed to polyvinyl chloride (PVC). The oils (technically known as plasticizers) used to make PVC flexible may permeate your cards and damage them after a long period of time. One good way to identify PVC sheets is by smell. PVC sheets will usually smell like vinyl, while sheets made of polypropylene or polyethylene should not have any odor at all. Unfortunately, card sheets made of polypropylene and polyethylene are somewhat flimsier and less transparent than PVC pages.

Damp, sunny, and/or hot conditions — no, this is not a weather forecast — are three elements to avoid in extremes if you are interested in preserving your collection. Too high (or less often, too low) humidity can cause gradual deterioration of a card. Direct, bright sun (or fluorescent light) will eventually bleach out the color of a card. Extreme heat accelerates the decomposition of cards. On the other hand, many cards have lasted more than 50 years without much scientific intervention. So be cautious, even if the above factors typically present a problem only in extremes. It never hurts to be prudent.

Collecting/Investing

Collecting individual players and collecting complete sets are both popular vehicles for investment and speculation. Most investors and speculators stock up on complete sets or on quantities of players they think have good investment potential. There is obviously no guarantee in this book, or anywhere else for that matter, that cards will outperform the stock market or other investment alternatives in the future. After all, sports cards do not pay quarterly dividends. And selling cards at the "going rate" is more difficult than selling stocks; instead of calling a broker and getting instant results, a card seller may have to contact several potential buyers to get the best price. Nevertheless, investors have noticed a favorable trend in the past performance of sports collectibles, and certain cards and sets have outperformed just about any other investment in recent years.

Some of the obvious questions are: Which cards? When to buy? When to sell? The best initial investment you can make is in your own education. The more you know about your collection and the hobby, the more informed the decisions you will be able to make. We're not selling investment tips. We're selling information about the current values of sports cards. It's up to you to use that information to your best advantage.

Nomenclature

Basketball sets, generally having been produced in the modern era from 1948 to present, can be described and identified by their year, maker, type of issue, and any other distinguishing characteristic. Regional issues are usually referred to by year, maker, and sometimes by title or theme of the set.

The following abbreviations are used for identifying major basketball sets:

B - Bowman (1948)
F - Fleer (1961-62, 1986-87 to 1990-91)
H - NBA Hoops (1989-90 to 1991-92)
S - Star Company (1983-84 to 1985-86)
SB - SkyBox (1990-91 to 1991-92)
T - Topps (1969-70 to 1981-82)
UD - Upper Deck (1991-92)

Glossary/Legend

Our glossary defines terms frequently used in the card collecting hobby. Many of these terms are also common to other types of sports memorabilia collecting. Some terms may have several meanings, depending on use and context.

ABA - American Basketball Association.

AS - All-Star or All-Star card. An All-Star card generally portrays an All-Star player of the previous year that says "All-Star" on its face.

ALP - Alphabetical.

BRICK - A group of cards, usually 50 or more having common characteristics, that is intended to be bought, sold, or traded as a unit.

CBA - Continental Basketball Association.

CO - Coach card, e.g., 1990-91 NBA Hoops cards #305-#331.

COLLECTOR - A person who engages in the hobby of collecting cards primarily for his own enjoyment, with any profit motive being secondary.

COLLECTOR ISSUE - A set produced for the sake of the card itself with no product or service sponsor. It derives its name from the fact that most of these sets are produced for sale directly to the hobby market.

COMBINATION CARD - A single card depicting two or more players (but not a team card).

COMMON CARD - The typical card of any set; it has no premium value accruing from subject matter, numerical scarcity, popular demand or anomaly.

CONVENTION ISSUE - A set produced in conjunction with a sports collectibles convention to commemorate or promote the show.

COUPON - See Tab.

DEALER - A person who engages in buying, selling, and trading sports collectibles or supplies. A dealer may also be a collector, but as a dealer, he anticipates a profit.

DIE-CUT - A card with part of its stock partially cut, allowing one or more parts to be folded or removed. After removal or appropriate folding, the remaining part of the card can frequently be made to stand up.

DISC - A circular-shaped card.

DISPLAY CARD - A sheet, usually containing three to nine cards, that is printed and used by the manufacturer to advertise and/or display the packages containing his products and cards. The backs of display cards are blank or contain advertisements.

FULL SHEET - A complete sheet of cards that has not been cut up into individual cards by the manufacturer. Also called an uncut sheet.

HOR - Horizontal pose on card as opposed to the standard vertical orientation found on most cards.

LEGITIMATE ISSUE - A set produced to promote or boost sales of a product or service, e.g., bubble gum, cereal, cigarettes, etc. Most collector issues are not legitimate issues in this sense.

LID - A circular-shaped card (possibly with tab) that forms the top of the container for the product being promoted.

NY - New York.

OBVERSE - The front, face, or pictured side of the card.

OLY - Olympic team card (1984-85 Star Company subset).

PANEL - An extended card composed of multiple individual cards. The most obvious basketball panels are found in the 1980-81 Topps set.

PREMIUM - A card, sometimes on photographic stock, that is purchased or obtained in conjunction with/or redemption for another card or product. The premium is not packaged in the same unit as the primary item.

REVERSE - The back side of the card.

STAR CARD - A card that portrays a player of some repute, usually determined by his ability, but sometimes referring to sheer popularity.

STICKER - A card with a removable layer

that can be affixed to another surface, for example the 1986-87 through 1989-90 Fleer bonus cards.

TC - Team checklist card (1990-91 NBA Hoops and SkyBox, for example).

TEAM CARD - A card that depicts an entire team, notably the 1989-90 and 1990-91 NBA Hoops Detroit Pistons championship cards and the 1991-91 NBA Hoops subset.

TEST SET - A set, usually containing a small number of cards, issued by a national producer and distributed in a limited section of the country or to a select group of people. Presumably, the purpose of a test set is to measure market appeal for a particular type of card. Also called a promo or prototype set.

TL - Team leader card.

TR - Traded card.

TRIMMED - A card cut down from its original size. Trimmed cards are undesirable to most collectors, and are therefore much less valuable than otherwise identical untrimmed cards. See the Condition Guide.

UER - Uncorrected error card.

VARIATION - One of two or more cards from the same series with the same number (or player with identical pose if the series is unnumbered) differing from one another in some aspect, including the printing, stock or other feature of the card. This is usually caused when the manufacturer becomes aware of an error or inconsistency in a particular card, fixes the mistake and resumes the print run. In this case there will be two variations of the same card. Sometimes one of the variations is relatively scarce. Variations can also result from accidental or deliberate design changes, information updates, photo substitutions, etc.

XRC - Extended Rookie Card. A player's first appearance on a card, but issued in a limited distribution, major set not distributed nationally nor in packs. In basketball sets, this term generally refers to 1983-84, 1984-85 and 1985-86 Star Company sets.

Basketball Card History

Basketball cards have been produced on and off since 1948 with the 72-card Bowman set of that year. However, one must skip ahead to 1957-58 to find the next basketball set, this time an 80-card set issued by Topps. Then skip ahead to 1961-62 to the 66-card Fleer issue. Finally in 1969, Topps began a 13-year run of producing basketball card sets which ended in 1981-82. Ironically, about the time the league's popularity had bottomed out and was about to begin its ascent to the lofty level it's at today.

Topps' run included several sets that are troublesome for today's collectors. The 1969-70, 1970-71 and 1976-77 sets are larger than standard size, thus making them hard to store and preserve. The 1980-81 set consists of standard-size panels containing three cards each. Completing and cataloging the 1980-81 set (which features the classic Larry Bird RC/Magic Johnson RC/Julius Erving panel) is challenging, to say the least.

In 1983, this basketball card void was filled by the Star Company, a small company which issued three attractive sets of basketball cards, along with a plethora of peripheral sets. Star's 1983-84 premiere offering was issued in four groups, with the first series (cards 1-100) very difficult to obtain, as many of the early team subsets were miscut and destroyed before release. The 1984-85 and 1985-86 sets were more widely and evenly distributed. Even so, players' initial appearances on any of the three Star Company sets are considered Extended Rookie Cards, not regular Rookie Cards, because of the relatively limited distribution.

Then, in 1986, Fleer took over the rights to produce cards for the NBA. Their 1986-87, 1987-88 and 1988-89 sets each contain 132 attractive, colorful cards depicting mostly stars and superstars. They were sold in the familiar wax pack format (12 cards and one sticker per pack). Fleer increased its set size to 168 in 1989-90, and was joined by NBA Hoops, which produced a 300-card first series (containing David Robinson's only Rookie Card) and a 352-card second series. The demand for all three Star Company sets, along with the first four Fleer sets and the premiere NBA Hoops set, skyrocketed during the early part of 1990.

The basketball card market stabilized somewhat in 1990-91, with both Fleer and Hoops stepping up production to meet demand. A new major set, SkyBox, also made a big splash in the market with its unique "high-tech" cards featuring computer-generated backgrounds. None of the three major 1990-91 sets have experienced significant price growth, although the increased competition apparently has led to higher quality and more innovative products.

Another major milestone in 1990-91 was the first-time inclusion of current rookies in update sets (NBA Hoops and SkyBox Series II, Fleer Update). The NBA Hoops and SkyBox issues contain just the 11 lottery picks, while Fleer's 100-card boxed set includes all rookies of any significance. A small company called "Star Pics" (not to be confused with Star Company) tried to fill this niche by printing a 70-card set in late

1990, but because the set was not licensed by the NBA, it is not considered a major set by the majority of collectors. It does, however, contain the first nationally distributed cards of 1990-91 rookies such as Derrick Coleman, Dennis Scott, Dee Brown and others.

The 1991-92 season brings with it the three established NBA card brands plus Upper Deck, known throughout the hobby for its high quality card stock and photography in other sports. Also, the draft pick set market that Star Pics opened in 1990-91 now has expanded to include several competitors. The basketball card market, perhaps the most seasonal of the major sports, still seems to have room for growth.

Business of Sports Card Collecting

Determining Value

Why are some cards more valuable than others? Obviously, the economic law of supply and demand is applicable to sports card collecting just as it is to any other field where a commodity is bought, sold, or traded.

Supply (the number of cards available on the market) is less than the total number of cards originally produced since attrition diminishes that original quantity. Each year a percentage of cards is thrown away, destroyed, or otherwise lost to collectors. This percentage is much smaller today than it was in the past because more and more people have become increasingly aware of the value of sports cards. For those who collect only Mint condition cards, the supply of older cards can be quite small indeed. Until recently, collectors were not so conscious of the need to preserve the condition of their cards. For this reason, it is difficult to know exactly how many 1948 Bowman basketball cards are currently available — Mint or otherwise. It is generally accepted that there are fewer 1948 Bowmans available than 1969-70 Topps or 1987-88 Fleer basketball cards. If demand were equal for each of these sets, the law of supply and demand would increase the price for the least available sets. But demand is based on many factors and changes constantly, making price correlation an inexact science.

The total number of cards produced for any given issue can only be approximated, as compared to other collectibles such as coins and stamps. The reason is simple: Card manufacturers are predominantly private companies which are not required to reveal such internal information, while governments are required to release figures regarding currency and postage stamp production. Even publicly owned companies only reveal dollar amounts, from which accurate production runs cannot be easily determined.

The demand for any given card is influenced by many factors. These include: (1) the age of the card; (2) the number of cards printed; (3) the player(s) portrayed on the card; (4) the attractiveness and popularity of the set; and often most importantly, (5) the physical condition of the card.

In general, (1) the older the card, (2) the fewer the number of the cards printed, (3) the more famous and/or successful the player, (4) the more attractive and popular the set, and (5) the better the condition of the card, the higher the value of the card will be. There are exceptions to all but one of these factors: the condition of the card. Given two cards similar in all respects except condition, the one in the best condition will always be valued higher.

While there are certain guidelines that help to establish the value of a card, the numerous exceptions and peculiarities make any simple, direct mathematical formula to determine card values impossible.

One certainty in the sports card hobby is the high demand for Rookie Cards, specifically for RCs of superstar players. A Rookie Card is defined as the first card from a major set of a particular player. Because minor league baseball players have signed contracts and are therefore professionals, baseball Rookie Cards are often issued before or during a player's first major league season. These cards usually are designated "Future Stars," "Major League Prospects," "Rated Rookies," or something similar on the front.

Basketball Rookie Cards, on the other hand, cannot be issued when a player is still in college. They can only be printed once a player has no more collegiate eligibility. Therefore, until 1990-91, basketball Rookie Cards were generally released in the year after the player's first (or even second or third, for late bloomers) professional season. And until recently, the fronts of basketball Rookie Cards did not have any special notation. But in the 1990-91 NBA Hoops set, rookies of the previous year have "Rookie Star" designations on the fronts. Also in 1990-91, the three major NBA card manufacturers (Fleer, NBA Hoops and SkyBox) each issued RCs for current rookies. The NBA Hoops and SkyBox Series II sets contain only the 11 lottery picks, while the Fleer Update set depicts all 1990-91 rookies of any significance.

Regional Variation

Two types of regional price variations exist. The first is the general variation on all cards bought and sold in one geographical area as compared to another. Card prices are slightly higher on the East and West coasts, and slightly lower in the middle of the country. Although prices may vary from the East to the West, or from the Southwest to the Midwest, the prices listed in this guide are nonetheless presented as a consensus of all sections of this large and diverse country.

Still, prices for a particular player's cards are usually higher in his home team's area than in other regions. This represents the second type of regional price variation in which local players are favored over those from distant areas. For example, a John Havlicek card is valued higher in Boston than in Los Angeles because Havlicek played in Boston; therefore, the demand there for Havlicek cards is higher than it is in Los Angeles. On the other hand, a Jerry West card is priced higher in LA (where he played and is still the Lakers general manager) than in Boston, for similar reasons. Sometimes even common player cards command a slight premium from hometown collectors.

Set Prices

A somewhat paradoxical situation often exists in the price of a complete set versus the combined cost of the individual cards in the set. In most cases, the sum of the prices for the individual cards is higher than the cost for the complete set. This is especially prevalent for cards issued during the past few years. The reasons for this apparent anomaly stem from the habits of collectors and from the inventory costs of dealers. Today, each card in a set is normally produced in the same quantity as all others in its set. However, many collectors pick up only cards of stars, superstars, and players from particular teams. As a result, the dealer is left with a shortage of certain player cards and an abundance of others. He therefore incurs an expense in simply "carrying" these less desirable cards in stock. On the other hand, if he sells a complete set, he gets rid of a large number of cards at one time. For this reason, he is usually willing to receive less money for a complete set. By doing this, he recovers all of his costs and also earns some profit. Set prices also do not include rare card varieties, unless specifically stated. Of course, the prices for sets do include one example of each type for the given set, but it is assumed to be the least expensive variety.

Scarce Series

Only a select few basketball sets contain scarce series: 1948 Bowman, 1970-71 and 1972-73 Topps and 1983-84 Star Company. The 1948 Bowman set was printed on two 36-card sheets, the second of which was issued in significantly lower quantities. The two Topps scarce series are only marginally tougher than the set as a whole. The Star Company scarcity actually is for particular team sets (the 76ers, Lakers, Celtics, Bucks and Mavericks) which, to different extents, were less widely distributed.

Grading Your Cards

Each hobby has its own grading terminology — stamps, coins, comic books, beer cans, right down the line. Collectors of sports cards are no exception. The one invariable criterion for determining the value of a card is its condition: the better the condition of the card, the more valuable it is. However, condition grading is very subjective. Individual card dealers and collectors differ in the strictness of their grading, but the stated condition of a card should be determined without regard to whether it is being bought or sold.

The physical defects which lower the condition of a card are usually quite apparent, but each individual places his own estimation (negative value in this case) on these defects. We present the Condition Guide for use in determining values listed in this Price Guide in the hopes that excess subjectivity can be minimized.

The defects listed in the Condition Guide below are those either created at the time of printing, such as uneven borders — or those defects that occur to a card under normal handling — corner sharpness, gloss, edge wear, light creases — and finally, environmental conditions, such as browning. Other defects to cards are caused by human carelessness and in all cases should be noted separately and in addition to the condition grade. Among the more common alterations are tape, tape stains, heavy creases, rubber band marks, water damage, smoke damage, trimming, paste, tears, writing, pin or tack holes, any back damage, and missing parts (tabs, tops, coupons, backgrounds).

Centering

It is important to define in words and pictures what is meant by certain frequently used hobby terms relating to grading cards. The adjacent pictures portray various stages of centering. Centering can range from well-centered to slightly off-centered to off-centered to badly off-centered to miscut.

Slightly Off-Centered: A slightly off-center card is one which upon close inspection is found to have one border bigger than the opposite border — approximately 60/40. This degree is only offensive to a purist.

Off-Centered: An off-center card has one border which is more than twice as wide as the opposite border — 70/30.

Badly Off-Centered: A badly off-center card has virtually no border on one side of the card — 80/20 to 90/10.

Miscut: A miscut card actually shows part of the adjacent card in its larger border and consequently a corresponding amount of the primary card is cut off.

Corner Wear

Degrees of corner wear generate several common terms used to facilitate accurate grading. The wear on card corners can be expressed as fuzzy corners, corner wear or slightly rounded corners, rounded corners or badly rounded corners.

Fuzzy Corners: Fuzzy corners still come to a right angle (to a point) but the point has begun to fray slightly.

Corner Wear or Slightly Rounded Corners: The slight fraying of the corners has increased to where there is no longer a point to the corner. Nevertheless, the corner is still reasonably sharp. There may be evidence of some slight loss of color in the corner also.

Rounded Corners: The corner is definitely no longer sharp but is not badly rounded.

Badly Rounded Corners: The corner is rounded to an objectionable degree. Excessive wear and rough handling are evident.

Creases

The third, and perhaps most frequent, common defect is the crease. Unfortunately, the degree of creasing in a card is very difficult to show in a drawing or picture. On giving the specific condition of an expensive card for sale, the seller should note any creases additionally. Creases can be categorized as to severity according to the following scale.

Light Crease: A light crease is a crease which is barely noticeable on close inspection.

In fact, when cards are in plastic sheets or holders, a light crease may not be visible until the card is removed from the sheet or holder. A light crease on the front is much more serious than a light crease on the card's back only.

Medium Crease: A medium crease is noticeable when held and studied at arm's length by the naked eye, but does not overly detract from the appearance of the card. It is an obvious crease, but not one that breaks the picture surface of the card.

Heavy Crease: A heavy crease is one which has torn or broken through the card's picture surface, e.g., puts a tear in the photo surface.

Alterations

Deceptive Trimming: Deceptive trimming occurs when someone alters the card in order (1) to shave off edge wear, (2) to improve the sharpness of the corners, or (3) to improve centering. Obviously, the trimmer's objective is to falsely increase the perceived value of the card to an unsuspecting buyer. The shrinkage is usually only evident if the trimmed card is compared to an adjacent full-sized card or if the trimmed card is itself measured.

Obvious Trimming: This type of trimming is noticeable — and unfortunate. It is usually performed by non-collectors who give no thought to the present or future value of their cards.

Deceptively Retouched Borders: This occurs when the borders (especially on those cards with dark borders) are touched up on the edges and corners with a magic marker of the matching color in order to make the card appear to be Mint.

Categorization of Defects

A "Micro Defect" would be fuzzy corners, slight off-centering, printer's lines, printer's spots, slightly out of focus, or slight loss of original gloss. A NrMt card may have one micro defect. An ExMt card may have two or more micro defects.

A "Minor Defect" would be corner wear or slight rounding, off-centering, light crease on back, wax or gum stains on reverse, loss of original gloss, writing or tape marks on back, or rubber band marks. An Excellent card may have minor defects.

A "Major Defect" would be rounded corner(s), badly off-centering, crease(s), deceptive trimming, deceptively retouched borders, pin hole, staple hole, incidental writing or tape marks on front, warping, water stains, or sun fading. A VG card may have one major defect. A Good card may have two or more major defects.

CENTERING

WELL-CENTERED

SLIGHTLY OFF-CENTERED

OFF-CENTERED

BADLY OFF-CENTERED

MISCUT

A "Catastrophic Defect" is the worst kind of defect and would include such defects as badly rounded corner(s), miscutting, heavy crease(s), obvious trimming, punch hole, tack hole, tear(s), corner missing or clipped, destructive writing on front. A Fair card may have one catastrophic defect. A Poor card has two or more catastrophic defects.

Condition Guide

MINT (M OR MT) - A card with no defects. The card has sharp corners, even borders, original gloss or shine on the surface, sharp focus of the picture, smooth edges, no signs of wear, and white borders. A Mint card (that is, a card that is worth a "Mint" price) does NOT have printers' lines or other printing defects or other serious quality control problems that should have been discovered by the producing card company before distribution. Note also that there is no allowance made for the age of the card.

NEAR MINT (NrMt) - A card with a micro defect. Any of the following would be sufficient to lower the grade of a card from Mint to the Near Mint category: layering at some of the corners (fuzzy corners), a very small amount of the original gloss lost, very minor wear on the edges, slightly off-center borders, slight wear visible only on close inspection, slight off-whiteness of the borders.

EXCELLENT-MINT (ExMt) - A card with micro defects, but no minor defects. Two or three of the following would be sufficient to lower the grade of a card from Mint to the Excellent-Mint category: layering at some of the corners (fuzzy corners), a very small amount of the original gloss lost, minor wear on the edges, slightly off-center borders, slight wear visible only on close inspection, slight off-whiteness of the borders.

EXCELLENT (Ex) - A card with minor defects. Any of the following would be sufficient to lower the grade of a card from Mint to the Excellent category: slight rounding at some of the corners, a small amount of the original gloss lost, minor wear on the edges, off-center borders, wear visible only on close inspection, off-whiteness of the borders.

VERY GOOD (VG) - A card that has been handled but not abused: Some rounding at all corners, slight layering or scuffing at one or two corners, slight notching on edges, gloss lost from the surface but not scuffed, borders might be somewhat uneven but some white is visible on all borders, noticeable yellowing or browning of borders, pictures may be slightly off focus.

GOOD (G) - A well-handled card, rounding and some layering at the corners, scuffing at the corners and minor scuffing on the face, borders noticeably uneven and browning, loss of gloss on the face, notching on the edges.

FAIR (F) - Round and layering corners, brown and dirty borders, frayed edges, noticeable scuffing on the face, white not visible on one or more borders, cloudy focus.

POOR (P) - An abused card: The lowest grade of card, frequently some major physical alteration has been performed on the card, collectible only as a filler until a better-condition replacement can be obtained.

Categories between these major condition grades are frequently used, such as Very Good to Excellent (VG-E), Fair to Good (F-G), etc. Such grades indicate a card with all qualities at least in the lower of the two categories, but with several qualities in the higher of the two categories. In the case of EX-MT, it essentially refers to a card which is halfway between Excellent and Mint.

Unopened Mint cards and factory-collated sets are considered Mint in their unknown (and presumed perfect) state. However, once opened or broken out, each of these cards is graded (and valued) in its own right by taking into account any quality control defects (such as off-centering, printer's lines, machine creases, or gum stains) that may be present in spite of the fact that the card has never been handled outside of the factory.

Cards before 1980 which are priced in the Price Guide in a top condition of NrMT, are obviously worth an additional premium when offered in strict Mint condition. This additional premium increases relative to the age and scarcity of the card. For example, Mint cards from the late '70s may bring only a 10% premium for Mint (above NrMT), whereas high demand cards from pre-World War II vintage sets can be sold for as much as double the NrMT price when offered in strict Mint condition.

Selling Your Cards

Just about every collector sells cards or will sell cards eventually. Someday you may be interested in selling your duplicates or maybe even your whole collection. You may sell to other collectors, friends, or dealers. You may even sell cards you purchased from a certain dealer back to that same dealer. In any event, it helps to know some of the mechanics of the typical transaction between buyer and seller.

Dealers will buy cards in order to resell them

to other collectors who are interested in the cards. Dealers will always pay a higher percentage for items which (in their opinion) can be resold quickly, and a much lower percentage for those items which are perceived as having low demand and hence are slow moving. In either case, dealers must buy at a price that allows for the expense of doing business and a fair margin for profit.

If you have cards for sale, the best advice we can give is that you get several offers for your cards and take the best offer, all things considered. Note, the "best" offer may not always be the one for the highest amount. And remember, if a dealer really wants your cards, he won't let you get away without making his best competitive offer. Another alternative is to take your cards to a nearby convention and either auction them off in the show auction or offer them for sale to some of the dealers present.

Many people think nothing of going into a department store and paying $15 for an item of clothing for which the store paid $5. But, if you were selling your $15 card to a dealer and he offered you only $5 for it, you might think his mark-up unreasonable. To complete the analogy: most retail stores (and card dealers) that pay $10 for $15 items eventually go out of business. An exception to this is when the dealer knows that a willing buyer for the merchandise you are attempting to sell is only a phone call away. Then an offer of up to 75 percent of the book value will still allow him to make a reasonable profit due to the short time he will need to hold the merchandise. Nevertheless, most cards and collections will bring offers in the range of 25 to 50 percent of retail price. Material from the past five to ten years or so is very plentiful. Don't be surprised if your best offer is only 20 percent of the book value for cards from these recent years.

Interesting Notes

The numerically first card of an issue is the single card most likely to experience excessive wear. Consequently, you will typically find the price on card #1 (in Mint condition) much higher than might otherwise be the case. Similarly, but to a lesser extent (because normally the less important, reverse side of the card is the one exposed), the numerically last card in an issue is also prone to abnormal wear. This extra wear and tear occurs because the first and last cards are exposed to the elements (human element included) more than any other cards. They are generally end cards in any "brick" formations,

rubber bandings, stackings on wet surfaces, and like situations.

Sports cards have no intrinsic value. The value of a card, like the value of other collectibles, can only be determined by you and your enjoyment in viewing and possessing these cardboard swatches.

Remember, the buyer ultimately determines the price of each sports card. You are the determining price factor because you have the ability to say "no" to the price of any card by not exchanging your hard-earned money for a given card. When the cost of a trading card exceeds the enjoyment you will receive from it, your answer should be "no." We assess and report the prices. You set them!

We are always interested in receiving the price input of collectors and dealers from around the country. We happily credit major contributors. We welcome your opinions, since your contributions assist us in ensuring a better guide each year. If you would like to join our survey list for the next editions of this book and others authored by Dr. Beckett, please send your name and address to Dr. James Beckett, 4887 Alpha Road, Suite 200, Dallas, Texas 75244.

Advertising

Within this guide you will find advertisements for sports memorabilia material, mail order, and retail sports collectibles establishments. All advertisements were accepted in good faith based on the reputation of the advertiser; however, neither the author, the publisher, the distributors, nor the other advertisers in the Price Guide accept any responsibility for any particular advertiser not complying with the terms of his or her ad.

Readers should also be aware that prices in advertisements are subject to change over the annual period before a new edition of this volume is issued each fall. When replying to an advertisement late in the sporting year following the fall release of this volume, the reader should take this into account, and contact the dealer by phone or in writing for up-to-date price quotes and availability. Should you come into contact with any of the advertisers in this guide as a result of their advertisement herein, please mention to them this source as your contact.

Recommended Reading

With the increase in popularity of the hobby in recent years, there has been a corresponding increase in available literature. Below is a list of the books and periodicals that receive our highest recommendation and that we hope will further your knowledge and enjoyment of our great hobby.

The Sport Americana Baseball Card Price Guide by Dr. James Beckett (Thirteenth Edition, $14.95, released 1991, published by Edgewater Book Company) — the most informative, up-to-date, and reliable Price Guide/checklist on its subject matter ever compiled. No serious hobbyist should be without it.

The Official Price Guide to Baseball Cards by Dr. James Beckett (Eleventh Edition, $5.95, released 1991, published by The House of Collectibles) — this work is an abridgment of the Sport Americana Price Guide immediately above, published in a convenient and economical pocket-size format and provides Dr. Beckett's pricing of the major baseball sets since 1948.

The Sport Americana Football Card Price Guide by Dr. James Beckett (Eighth Edition, $14.95, released 1991, published by Edgewater Book Company) — the most comprehensive Price Guide/checklist ever issued on football cards. No serious football card hobbyist should be without it.

The Official Price Guide to Football Cards by Dr. James Beckett (Tenth Edition, $5.95, released 1991, published by The House of Collectibles) — an abridgement of the Sport Americana Price Guide listed above in a convenient and economical pocket-size format providing Dr. Beckett's pricing of the major football sets since 1948.

The Sport Americana Hockey Card Price Guide by Dr. James Beckett (First Edition, $12.95, released 1991, published by Edgewater Book Company) — the most informative, up-to-date, and reliable Price Guide/checklist on its subject matter ever compiled. No serious hobbyist should be without it.

The Official Price Guide to Hockey Cards by Dr. James Beckett (Eleventh Edition, $5.95, released 1991, published by The House of Collectibles) — this work is an abridgment of the Sport Americana Price Guide immediately above, published in a convenient and economical pocket-size format and provides Dr. Beckett's pricing of the major hockey sets since 1951.

The Sport Americana Basketball Card Price Guide by Dr. James Beckett (First Edition, $12.95, released 1991, published by Edgewater Book Company) — the most informative, up-to-date, and reliable Price Guide/checklist on its subject matter ever compiled. No serious hobbyist should be without it.

The Official Price Guide to Basketball Cards by Dr. James Beckett (First Edition, $5.95, released 1991, published by The House of Collectibles) — this work is an abridgment of the Sport Americana Price Guide immediately above, published in a convenient and economical pocket-size format and provides Dr. Beckett's pricing of the major basketball sets since 1948.

The Sport Americana Price Guide to Baseball Collectibles by Dr. James Beckett (Second Edition, $12.95, released 1988, published by Edgewater Book Company) — the complete guide and checklist with up-to-date values for box cards, coins, decals, R-cards, bread labels, exhibits, discs, lids, fabric, pins, Canadian cards, stamps, stickers, and miscellaneous Topps issues.

The Sport Americana Alphabetical Baseball Card Checklist by Dr. James Beckett (Fourth Edition, $12.95, released 1990, published by Edgewater Book Company) — an alphabetical listing, by the last name of the player portrayed on the card, of virtually all major and minor league baseball cards produced through the 1990 major sets.

The Sport Americana Price Guide to the Non-Sports Cards 1930-1960 by Christopher Benjamin and Dennis W. Eckes ($14.95, released 1991, published by Edgewater Book Company) — the definitive guide to virtually all popular non-sports American tobacco and bubble gum cards issued between 1930 and 1960. In addition to cards, illustrations and prices for wrappers are also included.

The Sport Americana Price Guide to the Non-Sports Cards by Christopher Benjamin and Dennis W. Eckes (Third Edition, Part Two, $12.95, released 1988, co-published by Den's Collector's Den and Edgewater Book Company) — the definitive guide to all popular non-sports American tobacco and bubble gum cards. In addition to cards, illustrations and prices for wrappers are also included. Part Two covers non-sports cards from 1961 to 1987.

The Sport Americana Baseball Address List by Jack Smalling and Dennis W. Eckes (Sixth Edition, $12.95, released 1990, published by Edgewater Book Company) — the definitive guide for autograph hunters, giving addresses and deceased information for virtually all major league baseball players, managers, and even umpires, past and present.

The Sport Americana Baseball Card Team Checklist by Jeff Fritsch and Dennis W. Eckes (Fifth Edition, $12.95, released 1990, co-published by Den's Collector's Den and Edgewater Book Company) — includes all Topps, Bowman, Fleer, Play Ball, Goudey, Upper Deck and Donruss cards, with the players portrayed on the cards listed with the teams for whom they played. The book is invaluable to the collector who specializes in an individual team because it is the most complete baseball card team checklist available.

The Sport Americana Team Football and Basketball Card Checklist by Jane Fritsch, Jeff Fritsch, and Dennis W. Eckes (First Edition, $10.95, released 1990, published by Edgewater Book Company) — the book is invaluable to the collector who specializes in an individual team because it is the most complete football and basketball card team checklist available.

Beckett Baseball Card Monthly, published and edited by Dr. James Beckett — contains the most extensive and accepted monthly Price Guide, collectible glossy superstar covers, colorful feature articles, "who's Hot and who's not" section, Convention Calendar, tips for beginners, "Readers Write" letters to and responses from the editor, information on errors and varieties, autograph collecting tips, and profiles of the sport's Hottest stars. Published every month, *BBCM* is the hobby's largest paid circulation periodical.

Beckett Football Card Monthly, *Beckett Basketball Monthly*, *Beckett Hockey Monthly*, and *Beckett Focus on Future Stars* were built on the success of *BBCM*. These other publications contain many of the same features as *BBCM* and contain the most relied upon Price Guides to their respective segments of the sports card hobby.

Errata

There are thousands of names, tens of thousands of prices, and an untold number of words in this book. There are going to be a few typographical errors, a few misspellings, and possibly, a number or two out of place. If you catch a blooper, drop me a note directly or in care of the publisher, and we will fix it in the next year's edition.

Prices in this Guide

Prices found in this guide reflect current retail rates just prior to the printing of this book. They do not reflect the FOR SALE prices of the author, the publisher, the distributors, the advertisers, or any card dealers associated with this guide. No one is obligated in any way to buy, sell, or trade his or her cards based on these prices. The price listings were compiled by the author from actual buy/sell transactions at sports conventions, buy/sell advertisements in the hobby papers, for sale prices from dealer catalogs and price lists, and discussions with leading hobbyists in the U.S. and Canada. All prices are in U.S. dollars.

1955 Ashland Oil

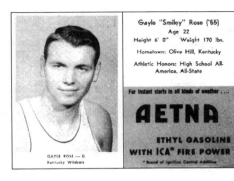

Gayle "Smiley" Rose ('55)
Age 22
Height 6' 0"   Weight 170 lbs.
Hometown: Olive Hill, Kentucky
Athletic Honors: High School All-
America, All-State

For instant starts in all kinds of weather . . .

AETNA

ETHYL GASOLINE
WITH ICA" FIRE POWER

GAYLE ROSE — G
Kentucky Wildcats

The 1955 Ashland/Aetna Oil Basketball set contains 96 black and white, unnumbered cards each measuring 2 5/8" by 3 3/4". There are two different backs for each card front, one with an Ashland Oil ad, the other with an Aetna Oil ad. The backs contain player vital statistics, his home town, and his graduation class. These thin-stocked cards are relatively difficult to obtain and have been numbered in the checklist below, by team and alphabetically within each team. The set contains 12 players each fron eight colleges: Eastern Kentucky 1-12, Kentucky 13-24, Louisville 25-36, Marshall 37-48, Morehead 49-60, Murray 61-72, Western Kentucky 73-84, and West Virginia 85-96. The cards of smaller school players within this set might well be in shorter supply than the cards of the larger schools. However, the prices below reflect the smaller demand for the cards of players from the smaller schools. The catalog designation for this set is UO18.

	NRMT	VG-E	GOOD
COMPLETE SET (96)	2750.00	1250.00	250.00
COMMON PLAYER (1-96)	25.00	12.50	2.50

		NRMT	VG-E	GOOD
☐ 1	Jack Adams	25.00	12.50	2.50
☐ 2	William Baxter	25.00	12.50	2.50
☐ 3	Jeffrey Brock	25.00	12.50	2.50
☐ 4	Paul Collins	25.00	12.50	2.50
☐ 5	Richard Culbertson	25.00	12.50	2.50
☐ 6	James Floyd	25.00	12.50	2.50
☐ 7	Harold Fraler	25.00	12.50	2.50
☐ 8	George Francis Jr.	25.00	12.50	2.50
☐ 9	Paul McBrayer CO	25.00	12.50	2.50
☐ 10	James Mitchell	25.00	12.50	2.50
☐ 11	Ronald Pellegrinon	25.00	12.50	2.50
☐ 12	Guy Strong	25.00	12.50	2.50
☐ 13	Earl Adkins	25.00	12.50	2.50
☐ 14	William Bibb	25.00	12.50	2.50
☐ 15	Jerry Bird	25.00	12.50	2.50
☐ 16	John Brewer	25.00	12.50	2.50
☐ 17	Robert Burrow	25.00	12.50	2.50
☐ 18	Gerry Calvert	25.00	12.50	2.50
☐ 19	William Evans	25.00	12.50	2.50
☐ 20	Phillip Grawemeyer	25.00	12.50	2.50
☐ 21	Ray Mills	25.00	12.50	2.50
☐ 22	Linville Puckett	25.00	12.50	2.50
☐ 23	Gayle Rose	35.00	17.50	3.50
☐ 24	Coach Adolph Rupp	250.00	125.00	25.00
☐ 25	William Darrah	25.00	12.50	2.50
☐ 26	Vladimir Gastevich	25.00	12.50	2.50
☐ 27	Allan Glaza	25.00	12.50	2.50
☐ 28	Herbert Harrah	25.00	12.50	2.50
☐ 29	Bernard Hickman CO	50.00	25.00	5.00
☐ 30	Richard Keffer	25.00	12.50	2.50
☐ 31	Gerald Moreman	25.00	12.50	2.50
☐ 32	James Morgan	25.00	12.50	2.50
☐ 33	John Prudhoe	25.00	12.50	2.50
☐ 34	Phillip Rollins	25.00	12.50	2.50
☐ 35	Roscoe Shackelford	25.00	12.50	2.50
☐ 36	Charles Tyra	50.00	25.00	5.00
☐ 37	Robert Ashley	25.00	12.50	2.50
☐ 38	Lewis Burns	25.00	12.50	2.50
☐ 39	Francis Crum	25.00	12.50	2.50
☐ 40	Raymond Frazier	25.00	12.50	2.50
☐ 41	Cam Henderson CO	35.00	17.50	3.50
☐ 42	Joseph Hunnicutt	25.00	12.50	2.50
☐ 43	Clarence Parkins	25.00	12.50	2.50
☐ 44	Jerry Pierson	25.00	12.50	2.50
☐ 45	David Robinson	25.00	12.50	2.50
☐ 46	Paul Underwood	25.00	12.50	2.50
☐ 47	Cebert Price	25.00	12.50	2.50
☐ 48	Charles Slack	25.00	12.50	2.50
☐ 49	David Breeze	25.00	12.50	2.50
☐ 50	Leonard Carpenter	25.00	12.50	2.50
☐ 51	Omar Fannin	25.00	12.50	2.50
☐ 52	Donnie Gaunce	25.00	12.50	2.50
☐ 53	Steve Hamilton	25.00	12.50	2.50
☐ 54	Bobby Laughlin CO	25.00	12.50	2.50
☐ 55	Jesse Mayabb	25.00	12.50	2.50
☐ 56	Jerry Riddle	25.00	12.50	2.50
☐ 57	Howard Shumate	25.00	12.50	2.50
☐ 58	Dan Swartz	25.00	12.50	2.50
☐ 59	Harlan Tolle	25.00	12.50	2.50
☐ 60	Donald Whitehouse	25.00	12.50	2.50
☐ 61	Rex Alexander CO	25.00	12.50	2.50
☐ 62	Jorgen Anderson	25.00	12.50	2.50
☐ 63	Jack Clutter	25.00	12.50	2.50
☐ 64	Howard Crittenden	25.00	12.50	2.50
☐ 65	James Gainey	25.00	12.50	2.50
☐ 66	Richard Kinder	25.00	12.50	2.50
☐ 67	Theo. Koenigsmark	25.00	12.50	2.50
☐ 68	Joseph Mikez	25.00	12.50	2.50
☐ 69	John Powless	25.00	12.50	2.50
☐ 70	Dolph Regelsky	25.00	12.50	2.50
☐ 71	Reinhard Tauck	25.00	12.50	2.50
☐ 72	Francis Watrous	25.00	12.50	2.50
☐ 73	Forrest Able	25.00	12.50	2.50
☐ 74	Tom Benbrook	25.00	12.50	2.50
☐ 75	Ronald Clark	25.00	12.50	2.50
☐ 76	Lynn Cole	25.00	12.50	2.50
☐ 77	Robert Daniels	25.00	12.50	2.50
☐ 78	Ed Diddle CO	125.00	60.00	12.50
☐ 79	Victor Harned	25.00	12.50	2.50
☐ 80	Dencil Miller	25.00	12.50	2.50
☐ 81	Ferrel Miller	25.00	12.50	2.50
☐ 82	George Orr	25.00	12.50	2.50
☐ 83	Jerry Weber	25.00	12.50	2.50
☐ 84	Jerry Whitsell	25.00	12.50	2.50
☐ 85	William Bergines	25.00	12.50	2.50
☐ 86	James Brennan	25.00	12.50	2.50
☐ 87	Marc Constantine	25.00	12.50	2.50
☐ 88	Michael Holt	25.00	12.50	2.50
☐ 89	Hot Rod Hundley	125.00	60.00	12.50
☐ 90	Clayce Kishbaugh	25.00	12.50	2.50
☐ 91	Ronald LaNeve	25.00	12.50	2.50
☐ 92	Gary Mullins	25.00	12.50	2.50
☐ 93	Fred Schaus CO	50.00	25.00	5.00
☐ 94	Frank Spadafore	25.00	12.50	2.50
☐ 95	Peter White	25.00	12.50	2.50
☐ 96	Paul Witting	25.00	12.50	2.50

1948 Bowman

The 1948 Bowman basketball card set of 72 cards was Bowman's only basketball issue. It was also the only major basketball issue until 1958. Cards in the set measure 2 1/16" by 2 1/2". The set is in color and features both player cards and diagram cards. The player cards in the second series are sometimes found without the red or blue printing on the card front, leaving only a gray background. These gray-front cards are more difficult to find, as they are printing errors where apparently the printer ran out of red or blue ink that was supposed to print on the player's uniform. The key rookie cards in this set are Joe Fulks, William "Red" Holzman, George Mikan, Jim Pollard, and Max Zaslofsky.

	NRMT	VG-E	GOOD
COMPLETE SET (72)	5400.00	2500.00	550.00
COMMON PLAYER (1-36)	30.00	15.00	3.00
COMMON PLAYER (37-72)	50.00	25.00	5.00
☐ 1 Ernie Calverley	100.00	20.00	4.00
Providence Steamrollers			
☐ 2 Ralph Hamilton	30.00	15.00	3.00
Ft. Wayne Pistons			
☐ 3 Gale Bishop	30.00	15.00	3.00
Philadelphia Warriors			
☐ 4 Fred Lewis CO	30.00	15.00	3.00
Indianapolis Jets			
☐ 5 Basketball Play	21.00	10.50	2.10
Single cut off post			
☐ 6 Bob Feerick	30.00	15.00	3.00
Washington Capitols			
☐ 7 John Logan	30.00	15.00	3.00
St. Louis Bombers			
☐ 8 Mel Riebe	30.00	15.00	3.00
Boston Celtics			
☐ 9 Andy Phillip	75.00	37.50	7.50
Chicago Stags			
☐ 10 Bob Davies	75.00	37.50	7.50
Rochester Royals			
☐ 11 Basketball Play	21.00	10.50	2.10
Single cut with			
return pass to post			
☐ 12 Kenny Sailors	30.00	15.00	3.00
Providence Steamrollers			
☐ 13 Paul Armstrong	30.00	15.00	3.00
Ft. Wayne Pistons			
☐ 14 Howard Dallmar	35.00	17.50	3.50
Philadelphia Warriors			
☐ 15 Bruce Hale	35.00	17.50	3.50
Indianapolis Jets			
☐ 16 Sid Hertzberg	30.00	15.00	3.00
Washington Capitols			
☐ 17 Basketball Play	21.00	10.50	2.10
Single cut			
☐ 18 Red Rocha	30.00	15.00	3.00
St. Louis Bombers			
☐ 19 Eddie Ehlers	30.00	15.00	3.00
Boston Celtics			
☐ 20 Ellis(Gene) Vance	30.00	15.00	3.00
Chicago Stags			
☐ 21 Andrew(Fuzzy) Levane	35.00	17.50	3.50
Rochester Royals			
☐ 22 Earl Shannon	30.00	15.00	3.00
Providence Steamrollers			
☐ 23 Basketball Play	21.00	10.50	2.10
Double cut off post			
☐ 24 Leo(Crystal) Klier	30.00	15.00	3.00
Ft. Wayne Pistons			
☐ 25 George Senesky	30.00	15.00	3.00
Philadelphia Warriors			
☐ 26 Price Brookfield	30.00	15.00	3.00
Indianapolis Jets			
☐ 27 John Norlander	30.00	15.00	3.00
Washington Capitols			
☐ 28 Don Putman	30.00	15.00	3.00
St. Louis Bombers			
☐ 29 Basketball Play	21.00	10.50	2.10
Double post			
☐ 30 Jack Garfinkel	30.00	15.00	3.00
Boston Celtics			
☐ 31 Chuck Gilmur	30.00	15.00	3.00
Chicago Stags			
☐ 32 William Holzman	200.00	100.00	20.00
Rochester Royals			
☐ 33 Jack Smiley	30.00	15.00	3.00
Ft. Wayne Pistons			
☐ 34 Joe Fulks	200.00	100.00	20.00
Philadelphia Warriors			
☐ 35 Basketball Play	21.00	10.50	2.10
Screen play			
☐ 36 Hal Tidrick	30.00	15.00	3.00
Indianapolis Jets			
☐ 37 Don(Swede) Carlson	50.00	25.00	5.00
Minneapolis Lakers			
☐ 38 Buddy Jeanette CO	60.00	30.00	6.00
Baltimore Bullets			
☐ 39 Ray Kuka	50.00	25.00	5.00
New York Knicks			
☐ 40 Stan Miasek	50.00	25.00	5.00
Chicago Stags			
☐ 41 Basketball Play	35.00	17.50	3.50
Double screen			
☐ 42 George Nostrand	50.00	25.00	5.00
Providence Steamrollers			
☐ 43 Chuck Halbert	60.00	30.00	6.00
Boston Celtics			
☐ 44 Arnie Johnson	50.00	25.00	5.00
Rochester Royals			
☐ 45 Bob Doll	50.00	25.00	5.00
St. Louis Bombers			
☐ 46 Horace McKinney	80.00	40.00	8.00
Washington Capitols			
☐ 47 Basketball Play	35.00	17.50	3.50
Out of bounds			
☐ 48 Ed Sadowski	50.00	25.00	5.00
Philadelphia Warriors			
☐ 49 Bob Kinney	50.00	25.00	5.00
Ft. Wayne Pistons			
☐ 50 Charles(Hawk) Black	50.00	25.00	5.00
Indianapolis Jets			
☐ 51 Jack Dwan	50.00	25.00	5.00
Minneapolis Lakers			
☐ 52 Cornelius Simmons	50.00	25.00	5.00
Baltimore Bullets			
☐ 53 Basketball Play	35.00	17.50	3.50
Out of bounds			
☐ 54 Bud Palmer	60.00	30.00	6.00
New York Knicks			
☐ 55 Max Zaslofsky	165.00	75.00	15.00
Chicago Stags			
☐ 56 Lee Roy Robbins	50.00	25.00	5.00
Providence Steamrollers			
☐ 57 Arthur Spector	50.00	25.00	5.00
Boston Celtics			
☐ 58 Arnie Risen	60.00	30.00	6.00
Rochester Royals			
☐ 59 Basketball Play	35.00	17.50	3.50
Out of bounds play			
☐ 60 Ariel Maughan	50.00	25.00	5.00
St. Louis Bombers			
☐ 61 Dick O'Keefe	50.00	25.00	5.00
Washington Capitols			
☐ 62 Herman Schaefer	50.00	25.00	5.00
Minneapolis Lakers			
☐ 63 John Mahnken	50.00	25.00	5.00
Baltimore Bullets			
☐ 64 Tommy Byrnes	50.00	25.00	5.00
New York Knicks			
☐ 65 Basketball Play	35.00	17.50	3.50
Held ball			
☐ 66 Jim Pollard	200.00	100.00	20.00
Minneapolis Lakers			
☐ 67 Lee Mogus	50.00	25.00	5.00
Baltimore Bullets			
☐ 68 Lee Knorek	50.00	25.00	5.00
New York Knicks			
☐ 69 George Mikan	2250.00	900.00	250.00
Minneapolis Lakers			
☐ 70 Walter Budko	50.00	25.00	5.00
Baltimore Bullets			
☐ 71 Basketball Play	35.00	17.50	3.50
Guards Play			
☐ 72 Carl Braun	125.00	30.00	6.00
New York Knicks			

1952 Bread for Health

The 1952 Bread for Health basketball (bread end label) set consists of 32 bread end labels (each measuring 2 3/4" by 2 3/4") of players in the National Basketball Association. While all the bakeries who issued this set are not at present known, Fisher's Bread in the New Jersey, New York and Pennsylvania area and NBC Bread in the Michigan area are two of the bakeries that have been confirmed to date. As with many of the bread label sets of the early '50s, an album to house the set was probably issued. Each label contains the B.E.B. copyright found on so many of the labels of this period. Labels which contain "Bread for Energy" at the bottom are not a part of the set but part of a series of movie, western and sports stars issued during the same approximate time period. The American Card Catalog does not designate a number to this series; however, based on its similarity to a corresponding football issue, it is referenced as D290-15A.

	NRMT	VG-E	GOOD
COMPLETE SET (32)	5000.00	2500.00	500.00
COMMON PLAYER (1-32)	125.00	60.00	12.50
☐ 1 Paul Armstrong	125.00	60.00	12.50
Ft.Wayne Pistons			
☐ 2 Boryla	125.00	60.00	12.50
New York Knicks			
☐ 3 Boven	125.00	60.00	12.50
Tri-Cities Blackhawks			
☐ 4 Walter Budko	125.00	60.00	12.50
Baltimore Bullets			
☐ 5 Cervi	125.00	60.00	12.50
Syracuse Nats			
☐ 6 Bob Davies	200.00	100.00	20.00
Rochester Royals			
☐ 7 Eddelman	125.00	60.00	12.50
Tri-Cities Blackhawks			
☐ 8 Ferrin	125.00	60.00	12.50
Minneapolis Lakers			
☐ 9 Joe Fulks	250.00	125.00	25.00
Philadelphia Warriors			
☐ 10 Harry Gallatan	200.00	100.00	20.00
New York Knicks			
☐ 11 Gilmer	125.00	60.00	12.50
Washington Caps			
☐ 12 Alex Groza	150.00	75.00	15.00
Indianapolis Olympians			
☐ 13 Bruce Hale	125.00	60.00	12.50
Indianapolis Olympians			
☐ 14 Hoffman	125.00	60.00	12.50
Baltimore Bullets			
☐ 15 Buddy Jeanette	150.00	75.00	15.00
Baltimore Bullets			
☐ 16 Bob Kinney	125.00	60.00	12.50
Boston Celtics			
☐ 17 Dante Lavelli	200.00	100.00	20.00
Boston Celtics			
☐ 18 Livingstone	125.00	60.00	12.50
Philadelphia Warriors			
☐ 19 Horace McKinney	150.00	75.00	15.00
Washington Caps			
☐ 20 Stan Miasek	125.00	60.00	12.50
Chicago Stags			
☐ 21 George Mikan	750.00	375.00	75.00
Minneapolis Lakers			
☐ 22 Vern Mikkelsen	200.00	100.00	20.00
Minneapolis Lakers			
☐ 23 Andy Phillip	200.00	100.00	20.00
Chicago Stags			
☐ 24 Arnie Risen	150.00	75.00	15.00
Rochester Royals			
☐ 25 Fred Schaus	150.00	75.00	15.00
Ft.Wayne Pistons			
☐ 26 Scolari	125.00	60.00	12.50
Washington Caps			
☐ 27 George Senesky	125.00	60.00	12.50
Philadelphia Warriors			
☐ 28 Seymour	125.00	60.00	12.50
Syracuse Nats			
☐ 29 Cornelius Simmons	125.00	60.00	12.50
New York Knicks			
☐ 30 Gene Vance	125.00	60.00	12.50
Tri-Cities Blackhawks			
☐ 31 Walker	125.00	60.00	12.50
Boston Celtics			
☐ 32 Max Zaszlofsky	200.00	100.00	20.00
New York Knicks			

1976 Buckman Discs

The 1976 Buckman Discs set contains 20 unnumbered discs approximately 3 3/8" in diameter. The discs have various color borders, and feature black and white drawings of the players with fascimile signatures. This set was distributed through Buckman's Ice Cream Village in Rochester, New York.

	NRMT	VG-E	GOOD
COMPLETE SET (20)	50.00	25.00	5.00
COMMON PLAYER (1-20)	1.00	.50	.10
☐ 1 Nate Archibald	3.00	1.50	.30
☐ 2 Rick Barry	5.00	2.50	.50
☐ 3 Tom Boerwinkle	1.00	.50	.10
☐ 4 Bill Bradley	7.50	3.75	.75
☐ 5 Dave Cowens	3.00	1.50	.30
☐ 6 Bob Dandridge	1.00	.50	.10
☐ 7 Walt Frazier	3.00	1.50	.30
☐ 8 Gail Goodrich	2.00	1.00	.20
☐ 9 John Havlicek	5.00	2.50	.50
☐ 10 Connie Hawkins	2.00	1.00	.20
☐ 11 Lou Hudson	1.50	.75	.15
☐ 12 Kareem Abdul Jabbar	15.00	7.50	1.50
☐ 13 Sam Lacey	1.00	.50	.10
☐ 14 Bob Lanier	2.00	1.00	.20
☐ 15 Bob Love	1.50	.75	.15
☐ 16 Bob McAdoo	2.00	1.00	.20
☐ 17 Earl Monroe	3.00	1.50	.30
☐ 18 Jerry Sloan	1.50	.75	.15
☐ 19 Norm Van Lier	1.00	.50	.10
☐ 20 Jo Jo White	1.50	.75	.15

1971-72 Bucks Linnett

These 10 charcoal drawings are skillfully executed facial portraits of Milwaukee Bucks players. They were drawn by noted sports artist Charles Linnett and measure approximately 8 1/2" by 11". In the lower right corner, a facsimile autograph of the player is written across the portrait. The backs are blank. The drawings are unnumbered and we have checklisted them below in alphabetical order.

	NRMT	VG-E	GOOD
COMPLETE SET (10)	20.00	10.00	2.00
COMMON PLAYER (1-10)	1.00	.50	.10
☐ 1 Kareem Abdul-Jabbar	12.50	6.25	1.25
☐ 2 Gary Brokaw	1.50	.75	.15
☐ 3 Bob Dandridge	2.00	1.00	.20
☐ 4 Mickey Davis	1.00	.50	.10
☐ 5 Steve Kuberski	1.00	.50	.10
☐ 6 Jon McGlocklin	1.50	.75	.15
☐ 7 Jim Price	1.00	.50	.10
☐ 8 Kevin Restani	1.00	.50	.10
☐ 9 George Thompson	1.00	.50	.10
☐ 10 Cornell Warner	1.00	.50	.10

1977-78 Bucks Action Photos

These glossy action photos (of Milwaukee Bucks) measure approximately 5" by 7" and are printed on very thin paper. The photos are in full color and without borders. The players are identified only by their facsimile autographs inscribed across the picture. The backs are blank.

	NRMT	VG-E	GOOD
COMPLETE SET (10)	20.00	10.00	2.00
COMMON PLAYER (1-10)	1.00	.50	.10
☐ 1 Kent Benson	2.00	1.00	.20
☐ 2 Junior Bridgeman	2.00	1.00	.20
☐ 3 Quinn Buckner	2.00	1.00	.20
☐ 4 Alex English	7.50	3.75	.75
☐ 5 John Gianelli	1.00	.50	.10
☐ 6 Ernie Grunfeld	2.00	1.00	.20
☐ 7 Marques Johnson	4.00	2.00	.40
☐ 8 Dave Meyers	2.00	1.00	.20
☐ 9 Lloyd Walton	1.00	.50	.10
☐ 10 Brian Winters	2.00	1.00	.20

1979 Bucks Open Pantry *

This set is an unnumbered, 12-card set featuring players from Milwaukee area professional sports teams with five Brewers baseball (1-5), five Bucks basketball (6-10), and two Packers football (11-12). Cards are black and white with red trim and measure approximately 5" by 6". Cards were sponsored by Open Pantry, Lake to Lake, and MACC (Milwaukee Athletes against Childhood Cancer). The cards are unnumbered and hence are listed and numbered below alphabetically within sport.

	NRMT	VG-E	GOOD
COMPLETE SET (12)	30.00	15.00	3.00
COMMON BASEBALL (1-5)	2.00	1.00	.20
COMMON BASKETBALL (6-10)	2.00	1.00	.20
COMMON FOOTBALL (11-12)	2.00	1.00	.20
☐ 1 Jerry Augustine	2.00	1.00	.20
☐ 2 Sal Bando	3.00	1.50	.30
☐ 3 Cecil Cooper	3.00	1.50	.30
☐ 4 Larry Hisle	2.00	1.00	.20
☐ 5 Lary Sorensen	2.00	1.00	.20
☐ 6 Kent Benson	3.00	1.50	.30
☐ 7 Junior Bridgeman	3.00	1.50	.30
☐ 8 Quinn Buckner	3.00	1.50	.30
☐ 9 Marques Johnson	5.00	2.50	.50
☐ 10 Jon McGlocklin	3.00	1.50	.30
☐ 11 Rich McGeorge	2.00	1.00	.20
☐ 12 Steve Wagner	2.00	1.00	.20

1979-80 Bucks Police/Spic'n'Span

This set contains 12 cards measuring 2 1/2" by 3 1/2" featuring the Milwaukee Bucks of the NBA. Backs contain safety tips ("Game Plan Tip"). The cards are numbered on the back next to the facsimile autograph. The cards feature full-color fronts and black printing on a white card stock back. The set was sponsored by Spic'N'Span. Also available was a coupon card.

	MINT	EXC	G-VG
COMPLETE SET (12)	100.00	50.00	10.00
COMMON PLAYER	6.00	3.00	.60
☐ 2 Junior Bridgeman	9.00	4.50	.90
☐ 4 Sidney Moncrief	20.00	10.00	2.00
☐ 6 Pat Cummings	7.50	3.75	.75
☐ 7 Dave Meyers	9.00	4.50	.90
☐ 8 Marques Johnson	15.00	7.50	1.50
☐ 11 Lloyd Walton	6.00	3.00	.60
☐ 21 Quinn Buckner	9.00	4.50	.90
☐ 31 Richard Washington	9.00	4.50	.90
☐ 32 Brian Winters	7.50	3.75	.75
☐ 42 Harvey Catchings	6.00	3.00	.60
☐ 54 Kent Benson	7.50	3.75	.75
☐ xx Coach Don Nelson and John Killilea, Assistant Coach	9.00	4.50	.90

1987-88 Bucks Polaroid

The 1987-88 Polaroid Milwaukee Bucks set contains 16 cards each measuring approximately 2 3/4" by 4". There are 14 player cards plus one coaching staff card and one title card. The cards were distributed in sheet form with perforations. The front borders are deep green and the backs feature biographical information.

	MINT	EXC	G-VG
COMPLETE SET (16)	20.00	10.00	2.00
COMMON PLAYER	1.00	.50	.10
☐ 2 Junior Bridgeman	2.00	1.00	.20
☐ 3 Pace Mannion	1.00	.50	.10
☐ 4 Sidney Moncrief	4.00	2.00	.40
☐ 10 John Lucas	2.00	1.00	.20
☐ 15 Craig Hodges	3.00	1.50	.30
☐ 21 Conner Henry	1.00	.50	.10
☐ 25 Paul Pressey	3.00	1.50	.30
☐ 34 Terry Cummings	5.00	2.50	.50
☐ 35 Jerry Reynolds	1.00	.50	.10
☐ 42 Larry Krystkowiak	1.00	.50	.10
☐ 43 Jack Sikma	3.00	1.50	.30
☐ 44 Paul Mokeski	1.00	.50	.10
☐ 45 Randy Breuer	1.00	.50	.10
☐ 54 John Stroeder	1.00	.50	.10
☐ xx Bucks Coaches Del Harris HEAD Frank Hamblen ASST Mack Calvin ASST Mike Dunleavy ASST Jeff Snedeker TR	1.00	.50	.10
☐ xx Title Card (discount offer detailed on back)	1.00	.50	.10

1988-89 Bucks Green Border

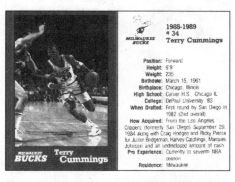

This 16-card set was issued in a panel of four rows of four cards each; after perforation, the cards measure approximately 2 3/4" by 4". The front features a color action player photo, with a thin black border on medium green background. In white lettering the team and player name are given below the picture. The back has the Milwaukee Bucks logo in the upper left corner and biographical information given in tabular format.

	MINT	EXC	G-VG
COMPLETE SET (16)	15.00	7.50	1.50
COMMON PLAYER (1-16)	.75	.35	.07
☐ 1 Kareem Abdul-Jabbar	5.00	2.50	.50
☐ 2 Randy Breuer	.75	.35	.07
☐ 3 Terry Cummings	2.00	1.00	.20
☐ 4 Jeff Grayer	1.00	.50	.10
☐ 5 Del Harris CO	.75	.35	.07
☐ 6 Tito Horford	1.00	.50	.10
☐ 7 Jay Humphries	1.00	.50	.10
☐ 8 Larry Krystkowiak	.75	.35	.07
☐ 9 Paul Mokeski	.75	.35	.07
☐ 10 Sidney Moncrief	2.00	1.00	.20
☐ 11 Ricky Pierce	2.00	1.00	.20
☐ 12 Paul Pressey	1.50	.75	.15
☐ 13 Fred Roberts	1.50	.75	.15
☐ 14 Jack Sikma	1.50	.75	.15
☐ 15 The Bradley Center	.75	.35	.07
☐ 16 1988-89 Coaching Staff Del Harris Frank Hamblen Mack Calvin Mike Dunleavy Jeff Snedeker (Trainer)	.75	.35	.07

1954-55 Bullets Gunther Beer

This 11-card set of Baltimore Bullets was sponsored by Gunther Beer. These black and white cards measure approximately 2 5/8" by 3 5/8". The front features a black and white posed player photo. The question "What's the good word," is written across the card top. A Gunther Beer bottle cap and the player's name are superimposed on the player's chest. The back has the words "Follow the Bullets with Gunther Beer" at the top, with biographical information and career summary below. A radio and TV notice on the bottom round out the card back. The cards are unnumbered and are checklisted below in alphabetical order. The cards are frequently found personally autographed. The catalog designation for this set is H805.

	NRMT	VG-E	GOOD
COMPLETE SET (11)	1350.00	600.00	100.00
COMMON PLAYER (1-11)	100.00	50.00	10.00
☐ 1 Leo Barnhorst	100.00	50.00	10.00
☐ 2 Clair Bee CO	300.00	150.00	30.00
☐ 3 Bill Bolger	100.00	50.00	10.00

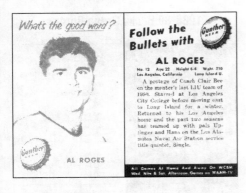

☐ 4 Ray Felix	150.00	75.00	15.00
☐ 5 Jim Fritsche	100.00	50.00	10.00
☐ 6 Rollen Hans	100.00	50.00	10.00
☐ 7 Paul Hoffman	100.00	50.00	10.00
☐ 8 Bob Houbregs	225.00	110.00	22.00
☐ 9 Ed Miller	100.00	50.00	10.00
☐ 10 Al Roges	100.00	50.00	10.00
☐ 11 Harold Uplinger	100.00	50.00	10.00

1973-74 Bullets Standups

These 12 player cards are issued in a album, with six players per 11 1/4" by 14" sheet. After perforation, the cards measure approximately 3 3/4" by 7 1/16". The cards are die cut, allowing the player pictures and bases to be pushed out and displayed as stand-ups. The fronts feature a color photo of the player, either dribbling or shooting the ball. The backs are blank. The cards are unnumbered and are checklisted below in alphabetical order. A card set, still intact in the album, would be valued at triple the values listed below.

	MINT	EXC	G-VG
COMPLETE SET (12)	35.00	17.50	3.50

COMMON PLAYER (1-12)	2.00	1.00	.20
☐ 1 Phil Chenier	3.00	1.50	.30
☐ 2 Archie Clark	4.00	2.00	.40
☐ 3 Elvin Hayes	12.00	6.00	1.20
☐ 4 Tom Kozelko	2.00	1.00	.20
☐ 5 Manny Leaks	2.00	1.00	.20
☐ 6 Louie Nelson	2.00	1.00	.20
☐ 7 Kevin Porter	4.00	2.00	.40
☐ 8 Mike Riordan	3.00	1.50	.30
☐ 9 Dave Stallworth	3.00	1.50	.30
☐ 10 Wes Unseld	9.00	4.50	.90
☐ 11 Nick Weatherspoon	2.00	1.00	.20
☐ 12 Walt Wesley	2.00	1.00	.20

1970-71 Bulls Hawthorne Milk

This five-card set was issued on the side panels of Hawthorne Milk cartons. The cards were intended to be cut from the carton and measure approximately 3 1/4" by 3 3/8" and feature on the front a posed head shot of the player within a circular picture frame. The second Weiss card measures 4 11/16" by 2 7/8". The backs are blank. The cards are unnumbered and are checklisted below in alphabetical order. The player photo is printed in blue but the outer border of the card is bright red.

	NRMT	VG-E	GOOD
COMPLETE SET (5)	250.00	125.00	25.00
COMMON PLAYER (1-5)	50.00	25.00	5.00
☐ 1 Bob Love	75.00	37.50	7.50
☐ 2 Jerry Sloan	75.00	37.50	7.50
☐ 3 Chet Walker	75.00	37.50	7.50
☐ 4 Bob Weiss	50.00	25.00	5.00
(regular size)			
☐ 5 Bob Weiss	50.00	25.00	5.00
(large size)			

1977-78 Bulls White Hen Pantry

These high gloss player photos are printed on very thin paper and measure 5" by 7". The fronts feature borderless color game action photos with a facsimile auto; the backs are blank. The photos are unnumbered and we have checklisted them below in alphabetical order.

	NRMT	VG-E	GOOD
COMPLETE SET (7)	15.00	7.50	1.50
COMMON PLAYER (1-7)	2.00	1.00	.20
☐ 1 Tom Boerwinkle	2.00	1.00	.20
☐ 2 Artis Gilmore	5.00	2.50	.50

		MINT	EXC	G-VG
☐ 3	Wilbur Holland	2.00	1.00	.20
☐ 4	Mickey Johnson	3.00	1.50	.30
☐ 5	Scott May	3.00	1.50	.30
☐ 6	John Mengelt	3.00	1.50	.30
☐ 7	Norm, Van Lier	3.00	1.50	.30

1979-80 Bulls Police

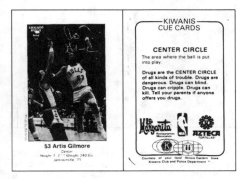

This set contains 16 cards measuring 2 5/8" by 4 1/8" featuring the Chicago Bulls. Cards in the set have rounded corners. Backs contain safety tips and are written in black ink with blue accent. The set was also sponsored by La Margarita Mexican Restaurants and Azteca Tortillas. The card backs are subtitled Kiwanis Cue Cards. Cards are unnumbered except for uniform number.

		MINT	EXC	G-VG
COMPLETE SET (16)		100.00	50.00	10.00
COMMON PLAYER		5.00	2.50	.50
☐ 1	Delmer Beshore	5.00	2.50	.50
☐ 13	Dwight Jones	5.00	2.50	.50
☐ 15	John Mengelt	7.50	3.75	.75

☐ 17	Scott May	7.50	3.75	.75
☐ 20	Dennis Awtrey	5.00	2.50	.50
☐ 24	Reggie Theus	9.00	4.50	.90
☐ 26	Coby Dietrick	5.00	2.50	.50
☐ 27	Ollie Johnson	5.00	2.50	.50
☐ 28	Sam Smith	5.00	2.50	.50
☐ 34	David Greenwood	7.50	3.75	.75
☐ 40	Ricky Sobers	7.50	3.75	.75
☐ 53	Artis Gilmore	12.00	6.00	1.20
☐ 54	Mark Landsberger	5.00	2.50	.50
☐ xx	Jerry Sloan CO	7.50	3.75	.75
☐ xx	Phil Johnson, assistant coach	5.00	2.50	.50
☐ xx	Luv-A-Bull	7.50	3.75	.75

1987-88 Bulls Entenmann's

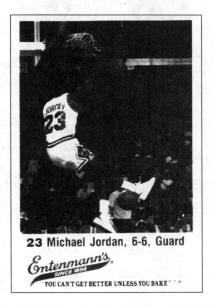

The 1987-88 Entenmann's Chicago Bulls set contains 12 blank-backed cards measuring approximately 2 5/8" by 4". There are 11 player cards and one coach card in this set. The cards are unnumbered except for uniform number; they are ordered below by uniform number.

		MINT	EXC	G-VG
COMPLETE SET (12)		70.00	35.00	7.00
COMMON PLAYER (1-12)		1.00	.50	.10
☐ 1	Rory Sparrow 2	1.00	.50	.10
☐ 2	Sedale Threatt 3	1.50	.75	.15
☐ 3	John Paxson 5	2.50	1.25	.25
☐ 4	Brad Sellers 6	1.50	.75	.15
☐ 5	Mike Brown 17	1.00	.50	.10
☐ 6	Michael Jordan 23	45.00	22.50	4.50
☐ 7	Granville Waiters 31	1.00	.50	.10
☐ 8	Scottie Pippen 33	15.00	7.50	1.50
☐ 9	Charles Oakley 34	2.50	1.25	.25
☐ 10	Dave Corzine 40	1.00	.50	.10
☐ 11	Horace Grant 54	5.00	2.50	.50
☐ 12	Doug Collins CO	2.00	1.00	.20

1988-89 Bulls Entenmann's

The 1988-89 Entenmann's Chicago Bulls set contains 12 blank-backed player cards each measuring approximately 2 5/8" by 4".

5 John Paxson, 6-2, Guard

54 Horace Grant 6-10, Forward — EQUAL SWEETENER NutraSweet

The cards are unnumbered except for uniform number; they are ordered and numbered below by uniform number.

	MINT	EXC	G-VG
COMPLETE SET (12)	40.00	20.00	4.00
COMMON PLAYER	.75	.35	.07
☐ 2 Brad Sellers	1.00	.50	.10
☐ 5 John Paxson	2.00	1.00	.20
☐ 11 Sam Vincent	1.50	.75	.15
☐ 14 Craig Hodges	1.50	.75	.15
☐ 15 Jack Haley	.75	.35	.07
☐ 22 Charles Davis	.75	.35	.07
☐ 23 Michael Jordan	24.00	12.00	2.40
☐ 24 Bill Cartwright	1.50	.75	.15
☐ 32 Will Perdue	1.25	.60	.12
☐ 33 Scottie Pippen	6.00	3.00	.60
☐ 40 Dave Corzine	.75	.35	.07
☐ 54 Horace Grant	2.50	1.25	.25

1989-90 Bulls Equal

This 11-card set was sponsored by Equal Brand sweetener, and its company logo appears in the lower right corner of the card face. It has been reported that 10,000 sets were given away to fans attending the April 17th Chicago Bulls home game. These oversized cards measure approximately 3" by 4 1/4". The front features a borderless color action photo. The player's number, name, height, and position are given in the white stripe below the picture. Except for the sponsor's trademark notice, the backs are blank. The cards are unnumbered and checklisted below in alphabetical order, with jersey number after the player's name.

	MINT	EXC	G-VG
COMPLETE SET (11)	25.00	12.50	2.50
COMMON PLAYER (1-11)	.65	.30	.06
☐ 1 B.J. Armstrong 10	1.50	.75	.15
☐ 2 Bill Cartwright 24	1.50	.75	.15
☐ 3 Charles Davis 22	.65	.30	.06
☐ 4 Horace Grant 54	2.50	1.25	.25
☐ 5 Craig Hodges 14	1.50	.75	.15
☐ 6 Michael Jordan 23	12.50	6.25	1.25
☐ 7 Stacey King 34	2.00	1.00	.20
☐ 8 Ed Nealy 45	.65	.30	.06

	MINT	EXC	G-VG
☐ 9 John Paxson 5	1.50	.75	.15
☐ 10 Will Perdue 32	1.00	.50	.10
☐ 11 Scottie Pippen 33	4.00	2.00	.40
☐ 12 Jeff Sanders 42	1.00	.50	.10

1990-91 Bulls Equal/Star

This 16-card set was sponsored by Equal brand sweetener and celebrates the 25th anniversary of the Chicago Bulls franchise. The set was produced (reportedly 10,000 complete sets) by Star Company and was distributed at the April 9th Chicago Bulls home game. The cards measure the standard size (2 1/2" by 3 1/2"). The fronts feature color action player photos for current Bull players, and blue-tinted photos for past Bull players. The team logo and the words "The Silver Season" overlay the top of the picture. The card background is in silver, and the player's name appears in a gray diagonal stripe traversing the bottom of the picture. The sponsor logo appears in blue print at the card bottom. The back has brief biographical information and statistics, in black print on a pink background. The cards are numbered on the back.

	MINT	EXC	G-VG
COMPLETE SET (16)	20.00	10.00	2.00
COMMON PLAYER (1-16)	.65	.30	.06
☐ 1 Michael Jordan	10.00	5.00	1.00
☐ 2 Tom Boerwinkle	.65	.30	.06
☐ 3 Bob Boozer	.65	.30	.06
☐ 4 Bill Cartwright	1.00	.50	.10
☐ 5 Artis Gilmore	1.50	.75	.15
☐ 6 Horace Grant	1.50	.75	.15
☐ 7 Phil Jackson CO	1.00	.50	.10
☐ 8 Johnny(Red) Kerr	1.00	.50	.10
☐ 9 Bob Love	1.00	.50	.10
☐ 10 Dick Motta CO	.65	.30	.06
☐ 11 John Paxson	1.00	.50	.10
☐ 12 Scottie Pippen	3.00	1.50	.30
☐ 13 Guy Rodgers	.65	.30	.06
☐ 14 Jerry Sloan	1.00	.50	.10
☐ 15 Norm Van Lier	.65	.30	.06
☐ 16 Chet Walker	1.00	.50	.10

1956 Busch Bavarian

These black and white photo-like cards were sponsored by Busch Bavarian Beer and feature members of the St. Louis Hawks. The cards are blank backed and measure approximately 4" by 5". The cards show a facsimile autograph of the player on a drop-out background.

	NRMT	VG-E	GOOD
COMPLETE SET (4)	400.00	200.00	40.00
COMMON PLAYER (1-4)	50.00	25.00	5.00
☐ 1 Cliff Hagan	100.00	50.00	10.00
☐ 2 Clyde Lovellette	100.00	50.00	10.00
☐ 3 John McCarthy	50.00	25.00	5.00
☐ 4 Bob Pettit	200.00	100.00	20.00

1975 Carvel Discs

The 1975 Carvel NBA Basketball Discs set contains 36 unnumbered discs approximately 3 3/8" in diameter. The blank-backed discs have various color borders, and feature black and white drawings of the players with fascimile signatures. Since the discs are unnumbered, they are ordered below in alphabetical order.

	NRMT	VG-E	GOOD
COMPLETE SET (36)	70.00	35.00	7.00
COMMON PLAYER (1-36)	.75	.35	.07
☐ 1 Nate Archibald	3.00	1.50	.30
☐ 2 Bill Bradley	6.00	3.00	.60
☐ 3 Don Chaney	1.50	.75	.15
☐ 4 Dave Cowens	3.00	1.50	.30
☐ 5 Bob Dandridge	1.00	.50	.10
☐ 6 Ernie DiGregorio	1.00	.50	.10
☐ 7 Walt Frazier	4.00	2.00	.40
☐ 8 John Gianelli	.75	.35	.07
☐ 9 Gail Goodrich	2.00	1.00	.20
☐ 10 Happy Hairston	.75	.35	.07
☐ 11 John Havlicek	6.00	3.00	.60
☐ 12 Spencer Haywood	1.50	.75	.15
☐ 13 Garfield Heard	.75	.35	.07
☐ 14 Lou Hudson	1.00	.50	.10
☐ 15 Kareem Abdul Jabbar	15.00	7.50	1.50
☐ 16 Phil Jackson	1.25	.60	.12
☐ 17 Sam Lacey	.75	.35	.07
☐ 18 Bob Lanier	2.00	1.00	.20
☐ 19 Bob Love	1.00	.50	.10
☐ 20 Bob McAdoo	2.00	1.00	.20
☐ 21 Jim McMillian	.75	.35	.07
☐ 22 Dean Meminger	1.00	.50	.10
☐ 23 Earl Monroe	3.00	1.50	.30
☐ 24 Don Nelson	2.00	1.00	.20
☐ 25 Jim Price	.75	.35	.07
☐ 26 Clifford Ray	.75	.35	.07
☐ 27 Charlie Scott	1.00	.50	.10
☐ 28 Paul Silas	1.25	.60	.12
☐ 29 Jerry Sloan	1.00	.50	.10
☐ 30 Randy Smith	1.00	.50	.10
☐ 31 Dick Van Arsdale	.75	.35	.07
☐ 32 Norm Van Lier	1.00	.50	.10
☐ 33 Chet Walker	1.50	.75	.15
☐ 34 Paul Westphal	1.50	.75	.15
☐ 35 JoJo White	2.00	1.00	.20
☐ 36 Hawthorne Wingo	.75	.35	.07

1991 Classic Draft

This 50-card set was produced by Classic Games, Inc. and features 48 players picked in the first two rounds of the 1991 NBA draft. A total of 450,000 sets were issued, and each set is accompanied by a letter of limited edition. The cards measure the standard size (2 1/2" by 3 1/2"). The front features a glossy color action photo of player. The back has statistics and biographical information. Special cards included in the set are a commemorative number one draft choice card of Larry Johnson and a "One-on-One" card of Billy Owens slam-dunking over Johnson.

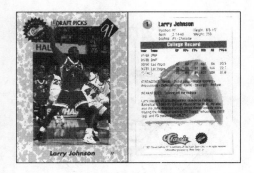

	MINT	EXC	G-VG
COMPLETE SET (50)	13.50		
COMMON PLAYER (1-50)	.10	.05	.01
☐ 1 Larry Johnson UNLV	3.50	1.75	.35
☐ 2 Billy Owens Syracuse	3.50	1.75	.35
☐ 3 Dikembe Mutombo Georgetown	1.75	.85	.17
☐ 4 Mark Macon Temple	1.00	.50	.10
☐ 5 Brian Williams Arizona	.75	.35	.07
☐ 6 Terrell Brandon Oregon	.75	.35	.07
☐ 7 Greg Anthony UNLV	1.00	.50	.10
☐ 8 Dale Davis Clemson	.40	.20	.04
☐ 9 Anthony Avent Seton Hall	.30	.15	.03
☐ 10 Chris Gatling Old Dominion	.30	.15	.03
☐ 11 Victor Alexander Iowa State	.40	.20	.04
☐ 12 Kevin Brooks Southwest Louisiana	.20	.10	.02
☐ 13 Eric Murdock Providence	.40	.20	.04
☐ 14 LeRon Ellis Syracuse	.20	.10	.02
☐ 15 Stanley Roberts LSU	.50	.25	.05
☐ 16 Rick Fox North Carolina	.75	.35	.07
☐ 17 Pete Chilcutt North Carolina	.25	.12	.02
☐ 18 Kevin Lynch Minnesota	.25	.12	.02
☐ 19 George Ackles UNLV	.25	.12	.02
☐ 20 Rodney Monroe North Carolina State	.50	.25	.05
☐ 21 Randy Brown New Mexico State	.15	.07	.01
☐ 22 Chad Gallagher Creighton	.20	.10	.02
☐ 23 Donald Hodge Temple	.20	.10	.02
☐ 24 Myron Brown Slippery Rock	.15	.07	.01
☐ 25 Mike Iuzzolino St. Francis	.20	.10	.02
☐ 26 Chris Corchiani North Carolina State	.30	.15	.03
☐ 27 Elliott Perry Memphis State	.20	.10	.02
☐ 28 Joe Wylie Miami (FL)	.10	.05	.01
☐ 29 Jimmy Oliver Purdue	.15	.07	.01
☐ 30 Doug Overton LaSalle	.20	.10	.02
☐ 31 Sean Green Iona	.10	.05	.01
☐ 32 Steve Hood James Madison	.20	.10	.02
☐ 33 Lamont Strothers Chris. Newport	.15	.07	.01
☐ 34 Alvaro Teheran Houston	.20	.10	.02
☐ 35 Bobby Phills Southern	.10	.05	.01
☐ 36 Richard Dumas Oklahoma State	.15	.07	.01
☐ 37 Keith Hughes Rutgers	.15	.07	.01
☐ 38 Isaac Austin Arizona State	.15	.07	.01
☐ 39 Greg Sutton Oral Roberts	.15	.07	.01
☐ 40 Joey Wright Texas	.20	.10	.02
☐ 41 Anthony Jones Oral Roberts	.10	.05	.01
☐ 42 Von McDade Milwaukee/Wisconsin	.10	.05	.01
☐ 43 Marcus Kennedy E. Michigan	.15	.07	.01
☐ 44 Larry Johnson UNLV Top Pick	1.75	.85	.17
☐ 45 Larry Johnson and Billy Owens UNLV and Syracuse	1.75	.85	.17
☐ 46 Anderson Hunt UNLV	.40	.20	.04
☐ 47 Darrin Chancellor S. Mississippi	.10	.05	.01
☐ 48 Damon Lopez Fordham	.10	.05	.01
☐ 49 Thomas Jordan Oklahoma State	.10	.05	.01
☐ 50 Tony Farmer Nebraska	.10	.05	.01

1978-79 Clippers Handyman

The 1978-79 Handyman San Diego Clippers set contains nine cards measuring approximately 2" by 4 1/4". The cards are "3-D" and are similar to the 1970s Kelloggs baseball sets. Each card has a coupon tab attached (included in the dimensions given above). Coach Gene Shue's card was apparently not distributed (as it was the grand prize winner of the contest) with the other cards but does exist. In addition there is a second version of the Lloyd Free card.

	NRMT	VG-E	GOOD
COMPLETE SET (9)	30.00	15.00	3.00
COMMON PLAYER (1-9)	2.50	1.25	.25
☐ 1 Randy Smith 9	3.50	1.75	.35
☐ 2 Nick Weatherspoon 12	2.50	1.25	.25
☐ 3 Freeman Williams 20	2.50	1.25	.25
☐ 4 Sidney Wicks 21	6.00	3.00	.60
☐ 5 Lloyd Free 24	4.50	2.25	.45
☐ 6 Swen Nater 31	4.50	2.25	.45

☐ 7	Jerome Whitehead 33	2.50	1.25	.25
☐ 8	Kermit Washington 42	3.50	1.75	.35
☐ 9	Kevin Kunnert 44	2.50	1.25	.25
☐ xx	Gene Shue CO	200.00	100.00	20.00

1990-91 Clippers Star

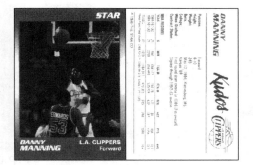

This 12-card set of Los Angeles Clippers was produced by the Star Company and measures the standard size (2 1/2" and 3 1/2"). The fronts feature color action shots, with red borders that wash out in the middle of the card face. The horizontally oriented backs are printed in red and blue on white and have biographical as well as statistical information. The cards are unnumbered and are checklisted below in alphabetical order. Benoit Benjamin and Mike Smrek were apparently planned for the set but were not released with the other cards listed below.

		MINT	EXC	G-VG
COMPLETE SET (12)		9.00	4.50	.90
COMMON PLAYER (1-12)		.60	.30	.06
☐ 1	Ken Bannister	.60	.30	.06
☐ 2	Winston Garland	.60	.30	.06
☐ 3	Tom Garrick	.60	.30	.06
☐ 4	Gary Grant	.75	.35	.07
☐ 5	Ron Harper	1.25	.60	.12
☐ 6	Bo Kimble	1.00	.50	.10
☐ 7	Danny Manning	1.50	.75	.15
☐ 8	Jeff Martin	.60	.30	.06
☐ 9	Ken Norman	1.25	.60	.12
☐ 10	Mike Schuler CO	.60	.30	.06
☐ 11	Charles Smith	1.25	.60	.12
☐ 12	Loy Vaught	1.00	.50	.10

1971 Colonels Marathon Oil

This set of Marathon Oil Pro Star Portraits consists of colorful portraits by distinguished artist Nicholas Volpe. Each (ABA Kentucky Colonels) portrait measures approximately 7 1/2" by 9 7/8" and features a painting of the player's face on a black background, with an action painting superimposed to the side. A facsimile autograph in white appears at the bottom of the portrait. At the bottom of each portrait is a postcard measuring 7 1/2" by 4" after perforation. While the back of the portrait has offers for a basketball photo album, autographed tumblers, and a poster, the postcard itself may be used to apply for a Marathon credit card. The portraits are unnumbered and checklisted below according to alphabetical order.

		NRMT	VG-E	GOOD
COMPLETE SET (11)		40.00	20.00	4.00
COMMON PLAYER (1-11)		3.00	1.50	.30
☐ 1	Darrell Carrier	4.00	2.00	.40
☐ 2	Bobby Croft	3.00	1.50	.30

☐ 3	Louie Dampier	5.00	2.50	.50
☐ 4	Les Hunter	4.00	2.00	.40
☐ 5	Dan Issel	12.00	6.00	1.20
☐ 6	Jim Ligon	3.00	1.50	.30
☐ 7	Cincy Powell	3.00	1.50	.30
☐ 8	Mike Pratt	3.00	1.50	.30
☐ 9	Walt Simon	3.00	1.50	.30
☐ 10	Sam Smith	3.00	1.50	.30
☐ 11	Howard Wright	3.00	1.50	.30

1989 Converse

This 14-card set was sponsored by Converse and measures the standard size (2 1/2" by 3 1/2"). The color action player photo on the front is outlined by a thin black border against a white background. At the top the words "Converse, Official Shoe of the NBA" is printed in blue lettering, as is the player's name and number below the picture. The NBA logo in the upper right corner rounds out the card face. The back presents brief biography, career highlights, and a tip from the player and Converse in the form of an anti-drug or alcohol message. The cards are unnumbered and checklisted below in alphabetical order. Mark Aguirre is misspelled Aquirre on the checklist card.

		MINT	EXC	G-VG
COMPLETE SET (14)		15.00	7.50	1.50
COMMON PLAYER (1-14)		.65	.30	.06
☐ 1	Mark Aguirre	.65	.30	.06
☐ 2	Larry Bird	5.00	2.50	.50
☐ 3	Rolando Blackman	.65	.30	.06
☐ 4	Tyrone Bogues	.65	.30	.06
☐ 5	Rex Chapman	1.00	.50	.10
☐ 6	Magic Johnson	5.00	2.50	.50
☐ 7	Bernard King	1.00	.50	.10
☐ 8	Bill Laimbeer	1.00	.50	.10
☐ 9	Karl Malone	2.00	1.00	.20
☐ 10	Kevin McHale	1.25	.60	.12
☐ 11	Mark Price	1.00	.50	.10
☐ 12	Jack Sikma	1.00	.50	.10
☐ 13	Reggie Theus	1.00	.50	.10
☐ 14	Title Card	.65	.30	.06
	(checklist back)			

1991 Courtside

The 1991 Courtside basketball set consists of 45 cards measuring the standard size (2 1/2" by 3 1/2"). All the 198,000 sets produced are numbered, and 30,000 autographed cards were randomly inserted in the 9,900 cases. The card front features a color action player photo. The player's name appears at the upper right corner of the card face, with the words "Courtside 1991" at the bottom.

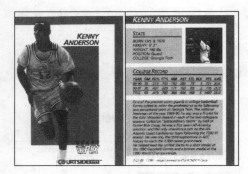

	MINT	EXC	G-VG
COMPLETE SET (45)	15.00	7.50	1.50
COMMON PLAYER (1-45)	.10	.05	.01

		MINT	EXC	G-VG
☐ 1	Larry Johnson First Draft Pick	1.75	.85	.17
☐ 2	George Ackles UNLV	.25	.12	.02
☐ 3	Kenny Anderson Georgia Tech	3.50	1.75	.35
☐ 4	Greg Anthony UNLV	1.00	.50	.10
☐ 5	Anthony Avent Seton Hall	.30	.15	.03
☐ 6	Terrell Brandon Oregon	.75	.35	.07
☐ 7	Kevin Brooks Southwestern Louisiana	.20	.10	.02
☐ 8	Marc Brown Siena	.10	.05	.01
☐ 9	Myron Brown Slippery Rock	.15	.07	.01
☐ 10	Randy Brown New Mexico State	.15	.07	.01
☐ 11	Darrin Chancellor Southern Mississippi	.10	.05	.01
☐ 12	Pete Chilcutt North Carolina	.25	.12	.02
☐ 13	Chris Corchiani N.C. State	.30	.15	.03
☐ 14	John Crotty Virginia	.10	.05	.01
☐ 15	Dale Davis Clemson	.40	.20	.04
☐ 16	Marty Dow San Diego State	.10	.05	.01
☐ 17	Richard Dumas Oklahoma State	.15	.07	.01
☐ 18	LeRon Ellis Syracuse	.20	.10	.02
☐ 19	Tony Farmer Nebraska	.10	.05	.01
☐ 20	Roy Fisher California	.10	.05	.01
☐ 21	Rick Fox North Carolina	.75	.35	.07
☐ 22	Chad Gallagher Creighton	.20	.10	.02
☐ 23	Chris Gatling Old Dominion	.30	.15	.03
☐ 24	Sean Green Iona	.15	.07	.01
☐ 25	Reggie Hanson Kentucky	.10	.05	.01
☐ 26	Donald Hodge Temple	.20	.10	.02
☐ 27	Steve Hood James Madison	.20	.10	.02
☐ 28	Keith Hughes Rutgers	.15	.07	.01
☐ 29	Mike Iuzzolino St.Francis	.20	.10	.02
☐ 30	Keith Jennings East Tenn. State	.20	.10	.02
☐ 31	Larry Johnson UNLV	3.50	1.75	.35
☐ 32	Treg Lee Ohio State	.10	.05	.01
☐ 33	Cedric Lewis Maryland	.15	.07	.01
☐ 34	Kevin Lynch Minnesota	.25	.12	.02
☐ 35	Mark Macon Temple	1.00	.50	.10
☐ 36	Jason Matthews Pittsburgh	.10	.05	.01
☐ 37	Eric Murdock Providence	.40	.20	.04
☐ 38	Jimmy Oliver Purdue	.15	.07	.01
☐ 39	Doug Overton La Salle	.20	.10	.02
☐ 40	Elliot Perry Memphis State	.20	.10	.02
☐ 41	Brian Shorter Pittsburgh	.20	.10	.02
☐ 42	Alvaro Teheran Houston	.20	.10	.02
☐ 43	Joey Wright Texas	.20	.10	.02
☐ 44	Joe Wylie Miami (FL)	.15	.07	.01
☐ 45	Larry Johnson Collegiate Player of the Year	1.75	.85	.17

1977-78 Dell Flipbooks

This set of flipbooks was produced by Pocket Money Basketball Co. These flipbooks measure approximately 4" by 3 1/8" and are 24 pages in length. They have color action player photos and career statistics. The booklets are unnumbered and are checklisted below in alphabetical order by subject. The front has a white stripe at the top, and a color head and shoulders shot of the player on a color background. The inside front cover has a table of contents, while the inside back cover has the logos of all 22 NBA teams. Each flipbook features a different play or move by the player; e.g., the Maravich flipbook is titled, "Pete The Pistol Maravich and his Fancy Dribble." When the odd-numbered pages are flipped in a smooth movement from front to back, they form a color "motion picture" of Maravich crossing over his dribble through his legs. The even-numbered pages present a variety of information on Maravich, his team (New Orleans Jazz), and the 1976-77 NBA season.

	NRMT	VG-E	GOOD
COMPLETE SET (6)	90.00	45.00	9.00
COMMON PLAYER (1-6)	10.00	5.00	1.00

		NRMT	VG-E	GOOD
☐ 1	Kareem Abdul-Jabbar	35.00	17.50	3.50
☐ 2	Dave Cowens	10.00	5.00	1.00
☐ 3	Julius Erving	20.00	10.00	2.00
☐ 4	Pete Maravich	15.00	7.50	1.50
☐ 5	David Thompson	10.00	5.00	1.00
☐ 6	Bill Walton	15.00	7.50	1.50

1948-49 Exhibits Sports Champions

This multi-sport 1948-49 Sports Champions Exhibits issue contains 49 cards. The cards measure 3 1/4" by 5 3/8". The cards are identifiable by a line of agate type below the facsimile autograph relating some information about the player's accomplishments. The cards, as with most exhibits, are blank backed. The catalog designation for this exhibit set is W469. The cards issued in 1949 are reportedly twice as difficult to find

as those issued in 1948. Cards issued only in 1949 are indicated with (49) in the checklist. Variations on Button and Scott exist in the agate line of type found on the bottom of the card.

	NRMT	VG-E	GOOD
COMPLETE SET (49)	1400.00	650.00	125.00
COMMON FOOTBALL	12.00	6.00	1.20
COMMON HOCKEY	15.00	7.50	1.50
COMMON BOXER	12.00	6.00	1.20
COMMON BASKETBALL	25.00	12.50	2.50
COMMON OTHER SPORTS	4.00	2.00	.40

☐ 1	Ted Allen horseshoes (49)	8.00	4.00	.80
☐ 2	Sammy Baugh football	50.00	25.00	5.00
☐ 3	Doug and Max Bentley hockey	30.00	15.00	3.00
☐ 4	Buddy Bomar bowling	4.00	2.00	.40
☐ 5A	Richard Button skating (white coat; signature in white)	12.00	6.00	1.20
☐ 5B	Richard Button skating (dark coat; signature in black)	12.00	6.00	1.20
☐ 6	Citation racehorse (49)	8.00	4.00	.80
☐ 7	John Cobb auto racing	15.00	7.50	1.50
☐ 8	Roy Conacher hockey (49)	30.00	15.00	3.00
☐ 9	Bob(Tarmac) Cook basketball	25.00	12.50	2.50
☐ 10	Ann Curtis swimming	4.00	2.00	.40
☐ 11	Ned Day (49)	8.00	4.00	.80
☐ 12	Jack Dempsey boxing	35.00	17.50	3.50
☐ 13	Harrison Dillard track (49)	12.00	6.00	1.20
☐ 14	Glenn Dobbs football (49)	30.00	15.00	3.00
☐ 15	Gil Dodds track	4.00	2.00	.40
☐ 16	Bill Durnan hockey	30.00	15.00	3.00
☐ 17	Chalmers(Bump) Elliott football	12.00	6.00	1.20
☐ 18	Joe Fulks basketball (49)	125.00	60.00	12.50
☐ 19	Edward Gauden track (49)	8.00	4.00	.80
☐ 20	Lucien Goudin fencing (49)	8.00	4.00	.80
☐ 21	Otto Graham football	35.00	17.50	3.50
☐ 22	Pat Harder football	15.00	7.50	1.50
☐ 23	Sonja Heine skating	6.00	3.00	.60
☐ 24	Ben Hogan golf (49)	30.00	15.00	3.00
☐ 25	Willie Hoppe billiards	4.00	2.00	.40
☐ 26	Jack Jacobs football	15.00	7.50	1.50
☐ 27	Jack Kramer tennis	8.00	4.00	.80
☐ 28	Gus Lewis handball (49)	8.00	4.00	.80
☐ 29	Guy Lombardo boat racing (49)	10.00	5.00	1.00
☐ 30	Joe Louis boxing	50.00	25.00	5.00
☐ 31	Sid Luckman football	35.00	17.50	3.50
☐ 32	Johnny Lujack football	30.00	15.00	3.00
☐ 33	Man of War racehorse	4.00	2.00	.40
☐ 34	Bob Mathias track (49)	20.00	10.00	2.00
☐ 35	Bob McDermott basketball	25.00	12.50	2.50
☐ 36	Gretchen Merrill skating	4.00	2.00	.40
☐ 37	George Mikan basketball	300.00	150.00	30.00
☐ 38	Dick Miles table tennis	4.00	2.00	.40
☐ 39	Marion Motley football (49)	40.00	20.00	4.00
☐ 40	Andy Phillip basketball (49)	90.00	45.00	9.00
☐ 41	Bobby Riggs tennis	8.00	4.00	.80
☐ 42A	Barbara Ann Scott skating (looking to side; signature in white)	6.00	3.00	.60
☐ 42A	Barbara Ann Scott skating (looking straight; signature in black)	6.00	3.00	.60
☐ 43	Ben Sklar marbles	4.00	2.00	.40
☐ 44	Clyde(Bulldog) Turner football	20.00	10.00	2.00
☐ 45	Steve Van Buren football	25.00	12.50	2.50
☐ 46	Andy Veripapa bowling	8.00	4.00	.80
☐ 47	Bob Waterfield football (49)	40.00	20.00	4.00
☐ 48	Murray Weir basketball (49)	90.00	45.00	9.00
☐ 49	Claude(Buddy) Young (hands on knees) football	12.00	6.00	1.20

1961-62 Fleer

The 1961 Fleer set was Fleer's only major basketball issue until the 1986-87 season. The cards in the set measure the standard, 2 1/2" by 3 1/2". Cards numbered 45 to 66 are action poses (designated IA) of players elsewhere in the set. No known scarcities exist, although the set is quite popular since it contains the first basketball cards of many of the game's all-time greats, e.g., Elgin Baylor, Wilt Chamberlain, Oscar Robertson, and Jerry West.

	NRMT	VG-E	GOOD
COMPLETE SET (66)	4250.00	2100.00	450.00
COMMON PLAYER (1-44)	14.00	7.00	1.40
COMMON PLAYER IA (45-66)	10.00	5.00	1.00
☐ 1 Al Attles Philadelphia Warriors	50.00	10.00	2.00
☐ 2 Paul Arizin Philadelphia Warriors	21.00	10.50	2.10
☐ 3 Elgin Baylor Los Angeles Lakers	250.00	125.00	25.00
☐ 4 Walt Bellamy Chicago Packers	21.00	10.50	2.10
☐ 5 Arlen Bockhorn Cincinnati Royals	14.00	7.00	1.40
☐ 6 Bob Boozer Cincinnati Royals	17.00	8.50	1.70
☐ 7 Carl Braun Boston Celtics	17.00	8.50	1.70
☐ 8 Wilt Chamberlain Philadelphia Warriors	1200.00	400.00	100.00
☐ 9 Larry Costello Syracuse Nationals	17.00	8.50	1.70
☐ 10 Bob Cousy Boston Celtics	100.00	50.00	10.00
☐ 11 Walter Dukes Detroit Pistons	14.00	7.00	1.40
☐ 12 Wayne Embrey Cincinnati Royals	21.00	10.50	2.10
☐ 13 Dave Gambee Syracuse Nationals	14.00	7.00	1.40
☐ 14 Tom Gola Philadelphia Warriors	21.00	10.50	2.10
☐ 15 Sihugo Green St. Louis Hawks	17.00	8.50	1.70
☐ 16 Hal Greer Syracuse Nationals	36.00	18.00	3.60
☐ 17 Richie Guerin New York Knicks	21.00	10.50	2.10
☐ 18 Cliff Hagan St. Louis Hawks	25.00	12.50	2.50
☐ 19 Tom Heinsohn Boston Celtics	40.00	20.00	4.00
☐ 20 Bailey Howell Detroit Pistons	21.00	10.50	2.10
☐ 21 Rod Hundley Los Angeles Lakers	17.00	8.50	1.70
☐ 22 K.C. Jones Boston Celtics	50.00	25.00	5.00
☐ 23 Sam Jones Boston Celtics	50.00	25.00	5.00
☐ 24 Phil Jordan New York Knicks	14.00	7.00	1.40
☐ 25 John Kerr Syracuse Nationals	17.00	8.50	1.70
☐ 26 Rudy LaRusso Los Angeles Lakers	17.00	8.50	1.70
☐ 27 George Lee Detroit Pistons	14.00	7.00	1.40
☐ 28 Bob Leonard Chicago Packers	14.00	7.00	1.40
☐ 29 Clyde Lovellette St. Louis Hawks	21.00	10.50	2.10
☐ 30 John McCarthy St. Louis Hawks	14.00	7.00	1.40
☐ 31 Tom Meschery Philadelphia Warriors	17.00	8.50	1.70
☐ 32 Willie Naulls New York Knicks	14.00	7.00	1.40
☐ 33 Don Ohl Detroit Pistons	17.00	8.50	1.70
☐ 34 Bob Pettit St. Louis Hawks	50.00	25.00	5.00
☐ 35 Frank Ramsey Boston Celtics	21.00	10.50	2.10
☐ 36 Oscar Robertson Cincinnati Royals	425.00	175.00	40.00
☐ 37 Guy Rodgers Philadelphia Warriors	17.00	8.50	1.70
☐ 38 Bill Russell Boston Celtics	425.00	175.00	40.00
☐ 39 Dolph Schayes Syracuse Nationals	25.00	12.50	2.50
☐ 40 Frank Selvy Los Angeles Lakers	14.00	7.00	1.40
☐ 41 Gene Shue Detroit Pistons	17.00	8.50	1.70
☐ 42 Jack Twyman Cincinnati Royals	21.00	10.50	2.10
☐ 43 Jerry West Los Angeles Lakers	600.00	300.00	60.00
☐ 44 Len Wilkens St. Louis Hawks	45.00	22.50	4.50
☐ 45 Paul Arizin IA Philadelphia Warriors	14.00	7.00	1.40
☐ 46 Elgin Baylor IA Los Angeles Lakers	90.00	45.00	9.00
☐ 47 Wilt Chamberlain IA Philadelphia Warriors	250.00	125.00	25.00
☐ 48 Larry Costello IA Syracuse Nationals	12.00	6.00	1.20
☐ 49 Bob Cousy IA Boston Celtics	35.00	17.50	3.50
☐ 50 Walter Dukes IA Detroit Pistons	10.00	5.00	1.00
☐ 51 Tom Gola IA Philadelphia Warriors	12.00	6.00	1.20
☐ 52 Richie Guerin IA New York Knicks	10.00	5.00	1.00
☐ 53 Cliff Hagan IA St. Louis Hawks	17.00	8.50	1.70
☐ 54 Tom Heinsohn IA Boston Celtics	21.00	10.50	2.10
☐ 55 Bailey Howell IA Detroit Pistons	12.00	6.00	1.20
☐ 56 John Kerr IA Syracuse Nationals	10.00	5.00	1.00
☐ 57 Rudy LaRusso IA Los Angeles Lakers	10.00	5.00	1.00
☐ 58 Clyde Lovellette IA St. Louis Hawks	14.00	7.00	1.40
☐ 59 Bob Pettit IA St. Louis Hawks	25.00	12.50	2.50
☐ 60 Frank Ramsey IA Boston Celtics	14.00	7.00	1.40
☐ 61 Oscar Robertson IA Cincinnati Royals	125.00	60.00	12.50
☐ 62 Bill Russell IA Boston Celtics	165.00	75.00	15.00
☐ 63 Dolph Schayes IA Syracuse Nationals	17.00	8.50	1.70
☐ 64 Gene Shue IA Detroit Pistons	10.00	5.00	1.00
☐ 65 Jack Twyman IA Cincinnati Royals	14.00	7.00	1.40
☐ 66 Jerry West IA Los Angeles Lakers	200.00	100.00	20.00

1974 Fleer "The Shots"

This 21-card set was produced by artist R.G. Laughlin for Fleer. The cards measure approximately 2 1/2" by 4". The front features an illustration of the shot depicted on the card. The illustration is in color, although crudely drawn. The back has a discussion of the shot. The cards are numbered on the back.

	NRMT	VG-E	GOOD
COMPLETE SET (21)	30.00	15.00	3.00
COMMON PLAYER (1-21)	2.00	1.00	.20
☐ 1 Two-Hand Set	3.00	1.50	.30
☐ 2 Overhead Set	2.00	1.00	.20
☐ 3 One-Hand Set	2.00	1.00	.20
☐ 4 Two-Hand Jumper	2.00	1.00	.20
☐ 5 One-Hand Jumper	2.00	1.00	.20
☐ 6 Twisting Jumper	2.00	1.00	.20
☐ 7 Hook Shot	2.00	1.00	.20
☐ 8 Driving Hook	2.00	1.00	.20

		MINT	EXC	G-VG
☐ 9	Layup	2.00	1.00	.20
☐ 10	Reverse Layup	2.00	1.00	.20
☐ 11	Underhand Layup	2.00	1.00	.20
☐ 12	Pivot Shots	2.00	1.00	.20
☐ 13	Step-Away	2.00	1.00	.20
☐ 14	Running One-Hander	2.00	1.00	.20
☐ 15	Stuff or Dunk	2.00	1.00	.20
☐ 16	Tap-In	2.00	1.00	.20
☐ 17	Bank Shot	2.00	1.00	.20
☐ 18	Free Throw	2.00	1.00	.20
☐ 19	Desperation Shot	2.00	1.00	.20
☐ 20	Blocked Shot	2.00	1.00	.20
☐ 21	The "Good" Shot	3.00	1.50	.30

1986-87 Fleer

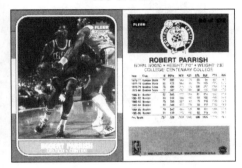

ROBERT PARRISH
BORN: 5/00/53 • HEIGHT: 7'0" • WEIGHT: 230
COLLEGE CENTENARY COLLEGE

This set of 132 cards features prominent players in the NBA. Cards measure the standard 2 1/2" by 3 1/2". The photo on the front is inside in red, white, and blue frame. A Fleer "Premier" logo is pictured in the upper corner of the obverse. The card backs are printed in red and blue on white card stock. The card numbers correspond to the alphabetical order of the player's names. Each retail wax pack contained 12 player cards, a piece of gum, and an insert sticker card. Several cards have special "Traded" notations on them if the player was traded after his picture was selected. Since only the Star Company had been issuing basketball cards nationally since 1983, most of the players in this Fleer set already had cards which are considered XRC's, extended rookie cards. However, since this Fleer set was the first nationally available set in packs since the 1981-82 Topps issue, most of the players in the set could be considered rookie cards. Therefore, the key rookie cards in this set, who had already had cards in previous Star sets are Charles Barkley, Clyde Drexler, Patrick Ewing, Michael Jordan, Akeem Olajuwon, and Dominique Wilkins. The key rookie cards in this set, who had not previously appeared on cards, are Karl Malone and Chris Mullin.

		MINT	EXC	G-VG
	COMPLETE SET (132)	650.00	325.00	65.00
	COMMON PLAYER (1-132)	.70	.35	.07
☐ 1	Kareem Abdul Jabbar	15.00	5.00	1.00
	Los Angeles Lakers			
☐ 2	Alvan Adams	.70	.35	.07
	Phoenix Suns			
☐ 3	Mark Aguirre	2.75	1.35	.27
	Dallas Mavericks			
☐ 4	Danny Ainge	4.50	2.25	.45
	Boston Celtics			
☐ 5	John Bagley	.90	.45	.09
	Cleveland Cavaliers			
☐ 6	Thurl Bailey	1.25	.60	.12
	Utah Jazz			
☐ 7	Charles Barkley	60.00	30.00	6.00
	Philadelphia 76ers			
☐ 8	Benoit Benjamin	3.00	1.50	.30
	Los Angeles Clippers			
☐ 9	Larry Bird	16.00	8.00	1.60
	Boston Celtics			
☐ 10	Otis Birdsong	.70	.35	.07
	New Jersey Nets			
☐ 11	Rolando Blackman	4.50	2.25	.45
	Dallas Mavericks			
☐ 12	Manute Bol	3.50	1.75	.35
	Washington Bullets			
☐ 13	Sam Bowie	1.25	.60	.12
	Portland Trail Blazers			
☐ 14	Joe Barry Carroll	.70	.35	.07
	Golden State Warriors			
☐ 15	Tom Chambers	18.00	9.00	1.80
	Seattle Supersonics			
☐ 16	Maurice Cheeks	1.10	.55	.11
	Philadelphia 76ers			
☐ 17	Michael Cooper	1.10	.55	.11
	Los Angeles Lakers			
☐ 18	Wayne Cooper	.70	.35	.07
	Denver Nuggets			
☐ 19	Pat Cummings	.70	.35	.07
	New York Knicks			
☐ 20	Terry Cummings	9.00	4.50	.90
	Milwaukee Bucks			
☐ 21	Adrian Dantley	1.00	.50	.10
	Utah Jazz			
☐ 22	Brad Davis	.70	.35	.07
	Dallas Mavericks			
☐ 23	Walter Davis	1.00	.50	.10
	Phoenix Suns			
☐ 24	Darryl Dawkins	.90	.45	.09
	New Jersey Nets			
☐ 25	Larry Drew	.90	.45	.09
	Sacramento Kings			
☐ 26	Clyde Drexler	36.00	18.00	3.60
	Portland Trail Blazers			
☐ 27	Joe Dumars	24.00	12.00	2.40
	Detroit Pistons			
☐ 28	Mark Eaton	1.25	.60	.12
	Utah Jazz			
☐ 29	James Edwards	.90	.45	.09
	Phoenix Suns			
☐ 30	Alex English	1.25	.60	.12
	Denver Nuggets			
☐ 31	Julius Erving	11.00	5.50	1.10
	Philadelphia 76ers			
☐ 32	Patrick Ewing	75.00	37.50	7.50
	New York Knicks			
☐ 33	Vern Fleming	1.25	.60	.12
	Indiana Pacers			
☐ 34	Sleepy Floyd	1.75	.85	.17
	Golden State Warriors			
☐ 35	World B. Free	.90	.45	.09
	Cleveland Cavaliers			
☐ 36	George Gervin	1.25	.60	.12
	Chicago Bulls			
☐ 37	Artis Gilmore	1.00	.50	.10
	San Antonio Spurs			
☐ 38	Mike Gminski	.90	.45	.09
	New Jersey Nets			
☐ 39	Rickey Green	.90	.45	.09
	Utah Jazz			
☐ 40	Sidney Green	.70	.35	.07
	Chicago Bulls			
☐ 41	David Greenwood	.70	.35	.07
	San Antonio Spurs			
☐ 42	Darrell Griffith	.90	.45	.09
	Utah Jazz			
☐ 43	Bill Hanzlik	.70	.35	.07
	Denver Nuggets			
☐ 44	Derek Harper	3.25	1.60	.32
	Dallas Mavericks			
☐ 45	Gerald Henderson	.70	.35	.07
	Seattle Supersonics			
☐ 46	Roy Hinson	1.00	.50	.10
	Philadelphia 76ers			
☐ 47	Craig Hodges	1.75	.85	.17
	Milwaukee Bucks			
☐ 48	Phil Hubbard	.70	.35	.07
	Cleveland Cavaliers			
☐ 49	Jay Humphries	1.00	.50	.10
	Phoenix Suns			
☐ 50	Dennis Johnson	1.00	.50	.10
	Boston Celtics			
☐ 51	Eddie Johnson	2.50	1.25	.25
	Sacramento Kings			
☐ 52	Frank Johnson	.70	.35	.07
	Washington Bullets			
☐ 53	Magic Johnson	16.00	8.00	1.60
	Los Angeles Lakers			
☐ 54	Marques Johnson	.90	.45	.09
	Los Angeles Clippers			
	(Decimal point missing, rookie year scoring avg.)			
☐ 55	Steve Johnson UER	1.00	.50	.10
	San Antonio Spurs			
	(photo actually David Greenwood)			

☐ 56 Vinnie Johnson Detroit Pistons	1.00	.50	.10
☐ 57 Michael Jordan Chicago Bulls	330.00	150.00	30.00
☐ 58 Clark Kellogg Indiana Pacers	.90	.45	.09
☐ 59 Albert King New Jersey Nets	.70	.35	.07
☐ 60 Bernard King New York Knicks	3.00	1.50	.30
☐ 61 Bill Laimbeer Detroit Pistons	1.10	.55	.11
☐ 62 Allen Leavell Houston Rockets	.70	.35	.07
☐ 63 Lafayette Lever Denver Nuggets	2.75	1.35	.27
☐ 64 Alton Lister Seattle Supersonics	.90	.45	.09
☐ 65 Lewis Lloyd Houston Rockets	.70	.35	.07
☐ 66 Maurice Lucas Los Angeles Lakers	.90	.45	.09
☐ 67 Jeff Malone Washington Bullets	5.00	2.50	.50
☐ 68 Karl Malone Utah Jazz	55.00	27.50	5.50
☐ 69 Moses Malone Washington Bullets	2.75	1.35	.27
☐ 70 Cedric Maxwell Los Angeles Clippers	.90	.45	.09
☐ 71 Rodney McCray Houston Rockets	1.25	.60	.12
☐ 72 Xavier McDaniel Seattle Supersonics	9.00	4.50	.90
☐ 73 Kevin McHale Boston Celtics	3.00	1.50	.30
☐ 74 Mike Mitchell San Antonio Spurs	.70	.35	.07
☐ 75 Sidney Moncrief Milwaukee Bucks	1.00	.50	.10
☐ 76 Johnny Moore San Antonio Spurs	.70	.35	.07
☐ 77 Chris Mullin Golden State Warriors	24.00	12.00	2.40
☐ 78 Larry Nance Phoenix Suns	3.00	1.50	.30
☐ 79 Calvin Natt Denver Nuggets	.90	.45	.09
☐ 80 Norm Nixon Los Angeles Clippers	.90	.45	.09
☐ 81 Charles Oakley Chicago Bulls	4.00	2.00	.40
☐ 82 Akeem Olajuwon Houston Rockets	55.00	27.50	5.50
☐ 83 Louis Orr New York Knicks	.70	.35	.07
☐ 84 Robert Parish Boston Celtics	2.50	1.25	.25
☐ 85 Jim Paxson Portland Trail Blazers	.70	.35	.07
☐ 86 Sam Perkins Dallas Mavericks	6.00	3.00	.60
☐ 87 Ricky Pierce Milwaukee Bucks	4.00	2.00	.40
☐ 88 Paul Pressey Milwaukee Bucks	1.50	.75	.15
☐ 89 Kurt Rambis Los Angeles Lakers	1.25	.60	.12
☐ 90 Robert Reid Houston Rockets	.70	.35	.07
☐ 91 Doc Rivers Atlanta Hawks	2.50	1.25	.25
☐ 92 Alvin Robertson San Antonio Spurs	4.00	2.00	.40
☐ 93 Cliff Robinson Philadelphia 76ers	.70	.35	.07
☐ 94 Tree Rollins Atlanta Hawks	.90	.45	.09
☐ 95 Dan Roundfield Washington Bullets	.70	.35	.07
☐ 96 Jeff Ruland Philadelphia 76ers	.90	.45	.09
☐ 97 Ralph Sampson Houston Rockets	2.25	1.10	.22
☐ 98 Danny Schayes Denver Nuggets	1.25	.60	.12
☐ 99 Byron Scott Los Angeles Lakers	4.50	2.25	.45
☐ 100 Purvis Short Golden State Warriors	.90	.45	.09
☐ 101 Jerry Sichting Boston Celtics	.70	.35	.07
☐ 102 Jack Sikma Milwaukee Bucks	1.00	.50	.10
☐ 103 Derek Smith Los Angeles Clippers	1.00	.50	.10
☐ 104 Larry Smith Golden State Warriors	.90	.45	.09
☐ 105 Rory Sparrow New York Knicks	.70	.35	.07
☐ 106 Steve Stipanovich Indiana Pacers	.90	.45	.09
☐ 107 Terry Teagle Golden State Warriors	1.25	.60	.12
☐ 108 Reggie Theus Sacramento Kings	.90	.45	.09
☐ 109 Isiah Thomas Detroit Pistons	33.00	15.00	3.00
☐ 110 LaSalle Thompson Sacramento Kings	1.00	.50	.10
☐ 111 Mychal Thompson Portland Trail Blazers	.90	.45	.09
☐ 112 Sedale Threatt Philadelphia 76ers	.90	.45	.09
☐ 113 Waymon Tisdale Indiana Pacers	4.50	2.25	.45
☐ 114 Andrew Toney Philadelphia 76ers	.70	.35	.07
☐ 115 Kelly Tripucka Detroit Pistons	1.00	.50	.10
☐ 116 Mel Turpin Cleveland Cavaliers	.70	.35	.07
☐ 117 Kiki Vandeweghe Portland Trail Blazers	1.75	.85	.17
☐ 118 Jay Vincent Dallas Mavericks	.70	.35	.07
☐ 119 Bill Walton Boston Celtics (Missing decimal points on four lines of FG Percentage)	2.00	1.00	.20
☐ 120 Spud Webb Atlanta Hawks	6.00	3.00	.60
☐ 121 Dominique Wilkins Atlanta Hawks	30.00	15.00	3.00
☐ 122 Gerald Wilkins New York Knicks	3.50	1.75	.35
☐ 123 Buck Williams New Jersey Nets	6.50	3.25	.65
☐ 124 Gus Williams Washington Bullets	.90	.45	.09
☐ 125 Herb Williams Indiana Pacers	1.25	.60	.12
☐ 126 Kevin Willis Atlanta Hawks	1.25	.60	.12
☐ 127 Randy Wittman Atlanta Hawks	.70	.35	.07
☐ 128 Al Wood Seattle Supersonics	.70	.35	.07
☐ 129 Mike Woodson Sacramento Kings	.70	.35	.07
☐ 130 Orlando Woolridge Chicago Bulls	3.00	1.50	.30
☐ 131 James Worthy Los Angeles Lakers	22.00	11.00	2.20
☐ 132 Checklist 1-132	1.00	.35	.07

1986-87 Fleer Sticker Inserts

This set of 11 stickers was inserted in the wax packs with the Fleer regular 132-card issue. The stickers are 2 1/2" by 3 1/2". The backs of the sticker cards are printed in blue and red on white card stock.

	MINT	EXC	G-VG
COMPLETE SET (11)	60.00	30.00	6.00
COMMON PLAYER (1-11)	.45	.22	.04
☐ 1 Kareem Abdul Jabbar Los Angeles Lakers	5.00	2.50	.50
☐ 2 Larry Bird Boston Celtics	5.00	2.50	.50
☐ 3 Adrian Dantley Utah Jazz	.45	.22	.04
☐ 4 Alex English Denver Nuggets	.65	.30	.06
☐ 5 Julius Erving Philadelphia 76ers	4.50	2.25	.45
☐ 6 Patrick Ewing New York Knicks	10.00	5.00	1.00
☐ 7 Magic Johnson Los Angeles Lakers	5.00	2.50	.50

Michael Jordan

		MINT	EXC	G-VG
☐ 8	Michael Jordan	40.00	20.00	4.00
	Chicago Bulls			
☐ 9	Akeem Olajuwon	6.00	3.00	.60
	Houston Rockets			
☐ 10	Isiah Thomas	4.50	2.25	.45
	Detroit Pistons			
☐ 11	Dominique Wilkins	4.50	2.25	.45
	Atlanta Hawks			

1987-88 Fleer

BILL LAIMBEER

The 1987-88 Fleer basketball set contains 132 standard size (2 1/2" by 3 1/2") cards featuring 131 of the NBA's better-known players, plus a checklist. The fronts are white with gray horizontal stripes. The backs are red, white, and blue and show each player's complete NBA statistics. The cards are numbered essentially in alphabetical order. This set was issued in wax packs, each containing 12 cards. The key rookie cards in this set are Brad Daugherty, A.C. Green, Ron Harper, Chuck Person, Terry Porter, Detlef Schrempf, and Hot Rod Williams.

		MINT	EXC	G-VG
COMPLETE SET (132)		240.00	100.00	20.00
COMMON PLAYER (1-132)		.35	.17	.03
☐ 1	Kareem Abdul Jabbar	10.00	2.50	.50
	Los Angeles Lakers			
☐ 2	Alvan Adams	.35	.17	.03
	Phoenix Suns			
☐ 3	Mark Aguirre	.75	.35	.07
	Dallas Mavericks			
☐ 4	Danny Ainge	1.00	.50	.10
	Boston Celtics			
☐ 5	John Bagley	.35	.17	.03
	Cleveland Cavaliers			
☐ 6	Thurl Bailey UER	.45	.22	.04
	Utah Jazz			
	(reverse negative)			
☐ 7	Greg Ballard	.35	.17	.03
	Golden State Warriors			
☐ 8	Gene Banks	.35	.17	.03
	Chicago Bulls			

		MINT	EXC	G-VG
☐ 9	Charles Barkley	15.00	7.50	1.50
	Philadelphia 76ers			
☐ 10	Benoit Benjamin	.75	.35	.07
	Los Angeles Clippers			
☐ 11	Larry Bird	11.00	5.50	1.10
	Boston Celtics			
☐ 12	Rolando Blackman	1.00	.50	.10
	Dallas Mavericks			
☐ 13	Manute Bol	.75	.35	.07
	Washington Bullets			
☐ 14	Tony Brown	.35	.17	.03
	New Jersey Nets			
☐ 15	Michael Cage	.60	.30	.06
	Los Angeles Clippers			
☐ 16	Joe Barry Carroll	.35	.17	.03
	Golden State Warriors			
☐ 17	Bill Cartwright	.50	.25	.05
	New York Knicks			
☐ 18	Terry Catledge	1.50	.75	.15
	Washington Bullets			
☐ 19	Tom Chambers	5.00	2.50	.50
	Seattle Supersonics			
☐ 20	Maurice Cheeks	.45	.22	.04
	Philadelphia 76ers			
☐ 21	Michael Cooper	.45	.22	.04
	Los Angeles Lakers			
☐ 22	Dave Corzine	.35	.17	.03
	Chicago Bulls			
☐ 23	Terry Cummings	1.25	.60	.12
	Milwaukee Bucks			
☐ 24	Adrian Dantley	.60	.30	.06
	Detroit Pistons			
☐ 25	Brad Daugherty	9.00	4.50	.90
	Cleveland Cavaliers			
☐ 26	Walter Davis	.45	.22	.04
	Phoenix Suns			
☐ 27	Johnny Dawkins	2.25	1.10	.22
	San Antonio Spurs			
☐ 28	James Donaldson	.60	.30	.06
	Dallas Mavericks			
☐ 29	Larry Drew	.35	.17	.03
	Los Angeles Clippers			
☐ 30	Clyde Drexler	10.00	5.00	1.00
	Portland Trail Blazers			
☐ 31	Joe Dumars	6.50	3.25	.65
	Detroit Pistons			
☐ 32	Mark Eaton	.45	.22	.04
	Utah Jazz			
☐ 33	Dale Ellis	3.00	1.50	.30
	Seattle Supersonics			
☐ 34	Alex English	.75	.35	.07
	Denver Nuggets			
☐ 35	Julius Erving	8.00	4.00	.80
	Philadelphia 76ers			
☐ 36	Mike Evans	.35	.17	.03
	Denver Nuggets			
☐ 37	Patrick Ewing	22.00	11.00	2.20
	New York Knicks			
☐ 38	Vern Fleming	.45	.22	.04
	Indiana Pacers			
☐ 39	Sleepy Floyd	.60	.30	.06
	Golden State Warriors			
☐ 40	Artis Gilmore	.45	.22	.04
	San Antonio Spurs			
☐ 41	Mike Gminski UER	.45	.22	.04
	New Jersey Nets			
	(reversed negative)			
☐ 42	A.C. Green	4.00	2.00	.40
	Los Angeles Lakers			
☐ 43	Rickey Green	.35	.17	.03
	Utah Jazz			
☐ 44	Sidney Green	.35	.17	.03
	Detroit Pistons			
☐ 45	David Greenwood	.35	.17	.03
	San Antonio Spurs			
☐ 46	Darrell Griffith	.45	.22	.04
	Utah Jazz			
☐ 47	Bill Hanzlik	.35	.17	.03
	Denver Nuggets			
☐ 48	Derek Harper	.75	.35	.07
	Dallas Mavericks			
☐ 49	Ron Harper	4.50	2.25	.45
	Cleveland Cavaliers			
☐ 50	Gerald Henderson	.35	.17	.03
	New York Knicks			
☐ 51	Roy Hinson	.35	.17	.03
	Philadelphia 76ers			
☐ 52	Craig Hodges	.50	.25	.05
	Milwaukee Bucks			
☐ 53	Phil Hubbard	.35	.17	.03
	Cleveland Cavaliers			
☐ 54	Dennis Johnson	.50	.25	.05
	Boston Celtics			
☐ 55	Eddie Johnson	.50	.25	.05
	Sacramento Kings			

☐ 56	Magic Johnson Los Angeles Lakers	11.00	5.50	1.10
☐ 57	Steve Johnson Portland Trail Blazers	.35	.17	.03
☐ 58	Vinnie Johnson Detroit Pistons	.75	.35	.07
☐ 59	Michael Jordan Chicago Bulls	100.00	50.00	10.00
☐ 60	Jerome Kersey Portland Trail Blazers	8.00	4.00	.80
☐ 61	Bill Laimbeer Detroit Pistons	.90	.45	.09
☐ 62	Lafayette Lever UER Denver Nuggets (Photo actually Otis Smith)	.45	.22	.04
☐ 63	Cliff Levingston Atlanta Hawks	1.00	.50	.10
☐ 64	Alton Lister Seattle Supersonics	.35	.17	.03
☐ 65	John Long Indiana Pacers	.35	.17	.03
☐ 66	John Lucas Milwaukee Bucks	.35	.17	.03
☐ 67	Jeff Malone Washington Bullets	1.25	.60	.12
☐ 68	Karl Malone Utah Jazz	15.00	7.50	1.50
☐ 69	Moses Malone Washington Bullets	1.50	.75	.15
☐ 70	Cedric Maxwell Houston Rockets	.45	.22	.04
☐ 71	Tim McCormick Philadelphia 76ers	.35	.17	.03
☐ 72	Rodney McCray Houston Rockets	.45	.22	.04
☐ 73	Xavier McDaniel Seattle Supersonics	1.75	.85	.17
☐ 74	Kevin McHale Boston Celtics	1.75	.85	.17
☐ 75	Nate McMillan Seattle Supersonics	.75	.35	.07
☐ 76	Sidney Moncrief Milwaukee Bucks	.50	.25	.05
☐ 77	Chris Mullin Golden State Warriors	6.50	3.25	.65
☐ 78	Larry Nance Phoenix Suns	.60	.30	.06
☐ 79	Charles Oakley Chicago Bulls	.60	.30	.06
☐ 80	Akeem Olajuwon Houston Rockets	15.00	7.50	1.50
☐ 81	Robert Parish Boston Celtics (Misspelled Parrish on both sides)	1.50	.75	.15
☐ 82	Jim Paxson Portland Trail Blazers	.35	.17	.03
☐ 83	John Paxson Chicago Bulls	3.50	1.75	.35
☐ 84	Sam Perkins Dallas Mavericks	1.25	.60	.12
☐ 85	Chuck Person Indiana Pacers	6.00	3.00	.60
☐ 86	Jim Peterson Houston Rockets	.45	.22	.04
☐ 87	Ricky Pierce Milwaukee Bucks	.75	.35	.07
☐ 88	Ed Pinckney Phoenix Suns	1.00	.50	.10
☐ 89	Terry Porter Portland Trail Blazers (College Wisconsin, should be Wisconsin - Stevens Point)	12.00	6.00	1.20
☐ 90	Paul Pressey Milwaukee Bucks	.45	.22	.04
☐ 91	Robert Reid Houston Rockets	.35	.17	.03
☐ 92	Doc Rivers Atlanta Hawks	.60	.30	.06
☐ 93	Alvin Robertson San Antonio Spurs	.60	.30	.06
☐ 94	Tree Rollins Atlanta Hawks	.45	.22	.04
☐ 95	Ralph Sampson Houston Rockets	.45	.22	.04
☐ 96	Mike Sanders Phoenix Suns	.35	.17	.03
☐ 97	Detlef Schrempf Dallas Mavericks	4.00	2.00	.40
☐ 98	Byron Scott Los Angeles Lakers	1.00	.50	.10
☐ 99	Jerry Sichting Boston Celtics	.35	.17	.03
☐ 100	Jack Sikma Milwaukee Bucks	.50	.25	.05
☐ 101	Larry Smith Golden State Warriors	.45	.22	.04
☐ 102	Rory Sparrow New York Knicks	.35	.17	.03
☐ 103	Steve Stipanovich Indiana Pacers	.45	.22	.04
☐ 104	Jon Sundvold San Antonio Spurs	.45	.22	.04
☐ 105	Reggie Theus Sacramento Kings	.50	.25	.05
☐ 106	Isiah Thomas Detroit Pistons	8.50	4.25	.85
☐ 107	LaSalle Thompson Sacramento Kings	.45	.22	.04
☐ 108	Mychal Thompson Los Angeles Lakers	.45	.22	.04
☐ 109	Otis Thorpe Sacramento Kings	4.25	2.10	.42
☐ 110	Sedale Threatt Chicago Bulls	.45	.22	.04
☐ 111	Waymon Tisdale Indiana Pacers	.75	.35	.07
☐ 112	Kelly Tripucka Utah Jazz	.45	.22	.04
☐ 113	Trent Tucker New York Knicks	.45	.22	.04
☐ 114	Terry Tyler Sacramento Kings	.35	.17	.03
☐ 115	Darnell Valentine Los Angeles Clippers	.35	.17	.03
☐ 116	Kiki Vandeweghe Portland Trail Blazers	.45	.22	.04
☐ 117	Darrell Walker Denver Nuggets	.45	.22	.04
☐ 118	Dominique Wilkins Atlanta Hawks	8.50	4.25	.85
☐ 119	Gerald Wilkins New York Knicks	.60	.30	.06
☐ 120	Buck Williams New Jersey Nets	1.50	.75	.15
☐ 121	Herb Williams Indiana Pacers	.45	.22	.04
☐ 122	John Williams Washington Bullets	1.25	.60	.12
☐ 123	John Williams Cleveland Cavaliers	3.25	1.60	.32
☐ 124	Kevin Willis Atlanta Hawks	.45	.22	.04
☐ 125	David Wingate Philadelphia 76ers	.45	.22	.04
☐ 126	Randy Wittman Atlanta Hawks	.35	.17	.03
☐ 127	Leon Wood New Jersey Nets	.35	.17	.03
☐ 128	Mike Woodson Los Angeles Clippers	.35	.17	.03
☐ 129	Orlando Woolridge New Jersey Nets	.60	.30	.06
☐ 130	James Worthy Los Angeles Lakers	5.00	2.50	.50
☐ 131	Danny Young Seattle Supersonics	.45	.22	.04
☐ 132	Checklist Card	.60	.20	.04

1987-88 Fleer Sticker Inserts

The 1987-88 Fleer Glossy Insert Stickers set is an 11-card standard size (2 1/2" by 3 1/2") bonus set issued as an insert with the regular 132-card set. The fronts are red, white, blue, and yellow. The backs are white and blue, and contain career highlights. One sticker was included in each wax pack. Featured are 11 NBA superstars. Virtually all cards from this set have wax-stained backs as a result of the packaging.

		MINT	EXC	G-VG
	COMPLETE SET (11)	25.00	12.50	2.50
	COMMON PLAYER (1-11)	.35	.17	.03
☐ 1	Magic Johnson Los Angeles Lakers	3.00	1.50	.30
☐ 2	Michael Jordan Chicago Bulls (In text, votes mis- spelled as voites)	17.00	8.50	1.70

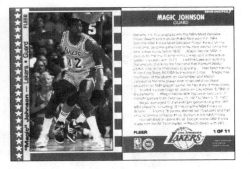

☐ 3 Akeem Olajuwon UER	3.00	1.50	.30
Houston Rockets			
(Misspelled Olajuwan			
on card back)			
☐ 4 Larry Bird	3.00	1.50	.30
Boston Celtics			
☐ 5 Kevin McHale	.65	.30	.06
Boston Celtics			
☐ 6 Charles Barkley	3.00	1.50	.30
Philadelphia 76ers			
☐ 7 Dominique Wilkins	2.00	1.00	.20
Atlanta Hawks			
☐ 8 Kareem Abdul Jabbar	3.00	1.50	.30
Los Angeles Lakers			
☐ 9 Mark Aguirre	.35	.17	.03
Dallas Mavericks			
☐ 10 Chuck Person	1.25	.60	.12
Indiana Pacers			
☐ 11 Alex English	.35	.17	.03
Denver Nuggets			

1988-89 Fleer

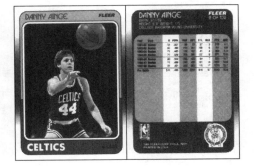

The 1988-89 Fleer basketball set contains 132 standard size (2 1/2" by 3 1/2") cards. There are 119 regular cards, plus 12 All-Star cards and a checklist. The outer borders are white and gray, while the inner borders correspond to the team colors. The backs are greenish, and show full NBA statistics with limited biographical information. The set is ordered alphabetically in team subsets (with a few exceptions due to late trades). The teams themselves are also presented in alphabetical order, Atlanta Hawks (1-6, 98, and 118), Boston Celtics (8-12), Charlotte Hornets (13-14), Chicago Bulls (15-17 and 19-21), Cleveland Cavaliers (22-26), Dallas Mavericks (27-32), Denver Nuggets (33-38), Detroit Pistons (39-45), Golden State Warriors (46-49), Houston Rockets (50-54 and 63), Indiana Pacers (55-60), Los Angeles Clippers (61), Los Angeles Lakers (64-70), Miami Heat (71-72), Milwaukee Bucks (73-76), New Jersey Nets (77-79 and 102), New York Knicks (18 and 80-84), Philadelphia 76ers (85-88), Phoenix Suns (89-91 and 106),

Portland Trail Blazers (92-96), Sacramento Kings (7, 97, and 99-100), San Antonio Spurs (101 and 103-105), Seattle Supersonics (62 and 107-110), Utah Jazz (111-115), Washington Bullets (116-117 and 119), and All-Stars (120-131). This set was issued in wax packs of 12 cards. The key rookie cards in this set are Kevin Duckworth, Horace Grant, Reggie Miller, Derrick McKey, Scottie Pippen, Mark Price, Dennis Rodman, and Kenny Smith. There is also a rookie card of John Stockton who had previously only appeared in a Star Company set.

	MINT	EXC	G-VG
COMPLETE SET (132)	115.00	50.00	10.00
COMMON PLAYER (1-132)	.17	.08	.01
☐ 1 Antoine Carr	.60	.30	.06
☐ 2 Cliff Levingston	.25	.12	.02
☐ 3 Doc Rivers	.25	.12	.02
☐ 4 Spud Webb	.75	.35	.07
☐ 5 Dominique Wilkins	3.75	1.85	.37
☐ 6 Kevin Willis	.25	.12	.02
☐ 7 Randy Wittman	.17	.08	.01
☐ 8 Danny Ainge	.50	.25	.05
☐ 9 Larry Bird	4.50	2.25	.45
☐ 10 Dennis Johnson	.30	.15	.03
☐ 11 Kevin McHale	.75	.35	.07
☐ 12 Robert Parish	.65	.30	.06
☐ 13 Tyrone Bogues	.75	.35	.07
☐ 14 Del Curry	.75	.35	.07
☐ 15 Dave Corzine	.17	.08	.01
☐ 16 Horace Grant	5.00	2.50	.50
☐ 17 Michael Jordan	30.00	15.00	3.00
☐ 18 Charles Oakley	.30	.15	.03
☐ 19 John Paxson	.50	.25	.05
☐ 20 Scottie Pippen UER	30.00	15.00	3.00
(Misspelled Pippin			
on card back)			
☐ 21 Brad Sellers	.40	.20	.04
☐ 22 Brad Daugherty	1.75	.85	.17
☐ 23 Ron Harper	.65	.30	.06
☐ 24 Larry Nance	.30	.15	.03
☐ 25 Mark Price	3.00	1.50	.30
☐ 26 Hot Rod Williams	.40	.20	.04
☐ 27 Mark Aguirre	.30	.15	.03
☐ 28 Rolando Blackman	.40	.20	.04
☐ 29 James Donaldson	.17	.08	.01
☐ 30 Derek Harper	.30	.15	.03
☐ 31 Sam Perkins	.60	.30	.06
☐ 32 Roy Tarpley	2.00	1.00	.20
☐ 33 Michael Adams	2.50	1.25	.25
☐ 34 Alex English	.40	.20	.04
☐ 35 Lafayette Lever	.30	.15	.03
☐ 36 Blair Rasmussen	.65	.30	.06
☐ 37 Danny Schayes	.25	.12	.02
☐ 38 Jay Vincent	.17	.08	.01
☐ 39 Adrian Dantley	.40	.20	.04
☐ 40 Joe Dumars	2.75	1.35	.27
☐ 41 Vinnie Johnson	.25	.12	.02
☐ 42 Bill Laimbeer	.30	.15	.03
☐ 43 Dennis Rodman	6.50	3.25	.65
☐ 44 John Salley	2.75	1.35	.27
☐ 45 Isiah Thomas	3.75	1.85	.37
☐ 46 Winston Garland	.40	.20	.04
☐ 47 Rod Higgins	.17	.08	.01
☐ 48 Chris Mullin	2.75	1.35	.27
☐ 49 Ralph Sampson	.30	.15	.03
☐ 50 Joe Barry Carroll	.17	.08	.01
☐ 51 Sleepy Floyd	.25	.12	.02
☐ 52 Rodney McCray	.25	.12	.02
☐ 53 Akeem Olajuwon	4.50	2.25	.45
☐ 54 Purvis Short	.17	.08	.01
☐ 55 Vern Fleming	.25	.12	.02
☐ 56 John Long	.17	.08	.01
☐ 57 Reggie Miller	10.00	5.00	1.00
☐ 58 Chuck Person	.90	.45	.09
☐ 59 Steve Stipanovich	.40	.20	.04
☐ 60 Waymon Tisdale	.40	.20	.04
☐ 61 Benoit Benjamin	.30	.15	.03
☐ 62 Michael Cage	.17	.08	.01
☐ 63 Mike Woodson	.17	.08	.01
☐ 64 Kareem Abdul-Jabbar	4.50	2.25	.45
☐ 65 Michael Cooper	.30	.15	.03
☐ 66 A.C. Green	.65	.30	.06
☐ 67 Magic Johnson	4.50	2.25	.45
☐ 68 Byron Scott	.35	.17	.03
☐ 69 Mychal Thompson	.25	.12	.02
☐ 70 James Worthy	2.50	1.25	.25
☐ 71 Duane Washington	.25	.12	.02
☐ 72 Kevin Williams	.17	.08	.01
☐ 73 Randy Breuer	.25	.12	.02
☐ 74 Terry Cummings	.50	.25	.05

□	75	Paul Pressey	.25	.12	.02
□	76	Jack Sikma	.30	.15	.03
□	77	John Bagley	.17	.08	.01
□	78	Roy Hinson	.17	.08	.01
□	79	Buck Williams	.60	.30	.06
□	80	Patrick Ewing	7.50	3.75	.75
□	81	Sidney Green	.17	.08	.01
□	82	Mark Jackson	1.50	.75	.15
□	83	Kenny Walker	.60	.30	.06
□	84	Gerald Wilkins	.30	.15	.03
□	85	Charles Barkley	4.50	2.25	.45
□	86	Maurice Cheeks	.30	.15	.03
□	87	Mike Gminski	.25	.12	.02
□	88	Cliff Robinson	.17	.08	.01
□	89	Armon Gilliam	2.00	1.00	.20
□	90	Eddie Johnson	.35	.17	.03
□	91	Mark West	.43		
□	92	Clyde Drexler	3.75	1.85	.37
□	93	Kevin Duckworth	3.00	1.50	.30
□	94	Steve Johnson	.17	.08	.01
□	95	Jerome Kersey	1.50	.75	.15
□	96	Terry Porter	2.00	1.00	.20
		(College Wisconsin, should be Wisconsin - Stevens Point)			
□	97	Joe Kleine	.30	.15	.03
□	98	Reggie Theus	.25	.12	.02
□	99	Otis Thorpe	.40	.20	.04
□	100	Kenny Smith	3.00	1.50	.30
		(College NC State, should be North Carolina)			
□	101	Greg Anderson	.60	.30	.06
□	102	Walter Berry	.25	.12	.02
□	103	Frank Brickowski	.30	.15	.03
□	104	Johnny Dawkins	.35	.17	.03
□	105	Alvin Robertson	.25	.12	.02
□	106	Tom Chambers	2.00	1.00	.20
		(Born 6/2/59, should be 6/21/59)			
□	107	Dale Ellis	.30	.15	.03
□	108	Xavier McDaniel	.65	.30	.06
□	109	Derrick McKey	1.50	.75	.15
□	110	Nate McMillan UER	.25	.12	.02
		(Photo actually Kevin Williams)			
□	111	Thurl Bailey	.25	.12	.02
□	112	Mark Eaton	.25	.12	.02
□	113	Bobby Hansen	.25	.12	.02
□	114	Karl Malone	4.50	2.25	.45
□	115	John Stockton	14.00	7.00	1.40
□	116	Bernard King	1.00	.50	.10
□	117	Jeff Malone	.50	.25	.05
□	118	Moses Malone	.65	.30	.06
□	119	John Williams	.25	.12	.02
□	120	Michael Jordan AS	8.00	4.00	.80
		Chicago Bulls			
□	121	Mark Jackson AS	.40	.20	.04
		New York Knicks			
□	122	Byron Scott AS	.25	.12	.02
		Los Angeles Lakers			
□	123	Magic Johnson AS	1.75	.85	.17
		Los Angeles Lakers			
□	124	Larry Bird AS	1.75	.85	.17
		Boston Celtics			
□	125	Dominique Wilkins AS	1.00	.50	.10
		Atlanta Hawks			
□	126	Akeem Olajuwon AS	1.50	.75	.15
		Houston Rockets			
□	127	John Stockton AS	2.25	1.10	.22
		Utah Jazz			
□	128	Alvin Robertson AS	.25	.12	.02
		San Antonio Spurs			
□	129	Charles Barkley AS	1.50	.75	.15
		Philadelphia 76ers (Back says Buck Williams is member of Jets, should be Nets)			
□	130	Patrick Ewing AS	1.75	.85	.17
		New York Knicks			
□	131	Mark Eaton AS	.25	.12	.02
		Utah Jazz			
□	132	Checklist Card	.30	.08	.01

1988-89 Fleer Sticker Inserts

The 1988-89 Fleer Glossy Insert Stickers set is an 11-card standard size (2 1/2" by 3 1/2") bonus set issued as an insert with the regular 132-card set. The fronts are baby blue, red, and white. The backs are blue and pink and contain career highlights. The stickers were packed randomly in the wax packs. The set is ordered alphabetically. Featured are 11 NBA superstars. Virtually all cards from this set have wax-stained backs as a result of the packaging.

			MINT	EXC	G-VG
		COMPLETE SET (11)	10.00	5.00	1.00
		COMMON PLAYER (1-11)	.25	.12	.02
□	1	Mark Aguirre	.25	.12	.02
		Dallas Mavericks			
□	2	Larry Bird	1.50	.75	.15
		Boston Celtics			
□	3	Clyde Drexler	1.25	.60	.12
		Portland Trail Blazers			
□	4	Alex English	.30	.15	.03
		Denver Nuggets			
□	5	Patrick Ewing	1.50	.75	.15
		New York Knicks			
□	6	Magic Johnson	1.50	.75	.15
		Los Angeles Lakers			
□	7	Michael Jordan	4.50	2.25	.45
		Chicago Bulls			
□	8	Karl Malone	1.25	.60	.12
		Utah Jazz			
□	9	Kevin McHale	.45	.22	.04
		Boston Celtics			
□	10	Isiah Thomas	1.00	.50	.10
		Detroit Pistons			
□	11	Dominique Wilkins	1.00	.50	.10
		Atlanta Hawks			

1989-90 Fleer

The 1989-90 Fleer basketball set consists of 168 cards measuring the standard size (2 1/2" by 3 1/2"). The fronts feature color action player photos, with various color borders between white inner and outer borders. The player's name and position appear in the upper left corner, with the team logo superimposed over the upper right corner of the picture. The horizontally oriented backs have black lettering on red, pink, and white background and present career statistics, biographical information, and a performance index. The set is ordered alphabetically in team subsets (with a few exceptions due to late trades). The teams themselves are also presented in alphabetical order, Atlanta Hawks (1-7), Boston Celtics (8-14), Charlotte Hornets (15-18), Chicago Bulls (19-23), Cleveland Cavaliers (25-31), Dallas Mavericks (32-37), Denver Nuggets (38-43), Detroit Pistons (44-51), Golden State Warriors (52-57), Houston Rockets (58-63), Indiana Pacers (64-68), Los Angeles Clippers (69-74), Los

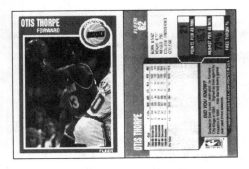

Angeles Lakers (75-80), Miami Heat (81-84), Milwaukee Bucks (85-91), Minnesota Timberwolves (92-94), New Jersey Nets (95-99), New York Knicks (100-107), Orlando Magic (108-111), Philadelphia 76ers (112-118), Phoenix Suns (119-125), Portland Trail Blazers (126-132), Sacramento Kings (133-139), San Antonio Spurs (140-144), Seattle Supersonics (24 and 145-150), Utah Jazz (151-156), Washington Bullets (157-162), and All-Star Game Combos (163-167). The key rookies in this set are Willie Anderson, Rex Chapman, Hersey Hawkins, Jeff Hornacek, Kevin Johnson, Reggie Lewis, Dan Majerle, Danny Manning, Vernon Maxwell, Ken Norman, Mitch Richmond, Rony Seikaly, Brian Shaw, Scott Skiles, Charles Smith, and Rod Strickland.

	MINT	EXC	G-VG
COMPLETE SET (168)	42.00	20.00	4.00
COMMON PLAYER (1-168)	.07	.03	.01

		MINT	EXC	G-VG
☐	1 John Battle	.35	.17	.03
☐	2 Jon Koncak	.20	.10	.02
☐	3 Cliff Levingston	.07	.03	.01
☐	4 Moses Malone	.35	.17	.03
☐	5 Glenn Rivers	.12	.06	.01
☐	6 Spud Webb UER	.25	.12	.02
	(Points per 48 minutes incorrect at 2.6)			
☐	7 Dominique Wilkins	.75	.35	.07
☐	8 Larry Bird	2.00	1.00	.20
☐	9 Dennis Johnson	.12	.06	.01
☐	10 Reggie Lewis	3.25	1.60	.32
☐	11 Kevin McHale	.40	.20	.04
☐	12 Robert Parish	.35	.17	.03
☐	13 Ed Pinckney	.17	.08	.01
☐	14 Brian Shaw	2.25	1.10	.22
☐	15 Rex Chapman	1.25	.60	.12
☐	16 Kurt Rambis	.12	.06	.01
☐	17 Robert Reid	.07	.03	.01
☐	18 Kelly Tripucka	.12	.06	.01
☐	19 Bill Cartwright	.12	.06	.01
	(First season 1978-80, should be 1979-80)			
☐	20 Horace Grant	.45	.22	.04
☐	21 Michael Jordan	8.00	4.00	.80
☐	22 John Paxson	.25	.12	.02
☐	23 Scottie Pippen	4.50	2.25	.45
☐	24 Brad Sellers	.07	.03	.01
☐	25 Brad Daugherty	.30	.15	.03
☐	26 Craig Ehlo	.35	.17	.03
☐	27 Ron Harper	.20	.10	.02
☐	28 Larry Nance	.12	.06	.01
☐	29 Mark Price	.50	.25	.05
☐	30 Mike Sanders	.07	.03	.01
☐	31A John Williams ERR	1.75	.85	.17
	Cleveland Cavaliers			
☐	31B John Williams COR	.25	.12	.02
	Cleveland Cavaliers			
☐	32 Rolando Blackman	.15	.07	.01
	(Career blocks and points listed as 1961 and 2127, should be 196 and 12,127)			
☐	33 Adrian Dantley	.20	.10	.02
☐	34 James Donaldson	.07	.03	.01
☐	35 Derek Harper	.12	.06	.01
☐	36 Sam Perkins	.25	.12	.02
☐	37 Herb Williams	.12	.06	.01
☐	38 Michael Adams	.30	.15	.03
☐	39 Walter Davis	.15	.07	.01
☐	40 Alex English	.25	.12	.02
☐	41 Lafayette Lever	.15	.07	.01

		MINT	EXC	G-VG
☐	42 Blair Rasmussen	.07	.03	.01
☐	43 Dan Schayes	.12	.06	.01
☐	44 Mark Aguirre	.15	.07	.01
☐	45 Joe Dumars	.60	.30	.06
☐	46 James Edwards	.12	.06	.01
☐	47 Vinnie Johnson	.15	.07	.01
☐	48 Bill Laimbeer	.20	.10	.02
☐	49 Dennis Rodman	.75	.35	.07
☐	50 Isiah Thomas	1.00	.50	.10
☐	51 John Salley	.35	.17	.03
☐	52 Manute Bol	.15	.07	.01
☐	53 Winston Garland	.07	.03	.01
☐	54 Rod Higgins	.07	.03	.01
☐	55 Chris Mullin	.75	.35	.07
☐	56 Mitch Richmond	4.50	2.25	.45
☐	57 Terry Teagle	.15	.07	.01
☐	58 Derrick Chievous	.12	.06	.01
	(Stats correctly say 81 games in '88-89, text says 82)			
☐	59 Sleepy Floyd	.12	.06	.01
☐	60 Tim McCormick	.07	.03	.01
☐	61 Akeem Olajuwon	1.25	.60	.12
☐	62 Otis Thorpe	.15	.07	.01
☐	63 Mike Woodson	.07	.03	.01
☐	64 Vern Fleming	.12	.06	.01
☐	65 Reggie Miller	1.25	.60	.12
☐	66 Chuck Person	.40	.20	.04
☐	67 Detlef Schrempf	.35	.17	.03
☐	68 Rik Smits	.45	.22	.04
☐	69 Benoit Benjamin	.15	.07	.01
☐	70 Gary Grant	.30	.15	.03
☐	71 Danny Manning	1.50	.75	.15
☐	72 Ken Norman	1.50	.75	.15
☐	73 Charles Smith	2.00	1.00	.20
☐	74 Reggie Williams	.17	.08	.01
☐	75 Michael Cooper	.15	.07	.01
☐	76 A.C. Green	.30	.15	.03
☐	77 Magic Johnson	2.00	1.00	.20
☐	78 Byron Scott	.25	.12	.02
☐	79 Mychal Thompson	.12	.06	.01
☐	80 James Worthy	.45	.22	.04
☐	81 Kevin Edwards	.25	.12	.02
☐	82 Grant Long	.17	.08	.01
☐	83 Rony Seikaly	1.75	.85	.17
☐	84 Rory Sparrow	.07	.03	.01
☐	85 Greg Anderson UER	.12	.06	.01
	(Stats show 1988-89 as 19888-89)			
☐	86 Jay Humphries	.12	.06	.01
☐	87 Larry Krystkowiak	.12	.06	.01
☐	88 Ricky Pierce	.17	.08	.01
☐	89 Paul Pressey	.12	.06	.01
☐	90 Alvin Robertson	.12	.06	.01
☐	91 Jack Sikma	.15	.07	.01
☐	92 Steve Johnson	.07	.03	.01
☐	93 Rick Mahorn	.17	.08	.01
☐	94 David Rivers	.12	.06	.01
☐	95 Joe Barry Carroll	.07	.03	.01
☐	96 Lester Conner UER	.07	.03	.01
	(Garden State in stats, should be Golden State)			
☐	97 Roy Hinson	.07	.03	.01
☐	98 Mike McGee	.12	.06	.01
☐	99 Chris Morris	.35	.17	.03
☐	100 Patrick Ewing	1.75	.85	.17
☐	101 Mark Jackson	.25	.12	.02
☐	102 Johnny Newman	.75	.35	.07
☐	103 Charles Oakley	.15	.07	.01
☐	104 Rod Strickland	1.25	.60	.12
☐	105 Trent Tucker	.07	.03	.01
☐	106 Kiki Vandeweghe	.12	.06	.01
☐	107A Gerald Wilkins	.15	.07	.01
	(U. of Tennessee)			
☐	107B Gerald Wilkins	.15	.07	.01
	(U. of Tenn.)			
☐	108 Terry Catledge	.12	.06	.01
☐	109 Dave Corzine	.07	.03	.01
☐	110 Scott Skiles	1.25	.60	.12
☐	111 Reggie Theus	.15	.07	.01
☐	112 Ron Anderson	.35	.17	.03
☐	113 Charles Barkley	1.25	.60	.12
☐	114 Scott Brooks	.15	.07	.01
☐	115 Maurice Cheeks	.15	.07	.01
☐	116 Mike Gminski	.12	.06	.01
☐	117 Hersey Hawkins	2.50	1.25	.25
	(Born 9/29/65, should be 9/6/65)			
☐	118 Chris Welp	.12	.06	.01
☐	119 Tom Chambers	.45	.22	.04
☐	120 Armon Gilliam	.25	.12	.02
☐	121 Jeff Hornacek	1.00	.50	.10
☐	122 Eddie Johnson	.15	.07	.01
☐	123 Kevin Johnson	9.00	4.50	.90
☐	124 Dan Majerle	1.50	.75	.15

☐ 125	Mark West	.07	.03	.01
☐ 126	Richard Anderson	.12	.06	.01
☐ 127	Mark Bryant	.17	.08	.01
☐ 128	Clyde Drexler	1.25	.60	.12
☐ 129	Kevin Duckworth	.40	.20	.04
☐ 130	Jerome Kersey	.45	.22	.04
☐ 131	Terry Porter	.50	.25	.05
☐ 132	Buck Williams	.25	.12	.02
☐ 133	Danny Ainge	.25	.12	.02
☐ 134	Ricky Berry	.20	.10	.02
☐ 135	Rodney McCray	.12	.06	.01
☐ 136	Jim Petersen	.07	.03	.01
☐ 137	Harold Pressley	.17	.08	.01
☐ 138	Kenny Smith	.25	.12	.02
☐ 139	Wyman Tisdale	.25	.12	.02
☐ 140	Willie Anderson	1.00	.50	.10
☐ 141	Frank Brickowski	.12	.06	.01
☐ 142	Terry Cummings	.25	.12	.02
☐ 143	Johnny Dawkins	.15	.07	.01
☐ 144	Vern Maxwell	1.25	.60	.12
☐ 145	Michael Cage	.07	.03	.01
☐ 146	Dale Ellis	.15	.07	.01
☐ 147	Alton Lister	.07	.03	.01
☐ 148	Xavier McDaniel	.25	.12	.02
☐ 149	Derrick McKey	.25	.12	.02
☐ 150	Nate McMillan	.07	.03	.01
☐ 151	Thurl Bailey	.12	.06	.01
☐ 152	Mark Eaton	.12	.06	.01
☐ 153	Darrell Griffith	.12	.06	.01
☐ 154	Eric Leckner	.17	.08	.01
☐ 155	Karl Malone	1.25	.60	.12
☐ 156	John Stockton	1.50	.75	.15
☐ 157	Mark Alarie	.15	.07	.01
☐ 158	Ledell Eackles	.35	.17	.03
☐ 159	Bernard King	.35	.17	.03
☐ 160	Jeff Malone	.20	.10	.02
☐ 161	Darrell Walker	.07	.03	.01
☐ 162A	John Williams ERR Washington Bullets	1.50	.75	.15
☐ 162A	John Williams COR Washington Bullets	.15	.07	.01
☐ 163	All Star Game Karl Malone John Stockton	.25	.12	.02
☐ 164	All Star Game Akeem Olajuwon Clyde Drexler	.30	.15	.03
☐ 165	All Star Game Dominique Wilkins Moses Malone	.20	.10	.02
☐ 166	All Star Game Brad Daugherty Mark Price (Bio says Nance had 204 blocks, should be 206)	.20	.10	.02
☐ 167	All Star Game Patrick Ewing Mark Jackson	.25	.12	.02
☐ 168	Checklist Card	.15	.01	.00

1989-90 Fleer All-Stars

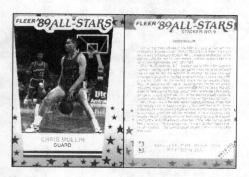

This set of 11 insert stickers features NBA All-Stars and measures the standard size (2 1/2" by 3 1/2"). The front has a color action player photo in the shape of a cup silhouette. An aqua stripe with dark blue stars traverses the card top, and the same pattern reappears about halfway down the card face. The words "Fleer '89 All-Stars" appear at the top of the picture, with the player's name and position immediately below the picture. The back has a star pattern similar to the front. A career summary is printed in blue on a white background. The stickers are numbered on the back and checklisted below accordingly. One was inserted in each wax pack.

		MINT	EXC	G-VG
	COMPLETE SET (11)	5.00	2.50	.50
	COMMON STICKER (1-11)	.15	.07	.01
☐ 1	Karl Malone Utah Jazz	.45	.22	.04
☐ 2	Akeem Olajuwon Houston Rockets	.45	.22	.04
☐ 3	Michael Jordan Chicago Bulls	2.50	1.25	.25
☐ 4	Charles Barkley Philadelphia 76ers	.45	.22	.04
☐ 5	Magic Johnson Los Angeles Lakers	.65	.30	.06
☐ 6	Isiah Thomas Detroit Pistons	.45	.22	.04
☐ 7	Patrick Ewing New York Knicks	.65	.30	.06
☐ 8	Dale Ellis Seattle Supersonics	.15	.07	.01
☐ 9	Chris Mullin Golden State Warriors	.40	.20	.04
☐ 10	Larry Bird Boston Celtics	.65	.30	.06
☐ 11	Tom Chambers Phoenix Suns	.40	.20	.04

1990-91 Fleer

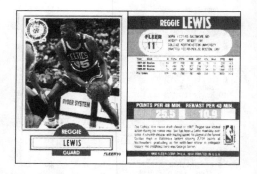

The 1990-91 Fleer set contains 198 cards measuring the standard size (2 1/2" by 3 1/2"). The front features a color action player photo, with a white inner border and a two-color (red on top and bottom, blue on sides) outer border on a white card face. The team logo is superimposed at the upper left corner of the picture, with the player's name and position appearing below the picture. The backs are printed in black, gray, and yellow, and present biographical and statistical information. The cards are numbered on the back. The set is ordered alphabetically in team subsets (with a few exceptions due to late trades). The teams themselves are also presented in alphabetical order, Atlanta Hawks (1-7), Boston Celtics (8-15), Charlotte Hornets (16-21), Chicago Bulls (22-30 and 120), Cleveland Cavaliers (31-37), Dallas Mavericks (38-45 and 50), Denver Nuggets (46-53), Detroit Pistons (54-61), Golden State Warriors (62-68), Houston Rockets (69-75), Indiana Pacers (76-83), Los Angeles Clippers (84-89), Los Angeles Lakers (90-97), Miami Heat (98-103), Milwaukee Bucks (104-110), Minnesota Timberwolves (111-116 and 140), New Jersey Nets (117-123 and 136), New York Knicks (124-131), Orlando Magic (132-135 and 137), Philadelphia 76ers (138-139 and 141-145),

Phoenix Suns (146-153), Portland Trail Blazers (154-161), Sacramento Kings (162-167 and 186-187), San Antonio Spurs (168-174), Seattle Supersonics (175-181), Utah Jazz (182-189 and 195), and Washington Bullets (164, 190-194, and 196). The description, All-American, is properly capitalized on the back of cards 134 and 144, but is not capitalized on cards 20, 29, 51, 53, 59, 70, 119, 130, 178, and 192. The key rookies in this set are Nick Anderson, Vlade Divac, Sherman Douglas, Sean Elliott, Danny Ferry, Tim Hardaway, Shawn Kemp, Glen Rice, and Pooh Richardson.

	MINT	EXC	G-VG
COMPLETE SET (198)	13.00	6.50	1.30
COMMON PLAYER (1-198)	.03	.01	.00

		MINT	EXC	G-VG
☐ 1	John Battle UER	.06	.03	.00
	(Drafted in '84,			
	should be '85)			
☐ 2	Cliff Levingston	.03	.01	.00
☐ 3	Moses Malone	.10	.05	.01
☐ 4	Kenny Smith	.06	.03	.00
☐ 5	Spud Webb	.08	.04	.01
☐ 6	Dominique Wilkins	.18	.09	.01
☐ 7	Kevin Willis	.03	.01	.00
☐ 8	Larry Bird	.30	.15	.03
☐ 9	Dennis Johnson	.08	.04	.01
☐ 10	Joe Kleine	.03	.01	.00
☐ 11	Reggie Lewis	.15	.07	.01
☐ 12	Kevin McHale	.10	.05	.01
☐ 13	Robert Parish	.10	.05	.01
☐ 14	Jim Paxson	.03	.01	.00
☐ 15	Ed Pinckney	.03	.01	.00
☐ 16	Tyrone Bogues	.03	.01	.00
☐ 17	Rex Chapman	.12	.06	.01
☐ 18	Dell Curry	.03	.01	.00
☐ 19	Armon Gilliam	.03	.01	.00
☐ 20	J.R. Reid	.25	.12	.02
☐ 21	Kelly Tripucka	.03	.01	.00
☐ 22	B.J. Armstrong	.25	.12	.02
☐ 23A	Bill Cartwright ERR	.25	.12	.02
	(No decimal points			
	in FGP and FTP)			
☐ 23B	Bill Cartwright COR	.06	.03	.00
☐ 24	Horace Grant	.15	.07	.01
☐ 25	Craig Hodges	.03	.01	.00
☐ 26	Michael Jordan	1.50	.75	.15
	(Led NBA in scoring			
	4 years, not 3)			
☐ 27	Stacey King	.15	.07	.01
	(Comma missing between			
	progressed and Stacy)			
☐ 28	John Paxson	.06	.03	.00
☐ 29	Will Perdue	.10	.05	.01
☐ 30	Scottie Pippen	.25	.12	.02
	(Born AR, not AK)			
☐ 31	Brad Daugherty	.10	.05	.01
☐ 32	Craig Ehlo	.03	.01	.00
☐ 33	Danny Ferry	.50	.25	.05
☐ 34	Steve Kerr	.08	.04	.01
☐ 35	Larry Nance	.06	.03	.00
☐ 36	Mark Price	.08	.04	.01
	(Drafted by Cleveland,			
	should be Dallas)			
☐ 37	Hot Rod Williams	.06	.03	.00
☐ 38	Rolando Blackman	.06	.03	.00
☐ 39A	Adrian Dantley ERR	.25	.12	.02
	(No decimal points			
	in FGP and FTP)			
☐ 39B	Adrian Dantley COR	.08	.04	.01
☐ 40	Brad Davis	.03	.01	.00
☐ 41	James Donaldson	.03	.01	.00
	(Text says in committed,			
	should be is committed)			
☐ 42	Derek Harper	.06	.03	.00
☐ 43	Sam Perkins	.10	.05	.01
	(First line of text			
	should be intact)			
☐ 44	Bill Wennington	.06	.03	.00
☐ 45	Herb Williams	.03	.01	.00
☐ 46	Michael Adams	.06	.03	.00
☐ 47	Walter Davis	.06	.03	.00
☐ 48	Alex English	.08	.04	.01
	(Stats missing from			
	'76-77 through '79-80)			
☐ 49	Bill Hanzlik	.03	.01	.00
☐ 50	Lafayette Lever	.06	.03	.00
	(Born AR, not AK)			
☐ 51	Todd Lichti	.15	.07	.01
☐ 52	Blair Rasmussen	.03	.01	.00
☐ 53	Dan Schayes	.06	.03	.00
☐ 54	Mark Aguirre	.08	.04	.01

		MINT	EXC	G-VG
☐ 55	Joe Dumars	.12	.06	.01
☐ 56	James Edwards	.03	.01	.00
☐ 57	Vinnie Johnson	.06	.03	.00
☐ 58	Bill Laimbeer	.10	.05	.01
☐ 59	Dennis Rodman	.10	.05	.01
☐ 60	John Salley	.06	.03	.00
☐ 61	Isiah Thomas	.18	.09	.01
☐ 62	Manute Bol	.03	.01	.00
☐ 63	Tim Hardaway	1.75	.85	.17
☐ 64	Rod Higgins	.03	.01	.00
☐ 65	Sarunas Marciulionis	.35	.17	.03
☐ 66	Chris Mullin	.15	.07	.01
☐ 67	Mitch Richmond	.30	.15	.03
☐ 68	Terry Teagle	.03	.01	.00
☐ 69	Anthony Bowie	.10	.05	.01
	(Seasons, not seeasons)			
☐ 70	Eric Floyd	.06	.03	.00
☐ 71	Buck Johnson	.03	.01	.00
☐ 72	Vernon Maxwell	.10	.05	.01
☐ 73	Akeem Olajuwon	.18	.09	.01
☐ 74	Otis Thorpe	.06	.03	.00
☐ 75	Mitchell Wiggins	.03	.01	.00
☐ 76	Vern Fleming	.03	.01	.00
☐ 77	George McCloud	.10	.05	.01
☐ 78	Reggie Miller	.15	.07	.01
☐ 79	Chuck Person	.10	.05	.01
☐ 80	Mike Sanders	.03	.01	.00
☐ 81	Detlef Schrempf	.08	.04	.01
☐ 82	Rik Smits	.06	.03	.00
☐ 83	Lasalle Thompson	.03	.01	.00
☐ 84	Benoit Benjamin	.06	.03	.00
☐ 85	Winston Garland	.03	.01	.00
☐ 86	Ron Harper	.06	.03	.00
☐ 87	Danny Manning	.10	.05	.01
☐ 88	Ken Norman	.08	.04	.01
☐ 89	Charles Smith	.10	.05	.01
☐ 90	Michael Cooper	.08	.04	.01
☐ 91	Vlade Divac	.60	.30	.06
☐ 92	A.C. Green	.08	.04	.01
☐ 93	Magic Johnson	.30	.15	.03
☐ 94	Byron Scott	.08	.04	.01
☐ 95	Mychal Thompson	.06	.03	.00
	(Missing '78-79 stats			
	from Portland)			
☐ 96	Orlando Woolridge	.03	.01	.00
☐ 97	James Worthy	.15	.07	.01
☐ 98	Sherman Douglas	.35	.17	.03
☐ 99	Kevin Edwards	.03	.01	.00
☐ 100	Grant Long	.03	.01	.00
☐ 101	Glen Rice	.35	.17	.03
☐ 102	Rony Seikaly	.12	.06	.01
	(Ron on front)			
☐ 103	Billy Thompson	.08	.04	.01
☐ 104	Jeff Grayer	.10	.05	.01
☐ 105	Jay Humphries	.03	.01	.00
☐ 106	Ricky Pierce	.06	.03	.00
☐ 107	Paul Pressey	.06	.03	.00
☐ 108	Fred Roberts	.08	.04	.01
☐ 109	Alvin Robertson	.06	.03	.00
☐ 110	Jack Sikma	.06	.03	.00
☐ 111	Randy Breuer	.03	.01	.00
☐ 112	Tony Campbell	.10	.05	.01
☐ 113	Tyrone Corbin	.06	.03	.00
☐ 114	Sam Mitchell	.15	.07	.01
	(Mercer University,			
	not Mercer College)			
☐ 115	Tod Murphy	.08	.04	.01
	Born Long Beach,			
	not Lakewood)			
☐ 116	Pooh Richardson	.60	.30	.06
☐ 117	Mookie Blaylock	.20	.10	.02
☐ 118	Sam Bowie	.06	.03	.00
☐ 119	Lester Conner	.03	.01	.00
☐ 120	Dennis Hopson	.08	.04	.01
☐ 121	Chris Morris	.08	.04	.01
☐ 122	Charles Shackleford	.08	.04	.01
☐ 123	Purvis Short	.03	.01	.00
☐ 124	Maurice Cheeks	.06	.03	.00
☐ 125	Patrick Ewing	.25	.12	.02
☐ 126	Mark Jackson	.06	.03	.00
☐ 127A	Johnny Newman ERR	.50	.25	.05
	(Jr. misprinted as J.			
	on card back)			
☐ 127B	Johnny Newman COR	.06	.03	.00
☐ 128	Charles Oakley	.08	.04	.01
☐ 129	Trent Tucker	.03	.01	.00
☐ 130	Kenny Walker	.03	.01	.00
☐ 131	Gerald Wilkins	.06	.03	.00
☐ 132	Nick Anderson	.35	.17	.03
☐ 133	Terry Catledge	.03	.01	.00
☐ 134	Sidney Green	.03	.01	.00
☐ 135	Otis Smith	.08	.04	.01
☐ 136	Reggie Theus	.06	.03	.00
☐ 137	Sam Vincent	.03	.01	.00

☐ 138	Ron Anderson	.06	.03	.00
☐ 139	Charles Barkley	.20	.10	.02
	(FG Percentage .545.)			
☐ 140	Scott Brooks	.03	.01	.00
	('89-89 Philadelphia in wrong typeface)			
☐ 141	Johnny Dawkins	.06	.03	.00
☐ 142	Mike Gminski	.06	.03	.00
☐ 143	Hersey Hawkins	.15	.07	.01
☐ 144	Rick Mahorn	.06	.03	.00
☐ 145	Derek Smith	.03	.01	.00
☐ 146	Tom Chambers	.12	.06	.01
☐ 147	Jeff Hornacek	.08	.04	.01
☐ 148	Eddie Johnson	.06	.03	.00
☐ 149	Kevin Johnson	.35	.17	.03
☐ 150A	Dan Majerle ERR	.30	.15	.03
	(Award in 1988; three-time selection)			
☐ 150B	Dan Majerle COR	.10	.05	.01
	(Award in 1989; three-time selection)			
☐ 151	Tim Perry	.08	.04	.01
☐ 152	Kurt Rambis	.06	.03	.00
☐ 153	Mark West	.03	.01	.00
☐ 154	Clyde Drexler	.18	.09	.01
☐ 155	Kevin Duckworth	.03	.01	.00
☐ 156	Byron Irvin	.12	.06	.01
☐ 157	Jerome Kersey	.08	.04	.01
☐ 158	Terry Porter	.10	.05	.01
☐ 159	Cliff Robinson	.30	.15	.03
☐ 160	Buck Williams	.08	.04	.01
☐ 161	Danny Young	.03	.01	.00
☐ 162	Danny Ainge	.08	.04	.01
☐ 163	Antoine Carr	.06	.03	.00
☐ 164	Pervis Ellison	.30	.15	.03
☐ 165	Rodney McCray	.06	.03	.00
☐ 166	Harold Pressley	.03	.01	.00
☐ 167	Wayman Tisdale	.08	.04	.01
☐ 168	Willie Anderson	.08	.04	.01
☐ 169	Frank Brickowski	.03	.01	.00
☐ 170	Terry Cummings	.08	.04	.01
☐ 171	Sean Elliott	.60	.30	.06
☐ 172	David Robinson	3.00	1.50	.30
☐ 173	Rod Strickland	.08	.04	.01
☐ 174	David Wingate	.03	.01	.00
☐ 175	Dana Barros	.15	.07	.01
☐ 176	Michael Cage	.03	.01	.00
	(Born AR, not AK)			
☐ 177	Dale Ellis	.08	.04	.01
☐ 178	Shawn Kemp	1.50	.75	.15
☐ 179	Xavier McDaniel	.08	.04	.01
☐ 180	Derrick McKey	.06	.03	.00
☐ 181	Nate McMillan	.03	.01	.00
☐ 182	Thurl Bailey	.06	.03	.00
☐ 183	Mike Brown	.08	.04	.01
☐ 184	Mark Eaton	.06	.03	.00
☐ 185	Theodore Edwards	.15	.07	.01
☐ 186	Bob Hansen	.03	.01	.00
☐ 187	Eric Leckner	.06	.03	.00
☐ 188	Karl Malone	.18	.09	.01
☐ 189	John Stockton	.18	.09	.01
☐ 190	Mark Alarie	.03	.01	.00
☐ 191	Ledell Eackles	.06	.03	.00
☐ 192A	Harvey Grant	1.00	.50	.10
	(First name on card front in black)			
☐ 192B	Harvey Grant	.15	.07	.01
	(First name on card front in white)			
☐ 193	Tom Hammonds	.12	.06	.01
☐ 194	Bernard King	.10	.05	.01
☐ 195	Jeff Malone	.08	.04	.01
☐ 196	Darrell Walker	.03	.01	.00
☐ 197	Checklist Card	.06	.01	.00
☐ 198	Checklist Card	.08	.01	.00

1990-91 Fleer All-Stars

These All-Star inserts measure the standard size (2 1/2" by 3 1/2"). The front features a color action player photo, framed by a basketball hoop and net on an aqua background. An orange stripe at the top represents the bottom of the backboard and has the words "Fleer '90 All-Stars." The player's name and position are given at the bottom between stars. The backs are printed in blue and pink with white borders and have career summaries. The cards are numbered on the back. These inserts were not included

in every wax pack and hence they are a little more difficult to find than the Fleer All-Star inserts of the previous years.

		MINT	EXC	G-VG
	COMPLETE SET (12)	5.50	2.75	.55
	COMMON PLAYER (1-12)	.15	.07	.01
☐ 1	Charles Barkley	.30	.15	.03
	Philadelphia 76ers			
☐ 2	Larry Bird	.40	.20	.04
	Boston Celtics			
☐ 3	Akeem Olajuwon	.30	.15	.03
	Houston Rockets			
☐ 4	Magic Johnson	.40	.20	.04
	Los Angeles Lakers			
☐ 5	Michael Jordan	1.50	.75	.15
	Chicago Bulls			
☐ 6	Isiah Thomas	.25	.12	.02
	Detroit Pistons			
☐ 7	Karl Malone	.30	.15	.03
	Utah Jazz			
☐ 8	Tom Chambers	.15	.07	.01
	Phoenix Suns			
☐ 9	John Stockton	.15	.07	.01
	Utah Jazz			
☐ 10	David Robinson	3.00	1.50	.30
	San Antonio Spurs			
☐ 11	Clyde Drexler	.25	.12	.02
	Portland Trail Blazers			
☐ 12	Patrick Ewing	.35	.17	.03
	New York Knicks			

1990-91 Fleer Rookie Sensations

These rookie sensation cards measure the standard size (2 1/2" by 3 1/2"). The fronts feature color action player photos, with white and red borders on an aqua background. A basketball overlays the lower left corner of the picture, with the words "Rookie Sensation" in yellow lettering, and the player's name appearing in white lettering in the bottom red border. The backs are printed in black and red on gray background (with white borders), and present summaries of their college careers and rookie seasons. The cards are numbered on the back. These inserts were found occasionally in cello packs and thus are considered a tougher insert set to complete.

	MINT	EXC	G-VG
COMPLETE SET (10)	42.00	15.00	3.00
COMMON PLAYER (1-10)	1.50	.75	.15
☐ 1 David Robinson San Antonio Spurs (Text has 1988-90 season, should be 1989-90)	21.00	7.00	1.50
☐ 2 Sean Elliott UER San Antonio Spurs (Misspelled Elliot on card front)	3.00	1.50	.30
☐ 3 Glen Rice Miami Heat	2.50	1.25	.25
☐ 4 J.R.Reid Charlotte Hornets	2.25	1.10	.22
☐ 5 Stacey King Chicago Bulls	1.50	.75	.15
☐ 6 Pooh Richardson Minnesota Timberwolves	3.00	1.50	.30
☐ 7 Nick Anderson Orlando Magic	2.50	1.25	.25
☐ 8 Tim Hardaway Golden State Warriors	10.00	5.00	1.00
☐ 9 Vlade Divac Los Angeles Lakers	3.00	1.50	.30
☐ 10 Sherman Douglas Miami Heat	2.50	1.25	.25

1990-91 Fleer Update

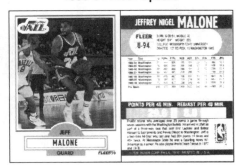

The cards are the same size (2 1/2" by 3 1/2") and design as the regular issue. The set numbering is arranged alphabetically by team as follows: Atlanta Hawks (1-5), Boston Celtics (6-10), Charlotte Hornets (11-13), Chicago Bulls (14-15), Cleveland Cavaliers (16-18), Dallas Mavericks (19-23), Cleveland Cavaliers (24-27), Detroit Pistons (28-30), Golden State Warriors (31-34), Houston Rockets (35-36), Indiana Pacers (37-39), Los Angeles Clippers (40-42), Los Angeles Lakers (43-46), Miami Heat (47-50), Milwaukee Bucks (51-55), Minnesota Timberwolves (56-58), New Jersey Nets (59-62), New York Knicks (63-66), Orlando Magic (67), Philadelphia 76ers (68-73), Phoenix Suns (74-77), Portland Trail Blazers (78-81), Sacramento Kings (82-87), San Antonio Spurs (88-91), Seattle Supersonics (92-93), Utah Jazz (94-96), and Washington Bullets (97-99). The key rookies in this set are Dee Brown (his only major card this year), Derrick Coleman, Kendall Gill, Gary Payton, Dennis Scott, and Lionel Simmons.

	MINT	EXC	G-VG
COMPLETE SET (100)	24.00	12.00	2.40
COMMON PLAYER (1-100)	.05	.02	.00
☐ U1 Jon Koncak	.10	.01	.00
☐ U2 Tim McCormick	.05	.02	.00
☐ U3 Glenn Rivers	.10	.05	.01
☐ U4 Rumeal Robinson	.25	.12	.02
☐ U5 Trevor Wilson	.15	.07	.01

☐ U6 Dee Brown	5.50	2.75	.55
☐ U7 Dave Popson	.10	.05	.01
☐ U8 Kevin Gamble	.35	.17	.03
☐ U9 Brian Shaw	.25	.12	.02
☐ U10 Michael Smith	.15	.07	.01
☐ U11 Kendall Gill	1.50	.75	.15
☐ U12 Johnny Newman	.10	.05	.01
☐ U13 Steve Scheffler	.10	.05	.01
☐ U14 Dennis Hopson	.10	.05	.01
☐ U15 Cliff Levingston	.05	.02	.00
☐ U16 Chucky Brown	.15	.07	.01
☐ U17 John Morton	.10	.05	.01
☐ U18 Gerald Paddio	.25	.12	.02
☐ U19 Alex English	.10	.05	.01
☐ U20 Fat Lever	.10	.05	.01
☐ U21 Rodney McCray	.05	.02	.00
☐ U22 Roy Tarpley	.10	.05	.01
☐ U23 Randy White	.35	.17	.03
☐ U24 Anthony Cook	.10	.05	.01
☐ U25 Chris Jackson	.90	.45	.09
☐ U26 Marcus Liberty	.25	.12	.02
☐ U27 Orlando Woolridge	.05	.02	.00
☐ U28 William Bedford	.15	.07	.01
☐ U29 Lance Blanks	.15	.07	.01
☐ U30 Scott Hastings	.10	.05	.01
☐ U31 Tyrone Hill	.35	.17	.03
☐ U32 Les Jepsen	.10	.05	.01
☐ U33 Steve Johnson	.05	.02	.00
☐ U34 Kevin Pritchard	.10	.05	.01
☐ U35 Dave Jamerson	.10	.05	.01
☐ U36 Kenny Smith	.10	.05	.01
☐ U37 Greg Dreiling	.10	.05	.01
☐ U38 Ken Williams	.20	.10	.02
☐ U39 Michael Williams	.35	.17	.03
☐ U40 Gary Grant	.05	.02	.00
☐ U41 Bo Kimble	.75	.35	.07
☐ U42 Loy Vaught	.25	.12	.02
☐ U43 Elden Campbell	1.00	.50	.10
☐ U44 Sam Perkins	.15	.07	.01
☐ U45 Tony Smith	.25	.12	.02
☐ U46 Terry Teagle	.05	.02	.00
☐ U47 Willie Burton	.75	.35	.07
☐ U48 Bimbo Coles	.20	.10	.02
☐ U49 Terry Davis	.10	.05	.01
☐ U50 Alec Kessler	.20	.10	.02
☐ U51 Greg Anderson	.05	.02	.00
☐ U52 Frank Brickowski	.05	.02	.00
☐ U53 Steve Henson	.10	.05	.01
☐ U54 Brad Lohaus	.10	.05	.01
☐ U55 Dan Schayes	.10	.05	.01
☐ U56 Gerald Glass	.25	.12	.02
☐ U57 Felton Spencer	.50	.25	.05
☐ U58 Doug West	.10	.05	.01
☐ U59 Jud Buechler	.10	.05	.01
☐ U60 Derrick Coleman	6.00	3.00	.60
☐ U61 Tate George	.15	.07	.01
☐ U62 Reggie Theus	.10	.05	.01
☐ U63 Greg Grant	.10	.05	.01
☐ U64 Jerrod Mustaf	.30	.15	.03
☐ U65 Eddie Lee Wilkins	.10	.05	.01
☐ U66 Michael Ansley	.10	.05	.01
☐ U67 Jerry Reynolds	.10	.05	.01
☐ U68 Dennis Scott	1.50	.75	.15
☐ U69 Manute Bol	.05	.02	.00
☐ U70 Armon Gilliam	.05	.02	.00
☐ U71 Brian Oliver	.20	.10	.02
☐ U72 Kenny Payne	.10	.05	.01
☐ U73 Jayson Williams	.15	.07	.01
☐ U74 Kenny Battle	.25	.12	.02
☐ U75 Cedric Ceballos	.60	.30	.06
☐ U76 Negele Knight	.60	.30	.06
☐ U77 Xavier McDaniel	.10	.05	.01
☐ U78 Alaa Abdelnaby	.20	.10	.02
☐ U79 Danny Ainge	.15	.07	.01
☐ U80 Mark Bryant	.05	.02	.00
☐ U81 Drazen Petrovic	.30	.15	.03
☐ U82 Anthony Bonner	.20	.10	.02
☐ U83 Duane Causwell	.15	.07	.01
☐ U84 Bobby Hansen	.05	.02	.00
☐ U85 Eric Leckner	.10	.05	.01
☐ U86 Travis Mays	.90	.45	.09
☐ U87 Lionel Simmons	2.75	1.35	.27
☐ U88 Sidney Green	.05	.02	.00
☐ U89 Tony Massenburg	.20	.10	.02
☐ U90 Paul Pressey	.05	.02	.00
☐ U91 Dwayne Schintzius	.40	.20	.04
☐ U92 Gary Payton	1.50	.75	.15
☐ U93 Olden Polynice	.05	.02	.00
☐ U94 Jeff Malone	.10	.05	.01
☐ U95 Walter Palmer	.10	.05	.01
☐ U96 Delaney Rudd	.10	.05	.01
☐ U97 Pervis Ellison	.20	.10	.02
☐ U98 A.J. English	.35	.17	.03
☐ U99 Greg Foster	.10	.05	.01
☐ U100 Checklist Card	.05	.01	.00

1991-92 Fleer

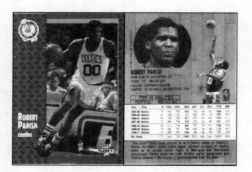

The 1991-92 Fleer basketball card set contains 240 cards measuring the standard size (2 1/2" by 3 1/2"). The fronts features color action player photos, bordered by a red stripe on the bottom, and gray and red stripes on the top. A 3/4" blue stripe checkered with black NBA logos runs the length of the card and serves as the left border of the picture. The team logo, player's name, and position are printed in white lettering in this stripe. The picture is bordered on the right side by a thin gray stripe and a thicker blue one. The backs present career summaries and are printed with black lettering on various pastel colors, superimposed over a wooden basketball floor background. The cards are numbered and checklisted below alphabetically within and according to teams as follows: Atlanta Hawks (1-7), Boston Celtics (8-16), Charlotte Hornets (17-24), Chicago Bulls (25-33), Cleveland Cavaliers (34-41), Dallas Mavericks (42-48), Denver Nuggets (49-56), Detroit Pistons (57-64), Golden State Warriors (65-72), Houston Rockets (73-80), Indiana Pacers (81-88), L.A. Clippers (86-96), L.A. Lakers (97-104), Miami Heat (105-112), Milwaukee Bucks (113-120), Minnesota Timberwolves (121-127), New Jersey Nets (128-134), New York Knicks (135-142), Orlando Magic (143-149), Philadelphia 76ers (150-157), Phoenix Suns (158-165), Portland Trail Blazers (166-173), Sacramento Kings (174-181), San Antonio Spurs (182-188), Seattle Supersonics (189-196), Utah Jazz (197-203), and Washington Bullets (204-209). Other subsets within the set are All-Stars (210-219), League Leaders (220-226), Slam Dunk (227-232), and All Star Game Highlights (233-238).

	MINT	EXC	G-VG
COMPLETE SET (240)	13.00	6.50	1.30
COMMON PLAYER (1-240)	.03	.01	.00

		MINT	EXC	G-VG
□ 1	John Battle	.06	.01	.00
□ 2	Jon Koncak	.03	.01	.00
□ 3	Rumeal Robinson	.08	.04	.01
□ 4	Spud Webb	.08	.04	.01
□ 5	Bob Weiss CO	.03	.01	.00
□ 6	Dominique Wilkins	.15	.07	.01
□ 7	Kevin Willis	.03	.01	.00
□ 8	Larry Bird	.25	.12	.02
□ 9	Dee Brown	.60	.30	.06
□ 10	Chris Ford CO	.03	.01	.00
□ 11	Kevin Gamble	.08	.04	.01
□ 12	Reggie Lewis	.12	.06	.01
□ 13	Kevin McHale	.10	.05	.01
□ 14	Robert Parish	.10	.05	.01
□ 15	Ed Pinckney	.03	.01	.00
□ 16	Brian Shaw	.10	.05	.01
□ 17	Tyrone Bogues	.03	.01	.00
□ 18	Rex Chapman	.08	.04	.01
□ 19	Dell Curry	.03	.01	.00
□ 20	Kendall Gill	.25	.12	.02
□ 21	Eric Leckner	.06	.03	.00
□ 22	Gene Littles CO	.03	.01	.00
□ 23	Johnny Newman	.06	.03	.00
□ 24	J.R. Reid	.08	.04	.01
□ 25	B.J. Armstrong	.08	.04	.01
□ 26	Bill Cartwright	.06	.03	.00
□ 27	Horace Grant	.10	.05	.01
□ 28	Phil Jackson CO	.03	.01	.00
□ 29	Michael Jordan	.75	.30	.06
□ 30	Cliff Levingston	.03	.01	.00
□ 31	John Paxson	.06	.03	.00
□ 32	Will Perdue	.06	.03	.00
□ 33	Scottie Pippen	.20	.10	.02
□ 34	Brad Daugherty	.10	.05	.01
□ 35	Craig Ehlo	.03	.01	.00
□ 36	Danny Ferry	.12	.06	.01
□ 37	Larry Nance	.06	.03	.00
□ 38	Mark Price	.08	.04	.01
□ 39	Darnell Valentine	.03	.01	.00
□ 40	Hot Rod Williams	.06	.03	.00
□ 41	Lenny Wilkens CO	.06	.03	.00
□ 42	Richie Adubato CO	.06	.03	.00
□ 43	Rolando Blackman	.08	.04	.01
□ 44	James Donaldson	.03	.01	.00
□ 45	Derek Harper	.06	.03	.00
□ 46	Rodney McCray	.06	.03	.00
□ 47	Randy White	.08	.04	.01
□ 48	Herb Williams	.03	.01	.00
□ 49	Chris Jackson	.18	.09	.01
□ 50	Marcus Liberty	.10	.05	.01
□ 51	Todd Lichti	.03	.01	.00
□ 52	Blair Rasmussen	.03	.01	.00
□ 53	Paul Westhead CO	.06	.03	.00
□ 54	Reggie Williams	.03	.01	.00
□ 55	Joe Wolf	.03	.01	.00
□ 56	Orlando Woolridge	.03	.01	.00
□ 57	Mark Aguirre	.08	.04	.01
□ 58	Chuck Daly CO	.03	.01	.00
□ 59	Joe Dumars	.10	.05	.01
□ 60	James Edwards	.03	.01	.00
□ 61	Vinnie Johnson	.06	.03	.00
□ 62	Bill Laimbeer	.08	.04	.01
□ 63	Dennis Rodman	.08	.04	.01
□ 64	Isiah Thomas	.15	.07	.01
□ 65	Tim Hardaway	.45	.22	.04
□ 66	Rod Higgins	.03	.01	.00
□ 67	Tyrone Hill	.10	.05	.01
□ 68	Sarunas Marciulionis	.08	.04	.01
□ 69	Chris Mullin	.12	.06	.01
□ 70	Don Nelson CO	.03	.01	.00
□ 71	Mitch Richmond	.12	.06	.01
□ 72	Tom Tolbert	.03	.01	.00
□ 73	Don Chaney CO	.03	.01	.00
□ 74	Eric Floyd	.03	.01	.00
□ 75	Buck Johnson	.03	.01	.00
□ 76	Vernon Maxwell	.08	.04	.01
□ 77	Hakeem Olajuwon	.18	.09	.01
□ 78	Kenny Smith	.06	.03	.00
□ 79	Larry Smith	.03	.01	.00
□ 80	Otis Thorpe	.06	.03	.00
□ 81	Vern Fleming	.03	.01	.00
□ 82	Bob Hill CO	.06	.03	.00
□ 83	Reggie Miller	.12	.06	.01
□ 84	Chuck Person	.08	.04	.01
□ 85	Detlef Schrempf	.08	.04	.01
□ 86	Rik Smits	.06	.03	.00
□ 87	LaSalle Thompson	.03	.01	.00
□ 88	Michael Williams	.06	.03	.00
□ 89	Gary Grant	.06	.03	.00
□ 90	Ron Harper	.08	.04	.01
□ 91	Bo Kimble	.12	.06	.01
□ 92	Danny Manning	.08	.04	.01
□ 93	Ken Norman	.08	.04	.01
□ 94	Olden Polynice	.03	.01	.00
□ 95	Mike Schuler CO	.03	.01	.00
□ 96	Charles Smith	.08	.04	.01
□ 97	Vlade Divac	.18	.09	.01
□ 98	Mike Dunleavy CO	.03	.01	.00
□ 99	A.C. Green	.06	.03	.00
□ 100	Magic Johnson	.25	.12	.02
□ 101	Sam Perkins	.08	.04	.01
□ 102	Byron Scott	.08	.04	.01
□ 103	Terry Teagle	.03	.01	.00
□ 104	James Worthy	.10	.05	.01
□ 105	Willie Burton	.15	.07	.01
□ 106	Bimbo Coles	.10	.05	.01
□ 107	Sherman Douglas	.10	.05	.01
□ 108	Kevin Edwards	.03	.01	.00
□ 109	Grant Long	.03	.01	.00
□ 110	Kevin Loughery CO	.03	.01	.00
□ 111	Glen Rice	.12	.06	.01
□ 112	Rony Seikaly	.08	.04	.01
□ 113	Frank Brickowski	.03	.01	.00
□ 114	Dale Ellis	.06	.03	.00
□ 115	Del Harris CO	.03	.01	.00
□ 116	Jay Humphries	.03	.01	.00
□ 117	Fred Roberts	.06	.03	.00
□ 118	Alvin Robertson	.06	.03	.00
□ 119	Dan Schayes	.06	.03	.00
□ 120	Jack Sikma	.06	.03	.00
□ 121	Tony Campbell	.06	.03	.00

122	Tyrone Corbin	.06 .03 .00
123	Sam Mitchell	.06 .03 .00
124	Tod Murphy	.03 .01 .00
125	Pooh Richardson	.15 .07 .01
126	Jim Rodgers CO	.06 .03 .00
127	Felton Spencer	.15 .07 .01
128	Mookie Blaylock	.08 .04 .01
129	Sam Bowie	.06 .03 .00
130	Derrick Coleman	.75 .35 .07
131	Chris Dudley	.03 .01 .00
132	Bill Fitch CO	.03 .01 .00
133	Chris Morris	.06 .03 .00
134	Drazen Petrovic	.06 .03 .00
135	Maurice Cheeks	.08 .04 .01
136	Patrick Ewing	.20 .10 .02
137	Mark Jackson	.06 .03 .00
138	Charles Oakley	.06 .03 .00
139	Pat Riley CO	.06 .03 .00
140	Trent Tucker	.03 .01 .00
141	Kiki Vandeweghe	.06 .03 .00
142	Gerald Wilkins	.06 .03 .00
143	Nick Anderson	.10 .05 .01
144	Terry Catledge	.03 .01 .00
145	Matt Guokas CO	.03 .01 .00
146	Jerry Reynolds	.03 .01 .00
147	Dennis Scott	.20 .10 .02
148	Scott Skiles	.08 .04 .01
149	Otis Smith	.03 .01 .00
150	Ron Anderson	.06 .03 .00
151	Charles Barkley	.18 .09 .01
152	Johnny Dawkins	.06 .03 .00
153	Armon Gilliam	.03 .01 .00
154	Hersey Hawkins	.10 .05 .01
155	Jim Lynam CO	.03 .01 .00
156	Rick Mahorn	.06 .03 .00
157	Brian Oliver	.08 .04 .01
158	Tom Chambers	.10 .05 .01
159	Cotton Fitzsimmons CO	.03 .01 .00
160	Jeff Hornacek	.06 .03 .00
161	Kevin Johnson	.25 .12 .02
162	Negele Knight	.15 .07 .01
163	Dan Majerle	.08 .04 .01
164	Xavier McDaniel	.08 .04 .01
165	Mark West	.03 .01 .00
166	Rick Adelman CO	.03 .01 .00
167	Danny Ainge	.08 .04 .01
168	Clyde Drexler	.17 .08 .01
169	Kevin Duckworth	.06 .03 .00
170	Jerome Kersey	.08 .04 .01
171	Terry Porter	.10 .05 .01
172	Cliff Robinson	.12 .06 .01
173	Buck Williams	.08 .04 .01
174	Antoine Carr	.03 .01 .00
175	Duane Causwell	.08 .04 .01
176	Jim Les	.08 .04 .01
177	Travis Mays	.15 .07 .01
178	Dick Motta CO	.03 .01 .00
179	Lionel Simmons	.35 .17 .03
180	Rory Sparrow	.03 .01 .00
181	Wayman Tisdale	.08 .04 .01
182	Willie Anderson	.08 .04 .01
183	Larry Brown CO	.03 .01 .00
184	Terry Cummings	.08 .04 .01
185	Sean Elliott	.15 .07 .01
186	Paul Pressey	.03 .01 .00
187	David Robinson	.75 .30 .06
188	Rod Strickland	.08 .04 .01
189	Benoit Benjamin	.06 .03 .00
190	Eddie Johnson	.06 .03 .00
191	K.C. Jones CO	.03 .01 .00
192	Shawn Kemp	.35 .17 .03
193	Derrick McKey	.06 .03 .00
194	Gary Payton	.25 .12 .02
195	Ricky Pierce	.06 .03 .00
196	Sedale Threatt	.03 .01 .00
197	Thurl Bailey	.06 .03 .00
198	Mark Eaton	.06 .03 .00
199	Theodore Edwards	.06 .03 .00
200	Jeff Malone	.08 .04 .01
201	Karl Malone	.18 .09 .01
202	Jerry Sloan CO	.03 .01 .00
203	John Stockton	.15 .07 .01
204	Ledell Eackles	.03 .01 .00
205	Pervis Ellison	.08 .04 .01
206	A.J. English	.10 .05 .01
207	Harvey Grant	.08 .04 .01
208	Bernard King	.10 .05 .01
209	Wes Unseld CO	.03 .01 .00
210	Kevin Johnson AS	.12 .06 .01
211	Michael Jordan AS	.35 .15 .03
212	Dominique Wilkins AS	.10 .05 .01
213	Charles Barkley AS	.12 .06 .01
214	Hakeem Olajuwon AS	.12 .06 .01
215	Patrick Ewing AS	.12 .06 .01
216	Tim Hardaway AS	.20 .10 .02

217	John Stockton AS	.10 .05 .01
218	Chris Mullin AS	.08 .04 .01
219	Karl Malone AS	.12 .06 .01
220	Michael Jordan LL	.35 .15 .03
221	John Stockton LL	.10 .05 .01
222	Alvin Robertson LL	.06 .03 .00
223	Hakeem Olajuwon LL	.12 .06 .01
224	Buck Williams LL	.08 .04 .01
225	David Robinson LL	.35 .15 .03
226	Reggie Miller LL	.08 .04 .01
227	Theodore Edwards SD	.06 .03 .00
228	Dee Brown SD	.30 .15 .03
229	Rex Chapman SD	.08 .04 .01
230	Kenny Smith SD	.06 .03 .00
231	Shawn Kemp SD	.20 .10 .02
232	Kendall Gill SD	.15 .07 .01
233	'91 All Star Game	.06 .03 .00
234	'91 All Star Game	.06 .03 .00
235	'91 All Star Game	.06 .03 .00
236	'91 All Star Game	.06 .03 .00
237	'91 All Star Game	.06 .03 .00
238	'91 All Star Game	.06 .03 .00
239	Checklist Card	.06 .01 .00
240	Checklist Card	.06 .01 .00

1991-92 Fleer Pro Visions

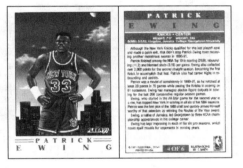

This 6-card set measures the standard size (2 1/2" by 3 1/2") and showcases outstanding NBA players. The front features a color player portrait by the renowned sports artist Terry Smith. The portrait is bordered on all sides by white, with the player's name in red lettering below the picture. The back presents biographical information and career summary in black lettering on a color background (with white borders). The cards are numbered on the back.

	MINT	EXC	G-VG
COMPLETE SET (6)	5.00	2.50	.50
COMMON PLAYER (1-6)	.60	.30	.06
1 David Robinson San Antonio Spurs	2.00	1.00	.20
2 Michael Jordan Chicago Bulls	2.00	1.00	.20
3 Charles Barkley Philadelphia 76ers	.60	.30	.06
4 Patrick Ewing New York Knicks	.65	.30	.06
5 Karl Malone Utah Jazz	.60	.30	.06
6 Magic Johnson Los Angeles Lakers	.75	.35	.07

1991-92 Fleer Rookie Sensations

This ten-card set showcases outstanding rookies and measures the standard size (2 1/2" by 3 1/2"). The front features a color player photo inside a basketball rim and net. The picture is

	3 Kevin McHale	.30	.15	.03
	Boston Celtics			
	4 Kevin Johnson	.75	.35	.07
	Phoenix Suns			
	5 Karl Malone	.60	.30	.06
	Utah Jazz			
	6 Alvin Robertson	.25	.12	.02
	Milwaukee Bucks			

bordered in magenta on all sides. The words "Rookie Sensations" appear above the picture, and player information is given below the picture. An orange basketball with the words "Fleer '91" appears in the upper left corner on both sides of the card. The back has a magenta border and includes highlights of the player's rookie season. The cards are numbered on the back.

	MINT	EXC	G-VG
COMPLETE SET (10)	12.00	6.00	1.20
COMMON PLAYER (1-10)	.90	.45	.09
☐ 1 Travis Mays	.90	.45	.09
☐ 2 Kendall Gill	1.25	.60	.12
☐ 3 Derrick Coleman	3.50	1.75	.35
☐ 4 Dennis Scott	1.25	.60	.12
☐ 5 Lionel Simmons	2.00	1.00	.20
☐ 6 Dee Brown	3.00	1.50	.30
☐ 7 Gary Payton	1.25	.60	.12
☐ 8 Chris Jackson	1.25	.60	.12
☐ 9 Willie Burton	.90	.45	.09
☐ 10 Felton Spencer	1.00	.50	.10

1991-92 Fleer Schoolyard Stars

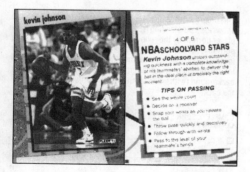

This six-card set measures the standard size (2 1/2" by 3 1/2"). The front features color action player photos. The photos are bordered on the left and bottom by a black stripe and a broken pink stripe. Yellow stripes traverse the card top and bottom, and the background is a gray cement-colored design. The back has a similar layout and presents a basketball tip in black lettering on white. The cards are numbered on the back.

	MINT	EXC	G-VG
COMPLETE SET (6)	2.50	1.25	.25
COMMON PLAYER (1-6)	.25	.12	.02
☐ 1 Chris Mullin	.35	.17	.03
Golden State Warriors			
☐ 2 Isiah Thomas	.45	.22	.04
Detroit Pistons			

1971-72 Floridians McDonald's

This nine-card set of ABA Miami Floridians was sponsored by McDonald's. The cards measure approximately 2 1/2" by 4", including a 1/2" tear-off tab at the bottom. The bottom tab admitted one 14-or-under to the game with each regular price adult ticket. The front features color action player photos with rounded corners and black borders. The back has player information, rules governing the free youth tickets, and an offer to receive an ABA basketball in exchange for a set of ten different Floridian tickets. The cards are unnumbered and are checklisted below in alphabetical order.

	NRMT	VG-E	GOOD
COMPLETE SET (9)	750.00	375.00	75.00
COMMON PLAYER (1-9)	75.00	37.50	7.50
☐ 1 Warren Armstrong	100.00	50.00	10.00
☐ 2 Mack Calvin	150.00	75.00	15.00
☐ 3 Ron Franz	75.00	37.50	7.50
☐ 4 Ira Harge	75.00	37.50	7.50
☐ 5 Larry Jones	75.00	37.50	7.50
☐ 6 Willie Long	75.00	37.50	7.50
☐ 7 Sam Robinson	75.00	37.50	7.50
☐ 8 George Tinsley	75.00	37.50	7.50
☐ 9 Lonnie Wright	75.00	37.50	7.50

1988 Foot Locker Slam Fest *

This nine-card set was produced by Foot Locker to commemorate the "Foot Locker Slam Fest" slam dunk contest, televised on ESPN on May 17, 1988. These standard size cards (2 1/2" by 3 1/2") feature color posed shots of the participants, who were professional athletes from sports other than basketball. The pictures have magenta and blue borders on a white card face. A colored banner with the words "Foot Locker" overlays the top of the picture. A line drawing of a referee overlays the lower left corner of the picture. The backs are printed in blue on white and promote the slam dunk contest and an in-store contest. The cards were given out in May at participating Foot Locker stores to customers. Between May 18 and July 31, customers could turn in the winner's card (Mike Conley) and

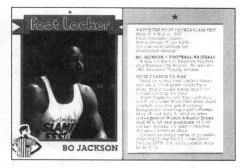

BO JACKSON

receive a free pair of Wilson athletic shoes and 50% off any purchase at Foot Locker. The cards are unnumbered and checklisted below in alphabetical order. Bo Jackson is obviously the key card in the set.

	MINT	EXC	G-VG
COMPLETE SET (9)	25.00	12.50	2.50
COMMON PLAYER (1-9)	1.00	.50	.10
☐ 1 Carl Banks Football	2.00	1.00	.20
☐ 2 Mike Conley Track and Field	3.50	1.75	.35
☐ 3 Thomas Hearns Boxing	1.00	.50	.10
☐ 4 Bo Jackson Baseball/Football	15.00	7.50	1.50
☐ 5 Keith Jackson Football	2.50	1.25	.25
☐ 6 Karch Kiraly Volleyball	2.50	1.25	.25
☐ 7 Ricky Sanders Football	1.00	.50	.10
☐ 8 Dwight Stones Track and Field	1.50	.75	.15
☐ 9 Devon White Baseball	2.00	1.00	.20

1989 Foot Locker Slam Fest *

MIKE POWELL

This ten-card set was produced by Foot Locker and Nike to commemorate the "Foot Locker Slam Fest" slam dunk contest, which was televised during halftimes of NBC college basketball games through March 12, 1989. These standard size cards (2 1/2" by 3 1/2") feature color posed shots of the participants, who were professional athletes from sports other than basketball. A banner with the words "Foot Locker" traverses the top of the card face. The cards were wrapped in cellophane and issued with one stick of gum. They were given out at participating Foot

Locker stores upon request with a purchase. The cards are unnumbered and checklisted below in alphabetical order.

	MINT	EXC	G-VG
COMPLETE SET (10)	7.50	3.75	.75
COMMON PLAYER (1-10)	.50	.25	.05
☐ 1 Mike Conley Track and Field	.75	.35	.07
☐ 2 Keith Jackson Football	1.00	.50	.10
☐ 3 Vince Coleman Baseball	1.00	.50	.10
☐ 4 Eric Dickerson Football	1.50	.75	.15
☐ 5 Steve Timmons Volleyball	1.00	.50	.10
☐ 6 Matt Biondi Swimming	.75	.35	.07
☐ 7 Carl Lewis Track and Field	1.50	.75	.15
☐ 8 Mike Quick Football	.50	.25	.05
☐ 9 Mike Powell Track and Field	1.00	.50	.10
☐ 10 Checklist Card	.50	.25	.05

1988 Fournier NBA Estrellas

The 32-card set was produced in Spain by Fournier and showcases 32 of the NBA hottest stars. The cards measure approximately 2 1/8" by 3 7/16" and have rounded corners. The front features borderless high glossy action player photos; in the white stripe below the picture, player statistics are given. The entire area of the card backs displays the NBA logo in red, white, and blue (indicating that the set was licensed by the NBA for distribution in Spain). The cards are numbered on the front in the upper left corner. The card backs were written in Spanish.

	MINT	EXC	G-VG
COMPLETE SET (33)	22.00	10.00	2.00
COMMON PLAYER (1-32)	.75	.35	.07
☐ 1 Larry Bird	3.00	1.50	.30
☐ 2 Robert Parish	1.00	.50	.10
☐ 3 Kevin McHale	.90	.45	.09
☐ 4 Magic Johnson	3.00	1.50	.30
☐ 5 Kareem Abdul Jabbar	2.50	1.25	.25
☐ 6 Byron Scott	.75	.35	.07
☐ 7 Isiah Thomas	2.00	1.00	.20
☐ 8 Adrian Dantley	1.00	.50	.10
☐ 9 Dominique Wilkins	2.00	1.00	.20
☐ 10 Spud Webb	.75	.35	.07
☐ 11 Clyde Drexler	2.00	1.00	.20
☐ 12 Terry Porter	.90	.45	.09
☐ 13 Mark Aguirre	.90	.45	.09
☐ 14 Tyrone Bogues	.75	.35	.07
☐ 15 Patrick Ewing	2.50	1.25	.25
☐ 16 Karl Malone	2.00	1.00	.20
☐ 17 Charles Barkley	2.00	1.00	.20
☐ 18 Ron Harper	.75	.35	.07

		NRMT	VG-E	GOOD
☐ 19	Alex English	1.00	.50	.10
☐ 20	Xavier McDaniel	.90	.45	.09
☐ 21	Jeff Malone	.90	.45	.09
☐ 22	Michael Jordan	6.00	3.00	.60
☐ 23	Akeem Olajuwon	2.00	1.00	.20
☐ 24	Ralph Sampson	.75	.35	.07
☐ 25	Buck Williams	.90	.45	.09
☐ 26	Chuck Person	.90	.45	.09
☐ 27	Alvin Robertson	.75	.35	.07
☐ 28	Tom Chambers	1.00	.50	.10
☐ 29	Paul Pressey	.75	.35	.07
☐ 30	Danny Manning	.90	.45	.09
☐ 31	Lasalle Thompson	.75	.35	.07
☐ 32	John Stockton	2.00	1.00	.20
☐ xx	Michael Jordan	6.00	3.00	.60
	Insert card			

☐ 24	Freddie(Curly) Neal	5.00	2.50	.50
☐ 25	Freddie(Curly) Neal	5.00	2.50	.50
	(Three paint brushes)			
☐ 26	Meadowlark Lemon	5.00	2.50	.50
	(Palming two balls)			
☐ 27	Mel Davis	3.00	1.50	.30
	(Leaning over with ball)			
☐ 28	Freddie"Curly" Neal	5.00	2.50	.50

1971-72 Globetrotters Cocoa Puffs 28

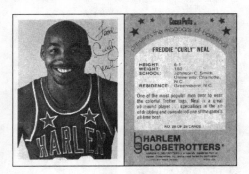

1971-72 Globetrotters 84

The 1971-72 Harlem Globetrotters set was produced by Fleer and sold in wax packs. The set contains 84 standard size (2 1/2" by 3 1/2") cards. The card fronts have full color pictures. The card backs have black printing on gray card stock and feature biographical sketches and other interesting information about the Globetrotters. The cards are numbered on back out of 84.

This 1971-72 Harlem Globetrotters set was produced for Cocoa Puffs cereal by Fleer and contains 28 standard size (2 1/2" by 3 1/2") cards. The card fronts have full color pictures with facsimile autographs. The card backs have black printing on gray card stock and feature biographical sketches and other interesting information about the Globetrotters. The cards are numbered on back out of 28.

		NRMT	VG-E	GOOD
COMPLETE SET (84)		175.00	85.00	18.00
COMMON CARD (1-84)		1.50	.75	.15
☐ 1	Bob"Showboat" Hall (full length)	6.00	1.00	.20
☐ 2	Bob"Showboat" Hall (kicking ball)	1.50	.75	.15
☐ 3	Bob"Showboat" Hall (passing behind back)	1.50	.75	.15
☐ 4	Pablo"Pabs" Robertson (ball in front)	1.50	.75	.15
☐ 5	Pablo"Pabs" Robertson (smiling)	1.50	.75	.15
☐ 6	Pablo"Pabs" Robertson (dribbling down)	1.50	.75	.15
☐ 7	Pablo"Pabs" Robertson (dribbling up)	1.50	.75	.15
☐ 8	Pablo"Pabs" Robertson (back-side)	1.50	.75	.15
☐ 9	Meadowlark Lemon (kicking behind back)	3.00	1.50	.30
☐ 10	Meadowlark Lemon (rolling ball on arm)	3.00	1.50	.30
☐ 11	Meadowlark Lemon (palming two balls)	3.00	1.50	.30
☐ 12	Meadowlark Lemon (ball on neck)	3.00	1.50	.30
☐ 13	Meadowlark Lemon (three balls)	3.00	1.50	.30
☐ 14	Meadowlark Lemon (three balls in front)	3.00	1.50	.30
☐ 15	Meadowlark Lemon (three balls)	3.00	1.50	.30
☐ 16	Meadowlark Lemon (dribbling two balls)	3.00	1.50	.30
☐ 17	Meadowlark Lemon (with cap)	3.00	1.50	.30
☐ 18	Curley, Meadowlark, and Mel	2.50	1.25	.25
☐ 19	Football Play (Meadowlark centering)	2.50	1.25	.25
☐ 20	Meadowlark Lemon (hooking)	2.50	1.25	.25
☐ 21	Hubert"Geese" Ausbie (balls between legs)	2.00	1.00	.20

		NRMT	VG-E	GOOD
COMPLETE SET (28)		100.00	50.00	10.00
COMMON CARD (1-28)		3.00	1.50	.30
☐ 1	Geese Ausbie and Curly Neal	6.00	1.50	.30
☐ 2	Neal and Meadowlark	4.00	2.00	.40
☐ 3	Meadowlark is Safe	5.00	2.50	.50
☐ 4	Meadowlark, Neal, and Geese Ausbie	5.00	2.50	.50
☐ 5	Mel Davis and Bill Meggett	3.00	1.50	.30
☐ 6	Ausbie, Meadowlark, and Curly Neal	4.00	2.00	.40
☐ 7	Ausbie, Meadowlark, and Curly Neal	4.00	2.00	.40
☐ 8	Mel Davis and Curly Neal	3.00	1.50	.30
☐ 9	Meadowlark, Neal, and Geese Ausbie	4.00	2.00	.40
☐ 10	Curly, Meadowlark, and Mel Davis	4.00	2.00	.40
☐ 11	Football Routine	3.00	1.50	.30
☐ 12	1970-71 Highlights	3.00	1.50	.30
☐ 13	Pabs Robertson	3.00	1.50	.30
☐ 14	Bobby Joe Mason	3.00	1.50	.30
☐ 15	Pabs Robertson	3.00	1.50	.30
☐ 16	Clarence Smith	3.00	1.50	.30
☐ 17	Clarence Smith	3.00	1.50	.30
☐ 18	Hubert(Geese) Ausbie	4.00	2.00	.40
☐ 19	Hubert(Geese) Ausbie (Two balls)	4.00	2.00	.40
☐ 20	Bobby Hunter	4.00	2.00	.40
☐ 21	Bobby Hunter (One leg up)	4.00	2.00	.40
☐ 22	Meadowlark Lemon (Three balls)	5.00	2.50	.50
☐ 23	Meadowlark Lemon	5.00	2.50	.50

☐ 22 Hubert"Geese" Ausbie .... (ball under arm)	2.00	1.00	.20
☐ 23 Hubert"Geese" Ausbie .... (ball on finger)	2.00	1.00	.20
☐ 24 Hubert"Geese" Ausbie .... (ball behind back)	2.00	1.00	.20
☐ 25 Hubert"Geese" Ausbie .... (no ball)	2.00	1.00	.20
☐ 26 Ausbie and Neal .... (with confetti)	2.50	1.25	.25
☐ 27 Freddie"Curly" Neal .... (artist)	2.50	1.25	.25
☐ 28 Freddie"Curly" Neal .... (sitting on ball)	2.50	1.25	.25
☐ 29 Freddie"Curly" Neal .... (two balls on head)	2.50	1.25	.25
☐ 30 Mel Davis and .... "Curly" Neal	2.00	1.00	.20
☐ 31 Freddie"Curly" Neal .... (smiling)	2.50	1.25	.25
☐ 32 Freddie"Curly" Neal .... (looking to side)	2.50	1.25	.25
☐ 33 Mel Davis .... (looking down)	1.50	.75	.15
☐ 34 Mel Davis .... (ready to shoot)	1.50	.75	.15
☐ 35 Mel Davis .... (ball in hand)	1.50	.75	.15
☐ 36 Mel Davis .... (ball over head)	1.50	.75	.15
☐ 37 Mel Davis and Bill .... Meggett (leap frog)	1.50	.75	.15
☐ 38 Mel Davis .... (ball on knee)	1.50	.75	.15
☐ 39 Bobby Joe Mason .... (ball under arm)	1.50	.75	.15
☐ 40 Bobby Joe Mason .... (ball between legs)	1.50	.75	.15
☐ 41 Bobby Joe Mason .... (passing behind back)	1.50	.75	.15
☐ 42 Mason and Stephens	1.50	.75	.15
☐ 43 Bobby Joe Mason .... (ball to side)	1.50	.75	.15
☐ 44 Bobby Joe Mason .... (ready to shoot)	1.50	.75	.15
☐ 45 Clarence Smith .... (three balls between legs)	1.50	.75	.15
☐ 46 Clarence Smith .... (on bike)	1.50	.75	.15
☐ 47 Clarence Smith .... (ball at ear)	1.50	.75	.15
☐ 48 Clarence Smith .... (dribbling on side)	1.50	.75	.15
☐ 49 Jerry Venable	1.50	.75	.15
☐ 50 Frank Stephens .... (hands in front)	1.50	.75	.15
☐ 51 Frank Stephens .... (ball on finger)	1.50	.75	.15
☐ 52 Frank Stephens .... (waiting for ball)	1.50	.75	.15
☐ 53 Frank Stephens .... (ball in hand)	1.50	.75	.15
☐ 54 Theodis Ray Lee .... (ball on hip)	1.50	.75	.15
☐ 55 Theodis Ray Lee .... (ball between knees)	1.50	.75	.15
☐ 56 Jerry Venable .... (palming ball)	1.50	.75	.15
☐ 57 Doug Himes .... (ball in air)	1.50	.75	.15
☐ 58 Doug Himes .... (ball behind back)	1.50	.75	.15
☐ 59 Bill Meggett .... (dribbling two balls)	1.50	.75	.15
☐ 60 Bill Meggett .... (ready to shoot)	1.50	.75	.15
☐ 61 Vincent White .... (ball on hip)	1.50	.75	.15
☐ 62 Vincent White .... (kicking ball)	1.50	.75	.15
☐ 63 Pablo and "Showboat" .... (arm in arm)	1.50	.75	.15
☐ 64 Meadowlark, Neal, ... and Ausbie (balls behind back)	2.50	1.25	.25
☐ 65 Curley Neal, ... Quarterback	2.50	1.25	.25
☐ 66 Ausbie, Meadowlark, ... and Neal (looking at ball)	2.50	1.25	.25
☐ 67 Neal and Meadowlark	3.00	1.50	.30
☐ 68 Football Routine	2.00	1.00	.20
☐ 69 Meadowlark To Neal .... To Ausbie	2.50	1.25	.25

☐ 70 Meadowlark Is Safe .... At The Plate	2.50	1.25	.25
☐ 71 1970-71 Highlights .... (baseball act)	2.50	1.25	.25
☐ 72 1970-71 Highlights .... (Lemon and Neal)	2.50	1.25	.25
☐ 73 Bobby Hunter .... (ball on hip)	2.00	1.00	.20
☐ 74 Bobby Hunter .... (ball in hand)	2.00	1.00	.20
☐ 75 Bobby Hunter .... (ball on shoulder)	2.00	1.00	.20
☐ 76 Bobby Hunter .... (ball in air)	2.00	1.00	.20
☐ 77 Bobby Hunter .... (passing between legs)	2.00	1.00	.20
☐ 78 Jackie Jackson .... (ball on hip)	2.00	1.00	.20
☐ 79 Jackie Jackson .... (ball behind back)	2.00	1.00	.20
☐ 80 Jackie Jackson .... (ball in air)	2.00	1.00	.20
☐ 81 Jackie Jackson .... (ball on finger)	2.00	1.00	.20
☐ 82 The Globetrotters	2.50	1.25	.25
☐ 83 The Globetrotters	2.50	1.25	.25
☐ 84 Dallas Thornton	3.00	1.50	.30
☐ xx Globetrotter Official .... Peel-off Team Emblem Sticker (unnumbered)	6.00	3.00	.60

1968-70 Hall of Fame Bookmarks

JOHN R. WOODEN
(1910-)
ELECTED 1969 COLLEGE PLAYER

These bookmarks commemorate individuals who were elected to the Basketball Hall of Fame. They measure approximately 2 7/16" by 6 3/8". The top of the front has a blue-tinted 2 1/8" by 2 5/16 "mug shot" of the individual on paper stock. In blue lettering the individual's name and a brief biography are printed below the picture. The backs are blank and the cards are unnumbered. The cards were probably issued year after year (with additions) by the Hall of Fame book store. The last five cards listed below were inducted in 1969 (47-48) and 1970 (49-51); there are some slight style and size differences in these later issue cards compared to the first 46 cards in the set.

	NRMT	VG-E	GOOD
COMPLETE SET (51)	30.00	15.00	3.00
COMMON PLAYER (1-46)	.30	.15	.03
COMMON PLAYER (47-51)	1.00	.50	.10

☐ 1 Forrest C. Allen		.50	.25	.05
☐ 2 Arnold J. Auerbach		.75	.35	.07
☐ 3 Clair F. Bee		.75	.35	.07
☐ 4 Bernhard Borgmann		.30	.15	.03
☐ 5 Walter A. Brown		.30	.15	.03
☐ 6 John W. Bunn		.30	.15	.03
☐ 7 Howard G. Cann		.30	.15	.03
☐ 8 H. Clifford Carlson		.30	.15	.03
☐ 9 Everett S. Dean		.30	.15	.03
☐ 10 Forrest S. DeBernardi		.30	.15	.03
☐ 11 Henry G. Dehnert		.30	.15	.03
☐ 12 Harold E. Foster		.30	.15	.03
☐ 13 Amory T. Gill		.30	.15	.03
☐ 14 Victor A. Hanson		.30	.15	.03
☐ 15 Edward J. Hickox		.30	.15	.03
☐ 16 Paul D. Hinkle		.30	.15	.03
☐ 17 Howard A. Hobson		.30	.15	.03
☐ 18 Nat Holman		.50	.25	.05
☐ 19 Charles D. Hyatt		.30	.15	.03
☐ 20 Henry P. Iba		.75	.35	.07
☐ 21 Edward S. Irish		.50	.25	.05
☐ 22 Alvin F. Julian		.30	.15	.03
☐ 23 Matthew P. Kennedy		.30	.15	.03
☐ 24 Robert A. Kurland		.75	.35	.07
☐ 25 Ward L. Lambert		.30	.15	.03
☐ 26 Joe Lapchick		.75	.35	.07
☐ 27 Kenneth D. Loeffler		.30	.15	.03
☐ 28 Angelo Luisetti		.75	.35	.07
☐ 29 Edward C. Macauley		.50	.25	.05
☐ 30 Branch McCracken		.30	.15	.03
☐ 31 George L. Mikan		3.00	1.50	.30
☐ 32 William G. Mokray		.30	.15	.03
☐ 33 Charles L. Murphy		.30	.15	.03
☐ 34 James Naismith		1.00	.50	.10
☐ 35 Andy Phillip		.50	.25	.05
☐ 36 John S. Roosma		.30	.15	.03
☐ 37 Adolph F. Rupp		1.00	.50	.10
☐ 38 John D. Russell		.30	.15	.03
☐ 39 Arthur A. Schabinger		.30	.15	.03
☐ 40 Amos Alonzo Stagg		.50	.25	.05
☐ 41 Charles H. Taylor		.30	.15	.03
☐ 42 John A. Thompson		.30	.15	.03
☐ 43 David Tobey		.30	.15	.03
☐ 44 Oswald Tower		.30	.15	.03
☐ 45 David H. Walsh		.30	.15	.03
☐ 46 John R. Wooden		.75	.35	.07
☐ 47 Bernard Carnevale		1.00	.50	.10
☐ 48 Robert E. Davies		2.00	1.00	.20
☐ 49 Robert J. Cousy		3.00	1.50	.30
☐ 50 Robert C. Pettit		3.00	1.50	.30
☐ 51 Abraham M. Saperstein		2.00	1.00	.20

1961 Hawks Essex Meats

The 1961 Essex Meats set contains 13 cards featuring the St. Louis Hawks only. These cards measure the standard 2 1/2" by 3 1/2". The fronts picture a posed black and white photo of the player with his name at the bottom of the card in bold-faced type. The backs of this white-stock card feature the player's name, brief physical data and biographical information. The

cards are unnumbered and give no indication of the producer on the card. The cards were also distributed by Bonnie Brands. The catalog designation for the set is F175.

	NRMT	VG-E	GOOD
COMPLETE SET (13)	250.00	125.00	25.00
COMMON PLAYER (1-13)	12.00	6.00	1.20

☐ 1 Barney Cable	12.00	6.00	1.20
☐ 2 Al Ferrari	12.00	6.00	1.20
☐ 3 Larry Foust	18.00	9.00	1.80
☐ 4 Cliff Hagen	35.00	17.50	3.50
☐ 5 Vern Hatton	12.00	6.00	1.20
☐ 6 Cleo Hill	12.00	6.00	1.20
☐ 7 Fred LaCour	12.00	6.00	1.20
☐ 8 Andrew Fuzzy Levane	12.00	6.00	1.20
☐ 9 Clyde Lovellette	35.00	17.50	3.50
☐ 10 John McCarthy	12.00	6.00	1.20
☐ 11 Shellie McMillon	12.00	6.00	1.20
☐ 12 Bob Pettit	100.00	50.00	10.00
☐ 13 Bobby Sims	12.00	6.00	1.20

1978-79 Hawks Coke/WPLO

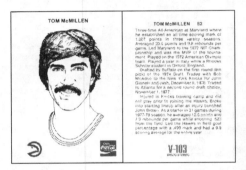

This 14-card set was sponsored by V-103/WPLO radio and Coca-Cola, and they were given out at 7-Eleven stores. The cards are printed on thin cardboard stock and measure approximately 3 by 4 1/4". The front features a black and white pen and ink drawing of the player's head, with the Hawks' and Coke logos in the lower corners in red. The back has a career summary and the sponsor's "V-103 Disco Stereo" at the bottom. The cards are unnumbered and are checklisted below in alphabetical order.

	NRMT	VG-E	GOOD
COMPLETE SET (14)	30.00	15.00	3.00
COMMON PLAYER (1-14)	1.50	.75	.15

☐ 1 Hubie Brown CO	2.50	1.25	.25
☐ 2 Charlie Criss	2.50	1.25	.25
☐ 3 John Drew	2.50	1.25	.25
☐ 4 Mike Fratello CO	3.50	1.75	.35
☐ 5 Jack Givens	2.50	1.25	.25
☐ 6 Steve Hawes	1.50	.75	.15
☐ 7 Armond Hill	1.50	.75	.15
☐ 8 Eddie Johnson	1.50	.75	.15
☐ 9 Frank Layden CO	3.50	1.75	.35
☐ 10 Butch Lee	2.00	1.00	.20
☐ 11 Tom McMillen	3.50	1.75	.35
☐ 12 Tree Rollins	3.50	1.75	.35
☐ 13 Dan Roundfield	2.50	1.25	.25
☐ 14 Rick Wilson	1.50	.75	.15

1979-80 Hawks Majik Market

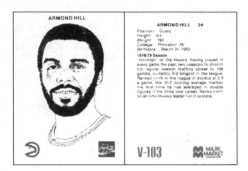

The 1979-80 Majik Market/Coca-Cola Atlanta Hawks set contains 15 cards on thin white stock. Cards are approximately 3" by 4 1/4". The fronts of the cards include a crude, black line drawing of the player, the player's name and, in red, a Coke logo and a stylized Hawks logo. The backs contain biographical data and a summary of the player's activity during the 1978-79 season. The Majik Market logo and the call letters V-103/WPLO are printed in red on the back of the cards. Most collectors consider the set quite unattractive and poorly produced. The cards are unnumbered and are checklisted below in alphabetical order.

	MINT	EXC	G-VG
COMPLETE SET (15)	50.00	25.00	5.00
COMMON PLAYER (1-15)	2.50	1.25	.25

		MINT	EXC	G-VG
☐ 1	Hubie Brown CO	3.50	1.75	.35
☐ 2	John Brown	3.50	1.75	.35
☐ 3	Charlie Criss	5.00	2.50	.50
☐ 4	John Drew	5.00	2.50	.50
☐ 5	Mike Fratello ACO	5.00	2.50	.50
☐ 6	Jack Givens	5.00	2.50	.50
☐ 7	Steve Hawes	2.50	1.25	.25
☐ 8	Armond Hill	2.50	1.25	.25
☐ 9	Eddie Johnson	2.50	1.25	.25
☐ 10	Jimmy McElroy	2.50	1.25	.25
☐ 11	Tom McMillen	6.00	3.00	.60
☐ 12	Sam Pellom	2.50	1.25	.25
☐ 13	Tree Rollins	6.00	3.00	.60
☐ 14	Dan Roundfield	3.50	1.75	.35
☐ 15	Brendan Suhr ACO	2.50	1.25	.25

1987-88 Hawks Pizza Hut

The 1987-88 Atlanta Hawks Team Photo Night (March 11, 1988) set was sponsored by Pizza Hut. This photo album was distributed to fans attending the Atlanta Hawks home game. It consists of three sheets, each measuring approximately 8 1/4" by 11" and joined together to form one continuous sheet. The first sheet features a team photo of the Hawks. While the second sheet presents two rows of five cards each, the third sheet presents seven additional player cards, with the remaining three slots filled in by Pizza Hut coupons. After perforation, the cards measure approximately 2 3/16" by 3 3/4". The card front features a color action player photo, with a red border on white card stock. The player's name and position are given below the picture, along with the team and Pizza Hut logos. The back presents career statistics in a horizontal format. The cards are unnumbered and checklisted below in the order they appear in the album.

	MINT	EXC	G-VG
COMPLETE SET (17)	15.00	7.50	1.50
COMMON PLAYER (1-17)	.75	.35	.07

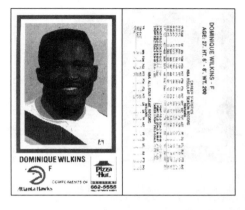

		MINT	EXC	G-VG
☐ 1	Mike Fratello CO	1.00	.50	.10
☐ 2	Brendan Suhr ASST	.75	.35	.07
☐ 3	Brian Hill ASST	.75	.35	.07
☐ 4	Don Chaney ASST	1.00	.50	.10
☐ 5	Joe O'Toole TR	.75	.35	.07
☐ 6	John Battle	1.00	.50	.10
☐ 7	Antoine Carr	1.00	.50	.10
☐ 8	Scott Hastings	.75	.35	.07
☐ 9	John Koncak	1.00	.50	.10
☐ 10	Cliff Levingston	1.00	.50	.10
☐ 11	Glenn Rivers	1.50	.75	.15
☐ 12	Tree Rollins	1.50	.75	.15
☐ 13	Chris Washburn	.75	.35	.07
☐ 14	Anthony(Spud) Webb	1.50	.75	.15
☐ 15	Dominique Wilkins	3.50	1.75	.35
☐ 16	Kevin Willis	1.50	.75	.15
☐ 17	Randy Wittman	.75	.35	.07

1989-90 Heat Publix

This 15-card set was distributed in Publix stores in the greater Miami area. The cards measure approximately 2" by 3 1/2". The front features a color action player photo, with the player's name and position in the stripe below the picture. The back has biographical and statistical information. The cards are unnumbered and are checklisted below in alphabetical order.

	MINT	EXC	G-VG
COMPLETE SET (15)	20.00	10.00	2.00
COMMON PLAYER (1-15)	1.00	.50	.10

		MINT	EXC	G-VG
☐ 1	Terry Davis	1.00	.50	.10
☐ 2	Sherman Douglas	2.00	1.00	.20
☐ 3	Kevin Edwards	1.50	.75	.15
☐ 4	Tony Fiorentino CO	1.00	.50	.10
☐ 5	Tellis Frank	1.00	.50	.10
☐ 6	Scott Haffner	1.00	.50	.10
☐ 7	Grant Long	1.50	.75	.15
☐ 8	Heat Mascot	1.00	.50	.10
☐ 9	Glen Rice	3.00	1.50	.30
☐ 10	Ron Rothstein CO	1.00	.50	.10
☐ 11	Rony Seikaly	3.00	1.50	.30
☐ 12	Rory Sparrow	1.00	.50	.10
☐ 13	Jon Sundvold	1.00	.50	.10
☐ 14	Billy Thompson	1.50	.75	.15
☐ 15	Dave Wohl CO	1.00	.50	.10

1990-91 Heat Publix

This 16-card set of Miami Heat was sponsored by Domino's, Dixie, and Bumble Bee. The cards were issued in a sheet that contains 16 player cards and four manufacturers' coupons; after perforation, the cards and coupons alike measure the

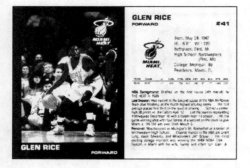

standard size (2 1/2" by 3 1/2"). The front features a color action player photo on a black background. The team logo appears in the upper right corner, while the player's name appears in white lettering below the picture. The back has biographical and statistical information. The cards are unnumbered and are checklisted below as they are listed on the panel, in alphabetical order with coaches at the end.

	MINT	EXC	G-VG
COMPLETE SET (16)	20.00	10.00	2.00
COMMON PLAYER (1-16)	1.00	.50	.10
☐ 1 Keith Askins	1.00	.50	.10
☐ 2 Willie Burton	3.00	1.50	.30
☐ 3 Vernell Coles	2.00	1.00	.20
☐ 4 Terry Davis	1.00	.50	.10
☐ 5 Sherman Douglas	2.00	1.00	.20
☐ 6 Kevin Edwards	1.50	.75	.15
☐ 7 Alec Kessler	1.50	.75	.15
☐ 8 Grant Long	1.00	.50	.10
☐ 9 Alan Ogg	1.50	.75	.15
☐ 10 Glen Rice	2.00	1.00	.20
☐ 11 Rony Seikaly	2.00	1.00	.20
☐ 12 Jon Sundvold	1.00	.50	.10
☐ 13 Billy Thompson	1.50	.75	.15
☐ 14 Ron Rothstein CO	1.00	.50	.10
☐ 15 Dave Wohl CO	1.00	.50	.10
☐ 16 Tony Fiorentino CO	1.00	.50	.10

1989-90 Hoops I

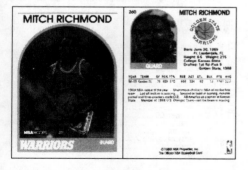

The 1989-90 Hoops sets contains 300 cards measuring the standard size (2 1/2" by 3 1/2"). The fronts feature color action player photos, bordered by a basketball lane in one of the team's colors. On a white card face the player's name appears in black lettering above the picture. The backs have head shots of the players, biographical information, and statistics, all printed on a pale yellow background with white borders. The cards are numbered on the backs. The key rookie in this set is David

Robinson's card #138 which only appeared in this first series of Hoops. Other notable rookies in this set are Willie Anderson, Rex Chapman, Hersey Hawkins, Jeff Hornacek, Kevin Johnson, Reggie Lewis, Dan Majerle, Danny Manning, Vernon Maxwell, Ken Norman, Mitch Richmond, Rony Seikaly, Brian Shaw, Scott Skiles, Charles Smith, and Rod Strickland. Beware of David Robinson counterfeit cards which are distinguishable primarily by comparison to a real card or under magnification.

	MINT	EXC	G-VG
COMPLETE SET (300)	62.00	25.00	5.00
COMMON PLAYER (1-300)	.03	.01	.00
COMMON PLAYER SP (1-300)	.20	.10	.02
☐ 1 Joe Dumars	.30	.10	.02
Detroit Pistons			
☐ 2 Wayne Rollins	.03	.01	.00
Cleveland Cavaliers			
☐ 3 Kenny Walker	.03	.01	.00
New York Knicks			
☐ 4 Mychal Thompson	.03	.01	.00
Los Angeles Lakers			
☐ 5 Alvin Robertson SP	.30	.15	.03
San Antonio Spurs			
☐ 6 Vinny Del Negro	.12	.06	.01
Sacramento Kings			
☐ 7 Greg Anderson SP	.25	.12	.02
San Antonio Spurs			
☐ 8 Rod Strickland	.50	.25	.05
New York Knicks			
☐ 9 Ed Pinckney	.10	.05	.01
Boston Celtics			
☐ 10 Dale Ellis	.08	.04	.01
Seattle Supersonics			
☐ 11 Chuck Daly	.10	.05	.01
Detroit Pistons			
☐ 12 Eric Leckner	.12	.06	.01
Utah Jazz			
☐ 13 Charles Davis	.03	.01	.00
Chicago Bulls			
☐ 14 Cotton Fitzsimmons CO	.03	.01	.00
Phoenix Suns			
(No NBA logo on back			
in bottom right)			
☐ 15 Byron Scott	.10	.05	.01
Los Angeles Lakers			
☐ 16 Derrick Chievous	.10	.05	.01
Houston Rockets			
☐ 17 Reggie Lewis	.80	.40	.08
Boston Celtics			
☐ 18 Jim Paxson	.03	.01	.00
Boston Celtics			
☐ 19 Tony Campbell	.40	.20	.04
Los Angeles Lakers			
☐ 20 Rolando Blackmon	.10	.05	.01
Dallas Mavericks			
☐ 21 Michael Jordan AS	.75	.35	.07
Chicago Bulls			
☐ 22 Cliff Levingston	.06	.03	.00
Atlanta Hawks			
☐ 23 Roy Tarpley	.12	.06	.01
Dallas Mavericks			
☐ 24 Harold Pressley	.12	.06	.01
Sacramento Kings			
(Cinderella misspelled			
as cindarella)			
☐ 25 Larry Nance	.08	.04	.01
Cleveland Cavaliers			
☐ 26 Chris Morris	.20	.10	.02
New Jersey Nets			
☐ 27 Bob Hansen	.03	.01	.00
Utah Jazz			
(Drafted in '84,			
should say '83)			
☐ 28 Mark Price AS	.06	.03	.00
Cleveland Cavaliers			
☐ 29 Reggie Miller	.35	.17	.03
Indiana Pacers			
☐ 30 Karl Malone	.35	.17	.03
Utah Jazz			
☐ 31 Sidney Lowe SP	.25	.12	.02
Charlotte Hornets			
☐ 32 Ron Anderson	.06	.03	.00
Philadelphia 76ers			
☐ 33 Mike Gminski	.06	.03	.00
Philadelphia 76ers			
☐ 34 Scott Brooks	.12	.06	.01
Philadelphia 76ers			
☐ 35 Kevin Johnson	3.00	1.50	.30
Phoenix Suns			
☐ 36 Mark Bryant	.12	.06	.01
Portland Trail Blazers			

☐ 37 Rik Smits	.25	.12	.02	
Indiana Pacers				
☐ 38 Tim Perry	.10	.05	.01	
Phoenix Suns				
☐ 39 Ralph Sampson	.08	.04	.01	
Golden State Warriors				
☐ 40 Danny Manning	.60	.30	.06	
Los Angeles Clippers				
(Missing 1988				
in draft info)				
☐ 41 Kevin Edwards	.15	.07	.01	
Miami Heat				
☐ 42 Paul Mokeski	.03	.01	.00	
Milwaukee Bucks				
☐ 43 Dale Ellis AS	.06	.03	.00	
Seattle Supersonics				
☐ 44 Walter Berry	.03	.01	.00	
Houston Rockets				
☐ 45 Chuck Person	.20	.10	.02	
Indiana Pacers				
☐ 46 Rick Mahorn	.12	.06	.01	
Detroit Pistons				
☐ 47 Joe Kleine	.03	.01	.00	
Boston Celtics				
☐ 48 Brad Daugherty AS	.06	.03	.00	
Cleveland Cavaliers				
☐ 49 Mike Woodson	.03	.01	.00	
Houston Rockets				
☐ 50 Brad Daugherty	.17	.08	.01	
Cleveland Cavaliers				
☐ 51 Shelton Jones SP	.30	.15	.03	
Philadelphia 76ers				
☐ 52 Michael Adams	.15	.07	.01	
Denver Nuggets				
☐ 53 Wes Unseld	.08	.04	.01	
Washington Bullets				
☐ 54 Rex Chapman	.65	.30	.06	
Charlotte Hornets				
☐ 55 Kelly Tripucka	.03	.01	.00	
Charlotte Hornets				
☐ 56 Rickey Green	.03	.01	.00	
Milwaukee Bucks				
☐ 57 Frank Johnson SP	.20	.10	.02	
Houston Rockets				
☐ 58 Johnny Newman	.30	.15	.03	
New York Knicks				
☐ 59 Billy Thompson	.17	.08	.01	
Miami Heat				
☐ 60 Stu Jackson CO	.06	.03	.00	
New York Knicks				
☐ 61 Walter Davis	.08	.04	.01	
Denver Nuggets				
☐ 62 Brian Shaw SP	2.25	1.10	.22	
Boston Celtics				
(Gary Grant led rookies				
in assists, not Shaw)				
☐ 63 Gerald Wilkins	.06	.03	.00	
New York Knicks				
☐ 64 Armon Gilliam	.12	.06	.01	
Phoenix Suns				
☐ 65 Maurice Cheeks SP	.35	.17	.03	
Philadelphia 76ers				
☐ 66 Jack Sikma	.08	.04	.01	
Milwaukee Bucks				
☐ 67 Harvey Grant	.30	.15	.03	
Washington Bullets				
☐ 68 Jim Lynam CO	.03	.01	.00	
Philadelphia 76ers				
☐ 69 Clyde Drexler AS	.12	.06	.01	
Portland Trail Blazers				
☐ 70 Xavier McDaniel	.08	.04	.01	
Seattle Supersonics				
☐ 71 Danny Young	.03	.01	.00	
Portland Trail Blazers				
☐ 72 Fennis Dembo	.10	.05	.01	
Detroit Pistons				
☐ 73 Mark Acres SP	.25	.12	.02	
Boston Celtics				
☐ 74 Brad Lohaus SP	.30	.15	.03	
Sacramento Kings				
☐ 75 Manute Bol	.08	.04	.01	
Golden State Warriors				
☐ 76 Purvis Short	.06	.03	.00	
Houston Rockets				
☐ 77 Allen Leavell	.03	.01	.00	
Houston Rockets				
☐ 78 Johnny Dawkins SP	.25	.12	.02	
San Antonio Spurs				
☐ 79 Paul Pressey	.06	.03	.00	
Milwaukee Bucks				
☐ 80 Patrick Ewing	.40	.20	.04	
New York Knicks				
☐ 81 Bill Wennington	.12	.06	.01	
Dallas Mavericks				

☐ 82 Dan Schayes	.06	.03	.00
Denver Nuggets			
☐ 83 Derek Smith	.03	.01	.00
Philadelphia 76ers			
☐ 84 Moses Malone AS	.08	.04	.01
Atlanta Hawks			
☐ 85 Jeff Malone	.10	.05	.01
Washington Bullets			
☐ 86 Otis Smith SP	.30	.15	.03
Golden State Warriors			
☐ 87 Trent Tucker	.03	.01	.00
New York Knicks			
☐ 88 Robert Reid	.03	.01	.00
Charlotte Hornets			
☐ 89 John Paxson	.15	.07	.01
Chicago Bulls			
☐ 90 Chris Mullin	.25	.12	.02
Golden State Warriors			
☐ 91 Tom Garrick	.10	.05	.01
Los Angeles Clippers			
☐ 92 Willis Reed CO SP	.30	.15	.03
New Jersey Nets			
(Gambling, should			
be Grambling)			
☐ 93 Dave Corzine SP	.20	.10	.02
Chicago Bulls			
☐ 94 Mark Alarie	.10	.05	.01
Washington Bullets			
☐ 95 Mark Aguirre	.08	.04	.01
Detroit Pistons			
☐ 96 Charles Barkley AS	.15	.07	.01
Philadelphia 76ers			
☐ 97 Sidney Green SP	.25	.12	.02
New York Knicks			
☐ 98 Kevin Willis	.06	.03	.00
Atlanta Hawks			
☐ 99 Dave Hoppen	.10	.05	.01
Charlotte Hornets			
☐ 100 Terry Cummings SP	.35	.17	.03
Milwaukee Bucks			
☐ 101 Dwayne Washington SP	.20	.10	.02
Miami Heat			
☐ 102 Larry Brown CO	.03	.01	.00
San Antonio Spurs			
☐ 103 Kevin Duckworth	.06	.03	.00
Portland Trail Blazers			
☐ 104 Uwe Blab SP	.30	.15	.03
Dallas Mavericks			
☐ 105 Terry Porter	.17	.08	.01
Portland Trail Blazers			
☐ 106 Craig Ehlo	.12	.06	.01
Cleveland Cavaliers			
☐ 107 Don Casey CO	.03	.01	.00
Los Angeles Clippers			
☐ 108 Pat Riley CO	.06	.03	.00
Los Angeles Lakers			
☐ 109 John Salley	.12	.06	.01
Detroit Pistons			
☐ 110 Charles Barkley	.35	.17	.03
Philadelphia 76ers			
☐ 111 Sam Bowie SP	.30	.15	.03
Portland Trail Blazers			
☐ 112 Earl Cureton	.10	.05	.01
Charlotte Hornets			
☐ 113 Craig Hodges	.10	.05	.01
Chicago Bulls			
(3-pointing shooting)			
☐ 114 Benoit Benjamin	.06	.03	.00
Los Angeles Clippers			
☐ 115A Spud Webb ERR SP	.50	.25	.05
Atlanta Hawks			
(Signed 9/27/89)			
☐ 115B Spud Webb COR	.10	.05	.01
Atlanta Hawks			
(Second series;			
signed 9/26/85)			
☐ 116 Karl Malone AS	.15	.07	.01
Utah Jazz			
☐ 117 Sleepy Floyd	.06	.03	.00
Houston Rockets			
☐ 118 John Williams	.08	.04	.01
Cleveland Cavaliers			
☐ 119 Michael Holton	.03	.01	.00
Charlotte Hornets			
☐ 120 Alex English	.12	.06	.01
Denver Nuggets			
☐ 121 Dennis Johnson	.10	.05	.01
Boston Celtics			
☐ 122 Wayne Cooper SP	.20	.10	.02
Denver Nuggets			
☐ 123A Don Chaney CO	.30	.15	.03
Houston Rockets			
(Line next to NBA			
coaching record)			

#	Player			
☐ 123B	Don Chaney CO (No line) Houston Rockets	.06	.03	.00
☐ 124	A.C. Green — Los Angeles Lakers	.06	.03	.00
☐ 125	Adrian Dantley — Dallas Mavericks	.12	.06	.01
☐ 126	Del Harris CO — Milwaukee Bucks	.03	.01	.00
☐ 127	Dick Harter CO — Charlotte Hornets	.03	.01	.00
☐ 128	Reggie Williams — Los Angeles Clippers	.10	.05	.01
☐ 129	Bill Hanzlik — Denver Nuggets	.03	.01	.00
☐ 130	Dominique Wilkins — Atlanta Hawks	.30	.15	.03
☐ 131	Herb Williams — Dallas Mavericks	.06	.03	.00
☐ 132	Steve Johnson SP — Portland Trail Blazers	.20	.10	.02
☐ 133	Alex English AS — Denver Nuggets	.06	.03	.00
☐ 134	Darrell Walker — Washington Bullets	.03	.01	.00
☐ 135	Bill Laimbeer — Detroit Pistons	.10	.05	.01
☐ 136	Fred Roberts — Milwaukee Bucks	.12	.06	.01
☐ 137	Hersey Hawkins — Philadelphia 76ers	.80	.40	.08
☐ 138	David Robinson — San Antonio Spurs	44.00	15.00	3.00
☐ 139	Brad Sellers SP — Chicago Bulls	.20	.10	.02
☐ 140	John Stockton — Utah Jazz	.35	.17	.03
☐ 141	Grant Long — Miami Heat	.12	.06	.01
☐ 142	Marc Iavaroni SP — Utah Jazz	.20	.10	.02
☐ 143	Steve Alford SP — Golden State Warriors	.35	.17	.03
☐ 144	Jeff Lamp SP — Los Angeles Lakers	.20	.10	.02
☐ 145	Buck Williams SP — New Jersey Nets (Won ROY in '81, should say '82)	.35	.17	.03
☐ 146	Mark Jackson AS — New York Knicks	.06	.03	.00
☐ 147	Jim Petersen — Sacramento Kings	.03	.01	.00
☐ 148	Steve Stipanovich SP — Indiana Pacers	.20	.10	.02
☐ 149	Sam Vincent SP — Chicago Bulls	.35	.17	.03
☐ 150	Larry Bird — Boston Celtics	.50	.25	.05
☐ 151	Jon Koncak — Atlanta Hawks	.10	.05	.01
☐ 152	Olden Polynice — Seattle Supersonics	.12	.06	.01
☐ 153	Randy Breuer — Milwaukee Bucks	.03	.01	.00
☐ 154	John Battle — Atlanta Hawks	.15	.07	.01
☐ 155	Mark Eaton — Utah Jazz	.06	.03	.00
☐ 156	Kevin McHale AS — Boston Celtics (No TM on Celtics logo on back)	.10	.05	.01
☐ 157	Jerry Sichting SP — Portland Trail Blazers	.20	.10	.02
☐ 158	Pat Cummings SP — Miami Heat	.20	.10	.02
☐ 159	Patrick Ewing AS — New York Knicks	.17	.08	.01
☐ 160	Mark Price — Cleveland Cavaliers	.20	.10	.02
☐ 161	Jerry Reynolds CO — Sacramento Kings	.03	.01	.00
☐ 162	Ken Norman — Los Angeles Clippers	.45	.22	.04
☐ 163	John Bagley SP — New Jersey Nets (Picked in '83, should say '82)	.20	.10	.02
☐ 164	Christian Welp SP — Philadelphia 76ers	.30	.15	.03
☐ 165	Reggie Theus SP — Atlanta Hawks	.30	.15	.03
☐ 166	Magic Johnson AS — Los Angeles Lakers	.17	.08	.01
☐ 167	John Long — Detroit Pistons (Picked in '79, should say '78)	.03	.01	.00
☐ 168	Larry Smith SP — Golden State Warriors	.20	.10	.02
☐ 169	Charles Shackleford — New Jersey Nets	.10	.05	.01
☐ 170	Tom Chambers — Phoenix Suns	.17	.08	.01
☐ 171A	John MacLeod CO SP — Dallas Mavericks ERR (NBA logo in wrong place)	.30	.15	.03
☐ 171B	John MacLeod CO — Dallas Mavericks COR (Second series)	.08	.04	.01
☐ 172	Ron Rothstein CO — Miami Heat	.03	.01	.00
☐ 173	Joe Wolf — Los Angeles Clippers	.10	.05	.01
☐ 174	Mark Eaton AS — Utah Jazz	.03	.01	.00
☐ 175	Jon Sundvold — Miami Heat	.03	.01	.00
☐ 176	Scott Hastings SP — Miami Heat	.20	.10	.02
☐ 177	Isiah Thomas AS — Detroit Pistons	.12	.06	.01
☐ 178	Akeem Olajuwon AS — Houston Rockets	.12	.06	.01
☑ 179	Mike Fratello CO — Atlanta Hawks	.03	.01	.00
☐ 180	Akeem Olajuwon — Houston Rockets	.35	.17	.03
☐ 181	Randolph Keys — Cleveland Cavaliers	.15	.07	.01
☐ 182	Richard Anderson — Portland Trail Blazers (Trail Blazers on front should be all caps)	.03	.01	.00
☐ 183	Dan Majerle — Phoenix Suns	.40	.20	.04
☐ 184	Derek Harper — Dallas Mavericks	.06	.03	.00
☐ 185	Robert Parish — Boston Celtics	.12	.06	.01
☐ 186	Ricky Berry SP — Sacramento Kings	.25	.12	.02
☐ 187	Michael Cooper — Los Angeles Lakers	.08	.04	.01
☐ 188	Vinnie Johnson — Detroit Pistons	.06	.03	.00
☐ 189	James Donaldson — Dallas Mavericks	.03	.01	.00
☐ 190	Clyde Drexler — Portland Trail Blazers (4th pick, should be 14th)	.30	.15	.03
☐ 191	Jay Vincent SP — San Antonio Spurs	.20	.10	.02
☐ 192	Nate McMillan — Seattle Supersonics	.03	.01	.00
☐ 193	Kevin Duckworth AS — Portland Trail Blazers	.06	.03	.00
☐ 194	Ledell Eackles — Washington Bullets	.20	.10	.02
☐ 195	Eddie Johnson — Phoenix Suns	.06	.03	.00
☐ 196	Terry Teagle — Golden State Warriors	.08	.04	.01
☐ 197	Tom Chambers AS — Phoenix Suns	.08	.04	.01
☐ 198	Joe Barry Carroll — New Jersey Nets	.03	.01	.00
☐ 199	Dennis Hopson — New Jersey Nets	.15	.07	.01
☐ 200	Michael Jordan — Chicago Bulls	2.50	1.25	.25
☐ 201	Jerome Lane — Denver Nuggets	.12	.06	.01
☐ 202	Greg Kite — Charlotte Hornets	.06	.03	.00
☐ 203	David Rivers SP — Los Angeles Lakers	.30	.15	.03
☐ 204	Sylvester Gray — Miami Heat	.10	.05	.01
☐ 205	Ron Harper — Cleveland Cavaliers	.10	.05	.01
☐ 206	Frank Brickowski — San Antonio Spurs	.06	.03	.00
☐ 207	Rory Sparrow — Miami Heat	.03	.01	.00
☐ 208	Gerald Henderson — Philadelphia 76ers	.03	.01	.00

☐ 209	Rod Higgins .... Golden State Warriors ('85-86 stats should also include San Antonio and Seattle)	.03	.01	.00
☐ 210	James Worthy .... Los Angeles Lakers	.20	.10	.02
☐ 211	Dennis Rodman .... Detroit Pistons	.15	.07	.01
☐ 212	Ricky Pierce .... Milwaukee Bucks	.10	.05	.01
☐ 213	Charles Oakley .... New York Knicks	.08	.04	.01
☐ 214	Steve Colter .... Washington Bullets	.03	.01	.00
☐ 215	Danny Ainge .... Sacramento Kings	.06	.03	.00
☐ 216	Lenny Wilkens CO .... Cleveland Cavaliers (No NBA logo on back in bottom right)	.08	.04	.01
☐ 217	Larry Nance AS .... Cleveland Cavaliers	.06	.03	.00
☐ 218	Tyrone Bogues .... Charlotte Hornets	.06	.03	.00
☐ 219	James Worthy AS .... Los Angeles Lakers	.10	.05	.01
☐ 220	Lafayette Lever .... Denver Nuggets	.08	.04	.01
☐ 221	Quintin Dailey SP .... Los Angeles Clippers	.20	.10	.02
☐ 222	Lester Conner .... New Jersey Nets	.03	.01	.00
☐ 223	Jose Ortiz .... Utah Jazz	.12	.06	.01
☐ 224	Michael Williams SP .... Detroit Pistons	1.00	.50	.10
☐ 225	Wyman Tisdale .... Sacramento Kings	.10	.05	.01
☐ 226	Mike Sanders SP .... Cleveland Cavaliers	.20	.10	.02
☐ 227	Jim Farmer SP .... Utah Jazz	.30	.15	.03
☐ 228	Mark West .... Phoenix Suns	.03	.01	.00
☐ 229	Jeff Hornacek .... Phoenix Suns	.30	.15	.03
☐ 230	Chris Mullin AS .... Golden State Warriors	.10	05	.01
☐ 231	Vern Fleming .... Indiana Pacers	.06	.03	.00
☐ 232	Kenny Smith .... Sacramento Kings	.10	.05	.01
☐ 233	Derrick McKey .... Seattle Supersonics	.08	.04	.01
☐ 234	Dominique Wilkins AS .... Atlanta Hawks	.12	.06	.01
☐ 235	Willie Andersen .... San Antonio Spurs	.40	.20	.04
☐ 236	Keith Lee SP .... New Jersey Nets	.30	.15	.03
☐ 237	Buck Johnson .... Houston Rockets	.25	.12	.02
☐ 238	Randy Wittman .... Indiana Pacers	.03	.01	.00
☐ 239	Terry Catledge SP .... Washington Bullets	.20	.10	.02
☐ 240	Bernard King .... Washington Bullets	.17	.08	.01
☐ 241	Darrell Griffith .... Utah Jazz	.06	.03	.00
☐ 242	Horace Grant .... Chicago Bulls	.20	.10	.02
☐ 243	Rony Seikaly .... Miami Heat	.65	.30	.06
☐ 244	Scottie Pippen .... Chicago Bulls	.90	.45	.09
☐ 245	Michael Cage .... Seattle Supersonics (Picked in '85, should say '84)	.03	.01	.00
☐ 246	Kurt Rambis .... Charlotte Hornets	.06	.03	.00
☐ 247	Morlon Wiley SP .... Dallas Mavericks	.30	.15	.03
☐ 248	Ronnie Grandison .... Boston Celtics	.12	.06	.01
☐ 249	Scott Skiles SP .... Indiana Pacers	1.00	.50	.10
☐ 250	Isiah Thomas .... Detroit Pistons	.30	.15	.03
☐ 251	Thurl Bailey .... Utah Jazz	.03	.01	.00
☐ 252	Glenn Rivers .... Atlanta Hawks	.06	.03	.00
☐ 253	Stuart Gray SP .... Indiana Pacers	.20	.10	.02
☐ 254	John Williams .... Washington Bullets	.06	.03	.00
☐ 255	Bill Cartwright .... Chicago Bulls	.06	.03	.00
☐ 256	Terry Cummings AS .... Milwaukee Bucks	.06	.03	.00
☐ 257	Rodney McCray .... Sacramento Kings	.06	.03	.00
☐ 258	Larry Krystkowiak .... Milwaukee Bucks	.12	.06	.01
☒ 259	Will Perdue .... Chicago Bulls	.17	.08	.01
☐ 260	Mitch Richmond .... Golden State Warriors	1.25	.60	.12
☐ 261	Blair Rasmussen .... Denver Nuggets	.03	.01	.00
☐ 262	Charles Smith .... Los Angeles Clippers	.80	.40	.08
☐ 263	Tyrone Corbin SP .... Phoenix Suns	.45	.22	.04
☐ 264	Kelvin Upshaw .... Boston Celtics	.08	.04	.01
☐ 265	Otis Thorpe .... Houston Rockets	.10	.05	.01
☐ 266	Phil Jackson CO .... Chicago Bulls	.03	.01	.00
☐ 267	Jerry Sloan CO .... Utah Jazz	.03	.01	.00
☐ 268	John Shasky .... Miami Heat	.08	.04	.01
☐ 269A	B. Bickerstaff CO SP .... Seattle Supersonics ERR (Born 2/11/44)	.30	.15	.03
☐ 269B	B. Bickerstaff CO .... Seattle Supersonics COR (Second series; Born 11/2/43)	.08	.04	.01
☐ 270	Magic Johnson .... Los Angeles Lakers	.50	.25	.05
☐ 271	Vernon Maxwell .... San Antonio Spurs	.35	.17	.03
☒ 272	Tim McCormick .... Houston Rockets	.03	.01	.00
☐ 273	Don Nelson CO .... Golden State Warriors	.03	.01	.00
☐ 274	Gary Grant .... Los Angeles Clippers	.15	.07	.01
☐ 275	Sidney Moncrief SP .... Milwaukee Bucks	.35	.17	.03
☐ 276	Roy Hinson .... New Jersey Nets	.03	.01	.00
☐ 277	Jimmy Rodgers CO .... Boston Celtics	.03	.01	.00
☐ 278	Antoine Carr .... Atlanta Hawks	.06	.03	.00
☐ 279A	Orlando Woolridge SP ...... Los Angeles Lakers ERR (No Trademark)	.30	.15	.03
☐ 279B	Orlando Woolridge .... Los Angeles Lakers COR (Second series)	.12	.06	.01
☐ 280	Kevin McHale .... Boston Celtics	.12	.06	.01
☐ 281	LaSalle Thompson .... Indiana Pacers	.03	.01	.00
☐ 282	Detlef Schrempf .... Indiana Pacers	.12	.06	.01
☐ 283	Doug Moe CO .... Denver Nuggets	.03	.01	.00
☐ 284A	James Edwards .... Detroit Pistons (Small black line next to card number)	.30	.15	.03
☐ 284B	James Edwards .... Detroit Pistons (No small black line)	.08	.04	.01
☐ 285	Jerome Kersey .... Portland Trail Blazers	.12	.06	.01
☐ 286	Sam Perkins .... Dallas Mavericks	.12	.06	.01
☐ 287	Sedale Threatt .... Seattle Supersonics	.03	.01	.00
☐ 288	Tim Kempton SP .... Charlotte Hornets	.30	.15	.03
☐ 289	Mark McNamara .... Los Angeles Lakers	.03	.01	.00
☐ 290	Moses Malone .... Atlanta Hawks	.12	.06	.01
☐ 291	Rick Adelman CO .... Portland Trail Blazers (Chemkata misspelled as Chemketa)	.06	.03	.00

☐ 292	Dick Versace CO	.03	.01	.00
	Indiana Pacers			
☐ 293	Alton Lister SP	.20	.10	.02
	Seattle Supersonics			
☐ 294	Winston Garland	.03	.01	.00
	Golden State Warriors			
☐ 295	Kiki Vandeweghe	.06	.03	.00
	New York Knicks			
☐ 296	Brad Davis	.03	.01	.00
	Dallas Mavericks			
☐ 297	John Stockton AS	.12	.06	.01
	Utah Jazz			
☐ 298	Jay Humphries	.03	.01	.00
	Milwaukee Bucks			
☐ 299	Dell Curry	.06	.03	.00
	Charlotte Hornets			
☐ 300	Mark Jackson	.08	.04	.01
	New York Knicks			

1989-90 Hoops II

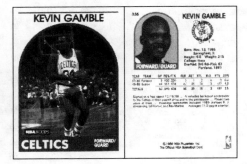

The design of the cards in the 53-card Hoops II set is identical to that of the first series. This set features the expansion teams (Minnesota and Orlando), traded players, a special NBA Championship card of the Detroit Pistons, and a David Robinson card. The cards are standard size (2 1/2" by 3 1/2") and numbered on the back in continuation of the first series. Cards numbered 301, 305, 307, 308, 318, 322, 328, 339, and 343 all have basketball misspelled as baasketball on the bottom of the card back. The key rookie in this set is Kevin Gamble. Since the original card number 353 Detroit Pistons World Champs was so difficult for collectors to find in packs, Hoops produced another edition of the card that was available direct from the company for free with additional copies available for only 35 cents per card.

	MINT	EXC	G-VG
COMPLETE SET (53)	12.00	6.00	1.20
COMMON PLAYER (301-353)	.06	.03	.00

☐ 301	Morlon Wiley	.08	.04	.01
	Orlando Magic			
☐ 302	Reggie Theus	.10	.05	.01
	Orlando Magic			
☐ 303	Otis Smith	.10	.05	.01
	Orlando Magic			
☐ 304	Tod Murphy	.20	.10	.02
	Minnesota Timberwolves			
☐ 305	Sidney Green	.06	.03	.00
	Orlando Magic			
☐ 306	Shelton Jones	.08	.04	.01
	Milwaukee Bucks			
☐ 307	Mark Acres	.06	.03	.00
	Orlando Magic			
☐ 308	Terry Catledge	.06	.03	.00
	Orlando Magic			
☐ 309	Larry Smith	.06	.03	.00
	Houston Rockets			
☐ 310	David Robinson IA	7.00	3.50	.70
	San Antonio Spurs			

☐ 311	Johnny Dawkins	.08	.04	.01
	Philadelphia 76ers			
☐ 312	Terry Cummings	.17	.08	.01
	San Antonio Spurs			
☐ 313	Sidney Lowe	.06	.03	.00
	Milwaukee Bucks			
☐ 314	Bill Musselman CO	.06	.03	.00
	Milwaukee Bucks			
☐ 315	Buck Williams	.17	.08	.01
	Portland Trail Blazers			
	(Won ROY in '81,			
	should say '82)			
☐ 316	Mel Turpin	.06	.03	.00
	Washington Bullets			
☐ 317	Scott Hastings	.06	.03	.00
	Detroit Pistons			
☐ 318	Scott Skiles	.35	.17	.03
	Orlando Magic			
☐ 319	Tyrone Corbin	.17	.08	.01
	Milwaukee Bucks			
☐ 320	Maurice Cheeks	.08	.04	.01
	San Antonio Spurs			
☐ 321	Matt Goukas CO	.06	.03	.00
	Orlando Magic			
☐ 322	Jeff Turner	.08	.04	.01
	Orlando Magic			
☐ 323	David Wingate	.06	.03	.00
	San Antonio Spurs			
☐ 324	Steve Johnson	.06	.03	.00
	Milwaukee Bucks			
☐ 325	Alton Lister	.06	.03	.00
	Golden State Warriors			
☐ 326	Ken Bannister	.08	.04	.01
	Los Angeles Clippers			
☐ 327	Bill Fitch CO	.06	.03	.00
	New Jersey Nets			
	(Copyright missing			
	on bottom of back)			
☐ 328	Sam Vincent	.10	.05	.01
	Orlando Magic			
☒ 329	Larry Drew	.06	.03	.00
	Los Angeles Lakers			
☐ 330	Rick Mahorn	.10	.05	.01
	Milwaukee Bucks			
☐ 331	Christian Welp	.08	.04	.01
	San Antonio Spurs			
☐ 332	Brad Lohaus	.08	.04	.01
	Milwaukee Bucks			
☐ 333	Frank Johnson	.06	.03	.00
	Orlando Magic			
☐ 334	Jim Farmer	.08	.04	.01
	Milwaukee Bucks			
☐ 335	Wayne Cooper	.06	.03	.00
	Portland Trail Blazers			
☐ 336	Mike Brown	.17	.08	.01
	Utah Jazz			
☐ 337	Sam Bowie	.10	.05	.01
	New Jersey Nets			
☐ 338	Kevin Gamble	1.00	.50	.10
	Boston Celtics			
☐ 339	Jerry Ice Reynolds	.15	.07	.01
	Orlando Magic			
☐ 340	Mike Sanders	.06	.03	.00
	Indiana Pacers			
☐ 341	Bill Jones	.10	.05	.01
	New Jersey Nets			
	(Center on front,			
	should be F)			
☐ 342	Greg Anderson	.08	.04	.01
	Milwaukee Bucks			
☐ 343	Dave Corzine	.06	.03	.00
	Orlando Magic			
☐ 344	Michael Williams	.30	.15	.03
	Phoenix Suns			
☐ 345	Jay Vincent	.06	.03	.00
	Philadelphia 76ers			
☐ 346	David Rivers	.08	.04	.01
	Milwaukee Bucks			
☒ 347	Caldwell Jones	.08	.04	.01
	San Antonio Spurs			
	(He was not starting			
	center on '83 Sixers)			
☐ 348	Brad Sellers	.06	.03	.00
	Seattle Supersonics			
☐ 349	Scott Roth	.10	.05	.01
	Milwaukee Bucks			
☐ 350	Alvin Robertson	.08	.04	.01
	Milwaukee Bucks			
☐ 351	Steve Kerr	.20	.10	.02
	Cleveland Cavaliers			
☐ 352	Stuart Gray	.06	.03	.00
	Charlotte Hornets			

☐ 353A	World Champions SP	12.50	6.25	1.25
	Detroit Pistons			
☐ 353B	World Champions	.50	.25	.05
	Detroit Pistons			
	(George Blaha mis-			
	spelled Blanha)			

1990 Hoops 100 Superstars

This 100-card set is a partial remake of the 1989-90 Hoops set, still measuring the standard size (2 1/2" by 3 1/2"). The pictures used are the same. The backs have a head shot in the same format as the front, as well as biographical and statistical information (only up through the 1988-89 season) on a pale yellow background. However, they differ from the Hoops issue in the yellow coloring on the card fronts and a new numbering system. The players are arranged by teams and the teams are placed in alphabetical order as follows: The cards are numbered on the back and arranged alphabetically according to teams as follows: Atlanta Hawks (1-4), Boston Celtics (5-8), Charlotte Hornets (9-11), Chicago Bulls (12-15), Cleveland Cavaliers (16-19), Dallas Mavericks (20-23), Denver Nuggets (24-26), Detroit Pistons (27-30), Golden State Warriors (31-34), Houston Rockets (35-38), Indiana Pacers (39-42), Los Angeles Clippers (43-46), Los Angeles Lakers (47-50), Miami Heat (51-53), Milwaukee Bucks (54-57), Minnesota Timberwolves (58-60), New Jersey Nets (61-63), New York Knicks (64-67), Orlando Magic (68-70), Philadelphia 76ers (71-74), Phoenix Suns (75-78), Portland Trail Blazers (79-82), Sacramento Kings (83-85), San Antonio Spurs (86-88), Seattle Supersonics (89-92), Utah Jazz (93-96), and Washington Bullets (97-100). This set was primarily sold through the Sears catalog.

	MINT	EXC	G-VG
COMPLETE SET (100)	17.00	8.50	1.70
COMMON PLAYER (1-100)	.05	.02	.00

☐ 1	Glenn Rivers	.10	.05	.01
☐ 2	Dominique Wilkins	.35	.17	.03
☐ 3	Spud Webb	.10	.05	.01
☐ 4	Moses Malone	.20	.10	.02
☐ 5	Reggie Lewis	.35	.17	.03
☐ 6	Larry Bird	.75	.35	.07
☐ 7	Kevin McHale	.15	.07	.01
☐ 8	Robert Parish	.15	.07	.01
☐ 9	Tyrone Bogues	.05	.02	.00
☐ 10	Rex Chapman	.35	.17	.03
☐ 11	Kelly Tripucka	.05	.02	.00
☐ 12	Michael Jordan	3.50	1.75	.35
☐ 13	Scottie Pippen	.50	.25	.05
☐ 14	John Paxson	.10	.05	.01
☐ 15	Bill Cartwright	.10	.05	.01
☐ 16	Mark Price	.10	.05	.01
☐ 17	Larry Nance	.10	.05	.01
☐ 18	Hot Rod Williams	.10	.05	.01
☐ 19	Brad Daugherty	.20	.10	.02
☐ 20	Derek Harper	.10	.05	.01
☐ 21	Rolando Blackman	.15	.07	.01
☐ 22	Sam Perkins	.15	.07	.01

☐ 23	James Donaldson	.05	.02	.00
☐ 24	Michael Adams	.10	.05	.01
☐ 25	Lafayette Lever	.10	.05	.01
☐ 26	Alex English	.10	.05	.01
☐ 27	Isiah Thomas	.35	.17	.03
☐ 28	Joe Dumars	.25	.12	.02
☐ 29	Bill Laimbeer	.10	.05	.01
☐ 30	Dennis Rodman	.20	.10	.02
☐ 31	Mitch Richmond	.50	.25	.05
☐ 32	Chris Mullin	.35	.17	.03
☐ 33	Manute Bol	.05	.02	.00
☐ 34	Rod Higgins	.05	.02	.00
☐ 35	Eric Floyd	.10	.05	.01
☐ 36	Otis Thorpe	.10	.05	.01
☐ 37	Buck Johnson	.10	.05	.01
☐ 38	Akeem Olajuwon	.35	.17	.03
☐ 39	Vern Fleming	.10	.05	.01
☐ 40	Reggie Miller	.35	.17	.03
☐ 41	Chuck Person	.25	.12	.02
☐ 42	Rik Smits	.10	.05	.01
☐ 43	Benoit Benjamin	.10	.05	.01
☐ 44	Charles Smith	.15	.07	.01
☐ 45	Gary Grant	.10	.05	.01
☐ 46	Danny Manning	.35	.17	.03
☐ 47	Magic Johnson	.75	.35	.07
☐ 48	Byron Scott	.15	.07	.01
☐ 49	A.C. Green	.10	.05	.01
☐ 50	James Worthy	.35	.17	.03
☐ 51	Kevin Edwards	.10	.05	.01
☐ 52	Rory Sparrow	.05	.02	.00
☐ 53	Rony Seikaly	.25	.12	.02
☐ 54	Jay Humphries	.05	.02	.00
☐ 55	Alvin Robertson	.10	.05	.01
☐ 56	Ricky Pierce	.10	.05	.01
☐ 57	Jack Sikma	.10	.05	.01
☐ 58	Tyrone Corbin	.10	.05	.01
☐ 59	Sidney Lowe	.05	.02	.00
☐ 60	Steve Johnson	.05	.02	.00
☐ 61	Dennis Hopson	.10	.05	.01
☐ 62	Chris Morris	.10	.05	.01
☐ 63	Roy Hinson	.05	.02	.00
☐ 64	Mark Jackson	.10	.05	.01
☐ 65	Gerald Wilkins	.10	.05	.01
☐ 66	Charles Oakley	.10	.05	.01
☐ 67	Patrick Ewing	.60	.30	.06
☐ 68	Reggie Theus	.10	.05	.01
☐ 69	Sam Vincent	.05	.02	.00
☐ 70	Terry Catledge	.05	.02	.00
☐ 71	Hersey Hawkins	.15	.07	.01
☐ 72	Johnny Dawkins	.10	.05	.01
☐ 73	Charles Barkley	.45	.22	.04
☐ 74	Mike Gminski	.10	.05	.01
☐ 75	Kevin Johnson	.60	.30	.06
☐ 76	Jeff Hornacek	.15	.07	.01
☐ 77	Tom Chambers	.25	.12	.02
☐ 78	Eddie Johnson	.10	.05	.01
☐ 79	Terry Porter	.15	.07	.01
☐ 80	Clyde Drexler	.35	.17	.03
☐ 81	Jerome Kersey	.15	.07	.01
☐ 82	Kevin Duckworth	.10	.05	.01
☐ 83	Danny Ainge	.15	.07	.01
☐ 84	Rodney McCray	.10	.05	.01
☐ 85	Wayman Tisdale	.15	.07	.01
☐ 86	Willie Anderson	.35	.17	.03
☐ 87	Terry Cummings	.15	.07	.01
☐ 88	David Robinson	3.50	1.75	.35
☐ 89	Dale Ellis	.10	.05	.01
☐ 90	Derrick McKey	.10	.05	.01
☐ 91	Xavier McDaniel	.15	.07	.01
☐ 92	Michael Cage	.05	.02	.00
☐ 93	John Stockton	.35	.17	.03
☐ 94	Karl Malone	.45	.22	.04
☐ 95	Thurl Bailey	.10	.05	.01
☐ 96	Mark Eaton	.10	.05	.01
☐ 97	Jeff Malone	.15	.07	.01
☐ 98	Darrell Walker	.05	.02	.00
☐ 99	Bernard King	.20	.10	.02
☐ 100	John Williams	.05	.02	.00

1990-91 Hoops I

The 1990-91 Hoops basketball set contains 336 cards measuring the standard size (2 1/2" by 3 1/2). On the front the color action player photo appears in the shape of a basketball lane, bordered by gold on the All-Star cards (1-26) and by silver on the regular issues (27-331, 336). The player's name and the stripe below

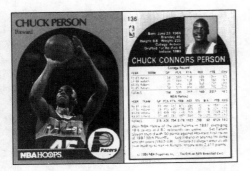

the picture are printed in one of the team's colors. The team logo at the lower right corner rounds out the card face. The back of the regular issue has a color head shot and biographical information as well as college and pro statistics, framed by a basketball lane. The cards are numbered on the back and arranged alphabetically according to teams as follows: Atlanta Hawks (27-37), Boston Celtics (38-48), Charlotte Hornets (49-59), Chicago Bulls (60-69), Cleveland Cavaliers (70-80), Dallas Mavericks (81-90), Denver Nuggets (91-100), Detroit Pistons (101-111), Golden State Warriors (112-122), Houston Rockets (123-131), Indiana Pacers (132-141), Los Angeles Clippers (142-152), Los Angeles Lakers (153-163), Miami Heat (164-172), Milwaukee Bucks (173-183), Minnesota Timberwolves (184-192), New Jersey Nets (193-201), New York Knicks (202-212), Orlando Magic (213-223), Philadelphia 76ers (224-232), Phoenix Suns (233-242), Portland Trail Blazers (243-252), Sacramento Kings (253-262), San Antonio Spurs (263-273), Seattle Supersonics (274-284), Utah Jazz (285-294), and Washington Bullets (295-304). The coaches cards number 305-331. Some of the All-Star cards (card numbers 2, 6, and 8) can be found with or without a printing mistake, i.e., no T in the the trademark logo on the card back. A few of the cards (card numbers 14, 66, 144, and 279) refer to the player as all America rather than All America. The following cards can be found with or without a black line under the card number, height, and birthplace: 20, 23, 24, 29, and 87. The key rookies in this set are Nick Anderson, Vlade Divac, Sherman Douglas, Sean Elliott, Danny Ferry, Tim Hardaway, Shawn Kemp, Glen Rice, and Pooh Richardson.

	MINT	EXC	G-VG
COMPLETE SET (336)	13.50	6.00	1.00
COMMON PLAYER (1-336)	.03	.01	.00
COMMON AS PLAYER (1-26)	.08	.04	.01
1 Charles Barkley AS SP	.15	.05	.01
Philadelphia 76ers			
2 Larry Bird AS SP	.20	.10	.02
Boston Celtics			
3 Joe Dumars AS SP	.12	.06	.01
Detroit Pistons			
4 Patrick Ewing AS SP	.20	.10	.02
New York Knicks			
(A-S blocks listed as			
1, should be 5)			
5 Michael Jordan AS SP	.75	.35	.07
Chicago Bulls			
(Won Slam Dunk in			
'87 and '88,			
not '86 and '88)			
6 Kevin McHale AS SP	.12	.06	.01
Boston Celtics			
7 Reggie Miller AS SP	.12	.06	.01
Indiana Pacers			
8 Robert Parish AS SP	.12	.06	.01
Boston Celtics			
9 Scottie Pippen AS SP	.12	.06	.01
Chicago Bulls			
10 Dennis Rodman AS SP	.10	.05	.01
Detroit Pistons			
11 Isiah Thomas AS SP	.15	.07	.01
Detroit Pistons			

12 Dom. Wilkins AS SP	.15	.07	.01
Atlanta Hawks			
13A All-Star Checklist SP	.50	.25	.05
ERR (No card number)			
13B All-Star Checklist SP	.12	.06	.01
COR (Card number on back)			
14 Rolando Blackman AS SP	.10	.05	.01
Dallas Mavericks			
15 Tom Chambers AS SP	.12	.06	.01
Phoenix Suns			
16 Clyde Drexler AS SP	.15	.07	.01
Portland Trail Blazers			
17 A.C. Green AS SP	.08	.04	.01
Los Angeles Lakers			
18 Magic Johnson AS SP	.20	.10	.02
Los Angeles Lakers			
19 Kevin Johnson AS SP	.20	.10	.02
Phoenix Suns			
20 Lafayette Lever AS SP	.08	.04	.01
Denver Nuggets			
21 Karl Malone AS SP	.15	.07	.01
Utah Jazz			
22 Chris Mullin AS SP	.12	.06	.01
Golden State Warriors			
23 Akeen Olajuwon AS SP	.15	.07	.01
Houston Rockets			
24 David Robinson AS SP	1.25	.60	.12
San Antonio Spurs			
25 John Stockton AS SP	.12	.06	.01
Utah Jazz			
26 James Worthy AS SP	.12	.06	.01
Los Angeles Lakers			
27 John Battle	.03	.01	.00
Atlanta Hawks			
28 Jon Koncak	.03	.01	.00
Atlanta Hawks			
29 Cliff Levingston SP	.08	.04	.01
Atlanta Hawks			
30 John Long SP	.08	.04	.01
Atlanta Hawks			
31 Moses Malone	.10	.05	.01
Atlanta Hawks			
32 Glenn Rivers	.06	.03	.00
Atlanta Hawks			
33 Kenny Smith SP	.10	.05	.01
Atlanta Hawks			
34 Alexander Volkov	.12	.06	.01
Atlanta Hawks			
35 Spud Webb	.08	.04	.01
Atlanta Hawks			
36 Dominique Wilkins	.17	.08	.01
Atlanta Hawks			
37 Kevin Willis	.03	.01	.00
Atlanta Hawks			
38 John Bagley	.03	.01	.00
Boston Celtics			
39 Larry Bird	.30	.15	.03
Boston Celtics			
40 Kevin Gamble	.12	.06	.01
Boston Celtics			
41 Dennis Johnson SP	.12	.06	.01
Boston Celtics			
42 Joe Kleine	.03	.01	.00
Boston Celtics			
43 Reggie Lewis	.18	.09	.01
Boston Celtics			
44 Kevin McHale	.10	.05	.01
Boston Celtics			
45 Robert Parish	.10	.05	.01
Boston Celtics			
46 Jim Paxson SP	.08	.04	.01
Boston Celtics			
47 Ed Pinckney	.03	.01	.00
Boston Celtics			
48 Brian Shaw	.20	.10	.02
Boston Celtics			
49 Richard Anderson SP	.08	.04	.01
Charlotte Hornets			
50 Tyrone Bogues	.03	.01	.00
Charlotte Hornets			
51 Rex Chapman	.12	.06	.01
Charlotte Hornets			
52 Dell Curry	.03	.01	.00
Charlotte Hornets			
53 Kenny Gattison	.10	.05	.01
Charlotte Hornets			
54 Armon Gilliam	.03	.01	.00
Charlotte Hornets			
55 Dave Hoppen	.06	.03	.00
Charlotte Hornets			
56 Randolph Keys	.03	.01	.00
Charlotte Hornets			
57 J.R. Reid	.25	.12	.02
Charlotte Hornets			

#	Player / Team			
58	Robert Reid SP	.08	.04	.01
	Charlotte Hornets			
59	Kelly Tripucka	.03	.01	.00
	Charlotte Hornets			
60	B.J. Armstrong	.25	.12	.02
	Chicago Bulls			
61	Bill Cartwright	.06	.03	.00
	Chicago Bulls			
62	Charles Davis SP	.08	.04	.01
	Chicago Bulls			
63	Horace Grant	.15	.07	.01
	Chicago Bulls			
64	Craig Hodges	.03	.01	.00
	Chicago Bulls			
65	Michael Jordan	1.50	.75	.15
	Chicago Bulls			
66	Stacey King	.20	.10	.02
	Chicago Bulls			
67	John Paxson	.06	.03	.00
	Chicago Bulls			
68	Will Perdue	.06	.03	.00
	Chicago Bulls			
69	Scottie Pippen	.25	.12	.02
	Chicago Bulls			
70	Winston Bennett	.10	.05	.01
	Cleveland Cavaliers			
71	Chucky Brown	.12	.06	.01
	Cleveland Cavaliers			
72	Derrick Chievous	.03	.01	.00
	Cleveland Cavaliers			
73	Brad Daugherty	.10	.05	.01
	Cleveland Cavaliers			
74	Craig Ehlo	.03	.01	.00
	Cleveland Cavaliers			
75	Steve Kerr	.08	.04	.01
	Cleveland Cavaliers			
76	Paul Mokeski SP	.08	.04	.01
	Cleveland Cavaliers			
77	John Morton	.12	.06	.01
	Cleveland Cavaliers			
78	Larry Nance	.06	.03	.00
	Cleveland Cavaliers			
79	Mark Price	.08	.04	.01
	Cleveland Cavaliers			
80	Hot Rod Williams	.08	.04	.01
	Cleveland Cavaliers			
81	Steve Alford	.08	.04	.01
	Dallas Mavericks			
82	Rolando Blackman	.08	.04	.01
	Dallas Mavericks			
83	Adrian Dantley SP	.12	.06	.01
	Dallas Mavericks			
84	Brad Davis	.03	.01	.00
	Dallas Mavericks			
85	James Donaldson	.03	.01	.00
	Dallas Mavericks			
86	Derek Harper	.06	.03	.00
	Dallas Mavericks			
87	Sam Perkins SP	.15	.07	.01
	Dallas Mavericks			
88	Roy Tarpley	.08	.04	.01
	Dallas Mavericks			
89	Bill Wennington SP	.08	.04	.01
	Dallas Mavericks			
90	Herb Williams	.03	.01	.00
	Dallas Mavericks			
91	Michael Adams	.06	.03	.00
	Denver Nuggets			
92	Joe Barry Carroll SP	.08	.04	.01
	Denver Nuggets			
93	Walter Davis	.06	.03	.00
	Denver Nuggets			
	(Born NC, not PA)			
94	Alex English SP	.15	.07	.01
	Denver Nuggets			
95	Bill Hanzlik	.03	.01	.00
	Denver Nuggets			
96	Jerome Lane	.06	.03	.00
	Denver Nuggets			
97	Lafayette Lever SP	.12	.06	.01
	Denver Nuggets			
98	Todd Lichti	.12	.06	.01
	Denver Nuggets			
99	Blair Rasmussen	.03	.01	.00
	Denver Nuggets			
100	Dan Schayes SP	.08	.04	.01
	Denver Nuggets			
101	Mark Aguirre	.08	.04	.01
	Detroit Pistons			
102	William Bedford	.12	.06	.01
	Detroit Pistons			
103	Joe Dumars	.12	.06	.01
	Detroit Pistons			
104	James Edwards	.03	.01	.00
	Detroit Pistons			
105	Scott Hastings	.03	.01	.00
	Detroit Pistons			
106	Gerald Henderson SP	.08	.04	.01
	Detroit Pistons			
107	Vinnie Johnson	.08	.04	.01
	Detroit Pistons			
108	Bill Laimbeer	.10	.05	.01
	Detroit Pistons			
109	Dennis Rodman	.10	.05	.01
	Detroit Pistons			
110	John Salley	.08	.04	.01
	Detroit Pistons			
111	Isiah Thomas	.18	.09	.01
	Detroit Pistons			
	(No position listed on the card)			
112	Manute Bol SP	.08	.04	.01
	Golden State Warriors			
113	Tim Hardaway	1.50	.75	.15
	Golden State Warriors			
114	Rod Higgins	.03	.01	.00
	Golden State Warriors			
115	Sarunas Marciulionis	.25	.12	.02
	Golden State Warriors			
116	Chris Mullin	.15	.07	.01
	Golden State Warriors			
	(Born Brooklyn, NY, not New York, NY)			
117	Jim Petersen	.03	.01	.00
	Golden State Warriors			
118	Mitch Richmond	.25	.12	.02
	Golden State Warriors			
119	Mike Smrek	.10	.05	.01
	Golden State Warriors			
120	Terry Teagle SP	.08	.04	.01
	Golden State Warriors			
121	Tom Tolbert	.10	.05	.01
	Golden State Warriors			
122	Christian Welp SP	.08	.04	.01
	Golden State Warriors			
123	Byron Dinkins SP	.15	.07	.01
	Houston Rockets			
124	Eric Floyd	.06	.03	.00
	Houston Rockets			
125	Buck Johnson	.08	.04	.01
	Houston Rockets			
126	Vernon Maxwell	.10	.05	.01
	Houston Rockets			
127	Akeem Olajuwon	.20	.10	.02
	Houston Rockets			
128	Larry Smith	.03	.01	.00
	Houston Rockets			
129	Otis Thorpe	.06	.03	.00
	Houston Rockets			
130	Mitchell Wiggins SP	.08	.04	.01
	Houston Rockets			
131	Mike Woodson	.03	.01	.00
	Houston Rockets			
132	Greg Dreiling	.10	.05	.01
	Indiana Pacers			
133	Vern Fleming	.03	.01	.00
	Indiana Pacers			
134	Rickey Green SP	.08	.04	.01
	Indiana Pacers			
135	Reggie Miller	.15	.07	.01
	Indiana Pacers			
136	Chuck Person	.10	.05	.01
	Indiana Pacers			
137	Mike Sanders	.03	.01	.00
	Indiana Pacers			
138	Detlef Schrempf	.08	.04	.01
	Indiana Pacers			
139	Rik Smits	.06	.03	.00
	Indiana Pacers			
140	LaSalle Thompson	.03	.01	.00
	Indiana Pacers			
141	Randy Wittman	.03	.01	.00
	Indiana Pacers			
142	Benoit Benjamin	.06	.03	.00
	Los Angeles Clippers			
143	Winston Garland	.03	.01	.00
	Los Angeles Clippers			
144	Tom Garrick	.03	.01	.00
	Los Angeles Clippers			
145	Gary Grant	.06	.03	.00
	Los Angeles Clippers			
146	Ron Harper	.08	.04	.01
	Los Angeles Clippers			
147	Danny Manning	.10	.05	.01
	Los Angeles Clippers			
148	Jeff Martin	.08	.04	.01
	Los Angeles Clippers			
149	Ken Norman	.10	.05	.01
	Los Angeles Clippers			

150 David Rivers SP Los Angeles Clippers	.08	.04	.01
151 Charles Smith Los Angeles Clippers	.10	.05	.01
152 Joe Wolf SP Los Angeles Clippers	.08	.04	.01
153 Michael Cooper SP Los Angeles Lakers	.12	.06	.01
154 Vlade Divac Los Angeles Lakers (Height 6'11", should be 7'1")	.60	.30	.06
155 Larry Drew Los Angeles Lakers	.03	.01	.00
156 A.C. Green Los Angeles Lakers	.08	.04	.01
157 Magic Johnson Los Angeles Lakers	.30	.15	.03
158 Mark McNamara SP Los Angeles Lakers	.08	.04	.01
159 Byron Scott Los Angeles Lakers	.08	.04	.01
160 Mychal Thompson Los Angeles Lakers	.03	.01	.00
161 Jay Vincent SP Los Angeles Lakers	.08	.04	.01
162 Orlando Woolridge SP Los Angeles Lakers	.08	.04	.01
163 James Worthy Los Angeles Lakers	.15	.07	.01
164 Sherman Douglas Miami Heat	.35	.17	.03
165 Kevin Edwards Miami Heat	.03	.01	.00
166 Tellis Frank SP Miami Heat	.12	.06	.01
167 Grant Long Miami Heat	.03	.01	.00
168 Glen Rice Miami Heat	.35	.17	.03
169A Rony Seikaly Miami Heat (Athens)	.15	.07	.01
169B Rony Seikaly Miami Heat (Beirut)	.15	.07	.01
170 Rory Sparrow SP Miami Heat	.08	.04	.01
171A Jon Sundvold Miami Heat (First series)	.08	.04	.01
171B Billy Thompson Miami Heat (Second series)	.08	.04	.01
172A Billy Thompson Miami Heat (First series)	.08	.04	.01
172B Jon Sundvold Miami Heat (Second series)	.08	.04	.01
173 Greg Anderson Milwaukee Bucks	.03	.01	.00
174 Jeff Grayer Milwaukee Bucks	.10	.05	.01
175 Jay Humphries Milwaukee Bucks	.03	.01	.00
176 Frank Kornet Milwaukee Bucks	.08	.04	.01
177 Larry Krystkowiak Milwaukee Bucks	.03	.01	.00
178 Brad Lohaus Milwaukee Bucks	.06	.03	.00
179 Ricky Pierce Milwaukee Bucks	.06	.03	.00
180 Paul Pressey SP Milwaukee Bucks	.08	.04	.01
181 Fred Roberts Milwaukee Bucks	.06	.03	.00
182 Alvin Robertson Milwaukee Bucks	.06	.03	.00
183 Jack Sikma Milwaukee Bucks	.06	.03	.00
184 Randy Breuer Minnesota Timberwolves	.03	.01	.00
185 Tony Campbell Minnesota Timberwolves	.08	.04	.01
186 Tyrone Corbin Minnesota Timberwolves	.06	.03	.00
187 Sidney Lowe SP Minnesota Timberwolves	.08	.04	.01
188 Sam Mitchell Minnesota Timberwolves	.12	.06	.01
189 Tod Murphy Minnesota Timberwolves	.08	.04	.01
190 Pooh Richardson Minnesota Timberwolves	.50	.25	.05
191 Scott Roth SP Minnesota Timberwolves	.08	.04	.01
192 Brad Sellers SP Minnesota Timberwolves	.08	.04	.01
193 Mookie Blaylock New Jersey Nets	.20	.10	.02
194 Sam Bowie New Jersey Nets	.06	.03	.00
195 Lester Conner New Jersey Nets	.03	.01	.00
196 Derrick Gervin New Jersey Nets	.12	.06	.01
197 Jack Haley New Jersey Nets	.08	.04	.01
198 Roy Hinson New Jersey Nets	.03	.01	.00
199 Dennis Hopson SP New Jersey Nets	.12	.06	.01
200 Chris Morris New Jersey Nets	.08	.04	.01
201 Puvis Short SP New Jersey Nets	.08	.04	.01
202 Maurice Cheeks New York Knicks	.08	.04	.01
203 Patrick Ewing New York Knicks	.30	.15	.03
204 Stuart Gray New York Knicks	.03	.01	.00
205 Mark Jackson New York Knicks	.06	.03	.00
206 Johnny Newman SP New York Knicks	.15	.07	.01
207 Charles Oakley New York Knicks	.08	.04	.01
208 Trent Tucker New York Knicks	.03	.01	.00
209 Kiki Vandeweghe New York Knicks	.06	.03	.00
210 Kenny Walker New York Knicks	.03	.01	.00
211 Eddie Lee Wilkins New York Knicks	.03	.01	.00
212 Gerald Wilkins New York Knicks	.06	.03	.00
213 Mark Acres Orlando Magic	.03	.01	.00
214 Nick Anderson Orlando Magic	.35	.17	.03
215 Michael Ansley Orlando Magic (Ranked first, not third)	.10	.05	.01
216 Terry Catledge Orlando Magic	.03	.01	.00
217 Dave Corzine SP Orlando Magic	.08	.04	.01
218 Sidney Green SP Orlando Magic	.08	.04	.01
219 Jerry Reynolds Orlando Magic	.03	.01	.00
220 Scott Skiles Orlando Magic	.10	.05	.01
221 Otis Smith Orlando Magic	.03	.01	.00
222 Reggie Theus SP Orlando Magic	.10	.05	.01
223A Sam Vincent Orlando Magic (First series, shows 12 Michael Jordan)	.75	.35	.07
223B Sam Vincent Orlando Magic (Second series, shows Sam dribbling)	.08	.04	.01
224 Ron Anderson Philadelphia 76ers	.06	.03	.00
225 Charles Barkley Philadelphia 76ers	.25	.12	.02
226 Scott Brooks SP Philadelphia 76ers (Born Lathron, Cal., not French Camp)	.08	.04	.01
227 Johnny Dawkins Philadelphia 76ers	.06	.03	.00
228 Mike Gminski Philadelphia 76ers	.06	.03	.00
229 Hersey Hawkins Philadelphia 76ers	.15	.07	.01
230 Rick Mahorn Philadelphia 76ers	.06	.03	.00
231 Derek Smith SP Philadelphia 76ers	.10	.05	.01
232 Bob Thornton Philadelphia 76ers	.08	.04	.01

#	Player			
233	Kenny Battle	.15	.07	.01
	Phoenix Suns			
234A	Tom Chambers	.17	.08	.01
	Phoenix Suns (First series; Forward on front)			
234B	Tom Chambers	.17	.08	.01
	Phoenix Suns (Second series; Guard on front)			
235	Greg Grant SP	.12	.06	.01
	Phoenix Suns			
236	Jeff Hornacek	.10	.05	.01
	Phoenix Suns			
237	Eddie Johnson	.06	.03	.00
	Phoenix Suns			
238A	Kevin Johnson	.35	.17	.03
	Phoenix Suns (First series; Guard on front)			
238B	Kevin Johnson	.35	.17	.03
	Phoenix Suns (Second series; Forward on front)			
239	Dan Majerle	.10	.05	.01
	Phoenix Suns			
240	Tim Perry	.03	.01	.00
	Phoenix Suns			
241	Kurt Rambis	.06	.03	.00
	Phoenix Suns			
242	Mark West	.03	.01	.00
	Phoenix Suns			
243	Mark Bryant	.03	.01	.00
	Portland Trail Blazers			
244	Wayne Cooper	.03	.01	.00
	Portland Trail Blazers			
245	Clyde Drexler	.18	.09	.01
	Portland Trail Blazers			
246	Kevin Duckworth	.06	.03	.00
	Portland Trail Blazers			
247	Jerome Kersey	.08	.04	.01
	Portland Trail Blazers			
248	Drazen Petrovic	.20	.10	.02
	Portland Trail Blazers			
249A	Terry Porter ERR	.30	.15	.03
	Portland Trail Blazers (No NBA symbol on back)			
249B	Terry Porter COR	.10	.05	.01
	Portland Trail Blazers			
250	Cliff Robinson	.25	.12	.02
	Portland Trail Blazers			
251	Buck Williams	.10	.05	.01
	Portland Trail Blazers			
252	Danny Young	.03	.01	.00
	Portland Trail Blazers			
253	Danny Ainge SP	.15	.07	.01
	Sacramento Kings			
254	Randy Allen SP	.12	.06	.01
	Sacramento Kings			
255	Antoine Carr	.06	.03	.00
	Sacramento Kings			
256	Vinny Del Negro SP	.10	.05	.01
	Sacramento Kings			
257	Pervis Ellison SP	.35	.17	.03
	Sacramento Kings			
258	Greg Kite SP	.08	.04	.01
	Sacramento Kings			
259	Rodney McCray SP	.10	.05	.01
	Sacramento Kings			
260	Harold Pressley SP	.10	.05	.01
	Sacramento Kings			
261	Ralph Sampson	.06	.03	.00
	Sacramento Kings			
262	Wayman Tisdale	.10	.05	.01
	Sacramento Kings			
263	Willie Anderson	.10	.05	.01
	San Antonio Spurs			
264	Uwe Blab SP	.08	.04	.01
	San Antonio Spurs			
265	Frank Brickowski SP	.08	.04	.01
	San Antonio Spurs			
266	Terry Cummings	.10	.05	.01
	San Antonio Spurs			
267	Sean Elliott	.50	.25	.05
	San Antonio Spurs			
268	Caldwell Jones SP	.10	.05	.01
	San Antonio Spurs			
269	Johnny Moore SP	.08	.04	.01
	San Antonio Spurs			
270	David Robinson	2.50	1.25	.25
	San Antonio Spurs			
271	Rod Strickland	.10	.05	.01
	San Antonio Spurs			
272	Reggie Williams	.06	.03	.00
	San Antonio Spurs			
273	David Wingate SP	.08	.04	.01
	San Antonio Spurs			
274	Dana Barros	.15	.07	.01
	Seattle Supersonics (Born April, not March)			
275	Michael Cage	.03	.01	.00
	Seattle Supersonics (Drafted '84, not '85)			
276	Quintin Dailey	.03	.01	.00
	Seattle Supersonics			
277	Dale Ellis	.08	.04	.01
	Seattle Supersonics			
278	Steve Johnson SP	.08	.04	.01
	Seattle Supersonics			
279	Shawn Kemp	1.10	.50	.10
	Seattle Supersonics			
280	Xavier McDaniel	.08	.04	.01
	Seattle Supersonics			
281	Derrick McKey	.06	.03	.00
	Seattle Supersonics			
282	Nate McMillan	.03	.01	.00
	Seattle Supersonics			
283	Olden Polynice	.03	.01	.00
	Seattle Supersonics			
284	Sedale Threatt	.03	.01	.00
	Seattle Supersonics			
285	Thurl Bailey	.06	.03	.00
	Utah Jazz			
286	Mike Brown	.03	.01	.00
	Utah Jazz			
287	Mark Eaton	.06	.03	.00
	Utah Jazz (72nd pick, not 82nd)			
288	Theodore Edwards	.15	.07	.01
	Utah Jazz			
289	Darrell Griffith	.06	.03	.00
	Utah Jazz			
290	Robert Hansen SP	.08	.04	.01
	Utah Jazz			
291	Eric Leckner SP	.12	.06	.01
	Utah Jazz			
292	Karl Malone	.18	.09	.01
	Utah Jazz			
293	Delaney Rudd	.08	.04	.01
	Utah Jazz			
294	John Stockton	.15	.07	.01
	Utah Jazz			
295	Mark Alarie	.03	.01	.00
	Washington Bullets			
296	Ledell Eackles SP	.12	.06	.01
	Washington Bullets			
297	Harvey Grant	.06	.03	.00
	Washington Bullets			
298A	Tom Hammonds	.20	.10	.02
	Washington Bullets (No rookie logo on front)			
298B	Tom Hammonds	.20	.10	.02
	Washington Bullets (Rookie logo on front)			
299	Charles Jones	.03	.01	.00
	Washington Bullets			
300	Bernard King	.10	.05	.01
	Washington Bullets			
301	Jeff Malone SP	.12	.06	.01
	Washington Bullets			
302	Mel Turpin SP	.08	.04	.01
	Washington Bullets			
303	Darrell Walker	.03	.01	.00
	Washington Bullets			
304	John Williams	.03	.01	.00
	Washington Bullets			
305	Bob Weiss CO	.03	.01	.00
	Atlanta Hawks			
306	Chris Ford CO	.03	.01	.00
	Boston Celtics			
307	Gene Littles CO	.03	.01	.00
	Charlotte Hornets			
308	Phil Jackson CO	.03	.01	.00
	Chicago Bulls			
309	Lenny Wilkens CO	.06	.03	.00
	Cleveland Cavaliers			
310	Richie Adubato CO	.03	.01	.00
	Dallas Mavericks			
311	Doug Moe CO SP	.08	.04	.01
	Denver Nuggets			
312	Chuck Daly CO	.03	.01	.00
	Detroit Pistons			
313	Don Nelson CO	.03	.01	.00
	Golden State Warriors			
314	Don Chaney CO	.03	.01	.00
	Houston Rockets			
315	Dick Versace CO	.03	.01	.00
	Indiana Pacers			
316	Mike Schuler CO	.03	.01	.00
	Los Angeles Clippers			

		MINT	EXC	G-VG
317	Pat Riley CO SP	.10	.05	.01
	Los Angeles Lakers			
318	Ron Rothstein CO	.03	.01	.00
	Miami Heat			
319	Del Harris CO	.03	.01	.00
	Milwaukee Bucks			
320	Bill Musselman CO	.03	.01	.00
	Minnesota Timberwolves			
321	Bill Fitch CO	.03	.01	.00
	New Jersey Nets			
322	Stu Jackson CO	.03	.01	.00
	New York Knicks			
323	Matt Guokas CO	.03	.01	.00
	Orlando Magic			
324	Jim Lynam CO	.03	.01	.00
	Philadelphia 76ers			
325	Cotton Fitzsimmons CO	.03	.01	.00
	Phoenix Suns			
326	Rick Adelman CO	.03	.01	.00
	Portland Trail Blazers			
327	Dick Motta CO	.03	.01	.00
	Sacramento Kings			
328	Larry Brown CO	.03	.01	.00
	San Antonio Spurs			
329	K.C. Jones CO	.06	.03	.00
	Seattle Supersonics			
330	Jerry Sloan CO	.03	.01	.00
	Utah Jazz			
331	Wes Unseld CO	.06	.03	.00
	Washington Bullets			
332	Checklist 1 SP	.08	.01	.00
333	Checklist 2 SP	.08	.01	.00
334	Checklist 3 SP	.08	.01	.00
335	Checklist 4 SP	.08	.01	.00
336	Danny Ferry SP	.85	.40	.08
	Cleveland Cavaliers			
NNO	David Robinson and All-Rookie Team	1.25	.60	.12

1990-91 Hoops II

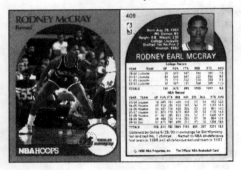

The design of the cards in the 104-card Hoops II set is identical to that of the first series. This set features NBA finals (337-342), coaches (343-354), team checklists (355-381), inside stuff (382-385), stay in school (386-387), don't foul out (388-389), lottery selections (390-400), and updates (401-438). The cards are standard size (2 1/2" by 3 1/2") and are numbered on the back in continuation of the first series. The key rookies in the set are the eleven lottery picks (390-400) led by Derrick Coleman and Lionel Simmons.

		MINT	EXC	G-VG
	COMPLETE SET (104)	10.00	5.00	1.00
	COMMON PLAYER (337-440)	.03	.01	.00
337	NBA Final Game 1	.08	.02	.00
338	NBA Final Game 2	.06	.03	.00
339	NBA Final Game 3	.06	.03	.00
340	NBA Final Game 4	.06	.03	.00
341A	NBA Final Game 5 ERR (No headline on back)	.10	.05	.01
341B	NBA Final Game 5 COR	.10	.05	.01
342	Championship Game (Player named as Sidney Green is really David Greenwood)	.15	.07	.01

		MINT	EXC	G-VG
343	K.C. Jones CO	.08	.04	.01
	Seattle Supersonics			
344	Wes Unseld CO	.08	.04	.01
	Washington Bullets			
345	Don Nelson CO	.06	.03	.00
	Golden State Warriors			
346	Bob Weiss CO	.06	.03	.00
	Atlanta Hawks			
347	Chris Ford CO	.06	.03	.00
	Boston Celtics			
348	Phil Jackson CO	.06	.03	.00
	Chicago Bulls			
349	Lenny Wilkens CO	.08	.04	.01
	Cleveland Cavaliers			
350	Don Chaney CO	.06	.03	.00
	Houston Rockets			
351	Mike Dunleavy CO	.06	.03	.00
	Los Angeles Lakers			
352	Matt Guokas Jr. CO	.06	.03	.00
	Orlando Magic			
353	Rick Adelman CO	.06	.03	.00
	Portland Trail Blazers			
354	Jerry Sloan CO	.06	.03	.00
	Utah Jazz			
355	Dominique Wilkins TC	.10	.05	.01
	Atlanta Hawks			
356	Larry Bird TC	.15	.07	.01
	Boston Celtics			
357	Rex Chapman TC	.08	.04	.01
	Charlotte Hornets			
358	Michael Jordan TC	.35	.17	.03
	Chicago Bulls			
359	Mark Price TC	.06	.03	.00
	Cleveland Cavaliers			
360	Rolando Blackman TC	.06	.03	.00
	Dallas Mavericks			
361	Michael Adams TC	.06	.03	.00
	Denver Nuggets			
362	Joe Dumars TC	.08	.04	.01
	Detroit Pistons (Gerald Henderson's name and number not listed)			
363	Chris Mullin TC	.08	.04	.01
	Golden State Warriors			
364	Akeem Olajuwon TC	.12	.06	.01
	Houston Rockets			
365	Reggie Miller TC	.10	.05	.01
	Indiana Pacers			
366	Danny Manning TC	.08	.04	.01
	Los Angeles Clippers			
367	Magic Johnson TC (Dunleavy listed as 439, should be 351)	.15	.07	.01
	Los Angeles Lakers			
368	Rony Seikaly TC	.08	.04	.01
	Miami Heat			
369	Alvin Robertson TC	.06	.03	.00
	Milwaukee Bucks			
370	Pooh Richardson TC	.08	.04	.01
	Minnesota Timberwolves			
371	Chris Morris TC	.06	.03	.00
	New Jersey Nets			
372	Patrick Ewing TC	.12	.06	.01
	New York Knicks			
373	Nick Anderson TC	.10	.05	.01
	Orlando Magic			
374	Charles Barkley TC	.12	.06	.01
	Philadelphia 76ers			
375	Kevin Johnson TC	.15	.07	.01
	Phoenix Suns			
376	Clyde Drexler TC	.10	.05	.01
	Portland Trail Blazers			
377	Wayman Tisdale TC	.06	.03	.00
	Sacramento Kings			
378A	David Robinson TC (basketball fully visible)	1.00	.50	.10
	San Antonio Spurs			
378A	David Robinson TC (basketball partially visible)	.60	.30	.06
	San Antonio Spurs			
379	Xavier McDaniel TC	.06	.03	.00
	Seattle Supersonics			
380	Karl Malone TC	.12	.06	.01
	Utah Jazz			
381	Bernard King TC	.08	.04	.01
	Washington Bullets Inside Stuff			
382	Michael Jordan Playground	.75	.35	.07
383	Lights, Camera, NBA Action (Karl Malone on horseback)	.12	.06	.01

		MINT	EXC	G-VG
☐ 384	European Imports .... (Vlade Divac and Sarunas Marciulionis)	.15	.07	.01
☐ 385	Super Streaks .... Stay In School (Magic Johnson and Michael Jordan)	.35	.17	.03
☐ 386	Johnny Newman .... Charlotte Hornets (Stay in School)	.08	.04	.01
☐ 387	Del Curry .... Charlotte Hornets (Stay in School)	.06	.03	.00
☐ 388	Patrick Ewing .... New York Knicks (Don't Foul Out)	.15	.07	.01
☐ 389	Isiah Thomas .... Detroit Pistons (Don't Foul Out)	.12	.06	.01
☐ 390	Derrick Coleman LS .... New Jersey Nets	3.25	1.60	.32
☐ 391	Gary Payton LS .... Seattle Supersonics	.75	.35	.07
☐ 392	Chris Jackson LS .... Denver Nuggets	.60	.30	.06
☐ 393	Dennis Scott LS .... Los Angeles Lakers	.75	.35	.07
☐ 394	Kendall Gill LS .... Charlotte Hornets	.75	.35	.07
☐ 395	Felton Spencer LS .... Minnesota Timberwolves	.40	.20	.04
☐ 396	Lionel Simmons LS .... Sacramento Kings	1.35	.65	.13
☐ 397	Bo Kimble LS .... Los Angeles Clippers	.40	.20	.04
☐ 398	Willie Burton LS .... Miami Heat	.40	.20	.04
☐ 399	Rumeal Robinson LS .... Atlanta Hawks	.17	.08	.01
☐ 400	Tyrone Hill LS .... Golden State Warriors	.25	.12	.02
☐ 401	Tim McCormick .... Atlanta Hawks	.03	.01	.00
☐ 402	Sidney Moncrief .... Atlanta Hawks	.06	.03	.00
☐ 403	Johnny Newman .... Charlotte Hornets	.08	.04	.01
☐ 404	Dennis Hopson .... Chicago Bulls	.08	.04	.01
☐ 405	Cliff Levingston .... Chicago Bulls	.03	.01	.00
☐ 406	Danny Ferry .... Cleveland Cavaliers	.30	.15	.03
☐ 407	Alex English .... Dallas Mavericks	.10	.05	.01
☐ 408	Lafayette Lever .... Dallas Mavericks	.08	.04	.01
☐ 409	Rodney McCray .... Dallas Mavericks	.06	.03	.00
☐ 410	Mike Dunleavy CO .... Los Angeles Lakers	.06	.03	.00
☐ 411	Orlando Woolridge .... Denver Nuggets	.06	.03	.00
☐ 412	Joe Wolf .... Denver Nuggets	.03	.01	.00
☐ 413	Tree Rollins .... Detroit Pistons	.03	.01	.00
☐ 414	Kenny Smith .... Houston Rockets	.06	.03	.00
☐ 415	Sam Perkins .... Los Angeles Lakers	.10	.05	.01
☐ 416	Terry Teagle .... Los Angeles Lakers	.03	.01	.00
☐ 417	Frank Brickowski .... Milwaukee Bucks	.03	.01	.00
☐ 418	Danny Schayes .... Milwaukee Bucks	.06	.03	.00
☐ 419	Scott Brooks .... Minnesota Timberwolves	.03	.01	.00
☐ 420	Reggie Theus .... New Jersey Nets	.06	.03	.00
☑ 421	Greg Grant .... New York Knicks	.06	.03	.00
☐ 422	Paul Westhead CO .... Denver Nuggets	.03	.01	.00
☐ 423	Greg Kite .... Orlando Magic	.03	.01	.00
☐ 424	Manute Bol .... Philadelphia 76ers	.03	.01	.00
☐ 425	Rickey Green .... Philadelphia 76ers	.03	.01	.00
☐ 426	Ed Nealy .... Phoenix Suns	.03	.01	.00
☐ 427	Danny Ainge .... Portland Trail Blazers	.08	.04	.01

		MINT	EXC	G-VG
☐ 428	Bobby Hansen .... Sacramento Kings	.03	.01	.00
☐ 429	Eric Leckner .... Charlotte Hornets	.06	.03	.00
☐ 430	Rory Sparrow .... Sacramento Kings	.03	.01	.00
☐ 431	Bill Wennington .... Sacramento Kings	.03	.01	.00
☐ 432	Paul Pressey .... San Antonio Spurs	.03	.01	.00
☐ 433	David Greenwood .... San Antonio Spurs	.03	.01	.00
☐ 434	Mark McNamara .... Orlando Magic	.03	.01	.00
☐ 435	Sidney Green .... Orlando Magic	.03	.01	.00
☐ 436	Dave Corzine .... Orlando Magic	.03	.01	.00
☐ 437	Jeff Malone .... Utah Jazz	.08	.04	.01
☐ 438	Pervis Ellison .... Washington Bullets	.12	.06	.01
☐ 439	Checklist 5	.06	.01	.00
☐ 440	Checklist 6	.06	.01	.00

1990-91 Hoops CollectABooks

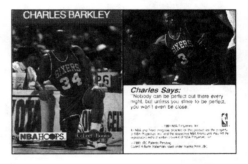

These card-size "books" measure approximately 2 1/2" by 3 3/8". Each book consists of eight pages, including the front and back covers. The front cover features a borderless color player photo, with the player's above the picture in the team's color stripe. Pages 2 and 3 have a color "mug shot" of the player, biographical information, team logo, and career highlights. A color stripe runs across the bottom of each page, with the team name in white lettering. Pages 4 and 5 has a "personal story" about the player. Page 6 has career statistics (college and pro), while page 7 features a borderless color action photo. The top half of the back cover has another color player photo, with a player quote below the picture. The set was issued in four different boxes, with 12 different mini-books in each box.

		MINT	EXC	G-VG
	COMPLETE SET (48)	12.00	6.00	1.20
	COMMON PLAYER (1-48)	.20	.10	.02
🂠 1	Sam Bowie .... New Jersey Nets	.20	.10	.02
🂠 2	Tom Chambers .... Phoenix Suns	.35	.17	.03
🂠 3	Clyde Drexler .... Portland Trail Blazers	.50	.25	.05
🂠 4	Michael Jordan .... Chicago Bulls	1.50	.75	.15
🂠 5	Karl Malone .... Utah Jazz	.50	.25	.05
🂠 6	Kevin McHale .... Boston Celtics	.35	.17	.03
🂠 7	Reggie Miller .... Indiana Pacers	.35	.17	.03
🂠 8	Mark Price .... Cleveland Cavaliers	.20	.10	.02
🂠 9	Mitch Richmond .... Golden State Warriors	.35	.17	.03
🂠 10	Doc Rivers .... Atlanta Hawks	.20	.10	.02

		MINT	EXC	G-VG
11	Rony Seikaly	.35	.17	.03
	Miami Heat			
12	Wayman Tisdale	.20	.10	.02
	Sacramento Kings			
13	Charles Barkley	.50	.25	.05
	Philadelphia 76ers			
14	Terry Cummings	.35	.17	.03
	San Antonio Spurs			
15	Patrick Ewing	.60	.30	.06
	New York Knicks			
16	Terry Porter	.35	.17	.03
	Portland Trail Blazers			
17	Danny Manning	.35	.17	.03
	Los Angeles Clippers			
18	Larry Nance	.20	.10	.02
	Cleveland Cavaliers			
19	Robert Parish	.35	.17	.03
	Boston Celtics			
20	Chuck Person	.35	.17	.03
	Indiana Pacers			
21	Ricky Pierce	.20	.10	.02
	Milwaukee Bucks			
22	John Stockton	.50	.25	.05
	Utah Jazz			
23	Isiah Thomas	.50	.25	.05
	Detroit Pistons			
24	Anthony(Spud) Webb	.20	.10	.02
	Atlanta Hawks			
25	Michael Adams	.20	.10	.02
	Denver Nuggets			
26	Muggsy Bogues	.20	.10	.02
	Charlotte Hornets			
27	Joe Dumars	.35	.17	.03
	Detroit Pistons			
28	Hersey Hawkins	.35	.17	.03
	Philadelphia 76ers			
29	Magic Johnson	.60	.30	.06
	Los Angeles Lakers			
30	Bernard King	.35	.17	.03
	Washington Bullets			
31	Chris Mullin	.50	.25	.05
	Golden State Warriors			
32	Charles Oakley	.20	.10	.02
	New York Knicks			
33	Alvin Robertson	.20	.10	.02
	Milwaukee Bucks			
34	David Robinson	1.00	.50	.10
	San Antonio Spurs			
35	Dominique Wilkins	.35	.17	.03
	Atlanta Hawks			
36	Buck Williams	.20	.10	.02
	Portland Trail Blazers			
37	Larry Bird	.60	.30	.06
	Boston Celtics			
38	Rolando Blackman	.20	.10	.02
	Dallas Mavericks			
39	Mark Eaton	.20	.10	.02
	Utah Jazz			
40	Kevin Johnson	.60	.30	.06
	Phoenix Suns			
41	J.R. Reid	.20	.10	.02
	Charlotte Hornets			
42	Xavier McDaniel	.20	.10	.02
	Seattle Supersonics			
43	Akeem Olajuwon	.50	.25	.05
	Houston Rockets			
44	Scottie Pippen	.50	.25	.05
	Chicago Bulls			
45	Pooh Richardson	.50	.25	.05
	Minnesota Timberwolves			
46	Dennis Rodman	.35	.17	.03
	Detroit Pistons			
47	Charles Smith	.35	.17	.03
	Los Angeles Clippers			
48	James Worthy	.50	.25	.05
	Los Angeles Lakers			

1991-92 Hoops I

The 1991-92 Hoops I basketball set contains 330 cards measuring the standard size (2 1/2" by 3 1/2"). The fronts feature color action player photos, with different color borders on a white card face. The player's name is printed in black lettering in the upper left corner, and the team logo is superimposed over the lower left corner of the picture. In a horizontal format the backs have color head shots and

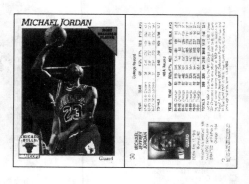

biographical information on the left side, while the right side presents college and pro statistics. The cards are numbered on the back and checklisted below alphabetically within and according to teams as follows: Atlanta Hawks (1-8), Boston Celtics (9-17), Charlotte Hornets (18-25), Chicago Bulls (26-34), Cleveland Cavaliers (35-42), Dallas Mavericks (43-50), Denver Nuggets (51-58), Detroit Pistons (59-66), Golden State Warriors (67-74), Houston Rockets (75-82), Indiana Pacers (83-90), Los Angeles Clippers (91-98), Los Angeles Lakers (99-106), Miami Heat (107-114), Milwaukee Bucks (115-122), Minnesota Timberwolves (123-130), New Jersey Nets (131-138), New York Knicks (139-146), Orlando Magic (147-154), Philadelphia 76ers (155-162), Phoenix Suns (163-170), Portland Trail Blazers (171-179), Sacramento Kings (180-187), San Antonio Spurs (188-196), Seattle Supersonics (197-204), Utah Jazz (205-212), and Washington Bullets (213-220). Other subsets included in this set are coaches (221-245), all-stars (246-271), teams (272-298), inserts (300-303), league leaders (304-311), milestones (312-316), NBA yearbook (317-323), and stay in school (324-326). Card number 300 is a Centennial card honoring James Naismith.

		MINT	EXC	G-VG
	COMPLETE SET (330)	15.00	7.50	1.50
	COMMON PLAYER (1-330)	.03	.01	.00
1	John Battle	.06	.03	.00
2	Moses Malone	.10	.05	.01
3	Sidney Moncrief	.06	.03	.00
4	Glenn Rivers	.06	.03	.00
5	Rumeal Robinson	.08	.04	.01
6	Spud Webb	.06	.03	.00
7	Dominique Wilkins	.15	.07	.01
8	Kevin Willis	.03	.01	.00
9	Larry Bird	.25	.12	.02
10	Dee Brown	.60	.30	.06
11	Kevin Gamble	.10	.05	.01
12	Joe Kleine	.03	.01	.00
13	Reggie Lewis	.12	.06	.01
14	Kevin McHale	.10	.05	.01
15	Robert Parish	.10	.05	.01
16	Ed Pinckney	.03	.01	.00
17	Brian Shaw	.10	.05	.01
18	Muggsy Bogues	.03	.01	.00
19	Rex Chapman	.08	.04	.01
20	Dell Curry	.03	.01	.00
21	Kendall Gill	.20	.10	.02
22	Mike Gminski	.03	.01	.00
23	Johnny Newman	.06	.03	.00
24	J.R. Reid	.08	.04	.01
25	Kelly Tripucka	.03	.01	.00
26	B.J. Armstrong	.10	.05	.01
27	Bill Cartwright	.06	.03	.00
28	Horace Grant	.12	.06	.01
29	Craig Hodges	.06	.03	.00
30	Michael Jordan	.75	.35	.07
31	Stacey King	.08	.04	.01
32	Cliff Levingston	.03	.01	.00
33	John Paxson	.06	.03	.00
34	Scottie Pippen	.20	.10	.02
35	Chucky Brown	.06	.03	.00
36	Brad Daugherty	.10	.05	.01
37	Craig Ehlo	.03	.01	.00
38	Danny Ferry	.12	.06	.01

#	Player			
39	Larry Nance	.06	.03	.00
40	Mark Price	.08	.04	.01
41	Darnell Valentine	.03	.01	.00
42	Hot Rod Williams	.06	.03	.00
43	Rolando Blackman	.08	.04	.01
44	Brad Davis	.03	.01	.00
45	James Donaldson	.03	.01	.00
46	Derek Harper	.06	.03	.00
47	Fat Lever	.06	.03	.00
48	Rodney McCray	.06	.03	.00
49	Roy Tarpley	.06	.03	.00
50	Herb Williams	.03	.01	.00
51	Michael Adams	.06	.03	.00
52	Chris Jackson	.20	.10	.02
53	Jerome Lane	.03	.01	.00
54	Todd Lichti	.03	.01	.00
55	Blair Rasmussen	.03	.01	.00
56	Reggie Williams	.03	.01	.00
57	Joe Wolf	.03	.01	.00
58	Orlando Woolridge	.06	.03	.00
59	Mark Aguirre	.06	.03	.00
60	Joe Dumars	.12	.06	.01
61	James Edwards	.03	.01	.00
62	Vinnie Johnson	.08	.04	.01
63	Bill Laimbeer	.08	.04	.01
64	Dennis Rodman	.08	.04	.01
65	John Salley	.06	.03	.00
66	Isiah Thomas	.15	.07	.01
67	Tim Hardaway	.45	.22	.04
68	Rod Higgins	.03	.01	.00
69	Tyrone Hill	.10	.05	.01
70	Alton Lister	.03	.01	.00
71	Sarunas Marciulionis	.08	.04	.01
72	Chris Mullin	.12	.06	.01
73	Mitch Richmond	.12	.06	.01
74	Tom Tolbert	.03	.01	.00
75	Eric Floyd	.06	.03	.00
76	Buck Johnson	.03	.01	.00
77	Vernon Maxwell	.08	.04	.01
78	Hakeem Olajuwon	.20	.10	.02
79	Kenny Smith	.06	.03	.00
80	Larry Smith	.03	.01	.00
81	Otis Thorpe	.06	.03	.00
82	David Wood	.12	.06	.01
83	Vern Fleming	.06	.03	.00
84	Reggie Miller	.12	.06	.01
85	Chuck Person	.10	.05	.01
86	Mike Sanders	.03	.01	.00
87	Detlef Schrempf	.08	.04	.01
88	Rik Smits	.06	.03	.00
89	LaSalle Thompson	.03	.01	.00
90	Micheal Williams	.06	.03	.00
91	Winston Garland	.03	.01	.00
92	Gary Grant	.03	.01	.00
93	Ron Harper	.08	.04	.01
94	Danny Manning	.08	.04	.01
95	Jeff Martin	.03	.01	.00
96	Ken Norman	.08	.04	.01
97	Olden Polynice	.03	.01	.00
98	Charles Smith	.10	.05	.01
99	Vlade Divac	.20	.10	.02
100	A.C. Green	.08	.04	.01
101	Magic Johnson	.25	.12	.02
102	Sam Perkins	.08	.04	.01
103	Byron Scott	.08	.04	.01
104	Terry Teagle	.03	.01	.00
105	Mychal Thompson	.03	.01	.00
106	James Worthy	.10	.05	.01
107	Willie Burton	.15	.07	.01
108	Bimbo Coles	.10	.05	.01
109	Terry Davis	.03	.01	.00
110	Sherman Douglas	.10	.05	.01
111	Kevin Edwards	.03	.01	.00
112	Alec Kessler	.08	.04	.01
113	Glen Rice	.12	.06	.01
114	Rony Seikaly	.08	.04	.01
115	Frank Brickowski	.03	.01	.00
116	Dale Ellis	.06	.03	.00
117	Jay Humphries	.03	.01	.00
118	Brad Lohaus	.03	.01	.00
119	Fred Roberts	.03	.01	.00
120	Alvin Robertson	.06	.03	.00
121	Dan Schayes	.03	.01	.00
122	Jack Sikma	.06	.03	.00
123	Randy Breuer	.03	.01	.00
124	Tony Campbell	.03	.01	.00
125	Tyrone Corbin	.03	.01	.00
126	Gerald Glass	.08	.04	.01
127	Sam Mitchell	.03	.01	.00
128	Tod Murphy	.03	.01	.00
129	Pooh Richardson	.15	.07	.01
130	Felton Spencer	.15	.07	.01
131	Mookie Blaylock	.08	.04	.01
132	Sam Bowie	.06	.03	.00
133	Jud Buechler	.06	.03	.00
134	Derrick Coleman	.75	.35	.07
135	Chris Dudley	.03	.01	.00
136	Chris Morris	.06	.03	.00
137	Drazen Petrovic	.03	.01	.00
138	Reggie Theus	.06	.03	.00
139	Maurice Cheeks	.08	.04	.01
140	Patrick Ewing	.20	.10	.02
141	Mark Jackson	.06	.03	.00
142	Charles Oakley	.06	.03	.00
143	Trent Tucker	.03	.01	.00
144	Kiki Vandeweghe	.06	.03	.00
145	Kenny Walker	.03	.01	.00
146	Gerald Wilkins	.06	.03	.00
147	Nick Anderson	.10	.05	.01
148	Michael Ansley	.03	.01	.00
149	Terry Catledge	.03	.01	.00
150	Jerry Reynolds	.03	.01	.00
151	Dennis Scott	.20	.10	.02
152	Scott Skiles	.08	.04	.01
153	Otis Smith	.03	.01	.00
154	Sam Vincent	.03	.01	.00
155	Ron Anderson	.03	.01	.00
156	Charles Barkley	.20	.10	.02
157	Manute Bol	.03	.01	.00
158	Johnny Dawkins	.06	.03	.00
159	Armon Gilliam	.03	.01	.00
160	Ricky Green	.03	.01	.00
161	Hersey Hawkins	.10	.05	.01
162	Rick Mahorn	.06	.03	.00
163	Tom Chambers	.10	.05	.01
164	Jeff Hornacek	.08	.04	.01
165	Kevin Johnson	.25	.12	.02
166	Andrew Lang	.03	.01	.00
167	Dan Majerle	.08	.04	.01
168	Xavier McDaniel	.08	.04	.01
169	Kurt Rambis	.06	.03	.00
170	Mark West	.03	.01	.00
171	Danny Ainge	.08	.04	.01
172	Mark Bryant	.03	.01	.00
173	Walter Davis	.06	.03	.00
174	Clyde Drexler	.17	.08	.01
175	Kevin Duckworth	.06	.03	.00
176	Jerome Kersey	.08	.04	.01
177	Terry Porter	.10	.05	.01
178	Cliff Robinson	.12	.06	.01
179	Buck Williams	.08	.04	.01
180	Anthony Bonner	.03	.01	.00
181	Antoine Carr	.03	.01	.00
182	Duane Causwell	.08	.04	.01
183	Bobby Hansen	.03	.01	.00
184	Travis Mays	.15	.07	.01
185	Lionel Simmons	.35	.17	.03
186	Rory Sparrow	.03	.01	.00
187	Wayman Tisdale	.08	.04	.01
188	Willie Anderson	.08	.04	.01
189	Terry Cummings	.08	.04	.01
190	Sean Elliott	.15	.07	.01
191	Sidney Green	.03	.01	.00
192	David Greenwood	.03	.01	.00
193	Paul Pressey	.06	.03	.00
194	David Robinson	.75	.35	.07
195	Dwayne Schintzius	.12	.06	.01
196	Rod Strickland	.08	.04	.01
197	Benoit Benjamin	.06	.03	.00
198	Michael Cage	.03	.01	.00
199	Eddie Johnson	.06	.03	.00
200	Shawn Kemp	.35	.17	.03
201	Derrick McKey	.06	.03	.00
202	Gary Payton	.25	.12	.02
203	Ricky Pierce	.06	.03	.00
204	Sedale Threatt	.03	.01	.00
205	Thurl Bailey	.06	.03	.00
206	Mike Brown	.03	.01	.00
207	Mark Eaton	.06	.03	.00
208	Blue Edwards	.03	.01	.00
209	Darrell Griffith	.06	.03	.00
210	Jeff Malone	.08	.04	.01
211	Karl Malone	.20	.10	.02
212	John Stockton	.15	.07	.01
213	Ledell Eackles	.03	.01	.00
214	Pervis Ellison	.08	.04	.01
215	A.J. English	.10	.05	.01
216	Harvey Grant	.08	.04	.01
217	Charles Jones	.03	.01	.00
218	Bernard King	.10	.05	.01
219	Darrell Walker	.03	.01	.00
220	John Williams	.03	.01	.00
221	Bob Weiss CO	.03	.01	.00
222	Chris Ford CO	.06	.03	.00
223	Gene Littles CO	.03	.01	.00
224	Phil Jackson CO	.06	.03	.00
225	Lenny Wilkens CO	.06	.03	.00
226	Richie Adubato CO	.03	.01	.00

227 Paul Westhead CO	.03	.01	.00
228 Chuck Daly CO	.06	.03	.00
229 Don Nelson CO	.06	.03	.00
230 Don Chaney CO	.06	.03	.00
231 Bob Hill CO	.06	.03	.00
232 Mike Schuler CO	.03	.01	.00
233 Mike Dunleavy CO	.03	.01	.00
234 Del Harris CO	.03	.01	.00
235 Bill Fitch CO	.03	.01	.00
236 Pat Riley CO	.06	.03	.00
237 Matt Guokas CO	.03	.01	.00
238 Jim Lynam CO	.03	.01	.00
239 Cotton Fitzsimmons CO	.03	.01	.00
240 Rick Adelman CO	.06	.03	.00
241 Dick Motta CO	.03	.01	.00
242 Larry Brown CO	.06	.03	.00
243 K.C. Jones CO	.06	.03	.00
244 Jerry Sloan CO	.03	.01	.00
245 Wes Unseld CO	.06	.03	.00
246 Charles Barkley AS	.12	.06	.01
247 Brad Daugherty AS	.08	.04	.01
248 Joe Dumars AS	.08	.04	.01
249 Patrick Ewing AS	.12	.06	.01
250 Hersey Hawkins AS	.06	.03	.00
251 Michael Jordan AS	.35	.17	.03
252 Bernard King AS	.08	.04	.01
253 Kevin McHale AS	.08	.04	.01
254 Robert Parish AS	.08	.04	.01
255 Ricky Pierce AS	.06	.03	.00
256 Alvin Robertson AS	.06	.03	.00
257 Dominique Wilkins AS	.10	.05	.01
258 Chris Ford CO AS	.06	.03	.00
259 Tom Chambers AS	.08	.04	.01
260 Clyde Drexler AS	.10	.05	.01
261 Kevin Duckworth AS	.06	.03	.00
262 Tim Hardaway AS	.25	.12	.02
263 Kevin Johnson AS	.12	.06	.01
264 Magic Johnson AS	.12	.06	.01
265 Karl Malone AS	.12	.06	.01
266 Chris Mullen AS	.10	.05	.01
267 Terry Porter AS	.08	.04	.01
268 David Robinson AS	.35	.17	.03
269 John Stockton AS	.10	.05	.01
270 James Worthy AS	.08	.04	.01
271 Rick Adelman CO AS	.06	.03	.00
272 Atlanta Hawks	.06	.03	.00
273 Boston Celtics	.06	.03	.00
274 Charlotte Hornets	.06	.03	.00
275 Chicago Bulls	.06	.03	.00
276 Cleveland Cavaliers	.06	.03	.00
277 Dallas Mavericks	.06	.03	.00
278 Denver Nuggets	.06	.03	.00
279 Detroit Pistons	.06	.03	.00
280 Golden State	.06	.03	.00
281 Houston Rockets	.06	.03	.00
282 Indiana Pacers	.06	.03	.00
283 Los Angeles Clippers	.06	.03	.00
284 Los Angeles Lakers	.06	.03	.00
285 Miami Heat	.06	.03	.00
286 Milwaukee Bucks	.06	.03	.00
287 Minnesota Timberwolves	.06	.03	.00
288 New Jersey Nets	.06	.03	.00
289 New York Knicks	.06	.03	.00
290 Orlando Magic	.06	.03	.00
291 Philadelphia 76ers	.06	.03	.00
292 Phoenix Suns	.06	.03	.00
293 Portland Trail Blazers	.06	.03	.00
294 Sacramento Kings	.06	.03	.00
295 San Antonio Spurs	.06	.03	.00
296 Seattle Supersonics	.06	.03	.00
297 Utah Jazz	.06	.03	.00
298 Washington Capitals	.06	.03	.00
299 Centennial Card	.10	.05	.01
James Naismith			
300 Kevin Johnson IS	.12	.06	.01
301 Reggie Miller IS	.08	.04	.01
302 Hakeem Olajuwon IS	.12	.06	.01
303 Robert Parish IS	.08	.04	.01
304 Scoring Leaders	.20	.10	.02
Michael Jordan			
Karl Malone			
305 3-Point FG Percent	.08	.04	.01
306 Free Throw Percent	.08	.04	.01
Reggie Miller			
Jeff Malone			
307 Blocks	.20	.10	.02
Hakeem Olajuwon			
David Robinson			
308 Steals	.08	.04	.01
Alvin Robertson			
John Stockton			
309 Rebounds	.15	.07	.01
David Robinson			
Dennis Rodman			

310 Assists	.15	.07	.01
John Stockton			
Magic Johnson			
311 Field Goal Percent	.08	.04	.01
Buck Williams			
Robert parish			
312 Larry Bird	.12	.06	.01
Milestone			
313 English/Malone	.08	.04	.01
Milestone			
314 Magic Johnson	.12	.06	.01
Milestone			
315 Michael Jordan	.35	.17	.03
Milestone			
316 Moses Malone	.08	.04	.01
Milestone			
317 Larry Bird	.12	.06	.01
NBA Yearbook			
318 Maurice Cheeks	.06	.03	.00
NBA Yearbook			
319 Magic Johnson	.12	.06	.01
NBA Yearbook			
320 Bernard King	.08	.04	.01
NBA Yearbook			
321 Moses Malone	.08	.04	.01
NBA Yearbook			
322 Robert Parish	.08	.04	.01
NBA Yearbook			
323 Adrian Dantley	.08	.04	.01
NBA Yearbook			
324 Will Smith	.08	.04	.01
Stay in School			
325 Kid N' Play	.06	.03	.00
Stay in School			
326 The Boys	.06	.03	.00
Stay in School			
327 David Robinson	.50	.25	.05
Don't ...			
328 Checklist 1	.06	.01	.00
329 Checklist 2	.06	.01	.00
330 Checklist 3	.06	.01	.00

1972-73 Icee Bear

The 1972-73 Icee Bear set contains 20 player cards each measuring approximately 3" by 5". The cards are printed on thin stock. The fronts feature color facial pictures, and the backs show brief biographical information. The set may have been printed in 1973-74 or perhaps later. There are three cards that are more difficult to find than the other 17; these three are listed as SP in the checklist below.

	NRMT	VG-E	GOOD
COMPLETE SET (20)	150.00	75.00	15.00
COMMON PLAYER (1-20)	2.50	1.25	.25
COMMON PLAYER SP	12.50	6.25	1.25
☐ 1 Dennis Awtrey	2.50	1.25	.25
☐ 2 Tom Boerwinkle	2.50	1.25	.25
☐ 3 Austin Carr SP	12.50	6.25	1.25
☐ 4 Wilt Chamberlain	25.00	12.50	2.50
☐ 5 Archie Clark SP	12.50	6.25	1.25

		MINT	EXC	G-VG
☐ 6	Dave DeBusschere	7.50	3.75	.75
☐ 7	Walt Frazier SP	25.00	12.50	2.50
☐ 8	John Havlicek	12.00	6.00	1.20
☐ 9	Connie Hawkins	4.50	2.25	.45
☐ 10	Kareem Abdul Jabbar	30.00	15.00	3.00
☐ 11	Bob Love	3.50	1.75	.35
☐ 12	Jerry Lucas	7.50	3.75	.75
☐ 13	Pete Maravich	9.00	4.50	.90
☐ 14	Calvin Murphy	3.50	1.75	.35
☐ 15	Oscar Robertson	15.00	7.50	1.50
☐ 16	Jerry Sloan	2.50	1.25	.25
☐ 17	Wes Unseld	6.00	3.00	.60
☐ 18	Dick Van Arsdale	2.50	1.25	.25
☐ 19	Jerry West	18.00	9.00	1.80
☐ 20	Sidney Wicks	4.50	2.25	.45

1988-89 Jazz Smokey

The 1988-89 Smokey Utah Jazz set contains eight 8" by 10" (approximately) cards featuring color action photos. The card backs feature a large fire safety cartoon and player information in the form of year-by-year statistics for each NBA regular season and playoffs. The cards are unnumbered and are ordered below alphabetically. The set was sponsored by the Utah Department of State Lands and Forestry and U.S.D.A. Forest Service. The player's name, number, and position are overprinted in white in the lower right corner of each obverse.

		MINT	EXC	G-VG
COMPLETE SET (8)		30.00	15.00	3.00
COMMON PLAYER (1-8)		3.00	1.50	.30
☐ 1	Thurl Bailey	4.00	2.00	.40
☐ 2	Mark Eaton	5.00	2.50	.50
☐ 3	Frank Layden CO	3.00	1.50	.30
☐ 4	Karl Malone	10.00	5.00	1.00
☐ 5	Marc Iavaroni	3.00	1.50	.30
☐ 6	John Stockton	8.00	4.00	.80
☐ 7	Smokey Bear	3.00	1.50	.30
☐ 8	Bobby Hansen	3.00	1.50	.30

1989 Jazz Old Home

This 13-card set of Utah Jazz was sponsored by Old Home bread, and its company logo appears on both sides of the card. The cards measure the standard size (2 1/2" by 3 1/2"). The color action player photo on the front has rounded corners, and it is superimposed on a background of yellow, green, and purple stripes of varying width. The player's name and team logo appear above the picture, and the words "1989 Collector's Series" below. The horizontally-oriented backs are printed in pink and red and present biographical and statistical information. The cards are numbered on the back.

	MINT	EXC	G-VG
COMPLETE SET (13)	65.00	32.50	6.50
COMMON PLAYER (1-13)	2.50	1.25	.25

		MINT	EXC	G-VG
☐ 1	Thurl Bailey	3.50	1.75	.35
☐ 2	Mike Brown	2.50	1.25	.25
☐ 3	Mark Eaton	4.50	2.25	.45
☐ 4	Darrell Griffith	3.50	1.75	.35
☐ 5	Bobby Hansen	2.50	1.25	.25
☐ 6	Marc Iavaroni	2.50	1.25	.25
☐ 7	Frank Layden CO	3.50	1.75	.35
☐ 8	Eric Leckner	2.50	1.25	.25
☐ 9	Jim Les	2.50	1.25	.25
☐ 10	Karl Malone	20.00	10.00	2.00
☐ 11	Jose Ortiz	3.50	1.75	.35
☐ 12	Scott Roth	2.50	1.25	.25
☐ 13	John Stockton	15.00	7.50	1.50

1990-91 Jazz Star

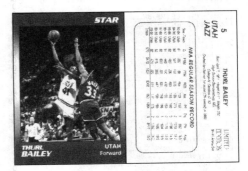

This 12-card set of Utah Jazz measures the standard size (2 1/2" and 3 1/2"). The fronts feature color action shots, with purple borders that wash out in the middle of the card face. The horizontally oriented backs are printed in purple on white and have various kinds of player information. The cards are numbered on the back and checklisted below accordingly.

		MINT	EXC	G-VG
COMPLETE SET (12)		9.00	4.50	.90
COMMON PLAYER (1-12)		.60	.30	.06
☐ 1	Karl Malone	2.50	1.25	.25
☐ 2	John Stockton	2.00	1.00	.20
☐ 3	Mark Eaton	.90	.45	.09
☐ 4	Theodore Edwards	.75	.35	.07
☐ 5	Thurl Bailey	.75	.35	.07
☐ 6	Mike Brown	.60	.30	.06
☐ 7	Jeff Malone	.90	.45	.09
☐ 8	Andy Toolson	.60	.30	.06
☐ 9	Darrell Griffith	.75	.35	.07
☐ 10	Delaney Rudd	.60	.30	.06
☐ 11	Walter Palmer	.60	.30	.06
☐ 12	Jerry Sloan CO	.75	.35	.07

1985-86 JMS Game

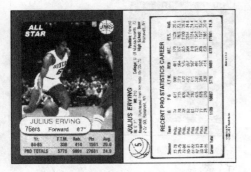

These standard size (2 1/2" by 3 1/2") cards were issued by J.M.S. in uncut team sheets as part of a table top game and featured nine players each from the Philadelphia 76ers (1-9), Boston Celtics (10-18), and Los Angeles Lakers (19-27). The front features a color action player photo, with a blue border on red background. Player information appears in a white capsule, and statistics are given below the picture in a pink box. In a horizontal format the back has a statistical breakdown year by year and brief biographical information. The cards are numbered on the back.

	MINT	EXC	G-VG
COMPLETE SET (27)	200.00	100.00	20.00
COMMON 76ERS (1-9)	4.00	2.00	.40
COMMON CELTICS (10-18)	4.00	2.00	.40
COMMON LAKERS (19-27)	4.00	2.00	.40
☐ 1 Maurice Cheeks	8.00	4.00	.80
☐ 2 Moses Malone	15.00	7.50	1.50
☐ 3 Bobby Jones	8.00	4.00	.80
☐ 4 Charles Barkley	35.00	17.50	3.50
☐ 5 Julius Erving	20.00	10.00	2.00
☐ 6 Clint Richardson	4.00	2.00	.40
☐ 8 Sedale Threatt	6.00	3.00	.60
☐ 7 Andrew Toney	6.00	3.00	.60
☐ 9 Clem Johnson	4.00	2.00	.40
☐ 10 Bill Walton	12.00	6.00	1.20
☐ 11 Danny Ainge	8.00	4.00	.80
☐ 12 Robert Parish	12.00	6.00	1.20
☐ 13 Kevin McHale	10.00	5.00	1.00
☐ 14 Larry Bird	25.00	12.50	2.50
☐ 15 Dennis Johnson	6.00	3.00	.60
☐ 16 Ray Williams	4.00	2.00	.40
☐ 17 Scott Wedman	4.00	2.00	.40
☐ 18 Greg Kite	4.00	2.00	.40
☐ 19 Michael Cooper	8.00	4.00	.80
☐ 20 Kareem Abdul Jabbar	20.00	10.00	2.00
☐ 21 Jamaal Wilkes	8.00	4.00	.80
☐ 22 Bob McAdoo	8.00	4.00	.80
☐ 23 James Worthy	15.00	7.50	1.50
☐ 24 Magic Johnson	25.00	12.50	2.50
☐ 25 Michael McGee	4.00	2.00	.40
☐ 26 Kurt Rambis	6.00	3.00	.60
☐ 27 Byron Scott	8.00	4.00	.80

1957-58 Kahn's

The 1957-58 Kahn's Basketball set contains 11 black and white cards. Cards are 3 3/16" by 3 15/16". The backs contain "How To" articles and instructional text. Cincinnati Royals players only are depicted.

	NRMT	VG-E	GOOD
COMPLETE SET (11)	1100.00	500.00	100.00
COMMON PLAYER (1-11)	75.00	37.50	7.50
☐ 1 Richard Duckett	75.00	37.50	7.50
☐ 2 George King	75.00	37.50	7.50

Compliments of Kahn's Wieners
"THE WIENER THE WORLD AWAITED"

☐ 3 Clyde Lovelette	150.00	75.00	15.00
☐ 4 Tom Marshall	75.00	37.50	7.50
☐ 5 J. Paxson	100.00	50.00	10.00
☐ 6 Dave Piontek	75.00	37.50	7.50
☐ 7 Richard Regan	75.00	37.50	7.50
☐ 8 Richard(Dick) Ricketts	75.00	37.50	7.50
☐ 9 Maurice Stokes	200.00	100.00	20.00
☐ 10 Jack Twyman	150.00	75.00	15.00
☐ 11 R. Wanzer	100.00	50.00	10.00

1958-59 Kahn's

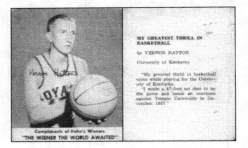

Compliments of Kahn's Wieners
"THE WIENER THE WORLD AWAITED"

The 1958-59 Kahn's Basketball set contains 10 black and white cards. Cards measure 3 1/4" by 3 15/16". The backs feature a short narrative entitled "My Greatest Thrill in Basketball" allegedly written by the player depicted on the front. Cincinnati Royals players only are depicted. The Sihugo Green card is supposedly a little tougher to find than the other cards in the set.

	NRMT	VG-E	GOOD
COMPLETE SET (10)	700.00	325.00	65.00
COMMON PLAYER (1-10)	65.00	32.50	6.50
☐ 1 Arlen Bockhorn	65.00	32.50	6.50
☐ 2 Archie Dees	65.00	32.50	6.50
☐ 3 Sihugo Green	85.00	42.50	8.50
☐ 4 Vern Hatton	65.00	32.50	6.50
☐ 5 Tom Marshall	65.00	32.50	6.50
☐ 6 Jack Paar	75.00	37.50	7.50
☐ 7 George Palmer	65.00	32.50	6.50
☐ 8 Jim Palmer	65.00	32.50	6.50
☐ 9 David V. Piontek	65.00	32.50	6.50
☐ 10 Jack Twyman	125.00	60.00	12.50

1959-60 Kahn's

The 1959-60 Kahn's Basketball set features 10 black and white cards. Cards are 3 1/4" by 4". The backs feature descriptive narratives allegedly written by the player depicted on the front. No statistics are featured on the backs. Cincinnati Royals players only are depicted.

	NRMT	VG-E	GOOD
COMPLETE SET (10)	500.00	250.00	50.00
COMMON PLAYER (1-10)	45.00	22.50	4.50
☐ 1 Arlen Bockhorn	45.00	22.50	4.50
☐ 2 Wayne Embry	65.00	32.50	6.50
☐ 3 Tom Marshall	45.00	22.50	4.50
☐ 4 Med Park	45.00	22.50	4.50
☐ 5 Dave Piontek	45.00	22.50	4.50
☐ 6 Hub Reed	45.00	22.50	4.50
☐ 7 Phil Rollins	45.00	22.50	4.50
☐ 8 Larry Staverman	45.00	22.50	4.50
☐ 9 Jack Twyman	90.00	45.00	9.00
☐ 10 Win Wilfong	45.00	22.50	4.50

1960-61 Kahn's

The 1960-61 Kahn's Basketball set features 12 black and white cards. Cards are 3 1/4" by 3 15/16". The backs contain statistical season-by-season records up through the 1959-60 season, player vital statistics, and a short biography of the player's career. Jerry West of the Lakers is the only non-Cincinnati Royals player depicted and his card does not have any statistical breakdown.

	NRMT	VG-E	GOOD
COMPLETE SET (12)	1100.00	500.00	100.00
COMMON PLAYER (1-12)	30.00	15.00	3.00
☐ 1 Arlen Bockhorn	30.00	15.00	3.00
☐ 2 Robert L. Boozer	30.00	15.00	3.00
☐ 3 Ralph E. Davis	30.00	15.00	3.00
☐ 4 Wayne Embry	35.00	17.50	3.50
☐ 5 Mike Farmer	30.00	15.00	3.00
☐ 6 Phil Jordan	30.00	15.00	3.00
☐ 7 Hub Reed	30.00	15.00	3.00
☐ 8 Oscar Robertson	350.00	175.00	35.00
☐ 9 Larry Staverman	30.00	15.00	3.00
☐ 10 Jack Twyman	60.00	30.00	6.00
☐ 11 Jerry West	500.00	250.00	50.00
☐ 12 Win Wilfong	30.00	15.00	3.00

1961-62 Kahn's

The 1961-62 Kahn's Basketball set consists of 13 black and white cards. Cards measure 3 3/16" by 4 1/16". Lakers' Jerry West is the only non-Cincinnati Royals player depicted and there is also a card of coach Charley Wolf. The backs of the cards are blank; this was the only year the Kahn's basketball cards were blank backed.

	NRMT	VG-E	GOOD
COMPLETE SET (13)	600.00	300.00	60.00
COMMON PLAYER (1-13)	20.00	10.00	2.00
☐ 1 Arlen Bockhorn	20.00	10.00	2.00
☐ 2 Bob Boozer	20.00	10.00	2.00
☐ 3 Joe Buckhalter	20.00	10.00	2.00
☐ 4 Wayne Embry	25.00	12.50	2.50
☐ 5 Bob Nordmann	20.00	10.00	2.00
☐ 6 Hub Reed	20.00	10.00	2.00
☐ 7 Oscar Robertson	175.00	85.00	18.00
☐ 8 Adrian Smith	20.00	10.00	2.00
☐ 9 Jack Twyman	40.00	20.00	4.00
☐ 10 Bob Wesenhahn	20.00	10.00	2.00
☐ 11 Jerry West	225.00	110.00	22.00
☐ 12 Charley Wolf CO	12.00	6.00	1.20
☐ 13 Dave Zeller	12.00	6.00	1.20

1962-63 Kahn's

The 1962-63 Kahn's Basketball set contains 11 black and white cards. Cards measure 3 1/4" by 4 3/16". Jerry West of the Lakers is the only non-Cincinnati Royals player depicted and there is also a card of Royals' coach Charley Wolf. The backs feature a short biography of the player depicted on the front of the card. The Jerry West card has a picture with no border around it. Cards of Bockhorn, Boozer, Reed, and Twyman are oriented horizontally.

	NRMT	VG-E	GOOD
COMPLETE SET (11)	500.00	250.00	50.00
COMMON PLAYER (1-11)	20.00	10.00	2.00
☐ 1 Arlen Bockhorn HOR	20.00	10.00	2.00
☐ 2 Bob Boozer HOR	20.00	10.00	2.00

			NRMT	VG-E	GOOD
☐	3	Wayne Embry	25.00	12.50	2.50
☐	4	Tom Hawkins	25.00	12.50	2.50
☐	5	Bud Olsen	20.00	10.00	2.00
☐	6	Hub Reed HOR	20.00	10.00	2.00
☐	7	Oscar Robertson	150.00	75.00	15.00
☐	8	Adrian Smith	20.00	10.00	2.00
☐	9	Jack Twyman HOR	40.00	20.00	4.00
☐	10	Jerry West	200.00	100.00	20.00
☐	11	Charley Wolf CO	20.00	10.00	2.00

1963-64 Kahn's

Compliments of Kahn's
"THE WIENER THE WORLD AWAITED"

The 1963-64 Kahn's Basketball set contains 13 black and white cards. Cards measure 3 1/4" by 4 3/16". This is the only Kahn's basketball set on which there is a distinctive white border on the fronts of the cards; in this respect the set is similar to the 1963 Kahn's baseball and football sets. A brief biography of the player is contained on the back of the card. Jerry West of the Lakers is the only non-Cincinnati Royals player depicted and there is also a card of coach Jack McMahon. The Jerry West card is identical to that of the previous year set except in smaller type and with the distinctive white border on the front. The cards of Bob Boozer and Jack Twyman are oriented horizontally.

		NRMT	VG-E	GOOD
COMPLETE SET (13)		450.00	225.00	45.00
COMMON PLAYER (1-13)		15.00	7.50	1.50

☐	1	Jay Arnette	15.00	7.50	1.50
☐	2	Arlen Bockhorn	15.00	7.50	1.50
☐	3	Bob Boozer HOR	15.00	7.50	1.50
☐	4	Wayne Embry	20.00	10.00	2.00
☐	5	Tom Hawkins	20.00	10.00	2.00
☐	6	Jerry Lucas	75.00	37.50	7.50
☐	7	Jack McMahon CO	15.00	7.50	1.50
☐	8	Bud Olsen	15.00	7.50	1.50
☐	9	Oscar Robertson	100.00	50.00	10.00
☐	10	Adrian Smith	15.00	7.50	1.50
☐	11	Thomas P. Thacker	15.00	7.50	1.50
☐	12	Jack Twyman HOR	30.00	15.00	3.00
☐	13	Jerry West	125.00	60.00	12.50

1964-65 Kahn's

The 1964-65 Kahn's Basketball set contains 12 full-color subjects on 14 distinct cards. Cards measure 3" by 3 5/8". These cards come in two types distinguishable by the color of the printing on the backs. Type I cards (1-3) have light maroon printing on the backs, while type II (4-12) have black printing on the backs. The fronts are completely devoid of any written material. There are two poses each of Jerry Lucas and Oscar Robertson.

		NRMT	VG-E	GOOD
COMPLETE SET (12)		400.00	200.00	40.00
COMMON PLAYER (1-3)		15.00	7.50	1.50
COMMON PLAYER (4-12)		15.00	7.50	1.50

☐	1	Harold(Happy) Hairston	18.00	9.00	1.80

☐	2	Jack McMahon CO	15.00	7.50	1.50
☐	3	George(Jif) Wilson	15.00	7.50	1.50
☐	4	Jay Arnette	15.00	7.50	1.50
☐	5	Arlen Bockhorn	15.00	7.50	1.50
☐	6	Wayne Embry	18.00	9.00	1.80
☐	7	Tom Hawkins	18.00	9.00	1.80
☐	8A	Jerry Lucas (windows open; right thumb hidden)	40.00	20.00	4.00
☐	8B	Jerry Lucas (no windows visible; right thumb barely visible)	40.00	20.00	4.00
☐	9	Bud Olsen	15.00	7.50	1.50
☐	10A	Oscar Robertson (facing side)	100.00	50.00	10.00
☐	10B	Oscar Robertson (facing front)	100.00	50.00	10.00
☐	11	Adrian Smith	15.00	7.50	1.50
☐	12	Jack Twyman	30.00	15.00	3.00

1965-66 Kahn's

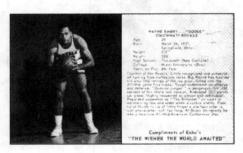

The 1965-66 Kahn's Basketball set contains four full-color cards featuring players of the Cincinnati Royals. Cards in this set measure approximately 3" by 3 9/16". This was the last of the Kahn's Basketball issues and the second in full color. The fronts are devoid of all written material, and the backs are printed in red ink. The "Compliments of Kahn's, The Wiener the World Awaited" slogan appears on the backs of the cards. The set is presumed complete with the following cards.

		NRMT	VG-E	GOOD
COMPLETE SET (4)		200.00	100.00	20.00
COMMON PLAYER (1-4)		25.00	12.50	2.50

☐	1	Wayne Embry	25.00	12.50	2.50
☐	2	Jerry Lucas	60.00	30.00	6.00
☐	3	Oscar Robertson	100.00	50.00	10.00
☐	4	Jack Twyman	40.00	20.00	4.00

1971 Keds KedKards *

This set is composed of crude artistic renditions of popular subjects from various sports from 1971 who were apparently celebrity endorsers of Keds shoes. The cards actually form a complete panel on the Keds tennis shoes box. The two different panels are actually different sizes; the Bing panel contains smaller cards. The smaller Bubba Smith shows him without beard and standing straight; the large Bubba shows him leaning over, with beard, and jersey number partially visible. The individual player card portions of the card panels measure approximately 2 15/16" by 2 3/4" and 2 5/16" by 2 3/16" respectively, although it should be noted that there are slight size differences among the individual cards even on the same panel. The panel background is colored in black and yellow.

	NRMT	VG-E	GOOD
COMPLETE SET (2)	50.00	25.00	5.00
COMMON PLAYER (1-2)	20.00	10.00	2.00
☐ 1 Dave Bing (Basketball) Clark Graebner (Tennis) Bubba Smith (Football) Jim Maloney (Baseball)	40.00	20.00	4.00
☐ 2 Willis Reed (Basketball) Stan Smith (Tennis) Bubba Smith (Football) Johnny Bench (Baseball)	20.00	10.00	2.00

1948 Kellogg's Pep *

MIKE TRESH

Catcher of Chicago White Sox. One of best throwers in major leagues and an artist on "squeeze play." A native of Detroit, Tresh is known as a "smart catcher" and annually works 100 or more games for White Sox.

Get Complete Series with Kellogg's PEP

These rather unattractive cards measure 1 7/16" by 1 5/8". The card front presents a black and white head-and-shoulders shot of the player, with a white border. The back has the player's name and a brief description of his accomplishments. The cards are unnumbered. There is only one basketball card in the set. The catalog designation for this set is F273-19.

	NRMT	VG-E	GOOD
COMPLETE SET (18)	700.00	350.00	70.00
COMMON BASEBALL (1-5)	20.00	10.00	2.00
COMMON FOOTBALL (6-10)	30.00	15.00	3.00
COMMON OTHERS (11-18)	10.00	5.00	1.00
☐ 1 Phil Cavaretta (baseball)	25.00	12.50	2.50

☐ 2 Orval Grove (baseball)	20.00	10.00	2.00
☐ 3 Mike Tresh (baseball)	20.00	10.00	2.00
☐ 4 Paul(Dizzy) Trout (baseball)	20.00	10.00	2.00
☐ 5 Dick Wakefield (baseball)	20.00	10.00	2.00
☐ 6 Lou Groza (football)	75.00	37.50	7.50
☐ 7 George McAfee (football)	45.00	22.50	4.50
☐ 8 Norm Standlee (football)	30.00	15.00	3.00
☐ 9A Charlie Trippi ERR (reversed negative)	45.00	22.50	4.50
☐ 9B Charlie Trippi COR (football)	45.00	22.50	4.50
☐ 10 Bob Waterfield (football)	75.00	37.50	7.50
☐ 11 Donald Budge (tennis)	15.00	7.50	1.50
☐ 12 James Ferrier (golf)	10.00	5.00	1.00
☐ 13 Mary Hardwick (tennis)	10.00	5.00	1.00
☐ 14 Adolph Kiefer (swimming)	10.00	5.00	1.00
☐ 15 Lloyd Mangrum (golf)	10.00	5.00	1.00
☐ 16 George Mikan (basketball)	200.00	100.00	20.00
☐ 17 Samuel Jackson Snead (golf)	20.00	10.00	2.00
☐ 18A Tony Zale ERR (reversed negative)	20.00	10.00	2.00
☐ 18B Tony Zale COR (boxing)	20.00	10.00	2.00

1985-86 Kings Smokey

This 15-card set features members of the Sacramento Kings of the NBA. The cards were originally distributed as a perforated sheet along with (and perforated to) a large team photo. The cards are numbered on the back in the upper right corner. The cards measure approximately 4" by 5 1/2". The card backs contain a fire safety cartoon but minimal information about the player.

	MINT	EXC	G-VG
COMPLETE SET (16)	15.00	7.50	1.50
COMMON PLAYER (1-16)	.75	.35	.07
☐ 1 Smokey Emblem	.75	.35	.07
☐ 2 Phil Johnson CO	.75	.35	.07
☐ 3 Frank Hamblen ASST Jerry Reynolds ASST Bill Jones TR	.75	.35	.07
☐ 4 Smokey Bear	.75	.35	.07
☐ 5 Michael Adams	3.00	1.50	.30
☐ 6 Larry Drew	1.00	.50	.10
☐ 7 Carl Henry	.75	.35	.07
☐ 8 Eddie Johnson	1.25	.60	.12
☐ 9 Rich Kelley	.75	.35	.07
☐ 10 Joe Kleine	1.00	.50	.10
☐ 11 Mark Olberding	.75	.35	.07
☐ 12 Reggie Theus	1.25	.60	.12

		MINT	EXC	G-VG
☐ 13	LaSalle Thompson	1.25	.60	.12
☐ 14	Otis Thorpe	3.00	1.50	.30
☐ 15	Terry Tyler	.75	.35	.07
☐ 16	Mike Woodson	1.00	.50	.10

1986-87 Kings Smokey

This 15-card set features members of the Sacramento Kings of the NBA. The cards were originally distributed as a perforated sheet along with (and perforated to) a large team photo. Since the cards are unnumbered, they are listed below in alphabetical order. The player's uniform number (given on both sides of the card) is also listed below. The cards measure approximately 2 3/8" by 3". The card backs contain a fire safety cartoon but minimal information about the player.

	MINT	EXC	G-VG
COMPLETE SET (15)	20.00	10.00	2.00
COMMON PLAYER	1.00	.50	.10

		MINT	EXC	G-VG
☐ 1	Don Buse ASST	1.00	.50	.10
☐ 2	Franklin Edwards 10	1.00	.50	.10
☐ 3	Eddie Johnson 8	2.00	1.00	.20
☐ 4	Bill Jones TR	1.00	.50	.10
☐ 5	Joe Kleine 35	1.50	.75	.15
☐ 6	Mark Olberding 53	1.00	.50	.10
☐ 7	Harold Pressley 21	1.50	.75	.15
☐ 8	Jerry Reynolds CO	1.00	.50	.10
☐ 9	Johnny Rogers 32	1.00	.50	.10
☐ 10	Derek Smith 18	1.50	.75	.15
☐ 11	Reggie Theus 24	2.00	1.00	.20
☐ 12	LaSalle Thompson 41	2.00	1.00	.20
☐ 13	Otis Thorpe 33	3.00	1.50	.30
☐ 14	Terry Tyler 40	1.00	.50	.10
☐ 15	Othell Wilson 2	1.00	.50	.10

1988-89 Kings Carl's Jr.

The 1988-89 Carl's Jr. Sacramento Kings set contains 12 cards each measuring approximately 2 1/2" by 3 1/2". There are 11 player cards and one coach card in this set. The cards are unnumbered except for uniform number; they are ordered below by uniform number. The cards were issued in three strips of four players plus a coupon for savings at Carl's Jr. restaurants before May 31, 1989. Since this set was issued in late spring of 1989, it does include comments and statistics about the 1988-89 season. The set was produced for Carl's Jr. by Sports Marketing Inc. of Redmond, Washington.

	MINT	EXC	G-VG
COMPLETE SET (12)	9.00	4.50	.90
COMMON PLAYER (1-12)	.60	.30	.06

		MINT	EXC	G-VG
☐ 2	Michael Jackson	.60	.30	.06
☐ 7	Danny Ainge	1.25	.60	.12
☐ 15	Vinnie Del Negro	.75	.35	.07
☐ 21	Harold Pressley	.75	.35	.07

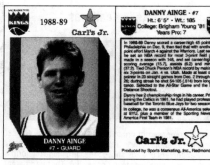

		MINT	EXC	G-VG
☐ 22	Rodney McCray	.75	.35	.07
☐ 23	Waymon Tisdale	1.25	.60	.12
☐ 30	Kenny Smith	1.25	.60	.12
☐ 34	Ricky Berry	.60	.30	.06
☐ 43	Jim Petersen	.60	.30	.06
☐ 50	Ben Gillery	.60	.30	.06
☐ 54	Brad Lohaus	.75	.35	.07
☐ xx	Jerry Reynolds CO	.60	.30	.06

1989-90 Kings Carl's Jr.

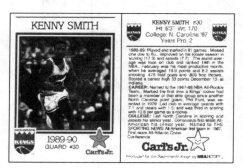

This 12-card set of Sacramento Kings was sponsored by Carl's Jr. restaurants and issued in three panels, each containing four player cards and one sponsor's coupon. After perforation, the player cards measure the standard size (2 1/2" by 3 1/2"). The front features a color action player photo, with red, white, and blue borders on white card stock. The player's name is written between a thin blue stripe and the top border. The team and sponsors' logos overlay the lower corners of the picture, with the year, position, and uniform number below the picture. The back has two team logos in the upper corners, with biographical information and career summary. The cards are unnumbered and checklisted below by uniform number. The cards were given away at three different games in strips of four player cards each. The set includes the rookie card of Pervis Ellison, the first pick of the 1989 NBA draft. The player groups on the panels were as follows: Michael Jackson, Vinny Del Negro, Wayman Tisdale, and Pervis Ellison; Danny Ainge, Kenny Smith, Randy Allen, and Ralph Sampson; and Harold Pressley, Rodney McCray, Greg Kite, and Jerry Reynolds.

	MINT	EXC	G-VG
COMPLETE SET (12)	7.00	3.50	.70
COMMON PLAYER	.50	.25	.05

		MINT	EXC	G-VG
☐ 2	Michael Jackson	.50	.25	.05
☐ 7	Danny Ainge	1.00	.50	.10
☐ 15	Vinny Del Negro	.50	.25	.05
☐ 21	Harold Pressley	.50	.25	.05

		MINT	EXC	G-VG
☐ 22	Rodney McCray	.75	.35	.07
☐ 23	Wayman Tisdale	1.00	.50	.10
☐ 30	Kenny Smith	1.00	.50	.10
☐ 32	Greg Kite	.50	.25	.05
☐ 40	Randy Allen	.50	.25	.05
☐ 42	Pervis Ellison	1.50	.75	.15
☐ 50	Ralph Sampson	.75	.35	.07
☐ xx	Jerry Reynolds CO	.50	.25	.05

1990-91 Kings Safeway

This 12-card set of Sacramento Kings was sponsored by Safeway stores and issued in three panels, each containing four player cards and one sponsor's coupon. After perforation, the player cards measure the standard size (2 1/2" by 3 1/2"). The front features a color action player photo, with red, white, and blue borders on white card stock. The player's name is written between a thin blue stripe and the top border. The team and sponsors' logos overlay the lower corners of the picture, with the year, position, and uniform number below the picture. The back has two team logos in the upper corners, with biographical information and career summary. The cards are unnumbered and are checklisted below in alphabetical order, with the uniform number after the player's name.

		MINT	EXC	G-VG
COMPLETE SET (12)		9.00	4.50	.90
COMMON PLAYER (1-12)		.50	.25	.05
☐ 1	Anthony Bonner 24	.75	.35	.07
☐ 2	Antoine Carr 35	.75	.35	.07
☐ 3	Duane Causwell 31	1.00	.50	.10
☐ 4	Steve Colter 21	.50	.25	.05
☐ 5	Bobby Hansen 20	.50	.25	.05
☐ 6	Eric Leckner 45	.50	.25	.05
☐ 7	Travis Mays 1	1.25	.60	.12
☐ 8	Dick Motta CO	.50	.25	.05
☐ 9	Lionel Simmons 22	2.50	1.25	.25
☐ 10	Rory Sparrow 2	.50	.25	.05
☐ 11	Wayman Tisdale 23	1.00	.50	.10
☐ 12	Bill Wennington 34	.50	.25	.05

1989-90 Knicks Marine Midland

This 14-card set of New York Knicks was sponsored by Marine Midland Bank. The cards were issued in one sheet with three rows of five cards each, and they measure the standard size (2 1/2" by 3 1/2") after perforation. The 15th slot is filled by the sponsor's advertisement. The front features a color action photo of the player, with orange borders. The upper left corner of the picture is cut out to provide space for the uniform number. The team logo overlays the lower right corner of the picture, and a row of miniature blue triangles run beneath the bottom orange border. In a horizontal format the back is divided

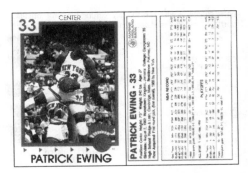

into two boxes and presents biographical (on blue) and statistical information. The cards are unnumbered and are checklisted below in alphabetical order, with the uniform number after the player's name.

		MINT	EXC	G-VG
COMPLETE SET (14)		20.00	10.00	2.00
COMMON PLAYER (1-14)		1.00	.50	.10
☐ 1	Greg Butler 54	1.00	.50	.10
☐ 2	Patrick Ewing 33	6.00	3.00	.60
☐ 3	Mark Jackson 13	2.00	1.00	.20
☐ 4	Stu Jackson CO	1.50	.75	.15
☐ 5	Charles Oakley 34	1.50	.75	.15
☐ 6	Pete Myers 8	1.00	.50	.10
☐ 7	Johnny Newman 4	2.00	1.00	.20
☐ 8	Brian Quinnett 23	1.00	.50	.10
☐ 9	Rod Strickland 11	2.00	1.00	.20
☐ 10	Trent Tucker 6	1.00	.50	.10
☐ 11	Kiki Vandeweghe 55	2.00	1.00	.20
☐ 12	Kenny Walker 7	1.50	.75	.15
☐ 13	Gerald Wilkins 21	1.50	.75	.15
☐ 14	Eddie Lee Wilkins 45	1.00	.50	.10

1961-62 Lakers Bell Brand

The unattractive cards in this ten-card set measure approximately 6" by 3 1/2" and feature members of the Los Angeles Lakers basketball team. Each player has two versions of his card, once in blue ink on white stock and again in brown ink on brown-tinted stock. The left half of the card features the player whereas the right side features a Laker schedule. The catalog designation is F391-2.

	NRMT	VG-E	GOOD
COMPLETE SET (10)	3000.00	1250.00	250.00
COMMON PLAYER (1-10)	200.00	100.00	20.00
☐ 1 Elgin Baylor	600.00	300.00	60.00
☐ 2 Ray Felix	200.00	100.00	20.00
☐ 3 Tom Hawkins	250.00	125.00	25.00
☐ 4 Rod Hundley	300.00	150.00	30.00
☐ 5 Howard Joliff	200.00	100.00	20.00
☐ 6 Rudy LaRusso	200.00	100.00	20.00
☐ 7 Fred Schaus CO	200.00	100.00	20.00
☐ 8 Frank Selvy	200.00	100.00	20.00
☐ 9 Jerry West	900.00	450.00	90.00
☐ 10 Wayne Yates	200.00	100.00	20.00

1979-80 Lakers/Kings Alta-Dena

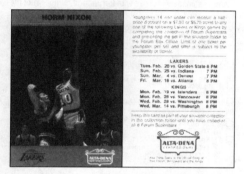

This 8-card set was sponsored by Alta-Dena Dairy, and its logo adorns the bottom of both sides of the card. The cards measure approximately 2 3/4" by 4" and feature color action player photos on the fronts. While the sides of the picture have no borders, green and red-orange stripes border the picture on its top and bottom. The player's name appears in black lettering in the top red-orange stripe. The team logo appears in the bottom red-orange stripe. The back has an offer for youngsters 14-and-under, who could present the complete eight-card set in the souvenir folder to the Forum Box Office and receive a half-price discount on certain tickets to any one of the Lakers and Kings games listed on the reverse of the card. The cards are unnumbered and are checklisted below in alphabetical order. This small set features Los Angeles Kings and Los Angeles Lakers as they were both owned by Jerry Buss. Cards 1-4 are Los Angeles Lakers (NBA) and Cards 5-8 are Los Angeles Kings (NHL).

	NRMT	VG-E	GOOD
COMPLETE SET (8)	20.00	10.00	2.00
COMMON PLAYER (1-8)	1.00	.50	.10
☐ 1 Adrian Dantley	2.50	1.25	.25
☐ 2 Don Ford	1.00	.50	.10
☐ 3 Kareem Abdul Jabbar	7.50	3.75	.75
☐ 4 Norm Nixon	1.50	.75	.15
☐ 5 Marcel Dionne	5.00	2.50	.50
☐ 6 Butch Goring	1.25	.60	.12
☐ 7 Mike Murphy	1.00	.50	.10
☐ 8 Dave Taylor	2.50	1.25	.25

1982-83 Lakers BASF

This 13-card set was produced by BASF audio and video tapes in a promotional tie-in with the Los Angeles Lakers. The cards measure approximately 5" by 7" and are unnumbered except for uniform number; they are listed below in alphabetical order for convenience. This set can be distinguished from the other two years of BASF Lakers sets in that it is the only year the set was also sponsored by Big Ben's and the only year there were no facsimile autographs on the back. The cards were distributed by Big Ben's and The Wherehouse (both chain record and tape stores in southern California), one player per week, with the final card scheduled for distribution during the week of the NBA championship series.

	MINT	EXC	G-VG
COMPLETE SET (13)	18.00	9.00	1.80
COMMON CARD (1-13)	.75	.35	.07
☐ 1 Kareem Abdul Jabbar	5.00	2.50	.50
☐ 2 Michael Cooper	1.00	.50	.10
☐ 3 Clay Johnson	.75	.35	.07
☐ 4 Earvin Johnson	5.00	2.50	.50
☐ 5 Eddie Jordan	.75	.35	.07
☐ 6 Mark Landsberger	.75	.35	.07
☐ 7 Bob McAdoo	1.25	.60	.12
☐ 8 Mike McGee	.75	.35	.07
☐ 9 Norm Nixon	1.25	.60	.12
☐ 10 Kurt Rambis	1.00	.50	.10
☐ 11 Jamaal Wilkes	1.00	.50	.10
☐ 12 James Worthy	3.00	1.50	.30
☐ 13 Team Card	.75	.35	.07
(team roster on back)			

1983-84 Lakers BASF

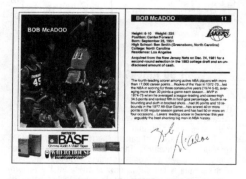

This 14-card set was produced by BASF audio and video tapes in a promotional tie-in with the Los Angeles Lakers. The cards measure approximately 5" by 7" and are unnumbered except for uniform number; they are listed below in alphabetical order for convenience. This set can be distinguished from the other two years of BASF Lakers sets in that it is the only year the set was referenced on the front of the card as "Switch to BASF".

	MINT	EXC	G-VG
COMPLETE SET (14)	12.50	6.25	1.25
COMMON PLAYER (1-14)	.50	.25	.05
☐ 1 Kareem Abdul Jabbar 33	2.50	1.25	.25
☐ 2 Michael Cooper 21	.75	.35	.07
☐ 3 Calvin Garrett 00	.50	.25	.05
☐ 4 Earvin Johnson 32	2.50	1.25	.25
☐ 5 Mitch Kupchak 25	.75	.35	.07
☐ 6 Bob McAdoo 11	.75	.35	.07
☐ 7 Mike McGee 40	.50	.25	.05
☐ 8 Swen Nater 41	.75	.35	.07
☐ 9 Kurt Rambis 31	.75	.35	.07
☐ 10 Byron Scott 4	1.25	.60	.12
☐ 11 Larry Spriggs 35	.50	.25	.05
☐ 12 Jamaal Wilkes 52	.75	.35	.07
☐ 13 James Worthy 42	1.50	.75	.15
☐ 14 Team Photo	.50	.25	.05

(team roster on back)

1984-85 Lakers BASF

This 12-card set was produced by BASF audio and video tapes in a promotional tie-in with the Los Angeles Lakers. The cards measure approximately 5" by 7" and are unnumbered except for uniform number; they are listed below in alphabetical order for convenience.

	MINT	EXC	G-VG
COMPLETE SET (12)	10.00	5.00	1.00
COMMON PLAYER (1-12)	.50	.25	.05
☐ 1 Kareem Abdul Jabbar 33	2.00	1.00	.20
☐ 2 Michael Cooper 21	.75	.35	.07
☐ 3 Earvin Johnson 32	2.00	1.00	.20
☐ 4 Mitch Kupchak 25	.75	.35	.07
☐ 5 Ronnie Lester 12	.50	.25	.05
☐ 6 Bob McAdoo 14	1.00	.50	.10
☐ 7 Mike McGee 40	.50	.25	.05
☐ 8 Kurt Rambis 31	.75	.35	.07
☐ 9 Byron Scott 4	1.00	.50	.10
☐ 10 Larry Spriggs 35	.50	.25	.05
☐ 11 James Worthy 42	1.25	.60	.12
☐ 12 Team Photo	.50	.25	.05

(team roster on back)

1989-90 Magic Pepsi

This eight-card set of Orlando Magic was sponsored by Pepsi. The cards measure the standard size (2 1/2" by 3 1/2") and feature on the front a posed color player photo, without borders

on the sides. While the player's name and team logo appears in the aqua stripe above the picture, the Pepsi logo and the words "'89/'90 Inaugural Season Collector's Card" appear in red stripe below the picture. Also an official sweepstakes entry sticker is attached to each card face. This sticker was to be peeled off and affixed to an official entry form available at participating stores. By collecting four stickers, one was entitled to enter the sweepstakes. The back presents 1988-89 statistics and career highlights, and is printed in black lettering on blue background, with a white stripe at the card bottom. The cards are unnumbered and are checklisted below in alphabetical order.

	MINT	EXC	G-VG
COMPLETE SET (8)	45.00	22.50	4.50
COMMON PLAYER (1-8)	5.00	2.50	.50
☐ 1 Nick Anderson	12.00	6.00	1.20
☐ 2 Michael Ansley	7.50	3.75	.75
☐ 3 Terry Catledge	7.50	3.75	.75
☐ 4 Dave Corzine	6.00	3.00	.60
☐ 5 Sidney Green	6.00	3.00	.60
☐ 6 Otis Smith	5.00	2.50	.50
☐ 7 Sam Vincent	6.00	3.00	.60
☐ 8 Stuff the Magic Dragon	6.00	3.00	.60
Mascot			

1988-89 Mavs Bud Light BLC

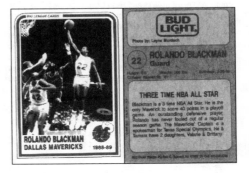

The 1988-89 Bud Light Dallas Mavericks set contains 14 cards comprised of 12 players and two coaches. The cards are standard sized (2 1/2" by 3 1/2"). The set is unnumbered except for uniform numbers on the card backs. This set was produced for distribution at the Mavericks "card night" promotion but may not have actually been used by the Mavericks. However the sets do exist within the hobby as the cards were apparently not destroyed. The set may have been rejected by the Mavericks because of the inclusion of Roy Tarpley and Mark Aguirre; however there is no indication that either the Tarpley or Aguirre cards is any harder to find than the others in the set. The set was produced for the Mavericks by Big League Cards of New Jersey.

	MINT	EXC	G-VG
COMPLETE SET (14)	12.50	6.25	1.25
COMMON PLAYER	.50	.25	.05
☐ 12 Derek Harper	1.00	.50	.10
☐ 15 Brad Davis	.75	.35	.07
☐ 20 Morlon Wiley	.50	.25	.05
☐ 22 Rolando Blackman	1.50	.75	.15
☐ 23 Bill Wennington	.50	.25	.05
☐ 24 Mark Aguirre	1.50	.75	.15
☐ 32 Detlef Schrempf	1.25	.60	.12
☐ 33 Uwe Blab	.50	.25	.05
☐ 40 James Donaldson	.75	.35	.07
☐ 41 Terry Tyler	.50	.25	.05
☐ 42 Roy Tarpley	3.50	1.75	.35
☐ 44 Sam Perkins	1.50	.75	.15
☐ xx Coaching Staff	.50	.25	.05
Richie Adubato			
Garfield Heard			
(unnumbered)			
☐ xx John MacLeod CO	.75	.35	.07
(unnumbered)			

1988-89 Mavs Bud Light Card Night

The 1988-89 Bud Light Dallas Mavericks set contains 13 cards comprised of 12 players and Head Coach John MacLeod. The cards are standard sized (2 1/2" by 3 1/2"). The set is unnumbered except for uniform numbers on the card backs. This set was produced for distribution at the Mavericks "card night" promotion and is apparently a rework of the set immediately above since Roy Tarpley and Mark Aguirre are not even in this set and many late season acquisitions are noted. It is not known what company produced these cards for the Mavericks and Bud Light.

	MINT	EXC	G-VG
COMPLETE SET (13)	10.00	5.00	1.00
COMMON PLAYER	.50	.25	.05
☐ 4 Adrian Dantley	1.50	.75	.15
☐ 12 Derek Harper	1.00	.50	.10
☐ 15 Brad Davis	.75	.35	.07
☐ 20 Morlon Wiley	.50	.25	.05
☐ 21 Anthony Jones	.50	.25	.05
☐ 22 Rolando Blackman	1.50	.75	.15
☐ 23 Bill Wennington	.50	.25	.05
☐ 32 Herb Williams	.75	.35	.07
☐ 33 Uwe Blab	.50	.25	.05
☐ 40 James Donaldson	.75	.35	.07
☐ 41 Terry Tyler	.50	.25	.05
☐ 44 Sam Perkins	1.50	.75	.15
☐ xx John MacLeod CO	.75	.35	.07
(unnumbered)			

1974 Nabisco Sugar Daddy *

This set of 25 tiny (approximately 1" by 2 3/4") cards features athletes from a variety of popular pro sports. The set is referred to as Pro Faces as the cards show an enlarged head photo with a small caricature body. Cards 1-10 are football players, cards 11-16 and 22 are hockey players, and cards 17-21 and 23-25 are basketball players.

	NRMT	VG-E	GOOD
COMPLETE SET (25)	100.00	50.00	10.00
COMMON PLAYER (1-25)	2.00	1.00	.20
☐ 1 Roger Staubach	15.00	7.50	1.50
☐ 2 Floyd Little	4.00	2.00	.40
☐ 3 Steve Owen	3.00	1.50	.30
☐ 4 Roman Gabriel	4.00	2.00	.40
☐ 5 Bobby Douglas	2.00	1.00	.20
☐ 6 John Gilliam	2.00	1.00	.20
☐ 7 Bob Lilly	6.00	3.00	.60
☐ 8 John Brockington	3.00	1.50	.30
☐ 9 Jim Plunkett	4.00	2.00	.40
☐ 10 Greg Landry	2.00	1.00	.20
☐ 11 Phil Esposito	6.00	3.00	.60
☐ 12 Dennis Hull	3.00	1.50	.30
☐ 13 Reg Fleming	2.00	1.00	.20
☐ 14 Garry Unger	3.00	1.50	.30
☐ 15 Derek Sanderson	3.00	1.50	.30
☐ 16 Jerry Korab	2.00	1.00	.20
☐ 17 Oscar Robertson	12.00	6.00	1.20
☐ 18 Spencer Haywood	4.00	2.00	.40
☐ 19 Jo Jo White	3.00	1.50	.30
☐ 20 Connie Hawkins	4.00	2.00	.40
☐ 21 Nate Thurmond	4.00	2.00	.40
☐ 22 Mickey Redmond	2.00	1.00	.20
☐ 23 Chet Walker	3.00	1.50	.30
☐ 24 Calvin Murphy	3.00	1.50	.30
☐ 25 Kareem Abdul Jabbar	12.00	6.00	1.20

1975 Nabisco Sugar Daddy *

This set of 25 tiny (approximately 1" by 2 3/4") cards features athletes from a variety of popular pro sports. Set is referred to as Sugar Daddy All-Stars. As with the set of the previous year, the cards show an enlarged head photo with a small caricature body with a flag background of stars and stripes. This set is referred on the back as Series No. 2 and has a red, white, and

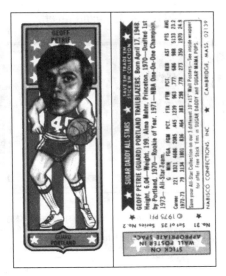

blue background behind the picture on the front of the card. Cards 1-10 are pro football players and the remainder are pro basketball (17-21, 23-25) and hockey (11-16, 22) players.

	NRMT	VG-E	GOOD
COMPLETE SET (25)	100.00	50.00	10.00
COMMON PLAYER (1-25)	2.00	1.00	.20

		NRMT	VG-E	GOOD
☐ 1	Roger Staubach	15.00	7.50	1.50
☐ 2	Floyd Little	4.00	2.00	.40
☐ 3	Alan Page	4.00	2.00	.40
☐ 4	Merlin Olson	6.00	3.00	.60
☐ 5	Wally Chambers	2.00	1.00	.20
☐ 6	John Gilliam	2.00	1.00	.20
☐ 7	Bob Lilly	6.00	3.00	.60
☐ 8	John Brockington	3.00	1.50	.30
☐ 9	Jim Plunkett	4.00	2.00	.40
☐ 10	Willie Lanier	4.00	2.00	.40
☐ 11	Phil Esposito	6.00	3.00	.60
☐ 13	Brad Park	4.00	2.00	.40
☐ 14	Tom Lysiak	2.00	1.00	.20
☐ 15	Bernie Parent	5.00	2.50	.50
☐ 16	Mickey Redmond	2.00	1.00	.20
☐ 17	Jerry Sloan	2.00	1.00	.20
☐ 18	Spencer Haywood	3.00	1.50	.30
☐ 19	Bob Lanier	4.00	2.00	.40
☐ 20	Connie Hawkins	3.00	1.50	.30
☐ 21	Geoff Petrie	2.00	1.00	.20
☐ 22	Don Awrey	2.00	1.00	.20
☐ 23	Chet Walker	3.00	1.50	.30
☐ 24	Bob McAdoo	4.00	2.00	.40
☐ 25	Kareem Abdul Jabbar	12.00	6.00	1.20

1976 Nabisco Sugar Daddy *

This set of 25 tiny (approximately 1" by 2 3/4") cards features action scenes from a variety of popular sports from around the world. The set is referred to as Sugar Daddy Sports World on the backs of the cards. The cards are in color with a relatively wide white border around the front of the cards.

	NRMT	VG-E	GOOD
COMPLETE SET (25)	50.00	25.00	5.00
COMMON PLAYER (1-25)	2.00	1.00	.20

		NRMT	VG-E	GOOD
☐ 1	Cricket	2.00	1.00	.20
☐ 2	Yachting	2.00	1.00	.20
☐ 3	Diving	2.00	1.00	.20
☐ 4	Football	5.00	2.50	.50
	(Sonny Jurgensen)			
☐ 5	Soccer	4.00	2.00	.40

☐ 6	Lacrosse	2.00	1.00	.20
☐ 7	Track and Field	2.00	1.00	.20
☐ 8	Motorcycle	2.00	1.00	.20
☐ 9	Hang Gliding	2.00	1.00	.20
☐ 10	Tennis	2.00	1.00	.20
☐ 11	Hockey	3.00	1.50	.30
☐ 12	Shot Put	2.00	1.00	.20
☐ 13	Basketball	3.00	1.50	.30
☐ 14	Track and Field	2.00	1.00	.20
☐ 15	Gymnastics	2.00	1.00	.20
☐ 16	Power Boat Racing	2.00	1.00	.20
☐ 17	Bike Racing	2.00	1.00	.20
☐ 18	Golf	2.00	1.00	.20
☐ 19	Hot Dog Ski	2.00	1.00	.20
☐ 20	Fishing	2.00	1.00	.20
☐ 21	Jai Alai	2.00	1.00	.20
☐ 22	Canoeing	2.00	1.00	.20
☐ 23	Gymnastics	3.00	1.50	.30
	(Cathy Rigby)			
☐ 24	Steeple Chase	2.00	1.00	.20
☐ 25	Baseball	5.00	2.50	.50
	(Bobby Murcer)			

1973-74 NBA Players Assn.

This set contains 36 full-color postcard format cards measuring approximately 3 3/8" by 5 5/8". The front features a borderless posed "action" shot of the player. The back has the player's name at the top, and the NBA Players Association logo. The cards are unnumbered and are checklisted below in alphabetical order. There are six tougher cards which are marked as SP in the checklist below.

	NRMT	VG-E	GOOD
COMPLETE SET (36)	200.00	100.00	20.00
COMMON PLAYER (1-36)	2.50	1.25	.25
COMMON PLAYER SP	10.00	5.00	1.00

		NRMT	VG-E	GOOD
☐ 1	Lucius Allen	2.50	1.25	.25
☐ 2	Dave Bing SP	20.00	10.00	2.00
☐ 3	Bill Bradley	15.00	7.50	1.50
☐ 4	Fred Carter SP	10.00	5.00	1.00
☐ 5	Austin Carr	2.50	1.25	.25
☐ 6	Dave Cowens	10.00	5.00	1.00
☐ 7	Dave DeBusschere	10.00	5.00	1.00
☐ 8	Ernie DiGregorio	2.50	1.25	.25
☐ 9	Gail Goodrich	5.00	2.50	.50
☐ 10	Hal Greer	5.00	2.50	.50
☐ 11	John Havlicek	12.00	6.00	1.20
☐ 12	Connie Hawkins	5.00	2.50	.50
☐ 13	Spencer Haywood	3.50	1.75	.35

		MINT	EXC	G-VG
☐ 14	Lou Hudson	3.50	1.75	.35
☐ 15	Bob Kauffman	2.50	1.25	.25
☐ 16	Bob Lanier	6.00	3.00	.60
☐ 17	Bob Love	3.50	1.75	.35
☐ 18	Jack Marin	2.50	1.25	.25
☐ 19	Jim McMillian	2.50	1.25	.25
☐ 20	Calvin Murphy	5.00	2.50	.50
☐ 21	Geoff Petrie	2.50	1.25	.25
☐ 22	Willis Reed SP	20.00	10.00	2.00
☐ 23	Rich Rinaldi	2.50	1.25	.25
☐ 24	Mike Riordan SP	10.00	5.00	1.00
☐ 25	Cazzie Russell	3.50	1.75	.35
☐ 26	Jerry Sloan	3.50	1.75	.35
☐ 27	Elmore Smith	2.50	1.25	.25
☐ 28	Dick Snyder	2.50	1.25	.25
☐ 29	Nate Thurmond	5.00	2.50	.50
☐ 30	Rudy Tomjanovich	2.50	1.25	.25
☐ 31	Wes Unseld	6.00	3.00	.60
☐ 32	Dick Van Arsdale SP	10.00	5.00	1.00
☐ 33	Tom Van Arsdale	2.50	1.25	.25
☐ 34	Chet Walker SP	12.00	6.00	1.20
☐ 35	Jo Jo White	3.50	1.75	.35
☐ 36	Len Wilkens	6.00	3.00	.60

1984-85 Nets Getty

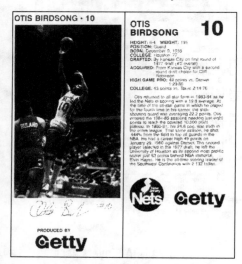

This 12-card set was produced by Getty and issued in four sheets, with three player cards per sheet. The sheets measure approximately 8" by 11". Although the sheets are not actually perforated, the black broken lines indicate that the cut cards measure 3 5/8" by 6 3/4". The front features a borderless color action shot, with the player's facsimile autograph below the picture. The player's name and number appear above the picture in block lettering. The New Jersey Nets and Getty logos appear at the bottom of each sheet. The cards are unnumbered and we have checklisted them below in alphabetical order.

		MINT	EXC	G-VG
	COMPLETE SET (12)	30.00	15.00	3.00
	COMMON PLAYER (1-12)	2.00	1.00	.20
☐ 1	Stan Albeck CO	2.00	1.00	.20
☐ 2	Otis Birdsong 10	3.00	1.50	.30
☐ 3	Darwin Cook 12	2.00	1.00	.20
☐ 4	Darryl Dawkins 53	4.00	2.00	.40
☐ 5	Mike Gminski 42	4.00	2.00	.40
☐ 6	Albert King 55	3.00	1.50	.30
☐ 7	Mike O'Koren 31	3.00	1.50	.30
☐ 8	Kelvin Ransey 14	2.00	1.00	.20
☐ 9	M.R. Richardson 20	3.00	1.50	.30
☐ 10	Jeff Turner 35	2.00	1.00	.20
☐ 11	Buck Williams 52	7.50	3.75	.75
☐ 12	Duncan (Mascot)	2.00	1.00	.20

1990-91 Nets Kayo/Breyers

This 14-card set of New Jersey Nets was sponsored by Kayo Cards and Breyers Ice Cream and measures the standard size (2 1/2" by 3 1/2"). The front features a color action player photo, with a thin red border. The left corner is cut out, and the word "Kayo" appears. The team logo overlays the left bottom corner of the picture, and the player's position and name are given below the picture in black and white lettering on red. The outer border is blue, which washes out as one moves toward the card bottom. The back has biographical information as well as college and pro statistics, enframed by a black border. As on the front, the red outer border washes out. The cards are numbered on the back.

		MINT	EXC	G-VG
	COMPLETE SET (14)	9.00	4.50	.90
	COMMON PLAYER (1-14)	.50	.25	.05
☐ 1	Mookie Blaylock	1.00	.50	.10
☐ 2	Sam Bowie	.75	.35	.07
☐ 3	Jud Buechler	.75	.35	.07
☐ 4	Derrick Coleman	4.00	2.00	.40
☐ 5	Lester Conner	.50	.25	.05
☐ 6	Chris Dudley	.50	.25	.05
☐ 7	Tate George	.75	.35	.07
☐ 8	Derrick Gervin	.75	.35	.07
☐ 9	Jack Haley	.50	.25	.05
☐ 10	Kirk Lee	.50	.25	.05
☐ 11	Chris Morris	.75	.35	.07
☐ 12	Reggie Theus	.75	.35	.07
☐ 13	Bill Fitch CO	.50	.25	.05
☐ 14	Nets Home Schedule	.50	.25	.05

1982-83 Nuggets Police

This set contains 14 cards measuring 2 5/8" by 4 1/8" featuring the Denver Nuggets. Backs contain safety tips and are printed with black ink. The set was sponsored by Colorado National Banks, the Denver Nuggets, and the metropolitan area police Juvenile Crime Prevention Bureaus. The cards are unnumbered except for uniform number.

		MINT	EXC	G-VG
	COMPLETE SET (14)	7.00	3.50	.70
	COMMON PLAYER	.35	.17	.03
☐ 2	Alex English	1.25	.60	.12
☐ 7	Billy McKinney	.50	.25	.05
☐ 21	Rob Williams	.35	.17	.03
☐ 22	Glen Gondrezick	.35	.17	.03
☐ 23	T.R. Dunn	.35	.17	.03
☐ 24	Bill Hanzlik	.50	.25	.05
☐ 25	Dave Robisch	.35	.17	.03
☐ 43	James Ray	.35	.17	.03
☐ 44	Dan Issel	1.00	.50	.10
☐ 53	Rich Kelley	.35	.17	.03
☐ 55	KiKi Vandeweghe	1.00	.50	.10

			MINT	EXC	G-VG
☐	xx	Carl Scheer, Pres. .... and General Mgr.	.35	.17	.03
☐	xx	Doug Moe CO	.50	.25	.05
☐	xx	Bill Ficke, ... Assistant Coach and Bob Travaglini TR	.35	.17	.03

1983-84 Nuggets Police

This set contains 14 cards measuring 2 5/8" by 4 1/8" featuring the Denver Nuggets. Backs contain safety tips with black printing. The team name written vertically on the front is distinctive in that "Denver" is in red and "Nuggets" is in blue. The cards are unnumbered except for uniform number.

		MINT	EXC	G-VG
COMPLETE SET (14)		6.00	3.00	.60
COMMON PLAYER		.30	.15	.03
☐ 2	Alex English	.90	.45	.09
☐ 5	Mike Evans	.30	.15	.03
☐ 21	Rob Williams	.30	.15	.03
☐ 23	T.R. Dunn	.30	.15	.03
☐ 24	Bill Hanzlik	.50	.25	.05
☐ 32	Howard Carter	.30	.15	.03
☐ 33	Ken Dennard	.30	.15	.03
☐ 34	Danny Schayes	.90	.45	.09
☐ 35	Richard Anderson	.50	.25	.05
☐ 44	Dan Issel	.90	.45	.09
☐ 55	KiKi Vandeweghe	.75	.35	.07
☐ xx	Carl Scheer, Pres. .... and General Mgr.	.30	.15	.03
☐ xx	Bill Ficke, ... Assistant Coach	.30	.15	.03
☐ xx	Doug Moe CO	.50	.25	.05

1985-86 Nuggets Police/Wendy's

The 1986 Wendy's Denver Nuggets set contains 12 cards each measuring approximately 2 1/2" by 5". A contest entry form tab is attached to each card (included in the dimensions above). The card fronts have color photos with navy and beige borders. The backs are black and white and have safety tips.

		MINT	EXC	G-VG
COMPLETE SET (12)		7.00	3.50	.70
COMMON PLAYER (1-12)		.50	.25	.05
☐ 1	Alex English	1.00	.50	.10
☐ 2	Mike Evans	.50	.25	.05
☐ 3	Bill Hanzlik	.50	.25	.05
☐ 4	Pete Williams	.50	.25	.05
☐ 5	Dan Schayes	1.00	.50	.10
☐ 6	Wayne Cooper	.50	.25	.05
☐ 7	Blair Rasmussen	.75	.35	.07
☐ 8	Elston Turner	.50	.25	.05
☐ 9	Lafayette(Fat) Lever	1.00	.50	.10
☐ 10	T.R. Dunn	.50	.25	.05
☐ 11	Willie White	.50	.25	.05
☐ 12	Calvin Natt	.75	.35	.07

1988-89 Nuggets Police/Pepsi

This 12-card set was sponsored by Pepsi, Pizza Hut, and The Children's Hospital of Denver. The cards measure approximately 2 5/8" by 4 1/8". The front features a borderless color action player photo. The player's number and name appear in white lettering in a purple stripe at the top of the card face, while team and sponsor logos appear in the white stripe at the bottom. The back is printed in blue on white and presents a safety tip from the player. The English and Lever variation cards differ only in the safety tip found on the back. The cards are unnumbered but they are numbered on the card front at the top by uniform number. The two Alex English cards and two Fat Lever cards are exactly the same except for the safety tip.

	MINT	EXC	G-VG
COMPLETE SET (12)	5.00	2.50	.50
COMMON PLAYER	.30	.15	.03

☐ 2A Alex English ....
  "If someone is hurt
  in an accident ..."
	.75	.35	.07

☐ 2B Alex English ....
  "You should never
  run around ..."
	.75	.35	.07

☐ 6 Walter Davis	.75	.35	.07

☐ 12A Fat Lever ....
  "Always wear a helmet
  when you're ..."
	.60	.30	.06

☐ 12B Fat Lever ....
  "If you're ever in
  danger, the most ..."
	.60	.30	.06

☐ 14 Michael Adams	.60	.30	.06
☐ 20 Elston Turner	.30	.15	.03
☐ 24 Bill Hanzlik	.30	.15	.03
☐ 34 Dan Schayes	.60	.30	.06
☐ 35 Jerome Lane	.50	.25	.05
☐ 41 Blair Rasmussen	.50	.25	.05
☐ 42 Wayne Cooper	.30	.15	.03

1989-90 Nuggets Police/Pepsi

This 12-card set was sponsored by Pepsi, 7/Eleven, and The Children's Hospital of Denver. Beginning in early February, the cards were given out in 7/Eleven stores with Pepsi products. They measure approximately 2 5/8" by 4 1/8". The front features a borderless color action player photo. Two stripes descend from the top of the picture on the right. The longer of the two has alternating black and yellow diagonal sections. In the white stripe appears the player's name and number. The team logo and sponsors' logos appear in the white stripe at the bottom of the card face. The back is printed in lavender on white card stock and presents a safety tip from the player. The cards are unnumbered and checklisted below in alphabetical order, with jersey number after the player's name.

	MINT	EXC	G-VG
COMPLETE SET (12)	5.00	2.50	.50
COMMON PLAYER (1-12)	.30	.15	.03
☐ 1 Michael Adams 14	.60	.30	.06
☐ 2 Walter Davis 6	.60	.30	.06
☐ 3 T.R. Dunn 23	.30	.15	.03
☐ 4 Alex English 2	.75	.35	.07
☐ 5 Bill Hanzlik 24	.30	.15	.03
☐ 6 Eddie Hughes 1	.30	.15	.03
☐ 7 Tim Kempton 45	.30	.15	.03
☐ 8 Jerome Lane 35	.40	.20	.04
☐ 9 Lafayette Lever 12	.60	.30	.06
☐ 10 Todd Lichti 21	.60	.30	.06
☐ 11 Blair Rasmussen 41	.50	.25	.05
☐ 12 Dan Schayes 34	.60	.30	.06

1971 Pacers Marathon Oil

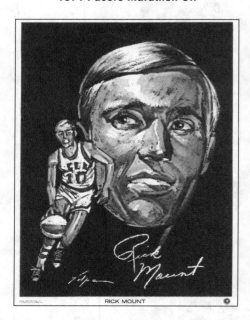

RICK MOUNT

This set of Marathon Oil Pro Star Portraits consists of colorful portraits by distinguished artist Nicholas Volpe. Each portrait measures approximately 7 1/2" by 9 7/8" and features a painting of the player's face on a black background, with an action painting superimposed to the side. A facsimile autograph in white appears at the bottom of the portrait. At the bottom of each portrait is a postcard measuring 7 1/2" by 4" after perforation. While the back of the portrait has offers for a basketball photo album, autographed tumblers, and a poster, the postcard itself may be used to apply for a Marathon credit card. The portraits are unnumbered and checklisted below according to alphabetical order.

	NRMT	VG-E	GOOD
COMPLETE SET (9)	35.00	17.50	3.50
COMMON PLAYER (1-9)	3.00	1.50	.30
☐ 1 Roger Brown	4.00	2.00	.40
☐ 2 Mel Daniels	5.00	2.50	.50
☐ 3 Earle Higgins	3.00	1.50	.30
☐ 4 Bill Keller	4.00	2.00	.40
☐ 5 Bob Leonard	4.00	2.00	.40
☐ 6 Freddie Lewis	4.00	2.00	.40
☐ 7 Rick Mount	5.00	2.50	.50
☐ 8 Bob Netolicky	4.00	2.00	.40
☐ 9 Howard Wright	3.00	1.50	.30

1990-91 Panini NBA

This set of 180 basketball stickers was produced and distributed by Panini. The stickers measure 1 7/8" by 2 15/16" and are issued in sheets consisting of three rows of four stickers each. The sheets were included with the sticker album itself. The stickers feature color action photos of the players on a white background. The team name is given in a light blue stripe below the picture, with a basketball icon to the right. The player's name appears at the bottom of the sticker. The stickers are numbered on the back. Stickers 1-162 showcase NBA players

UTAH JAZZ
JOHN STOCKTON

according to their teams as follows: Los Angeles Lakers (1-6), Portland Trail Blazers (7-12), Phoenix Suns (13-18), Seattle Supersonics (19-24), Golden State Warriors (25-30), Los Angeles Clippers (31-36), Sacramento Kings (37-42), San Antonio Spurs (43-48), Utah Jazz (49-54), Dallas Mavericks (55-60), Denver Nuggets (61-66), Houston Rockets (67-72), Minnesota Timberwolves (73-78), Charlotte Hornets (79-84), Detroit Pistons (85-90), Chicago Bulls (91-96), Milwaukee Bucks (97-102), Cleveland Cavaliers (103-108), Indiana Pacers (109-114), Atlanta Hawks (115-120), Orlando Magic (121-126), Philadelphia 76ers (127-132), Boston Celtics (133-138), New York Knicks (139-144), Washington Bullets (145-150), Miami Heat (151-156), and New Jersey Nets (157-162). The remaining 18 stickers are lettered A-R and feature 1990 NBA All-Stars (A-J); Jordan, Bird, and Olajuwon (K-M); and the 1990 NBA Finals (N-R).

	MINT	EXC	G-VG
COMPLETE SET (180)	9.00	4.50	.90
COMMON PLAYER (1-162)	.03	.01	.00
COMMON STICKER (A-R)	.05	.02	.00

		MINT	EXC	G-VG
☐ 1	Magic Johnson	.30	.15	.03
☐ 2	Mychal Thompson	.03	.01	.00
☐ 3	Vlade Divac	.12	.06	.01
☐ 4	Byron Scott	.06	.03	.00
☐ 5	James Worthy	.12	.06	.01
☐ 6	A.C. Green	.06	.03	.00
☐ 7	Jerome Kersey	.08	.04	.01
☐ 8	Clyde Drexler	.20	.10	.02
☐ 9	Buck Williams	.06	.03	.00
☐ 10	Kevin Duckworth	.06	.03	.00
☐ 11	Terry Porter	.08	.04	.01
☐ 12	Cliff Robinson	.08	.04	.01
☐ 13	Tom Chambers	.10	.05	.01
☐ 14	Dan Majerle	.08	.04	.01
☐ 15	Mark West	.03	.01	.00
☐ 16	Kevin Johnson	.20	.10	.02
☐ 17	Jeff Hornacek	.06	.03	.00
☐ 18	Kurt Rambis	.06	.03	.00
☐ 19	Nate McMillan	.03	.01	.00
☐ 20	Shawn Kemp	.25	.12	.02
☐ 21	Dale Ellis	.06	.03	.00
☐ 22	Michael Cage	.03	.01	.00
☐ 23	Xavier McDaniel	.06	.03	.00
☐ 24	Derrick McKey	.03	.01	.00
☐ 25	Manute Bol	.03	.01	.00
☐ 26	Chris Mullin	.10	.05	.01
☐ 27	Terry Teagle	.03	.01	.00
☐ 28	Tim Hardaway	.30	.15	.03
☐ 29	Sarunas Marciulionis	.10	.05	.01
☐ 30	Mitch Richmond	.15	.07	.01
☐ 31	Gary Grant	.03	.01	.00
☐ 32	Danny Manning	.10	.05	.01
☐ 33	Benoit Benjamin	.06	.03	.00
☐ 34	Ron Harper	.06	.03	.00
☐ 35	Ken Norman	.06	.03	.00
☐ 36	Charles Smith	.06	.03	.00
☐ 37	Harold Pressley	.03	.01	.00
☐ 38	Antoine Carr	.03	.01	.00
☐ 39	Danny Ainge	.06	.03	.00
☐ 40	Wayman Tisdale	.06	.03	.00
☐ 41	Ralph Sampson	.06	.03	.00
☐ 42	Vinny Del Negro	.03	.01	.00
☐ 43	David Robinson	.60	.30	.06
☐ 44	Sean Elliott	.15	.07	.01
☐ 45	Terry Cummings	.06	.03	.00
☐ 46	Willie Anderson	.06	.03	.00
☐ 47	Rod Strickland	.06	.03	.00
☐ 48	Frank Brickowski	.03	.01	.00
☐ 49	Karl Malone	.15	.07	.01
☐ 50	Darrell Griffith	.06	.03	.00
☐ 51	John Stockton	.12	.06	.01
☐ 52	Theodore Edwards	.08	.04	.01
☐ 53	Mark Eaton	.06	.03	.00
☐ 54	Thurl Bailey	.06	.03	.00
☐ 55	Rolando Blackman	.06	.03	.00
☐ 56	Sam Perkins	.08	.04	.01
☐ 57	James Donaldson	.03	.01	.00
☐ 58	Herb Williams	.03	.01	.00
☐ 59	Roy Tarpley	.06	.03	.00
☐ 60	Derek Harper	.06	.03	.00
☐ 61	Michael Adams	.06	.03	.00
☐ 62	Blair Rasmussen	.03	.01	.00
☐ 63	Jerome Lane	.03	.01	.00
☐ 64	Walter Davis	.06	.03	.00
☐ 65	Todd Lichti	.06	.03	.00
☐ 66	Joe Barry Carroll	.03	.01	.00
☐ 67	Vernon Maxwell	.06	.03	.00
☐ 68	Otis Thorpe	.06	.03	.00
☐ 69	Akeem Olajuwon	.20	.10	.02
☐ 70	Buck Johnson	.03	.01	.00
☐ 71	Eric Floyd	.03	.01	.00
☐ 72	Mitchell Wiggins	.03	.01	.00
☐ 73	Tony Campbell	.06	.03	.00
☐ 74	Tod Murphy	.06	.03	.00
☐ 75	Tyrone Corbin	.06	.03	.00
☐ 76	Sam Mitchell	.06	.03	.00
☐ 77	Randy Breuer	.03	.01	.00
☐ 78	Pooh Richardson	.20	.10	.02
☐ 79	Rex Chapman	.15	.07	.01
☐ 80	Dell Curry	.03	.01	.00
☐ 81	Tyrone Bogues	.03	.01	.00
☐ 82	J.R. Reid	.12	.06	.01
☐ 83	Armon Gilliam	.03	.01	.00
☐ 84	Kelly Tripucka	.03	.01	.00
☐ 85	Dennis Rodman	.08	.04	.01
☐ 86	Joe Dumars	.08	.04	.01
☐ 87	Isiah Thomas	.15	.07	.01
☐ 88	Bill Laimbeer	.08	.04	.01
☐ 89	Vinnie Johnson	.06	.03	.00
☐ 90	James Edwards	.03	.01	.00
☐ 91	Michael Jordan	1.00	.50	.10
☐ 92	Stacey King	.10	.05	.01
☐ 93	Scottie Pippen	.15	.07	.01
☐ 94	John Paxson	.06	.03	.00
☐ 95	Horace Grant	.08	.04	.01
☐ 96	Craig Hodges	.03	.01	.00
☐ 97	Brad Lohaus	.06	.03	.00
☐ 98	Jack Sikma	.06	.03	.00
☐ 99	Ricky Pierce	.06	.03	.00
☐ 100	Greg Anderson	.03	.01	.00
☐ 101	Alvin Robertson	.06	.03	.00
☐ 102	Jay Humphries	.03	.01	.00
☐ 103	Mark Price	.06	.03	.00
☐ 104	Winston Bennett	.06	.03	.00
☐ 105	Brad Daugherty	.08	.04	.01
☐ 106	Craig Ehlo	.03	.01	.00
☐ 107	Larry Nance	.06	.03	.00
☐ 108	Hot Rod Williams	.06	.03	.00
☐ 109	Rik Smits	.06	.03	.00
☐ 110	Chuck Person	.08	.04	.01
☐ 111	Reggie Miller	.10	.05	.01
☐ 112	LaSalle Thompson	.03	.01	.00
☐ 113	Detlef Schrempf	.08	.04	.01
☐ 114	Vern Fleming	.03	.01	.00
☐ 115	Moses Malone	.12	.06	.01
☐ 116	Glenn Rivers	.06	.03	.00
☐ 117	Dominique Wilkins	.15	.07	.01
☐ 118	Spud Webb	.06	.03	.00
☐ 119	Kevin Willis	.03	.01	.00
☐ 120	Kenny Smith	.06	.03	.00
☐ 121	Otis Smith	.03	.01	.00
☐ 122	Sidney Green	.03	.01	.00
☐ 123	Nick Anderson	.15	.07	.01
☐ 124	Scott Skiles	.08	.04	.01
☐ 125	Jerry Reynolds	.03	.01	.00
☐ 126	Terry Catledge	.03	.01	.00
☐ 127	Charles Barkley	.17	.08	.01
☐ 128	Ron Anderson	.06	.03	.00
☐ 129	Hersey Hawkins	.08	.04	.01
☐ 130	Mike Gminski	.06	.03	.00
☐ 131	Johnny Dawkins	.03	.01	.00
☐ 132	Rick Mahorn	.06	.03	.00
☐ 133	Michael Smith	.10	.05	.01
☐ 134	Reggie Lewis	.10	.05	.01
☐ 135	Larry Bird	.25	.12	.02
☐ 136	Kevin McHale	.10	.05	.01
☐ 137	Joe Kleine	.03	.01	.00

☐ 138 Robert Parish	.10	.05	.01
☐ 139 Maurice Cheeks	.06	.03	.00
☐ 140 Patrick Ewing	.20	.10	.02
☐ 141 Charles Oakley	.06	.03	.00
☐ 142 Gerald Wilkins	.06	.03	.00
☐ 143 Kenny Walker	.03	.01	.00
☐ 144 Mark Jackson	.06	.03	.00
☐ 145 Mark Alarie	.03	.01	.00
☐ 146 John Williams	.03	.01	.00
☐ 147 Darrell Walker	.03	.01	.00
☐ 148 Bernard King	.08	.04	.01
☐ 149 Harvey Grant	.06	.03	.00
☐ 150 Ledell Eackles	.06	.03	.00
☐ 151 Glen Rice	.10	.05	.01
☐ 152 Kevin Edwards	.03	.01	.00
☐ 153 Tellis Frank	.03	.01	.00
☐ 154 Rony Seikaly	.08	.04	.01
☐ 155 Billy Thompson	.06	.03	.00
☐ 156 Sherman Douglas	.10	.05	.01
☐ 157 Roy Hinson	.03	.01	.00
☐ 158 Chris Morris	.06	.03	.00
☐ 159 Lester Conner	.03	.01	.00
☐ 160 Sam Bowie	.06	.03	.00
☐ 161 Purvis Short	.06	.03	.00
☐ 162 Mookie Blaylock	.10	.05	.01
☐ A John Stockton AS	.15	.07	.01
☐ B Earvin Johnson AS	.25	.12	.02
☐ C A.C. Green AS	.08	.04	.01
☐ D Akeem Olajuwon AS	.15	.07	.01
☐ E James Worthy AS	.12	.06	.01
☐ F Isiah Thomas AS	.15	.07	.01
☐ G Michael Jordan AS	.60	.30	.06
☐ H Larry Bird AS	.25	.12	.02
☐ I Patrick Ewing AS	.20	.10	.02
☐ J Charles Barkley AS	.15	.07	.01
☐ K Michael Jordan	.60	.30	.06
☐ L Larry Bird	.25	.12	.02
☐ M Akeem Olajuwon	.15	.07	.01
☐ N NBA Finals	.05	.02	.00
☐ O NBA Finals	.05	.02	.00
☐ P NBA Finals	.05	.02	.00
☐ Q NBA Finals	.05	.02	.00
☐ R NBA Finals	.05	.02	.00

1968-70 Partridge Meats *

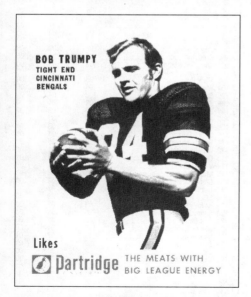

This black and white (with a little bit of red trim) photo-like card set features players from all three Cincinnati major league sports teams of that time, Reds baseball (1-8), Bengals football (9-12), and Royals basketball (13-14). The cards measure approximately 4" by 5", although there are other sizes sometimes

found which are attributable to other years of issue. The cards are blank backed.

	NRMT	VG-E	GOOD
COMPLETE SET (14)	600.00	300.00	60.00
COMMON BASEBALL (1-8)	15.00	7.50	1.50
COMMON FOOTBALL (9-12)	15.00	7.50	1.50
COMMON BASKETBALL (13-14)	25.00	12.50	2.50
☐ 1 Johnny Bench	200.00	100.00	20.00
☐ 2 Jimmy Bragan	15.00	7.50	1.50
☐ 3 Tommy Helms	15.00	7.50	1.50
☐ 4 Gary Nolan	15.00	7.50	1.50
☐ 5 Don Pavletich	15.00	7.50	1.50
☐ 6 Mel Queen	15.00	7.50	1.50
☐ 7 Pete Rose	200.00	100.00	20.00
☐ 8 Jim Stewart	15.00	7.50	1.50
☐ 9 Bob Johnson	15.00	7.50	1.50
☐ 10 Paul Robinson	15.00	7.50	1.50
☐ 11 John Stofa	15.00	7.50	1.50
☐ 12 Bob Trumpy	25.00	12.50	2.50
☐ 13 Adrian Smith	25.00	12.50	2.50
☐ 14 Tom Van Arsdale	25.00	12.50	2.50

1977-78 Pepsi All-Stars

This set of eight photos was sponsored by Pepsi. The borderless color player photos measure approximately 8" by 10" and are printed on thick cardboard stock. All the photos depict players either shooting or dunking the ball. The Pepsi logo and the player's name appear in the upper right corner. In blue print the back presents various statistics. The photos are unnumbered and are checklisted below in alphabetical order.

	NRMT	VG-E	GOOD
COMPLETE SET (8)	40.00	20.00	4.00
COMMON PLAYER (1-8)	5.00	2.50	.50
☐ 1 Rick Barry	5.00	2.50	.50
☐ 2 Dave Cowens	5.00	2.50	.50
☐ 3 Julius Erving	10.00	5.00	1.00
☐ 4 Kareem Abdul Jabbar	15.00	7.50	1.50
☐ 5 Pete Maravich	9.00	4.50	.90
☐ 6 Bob McAdoo	5.00	2.50	.50
☐ 7 David Thompson	5.00	2.50	.50
☐ 8 Bill Walton	7.50	3.75	.75

1981-82 Philip Morris *

This 18-card set was included in the Champions of American Sport program and features major stars from a variety of sports. The cards are standard size, 2 1/2" by 3 1/2". The cards are either reproductions of works of art (paintings) or famous photographs of the time. The cards are frequently found with a perforated edge on at least one side. There is no recognition anywhere on the cards with respect to who produced them.

Bill Russell
"Dominating force in professional basketball of 1950's:

1956 signed on with Boston Celtics;
Named to East All-Star team 11 times;
Won Most Valuable Player Award 5 times;
1963 became captain of team;
1966 first black to be head coach of an NBA team.

Bill Russell in a Match with the New York Knicks, James Drake, 1969, photograph, Collection Sports Illustrated @ TIME, Inc. 1969

	MINT	EXC	G-VG
COMPLETE SET (18)	45.00	20.00	4.00
COMMON CARD (1-18)	1.00	.50	.10
☐ 1 Muhammed Ali	5.00	2.50	.50
☐ 2 Arthur Ashe	1.00	.50	.10
☐ 3 Peggy Fleming	1.00	.50	.10
☐ 4 A.J. Foyt	4.00	2.00	.40
☐ 5 Eric Heiden	1.00	.50	.10
☐ 6 Bobby Hull	8.00	4.00	.80
☐ 7 Sandy Koufax	8.00	4.00	.80
☐ 8 Joe Louis	3.00	1.50	.30
☐ 9 Bob Mathias	1.00	.50	.10
☐ 10 Willie Mays	9.00	4.50	.90
☐ 11 Joe Namath	9.00	4.50	.90
☐ 12 Jack Nicklaus	4.00	2.00	.40
☐ 13 Knute Rockne	5.00	2.50	.50
☐ 14 Bill Russell	9.00	4.50	.90
☐ 15 Jim Ryun	1.00	.50	.10
☐ 16 Willie Shoemaker	3.00	1.50	.30
☐ 17 Casey Stengel	4.00	2.00	.40
☐ 18 Johnny Unitas	8.00	4.00	.80

1990-91 Pistons Unocal

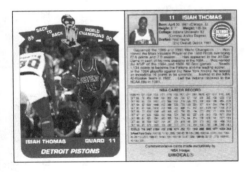

This 16-card set was produced by Hoops for UNOCAL 76 to commemorate the Piston's back to back championship seasons. A photo album to hold the cards was available for 2.76 at all participating UNOCAL 76 filling stations. Beginning on December 1, 1990 and continuing through the end of March, one card was given away each week with a fuel purchase at participating stations. The cards measure the standard size (2 1/2" by 3 1/2") and feature color action player photos on white card stock. A blue banner is draped along the top of the picture, and it reads "89-90 Back to Back World Champions." A Lawrence O'Brien trophy is superimposed at the middle of the banner. Player information and the team name are given in a reddish-orange stripe below the picture. On a blue background, the backs have a head shot of the player in the upper left corner, biographical information, and statistics for the player's NBA career. The cards are unnumbered.

	MINT	EXC	G-VG
COMPLETE SET (16)	9.00	4.50	.90
COMMON PLAYER (1-16)	.50	.25	.05
☐ 1 Mark Aguirre	.75	.35	.07
☐ 2 Chuck Daly CO	.50	.25	.05
☐ 3 Joe Dumars	1.00	.50	.10
☐ 4 James Edwards	.50	.25	.05
☐ 5 Vinnie Johnson	.75	.35	.07
☐ 6 Vinnie Johnson (The Shot)	.75	.35	.07
☐ 7 Bill Laimbeer	1.00	.50	.10
☐ 8 Lawrence O'Brien Trophy	.50	.25	.05
☐ 9 Dennis Rodman	1.00	.50	.10
☐ 10 John Salley	.75	.35	.07
☐ 11 Isiah Thomas	1.50	.75	.15
☐ 12 Isiah Thomas MVP	1.50	.75	.15
☐ 13 Celebration Card	.50	.25	.05
☐ 14 Team Photo	.50	.25	.05
☐ 15 Two Championship Rings	.50	.25	.05
☐ 16 1990 World Champions	.50	.25	.05

1990-91 Pistons Star

This 14-card set was produced by Star Company and sponsored by Home Respiratory Health Care, Inc., and the HRHC logo adorns the top of each card back. The cards measure the standard size (2 1/2" by 3 1/2"). The front features a color action photo of the player, on a royal blue background that washes out in the middle of the card. In white lettering the player's name, team, and position appear below the picture. In blue lettering the back presents biographical and statistical information in a horizontal format. The cards are numbered on the back.

	MINT	EXC	G-VG
COMPLETE SET (14)	9.00	4.50	.90
COMMON PLAYER (1-14)	.50	.25	.05
☐ 1 Mark Aguirre	.75	.35	.07
☐ 2 William Bedford	.50	.25	.05
☐ 3 Joe Dumars	1.00	.50	.10
☐ 4 James Edwards	.50	.25	.05
☐ 5 Dave Greenwood	.50	.25	.05
☐ 6 Scott Hastings	.50	.25	.05
☐ 7 Gerald Henderson	.50	.25	.05
☐ 8 Vinnie Johnson	.75	.35	.07
☐ 9 Bill Laimbeer	1.00	.50	.10
☐ 10 Dennis Rodman	1.00	.50	.10
☐ 11 John Salley	.75	.35	.07
☐ 12 Isiah Thomas	1.50	.75	.15
☐ 13 Chuck Daly CO	.50	.25	.05
☐ 14 Maia A. Porche PRES	.50	.25	.05

1985 Prism Stickers

These metallic stickers measure approximately 2 11/16" by 4". The front features a colorful drawn picture of the player, with the

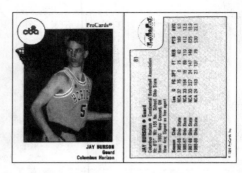

player's name in block lettering and in a facsimile autograph. The picture has rounded corners and a silver border. The backs are blank. The stickers are unnumbered and are checklisted below in alphabetical order by subject.

	MINT	EXC	G-VG
COMPLETE SET (8)	30.00	15.00	3.00
COMMON PLAYER (1-8)	2.00	1.00	.20
☐ 1 Bird vs. Worthy	6.00	3.00	.60
☐ 2 Patrick Ewing	6.00	3.00	.60
☐ 3 Moses Malone	4.00	2.00	.40
☐ 4 Malone vs. Jabbar	6.00	3.00	.60
☐ 5 Sidney Moncrief	3.00	1.50	.30
☐ 6 Isiah Thomas	5.00	2.50	.50
☐ 7 Kelly Tripucka	2.00	1.00	.20
☐ 8 Buck Williams	3.00	1.50	.30

1989-90 ProCards CBA

The 1989-90 ProCards CBA basketball set contains 207 cards measuring the standard size (2 1/2" by 3 1/2"). The fronts feature posed or action color player photos on a light tan background. Overlaying the upper left corner of the picture is a white circle (representing a basketball), with the CBA logo on it. Just below the circle a basketball rim and net are drawn. The player's name, position, and team are given in black lettering in the lower right corner of the card face. On a gray background with black borders and lettering the horizontally oriented backs present biographical and statistical information. The team logo appears in the cut-out section at the upper right corner. The cards are numbered on the back and arranged according to teams as follows: Sioux Falls SkyForce (1-13), Wichita Falls Texans (14-25), Rapid City Thrillers (26-37), Quad City Thunder (38-50), Pensacola Tornados (51-60), Omaha Racers (61-74, 206-7), Columbus Horizon (75-86), Rockford Lightning (87-100), Albany Patroons (101-114), Santa Barbara Islanders (115-127), Grand Rapids Hoops (128-140), Tulsa Fast Breakers

(141-153), LaCrosse Catbirds (154-165), Topeka Sizzlers (166-178), Cedar Rapids Silver Bullets (179-192), and San Jose Jammers (193-205).

	MINT	EXC	G-VG
COMPLETE SET (207)	70.00	35.00	7.00
COMMON PLAYER (1-207)	.25	.12	.02
☐ 1 Sioux Falls Checklist	.35	.17	.03
☐ 2 Ben Wilson	.35	.17	.03
☐ 3 Leonard Harris	.35	.17	.03
☐ 4 Laurent Crawford	.25	.12	.02
☐ 5 Steve Grayer	.35	.17	.03
☐ 6 Jim Lampley	.50	.25	.05
☐ 7 Eric Brown	.25	.12	.02
☐ 8 Dennis Nutt	.35	.17	.03
☐ 9 Ralph Lewis	.25	.12	.02
☐ 10 Lashun McDaniel	.25	.12	.02
☐ 11 Leo Parent	.25	.12	.02
☐ 12 Ron Ekker	.35	.17	.03
☐ 13 Terry Gould	.25	.12	.02
☐ 14 Wichita Falls Checklist	.35	.17	.03
☐ 15 Mark Peterson	.25	.12	.02
☐ 16 Greg Van Soelen	.25	.12	.02
☐ 17 Maurice Selvin	.25	.12	.02
☐ 18 Michael Tait	.35	.17	.03
☐ 19 Deon Hunter	.35	.17	.03
☐ 20 Randy Henry	.25	.12	.02
☐ 21 Kenny McClary	.25	.12	.02
☐ 22 Earl Walker	.25	.12	.02
☐ 23 Jeff Hodge	.25	.12	.02
☐ 24 Martin Nessley	.35	.17	.03
☐ 25 On Court Staff	.25	.12	.02
☐ 26 Rapid City Checklist	.35	.17	.03
☐ 27 Daren Queenan	.25	.12	.02
☐ 28 Carey Scurry	.25	.12	.02
☐ 29 Keith Smart	.75	.35	.07
☐ 30 Jim Thomas	.50	.25	.05
☐ 31 Pearl Washington	.50	.25	.05
☐ 32 Chris Childs	.25	.12	.02
☐ 33 Jarvis Basnight	.50	.25	.05
☐ 34 Dwight Boyd	.25	.12	.02
☐ 35 Raymond Brown	.25	.12	.02
☐ 36 Sylvester Gray	.35	.17	.03
☐ 37 Eric Musselman	.35	.17	.03
☐ 38 Quad City Checklist	.35	.17	.03
☐ 39 Kenny Gattison	.75	.35	.07
☐ 40 Lafester Rhodes	.35	.17	.03
☐ 41 Perry Young	.50	.25	.05
☐ 42 Wiley Brown	.35	.17	.03
☐ 43 Jose Slaughter	.35	.17	.03
☐ 44 Gerald Greene	.25	.12	.02
☐ 45 Lloyd Daniels	1.25	.60	.12
☐ 46 Bill Jones	.35	.17	.03
☐ 47 Sean Couch	.25	.12	.02
☐ 48 Marty Eggleston	.25	.12	.02
☐ 49 Mauro Panaggio	.35	.17	.03
☐ 50 Dan Panaggio	.25	.12	.02
☐ 51 Pensacola Checklist	.35	.17	.03
☐ 52 Joe Mullaney	.35	.17	.03
☐ 53 Mark Wade	.50	.25	.05
☐ 54 Larry Houzer	.25	.12	.02
☐ 55 Clifford Lett	.35	.17	.03
☐ 56 Tony Dawson	.25	.12	.02
☐ 57 Johnathan Edwards	.25	.12	.02
☐ 58 Jim Farmer	.50	.25	.05
☐ 59 Dwayne Taylor	.25	.12	.02
☐ 60 Bob McCann	.35	.17	.03
☐ 61 Omaha Checklist	.35	.17	.03
☐ 62 Silks/Rodie	.25	.12	.02
☐ 63 Racers Front Ofice	.25	.12	.02

☐ 64	Rodie-Team Mascot	.25	.12	.02
☐ 65	Tim Price	.25	.12	.02
☐ 66	Barry Glanzer	.25	.12	.02
☐ 67	Greg Wiltjer	.25	.12	.02
☐ 68	Ron Kellogg	.25	.12	.02
☐ 69	Tat Hunter	.25	.12	.02
☐ 70	Reginald Turner	.25	.12	.02
☐ 71	Jerry Adams	.25	.12	.02
☐ 72	Roland Gray	.25	.12	.02
☐ 73	Tim Legler	.35	.17	.03
☐ 74	Corey Gaines	.35	.17	.03
☐ 75	Columbus Checklist	.35	.17	.03
☐ 76	Gary Youmans	.25	.12	.02
☐ 77	Kelvin Ransey	.50	.25	.05
☐ 78	Chip Engelland	.35	.17	.03
☐ 79	Brian Martin	.25	.12	.02
☐ 80	Ray Hall	.25	.12	.02
☐ 81	Jay Burson	1.25	.60	.12
☐ 82	Bill Martin	.35	.17	.03
☐ 83	Eric Mudd	.25	.12	.02
☐ 84	Tom Schafer	.35	.17	.03
☐ 85	Steve Harris	.35	.17	.03
☐ 86	Eric Newsome	.25	.12	.02
☐ 87	Rockford Checklist	.35	.17	.03
☐ 88	Charley Rosen	.25	.12	.02
☐ 89	Tom Hart	.25	.12	.02
☐ 90	Team Picture	.25	.12	.02
☐ 91	Brent Carmichael	.25	.12	.02
☐ 92	Fred Cofield	.25	.12	.02
☐ 93	Darren Guest	.25	.12	.02
☐ 94	Bobby Parks	.35	.17	.03
☐ 95	Elsyon Turner	.35	.17	.03
☐ 96	Adrian McKinnon	.25	.12	.02
☐ 97	Gary Massey	.25	.12	.02
☐ 98	Tim Dillon	.25	.12	.02
☐ 99	Herb Blunt	.25	.12	.02
☐ 100	Greg Grissom	.35	.17	.03
☐ 101	Albany Checklist	.35	.17	.03
☐ 102	Leroy Witherspoon	.25	.12	.02
☐ 103	Vince Askew	.50	.25	.05
☐ 104	Clinton Smith	.25	.12	.02
☐ 105	Andre Patterson	.25	.12	.02
☐ 106	Jim Ferrer	.25	.12	.02
☐ 107	Willie Glass	.50	.25	.05
☐ 108	Darryl Joe	.35	.17	.03
☐ 109	Mario Elie	2.00	1.00	.20
☐ 110	Dave Popson	.50	.25	.05
☐ 111	Danny Pearson	.25	.12	.02
☐ 112	Doc Nunnally	.25	.12	.02
☐ 113	Gene Espeland	.25	.12	.02
☐ 114	Gerald Oliver	.25	.12	.02
☐ 115	Santa Barbara CL	.35	.17	.03
☐ 116	Luther Burks	.25	.12	.02
☐ 117	Brian Christensen	.35	.17	.03
☐ 118	Kevin Francewar	.25	.12	.02
☐ 119	Leon Wood	.50	.25	.05
☐ 120	Derrick Gervin	1.25	.60	.12
☐ 121	Larry Spriggs	.75	.35	.07
☐ 122	Michael Phelps	.50	.25	.05
☐ 123	Mike Ratliff	.35	.17	.03
☐ 124	Steffond Johnson	.50	.25	.05
☐ 125	Mitch McMullen	.25	.12	.02
☐ 126	Sonny Allen	.35	.17	.03
☐ 127	Don Ford	.35	.17	.03
☐ 128	Grand Rapids Checklist	.35	.17	.03
☐ 129	Lorenzo Sutton	.35	.17	.03
☐ 130	Willie Simmons	.25	.12	.02
☐ 131	Kenny Fields	.50	.25	.05
☐ 132	Winston Crite	.35	.17	.03
☐ 133	Eric McLaughlin	.25	.12	.02
☐ 134	Tony Brown	.35	.17	.03
☐ 135	Ricky Wilson	.35	.17	.03
☐ 136	Milt Newton	.50	.25	.05
☐ 137	Albert Springs	.25	.12	.02
☐ 138	Herbert Crook	.50	.25	.05
☐ 139	Mike Mashak	.25	.12	.02
☐ 140	Jim Sleeper	.25	.12	.02
☐ 141	Tulsa Checklist	.35	.17	.03
☐ 142	Terry Faggins	.25	.12	.02
☐ 143	Ozell Jones	.35	.17	.03
☐ 144	Brian Rahilly	.25	.12	.02
☐ 145	Duane Washington	.35	.17	.03
☐ 146	Ron Spivey	.25	.12	.02
☐ 147	Henry Bibby	.50	.25	.05
☐ 148	Al Gipson	.35	.17	.03
☐ 149	Greg Jones	.25	.12	.02
☐ 150	Andre Moore	.25	.12	.02
☐ 151	Tracy Moore	.25	.12	.02
☐ 152	Steve Bontranger	.25	.12	.02
☐ 153	Bubby Breaker Team Mascot	.25	.12	.02
☐ 154	Lacrosse Checklist	.35	.17	.03
☐ 155	Mike Williams	.25	.12	.02

☐ 156	Vince Hamilton	.25	.12	.02
☐ 157	John Harris	.25	.12	.02
☐ 158	Tony White	.25	.12	.02
☐ 159	Todd Alexander	.25	.12	.02
☐ 160	Richard Johnson	.35	.17	.03
☐ 161	Leo Rautins	.35	.17	.03
☐ 162	Dwayne McClain	.50	.25	.05
☐ 163	Carlos Clark	.35	.17	.03
☐ 164	Vada Martin	.25	.12	.02
☐ 165	Flip Saunders	.25	.12	.02
☐ 166	Topeka Checklist	.35	.17	.03
☐ 167	Cedric Hunter	.35	.17	.03
☐ 168	Elfrem Jackson	.25	.12	.02
☐ 169	Glen Clem	.25	.12	.02
☐ 170	Mike Richmond	.25	.12	.02
☐ 171	Jim Rowinski	.35	.17	.03
☐ 172	Craig Jackson	.25	.12	.02
☐ 173	Tony Mack	.25	.12	.02
☐ 174	Hubert Henderson	.25	.12	.02
☐ 175	Kevin Nixon	.25	.12	.02
☐ 176	Haywoode Workman	.35	.17	.03
☐ 177	Porter Cutrell	.25	.12	.02
☐ 178	Mike Riley	.25	.12	.02
☐ 179	Cedar Rapids Checklist	.35	.17	.03
☐ 180	Bullet Bear	.25	.12	.02
☐ 181	George Whittaker	.25	.12	.02
☐ 182	Tom Domako	.25	.12	.02
☐ 183	Al Lorenzen	.35	.17	.03
☐ 184	Darryl Johnson	.25	.12	.02
☐ 185	Mel Braxton	.25	.12	.02
☐ 186	Orlando Graham	.25	.12	.02
☐ 187	Reggie Owens	.35	.17	.03
☐ 188	John Starks	.50	.25	.05
☐ 189	Kenny Drummond	.25	.12	.02
☐ 190	Mark Plansky	.35	.17	.03
☐ 191	Anthony Blakley	.35	.17	.03
☐ 192	Everette Stephens	.35	.17	.03
☐ 193	San Jose Checklist	.35	.17	.03
☐ 194	Cory Russell	.25	.12	.02
☐ 195	Jim Ellis	.25	.12	.02
☐ 196	Butch Hays	.25	.12	.02
☐ 197	Mike Doktorczyk	.25	.12	.02
☐ 198	Scooter Barry	.75	.35	.07
☐ 199	Monroe Douglass	.35	.17	.03
☐ 200	Scott Fisher	.25	.12	.02
☐ 201	David Boone	.25	.12	.02
☐ 202	Jervis Cole	.25	.12	.02
☐ 203	Freddie Banks	.35	.17	.03
☐ 204	Richard Morton	.25	.12	.02
☐ 205	Dan Williams	.25	.12	.02
☐ 206	Mike Thibault CO	.25	.12	.02
☐ 207	Omaha Coaches Omaha Racers	.25	.12	.02

1990-91 ProCards CBA

These standard size (2 1/2" by 3 1/2") cards are numbered and checklisted below according to teams as follows: Omaha Racers (1-16), Cedar Rapids Silver Bullets (17-29), Pensacola Tornados (30-44), Rockford Lightning (45-59), Lacrosse Catbirds (60-71), Rapid City Thrillers (72-81), Sioux Falls Skyforce (82-96), Oklahoma City Cavalry (97-107), Tulsa Fast Breakers (108-118), Wichita Falls Texans (119-134), Quad City Thunder (135-148), Albany Patroons (149-162), Grand Rapids

Hoops (163-171), Columbus Horizon (172-183), Yakima Sun Kings (184-192), and San Jose Jammers (193-203).

	MINT	EXC	G-VG
COMPLETE SET (203)	55.00	27.50	5.50
COMMON PLAYER (1-203)	.25	.12	.02

		MINT	EXC	G-VG
☐ 1	Jim Les	1.00	.50	.10
☐ 2	Ron Moore	.25	.12	.02
☐ 3	Rod Mason	.25	.12	.02
☐ 4	Paul Weakly	.25	.12	.02
☐ 5	Brian Howard	.25	.12	.02
☐ 6	Pat Bolden	.25	.12	.02
☐ 7	Mike Thibault	.25	.12	.02
☐ 8	Tim Legler	.35	.17	.03
☐ 9	Cedric Hunter	.35	.17	.03
☐ 10	Mark Peterson	.25	.12	.02
☐ 11	Greg Wiltjer	.25	.12	.02
☐ 12	The Idelman's	.25	.12	.02
☐ 13	The Silks and Rodie	.25	.12	.02
☐ 14	Basketball Staff	.25	.12	.02
☐ 15	Front Office Staff	.25	.12	.02
☐ 16	Omaha Checklist	.35	.17	.03
☐ 17	Calvin Duncan	.25	.12	.02
☐ 18	Pat Durham	.35	.17	.03
☐ 19	Steve Grayer	.35	.17	.03
☐ 20	Roy Marble	.75	.35	.07
☐ 21	Tony Martin	.35	.17	.03
☐ 22	Shawn McDaniel	.25	.12	.02
☐ 23	Peter Thibeaux	.35	.17	.03
☐ 24	Clarence Thompson	.25	.12	.02
☐ 25	Demone Webster	.25	.12	.02
☐ 26	A.J. Wynder	.25	.12	.02
☐ 27	Steve Kahl	.25	.12	.02
☐ 28	Steve Bontrager	.25	.12	.02
☐ 29	Cedar Rapids Checklist	.35	.17	.03
☐ 30	Skeeter Henry	.35	.17	.03
☐ 31	Eugene McDowell	.35	.17	.03
☐ 32	Bruce Wheatley	.25	.12	.02
☐ 33	Mark Wade	.35	.17	.03
☐ 34	Cheyenne Gibson	.25	.12	.02
☐ 35	Clifford Lett	.35	.17	.03
☐ 36	Larry Houzer	.25	.12	.02
☐ 37	Tony Dawson	.35	.17	.03
☐ 38	Richard Hollis	.35	.17	.03
☐ 39	Ed Leonard and Joe Corona	.25	.12	.02
☐ 40	Front Office Staff	.25	.12	.02
☐ 41	Torry the Tornado	.25	.12	.02
☐ 42	Fred Bryan	.25	.12	.02
☐ 43	Jim Goodman	.25	.12	.02
☐ 44	Pensacola Checklist	.35	.17	.03
☐ 45	Joe Fredrick	.25	.12	.02
☐ 46	Everette Stephens	.35	.17	.03
☐ 47	Mario Donaldson	.25	.12	.02
☐ 48	Dan Godfread	.25	.12	.02
☐ 49	Haakon Austefjord	.25	.12	.02
☐ 50	Gary Massey	.25	.12	.02
☐ 51	Chris Childs	.25	.12	.02
☐ 52	Gerry Wright	.25	.12	.02
☐ 53	Marty Conlon	.35	.17	.03
☐ 54	Tony Costner	.25	.12	.02
☐ 55	Steve Hayes	.35	.17	.03
☐ 56	Tom Hart	.25	.12	.02
☐ 57	Paul Kulick	.25	.12	.02
☐ 58	Rockford Team Photo	.25	.12	.02
☐ 59	Rockford Checklist	.35	.17	.03
☐ 60	Mike Williams	.25	.12	.02
☐ 61	Brian Rahilly	.25	.12	.02
☐ 62	Bill Martin	.35	.17	.03
☐ 63	Vince Hamilton	.25	.12	.02
☐ 64	Dwayne McClain	.50	.25	.05
☐ 65	Bart Kofoed	.35	.17	.03
☐ 66	Dominic Pressley	.35	.17	.03
☐ 67	Herb Dixon	.25	.12	.02
☐ 68	Todd Mitchell	.50	.25	.05
☐ 69	Ben Mitchell	.25	.12	.02
☐ 70	Flip Saunders	.25	.12	.02
☐ 71	Lacrosse Checklist	.35	.17	.03
☐ 72	Keith Smart	.75	.35	.07
☐ 73	Stephen Thompson	1.25	.60	.12
☐ 74	Brian Rowsom	.35	.17	.03
☐ 75	Tony Martin	.25	.12	.02
☐ 76	Joe Ward	.25	.12	.02
☐ 77	Fennis Dembo	.75	.35	.07
☐ 78	Glenn Puddy	.35	.17	.03
☐ 79	Lanard Copeland	.75	.35	.07
☐ 80	Carl Brown	.25	.12	.02
☐ 81	Rapid City Checklist	.35	.17	.03
☐ 82	Dennis Nutt	.35	.17	.03
☐ 83	Leonard Harris	.25	.12	.02
☐ 84	Tharon Mayes	.25	.12	.02
☐ 85	Melvin McCants	.50	.25	.05
☐ 86	Tracy Mitchell	.50	.25	.05
☐ 87	Ken Redfield	.25	.12	.02
☐ 88	Frank Ross	.25	.12	.02
☐ 89	Michael Phelps	.35	.17	.03
☐ 90	Brian Christensen	.25	.12	.02
☐ 91	Kevin McKenna	.25	.12	.02
☐ 92	Steve Raab	.25	.12	.02
☐ 93	Clay Moser	.25	.12	.02
☐ 94	Tony Khing	.25	.12	.02
☐ 95	Little Dude	.25	.12	.02
☐ 96	Sioux Falls Checklist	.35	.17	.03
☐ 97	Perry Young	.35	.17	.03
☐ 98	Ozell Jones	.35	.17	.03
☐ 99	Willie Simmons	.25	.12	.02
☐ 100	Alvin Heggs	.25	.12	.02
☐ 101	Kelsey Weems	.35	.17	.03
☐ 102	Anthony Frederick	.25	.12	.02
☐ 103	Royce Jeffries	.25	.12	.02
☐ 104	Darryl McDonald	.25	.12	.02
☐ 105	Sgt. Slammer	.35	.17	.03
☐ 106	Charley Rosen	.25	.12	.02
☐ 107	Oklahoma City Checklist	.35	.17	.03
☐ 108	Keith Wilson	.25	.12	.02
☐ 109	James Carter	.25	.12	.02
☐ 110	Tracy Moore	.25	.12	.02
☐ 111	Mark Plansky	.35	.17	.03
☐ 112	Charles Bradley	.25	.12	.02
☐ 113	Leroy Combs	.25	.12	.02
☐ 114	Anthony Mason	.25	.12	.02
☐ 115	Gary Voce	.25	.12	.02
☐ 116	Jim Lampley	.35	.17	.03
☐ 117	Henry Bibby	.35	.17	.03
☐ 118	Tulsa Checklist	.35	.17	.03
☐ 119	Texans Logo	.25	.12	.02
☐ 120	Ennis Whatley	.50	.25	.05
☐ 121	Mike Mitchell	.35	.17	.03
☐ 122	Derrick Taylor	.35	.17	.03
☐ 123	Kenny Atkinson	.25	.12	.02
☐ 124	Jaren Jackson	.35	.17	.03
☐ 125	Cedric Ball	.25	.12	.02
☐ 126	Chris Munk	.25	.12	.02
☐ 127	Mark Becker	.25	.12	.02
☐ 128	Rodney Blake	.25	.12	.02
☐ 129	Kurt Portmann	.25	.12	.02
☐ 130	Henry James	.25	.12	.02
☐ 131	John Treloar	.25	.12	.02
☐ 132	Dave Whitney	.35	.17	.03
☐ 133	Mike Davis	.25	.12	.02
☐ 134	Wichita Falls Checklist	.35	.17	.03
☐ 135	Milt Wagner	.50	.25	.05
☐ 136	Phil Henderson	.75	.35	.07
☐ 137	Tony Harris	.25	.12	.02
☐ 138	Steve Bardo	.50	.25	.05
☐ 139	A.J. Wynder	.25	.12	.02
☐ 140	Joel DeBortoli	.25	.12	.02
☐ 141	Tim Anderson	.25	.12	.02
☐ 142	Ron Draper	.25	.12	.02
☐ 143	Barry Sumpter	.35	.17	.03
☐ 144	Demone Webster	.25	.12	.02
☐ 145	Thunderbird Dance Team	.25	.12	.02
☐ 146	Mauro Panaggio	.35	.17	.03
☐ 147	Dan Panaggio	.25	.12	.02
☐ 148	Quad City Checklist	.35	.17	.03
☐ 149	Albert King	.50	.25	.05
☐ 150	Keith Smith	.25	.12	.02
☐ 151	Mario Elie	1.50	.75	.15
☐ 152	Albert Springs	.25	.12	.02
☐ 153	Jeff Fryer	.35	.17	.03
☐ 154	Clinton Smith	.25	.12	.02
☐ 155	Vincent Askew	.50	.25	.05
☐ 156	Paul Graham	.25	.12	.02
☐ 157	Ben McDonald	.25	.12	.02
☐ 158	Willie McDuffie	.25	.12	.02
☐ 159	George Karl	.35	.17	.03
☐ 160	Terry Stotts	.35	.17	.03
☐ 161	Doc Nunnally	.25	.12	.02
☐ 162	Albany Checklist	.35	.17	.03
☐ 163	Reggie Fox	.25	.12	.02
☐ 164	Ron Draper	.25	.12	.02
☐ 165	Sedric Toney	.25	.12	.02
☐ 166	Alex Austin	.25	.12	.02
☐ 167	Robert Brickey	.50	.25	.05
☐ 168	Ricky Blanton	.50	.25	.05
☐ 169	Stan Kimbrough	.25	.12	.02
☐ 170	Ron Cavenall	.35	.17	.03
☐ 171	Grand Rapids Checklist	.35	.17	.03
☐ 172	Darren Henrie	.25	.12	.02
☐ 173	Duane Washington	.35	.17	.03
☐ 174	Barry Stevens	.25	.12	.02
☐ 175	Craig Neal	.35	.17	.03

☐	176	Ron Spivey	.25	.12	.02

			NRMT	VG-E	GOOD
☐ 176	Ron Spivey	.25	.12	.02
☐ 177	Kerry Hammonds	.25	.12	.02
☐ 178	Brian Martin	.25	.12	.02
☐ 179	Jerome Henderson	.25	.12	.02
☐ 180	John McIntyre	.25	.12	.02
☐ 181	Chris Childs	.25	.12	.02
☐ 182	The Jacobson's	.25	.12	.02
☐ 183	Columbus Checklist	.35	.17	.03
☐ 184	Luther Burks	.25	.12	.02
☐ 185	Lee Campbell	.25	.12	.02
☐ 186	Corey Gaines	.35	.17	.03
☐ 187	Mike Higgins	.25	.12	.02
☐ 188	Ron Kellogg	.25	.12	.02
☐ 189	Bart Kofoed	.35	.17	.03
☐ 190	Jim Rowinski	.25	.12	.02
☐ 191	Riley Smith	.25	.12	.02
☐ 192	Yakima Checklist	.35	.17	.03
☐ 193	Mike Yoest	.25	.12	.02
☐ 194	Freddie Banks	.35	.17	.03
☐ 195	Scooter Barry	.75	.35	.07
☐ 196	Richard Morton	.35	.17	.03
☐ 197	Kelby Stuckey	.25	.12	.02
☐ 198	Jervis Cole	.25	.12	.02
☐ 199	Kenny McClary	.25	.12	.02
☐ 200	Joe Wallace	.25	.12	.02
☐ 201	Mark Tillmon	.50	.25	.05
☐ 202	Greg Butler	.50	.25	.05
☐ 203	San Jose Checklist	.35	.17	.03

1954 Quaker Sports Oddities *

This 27-card set features strange moments in sports and was issued as an insert inside Quaker Puffed Rice cereal boxes. Fronts of the cards are drawings depicting the person or the event. In a stripe at the top of the card face appear the words "Sports Oddities." Two colorful drawings fill the remaining space: the left half is a portrait, while the right half is action-oriented. A variety of sports are included. The cards measure approximately 2 1/4" by 3 1/2" and have rounded corners. The last line on the back of each card declares, "It's Odd but True."

	NRMT	VG-E	GOOD
COMPLETE SET (27)	250.00	125.00	25.00
COMMON CARD (1-27)	3.00	1.50	.30
☐ 1 Johnny Miller	7.50	3.75	.75
(Incredible Punt)			
☐ 2 Fred Snite Sr.	3.00	1.50	.30
(Two Holes-In-One)			
☐ 3 George Quam	3.00	1.50	.30
(One Arm Handball)			
☐ 4 John B. Maypole	3.00	1.50	.30
(Speedboating)			
☐ 5 Harold(Bunny) Levitt	12.50	6.25	1.25
(Free Throws)			
☐ 6 Wake Forest College	7.50	3.75	.75
(Six Forward Passes)			
☐ 7 Amos Alonzo Stagg	25.00	12.50	2.50
(Three TD's No Score)			
☐ 8 Catherine Fellmuth	3.00	1.50	.30
☐ 9 Bill Wilson	3.00	1.50	.30
☐ 10 Chicago Blackhawks	7.50	3.75	.75
☐ 11 Betty Robinson	3.00	1.50	.30
☐ 12 Dartmouth College/	7.50	3.75	.75
University of Utah			
(1944 NCAA Basketball)			
☐ 13 Ab Jenkins	3.00	1.50	.30
☐ 14 Capt.Eddie Rickenbacker	5.00	2.50	.50
☐ 15 Jackie LaVine	3.00	1.50	.30
☐ 16 Jackie Riley	3.00	1.50	.30
☐ 17 Carol Stokholm	3.00	1.50	.30
☐ 18 Jimmy Smilgoff	3.00	1.50	.30
☐ 19 George Halas	30.00	15.00	3.00
☐ 20 Joyce Rosenblom	3.00	1.50	.30
☐ 21 Squatter's Rights	3.00	1.50	.30
☐ 22 Richard Dwyer	3.00	1.50	.30
☐ 23 Harlem Globetrotters	30.00	15.00	3.00
☐ 24 Everett Dean	15.00	7.50	1.50
(basketball)			
☐ 25 Texas University/	6.00	3.00	.60
Northwestern University			
☐ 26 Bronko Nagurski	90.00	45.00	9.00
(All-American Team)			
☐ 27 Yankee Stadium	9.00	4.50	.90
(No Homers Out)			

1968-69 Rockets Jack in the Box

This 14-card set of San Diego Rockets was sponsored by Jack-in-the-Box and available at their restaurants in the greater San Diego area. There is some question of whether or not this set was substantially reissued the following year. The cards measure approximately 2" by 3" and have the appearance of wallet-size photos. The fronts have posed color head and shoulders shots, with the player's name, team name, team logo, and sponsor's logo below the picture. The backs are blank. The cards are unnumbered and are checklisted below in alphabetical order. The two cards in the set that are more difficult to find are marked by SP in the checklist below.

	NRMT	VG-E	GOOD
COMPLETE SET (14)	80.00	40.00	8.00
COMMON PLAYER (1-14)	2.00	1.00	.20
COMMON PLAYER SP	15.00	7.50	1.50
☐ 1 Rick Adelman	6.00	3.00	.60
☐ 2 Harry Barnes SP	15.00	7.50	1.50
☐ 3 Jim Barnett	3.00	1.50	.30
☐ 4 John Block	2.00	1.00	.20
☐ 5 Henry Finkel SP	15.00	7.50	1.50
☐ 6 Elvin Hayes	15.00	7.50	1.50
☐ 7 Toby Kimball	2.00	1.00	.20
☐ 8 Don Kojis	2.00	1.00	.20
☐ 9 Stuart Lantz	2.00	1.00	.20
☐ 10 Pat Riley	12.00	6.00	1.20
☐ 11 Bobby Smith	4.00	2.00	.40
☐ 12 John Q. Trapp	2.00	1.00	.20
☐ 13 Art Williams	2.00	1.00	.20
☐ 14 Bernie Williams	3.00	1.50	.30

1978-79 Royal Crown Cola

This 40-card set was sponsored by RC Cola, and its logo appears at the top of the card face. The cards were supposedly only issued in the southern New England area. The cards were intended to be placed in six-packs of Royal Crown Cola, one per six-pack. The cards measure approximately 3 1/8" by 6". The front features a black and white head shot of the player framed by a basketball hoop net with red and blue trim. The cards are unnumbered and are checklisted below in alphabetical order. The cards were apparently only licensed by the NBA Players Association since there are no team logos or team markings anywhere on the cards.

		NRMT	VG-E	GOOD
COMPLETE SET (40)		400.00	200.00	40.00
COMMON PLAYER (1-40)		6.00	3.00	.60
☐ 1	Kareem Abdul Jabbar	50.00	25.00	5.00
☐ 2	Nate Archibald	15.00	7.50	1.50
☐ 3	Rick Barry	18.00	9.00	1.80
☐ 4	Jim Chones	6.00	3.00	.60
☐ 5	Doug Collins	7.50	3.75	.75
☐ 6	Dave Cowens	15.00	7.50	1.50
☐ 7	Adrian Dantley	12.00	6.00	1.20
☐ 8	Walter Davis	10.00	5.00	1.00
☐ 9	John Drew	7.50	3.75	.75
☐ 10	Julius Erving	30.00	15.00	3.00
☐ 11	Walt Frazier	15.00	7.50	1.50
☐ 12	George Gervin	10.00	5.00	1.00
☐ 13	Artis Gilmore	10.00	5.00	1.00
☐ 14	Elvin Hayes	15.00	7.50	1.50
☐ 15	Dan Issel	10.00	5.00	1.00
☐ 16	Marques Johnson	7.50	3.75	.75
☐ 17	Bernard King	12.50	6.25	1.25
☐ 18	Bob Lanier	10.00	5.00	1.00
☐ 19	Maurice Lucas	7.50	3.75	.75
☐ 20	Pete Maravich	18.00	9.00	1.80
☐ 21	Bob McAdoo	7.50	3.75	.75
☐ 22	George McGinnis	7.50	3.75	.75
☐ 23	Eric Money	6.00	3.00	.60
☐ 24	Earl Monroe	12.00	6.00	1.20
☐ 25	Calvin Murphy	7.50	3.75	.75
☐ 26	Robert Parish	18.00	9.00	1.80
☐ 27	Billy Paultz	5.00	2.50	.50
☐ 28	Jack Sikma	7.50	3.75	.75
☐ 29	Rickey Sobers	6.00	3.00	.60
☐ 30	David Thompson	7.50	3.75	.75

☐ 31	Rudy Tomjanovich	6.00	3.00	.60
☐ 32	Wes Unseld	10.00	5.00	1.00
☐ 33	Norm Van Lier	6.00	3.00	.60
☐ 34	Bill Walton	10.00	5.00	1.00
☐ 35	Marvin Webster	6.00	3.00	.60
☐ 36	Scott Wedman	6.00	3.00	.60
☐ 37	Paul Westphal	7.50	3.75	.75
☐ 38	Jo Jo White	7.50	3.75	.75
☐ 39	John Williamson	6.00	3.00	.60
☐ 40	Brian Winters	6.00	3.00	.60

1952 Royal Desserts

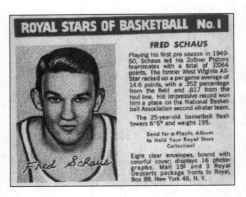

The 1952 Royal Desserts Stars of Basketball set contains eight horizontally oriented cards. The cards formed the backs of Royal Desserts packages of the period; consequently many cards are found with uneven edges stemming from the method of cutting the cards off the box. Each card has its number and the statement "Royal Stars of Basketball" in a red rectangle at the top. Cards measure approximately 2 5/8" by 3 1/4". The cards fronts have a stripe at the top and are divided into halves. The left half has a light-blue tinted head shot of the player and a facsimile autograph, while the right half has career summary. The blue tinted picture contains a facsimile autograph of the player. An album was presumably available as it is advertised on the card. The catalog designation for this scarce set is F219-2.

		NRMT	VG-E	GOOD
COMPLETE SET (8)		2350.00	1000.00	200.00
COMMON PLAYER (1-8)		150.00	75.00	15.00
☐ 1	Fred Schaus	150.00	75.00	15.00
☐ 2	Dick McGuire	200.00	100.00	20.00
☐ 3	Jack Nichols	150.00	75.00	15.00
☐ 4	Frank Brian	150.00	75.00	15.00
☐ 5	Joe Fulks	300.00	150.00	30.00
☐ 6	George Mikan	1000.00	400.00	80.00
☐ 7	Jim Pollard	300.00	150.00	30.00
☐ 8	Harry E. Jeanette	150.00	75.00	15.00

1975-76 76ers McDonald's Standups

The 1975-76 McDonalds Philadelphia 76ers set contains six blank-backed cards measuring approximately 3 3/4" by 7". The cards are die cut, allowing the player pictures to be punched out and displayed. The cards are unnumbered and checklisted below in alphabetical order.

	NRMT	VG-E	GOOD
COMPLETE SET (6)	18.00	9.00	1.80
COMMON PLAYER (1-6)	2.00	1.00	.20

(33) HERSEY HAWKINS
Guard

		MINT	EXC	G-VG
☐ 1	Fred Carter	2.00	1.00	.20
☐ 2	Harvey Catchings	2.00	1.00	.20
☐ 3	Doug Collins	4.00	2.00	.40
☐ 4	Billy Cunningham	6.00	3.00	.60
☐ 5	George McGinnis	4.00	2.00	.40
☐ 6	Steve Mix	2.00	1.00	.20

☐ 13	Big Shot	.35	.17	.03
	Team Mascot			
☐ 14	Jim Lynam CO	.35	.17	.03
☐ 15	Fred Carter CO	.35	.17	.03
☐ 16	Buzz Braman CO	.35	.17	.03

1989-90 76ers Kodak

This team photo album was jointly sponsored by Jack's Cameras and Kodak. The photo album consists of three sheets, each measuring approximately 8" by 11" and joined together to form one continuous sheet. The first sheet features a team photo of the Philadelphia 76ers. While the second sheet presents two rows of five cards each, the third sheet presents six additional player cards, with the remaining four slots filled in by coupons redeemable at Jack's Cameras. After perforation, the cards measure 2 3/16" by 3 3/4". The card front features a color action player photo, with a red border on white card stock. The player's name and position are given below the picture, and the 76ers logo is sandwiched between the sponsors' logos. The backs have the Philadelphia 76ers logo in blue and red print. The cards are presented in the album in alphabetical order, with coaches at the end, and we have checklisted them below accordingly, placing the uniform number to the right of the name.

		MINT	EXC	G-VG
COMPLETE SET (16)		7.00	3.50	.70
COMMON PLAYER (1-16)		.35	.17	.03
☐ 1	Ron Anderson 20	.50	.25	.05
☐ 2	Charles Barkley 34	1.50	.75	.15
☐ 3	Scott Brooks 1	.35	.17	.03
☐ 4	Lanard Copeland 7	.35	.17	.03
☐ 5	Johnny Dawkins 12	.50	.25	.05
☐ 6	Mike Gminski 42	.50	.25	.05
☐ 7	Hersey Hawkins 33	.90	.45	.09
☐ 8	Rick Mahorn 44	.50	.25	.05
☐ 9	Kurt Nimphius 40	.35	.17	.03
☐ 10	Kenny Payne 21	.35	.17	.03
☐ 11	Derek Smith 18	.50	.25	.05
☐ 12	Bob Thornton 23	.35	.17	.03

1990-91 SkyBox

The 1990-91 Sky Box set contains 300 cards featuring NBA players. The cards measure the standard size (2 1/2" by 3 1/2"). The front features an action shot of the player on a computed-generated background consisting of various color stripes and geometric shapes. The player's name appears in a black stripe below the photo, with the team logo superimposed at the left lower corner. The photo is bordered in gold. The back presents head shots of the player, with gold borders on white background. Player statistics are given in a box below the photo. The cards are numbered on the back and checklisted below alphabetically according to team names as follows: Atlanta Hawks (1-12), Boston Celtics (13-24), Charlotte Hornets (25-36), Chicago Bulls (37-47), Cleveland Cavaliers (48-58), Dallas Mavericks (59-70), Denver Nuggets (71-81), Detroit Pistons (82-93), Golden State Warriors (94-104), Houston Rockets (105-113),

Indiana Pacers (114-123), Los Angeles Clippers (124-133), Los Angeles Lakers (134-143), Miami Heat (144-154), Milwaukee Bucks (155-166), Minnesota Timberwolves (167-175), New Jersey Nets (176-185), New York Knicks (186-197), Orlando Magic (198-209), Philadelphia 76ers (210-219), Phoenix Suns (220-230), Portland Trail Blazers (231-241), Sacramento Kings (242-251), San Antonio Spurs (252-262), Seattle Supersonics (263-273), Utah Jazz (274-284), and Washington Bullets (285-294). The key rookies in this set are Nick Anderson, Vlade Divac, Sherman Douglas, Sean Elliott, Danny Ferry, Tim Hardaway, Shawn Kemp, Glen Rice, and Pooh Richardson. Cards that were deleted by Sky Box for the second series are marked in the checklist below by SP.

	MINT	EXC	G-VG
COMPLETE SET (300)	28.00	14.00	2.80
COMMON PLAYER (1-300)	.04	.02	.00
☐ 1 John Battle Atlanta Hawks	.10	.02	.00
☐ 2 Duane Ferrell SP Atlanta Hawks	.20	.10	.02
☐ 3 Jon Koncak Atlanta Hawks	.04	.02	.00
☐ 4 Cliff Levingston SP Atlanta Hawks	.10	.05	.01
☐ 5 John Long SP Atlanta Hawks	.10	.05	.01
☐ 6 Moses Malone Atlanta Hawks	.18	.09	.01
☐ 7 Glenn Rivers Atlanta Hawks	.07	.03	.01
☐ 8 Kenny Smith SP Atlanta Hawks	.12	.06	.01
☐ 9 Alexander Volkov Atlanta Hawks	.20	.10	.02
☐ 10 Spud Webb Atlanta Hawks	.12	.06	.01
☐ 11 Dominique Wilkins Atlanta Hawks	.25	.12	.02
☐ 12 Kevin Willis Atlanta Hawks	.04	.02	.00
☐ 13 John Bagley Boston Celtics	.04	.02	.00
☐ 14 Larry Bird Boston Celtics	.45	.22	.04
☐ 15 Kevin Gamble Boston Celtics	.25	.12	.02
☐ 16 Dennis Johnson SP Boston Celtics	.17	.08	.01
☐ 17 Joe Kleine Boston Celtics	.04	.02	.00
☐ 18 Reggie Lewis Boston Celtics	.30	.15	.03
☐ 19 Kevin McHale Boston Celtics	.20	.10	.02
☐ 20 Robert Parish Boston Celtics	.20	.10	.02
☐ 21 Jim Paxson SP Boston Celtics	.10	.05	.01
☐ 22 Ed Pinckney Boston Celtics	.04	.02	.00
☐ 23 Brian Shaw Boston Celtics	.25	.12	.02
☐ 24 Michael Smith Boston Celtics	.20	.10	.02
☐ 25 Richard Anderson SP Charlotte Hornets	.10	.05	.01
☐ 26 Tyrone Bogues Charlotte Hornets	.04	.02	.00
☐ 27 Rex Chapman Charlotte Hornets	.17	.08	.01
☐ 28 Dell Curry Charlotte Hornets	.04	.02	.00
☐ 29 Armon Gilliam Charlotte Hornets	.04	.02	.00
☐ 30 Michael Holton SP Charlotte Hornets	.10	.05	.01
☐ 31 Dave Hoppen Charlotte Hornets	.07	.03	.01
☐ 32 J.R. Reid Charlotte Hornets	.40	.20	.04
☐ 33 Robert Reid SP Charlotte Hornets	.10	.05	.01
☐ 34 Brian Rowsom SP Charlotte Hornets	.17	.08	.01
☐ 35 Kelly Tripucka Charlotte Hornets	.04	.02	.00
☐ 36 Michael Williams SP Charlotte Hornets	.30	.15	.03
☐ 37 B.J. Armstrong Chicago Bulls	.35	.17	.03
☐ 38 Bill Cartwright Chicago Bulls	.07	.03	.01
☐ 39 Horace Grant Chicago Bulls	.20	.10	.02
☐ 40 Craig Hodges Chicago Bulls	.07	.03	.01
☐ 41 Michael Jordan Chicago Bulls	2.00	1.00	.20
☐ 42 Stacey King Chicago Bulls	.25	.12	.02
☐ 43 Ed Nealy SP Chicago Bulls	.10	.05	.01
☐ 44 John Paxson Chicago Bulls	.07	.03	.01
☐ 45 Will Perdue Chicago Bulls	.10	.05	.01
☐ 46 Scottie Pippen Chicago Bulls	.35	.17	.03
☐ 47 Jeff Sanders SP Chicago Bulls	.17	.08	.01
☐ 48 Winston Bennett Cleveland Cavaliers	.15	.07	.01
☐ 49 Chucky Brown Cleveland Cavaliers	.20	.10	.02
☐ 50 Brad Daugherty Cleveland Cavaliers	.20	.10	.02
☐ 51 Craig Ehlo Cleveland Cavaliers	.07	.03	.01
☐ 52 Steve Kerr Cleveland Cavaliers	.07	.03	.01
☐ 53 Paul Mokeski SP Cleveland Cavaliers	.10	.05	.01
☐ 54 John Morton Cleveland Cavaliers	.20	.10	.02
☐ 55 Larry Nance Cleveland Cavaliers	.07	.03	.01
☐ 56 Mark Price Cleveland Cavaliers	.12	.06	.01
☐ 57 Tree Rollins SP Cleveland Cavaliers	.12	.06	.01
☐ 58 Hot Rod Williams Cleveland Cavaliers	.12	.06	.01
☐ 59 Steve Alford Dallas Mavericks	.07	.03	.01
☐ 60 Rolando Blackman Dallas Mavericks	.10	.05	.01
☐ 61 Adrian Dantley SP Dallas Mavericks	.17	.08	.01
☐ 62 Brad Davis Dallas Mavericks	.04	.02	.00
☐ 63 James Donaldson Dallas Mavericks	.04	.02	.00
☐ 64 Derek Harper Dallas Mavericks	.07	.03	.01
☐ 65 Anthony Jones SP Dallas Mavericks	.17	.08	.01
☐ 66 Sam Perkins SP Dallas Mavericks	.20	.10	.02
☐ 67 Roy Tarpley Dallas Mavericks	.07	.03	.01
☐ 68 Bill Wennington SP Dallas Mavericks	.15	.07	.01
☐ 69 Randy White Dallas Mavericks	.30	.15	.03
☐ 70 Herb Williams Dallas Mavericks	.04	.02	.00
☐ 71 Michael Adams Denver Nuggets	.07	.03	.01
☐ 72 Joe Barry Carroll SP Denver Nuggets	.10	.05	.01
☐ 73 Walter Davis Denver Nuggets	.07	.03	.01
☐ 74 Alex English SP Denver Nuggets	.25	.12	.02
☐ 75 Bill Hanzlik Denver Nuggets	.04	.02	.00
☐ 76 Tim Kempton SP Denver Nuggets	.12	.06	.01
☐ 77 Jerome Lane Denver Nuggets	.07	.03	.01
☐ 78 Lafayette Lever SP Denver Nuggets	.15	.07	.01
☐ 79 Todd Lichti Denver Nuggets	.20	.10	.02
☐ 80 Blair Rasmussen Denver Nuggets	.04	.02	.00
☐ 81 Dan Schayes SP Denver Nuggets	.12	.06	.01
☐ 82 Mark Aguirre Detroit Pistons	.10	.05	.01
☐ 83 William Bedford Detroit Pistons	.20	.10	.02

84 Joe Dumars	.18	.09	.01
Detroit Pistons			
85 James Edwards	.04	.02	.00
Detroit Pistons			
86 David Greenwood SP	.10	.05	.01
Detroit Pistons			
87 Scott Hastings	.04	.02	.00
Detroit Pistons			
88 Gerald Henderson SP	.10	.05	.01
Detroit Pistons			
89 Vinnie Johnson	.10	.05	.01
Detroit Pistons			
90 Bill Laimbeer	.12	.06	.01
Detroit Pistons			
91A Dennis Rodman	.18	.09	.01
Detroit Pistons			
(Sky Box logo in upper right corner)			
91B Dennis Rodman	.18	.09	.01
Detroit Pistons			
(Sky Box logo in upper left corner)			
92 John Salley	.10	.05	.01
Detroit Pistons			
93 Isiah Thomas	.30	.15	.03
Detroit Pistons			
94 Manute Bol SP	.12	.06	.01
Golden State Warriors			
95 Tim Hardaway	2.75	1.35	.27
Golden State Warriors			
96 Rod Higgins	.04	.02	.00
Golden State Warriors			
97 Sarunas Marciulionis	.35	.17	.03
Golden State Warriors			
98 Chris Mullin	.25	.12	.02
Golden State Warriors			
99 Jim Petersen	.04	.02	.00
Golden State Warriors			
100 Mitch Richmond	.35	.17	.03
Golden State Warriors			
101 Mike Smrek	.10	.05	.01
Golden State Warriors			
102 Terry Teagle SP	.10	.05	.01
Golden State Warriors			
103 Tom Tolbert	.10	.05	.01
Golden State Warriors			
104 Kelvin Upshaw SP	.15	.07	.01
Golden State Warriors			
105 Anthony Bowie SP	.30	.15	.03
Houston Rockets			
106 Adrian Caldwell	.10	.05	.01
Houston Rockets			
107 Eric Floyd	.07	.03	.01
Houston Rockets			
108 Buck Johnson	.07	.03	.01
Houston Rockets			
109 Vernon Maxwell	.17	.08	.01
Houston Rockets			
110 Akeem Olajuwon	.30	.15	.03
Houston Rockets			
111 Larry Smith	.04	.02	.00
Houston Rockets			
112A Otis Thorpe ERR	1.25	.60	.12
Houston Rockets			
(Front photo actually Mitchell Wiggins)			
112B Otis Thorpe COR	.12	.06	.01
Houston Rockets			
113A M. Wiggins ERR SP	1.25	.60	.12
Houston Rockets			
(Front photo actually Otis Thorpe)			
113B M. Wiggins COR SP	.25	.12	.02
Houston Rockets			
114 Vern Fleming	.04	.02	.00
Indiana Pacers			
115 Rickey Green SP	.10	.05	.01
Indiana Pacers			
116 George McCloud	.18	.09	.01
Indiana Pacers			
117 Reggie Miller	.30	.15	.03
Indiana Pacers			
118A Dyron Nix ERR SP	5.00	2.50	.50
Indiana Pacers			
(Back photo actually Wayman Tisdale)			
118B Dyron Nix COR SP	.30	.15	.03
Indiana Pacers			
119 Chuck Person	.15	.07	.01
Indiana Pacers			
120 Mike Sanders	.04	.02	.00
Indiana Pacers			
121 Detlef Schrempf	.12	.06	.01
Indiana Pacers			

122 Rik Smits	.10	.05	.01
Indiana Pacers			
123 LaSalle Thompson	.04	.02	.00
Indiana Pacers			
124 Benoit Benjamin	.07	.03	.01
Los Angeles Clippers			
125 Winston Garland	.04	.02	.00
Los Angeles Clippers			
126 Tom Garrick	.07	.03	.01
Los Angeles Clippers			
127 Gary Grant	.07	.03	.01
Los Angeles Clippers			
128 Ron Harper	.15	.07	.01
Los Angeles Clippers			
129 Danny Manning	.17	.08	.01
Los Angeles Clippers			
130 Jeff Martin	.15	.07	.01
Los Angeles Clippers			
131 Ken Norman	.17	.08	.01
Los Angeles Clippers			
132 Charles Smith	.18	.09	.01
Los Angeles Clippers			
133 Joe Wolf SP	.10	.05	.01
Los Angeles Clippers			
134 Michael Cooper SP	.15	.07	.01
Los Angeles Lakers			
135 Vlade Divac	1.00	.50	.10
Los Angeles Lakers			
136 Larry Drew	.04	.02	.00
Los Angeles Lakers			
137 A.C. Green	.10	.05	.01
Los Angeles Lakers			
138 Magic Johnson	.45	.22	.04
Los Angeles Lakers			
139 Mark McNamara SP	.10	.05	.01
Los Angeles Lakers			
140 Byron Scott	.12	.06	.01
Los Angeles Lakers			
141 Mychal Thompson	.07	.03	.01
Los Angeles Lakers			
142 Orlando Woolridge SP	.12	.06	.01
Los Angeles Lakers			
143 James Worthy	.20	.10	.02
Los Angeles Lakers			
144 Terry Davis	.10	.05	.01
Miami Heat			
145 Sherman Douglas	.60	.30	.06
Miami Heat			
146 Kevin Edwards	.07	.03	.01
Miami Heat			
147 Tellis Frank SP	.17	.08	.01
Miami Heat			
148 Scott Haffner SP	.17	.08	.01
Miami Heat			
149 Grant Long	.10	.05	.01
Miami Heat			
150 Glen Rice	.60	.30	.06
Miami Heat			
151 Rony Seikaly	.20	.10	.02
Miami Heat			
152 Rory Sparrow SP	.12	.06	.01
Miami Heat			
153 Jon Sundvold	.04	.02	.00
Miami Heat			
154 Billy Thompson	.07	.03	.01
Miami Heat			
155 Greg Anderson	.04	.02	.00
Milwaukee Bucks			
156 Ben Coleman SP	.20	.10	.02
Milwaukee Bucks			
157 Jeff Grayer	.17	.08	.01
Milwaukee Bucks			
158 Jay Humphries	.04	.02	.00
Milwaukee Bucks			
159 Frank Kornet	.10	.05	.01
Milwaukee Bucks			
160 Larry Krystkowiak	.04	.02	.00
Milwaukee Bucks			
161 Brad Lohaus	.07	.03	.01
Milwaukee Bucks			
162 Ricky Pierce	.07	.03	.01
Milwaukee Bucks			
163 Paul Pressey SP	.12	.06	.01
Milwaukee Bucks			
164 Fred Roberts	.07	.03	.01
Milwaukee Bucks			
165 Alvin Robertson	.07	.03	.01
Milwaukee Bucks			
166 Jack Sikma	.07	.03	.01
Milwaukee Bucks			
167 Randy Breuer	.04	.02	.00
Minnesota Timberwolves			
168 Tony Campbell	.12	.06	.01
Minnesota Timberwolves			

169 Tyrone Corbin	.10	.05	.01
Minnesota Timberwolves			
170 Sidney Lowe SP	.10	.05	.01
Minnesota Timberwolves			
171 Sam Mitchell	.20	.10	.02
Minnesota Timberwolves			
172 Tod Murphy	.07	.03	.01
Minnesota Timberwolves			
173 Pooh Richardson	.80	.40	.08
Minnesota Timberwolves			
174 Donald Royal SP	.17	.08	.01
Minnesota Timberwolves			
175 Brad Sellers SP	.10	.05	.01
Minnesota Timberwolves			
176 Mookie Blaylock	.25	.12	.02
New Jersey Nets			
177 Sam Bowie	.07	.03	.01
New Jersey Nets			
178 Lester Conner	.04	.02	.00
New Jersey Nets			
179 Derrick Gervin	.15	.07	.01
New Jersey Nets			
180 Jack Haley	.10	.05	.01
New Jersey Nets			
181 Roy Hinson	.04	.02	.00
New Jersey Nets			
182 Dennis Hopson SP	.15	.07	.01
New Jersey Nets			
183 Chris Morris	.15	.07	.01
New Jersey Nets			
184 Pete Myers SP	.15	.07	.01
New Jersey Nets			
185 Purvis Short SP	.10	.05	.01
New Jersey Nets			
186 Maurice Cheeks	.10	.05	.01
New York Knicks			
187 Patrick Ewing	.45	.22	.04
New York Knicks			
188 Stuart Gray	.04	.02	.00
New York Knicks			
189 Mark Jackson	.10	.05	.01
New York Knicks			
190 Johnny Newman SP	.25	.12	.02
New York Knicks			
191 Charles Oakley	.10	.05	.01
New York Knicks			
192 Brian Quinnett	.15	.07	.01
New York Knicks			
193 Trent Tucker	.04	.02	.00
New York Knicks			
194 Kiki Vandeweghe	.07	.03	.01
New York Knicks			
195 Kenny Walker	.07	.03	.01
New York Knicks			
196 Eddie Lee Wilkins	.04	.02	.00
New York Knicks			
197 Gerald Wilkins	.07	.03	.01
New York Knicks			
198 Mark Acres	.07	.03	.01
Orlando Magic			
199 Nick Anderson	.60	.30	.06
Orlando Magic			
200 Michael Ansley	.15	.07	.01
Orlando Magic			
201 Terry Catledge	.04	.02	.00
Orlando Magic			
202 Dave Corzine SP	.10	.05	.01
Orlando Magic			
203 Sidney Green SP	.10	.05	.01
Orlando Magic			
204 Jerry Reynolds	.07	.03	.01
Orlando Magic			
205 Scott Skiles	.15	.07	.01
Orlando Magic			
206 Otis Smith	.07	.03	.01
Orlando Magic			
207 Reggie Theus SP	.12	.06	.01
Orlando Magic			
208 Jeff Turner	.04	.02	.00
Orlando Magic			
209 Sam Vincent	.07	.03	.01
Orlando Magic			
210 Ron Anderson	.07	.03	.01
Philadelphia 76ers			
211 Charles Barkley	.30	.15	.03
Philadelphia 76ers			
212 Scott Brooks SP	.10	.05	.01
Philadelphia 76ers			
213 Lanard Copeland SP	.15	.07	.01
Philadelphia 76ers			
214 Johnny Dawkins	.07	.03	.01
Philadelphia 76ers			
215 Mike Gminski	.07	.03	.01
Philadelphia 76ers			

216 Hersey Hawkins	.20	.10	.02
Philadelphia 76ers			
217 Rick Mahorn	.07	.03	.01
Philadelphia 76ers			
218 Derek Smith SP	.12	.06	.01
Philadelphia 76ers			
219 Bob Thornton	.10	.05	.01
Philadelphia 76ers			
220 Tom Chambers	.18	.09	.01
Phoenix Suns			
221 Greg Grant SP	.17	.08	.01
Phoenix Suns			
222 Jeff Hornacek	.12	.06	.01
Phoenix Suns			
223 Eddie Johnson	.07	.03	.01
Phoenix Suns			
224A Kevin Johnson	.50	.25	.05
Phoenix Suns			
(Sky Box logo in upper right corner)			
224B Kevin Johnson	.50	.25	.05
Phoenix Suns			
(Sky Box logo in upper left corner)			
225 Andrew Lang	.15	.07	.01
Phoenix Suns			
226 Dan Majerle	.20	.10	.02
Phoenix Suns			
227 Mike McGee SP	.10	.05	.01
Phoenix Suns			
228 Tim Perry	.07	.03	.01
Phoenix Suns			
229 Kurt Rambis	.07	.03	.01
Phoenix Suns			
230 Mark West	.04	.02	.00
Phoenix Suns			
231 Mark Bryant	.07	.03	.01
Portland Trail Blazers			
232 Wayne Cooper	.04	.02	.00
Portland Trail Blazers			
233 Clyde Drexler	.30	.15	.03
Portland Trail Blazers			
234 Kevin Duckworth	.07	.03	.01
Portland Trail Blazers			
235 Byron Irvin SP	.30	.15	.03
Portland Trail Blazers			
236 Jerome Kersey	.18	.09	.01
Portland Trail Blazers			
237 Drazen Petrovic	.30	.15	.03
Portland Trail Blazers			
238 Terry Porter	.20	.10	.02
Portland Trail Blazers			
239 Cliff Robinson	.60	.30	.06
Portland Trail Blazers			
240 Buck Williams	.12	.06	.01
Portland Trail Blazers			
241 Danny Young	.04	.02	.00
Portland Trail Blazers			
242 Danny Ainge SP	.17	.08	.01
Sacramento Kings			
243 Randy Allen SP	.17	.08	.01
Sacramento Kings			
244A Antoine Carr SP	.17	.08	.01
Sacramento Kings			
(Wearing Atlanta jersey on back)			
244B Antoine Carr	.10	.05	.01
Sacramento Kings			
(Wearing Sacramento jersey on back)			
245 Vinny Del Negro SP	.15	.07	.01
Sacramento Kings			
246 Pervis Ellison	.40	.20	.04
Sacramento Kings			
247 Greg Kite SP	.10	.05	.01
Sacramento Kings			
248 Rodney McCray SP	.12	.06	.01
Sacramento Kings			
249 Harold Pressley SP	.12	.06	.01
Sacramento Kings			
250 Ralph Sampson	.07	.03	.01
Sacramento Kings			
251 Wayman Tisdale	.12	.06	.01
Sacramento Kings			
252 Willie Anderson	.20	.10	.02
San Antonio Spurs			
253 Uwe Blab SP	.15	.07	.01
San Antonio Spurs			
254 Frank Brickowski SP	.12	.06	.01
San Antonio Spurs			
255 Terry Cummings	.15	.07	.01
San Antonio Spurs			
256 Sean Elliott	.80	.40	.08
San Antonio Spurs			

☐ 257	Caldwell Jones SP	.12	.06	.01
	San Antonio Spurs			
☐ 258	Johnny Moore SP	.10	.05	.01
	San Antonio Spurs			
☐ 259	Zarko Paspalj SP	.17	.08	.01
	San Antonio Spurs			
☐ 260	David Robinson	3.50	1.75	.35
	San Antonio Spurs			
☐ 261	Rod Strickland	.15	.07	.01
	San Antonio Spurs			
☐ 262	David Wingate SP	.10	.05	.01
	San Antonio Spurs			
☐ 263	Dana Barros	.25	.12	.02
	Seattle Supersonics			
☐ 264	Michael Cage	.04	.02	.00
	Seattle Supersonics			
☐ 265	Quintin Dailey	.04	.02	.00
	Seattle Supersonics			
☐ 266	Dale Ellis	.10	.05	.01
	Seattle Supersonics			
☐ 267	Steve Johnson SP	.10	.05	.01
	Seattle Supersonics			
☐ 268	Shawn Kemp	2.50	1.25	.25
	Seattle Supersonics			
☐ 269	Xavier McDaniel	.12	.06	.01
	Seattle Supersonics			
☐ 270	Derrick McKey	.07	.03	.01
	Seattle Supersonics			
☐ 271A	Nate McMillan ERR SP	.15	.07	.01
	Seattle Supersonics			
	(Back photo actually			
	Olden Polynice;			
	first series)			
☐ 271B	Nate McMillan COR	.10	.05	.01
	Seattle Supersonics			
	(second series)			
☐ 272	Olden Polynice	.12	.06	.01
	Seattle Supersonics			
☐ 273	Sedale Threatt	.04	.02	.00
	Seattle Supersonics			
☐ 274	Thurl Bailey	.07	.03	.01
	Utah Jazz			
☐ 275	Mike Brown	.10	.05	.01
	Utah Jazz			
☐ 276	Mark Eaton	.07	.03	.01
	Utah Jazz			
☐ 277	Theodore Edwards	.25	.12	.02
	Utah Jazz			
☐ 278	Darrell Griffith	.07	.03	.01
	Utah Jazz			
☐ 279	Bobby Hansen SP	.10	.05	.01
	Utah Jazz			
☐ 280	Eric Johnson	.15	.07	.01
	Utah Jazz			
☐ 281	Eric Leckner SP	.15	.07	.01
	Utah Jazz			
☐ 282	Karl Malone	.30	.15	.03
	Utah Jazz			
☐ 283	Delaney Rudd	.07	.03	.01
	Utah Jazz			
☐ 284	John Stockton	.25	.12	.02
	Utah Jazz			
☐ 285	Mark Alarie	.04	.02	.00
	Washington Bullets			
☐ 286	Steve Colter SP	.10	.05	.01
	Washington Bullets			
☐ 287	Ledell Eackles SP	.15	.07	.01
	Washington Bullets			
☐ 288	Harvey Grant	.17	.08	.01
	Washington Bullets			
☐ 289	Tom Hammonds	.25	.12	.02
	Washington Bullets			
☐ 290	Charles Jones	.04	.02	.00
	Washington Bullets			
☐ 291	Bernard King	.18	.09	.01
	Washington Bullets			
☐ 292	Jeff Malone SP	.17	.08	.01
	Washington Bullets			
☐ 293	Darrell Walker	.04	.02	.00
	Washington Bullets			
☐ 294	John Williams	.04	.02	.00
	Washington Bullets			
☐ 295	Checklist 1 SP	.10	.01	.00
☐ 296	Checklist 2 SP	.10	.01	.00
☐ 297	Checklist 3 SP	.10	.01	.00
☐ 298	Checklist 4 SP	.10	.01	.00
☐ 299	Checklist 5 SP	.10	.01	.00
☐ 300	Danny Ferry SP	1.00	.50	.10
	Cleveland Cavaliers			

1991 SkyBox II

This 123-card set measures the standard size (2 1/2" by 3 1/2") and has the same design as the regular issue 1990-91 Sky Box. The backs of the coaches' cards each feature a quote. The cards are numbered on the back in continuation of the first series and checklisted below as follows: coaches (301-327), team checklists (328-354), lottery picks (355-365), updates (366-420), and card checklists (421-423). The key rookies in the set are the eleven lottery picks (355-365) led by Derrick Coleman, Gary Payton, Dennis Scott, and Lionel Simmons.

		MINT	EXC	G-VG
COMPLETE SET (123)		13.50	6.00	1.00
COMMON PLAYER (301-423)		.04	.02	.00
☐ 301	Bob Weiss CO	.04	.02	.00
	Atlanta Hawks			
☐ 302	Chris Ford CO	.04	.02	.00
	Boston Celtics			
☐ 303	Gene Littles CO	.04	.02	.00
	Charlotte Hornets			
☐ 304	Phil Jackson CO	.04	.02	.00
	Chicago Bulls			
☐ 305	Lenny Wilkens CO	.07	.03	.01
	Cleveland Cavaliers			
☐ 306	Richie Abudato CO	.04	.02	.00
	Dallas Mavericks			
☐ 307	Paul Westhead CO	.04	.02	.00
	Denver Nuggets			
☐ 308	Chuck Daly CO	.04	.02	.00
	Detroit Pistons			
☐ 309	Don Nelson CO	.04	.02	.00
	Golden State Warriors			
☐ 310	Don Chaney CO	.04	.02	.00
	Houston Rockets			
☐ 311	Dick Versace CO	.04	.02	.00
	Indiana Pacers			
☐ 312	Mike Schuler CO	.04	.02	.00
	Los Angeles Clippers			
☐ 313	Mike Dunleavy CO	.04	.02	.00
	Los Angeles Lakers			
☐ 314	Ron Rothstein CO	.04	.02	.00
	Miami Heat			
☐ 315	Del Harris CO	.04	.02	.00
	Milwaukee Bucks			
☐ 316	Bill Musselman CO	.04	.02	.00
	Minnesota Timberwolves			
☐ 317	Bill Fitch CO	.04	.02	.00
	Houston Rockets			
☐ 318	Stu Jackson CO	.04	.02	.00
	New York Knicks			
☐ 319	Matt Guokas CO	.04	.02	.00
	Orlando Magic			
☐ 320	Jim Lynam CO	.04	.02	.00
	Philadelphia 76ers			
☐ 321	Cotton Fitzsimmons CO	.04	.02	.00
	Phoenix Suns			
☐ 322	Rick Adelman CO	.04	.02	.00
	Portland Trail Blazers			
☐ 323	Dick Motta CO	.04	.02	.00
	Sacramento Kings			
☐ 324	Larry Brown CO	.04	.02	.00
	San Antonio Spurs			
☐ 325	K.C. Jones CO	.04	.02	.00
	Seattle Supersonics			
☐ 326	Jerry Sloan CO	.04	.02	.00
	Utah Jazz			

☑ 327	Wes Unseld CO	.07	.03	.01
	Washington Bullets			
☐ 328	Atlanta Hawks TC	.04	.02	.00
☐ 329	Boston Celtics TC	.04	.02	.00
☐ 330	Charlotte Hornets TC	.04	.02	.00
☐ 331	Chicago Bulls TC	.04	.02	.00
☐ 332	Cleveland Cavaliers TC	.04	.02	.00
☐ 333	Dallas Mavericks TC	.04	.02	.00
☒ 334	Denver Nuggets TC	.04	.02	.00
☐ 335	Detroit Pistons TC	.04	.02	.00
☐ 336	Golden State Warriors TC	.04	.02	.00
☐ 337	Houston Rockets TC	.04	.02	.00
☐ 338	Indiana Pacers TC	.04	.02	.00
☐ 339	Los Angeles Clippers TC	.04	.02	.00
☐ 340	Los Angeles Lakers TC	.04	.02	.00
☑ 341	Miami Heat TC	.04	.02	.00
☐ 342	Milwaukee Bucks TC	.04	.02	.00
☐ 343	Minnesota Timberwolves TC	.04	.02	.00
☐ 344	New Jersey Nets TC	.04	.02	.00
☐ 345	New York Knicks TC	.04	.02	.00
☐ 346	Orlando Magic TC	.04	.02	.00
☐ 347	Philadelphia 76ers TC	.04	.02	.00
☐ 348	Phoenix Suns TC	.04	.02	.00
☐ 349	Portland Trail Blazers TC	.04	.02	.00
☐ 350	Sacramento Kings TC	.04	.02	.00
☑ 351	San Antonio Spurs TC	.04	.02	.00
☐ 352	Seattle SuperSonics TC	.04	.02	.00
☐ 353	Utah Jazz TC	.04	.02	.00
☐ 354	Washington Bullets TC	.04	.02	.00
☐ 355	Rumeal Robinson LP	.20	.10	.02
	Atlanta Hawks			
☐ 356	Kendall Gill LP	1.00	.50	.10
	Charlotte Hornets			
☐ 357	Chris Jackson LP	.90	.45	.09
	Denver Nuggets			
☐ 358	Tyrone Hill LP	.30	.15	.03
	Golden State Warriors			
☐ 359	Bo Kimble LP	.60	.30	.06
	Los Angeles Clippers			
☐ 360	Willie Burton LP	.60	.30	.06
	Miami Heat			
☐ 361	Felton Spencer LP	.50	.25	.05
	Minnesota Timberwolves			
☐ 362	Derrick Coleman LP	5.50	2.75	.55
	New Jersey Nets			
☑ 363	Dennis Scott LP	1.00	.50	.10
	Orlando Magic			
☐ 364	Lionel Simmons LP	2.00	1.00	.20
	Sacramento Kings			
☐ 365	Gary Payton LP	1.00	.50	.10
	Seattle Supersonics			
☑ 366	Tim McCormick	.04	.02	.00
	Atlanta Hawks			
☑ 367	Sidney Moncrief	.07	.03	.01
	Atlanta Hawks			
☑ 368	Kenny Gattison	.17	.08	.01
	Charlotte Hornets			
☐ 369	Randolph Keys	.10	.05	.01
	Charlotte Hornets			
☐ 370	Johnny Newman	.17	.08	.01
	Charlotte Hornets			
☐ 371	Dennis Hopson	.07	.03	.01
	Chicago Bulls			
☐ 372	Cliff Levingston	.04	.02	.00
	Chicago Bulls			
☐ 373	Derrick Chievous	.07	.03	.01
	Cleveland Cavaliers			
☐ 374	Danny Ferry	.35	.17	.03
	Cleveland Cavaliers			
☐ 375	Alex English	.15	.07	.01
	Dallas Mavericks			
☐ 376	Lafayette Lever	.10	.05	.01
	Dallas Mavericks			
☐ 377	Rodney McCray	.07	.03	.01
	Dallas Mavericks			
☐ 378	T.R. Dunn	.04	.02	.00
	Denver Nuggets			
☑ 379	Corey Gaines	.10	.05	.01
	Denver Nuggets			
☐ 380	Avery Johnson	.10	.05	.01
	San Antonio Spurs			
☐ 381	Joe Wolf	.07	.03	.01
	Denver Nuggets			
☐ 382	Orlando Woolridge	.07	.03	.01
	Denver Nuggets			
☐ 383	Wayne Rollins	.04	.02	.00
	Detroit Pistons			
☐ 384	Steve Johnson	.04	.02	.00
	Seattle Supersonics			
☐ 385	Kenny Smith	.07	.03	.01
	Houston Rockets			
☐ 386	Mike Woodson	.04	.02	.00
	Cleveland Cavaliers			
☑ 387	Greg Dreiling	.12	.06	.01
	Indiana Pacers			
☐ 388	Michael Williams	.17	.08	.01
	Indiana Pacers			
☐ 389	Randy Wittman	.04	.02	.00
	Indiana Pacers			
☐ 390	Ken Bannister	.04	.02	.00
	Los Angeles Clippers			
☐ 391	Sam Perkins	.17	.08	.01
	Los Angeles Lakers			
☐ 392	Terry Teagle	.04	.02	.00
	Los Angeles Lakers			
☐ 393	Milt Wagner	.10	.05	.01
	Miami Heat			
☐ 394	Frank Brickowski	.04	.02	.00
	Milwaukee Bucks			
☐ 395	Dan Schayes	.07	.03	.01
	Milwaukee Bucks			
☐ 396	Scott Brooks	.04	.02	.00
	Minnesota Timberwolves			
☑ 397	Doug West	.15	.07	.01
	Minnesota Timberwolves			
☐ 398	Chris Dudley	.12	.06	.01
	New Jersey Nets			
☐ 399	Reggie Theus	.10	.05	.01
	New Jersey Nets			
☐ 400	Greg Grant	.04	.02	.00
	Chicago Bulls			
☐ 401	Greg Kite	.04	.02	.00
	Orlando Magic			
☐ 402	Mark McNamara	.04	.02	.00
	Orlando Magic			
☐ 403	Manute Bol	.07	.03	.01
	Philadelphia 76ers			
☐ 404	Rickey Green	.04	.02	.00
	Philadelphia 76ers			
☑ 405	Kenny Battle	.25	.12	.02
	Denver Nuggets			
☐ 406	Ed Nealy	.04	.02	.00
	Phoenix Suns			
☐ 407	Danny Ainge	.17	.08	.01
	Portland Trail Blazers			
☐ 408	Steve Colter	.04	.02	.00
	Sacramento Kings			
☐ 409	Bobby Hansen	.04	.02	.00
	Sacramento Kings			
☐ 410	Eric Leckner	.07	.03	.01
	Charlotte Hornets			
☐ 411	Rory Sparrow	.04	.02	.00
	Sacramento Kings			
☑ 412	Bill Wennington	.04	.02	.00
	Sacramento Kings			
☐ 413	Sidney Green	.04	.02	.00
	San Antonio Spurs			
☐ 414	David Greenwood	.04	.02	.00
	San Antonio Spurs			
☐ 415	Paul Pressey	.04	.02	.00
	San Antonio Spurs			
☐ 416	Reggie Williams	.07	.03	.01
	San Antonio Spurs			
☐ 417	Dave Corzine	.04	.02	.00
	Orlando Magic			
☐ 418	Jeff Malone	.17	.08	.01
	Utah Jazz			
☑ 419	Pervis Ellison	.17	.08	.01
	Washington Bullets			
☐ 420	Byron Irvin	.12	.06	.01
	Washington Bullets			
☐ 421	Checklist 1	.07	.01	.00
☐ 422	Checklist 2	.07	.01	.00
☐ 423	Checklist 3	.07	.01	.00

1979-80 Spurs Police

This set contains 15 cards measuring 2 5/8" by 4 1/8" featuring the San Antonio Spurs. Backs contain safety tips, "Tips from the Spurs." The set was also sponsored by Handy Dan and were put out by Express News and Handy Dan in conjunction with the Police Department.

	MINT	EXC	G-VG
COMPLETE SET (15)	4.00	2.00	.40
COMMON PLAYER	.30	.15	.03
☐ 1 Mike Evans	.30	.15	.03

#44 George Gervin
6'-7" Guard
185 lbs Eastern Michigan '72

☐ 2	Billy Paultz	.40	.20	.04
☐ 12	Mike Gale	.30	.15	.03
☐ 13	James Silas	.40	.20	.04
☐ 21	Irv Kiffin	.30	.15	.03
☐ 30	Paul Griffin	.30	.15	.03
☐ 31	Kevin Restani	.30	.15	.03
☐ 35	Larry Kenon	.40	.20	.04
☐ 44	George Gervin	1.00	.50	.10
☐ 53	Mark Olberding	.30	.15	.03
☐ 54	Wiley Peck	.30	.15	.03
☐ xx	Bob Bass	.30	.15	.03
☐ xx	George Karl	.40	.20	.04
☐ xx	Bernie LaReau	.30	.15	.03
☐ xx	Doug Moe	.50	.25	.05

1988-89 Spurs Police/Diamond Shamrock

This eight-card set of San Antonio Spurs is one of two that were sponsored by Diamond Shamrock, a regional oil retailer and convenience store chain headquartered in San Antonio. One set had a tear-off tab, and one card was given out each week at San Antonio Diamond Shamrock CornerStore locations with each 3.00 purchase or purchase of eight gallons of gas. It is reported that 100,000 sets were printed. This promotion included weekly drawings for pairs of tickets and a final drawing to determine the winners of the Grand Prize and other prizes. The other set was donated to the San Antonio Police Department and distributed to kids in the San Antonio area by patrolmen on the night shift; 50,000 sets were produced. The cards measure approximately 2 1/2" by 3 9/16" and except for the tear-off tab, the two sets are identical. The front features a color action player photo with a white border (only the Robinson card has a posed shot). The card front has a distinctive black background with a white pinstripe pattern. Three color bands (aqua, red, and orange) overlay the top of the picture, with the team logo in the middle. The player's name is given in the aqua band below the picture. The back has biographical information and a player

safety tip in a gray box. The San Antonio Police and sponsor logos appear at the bottom. The cards are unnumbered and checklisted below in alphabetical order, with jersey number after the player's name. The set may have received additional multiple printings in order to capitalize on the popularity of David Robinson.

	MINT	EXC	G-VG
COMPLETE SET (8)	12.00	6.00	1.20
COMMON PLAYER (1-8)	.50	.25	.05
☐ 1 Greg Anderson 33	.50	.25	.05
☐ 2 Willie Anderson 40	1.50	.75	.15
☐ 3 Frank Brickowski 43	.75	.35	.07
☐ 4 Larry Brown CO	.75	.35	.07
☐ 5 Dallas Comegys 22	.75	.35	.07
☐ 6 Johnny Dawkins 24	.75	.35	.07
☐ 7 Alvin Robertson 21	.75	.35	.07
☐ 8 David Robinson 50	7.50	3.75	.75

1983-84 Star NBA

This set of 276 cards was issued in four series during the first six months of 1984. The set features players by team throughout the NBA. Several teams in the first series (1-100) are difficult to obtain due to extensive miscuts (all of which were destroyed according to the company) in the original production process for those teams. Cards measure 2 1/2" by 3 1/2" and have a colored border around the fronts of the cards according to the team with corresponding color printing on the backs. Cards are numbered according to team order, e.g., Philadelphia 76ers (1-12), Los Angeles Lakers (13-25), Boston Celtics (26-37), Milwaukee Bucks (38-48), Dallas Mavericks (49-60), New York Knicks (61-72), Houston Rockets (73-84), Detroit Pistons (85-96), Portland Trail Blazers (97-108), Phoenix Suns (109-120), San Diego Clippers (121-132), Utah Jazz (133-144), New Jersey Nets (145-156), Indiana Pacers (157-168), Chicago Bulls (169-180), Denver Nuggets (181-192), Seattle Supersonics (193-203), Washington Bullets (204-215), Kansas City Kings (216-227), Cleveland Cavaliers (228-240), San Antonio Spurs (241-251), Golden State Warriors (252-263), and Atlanta Hawks (264-275). The key extended rookie cards in this set are Mark Aguirre, Rolando Blackman, Tom Chambers, Clyde Drexler, Dale Ellis, Derek Harper, Isiah Thomas, Dominique Wilkins, and James Worthy. A promotional card of Sidney Moncrief was produced in limited quantities, but it was numbered 39 rather than 38 as it was in the regular set.

	MINT	EXC	G-VG
COMPLETE SET (276)	2250.00	1000.00	225.00
COMMON 76ER (1-12)	5.00	2.50	.50
COMMON LAKERS (13-25)	3.25	1.60	.32
COMMON CELTICS (26-37)	12.00	6.00	1.20
COMMON BUCKS (38-48)	3.25	1.60	.32
COMMON MAVS (49-60)	40.00	20.00	4.00
COMMON PLAYER (61-275)	1.50	.75	.15

#	Player			
☐ 1	Julius Erving	75.00	37.50	7.50
☐ 2	Maurice Cheeks	10.00	5.00	1.00
☐ 3	Franklin Edwards	5.00	2.50	.50
☐ 4	Marc Iavaroni	5.00	2.50	.50
☐ 5	Clemon Johnson	5.00	2.50	.50
☐ 6	Bobby Jones	7.50	3.75	.75
☐ 7	Moses Malone	24.00	12.00	2.40
☐ 8	Leo Rautins	5.00	2.50	.50
☐ 9	Clint Richardson	5.00	2.50	.50
☐ 10	Sedale Threatt	10.00	5.00	1.00
☐ 11	Andrew Toney	10.00	5.00	1.00
☐ 12	Sam Williams	5.00	2.50	.50
☐ 13	Magic Johnson	90.00	45.00	9.00
☐ 14	Kareem Abdul Jabbar	50.00	25.00	5.00
☐ 15	Michael Cooper	6.00	3.00	.60
☐ 16	Calvin Garrett	3.50	1.75	.35
☐ 17	Mitch Kupchak	3.50	1.75	.35
☐ 18	Bob McAdoo	6.00	3.00	.60
☐ 19	Mike McGee	5.00	2.50	.50
☐ 20	Swen Nater	3.50	1.75	.35
☐ 21	Kurt Rambis	12.00	6.00	1.20
☐ 22	Byron Scott	25.00	12.50	2.50
☐ 23	Larry Spriggs	3.50	1.75	.35
☐ 24	Jamaal Wilkes	5.00	2.50	.50
☐ 25	James Worthy	90.00	45.00	9.00
☐ 26	Larry Bird	120.00	60.00	12.00
☐ 27	Danny Ainge	45.00	22.50	4.50
☐ 28	Quinn Buckner	15.00	7.50	1.50
☐ 29	M.L. Carr	15.00	7.50	1.50
☐ 30	Carlos Clark	12.00	6.00	1.20
☐ 31	Gerald Henderson	15.00	7.50	1.50
☐ 32	Dennis Johnson	15.00	7.50	1.50
☐ 33	Cedric Maxwell	15.00	7.50	1.50
☐ 34	Kevin McHale	50.00	25.00	5.00
☐ 35	Robert Parish	45.00	22.50	4.50
☐ 36	Scott Wedman	15.00	7.50	1.50
☐ 37	Greg Kite	15.00	7.50	1.50
☐ 38	Sidney Moncrief	12.00	6.00	1.20
☐ 39A	Sidney Moncrief	75.00	37.50	7.50
	(Promotional card)			
☐ 39B	Nate Archibald	7.50	3.75	.75
☐ 40	Randy Breuer	6.00	3.00	.60
☐ 41	Junior Bridgeman	4.50	2.25	.45
☐ 42	Harvey Catchings	3.50	1.75	.35
☐ 43	Kevin Grevey	3.50	1.75	.35
☐ 44	Marques Johnson	6.00	3.00	.60
☐ 45	Bob Lanier	7.50	3.75	.75
☐ 46	Alton Lister	7.50	3.75	.75
☐ 47	Paul Mokeski	5.00	2.50	.50
☐ 48	Paul Pressey	12.00	6.00	1.20
☐ 49	Mark Aguirre	100.00	50.00	10.00
☐ 50	Rolando Blackman	100.00	50.00	10.00
☐ 51	Pat Cummings	50.00	25.00	5.00
☐ 52	Brad Davis	50.00	25.00	5.00
☐ 53	Dale Ellis	90.00	45.00	9.00
☐ 54	Bill Garnett	40.00	20.00	4.00
☐ 55	Derek Harper	90.00	45.00	9.00
☐ 56	Kurt Nimphius	40.00	20.00	4.00
☐ 57	Jim Spanarkel	40.00	20.00	4.00
☐ 58	Elston Turner	40.00	20.00	4.00
☐ 59	Jay Vincent	50.00	25.00	5.00
☐ 60	Mark West	50.00	25.00	5.00
☐ 61	Bernard King	15.00	7.50	1.50
☐ 62	Bill Cartwright	4.50	2.25	.45
☐ 63	Len Elmore	2.25	1.10	.22
☐ 64	Eric Fernsten	1.50	.75	.15
☐ 65	Ernie Grunfeld	2.25	1.10	.22
☐ 66	Louis Orr	1.50	.75	.15
☐ 67	Leonard Robinson	2.25	1.10	.22
☐ 68	Rory Sparrow	3.50	1.75	.35
☐ 69	Trent Tucker	3.50	1.75	.35
☐ 70	Darrell Walker	3.50	1.75	.35
☐ 71	Marvin Webster	1.50	.75	.15
☐ 72	Ray Williams	1.50	.75	.15
☐ 73	Ralph Sampson	6.50	3.25	.65
☐ 74	James Bailey	1.50	.75	.15
☐ 75	Phil Ford	2.25	1.10	.22
☐ 76	Elvin Hayes	5.00	2.50	.50
☐ 77	Caldwell Jones	2.25	1.10	.22
☐ 78	Major Jones	1.50	.75	.15
☐ 79	Allen Leavell	1.50	.75	.15
☐ 80	Lewis Lloyd	1.50	.75	.15
☐ 81	Rodney McCray	5.00	2.50	.50
☐ 82	Robert Reid	1.50	.75	.15
☐ 83	Terry Teagle	6.50	3.25	.65
☐ 84	Wally Walker	1.50	.75	.15
☐ 85	Kelly Tripucka	5.00	2.50	.50
☐ 86	Kent Benson	2.25	1.10	.22
☐ 87	Earl Cureton	2.25	1.10	.22
☐ 88	Lionel Hollins	1.50	.75	.15
☐ 89	Vinnie Johnson	4.00	2.00	.40
☐ 90	Bill Laimbeer	7.00	3.50	.70
☐ 91	Cliff Levingston	6.50	3.25	.65
☐ 92	John Long	1.50	.75	.15
☐ 93	David Thirdkill	1.50	.75	.15
☐ 94	Isiah Thomas	135.00	65.00	13.50
☐ 95	Ray Tolbert	2.25	1.10	.22
☐ 96	Terry Tyler	1.50	.75	.15
☐ 97	Jim Paxson	2.25	1.10	.22
☐ 98	Kenny Carr	1.50	.75	.15
☐ 99	Wayne Cooper	1.50	.75	.15
☐ 100	Clyde Drexler	150.00	75.00	15.00
☐ 101	Jeff Lamp	2.25	1.10	.22
☐ 102	Lafayette Lever	12.00	6.00	1.20
☐ 103	Calvin Natt	2.25	1.10	.22
☐ 104	Audie Norris	1.50	.75	.15
☐ 105	Tom Piotrowski	1.50	.75	.15
☐ 106	Mychal Thompson	2.50	1.25	.25
☐ 107	Darnell Valentine	2.25	1.10	.22
☐ 108	Pete Verhoeven	1.50	.75	.15
☐ 109	Walter Davis	2.75	1.35	.27
☐ 110	Alvan Adams	2.25	1.10	.22
☐ 111	James Edwards	2.25	1.10	.22
☐ 112	Rod Foster	2.25	1.10	.22
☐ 113	Maurice Lucas	2.25	1.10	.22
☐ 114	Kyle Macy	2.25	1.10	.22
☐ 115	Larry Nance	15.00	7.50	1.50
☐ 116	Charles Pittman	1.50	.75	.15
☐ 117	Rick Robey	2.25	1.10	.22
☐ 118	Mike Sanders	2.25	1.10	.22
☐ 119	Alvin Scott	1.50	.75	.15
☐ 120	Paul Westphal	2.50	1.25	.25
☐ 121	Bill Walton	5.00	2.50	.50
☐ 122	Michael Brooks	1.50	.75	.15
☐ 123	Terry Cummings	27.00	13.50	2.70
☐ 124	James Donaldson	6.00	3.00	.60
☐ 125	Craig Hodges	7.00	3.50	.70
☐ 126	Greg Kelser	2.25	1.10	.22
☐ 127	Hank McDowell	1.50	.75	.15
☐ 128	Billy McKinney	2.25	1.10	.22
☐ 129	Norm Nixon	2.25	1.10	.22
☐ 130	Ricky Pierce	15.00	7.50	1.50
☐ 131	Derek Smith	4.00	2.00	.40
☐ 132	Jerome Whitehead	1.50	.75	.15
☐ 133	Adrian Dantley	4.00	2.00	.40
☐ 134	Mitch Anderson	1.50	.75	.15
☐ 135	Thurl Bailey	6.00	3.00	.60
☐ 136	Tom Boswell	1.50	.75	.15
☐ 137	John Drew	2.25	1.10	.22
☐ 138	Mark Eaton	7.00	3.50	.70
☐ 139	Jerry Eaves	1.50	.75	.15
☐ 140	Rickey Green	3.50	1.75	.35
☐ 141	Darrell Griffith	2.50	1.25	.25
☐ 142	Bobby Hansen	2.50	1.25	.25
☐ 143	Rich Kelley	1.50	.75	.15
☐ 144	Jeff Wilkins	1.50	.75	.15
☐ 145	Buck Williams	25.00	12.50	2.50
☐ 146	Otis Birdsong	2.25	1.10	.22
☐ 147	Darwin Cook	1.50	.75	.15
☐ 148	Darryl Dawkins	2.25	1.10	.22
☐ 149	Mike Gminski	2.25	1.10	.22
☐ 150	Reggie Johnson	1.50	.75	.15
☐ 151	Albert King	2.25	1.10	.22
☐ 152	Mike O'Koren	1.50	.75	.15
☐ 153	Kelvin Ransey	1.50	.75	.15
☐ 154	M.R. Richardson	2.25	1.10	.22
☐ 155	Clarence Walker	1.50	.75	.15
☐ 156	Bill Willoughby	1.50	.75	.15
☐ 157	Steve Stipanovich	2.50	1.25	.25
☐ 158	Butch Carter	1.50	.75	.15
☐ 159	Edwin Leroy Combs	1.50	.75	.15
☐ 160	George L. Johnson	1.50	.75	.15
☐ 161	Clark Kellogg	2.25	1.10	.22
☐ 162	Sidney Lowe	2.25	1.10	.22
☐ 163	Kevin McKenna	1.50	.75	.15
☐ 164	Jerry Sichting	2.25	1.10	.22
☐ 165	Brook Steppe	1.50	.75	.15
☐ 166	Jimmy Thomas	1.50	.75	.15
☐ 167	Granville Waiters	1.50	.75	.15
☐ 168	Herb Williams	6.00	3.00	.60
☐ 169	Dave Corzine	1.50	.75	.15
☐ 170	Wallace Bryant	1.50	.75	.15
☐ 171	Quintin Dailey	2.50	1.25	.25
☐ 172	Sidney Green	3.00	1.50	.30
☐ 173	David Greenwood	1.50	.75	.15
☐ 174	Rod Higgins	3.00	1.50	.30
☐ 175	Clarence Johnson	1.50	.75	.15
☐ 176	Ronnie Lester	1.50	.75	.15
☐ 177	Jawann Oldham	1.50	.75	.15
☐ 178	Ennis Whatley	1.50	.75	.15
☐ 179	Mitchell Wiggins	2.25	1.10	.22
☐ 180	Orlando Woolridge	15.00	7.50	1.50
☐ 181	Kiki Vandeweghe	10.00	5.00	1.00
☐ 182	Richard Anderson	2.25	1.10	.22
☐ 183	Howard Carter	1.50	.75	.15
☐ 184	T.R. Dunn	1.50	.75	.15
☐ 185	Keith Edmonson	1.50	.75	.15
☐ 186	Alex English	5.00	2.50	.50
☐ 187	Mike Evans	1.50	.75	.15
☐ 188	Bill Hanzlik	2.50	1.25	.25

☐	189 Dan Issel	2.75	1.35	.27
☐	190 Anthony Roberts	1.50	.75	.15
☐	191 Danny Schayes	7.00	3.50	.70
☐	192 Rob Williams	1.50	.75	.15
☐	193 Jack Sikma	3.00	1.50	.30
☐	194 Fred Brown	2.25	1.10	.22
☐	195 Tom Chambers	75.00	37.50	7.50
☐	196 Steve Hawes	1.50	.75	.15
☐	197 Steve Hayes	1.50	.75	.15
☐	198 Reggie King	1.50	.75	.15
☐	199 Scooter McCray	2.25	1.10	.22
☐	200 Jon Sundvold	2.25	1.10	.22
☐	201 Danny Vranes	2.25	1.10	.22
☐	202 Gus Williams	2.25	1.10	.22
☐	203 Al Wood	2.25	1.10	.22
☐	204 Jeff Ruland	2.50	1.25	.25
☐	205 Greg Ballard	1.50	.75	.15
☐	206 Charles Davis	1.50	.75	.15
☐	207 Darren Daye	2.25	1.10	.22
☐	208 Michael Gibson	1.50	.75	.15
☐	209 Frank Johnson	1.50	.75	.15
☐	210 Joe Kopicki	1.50	.75	.15
☐	211 Rick Mahorn	2.50	1.25	.25
☐	212 Jeff Malone	22.00	11.00	2.20
☐	213 Tom McMillen	2.25	1.10	.22
☐	214 Ricky Sobers	1.50	.75	.15
☐	215 Bryan Warrick	1.50	.75	.15
☐	216 Billy Knight	1.50	.75	.15
☐	217 Don Buse	1.50	.75	.15
☐	218 Larry Drew	2.50	1.25	.25
☐	219 Eddie Johnson	10.00	5.00	1.00
☐	220 Joe Meriweather	1.50	.75	.15
☐	221 Larry Micheaux	1.50	.75	.15
☐	222 Ed Nealy	2.25	1.10	.22
☐	223 Mark Olberding	1.50	.75	.15
☐	224 Dave Robisch	1.50	.75	.15
☐	225 Reggie Theus	2.50	1.25	.25
☐	226 LaSalle Thompson	5.00	2.50	.50
☐	227 Mike Woodson	2.25	1.10	.22
☐	228 World B. Free	2.25	1.10	.22
☐	229 John Bagley	2.25	1.10	.22
☐	230 Jeff Cook	1.50	.75	.15
☐	231 Geoff Crompton	1.50	.75	.15
☐	232 John Garris	1.50	.75	.15
☐	233 Stewart Granger	1.50	.75	.15
☐	234 Roy Hinson	3.50	1.75	.35
☐	235 Phil Hubbard	1.50	.75	.15
☐	236 Geoff Huston	1.50	.75	.15
☐	237 Ben Poquette	1.50	.75	.15
☐	238 Cliff Robinson	2.25	1.10	.22
☐	239 Lonnie Shelton	1.50	.75	.15
☐	240 Paul Thompson	1.50	.75	.15
☐	241 George Gervin	5.00	2.50	.50
☐	242 Gene Banks	1.50	.75	.15
☐	243 Ron Brewer	1.50	.75	.15
☐	244 Artis Gilmore	3.00	1.50	.30
☐	245 Edgar Jones	1.50	.75	.15
☐	246 John Lucas	2.25	1.10	.22
☐	247A Mike Mitchell ERR (Photo actually Mark McNamara)	6.50	3.25	.65
☐	247B Mike Mitchell COR	2.25	1.10	.22
☐	248A Mark McNamara ERR (Photo actually Mike Mitchell)	6.50	3.25	.65
☐	248B Mark McNamara COR	2.25	1.10	.22
☐	249 Johnny Moore	2.25	1.10	.22
☐	250 John Paxson	12.00	6.00	1.20
☐	251 Fred Roberts	7.00	3.50	.70
☐	252 Joe Barry Carroll	2.25	1.10	.22
☐	253 Mike Bratz	1.50	.75	.15
☐	254 Don Collins	1.50	.75	.15
☐	255 Lester Conner	1.50	.75	.15
☐	256 Chris Engler	1.50	.75	.15
☐	257 Sleepy Floyd	8.00	4.00	.80
☐	258 Wallace Johnson	1.50	.75	.15
☐	259 Pace Mannion	1.50	.75	.15
☐	260 Purvis Short	2.25	1.10	.22
☐	261 Larry Smith	2.25	1.10	.22
☐	262 Darren Tillis	1.50	.75	.15
☐	263 Dominique Wilkins	125.00	60.00	12.50
☐	264 Rickey Brown	1.50	.75	.15
☐	265 Johnny Davis	1.50	.75	.15
☐	266 Mike Glenn	1.50	.75	.15
☐	267 Scott Hastings	3.00	1.50	.30
☐	268 Eddie Johnson	1.50	.75	.15
☐	269 Mark Landsberger	1.50	.75	.15
☐	270 Billy Paultz	1.50	.75	.15
☐	271 Doc Rivers	10.00	5.00	1.00
☐	272 Tree Rollins	2.25	1.10	.22
☐	273 Dan Roundfield	2.25	1.10	.22
☐	274 Sly Williams	1.50	.75	.15
☐	275 Randy Wittman	3.00	1.50	.30

1984-85 Star NBA

This set of 288 cards was issued in three series during the first five months of 1985 by the Star Company. The set features players by team throughout the NBA. Cards measure 2 1/2" by 3 1/2" and have a colored border around the fronts of the cards according to the team with corresponding color printing on the backs. Card are organized numerically by team, i.e., Boston Celtics (1-12), Los Angeles Clippers (13-24), New York Knicks (25-37), Phoenix Suns ((38-51), Indiana Pacers (52-63), San Antonio Spurs (64-75), Atlanta Hawks (76-87), New Jersey Nets (88-100), Chicago Bulls (101-112), Seattle Supersonics (113-124), Milwaukee Bucks (125-136), Denver Nuggets (137-148), Golden State Warriors (149-160), Portland Trail Blazers (161-171), Los Angeles Lakers (172-184), Washington Bullets (185-194), Philadelphia 76ers (201-212), Cleveland Cavaliers (213-224), Utah Jazz (225-236), Houston Rockets (237-249), Dallas Mavericks (250-260), Detroit Pistons (261-269), and Sacramento Kings (270-280). The set also features a special subseries (195-200) honoring Gold Medal-winning players from the 1984 Olympic basketball competition as well as a subseries of NBA specials (281-288). The key extended rookies cards in this set are Charles Barkley, Michael Jordan, Akeem Olajuwon and John Stockton.

		MINT	EXC	G-VG
	COMPLETE SET (288)	2400.00	1200.00	250.00
	COMMON PLAYER (1-288)	1.50	.75	.15
☐	1 Larry Bird	60.00	30.00	6.00
☐	2 Danny Ainge	6.50	3.25	.65
☐	3 Quinn Buckner	2.25	1.10	.22
☐	4 Rick Carlisle	2.25	1.10	.22
☐	5 M.L. Carr	2.25	1.10	.22
☐	6 Dennis Johnson	2.50	1.25	.25
☐	7 Greg Kite	2.25	1.10	.22
☐	8 Cedric Maxwell	2.25	1.10	.22
☐	9 Kevin McHale	10.00	5.00	1.00
☐	10 Robert Parish	8.00	4.00	.80
☐	11 Scott Wedman	2.25	1.10	.22
☐	12 Larry Bird 1983-84 NBA MVP	25.00	10.00	2.00
☐	13 Marques Johnson	2.50	1.25	.25
☐	14 Junior Bridgeman	2.25	1.10	.22
☐	15 Michael Cage	4.00	2.00	.40
☐	16 Harvey Catchings	1.50	.75	.15
☐	17 James Donaldson	2.25	1.10	.22
☐	18 Lancaster Gordon	2.25	1.10	.22
☐	19 Jay Murphy	1.50	.75	.15
☐	20 Norm Nixon	2.25	1.10	.22
☐	21 Derek Smith	2.25	1.10	.22
☐	22 Bill Walton	4.00	2.00	.40
☐	23 Bryan Warrick	1.50	.75	.15
☐	24 Rory White	1.50	.75	.15
☐	25 Bernard King	8.00	4.00	.80
☐	26 James Bailey	1.50	.75	.15
☐	27 Ken Bannister	1.50	.75	.15
☐	28 Butch Carter	1.50	.75	.15
☐	29 Bill Cartwright	3.50	1.75	.35
☐	30 Pat Cummings	2.25	1.10	.22
☐	31 Ernie Grunfeld	2.25	1.10	.22
☐	32 Louis Orr	1.50	.75	.15
☐	33 Leonard Robinson	2.25	1.10	.22

#	Player			
☐ 34	Rory Sparrow	2.25	1.10	.22
☐ 35	Trent Tucker	2.25	1.10	.22
☐ 36	Darrell Walker	2.25	1.10	.22
☐ 37	Eddie Wilkins	2.25	1.10	.22
☐ 38	Alvan Adams	2.25	1.10	.22
☐ 39	Walter Davis	2.50	1.25	.25
☐ 40	James Edwards	2.25	1.10	.22
☐ 41	Rod Foster	1.50	.75	.15
☐ 42	Michael Holton	2.25	1.10	.22
☐ 43	Jay Humphries	4.50	2.25	.45
☐ 44	Charles Jones	1.50	.75	.15
☐ 45	Maurice Lucas	2.25	1.10	.22
☐ 46	Kyle Macy	2.25	1.10	.22
☐ 47	Larry Nance	4.50	2.25	.45
☐ 48	Charles Pittman	1.50	.75	.15
☐ 49	Rick Robey	2.25	1.10	.22
☐ 50	Mike Sanders	2.25	1.10	.22
☐ 51	Alvin Scott	1.50	.75	.15
☐ 52	Clark Kellogg	1.50	.75	.15
☐ 53	Tony Brown	1.50	.75	.15
☐ 54	Devin Durrant	1.50	.75	.15
☐ 55	Vern Fleming	6.50	3.25	.65
☐ 56	Bill Garnett	1.50	.75	.15
☐ 57	Stuart Gray UER (Photo actually Tony Brown)	2.50	1.25	.25
☐ 58	Jerry Sichting	1.50	.75	.15
☐ 59	Terence Stansbury	2.25	1.10	.22
☐ 60	Steve Stipanovich	2.25	1.10	.22
☐ 61	Jimmy Thomas	1.50	.75	.15
☐ 62	Granville Waiters	1.50	.75	.15
☐ 63	Herb Williams	2.25	1.10	.20
☐ 64	Artis Gilmore	2.50	1.25	.25
☐ 65	Gene Banks	1.50	.75	.15
☐ 66	Ron Brewer	1.50	.75	.15
☐ 67	George Gervin	4.50	2.25	.45
☐ 68	Edgar Jones	1.50	.75	.15
☐ 69	Ozell Jones	1.50	.75	.15
☐ 70	Mark McNamara	1.50	.75	.15
☐ 71	Mike Mitchell	1.50	.75	.15
☐ 72	Johnny Moore	1.50	.75	.15
☐ 73	John Paxson	4.00	2.00	.40
☐ 74	Fred Roberts	3.00	1.50	.30
☐ 75	Alvin Robertson	14.00	7.00	1.40
☐ 76	Dominique Wilkins	42.00	18.00	3.50
☐ 77	Rickey Brown	1.50	.75	.15
☐ 78	Antoine Carr	6.00	3.00	.60
☐ 79	Mike Glenn	1.50	.75	.15
☐ 80	Scott Hastings	2.25	1.10	.22
☐ 81	Eddie Johnson	1.50	.75	.15
☐ 82	Cliff Levingston	2.50	1.25	.25
☐ 83	Leo Rautins	1.50	.75	.15
☐ 84	Doc Rivers	3.75	1.85	.37
☐ 85	Tree Rollins	2.25	1.10	.22
☐ 86	Randy Wittman	1.50	.75	.15
☐ 87	Sly Williams	1.50	.75	.15
☐ 88	Darryl Dawkins	2.25	1.10	.22
☐ 89	Otis Birdsong	2.25	1.10	.22
☐ 90	Darwin Cook	1.50	.75	.15
☐ 91	Mike Gminski	2.25	1.10	.22
☐ 92	George L. Johnson	1.50	.75	.15
☐ 93	Albert King	1.50	.75	.15
☐ 94	Mike O'Koren	1.50	.75	.15
☐ 95	Kelvin Ransey	1.50	.75	.15
☐ 96	M.R. Richardson	1.50	.75	.15
☐ 97	Wayne Sappleton	1.50	.75	.15
☐ 98	Jeff Turner	2.25	1.10	.22
☐ 99	Buck Williams	8.00	4.00	.80
☐ 100	Michael Wilson	1.50	.75	.15
☐ 101	Michael Jordan	750.00	375.00	75.00
☐ 102	Dave Corzine	1.50	.75	.15
☐ 103	Quintin Dailey	1.50	.75	.15
☐ 104	Sidney Green	1.50	.75	.15
☐ 105	David Greenwood	1.50	.75	.15
☐ 106	Rod Higgins	1.50	.75	.15
☐ 107	Steve Johnson	2.50	1.25	.25
☐ 108	Caldwell Jones	2.25	1.10	.22
☐ 109	Wes Matthews	1.50	.75	.15
☐ 110	Jawann Oldham	1.50	.75	.15
☐ 111	Ennis Whatley	1.50	.75	.15
☐ 112	Orlando Woolridge	3.50	1.75	.35
☐ 113	Tom Chambers	18.00	9.00	1.80
☐ 114	Cory Blackwell	2.25	1.10	.22
☐ 115	Frank Brickowski	5.00	2.50	.50
☐ 116	Gerald Henderson	1.50	.75	.15
☐ 117	Reggie King	1.50	.75	.15
☐ 118	Tim McCormick	3.00	1.50	.30
☐ 119	John Schweitz	1.50	.75	.15
☐ 120	Jack Sikma	2.50	1.25	.25
☐ 121	Ricky Sobers	1.50	.75	.15
☐ 122	Jon Sundvold	1.50	.75	.15
☐ 123	Danny Vranes	1.50	.75	.15
☐ 124	Al Wood	1.50	.75	.15
☐ 125	Terry Cummings (Robert Cummings on card back)	7.00	3.50	.70
☐ 126	Randy Breuer	2.25	1.10	.22
☐ 127	Charles Davis	1.50	.75	.15
☐ 128	Mike Dunleavy	3.00	1.50	.30
☐ 129	Kenny Fields	2.25	1.10	.22
☐ 130	Kevin Grevey	1.50	.75	.15
☐ 131	Craig Hodges	3.00	1.50	.30
☐ 132	Alton Lister	2.25	1.10	.22
☐ 133	Larry Micheaux	1.50	.75	.15
☐ 134	Paul Mokeski	1.50	.75	.15
☐ 135	Sidney Moncrief	3.00	1.50	.30
☐ 136	Paul Pressey	2.25	1.10	.22
☐ 137	Alex English	3.50	1.75	.35
☐ 138	Wayne Cooper	1.50	.75	.15
☐ 139	T.R. Dunn	1.50	.75	.15
☐ 140	Mike Evans	1.50	.75	.15
☐ 141	Bill Hanzlik	2.25	1.10	.22
☐ 142	Dan Issel	2.25	1.10	.22
☐ 143	Joe Kopicki	1.50	.75	.15
☐ 144	Lafayette Lever	2.50	1.25	.25
☐ 145	Calvin Natt	2.25	1.10	.22
☐ 146	Danny Schayes	2.50	1.25	.25
☐ 147	Elston Turner	1.50	.75	.15
☐ 148	Willie White	1.50	.75	.15
☐ 149	Purvis Short	2.25	1.10	.22
☐ 150	Chuck Aleksinas	1.50	.75	.15
☐ 151	Mike Bratz	1.50	.75	.15
☐ 152	Steve Burtt	1.50	.75	.15
☐ 153	Lester Conner	1.50	.75	.15
☐ 154	Sleepy Floyd	3.00	1.50	.30
☐ 155	Mickey Johnson	1.50	.75	.15
☐ 156	Gary Plummer	1.50	.75	.15
☐ 157	Larry Smith	2.25	1.10	.22
☐ 158	Peter Thibeaux	1.50	.75	.15
☐ 159	Jerome Whitehead	1.50	.75	.15
☐ 160	Othell Wilson	1.50	.75	.15
☐ 161	Kiki Vandeweghe	3.50	1.75	.35
☐ 162	Sam Bowie	6.50	3.25	.65
☐ 163	Kenny Carr	1.50	.75	.15
☐ 164	Steve Colter	2.25	1.10	.22
☐ 165	Clyde Drexler	60.00	30.00	6.00
☐ 166	Audie Norris	1.50	.75	.15
☐ 167	Jim Paxson	1.50	.75	.15
☐ 168	Tom Scheffler	1.50	.75	.15
☐ 169	Bernard Thompson	1.50	.75	.15
☐ 170	Mychal Thompson	2.25	1.10	.22
☐ 171	Darnell Valentine	1.50	.75	.15
☐ 172	Magic Johnson	45.00	22.50	4.50
☐ 173	Kareem Abdul Jabbar	33.00	15.00	3.00
☐ 174	Michael Cooper	2.50	1.25	.25
☐ 175	Earl Jones	1.50	.75	.15
☐ 176	Mitch Kupchak	2.25	1.10	.22
☐ 177	Ronnie Lester	1.50	.75	.15
☐ 178	Bob McAdoo	2.50	1.25	.25
☐ 179	Mike McGee	1.50	.75	.15
☐ 180	Kurt Rambis	3.00	1.50	.30
☐ 181	Byron Scott	4.00	2.00	.40
☐ 182	Larry Spriggs	1.50	.75	.15
☐ 183	Jamaal Wilkes	2.25	1.10	.22
☐ 184	James Worthy	22.00	11.00	2.20
☐ 185	Gus Williams	2.25	1.10	.22
☐ 186	Greg Ballard	1.50	.75	.15
☐ 187	Dudley Bradley	1.50	.75	.15
☐ 188	Darren Daye	1.50	.75	.15
☐ 189	Frank Johnson	1.50	.75	.15
☐ 190	Charles Jones	1.50	.75	.15
☐ 191	Rick Mahorn	2.50	1.25	.25
☐ 192	Jeff Malone	6.00	3.00	.60
☐ 193	Tom McMillen	2.25	1.10	.22
☐ 194	Jeff Ruland	2.25	1.10	.22
☐ 195	Michael Jordan	330.00	150.00	30.00
☐ 196	Vern Fleming	4.50	2.25	.45
☐ 197	Sam Perkins	12.00	6.00	1.20
☐ 198	Alvin Robertson	8.00	4.00	.80
☐ 199	Jeff Turner	2.25	1.10	.22
☐ 200	Leon Wood	2.25	1.10	.22
☐ 201	Moses Malone	8.00	4.00	.80
☐ 202	Charles Barkley	165.00	75.00	15.00
☐ 203	Maurice Cheeks	2.50	1.25	.25
☐ 204	Julius Erving	33.00	15.00	3.00
☐ 205	Clemon Johnson	1.50	.75	.15
☐ 206	George Johnson	1.50	.75	.15
☐ 207	Bobby Jones	2.25	1.10	.22
☐ 208	Clint Richardson	1.50	.75	.15
☐ 209	Sedale Threatt	2.25	1.10	.22
☐ 210	Andrew Toney	2.25	1.10	.22
☐ 211	Sam Williams	1.50	.75	.15
☐ 212	Leon Wood	2.25	1.10	.22
☐ 213	Mel Turpin	2.50	1.25	.25
☐ 214	Ron Anderson	6.50	3.25	.65
☐ 215	John Bagley	1.50	.75	.15
☐ 216	Johnny Davis	1.50	.75	.15

☐ 217	World B. Free	2.25	1.10	.22
☐ 218	Roy Hinson	2.25	1.10	.22
☐ 219	Phil Hubbard	1.50	.75	.15
☐ 220	Edgar Jones	1.50	.75	.15
☐ 221	Ben Poquette	1.50	.75	.15
☐ 222	Lonnie Shelton	1.50	.75	.15
☐ 223	Mark West	2.25	1.10	.22
☐ 224	Kevin Williams	1.50	.75	.15
☐ 225	Mark Eaton	2.50	1.25	.25
☐ 226	Mitchell Anderson	1.50	.75	.15
☐ 227	Thurl Bailey	2.50	1.25	.25
☐ 228	Adrian Dantley	2.50	1.25	.25
☐ 229	Rickey Green	2.25	1.10	.22
☐ 230	Darrell Griffith	2.25	1.10	.22
☐ 231	Rich Kelley	1.50	.75	.15
☐ 232	Pace Mannion	1.50	.75	.15
☐ 233	Billy Paultz	3.00	1.50	.30
☐ 234	Fred Roberts	1.50	.75	.15
☐ 235	John Stockton	115.00	50.00	10.00
☐ 236	Jeff Wilkins	1.50	.75	.15
☐ 237	Akeem Olajuwon	165.00	75.00	15.00
☐ 238	Craig Ehlo	4.00	2.00	.40
☐ 239	Lionel Hollins	1.50	.75	.15
☐ 240	Allen Leavell	1.50	.75	.15
☐ 241	Lewis Lloyd	1.50	.75	.15
☐ 242	John Lucas	2.25	1.10	.22
☐ 243	Rodney McCray	2.50	1.25	.25
☐ 244	Hank McDowell	1.50	.75	.15
☐ 245	Larry Micheaux	1.50	.75	.15
☐ 246	Jim Peterson	3.00	1.50	.30
☐ 247	Robert Reid	1.50	.75	.15
☐ 248	Ralph Sampson	3.50	1.75	.35
☐ 249	Mitchell Wiggins	1.50	.75	.15
☐ 250	Mark Aguirre	5.00	2.50	.50
☐ 251	Rolando Blackman	5.00	2.50	.50
☐ 252	Wallace Bryant	1.50	.75	.15
☐ 253	Brad Davis	2.25	1.10	.22
☐ 254	Dale Ellis	4.00	2.00	.40
☐ 255	Derek Harper	4.00	2.00	.40
☐ 256	Kurt Nimphius	1.50	.75	.15
☐ 257	Sam Perkins	24.00	12.00	2.40
☐ 258	Charlie Sitton	1.50	.75	.15
☐ 259	Tom Sluby	1.50	.75	.15
☐ 260	Jay Vincent	2.25	1.10	.22
☐ 261	Isiah Thomas	45.00	22.50	4.50
☐ 262	Kent Benson	2.25	1.10	.22
☐ 263	Earl Cureton	1.50	.75	.15
☐ 264	Vinnie Johnson	3.00	1.50	.30
☐ 265	Bill Laimbeer	3.50	1.75	.35
☐ 266	John Long	1.50	.75	.15
☐ 267	Dan Roundfield	2.25	1.10	.22
☐ 268	Kelly Tripucka	2.25	1.10	.22
☐ 269	Terry Tyler	1.50	.75	.15
☐ 270	Reggie Theus	2.25	1.10	.22
☐ 271	Don Buse	1.50	.75	.15
☐ 272	Larry Drew	1.50	.75	.15
☐ 273	Eddie Johnson	3.00	1.50	.30
☐ 274	Billy Knight	1.50	.75	.15
☐ 275	Joe Meriweather	1.50	.75	.15
☐ 276	Mark Olberding	1.50	.75	.15
☐ 277	LaSalle Thompson	2.50	1.25	.25
☐ 278	Otis Thorpe	15.00	7.50	1.50
☐ 279	Pete Verhoeven	1.50	.75	.15
☐ 280	Mike Woodson	1.50	.75	.15
☐ 281	Julius Erving	18.00	9.00	1.80
☐ 282	Kareem Abdul Jabbar	24.00	12.00	2.40
☐ 283	Dan Issel	2.50	1.25	.25
☐ 284	Bernard King	5.00	2.50	.50
☐ 285	Moses Malone	5.00	2.50	.50
☐ 286	Mark Eaton	2.50	1.25	.25
☐ 287	Isiah Thomas	22.00	11.00	2.20
☐ 288	Michael Jordan	330.00	150.00	30.00

1985-86 Star NBA

This 172-card set was produced by the Star Company and
features players in the NBA. Cards are numbered in team order
and measure the standard 2 1/2" by 3 1/2". The team ordering
is as follows, Philadelphia 76ers (1-9), Detroit Pistons (10-17),
Houston Rockets (18-25), Los Angeles Lakers (26-33), Phoenix
Suns (34-41), Atlanta Hawks (42-49), Denver Nuggets (50-57),
New Jersey Nets (58-65), Seattle Supersonics (66-73),
Sacramento Kings (74-80), Indiana Pacers (81-87), Los Angeles
Clippers (88-94), Boston Celtics (95-102), Portland Trail Blazers
(103-109), Washington Bullets (110-116), Chicago Bulls (117-

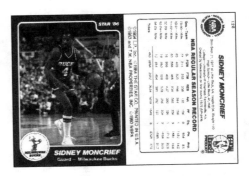

123), Milwaukee Bucks (124-130), Golden State Warriors
(131-136), Utah Jazz (137-144), San Antonio Spurs (145-
151), Cleveland Cavaliers (152-158), Dallas Mavericks (159-
165), and New York Knicks (166-172). Players on each team
have the same color border on the front. Cards were issued in
two series, 1-94 and 95-172. Card backs are very similar to the
other Star basketball sets except that the player statistics go up
through the 1984-85 season. The key extended rookie cards in
this set are Patrick Ewing and Jerome Kersey.

		MINT	EXC	G-VG
	COMPLETE SET (172)	1100.00	500.00	100.00
	COMMON PLAYER (1-172)	1.50	.75	.15
☐ 1	Maurice Cheeks	3.00	1.50	.30
☐ 2	Charles Barkley	50.00	25.00	5.00
☐ 3	Julius Erving	18.00	9.00	1.80
☐ 4	Clemon Johnson	1.50	.75	.15
☐ 5	Bobby Jones	2.25	1.10	.22
☐ 6	Moses Malone	5.00	2.50	.50
☐ 7	Sedale Threatt	2.25	1.10	.22
☐ 8	Andrew Toney	2.25	1.10	.22
☐ 9	Leon Wood	1.50	.75	.15
☐ 10	Isiah Thomas UER	30.00	15.00	3.00
	(No Pistons logo			
	on card front)			
☐ 11	Kent Benson	2.25	1.10	.22
☐ 12	Earl Cureton	1.50	.75	.15
☐ 13	Vinnie Johnson	2.50	1.25	.25
☐ 14	Bill Laimbeer	3.00	1.50	.30
☐ 15	John Long	1.50	.75	.15
☐ 16	Rick Mahorn	2.50	1.25	.25
☐ 17	Kelly Tripucka	2.25	1.10	.22
☐ 18	Akeem Olajuwon	50.00	25.00	5.00
☐ 19	Allen Leavell	1.50	.75	.15
☐ 20	Lewis Lloyd	1.50	.75	.15
☐ 21	John Lucas	2.25	1.10	.22
☐ 22	Rodney McCray	2.25	1.10	.22
☐ 23	Robert Reid	1.50	.75	.15
☐ 24	Ralph Sampson	2.50	1.25	.25
☐ 25	Mitchell Wiggins	1.50	.75	.15
☐ 26	Kareem Abdul Jabbar	30.00	15.00	3.00
☐ 27	Michael Cooper	2.50	1.25	.25
☐ 28	Magic Johnson	45.00	22.50	4.50
☐ 29	Mitch Kupchak	1.50	.75	.15
☐ 30	Maurice Lucas	2.50	1.25	.25
☐ 31	Kurt Rambis	3.50	1.75	.35
☐ 32	Byron Scott	18.00	9.00	1.80
☐ 33	James Worthy	2.50	1.25	.25
☐ 34	Larry Nance	2.50	1.25	.25
☐ 35	Alvan Adams	2.25	1.10	.22
☐ 36	Walter Davis	2.25	1.10	.22
☐ 37	James Edwards	2.25	1.10	.22
☐ 38	Jay Humphries	2.25	1.10	.22
☐ 39	Charles Pittman	1.50	.75	.15
☐ 40	Rick Robey	2.25	1.10	.22
☐ 41	Mike Sanders	1.50	.75	.15
☐ 42	Dominique Wilkins	30.00	15.00	3.00
☐ 43	Scott Hastings	2.25	1.10	.22
☐ 44	Eddie Johnson	1.50	.75	.15
☐ 45	Cliff Levingston	2.25	1.10	.22
☐ 46	Tree Rollins	2.25	1.10	.22
☐ 47	Doc Rivers	3.00	1.50	.30
☐ 48	Kevin Willis	5.00	2.50	.50
☐ 49	Randy Wittman	2.25	1.10	.22
☐ 50	Alex English	3.00	1.50	.30
☐ 51	Wayne Cooper	1.50	.75	.15
☐ 52	T.R. Dunn	1.50	.75	.15

☐ 53	Mike Evans	1.50	.75	.15
☐ 54	Lafayette Lever	2.50	1.25	.25
☐ 55	Calvin Natt	2.25	1.10	.22
☐ 56	Danny Schayes	2.25	1.10	.22
☐ 57	Elston Turner	1.50	.75	.15
☐ 58	Buck Williams	5.00	2.50	.50
☐ 59	Otis Birdsong	1.50	.75	.15
☐ 60	Darwin Cook	1.50	.75	.15
☐ 61	Darryl Dawkins	2.25	1.10	.22
☐ 62	Mike Gminski	2.25	1.10	.22
☐ 63	Mickey Johnson	1.50	.75	.15
☐ 64	Mike O'Koren	1.50	.75	.15
☐ 65	Michael R. Richardson	2.25	1.10	.22
☐ 66	Tom Chambers	12.00	6.00	1.20
☐ 67	Gerald Henderson	2.25	1.10	.22
☐ 68	Tim McCormick	2.25	1.10	.22
☐ 69	Jack Sikma	2.50	1.25	.25
☐ 70	Ricky Sobers	1.50	.75	.15
☐ 71	Danny Vranes	1.50	.75	.15
☐ 72	Al Wood	1.50	.75	.15
☐ 73	Danny Young	3.00	1.50	.30
☐ 74	Reggie Theus	2.25	1.10	.22
☐ 75	Larry Drew	1.50	.75	.15
☐ 76	Eddie Johnson	3.00	1.50	.30
☐ 77	Mark Olberding	1.50	.75	.15
☐ 78	LaSalle Thompson	2.25	1.10	.22
☐ 79	Otis Thorpe	4.50	2.25	.45
☐ 80	Mike Woodson	1.50	.75	.15
☐ 81	Clark Kellogg	1.50	.75	.15
☐ 82	Quinn Buckner	2.25	1.10	.22
☐ 83	Vern Fleming	2.25	1.10	.22
☐ 84	Bill Garnett	1.50	.75	.15
☐ 85	Terence Stansbury	1.50	.75	.15
☐ 86	Steve Stipanovich	2.25	1.10	.22
☐ 87	Herb Williams	2.25	1.10	.22
☐ 88	Marques Johnson	2.50	1.25	.25
☐ 89	Michael Cage	2.25	1.10	.22
☐ 90	Franklin Edwards	1.50	.75	.15
☐ 91	Cedric Maxwell	2.25	1.10	.22
☐ 92	Derek Smith	2.25	1.10	.22
☐ 93	Rory White	1.50	.75	.15
☐ 94	Jamaal Wilkes	2.25	1.10	.22
☐ 95A	Larry Bird (Green border)	42.00	20.00	4.00
☐ 95B	Larry Bird (White border)	42.00	20.00	4.00
☐ 96A	Danny Ainge (Green border)	4.00	2.00	.40
☐ 96B	Danny Ainge (White border)	4.00	2.00	.40
☐ 97A	Dennis Johnson (Green border)	2.50	1.25	.25
☐ 97B	Dennis Johnson (White border)	2.50	1.25	.25
☐ 98A	Kevin McHale (Green border)	7.00	3.50	.70
☐ 98B	Kevin McHale (White border)	7.00	3.50	.70
☐ 99A	Robert Parish ERR (Green border; no number on back)	5.00	2.50	.50
☐ 99B	Robert Parish COR (White border)	5.00	2.50	.50
☐ 100A	Jerry Sichting (Green border)	1.50	.75	.15
☐ 100B	Jerry Sichting (White border)	1.50	.75	.15
☐ 101A	Bill Walton (Green border)	3.00	1.50	.30
☐ 101B	Bill Walton (White border)	3.00	1.50	.30
☐ 102A	Scott Wedman (Green border)	2.25	1.10	.22
☐ 102B	Scott Wedman (White border)	2.25	1.10	.22
☐ 103	Kiki Vandeweghe	3.00	1.50	.30
☐ 104	Sam Bowie	3.00	1.50	.30
☐ 105	Kenny Carr	1.50	.75	.15
☐ 106	Clyde Drexler	33.00	15.00	3.00
☐ 107	Jerome Kersey	27.00	13.50	2.70
☐ 108	Jim Paxson	1.50	.75	.15
☐ 109	Mychal Thompson	2.25	1.10	.22
☐ 110	Gus Williams	2.25	1.10	.22
☐ 111	Darren Daye	1.50	.75	.15
☐ 112	Jeff Malone	4.00	2.00	.40
☐ 113	Tom McMillen	2.25	1.10	.22
☐ 114	Cliff Robinson	1.50	.75	.15
☐ 115	Dan Roundfield	1.50	.75	.15
☐ 116	Jeff Ruland	2.25	1.10	.22
☐ 117	Michael Jordan	280.00	125.00	25.00
☐ 118	Gene Banks	1.50	.75	.15
☐ 119	Dave Corzine	1.50	.75	.15
☐ 120	Quintin Dailey	1.50	.75	.15
☐ 121	George Gervin	3.50	1.75	.35

☐ 122	Jawann Oldham	1.50	.75	.15
☐ 123	Orlando Woolridge	2.50	1.25	.25
☐ 124	Terry Cummings	4.50	2.25	.45
☐ 125	Craig Hodges	2.50	1.25	.25
☐ 126	Alton Lister	1.50	.75	.15
☐ 127	Paul Mokeski	1.50	.75	.15
☐ 128	Sidney Moncrief	2.50	1.25	.25
☐ 129	Ricky Pierce	4.00	2.00	.40
☐ 130	Paul Pressey	2.25	1.10	.22
☐ 131	Purvis Short	2.25	1.10	.22
☐ 132	Joe Barry Carroll	2.25	1.10	.22
☐ 133	Lester Conner	1.50	.75	.15
☐ 134	Sleepy Floyd	2.50	1.25	.25
☐ 135	Geoff Huston	1.50	.75	.15
☐ 136	Larry Smith	2.25	1.10	.22
☐ 137	Jerome Whitehead	1.50	.75	.15
☐ 138	Adrian Dantley	2.50	1.25	.25
☐ 139	Mitchell Anderson	1.50	.75	.15
☐ 140	Thurl Bailey	2.25	1.10	.22
☐ 141	Mark Eaton	2.25	1.10	.22
☐ 142	Rickey Green	2.25	1.10	.22
☐ 143	Darrell Griffith	2.25	1.10	.22
☐ 144	John Stockton	36.00	15.00	3.00
☐ 145	Artis Gilmore	2.25	1.10	.22
☐ 146	Marc Iavaroni	1.50	.75	.15
☐ 147	Steve Johnson	1.50	.75	.15
☐ 148	Mike Mitchell	1.50	.75	.15
☐ 149	Johnny Moore	1.50	.75	.15
☐ 150	Alvin Robertson	4.00	2.00	.40
☐ 151	Jon Sundvold	1.50	.75	.15
☐ 152	World B. Free	2.25	1.10	.22
☐ 153	John Bagley	1.50	.75	.15
☐ 154	Johnny Davis	1.50	.75	.15
☐ 155	Roy Hinson	2.25	1.10	.22
☐ 156	Phil Hubbard	1.50	.75	.15
☐ 157	Ben Poquette	1.50	.75	.15
☐ 158	Mel Turpin	1.50	.75	.15
☐ 159	Rolando Blackman	4.00	2.00	.40
☐ 160	Mark Aguirre	3.50	1.75	.35
☐ 161	Brad Davis	1.50	.75	.15
☐ 162	Dale Ellis	3.50	1.75	.35
☐ 163	Derek Harper	3.50	1.75	.35
☐ 164	Sam Perkins	6.50	3.25	.65
☐ 165	Jay Vincent	2.25	1.10	.22
☐ 166	Patrick Ewing	210.00	90.00	18.00
☐ 167	Bill Cartwright	3.00	1.50	.30
☐ 168	Pat Cummings	1.50	.75	.15
☐ 169	Ernie Grunfeld	2.25	1.10	.22
☐ 170	Rory Sparrow	1.50	.75	.15
☐ 171	Trent Tucker	1.50	.75	.15
☐ 172	Darrell Walker	1.50	.75	.15

1983 Star All-Star Game

DAVID THOMPSON
WEST ALL-STAR

This was the first NBA set issued by the Star Company. The set contains 30 cards measuring 2 1/2" by 3 1/2". The cards have a blue border on the front of each card and blue print is used on the back of each card. The set commemorates the 1983 NBA All-Star Game held in Los Angeles. Many of the cards feature players in their special all-star uniforms. There are two unnumbered cards in the set listed at the end of the list below.

	MINT	EXC	G-VG
COMPLETE SET (32)	75.00	37.50	7.50
COMMON PLAYER (1-30)	1.50	.75	.15

☐ 1 Checklist (Julius Erving on front)	6.00	3.00	.60
☐ 2 Larry Bird	12.00	6.00	1.20
☐ 3 Maurice Cheeks	2.25	1.10	.22
☐ 4 Julius Erving	9.00	4.50	.90
☐ 5 Marques Johnson	2.25	1.10	.22
☐ 6 Bill Laimbeer	4.00	2.00	.40
☐ 7 Moses Malone	4.00	2.00	.40
☐ 8 Sidney Moncrief	2.25	1.10	.22
☐ 9 Robert Parish	4.00	2.00	.40
☐ 10 Reggie Theus	2.25	1.10	.22
☐ 11 Isiah Thomas	25.00	12.50	2.50
☐ 12 Andrew Toney	1.50	.75	.15
☐ 13 Buck Williams	6.00	3.00	.60
☐ 14 Kareem Abdul Jabbar	9.00	4.50	.90
☐ 15 Alex English	3.00	1.50	.30
☐ 16 George Gervin	3.00	1.50	.30
☐ 17 Artis Gilmore	3.00	1.50	.30
☐ 18 Magic Johnson	12.00	6.00	1.20
☐ 19 Maurice Lucas	1.50	.75	.15
☐ 20 Jim Paxson	1.50	.75	.15
☐ 21 Jack Sikma	1.50	.75	.15
☐ 22 David Thompson	2.25	1.10	.22
☐ 23 Kiki Vandeweghe	2.25	1.10	.22
☐ 24 Jamaal Wilkes	2.25	1.10	.22
☐ 25 Gus Williams	2.25	1.10	.22
☐ 26 All-Star MVPs (Dr. J, '77, '83)	4.00	2.00	.40
☐ 27 One Player, Single Game Records (Theus and Malone)	2.25	1.10	.22
☐ 28 All-Star All-Time Leaders (East Coast Line)	2.25	1.10	.22
☐ 29 East Box Score (Boston Bombers: Bird and Parish)	7.50	3.75	.75
☐ 30 West Box Score (Moncrief Soars)	1.50	.75	.15
☐ xx Gilmore and English (Ad on back)	2.25	1.10	.22
☐ xx Kareem Abdul Jabbar (Uncut sheet offer on back)	5.00	2.50	.50

1983-84 Star All-Rookies

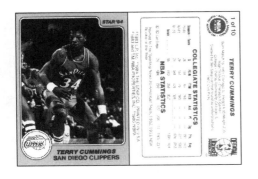

TERRY CUMMINGS
SAN DIEGO CLIPPERS

This set features the 10 members of the 1982-83 NBA All-Rookie Team. Cards measure 2 1/2" by 3 1/2" and have a yellow border around the fronts of the cards. The set was issued in late Summer of 1983 and features the Star '84 logo on the front of each card.

	MINT	EXC	G-VG
COMPLETE SET (10)	90.00	45.00	9.00
COMMON PLAYER (1-10)	2.00	1.00	.20
☐ 1 Terry Cummings	30.00	15.00	3.00
☐ 2 Quintin Dailey	3.00	1.50	.30
☐ 3 Roderick Higgins	2.00	1.00	.20
☐ 4 Clark Kellogg	4.00	2.00	.40
☐ 5 Lafayette Lever	10.00	5.00	1.00
☐ 6 Paul Pressey	5.00	2.50	.50
☐ 7 Trent Tucker	3.00	1.50	.30
☐ 8 Dominique Wilkens	35.00	17.50	3.50

☐ 9 Rob Williams	2.00	1.00	.20
☐ 10 James Worthy	30.00	15.00	3.00

1983-84 Star Sixers Champs

JULIUS SCOOPS
Julius Erving

This set of 25 cards is devoted to Philadelphia's NBA Championship victory over the Los Angeles Lakers in 1983. Cards measure 2 1/2" by 3 1/2" and have a red border around the fronts of the cards and red printing on the backs. The set was issued in late Summer of 1983 and features the Star '84 logo on the front of each card.

	MINT	EXC	G-VG
COMPLETE SET (25)	45.00	22.50	4.50
COMMON PLAYER (1-25)	1.50	.75	.15
☐ 1 Sixers 1982-83 NBA World Champs (Checklist back)	2.25	1.10	.22
☐ 2 Billy Cunningham Head Coach	2.25	1.10	.22
☐ 3 Clash of the Titans Malone vs. Jabbar	5.00	2.50	.50
☐ 4 The Quest Begins Julius Erving	5.00	2.50	.50
☐ 5 Philly Super-Sub Clint Richardson	1.50	.75	.15
☐ 6 Laker Killer Andrew Toney	1.50	.75	.15
☐ 7 Phila. 113, LA 107 Game 1 Boxscore	1.50	.75	.15
☐ 8 Secretary of Defense Bobby Jones	2.25	1.10	.22
☐ 9 Mo Can Go Maurice Cheeks	2.25	1.10	.22
☐ 10 Doc for 2 Julius Erving	5.00	2.50	.50
☐ 11 Toney on the Drive Andrew Toney	1.50	.75	.15
☐ 12 Phila. 103, LA 93 Game 2 Boxscore	1.50	.75	.15
☐ 13 Serious Sixers (Pre-Game Lineup)	1.50	.75	.15
☐ 14 Moses Leads Sixers Moses Malone	3.50	1.75	.35
☐ 15 Bench Strength Clemon Johnson	1.50	.75	.15
☐ 16 One Mo Time Maurice Cheeks	2.25	1.10	.22
☐ 17 Phila. 111, LA 94 Game 3 Boxscore	1.50	.75	.15
☐ 18 Julius Scoops Julius Erving	5.00	2.50	.50
☐ 19 Sixth Man of Year Bobby Jones	2.25	1.10	.22
☐ 20 Coast to Coast Moses Malone	3.50	1.75	.35
☐ 21 World Champs Phila. 115, LA 108 Game 4 Boxscore	1.50	.75	.15
☐ 22 Doc Gets the Ring (Julius Erving) Series Stats	3.50	1.75	.35
☐ 23 Philly in a Sweep Prior World Champs	1.50	.75	.15

		MINT	EXC	G-VG
☐ 24	Basking in Glory .... Profile: Dr.J	5.00	2.50	.50
☐ 25	The NBA's MVP .... Profile: Moses Malone	3.00	1.50	.30

1984 Star All-Star Game

ANDREW TONEY
East All-Star

This set of 25 cards features players in the 34th Annual 1984 NBA All-Star Game held in Denver. Cards measure 2 1/2" by 3 1/2" and have a white border around the fronts of the cards and blue printing on the backs. Cards feature the Star '84 logo on the front. The cards are ordered with the East All-Stars on cards 2-13 and the West All-Stars on cards 14-25.

		MINT	EXC	G-VG
COMPLETE SET (25)		75.00	37.50	7.50
COMMON PLAYER (1-25)		1.50	.75	.15
☐ 1	1984 NBA All-Star Game Checklist (Isiah Thomas)	3.50	1.75	.35
☐ 2	Larry Bird	15.00	7.50	1.50
☐ 3	Otis Birdsong	1.50	.75	.15
☐ 4	Julius Erving	6.00	3.00	.60
☐ 5	Bernard King	4.00	2.00	.40
☐ 6	Bill Laimbeer	3.00	1.50	.30
☐ 7	Kevin McHale	4.00	2.00	.40
☐ 8	Sidney Moncrief	2.25	1.10	.22
☐ 9	Robert Parish	4.00	2.00	.40
☐ 10	Jeff Ruland	1.50	.75	.15
☐ 11	Isiah Thomas	7.50	3.75	.75
☐ 12	Andrew Toney	1.50	.75	.15
☐ 13	Kelly Tripucka	1.50	.75	.15
☐ 14	Kareem Abdul Jabbar	7.50	3.75	.75
☐ 15	Mark Aguirre	2.25	1.10	.22
☐ 16	Adrian Dantley	3.00	1.50	.30
☐ 17	Walter Davis	2.25	1.10	.22
☐ 18	Alex English	3.00	1.50	.30
☐ 19	George Gervin	4.00	2.00	.40
☐ 20	Rickey Green	1.50	.75	.15
☐ 21	Magic Johnson	15.00	7.50	1.50
☐ 22	Jim Paxson	1.50	.75	.15
☐ 23	Ralph Sampson	2.25	1.10	.22
☐ 24	Jack Sikma	2.25	1.10	.22
☐ 25	Kiki Vandeweghe	2.25	1.10	.22

1984 Star Police Denver ASG

This 34-card set was distributed as individual cards by the Denver Police in the months following the NBA All-Star Game (ASG) held in Denver. The set was composed of participants in the All-Star Game (1-25) and the Slam Dunk contest (26-34). Cards measure 2 1/2" by 3 1/2" and have a white border around the fronts of the cards and blue printing on the backs. Cards feature Star '84 logo on the fronts and safety tips on the backs. Supposedly 10,000 sets were produced.

KEVIN McHALE
East All-Star

		MINT	EXC	G-VG
COMPLETE SET (34)		165.00	75.00	15.00
COMMON PLAYER (1-34)		3.00	1.50	.30
☐ 1	Checklist Card	3.00	1.50	.30
☐ 2	Larry Bird	30.00	15.00	3.00
☐ 3	Otis Birdsong	3.00	1.50	.30
☐ 4	Julius Erving	12.00	6.00	1.20
☐ 5	Bernard King	8.00	4.00	.80
☐ 6	Bill Laimbeer	6.00	3.00	.60
☐ 7	Kevin McHale	8.00	4.00	.80
☐ 8	Sidney Moncrief	4.50	2.25	.45
☐ 9	Robert Parish	8.00	4.00	.80
☐ 10	Jeff Ruland	3.00	1.50	.30
☐ 11	Isiah Thomas	15.00	7.50	1.50
☐ 12	Andrew Toney	3.00	1.50	.30
☐ 13	Kelly Tripucka	3.00	1.50	.30
☐ 14	Kareem Abdul Jabbar	15.00	7.50	1.50
☐ 15	Mark Aguirre	4.50	2.25	.45
☐ 16	Adrian Dantley	6.00	3.00	.60
☐ 17	Walter Davis	4.50	2.25	.45
☐ 18	Alex English	6.00	3.00	.60
☐ 19	George Gervin	8.00	4.00	.80
☐ 20	Rickey Green	3.00	1.50	.30
☐ 21	Magic Johnson	30.00	15.00	3.00
☐ 22	Jim Paxson	3.00	1.50	.30
☐ 23	Ralph Sampson	4.50	2.25	.45
☐ 24	Jack Sikma	4.50	2.25	.45
☐ 25	KiKi Vandeweghe	4.50	2.25	.45
☐ 26	Michael Cooper	4.50	2.25	.45
☐ 27	Clyde Drexler	15.00	7.50	1.50
☐ 28	Julius Erving	12.00	6.00	1.20
☐ 29	Darrell Griffith	4.50	2.25	.45
☐ 30	Edgar Jones	3.00	1.50	.30
☐ 31	Larry Nance	3.00	1.50	.30
☐ 32	Ralph Sampson	4.50	2.25	.45
☐ 33	Dominique Wilkins	12.00	6.00	1.20
☐ 34	Orlando Woolridge	3.00	1.50	.30

1984 Star Slam Dunk

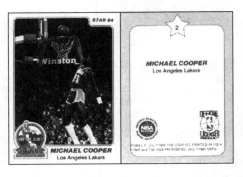

MICHAEL COOPER
Los Angeles Lakers

An 11-card set highlighting the revival of the Slam Dunk contest (during the 1984 All-Star Weekend in Denver) was produced by the Star Company in 1984. Cards measure 2 1/2" by 3 1/2" and have a white border around the fronts of the cards and blue printing on the backs. Cards feature the Star '84 logo on the front.

	MINT	EXC	G-VG
COMPLETE SET (11)	90.00	45.00	9.00
COMMON PLAYER (1-11)	2.00	1.00	.20
☐ 1 Group Photo (checklist back)	9.00	2.00	.40
☐ 2 Michael Cooper	6.00	3.00	.60
☐ 3 Clyde Drexler	30.00	15.00	3.00
☐ 4 Julius Erving	20.00	10.00	2.00
☐ 5 Darrell Griffith	4.00	2.00	.40
☐ 6 Edgar Jones	2.00	1.00	.20
☐ 7 Larry Nance	6.00	3.00	.60
☐ 8 Ralph Sampson	4.00	2.00	.40
☐ 9 Dominique Wilkens	25.00	12.50	2.50
☐ 10 Orlando Woolridge	6.00	3.00	.60
☐ 11 Larry Nance, 1984 Slam Dunk Champ	6.00	3.00	.60

☐ 17 Game 6 (Parish sandwich)	2.25	1.10	.22
☐ 18 Game 6 (Kareem Abdul Jabbar)	3.50	1.75	.35
☐ 19 LA 119, Boston 108 (Dennis Johnson)	2.25	1.10	.22
☐ 20 Game 7 (Kareem sky hook)	4.50	2.25	.45
☐ 21 Game 7 (K.C. Jones)	1.50	.75	.15
☐ 22 World Champs; Boston 111, LA 102 (M.L. Carr)	1.50	.75	.15
☐ 23 Prior Celtic Championships (Red Auerbach)	2.25	1.10	.22
☐ 24 Bird: Championship Series MVP	7.50	3.75	.75
☐ 25 The Road to the Title (Boston Garden)	2.25	1.10	.22

1984 Star Celtics Champs

This set of 25 cards is devoted to Boston's NBA Championship victory over the Los Angeles Lakers in 1984. Cards measure 2 1/2" by 3 1/2" and have a green border around the fronts of the cards and green printing on the backs. The set was issued in Summer of 1984 and features the Star '84 logo on the front of each card.

	MINT	EXC	G-VG
COMPLETE SET (25)	60.00	30.00	6.00
COMMON PLAYER (1-25)	1.50	.75	.15
☐ 1 Celtics Champs (Auerbach/Maxwell) (Checklist back)	2.25	1.10	.22
☐ 2 Game 1 (Jabbar over Parish)	3.50	1.75	.35
☐ 3 Game 1 (McHale drives)	3.50	1.75	.35
☐ 4 LA 115, Boston 109 (Larry Bird)	6.00	3.00	.60
☐ 5 Game 2 (Magic Johnson)	6.00	3.00	.60
☐ 6 Game 2 (K.C. Jones and Danny Ainge)	2.25	1.10	.22
☐ 7 Boston 124, LA 121 (OT) (Larry Bird)	4.50	2.25	.45
☐ 8 Game 3 (Jabbar and McHale)	3.50	1.75	.35
☐ 9 Game 3 (J.Worthy)	3.50	1.75	.35
☐ 10 LA 137, Boston 104 (Magic Johnson)	6.00	3.00	.60
☐ 11 Game 4 (Magic blocks Bird)	7.50	3.75	.75
☐ 12 Game 4 (Ainge scuffle)	1.50	.75	.15
☐ 13 Boston 129, LA 125 Overtime (Carr and Maxwell)	1.50	.75	.15
☐ 14 Game 5 (Larry Bird)	5.00	2.50	.50
☐ 15 Game 5 (Pat Riley)	2.25	1.10	.22
☐ 16 Boston 121, LA 103 (Kareem Abdul Jabbar)	3.50	1.75	.35

1984 Star Award Winners

This 24-card set was produced for the NBA to be given away at the Awards Banquet which took place following the conclusion of the 1983-84 season. Cards highlighted award winners from the 1983-84 season. Cards measure 2 1/2" by 3 1/2" and have a blue border around the fronts of the cards and pink and blue printing on the backs. The set was issued in June of 1984 and features the Star '84 logo on the front of each card.

	MINT	EXC	G-VG
COMPLETE SET (24)	60.00	30.00	6.00
COMMON PLAYER (1-24)	1.50	.75	.15
☐ 1 1984 Award Winners Checklist	2.25	1.10	.22
☐ 2 Coach: Frank Layden	1.50	.75	.15
☐ 3 Rookie of the Year: Ralph Sampson	2.25	1.10	.22
☐ 4 Comeback Player of the Year; Adrian Dantley	2.25	1.10	.22
☐ 5 Sixth Man: Kevin McHale	3.50	1.75	.35
☐ 6 Pivotal Player of the Year; Magic Johnson	9.00	4.50	.90
☐ 7 Defensive Player: Sidney Moncrief	2.25	1.10	.22
☐ 8 MVP: Larry Bird	9.00	4.50	.90
☐ 9 Slam Dunk Champ; Larry Nance	3.00	1.50	.30
☐ 10 Statistical Leaders	1.50	.75	.15
☐ 11 Statistical Leaders II	1.50	.75	.15
☐ 12 All-Star Game MVP; Isiah Thomas	5.00	2.50	.50
☐ 13 Leading Scorer; Adrian Dantley	2.25	1.10	.22
☐ 14 Field Goal Percent Leader; Artis Gilmore	2.25	1.10	.22
☐ 15 Free Throw Percent Leader; Larry Bird	7.50	3.75	.75
☐ 16 Three Point Field Goal Percent Leader; Darrell Griffith	2.25	1.10	.22

		MINT	EXC	G-VG
☐ 17	Assists Leader; .... Magic Johnson	7.50	3.75	.75
☐ 18	Steals Leader; .... Rickey Green	1.50	.75	.15
☐ 19	Most Blocked Shots; .... Mark Eaton	1.50	.75	.15
☐ 20	Leading Rebounder; .... Moses Malone	3.50	1.75	.35
☐ 21	Most Career Points; .... Kareem Abdul Jabbar	4.50	2.25	.45
☐ 22	NBA All-Defensive Team	3.00	1.50	.30
☐ 23	NBA All Rookie Team	3.00	1.50	.30
☐ 24	NBA All-NBA Team	3.00	1.50	.30

1984 Star Larry Bird

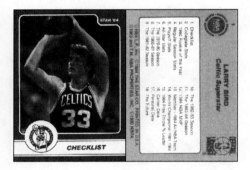

This set contains 18 cards highlighting the career of basketball great Larry Bird. Cards measure 2 1/2" by 3 1/2" and have a green border around the fronts of the cards and green printing on the backs. Cards feature Star '84 logo on the front as they were released in May of 1984.

		MINT	EXC	G-VG
COMPLETE SET (18)		50.00	25.00	5.00
COMMON PLAYER (1-18)		4.00	2.00	.40
☐ 1	Checklist	5.00	2.50	.50
☐ 2	Collegiate Stats	4.00	2.00	.40
☐ 3	1980 Rookie .... of the Year	4.00	2.00	.40
☐ 4	Regular Season Stats	4.00	2.00	.40
☐ 5	Playoff Stats	4.00	2.00	.40
☐ 6	All-Star Stats	4.00	2.00	.40
☐ 7	The 1979-80 Season	4.00	2.00	.40
☐ 8	The 1980-81 Season	4.00	2.00	.40
☐ 9	The 1981-82 Season	4.00	2.00	.40
☐ 10	The 1982-83 Season	4.00	2.00	.40
☐ 11	The 1983-84 Season	4.00	2.00	.40
☐ 12	The 1984 NBA MVP	4.00	2.00	.40
☐ 13	Member - 1984 .... All NBA Team	4.00	2.00	.40
☐ 14	World Champions 1981, 1984	4.00	2.00	.40
☐ 15	1984 Free Throw .... Percentage Leader	4.00	2.00	.40
☐ 16	Career Data	4.00	2.00	.40
☐ 17	Personal Data	4.00	2.00	.40
☐ 18	The Future	5.00	2.50	.50

1984 Star Mr. Z's Trail Blazers

This five-card set was produced by Star Co. as a promotion for Mr. Z's frozen pizzas. The cards measure approximately 5" by 7" and feature on the fronts glossy color action player photos, with rounded corners as well as white and black borders on a dark red background. The team logo is superimposed over the picture at the intersection of the left side and bottom borders. The sponsor logo "Mr. Z's" appears in the upper right corner of

the front, and player information is given below the picture. The backs have an advertisement for Blazer merchandise. The cards are unnumbered and are checklisted below in alphabetical order. Originally the set was planned to feature the whole team (12 players) but only five players were issued. Individual cards were given out in Mr. Z's frozen pizzas. Supposedly 10,000 cards of each player were produced. The cards were issued beginning in January 1984.

		MINT	EXC	G-VG
COMPLETE SET (5)		400.00	200.00	40.00
COMMON PLAYER (1-5)		50.00	25.00	5.00
☐ 1	Kenny Carr	50.00	25.00	5.00
☐ 2	Clyde Drexler	250.00	125.00	25.00
☐ 3	Audie Norris	50.00	25.00	5.00
☐ 4	Mychal Thompson	60.00	30.00	6.00
☐ 5	Darnell Valentine	50.00	25.00	5.00

1984-85 Star Arena

These sets were produced to be sold in the arena of each of the five teams. Each set is different from the team's regular issue set in that the photography and and card backs are different. Shortly after distribution began, Bob Lanier announced his retirement plans and hence his cards were withdrawn from the Milwaukee set. Cards measure 2 1/2" by 3 1/2" and have a colored border around the fronts of the cards according to the team with corresponding color printing on the backs. Celtics feature Star '85 logo on the front while the other four teams feature the Star '84 logo on the front. The cards are ordered below by teams, for example, Boston Celtics A, Dallas Mavericks B, Milwaukee Bucks C, Los Angeles Lakers D, and Philadelphia 76ers E.

	MINT	EXC	G-VG
COMPLETE SET (49)	175.00	85.00	18.00
COMMON PLAYER	1.50	.75	.15

	MINT	EXC	G-VG

☐ A1 Larry Bird	20.00	10.00	2.00
☐ A2 Danny Ainge	4.00	2.00	.40
☐ A3 Rick Carlisle	1.50	.75	.15
☐ A4 Dennis Johnson	3.00	1.50	.30
☐ A5 Cedric Maxwell	3.00	1.50	.30
☐ A6 Kevin McHale	5.00	2.50	.50
☐ A7 Robert Parish	6.00	3.00	.60
☐ A8 Scott Wedman	1.50	.75	.15
☐ A9 World Champs 1981, 1984	1.50	.75	.15
☐ B1 Mark Aguirre	4.00	2.00	.40
☐ B2 Rolando Blackman	4.00	2.00	.40
☐ B3 Brad Davis	1.50	.75	.15
☐ B4 Dale Ellis	4.00	2.00	.40
☐ B5 Bill Garnett	1.50	.75	.15
☐ B6 Derek Harper UER (Mike Harper on both sides with Mike's birthdate, etc.)	3.00	1.50	.30
☐ B7 Kurt Nimphius	1.50	.75	.15
☐ B8 Jim Spanarkel	1.50	.75	.15
☐ B9 Elston Turner	1.50	.75	.15
☐ B10 Jay Vincent	2.25	1.10	.22
☐ B11 Mark West	3.00	1.50	.30
☐ C1 Nate Archibald	5.00	2.50	.50
☐ C2 Junior Bridgeman	2.25	1.10	.22
☐ C3 Mike Dunleavy	3.00	1.50	.30
☐ C4 Kevin Grevey	2.25	1.10	.22
☐ C5 Marques Johnson	4.00	2.00	.40
☐ C6 Bob Lanier SP	700.00	350.00	70.00
☐ C7 Alton Lister	1.50	.75	.15
☐ C8 Sidney Moncrief	3.00	1.50	.30
☐ C9 Paul Pressey	3.00	1.50	.30
☐ D1 Kareem Abdul Jabbar	10.00	5.00	1.00
☐ D2 Michael Cooper	4.00	2.00	.40
☐ D3 Magic Johnson	20.00	10.00	2.00
☐ D4 Mike McGee	1.50	.75	.15
☐ D5 Swen Nater	2.25	1.10	.22
☐ D6 Kurt Rambis	3.00	1.50	.30
☐ D7 Byron Scott	5.00	2.50	.50
☐ D8 James Worthy	10.00	5.00	1.00
☐ D9 Laker All-Stars	3.00	1.50	.30
☐ D10 Kareem Abdul Jabbar NBA Scoring Leader	10.00	5.00	1.00
☐ E1 Julius Erving	10.00	5.00	1.00
☐ E2 Maurice Cheeks	3.00	1.50	.30
☐ E3 Franklin Edwards	1.50	.75	.15
☐ E4 Marc Iavaroni	1.50	.75	.15
☐ E5 Clemon Johnson	1.50	.75	.15
☐ E6 Bobby Jones	3.00	1.50	.30
☐ E7 Moses Malone	7.50	3.75	.75
☐ E8 Clint Richardson	1.50	.75	.15
☐ E9 Andrew Toney	1.50	.75	.15
☐ E10 Sam Williams	1.50	.75	.15

	MINT	EXC	G-VG
COMPLETE SET (50)	300.00	150.00	30.00
COMMON PLAYER (1-25)	3.00	1.50	.30
COMMON PLAYER (26-50)	3.00	1.50	.30
☐ 1 Kareem Abdul Jabbar	15.00	7.50	1.50
☐ 2 Jeff Ruland	3.00	1.50	.30
☐ 3 Mark Aguirre	5.00	2.50	.50
☐ 4 Julius Erving	15.00	7.50	1.50
☐ 5 Kelly Tripucka	3.00	1.50	.30
☐ 6 Buck Williams	7.50	3.75	.75
☐ 7 Sidney Moncrief	5.00	2.50	.50
☐ 8 World B. Free	4.00	2.00	.40
☐ 9 Bill Walton	6.00	3.00	.60
☐ 10 Purvis Short	3.00	1.50	.30
☐ 11 Rickey Green	3.00	1.50	.30
☐ 12 Dominique Wilkins	12.00	6.00	1.20
☐ 13 Jim Paxson	3.00	1.50	.30
☐ 14 Ralph Sampson	4.00	2.00	.40
☐ 15 Magic Johnson	20.00	10.00	2.00
☐ 16 Reggie Theus	4.00	2.00	.40
☐ 17 Moses Malone	9.00	4.50	.90
☐ 18 Larry Bird	20.00	10.00	2.00
☐ 19 Larry Nance	4.00	2.00	.40
☐ 20 Clark Kellogg	3.00	1.50	.30
☐ 21 Jack Sikma	4.00	2.00	.40
☐ 22 Alex English	6.00	3.00	.60
☐ 23 Bernard King	6.00	3.00	.60
☐ 24 Dave Corzine	3.00	1.50	.30
☐ 25 George Gervin	6.00	3.00	.60
☐ 26 Michael Jordan	125.00	60.00	12.50
☐ 27 Rolando Blackman	5.00	2.50	.50
☐ 28 Dan Issel	5.00	2.50	.50
☐ 29 Maurice Cheeks	4.00	2.00	.40
☐ 30 Isiah Thomas	10.00	5.00	1.00
☐ 31 Robert Parish	7.50	3.75	.75
☐ 32 Mark Eaton	4.00	2.00	.40
☐ 33 Sam Perkins	12.00	6.00	1.20
☐ 34 Artis Gilmore	5.00	2.50	.50
☐ 35 Andrew Toney	3.00	1.50	.30
☐ 36 Adrian Dantley	6.00	3.00	.60
☐ 37 Terry Cummings	12.00	6.00	1.20
☐ 38 Orlando Woolridge	5.00	2.50	.50
☐ 39 Tom Chambers	12.00	6.00	1.20
☐ 40 Gus Williams	4.00	2.00	.40
☐ 41 Charles Barkley	25.00	12.50	2.50
☐ 42 Kevin McHale	6.00	3.00	.60
☐ 43 Otis Birdsong	3.00	1.50	.30
☐ 44 Sam Bowie	4.00	2.00	.40
☐ 45 Darrell Griffith	4.00	2.00	.40
☐ 46 Kiki Vandeweghe	5.00	2.50	.50
☐ 47 Akeem Olajuwon	20.00	10.00	2.00
☐ 48 Marques Johnson	4.00	2.00	.40
☐ 49 James Worthy	10.00	5.00	1.00
☐ 50 Mel Turpin	3.00	1.50	.30

1984-85 Star Court Kings

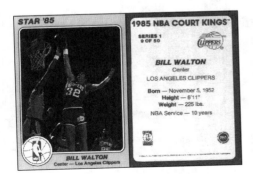

This 50-card set was issued as two series of 25. Cards measure 5" by 7" and have a yellow (first series 1-25) or blue (second series 26-50) colored border around the fronts of the cards and blue and yellow printing on the backs. These large cards feature the Star '85 logo on the front.

1984-85 Star Julius Erving

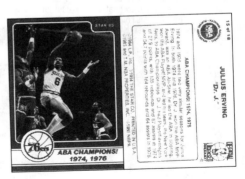

This set contains 18 cards highlighting the career of basketball great Julius Erving. Cards measure 2 1/2" by 3 1/2" and have a red border around the fronts of the cards and red printing on the backs. Cards feature Star '85 logo on the front although they were released in the Summer of 1984.

	MINT	EXC	G-VG
COMPLETE SET (18)	50.00	25.00	5.00
COMMON PLAYER (1-18)	4.00	2.00	.40
□ 1 Checklist	5.00	2.50	.50
□ 2 NBA Regular Season Stats	4.00	2.00	.40
□ 3 ABA Regular Season Stats	4.00	2.00	.40
□ 4 NBA All-Star Eight Times	4.00	2.00	.40
□ 5 ABA All-Star Five Times	4.00	2.00	.40
□ 6 NBA Playoff Stats	4.00	2.00	.40
□ 7 ABA Playoff Stats	4.00	2.00	.40
□ 8 NBA MVP, 1981	4.00	2.00	.40
□ 9 ABA MVP, 1974, 1975, and 1976	4.00	2.00	.40
□ 10 Collegiate Stats	4.00	2.00	.40
□ 11 NBA All-Star MVP, 1977 and 1983	4.00	2.00	.40
□ 12 NBA Career Highlights	4.00	2.00	.40
□ 13 ABA Career Highlights	4.00	2.00	.40
□ 14 1983 World Champs	4.00	2.00	.40
□ 15 ABA Champions 1974 and 1976	4.00	2.00	.40
□ 16 All-Time Scoring	4.00	2.00	.40
□ 17 Personal Data	4.00	2.00	.40
□ 18 The Future	5.00	2.50	.50

1985 Star Bucks Card Night

This 13-card set was given away during the Milwaukee Bucks "Card Night" on January 21, 1985. Card number 10 Larry Micheaux was withdrawn at the request of the Bucks management due to his Free Agent signing after the printing of the cards. Cards measure 2 1/2" by 3 1/2" and have a green border around the fronts of the cards and green printing on the backs. Cards feature Star '85 logo on the fronts.

	MINT	EXC	G-VG
COMPLETE SET (13)	75.00	37.50	7.50
COMMON PLAYER (1-13)	1.50	.75	.15
□ 1 Don Nelson CO	3.50	1.75	.35
□ 2 Randy Breuer	2.25	1.10	.22
□ 3 Terry Cummings	9.00	4.50	.90
□ 4 Charlie Davis	1.50	.75	.15
□ 5 Mike Dunleavy	3.50	1.75	.35
□ 6 Kenny Fields	2.25	1.10	.22
□ 7 Kevin Grevey	2.25	1.10	.22
□ 8 Craig Hodges	3.50	1.75	.35
□ 9 Alton Lister	2.25	1.10	.22
□ 10 Larry Micheaux	50.00	25.00	5.00
□ 11 Paul Mokeski	2.25	1.10	.22
□ 12 Sidney Moncrief	5.00	2.50	.50
□ 13 Paul Pressey	3.50	1.75	.35

1985 Star Slam Dunk Supers

This ten-card set uses actual photography from the 1985 Slam Dunk contest in Indianapolis held during the NBA All-Star Weekend. Cards measure 5" by 7" and have a red border around the fronts of the cards and red printing on the backs. Cards feature Star '85 logo on the fronts.

	MINT	EXC	G-VG
COMPLETE SET (10)	165.00	75.00	15.00
COMMON PLAYER (1-10)	3.00	1.50	.30
□ 1 Checklist Card	3.00	1.50	.30
□ 2 Clyde Drexler	25.00	12.50	2.50
□ 3 Julius Erving	12.00	6.00	1.20
□ 4 Darrel Griffith	4.00	2.00	.40
□ 5 Michael Jordan	100.00	50.00	10.00
□ 6 Larry Nance	5.00	2.50	.50
□ 7 Terence Stansbury	3.00	1.50	.30
□ 8 Dominique Wilkins	15.00	7.50	1.50
□ 9 Orlando Woolridge	4.00	2.00	.40
□ 10 Dominique Wilkins (1985 Slam Dunk Champion)	12.00	6.00	1.20

1985 Star Gatorade Slam Dunk

This nine-card set was given to the people who attended the 1985 All-Star Weekend Banquet at Indianapolis. Since Terence Stansbury was a late substitute in the Slam Dunk contest for Charles Barkley, both cards were produced, but the Barkley card was never released. Cards measure 2 1/2" by 3 1/2" and have a green border around the fronts of the cards and green printing on the backs. Cards feature the Star '85 and Gatorade logos on the fronts.

	MINT	EXC	G-VG
COMPLETE SET (9)	135.00	60.00	12.00
COMMON PLAYER (1-9)	3.00	1.50	.30

		MINT	EXC	G-VG
☐ 1	Gatorade 2nd Annual .... Slam Dunk Championship (checklist back)	3.00	1.50	.30
☐ 2	Larry Nance	5.00	2.50	.50
☐ 3	Terence Stansbury	3.00	1.50	.30
☐ 4	Clyde Drexler	25.00	12.50	2.50
☐ 5	Julius Erving	12.00	6.00	1.20
☐ 6	Darrell Griffith	4.00	2.00	.40
☐ 7	Michael Jordan	100.00	50.00	10.00
☐ 8	Dominique Wilkins	15.00	7.50	1.50
☐ 9	Orlando Woolridge	4.00	2.00	.40

1985 Star Lite All-Stars

This 13-card set was given to the people who attended the 1985 All-Star Weekend Banquet at Indianapolis. Cards measure 2 1/2" by 3 1/2" and have a blue border around the fronts of the cards and blue printing on the backs. Cards feature the Star '85 and Lite Beer logos on the fronts. Players featured are the 1985 NBA All-Star starting line-ups and coaches.

		MINT	EXC	G-VG
COMPLETE SET (13)		150.00	75.00	15.00
COMMON PLAYER (1-13)		3.00	1.50	.30
☐ 1	1985 NBA All-Stars .... Starting Line-Ups	3.00	1.50	.30
☐ 2	Larry Bird	20.00	10.00	2.00
☐ 3	Julius Erving	9.00	4.50	.90
☐ 4	Michael Jordan	100.00	50.00	10.00
☐ 5	Moses Malone	6.00	3.00	.60
☐ 6	Isiah Thomas	10.00	5.00	1.00
☐ 7	K.C. Jones CO	3.00	1.50	.30
☐ 8	Kareem Abdul Jabbar	9.00	4.50	.90
☐ 9	Adrian Dantley	4.00	2.00	.40
☐ 10	George Gervin	5.00	2.50	.50
☐ 11	Magic Johnson	20.00	10.00	2.00
☐ 12	Ralph Sampson	3.00	1.50	.30
☐ 13	Pat Riley CO	4.00	2.00	.40

1985 Star Schick Legends

This 24-card set was given to the people who attended the 1985 All-Star Weekend Banquet at Indianapolis. Cards measure 2 1/2" by 3 1/2" and have a yellow border around the fronts of the cards and yellow and black printing on the backs. Cards feature the Star '85 and Schick logos on the fronts. Players featured were participants in the Schick NBA Legends Classic.

		MINT	EXC	G-VG
COMPLETE SET (25)		50.00	25.00	5.00
COMMON PLAYER (1-25)		1.50	.75	.15
☐ 1	Schick NBA Legends .... Checklist	2.25	1.10	.22
☐ 2	Rick Barry	6.00	3.00	.60
☐ 3	Zelmo Beaty	1.50	.75	.15

		MINT	EXC	G-VG
☐ 4	Walt Bellamy	1.50	.75	.15
☐ 5	Dave Bing	4.00	2.00	.40
☐ 6	Roger Brown	1.50	.75	.15
☐ 7	Bob Cousy	10.00	5.00	1.00
☐ 8	Mel Daniels	1.50	.75	.15
☐ 9	Bob Davies	2.25	1.10	.22
☐ 10	Dave DeBusschere	4.00	2.00	.40
☐ 11	Walt Frazier	5.00	2.50	.50
☐ 12	John Havlicek	7.50	3.75	.75
☐ 13	Connie Hawkins	3.00	1.50	.30
☐ 14	Tom Heinsohn	4.00	2.00	.40
☐ 15	Red Holzman	2.25	1.10	.22
☐ 16	Johnny Kerr	1.50	.75	.15
☐ 17	Bobby Leonard	1.50	.75	.15
☐ 18	Pete Maravich	12.00	6.00	1.20
☐ 19	Earl Monroe	4.00	2.00	.40
☐ 20	Bob Pettit	6.00	3.00	.60
☐ 21	Oscar Robertson	10.00	5.00	1.00
☐ 22	Nate Thurmond	4.00	2.00	.40
☐ 23	Dick Van Arsdale	1.50	.75	.15
☐ 24	Tom Van Arsdale	1.50	.75	.15
☐ 25	George Yardley	1.50	.75	.15

1985 Star Team Supers

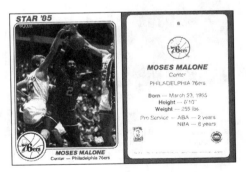

This 40-card set is actually eight team sets of five each except for the Sixers having 10 players included. Cards measure 5" by 7" and have a colored border around the fronts of the cards according to the team with corresponding color printing on the backs. Cards feature Star '85 logo on the front. Cards are numbered below by assigning a team prefix based on the initials of the team, for example, BC for Boston Celtics.

		MINT	EXC	G-VG
COMPLETE SET (40)		350.00	175.00	35.00
COMMON PLAYER		3.00	1.50	.30
☐ BC1	Larry Bird	25.00	12.50	2.50
☐ BC2	Robert Parish	7.50	3.75	.75
☐ BC3	Kevin McHale	6.00	3.00	.60
☐ BC4	Dennis Johnson	5.00	2.50	.50
☐ BC5	Danny Ainge	5.00	2.50	.50
☐ CB1	Michael Jordan	125.00	60.00	12.50

☐	CB2	Orlando Woolridge	4.00	2.00	.40
☐	CB3	Quintin Dailey	3.00	1.50	.30
☐	CB4	Dave Corzine	3.00	1.50	.30
☐	CB5	Steve Johnson	3.00	1.50	.30
☐	DP1	Isiah Thomas	15.00	7.50	1.50
☐	DP2	Kelly Tripucka	4.00	2.00	.40
☐	DP3	Vinnie Johnson	6.00	3.00	.60
☐	DP4	Bill Laimbeer	7.50	3.75	.75
☐	DP5	John Long	3.00	1.50	.30
☐	HR1	Ralph Sampson	4.00	2.00	.40
☐	HR2	Akeem Olajuwon	40.00	20.00	4.00
☐	HR3	Lewis Lloyd	3.00	1.50	.30
☐	HR4	Rodney McCray	5.00	2.50	.50
☐	HR5	Lionel Hollins	4.00	2.00	.40
☐	LA1	Kareem Abdul Jabbar	15.00	7.50	1.50
☐	LA2	Magic Johnson	25.00	12.50	2.50
☐	LA3	James Worthy	12.00	6.00	1.20
☐	LA4	Byron Scott	6.00	3.00	.60
☐	LA5	Bob McAdoo	5.00	2.50	.50
☐	MB1	Terry Cummings	12.00	6.00	1.20
☐	MB2	Sidney Moncrief	6.00	3.00	.60
☐	MB3	Paul Pressey	5.00	2.50	.50
☐	MB4	Mike Dunleavy	4.00	2.00	.40
☐	MB5	Alton Lister	3.00	1.50	.30
☐	PS1	Julius Erving	15.00	7.50	1.50
☐	PS2	Maurice Cheeks	4.00	2.00	.40
☐	PS3	Bobby Jones	5.00	2.50	.50
☐	PS4	Clemon Johnson	3.00	1.50	.30
☐	PS5	Leon Wood	3.00	1.50	.30
☐	PS6	Moses Malone	9.00	4.50	.90
☐	PS7	Andrew Toney	3.00	1.50	.30
☐	PS8	Charles Barkley	50.00	25.00	5.00
☐	PS9	Clint Richardson	3.00	1.50	.30
☐	PS10	Sedale Threatt	4.00	2.00	.40

1985 Star Coaches

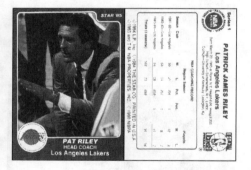

PAT RILEY
HEAD COACH
Los Angeles Lakers

The 1984-85 Star NBA Coaches set is a ten-card set depicting some of the NBA's best known coaches. The set's basic design is identical to those of the Star Company's regular NBA sets. The cards measure approximately 2 1/2" by 3 1/2". The front borders are royal blue, and the backs show each man's coaching records. Statistics for ex-players are NOT included. The cards show a Star '85 logo in the upper right corner. Coaching statistics on the card backs only go up through the 1983-84 NBA season.

		MINT	EXC	G-VG
	COMPLETE SET (10)	15.00	7.50	1.50
	COMMON PLAYER (1-10)	1.50	.75	.15
☐	1 John Bach	1.50	.75	.15
☐	2 Hubie Brown	2.25	1.10	.22
☐	3 Cotton Fitzsimmons	2.25	1.10	.22
☐	4 Kevin Loughery	1.50	.75	.15
☐	5 John MacLeod	2.25	1.10	.22
☐	6 Doug Moe	2.25	1.10	.22
☐	7 Don Nelson	3.00	1.50	.30
☐	8 Jack Ramsay	2.25	1.10	.22
☐	9 Pat Riley	4.00	2.00	.40
☐	10 Lenny Wilkens	3.00	1.50	.30
	(Name misspelled on card back)			

1985 Star Crunch'n'Munch All-Stars

MAGIC JOHNSON
West All-Star

The 1985 Star Crunch 'n Munch NBA All-Stars set is an 11-card set featuring the ten starting players in the 1985 NBA All-Star Game, plus a checklist card. The set's basic design is identical to those of the Star Company's regular NBA sets. The cards measure approximately 2 1/2" by 3 1/2". The cards show a Star '85 logo in the upper right corner. The front borders are yellowish orange, and the backs show each player's All-Star Game record.

		MINT	EXC	G-VG
	COMPLETE SET (11)	150.00	75.00	15.00
	COMMON PLAYER (1-11)	2.00	1.00	.20
☐	1 Checklist Card	5.00	1.00	.20
☐	2 Larry Bird	20.00	10.00	2.00
☐	3 Julius Erving	10.00	5.00	1.00
☐	4 Michael Jordan	100.00	50.00	10.00
☐	5 Moses Malone	7.50	3.75	.75
☐	6 Isiah Thomas	10.00	5.00	1.00
☐	7 Kareem Abdul Jabbar	10.00	5.00	1.00
☐	8 Adrian Dantley	4.00	2.00	.40
☐	9 George Gervin	5.00	2.50	.50
☐	10 Magic Johnson	20.00	10.00	2.00
☐	11 Ralph Sampson	2.00	1.00	.20

1985 Star Kareem

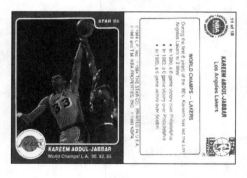

KAREEM ABDUL-JABBAR
World Champs! L.A. '80, '82, '85

The 1985 Star Kareem Abdul Jabbar set is an 18-card tribute highlighting the career of Abdul Jabbar. The pictures on the fronts show recent pictures of Kareem, but the backs provide various statistics and tidbits of information about Abdul Jabbar. The set's basic design is identical to those of the Star Company's regular NBA sets. The cards show a Star '85 logo in the upper right corner. The cards measure approximately 2 1/2" by 3 1/2". The front borders are Lakers' purple.

	MINT	EXC	G-VG
COMPLETE SET (18)	50.00	25.00	5.00
COMMON PLAYER (1-18)	4.00	2.00	.40
☐ 1 Checklist Card	5.00	2.50	.50
☐ 2 Collegiate Stats	4.00	2.00	.40
☐ 3 Regular Season Stats	4.00	2.00	.40
☐ 4 Playoff Stats	4.00	2.00	.40
☐ 5 All Star Stats	4.00	2.00	.40
☐ 6 All-Time Scoring King	4.00	2.00	.40
☐ 7 NBA MVP 71/72/74	4.00	2.00	.40
☐ 8 NBA MVP 76/77/80	4.00	2.00	.40
☐ 9 Defensive Star	4.00	2.00	.40
☐ 10 World Champs 71	4.00	2.00	.40
☐ 11 World Champs 80/82/85	4.00	2.00	.40
☐ 12 All-Time Records	4.00	2.00	.40
☐ 13 Rookie-of-the-Year 70	4.00	2.00	.40
☐ 14 Playoff MVP 71/85	4.00	2.00	.40
☐ 15 The League Leader	4.00	2.00	.40
☐ 16 Career Highlights	4.00	2.00	.40
☐ 17 Personal Data	4.00	2.00	.40
☐ 18 The Future	5.00	2.50	.50

1985 Star ROY's

The 1985 Star Rookies of the Year set is an 11-card set depicting each of the NBA's ROY award winners from the 1974-75 through 1984-85 seasons. Michael Jordan's card only shows his collegiate statistics; all others provide NBA statistics (but only up through the 1983-84 NBA season). Cards of Darrell Griffith and Keith Wilkes show the Star '86 logo in the upper right corner; all others in the set show Star '85. The set's basic design is identical to those of the Star Company's regular NBA sets, and the front borders are off-white. The cards measure approximately 2 1/2" by 3 1/2".

	MINT	EXC	G-VG
COMPLETE SET (11)	150.00	75.00	15.00
COMMON PLAYER (1-11)	1.50	.75	.15
☐ 1 Michael Jordan	100.00	50.00	10.00
☐ 2 Ralph Sampson	3.00	1.50	.30
☐ 3 Terry Cummings	15.00	7.50	1.50
☐ 4 Buck Williams	9.00	4.50	.90
☐ 5 Darrell Griffith	4.00	2.00	.40
☐ 6 Larry Bird	30.00	15.00	3.00
☐ 7 Phil Ford	2.25	1.10	.22
☐ 8 Walter Davis	5.00	2.50	.50
☐ 9 Adrian Dantley	5.00	2.50	.50
☐ 10 Alvan Adams	1.50	.75	.15
☐ 11 Keith Wilkes	3.50	1.75	.35

1985-86 Star All-Rookie Team

The 1985-86 Star NBA All-Rookie Team is an 11-card set features 11 top rookies from the previous (1984-85) season. The set's basic design is identical to those of the Star Company's

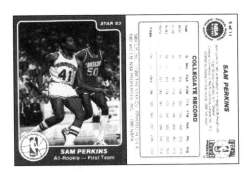

regular NBA sets. The cards measure approximately 2 1/2" by 3 1/2". The front borders are red, and the backs include each player's collegiate statistics. Alvin Robertson's card shows the Star '86 logo in the upper right corner; all others in the set show Star '85. The statistics on the card backs provide only college records.

	MINT	EXC	G-VG
COMPLETE SET (11)	250.00	125.00	25.00
COMMON PLAYER (1-11)	1.50	.75	.15
☐ 1 Akeem Olajuwon	50.00	25.00	5.00
☐ 2 Michael Jordan	100.00	50.00	10.00
☐ 3 Charles Barkley	60.00	30.00	6.00
☐ 4 Sam Bowie	6.00	3.00	.60
☐ 5 Sam Perkins	12.00	6.00	1.20
☐ 6 Vern Fleming	3.00	1.50	.30
☐ 7 Otis Thorpe	12.00	6.00	1.20
☐ 8 John Stockton	60.00	30.00	6.00
☐ 9 Kevin Willis	6.00	3.00	.60
☐ 10 Tim McCormick	1.50	.75	.15
☐ 11 Alvin Robertson	8.00	4.00	.80

1985-86 Star Lakers Champs

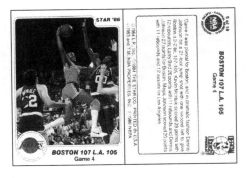

The 1985-86 Star Lakers NBA Champs set is an 18-card set commemorating the Los Angeles Lakers' 1985 NBA Championship. Each card depicts one scene from the Championship series. The front borders are off-white. The backs feature game and series summaries, plus other related information. The set's basic design is identical to those of the Star Company's regular NBA sets. The cards show a Star '86 logo in the upper right corner. The cards measure approximately 2 1/2" by 3 1/2". The cards are numbered in the upper left corner of the reverse.

	MINT	EXC	G-VG
COMPLETE SET (18)	70.00	35.00	7.00
COMMON PLAYER (1-18)	1.50	.75	.15

		MINT	EXC	G-VG
☐ 1	Lakers 1985 NBA Champs ...... (Kareem and Buss with trophy)¡	6.00	3.00	.60
☐ 2	Boston 148, L.A. 114 .... (Bird under basket)	7.50	3.75	.75
☐ 3	L.A. 109, Boston 102 .... (Dennis Johnson)	3.00	1.50	.30
☐ 4	L.A. 136, Boston 111 .... (Danny Ainge)	3.00	1.50	.30
☐ 5	Boston 107, L.A. 105 .... (Byron Scott driving)	3.00	1.50	.30
☐ 6	L.A. 120, Boston 111 .... (McHale under basket)	4.00	2.00	.40
☐ 7	L.A. 111, Boston 100 .... (Magic driving)	7.50	3.75	.75
☐ 8	Kareem 1985 Series MVP	5.00	2.50	.50
☐ 9	Playoff Highs .... (Larry Bird)	7.50	3.75	.75
☐ 10	Top Playoff Scorers .... (Kareem holding ball)	5.00	2.50	.50
☐ 11	Title Fight .... (Ainge/Michael Cooper)	3.00	1.50	.30
☐ 12	Laker Series Stats .... (Riley in huddle)	3.00	1.50	.30
☐ 13	Boston Series Stats .... (K.C. Jones in huddle)	2.25	1.10	.22
☐ 14	L.A. Playoff Stats .... (Magic driving)	7.50	3.75	.75
☐ 15	Boston Playoff Stats .... (action under basket)	1.50	.75	.15
☐ 16	Road To The Title	1.50	.75	.15
☐ 17	Prior World Champs I .... (riding on float)	1.50	.75	.15
☐ 18	Prior World Champs II .... (with Ronald Reagan)	15.00	7.50	1.50

		MINT	EXC	G-VG
☐ 14	Patrick Ewing	40.00	20.00	4.00
☐ 15	George Gervin	5.00	2.50	.50
☐ 16	Darrell Griffith	3.00	1.50	.30
☐ 17	Magic Johnson	20.00	10.00	2.00
☐ 18	Michael Jordan	100.00	50.00	10.00
☐ 19	Clark Kellogg	1.50	.75	.15
☐ 20	Bernard King	5.00	2.50	.50
☐ 21	Moses Malone	6.00	3.00	.60
☐ 22	Kevin McHale	5.00	2.50	.50
☐ 23	Sidney Moncrief	3.50	1.75	.35
☐ 24	Larry Nance	2.25	1.10	.22
☐ 25	Akeem Olajuwon	20.00	10.00	2.00
☐ 26	Robert Parish	6.00	3.00	.60
☐ 27	Ralph Sampson	3.00	1.50	.30
☐ 28	Isiah Thomas	10.00	5.00	1.00
☐ 29	Andrew Toney	1.50	.75	.15
☐ 30	Kelly Tripucka	1.50	.75	.15
☐ 31	Kiki Vandeweghe	3.00	1.50	.30
☐ 32	Dominique Wilkins	10.00	5.00	1.00
☐ 33	James Worthy	7.50	3.75	.75

1986 Star Michael Jordan

The 1986 Star Michael Jordan set contains 10 cards highlighting the career of Michael Jordan. The card backs contain various information about Jordan. The set's basic design is identical to those of the Star Company's regular NBA sets. The front borders are red. The cards show a Star '86 logo in the upper right corner. The cards measure approximately 2 1/2" by 3 1/2". The cards are numbered in the upper left corner of the reverse.

		MINT	EXC	G-VG
COMPLETE SET (10)		500.00	250.00	50.00
COMMON PLAYER (1-10)		75.00	37.50	7.50
☐ 1	Michael Jordan	75.00	37.50	7.50
☐ 2	Collegiate Stats	75.00	37.50	7.50
☐ 3	1984 Olympian	75.00	37.50	7.50
☐ 4	Pro Stats	75.00	37.50	7.50
☐ 5	1985 All-Star	75.00	37.50	7.50
☐ 6	1985 Rookie of Year	75.00	37.50	7.50
☐ 7	Career Highlights	75.00	37.50	7.50
☐ 8	The 1986 Playoffs	75.00	37.50	7.50
☐ 9	Personal Data	75.00	37.50	7.50
☐ 10	The Future	75.00	37.50	7.50

1986 Star Court Kings

The 1986 Star Court Kings set contains 33 cards which feature many of the NBA's top players. The set's basic design is identical to those of the Star Company's regular NBA sets. The front borders are yellow, and the backs have career narrative summaries of each player but no statistics. The cards show a Star '86 logo in the upper right corner. The cards measure approximately 2 1/2" by 3 1/2". The cards are numbered in the upper left corner of the reverse.

		MINT	EXC	G-VG
COMPLETE SET (33)		250.00	125.00	25.00
COMMON PLAYER (1-33)		1.50	.75	.15
☐ 1	Mark Aguirre	3.00	1.50	.30
☐ 2	Kareem Abdul Jabbar	9.00	4.50	.90
☐ 3	Charles Barkley	20.00	10.00	2.00
☐ 4	Larry Bird	20.00	10.00	2.00
☐ 5	Rolando Blackman	3.00	1.50	.30
☐ 6	Tom Chambers	6.00	3.00	.60
☐ 7	Maurice Cheeks	2.25	1.10	.22
☐ 8	Terry Cummings	7.50	3.75	.75
☐ 9	Adrian Dantley	3.50	1.75	.35
☐ 10	Darryl Dawkins	2.25	1.10	.22
☐ 11	Mark Eaton	2.25	1.10	.22
☐ 12	Alex English	5.00	2.50	.50
☐ 13	Julius Erving	9.00	4.50	.90

1986 Star Lifebuoy Bucks

The 1986 Star Lifebuoy Milwaukee Bucks set contains 13 cards, one for each of the 12 players plus a coaching staff card. The set's basic design is identical to those of the Star Company's regular NBA sets. The front borders are lime green, and the backs show each player's NBA statistics (collegiate for number 13 Jerry Reynolds). The cards show a Star '86 logo in the upper right corner. The cards measure approximately 2 1/2" by 3 1/2". The cards are numbered in the upper left corner of the reverse.

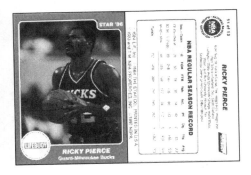

		MINT	EXC	G-VG
☐ 11	Micheal Ray Richardson	3.00	1.50	.30
☐ 12	Jeff Turner	1.50	.75	.15
☐ 13	Buck Williams	6.00	3.00	.60
☐ 14	Title Card	1.50	.75	.15
	(checklist on back)			

	MINT	EXC	G-VG
COMPLETE SET (13)	18.00	9.00	1.80
COMMON PLAYER (1-13)	1.50	.75	.15

		MINT	EXC	G-VG
☐ 1	Don Nelson CO	2.25	1.10	.22
☐ 2	Randy Breuer	2.25	1.10	.22
☐ 3	Terry Cummings	6.00	3.00	.60
☐ 4	Charlie Davis	1.50	.75	.15
☐ 5	Kenny Fields	2.25	1.10	.22
☐ 6	Craig Hodges	3.00	1.50	.30
☐ 7	Jeff Lamp	1.50	.75	.15
☐ 8	Alton Lister	2.25	1.10	.22
☐ 9	Paul Mokeski	1.50	.75	.15
☐ 10	Sidney Moncrief	4.00	2.00	.40
☐ 11	Ricky Pierce	5.00	2.50	.50
☐ 12	Paul Pressey	3.00	1.50	.30
☐ 13	Jerry Reynolds	1.50	.75	.15

1986 Star Lifebuoy Nets

The 1986 Star Lifebuoy New Jersey Nets set contains 14 cards, one for each of the 12 players, one for Head Coach Dave Wohl, and a checklist card. The set's basic design is identical to those of the Star Company's regular NBA sets. The front borders are royal blue, and the backs show each player's NBA statistics. The cards show a Star '86 logo in the upper right corner. The cards measure approximately 2 1/2" by 3 1/2". The cards are numbered in the upper left corner of the reverse.

	MINT	EXC	G-VG
COMPLETE SET (14)	15.00	7.50	1.50
COMMON PLAYER (1-14)	1.50	.75	.15

		MINT	EXC	G-VG
☐ 1	Dave Wohl CO	1.50	.75	.15
☐ 2	Otis Birdsong	2.25	1.10	.22
☐ 3	Bobby Cattage	1.50	.75	.15
☐ 4	Darwin Cook	1.50	.75	.15
☐ 5	Darryl Dawkins	3.00	1.50	.30
☐ 6	Mike Gminski	3.00	1.50	.30
☐ 7	Mickey Johnson	2.25	1.10	.22
☐ 8	Albert King	2.25	1.10	.22
☐ 9	Mike O'Koren	2.25	1.10	.22
☐ 10	Kelvin Ransey	1.50	.75	.15

1986 Star Best of the Old/New

According to the producer, only 440 of these sets were produced by Star Company, who distributed them to dealers who bought 1985-86 complete sets. Dealers received one set for every five regular sets purchased. The cards measure the standard size (2 1/2" by 3 1/2"). The cards are unnumbered and checklisted below in alphabetical order. The Best of the New are numbered 1-4 and the Best of the Old are numbered 5-8.

	MINT	EXC	G-VG
COMPLETE SET (8)	1800.00	750.00	150.00
COMMON PLAYER (1-4)	40.00	20.00	4.00
COMMON PLAYER (5-8)	40.00	20.00	4.00

		MINT	EXC	G-VG
☐ 1	Patrick Ewing	300.00	150.00	30.00
☐ 2	Michael Jordan	900.00	450.00	90.00
☐ 3	Akeem Olajuwon	250.00	125.00	25.00
☐ 4	Ralph Sampson	40.00	20.00	4.00
☐ 5	Kareem Abdul Jabbar	125.00	60.00	12.50
☐ 6	Julius Erving	125.00	60.00	12.50
☐ 7	George Gervin	40.00	20.00	4.00
☐ 8	Bill Walton	60.00	30.00	6.00

1990 Star Pics

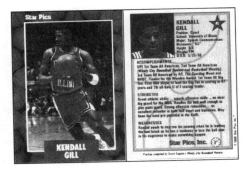

This premier edition showcases sixty of college basketball's top pro prospects. The cards measure the standard size (2 1/2" by 3 1/2"). The front features a color action player photo, with the player shown in his college uniform. A white border separates the picture from the surrounding "basketball" background. The player's name appears in an aqua box at the bottom. The back has a head shot of the player in the upper left corner and the card number in a red star in the upper right corner. On a tan-colored basketball court design, the back presents biography, accomplishments, and a mini-scouting report that assesses a player's strengths and weaknesses. The more limited "Medallion" edition is valued at approximately double the prices listed below.

	MINT	EXC	G-VG
COMPLETE SET (70)	33.00	15.00	3.00
COMMON PLAYER (1-70)	.10	.05	.01

		MINT	EXC	G-VG
☐ 1	Checklist Card	.10	.05	.01
☐ 2	David Robinson	6.00	3.00	.60
	(Mr. Robinson)			
☐ 3	Antonio Davis	.10	.05	.01
	UTEP			

☐ 4 Steve Bardo Illinois	.15	.07	.01
☐ 5 Jayson Williams St. John's	.20	.10	.02
☐ 6 Alaa Abdelnaby Duke	.25	.12	.02
☐ 7 Trevor Wilson UCLA	.15	.07	.01
☐ 8 Dee Brown Jacksonville	7.50	3.75	.75
☐ 9 Dennis Scott Georgia Tech	1.75	.85	.17
☐ 10 Danny Ferry (Flashback)	.50	.25	.05
☐ 11 Stevie Thompson Syracuse	.15	.07	.01
☐ 12 Anthony Bonner St. Louis	.25	.12	.02
☐ 13 Keith Robinson Notre Dame	.10	.05	.01
☐ 14 Sean Higgins Michigan	.30	.15	.03
☐ 15 Bo Kimble Loyola Marymount	1.00	.50	.10
☐ 16 David Jamerson Ohio University	.20	.10	.02
☐ 17 Anthony Pullard McNeese State	.10	.05	.01
☐ 18 Phil Henderson Duke	.15	.07	.01
☐ 19 Mike Mitchell Colorado State	.10	.05	.01
☐ 20 Vanderbilt Team	.10	.05	.01
☐ 21 Gary Payton Oregon State	1.75	.85	.17
☐ 22 Tony Massenburg Maryland	.25	.12	.02
☐ 23 Cedric Ceballos Cal State-Fullerton	.75	.35	.07
☐ 24 Dwayne Schintzius Florida	.50	.25	.05
☐ 25 Bimbo Coles Virginia Tech	.25	.12	.02
☐ 26 Scott Williams North Carolina	.25	.12	.02
☐ 27 Willie Burton Minnesota	1.00	.50	.10
☐ 28 Tate George U Conn	.20	.10	.02
☐ 29 Mark Stevenson Duquesne	.10	.05	.01
☐ 30 UNLV Team	.75	.35	.07
☐ 31 Earl Wise Tennessee Tech	.10	.05	.01
☐ 32 Alec Kessler Georgia	.25	.12	.02
☐ 33 Les Jepsen Iowa	.15	.07	.01
☐ 34 Boo Harvey St. John's	.15	.07	.01
☐ 35 Elden Campbell Clemson	1.25	.60	.12
☐ 36 Jud Buechler Arizona	.15	.07	.01
☐ 37 Loy Vaught Michigan	.30	.15	.03
☐ 38 Tyrone Hill Xavier	.50	.25	.05
☐ 39 Toni Kukoc Jugoplastika	.50	.25	.05
☐ 40 Jim Calhoun CO U Conn	.10	.05	.01
☐ 41 Felton Spencer Louisville	.75	.35	.07
☐ 42 Dan Godfread Evansville	.10	.05	.01
☐ 43 Derrick Coleman Syracuse	9.00	4.50	.90
☐ 44 Terry Mills Michigan	.40	.20	.04
☐ 45 Kendall Gill Illinois	1.75	.85	.17
☐ 46 A.J. English Virginia Union	.40	.20	.04
☐ 47 Duane Causwell Temple	.30	.15	.03
☐ 48 Jerrod Mustaf Maryland	.40	.20	.04
☐ 49 Alan Ogg Alabama Birmingham	.10	.05	.01
☐ 50 Pervis Ellison (Flashback)	.30	.15	.03
☐ 51 Matt Bullard Iowa	.10	.05	.01

☐ 52 Melvin Newbern Minnesota	.15	.07	.01
☐ 53 Marcus Liberty Illinois	.30	.15	.03
☐ 54 Walter Palmer Dartmouth	.15	.07	.01
☐ 55 Negele Knight Dayton	1.00	.50	.10
☐ 56 Steve Henson Kansas State	.15	.07	.01
☐ 57 Greg Foster UTEP	.15	.07	.01
☐ 58 Brian Oliver Georgia Tech	.25	.12	.02
☐ 59 Travis Mays Texas	1.25	.60	.12
☐ 60 All-Rookie Team	1.00	.50	.10
☐ 61 Steve Scheffler Purdue	.15	.07	.01
☐ 62 Chris Jackson LSU	1.25	.60	.12
☐ 63 Derek Strong Xavier	.10	.05	.01
☐ 64 David Butler UNLV	.15	.07	.01
☐ 65 Kevin Pritchard Kansas	.15	.07	.01
☐ 66 Lionel Simmons LaSalle	3.50	1.75	.35
☐ 67 Gerald Glass Mississippi	.30	.15	.03
☐ 68 Tony Harris New Orleans	.10	.05	.01
☐ 69 Lance Blanks Texas	.20	.10	.02
☐ 70 Draft Overview	.10	.05	.01

1991 Star Pics

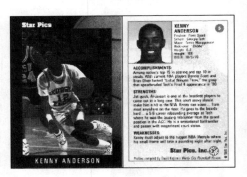

KENNY ANDERSON

This 72-card set was produced by Star Pics, subtitled "Pro Prospects," and features 45 of the 54 players picked in the 1991 NBA draft. The cards measure the standard size (2 1/2" by 3 1/2"). The front features a color action photo of player in his college uniform. This picture overlays a black background with a basketball partially in view. The back has a color head shot of the player in the upper left corner and an orange border. On a two color jersey background, the back presents biographical information, accomplishments, and a mini scouting report assessing the player's strengths and weaknesses. The cards are numbered on the back.

	MINT	EXC	G-VG
COMPLETE SET (72)	15.00	7.50	1.50
COMMON PLAYER (1-72)	.10	.05	.01
☐ 1 Draft Overview	.10	.05	.01
☐ 2 Derrick Coleman Flashback	1.00	.50	.10
☐ 3 Treg Lee Ohio State	.10	.05	.01
☐ 4 Rich King Nebraska	.30	.15	.03
☐ 5 Kenny Anderson Georgia Tech	3.50	1.75	.35

☐ 6 John Crotty Virginia	.10	.05	.01
☐ 7 Mark Randall Kansas	.25	.12	.02
☐ 8 Kevin Brooks Southwestern Lousiana	.20	.10	.02
☐ 9 Lamont Strothers Christopher Newport	.15	.07	.01
☐ 10 Tim Hardaway Flashback	.75	.35	.07
☐ 11 Eric Murdock Providence	.40	.20	.04
☐ 12 Melvin Cheatum Alabama	.10	.05	.01
☐ 13 Pete Chilcutt North Carolina	.25	.12	.02
☐ 14 Zan Tabak Jugoplastika	.20	.10	.02
☐ 15 Greg Anthony UNLV	1.00	.50	.10
☐ 16 George Ackles UNLV	.25	.12	.02
☐ 17 Stacey Augmon UNLV	1.00	.50	.10
☐ 18 Larry Johnson UNLV	3.50	1.75	.35
☐ 19 Alvaro Teheran Houston	.20	.10	.02
☐ 20 Reggie Miller Flashback	.30	.15	.03
☐ 21 Steve Smith Michigan State	1.75	.85	.17
☐ 22 Sean Green Iona	.10	.05	.01
☐ 23 Johnny Pittman Oklahoma State	.15	.07	.01
☐ 24 Anthony Avent Seton Hall	.30	.15	.03
☐ 25 Chris Gatling Old Dominion	.30	.15	.03
☐ 26 Mark Macon Temple	1.00	.50	.10
☐ 27 Joey Wright Texas	.20	.10	.02
☐ 28 Von McDade Wisconsn (Mil)	.10	.05	.01
☐ 29 Bobby Phills Southern U	.10	.05	.01
☐ 30 Larry Fleisher HOF and Lawyer (In Memoriam)	.10	.05	.01
☐ 31 Luc Longley New Mexico	1.00	.50	.10
☐ 32 Jean Derouillere Kansas State	.10	.05	.01
☐ 33 Doug Smith Missouri	1.75	.85	.17
☐ 34 Chad Gallagher Creighton	.20	.10	.02
☐ 35 Marty Dow San Diego State	.10	.05	.01
☐ 36 Tony Farmer Nebraska	.10	.05	.01
☐ 37 John Taft Marshall	.10	.05	.01
☐ 38 Reggie Hanson Kentucky	.10	.05	.01
☐ 39 Terrell Brandon Oregon	.75	.35	.07
☐ 40 Dee Brown Flashback	1.25	.60	.12
☐ 41 Doug Overton La Salle	.20	.10	.02
☐ 42 Joe Wylie Miami	.10	.05	.01
☐ 43 Myron Brown Slippery Rock	.15	.07	.01
☐ 44 Steve Hood James Madison	.20	.10	.02
☐ 45 Randy Brown New Mexico State	.15	.07	.01
☐ 46 Chris Corchiani NC State	.30	.15	.03
☐ 47 Kevin Lynch Minnesota	.25	.12	.02
☐ 48 Donald Hodge Temple	.20	.10	.02
☐ 49 LaBradford Smith Louisville	.50	.25	.05
☐ 50 Shawn Kemp Flashback	.75	.35	.07
☐ 51 Brian Shorter Pittsburgh	.20	.10	.02
☐ 52 Gary Waites Alabama	.10	.05	.01

☐ 53 Mike Iuzzolino St. Francis	.20	.10	.02
☐ 54 LeRon Ellis Syracuse	.25	.12	.02
☐ 55 Perry Carter Ohio State	.10	.05	.01
☐ 56 Keith Hughes Rutgers	.15	.07	.01
☐ 57 John Turner Phillips University	.30	.15	.03
☐ 58 Marcus Kennedy Eastern Michigan	.15	.07	.01
☐ 59 Randy Ayers CO Ohio State	.10	.05	.01
☐ 60 All Rookie Team	.75	.35	.07
☐ 61 Jackie Jones Oklahoma	.10	.05	.01
☐ 62 Shaun Vandiver Colorado	.30	.15	.03
☐ 63 Dale Davis Clemson	.40	.20	.04
☐ 64 Jimmy Oliver Purdue	.15	.07	.01
☐ 65 Elliot Perry Memphis State	.20	.10	.02
☐ 66 Jerome Harmon Louisville	.20	.10	.02
☐ 67 Darrin Chancellor Southern Mississippi	.10	.05	.01
☐ 68 Roy Fisher California (Berkeley)	.10	.05	.01
☐ 69 Rick Fox North Carolina	.75	.35	.07
☐ 70 Kenny Anderson Special Second Card	1.75	.85	.17
☐ 71 Richard Dumas Oklahoma State	.15	.07	.01
☐ 72 Checklist Card	.10	.05	.01

1968-69 Suns Carnation Milk

This 12-card set of Phoenix Suns was sponsored by Carnation Milk and was issued as panels on the sides of milk cartons. The fronts feature a player pose and brief biographical information near the photo. The bottom of the panels indicate "WIN, 440 Home Game tickets to be given away." The cards measure approximately 3 1/2" by 7 1/2". The backs are blank. The cards are unnumbered and are checklisted below in alphabetical order. Bob Warlick was only with the Phoenix Suns during the last half of the 1968-69 season.

	NRMT	VG-E	GOOD
COMPLETE SET (12)	300.00	150.00	30.00
COMMON PLAYER (1-12)	20.00	10.00	2.00
☐ 1 Jim Fox	20.00	10.00	2.00
☐ 2 Gail Goodrich	60.00	30.00	6.00
☐ 3 Gary Gregor	20.00	10.00	2.00
☐ 4 Neil Johnson	20.00	10.00	2.00
☐ 5 John Kerr CO	25.00	12.50	2.50
☐ 6 Dave Lattin	25.00	12.50	2.50
☐ 7 Stan McKenzie	20.00	10.00	2.00
☐ 8 McCoy McLemore	20.00	10.00	2.00
☐ 9 Dick Snyder	20.00	10.00	2.00
☐ 10 Dick Van Arsdale	30.00	15.00	3.00
☐ 11 Bob Warlick	20.00	10.00	2.00
☐ 12 George Wilson	20.00	10.00	2.00

1969-70 Suns Carnation Milk

This ten-card set features members of the Phoenix Suns and was produced by Carnation Milk. The cards show white backgrounds with blue and white drawings of the players. Playing tips (in red type) are found at the bottom of each card. Player statistics were on the opposite milk carton panel and hence were not saved in most cases. The cards measure approximately 3 1/2" by 7 1/2". The backs are blank. The cards are unnumbered and are checklisted below in alphabetical order.

	NRMT	VG-E	GOOD
COMPLETE SET (10)	300.00	150.00	30.00
COMMON PLAYER (1-10)	20.00	10.00	2.00
☐ 1 Jerry Chambers	20.00	10.00	2.00
☐ 2 Jim Fox	20.00	10.00	2.00
☐ 3 Gail Goodrich	60.00	30.00	6.00
☐ 4 Connie Hawkins	50.00	25.00	5.00
☐ 5 Stan McKenzie	20.00	10.00	2.00
☐ 6 Paul Silas	40.00	20.00	4.00
☐ 7 Dick Snyder	20.00	10.00	2.00
☐ 8 Dick Van Arsdale	30.00	15.00	3.00
☐ 9 Neal Walk	25.00	12.50	2.50
☐ 10 Gene Williams	20.00	10.00	2.00

1970-71 Suns Carnation Milk

This 11-card set features members of the Phoenix Suns and was produced by Carnation Milk. The cards have solid red backgrounds or orange backgrounds if the cards were from diet milk cartons. Apparently the entire set was issued in both color backgrounds. The cards measure approximately 3 1/2" by 7 1/2". The backs are blank. The cards are unnumbered and are checklisted below in alphabetical order.

	NRMT	VG-E	GOOD
COMPLETE SET (11)	300.00	150.00	30.00
COMMON PLAYER (1-11)	20.00	10.00	2.00
☐ 1 Mel Counts	25.00	12.50	2.50
☐ 2 Lamar Green	20.00	10.00	2.00
☐ 3 Art Harris	20.00	10.00	2.00
☐ 4 Clem Haskins	30.00	15.00	3.00
☐ 5 Connie Hawkins	50.00	25.00	5.00
☐ 6 Gus Johnson	40.00	20.00	4.00
☐ 7 Otto Moore	20.00	10.00	2.00
☐ 8 Paul Silas	40.00	20.00	4.00
☐ 9 Dick Van Arsdale	30.00	15.00	3.00
☐ 10 Bill VanBredaKolff CO	20.00	10.00	2.00
☐ 11 Neal Walk	25.00	12.50	2.50

1970-71 Suns A1 Premium Beer

The scarce cards are black and white and come with unperforated tabs. The cards were actually the price tabs for six-packs of beer. The set features members of the Phoenix Suns exclusively. There are three variations primarily based on the price marked on the tab. Apparently the 98 cents variations are tougher to find.

	NRMT	VG-E	GOOD
COMPLETE SET (13)	900.00	450.00	90.00
COMMON PLAYER (1-10)	60.00	30.00	6.00
☐ 1A Mel Counts (95 cents)	75.00	37.50	7.50
☐ 1B Mel Counts (98 cents)	100.00	50.00	10.00
☐ 2 Lamar Green	60.00	30.00	6.00
☐ 3 Clem Haskins	75.00	37.50	7.50
☐ 4 Connie Hawkins	125.00	60.00	12.50
☐ 5 Greg Howard	60.00	30.00	6.00
☐ 6 Paul Silas	75.00	37.50	7.50
☐ 7 Fred Taylor	60.00	30.00	6.00
☐ 8A Dick Van Arsdale ERR (reversed negative)	100.00	50.00	10.00
☐ 8B Dick Van Arsdale COR	75.00	37.50	7.50
☐ 9A Neal Walk (95 cents)	75.00	37.50	7.50
☐ 9B Neal Walk (no price)	100.00	50.00	10.00
☐ 10 John Wetzel	60.00	30.00	6.00

1975-76 Suns Phoenix

The 1975-76 Phoenix Suns set contains 16 cards, including 12 player cards. The fronts feature black and white pictures, and the backs are blank. The dimensions are approximately 3 1/2" by 4 3/8". The set commemorates the Suns' Western Conference Championship.

	NRMT	VG-E	GOOD
COMPLETE SET (16)	12.00	6.00	1.20
COMMON PLAYER (1-16)	.50	.25	.05
☐ 1 Alvan Adams	1.00	.50	.10
☐ 2 Dennis Awtrey	.50	.25	.05
☐ 3 Al Bianchi	.75	.35	.07
☐ 4 Jerry Colangelo	.50	.25	.05
☐ 5 Keith Erickson	.75	.35	.07
☐ 6 Nate Hawthorne	.50	.25	.05
☐ 7 Garfield Heard	.75	.35	.07
☐ 8 Phil Lumpkin	.50	.25	.05
☐ 9 John MacLeod CO	1.00	.50	.10
☐ 10 Curtis Perry	.75	.35	.07
☐ 11 Joe Proski, trainer	.50	.25	.05
☐ 12 Pat Riley	2.00	1.00	.20
☐ 13 Ricky Sobers	1.00	.50	.10
☐ 14 Dick Van Arsdale	.75	.35	.07

☐ 15 Paul Westphal	1.25	.60	.12
☐ 16 John Wetzel	.50	.25	.05

1976-77 Suns Phoenix

The 1976-77 Phoenix Suns set contains 12 horizontal player cards measuring 3 1/2" by 4 3/8". The fronts have circular black and white photos framed by the Suns' orange and purple logo. The backs are blank.

	NRMT	VG-E	GOOD
COMPLETE SET (12)	9.00	4.50	.90
COMMON PLAYER (1-12)	.60	.30	.06
☐ 1 Alvan Adams	1.00	.50	.10
☐ 2 Dennis Awtrey	.60	.30	.06
☐ 3 Keith Erickson	.75	.35	.07
☐ 4 Butch Feher	.60	.30	.06
☐ 5 Garfield Heard	.75	.35	.07
☐ 6 Ron Lee	.60	.30	.06
☐ 7 Curtis Perry	.75	.35	.07
☐ 8 Ricky Sobers	.75	.35	.07
☐ 9 Ira Terrell	.75	.35	.07
☐ 10 Dick Van Arsdale	.75	.35	.07
☐ 11 Tom Van Arsdale	.75	.35	.07
☐ 12 Paul Westphal	1.50	.75	.15

1977-78 Suns Humpty Dumpty Discs

The 1977-78 Humpty Dumpty Phoenix Suns set contains 12 discs measuring approximately 3 1/4" in diameter. The blankbacked discs are printed on thick stock. The fronts feature small black and white facial photos surrounded by a purple border with orange trim. Players are numbered below in alphabetical order by subject.

	NRMT	VG-E	GOOD
COMPLETE SET (12)	15.00	7.50	1.50
COMMON PLAYER	.75	.35	.07
☐ 1 Alvan Adams	2.00	1.00	.20
☐ 2 Dennis Awtrey	.75	.35	.07
☐ 3 Mike Bratz	.75	.35	.07
☐ 4 Don Buse	1.00	.50	.10
☐ 5 Walter Davis	3.00	1.50	.30
☐ 6 Bayard Forrest	.75	.35	.07
☐ 7 Garfield Heard	1.25	.60	.12
☐ 8 Ron Lee	.75	.35	.07
☐ 9 Curtis Perry	1.00	.50	.10
☐ 10 Alvin Scott	.75	.35	.07
☐ 11 Ira Terrell	1.00	.50	.10
☐ 12 Paul Westphal	2.50	1.25	.25

1980-81 Suns Pepsi

The 1980-81 Pepsi Phoenix Suns set contains 12 numbered cards attached to a bumper sticker-sized promotional flyer/entry blank. The cards themselves are approximately 2 1/2" by 3 1/2". The fronts feature color photos, and the backs include statistics and biographical information. The cards were part of a promotion featuring the fans' selection of their Suns' dream team.

	MINT	EXC	G-VG
COMPLETE SET (12)	10.00	5.00	1.00
COMMON PLAYER (1-12)	.50	.25	.05
☐ 1 Walter Davis	1.50	.75	.15
☐ 2 Alvin Scott	.50	.25	.05
☐ 3 Johnny High	.50	.25	.05
☐ 4 Dennis Johnson	1.50	.75	.15
☐ 5 Alvan Adams	1.00	.50	.10
☐ 6 Rich Kelley	.75	.35	.07
☐ 7 Truck Robinson	1.00	.50	.10
☐ 8 Joel Kramer	.50	.25	.05
☐ 9 Jeff Cook	.50	.25	.05
☐ 10 Mike Niles	.50	.25	.05
☐ 11 Kyle Macy	1.00	.50	.10
☐ 12 John MacLeod CO	.75	.35	.07

1982-83 Suns Giant Service

The 1982-83 Giant Self Service Stations Phoenix Suns set contains three cards each measuring approximately 3 1/4" by 4 1/2". The fronts have color photos while the backs show detailed career highlights and statistics. Each card has a safety tip on back. Apparently during the course of the promotion, one card was given out each month until the end of the season,

Walter Davis in January, Maurice Lucas in February, and Larry Nance in March. In addition to being available at gas stations, the cards were also distributed at the Phoenix Suns' Arena on "Giant Service Station Night."

	MINT	EXC	G-VG
COMPLETE SET (3)	12.00	6.00	1.20
COMMON PLAYER (1-3)	5.00	2.50	.50
☐ 1 Walter Davis January	5.00	2.50	.50
☐ 2 Maurice Lucas February	5.00	2.50	.50
☐ 3 Larry Nance March	5.00	2.50	.50

1984-85 Suns Police

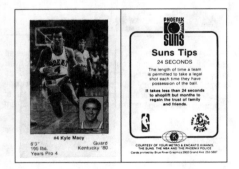

This set contains 16 cards measuring 2 5/8" by 4 1/8" featuring the Phoenix Suns. This set was issued in the Summer of 1984. Backs contain safety tips ("Suns Tips") and are written in purple print with an orange accent color. The set was sponsored by Kiwanis, the Suns, the NBA, and the Phoenix Police. The cards are unnumbered except for uniform number.

	MINT	EXC	G-VG
COMPLETE SET (16)	25.00	12.50	2.50
COMMON PLAYER	1.25	.60	.12
☐ 4 Kyle Macy	2.00	1.00	.20
☐ 6 Walter Davis	3.00	1.50	.30
☐ 7 Mike Sanders	1.50	.75	.15
☐ 8 Rick Robey	1.50	.75	.15
☐ 10 Rod Foster	1.50	.75	.15
☐ 14 Alvin Scott	1.25	.60	.12
☐ 21 Maurice Lucas	2.00	1.00	.20
☐ 22 Larry Nance	3.00	1.50	.30
☐ 32 Charles Pittman	1.25	.60	.12
☐ 33 Alvan Adams	2.50	1.25	.25
☐ 44 Paul Westphal	3.00	1.50	.30
☐ 53 James Edwards	2.50	1.25	.25
☐ xx Suns Mascot	1.25	.60	.12

☐ xx John MacLeod CO	2.00	1.00	.20
☐ xx Al Bianchi, Assistant Coach	1.25	.60	.12
☐ xx Joe Proski, Trainer	1.25	.60	.12

1987-88 Suns Circle K

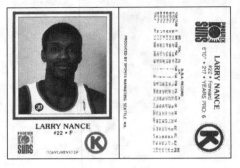

This ten-card set was sponsored by Circle K stores. The cards were issued in two strips of five player cards each, plus a coupon. After perforation, the cards measure the standard size (2 1/2" by 3 1/2"). The front features a posed color player photo, with white and purple borders on white card stock. Player information is given below the picture, and team and sponsor logos in the lower corners round out the card face. In a horizontal format the back has biographical and statistical information. The cards are unnumbered and are checklist below in alphabetical order, with the uniform number after the player's name.

	MINT	EXC	G-VG
COMPLETE SET (10)	15.00	7.50	1.50
COMMON PLAYER (1-10)	1.00	.50	.10
☐ 1 Alvan Adams 33	2.00	1.00	.20
☐ 2 Herb Brown CO	1.00	.50	.10
☐ 3 Jeff Cook 45	1.00	.50	.10
☐ 4 Walter Davis 6	2.50	1.25	.25
☐ 5 James Edwards 53	2.00	1.00	.20
☐ 6 Jeff Hornacek 14	4.00	2.00	.40
☐ 7 Larry Nance 22	2.00	1.00	.20
☐ 8 Mike Sanders 11	1.00	.50	.10
☐ 9 Bernard Thompson 7	1.00	.50	.10
☐ 10 John Wetzel CO	1.00	.50	.10

1990-91 Suns Smokey

This five-card set of Phoenix Suns was sponsored by the USDA Forest Service in cooperation with several other federal agencies. The cards are oversized and measure approximately 3" by 5". The front features a color action player photo, with the Smokey Bear logo superimposed on the top left edge of the picture and the team logo on the bottom right edge. The picture is bordered in purple and has a shadow format. The team name and player's name are given in purple lettering on a peach-colored background. The back presents brief biographical information and features a fire prevention cartoon starring Smokey the Bear. The cards are unnumbered and are checklisted below in alphabetical order. Eddie Johnson was apparently pulled from distribution after he was traded and hence his card is a little tougher to find than the other four players.

	MINT	EXC	G-VG
COMPLETE SET (5)	15.00	7.50	1.50
COMMON PLAYER (1-5)	3.00	1.50	.30
☐ 1 Tom Chambers	4.00	2.00	.40
☐ 2 Jeff Hornacek	3.00	1.50	.30
☐ 3 Eddie Johnson SP	5.00	2.50	.50
☐ 4 Kevin Johnson	5.00	2.50	.50
☐ 5 Dan Majerle	3.00	1.50	.30

1969-70 Supersonics Sunbeam Bread

This 11-card set consists of cards measuring 2 3/4" by 2 3/4". The cards were attached to plastic bread ties and issued on loaves of Sunbeam Bread. The front features a color posed photo of player shot from the waist up. The team and player name are given in white lettering in the picture. The photo has a thin red border, with the words "Sunbeam Enriched Bread" across the top of the card face. The words "Sonic Stars" are written vertically along the right side of the picture. Cards show the team's schedule for the 1969-70 season.

	NRMT	VG-E	GOOD
COMPLETE SET (11)	75.00	37.50	7.50
COMMON PLAYER (1-11)	6.00	3.00	.60
☐ 1 Lucius Allen	9.00	4.50	.90
☐ 2 Bob Boozer	6.00	3.00	.60
☐ 3 Barry Clemens	6.00	3.00	.60
☐ 4 Art Harris	6.00	3.00	.60
☐ 5 Tom Meschery	6.00	3.00	.60
☐ 6 Erwin Mueller	6.00	3.00	.60
☐ 7 Dorie Murrey	6.00	3.00	.60
☐ 8 Bob Rule	6.00	3.00	.60
☐ 9 John Tresvant	6.00	3.00	.60
☐ 10 Len Wilkens	12.00	6.00	1.20
(Player/coach)			
☐ 11 Sonics Coliseum	6.00	3.00	.60

1970-71 Supersonics Sunbeam Bread

This 11-card set consists of cards measuring 2 3/4" by 2 3/4". The cards were attached to plastic bread ties and issued on loaves of Sunbeam Bread. The front features a color posed photo of player shot from the waist up. The team and player name are given in white lettering in the picture. The photo has a thin red border, with the words "Sunbeam Enriched Bread" across the top of the card face. The words "Sonic Stars" are written vertically along the right side of the picture. The back has a career summary of the player and an offer to complete a set of

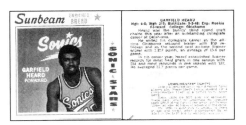

four different Sonic players (including Wilkens) for a complimentary ticket to a 1970-71 Seattle Supersonics home game.

	NRMT	VG-E	GOOD
COMPLETE SET (11)	75.00	37.50	7.50
COMMON PLAYER (1-11)	6.00	3.00	.60
☐ 1 Tom Black	6.00	3.00	.60
☐ 2 Barry Clemens	6.00	3.00	.60
☐ 3 Pete Cross	6.00	3.00	.60
☐ 4 Jake Ford	6.00	3.00	.60
☐ 5 Garfield Heard	9.00	4.50	.90
☐ 6 Don Kojis	6.00	3.00	.60
☐ 7 Tom Meschery	6.00	3.00	.60
☐ 8 Dick Snyder	6.00	3.00	.60
☐ 9 Len Wilkens	12.00	6.00	1.20
(Player/Coach)			
☐ 10 Lee Winfield	6.00	3.00	.60
☐ 11 Seattle Coliseum	6.00	3.00	.60

1971-72 Supersonics Sunbeam Bread

This 11-card set consists of cards measuring 2 3/4" by 2 3/4". The cards were attached to plastic bread ties and issued on loaves of Sunbeam Bread. The front features a color posed photo of player shot from the waist up. The team and player name are given in white lettering in the picture. The photo has a thin red border, with the words "Sunbeam Enriched Bread" across the top of the card face. The words "Sonic Stars" are written vertically along the right side of the picture.

	NRMT	VG-E	GOOD
COMPLETE SET (11)	75.00	37.50	7.50
COMMON PLAYER (1-11)	6.00	3.00	.60
☐ 1 Pete Cross	6.00	3.00	.60
☐ 2 Jake Ford	6.00	3.00	.60
☐ 3 Spencer Haywood	12.00	6.00	1.20
☐ 4 Garfield Heard	9.00	4.50	.90
☐ 5 Don Kojis	6.00	3.00	.60
☐ 6 Bob Rule	6.00	3.00	.60
☐ 7 Don Smith	6.00	3.00	.60
☐ 8 Dick Snyder	6.00	3.00	.60
☐ 9 Len Wilkens	12.00	6.00	1.20
(Player/Coach)			
☐ 10 Lee Winfield	6.00	3.00	.60
☐ 11 Sonics Coliseum	6.00	3.00	.60

1973-74 Supersonics Shur-Fresh

The 1973-74 Shur-Fresh Seattle Supersonics set contains 12 cards measuring 2 3/4" square. There are ten player cards and two coach cards. The cards have plastic bread ties attached to them. The fronts have color photos and the backs have biographical information. Cards are unnumbered so they are listed below in alphabetical order.

	NRMT	VG-E	GOOD
COMPLETE SET (12)	100.00	50.00	10.00
COMMON PLAYER (1-12)	6.00	3.00	.60

☐ 1 John Brisker	6.00	3.00	.60
☐ 2 Fred Brown	12.00	6.00	1.20
☐ 3 Emmette Bryant	6.00	3.00	.60
☐ 4 Jim Fox	6.00	3.00	.60
☐ 5 Dick Gibbs	6.00	3.00	.60
☐ 6 Spencer Haywood	12.00	6.00	1.20
☐ 7 Bill Russell CO	40.00	20.00	4.00
☐ 8 Jim McDaniels	6.00	3.00	.60
☐ 9 Kennedy McIntosh	6.00	3.00	.60
☐ 10 Dick Snyder	6.00	3.00	.60
☐ 11 Bud Stallworth	6.00	3.00	.60
☐ 12 Lee Winfield	6.00	3.00	.60

1978-79 Supersonics Police

This set contains 16 unnumbered cards measuring 2 5/8" by 4 1/8" featuring the Seattle Supersonics. The set was sponsored by the Washington State Crime Prevention Association, Kiwanis Club, and local law enforcement agencies. The year of issue is printed in the lower right corner of the reverse. Backs contain safety tips ("Tips from the Sonics") and are written in black ink with blue accent. The uniform number is added parenthetically in the checklist below where applicable.

	NRMT	VG-E	GOOD
COMPLETE SET (16)	15.00	7.50	1.50
COMMON PLAYER (1-16)	.75	.35	.07
☐ 1 Fred Brown (32)	1.25	.60	.12
☐ 2 Joe Hassett (10)	.75	.35	.07
☐ 3 Dennis Johnson (24)	1.50	.75	.15
☐ 4 John Johnson (27)	1.00	.50	.10
☐ 5 Tom LaGarde (23)	.75	.35	.07
☐ 6 Lonnie Shelton (8)	1.00	.50	.10
☐ 7 Jack Sikma (43)	1.50	.75	.15
☐ 8 Paul Silas (35)	1.25	.60	.12
☐ 9 Dick Snyder (11)	.75	.35	.07
☐ 10 Wally Walker (42)	.75	.35	.07
☐ 11 Gus Williams (1)	1.50	.75	.15
☐ 12 Len Wilkens CO	1.50	.75	.15
☐ 13 Les Habegger ASST	.75	.35	.07
☐ 14 Frank Furtado, trainer	.75	.35	.07
☐ 15 T. Wheedle, mascot	.75	.35	.07
☐ 16 Team Photo	.75	.35	.07

1979-80 Supersonics Police

This set contains 16 numbered cards measuring 2 5/8" by 4 1/8" featuring the Seattle Supersonics. Backs contain safety tips ("Tips for the Sonics") and are written in blue ink with red accent. The cards are numbered and dated in the lower right corner of the obverse. The set was sponsored by the Washington State Crime Prevention Association, Kiwanis, Coca Cola, Rainier Bank, and local area law enforcement agencies.

	MINT	EXC	G-VG
COMPLETE SET (16)	12.00	6.00	1.20
COMMON PLAYER (1-16)	.50	.25	.05
☐ 1 Gus Williams	1.25	.60	.12
☐ 2 James Bailey	.75	.35	.07
☐ 3 Jack Sikma	1.25	.60	.12
☐ 4 Tom LaGarde	.50	.25	.05
☐ 5 Paul Silas	1.00	.50	.10
☐ 6 Lonnie Shelton	.75	.35	.07
☐ 7 T. Wheedle (mascot)	.50	.25	.05
☐ 8 Vinnie Johnson	1.25	.60	.12
☐ 9 Dennis Johnson	1.25	.60	.12
☐ 10 Wally Walker	.50	.25	.05
☐ 11 Les Habegger,ASST	.50	.25	.05
☐ 12 Frank Furtado, trainer	.50	.25	.05
☐ 13 Fred Brown	1.00	.50	.10
☐ 14 John Johnson	.75	.35	.07
☐ 15 Team Photo	.50	.25	.05
☐ 16 Len Wilkens CO	1.25	.60	.12

1983-84 Supersonics Police

This set contains 16 cards measuring 2 5/8" by 4 1/8" featuring the Seattle Supersonics. Backs contain safety tips ("Tips from the Sonics") and are written in blue ink with a red accent. Set was also sponsored by the Washington State Crime Prevention Association, Kiwanis, Coca Cola, Ernst Home Centers, and area law enforcement agencies. The year of issue is given at the bottom right corner of the obverse. The cards are numbered on the back.

	MINT	EXC	G-VG
COMPLETE SET (16)	6.00	3.00	.60
COMMON PLAYER (1-16)	.35	.17	.03
☐ 1 Reggie King	.35	.17	.03
☐ 2 Frank Furtado, trainer	.35	.17	.03
☐ 3 Tom Chambers	1.00	.50	.10
☐ 4 Dave Harshman, ASST	.35	.17	.03
☐ 5 Gus Williams	.75	.35	.07
☐ 6 T. Wheedle, mascot	.35	.17	.03
☐ 7 Scooter McCray	.35	.17	.03
☐ 8 Jack Sikma	.75	.35	.07
☐ 9 Al Wood	.35	.17	.03
☐ 10 Bob Blackburn, ...	.35	.17	.03
Voice of the Sonics			
☐ 11 Danny Vranes	.35	.17	.03
☐ 12 Charles Bradley	.35	.17	.03
☐ 13 Steve Hawes	.35	.17	.03
☐ 14 Jon Sundvold	.50	.25	.05
☐ 15 Fred Brown	.75	.35	.07
☐ 16 Lenny Wilkens CO	1.00	.50	.10

1990-91 Supersonics Kayo

This 14-card set was produced by Kayo Cards as a give-away to fans attending the April 13, 1991 Seattle Supersonics home game. A total of 10,000 sets supposedly were produced. The cards are numbered on the back. Cards are standard size, 2 1/2" by 3 1/2".

	MINT	EXC	G-VG
COMPLETE SET (14)	7.00	3.50	.70
COMMON PLAYER (1-14)	.30	.15	.03
☐ 1 Shawn Kemp	2.50	1.25	.25
☐ 2 Scott Meents	.40	.20	.04
☐ 3 Derrick McKey	.40	.20	.04
☐ 4 Michael Cage	.30	.15	.03
☐ 5 Benoit Benjamin	.50	.25	.05
☐ 6 Dave Corzine	.30	.15	.03
☐ 7 K.C. Jones CO	.50	.25	.05
☐ 8 Quintin Dailey	.30	.15	.03
☐ 9 Ricky Pierce	.60	.30	.06
☐ 10 Eddie Johnson	.50	.25	.05
☐ 11 Nate McMillan	.30	.15	.03
☐ 12 Gary Payton	1.50	.75	.15
☐ 13 Sedale Threatt	.30	.15	.03
☐ 14 Dana Barros	.40	.20	.04

1990-91 Supersonics Smokey

This 16-card set was sponsored by the USDA Forest Service in conjunction with other federal agencies. The cards were issued in a panel of 4 rows of 4 cards each. After perforation, they measure the standard size (2 1/2" by 3 1/2"). The front features a color action player photo, with the Smokey the Bear logo in the lower left corner. The front is done in the team's colors: border and lettering in yellow on a green background. The team name is inscribed above the picture, with the player's name below. The back presents biographical information and a fire prevention cartoon starring Smokey.

	MINT	EXC	G-VG
COMPLETE SET (16)	10.00	5.00	1.00
COMMON PLAYER (1-16)	.50	.25	.05
☐ 1 Dana Barros	.60	.30	.06
☐ 2 Michael Cage	.50	.25	.05
☐ 3 Dave Corzine	.50	.25	.05
☐ 4 Quintin Dailey	.50	.25	.05
☐ 5 Dale Ellis	1.00	.50	.10
☐ 6 K.C. Jones CO	1.00	.50	.10
☐ 7 Shawn Kemp	2.00	1.00	.20
☐ 8 Bob Kloppenburg CO	.50	.25	.05
☐ 9 Xavier McDaniel	1.00	.50	.10
☐ 10 Derrick McKey	.75	.35	.07
☐ 11 Nate McMillan	.50	.25	.05
☐ 12 Scott Meents	.60	.30	.06
☐ 13 Kip Moota CO	.50	.25	.05
☐ 14 Gary Payton	1.00	.50	.10
☐ 15 Olden Polynice	.50	.25	.05
☐ 16 Sedale Threatt	.60	.30	.06

1980-81 TCMA CBA

The 1980-81 Continental Basketball Association set, produced by TCMA, features 45 black and white photos of the players along with the team name in red along the side of the front of the card. The backs contain brief biographical data and statistics, the CBA logo, the team logo and the card number. A 1981 TCMA copyright date also appears on the back. The cards are numbered on back and are printed on white cardboard backs. Cards measure the standard 2 1/2" by 3 1/2".

	MINT	EXC	G-VG
COMPLETE SET (45)	45.00	22.50	4.50
COMMON PLAYER (1-45)	.75	.35	.07

		MINT	EXC	G-VG
☐	1 Chubby Cox	1.25	.60	.12
☐	2 Sylvester Cuyler	.75	.35	.07
☐	3 Harry Davis	.75	.35	.07
☐	4 Danny Salisbury	.75	.35	.07
☐	5 Cazzie Russell	3.00	1.50	.30
☐	6 Al Green	.75	.35	.07
☐	7 Rick Wilson	.75	.35	.07
☐	8 Jim Brogan	.75	.35	.07
☐	9 Andre McCarter	1.50	.75	.15
☐	10 Jerry Baskerville	.75	.35	.07
☐	11 James Woods	.75	.35	.07
☐	12 Geoff Crompton	1.25	.60	.12
☐	13 Korky Nelson	.75	.35	.07
☐	14 George Karl (Coach Montana)	1.50	.75	.15
☐	15 Stan Pietkiewicz	.75	.35	.07
☐	16 Raymond Townsend	1.50	.75	.15
☐	17 Lenny Horton	.75	.35	.07
☐	18 Carl Bailey	.75	.35	.07
☐	19 Ken Jones	.75	.35	.07
☐	20 Rory Sparrow	3.00	1.50	.30
☐	21 Mauro Panaggio (Coach Rochester)	.75	.35	.07
☐	22 Glenn Hagan	.75	.35	.07
☐	23 Larry Fogle	1.25	.60	.12
☐	24 Wayne Abrams	.75	.35	.07
☐	25 Jerry Christian	.75	.35	.07
☐	26 Edgar Jones	1.25	.60	.12
☐	27 Jerry Radocha	.75	.35	.07
☐	28 Greg Jackson	.75	.35	.07
☐	29 Eddie Mast (Player/Coach, Lehigh Valley)	.75	.35	.07
☐	30 Ron Davis	.75	.35	.07
☐	31 Tico Brown	.75	.35	.07
☐	32 Freeman Blade	.75	.35	.07
☐	33 Bill Klucas (Coach Anchorage)	.75	.35	.07
☐	34 Melvin Davis	1.25	.60	.12
☐	35 James Hardy	.75	.35	.07
☐	36 Brad Davis	3.00	1.50	.30
☐	37 Andre Wakefield	.75	.35	.07
☐	38 Brett Vroman	.75	.35	.07
☐	39 Larry Knight	.75	.35	.07
☐	40 Mel Bennett	.75	.35	.07
☐	41 Stan Eckwood	.75	.35	.07
☐	42 Andrew Parker	.75	.35	.07
☐	43 Billy Ray(Dunk) Bates	3.00	1.50	.30
☐	44 Matt Teahan	.75	.35	.07
☐	45 Carlton Green	.75	.35	.07

		MINT	EXC	G-VG
☐	13 Ed Macauley	2.00	1.00	.20
☐	14 Clyde Lovellette	2.00	1.00	.20
☐	15 Slater(Dugie) Martin	2.00	1.00	.20
☐	16 Bill Russell	15.00	7.50	1.50
☐	17 Oscar Robertson	7.50	3.75	.75
☐	18 Bill Bradley	6.00	3.00	.60
☐	19 Elgin Baylor	5.00	2.50	.50
☐	20 Bill Sharman	3.00	1.50	.30
☐	21 Tom(Satch) Sanders	1.00	.50	.10
☐	22 Dave Bing	3.00	1.50	.30
☐	23 Carl Braun	1.00	.50	.10
☐	24 Frank Selvy	1.00	.50	.10
☐	25 George Yardley	1.00	.50	.10
☐	26 Dick McGuire	1.00	.50	.10
☐	27 Leroy Ellis	1.00	.50	.10
☐	28 Jack Twyman	2.00	1.00	.20
☐	29 Nate Thurmond	3.00	1.50	.30
☐	30 Walt(Clyde) Frazier	4.00	2.00	.40
☐	31 John(Red) Kerr	1.00	.50	.10
☐	32 Jerry West	10.00	5.00	1.00
☐	33 John Egan	1.00	.50	.10
☐	34 Jim Loscutoff	1.00	.50	.10
☐	35 Bob Leonard	1.00	.50	.10
☐	36 Rick Barry	5.00	2.50	.50
☐	37 Gene Shue	1.00	.50	.10
☐	38 Jerry Lucas	4.00	2.00	.40
☐	39 Dave DeBusschere	3.00	1.50	.30
☐	40 John Green, Charles Tyra, Carl Braun, Richie Guerin, and John George	1.00	.50	.10
☐	41 Bob Cousy	7.50	3.75	.75
☐	42 Walter Bellamy	1.00	.50	.10
☐	43 Billy Cunningham	3.00	1.50	.30
☐	44 Wilt Chamberlain	15.00	7.50	1.50

1981 TCMA NBA

This 44-card set features some of the all-time great basketball players. The front features a color posed photo of the player, while the back has name, career summary, and career highlights. The cards are numbered on the back and checklisted below accordingly. The cards are standard size, 2 1/2" by 3 1/2".

	MINT	VG-E	F-G
COMPLETE SET (44)	100.00	50.00	10.00
COMMON PLAYER (1-44)	1.00	.50	.10

		MINT	VG-E	F-G
☐	1 Alex Hannum	1.00	.50	.10
☐	2 Larry Foust	1.00	.50	.10
☐	3 George Mikan	10.00	5.00	1.00
☐	4 Mel(Hutch) Hutchins	1.00	.50	.10
☐	5 Bob Pettit	6.00	3.00	.60
☐	6 Willis Reed	5.00	2.50	.50
☐	7 Adolph Schayes	3.00	1.50	.30
☐	8 Vern Mikkelsen	2.00	1.00	.20
☐	9 Cazzie Russell	2.00	1.00	.20
☐	10 Dick Van Arsdale	1.00	.50	.10
☐	11 Lenny Wilkens	3.00	1.50	.30
☐	12 Ray Felix	1.00	.50	.10

1981-82 TCMA CBA

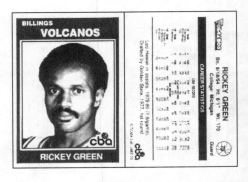

This 90-card set features black and white photos surrounded by a red frame line in which the player's name and team are printed. The Continental Basketball Association (CBA) logo appears in black on the front of the card. The back of the card contains the card number, career statistics, brief biographical data, and the team and CBA logos. A TCMA copyright date appears on the back. Cards measure the standard 2 1/2" by 3 1/2".

	MINT	EXC	G-VG
COMPLETE SET (90)	75.00	37.50	7.50
COMMON PLAYER (1-90)	.75	.35	.07
□ 1 1981 CBA Champions Rochester Zeniths (previous champions listed on back)	1.50	.75	.15
□ 2 Wayne Abrams	.75	.35	.07
□ 3 Pete Taylor	.75	.35	.07
□ 4 George Torres	.75	.35	.07
□ 5 Henry Bibby	3.00	1.50	.30
□ 6 Rufus Harris	.75	.35	.07
□ 7 Donnie Koonce	.75	.35	.07
□ 8 Jeff Wilkins	1.25	.60	.12
□ 9 Kurt Nimphius	1.50	.75	.15
□ 10 Billy Ray Bates	3.00	1.50	.30
□ 11 James Lee	1.25	.60	.12
□ 12 Marlon Redmond	.75	.35	.07
□ 13 Gary Mazza (Coach Alberta)	.75	.35	.07
□ 14 Tony Fuller	.75	.35	.07
□ 15 Brad Davis	3.00	1.50	.30
□ 16 Joe Cooper	1.25	.60	.12
□ 17 Andra Griffin	.75	.35	.07
□ 18 Rudy White	1.25	.60	.12
□ 19 Ricky Williams	.75	.35	.07
□ 20 Glenn Hagan	.75	.35	.07
□ 21 Ernie Graham	.75	.35	.07
□ 22 Kevin Graham	.75	.35	.07
□ 23 Billy Reid	.75	.35	.07
□ 24 Mauro Panaggio (Coach Rochester)	.75	.35	.07
□ 25 Bo Ellis	3.00	1.50	.30
□ 26 Ollie Matson	.75	.35	.07
□ 27 Tony Turner	.75	.35	.07
□ 28 Leo Papile (Coach Quincy)	.75	.35	.07
□ 29 Larry Holmes	.75	.35	.07
□ 30 Steve Hayes	2.00	1.00	.20
□ 31 Carl Bailey	.75	.35	.07
□ 32 Tico Brown	.75	.35	.07
□ 33 Percy Davis	.75	.35	.07
□ 34 Al Leslie	.75	.35	.07
□ 35 Ken Dennard	1.25	.60	.12
□ 36 Larry Spriggs	3.00	1.50	.30
□ 37 John Smith	.75	.35	.07
□ 38 Kenny Natt	1.50	.75	.15
□ 39 Harry Heineken	.75	.35	.07
□ 40 Lowes Moore	1.25	.60	.12
□ 41 Curtis Berry	1.25	.60	.12
□ 42 Freeman Blade (Coach Anchorage)	.75	.35	.07
□ 43 Larry Lawrence	.75	.35	.07
□ 44 Purvis Miller	1.25	.60	.12
□ 45 Ron Valentine	.75	.35	.07
□ 46 Charles Floyd	.75	.35	.07
□ 47 Greg Cornelius	.75	.35	.07
□ 48 Clay Johnson	1.25	.60	.12
□ 49 Bill Klucas (Coach Billings)	.75	.35	.07
□ 50 Cazzie Russell (Player/Coach Lancaster)	2.50	1.25	.25
□ 51 Craig Shelton	1.25	.60	.12
□ 52 Dave Britton	.75	.35	.07
□ 53 Ken Green	.75	.35	.07
□ 54 Stan Pawlak (Coach Atlantic City)	.75	.35	.07
□ 55 Rich Yonakor	1.25	.60	.12
□ 56 Darryl Gladden	.75	.35	.07
□ 57 Norman Black	.75	.35	.07
□ 58 Pete Harris	.75	.35	.07
□ 59 Anthony Roberts	1.25	.60	.12
□ 60 Jawann Oldham	2.50	1.25	.25
□ 61 Sam Clancy	2.50	1.25	.25
□ 62 Andre McCarter	1.25	.60	.12
□ 63 Joe Merten	.75	.35	.07
□ 64 Eddie Moss	.75	.35	.07
□ 65 Brad Branson	.75	.35	.07
□ 66 Lenny Horton	.75	.35	.07
□ 67 Jerome Henderson	.75	.35	.07
□ 68 Terry Stotts	.75	.35	.07
□ 69 Tony Wells	.75	.35	.07
□ 70 Rickey Green	3.00	1.50	.30
□ 71 Don Newman	.75	.35	.07
□ 72 Randy Owens	.75	.35	.07
□ 73 Erv Giddings	.75	.35	.07
□ 74 Barry Young	.75	.35	.07
□ 75 Jim Brogan	.75	.35	.07
□ 76 Richard Johnson	.75	.35	.07
□ 77 George Karl (Coach Montana)	1.50	.75	.15
□ 78 U.S. Reed	1.25	.60	.12
□ 79 Fran Greenberg (Public Relations Director)	.75	.35	.07
□ 80 Ron Davis	.75	.35	.07
□ 81 Larry Fogle	1.25	.60	.12
□ 82 Clarence Kea	.75	.35	.07
□ 83 Steve Craig	.75	.35	.07
□ 84 Harry Davis	.75	.35	.07
□ 85 Jacky Dorsey	1.25	.60	.12
□ 86 Herb Gray	.75	.35	.07
□ 87 Randy Johnson	.75	.35	.07
□ 88 Jim Drucker (Commissioner)	1.25	.60	.12
□ 89 Lynbert Johnson	1.25	.60	.12
□ 90 Checklist 1-90	1.25	.60	.12

1982-83 TCMA CBA

This third Continental Basketball Association set from TCMA features 90 black and white cards with red frame lines. The CBA logo, the player's name, physical data, team name, and team logo appear on the front, as does the card number. The back of the cards form a large puzzle. The cards were apparently issued in two series of 45 cards each. Cards measure the standard 2 1/2" by 3 1/2".

	MINT	EXC	G-VG
COMPLETE SET (90)	75.00	37.50	7.50
COMMON PLAYER (1-45)	.75	.35	.07
COMMON PLAYER (46-90)	.75	.35	.07
□ 1 Cazzie Russell (Coach Lancaster)	2.50	1.25	.25
□ 2 Boot Bond	.75	.35	.07
□ 3 Ron Charles	.75	.35	.07
□ 4 Charles Pittman	1.25	.60	.12
□ 5 Calvin Garrett	1.25	.60	.12
□ 6 Willie Jones	.75	.35	.07
□ 7 Riley Clarida	.75	.35	.07
□ 8 Jim Johnstone	.75	.35	.07
□ 9 Bobby Potts	.75	.35	.07
□ 10 Lowes Moore	1.25	.60	.12
□ 11 Dwight Anderson	2.50	1.25	.25
□ 12 John Coughran	.75	.35	.07
□ 13 Mike Evans	1.25	.60	.12
□ 14 Alan Hardy	.75	.35	.07
□ 15 Willie Smith	.75	.35	.07
□ 16 Oliver Mack	1.25	.60	.12
□ 17 Checklist 1-45	1.25	.60	.12
□ 18 Picture 1 (action under basket)	.75	.35	.07
□ 19 James Lee	1.25	.60	.12
□ 20 Kenny Natt	1.25	.60	.12
□ 21 Cyrus Mann	.75	.35	.07
□ 22 Bobby Cattage	.75	.35	.07
□ 23 Garry Witts	.75	.35	.07
□ 24 Bill Klucas (Coach Billings)	.75	.35	.07
□ 25 Al Smith	.75	.35	.07
□ 26 B.B. Fontenet	.75	.35	.07
□ 27 Chris Giles	.75	.35	.07
□ 28 Barry Young	.75	.35	.07

		MINT	EXC	G-VG
☐ 29	Horace Wyatt	.75	.35	.07
☐ 30	Robert Smith	1.25	.60	.12
☐ 31	Ron Baxter	1.25	.60	.12
☐ 32	Charlie Jones	.75	.35	.07
☐ 33	Tico Brown	.75	.35	.07
☐ 34	John McCullough	.75	.35	.07
☐ 35	Dan Callandrillo	1.25	.60	.12
☐ 36	John Leonard	.75	.35	.07
☐ 37	Sam Worthen	1.25	.60	.12
☐ 38	Dale Wilkinson	.75	.35	.07
☐ 39	Gary Johnson	.75	.35	.07
☐ 40	Dean Meminger	1.25	.60	.12
	(Coach Albany)			
☐ 41	Lloyd Terry	.75	.35	.07
☐ 42	Mike Schultz	.75	.35	.07
☐ 43	Darryl Gladden	.75	.35	.07
☐ 44	Clarence Kea	.75	.35	.07
☐ 45	Charlie Floyd	.75	.35	.07
☐ 46	Skip Dillard	1.25	.60	.12
☐ 47	Craig Tucker	.75	.35	.07
☐ 48	Gib Hinz	.75	.35	.07
☐ 49	Tom Sienkiewicz	.75	.35	.07
☐ 50	Larry Spriggs	2.00	1.00	.20
☐ 51	Perry Moss	.75	.35	.07
☐ 52	Gerald Sims	.75	.35	.07
☐ 53	Alan Taylor	.75	.35	.07
☐ 54	James Terry	.75	.35	.07
☐ 55	John Nillen	.75	.35	.07
	(Coach Ohio)			
☐ 56	Steve Burks	.75	.35	.07
☐ 57	Anthony Martin	.75	.35	.07
☐ 58	Purvis Miller	1.25	.60	.12
☐ 59	Kevin Smith	.75	.35	.07
☐ 60	John Neumann	1.25	.60	.12
	(Coach Maine)			
☐ 61	Mike Davis	.75	.35	.07
☐ 62	Gary Carter	.75	.35	.07
☐ 63	Checklist 46-90	1.25	.60	.12
☐ 64	Picture 2	.75	.35	.07
	(action under basket)			
☐ 65	Charles Thompson	.75	.35	.07
☐ 66	John Douglas	.75	.35	.07
☐ 67	John Schweitz	.75	.35	.07
☐ 68	Kevin Figaro	.75	.35	.07
☐ 69	John Smith	.75	.35	.07
☐ 70	Joe Cooper	1.25	.60	.12
☐ 71	Tony Brown	.75	.35	.07
☐ 72	Mike Wilson	.75	.35	.07
☐ 73	Wayne Abrams	.75	.35	.07
☐ 74	T.X. Martin	.75	.35	.07
☐ 75	Joe Merten	.75	.35	.07
☐ 76	Joe Kopicki	.75	.35	.07
☐ 77	Carl Nicks	1.25	.60	.12
☐ 78	Wayne Kreklow	.75	.35	.07
☐ 79	Tony Guy	1.25	.60	.12
☐ 80	Dave Harshman	.75	.35	.07
	(Coach Wisconsin)			
☐ 81	Bob Davis	.75	.35	.07
☐ 82	Gary Mazza	.75	.35	.07
	(Coach Detroit)			
☐ 83	Randy Owens	.75	.35	.07
☐ 84	David Burns	.75	.35	.07
☐ 85	Erv Giddings	.75	.35	.07
☐ 86	Jo Jo Hunter	1.25	.60	.12
☐ 87	Frankie Sanders	.75	.35	.07
☐ 88	Dave Richardson	.75	.35	.07
☐ 89	Lionel Garrett	.75	.35	.07
☐ 90	Marvin Barnes	2.00	1.00	.20

		MINT	EXC	G-VG
☐ 2	1982-83 Lancaster	1.00	.50	.10
	Lightning Team Picture			
☐ 3	Dr. Seymour Kilstein,	1.00	.50	.10
	President			
☐ 4	Cazzie Russell,	3.00	1.50	.30
	Head Coach			
☐ 5	Coach Russell IA	3.00	1.50	.30
☐ 6	Ed Koback, Operations	2.00	1.00	.20
☐ 7	Bob Danforth,	1.00	.50	.10
	Marketing			
☐ 8	Henry Bibby In Action	2.00	1.00	.20
☐ 9	Joe Cooper	1.50	.75	.15
☐ 10	Joe Cooper In Action	1.50	.75	.15
☐ 11	Curtis Berry	1.50	.75	.15
☐ 12	Berry In Action	1.50	.75	.15
☐ 13	James Lee	1.50	.75	.15
☐ 14	Lee In Action	1.50	.75	.15
☐ 15	Sherod In Action	1.50	.75	.15
☐ 16	Charlie Floyd	1.00	.50	.10
☐ 17	Charlie Floyd In Action	1.00	.50	.10
☐ 18	Darryl Gladden	1.00	.50	.10
☐ 19	Gladden In Action	1.00	.50	.10
☐ 20	Tom Sienkiewicz	1.00	.50	.10
☐ 21	Sienkiewicz In Action	1.00	.50	.10
☐ 22	Stan Williams	1.00	.50	.10
☐ 23	Willie Redden	1.00	.50	.10
☐ 24	Reginald Gaines	1.00	.50	.10
☐ 25	Gary(Cat) Johnson	1.50	.75	.15
☐ 26	Cat Johnson IA	1.50	.75	.15
☐ 27	Keith Hilliard	1.00	.50	.10
☐ 28	Hilliard In Action	1.00	.50	.10
☐ 29	Donald Seals	1.00	.50	.10
☐ 30	Rufus Harris	1.00	.50	.10

1989-90 Timberwolves Burger King

1982-83 TCMA Lancaster CBA

This set features 30 black and white standard-sized (2 1/2" by 3 1/2") cards with blue border on front. The card backs contain statistics and are numbered on the back. Many of the poses are in action shots. The set is printed on dark cardboard. All cards feature players or personnel of the Lancaster Lightning (Continental Basketball Association) team which won the 1981-82 CBA Championship. The set was produced by TCMA.

	MINT	EXC	G-VG
COMPLETE SET (30)	30.00	15.00	3.00
COMMON PLAYER (1-30)	1.00	.50	.10
☐ 1 Lightning Wins 1982	1.00	.50	.10
CBA Championship			

This seven-card set was sponsored by Burger King to commemorate the inaugural season of the Minnesota Timberwolves. The cards were issued with a (9" by 12") Player Cards Collector Set, which included on the inside a 1989-90 game schedule and slots to hold the cards. The standard size (2 1/2" by 3 1/2") cards feature on the fronts color action player photos, with dark blue borders on white card stock. A banner reading "Inaugural Season" overlays the top of the picture. The team name and logo at the top and player identification below the picture round out the card face. The backs have biographical and statistical information, with the team logo and a blue stripe (with player's name in white) appearing at the top of the cards. The cards are unnumbered. Brad Lohaus is considered somewhat tougher to find since he was supposedly pulled from the set and replaced by Randy Breuer during the promotion.

	MINT	EXC	G-VG
COMPLETE SET (7)	7.50	3.75	.75
COMMON PLAYER	.75	.35	.07
☐ 19 Tony Campbell	1.00	.50	.10
☐ 23 Tyrone Corbin	1.00	.50	.10
☐ 24 Pooh Richardson	3.00	1.50	.30
☐ 35 Sidney Lowe	.75	.35	.07
☐ 42 Sam Mitchell	.75	.35	.07
☐ 45 Randy Breuer	1.00	.50	.10
☐ 54 Brad Lohaus	1.50	.75	.15

1948 Topps Magic Photos *

The 1948 Topps Magic Photos set contains 252 small (approximately 7/8" by 1 7/16") individual cards featuring sport and non-sport subjects. They were issued in 19 lettered series with cards numbered within each series. The fronts were developed from a "blank" appearance by using moisture and sunlight. Due to varying degrees of photographic sensitivity, the clarity of these cards ranges from fully developed to poorly developed. This set contains Topps' first baseball cards. A premium album holding 126 cards was also issued. The set is sometimes confused with Topps' 1956 Hocus-Focus set, although the cards in this set are slightly smaller than those in the Hocus-Focus set. The checklist below is presented by series. Poorly developed cards are considered in lesser condition and hence have lesser value. The catalog designation for this set is R714-27. Each type of card subject has a letter prefix as follows: Boxing Champions (A), All-American Basketball (B), All-American Football (C), Wrestling Champions (D), Track and Field Champions (E), Stars of Stage and Screen (F), American Dogs (G), General Sports (H), Movie Stars (J), Baseball Hall of Fame (K), Aviation Pioneers (L), Famous Landmarks (M), American Inventors (N), American Military Leaders (O), American Explorers (P), Basketball Thrills (Q), Football Thrills (R), Figures of the Wild West (S), and General Sports (T).

	NRMT	VG-E	GOOD
COMPLETE SET	2500.00	1000.00	200.00
COMMON CARD A/B/C/D/K	15.00	7.50	1.50
COMMON CARD Q/R	7.50	3.75	.75
COMMON CARD E/F/J/L	5.00	2.50	.50
COMMON CARD OTHERS	2.00	1.00	.20
☐ A1 Tommy Burns	15.00	7.50	1.50
☐ A2 John L. Sullivan	35.00	17.50	3.50
☐ A3 James J. Corbett	30.00	15.00	3.00
☐ A4 Bob Fitzsimmons	20.00	10.00	2.00
☐ A5 James J. Jeffries	25.00	12.50	2.50
☐ A6 Jack Johnson	30.00	15.00	3.00
☐ A7 Jess Willard	20.00	10.00	2.00
☐ A8 Jack Dempsey	35.00	17.50	3.50
☐ A9 Gene Tunney	35.00	17.50	3.50
☐ A10 Max Schmeling	20.00	10.00	2.00
☐ A11 Jack Sharkey	15.00	7.50	1.50
☐ A12 Primo Carnera	15.00	7.50	1.50
☐ A13 Max Baer	20.00	10.00	2.00
☐ A14 James J. Braddock	20.00	10.00	2.00
☐ A15 Joe Louis	35.00	17.50	3.50
☐ A16 Gus Lesnevich	15.00	7.50	1.50
☐ A17 Tony Zale	15.00	7.50	1.50
☐ A18 Ike Williams	15.00	7.50	1.50
☐ A19 Ray Robinson	30.00	15.00	3.00
☐ A20 Willie Pep	15.00	7.50	1.50
☐ A21 Rinty Monaghan	15.00	7.50	1.50
☐ A22 Manuel Ortiz	15.00	7.50	1.50
☐ A23 Marcel Cerdan	15.00	7.50	1.50
☐ A24 Buddy Baer	15.00	7.50	1.50

☐ B1 Ralph Beard	25.00	12.50	2.50
☐ B2 Murray Wier	25.00	12.50	2.50
☐ B3 Ed Macauley	35.00	17.50	3.50
☐ B4 Kevin O'Shea	15.00	7.50	1.50
☐ B5 Jim McIntyre	15.00	7.50	1.50
☐ B6 Manhattan Beats	15.00	7.50	1.50
Dartmouth			
☐ C1 Barney Poole	15.00	7.50	1.50
☐ C2 Pete Elliott	15.00	7.50	1.50
☐ C3 Doak Walker	30.00	15.00	3.00
☐ C4 Bill Swiacki	15.00	7.50	1.50
☐ C5 Bill Fischer	15.00	7.50	1.50
☐ C6 Johnny Lujack	30.00	15.00	3.00
☐ C7 Chas. P. Bednarik	30.00	15.00	3.00
☐ C8 Joe Steffy	15.00	7.50	1.50
☐ C9 George Connor	25.00	12.50	2.50
☐ C10 Steve Suhey	15.00	7.50	1.50
☐ C11 Bob Chappins	15.00	7.50	1.50
☐ C12 Columbia 23/Navy 14	15.00	7.50	1.50
☐ C13 Army-Notre Dame	15.00	7.50	1.50
☐ D1 Frank Gotch	20.00	10.00	2.00
☐ D2 Hackenschmidt	15.00	7.50	1.50
☐ D3 Stanuslaus Zbyszko	15.00	7.50	1.50
☐ D4 Jim Browning	20.00	10.00	2.00
☐ D5 Jim Londos	20.00	10.00	2.00
☐ D6 Strangler Lewis	20.00	10.00	2.00
☐ D7 George Becker	15.00	7.50	1.50
☐ D8 Ernie Dusek	15.00	7.50	1.50

☐ D9	Rudy Dusek	15.00	7.50	1.50
☐ D10	Dean Detton	15.00	7.50	1.50
☐ D11	Masked Marvel	20.00	10.00	2.00
☐ D12	Maurice Tillet	15.00	7.50	1.50
☐ D13	Olaf Swenson	15.00	7.50	1.50
☐ D14	Tony Galento	20.00	10.00	2.00
☐ D15	Frank Sexton	15.00	7.50	1.50
☐ D16	George Calza	15.00	7.50	1.50
☐ D17	Arm Lock	15.00	7.50	1.50
☐ D18	Flying Dropkick	15.00	7.50	1.50
☐ D19	Primo Carnera	20.00	10.00	2.00
☐ D20	Gino Garabaldi	15.00	7.50	1.50
☐ D21	"Lord"Jan Blears	25.00	12.50	2.50
☐ D22	Joe Savoldi	15.00	7.50	1.50
☐ D23	Dick Shikat	15.00	7.50	1.50
☐ D24	Wadleslaw	15.00	7.50	1.50
☐ D25	Steinke	15.00	7.50	1.50
☐ E1	Jesse Owens	20.00	10.00	2.00
☐ E2	Leo Steers	5.00	2.50	.50
☐ E3	Ben Eastman	5.00	2.50	.50
☐ E4	Harrison Dillard	10.00	5.00	1.00
☐ E5	Greg Rice	5.00	2.50	.50
☐ E6	Kolehmainen	5.00	2.50	.50
☐ E7	Gunner Hagg	5.00	2.50	.50
☐ E8	Chas. Pores	5.00	2.50	.50
☐ E9	Grover Kelmmer	5.00	2.50	.50
☐ E10	Boyd Brown	5.00	2.50	.50
☐ E11	Pat Ryan	5.00	2.50	.50
☐ E12	Charlie Fonville	5.00	2.50	.50
☐ E13	C. Warmerdam	10.00	5.00	1.00
☐ E14	Army-Navy Tie	5.00	2.50	.50
☐ E15	Haaken Lidman	5.00	2.50	.50
	(Sweden)			
☐ E16	Morris-Army Wins	5.00	2.50	.50
☐ E17	M. Jarvinen,	5.00	2.50	.50
	Javelin			
☐ F1	Clark Gable	20.00	10.00	2.00
☐ F2	Barbara Stanwyck	10.00	5.00	1.00
☐ F3	Lana Turner	10.00	5.00	1.00
☐ F4	Ingrid Bergman	10.00	5.00	1.00
☐ F5	Betty Grable	10.00	5.00	1.00
☐ F6	Tyrone Power	10.00	5.00	1.00
☐ F7	Olivia DeHavilland	7.50	3.75	.75
☐ F8	Joan Fontaine	7.50	3.75	.75
☐ F9	June Allyson	7.50	3.75	.75
☐ F10	Dorothy Lamour	7.50	3.75	.75
☐ F11	William Powell	7.50	3.75	.75
☐ F12	Sylvia Sidney	5.00	2.50	.50
☐ F13	Van Johnson	7.50	3.75	.75
☐ F14	Virginia Mayo	7.50	3.75	.75
☐ F15	Claudette Colbert	7.50	3.75	.75
☐ F16	Eve Arden	7.50	3.75	.75
☐ F17	Lynn Bari	5.00	2.50	.50
☐ F18	Maureen O'Hara	7.50	3.75	.75
☐ F19	Jean Arthur	7.50	3.75	.75
☐ F20	Hazel Brooks	5.00	2.50	.50
☐ F21	Martha Vickers	5.00	2.50	.50
☐ F22	Noreen Nash	5.00	2.50	.50
☐ G1	Terrier	2.00	1.00	.20
☐ G2	Chow	2.00	1.00	.20
☐ G3	Cairn Terrier	2.00	1.00	.20
☐ G4	White Sealyham	2.00	1.00	.20
☐ G5	St. Bernard	2.00	1.00	.20
☐ G6	Boston Bull	2.00	1.00	.20
☐ G7	Greyhound	2.00	1.00	.20
☐ G8	Dalmation	2.00	1.00	.20
☐ G9	Pointer	2.00	1.00	.20
☐ G10	Cocker Spaniel	2.00	1.00	.20
☐ G11	English Bulldog	2.00	1.00	.20
☐ G12	Champion Pointer	2.00	1.00	.20
☐ G13	Setter	2.00	1.00	.20
☐ G14	Boxer	2.00	1.00	.20
☐ G15	Russian Wolfhound	2.00	1.00	.20
☐ G16	Doberman	2.00	1.00	.20
☐ G17	Collie	2.00	1.00	.20
☐ H1	Mr. and Mrs. George	.50	.25	.05
	Remington			
☐ H2	Bernice Dossey	.50	.25	.05
☐ J1	Johnny Mack Brown	7.50	3.75	.75
☐ J2	Andy Clyde	5.00	2.50	.50
☐ J3	Roddy McDowall	10.00	5.00	1.00
☐ J4	Keye Luke	7.50	3.75	.75
☐ J5	Jackie Coogan	7.50	3.75	.75
☐ J6	Joe Kirkwood Jr.	5.00	2.50	.50
☐ J7	Jackie Cooper	7.50	3.75	.75
☐ J8	Arthur Lake	5.00	2.50	.50
☐ J9	Sam Levine	7.50	3.75	.75
☐ J10	Binnie Barnes	5.00	2.50	.50
☐ J11	Gertrude Niesen	5.00	2.50	.50
☐ J12	Rory Calhoun	7.50	3.75	.75
☐ J13	June Lockhart	7.50	3.75	.75
☐ J14	Hedy Lamarr	7.50	3.75	.75
☐ J15	Robert Cummings	7.50	3.75	.75
☐ J16	Brian Aherne	5.00	2.50	.50

☐ J17	William Bendix	7.50	3.75	.75
☐ J18	Roland Winters	5.00	2.50	.50
☐ J19	Michael O'Shea	5.00	2.50	.50
☐ J20	Lois Butler	5.00	2.50	.50
☐ J21	Renie Riano	5.00	2.50	.50
☐ J22	Jimmy Wakely	5.00	2.50	.50
☐ J23	Audie Murphy	10.00	5.00	1.00
☐ J24	Leo Gorcey	7.50	3.75	.75
☐ J25	Leon Errol	7.50	3.75	.75
☐ J26	Lon Chaney	10.00	5.00	1.00
☐ J27	William Frawley	7.50	3.75	.75
☐ J28	Billy Benedict	5.00	2.50	.50
☐ J29	Rod Cameron	5.00	2.50	.50
☐ J30	James Gleason	5.00	2.50	.50
☐ J31	Gilbert Roland	7.50	3.75	.75
☐ J32	Raymond Hatton	5.00	2.50	.50
☐ J33	Joe Yule	5.00	2.50	.50
☐ J34	Eddie Albert	7.50	3.75	.75
☐ J35	Barry Sullivan	7.50	3.75	.75
☐ J36	Richard Basehart	7.50	3.75	.75
☐ J37	Claire Trevor	7.50	3.75	.75
☐ J38	Constance Bennett	7.50	3.75	.75
☐ J39	Gale Storm	7.50	3.75	.75
☐ J40	Elyse Knox	5.00	2.50	.50
☐ J41	Jane Wyatt	7.50	3.75	.75
☐ J42	Whip Wilson	5.00	2.50	.50
☐ J43	Charles Bickford	7.50	3.75	.75
☐ J44	Guy Madison	7.50	3.75	.75
☐ J45	Barton MacLane	5.00	2.50	.50
☐ K1	Lou Boudreau	30.00	15.00	3.00
☐ K2	Cleveland Indians	15.00	7.50	1.50
☐ K3	Bob Elliott	15.00	7.50	1.50
☐ K4	Cleveland Indians 4-3	15.00	7.50	1.50
☐ K5	Cleveland Indians 4-1	15.00	7.50	1.50
	(Boudreau scoring)			
☐ K6	Babe Ruth 714	150.00	75.00	15.00
☐ K7	Tris Speaker 793	30.00	15.00	3.00
☐ K8	Rogers Hornsby	40.00	20.00	4.00
☐ K9	Connie Mack	35.00	17.50	3.50
☐ K10	Christy Mathewson	45.00	22.50	4.50
☐ K11	Hans Wagner	50.00	25.00	5.00
☐ K12	Grover Alexander	30.00	15.00	3.00
☐ K13	Ty Cobb	90.00	45.00	9.00
☐ K14	Lou Gehrig	90.00	45.00	9.00
☐ K15	Walter Johnson	45.00	22.50	4.50
☐ K16	Cy Young	45.00	22.50	4.50
☐ K17	George Sisler 257	30.00	15.00	3.00
☐ K18	Tinker and Evers	25.00	12.50	2.50
☐ K19	Third Base,	15.00	7.50	1.50
	Cleveland Indians			
☐ L1	Colonial Airlines	5.00	2.50	.50
☐ L2	James Doolittle	7.50	3.75	.75
☐ L3	Wiley Post	7.50	3.75	.75
☐ L4	Eddie Rickenbacker	7.50	3.75	.75
☐ L5	Amelia Earhart	10.00	5.00	1.00
☐ L6	Charles Lindbergh	10.00	5.00	1.00
☐ L7	Doug Corrigan	7.50	3.75	.75
☐ L8	Chas. A. Levine	5.00	2.50	.50
☐ L9	Wright Brothers	7.50	3.75	.75
☐ M1	Niagara Falls	2.00	1.00	.20
☐ M2	Empire State Building	2.00	1.00	.20
☐ M3	Leaning Tower of Pisa	2.00	1.00	.20
☐ M4	Eiffel Tower	2.00	1.00	.20
☐ M5	Lincoln Memorial	2.00	1.00	.20
☐ M6	Statue of Liberty	3.00	1.50	.30
☐ M7	Geyser, Yellowstone	2.00	1.00	.20
☐ M8	Sphinx	2.00	1.00	.20
☐ M9	Washington Monument	2.00	1.00	.20
☐ N1	Eli Whitney	2.00	1.00	.20
☐ N2	Thomas A. Edison	3.00	1.50	.30
☐ N3	C.E. Duryea	2.00	1.00	.20
☐ N4	Benjamin Franklin	4.00	2.00	.40
☐ N5	V.K. Zworykin	2.00	1.00	.20
☐ N6	Robert Fulton	2.00	1.00	.20
☐ N7	Samuel Morse	2.00	1.00	.20
☐ N8	Alexander Graham Bell	4.00	2.00	.40
☐ O1	Joseph Stillwell	2.00	1.00	.20
☐ O2	Adm. Chester Nimitz	3.00	1.50	.30
☐ O3	George Patton	5.00	2.50	.50
☐ O4	General John Pershing	3.00	1.50	.30
☐ O5	Adm. David Farragut	3.00	1.50	.30
☐ O6	Jonathan Wainright	2.00	1.00	.20
☐ O7	Douglas MacArthur	5.00	2.50	.50
☐ O8	General Omar Bradley	3.00	1.50	.30
☐ O9	George Dewey	2.00	1.00	.20
☐ O10	Gen. Dw. Eisenhower	7.50	3.75	.75
☐ P1	Adm. Robert Peary	2.00	1.00	.20
☐ P2	Richard E. Byrd	2.00	1.00	.20
☐ Q1	St. Louis Univ.	7.50	3.75	.75
☐ Q2	Long Island Univ.	7.50	3.75	.75
☐ Q3	Notre Dame	12.00	6.00	1.20
☐ Q4	Kentucky 58-42	7.50	3.75	.75
☐ Q5	DePaul 75-64	7.50	3.75	.75
☐ R1	Wally Triplett	7.50	3.75	.75

		NRMT	VG-E	GOOD
☐ R2	Gil Stevenson	10.00	5.00	1.00
☐ R3	Northwestern	7.50	3.75	.75
☐ R4	Yale vs. Columbia	7.50	3.75	.75
☐ R5	Cornell	7.50	3.75	.75
☐ S1	General Custer	4.00	2.00	.40
☐ S2	Buffalo Bill Cody	5.00	2.50	.50
☐ S3	Sitting Bull	3.00	1.50	.30
☐ S4	Annie Oakley	4.00	2.00	.40
☐ S5	Jessie James	5.00	2.50	.50
☐ S6	Geronimo	3.00	1.50	.30
☐ S7	Billy the Kid	4.00	2.00	.40
☐ T1	Soccer	3.00	1.50	.30
☐ T2	Motor Boat Racing	3.00	1.50	.30
☐ T3	Ice Hockey	5.00	2.50	.50
☐ T4	Water Skiing	3.00	1.50	.30
☐ T5	Gallorette	2.00	1.00	.20
☐ T6	Headlock	2.00	1.00	.20
☐ T7	Tennis	3.00	1.50	.30

1957-58 Topps

The 1957-58 Topps basketball set of 80 cards was Topps first basketball issue. Topps did not release another basketball set until 1969. The set contains the only card of Maurice Stokes. Cards in the set measure approximately 2 1/2" by 3 1/2". A number of the cards in the set were double printed and hence more plentiful; these are designated DP in the checklist below. In fact there are 49 double prints, 30 single prints, and one quadruple print in the set. Card backs give statistical information from the 1956-57 NBA season. The key rookie cards in this set are Bob Cousy, Tom Heinsohn, Bob Pettit, and Bill Russell.

		NRMT	VG-E	GOOD
COMPLETE SET (80)		4500.00	2250.00	500.00
COMMON PLAYER (1-80)		25.00	12.50	2.50
COMMON PLAYER DP		20.00	10.00	2.00
☐ 1	Nat Clifton DP Detroit Pistons	125.00	30.00	6.00
☐ 2	George Yardley DP Detroit Pistons	35.00	17.50	3.50
☐ 3	Neil Johnston DP Philadelphia Warriors	40.00	20.00	4.00
☐ 4	Carl Braun DP New York Knicks	30.00	15.00	3.00
☐ 5	Bill Sharman DP Boston Celtics	100.00	50.00	10.00
☐ 6	George King DP Cincinnati Royals	30.00	15.00	3.00
☐ 7	Kenny Sears DP New York Knicks	30.00	15.00	3.00
☐ 8	Dick Ricketts DP Cincinnati Royals	25.00	12.50	2.50
☐ 9	Jack Nichols DP Boston Celtics	20.00	10.00	2.00
☐ 10	Paul Arizin DP Philadelphia Warriors	60.00	30.00	6.00
☐ 11	Chuck Noble DP Detroit Pistons	20.00	10.00	2.00
☐ 12	Slater Martin DP St. Louis Hawks	40.00	20.00	4.00
☐ 13	Dolph Schayes DP Syracuse Nationals	60.00	30.00	6.00

		NRMT	VG-E	GOOD
☐ 14	Dick Atha DP Detroit Pistons	20.00	10.00	2.00
☐ 15	Frank Ramsey DP Boston Celtics	60.00	30.00	6.00
☐ 16	Dick McGuire DP Detroit Pistons	35.00	17.50	3.50
☐ 17	Bob Cousy DP Boston Celtics	270.00	125.00	25.00
☐ 18	Larry Foust DP Minneapolis Lakers	30.00	15.00	3.00
☐ 19	Tom Heinsohn Boston Celtics	160.00	80.00	16.00
☐ 20	Bill Thieben DP Detroit Pistons	20.00	10.00	2.00
☐ 21	Don Meineke DP Cincinnati Royals	20.00	10.00	2.00
☐ 22	Tom Marshall Cincinnati Royals	25.00	12.50	2.50
☐ 23	Dick Garmaker Minneapolis Lakers	25.00	12.50	2.50
☐ 24	Bob Pettit QP St. Louis Hawks	135.00	60.00	12.00
☐ 25	Jim Krebs DP Minneapolis Lakers	30.00	15.00	3.00
☐ 26	Gene Shue DP Detroit Pistons	40.00	20.00	4.00
☐ 27	Ed Macauley DP St. Louis Hawks	40.00	20.00	4.00
☐ 28	Vern Mikkelsen Minneapolis Lakers	35.00	17.50	3.50
☐ 29	Willie Naulls New York Knicks	35.00	17.50	3.50
☐ 30	Walter Dukes DP Detroit Pistons	30.00	15.00	3.00
☐ 31	Dave Piontek DP Cincinnati Royals	20.00	10.00	2.00
☐ 32	John Kerr Syracuse Nationals	35.00	17.50	3.50
☐ 33	Larry Costello DP Syracuse Nationals	35.00	17.50	3.50
☐ 34	Woody Sauldsberry DP Philadelphia Warriors	20.00	10.00	2.00
☐ 35	Ray Felix New York Knicks	25.00	12.50	2.50
☐ 36	Ernie Beck Philadelphia Warriors	25.00	12.50	2.50
☐ 37	Cliff Hagan St. Louis Hawks	60.00	30.00	6.00
☐ 38	Guy Sparrow DP New York Knicks	20.00	10.00	2.00
☐ 39	Jim Loscutoff Boston Celtics	35.00	17.50	3.50
☐ 40	Arnie Risen DP Boston Celtics	30.00	15.00	3.00
☐ 41	Joe Graboski Philadelphia Warriors	25.00	12.50	2.50
☐ 42	Maurice Stokes DP Cincinnati Royals (Text refers to N.F.L. Record) UER	75.00	37.50	7.50
☐ 43	Rod Hundley DP Minneapolis Lakers	45.00	22.50	4.50
☐ 44	Tom Gola DP Philadelphia Warriors	50.00	25.00	5.00
☐ 45	Med Park St. Louis Hawks	25.00	12.50	2.50
☐ 46	Mel Hutchins DP New York Knicks	20.00	10.00	2.00
☐ 47	Larry Friend DP New York Knicks	20.00	10.00	2.00
☐ 48	Lennie Rosenbluth DP Philadelphia Warriors	30.00	15.00	3.00
☐ 49	Walt Davis Philadelphia Warriors	25.00	12.50	2.50
☐ 50	Richie Regan Cincinnati Royals	25.00	12.50	2.50
☐ 51	Frank Selvy DP St. Louis Hawks	30.00	15.00	3.00
☐ 52	Art Spoelstra DP Minneapolis Lakers	20.00	10.00	2.00
☐ 53	Bob Hopkins Syracuse Nationals	30.00	15.00	3.00
☐ 54	Earl Lloyd Syracuse Nationals	30.00	15.00	3.00
☐ 55	Phil Jordan DP New York Knicks	20.00	10.00	2.00
☐ 56	Bob Houbregs DP Detroit Pistons	35.00	17.50	3.50
☐ 57	Lou Tsioropoulas DP Boston Celtics	20.00	10.00	2.00
☐ 58	Ed Conlin Syracuse Nationals	25.00	12.50	2.50
☐ 59	Al Bianchi Syracuse Nationals	35.00	17.50	3.50

		NRMT	VG-E	GOOD
☐ 60	George Dempsey Philadelphia Warriors	25.00	12.50	2.50
☐ 61	Chuck Share St. Louis Hawks	25.00	12.50	2.50
☐ 62	Harry Gallatin DP Detroit Pistons	40.00	20.00	4.00
☐ 63	Bob Harrison Syracuse Nationals	25.00	12.50	2.50
☐ 64	Bob Burrow DP Minneapolis Lakers	20.00	10.00	2.00
☐ 65	Win Wilfong DP St. Louis Hawks	20.00	10.00	2.00
☐ 66	Jack McMahon DP St. Louis Hawks	30.00	15.00	3.00
☐ 67	Jack George Philadelphia Warriors	25.00	12.50	2.50
☐ 68	Charlie Tyra DP New York Knicks	20.00	10.00	2.00
☐ 69	Ron Sobie New York Knicks	25.00	12.50	2.50
☐ 70	Jack Coleman St. Louis Hawks	25.00	12.50	2.50
☐ 71	Jack Twyman DP Cincinnati Royals	60.00	30.00	6.00
☐ 72	Paul Seymour Syracuse Nationals	25.00	12.50	2.50
☐ 73	Jim Paxson DP Cincinnati Royals	30.00	15.00	3.00
☐ 74	Bob Leonard Minneapolis Lakers	30.00	15.00	3.00
☐ 75	Andy Phillip Boston Celtics	30.00	15.00	3.00
☐ 76	Joe Holup Syracuse Nationals	25.00	12.50	2.50
☐ 77	Bill Russell Boston Celtics	1650.00	750.00	150.00
☐ 78	Clyde Lovellette DP Cincinnati Royals	60.00	30.00	6.00
☐ 79	Ed Fleming DP Minneapolis Lakers	20.00	10.00	2.00
☐ 80	Dick Schnittker Minneapolis Lakers	40.00	15.00	3.00

		NRMT	VG-E	GOOD
☐ 5	John Havlicek Boston Celtics	500.00	250.00	50.00
☐ 6	Cazzie Russell New York Knicks	250.00	125.00	25.00
☐ 7	Willis Reed New York Knicks	400.00	200.00	40.00
☐ 8	Bill Bradley New York Knicks	600.00	300.00	60.00
☐ 9	Odie Smith Cincinnati Royals	200.00	100.00	20.00
☐ 10	Dave Bing Detroit Pistons	300.00	150.00	30.00
☐ 11	Dave DeBusschere Detroit Pistons	400.00	200.00	40.00
☐ 12	Earl Monroe Baltimore Bullets	400.00	200.00	40.00
☐ 13	Nate Thurmond San Francisco Warriors	300.00	150.00	30.00
☐ 14	Jim King San Francisco Warriors	200.00	100.00	20.00
☐ 15	Len Wilkens St. Louis Hawks	400.00	200.00	40.00
☐ 16	Bill Bridges St. Louis Hawks	200.00	100.00	20.00
☐ 17	Zelmo Beaty St. Louis Hawks	200.00	100.00	20.00
☐ 18	Elgin Baylor Los Angeles Lakers	500.00	250.00	50.00
☐ 19	Jerry West Los Angeles Lakers	900.00	450.00	90.00
☐ 20	Jerry Sloan Chicago Bulls	200.00	100.00	20.00
☐ 21	Jerry Lucas Cincinnati Royals	500.00	250.00	50.00
☐ 22	Oscar Robertson Cincinnati Royals	750.00	375.00	75.00

1968-69 Topps Test

JERRY SLOAN
CHICAGO BULLS • HT: 6'6"

This set was apparently a limited test issue produced by Topps. The cards measure the standard size (2 1/2" by 3 1/2"). The front features a black and white "action" pose of the player, on white card stock. The player's name, team, and height are given below the picture. The horizontally oriented card backs form a composite of Wilt Chamberlain. The cards are numbered on the back. The set is dated as 1968-69 since Earl Monroe's first season was 1967-68.

	NRMT	VG-E	GOOD
COMPLETE SET (22)	7500.00	3500.00	700.00
COMMON PLAYER (1-22)	200.00	100.00	20.00
☐ 1 Unknown	000.00	00.00	00.00
☐ 2 Hal Greer Philadelphia 76ers	300.00	150.00	30.00
☐ 3 Chet Walker Philadelphia 76ers	250.00	125.00	25.00
☐ 4 Unknown	000.00	00.00	00.00

1969-70 Topps

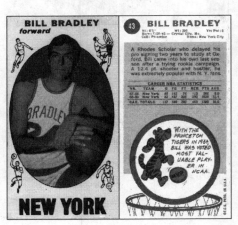

The 1969-70 Topps set of 99 cards was Topps' first basketball issue since 1958. These tall cards measure 2 1/2" by 4 11/16". The cards are much larger than the standard card size, perhaps rather appropriate considering the dimensions of most basketball players. The set features the first card of Lew Alcindor (later Kareem Abdul Jabbar). Other notable rookie cards in the set are Bill Bradley, Billy Cunningham, Dave DeBusschere, Walt Frazier, John Havlicek, Elvin Hayes, Jerry Lucas, Earl Monroe, Willis Reed, and Wes Unseld. The set was printed on a sheet of 99 cards (nine rows of eleven across) with the checklist card occupying the lower right corner of the sheet.

	NRMT	VG-E	GOOD
COMPLETE SET (99)	2200.00	1000.00	225.00
COMMON PLAYER (1-99)	3.00	1.50	.30
☐ 1 Wilt Chamberlain Los Angeles Lakers	200.00	50.00	10.00

#	Player / Team			
☐ 2	Gail Goodrich — Phoenix Suns	15.00	7.50	1.50
☐ 3	Cazzie Russell — New York Knicks	10.00	5.00	1.00
☐ 4	Darrall Imhoff — Philadelphia 76ers	3.00	1.50	.30
☐ 5	Bailey Howell — Boston Celtics	3.00	1.50	.30
☐ 6	Lucius Allen — Seattle Supersonics	5.00	2.50	.50
☐ 7	Tom Boerwinkle — Chicago Bulls	4.00	2.00	.40
☐ 8	Jimmy Walker — Detroit Pistons	4.00	2.00	.40
☐ 9	John Block — San Diego Rockets	3.00	1.50	.30
☐ 10	Nate Thurmond — San Francisco Warriors	15.00	7.50	1.50
☐ 11	Gary Gregor — Atlanta Hawks	3.00	1.50	.30
☐ 12	Gus Johnson — Baltimore Bullets	8.00	4.00	.80
☐ 13	Luther Rackley — Cincinnati Royals	3.00	1.50	.30
☐ 14	Jon McGlocklin — Milwaukee Bucks	4.00	2.00	.40
☐ 15	Connie Hawkins — Phoenix Suns	18.00	9.00	1.80
☐ 16	Johnny Egan — Los Angeles Lakers	3.00	1.50	.30
☐ 17	Jim Washington — Philadelphia 76ers	3.00	1.50	.30
☐ 18	Dick Barnett — New York Knicks	5.00	2.50	.50
☐ 19	Tom Meschery — Seattle Supersonics	3.00	1.50	.30
☐ 20	John Havlicek — Boston Celtics	150.00	75.00	15.00
☐ 21	Eddie Miles — Detroit Pistons	3.00	1.50	.30
☐ 22	Walt Wesley — Chicago Bulls	3.00	1.50	.30
☐ 23	Rick Adelman — San Diego Rockets	7.00	3.50	.70
☐ 24	Al Attles — San Francisco Warriors	4.00	2.00	.40
☐ 25	Lew Alcindor — Milwaukee Bucks	800.00	350.00	70.00
☐ 26	Jack Marin — Baltimore Bullets	4.00	2.00	.40
☐ 27	Walt Hazzard — Atlanta Hawks	7.00	3.50	.70
☐ 28	Connie Dierking — Cincinnati Royals	3.00	1.50	.30
☐ 29	Keith Erickson — Los Angeles Lakers	4.00	2.00	.40
☐ 30	Bob Rule — Seattle Supersonics	4.00	2.00	.40
☐ 31	Dick Van Arsdale — Phoenix Suns	4.00	2.00	.40
☐ 32	Archie Clark — Philadelphia 76ers	5.00	2.50	.50
☐ 33	Terry Dischinger — Detroit Pistons	4.00	2.00	.40
☐ 34	Henry Finkel — Boston Celtics	3.00	1.50	.30
☐ 35	Elgin Baylor — Los Angeles Lakers	55.00	27.50	5.50
☐ 36	Ron Williams — San Francisco Warriors	3.00	1.50	.30
☐ 37	Loy Petersen — Chicago Bulls	3.00	1.50	.30
☐ 38	Guy Rodgers — Milwaukee Bucks	4.00	2.00	.40
☐ 39	Toby Kimball — San Diego Rockets	3.00	1.50	.30
☐ 40	Billy Cunningham — Philadelphia 76ers	33.00	15.00	3.00
☐ 41	Joe Caldwell — Atlanta Hawks	4.00	2.00	.40
☐ 42	Leroy Ellis — Baltimore Bullets	4.00	2.00	.40
☐ 43	Bill Bradley — New York Knicks	240.00	100.00	20.00
☐ 44	Len Wilkens — Seattle Supersonics (Misspelled Wilkins on card back)	9.00	4.50	.90
☐ 45	Jerry Lucas — San Francisco Warriors	42.00	18.00	4.00
☐ 46	Neal Walk — Phoenix Suns	4.00	2.00	.40
☐ 47	Emmette Bryant — Boston Celtics	3.00	1.50	.30
☐ 48	Bob Kauffman — Chicago Bulls	4.00	2.00	.40
☐ 49	Mel Counts — Los Angeles Lakers	4.00	2.00	.40
☐ 50	Oscar Robertson — Cincinnati Royals	65.00	32.50	6.50
☐ 51	Jim Barnett — San Diego Rockets	4.00	2.00	.40
☐ 52	Don Smith — Milwaukee Bucks	3.00	1.50	.30
☐ 53	Jim Davis — Atlanta Hawks	3.00	1.50	.30
☐ 54	Wally Jones — Philadelphia 76ers	3.00	1.50	.30
☐ 55	Dave Bing — Detroit Pistons	22.00	11.00	2.20
☐ 56	Wes Unseld — Baltimore Bullets	33.00	15.00	3.00
☐ 57	Joe Ellis — San Francisco Warriors	3.00	1.50	.30
☐ 58	John Tresvant — Seattle Supersonics	3.00	1.50	.30
☐ 59	Larry Siegfried — Boston Celtics	4.00	2.00	.40
☐ 60	Willis Reed — New York Knicks	37.50	17.50	3.50
☐ 61	Paul Silas — Phoenix Suns	8.00	4.00	.80
☐ 62	Bob Weiss — Chicago Bulls	6.00	3.00	.60
☐ 63	Willie McCarter — Los Angeles Lakers	3.00	1.50	.30
☐ 64	Don Kojis — San Diego Rockets	3.00	1.50	.30
☐ 65	Lou Hudson — Atlanta Hawks	6.00	3.00	.60
☐ 66	Jim King — Cincinnati Royals	3.00	1.50	.30
☐ 67	Luke Jackson — Philadelphia 76ers	3.00	1.50	.30
☐ 68	Len Chappell — Milwaukee Bucks	4.00	2.00	.40
☐ 69	Ray Scott — Baltimore Bullets	3.00	1.50	.30
☐ 70	Jeff Mullins — San Francisco Warriors	4.00	2.00	.40
☐ 71	Howie Komives — Detroit Pistons	3.00	1.50	.30
☐ 72	Tom Sanders — Boston Celtics	5.00	2.50	.50
☐ 73	Dick Snyder — Seattle Supersonics	3.00	1.50	.30
☐ 74	Dave Stallworth — New York Knicks	4.00	2.00	.40
☐ 75	Elvin Hayes — San Diego Rockets	65.00	32.50	6.50
☐ 76	Art Harris — Phoenix Suns	3.00	1.50	.30
☐ 77	Don Ohl — Atlanta Hawks	3.00	1.50	.30
☐ 78	Bob Love — Chicago Bulls	9.00	4.50	.90
☐ 79	Tom Van Arsdale — Cincinnati Royals	4.00	2.00	.40
☐ 80	Earl Monroe — Baltimore Bullets	38.00	17.50	3.50
☐ 81	Greg Smith — Milwaukee Bucks	3.00	1.50	.30
☐ 82	Don Nelson — Boston Celtics	16.00	8.00	1.60
☐ 83	Happy Hairston — Detroit Pistons	5.00	2.50	.50
☐ 84	Hal Greer — Philadelphia 76ers	7.00	3.50	.70
☐ 85	Dave DeBusschere — New York Knicks	40.00	20.00	4.00
☐ 86	Bill Bridges — Atlanta Hawks	5.00	2.50	.50
☐ 87	Herm Gilliam — Cincinnati Royals	4.00	2.00	.40
☐ 88	Jim Fox — Phoenix Suns	3.00	1.50	.30
☐ 89	Bob Boozer — Seattle Supersonics	3.00	1.50	.30
☐ 90	Jerry West — Los Angeles Lakers	85.00	42.50	8.50
☐ 91	Chet Walker — Chicago Bulls	9.00	4.50	.90
☐ 92	Flynn Robinson — Milwaukee Bucks	3.00	1.50	.30
☐ 93	Clyde Lee — San Francisco Warriors	3.00	1.50	.30
☐ 94	Kevin Loughery — Baltimore Bullets	5.00	2.50	.50

		NRMT	VG-E	GOOD
☐ 95	Walt Bellamy Detroit Pistons	4.00	2.00	.40
☐ 96	Art Williams San Diego Rockets	3.00	1.50	.30
☐ 97	Adrian Smith Cincinnati Royals	3.00	1.50	.30
☐ 98	Walt Frazier New York Knicks	65.00	32.50	6.50
☐ 99	Checklist Card	240.00	20.00	4.00

1969-70 Topps Poster Inserts

The 1969-70 Topps basketball cartoon poster inserts are clever color cartoon drawings of NBA players, with ruler markings on the left edge of the insert. These paper-thin posters measure approximately 2 1/2" by 9 7/8". The player's height is indicated in an arrow pointing towards the ruler, and the top of the player's head corresponds to this line on the ruler. The inserts are numbered and contain the player's name and team in an oval near the bottom of the insert. As might be expected, these inserts make the players look both taller and thinner than they actually are. Insert number 5 was never issued; it was intended to be Bill Russell. The inserts came with gum packages of Topps regular issue basketball cards of that year.

		NRMT	VG-E	GOOD
COMPLETE SET (23)		400.00	200.00	40.00
COMMON PLAYER (1-24)		6.00	3.00	.60
☐ 1	Walt Bellamy Detroit Pistons	6.00	3.00	.60
☐ 2	Jerry West Los Angeles Lakers	35.00	17.50	3.50
☐ 3	Bailey Howell Boston Celtics	6.00	3.00	.60
☐ 4	Elvin Hayes San Diego Rockets	20.00	10.00	2.00
☐ 5	Never Issued	0.00	0.00	.00
☐ 6	Bob Rule Seattle Supersonics	6.00	3.00	.60
☐ 7	Gail Goodrich Phoenix Suns	8.00	4.00	.80
☐ 8	Jeff Mullins San Francisco Warriors	6.00	3.00	.60
☐ 9	John Havlicek Boston Celtics	27.00	13.50	2.70

☐ 10	Lew Alcindor Milwaukee Bucks	85.00	42.50	8.50
☐ 11	Wilt Chamberlain Los Angeles Lakers	70.00	35.00	7.00
☐ 12	Nate Thurmond San Francisco Warriors	9.00	4.50	.90
☐ 13	Hal Greer Philadelphia 76ers	6.00	3.00	.60
☐ 14	Lou Hudson Atlanta Hawks	6.00	3.00	.60
☐ 15	Jerry Lucas San Francisco Warriors	15.00	7.50	1.50
☐ 16	Dave Bing Detroit Pistons	10.00	5.00	1.00
☐ 17	Walt Frazier New York Knicks	15.00	7.50	1.50
☐ 18	Gus Johnson Baltimore Bullets	6.00	3.00	.60
☐ 19	Willis Reed New York Knicks	15.00	7.50	1.50
☐ 20	Earl Monroe Baltimore Bullets	12.00	6.00	1.20
☐ 21	Billy Cunningham Philadelphia 76ers	12.00	6.00	1.20
☐ 22	Wes Unseld Baltimore Bullets	12.00	6.00	1.20
☐ 23	Bob Boozer Seattle Supersonics	6.00	3.00	.60
☐ 24	Oscar Robertson Cincinnati Royals	30.00	15.00	3.00

1970-71 Topps

The 1970-71 Topps basketball card set of 175 full-color cards continued the larger-size card. These tall cards measure 2 1/2" by 4 11/16". Cards numbered 106 to 115 contained the previous season's NBA first and second team All-Star selections. The first six cards in the set (1-6) feature the statistical league leaders from the previous season. The last eight cards in the set (168-175) summarize the results of the previous season's NBA championship playoff series won by the Knicks over the Lakers. The key rookie cards in this set are Pete Maravich and Pat Riley.

		NRMT	VG-E	GOOD
COMPLETE SET (175)		1350.00	650.00	150.00
COMMON PLAYER (1-110)		1.75	.85	.17
COMMON PLAYER (111-175)		2.25	1.10	.22
☐ 1	NBA Scoring Leaders Lew Alcindor Jerry West Elvin Hayes	25.00	7.50	1.50
☐ 2	NBA Scoring Average Leaders Jerry West Lew Alcindor Elvin Hayes	10.00	5.00	1.00

☐ 3 NBA FG Pct Leaders Johnny Green Darrall Imhoff Lou Hudson	3.50	1.75	.35
☐ 4 NBA FT Pct Leaders Flynn Robinson Chet Walker Jeff Mullins	3.50	1.75	.35
☐ 5 NBA Rebound Leaders Elvin Hayes Wes Unseld Lew Alcindor	9.00	4.50	.90
☐ 6 NBA Assist Leaders Len Wilkens Walt Frazier Clem Haskins	4.00	2.00	.40
☐ 7 Bill Bradley New York Knicks	100.00	50.00	10.00
☐ 8 Ron Williams San Francisco Warriors	1.75	.85	.17
☐ 9 Otto Moore Detroit Pistons	1.75	.85	.17
☐ 10 John Havlicek Boston Celtics	80.00	40.00	8.00
☐ 11 George Wilson Buffalo Braves	1.75	.85	.17
☐ 12 John Trapp San Diego Rockets	1.75	.85	.17
☐ 13 Pat Riley Portland Trail Blazers	30.00	15.00	3.00
☐ 14 Jim Washington Philadelphia 76ers	1.75	.85	.17
☐ 15 Bob Rule Seattle Supersonics	1.75	.85	.17
☐ 16 Bob Weiss Chicago Bulls	2.25	1.10	.22
☐ 17 Neil Johnson Phoenix Suns	1.75	.85	.17
☐ 18 Walt Bellamy Atlanta Hawks	2.50	1.25	.25
☐ 19 McCoy McLemore Cleveland Cavaliers	1.75	.85	.17
☐ 20 Earl Monroe Baltimore Bullets	15.00	7.50	1.50
☐ 21 Wally Anderzunas Cincinnati Royals	1.75	.85	.17
☐ 22 Guy Rodgers Milwaukee Bucks	2.25	1.10	.22
☐ 23 Rick Roberson Los Angeles Lakers	1.75	.85	.17
☐ 24 Checklist 1-110	45.00	4.00	.80
☐ 25 Jimmy Walker Detroit Pistons	1.75	.85	.17
☐ 26 Mike Riordan New York Knicks	3.00	1.50	.30
☐ 27 Henry Finkel Boston Celtics	1.75	.85	.17
☐ 28 Joe Ellis San Francisco Warriors	1.75	.85	.17
☐ 29 Mike Davis Buffalo Braves	1.75	.85	.17
☐ 30 Lou Hudson Atlanta Hawks	3.00	1.50	.30
☐ 31 Lucius Allen Seattle Supersonics	3.00	1.50	.30
☐ 32 Toby Kimball San Diego Rockets	1.75	.85	.17
☐ 33 Luke Jackson Philadelphia 76ers	1.75	.85	.17
☐ 34 Johnny Egan Cleveland Cavaliers	1.75	.85	.17
☐ 35 Leroy Ellis Portland Trail Blazers	2.25	1.10	.22
☐ 36 Jack Marin Baltimore Bullets	2.25	1.10	.22
☐ 37 Joe Caldwell Atlanta Hawks	2.50	1.25	.25
☐ 38 Keith Erickson Los Angeles Lakers	2.25	1.10	.22
☐ 39 Don Smith Milwaukee Bucks	1.75	.85	.17
☐ 40 Flynn Robinson Cincinnati Royals	1.75	.85	.17
☐ 41 Bob Boozer Seattle Supersonics	1.75	.85	.17
☐ 42 Howie Komives Detroit Pistons	1.75	.85	.17
☐ 43 Dick Barnett New York Knicks	2.50	1.25	.25
☐ 44 Stu Lantz San Diego Rockets	1.75	.85	.17
☐ 45 Dick Van Arsdale Phoenix Suns	2.25	1.10	.22
☐ 46 Jerry Lucas San Francisco Warriors	15.00	7.50	1.50
☐ 47 Don Chaney Boston Celtics	10.00	5.00	1.00
☐ 48 Ray Scott Buffalo Braves	1.75	.85	.17
☐ 49 Dick Cunningham Milwaukee Bucks	1.75	.85	.17
☐ 50 Wilt Chamberlain Los Angeles Lakers	110.00	55.00	11.00
☐ 51 Kevin Loughery Baltimore Bullets	3.00	1.50	.30
☐ 52 Stan McKenzie Portland Trail Blazers	1.75	.85	.17
☐ 53 Fred Foster Cincinnati Royals	1.75	.85	.17
☐ 54 Jim Davis Atlanta Hawks	1.75	.85	.17
☐ 55 Walt Wesley Cleveland Cavaliers	1.75	.85	.17
☐ 56 Bill Hewitt Detroit Pistons	1.75	.85	.17
☐ 57 Darrall Imhoff Philadelphia 76ers	1.75	.85	.17
☐ 58 John Block San Diego Rockets	1.75	.85	.17
☐ 59 Al Attles San Francisco Warriors	2.50	1.25	.25
☐ 60 Chet Walker Chicago Bulls	3.50	1.75	.35
☐ 61 Luther Rackley Cleveland Cavaliers	1.75	.85	.17
☐ 62 Jerry Chambers Atlanta Hawks	1.75	.85	.17
☐ 63 Bob Dandridge Milwaukee Bucks	5.00	2.50	.50
☐ 64 Dick Snyder Seattle Supersonics	1.75	.85	.17
☐ 65 Elgin Baylor Los Angeles Lakers	33.00	15.00	3.00
☐ 66 Connie Dierking Cincinnati Royals	1.75	.85	.17
☐ 67 Steve Kuberski Boston Celtics	1.75	.85	.17
☐ 68 Tom Boerwinkle Chicago Bulls	1.75	.85	.17
☐ 69 Paul Silas Phoenix Suns	3.50	1.75	.35
☐ 70 Elvin Hayes San Diego Rockets	24.00	12.00	2.40
☐ 71 Bill Bridges Atlanta Hawks	2.25	1.10	.22
☐ 72 Wes Unseld Baltimore Bullets	8.50	4.25	.85
☐ 73 Herm Gilliam Buffalo Braves	1.75	.85	.17
☐ 74 Bobby Smith Cleveland Cavaliers	2.50	1.25	.25
☐ 75 Lew Alcindor Milwaukee Bucks	225.00	110.00	22.00
☐ 76 Jeff Mullins San Francisco Warriors	2.25	1.10	.22
☐ 77 Happy Hairston Los Angeles Lakers	2.25	1.10	.22
☐ 78 Dave Stallworth New York Knicks	2.25	1.10	.22
☐ 79 Fred Hetzel Portland Trail Blazers	1.75	.85	.17
☐ 80 Len Wilkens Seattle Supersonics	6.00	3.00	.60
☐ 81 Johnny Green Cincinnati Royals	2.50	1.25	.25
☐ 82 Erwin Mueller Detroit Pistons	1.75	.85	.17
☐ 83 Wally Jones Philadelphia 76ers	1.75	.85	.17
☐ 84 Bob Love Chicago Bulls	3.50	1.75	.35
☐ 85 Dick Garrett Buffalo Braves	2.25	1.10	.22
☐ 86 Don Nelson Boston Celtics	7.00	3.50	.70
☐ 87 Neal Walk Phoenix Suns	1.75	.85	.17
☐ 88 Larry Siegfried San Diego Rockets	2.25	1.10	.22
☐ 89 Gary Gregor Portland Trail Blazers	1.75	.85	.17
☐ 90 Nate Thurmond San Francisco Warriors	5.00	2.50	.50
☐ 91 John Warren Cleveland Cavaliers	1.75	.85	.17
☐ 92 Gus Johnson Baltimore Bullets	2.50	1.25	.25
☐ 93 Gail Goodrich Los Angeles Lakers	4.00	2.00	.40

□ 94	Dorrie Murrey Portland Trail Blazers	1.75	.85	.17
□ 95	Cazzie Russell New York Knicks	3.50	1.75	.35
□ 96	Terry Dischinger Detroit Pistons	2.25	1.10	.22
□ 97	Norm Van Lier Cincinnati Royals	4.00	2.00	.40
□ 98	Jim Fox Chicago Bulls	1.75	.85	.17
□ 99	Tom Meschery Seattle Supersonics	1.75	.85	.17
□ 100	Oscar Robertson Milwaukee Bucks	40.00	20.00	4.00
□ 101A	Checklist 111-175 (1970-71 in black)	27.00	3.00	.60
□ 101B	Checklist 111-175 (1970-71 in white)	27.00	3.00	.60
□ 102	Rich Johnson Boston Celtics	1.75	.85	.17
□ 103	Mel Counts Phoenix Suns	1.75	.85	.17
□ 104	Bill Hosket Buffalo Braves	1.75	.85	.17
□ 105	Archie Clark Philadelphia 76ers	2.50	1.25	.25
□ 106	Walt Frazier AS New York Knicks	8.50	4.25	.85
□ 107	Jerry West AS Los Angeles Lakers	27.00	13.50	2.70
□ 108	Bill Cunningham AS Philadelphia 76ers	4.00	2.00	.40
□ 109	Connie Hawkins AS Phoenix Suns	3.00	1.50	.30
□ 110	Willis Reed AS New York Knicks	4.00	2.00	.40
□ 111	Nate Thurmond AS San Francisco Warriors	3.50	1.75	.35
□ 112	John Havlicek AS Boston Celtics	27.00	13.50	2.70
□ 113	Elgin Baylor AS Los Angeles Lakers	14.00	7.00	1.40
□ 114	Oscar Robertson AS Milwaukee Bucks	21.00	10.50	2.10
□ 115	Lou Hudson AS Atlanta Hawks	3.50	1.75	.35
□ 116	Emmette Bryant Buffalo Braves	2.25	1.10	.22
□ 117	Greg Howard Phoenix Suns	2.25	1.10	.22
□ 118	Rick Adelman Portland Trail Blazers	2.75	1.35	.27
□ 119	Barry Clemens Seattle Supersonics	2.25	1.10	.22
□ 120	Walt Frazier New York Knicks	24.00	12.00	2.40
□ 121	Jim Barnes Boston Celtics	2.75	1.35	.27
□ 122	Bernie Williams San Diego Rockets	2.25	1.10	.22
□ 123	Pete Maravich Atlanta Hawks	175.00	85.00	18.00
□ 124	Matt Guokas Philadelphia 76ers	5.00	2.50	.50
□ 125	Dave Bing Detroit Pistons	7.50	3.75	.75
□ 126	John Tresvant Los Angeles Lakers	2.25	1.10	.22
□ 127	Shaler Halimon Chicago Bulls	2.25	1.10	.22
□ 128	Don Ohl Cleveland Cavaliers	2.25	1.10	.22
□ 129	Fred Carter Baltimore Bullets	2.75	1.35	.27
□ 130	Connie Hawkins Phoenix Suns	5.50	2.75	.55
□ 131	Jim King Cincinnati Royals	2.25	1.10	.22
□ 132	Ed Manning Portland Trail Blazers	2.75	1.35	.27
□ 133	Adrian Smith San Francisco Warriors	2.25	1.10	.22
□ 134	Walt Hazzard Atlanta Hawks	3.00	1.50	.30
□ 135	Dave DeBusschere New York Knicks	15.00	7.50	1.50
□ 136	Don Kojis Seattle Supersonics	2.25	1.10	.22
□ 137	Calvin Murphy San Diego Rockets	15.00	7.50	1.50
□ 138	Nate Bowman Buffalo Braves	2.25	1.10	.22
□ 139	Jon McGlocklin Milwaukee Bucks	2.75	1.35	.27
□ 140	Billy Cunningham Philadelphia 76ers	12.00	6.00	1.20
□ 141	Willie McCarter Los Angeles Lakers	2.25	1.10	.22
□ 142	Jim Barnett Portland Trail Blazers	2.75	1.35	.27
□ 143	Jo Jo White Boston Celtics	12.00	6.00	1.20
□ 144	Clyde Lee San Francisco Warriors	2.25	1.10	.22
□ 145	Tom Van Arsdale Cincinnati Royals	2.75	1.35	.27
□ 146	Len Chappell Cleveland Cavaliers	2.25	1.10	.22
□ 147	Lee Winfield Seattle Supersonics	2.25	1.10	.22
□ 148	Jerry Sloan Chicago Bulls	7.00	3.50	.70
□ 149	Art Harris Phoenix Suns	2.25	1.10	.22
□ 150	Willis Reed New York Knicks	16.00	8.00	1.60
□ 151	Art Williams San Diego Rockets	2.25	1.10	.22
□ 152	Don May Buffalo Braves	2.25	1.10	.22
□ 153	Loy Petersen Cleveland Cavaliers	2.25	1.10	.22
□ 154	Dave Gambee San Francisco Warriors	2.25	1.10	.22
□ 155	Hal Greer Philadelphia 76ers	5.00	2.50	.50
□ 156	Dave Newmark Atlanta Hawks	2.25	1.10	.22
□ 157	Jimmy Collins Chicago Bulls	2.25	1.10	.22
□ 158	Bill Turner Cincinnati Royals	2.25	1.10	.22
□ 159	Eddie Miles Baltimore Bullets	2.25	1.10	.22
□ 160	Jerry West Los Angeles Lakers	50.00	25.00	5.00
□ 161	Bob Quick Detroit Pistons	2.25	1.10	.22
□ 162	Fred Crawford Buffalo Braves	2.25	1.10	.22
□ 163	Tom Sanders Boston Celtics	2.75	1.35	.27
□ 164	Dale Schlueter Portland Trail Blazers	2.25	1.10	.22
□ 165	Clem Haskins Phoenix Suns	3.50	1.75	.35
□ 166	Greg Smith Milwaukee Bucks	2.25	1.10	.22
□ 167	Rod Thorn Seattle Supersonics	3.50	1.75	.35
□ 168	Playoff Game 1 (Willis Reed)	5.00	2.50	.50
□ 169	Playoff Game 2 (Dick Garrett)	4.00	2.00	.40
□ 170	Playoff Game 3 (Dave DeBusschere)	5.00	2.50	.50
□ 171	Playoff Game 4 (Jerry West)	10.00	5.00	1.00
□ 172	Playoff Game 5 (Bill Bradley)	10.00	5.00	1.00
□ 173	Playoff Game 6 (W. Chamberlain)	10.00	5.00	1.00
□ 174	Playoff Game 7 (Walt Frazier)	6.00	3.00	.60
□ 175	Knicks Celebrate New York Knicks, World Champs	13.50	4.00	.80

1970-71 Topps Poster Inserts

This set of 24 large (8" by 10") thin paper posters was issued with the 1970-71 Topps regular basketball cards. The posters are in full color and contain the player's name and his team near the upper left of the poster. The number appears in the border at the lower right, and a Topps copyright date and a 1968 National Basketball Player's Association copyright date appears in the border at the left.

1971-72 Topps

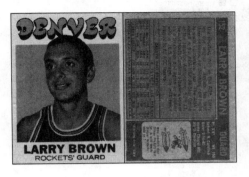

LARRY BROWN
ROCKETS' GUARD

The 1971-72 Topps basketball set of 233 witnessed a return to the standard-sized card, i.e., 2 1/2" by 3 1/2". National Basketball Association (NBA) players are depicted on cards 1 to 144 and American Basketball Association (ABA) players are depicted on cards 145 to 233. The set was produced on two sheets. The second production sheet contained the ABA players (145-233) as well as 31 double-printed cards (essentially NBA players) from the first sheet. These DP's are indicated in the checklist below. Special subseries within this set include NBA Playoffs (133-137), NBA Statistical Leaders (138-143), and ABA Statistical Leaders (146-151). The key rookie cards in this set are Nate Archibald, Rick Barry, Dave Cowens, Dan Issel, and Bob Lanier.

	NRMT	VG-E	GOOD
COMPLETE SET (233)	775.00	375.00	75.00
COMMON PLAYER (1-233)	.90	.45	.09
☐ 1 Oscar Robertson	50.00	12.50	2.50
Milwaukee Bucks			
☐ 2 Bill Bradley	50.00	25.00	5.00
New York Knicks			
☐ 3 Jim Fox	.90	.45	.09
Chicago Bulls			
☐ 4 John Johnson	2.00	1.00	.20
Cleveland Cavaliers			
☐ 5 Luke Jackson	.90	.45	.09
Philadelphia 76ers			
☐ 6 Don May DP	.90	.45	.09
Atlanta Hawks			
☐ 7 Kevin Loughery	1.75	.85	.17
Baltimore Bullets			
☐ 8 Terry Dischinger	1.25	.60	.12
Detroit Pistons			
☐ 9 Neal Walk	1.00	.50	.10
Phoenix Suns			
☐ 10 Elgin Baylor	27.00	13.50	2.70
Los Angeles Lakers			
☐ 11 Rick Adelman	1.50	.75	.15
Portland Trail Blazers			
☐ 12 Clyde Lee	.90	.45	.09
Golden State Warriors			
☐ 13 Jerry Chambers	.90	.45	.09
Buffalo Braves			
☐ 14 Fred Carter	.90	.45	.09
Baltimore Bullets			
☐ 15 Tom Boerwinkle DP	.90	.45	.09
Chicago Bulls			
☐ 16 John Block	.90	.45	.09
Houston Rockets			
☐ 17 Dick Barnett	1.25	.60	.12
New York Knicks			
☐ 18 Henry Finkel	.90	.45	.09
Boston Celtics			
☐ 19 Norm Van Lier	1.50	.75	.15
Cincinnati Royals			
☐ 20 Spencer Haywood	6.50	3.25	.65
Seattle Supersonics			
☐ 21 George Johnson	.90	.45	.09
Baltimore Bullets			
☐ 22 Bobby Lewis	.90	.45	.09
Cleveland Cavaliers			
☐ 23 Bill Hewitt	.90	.45	.09
Detroit Pistons			

CHET WALKER — CHICAGO

	NRMT	VG-E	GOOD
COMPLETE SET (24)	150.00	75.00	15.00
COMMON PLAYER (1-24)	1.50	.75	.15
☐ 1 Walt Frazier	7.50	3.75	.75
New York Knicks			
☐ 2 Joe Caldwell	1.50	.75	.15
Atlanta Hawks			
☐ 3 Willis Reed	7.50	3.75	.75
New York Knicks			
☐ 4 Elvin Hayes	10.00	5.00	1.00
San Diego Rockets			
☐ 5 Jeff Mullins	1.50	.75	.15
San Francisco Warriors			
☐ 6 Oscar Robertson	20.00	10.00	2.00
Cincinnati Royals			
☐ 7 Dave Bing	5.00	2.50	.50
Detroit Pistons			
☐ 8 Jerry Sloan	1.50	.75	.15
Chicago Bulls			
☐ 9 Leroy Ellis	1.50	.75	.15
Portland Trail Blazers			
☐ 10 Hal Greer	3.50	1.75	.35
Philadelphia 76ers			
☐ 11 Emmette Bryant	1.50	.75	.15
Buffalo Braves			
☐ 12 Bob Rule	1.50	.75	.15
Seattle Supersonics			
☐ 13 Lew Alcindor	45.00	22.50	4.50
Milwaukee Bucks			
☐ 14 Chet Walker	2.50	1.25	.25
Chicago Bulls			
☐ 15 Jerry West	22.50	10.00	2.00
Los Angeles Lakers			
☐ 16 Billy Cunningham	5.00	2.50	.50
Philadelphia 76ers			
☐ 17 Wilt Chamberlain	33.00	15.00	3.00
Los Angeles Lakers			
☐ 18 John Havlicek	20.00	10.00	2.00
Boston Celtics			
☐ 19 Lou Hudson	1.50	.75	.15
Atlanta Hawks			
☐ 20 Earl Monroe	5.00	2.50	.50
Baltimore Bullets			
☐ 21 Wes Unseld	5.00	2.50	.50
Baltimore Bullets			
☐ 22 Connie Hawkins	3.50	1.75	.35
Phoenix Suns			
☐ 23 Tom Van Arsdale	1.50	.75	.15
Cincinnati Royals			
☐ 24 Len Chappell	1.50	.75	.15
Cleveland Cavaliers			

☐ 24 Walt Hazzard DP	1.25	.60	.12
Buffalo Braves			
☐ 25 Happy Hairston	1.25	.60	.12
Los Angeles Lakers			
☐ 26 George Wilson	.90	.45	.09
Buffalo Braves			
☐ 27 Lucius Allen	1.50	.75	.15
Milwaukee Bucks			
☐ 28 Jim Washington	.90	.45	.09
Philadelphia 76ers			
☐ 29 Nate Archibald	21.00	10.50	2.10
Cincinnati Royals			
☐ 30 Willis Reed	7.50	3.75	.75
New York Knicks			
☐ 31 Erwin Mueller	.90	.45	.09
Detroit Pistons			
☐ 32 Art Harris	.90	.45	.09
Phoenix Suns			
☐ 33 Pete Cross	.90	.45	.09
Seattle Supersonics			
☐ 34 Geoff Petrie	3.50	1.75	.35
Portland Trail Blazers			
☐ 35 John Havlicek	36.00	18.00	3.60
Boston Celtics			
☐ 36 Larry Siegfried	.90	.45	.09
Houston Rockets			
☐ 37 John Tresvant DP	.90	.45	.09
Baltimore Bullets			
☐ 38 Ron Williams	.90	.45	.09
Golden State Warriors			
☐ 39 Lamar Green DP	.90	.45	.09
Phoenix Suns			
☐ 40 Bob Rule DP	.90	.45	.09
Seattle Supersonics			
☐ 41 Jim McMillian	1.75	.85	.17
Los Angeles Lakers			
☐ 42 Wally Jones	.90	.45	.09
Philadelphia 76ers			
☐ 43 Bob Boozer	.90	.45	.09
Milwaukee Bucks			
☐ 44 Eddie Miles	.90	.45	.09
Baltimore Bullets			
☐ 45 Bob Love DP	1.75	.85	.17
Chicago Bulls			
☐ 46 Claude English	.90	.45	.09
Portland Trail Blazers			
☐ 47 Dave Cowens	38.00	17.50	3.50
Boston Celtics			
☐ 48 Emmette Bryant	.90	.45	.09
Buffalo Braves			
☐ 49 Dave Stallworth	1.25	.60	.12
New York Knicks			
☐ 50 Jerry West	42.00	20.00	4.00
Los Angeles Lakers			
☐ 51 Joe Ellis	.90	.45	.09
Golden State Warriors			
☐ 52 Walt Wesley DP	.90	.45	.09
Cleveland Cavaliers			
☐ 53 Howie Komives	.90	.45	.09
Detroit Pistons			
☐ 54 Paul Silas	1.75	.85	.17
Phoenix Suns			
☐ 55 Pete Maravich DP	45.00	22.50	4.50
Atlanta Hawks			
☐ 56 Gary Gregor	.90	.45	.09
Portland Trail Blazers			
☐ 57 Sam Lacey	1.75	.85	.17
Cincinnati Royals			
☐ 58 Calvin Murphy DP	4.50	2.25	.45
Houston Rockets			
☐ 59 Bob Dandridge	1.25	.60	.12
Milwaukee Bucks			
☐ 60 Hal Greer	2.75	1.35	.27
Philadelphia 76ers			
☐ 61 Keith Erickson	1.25	.60	.12
Los Angeles Lakers			
☐ 62 Joe Cooke	.90	.45	.09
Cleveland Cavaliers			
☐ 63 Bob Lanier	24.00	12.00	2.40
Detroit Pistons			
☐ 64 Don Kojis	.90	.45	.09
Seattle Supersonics			
☐ 65 Walt Frazier	14.00	7.00	1.40
New York Knicks			
☐ 66 Chet Walker DP	1.75	.85	.17
Chicago Bulls			
☐ 67 Dick Garrett	.90	.45	.09
Buffalo Braves			
☐ 68 John Trapp	.90	.45	.09
Houston Rockets			
☐ 69 Jo Jo White	4.00	2.00	.40
Boston Celtics			
☐ 70 Wilt Chamberlain	70.00	35.00	7.00
Los Angeles Lakers			

☐ 71 Dave Sorenson	.90	.45	.09
Cleveland Cavaliers			
☐ 72 Jim King	.90	.45	.09
Chicago Bulls			
☐ 73 Cazzie Russell	2.25	1.10	.22
Golden State Warriors			
☐ 74 Jon McGlocklin	1.50	.75	.15
Milwaukee Bucks			
☐ 75 Tom Van Arsdale	.90	.45	.09
Cincinnati Royals			
☐ 76 Dale Schlueter	.90	.45	.09
Portland Trail Blazers			
☐ 77 Gus Johnson DP	1.50	.75	.15
Baltimore Bullets			
☐ 78 Dave Bing	3.50	1.75	.35
Detroit Pistons			
☐ 79 Billy Cunningham	5.50	2.75	.55
Philadelphia 76ers			
☐ 80 Len Wilkens	3.50	1.75	.35
Seattle Supersonics			
☐ 81 Jerry Lucas DP	9.00	4.50	.90
New York Knicks			
☐ 82 Don Chaney	2.75	1.35	.27
Boston Celtics			
☐ 83 McCoy McLemore	.90	.45	.09
Milwaukee Bucks			
☐ 84 Bob Kauffman DP	.90	.45	.09
Buffalo Braves			
☐ 85 Dick Van Arsdale	.90	.45	.09
Phoenix Suns			
☐ 86 Johnny Green	.90	.45	.09
Cincinnati Royals			
☐ 87 Jerry Sloan	2.25	1.10	.22
Chicago Bulls			
☐ 88 Luther Rackley DP	.90	.45	.09
Cleveland Cavaliers			
☐ 89 Shaler Halimon	.90	.45	.09
Portland Trail Blazers			
☐ 90 Jimmy Walker	.90	.45	.09
Detroit Pistons			
☐ 91 Rudy Tomjanovich	3.25	1.60	.32
Houston Rockets			
☐ 92 Levi Fontaine	.90	.45	.09
Golden State Warriors			
☐ 93 Bobby Smith	.90	.45	.09
Cleveland Cavaliers			
☐ 94 Bob Arnzen	.90	.45	.09
Cincinnati Royals			
☐ 95 Wes Unseld DP	5.50	2.75	.55
Baltimore Bullets			
☐ 96 Clem Haskins DP	1.25	.60	.12
Phoenix Suns			
☐ 97 Jim Davis	.90	.45	.09
Atlanta Hawks			
☐ 98 Steve Kuberski	.90	.45	.09
Boston Celtics			
☐ 99 Mike Davis DP	.90	.45	.09
Buffalo Braves			
☐ 100 Lew Alcindor	100.00	50.00	10.00
Milwaukee Bucks			
☐ 101 Willie McCarter	.90	.45	.09
Los Angeles Lakers			
☐ 102 Charlie Paulk	.90	.45	.09
Chicago Bulls			
☐ 103 Lee Winfield	.90	.45	.09
Seattle Supersonics			
☐ 104 Jim Barnett	.90	.45	.09
Golden State Warriors			
☐ 105 Connie Hawkins DP	3.50	1.75	.35
Phoenix Suns			
☐ 106 Archie Clark DP	1.25	.60	.12
Philadelphia 76ers			
☐ 107 Dave DeBusschere	9.00	4.50	.90
New York Knicks			
☐ 108 Stu Lantz DP	.90	.45	.09
Houston Rockets			
☐ 109 Don Smith	.90	.45	.09
Seattle Supersonics			
☐ 110 Lou Hudson	1.75	.85	.17
Atlanta Hawks			
☐ 111 Leroy Ellis	.90	.45	.09
Portland Trail Blazers			
☐ 112 Jack Marin	1.25	.60	.12
Baltimore Bullets			
☐ 113 Matt Guokas	1.75	.85	.17
Cincinnati Royals			
☐ 114 Don Nelson	3.50	1.75	.35
Boston Celtics			
☐ 115 Jeff Mullins DP	1.25	.60	.12
Golden State Warriors			
☐ 116 Walt Bellamy	1.75	.85	.17
Atlanta Hawks			
☐ 117 Bob Quick	.90	.45	.09
Detroit Pistons			

#	Card			
☐ 118	John Warren / Cleveland Cavaliers	.90	.45	.09
☐ 119	Barry Clemens / Seattle Supersonics	.90	.45	.09
☐ 120	Elvin Hayes DP / Houston Rockets	14.00	7.00	1.40
☐ 121	Gail Goodrich / Los Angeles Lakers	2.50	1.25	.25
☐ 122	Ed Manning / Portland Trail Blazers	1.25	.60	.12
☐ 123	Herm Gilliam DP / Atlanta Hawks	.90	.45	.09
☐ 124	Dennis Awtrey / Philadelphia 76ers	.90	.45	.09
☐ 125	John Hummer DP / Buffalo Braves	.90	.45	.09
☐ 126	Mike Riordan / New York Knicks	1.25	.60	.12
☐ 127	Mel Counts / Phoenix Suns	.90	.45	.09
☐ 128	Bob Weiss DP / Chicago Bulls	1.25	.60	.12
☐ 129	Greg Smith DP / Milwaukee Bucks	.90	.45	.09
☐ 130	Earl Monroe / Baltimore Bullets	7.50	3.75	.75
☐ 131	Nate Thurmond DP / Golden State Warriors	3.00	1.50	.30
☐ 132	Bill Bridges DP / Atlanta Hawks	1.25	.60	.12
☐ 133	NBA Playoffs G1 / Alcindor scores 31	7.50	3.75	.75
☐ 134	NBA Playoffs G2 / Bucks make it / Two Straight	2.00	1.00	.20
☐ 135	NBA Playoffs G3 / Dandridge makes / It 3 in a Row	2.00	1.00	.20
☐ 136	NBA Playoffs G4 / A Clean Sweep / (Oscar Robertson)	5.00	2.50	.50
☐ 137	NBA Champs Celebrate / Bucks sweep Bullets	2.00	1.00	.20
☐ 138	NBA Scoring Leaders / Lew Alcindor / Elvin Hayes / John Havlicek	8.50	4.25	.85
☐ 139	NBA Scoring Average / Leaders / Lew Alcindor / John Havlicek / Elvin Hayes	8.50	4.25	.85
☐ 140	NBA FG Pct Leaders / Johnny Green / Lew Alcindor / Wilt Chamberlain	7.50	3.75	.75
☐ 141	NBA FT Pct Leaders / Chet Walker / Oscar Robertson / Ron Williams	2.50	1.25	.25
☐ 142	NBA Rebound Leaders / Wilt Chamberlain / Elvin Hayes / Lew Alcindor	11.00	5.50	1.10
☐ 143	NBA Assist Leaders / Norm Van Lier / Oscar Robertson / Jerry West	5.00	2.50	.50
☐ 144A	NBA Checklist 1-144 / (copyright notation / extends up to / card 110)	12.50	1.00	.20
☐ 144B	NBA Checklist 1-144 / (copyright notation / extends up to / card 108)	12.50	1.00	.20
☐ 145	ABA Checklist 145-233	12.50	1.00	.20
☐ 146	ABA Scoring Leaders / Dan Issel / John Brisker / Charlie Scott	3.00	1.50	.30
☐ 147	ABA Scoring Average / Leaders / Dan Issel / Rick Barry / John Brisker	7.50	3.75	.75
☐ 148	ABA 2pt FG Pct Leaders / Zelmo Beaty / Bill Paultz / Roger Brown	2.00	1.00	.20
☐ 149	ABA FT Pct Leaders / Rick Barry / Darrell Carrier / Billy Keller	6.00	3.00	.60
☐ 150	ABA Rebound Leaders / Mel Daniels / Julius Keye / Mike Lewis	2.00	1.00	.20
☐ 151	ABA Assist Leaders / Bill Melchionni / Mack Calvin / Charlie Scott	2.00	1.00	.20
☐ 152	Larry Brown / Denver Rockets	8.50	4.25	.85
☐ 153	Bob Bedell / Dallas Chaparrals	.90	.45	.09
☐ 154	Merv Jackson / Utah Stars	.90	.45	.09
☐ 155	Joe Caldwell / Carolina Cougars	1.50	.75	.15
☐ 156	Billy Paultz / New York Nets	1.25	.60	.12
☐ 157	Les Hunter / Kentucky Colonels	.90	.45	.09
☐ 158	Charlie Williams / Memphis Pros	.90	.45	.09
☐ 159	Stew Johnson / Pittsburgh Condors	.90	.45	.09
☐ 160	Mack Calvin / Florida Floridians	1.75	.85	.17
☐ 161	Don Sidle / Indiana Pacers	.90	.45	.09
☐ 162	Mike Barrett / Virginia Squires	.90	.45	.09
☐ 163	Tom Workman / Denver Rockets	.90	.45	.09
☐ 164	Joe Hamilton / Dallas Chaparrals	.90	.45	.09
☐ 165	Zelmo Beaty / Utah Stars	3.00	1.50	.30
☐ 166	Dan Hester / Kentucky Colonels	.90	.45	.09
☐ 167	Bob Verga / Carolina Cougars	.90	.45	.09
☐ 168	Wilbert Jones / Memphis Pros	.90	.45	.09
☐ 169	Skeeter Swift / Pittsburgh Condors	.90	.45	.09
☐ 170	Rick Barry / New York Nets	80.00	40.00	8.00
☐ 171	Billy Keller / Indiana Pacers	1.25	.60	.12
☐ 172	Ron Franz / Florida Floridians	.90	.45	.09
☐ 173	Roland Taylor / Virginia Squires	.90	.45	.09
☐ 174	Julian Hammond / Denver Rockets	.90	.45	.09
☐ 175	Steve Jones / Dallas Chaparrals	2.50	1.25	.25
☐ 176	Gerald Govan / Memphis Pros	.90	.45	.09
☐ 177	Darrell Carrier / Kentucky Colonels	1.25	.60	.12
☐ 178	Ron Boone / Utah Stars	1.75	.85	.17
☐ 179	George Peeples / Carolina Cougars	.90	.45	.09
☐ 180	John Brisker / Pittsburgh Condors	1.25	.60	.12
☐ 181	Doug Moe / Virginia Squires	10.00	5.00	1.00
☐ 182	Ollie Taylor / New York Nets	1.25	.60	.12
☐ 183	Bob Netolicky / Indiana Pacers	1.25	.60	.12
☐ 184	Sam Robinson / Florida Floridians	.90	.45	.09
☐ 185	James Jones / Memphis Pros	1.25	.60	.12
☐ 186	Julius Keye / Denver Rockets	.90	.45	.09
☐ 187	Wayne Hightower / Dallas Chaparrals	.90	.45	.09
☐ 188	Warren Armstrong / Indiana Pacers	1.25	.60	.12
☐ 189	Mike Lewis / Pittsburgh Condors	1.25	.60	.12
☐ 190	Charlie Scott / Virginia Squires	3.50	1.75	.35
☐ 191	Jim Ard / New York Nets	.90	.45	.09
☐ 192	George Lehmann / Carolina Cougars	.90	.45	.09
☐ 193	Ira Harge / Florida Floridians	.90	.45	.09
☐ 194	Willie Wise / Utah Stars	2.50	1.25	.25

		NRMT	VG-E	GOOD
☐ 195	Mel Daniels Indiana Pacers	3.50	1.75	.35
☐ 196	Larry Cannon Denver Rockets	.90	.45	.09
☐ 197	Jim Eakins Virginia Squires	.90	.45	.09
☐ 198	Rich Jones Dallas Chaparrals	.90	.45	.09
☐ 199	Bill Melchionni New York Nets	1.25	.60	.12
☐ 200	Dan Issel Kentucky Colonels	18.00	9.00	1.80
☐ 201	George Stone Utah Stars	.90	.45	.09
☐ 202	George Thompson Pittsburgh Condors	.90	.45	.09
☐ 203	Craig Raymond Memphis Pros	.90	.45	.09
☐ 204	Freddie Lewis Indiana Pacers	1.75	.85	.17
☐ 205	George Carter Virginia Squires	.90	.45	.09
☐ 206	Lonnie Wright Florida Floridians	.90	.45	.09
☐ 207	Cincy Powell Kentucky Colonels	.90	.45	.09
☐ 208	Larry Miller Carolina Cougars	1.25	.60	.12
☐ 209	Sonny Dove New York Nets	.90	.45	.09
☐ 210	Byron Beck Denver Rockets	1.25	.60	.12
☐ 211	John Beasley Dallas Chaparrals	.90	.45	.09
☐ 212	Lee Davis Memphis Pros	.90	.45	.09
☐ 213	Rick Mount Indiana Pacers	3.50	1.75	.35
☐ 214	Walt Simon Kentucky Colonels	.90	.45	.09
☐ 215	Glen Combs Utah Stars	1.25	.60	.12
☐ 216	Neil Johnson Virginia Squires	.90	.45	.09
☐ 217	Manny Leaks New York Nets	.90	.45	.09
☐ 218	Chuck Williams Pittsburgh Condors	.90	.45	.09
☐ 219	Warren Davis Florida Floridians	.90	.45	.09
☐ 220	Donnie Freeman Dallas Chaparrals	1.75	.85	.17
☐ 221	Randy Mahaffey Carolina Cougars	.90	.45	.09
☐ 222	John Barnhill Denver Rockets	.90	.45	.09
☐ 223	Al Cueto Memphis Pros	.90	.45	.09
☐ 224	Louie Dampier Kentucky Colonels	3.00	1.50	.30
☐ 225	Roger Brown Indiana Pacers	2.00	1.00	.20
☐ 226	Joe DePre New York Nets	.90	.45	.09
☐ 227	Ray Scott Virginia Squires	.90	.45	.09
☐ 228	Arvesta Kelly Pittsburgh Condors	.90	.45	.09
☐ 229	Vann Williford Carolina Cougars	.90	.45	.09
☐ 230	Larry Jones Florida Floridians	1.25	.60	.12
☐ 231	Gene Moore Dallas Chaparrals	.90	.45	.09
☐ 232	Ralph Simpson Denver Rockets	2.00	1.00	.20
☐ 233	Red Robbins Utah Stars	1.50	.75	.15

1971-72 Topps Insert Sticker Panels

The 1971-72 Topps Insert Sticker Panels set contains 26 card-sized (2 1/2" by 3 1/2") panels each with three player stickers. There are also three logo sticker panels. Each player sticker has a black border surrounding a color photo with a yellow player's name, and white team name. The NBA players are numbered by the number indicated; stickers of ABA players have the suffix

"A" added to their numbers in order to differentiate them. The logo stickers are hard to find in good shape. The stickers were printed on a sheet of 77 (7 rows and 11 columns). There are a number of oddities with respect to the distribution on the sheet and hence also to the availability of respective cards in the set. The most difficult cards in the set (34, 37, 40, 43, 1A, 4A, 7A, 10A, 13A, 16A, 19A, 23A, and 24A) appeared on the sheet only twice; they are designated as short prints (SP) in the checklist below. Cards 1, 4, 7, 10, 13, 16, 19, 22, 25, 28, and 31 were all printed three times on the sheet and are hence 50 percent more available than the SP's. The rest of the sheet is comprised of 4 copies of card 22A and 14 copies of card 46; they are referenced as DP and QP respectively.

		NRMT	VG-E	GOOD
COMPLETE SET (26)		425.00	200.00	42.00
COMMON CARD		2.00	1.00	.20
☐ 1	Lou Hudson 2 Bob Rule 3 Calvin Murphy	6.00	3.00	.60
☐ 4	Walt Wesley 5 Jo Jo White 6 Bob Dandridge	2.50	1.25	.25
☐ 7	Nate Thurmond 8 Earl Monroe 9 Spencer Haywood	9.00	4.50	.90
☐ 10	Dave DeBusschere 11 Bob Lanier 12 Tom Van Arsdale	10.00	5.00	1.00
☐ 13	Hal Greer 14 Johnny Green 15 Elvin Hayes	12.00	6.00	1.20
☐ 16	Jimmy Walker 17 Don May 18 Archie Clark	2.50	1.25	.25
☐ 19	Happy Hairston 20 Leroy Ellis 21 Jerry Sloan	2.50	1.25	.25
☐ 22	Pete Maravich 23 Bob Kauffman 24 John Havlicek	55.00	27.50	5.50
☐ 25	Walt Frazier 26 Dick Van Arsdale 27 Dave Bing	12.00	6.00	1.20
☐ 28	Bob Love 29 Ron Williams 30 Dave Cowens	10.00	5.00	1.00
☐ 31	Jerry West 32 Willis Reed 33 Chet Walker	55.00	27.50	5.50
☐ 34	Oscar Robertson SP 35 Wes Unseld 36 Bobby Smith	40.00	20.00	4.00
☐ 37	Connie Hawkins SP 38 Jeff Mullins 39 Lew Alcindor	90.00	45.00	9.00
☐ 40	Billy Cunningham SP 41 Walt Bellamy 42 Geoff Petrie	7.50	3.75	.75
☐ 43	Wilt Chamberlain SP 44 Gus Johnson 45 Norm Van Lier	55.00	27.50	5.50
☐ 46	NBA Team QP Logo Stickers	2.00	1.00	.20
☐ 1A	James Jones SP 2A Willie Wise 3A Dan Issel	7.50	3.75	.75
☐ 4A	Mack Calvin SP 5A Roger Brown 6A Bob Verga	2.00	1.00	.20
☐ 7A	Bill Melchionni SP 8A Mel Daniels 9A Donnie Freeman	2.00	1.00	.20

☐ 10A Joe Caldwell SP	2.00	1.00	.20
11A Louie Dampier			
12A Mike Lewis			
☐ 13A Rick Barry SP	15.00	7.50	1.50
14A Larry Jones			
15A Julius Keye			
☐ 16A Larry Cannon SP	2.00	1.00	.20
17A Zelmo Beatty			
18A Charlie Scott			
☐ 19A Steve Jones SP	2.00	1.00	.20
20A George Carter			
21A John Brisker			
☐ 22A ABA Team DP	2.00	1.00	.20
Logo Stickers			
☐ 23A ABA Team SP	25.00	12.50	2.50
Logo Stickers			
☐ 24A ABA Team SP	25.00	12.50	2.50
Logo Stickers			

1972-73 Topps

ARTIS GILMORE   CENTER

The 1972-73 Topps set of 264 cards contains NBA players (1-176) and ABA players (177-264). The cards in the set measure the standard 2 1/2" by 3 1/2". All-Star selections are depicted for the NBA on cards numbered 161 to 170 and for the ABA on cards numbered 249 to 258. Special subseries within this set include NBA Playoffs (154-159), NBA Statistical Leaders (171-176), ABA Playoffs (241-247), and ABA Statistical Leaders (259-264). The key rookie cards in this set are Julius Erving and Artis Gilmore.

	NRMT	VG-E	GOOD
COMPLETE SET (264)	775.00	375.00	75.00
COMMON PLAYER (1-264)	.60	.30	.06
☐ 1 Wilt Chamberlain	70.00	20.00	4.00
Los Angeles Lakers			
☐ 2 Stan Love	.60	.30	.06
Baltimore Bullets			
☐ 3 Geoff Petrie	1.00	.50	.10
Portland Trail Blazers			
☐ 4 Curtis Perry	1.00	.50	.10
Milwaukee Bucks			
☐ 5 Pete Maravich	24.00	12.00	2.40
Atlanta Hawks			
☐ 6 Gus Johnson	1.25	.60	.12
Phoenix Suns			
☐ 7 Dave Cowens	12.00	6.00	1.20
Boston Celtics			
☐ 8 Randy Smith	1.25	.60	.12
Buffalo Braves			
☐ 9 Matt Guokas	1.00	.50	.10
Kansas City-Omaha Kings			
☐ 10 Spencer Haywood	1.75	.85	.17
Seattle Supersonics			
☐ 11 Jerry Sloan	1.75	.85	.17
Chicago Bulls			
☐ 12 Dave Sorenson	.60	.30	.06
Cleveland Cavaliers			
☐ 13 Howie Komives	.60	.30	.06
Detroit Pistons			
☐ 14 Joe Ellis	.60	.30	.06
Golden State Warriors			
☐ 15 Jerry Lucas	6.00	3.00	.60
New York Knicks			

☐ 16 Stu Lantz	.60	.30	.06
Detroit Pistons			
☐ 17 Bill Bridges	.75	.35	.07
Philadelphia 76ers			
☐ 18 Leroy Ellis	.60	.30	.06
Los Angeles Lakers			
☐ 19 Art Williams	.60	.30	.06
Boston Celtics			
☐ 20 Sidney Wicks	6.50	3.25	.65
Portland Trail Blazers			
☐ 21 Wes Unseld	4.50	2.25	.45
Baltimore Bullets			
☐ 22 Jim Washington	.60	.30	.06
Atlanta Hawks			
☐ 23 Fred Hilton	.60	.30	.06
Buffalo Braves			
☐ 24 Curtis Rowe	3.00	1.50	.30
Detroit Pistons			
☐ 25 Oscar Robertson	18.00	9.00	1.80
Milwaukee Bucks			
☐ 26 Larry Steele	1.00	.50	.10
Portland Trail Blazers			
☐ 27 Charlie Davis	.60	.30	.06
Cleveland Cavaliers			
☐ 28 Nate Thurmond	2.00	1.00	.20
Golden State Warriors			
☐ 29 Fred Carter	.60	.30	.06
Philadelphia 76ers			
☐ 30 Connie Hawkins	2.00	1.00	.20
Phoenix Suns			
☐ 31 Calvin Murphy	2.00	1.00	.20
Houston Rockets			
☐ 32 Phil Jackson	6.00	3.00	.60
New York Knicks			
☐ 33 Lee Winfield	.60	.30	.06
Seattle Supersonics			
☐ 34 Jim Fox	.60	.30	.06
Seattle Supersonics			
☐ 35 Dave Bing	2.50	1.25	.25
Detroit Pistons			
☐ 36 Gary Gregor	.60	.30	.06
Portland Trail Blazers			
☐ 37 Mike Riordan	.75	.35	.07
Baltimore Bullets			
☐ 38 George Trapp	.60	.30	.06
Atlanta Hawks			
☐ 39 Mike Davis	.60	.30	.06
Buffalo Braves			
☐ 40 Bob Rule	.60	.30	.06
Philadelphia 76ers			
☐ 41 John Block	.60	.30	.06
Philadelphia 76ers			
☐ 42 Bob Dandridge	.75	.35	.07
Milwaukee Bucks			
☐ 43 John Johnson	1.00	.50	.10
Cleveland Cavaliers			
☐ 44 Rick Barry	25.00	12.50	2.50
Golden State Warriors			
☐ 45 Jo Jo White	1.75	.85	.17
Boston Celtics			
☐ 46 Cliff Meely	.60	.30	.06
Houston Rockets			
☐ 47 Charlie Scott	1.00	.50	.10
Phoenix Suns			
☐ 48 Johnny Green	.60	.30	.06
Kansas City-Omaha Kings			
☐ 49 Pete Cross	.60	.30	.06
Kansas City-Omaha Kings			
☐ 50 Gail Goodrich	1.75	.85	.17
Los Angeles Lakers			
☐ 51 Jim Davis	.60	.30	.06
Detroit Pistons			
☐ 52 Dick Barnett	.75	.35	.07
New York Knicks			
☐ 53 Bob Christian	.60	.30	.06
Atlanta Hawks			
☐ 54 Jon McGlocklin	.75	.35	.07
Milwaukee Bucks			
☐ 55 Paul Silas	1.25	.60	.12
Boston Celtics			
☐ 56 Hal Greer	2.00	1.00	.20
Philadelphia 76ers			
☐ 57 Barry Clemens	.60	.30	.06
Seattle Supersonics			
☐ 58 Nick Jones	.60	.30	.06
Golden State Warriors			
☐ 59 Cornell Warner	.60	.30	.06
Buffalo Braves			
☐ 60 Walt Frazier	9.00	4.50	.90
New York Knicks			
☐ 61 Dorrie Murray	.60	.30	.06
Baltimore Bullets			
☐ 62 Dick Cunningham	.60	.30	.06
Houston Rockets			

☐ 63	Sam Lacey Kansas City-Omaha Kings	.75	.35	.07
☐ 64	John Warren Cleveland Cavaliers	.60	.30	.06
☐ 65	Tom Boerwinkle Chicago Bulls	.60	.30	.06
☐ 66	Fred Foster Detroit Pistons	.60	.30	.06
☐ 67	Mel Counts Phoenix Suns	.60	.30	.06
☐ 68	Toby Kimball Milwaukee Bucks	.60	.30	.06
☐ 69	Dale Schlueter Portland Trail Blazers	.60	.30	.06
☐ 70	Jack Marin Houston Rockets	.75	.35	.07
☐ 71	Jim Barnett Golden State Warriors	.60	.30	.06
☐ 72	Clem Haskins Phoenix Suns	.75	.35	.07
☐ 73	Earl Monroe New York Knicks	5.50	2.75	.55
☐ 74	Tom Sanders Boston Celtics	.75	.35	.07
☐ 75	Jerry West Los Angeles Lakers	25.00	12.50	2.50
☐ 76	Elmore Smith Buffalo Braves	1.00	.50	.10
☐ 77	Don Adams Atlanta Hawks	.60	.30	.06
☐ 78	Wally Jones Milwaukee Bucks	.60	.30	.06
☐ 79	Tom Van Arsdale Kansas City-Omaha Kings	.60	.30	.06
☐ 80	Bob Lanier Detroit Pistons	6.50	3.25	.65
☐ 81	Len Wilkens Seattle Supersonics	2.50	1.25	.25
☐ 82	Neal Walk Phoenix Suns	.60	.30	.06
☐ 83	Kevin Loughery Philadelphia 76ers	1.00	.50	.10
☐ 84	Stan McKenzie Portland Trail Blazers	.60	.30	.06
☐ 85	Jeff Mullins Golden State Warriors	.75	.35	.07
☐ 86	Otto Moore Houston Rockets	.60	.30	.06
☐ 87	John Tresvant Baltimore Bullets	.60	.30	.06
☐ 88	Dean Meminger New York Knicks	1.00	.50	.10
☐ 89	Jim McMillian Los Angeles Lakers	.75	.35	.07
☐ 90	Austin Carr Cleveland Cavaliers	3.50	1.75	.35
☐ 91	Clifford Ray Chicago Bulls	1.75	.85	.17
☐ 92	Don Nelson Boston Celtics	2.50	1.25	.25
☐ 93	Mahdi Abdul Rahman Buffalo Braves (formerly Walt Hazzard)	1.00	.50	.10
☐ 94	Willie Norwood Detroit Pistons	.60	.30	.06
☐ 95	Dick Van Arsdale Phoenix Suns	.60	.30	.06
☐ 96	Don May Atlanta Hawks	.60	.30	.06
☐ 97	Walt Bellamy Atlanta Hawks	1.25	.60	.12
☐ 98	Garfield Heard Seattle Supersonics	1.00	.50	.10
☐ 99	Dave Wohl Philadelphia 76ers	.60	.30	.06
☐ 100	Kareem Abdul Jabbar Milwaukee Bucks	65.00	32.50	6.50
☐ 101	Ron Knight Portland Trail Blazers	.60	.30	.06
☐ 102	Phil Chenier Baltimore Bullets	2.25	1.10	.22
☐ 103	Rudy Tomjanovich Houston Rockets	.75	.35	.07
☐ 104	Flynn Robinson Los Angeles Lakers	.60	.30	.06
☐ 105	Dave DeBusschere New York Knicks	6.50	3.25	.65
☐ 106	Dennis Layton Phoenix Suns	.60	.30	.06
☐ 107	Bill Hewitt Detroit Pistons	.60	.30	.06
☐ 108	Dick Garrett Buffalo Braves	.60	.30	.06
☐ 109	Walt Wesley Cleveland Cavaliers	.60	.30	.06
☐ 110	John Havlicek Boston Celtics	25.00	12.50	2.50
☐ 111	Norm Van Lier Chicago Bulls	.75	.35	.07
☐ 112	Cazzie Russell Golden State Warriors	1.50	.75	.15
☐ 113	Herm Gilliam Atlanta Hawks	.60	.30	.06
☐ 114	Greg Smith Houston Rockets	.60	.30	.06
☐ 115	Nate Archibald Kansas City-Omaha Kings	5.00	2.50	.50
☐ 116	Don Kojis Kansas City-Omaha Kings	.60	.30	.06
☐ 117	Rick Adelman Portland Trail Blazers	.75	.35	.07
☐ 118	Luke Jackson Philadelphia 76ers	.60	.30	.06
☐ 119	Lamar Green Phoenix Suns	.60	.30	.06
☐ 120	Archie Clark Baltimore Bullets	.75	.35	.07
☐ 121	Happy Hairston Los Angeles Lakers	.75	.35	.07
☐ 122	Bill Bradley New York Knicks	30.00	15.00	3.00
☐ 123	Ron Williams Golden State Warriors	.60	.30	.06
☐ 124	Jimmy Walker Houston Rockets	.60	.30	.06
☐ 125	Bob Kauffman Buffalo Braves	.60	.30	.06
☐ 126	Rick Roberson Cleveland Cavaliers	.60	.30	.06
☐ 127	Howard Porter Chicago Bulls	1.50	.75	.15
☐ 128	Mike Newlin Houston Rockets	1.00	.50	.10
☐ 129	Willis Reed New York Knicks	5.00	2.50	.50
☐ 130	Lou Hudson Atlanta Hawks	1.00	.50	.10
☐ 131	Don Chaney Boston Celtics	2.25	1.10	.22
☐ 132	Dave Stallworth Baltimore Bullets	.75	.35	.07
☐ 133	Charlie Yelverton Portland Trail Blazers	.75	.35	.07
☐ 134	Ken Durrett Kansas City-Omaha Kings	.75	.35	.07
☐ 135	John Brisker Seattle Supersonics	.75	.35	.07
☐ 136	Dick Snyder Seattle Supersonics	.75	.35	.07
☐ 137	Jim McDaniels Seattle Supersonics	.75	.35	.07
☐ 138	Clyde Lee Golden State Warriors	.75	.35	.07
☐ 139	Dennis Awtrey Philadelphia 76ers (Misspelled Awtry on card front)	.75	.35	.07
☐ 140	Keith Erickson Los Angeles Lakers	.75	.35	.07
☐ 141	Bob Weiss Chicago Bulls	.75	.35	.07
☐ 142	Butch Beard Cleveland Cavaliers	1.25	.60	.12
☐ 143	Terry Dischinger Portland Trail Blazers	1.00	.50	.10
☐ 144	Pat Riley Los Angeles Lakers	6.50	3.25	.65
☐ 145	Lucius Allen Milwaukee Bucks	1.00	.50	.10
☐ 146	John Mengelt Kansas City-Omaha Kings	1.00	.50	.10
☐ 147	John Hummer Buffalo Braves	.75	.35	.07
☐ 148	Bob Love Chicago Bulls	1.50	.75	.15
☐ 149	Bobby Smith Cleveland Cavaliers	.75	.35	.07
☐ 150	Elvin Hayes Baltimore Bullets	9.00	4.50	.90
☐ 151	Nate Williams Kansas City-Omaha Kings	.75	.35	.07
☐ 152	Chet Walker Chicago Bulls	1.50	.75	.15
☐ 153	Steve Kuberski Boston Celtics	.75	.35	.07
☐ 154	NBA Playoffs G1 Knicks win Opener (Earl Monroe)	1.75	.85	.17

#	Card			
155	NBA Playoffs G2 Lakers Come Back (under the basket)	1.50	.75	.15
156	NBA Playoffs G3 Two in a Row (under the basket)	1.50	.75	.15
157	NBA Playoffs G4 Ellis provides bench strength	1.50	.75	.15
158	NBA Playoffs G5 Jerry drives in (Jerry West)	4.00	2.00	.40
159	NBA Champs-Lakers (Wilt rebounding)	4.00	2.00	.40
160	NBA Checklist 1-176 UER (135 Jim King)	10.00	1.00	.20
161	John Havlicek AS Boston Celtics	8.00	4.00	.80
162	Spencer Haywood AS Seattle Supersonics	1.00	.50	.10
163	Kareem Ab. Jabbar AS Milwaukee Bucks	22.00	11.00	2.20
164	Jerry West AS Los Angeles Lakers	12.00	6.00	1.20
165	Walt Frazier AS New York Knicks	4.50	2.25	.45
166	Bob Love AS Chicago Bulls	1.00	.50	.10
167	Billy Cunningham AS Philadelphia 76ers	2.00	1.00	.20
168	Wilt Chamberlain AS Los Angeles Lakers	22.00	11.00	2.20
169	Nate Archibald AS Kansas City-Omaha Kings	2.00	1.00	.20
170	Archie Clark AS Baltimore Bullets	1.00	.50	.10
171	NBA Scoring Leaders Kareem Abdul Jabbar John Havlicek Nate Archibald	6.00	3.00	.60
172	NBA Scoring Average Leaders Kareem Abdul Jabbar Nate Archibald John Havlicek	6.00	3.00	.60
173	NBA FG Pct Leaders Wilt Chamberlain Kareem Abdul Jabbar Walt Bellamy	6.00	3.00	.60
174	NBA FT Pct Leaders Jack Marin Calvin Murphy Gail Goodrich	1.50	.75	.15
175	NBA Rebound Leaders Wilt Chamberlain Kareem Abdul Jabbar Wes Unseld	6.50	3.25	.65
176	NBA Assist Leaders Len Wilkens Jerry West Nate Archibald	2.50	1.25	.25
177	Roland Taylor Virginia Squires	.75	.35	.07
178	Art Becker San Diego Conquistadors	.75	.35	.07
179	Mack Calvin Carolina Cougars	1.00	.50	.10
180	Artis Gilmore Kentucky Colonels	18.00	9.00	1.80
181	Collis Jones Dallas Chaparrals	.75	.35	.07
182	John Roche New York Nets	1.25	.60	.12
183	George McGinnis Indiana Pacers	7.50	3.75	.75
184	Johnny Neumann Memphis Tams	.75	.35	.07
185	Willie Wise Utah Stars	1.00	.50	.10
186	Bernie Williams Virginia Squires	.75	.35	.07
187	Byron Beck Denver Rockets	.75	.35	.07
188	Larry Miller San Diego Conquistadors	.75	.35	.07
189	Cincy Powell Kentucky Colonels	.75	.35	.07
190	Donnie Freeman Dallas Chaparrals	1.00	.50	.10
191	John Baum New York Nets	.75	.35	.07
192	Billy Keller Indiana Pacers	1.00	.50	.10
193	Wilbert Jones Memphis Tams	.75	.35	.07
194	Glen Combs Utah Stars	.75	.35	.07
195	Julius Erving Virginia Squires (Forward on front, but Center on back)	270.00	125.00	25.00
196	Al Smith Denver Rockets	.75	.35	.07
197	George Carter New York Nets	.75	.35	.07
198	Louie Dampier Kentucky Colonels	1.00	.50	.10
199	Rich Jones Dallas Chaparrals	.75	.35	.07
200	Mel Daniels Indiana Pacers	1.00	.50	.10
201	Gene Moore San Diego Conquistadors	.75	.35	.07
202	Randy Denton Memphis Tams	.75	.35	.07
203	Larry Jones Utah Stars	.75	.35	.07
204	Jim Ligon Virginia Squires	.75	.35	.07
205	Warren Jabali Denver Rockets	1.00	.50	.10
206	Joe Caldwell Carolina Cougars	1.00	.50	.10
207	Darrell Carrier Kentucky Colonels	.75	.35	.07
208	Gene Kennedy Dallas Chaparrals	.75	.35	.07
209	Ollie Taylor San Diego Conquistadors	.75	.35	.07
210	Roger Brown Indiana Pacers	1.00	.50	.10
211	George Lehmann Memphis Tams	.75	.35	.07
212	Red Robbins San Diego Conquistadors	.75	.35	.07
213	Jim Eakins Virginia Squires	.75	.35	.07
214	Willie Long Denver Rockets	.75	.35	.07
215	Billy Cunningham Carolina Cougars	4.50	2.25	.45
216	Steve Jones Dallas Chaparrals	1.00	.50	.10
217	Les Hunter San Diego Conquistadors	.75	.35	.07
218	Billy Paultz New York Nets	.75	.35	.07
219	Freddie Lewis Indiana Pacers	1.00	.50	.10
220	Zelmo Beaty Utah Stars	1.00	.50	.10
221	George Thompson Memphis Tams	.75	.35	.07
222	Neil Johnson Virginia Squires	.75	.35	.07
223	Dave Robisch Denver Rockets	1.00	.50	.10
224	Walt Simon Kentucky Colonels	.75	.35	.07
225	Bill Melchionni New York Nets	1.00	.50	.10
226	Wendell Ladner Memphis Tams	1.00	.50	.10
227	Joe Hamilton Dallas Chaparrals	.75	.35	.07
228	Bob Netolicky Dallas Chaparrals	.75	.35	.07
229	James Jones Utah Stars	1.00	.50	.10
230	Dan Issel Kentucky Colonels	4.50	2.25	.45
231	Charlie Williams San Diego Conquistadors	.75	.35	.07
232	Willie Sojourner Virginia Squires	.75	.35	.07
233	Merv Jackson Utah Stars	.75	.35	.07
234	Mike Lewis Carolina Cougars	1.00	.50	.10
235	Ralph Simpson Denver Rockets	1.00	.50	.10
236	Darnell Hillman Indiana Pacers	1.00	.50	.10
237	Rick Mount Kentucky Colonels	1.25	.60	.12
238	Gerald Govan Memphis Tams	.75	.35	.07
239	Ron Boone Utah Stars	1.00	.50	.10

		NRMT	VG-E	GOOD
☐ 240	Tom Washington New York Nets	.75	.35	.07
☐ 241	ABA Playoffs G1 Pacers take lead (under the basket)	1.50	.75	.15
☐ 242	ABA Playoffs G2 Barry evens things	2.00	1.00	.20
☐ 243	ABA Playoffs G3 McGinnis blocks a jumper	1.50	.75	.15
☐ 244	ABA Playoffs G4 Rick (Barry) scores on fast break	2.00	1.00	.20
☐ 245	ABA Playoffs G5 Keller becomes Net killer	1.50	.75	.15
☐ 246	ABA Playoffs G6 Tight Defense	1.50	.75	.15
☐ 247	ABA Champs: Pacers	1.50	.75	.15
☐ 248	ABA Checklist 177-264 UER (236 John Brisker)	10.00	1.00	.20
☐ 249	Dan Issel AS Kentucky Colonels	2.00	1.00	.20
☐ 250	Rick Barry AS New York Nets	10.00	5.00	1.00
☐ 251	Artis Gilmore AS Kentucky Colonels	4.50	2.25	.45
☐ 252	Donnie Freeman AS Dallas Chaparrals	1.00	.50	.10
☐ 253	Bill Melchionni AS New York Nets	1.00	.50	.10
☐ 254	Willie Wise AS Utah Stars	1.00	.50	.10
☐ 255	Julius Erving AS Virginia Squires	65.00	32.50	6.50
☐ 256	Zelmo Beaty AS Utah Stars	1.00	.50	.10
☐ 257	Ralph Simpson AS Denver Rockets	1.00	.50	.10
☐ 258	Charlie Scott AS Virginia Squires	1.00	.50	.10
☐ 259	ABA Scoring Average Leaders Charlie Scott Rick Barry Dan Issel	1.75	.85	.17
☐ 260	ABA 2pt FG Pct. Leaders Artis Gilmore Tom Washington Larry Jones	1.75	.85	.17
☐ 261	ABA 3pt FG Pct. Leaders Glen Combs Louie Dampier Warren Jabali	1.50	.75	.15
☐ 262	ABA FT Pct Leaders Rick Barry Mack Calvin Steve Jones	1.50	.75	.15
☐ 263	ABA Rebound Leaders Artis Gilmore Julius Erving Mel Daniels	5.00	2.50	.50
☐ 264	ABA Assist Leaders Bill Melchionni Larry Brown Louie Dampier	1.50	.75	.15

1973-74 Topps

The 1973-74 Topps set of 264 contains NBA players on cards numbered 1 to 176 and ABA players on cards numbered 177 to 264. The cards in the set measure the standard 2 1/2" by 3 1/2". All-Star selections (first and second team) for both leagues are noted on the respective player's regular cards. Card backs are printed in red and green on gray card stock. The backs feature year-by-year ABA and NBA statistics. Subseries within the set include NBA Playoffs (62-68), NBA League Leaders (153-158), ABA Playoffs (202-208), and ABA League Leaders (234-239). The only notable rookie card in this set is Bob McAdoo.

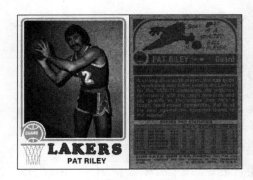

LAKERS
PAT RILEY

		NRMT	VG-E	GOOD
	COMPLETE SET (264)	375.00	175.00	35.00
	COMMON PLAYER (1-132)	.45	.22	.04
	COMMON PLAYER (133-264)	.45	.22	.04
☐ 1	Nate Archibald AS1 Kansas City-Omaha Kings	5.00	1.25	.25
☐ 2	Steve Kuberski Boston Celtics	.45	.22	.04
☐ 3	John Mengelt Detroit Pistons	.60	.30	.06
☐ 4	Jim McMillian Los Angeles Lakers	.60	.30	.06
☐ 5	Nate Thurmond Golden State Warriors	1.75	.85	.17
☐ 6	Dave Wohl Buffalo Braves	.45	.22	.04
☐ 7	John Brisker Seattle Supersonics	.45	.22	.04
☐ 8	Charlie Davis Portland Trail Blazers	.45	.22	.04
☐ 9	Lamar Green Phoenix Suns	.45	.22	.04
☐ 10	Walt Frazier AS2 New York Knicks	6.50	3.25	.65
☐ 11	Bob Christian Atlanta Hawks	.45	.22	.04
☐ 12	Cornell Warner Cleveland Cavaliers	.45	.22	.04
☐ 13	Calvin Murphy Houston Rockets	1.75	.85	.17
☐ 14	Dave Sorenson Philadelphia 76ers	.45	.22	.04
☐ 15	Archie Clark Capital Bullets	.60	.30	.06
☐ 16	Clifford Ray Chicago Bulls	.60	.30	.06
☐ 17	Terry Driscoll Milwaukee Bucks	.45	.22	.04
☐ 18	Matt Guokas Kansas City-Omaha Kings	.60	.30	.06
☐ 19	Elmore Smith Buffalo Braves	.60	.30	.06
☐ 20	John Havlicek AS1 Boston Celtics	15.00	7.50	1.50
☐ 21	Pat Riley Los Angeles Lakers	4.50	2.25	.45
☐ 22	George Trapp Detroit Pistons	.45	.22	.04
☐ 23	Ron Williams Golden State Warriors	.45	.22	.04
☐ 24	Jim Fox Seattle Supersonics	.45	.22	.04
☐ 25	Dick Van Arsdale Phoenix Suns	.45	.22	.04
☐ 26	John Tresvant Capital Bullets	.45	.22	.04
☐ 27	Rick Adelman Portland Trail Blazers	.60	.30	.06
☐ 28	Eddie Mast Atlanta Hawks	.45	.22	.04
☐ 29	Jim Cleamons Cleveland Cavaliers	.45	.22	.04
☐ 30	Dave DeBusschere AS2 New York Knicks	5.50	2.75	.55
☐ 31	Norm Van Lier Chicago Bulls	.60	.30	.06
☐ 32	Stan McKenzie Houston Rockets	.45	.22	.04
☐ 33	Bob Dandridge Milwaukee Bucks	.60	.30	.06

#	Player / Team			
☐ 34	Leroy Ellis — Philadelphia 76ers	.45	.22	.04
☐ 35	Mike Riordan — Capital Bullets	.60	.30	.06
☐ 36	Fred Hilton — Buffalo Braves	.45	.22	.04
☐ 37	Toby Kimball — Kansas City-Omaha Kings	.45	.22	.04
☐ 38	Jim Price — Los Angeles Lakers	.45	.22	.04
☐ 39	Willie Norwood — Detroit Pistons	.45	.22	.04
☐ 40	Dave Cowens AS2 — Boston Celtics	5.50	2.75	.55
☐ 41	Cazzie Russell — Golden State Warriors	1.00	.50	.10
☐ 42	Lee Winfield — Seattle Supersonics	.45	.22	.04
☐ 43	Connie Hawkins — Phoenix Suns	1.75	.85	.17
☐ 44	Mike Newlin — Houston Rockets	.45	.22	.04
☐ 45	Chet Walker — Chicago Bulls	1.00	.50	.10
☐ 46	Walt Bellamy — Atlanta Hawks	1.00	.50	.10
☐ 47	John Johnson — Portland Trail Blazers	.60	.30	.06
☐ 48	Henry Bibby — New York Knicks	1.25	.60	.12
☐ 49	Bobby Smith — Cleveland Cavaliers	.45	.22	.04
☐ 50	Kareem Ab.Jabbar AS1 — Milwaukee Bucks	45.00	22.50	4.50
☐ 51	Mike Price — Philadelphia 76ers	.45	.22	.04
☐ 52	John Hummer — Buffalo Braves	.45	.22	.04
☐ 53	Kevin Porter — Capital Bullets	2.00	1.00	.20
☐ 54	Nate Williams — Kansas City-Omaha Kings	.45	.22	.04
☐ 55	Gail Goodrich — Los Angeles Lakers	1.50	.75	.15
☐ 56	Fred Foster — Detroit Pistons	.45	.22	.04
☐ 57	Don Chaney — Boston Celtics	1.50	.75	.15
☐ 58	Bud Stallworth — Seattle Supersonics	.45	.22	.04
☐ 59	Clem Haskins — Phoenix Suns	.60	.30	.06
☐ 60	Bob Love AS2 — Chicago Bulls	1.00	.50	.10
☐ 61	Jimmy Walker — Houston Rockets	.45	.22	.04
☐ 62	NBA Eastern Semis — Knicks shoot down Bullets in 5	1.00	.50	.10
☐ 63	NBA Eastern Semis — Celts oust Hawks 2nd Straight Year	1.00	.50	.10
☐ 64	NBA Western Semis — Lakers outlast Bulls at Wire (W.Chamberlain)	3.25	1.60	.32
☐ 65	NBA Western Semis — Warriors overwhelm Milwaukee	1.00	.50	.10
☐ 66	NBA Eastern Finals — Knicks stun Celtics at Boston (W.Reed/Finkel)	2.00	1.00	.20
☐ 67	NBA Western Finals — Lakers Breeze Past Golden State	1.00	.50	.10
☐ 68	NBA Championship — Knicks Do It, Repeat '70 Miracle (W.Frazier/Erickson)	2.25	1.10	.22
☐ 69	Larry Steele — Portland Trail Blazers	.45	.22	.04
☐ 70	Oscar Robertson — Milwaukee Bucks	16.00	8.00	1.60
☐ 71	Phil Jackson — New York Knicks	1.50	.75	.15
☐ 72	John Wetzel — Atlanta Hawks	.45	.22	.04
☐ 73	Steve Patterson — Cleveland Cavaliers	.75	.35	.07
☐ 74	Manny Leaks — Philadelphia 76ers	.45	.22	.04
☐ 75	Jeff Mullins — Golden State Warriors	.60	.30	.06
☐ 76	Stan Love — Capital Bullets	.45	.22	.04
☐ 77	Dick Garrett — Buffalo Braves	.45	.22	.04
☐ 78	Don Nelson — Boston Celtics	1.50	.75	.15
☐ 79	Chris Ford — Detroit Pistons	3.50	1.75	.35
☐ 80	Wilt Chamberlain — Los Angeles Lakers	45.00	22.50	4.50
☐ 81	Dennis Layton — Phoenix Suns	.45	.22	.04
☐ 82	Bill Bradley — New York Knicks	22.00	11.00	2.20
☐ 83	Jerry Sloan — Chicago Bulls	1.50	.75	.15
☐ 84	Cliff Meely — Houston Rockets	.45	.22	.04
☐ 85	Sam Lacey — Kansas City-Omaha Kings	.60	.30	.06
☐ 86	Dick Snyder — Seattle Supersonics	.45	.22	.04
☐ 87	Jim Washington — Atlanta Hawks	.45	.22	.04
☐ 88	Lucius Allen — Milwaukee Bucks	.75	.35	.07
☐ 89	LaRue Martin — Portland Trail Blazers	.45	.22	.04
☐ 90	Rick Barry — Golden State Warriors	14.00	7.00	1.40
☐ 91	Fred Boyd — Philadelphia 76ers	.45	.22	.04
☐ 92	Barry Clemens — Cleveland Cavaliers	.45	.22	.04
☐ 93	Dean Meminger — New York Knicks	.60	.30	.06
☐ 94	Henry Finkel — Boston Celtics	.45	.22	.04
☐ 95	Elvin Hayes — Capital Bullets	7.00	3.50	.70
☐ 96	Stu Lantz — Detroit Pistons	.45	.22	.04
☐ 97	Bill Hewitt — Buffalo Braves	.45	.22	.04
☐ 98	Neal Walk — Phoenix Suns	.45	.22	.04
☐ 99	Garfield Heard — Chicago Bulls	.60	.30	.06
☐ 100	Jerry West AS1 — Los Angeles Lakers	22.00	11.00	2.20
☐ 101	Otto Moore — Houston Rockets	.45	.22	.04
☐ 102	Don Kojis — Kansas City-Omaha Kings	.45	.22	.04
☐ 103	Fred Brown — Seattle Supersonics	3.25	1.60	.32
☐ 104	Dwight Davis — Cleveland Cavaliers	.45	.22	.04
☐ 105	Willis Reed — New York Knicks	4.50	2.25	.45
☐ 106	Herm Gilliam — Atlanta Hawks	.45	.22	.04
☐ 107	Mickey Davis — Milwaukee Bucks	.45	.22	.04
☐ 108	Jim Barnett — Golden State Warriors	.45	.22	.04
☐ 109	Ollie Johnson — Portland Trail Blazers	.45	.22	.04
☐ 110	Bob Lanier — Detroit Pistons	3.25	1.60	.32
☐ 111	Fred Carter — Philadelphia 76ers	.45	.22	.04
☐ 112	Paul Silas — Boston Celtics	1.00	.50	.10
☐ 113	Phil Chenier — Capital Bullets	.75	.35	.07
☐ 114	Dennis Awtrey — Chicago Bulls	.45	.22	.04
☐ 115	Austin Carr — Cleveland Cavaliers	.75	.35	.07
☐ 116	Bob Kauffman — Buffalo Braves	.45	.22	.04
☐ 117	Keith Erickson — Los Angeles Lakers	.45	.22	.04
☐ 118	Walt Wesley — Phoenix Suns	.45	.22	.04
☐ 119	Steve Bracey — Atlanta Hawks	.45	.22	.04
☐ 120	Spencer Haywood AS1 — Seattle Supersonics	1.50	.75	.15
☐ 121	NBA Checklist 1-176	7.50	.75	.15
☐ 122	Jack Marin — Houston Rockets	.60	.30	.06
☐ 123	Jon McGlocklin — Milwaukee Bucks	.60	.30	.06

#	Player / Description			
124	Johnny Green — Kansas City-Omaha Kings	.45	.22	.04
125	Jerry Lucas — New York Knicks	5.00	2.50	.50
126	Paul Westphal — Boston Celtics	6.50	3.25	.65
127	Curtis Rowe — Detroit Pistons	.75	.35	.07
128	Mahdi Abdul Rahman — Seattle Supersonics (formerly Walt Hazzard)	.75	.35	.07
129	Lloyd Neal — Portland Trail Blazers	.75	.35	.07
130	Pete Maravich AS1 — Atlanta Hawks	16.00	8.00	1.60
131	Don May — Philadelphia 76ers	.45	.22	.04
132	Bob Weiss — Chicago Bulls	.60	.30	.06
133	Dave Stallworth — Capital Bullets	.60	.30	.06
134	Dick Cunningham — Milwaukee Bucks	.45	.22	.04
135	Bob McAdoo — Buffalo Braves	16.00	8.00	1.60
136	Butch Beard — Golden State Warriors	.60	.30	.06
137	Happy Hairston — Los Angeles Lakers	.60	.30	.06
138	Bob Rule — Cleveland Cavaliers	.45	.22	.04
139	Don Adams — Detroit Pistons	.45	.22	.04
140	Charlie Scott — Phoenix Suns	.75	.35	.07
141	Ron Riley — Kansas City-Omaha Kings	.45	.22	.04
142	Earl Monroe — New York Knicks	4.50	2.25	.45
143	Clyde Lee — Golden State Warriors	.45	.22	.04
144	Rick Roberson — Portland Trail Blazers	.45	.22	.04
145	Rudy Tomjanovich — Houston Rockets (Printed without Houston on basket)	.60	.30	.06
146	Tom Van Arsdale — Philadelphia 76ers	.45	.22	.04
147	Art Williams — Boston Celtics	.45	.22	.04
148	Curtis Perry — Milwaukee Bucks	.45	.22	.04
149	Rich Rinaldi — Capital Bullets	.45	.22	.04
150	Lou Hudson — Atlanta Hawks	1.00	.50	.10
151	Mel Counts — Los Angeles Lakers	.45	.22	.04
152	Jim McDaniels — Seattle Supersonics	.45	.22	.04
153	NBA Scoring Leaders — Nate Archibald, Kareem Abdul Jabbar, Spencer Haywood	3.50	1.75	.35
154	NBA Scoring Average Leaders — Nate Archibald, Kareem Abdul Jabbar, Spencer Haywood	3.50	1.75	.35
155	NBA FG Pct Leaders — Wilt Chamberlain, Matt Guokas, Kareem Abdul Jabbar	4.50	2.25	.45
156	NBA FT Pct Leaders — Rick Barry, Calvin Murphy, Mike Newlin	1.50	.75	.15
157	NBA Rebound Leaders — Wilt Chamberlain, Nate Thurmond, Dave Cowens	3.50	1.75	.35
158	NBA Assist Leaders — Nate Archibald, Len Wilkens, Dave Bing	1.50	.75	.15
159	Don Smith — Houston Rockets	.45	.22	.04
160	Sidney Wicks — Portland Trail Blazers	1.75	.85	.17
161	Howie Komives — Buffalo Braves	.45	.22	.04
162	John Gianelli — New York Knicks	.45	.22	.04
163	Jeff Halliburton — Philadelphia 76ers	.45	.22	.04
164	Kennedy McIntosh — Seattle Supersonics	.45	.22	.04
165	Len Wilkens — Cleveland Cavaliers	1.75	.85	.17
166	Corky Calhoun — Phoenix Suns	.45	.22	.04
167	Howard Porter — Chicago Bulls	.60	.30	.06
168	Jo Jo White — Boston Celtics	1.50	.75	.15
169	John Block — Kansas City-Omaha Kings	.45	.22	.04
170	Dave Bing — Detroit Pistons	2.00	1.00	.20
171	Joe Ellis — Golden State Warriors	.45	.22	.04
172	Chuck Terry — Milwaukee Bucks	.45	.22	.04
173	Randy Smith — Buffalo Braves	.75	.35	.07
174	Bill Bridges — Los Angeles Lakers	.60	.30	.06
175	Geoff Petrie — Portland Trail Blazers	.75	.35	.07
176	Wes Unseld — Capital Bullets	3.50	1.75	.35
177	Skeeter Swift — San Antonio Spurs	.45	.22	.04
178	Jim Eakins — Virginia Squires	.45	.22	.04
179	Steve Jones — Carolina Cougars	.60	.30	.06
180	George McGinnis AS1 — Indiana Pacers	2.00	1.00	.20
181	Al Smith — Denver Rockets	.45	.22	.04
182	Tom Washington — New York Nets	.45	.22	.04
183	Louie Dampier — Kentucky Colonels	.60	.30	.06
184	Simmie Hill — San Diego Conquistadors	.45	.22	.04
185	George Thompson — Memphis Tams	.45	.22	.04
186	Cincy Powell — Utah Stars	.45	.22	.04
187	Larry Jones — San Antonio Spurs	.45	.22	.04
188	Neil Johnson — Virginia Squires	.45	.22	.04
189	Tom Owens — Carolina Cougars	.60	.30	.06
190	Ralph Simpson AS2 — Denver Rockets	.60	.30	.06
191	George Carter — Virginia Squires	.45	.22	.04
192	Rick Mount — Kentucky Colonels	.60	.30	.06
193	Red Robbins — San Diego Conquistadors	.45	.22	.04
194	George Lehmann — Memphis Tams	.45	.22	.04
195	Mel Daniels AS2 — Indiana Pacers	.60	.30	.06
196	Bob Warren — Utah Stars	.45	.22	.04
197	Gene Kennedy — San Antonio Spurs	.45	.22	.04
198	Mike Barr — Virginia Squires	.45	.22	.04
199	Dave Robisch — Denver Rockets	.45	.22	.04
200	Billy Cunningham AS1 — Carolina Cougars	3.50	1.75	.35
201	John Roche — New York Nets	.60	.30	.06
202	ABA Western Semis — Pacers Oust Injured Rockets	1.00	.50	.10
203	ABA Western Semis — Stars sweep Q's in Four Straight	1.00	.50	.10
204	ABA Eastern Semis — Kentucky overcomes Squires and Dr. J. (Issel jump shot)	1.25	.60	.12
205	ABA Eastern Semis — Cougars in strong finish over Nets	1.00	.50	.10
206	ABA Western Finals — Pacers nip bitter rival, Stars	1.00	.50	.10

			NRMT	VG-E	GOOD

☐ 207 ABA Eastern Finals .... 1.75 .85 .17
Colonels prevail
in grueling Series
(Gilmore shooting)
☐ 208 ABA Championship .... 1.00 .50 .10
McGinnis leads
Pacers to Title
(center jump)
☐ 209 Glen Combs .... .45 .22 .04
Utah Stars
☐ 210 Dan Issel AS2 .... 2.50 1.25 .25
Kentucky Colonels
☐ 211 Randy Denton .... .45 .22 .04
Memphis Tams
☐ 212 Freddie Lewis .... .60 .30 .06
Indiana Pacers
☐ 213 Stew Johnson .... .45 .22 .04
San Diego Conquistadors
☐ 214 Roland Taylor .... .45 .22 .04
Virginia Squires
☐ 215 Rich Jones .... .45 .22 .04
San Antonio Spurs
☐ 216 Billy Paultz .... .60 .30 .06
New York Nets
☐ 217 Ron Boone .... .60 .30 .06
Utah Stars
☐ 218 Walt Simon .... .45 .22 .04
Kentucky Colonels
☐ 219 Mike Lewis .... .45 .22 .04
Carolina Cougars
☐ 220 Warren Jabali AS1 .... .60 .30 .06
Denver Rockets
☐ 221 Wilbert Jones .... .45 .22 .04
Memphis Tams
☐ 222 Don Buse .... 1.25 .60 .12
Indiana Pacers
☐ 223 Gene Moore .... .45 .22 .04
San Diego Conquistadors
☐ 224 Joe Hamilton .... .45 .22 .04
San Antonio Spurs
☐ 225 Zelmo Beaty .... .60 .30 .06
Utah Stars
☐ 226 Brian Taylor .... .75 .35 .07
New York Nets
☐ 227 Julius Keye .... .45 .22 .04
Denver Rockets
☐ 228 Mike Gale .... .45 .22 .04
Kentucky Colonels
☐ 229 Warren Davis .... .45 .22 .04
Memphis Tams
☐ 230 Mack Calvin AS2 .... .60 .30 .06
Carolina Cougars
☐ 231 Roger Brown .... .60 .30 .06
Indiana Pacers
☐ 232 Chuck Williams .... .45 .22 .04
San Diego Conquistadors
☐ 233 Gerald Govan .... .45 .22 .04
Utah Stars
☐ 234 ABA Scoring Average .... 4.50 2.25 .45
Leaders
Julius Erving
George McGinnis
Dan Issel
☐ 235 ABA 2 Pt. Pct. .... 1.00 .50 .10
Leaders
Artis Gilmore
Gene Kennedy
Tom Owens
☐ 236 ABA 3 Pt. Pct. .... 1.00 .50 .10
Leaders
Glen Combs
Roger Brown
Louie Dampier
☐ 237 ABA F.T. Pct. Leaders .... 1.00 .50 .10
Billy Keller
Ron Boone
Bob Warren
☐ 238 ABA Rebound Leaders .... 1.00 .50 .10
Artis Gilmore
Mel Daniels
Bill Paultz
☐ 239 ABA Assist Leaders .... 1.00 .50 .10
Bill Melchionni
Chuck Williams
Warren Jabali
☐ 240 Julius Erving AS2 .... 75.00 37.50 7.50
Virginia Squires
☐ 241 Jimmy O'Brien .... .45 .22 .04
Kentucky Colonels
☐ 242 ABA Checklist 177-264 .... 7.50 .75 .15
☐ 243 Johnny Neumann .... .45 .22 .04
Memphis Tams
☐ 244 Darnell Hillman .... .45 .22 .04
Indiana Pacers

☐ 245 Willie Wise .... .60 .30 .06
Utah Stars
☐ 246 Collis Jones .... .45 .22 .04
San Antonio Spurs
☐ 247 Ted McClain .... .45 .22 .04
Carolina Cougars
☐ 248 George Irvine .... .60 .30 .06
Virginia Squires
☐ 249 Bill Melchionni .... .60 .30 .06
New York Nets
☐ 250 Artis Gilmore AS1 .... 4.50 2.25 .45
Kentucky Colonels
☐ 251 Willie Long .... .45 .22 .04
Denver Rockets
☐ 252 Larry Miller .... .60 .30 .06
San Diego Conquistadors
☐ 253 Lee Davis .... .45 .22 .04
Memphis Tams
☐ 254 Donnie Freeman .... .60 .30 .06
Indiana Pacers
☐ 255 Joe Caldwell .... .60 .30 .06
Carolina Cougars
☐ 256 Bob Netolicky .... .45 .22 .04
San Antonio Spurs
☐ 257 Bernie Williams .... .45 .22 .04
Virginia Squires
☐ 258 Byron Beck .... .45 .22 .04
Denver Rockets
☐ 259 Jim Chones .... .75 .35 .07
New York Nets
☐ 260 James Jones AS1 .... .60 .30 .06
Utah Stars
☐ 261 Wendell Ladner .... .45 · .22 .04
Kentucky Colonels
☐ 262 Ollie Taylor .... .45 .22 .04
San Diego Conquistadors
☐ 263 Les Hunter .... .45 .22 .04
Memphis Tams
☐ 264 Billy Keller .... .70 .35 .07
Indiana Pacers

1974-75 Topps

The 1974-75 Topps set of 264 cards contains NBA players on cards numbered 1 to 176 and ABA players on cards numbered 177 to 264. For the first time Team Leader (TL) cards are provided for each team. The cards in the set measure the standard 2 1/2" by 3 1/2". All-Star selections (first and second team) for both leagues are noted on the respective player's regular cards. The card backs are printed in blue and red on gray card stock. Subseries within the set include NBA Team Leaders (81-98), NBA Statistical Leaders (144-149), NBA Playoffs (161-164), ABA Statistical Leaders (207-212), ABA Team Leaders (221-230), and ABA Playoffs (246-249). The key rookie cards in this set are George Gervin and Bill Walton.

	NRMT	VG-E	GOOD
COMPLETE SET (264)	325.00	160.00	32.00
COMMON PLAYER (1-132)	.40	.20	.04
COMMON PLAYER (133-264)	.40	.20	.04
☐ 1 Kareem Ab.Jabbar AS1 .... Milwaukee Bucks	45.00	12.50	2.50

☐ 2	Don May .... Philadelphia 76ers	.40	.20	.04
☐ 3	Bernie Fryer .... Portland Trail Blazers	.60	.30	.06
☐ 4	Don Adams .... Detroit Pistons	.40	.20	.04
☐ 5	Herm Gilliam .... Atlanta Hawks	.40	.20	.04
☐ 6	Jim Chones .... Cleveland Cavaliers	.40	.20	.04
☐ 7	Rick Adelman .... Chicago Bulls	.60	.30	.06
☐ 8	Randy Smith .... Buffalo Braves	.40	.20	.04
☐ 9	Paul Silas .... Boston Celtics	.75	.35	.07
☐ 10	Pete Maravich .... New Orleans Jazz	12.50	6.25	1.25
☐ 11	Ron Behagen .... Kansas City-Omaha Kings	.40	.20	.04
☐ 12	Kevin Porter .... Washington Bullets	.60	.30	.06
☐ 13	Bill Bridges .... Los Angeles Lakers (On back team shown as Los And., should be Los Ang.)	.40	.20	.04
☐ 14	Charles Johnson .... Golden State Warriors	.40	.20	.04
☐ 15	Bob Love .... Chicago Bulls	.75	.35	.07
☐ 16	Henry Bibby .... New York Knicks	.60	.30	.06
☐ 17	Neal Walk .... Phoenix Suns	.40	.20	.04
☐ 18	John Brisker .... Seattle Supersonics	.40	.20	.04
☐ 19	Lucius Allen .... Milwaukee Bucks	.60	.30	.06
☐ 20	Tom Van Arsdale .... Philadelphia 76ers	.40	.20	.04
☐ 21	Larry Steele .... Portland Trail Blazers	.40	.20	.04
☐ 22	Curtis Rowe .... Detroit Pistons	.60	.30	.06
☐ 23	Dean Meminger .... Atlanta Hawks	.40	.20	.04
☐ 24	Steve Patterson .... Cleveland Cavaliers	.40	.20	.04
☐ 25	Earl Monroe .... New York Knicks	3.50	1.75	.35
☐ 26	Jack Marin .... Buffalo Braves	.40	.20	.04
☐ 27	Jo Jo White .... Boston Celtics	1.00	.50	.10
☐ 28	Rudy Tomjanovich .... Houston Rockets	.40	.20	.04
☐ 29	Otto Moore .... Kansas City-Omaha Kings	.40	.20	.04
☐ 30	Elvin Hayes AS2 .... Washington Bullets	5.50	2.75	.55
☐ 31	Pat Riley .... Los Angeles Lakers	3.25	1.60	.32
☐ 32	Clyde Lee .... Golden State Warriors	.40	.20	.04
☐ 33	Bob Weiss .... Chicago Bulls	.60	.30	.06
☐ 34	Jim Fox .... Seattle Supersonics	.40	.20	.04
☐ 35	Charlie Scott .... Phoenix Suns	.60	.30	.06
☐ 36	Cliff Meely .... Houston Rockets	.40	.20	.04
☐ 37	Jon McGlocklin .... Milwaukee Bucks	.40	.20	.04
☐ 38	Jim McMillian .... Buffalo Braves	.40	.20	.04
☐ 39	Bill Walton .... Portland Trail Blazers	33.00	15.00	3.00
☐ 40	Dave Bing AS2 .... Detroit Pistons	2.00	1.00	.20
☐ 41	Jim Washington .... Atlanta Hawks	.40	.20	.04
☐ 42	Jim Cleamons .... Cleveland Cavaliers	.40	.20	.04
☐ 43	Mel Davis .... New York Knicks	.40	.20	.04
☐ 44	Garfield Heard .... Buffalo Braves	.40	.20	.04
☐ 45	Jimmy Walker .... Kansas City-Omaha Kings	.40	.20	.04
☐ 46	Don Nelson .... Boston Celtics	1.25	.60	.12
☐ 47	Jim Barnett .... New Orleans Jazz	.40	.20	.04

☐ 48	Manny Leaks .... Washington Bullets	.40	.20	.04
☐ 49	Elmore Smith .... Los Angeles Lakers	.40	.20	.04
☐ 50	Rick Barry AS1 .... Golden State Warriors	10.00	5.00	1.00
☐ 51	Jerry Sloan .... Chicago Bulls	.60	.30	.06
☐ 52	John Hummer .... Seattle Supersonics	.40	.20	.04
☐ 53	Keith Erickson .... Phoenix Suns	.40	.20	.04
☐ 54	George E. Johnson .... Houston Rockets	.40	.20	.04
☐ 55	Oscar Robertson .... Milwaukee Bucks	12.50	6.25	1.25
☐ 56	Steve Mix .... Philadelphia 76ers	.75	.35	.07
☐ 57	Rick Roberson .... Portland Trail Blazers	.40	.20	.04
☐ 58	John Mengelt .... Detroit Pistons	.40	.20	.04
☐ 59	Dwight Jones .... Atlanta Hawks	.40	.20	.04
☐ 60	Austin Carr .... Cleveland Cavaliers	.60	.30	.06
☐ 61	Nick Weatherspoon .... Washington Bullets	.40	.20	.04
☐ 62	Clem Haskins .... Phoenix Suns	.60	.30	.06
☐ 63	Don Kojis .... Kansas City-Omaha Kings	.40	.20	.04
☐ 64	Paul Westphal .... Boston Celtics	1.00	.50	.10
☐ 65	Walt Bellamy .... New Orleans Jazz	.75	.35	.07
☐ 66	John Johnson .... Portland Trail Blazers	.40	.20	.04
☐ 67	Butch Beard .... Golden State Warriors	.40	.20	.04
☐ 68	Happy Hairston .... Los Angeles Lakers	.60	.30	.06
☐ 69	Tom Boerwinkle .... Chicago Bulls	.40	.20	.04
☐ 70	Spencer Haywood AS2 ..... Seattle Supersonics	1.25	.60	.12
☐ 71	Gary Melchionni .... Phoenix Suns	.40	.20	.04
☐ 72	Ed Ratleff .... Houston Rockets	.40	.20	.04
☐ 73	Mickey Davis .... Milwaukee Bucks	.40	.20	.04
☐ 74	Dennis Awtrey .... New Orleans Jazz	.40	.20	.04
☐ 75	Fred Carter .... Philadelphia 76ers	.40	.20	.04
☐ 76	George Trapp .... Detroit Pistons	.40	.20	.04
☐ 77	John Wetzel .... Atlanta Hawks	.40	.20	.04
☐ 78	Bobby Smith .... Cleveland Cavaliers	.40	.20	.04
☐ 79	John Gianelli .... New York Knicks	.40	.20	.04
☐ 80	Bob McAdoo AS2 .... Buffalo Braves	3.50	1.75	.35
☐ 81	Atlanta Hawks TL .... Pete Maravich Lou Hudson Walt Bellamy Pete Maravich	2.00	1.00	.20
☐ 82	Boston Celtics TL .... John Havlicek Jo Jo White Dave Cowens Jo Jo White	3.25	1.60	.32
☐ 83	Buffalo Braves TL .... Bob McAdoo Ernie DiGregorio Bob McAdoo Ernie DiGregorio	1.00	.50	.10
☐ 84	Chicago Bulls TL .... Bob Love Chet Walker Clifford Ray Norm Van Lier	1.00	.50	.10
☐ 85	Cleveland Cavs TL .... Austin Carr Austin Carr Dwight Davis Len Wilkens	.80	.40	.08
☐ 86	Detroit Pistons TL .... Bob Lanier Stu Lantz Bob Lanier Dave Bing	1.00	.50	.10

☐ 87	Golden State Warriors Leaders Rick Barry Rick Barry Nate Thurmond Rick Barry	2.00	1.00	.20	☐ 115	Dick Snyder Cleveland Cavaliers	.40	.20	.04
☐ 88	Houston Rockets TL Rudy Tomjanovich Calvin Murphy Don Smith Calvin Murphy	.80	.40	.08	☐ 116	Nate Williams Kansas City-Omaha Kings	.40	.20	.04
					☐ 117	Matt Guokas Buffalo Braves	.60	.30	.06
					☐ 118	Henry Finkel Boston Celtics	.40	.20	.04
					☐ 119	Curtis Perry New Orleans Jazz	.40	.20	.04
☐ 89	Kansas City Omaha TL Jimmy Walker Jimmy Walker Sam Lacey Jimmy Walker	.80	.40	.08	☐ 120	Gail Goodrich AS1 Los Angeles Lakers	1.25	.60	.12
					☐ 121	Wes Unseld Washington Bullets	2.75	1.35	.27
☐ 90	Los Angeles Lakers TL Gail Goodrich Gail Goodrich Happy Hairston Gail Goodrich	1.00	.50	.10	☐ 122	Howard Porter New York Knicks	.40	.20	.04
					☐ 123	Jeff Mullins Golden State Warriors	.60	.30	.06
					☐ 124	Mike Bantom Phoenix Suns	.60	.30	.06
☐ 91	Milwaukee Bucks TL Kareem Abdul Jabbar Oscar Robertson Kareem Abdul Jabbar Oscar Robertson	5.00	2.50	.50	☐ 125	Fred Brown Seattle Supersonics	.75	.35	.07
					☐ 126	Bob Dandridge Milwaukee Bucks	.60	.30	.06
☐ 92	New Orleans Jazz Emblem; Expansion Draft Picks on Back	.80	.40	.08	☐ 127	Mike Newlin Houston Rockets	.40	.20	.04
					☐ 128	Greg Smith Portland Trail Blazers	.40	.20	.04
					☐ 129	Doug Collins Philadelphia 76ers	5.00	2.50	.50
☐ 93	New York Knicks TL Walt Frazier Bill Bradley Dave DeBusschere Walt Frazier	3.50	1.75	.35	☐ 130	Lou Hudson Atlanta Hawks	.60	.30	.06
					☐ 131	Bob Lanier Detroit Pistons	2.50	1.25	.25
☐ 94	Philadelphia 76ers TL Fred Carter Tom Van Arsdale Leroy Ellis Fred Carter	.80	.40	.08	☐ 132	Phil Jackson New York Knicks	1.25	.60	.12
					☐ 133	Don Chaney Boston Celtics	1.00	.50	.10
☐ 95	Phoenix Suns TL Charlie Scott Dick Van Arsdale Neal Walk Neal Walk	.80	.40	.08	☐ 134	Jim Brewer Cleveland Cavaliers	.40	.20	.04
					☐ 135	Ernie DiGregorio Buffalo Braves	1.00	.50	.10
					☐ 136	Steve Kuberski New Orleans Jazz	.40	.20	.04
☐ 96	Portland Trail Blazers Team Leaders Geoff Petrie Geoff Petrie Rick Roberson Sidney Wicks	1.00	.50	.10	☐ 137	Jim Price Los Angeles Lakers	.40	.20	.04
					☐ 138	Mike D'Antoni Kansas City-Omaha Kings	.40	.20	.04
					☐ 139	John Brown Atlanta Hawks	.40	.20	.04
☐ 97	Seattle Supersonics TL Spencer Haywood Dick Snyder Spencer Haywood Fred Brown	.80	.40	.08	☐ 140	Norm Van Lier AS2 Chicago Bulls	.60	.30	.06
					☐ 141	NBA Checklist 1-176	5.00	.50	.10
					☐ 142	Don Watts Seattle Supersonics	.75	.35	.07
☐ 98	Capitol Bullets TL Phil Chenier Phil Chenier Elvin Hayes Kevin Porter	.80	.40	.08	☐ 143	Walt Wesley Washington Bullets	.40	.20	.04
					☐ 144	NBA Scoring Leaders Bob McAdoo Kareem Abdul Jabbar Pete Maravich	3.25	1.60	.32
☐ 99	Sam Lacey Kansas City-Omaha Kings	.40	.20	.04	☐ 145	NBA Scoring Average Leaders Bob McAdoo Pete Maravich Kareem Abdul Jabbar	3.25	1.60	.32
☐ 100	John Havlicek AS1 Boston Celtics	12.50	6.25	1.25					
☐ 101	Stu Lantz New Orleans Jazz	.40	.20	.04	☐ 146	NBA F.G. Pct. Leaders Bob McAdoo Kareem Abdul Jabbar Rudy Tomjanovich	2.75	1.35	.27
☐ 102	Mike Riordan Washington Bullets	.40	.20	.04					
☐ 103	Larry Jones Philadelphia 76ers	.40	.20	.04	☐ 147	NBA F.T. Pct. Leaders Ernie DiGregorio Rick Barry Jeff Mullins	1.00	.50	.10
☐ 104	Connie Hawkins Los Angeles Lakers	1.50	.75	.15					
☐ 105	Nate Thurmond Golden State Warriors	1.50	.75	.15	☐ 148	NBA Rebound Leaders Elvin Hayes Dave Cowens Bob McAdoo	1.25	.60	.12
☐ 106	Dick Gibbs Seattle Supersonics	.40	.20	.04					
☐ 107	Corky Calhoun Phoenix Suns	.40	.20	.04	☐ 149	NBA Assist Leaders Ernie DiGregorio Calvin Murphy Len Wilkens	1.00	.50	.10
☐ 108	Dave Wohl Houston Rockets	.40	.20	.04					
☐ 109	Cornell Warner Milwaukee Bucks	.40	.20	.04	☐ 150	Walt Frazier AS1 New York Knicks	5.50	2.75	.55
☐ 110	Geoff Petrie UER Portland Trail Blazers (Misspelled Patrie on card front)	.60	.30	.06	☐ 151	Cazzie Russell Golden State Warriors	1.00	.50	.10
					☐ 152	Calvin Murphy Houston Rockets	1.00	.50	.10
☐ 111	Leroy Ellis Philadelphia 76ers	.40	.20	.04	☐ 153	Bob Kauffman Atlanta Hawks	.40	.20	.04
☐ 112	Chris Ford Detroit Pistons	1.25	.60	.12	☐ 154	Fred Boyd Philadelphia 76ers	.40	.20	.04
☐ 113	Bill Bradley New York Knicks	17.00	8.50	1.70	☐ 155	Dave Cowens Boston Celtics	4.50	2.25	.45
☐ 114	Clifford Ray Chicago Bulls	.60	.30	.06					

☐ 156	Willie Norwood	.40	.20	.04
	Detroit Pistons			
☐ 157	Lee Winfield	.40	.20	.04
	Buffalo Braves			
☐ 158	Dwight Davis	.40	.20	.04
	Cleveland Cavaliers			
☐ 159	George T. Johnson	.40	.20	.04
	Golden State Warriors			
☐ 160	Dick Van Arsdale	.40	.20	.04
	Phoenix Suns			
☐ 161	NBA Eastern Semis	.80	.40	.08
	Celts over Braves			
	Knicks edge Bullet			
☐ 162	NBA Western Semis	.80	.40	.08
	Bucks over Lakers			
	Bulls edge Pistons			
☐ 163	NBA Div. Finals	.80	.40	.08
	Celts over Knicks			
	Bucks sweep Bulls			
☐ 164	NBA Championship	.80	.40	.08
	Celtics over Bucks			
☐ 165	Phil Chenier	.60	.30	.06
	Washington Bullets			
☐ 166	Ken Washington	.40	.20	.04
	Los Angeles Lakers			
☐ 167	Dale Schlueter	.40	.20	.04
	Atlanta Hawks			
☐ 168	John Block	.40	.20	.04
	New Orleans Jazz			
☐ 169	Don Smith	.40	.20	.04
	Houston Rockets			
☐ 170	Nate Archibald	2.25	1.10	.22
	Kansas City-Omaha Kings			
☐ 171	Chet Walker	.75	.35	.07
	Chicago Bulls			
☐ 172	Archie Clark	.60	.30	.06
	Washington Bullets			
☐ 173	Kennedy McIntosh	.40	.20	.04
	Seattle Supersonics			
☐ 174	George Thompson	.40	.20	.04
	Milwaukee Bucks			
☐ 175	Sidney Wicks	1.25	.60	.12
	Portland Trail Blazers			
☐ 176	Jerry West	17.00	8.50	1.70
	Los Angeles Lakers			
☐ 177	Dwight Lamar	.40	.20	.04
	San Diego Conquistadors			
☐ 178	George Carter	.40	.20	.04
	Virginia Squires			
☐ 179	Wil Robinson	.40	.20	.04
	Memphis Sounds			
☐ 180	Artis Gilmore AS1	2.75	1.35	.27
	Kentucky Colonels			
☐ 181	Brian Taylor	.40	.20	.04
	New York Nets			
☐ 182	Darnell Hillman	.40	.20	.04
	Indiana Pacers			
☐ 183	Dave Robisch	.40	.20	.04
	Denver Nuggets			
☐ 184	Gene Littles	1.25	.60	.12
	St. Louis Spirits			
☐ 185	Willie Wise AS2	.60	.30	.06
	Utah Stars			
☐ 186	James Silas	1.00	.50	.10
	San Antonio Spurs			
☐ 187	Caldwell Jones	2.00	1.00	.20
	San Diego Conquistadors			
☐ 188	Roland Taylor	.40	.20	.04
	Virginia Squires			
☐ 189	Randy Denton	.40	.20	.04
	Memphis Sounds			
☐ 190	Dan Issel AS2	2.25	1.10	.22
	Kentucky Colonels			
☐ 191	Mike Gale	.40	.20	.04
	New York Nets			
☐ 192	Mel Daniels	.60	.30	.06
	Memphis Sounds			
☐ 193	Steve Jones	.60	.30	.06
	Denver Nuggets			
☐ 194	Marv Roberts	.40	.20	.04
	St. Louis Spirits			
☐ 195	Ron Boone AS2	.40	.20	.04
	Utah Stars			
☐ 196	George Gervin	24.00	12.00	2.40
	San Antonio Spurs			
☐ 197	Flynn Robinson	.40	.20	.04
	San Diego Conquistadors			
☐ 198	Cincy Powell	.40	.20	.04
	Virginia Squires			
☐ 199	Glen Combs	.40	.20	.04
	Memphis Sounds			
☐ 200	Julius Erving AS1	42.00	20.00	4.00
	New York Nets			
	(Misspelled Irving			
	on card back)			

☐ 201	Billy Keller	.40	.20	.04
	Indiana Pacers			
☐ 202	Willie Long	.40	.20	.04
	Denver Nuggets			
☐ 203	ABA Checklist 177-264	5.00	.50	.10
☐ 204	Joe Caldwell	.60	.30	.06
	St. Louis Spirits			
☐ 205	Swen Nater AS2	1.50	.75	.15
	San Antonio Spurs			
☐ 206	Rick Mount	.60	.30	.06
	Utah Stars			
☐ 207	ABA Scoring	2.75	1.35	.27
	Avg. Leaders			
	Julius Erving			
	George McGinnis			
	Dan Issel			
☐ 208	ABA 2 Pt. F.G.	.80	.40	.08
	Pct. Leaders			
	Swen Nater			
	James Jones			
	Tom Owens			
☐ 209	ABA 3 Pt. F.G.	.80	.40	.08
	Pct. Leaders			
	Louie Dampier			
	Billy Keller			
	Roger Brown			
☐ 210	ABA F.T. Pct. Leaders	.80	.40	.08
	James Jones			
	Mack Calvin			
	Ron Boone			
☐ 211	ABA Rebound Leaders	.80	.40	.08
	Artis Gilmore			
	George McGinnis			
	Caldwell Jones			
☐ 212	ABA Assist Leaders	.80	.40	.08
	Al Smith			
	Chuck Williams			
	Louie Dampier			
☐ 213	Larry Miller	.60	.30	.06
	Virginia Squires			
☐ 214	Stew Johnson	.40	.20	.04
	San Diego Conquistadors			
☐ 215	Larry Finch	1.50	.75	.15
	Memphis Sounds			
☐ 216	Larry Kenon	1.50	.75	.15
	New York Nets			
☐ 217	Joe Hamilton	.40	.20	.04
	Kentucky Colonels			
☐ 218	Gerald Govan	.40	.20	.04
	Utah Stars			
☐ 219	Ralph Simpson	.40	.20	.04
	Denver Nuggets			
☐ 220	George McGinnis AS1	1.50	.75	.15
	Indiana Pacers			
☐ 221	Carolina Cougars TL	.80	.40	.08
	Billy Cunningham			
	Mack Calvin			
	Tom Owens			
	Joe Caldwell			
☐ 222	Denver Nuggets TL	.80	.40	.08
	Ralph Simpson			
	Byron Beck			
	Dave Robisch			
	Al Smith			
☐ 223	Indiana Pacers TL	.80	.40	.08
	George McGinnis			
	Billy Keller			
	George McGinnis			
	Freddie Lewis			
☐ 224	Kentucky Colonels TL	1.50	.75	.15
	Dan Issel			
	Louie Dampier			
	Artis Gilmore			
	Louie Dampier			
☐ 225	Memphis Sounds TL	.80	.40	.08
	George Thompson			
	Larry Finch			
	Randy Denton			
	George Thompson			
☐ 226	New York Nets TL	3.75	1.85	.37
	Julius Erving			
	John Roche			
	Larry Kenon			
	Julius Erving			
☐ 227	San Antonio Spurs TL	2.50	1.25	.25
	George Gervin			
	George Gervin			
	Swen Nater			
	James Silas			
☐ 228	San Diego Conq. TL	.80	.40	.08
	Dwight Lamar			
	Stew Johnson			
	Caldwell Jones			
	Chuck Williams			

☐ 229 Utah Stars TL .... Willie Wise James Jones Gerald Goven James Jones	.80	.40	.08
☐ 230 Virginia Squires TL .... George Carter George Irvine Jim Eakins Roland Taylor	.80	.40	.08
☐ 231 Bird Averitt .... Kentucky Colonels	.40	.20	.04
☐ 232 John Roche .... Kentucky Colonels	.60	.30	.06
☐ 233 George Irvine .... Virginia Squires	.40	.20	.04
☐ 234 John Williamson .... New York Nets	1.50	.75	.15
☐ 235 Billy Cunningham .... St. Louis Spirits	2.75	1.35	.27
☐ 236 Jimmy O'Brien .... San Diego Conquistadors	.40	.20	.04
☐ 237 Wilbert Jones .... Kentucky Colonels	.40	.20	.04
☐ 238 Johnny Neumann .... Utah Stars	.40	.20	.04
☐ 239 Al Smith .... Denver Nuggets	.40	.20	.04
☐ 240 Roger Brown .... Memphis Sounds	.60	.30	.06
☐ 241 Chuck Williams .... Kentucky Colonels	.40	.20	.04
☐ 242 Rich Jones .... San Antonio Spurs	.40	.20	.04
☐ 243 Dave Twardzik .... Virginia Squires	.75	.35	.07
☐ 244 Wendell Ladner .... New York Nets	.40	.20	.04
☐ 245 Mack Calvin AS1 .... St. Louis Spirits	.60	.30	.06
☐ 246 ABA Eastern Semis .... Nets over Squires Colonels sweep Cougars	.80	.40	.08
☐ 247 ABA Western Semis .... Stars over Conquistadors Pacers over Spurs	.80	.40	.08
☐ 248 ABA Div. Finals .... Nets sweep Colonels Stars edge Pacers	.80	.40	.08
☐ 249 ABA Championship .... Nets over Stars	.80	.40	.08
☐ 250 Wilt Chamberlain .... San Diego Conquistadors	45.00	22.50	4.50
☐ 251 Ron Robinson .... Memphis Sounds	.40	.20	.04
☐ 252 Zelmo Beaty .... Utah Stars	.60	.30	.06
☐ 253 Donnie Freeman .... Indiana Pacers	.60	.30	.06
☐ 254 Mike Green .... Denver Nuggets	.40	.20	.04
☐ 255 Louie Dampier AS2 .... Kentucky Colonels	.60	.30	.06
☐ 256 Tom Owens .... St. Louis Spirits	.40	.20	.04
☐ 257 George Karl .... San Antonio Spurs	.75	.35	.07
☐ 258 Jim Eakins .... Virginia Squires	.40	.20	.04
☐ 259 Travis Grant .... San Diego Conquistadors	.40	.20	.04
☐ 260 James Jones AS1 .... Utah Stars	.60	.30	.06
☐ 261 Mike Jackson .... Memphis Sounds	.40	.20	.04
☐ 262 Billy Paultz .... New York Nets	.40	.20	.04
☐ 263 Freddie Lewis .... Memphis Sounds	.60	.30	.06
☐ 264 Byron Beck .... Denver Nuggets (Back refers to ANA, should be ABA)	.60	.30	.06

1975-76 Topps

The 1975-76 Topps basketball card set of 330 was the largest basketball set ever produced to that time. NBA players are depicted on cards 1-220 and ABA players on cards 221-330. The cards in the set measure the standard 2 1/2" by 3 1/2". Team Leader (TL) cards are provided for each team on cards 116-133 and 278-287. Other subseries in this set include NBA Statistical Leaders (1-6), NBA Playoffs (188-189), NBA Team Checklists (203-220), ABA Statistical Leaders (221-226), ABA Playoffs (309-310), and ABA Team Checklists (321-330). All-Star selections (first and second team) for both leagues are noted on the respective player's regular cards. Card backs are printed in blue and green on gray card stock. The set is particularly hard to sort numerically, as the small card number on the back is printed in blue on a dark green background. The set was printed on three large sheets each containing 110 different cards. Investigation of the second (series) sheet reveals that indeed 22 of the cards were double printed; they are marked DP in the checklist below. The key rookie card in this set is Moses Malone.

	NRMT	VG-E	GOOD
COMPLETE SET (330)	425.00	200.00	40.00
COMMON PLAYER (1-110)	.45	.22	.04
COMMON PLAYER (111-220)	.45	.22	.04
COMMON PLAYER (221-330)	.55	.27	.05
☐ 1 NBA Scoring Average .... Leaders Bob McAdoo Rick Barry Kareem Abdul Jabbar	7.50	3.75	.75
☐ 2 NBA Field Goal .... Percentage Leaders Don Nelson Butch Beard Rudy Tomjanovich	.90	.45	.09
☐ 3 NBA Free Throw .... Percentage Leaders Rick Barry Calvin Murphy Bill Bradley	2.75	1.35	.27
☐ 4 NBA Rebounds Leaders .... Wes Unseld Dave Cowens Sam Lacey	.90	.45	.09
☐ 5 NBA Assists Leaders .... Kevin Porter Dave Bing Nate Archibald	1.25	.60	.12
☐ 6 NBA Steals Leaders .... Rick Barry Walt Frazier Larry Steele	1.75	.85	.17
☐ 7 Tom Van Arsdale .... Atlanta Hawks	.45	.22	.04
☐ 8 Paul Silas .... Boston Celtics	.75	.35	.07
☐ 9 Jerry Sloan .... Chicago Bulls	.75	.35	.07
☐ 10 Bob McAdoo AS1 .... Buffalo Braves	3.25	1.60	.32

☐ 11	Dwight Davis	.45	.22	.04
	Golden State Warriors			
☐ 12	John Mengelt	.45	.22	.04
	Detroit Pistons			
☐ 13	George Johnson	.45	.22	.04
	Golden State Warriors			
☐ 14	Ed Ratleff	.45	.22	.04
	Houston Rockets			
☐ 15	Nate Archibald AS1	2.00	1.00	.20
	Kansas City Kings			
☐ 16	Elmore Smith	.45	.22	.04
	Milwaukee Bucks			
☐ 17	Bob Dandridge	.60	.30	.06
	Milwaukee Bucks			
☐ 18	Louie Nelson	.45	.22	.04
	New Orleans Jazz			
☐ 19	Neal Walk	.45	.22	.04
	New York Knicks			
☐ 20	Billy Cunningham	3.00	1.50	.30
	Philadelphia 76ers			
☐ 21	Gary Melchionni	.45	.22	.04
	Phoenix Suns			
☐ 22	Barry Clemens	.45	.22	.04
	Portland Trail Blazers			
☐ 23	Jimmy Jones	.45	.22	.04
	Washington Bullets			
☐ 24	Tom Burleson	1.25	.60	.12
	Seattle Supersonics			
☐ 25	Lou Hudson	.60	.30	.06
	Atlanta Hawks			
☐ 26	Henry Finkel	.45	.22	.04
	Boston Celtics			
☐ 27	Jim McMillian	.45	.22	.04
	Buffalo Braves			
☐ 28	Matt Guokas	.60	.30	.06
	Chicago Bulls			
☐ 29	Fred Foster DP	.45	.22	.04
	Cleveland Cavaliers			
☐ 30	Bob Lanier	3.00	1.50	.30
	Detroit Pistons			
☐ 31	Jimmy Walker	.45	.22	.04
	Kansas City Kings			
☐ 32	Cliff Meely	.45	.22	.04
	Houston Rockets			
☐ 33	Butch Beard	.45	.22	.04
	Cleveland Cavaliers			
☐ 34	Cazzie Russell	.75	.35	.07
	Los Angeles Lakers			
☐ 35	Jon McGlocklin	.45	.22	.04
	Milwaukee Bucks			
☐ 36	Bernie Fryer	.45	.22	.04
	New Orleans Jazz			
☐ 37	Bill Bradley	17.00	8.50	1.70
	New York Knicks			
☐ 38	Fred Carter	.45	.22	.04
	Philadelphia 76ers			
☐ 39	Dennis Awtrey DP	.45	.22	.04
	Phoenix Suns			
☐ 40	Sidney Wicks	1.00	.50	.10
	Portland Trail Blazers			
☐ 41	Fred Brown	.60	.30	.06
	Seattle Supersonics			
☐ 42	Rowland Garrett	.45	.22	.04
	Chicago Bulls			
☐ 43	Herm Gilliam	.45	.22	.04
	Atlanta Hawks			
☐ 44	Don Nelson	1.00	.50	.10
	Boston Celtics			
☐ 45	Ernie DiGregorio	.60	.30	.06
	Buffalo Braves			
☐ 46	Jim Brewer	.45	.22	.04
	Cleveland Cavaliers			
☐ 47	Chris Ford	.75	.35	.07
	Detroit Pistons			
☐ 48	Nick Weatherspoon	.45	.22	.04
	Washington Bullets			
☐ 49	Zaid Abdul Aziz	.45	.22	.04
	Houston Rockets			
☐ 50	Keith Wilkes	7.00	3.50	.70
	Golden State Warriors			
☐ 51	Ollie Johnson DP	.45	.22	.04
	Kansas City Kings			
☐ 52	Lucius Allen	.60	.30	.06
	Los Angeles Lakers			
☐ 53	Mickey Davis	.45	.22	.04
	Milwaukee Bucks			
☐ 54	Otto Moore	.45	.22	.04
	New Orleans Jazz			
☐ 55	Walt Frazier AS1	6.00	3.00	.60
	New York Knicks			
☐ 56	Steve Mix	.45	.22	.04
	Philadelphia 76ers			
☐ 57	Nate Hawthorne	.45	.22	.04
	Phoenix Suns			

☐ 58	Lloyd Neal	.45	.22	.04
	Portland Trail Blazers			
☐ 59	Don Watts	.45	.22	.04
	Seattle Supersonics			
☐ 60	Elvin Hayes	6.00	3.00	.60
	Washington Bullets			
☐ 61	Checklist 1-110	4.50	.50	.10
☐ 62	Mike Sojourner	.45	.22	.04
	Atlanta Hawks			
☐ 63	Randy Smith	.60	.30	.06
	Buffalo Braves			
☐ 64	John Block DP	.45	.22	.04
	Chicago Bulls			
☐ 65	Charlie Scott	.60	.30	.06
	Boston Celtics			
☐ 66	Jim Chones	.45	.22	.04
	Cleveland Cavaliers			
☐ 67	Rick Adelman	.75	.35	.07
	Kansas City Kings			
☐ 68	Curtis Rowe	.60	.30	.06
	Detroit Pistons			
☐ 69	Derrek Dickey	.45	.22	.04
	Golden State Warriors			
☐ 70	Rudy Tomjanovich	.45	.22	.04
	Houston Rockets			
☐ 71	Pat Riley	3.25	1.60	.32
	Los Angeles Lakers			
☐ 72	Cornell Warner	.45	.22	.04
	Milwaukee Bucks			
☐ 73	Earl Monroe	3.50	1.75	.35
	New York Knicks			
☐ 74	Allan Bristow	1.00	.50	.10
	Philadelphia 76ers			
☐ 75	Pete Maravich DP	11.00	5.50	1.10
	New Orleans Jazz			
☐ 76	Curtis Perry	.45	.22	.04
	Phoenix Suns			
☐ 77	Bill Walton	12.50	6.25	1.25
	Portland Trail Blazers			
☐ 78	Leonard Gray	.45	.22	.04
	Seattle Supersonics			
☐ 79	Kevin Porter	.60	.30	.06
	Washington Bullets			
☐ 80	John Havlicek AS2	12.00	6.00	1.20
	Boston Celtics			
☐ 81	Dwight Jones	.45	.22	.04
	Atlanta Hawks			
☐ 82	Jack Marin	.45	.22	.04
	Buffalo Braves			
☐ 83	Dick Snyder	.45	.22	.04
	Cleveland Cavaliers			
☐ 84	George Trapp	.45	.22	.04
	Detroit Pistons			
☐ 85	Nate Thurmond	.90	.45	.09
	Chicago Bulls			
☐ 86	Charles Johnson	.45	.22	.04
	Golden State Warriors			
☐ 87	Ron Riley	.45	.22	.04
	Houston Rockets			
☐ 88	Stu Lantz	.45	.22	.04
	Los Angeles Lakers			
☐ 89	Scott Wedman	1.00	.50	.10
	Kansas City Kings			
☐ 90	Kareem Abdul Jabbar	38.00	17.50	3.50
	Los Angeles Lakers			
☐ 91	Aaron James	.45	.22	.04
	New Orleans Jazz			
☐ 92	Jim Barnett	.45	.22	.04
	New York Knicks			
☐ 93	Clyde Lee	.45	.22	.04
	Philadelphia 76ers			
☐ 94	Larry Steele	.45	.22	.04
	Portland Trail Blazers			
☐ 95	Mike Riordan	.45	.22	.04
	Washington Bullets			
☐ 96	Archie Clark	.60	.30	.06
	Seattle Supersonics			
☐ 97	Mike Bantom	.45	.22	.04
	Phoenix Suns			
☐ 98	Bob Kauffman	.45	.22	.04
	Atlanta Hawks			
☐ 99	Kevin Stacom	.60	.30	.06
	Boston Celtics			
☐ 100	Rick Barry AS1	7.50	3.75	.75
	Golden State Warriors			
☐ 101	Ken Charles	.45	.22	.04
	Buffalo Braves			
☐ 102	Tom Boerwinkle	.45	.22	.04
	Chicago Bulls			
☐ 103	Mike Newlin	.45	.22	.04
	Houston Rockets			
☐ 104	Leroy Ellis	.45	.22	.04
	Philadelphia 76ers			
☐ 105	Austin Carr	.75	.35	.07
	Cleveland Cavaliers			

#	Player	Team			
☐ 106	Ron Behagen	New Orleans Jazz	.45	.22	.04
☐ 107	Jim Price	Milwaukee Bucks	.45	.22	.04
☐ 108	Bud Stallworth	New Orleans Jazz	.45	.22	.04
☐ 109	Earl Williams	Detroit Pistons	.45	.22	.04
☐ 110	Gail Goodrich	Los Angeles Lakers	.90	.45	.09
☐ 111	Phil Jackson	New York Knicks	1.00	.50	.10
☐ 112	Rod Derline	Seattle Supersonics	.45	.22	.04
☐ 113	Keith Erickson	Phoenix Suns	.45	.22	.04
☐ 114	Phil Lumpkin	Phoenix Suns	.45	.22	.04
☐ 115	Wes Unseld	Washington Bullets	3.00	1.50	.30
☐ 116	Atlanta Hawks TL	Lou Hudson / Lou Hudson / John Drew / Dean Meminger	.90	.45	.09
☐ 117	Boston Celtics TL	Dave Cowens / Kevin Stacom / Paul Silas / Jo Jo White	1.25	.60	.12
☐ 118	Buffalo Braves TL	Bob McAdoo / Jack Marin / Bob McAdoo / Randy Smith	.90	.45	.09
☐ 119	Chicago Bulls TL	Bob Love / Chet Walker / Nate Thurmond / Norm Van Lier	1.25	.60	.12
☐ 120	Cleveland Cavs TL	Bobby Smith / Dick Snyder / Jim Chones / Jim Cleamons	.90	.45	.09
☐ 121	Detroit Pistons TL	Bob Lanier / John Mengelt / Bob Lanier / Dave Bing	1.25	.60	.12
☐ 122	Golden State TL	Rick Barry / Rick Barry / Clifford Ray / Rick Barry	2.00	1.00	.20
☐ 123	Houston Rockets TL	Rudy Tomjanovich / Calvin Murphy / Kevin Kunnert / Mike Newlin	.90	.45	.09
☐ 124	Kansas City Kings TL	Nate Archibald / Ollie Johnson / Sam Lacey / (Lacy on front) / Nate Archibald	1.25	.60	.12
☐ 125	Los Angeles Lakers TL	Gail Goodrich / Cazzie Russell / Happy Hairston / Gail Goodrich	1.25	.60	.12
☐ 126	Milwaukee Bucks TL	Kareem Abdul Jabbar / Mickey Davis / Kareem Abdul Jabbar / Kareem Abdul Jabbar	3.50	1.75	.35
☐ 127	New Orleans Jazz TL	Pete Maravich / Stu Lantz / E.C. Coleman / Pete Maravich	2.00	1.00	.20
☐ 128	New York Knicks TL DP	Walt Frazier / Bill Bradley / John Gianelli / Walt Frazier	2.50	1.25	.25
☐ 129	Phila. 76ers TL DP	Fred Carter / Doug Collins / Billy Cunningham / Billy Cunningham	1.25	.60	.12
☐ 130	Phoenix Suns TL DP	Charlie Scott / Keith Erickson / Curtis Perry / Dennis Awtrey	.90	.45	.09
☐ 131	Portland Blazers TL DP	Sidney Wicks / Geoff Petrie / Sidney Wicks / Geoff Petrie	.90	.45	.09
☐ 132	Seattle Sonics TL	Spencer Haywood / Archie Clark / Spencer Haywood / Don Watts	.90	.45	.09
☐ 133	Washington Bullets TL	Elvin Hayes / Clem Haskins / Wes Unseld / Kevin Porter	1.25	.60	.12
☐ 134	John Drew	Atlanta Hawks	1.50	.75	.15
☐ 135	Jo Jo White AS2	Boston Celtics	1.00	.50	.10
☐ 136	Garfield Heard	Buffalo Braves	.45	.22	.04
☐ 137	Jim Cleamons	Cleveland Cavaliers	.45	.22	.04
☐ 138	Howard Porter	Detroit Pistons	.45	.22	.04
☐ 139	Phil Smith	Golden State Warriors	.75	.35	.07
☐ 140	Bob Love	Chicago Bulls	.75	.35	.07
☐ 141	John Gianelli DP	New York Knicks	.45	.22	.04
☐ 142	Larry McNeill	Kansas City Kings	.45	.22	.04
☐ 143	Brian Winters	Milwaukee Bucks	1.00	.50	.10
☐ 144	George Thompson	Milwaukee Bucks	.45	.22	.04
☐ 145	Kevin Kunnert	Houston Rockets	.45	.22	.04
☐ 146	Henry Bibby	New Orleans Jazz	.60	.30	.06
☐ 147	John Johnson	Portland Trail Blazers	.45	.22	.04
☐ 148	Doug Collins	Philadelphia 76ers	2.25	1.10	.22
☐ 149	John Brisker	Seattle Supersonics	.45	.22	.04
☐ 150	Dick Van Arsdale	Phoenix Suns	.45	.22	.04
☐ 151	Leonard Robinson	Washington Bullets	2.25	1.10	.22
☐ 152	Dean Meminger	Atlanta Hawks	.60	.30	.06
☐ 153	Phil Hankinson	Boston Celtics	.45	.22	.04
☐ 154	Dale Schlueter	Buffalo Braves	.45	.22	.04
☐ 155	Norm Van Lier	Chicago Bulls	.60	.30	.06
☐ 156	Campy Russell	Cleveland Cavaliers	1.00	.50	.10
☐ 157	Jeff Mullins	Golden State Warriors	.60	.30	.06
☐ 158	Sam Lacey	Kansas City Kings	.45	.22	.04
☐ 159	Happy Hairston	Los Angeles Lakers	.60	.30	.06
☐ 160	Dave Bing DP	Detroit Pistons	1.75	.85	.17
☐ 161	Kevin Restani	Milwaukee Bucks	.45	.22	.04
☐ 162	Dave Wohl	Houston Rockets	.45	.22	.04
☐ 163	E.C. Coleman	New Orleans Jazz	.45	.22	.04
☐ 164	Jim Fox	Seattle Supersonics	.45	.22	.04
☐ 165	Geoff Petrie	Portland Trail Blazers	.75	.35	.07
☐ 166	Hawthorne Wingo DP	New York Knicks (MIsspelled Harthorne on card front) UER	.45	.22	.04
☐ 167	Fred Boyd	Philadelphia 76ers	.45	.22	.04
☐ 168	Willie Norwood	Phoenix Suns	.45	.22	.04
☐ 169	Bob Wilson	Chicago Bulls	.45	.22	.04
☐ 170	Dave Cowens	Boston Celtics	3.75	1.85	.37
☐ 171	Tom Henderson	Atlanta Hawks	.45	.22	.04
☐ 172	Jim Washington	Buffalo Braves	.45	.22	.04

☐ 173	Clem Haskins .... Washington Bullets	.60	.30	.06
☐ 174	Jim Davis .... Detroit Pistons	.45	.22	.04
☐ 175	Bobby Smith DP .... Cleveland Cavaliers	.45	.22	.04
☐ 176	Mike D'Antoni .... Kansas City Kings	.45	.22	.04
☐ 177	Zelmo Beaty .... Los Angeles Lakers	.60	.30	.06
☐ 178	Gary Brokaw .... Milwaukee Bucks	.60	.30	.06
☐ 179	Mel Davis .... New York Knicks	.45	.22	.04
☐ 180	Calvin Murphy .... Houston Rockets	1.00	.50	.10
☐ 181	Checklist 111-220 DP	4.50	.50	.10
☐ 182	Nate Williams .... New Orleans Jazz	.45	.22	.04
☐ 183	LaRue Martin .... Portland Trail Blazers	.45	.22	.04
☐ 184	George McGinnis .... Philadelphia 76ers	1.25	.60	.12
☐ 185	Clifford Ray .... Golden State Warriors	.45	.22	.04
☐ 186	Paul Westphal .... Phoenix Suns	1.50	.75	.15
☐ 187	Talvin Skinner .... Seattle Supersonics	.45	.22	.04
☐ 188	NBA Playoff Semis DP .... Warriors edge Bulls Bullets over Celts	.90	.45	.09
☐ 189	NBA Playoff Finals .... Warriors sweep Bullets (C.Ray blocks shot)	.90	.45	.09
☐ 190	Phil Chenier AS2 DP .... Washington Bullets	.60	.30	.06
☐ 191	John Brown .... Atlanta Hawks	.45	.22	.04
☐ 192	Lee Winfield .... Buffalo Braves	.45	.22	.04
☐ 193	Steve Patterson .... Cleveland Cavaliers	.45	.22	.04
☐ 194	Charles Dudley .... Golden State Warriors	.45	.22	.04
☐ 195	Connie Hawkins DP .... Los Angeles Lakers	1.00	.50	.10
☐ 196	Leon Benbow .... Chicago Bulls	.45	.22	.04
☐ 197	Don Kojis .... Kansas City Kings	.45	.22	.04
☐ 198	Ron Williams .... Milwaukee Bucks	.45	.22	.04
☐ 199	Mel Counts .... New Orleans Jazz	.45	.22	.04
☐ 200	Spencer Haywood AS2 .... Seattle Supersonics	1.00	.50	.10
☐ 201	Greg Jackson .... Phoenix Suns	.45	.22	.04
☐ 202	Tom Kozelko DP .... Washington Bullets	.45	.22	.04
☐ 203	Atlanta Hawks .... Checklist	.90	.20	.04
☐ 204	Boston Celtics .... Checklist	.90	.20	.04
☐ 205	Buffalo Braves .... Checklist	.90	.20	.04
☐ 206	Chicago Bulls .... Checklist	.90	.20	.04
☐ 207	Cleveland Cavs .... Checklist	.90	.20	.04
☐ 208	Detroit Pistons .... Checklist	.90	.20	.04
☐ 209	Golden State .... Checklist	.90	.20	.04
☐ 210	Houston Rockets .... Checklist	.90	.20	.04
☐ 211	Kansas City Kings DP .... Checklist	.90	.20	.04
☐ 212	Los Angeles Lakers DP .... Checklist	.90	.20	.04
☐ 213	Milwaukee Bucks .... Checklist	.90	.20	.04
☐ 214	New Orleans Jazz .... Checklist	.90	.20	.04
☐ 215	New York Knicks .... Checklist	.90	.20	.04
☐ 216	Philadelphia 76ers .... Checklist	.90	.20	.04
☐ 217	Phoenix Suns DP .... Checklist	.90	.20	.04
☐ 218	Portland Blazers .... Checklist	.90	.20	.04
☐ 219	Seattle Sonics DP .... Checklist	.90	.20	.04
☐ 220	Washington Bullets .... Checklist	.90	.20	.04
☐ 221	ABA Scoring .... Average Leaders George McGinnis Julius Erving Ron Boone	2.50	1.25	.25
☐ 222	ABA 2 Pt. Field Goal .... Percentage Leaders Bobby Jones Artis Gilmore Moses Malone	2.50	1.25	.25
☐ 223	ABA 3 Pt. Field Goal .... Percentage Leaders Billy Shepherd Louis Dampier Al Smith	.90	.45	.09
☐ 224	ABA Free Throw .... Percentage Leaders Mack Calvin James Silas Dave Robisch	.90	.45	.09
☐ 225	ABA Rebounds Leaders ...... Swen Nater Artis Gilmore Marvin Barnes	.90	.45	.09
☐ 226	ABA Assists Leaders .... Mack Calvin Chuck Williams George McGinnis	.90	.45	.09
☐ 227	Mack Calvin AS1 .... Virginia Squires	.75	.35	.07
☐ 228	Billy Knight AS1 .... Indiana Pacers	1.25	.60	.12
☐ 229	Bird Averitt .... Kentucky Colonels	.55	.27	.05
☐ 230	George Carter .... Memphis Sounds	.55	.27	.05
☐ 231	Swen Nater AS2 .... New York Nets	.75	.35	.07
☐ 232	Steve Jones .... St. Louis Spirits	.75	.35	.07
☐ 233	George Gervin .... San Antonio Spurs	7.50	3.75	.75
☐ 234	Lee Davis .... San Diego Sails	.55	.27	.05
☐ 235	Ron Boone AS1 .... Utah Stars	.55	.27	.05
☐ 236	Mike Jackson .... Virginia Squires	.55	.27	.05
☐ 237	Kevin Joyce .... Indiana Pacers	.55	.27	.05
☐ 238	Marv Roberts .... Kentucky Colonels	.55	.27	.05
☐ 239	Tom Owens .... Memphis Sounds	.55	.27	.05
☐ 240	Ralph Simpson .... Denver Nuggets	.75	.35	.07
☐ 241	Gus Gerard .... St. Louis Spirits	.55	.27	.05
☐ 242	Brian Taylor AS2 .... New York Nets	.75	.35	.07
☐ 243	Rich Jones .... San Antonio Spurs	.55	.27	.05
☐ 244	John Roche .... Utah Stars	.75	.35	.07
☐ 245	Travis Grant .... San Diego Sails	.55	.27	.05
☐ 246	Dave Twardzik .... Virginia Squires	.75	.35	.07
☐ 247	Mike Green .... Virginia Squires	.55	.27	.05
☐ 248	Billy Keller .... Indiana Pacers	.55	.27	.05
☐ 249	Stew Johnson .... Memphis Sounds	.55	.27	.05
☐ 250	Artis Gilmore AS1 .... Kentucky Colonels	2.00	1.00	.20
☐ 251	John Williamson .... New York Nets	.75	.35	.07
☐ 252	Marvin Barnes AS2 .... St. Louis Spirits	3.00	1.50	.30
☐ 253	James Silas AS2 .... San Antonio Spurs	.75	.35	.07
☐ 254	Moses Malone .... Utah Stars	75.00	37.50	7.50
☐ 255	Willie Wise .... Virginia Squires	.75	.35	.07
☐ 256	Dwight Lamar .... San Diego Sails	.55	.27	.05
☐ 257	Checklist 221-330	4.50	.50	.10
☐ 258	Byron Beck .... Denver Nuggets	.55	.27	.05
☐ 259	Len Elmore .... Indiana Pacers	2.00	1.00	.20

☐ 260 Dan Issel Kentucky Colonels	2.00	1.00	.20
☐ 261 Rick Mount Memphis Sounds	.75	.35	.07
☐ 262 Billy Paultz New York Nets	.55	.27	.05
☐ 263 Donnie Freeman San Antonio Spurs	.55	.27	.05
☐ 264 George Adams San Diego Sails	.55	.27	.05
☐ 265 Don Chaney St. Louis Spirits	1.00	.50	.10
☐ 266 Randy Denton Utah Stars	.55	.27	.05
☐ 267 Don Washington Denver Nuggets	.55	.27	.05
☐ 268 Roland Taylor Denver Nuggets	.55	.27	.05
☐ 269 Charlie Edge Indiana Pacers	.55	.27	.05
☐ 270 Louie Dampier Kentucky Colonels	.75	.35	.07
☐ 271 Collis Jones Memphis Sounds	.55	.27	.05
☐ 272 Al Skinner New York Nets	.55	.27	.05
☐ 273 Coby Dietrick San Antonio Spurs	.55	.27	.05
☐ 274 Tim Bassett San Diego Sails	.55	.27	.05
☐ 275 Freddie Lewis St. Louis Spirits	.75	.35	.07
☐ 276 Gerald Govan Utah Stars	.55	.27	.05
☐ 277 Ron Thomas Kentucky Colonels	.55	.27	.05
☐ 278 Denver Nuggets TL Ralph Simpson Mack Calvin Mike Green Mack Calvin	.90	.45	.09
☐ 279 Indiana Pacers TL George McGinnis Billy Keller George McGinnis George McGinnis	.90	.45	.09
☐ 280 Kentucky Colonels TL Artis Gilmore Louie Dampier Artis Gilmore Louie Dampier	1.25	.60	.12
☐ 281 Memphis Sounds TL George Carter Larry Finch Tom Owens Chuck Williams	.90	.45	.09
☐ 282 New York Nets TL Julius Erving John Williamson Julius Erving Julius Erving	3.25	1.60	.32
☐ 283 St. Louis Spirits TL Marvin Barnes Freddie Lewis Marvin Barnes Freddie Lewis	.90	.45	.09
☐ 284 San Antonio Spurs TL George Gervin James Silas Swen Nater James Silas	.90	.45	.09
☐ 285 San Diego Sails TL Travis Grant Jimmy O'Brien Caldwell Jones Jimmy O'Brien	.90	.45	.09
☐ 286 Utah Stars TL Ron Boone Ron Boone Moses Malone Al Smith	5.00	2.50	.50
☐ 287 Virginia Squires TL Willie Wise Red Robbins Dave Vaughn Dave Twardzik	.90	.45	.09
☐ 288 Claude Terry Denver Nuggets	.55	.27	.05
☐ 289 Wilbert Jones Kentucky Colonels	.55	.27	.05
☐ 290 Darnell Hillman Indiana Pacers	.55	.27	.05
☐ 291 Bill Melchionni New York Nets	.75	.35	.07
☐ 292 Mel Daniels Memphis Sounds	.75	.35	.07
☐ 293 Fly Williams St. Louis Spirits	.90	.45	.09
☐ 294 Larry Kenon San Antonio Spurs	.75	.35	.07
☐ 295 Red Robbins Virginia Squires	.55	.27	.05
☐ 296 Warren Jabali San Diego Sails	.55	.27	.05
☐ 297 Jim Eakins Utah Stars	.55	.27	.05
☐ 298 Bobby Jones Denver Nuggets	7.50	3.75	.75
☐ 299 Don Buse Indiana Pacers	.55	.27	.05
☐ 300 Julius Erving AS1 New York Nets	42.00	20.00	4.00
☐ 301 Billy Shepherd Memphis Sounds	.55	.27	.05
☐ 302 Maurice Lucas St. Louis Spirits	7.50	3.75	.75
☐ 303 George Karl San Antonio Spurs	.75	.35	.07
☐ 304 Jim Bradley Kentucky Colonels	.55	.27	.05
☐ 305 Caldwell Jones San Diego Sails	.90	.45	.09
☐ 306 Al Smith Utah Stars	.55	.27	.05
☐ 307 Jan Van Breda Kolff Virginia Squires	.75	.35	.07
☐ 308 Darrell Elston Virginia Squires	.55	.27	.05
☐ 309 ABA Playoff Semis Colonels over Spirits; Pacers edge Nuggets	.90	.45	.09
☐ 310 ABA Playoff Finals Colonels over Pacers (Gilmore hooking)	1.25	.60	.12
☐ 311 Ted McClain Kentucky Colonels	.55	.27	.05
☐ 312 Willie Sojourner New York Nets	.55	.27	.05
☐ 313 Bob Warren San Antonio Spurs	.55	.27	.05
☐ 314 Bob Netolicky Indiana Pacers	.55	.27	.05
☐ 315 Chuck Williams Memphis Sounds	.55	.27	.05
☐ 316 Gene Kennedy St. Louis Spirits	.55	.27	.05
☐ 317 Jimmy O'Brien San Diego Sails	.55	.27	.05
☐ 318 Dave Robisch Denver Nuggets	.55	.27	.05
☐ 319 Wali Jones Utah Stars	.55	.27	.05
☐ 320 George Irvine Denver Nuggets	.55	.27	.05
☐ 321 Denver Nuggets Checklist	.90	.20	.04
☐ 322 Indiana Pacers Checklist	.90	.20	.04
☐ 323 Kentucky Colonels Checklist	.90	.20	.04
☐ 324 Memphis Sounds Checklist	.90	.20	.04
☐ 325 New York Nets Checklist	.90	.20	.04
☐ 326 St. Louis Spirits Checklist (Spirits of St. Louis on card back)	.90	.20	.04
☐ 327 San Antonio Spurs Checklist	.90	.20	.04
☐ 328 San Diego Sails Checklist	.90	.20	.04
☐ 329 Utah Stars Checklist	.90	.20	.04
☐ 330 Virginia Squires Checklist	1.50	.25	.05

1975-76 Topps Team Checklist

These team checklists were issued in three panels, with nine teams per panel. Each panel measures approximately 7 1/2" by 10 1/2" and are joined together to form one continuous sheet.

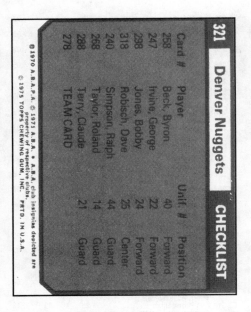

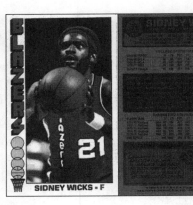

SIDNEY WICKS - F

The checklists are printed in blue and green on white card stock and list all NBA and ABA teams. They are numbered on the front and listed alphabetically according to the city names. The backs are blank. Since there was only room for 27 teams on the three-part sheet, Topps apparently left off card 324 Memphis Sounds, which is in the regular set.

	NRMT	VG-E	GOOD
COMPLETE SET	50.00	25.00	5.00
COMMON TEAM	2.00	1.00	.20
☐ 203 Atlanta Hawks	2.00	1.00	.20
☐ 204 Boston Celtics	2.00	1.00	.20
☐ 205 Buffalo Braves	2.00	1.00	.20
☐ 206 Chicago Bulls	2.00	1.00	.20
☐ 207 Cleveland Cavaliers	2.00	1.00	.20
☐ 208 Detroit Pistons	2.00	1.00	.20
☐ 209 Golden State Warriors	2.00	1.00	.20
☐ 210 Houston Rockets	2.00	1.00	.20
☐ 211 Kansas City Kings	2.00	1.00	.20
☐ 212 Los Angeles Lakers	2.00	1.00	.20
☐ 213 Milwaukee Bucks	2.00	1.00	.20
☐ 214 New Orleans Jazz	2.00	1.00	.20
☐ 215 New York Knicks	2.00	1.00	.20
☐ 216 Philadelphia 76ers	2.00	1.00	.20
☐ 217 Phoenix Suns	2.00	1.00	.20
☐ 218 Portland Trail Blazers	2.00	1.00	.20
☐ 219 Seattle SuperSonics	2.00	1.00	.20
☐ 220 Washington Bullets	2.00	1.00	.20
☐ 321 Denver Nuggets	2.00	1.00	.20
☐ 322 Indiana Pacers	2.00	1.00	.20
☐ 323 Kentucky Colonels	2.00	1.00	.20
☐ 325 New York Nets	2.00	1.00	.20
☐ 326 Spirits of St. Louis	2.00	1.00	.20
☐ 327 San Antonio Spurs	2.00	1.00	.20
☐ 328 San Diego Sails	2.00	1.00	.20
☐ 329 Utah Stars	2.00	1.00	.20
☐ 330 Virginia Squires	2.00	1.00	.20

1976-77 Topps

The 1976-77 Topps set witnesses a return to the larger-sized cards, with each card measuring approximately 3 1/8" by 5 1/4". Cards numbered 126-135 are the previous season's NBA All-Star selections. The set is complete at 144 cards. The cards were

printed on two large sheets, each with eight rows and nine columns. The checklist card was located in the lower right corner of the second sheet. The key rookie card in this set is David Thompson.

	NRMT	VG-E	GOOD
COMPLETE SET (144)	160.00	80.00	16.00
COMMON PLAYER (1-144)	.45	.22	.04
☐ 1 Julius Erving	28.00	7.00	1.40
New York Nets			
☐ 2 Dick Snyder	.45	.22	.04
Cleveland Cavaliers			
☐ 3 Paul Silas	.60	.30	.06
Boston Celtics			
☐ 4 Keith Erickson	.45	.22	.04
Phoenix Suns			
☐ 5 Wes Unseld	2.00	1.00	.20
Washington Bullets			
☐ 6 Butch Beard	.45	.22	.04
New York Knicks			
☐ 7 Lloyd Neal	.45	.22	.04
Portland Trail Blazers			
☐ 8 Tom Henderson	.45	.22	.04
Atlanta Hawks			
☐ 9 Jim McMillian	.45	.22	.04
Buffalo Braves			
☐ 10 Bob Lanier	1.75	.85	.17
Detroit Pistons			
☐ 11 Junior Bridgeman	1.50	.75	.15
Milwaukee Bucks			
☐ 12 Corky Calhoun	.45	.22	.04
Los Angeles Lakers			
☐ 13 Billy Keller	.45	.22	.04
Indiana Pacers			
☐ 14 Mickey Johnson	.45	.22	.04
Chicago Bulls			
☐ 15 Fred Brown	.60	.30	.06
Seattle Supersonics			
☐ 16 Jamaal Wilkes	2.00	1.00	.20
Golden State Warriors			
☐ 17 Louie Nelson	.45	.22	.04
New Orleans Jazz			
☐ 18 Ed Ratleff	.45	.22	.04
Houston Rockets			
☐ 19 Billy Paultz	.45	.22	.04
San Antonio Spurs			
☐ 20 Nate Archibald	1.75	.85	.17
Kansas City Kings			
☐ 21 Steve Mix	.45	.22	.04
Philadelphia 76ers			
☐ 22 Ralph Simpson	.45	.22	.04
Denver Nuggets			
☐ 23 Campy Russell	.60	.30	.06
Cleveland Cavaliers			
☐ 24 Charlie Scott	.60	.30	.06
Boston Celtics			
☐ 25 Artis Gilmore	1.50	.75	.15
Chicago Bulls			
☐ 26 Dick Van Arsdale	.45	.22	.04
Phoenix Suns			
☐ 27 Phil Chenier	.45	.22	.04
Washington Bullets			
☐ 28 Spencer Haywood	.75	.35	.07
New York Knicks			
☐ 29 Chris Ford	.60	.30	.06
Detroit Pistons			

30	Dave Cowens	3.50	1.75	.35
	Boston Celtics			
31	Sidney Wicks	.75	.35	.07
	Portland Trail Blazers			
32	Jim Price	.45	.22	.04
	Milwaukee Bucks			
33	Dwight Jones	.45	.22	.04
	Houston Rockets			
34	Lucius Allen	.60	.30	.06
	Los Angeles Lakers			
35	Marvin Barnes	.75	.35	.07
	Detroit Pistons			
36	Henry Bibby	.60	.30	.06
	New Orleans Jazz			
37	Joe Merriweather	1.00	.50	.10
	Atlanta Hawks			
38	Doug Collins	1.50	.75	.15
	Philadelphia 76ers			
39	Garfield Heard	.45	.22	.04
	Phoenix Suns			
40	Randy Smith	.45	.22	.04
	Buffalo Braves			
41	Tom Burleson	.45	.22	.04
	Seattle Supersonics			
42	Dave Twardzik	.60	.30	.06
	Portland Trail Blazers			
43	Bill Bradley	16.00	8.00	1.60
	New York Knicks			
44	Calvin Murphy	.75	.35	.07
	Houston Rockets			
45	Bob Love	.75	.35	.07
	Chicago Bulls			
46	Brian Winters	.60	.30	.06
	Milwaukee Bucks			
47	Glenn McDonald	.45	.22	.04
	Boston Celtics			
48	Checklist Card	6.00	.50	.10
49	Bird Averitt	.45	.22	.04
	Buffalo Braves			
50	Rick Barry	7.50	3.75	.75
	Golden State Warriors			
51	Ticky Burden	.45	.22	.04
	New York Knicks			
52	Rich Jones	.45	.22	.04
	New York Nets			
53	Austin Carr	.75	.35	.07
	Cleveland Cavaliers			
54	Steve Kuberski	.45	.22	.04
	Boston Celtics			
55	Paul Westphal	.75	.35	.07
	Phoenix Suns			
56	Mike Riordan	.45	.22	.04
	Washington Bullets			
57	Bill Walton	7.50	3.75	.75
	Portland Trail Blazers			
58	Eric Money	.45	.22	.04
	Detroit Pistons			
59	John Drew	.60	.30	.06
	Atlanta Hawks			
60	Pete Maravich	7.50	3.75	.75
	New Orleans Jazz			
61	John Shumate	1.75	.85	.17
	Buffalo Braves			
62	Mack Calvin	.60	.30	.06
	Los Angeles Lakers			
63	Bruce Seals	.45	.22	.04
	Seattle Supersonics			
64	Walt Frazier	5.00	2.50	.50
	New York Knicks			
65	Elmore Smith	.45	.22	.04
	Milwaukee Bucks			
66	Rudy Tomjanovich	.45	.22	.04
	Houston Rockets			
67	Sam Lacey	.45	.22	.04
	Kansas City Kings			
68	George Gervin	5.00	2.50	.50
	San Antonio Spurs			
69	Gus Williams	4.00	2.00	.40
	Golden State Warriors			
70	George McGinnis	1.00	.50	.10
	Philadelphia 76ers			
71	Len Elmore	.45	.22	.04
	Indiana Pacers			
72	Jack Marin	.45	.22	.04
	Chicago Bulls			
73	Brian Taylor	.60	.30	.06
	New York Nets			
74	Jim Brewer	.45	.22	.04
	Cleveland Cavaliers			
75	Alvan Adams	2.00	1.00	.20
	Phoenix Suns			
76	Dave Bing	2.00	1.00	.20
	Washington Bullets			
77	Phil Jackson	.75	.35	.07
	New York Knicks			
78	Geoff Petrie	.60	.30	.06
	Portland Trail Blazers			
79	Mike Sojourner	.45	.22	.04
	Atlanta Hawks			
80	James Silas	.45	.22	.04
	San Antonio Spurs			
81	Bob Dandridge	.60	.30	.06
	Milwaukee Bucks			
82	Ernie DiGregorio	.60	.30	.06
	Buffalo Braves			
83	Cazzie Russell	1.00	.50	.10
	Los Angeles Lakers			
84	Kevin Porter	.60	.30	.06
	Detroit Pistons			
85	Tom Boerwinkle	.45	.22	.04
	Chicago Bulls			
86	Darnell Hillman	.45	.22	.04
	Indiana Pacers			
87	Herm Gilliam	.45	.22	.04
	Seattle Supersonics			
88	Nate Williams	.45	.22	.04
	New Orleans Jazz			
89	Phil Smith	.45	.22	.04
	Golden State Warriors			
90	John Havlicek	10.00	5.00	1.00
	Boston Celtics			
91	Kevin Kunnert	.45	.22	.04
	Houston Rockets			
92	Jimmy Walker	.45	.22	.04
	Kansas City Kings			
93	Billy Cunningham	2.50	1.25	.25
	Philadelphia 76ers			
94	Dan Issel	1.50	.75	.15
	Denver Nuggets			
95	Ron Boone	.45	.22	.04
	Kansas City Kings			
96	Lou Hudson	.75	.35	.07
	Atlanta Hawks			
97	Jim Chones	.45	.22	.04
	Cleveland Cavaliers			
98	Earl Monroe	2.50	1.25	.25
	New York Knicks			
99	Tom Van Arsdale	.45	.22	.04
	Buffalo Braves			
100	Kareem Abdul Jabbar	25.00	12.50	2.50
	Los Angeles Lakers			
101	Moses Malone	21.00	10.50	2.10
	Portland Trail Blazers			
102	Ricky Sobers	.75	.35	.07
	Phoenix Suns			
103	Swen Nater	.60	.30	.06
	Milwaukee Bucks			
104	Leonard Robinson	.60	.30	.06
	Washington Bullets			
105	Don Watts	.45	.22	.04
	Seattle Supersonics			
106	Otto Moore	.45	.22	.04
	New Orleans Jazz			
107	Maurice Lucas	1.50	.75	.15
	Portland Trail Blazers			
108	Norm Van Lier	.60	.30	.06
	Chicago Bulls			
109	Clifford Ray	.45	.22	.04
	Golden State Warriors			
110	David Thompson	12.00	6.00	1.20
	Denver Nuggets			
111	Fred Carter	.45	.22	.04
	Philadelphia 76ers			
112	Caldwell Jones	.75	.35	.07
	Philadelphia 76ers			
113	John Williamson	.60	.30	.06
	New York Nets			
114	Bobby Smith	.45	.22	.04
	Cleveland Cavaliers			
115	Jo Jo White	1.00	.50	.10
	Boston Celtics			
116	Curtis Perry	.45	.22	.04
	Phoenix Suns			
117	John Gianelli	.45	.22	.04
	New York Knicks			
118	Curtis Rowe	.60	.30	.06
	Detroit Pistons			
119	Lionel Hollins	1.25	.60	.12
	Portland Trail Blazers			
120	Elvin Hayes	5.00	2.50	.50
	Washington Bullets			
121	Ken Charles	.45	.22	.04
	Atlanta Hawks			
122	Dave Meyers	2.50	1.25	.25
	Milwaukee Bucks			
123	Jerry Sloan	.60	.30	.06
	Chicago Bulls			
124	Billy Knight	.60	.30	.06
	Indiana Pacers			

		NRMT	VG-E	GOOD
□ 125	Gail Goodrich Los Angeles Lakers	1.00	.50	.10
□ 126	Kareem Ab. Jabbar AS Los Angeles Lakers	12.00	6.00	1.20
□ 127	Julius Erving AS New York Nets	12.00	6.00	1.20
□ 128	George McGinnis AS Philadelphia 76ers	.75	.35	.07
□ 129	Nate Archibald AS Kansas City Kings	1.00	.50	.10
□ 130	Pete Maravich AS New Orleans Jazz	3.50	1.75	.35
□ 131	Dave Cowens AS Boston Celtics	2.00	1.00	.20
□ 132	Rick Barry AS Golden State Warriors	3.00	1.50	.30
□ 133	Elvin Hayes AS Washington Bullets	2.00	1.00	.20
□ 134	James Silas AS San Antonio Spurs	.60	.30	.06
□ 135	Randy Smith AS Buffalo Braves	.60	.30	.06
□ 136	Leonard Gray Seattle Supersonics	.60	.30	.06
□ 137	Charles Johnson Golden State Warriors	.45	.22	.04
□ 138	Ron Behagen New Orleans Jazz	.45	.22	.04
□ 139	Mike Newlin Houston Rockets	.45	.22	.04
□ 140	Bob McAdoo Buffalo Braves	2.50	1.25	.25
□ 141	Mike Gale San Antonio Spurs	.45	.22	.04
□ 142	Scott Wedman Kansas City Kings	.60	.30	.06
□ 143	Lloyd Free Philadelphia 76ers	3.00	1.50	.30
□ 144	Bobby Jones Denver Nuggets	1.50	.75	.15

1977-78 Topps

The 1977-78 Topps basketball card set of 132 is printed on standard-sized cards, that is, the cards in the set measure the standard 2 1/2" by 3 1/2". Card backs are printed in green and black on either white or gray card stock. The white card stock is considered more desirable by most collectors and may even be a little tougher to find. The key rookie cards in this set are Adrian Dantley and Robert Parish.

		NRMT	VG-E	GOOD
COMPLETE SET (132)		105.00	45.00	9.00
COMMON PLAYER (1-132)		.18	.09	.01
□ 1	Kareem Abdul Jabbar Los Angeles Lakers	20.00	6.00	1.20
□ 2	Henry Bibby Philadelphia 76ers	.30	.15	.03
□ 3	Curtis Rowe Boston Celtics	.30	.15	.03
□ 4	Norm Van Lier Chicago Bulls	.30	.15	.03
□ 5	Darnell Hillman New Jersey Nets	.18	.09	.01

		NRMT	VG-E	GOOD
□ 6	Earl Monroe New York Knicks	2.00	1.00	.20
□ 7	Leonard Gray Washington Bullets	.18	.09	.01
□ 8	Bird Averitt Buffalo Braves	.18	.09	.01
□ 9	Jim Brewer Cleveland Cavaliers	.18	.09	.01
□ 10	Paul Westphal Phoenix Suns	.50	.25	.05
□ 11	Bob Gross Portland Trail Blazers	.40	.20	.04
□ 12	Phil Smith Golden State Warriors	.18	.09	.01
□ 13	Dan Roundfield Indiana Pacers	1.00	.50	.10
□ 14	Brian Taylor Denver Nuggets	.30	.15	.03
□ 15	Rudy Tomjanovich Houston Rockets	.18	.09	.01
□ 16	Kevin Porter Detroit Pistons	.18	.09	.01
□ 17	Scott Wedman Kansas City Kings	.30	.15	.03
□ 18	Lloyd Free Philadelphia 76ers	.60	.30	.06
□ 19	Tom Boswell Boston Celtics	.18	.09	.01
□ 20	Pete Maravich New Orleans Jazz	5.00	2.50	.50
□ 21	Cliff Poindexter Chicago Bulls	.18	.09	.01
□ 22	Bubbles Hawkins New Jersey Nets	.30	.15	.03
□ 23	Kevin Grevey Washington Bullets	.60	.30	.06
□ 24	Ken Charles Atlanta Hawks	.18	.09	.01
□ 25	Bob Dandridge Washington Bullets	.30	.15	.03
□ 26	Lonnie Shelton New York Knicks	.40	.20	.04
□ 27	Don Chaney Los Angeles Lakers	.30	.15	.03
□ 28	Larry Kenon San Antonio Spurs	.30	.15	.03
□ 29	Checklist Card	2.00	.20	.04
□ 30	Fred Brown Seattle Supersonics	.30	.15	.03
□ 31	John Gianelli Cleveland Cavaliers (Listed as Cavaliers, should be Buffalo Braves)	.18	.09	.01
□ 32	Austin Carr Cleveland Cavaliers	.30	.15	.03
□ 33	Jamaal Wilkes Los Angeles Lakers	1.00	.50	.10
□ 34	Caldwell Jones Philadelphia 76ers	.30	.15	.03
□ 35	Jo Jo White Boston Celtics	.60	.30	.06
□ 36	Scott May Chicago Bulls	1.75	.85	.17
□ 37	Mike Newlin Houston Rockets	.18	.09	.01
□ 38	Mel Davis New Jersey Nets	.18	.09	.01
□ 39	Lionel Hollins Portland Trail Blazers	.30	.15	.03
□ 40	Elvin Hayes Washington Bullets	2.50	1.25	.25
□ 41	Dan Issel Denver Nuggets	.90	.45	.09
□ 42	Ricky Sobers Phoenix Suns	.18	.09	.01
□ 43	Don Ford Los Angeles Lakers	.18	.09	.01
□ 44	John Williamson Indiana Pacers	.30	.15	.03
□ 45	Bob McAdoo New York Knicks	1.50	.75	.15
□ 46	Geoff Petrie Atlanta Hawks	.30	.15	.03
□ 47	M.L. Carr Detroit Pistons	.90	.45	.09
□ 48	Brian Winters Milwaukee Bucks	.30	.15	.03
□ 49	Sam Lacey Kansas City Kings	.18	.09	.01
□ 50	George McGinnis Philadelphia 76ers	.60	.30	.06
□ 51	Don Watts Seattle Supersonics	.18	.09	.01
□ 52	Sidney Wicks Boston Celtics	.50	.25	.05

☐ 53	Wilbur Holland .... Chicago Bulls	.18	.09	.01
☐ 54	Tim Bassett .... New Jersey Nets	.18	.09	.01
☐ 55	Phil Chenier .... Washington Bullets	.30	.15	.03
☐ 56	Adrian Dantley .... Buffalo Braves	12.50	6.25	1.25
☐ 57	Jim Chones .... Cleveland Cavaliers	.18	.09	.01
☐ 58	John Lucas .... Houston Rockets	1.50	.75	.15
☐ 59	Cazzie Russell .... Los Angeles Lakers	.40	.20	.04
☐ 60	David Thompson .... Denver Nuggets	1.75	.85	.17
☐ 61	Bob Lanier .... Detroit Pistons	1.25	.60	.12
☐ 62	Dave Twardzik .... Portland Trail Blazers	.18	.09	.01
☐ 63	Wilbert Jones .... Indiana Pacers	.18	.09	.01
☐ 64	Clifford Ray .... Golden State Warriors	.18	.09	.01
☐ 65	Doug Collins .... Philadelphia 76ers	.60	.30	.06
☐ 66	Tom McMillen .... New York Knicks	2.25	1.10	.22
☐ 67	Rich Kelley .... New Orleans Jazz	.18	.09	.01
☐ 68	Mike Bantom .... New Jersey Nets	.18	.09	.01
☐ 69	Tom Boerwinkle .... Chicago Bulls	.18	.09	.01
☐ 70	John Havlicek .... Boston Celtics	6.00	3.00	.60
☐ 71	Marvin Webster .... Seattle Supersonics	.50	.25	.05
☐ 72	Curtis Perry .... Phoenix Suns	.18	.09	.01
☐ 73	George Gervin .... San Antonio Spurs	2.75	1.35	.27
☐ 74	Leonard Robinson .... New Orleans Jazz	.30	.15	.03
☐ 75	Wes Unseld .... Washington Bullets	1.25	.60	.12
☐ 76	Dave Meyers .... Milwaukee Bucks	.60	.30	.06
☐ 77	Gail Goodrich .... New Orleans Jazz	.60	.30	.06
☐ 78	Richard Washington .... Kansas City Kings	.60	.30	.06
☐ 79	Mike Gale .... San Antonio Spurs	.18	.09	.01
☐ 80	Maurice Lucas .... Portland Trail Blazers	.90	.45	.09
☐ 81	Harvey Catchings .... Philadelphia 76ers	.18	.09	.01
☐ 82	Randy Smith .... Buffalo Braves	.18	.09	.01
☐ 83	Campy Russell .... Cleveland Cavaliers	.18	.09	.01
☐ 84	Kevin Kunnert .... Houston Rockets	.18	.09	.01
☐ 85	Lou Hudson .... Atlanta Hawks	.30	.15	.03
☐ 86	Mickey Johnson .... Chicago Bulls	.30	.15	.03
☐ 87	Lucius Allen .... Kansas City Kings	.30	.15	.03
☐ 88	Spencer Haywood .... New York Knicks	.50	.25	.05
☐ 89	Gus Williams .... Golden State Warriors	.90	.45	.09
☐ 90	Dave Cowens .... Boston Celtics	2.50	1.25	.25
☐ 91	Al Skinner .... New Jersey Nets	.18	.09	.01
☐ 92	Swen Nater .... Buffalo Braves	.30	.15	.03
☐ 93	Tom Henderson .... Washington Bullets	.18	.09	.01
☐ 94	Don Buse .... Indiana Pacers	.18	.09	.01
☐ 95	Alvan Adams .... Phoenix Suns	.60	.30	.06
☐ 96	Mack Calvin .... Denver Nuggets	.30	.15	.03
☐ 97	Tom Burleson .... Kansas City Kings	.18	.09	.01
☐ 98	John Drew .... Atlanta Hawks	.30	.15	.03
☐ 99	Mike Green .... Seattle Supersonics	.18	.09	.01
☐ 100	Julius Erving .... Philadelphia 76ers	16.00	8.00	1.60
☐ 101	John Mengelt .... Chicago Bulls	.18	.09	.01
☐ 102	Howard Porter .... Detroit Pistons	.18	.09	.01
☐ 103	Billy Paultz .... San Antonio Spurs	.18	.09	.01
☐ 104	John Shumate .... Buffalo Braves	.60	.30	.06
☐ 105	Calvin Murphy .... Houston Rockets	.60	.30	.06
☐ 106	Elmore Smith .... Cleveland Cavaliers	.18	.09	.01
☐ 107	Jim McMillian .... New York Knicks	.18	.09	.01
☐ 108	Kevin Stacom .... Boston Celtics	.18	.09	.01
☐ 109	Jan Van Breda Kolff .... New Jersey Nets	.18	.09	.01
☐ 110	Billy Knight .... Indiana Pacers	.18	.09	.01
☐ 111	Robert Parish .... Golden State Warriors	35.00	17.50	3.50
☐ 112	Larry Wright .... Washington Bullets	.18	.09	.01
☐ 113	Bruce Seals .... Seattle Supersonics	.18	.09	.01
☐ 114	Junior Bridgeman .... Milwaukee Bucks	.30	.15	.03
☐ 115	Artis Gilmore .... Chicago Bulls	1.25	.60	.12
☐ 116	Steve Mix .... Philadelphia 76ers	.18	.09	.01
☐ 117	Ron Lee .... Phoenix Suns	.18	.09	.01
☐ 118	Bobby Jones .... Denver Nuggets	.60	.30	.06
☐ 119	Ron Boone .... Kansas City Kings	.18	.09	.01
☐ 120	Bill Walton .... Portland Trail Blazers	5.00	2.50	.50
☐ 121	Chris Ford .... Detroit Pistons	.35	.17	.03
☐ 122	Earl Tatum .... Los Angeles Lakers	.18	.09	.01
☐ 123	E.C. Coleman .... New Orleans Jazz	.18	.09	.01
☐ 124	Moses Malone .... Houston Rockets	7.50	3.75	.75
☐ 125	Charlie Scott .... Boston Celtics	.30	.15	.03
☐ 126	Bobby Smith .... Cleveland Cavaliers	.18	.09	.01
☐ 127	Nate Archibald .... New Jersey Nets	.90	.45	.09
☐ 128	Mitch Kupchak .... Washington Bullets	1.25	.60	.12
☐ 129	Walt Frazier .... New York Knicks	3.00	1.50	.30
☐ 130	Rick Barry .... Golden State Warriors	4.50	2.25	.45
☐ 131	Ernie DiGregorio .... Buffalo Braves	.30	.15	.03
☐ 132	Darryl Dawkins .... Philadelphia 76ers	3.00	1.00	.20

1978-79 Topps

The 1978-79 Topps basketball card set contains 132 cards. The cards in the set measure the standard 2 1/2" by 3 1/2". Card backs are printed in orange and brown on gray card stock. The key rookie cards in this set are Walter Davis, Dennis Johnson, Marques Johnson, Bernard King, and Jack Sikma.

		NRMT	VG-E	GOOD
	COMPLETE SET (132)	95.00	40.00	8.00
	COMMON PLAYER (1-132)	.15	.07	.01
☐ 1	Bill Walton .... Portland Trail Blazers	9.00	2.00	.40
☐ 2	Doug Collins .... Philadelphia 76ers	.40	.20	.04
☐ 3	Jamaal Wilkes .... Los Angeles Lakers	.65	.30	.06
☐ 4	Wilbur Holland .... Chicago Bulls	.15	.07	.01

☐ 5 Bob McAdoo	.90	.45	.09
New York Knicks			
☐ 6 Lucius Allen	.30	.15	.03
Kansas City Kings			
☐ 7 Wes Unseld	1.00	.50	.10
Washington Bullets			
☐ 8 Dave Meyers	.30	.15	.03
Milwaukee Bucks			
☐ 9 Austin Carr	.30	.15	.03
Cleveland Cavaliers			
☐ 10 Walter Davis	6.50	3.25	.65
Phoenix Suns			
☐ 11 John Williamson	.30	.15	.03
New Jersey Nets			
☐ 12 E.C. Coleman	.15	.07	.01
Golden State Warriors			
☐ 13 Calvin Murphy	.40	.20	.04
Houston Rockets			
☐ 14 Bobby Jones	.40	.20	.04
Denver Nuggets			
☐ 15 Chris Ford	.30	.15	.03
Detroit Pistons			
☐ 16 Kermit Washington	.40	.20	.04
Boston Celtics			
☐ 17 Butch Beard	.15	.07	.01
New York Knicks			
☐ 18 Steve Mix	.15	.07	.01
Philadelphia 76ers			
☐ 19 Marvin Webster	.15	.07	.01
Seattle Supersonics			
☐ 20 George Gervin	2.50	1.25	.25
San Antonio Spurs			
☐ 21 Steve Hawes	.15	.07	.01
Atlanta Hawks			
☐ 22 Johnny Davis	.15	.07	.01
Portland Trail Blazers			
☐ 23 Swen Nater	.30	.15	.03
San Diego Clippers			
☐ 24 Lou Hudson	.30	.15	.03
Los Angeles Lakers			
☐ 25 Elvin Hayes	2.50	1.25	.25
Washington Bullets			
☐ 26 Nate Archibald	.65	.30	.06
San Diego Clippers			
☐ 27 James Edwards	2.25	1.10	.22
Indiana Pacers			
☐ 28 Howard Porter	.15	.07	.01
New Jersey Nets			
☐ 29 Quinn Buckner	1.50	.75	.15
Milwaukee Bucks			
☐ 30 Leonard Robinson	.30	.15	.03
New Orleans Jazz			
☐ 31 Jim Cleamons	.15	.07	.01
New York Knicks			
☐ 32 Campy Russell	.15	.07	.01
Cleveland Cavaliers			
☐ 33 Phil Smith	.15	.07	.01
Golden State Warriors			
☐ 34 Darryl Dawkins	.90	.45	.09
Philadelphia 76ers			
☐ 35 Don Buse	.15	.07	.01
Phoenix Suns			
☐ 36 Mickey Johnson	.15	.07	.01
Chicago Bulls			
☐ 37 Mike Gale	.15	.07	.01
San Antonio Spurs			
☐ 38 Moses Malone	5.00	2.50	.50
Houston Rockets			
☐ 39 Gus Williams	.60	.30	.06
Seattle Supersonics			
☐ 40 Dave Cowens	2.00	1.00	.20
Boston Celtics			
☐ 41 Bobby Wilkerson	.40	.20	.04
Denver Nuggets			
☐ 42 Wilbert Jones	.15	.07	.01
San Diego Clippers			
☐ 43 Charlie Scott	.30	.15	.03
Los Angeles Lakers			
☐ 44 John Drew	.30	.15	.03
Atlanta Hawks			
☐ 45 Earl Monroe	1.75	.85	.17
New York Knicks			
☐ 46 John Shumate	.30	.15	.03
Detroit Pistons			
☐ 47 Earl Tatum	.15	.07	.01
Indiana Pacers			
☐ 48 Mitch Kupchak	.30	.15	.03
Washington Bullets			
☐ 49 Ron Boone	.15	.07	.01
Kansas City Kings			
☐ 50 Maurice Lucas	.60	.30	.06
Portland Trail Blazers			
☐ 51 Louie Dampier	.30	.15	.03
San Antonio Spurs			
☐ 52 Aaron James	.15	.07	.01
New Orleans Jazz			
☐ 53 John Mengelt	.15	.07	.01
Chicago Bulls			
☐ 54 Garfield Heard	.15	.07	.01
Phoenix Suns			
☐ 55 George Johnson	.15	.07	.01
New Jersey Nets			
☐ 56 Junior Bridgeman	.30	.15	.03
Milwaukee Bucks			
☐ 57 Elmore Smith	.15	.07	.01
Cleveland Cavaliers			
☐ 58 Rudy Tomjanovich	.15	.07	.01
Houston Rockets			
☐ 59 Fred Brown	.30	.15	.03
Seattle Supersonics			
☐ 60 Rick Barry UER	3.50	1.75	.35
Golden State Warriors			
(reversed negative)			
☐ 61 Dave Bing	.90	.45	.09
Boston Celtics			
☐ 62 Anthony Roberts	.15	.07	.01
Denver Nuggets			
☐ 63 Norm Nixon	2.50	1.25	.25
Los Angeles Lakers			
☐ 64 Leon Douglas	.15	.07	.01
Detroit Pistons			
☐ 65 Henry Bibby	.30	.15	.03
Philadelphia 76ers			
☐ 66 Lonnie Shelton	.30	.15	.03
New York Knicks			
☐ 67 Checklist Card	1.75	.15	.03
☐ 68 Tom Henderson	.15	.07	.01
Washington Bullets			
☐ 69 Dan Roundfield	.30	.15	.03
Indiana Pacers			
☐ 70 Armond Hill	.15	.07	.01
Atlanta Hawks			
☐ 71 Larry Kenon	.30	.15	.03
San Antonio Spurs			
☐ 72 Billy Knight	.15	.07	.01
San Diego Clippers			
☐ 73 Artis Gilmore	.90	.45	.09
Chicago Bulls			
☐ 74 Lionel Hollins	.30	.15	.03
Portland Trail Blazers			
☐ 75 Bernard King	25.00	12.50	2.50
New Jersey Nets			
☐ 76 Brian Winters	.30	.15	.03
Milwaukee Bucks			
☐ 77 Alvan Adams	.30	.15	.03
Phoenix Suns			
☐ 78 Dennis Johnson	6.50	3.25	.65
Seattle Supersonics			
☐ 79 Scott Wedman	.30	.15	.03
Kansas City Kings			
☐ 80 Pete Maravich	3.75	1.85	.37
New Orleans Jazz			
☐ 81 Dan Issel	.65	.30	.06
Denver Nuggets			
☐ 82 M.L. Carr	.30	.15	.03
Detroit Pistons			
☐ 83 Walt Frazier	2.50	1.25	.25
Cleveland Cavaliers			
☐ 84 Dwight Jones	.15	.07	.01
Houston Rockets			
☐ 85 Jo Jo White	.50	.25	.05
Boston Celtics			
☐ 86 Robert Parish	7.00	3.50	.70
Golden State Warriors			
☐ 87 Charlie Criss	.40	.20	.04
Atlanta Hawks			

☐ 88	Jim McMillian	.15	.07	.01
	New York Knicks			
☐ 89	Chuck Williams	.15	.07	.01
	San Diego Clippers			
☐ 90	George McGinnis	.40	.20	.04
	Philadelphia 76ers			
☐ 91	Billy Paultz	.15	.07	.01
	San Antonio Spurs			
☐ 92	Bob Dandridge	.30	.15	.03
	Washington Bullets			
☐ 93	Ricky Sobers	.30	.15	.03
	Indiana Pacers			
☐ 94	Paul Silas	.30	.15	.03
	Seattle Supersonics			
☐ 95	Gail Goodrich	.40	.20	.04
	New Orleans Jazz			
☐ 96	Tim Bassett	.15	.07	.01
	New Jersey Nets			
☐ 97	Ron Lee	.15	.07	.01
	Phoenix Suns			
☐ 98	Bob Gross	.15	.07	.01
	Portland Trail Blazers			
☐ 99	Sam Lacey	.15	.07	.01
	Kansas City Kings			
☐ 100	David Thompson	1.50	.75	.15
	Denver Nuggets			
	(College North Carolina, should be NC State)			
☐ 101	John Gianelli	.15	.07	.01
	Milwaukee Bucks			
☐ 102	Norm Van Lier	.30	.15	.03
	Chicago Bulls			
☐ 103	Caldwell Jones	.30	.15	.03
	Philadelphia 76ers			
☐ 104	Eric Money	.15	.07	.01
	Detroit Pistons			
☐ 105	Jim Chones	.15	.07	.01
	Cleveland Cavaliers			
☐ 106	John Lucas	.40	.20	.04
	Houston Rockets			
☐ 107	Spencer Haywood	.40	.20	.04
	New York Knicks			
☐ 108	Eddie Johnson	.50	.25	.05
	Atlanta Hawks			
☐ 109	Sidney Wicks	.40	.20	.04
	Boston Celtics			
☐ 110	Kareem Abdul Jabbar	16.00	8.00	1.60
	Los Angeles Lakers			
☐ 111	Sonny Parker	.15	.07	.01
	Golden State Warriors			
☐ 112	Randy Smith	.30	.15	.03
	San Diego Clippers			
☐ 113	Kevin Grevey	.30	.15	.03
	Washington Bullets			
☐ 114	Rich Kelley	.15	.07	.01
	New Orleans Jazz			
☐ 115	Scott May	.30	.15	.03
	Chicago Bulls			
☐ 116	Lloyd Free	.30	.15	.03
	Philadelphia 76ers			
☐ 117	Jack Sikma	6.50	3.25	.65
	Seattle Supersonics			
☐ 118	Kevin Porter	.30	.15	.03
	New Jersey Nets			
☐ 119	Darnell Hillman	.15	.07	.01
	Denver Nuggets			
☐ 120	Paul Westphal	.40	.20	.04
	Phoenix Suns			
☐ 121	Richard Washington	.30	.15	.03
	Kansas City Kings			
☐ 122	Dave Twardzik	.15	.07	.01
	Portland Trail Blazers			
☐ 123	Mike Bantom	.15	.07	.01
	Indiana Pacers			
☐ 124	Mike Newlin	.15	.07	.01
	Houston Rockets			
☐ 125	Bob Lanier	.90	.45	.09
	Detroit Pistons			
☐ 126	Marques Johnson	4.50	2.25	.45
	Milwaukee Bucks			
☐ 127	Foots Walker	.40	.20	.04
	Cleveland Cavaliers			
☐ 128	Cedric Maxwell	2.00	1.00	.20
	Boston Celtics			
☐ 129	Ray Williams	.75	.35	.07
	New York Knicks			
☐ 130	Julius Erving	14.00	7.00	1.40
	Philadelphia 76ers			
☐ 131	Clifford Ray	.15	.07	.01
	Golden State Warriors			
☐ 132	Adrian Dantley	2.75	1.35	.27
	Los Angeles Lakers			

1979-80 Topps

The 1979-80 Topps basketball card set contains 132 cards of NBA players. All-Star selections are designated as AS1 for first team selections and AS2 for second team selections and are denoted on the front of the player's regular card. Past U.S Olympic basketball team members are indicated in the checklist below by having the year of their participation followed by an "O" to signify that the player was an Olympic team member. The cards in the set measure the standard 2 1/2" by 3 1/2". Card backs are printed in red and black on gray card stock. Notable rookie cards in this set include Alex English and Reggie Theus.

		MINT	EXC	G-VG
COMPLETE SET (132)		70.00	35.00	7.00
COMMON PLAYER (1-132)		.12	.06	.01
☐ 1	George Gervin	2.75	.75	.15
	San Antonio Spurs			
☐ 2	Mitch Kupchak	.25	.12	.02
	Washington Bullets			
☐ 3	Henry Bibby	.25	.12	.02
	Philadelphia 76ers			
☐ 4	Bob Gross	.12	.06	.01
	Portland Trail Blazers			
☐ 5	Dave Cowens	1.50	.75	.15
	Boston Celtics			
☐ 6	Dennis Johnson	1.50	.75	.15
	Seattle Supersonics			
☐ 7	Scott Wedman	.25	.12	.02
	Kansas City Kings			
☐ 8	Earl Monroe	1.00	.50	.10
	New York Knicks			
☐ 9	Mike Bantom 720	.12	.06	.01
	Indiana Pacers			
☐ 10	Kareem Ab. Jabbar AS	14.00	7.00	1.40
	Los Angeles Lakers			
☐ 11	Jo Jo White 680	.40	.20	.04
	Golden State Warriors			
☐ 12	Spencer Haywood	.30	.15	.03
	Utah Jazz			
☐ 13	Kevin Porter	.25	.12	.02
	Detroit Pistons			
☐ 14	Bernard King	5.50	2.75	.55
	New Jersey Nets			
☐ 15	Mike Newlin	.12	.06	.01
	Houston Rockets			
☐ 16	Sidney Wicks	.40	.20	.04
	San Diego Clippers			
☐ 17	Dan Issel	.65	.30	.06
	Denver Nuggets			
☐ 18	Tom Henderson 720	.12	.06	.01
	Washington Bullets			
☐ 19	Jim Chones	.12	.06	.01
	Cleveland Cavaliers			
☐ 20	Julius Erving	12.50	6.25	1.25
	Philadelphia 76ers			
☐ 21	Brian Winters	.12	.06	.01
	Milwaukee Bucks			
☐ 22	Billy Paultz	.12	.06	.01
	San Antonio Spurs			
☐ 23	Cedric Maxwell	.40	.20	.04
	Boston Celtics			
☐ 24	Eddie Johnson	.12	.06	.01
	Atlanta Hawks			
☐ 25	Artis Gilmore	.75	.35	.07
	Chicago Bulls			

☐ 26	Maurice Lucas	.40	.20	.04
	Portland Trail Blazers			
☐ 27	Gus Williams	.50	.25	.05
	Seattle Supersonics			
☐ 28	Sam Lacey	.12	.06	.01
	Kansas City Kings			
☐ 29	Toby Knight	.12	.06	.01
	New York Knicks			
☐ 30	Paul Westphal AS1	.30	.15	.03
	Phoenix Suns			
☐ 31	Alex English	14.00	7.00	1.40
	Indiana Pacers			
☐ 32	Gail Goodrich	.40	.20	.04
	Utah Jazz			
☐ 33	Caldwell Jones	.25	.12	.02
	Philadelphia 76ers			
☐ 34	Kevin Grevey	.12	.06	.01
	Washington Bullets			
☐ 35	Jamaal Wilkes	.50	.25	.05
	Los Angeles Lakers			
☐ 36	Sonny Parker	.12	.06	.01
	Golden State Warriors			
☐ 37	John Gianelli	.12	.06	.01
	New Jersey Nets			
☐ 38	John Long	.75	.35	.07
	Detroit Pistons			
☐ 39	George Johnson	.12	.06	.01
	New Jersey Nets			
☐ 40	Lloyd Free AS2	.25	.12	.02
	San Diego Clippers			
☐ 41	Rudy Tomjanovich	.12	.06	.01
	Houston Rockets			
☐ 42	Foots Walker	.12	.06	.01
	Cleveland Cavaliers			
☐ 43	Dan Roundfield	.25	.12	.02
	Atlanta Hawks			
☐ 44	Reggie Theus	4.50	2.25	.45
	Chicago Bulls			
☐ 45	Bill Walton	3.00	1.50	.30
	San Diego Clippers			
☐ 46	Fred Brown	.25	.12	.02
	Seattle Supersonics			
☐ 47	Darnell Hillman	.12	.06	.01
	Kansas City Kings			
☐ 48	Ray Williams	.25	.12	.02
	New York Knicks			
☐ 49	Larry Kenon	.25	.12	.02
	San Antonio Spurs			
☐ 50	David Thompson	1.25	.60	.12
	Denver Nuggets			
☐ 51	Billy Knight	.12	.06	.01
	Indiana Pacers			
☐ 52	Alvan Adams	.25	.12	.02
	Phoenix Suns			
☐ 53	Phil Smith	.12	.06	.01
	Golden State Warriors			
☐ 54	Adrian Dantley 760	1.50	.75	.15
	Los Angeles Lakers			
☐ 55	John Williamson	.25	.12	.02
	New Jersey Nets			
☐ 56	Campy Russell	.12	.06	.01
	Cleveland Cavaliers			
☐ 57	Armond Hill	.12	.06	.01
	Atlanta Hawks			
☐ 58	Bob Lanier	.75	.35	.07
	Detroit Pistons			
☐ 59	Mickey Johnson	.12	.06	.01
	Chicago Bulls			
☐ 60	Pete Maravich	3.25	1.60	.32
	Utah Jazz			
☐ 61	Nick Weatherspoon	.12	.06	.01
	San Diego Clippers			
☐ 62	Robert Reid	.90	.45	.09
	Houston Rockets			
☐ 63	Mychal Thompson	3.25	1.60	.32
	Portland Trail Blazers			
☐ 64	Doug Collins 720	.30	.15	.03
	Philadelphia 76ers			
☐ 65	Wes Unseld	1.00	.50	.10
	Washington Bullets			
☐ 66	Jack Sikma	1.50	.75	.15
	Seattle Supersonics			
☐ 67	Bobby Wilkerson	.12	.06	.01
	Denver Nuggets			
☐ 68	Bill Robinzine	.12	.06	.01
	Kansas City Kings			
☐ 69	Joe Meriweather	.12	.06	.01
	New York Knicks			
☐ 70	Marques Johnson AS1	1.00	.50	.10
	Milwaukee Bucks			
☐ 71	Ricky Sobers	.12	.06	.01
	Indiana Pacers			
☐ 72	Clifford Ray	.12	.06	.01
	Golden State Warriors			
☐ 73	Tim Bassett	.12	.06	.01
	New Jersey Nets			
☐ 74	James Silas	.12	.06	.01
	San Antonio Spurs			
☐ 75	Bob McAdoo	.75	.35	.07
	Boston Celtics			
☐ 76	Austin Carr	.25	.12	.02
	Cleveland Cavaliers			
☐ 77	Don Ford	.12	.06	.01
	Los Angeles Lakers			
☐ 78	Steve Hawes	.12	.06	.01
	Atlanta Hawks			
☐ 79	Ron Brewer	.35	.17	.03
	Portland Trail Blazers			
☐ 80	Walter Davis	1.50	.75	.15
	Phoenix Suns			
☐ 81	Calvin Murphy	.40	.20	.04
	Houston Rockets			
☐ 82	Tom Boswell	.12	.06	.01
	Denver Nuggets			
☐ 83	Lonnie Shelton	.12	.06	.01
	Seattle Supersonics			
☐ 84	Terry Tyler	.30	.15	.03
	Detroit Pistons			
☐ 85	Randy Smith	.12	.06	.01
	San Diego Clippers			
☐ 86	Rich Kelley	.12	.06	.01
	Utah Jazz			
☐ 87	Otis Birdsong	.60	.30	.06
	Kansas City Kings			
☐ 88	Marvin Webster	.25	.12	.02
	New York Knicks			
☐ 89	Eric Money	.12	.06	.01
	Philadelphia 76ers			
☐ 90	Elvin Hayes AS1	1.75	.85	.17
	Washington Bullets			
☐ 91	Junior Bridgeman	.25	.12	.02
	Milwaukee Bucks			
☐ 92	Johnny Davis	.12	.06	.01
	Indiana Pacers			
☐ 93	Robert Parish	3.75	1.85	.37
	Golden State Warriors			
☐ 94	Eddie Jordan	.12	.06	.01
	New Jersey Nets			
☐ 95	Leonard Robinson	.25	.12	.02
	Phoenix Suns			
☐ 96	Rick Robey	.35	.17	.03
	Boston Celtics			
☐ 97	Norm Nixon	.40	.20	.04
	Los Angeles Lakers			
☐ 98	Mark Olberding	.12	.06	.01
	San Antonio Spurs			
☐ 99	Wilbur Holland	.12	.06	.01
	Utah Jazz			
☐ 100	Moses Malone AS1	4.00	2.00	.40
	Houston Rockets			
☐ 101	Checklist Card	1.50	.10	.02
☐ 102	Tom Owens	.12	.06	.01
	Portland Trail Blazers			
☐ 103	Phil Chenier	.12	.06	.01
	Washington Bullets			
☐ 104	John Johnson	.25	.12	.02
	Seattle Supersonics			
☐ 105	Darryl Dawkins	.50	.25	.05
	Philadelphia 76ers			
☐ 106	Charlie Scott 680	.25	.12	.02
	Denver Nuggets			
☐ 107	M.L. Carr	.25	.12	.02
	Detroit Pistons			
☐ 108	Phil Ford 760	1.50	.75	.15
	Kansas City Kings			
☐ 109	Swen Nater	.25	.12	.02
	San Diego Clippers			
☐ 110	Nate Archibald	.65	.30	.06
	Boston Celtics			
☐ 111	Aaron James	.12	.06	.01
	Utah Jazz			
☐ 112	Jim Cleamons	.12	.06	.01
	New York Knicks			
☐ 113	James Edwards	.60	.30	.06
	Indiana Pacers			
☐ 114	Don Buse	.12	.06	.01
	Phoenix Suns			
☐ 115	Steve Mix	.12	.06	.01
	Philadelphia 76ers			
☐ 116	Charles Johnson	.12	.06	.01
	Washington Bullets			
☐ 117	Elmore Smith	.12	.06	.01
	Cleveland Cavaliers			
☐ 118	John Drew	.25	.12	.02
	Atlanta Hawks			
☐ 119	Lou Hudson	.25	.12	.02
	Los Angeles Lakers			
☐ 120	Rick Barry	3.25	1.60	.32
	Houston Rockets			

☐ 121	Kent Benson .... Milwaukee Bucks	.50	.25	.05
☐ 122	Mike Gale .... San Antonio Spurs	.12	.06	.01
☐ 123	Jan Van Breda Kolff .... New Jersey Nets	.12	.06	.01
☐ 124	Chris Ford .... Boston Celtics	.30	.15	.03
☐ 125	George McGinnis .... Denver Nuggets	.40	.20	.04
☐ 126	Leon Douglas .... Detroit Pistons	.12	.06	.01
☐ 127	John Lucas .... Golden State Warriors	.25	.12	.02
☐ 128	Kermit Washington .... San Diego Clippers	.12	.06	.01
☐ 129	Lionel Hollins .... Portland Trail Blazers	.25	.12	.02
☐ 130	Bob Dandridge AS2 .... Washington Bullets	.25	.12	.02
☐ 131	James McElroy .... Utah Jazz	.12	.06	.01
☐ 132	Bobby Jones 720 .... Philadelphia 76ers	.30	.15	.03

1980-81 Topps

The 1980-81 Topps basketball card set contains 264 different individual players (1 1/6" by 2 1/2") on 176 different panels of three (2 1/2" by 3 1/2"). The cards come with three individual players per standard card. A perforation line segments each card into three players. In all, there are 176 different complete cards; however, the same player will be on more than one card. The variations stem from the fact that the cards in this set were printed on two separate sheets. In the checklist below, the first 88 cards comprise a complete set of all 264 players. The second 88 cards (89-176) provide a slight rearrangement of players within the card, but still contain the same 264 players. The cards are numbered within each series of 88 by any ordering of the left-hand player's number when the card is viewed from the back. In the checklist below, SD refers to a "Slam Dunk" star card. The letters AS in the checklist refer to an All-Star selection pictured on the front of the checklist card. Prices given below are for complete panels, as that is the typical way these cards are collected; cards which have been separated into the three parts are relatively valueless. There are a number of team leader (TL) cards which depict the team's leader in assists scoring or rebounds. The key card in this set is the combination of Larry Bird, Julius Erving, and Magic Johnson which features together both rookie type cards of Bird and Johnson. Since this confusing set was issued in three-player panels, there are no single-player rookie cards as the other basketball have. However the following players made their first card appearance in this set: James Bailey, Greg Ballard, Larry Bird, Dudley Bradley, Mike Bratz, Joe Bryant, Kenny Carr, Bill Cartwright, Maurice Cheeks, Michael Cooper, Wayne Cooper, David Greenwood, Phil Hubbard, Geoff Huston, Abdul Jeelani, Magic Johnson, Reggie King, Tom

LaGarde, Mark Landsberger, Allen Leavell, Sidney Moncrief, Calvin Natt, Roger Phegley, Ben Poquette, Micheal Ray Richardson, Cliff Robinson, Purvis Short, Jerome Whitehead, and Freeman Williams.

		MINT	EXC	G-VG
COMPLETE SET (1-176)		400.00	200.00	40.00
COMMON PANEL		.15	.07	.01
☐ 1	3 Dan Roundfield AS .... 181 Julius Erving 258 Ron Brewer SD	4.50	2.25	.45
☐ 2	7 Moses Malone AS .... 185 Steve Mix 92 Robert Parish TL	.90	.45	.09
☐ 3	12 Gus Williams AS .... 67 Geoff Huston 5 John Drew AS	.15	.07	.01
☐ 4	24 Steve Hawes .... 32 Nate Archibald TL 248 Elvin Hayes	.50	.25	.05
☐ 5	29 Dan Roundfield .... 73 Dan Issel TL 152 Brian Winters	.15	.07	.01
☐ 6	34 Larry Bird .... 174 Julius Erving TL 139 Magic Johnson	250.00	125.00	25.00
☐ 7	36 Dave Cowens .... 186 Paul Westphal TL 142 Jamaal Wilkes	.40	.20	.04
☐ 8	38 Pete Maravich .... 264 Lloyd Free SD 194 Dennis Johnson	.90	.45	.09
☐ 9	40 Rick Robey .... 234 Ad.Dantley TL 26 Eddie Johnson	.25	.12	.02
☐ 10	47 Scott May .... 196 K.Washington TL 177 Henry Bibby	.15	.07	.01
☐ 11	55 Don Ford .... 145 Quinn Buckner TL 138 Brad Holland	.15	.07	.01
☐ 12	58 Campy Russell .... 247 Kevin Grevey 52 Dave Robisch TL	.15	.07	.01
☐ 13	60 Foots Walker .... 113 Mick.Johnson TL 130 Bill Robinzine	.15	.07	.01
☐ 14	61 Austin Carr .... 8 Kareem A.Jabbar AS 200 Calvin Natt	2.25	1.10	.22
☐ 15	63 Jim Cleamons .... 256 Robert Reid SD 22 Charlie Criss	.15	.07	.01
☐ 16	69 Tom LaGarde .... 215 Swen Nater TL 213 James Silas	.15	.07	.01
☐ 17	71 Jerome Whitehead .... 259 Artis Gilmore SD 184 Caldwell Jones	.20	.10	.02
☐ 18	74 John Roche TL .... 99 Clifford Ray 235 Ben Poquette TL	.15	.07	.01
☐ 19	75 Alex English .... 2 Marques Johnson AS 68 Jeff Judkins	1.50	.75	.15
☐ 20	82 Terry Tyler TL .... 21 Armond Hill TL 171 M.R. Richardson	.15	.07	.01
☐ 21	84 Kent Benson .... 212 John Shumate 229 Paul Westphal	.15	.07	.01
☐ 22	86 Phil Hubbard .... 93 Robert Parish TL 126 Tom Burleson	.50	.25	.05
☐ 23	88 John Long .... 1 Julius Erving AS 49 Ricky Sobers	1.75	.85	.17
☐ 24	90 Eric Money .... 57 Dave Robisch 254 Rick Robey SD	.15	.07	.01
☐ 25	95 Wayne Cooper .... 226 John Johnson TL 45 David Greenwood	.15	.07	.01
☐ 26	97 Robert Parish .... 187 Leon.Robinson TL 46 Dwight Jones	1.50	.75	.15
☐ 27	98 Sonny Parker .... 197 Dave Twardzik TL 39 Cedric Maxwell	.20	.10	.02
☐ 28	105 Rick Barry .... 122 Otis Birdsong TL 48 John Mengelt	.65	.30	.06

☐ 29 106 Allen Leavell .15 .07 .01
   53 Foots Walker TL
   223 Freeman Williams

☐ 30 108 Calvin Murphy .90 .45 .09
   176 Maur.Cheeks TL
   87 Greg Kelser

☐ 31 110 Robert Reid .40 .20 .04
   243 Wes Unseld TL
   50 Reggie Theus

☐ 32 111 Rudy Tomjanovich .15 .07 .01
   13 Eddie Johnson AS
   179 Doug Collins

☐ 33 112 Mickey Johnson TL .35 .17 .03
   28 Wayne Rollins
   15 M.R.Richardson AS

☐ 34 115 Mike Bantom .25 .12 .02
   6 Adrian Dantley AS
   227 James Bailey

☐ 35 116 Dudley Bradley .15 .07 .01
   155 Eddie Jordan TL
   239 Allan Bristow

☐ 36 118 James Edwards .15 .07 .01
   153 Mike Newlin TL
   182 Lionel Hollins

☐ 37 119 Mickey Johnson .15 .07 .01
   154 Geo.Johnson TL
   193 Leonard Robinson

☐ 38 120 Billy Knight .15 .07 .01
   16 Paul Westphal AS
   59 Randy Smith

☐ 39 121 George McGinnis .15 .07 .01
   83 Eric Money TL
   65 Mike Bratz

☐ 40 124 Phil Ford TL .15 .07 .01
   101 Phil Smith
   224 Gus Williams TL

☐ 41 127 Phil Ford .15 .07 .01
   19 John Drew TL
   209 Larry Kenon

☐ 42 131 Scott Wedman .15 .07 .01
   164 B.Cartwright TL
   23 John Drew

☐ 43 132 Kar.A.Jabbar TL 2.00 1.00 .20
   56 Mike Mitchell
   81 Terry Tyler TL

☐ 44 135 Kareem A.Jabbar 5.00 2.50 .50
   79 David Thompson
   216 Brian Taylor TL

☐ 45 137 Michael Cooper 2.00 1.00 .20
   103 Moses Malone TL
   148 George Johnson

☐ 46 140 Mark Landsberger .65 .30 .06
   10 Bob Lanier AS
   222 Bill Walton

☐ 47 141 Norm Nixon .15 .07 .01
   123 Sam Lacey TL
   54 Kenny Carr

☐ 48 143 Marq.Johnson TL 20.00 10.00 2.00
   30 Larry Bird TL
   232 Jack Sikma

☐ 49 146 Junior Bridgeman 20.00 10.00 2.00
   31 Larry Bird TL
   198 Ron Brewer

☐ 50 147 Quinn Buckner 2.00 1.00 .20
   133 Kar.Ab.Jabbar TL
   207 Mike Gale

☐ 51 149 Marques Johnson 1.75 .85 .17
   262 Julius Erving SD
   62 Abdul Jeelani

☐ 52 151 Sidney Moncrief 2.25 1.10 .22
   260 Lon.Shelton SD
   220 Paul Silas

☐ 53 156 George Johnson .15 .07 .01
   9 Bill Cartwright AS
   199 Bob Gross

☐ 54 158 Maurice Lucas .15 .07 .01
   261 James Edwards SD
   157 Eddie Jordan

☐ 55 159 Mike Newlin .15 .07 .01
   134 Norm Nixon TL
   180 Darryl Dawkins

☐ 56 160 Roger Phegley .15 .07 .01
   206 James Silas TL
   91 Terry Tyler

☐ 57 161 Cliff Robinson .15 .07 .01
   51 Mike Mitchell TL
   80 Bobby Wilkerson

☐ 58 162 Jan V.Breda Kolff .25 .12 .02
   204 George Gervin TL
   117 Johnny Davis

☐ 59 165 M.R.Richardson TL .25 .12 .02
   214 Lloyd Free TL
   44 Artis Gilmore

☐ 60 166 Bill Cartwright 2.25 1.10 .22
   244 Kevin Porter TL
   25 Armond Hill

☐ 61 168 Toby Knight .40 .20 .04
   14 Lloyd Free AS
   240 Adrian Dantley

☐ 62 169 Joe Meriweather .15 .07 .01
   218 Lloyd Free
   42 D.Greenwood TL

☐ 63 170 Earl Monroe .35 .17 .03
   27 James McElroy
   85 Leon Douglas

☐ 64 172 Marvin Webster .15 .07 .01
   175 Caldw.Jones TL
   129 Sam Lacey

☐ 65 173 Ray Williams .15 .07 .01
   94 John Lucas TL
   202 Dave Twardzik

☐ 66 178 Maurice Cheeks 25.00 12.50 2.50
   18 Magic Johnson AS
   237 Ron Boone

☐ 67 183 Bobby Jones .15 .07 .01
   37 Chris Ford
   66 Joe Hassett

☐ 68 189 Alvan Adams .25 .12 .02
   163 B.Cartwright TL
   76 Dan Issel

☐ 69 190 Don Buse .25 .12 .02
   242 Elvin Hayes TL
   35 M.L. Carr

☐ 70 191 Walter Davis .35 .17 .03
   11 George Gervin AS
   136 Jim Chones

☐ 71 192 Rich Kelley .35 .17 .03
   102 Moses Malone TL
   64 Winford Boynes

☐ 72 201 Tom Owens .40 .20 .04
   225 Jack Sikma TL
   100 Purvis Short

☐ 73 208 George Gervin .50 .25 .05
   72 Dan Issel TL
   249 Mitch Kupchak

☐ 74 217 Joe Bryant 1.25 .60 .12
   263 Bobby Jones SD
   107 Moses Malone

☐ 75 219 Swen Nater .15 .07 .01
   17 Calvin Murphy AS
   70 Rich.Washington

☐ 76 221 Brian Taylor .15 .07 .01
   253 John Shumate SD
   167 Larry Demic

☐ 77 228 Fred Brown .15 .07 .01
   205 Larry Kenon TL
   203 Kerm.Washington

☐ 78 230 John Johnson .25 .12 .02
   4 Walter Davis AS
   33 Nate Archibald

☐ 79 231 Lonnie Shelton .15 .07 .01
   104 Allen Leavell TL
   96 John Lucas

☐ 80 233 Gus Williams .15 .07 .01
   20 Dan Roundfield TL
   211 Kevin Restani

☐ 81 236 Allan Bristow TL .15 .07 .01
   210 Mark Olberding
   255 James Bailey SD

☐ 82 238 Tom Boswell .25 .12 .02
   109 Billy Paultz
   150 Bob Lanier

☐ 83 241 Ben Poquette .15 .07 .01
   188 Paul Westphal TL
   77 Charlie Scott

☐ 84 245 Greg Ballard .15 .07 .01
   43 Reggie Theus TL
   252 John Williamson

☐ 85 246 Bob Dandridge .15 .07 .01
   41 Reggie Theus TL
   128 Reggie King

☐ 86 250 Kevin Porter .15 .07 .01
   114 Johnny Davis TL
   125 Otis Birdsong

☐ 87 251 Wes Unseld .25 .12 .02
   195 Tom Owens TL
   78 John Roche

☐ 88 257 Elvin Hayes SD .50 .25 .05
   144 Marq.Johnson TL
   89 Bob McAdoo

☐ 89 3 Dan Roundfield .15 .07 .01
   218 Lloyd Free
   42 D.Greenwood TL

☐ 90 7 Moses Malone .65 .30 .06
   247 Kevin Grevey
   52 Dave Robisch TL

☐ 91 12 Gus Williams	.15	.07	.01
210 Mark Olberding			
255 James Bailey SD			
☐ 92 24 Steve Hawes	.15	.07	.01
226 John Johnson TL			
45 David Greenwood			
☐ 93 29 Dan Roundfield	.15	.07	.01
113 Mick.Johnson TL			
130 Bill Robinzine			
☐ 94 34 Larry Bird	35.00	17.50	3.50
164 B.Cartwright TL			
23 John Drew			
☐ 95 36 Dave Cowens	.35	.17	.03
16 Paul Westphal AS			
59 Randy Smith			
☐ 96 38 Pete Maravich	.65	.30	.06
187 Leon.Robinson TL			
46 Dwight Jones			
☐ 97 40 Rick Robey	.15	.07	.01
37 Chris Ford			
66 Joe Hassett			
☐ 98 47 Scott May	20.00	10.00	2.00
30 Larry Bird TL			
232 Jack Sikma			
☐ 99 55 Don Ford	.25	.12	.02
144 Marq.Johnson TL			
89 Bob McAdoo			
☐ 100 58 Campy Russell	.15	.07	.01
21 Armond Hill TL			
171 M.R.Richardson			
☐ 101 60 Foots Walker	.15	.07	.01
122 Otis Birdsong TL			
48 John Mengelt			
☐ 102 61 Austin Carr	.15	.07	.01
56 Mike Mitchell			
81 Terry Tyler TL			
☐ 103 63 Jim Cleamons	.15	.07	.01
261 James Edwards SD			
157 Eddie Jordan			
☐ 104 69 Tom LaGarde	.25	.12	.02
109 Billy Paultz			
150 Bob Lanier			
☐ 105 71 Jerome Whitehead	.15	.07	.01
17 Calvin Murphy AS			
70 Rich.Washington			
☐ 106 74 John Roche TL	.35	.17	.03
28 Wayne Rollins			
15 M.R.Richardson AS			
☐ 107 75 Alex English	1.75	.85	.17
102 Moses Malone TL			
64 Winford Boynes			
☐ 108 82 Terry Tyler TL	.35	.17	.03
79 David Thompson			
216 Brian Taylor TL			
☐ 109 84 Kent Benson	.20	.10	.02
259 Artis Gilmore SD			
184 Caldwell Jones			
☐ 110 86 Phil Hubbard	.15	.07	.01
195 Tom Owens TL			
78 John Roche			
☐ 111 88 John Long	24.00	12.00	2.40
18 Magic Johnson AS			
237 Ron Boone			
☐ 112 90 Eric Money	.15	.07	.01
215 Swen Nater TL			
213 James Silas			
☐ 113 95 Wayne Cooper	.15	.07	.01
154 Geo.Johnson TL			
193 Leon.Robinson			
☐ 114 97 Robert Parish	1.75	.85	.17
103 Moses Malone TL			
148 George Johnson			
☐ 115 98 Sonny Parker	.15	.07	.01
94 John Lucas TL			
202 Dave Twardzik			
☐ 116 105 Rick Barry	.65	.30	.06
123 Sam Lacey TL			
54 Kenny Carr			
☐ 117 106 Allen Leavell	.20	.10	.02
197 Dave Twardzik TL			
39 Cedric Maxwell			
☐ 118 108 Calvin Murphy	.20	.10	.02
51 Mike Mitchell TL			
80 Bobby Wilkerson			
☐ 119 110 Robert Reid	.15	.07	.01
153 Mike Newlin TL			
182 Lionel Hollins			
☐ 120 111 Rudy Tomjanovich	.15	.07	.01
73 Dan Issel TL			
152 Brian Winters			
☐ 121 112 Mick.Johnson TL	.35	.17	.03
264 Lloyd Free SD			
194 Dennis Johnson			
☐ 122 115 Mike Bantom	.25	.12	.02
204 George Gervin TL			
117 Johnny Davis			
☐ 123 116 Dudley Bradley	.15	.07	.01
186 Paul Westphal TL			
142 Jamaal Wilkes			
☐ 124 118 James Edwards	.50	.25	.05
32 Nate Archibald TL			
248 Elvin Hayes			
☐ 125 119 Mickey Johnson	.15	.07	.01
72 Dan Issel TL			
249 Mitch Kupchak			
☐ 126 120 Billy Knight	.15	.07	.01
104 Allen Leavell TL			
96 John Lucas			
☐ 127 121 George McGinnis	.65	.30	.06
10 Bob Lanier AS			
222 Bill Walton			
☐ 128 124 Phil Ford TL	.25	.12	.02
234 Adr.Dantley TL			
26 Eddie Johnson			
☐ 129 127 Phil Ford	.15	.07	.01
43 Reggie Theus TL			
252 John Williamson			
☐ 130 131 Scott Wedman	.15	.07	.01
244 Kevin Porter TL			
25 Armond Hill			
☐ 131 132 Kar.A.Jabbar TL	2.25	1.10	.22
93 Robert Parish TL			
126 Tom Burleson			
☐ 132 135 Kareem A.Jabbar	5.00	2.50	.50
253 John Shumate SD			
167 Larry Demic			
☐ 133 137 Michael Cooper	2.00	1.00	.20
212 John Shumate			
229 Paul Westphal			
☐ 134 140 Mark Landsberger	.25	.12	.02
214 Lloyd Free TL			
44 Artis Gilmore			
☐ 135 141 Norm Nixon	.25	.12	.02
242 Elvin Hayes TL			
35 M.L. Carr			
☐ 136 143 Marq.Johnson TL	.15	.07	.01
57 Dave Robisch			
254 Rick Robey SD			
☐ 137 146 Junior Bridgeman	1.75	.85	.17
1 Julius Erving AS			
49 Ricky Sobers			
☐ 138 147 Quinn Buckner	.15	.07	.01
2 Marques Johnson AS			
68 Jeff Judkins			
☐ 139 149 Marques Johnson	.25	.12	.02
83 Eric Money TL			
65 Mike Bratz			
☐ 140 151 Sidney Moncrief	4.00	2.00	.40
133 Kar.Ab.Jabbar TL			
207 Mike Gale			
☐ 141 156 George Johnson	.15	.07	.01
175 Caldw.Jones TL			
129 Sam Lacey			
☐ 142 158 Maurice Lucas	1.75	.85	.17
262 Julius Erving SD			
62 Abdul Jeelani			
☐ 143 159 Mike Newlin	.50	.25	.05
243 Wes Unseld TL			
50 Reggie Theus			
☐ 144 160 Roger Phegley	.15	.07	.01
145 Quinn Buckner TL			
138 Brad Holland			
☐ 145 161 Cliff Robinson	.15	.07	.01
114 Johnny Davis TL			
125 Otis Birdsong			
☐ 146 162 Jan V.Breda Kolff	40.00	20.00	4.00
174 Julius Erving TL			
139 Magic Johnson			
☐ 147 165 M.R.Richardson TL	.50	.25	.05
185 Steve Mix			
92 Robert Parish TL			
☐ 148 166 Bill Cartwright AS	2.25	1.10	.22
13 Eddie Johnson AS			
179 Doug Collins			
☐ 149 168 Toby Knight	.15	.07	.01
188 Paul Westphal TL			
77 Charlie Scott			
☐ 150 169 Joe Meriweather	.15	.07	.01
196 K.Washington TL			
177 Henry Bibby			
☐ 151 170 Earl Monroe	.35	.17	.03
206 James Silas TL			
91 Terry Tyler			
☐ 152 172 Marvin Webster	.15	.07	.01
155 Eddie Jordan TL			
239 Allan Bristow			

☐ 153	173 Ray Williams .... 225 Jack Sikma TL 100 Purvis Short	.35	.17	.03
☐ 154	178 Maurice Cheeks .... 11 George Gervin AS 136 Jim Chones	3.00	1.50	.30
☐ 155	183 Bobby Jones .... 99 Clifford Ray 235 Ben Poquette TL	.15	.07	.01
☐ 156	189 Alvan Adams .... 14 Lloyd Free AS 240 Adrian Dantley	.40	.20	.04
☐ 157	190 Don Buse .... 6 Adrian Dantley AS 227 James Bailey	.25	.12	.02
☐ 158	191 Walter Davis .... 9 Bill Cartwright AS 199 Bob Gross	.35	.17	.03
☐ 159	192 Rich Kelley .... 263 Bobby Jones SD 107 Moses Malone	1.25	.60	.12
☐ 160	201 Tom Owens .... 134 Norm Nixon TL 180 Darryl Dawkins	.20	.10	.02
☐ 161	208 George Gervin .... 53 Foots Walker TL 223 Freeman Williams	.50	.25	.05
☐ 162	217 Joe Bryant .... 8 Kareem A.Jabbar AS 200 Calvin Natt	2.25	1.10	.22
☐ 163	219 Swen Nater .... 101 Phil Smith 224 Gus Williams TL	.15	.07	.01
☐ 164	221 Brian Taylor .... 256 Robert Reid SD 22 Charlie Criss	.15	.07	.01
☐ 165	228 Fred Brown .... 31 Larry Bird TL 198 Ron Brewer	20.00	10.00	2.00
☐ 166	230 John Johnson .... 163 B.Cartwright TL 76 Dan Issel	.25	.12	.02
☐ 167	231 Lonnie Shelton .... 205 Larry Kenon TL 203 Kerm.Washington	.15	.07	.01
☐ 168	233 Gus Williams .... 41 Reggie Theus TL 128 Reggie King	.15	.07	.01
☐ 169	236 Allan Bristow TL .... 260 Lon.Shelton SD 220 Paul Silas	.15	.07	.01
☐ 170	238 Tom Boswell .... 27 James McElroy 85 Leon Douglas	.15	.07	.01
☐ 171	241 Ben Poquette .... 176 Maur.Cheeks TL 87 Greg Kelser	.90	.45	.09
☐ 172	245 Greg Ballard .... 4 Walter Davis AS 33 Nate Archibald	.25	.12	.02
☐ 173	246 Bob Dandridge .... 19 John Drew TL 209 Larry Kenon	.15	.07	.01
☐ 174	250 Kevin Porter .... 20 Dan Roundfield TL 211 Kevin Restani	.15	.07	.01
☐ 175	251 Wes Unseld .... 67 Geoff Huston 5 John Drew AS	.30	.15	.03
☐ 176	257 Elvin Hayes SD .... 181 Julius Erving 258 Ron Brewer SD	4.50	2.25	.45

1980-81 Topps Team Posters

This set of 16 numbered team mini-posters was issued in regular packs of 1980-81 Topps basketball cards. The small posters feature a full-color posed team picture, with the team name in the frame line. These posters are on thin, white paper stock and measure approximately 4 7/8" by 6 7/8" when unfolded.

	MINT	EXC	G-VG
COMPLETE SET (16)	5.00	2.50	.50
COMMON TEAM (1-16)	.40	.20	.04

		MINT	EXC	G-VG
☐ 1	Atlanta Hawks	.40	.20	.04
☐ 2	Boston Celtics	.40	.20	.04
☐ 3	Chicago Bulls	.40	.20	.04
☐ 4	Cleveland Cavaliers	.40	.20	.04
☐ 5	Detroit Pistons	.40	.20	.04
☐ 6	Houston Rockets	.40	.20	.04
☐ 7	Indiana Pacers	.40	.20	.04
☐ 8	Los Angeles Lakers	.40	.20	.04
☐ 9	Milwaukee Bucks	.40	.20	.04
☐ 10	New Jersey Nets	.40	.20	.04
☐ 11	New York Knicks	.40	.20	.04
☐ 12	Philadelphia 76ers	.40	.20	.04
☐ 13	Phoenix Suns	.40	.20	.04
☐ 14	Portland Blazers	.40	.20	.04
☐ 15	Seattle Sonics	.40	.20	.04
☐ 16	Washington Bullets	.40	.20	.04

1981 Topps Thirst Break *

This 56-card set is actually a set of gum wrappers. These wrappers were issued in Thirst Break Orange Gum, which was reportedly only distributed in Pennsylvania and Ohio. Each of these small gum wrappers has a cartoon-type image of a particular great moment in sports. As the checklist below shows, many different sports are represented in this set. The wrappers each measure approximately 2 9/16" by 1 5/8". The wrappers are numbered in small print at the top. The backs of the wrappers are blank. The "1981 Topps" copyright is at the bottom of each card.

	MINT	EXC	G-VG
COMPLETE SET (56)	75.00	37.50	7.50
COMMON PLAYER (1-56)	.75	.35	.07
☐ 1 Shortest Baseball Game	.75	.35	.07
☐ 2 Lefty Gomez	1.50	.75	.15
World Series Fact			
☐ 3 Bob Gibson	2.50	1.25	.25
World Series			
Strikeout Record			
☐ 4 Hoyt Wilhelm	1.50	.75	.15
1070 Games			
☐ 5 Babe Ruth	6.00	3.00	.60
Best Clutch Hitter			
☐ 6 Toby Harrah	.75	.35	.07
Fielding Fact			
☐ 7 Carl Hubbell	1.25	.60	.12
24 Consecutive Wins			
☐ 8 Harvey Haddix	.75	.35	.07
12 Perfect Innings			
☐ 9 Steve Carlton	2.50	1.25	.25
Strikeout Fact			
☐ 10 Nolan Ryan,	5.00	2.50	.50
Tom Seaver, and			
Steve Carlton			
☐ 11 Lou Brock	2.50	1.25	.25
Stolen Base Record			
☐ 12 Mickey Mantle	6.00	3.00	.60
565 ft. Home Run			
☐ 13 Tom Seaver	2.50	1.25	.25
Strikeout Record			
☐ 14 Don Drysdale	1.50	.75	.15
Scoreless Innings			
☐ 15 Billy Williams	1.50	.75	.15
Consecutive Games			
☐ 16 Wilt Chamberlain	3.50	1.75	.35
100 Points One Game			
☐ 17 Wilt Chamberlain	3.50	1.75	.35
50.4 Avg/Game			
☐ 18 Wilt Chamberlain	3.50	1.75	.35
No Foulout Record			
☐ 19 Kevin Porter	.75	.35	.07
Assist Record			
☐ 20 Christy Mathewson	1.50	.75	.15
World Series Shutout			
☐ 21 Hank Aaron	3.50	1.75	.35
Home Run Record			
☐ 22 Ron Blomberg	.75	.35	.07
First DH in Majors			
☐ 23 Joe Nuxhall	.75	.35	.07
Youngest Player			
☐ 24 Reggie Jackson	3.00	1.50	.30
World Series Home Runs			
☐ 25 John Havlicek	2.50	1.25	.25
Most Games Played			
☐ 26 Oscar Robertson	2.50	1.25	.25
Free Throw Record			
☐ 27 Calvin Murphy	1.25	.60	.12
Free Throw Fact			
☐ 28 Clarence(Bevo) Francis	.75	.35	.07
Basketball Fact			
☐ 29 Garo Yepremian	.75	.35	.07
20 Consecutive			
Field Goals			
☐ 30 Bert Jones	.75	.35	.07
17 Consecutive Passes			
☐ 31 Norm Van Brocklin	1.50	.75	.15
Yardage Record			
☐ 32 Fran Tarkenton	2.50	1.25	.25
Touchdown Record			
☐ 33 Johnny Unitas	3.00	1.50	.30
Football Fact			
☐ 34 Bob Beamon	.75	.35	.07
Long Jump Record			
☐ 35 Jesse Owens	1.25	.60	.12
Track Records			
☐ 36 Bart Starr	2.50	1.25	.25
Passing Fact			
☐ 37 O.J. Simpson	3.00	1.50	.30
Touchdown Record			
☐ 38 Jim Brown	3.50	1.75	.35
Football Fact			
☐ 39 Jim Marshall	1.25	.60	.12
256 Consecutive Games			
☐ 40 George Blanda	2.00	1.00	.20
Extra Point Fact			
☐ 41 Jack Tatum	.75	.35	.07
Football Record			
☐ 42 Tim Brown	.75	.35	.07
Touchdown Record			
☐ 43 Gerry Cheevers	2.00	1.00	.20
Hockey Fact			
☐ 44 Dave Schultz	.75	.35	.07
Hockey Penalty Record			

	MINT	EXC	G-VG
☐ 45 Mark Spitz	1.00	.50	.10
9 Olympic Gold Medals			
☐ 46 Byron Nelson	.75	.35	.07
Golf Fact			
☐ 47 Soccer Attendance	.75	.35	.07
Record, 1950 World Cup			
☐ 48 Tom Dempsey	.75	.35	.07
Field Goal Record			
☐ 49 Gale Sayers	2.00	1.00	.20
Football Fact			
☐ 50 Bobby Hull	2.50	1.25	.25
Hockey Fact			
☐ 51 Bobby Hull	2.50	1.25	.25
Hockey Fact			
☐ 52 Bobby Hull	2.50	1.25	.25
Assist Record			
☐ 53 Giorgio Chinaglia	.75	.35	.07
Soccer Fact			
☐ 54 Muhammad Ali	2.50	1.25	.25
Boxing Record			
☐ 55 Gene Tunney and	1.25	.60	.12
Rocky Marciano			
☐ 56 Roger Bannister	.75	.35	.07
4 Minute Mile			

1981-82 Topps

The 1981-82 Topps basketball card set contains a total of 198 cards. The cards in the set measure the standard 2 1/2" by 3 1/2". These cards, however, are numbered depending upon the regional distribution used in the issue. A 66-card national set was issued to all parts of the country; however, subsets of 44 cards each were issued in the east, mid-west, and west. Card numbers over 66 are prefaced on the card by the region in which they were distributed, e.g., East 96. The cards themselves feature the Topps logo in the frame line and a quarter-round sunburst in the lower left-hand corner which lists the name, position, and team of the player depicted. Cards 44-66 are Team Leader (TL) cards picturing each team's statistical leaders. The back, printed in orange and brown on gray stock, features standard Topps biographical data and career statistics. There are a number of Super Action (SA) cards in the set. The notable rookie cards in this set are Joe Barry Carroll, Mike Dunleavy, Mike Gminski, Darrell Griffith, Vinnie Johnson, Bill Laimbeer, Rick Mahorn, Kevin McHale, and Larry Smith.

	MINT	EXC	G-VG
COMPLETE SET (198)	95.00	45.00	9.00
COMMON CARD (1-44)	.10	.05	.01
COMMON CARD (45-66)	.15	.07	.01
COMMON CARD (67-110)	.15	.07	.01
☐ 1 John Drew	.20	.10	.02
Atlanta Hawks			
☐ 2 Dan Roundfield	.10	.05	.01
Atlanta Hawks			
☐ 3 Nate Archibald	.40	.20	.04
Boston Celtics			
☐ 4 Larry Bird	22.00	11.00	2.20
Boston Celtics			
☐ 5 Cedric Maxwell	.20	.10	.02
Boston Celtics			

☐ 6	Robert Parish .... Boston Celtics	2.00	1.00	.20
☐ 7	Artis Gilmore .... Chicago Bulls	.40	.20	.04
☐ 8	Ricky Sobers .... Chicago Bulls	.10	.05	.01
☐ 9	Mike Mitchell .... Cleveland Cavaliers	.10	.05	.01
☐ 10	Tom LaGarde .... Dallas Mavericks	.10	.05	.01
☐ 11	Dan Issel .... Denver Nuggets	.40	.20	.04
☐ 12	David Thompson .... Denver Nuggets	.40	.20	.04
☐ 13	Lloyd Free .... Golden State Warriors	.20	.10	.02
☐ 14	Moses Malone .... Houston Rockets	2.25	1.10	.22
☐ 15	Calvin Murphy .... Houston Rockets	.25	.12	.02
☐ 16	Johnny Davis .... Indiana Pacers	.10	.05	.01
☐ 17	Otis Birdsong .... Kansas City Kings	.10	.05	.01
☐ 18	Phil Ford .... Kansas City Kings	.25	.12	.02
☐ 19	Scott Wedman .... Cleveland Cavaliers	.20	.10	.02
☐ 20	Kareem Abdul Jabbar .... Los Angeles Lakers	8.50	4.25	.85
☐ 21	Magic Johnson .... Los Angeles Lakers	22.00	11.00	2.20
☐ 22	Norm Nixon .... Los Angeles Lakers	.25	.12	.02
☐ 23	Jamaal Wilkes .... Los Angeles Lakers	.30	.15	.03
☐ 24	Marques Johnson .... Milwaukee Bucks	.30	.15	.03
☐ 25	Bob Lanier .... Milwaukee Bucks	.40	.20	.04
☐ 26	Bill Cartwright .... New York Knicks	.65	.30	.06
☐ 27	M.R. Richardson .... New York Knicks	.20	.10	.02
☐ 28	Ray Williams .... New York Knicks	.10	.05	.01
☐ 29	Darryl Dawkins .... Philadelphia 76ers	.30	.15	.03
☐ 30	Julius Erving .... Philadelphia 76ers	7.50	3.75	.75
☐ 31	Lionel Hollins .... Philadelphia 76ers	.10	.05	.01
☐ 32	Bobby Jones .... Philadelphia 76ers	.20	.10	.02
☐ 33	Walter Davis .... Phoenix Suns	.40	.20	.04
☐ 34	Dennis Johnson .... Phoenix Suns	.50	.25	.05
☐ 35	Leonard Robinson .... Phoenix Suns	.10	.05	.01
☐ 36	Mychal Thompson .... Portland Trail Blazers	.15	.07	.01
☐ 37	George Gervin .... San Antonio Spurs	.90	.45	.09
☐ 38	Swen Nater .... San Diego Clippers	.10	.05	.01
☐ 39	Jack Sikma .... Seattle Supersonics	.40	.20	.04
☐ 40	Adrian Dantley .... Utah Jazz	.60	.30	.06
☐ 41	Darrell Griffith .... Utah Jazz	1.50	.75	.15
☐ 42	Elvin Hayes .... Houston Rockets	.90	.45	.09
☐ 43	Fred Brown .... Seattle Supersonics	.25	.12	.02
☐ 44	Atlanta Hawks TL .... John Drew Dan Roundfield Eddie Johnson	.15	.07	.01
☐ 45	Boston Celtics TL .... Larry Bird Larry Bird Nate Archibald	2.75	1.35	.27
☐ 46	Chicago Bulls TL .... Reggie Theus Artis Gilmore Reggie Theus	.15	.07	.01
☐ 47	Cleveland Cavs TL .... Mike Mitchell Kenny Carr Mike Bratz	.15	.07	.01
☐ 48	Dallas Mavericks TL .... Jim Spanarkel Tom LaGarde Brad Davis	.15	.07	.01
☐ 49	Denver Nuggets TL .... David Thompson Dan Issel Kenny Higgs	.25	.12	.02
☐ 50	Detroit Pistons TL .... John Long Phil Hubbard Ron Lee	.15	.07	.01
☐ 51	Golden State TL .... Lloyd Free Larry Smith John Lucas	.15	.07	.01
☐ 52	Houston Rockets TL .... Moses Malone Moses Malone Allen Leavell	.60	.30	.06
☐ 53	Indiana Pacers TL .... Billy Knight James Edwards Johnny Davis	.15	.07	.01
☐ 54	Kansas City Kings TL .... Otis Birdsong Reggie King Phil Ford	.15	.07	.01
☐ 55	Los Angeles Lakers TL .... Kareem Abdul Jabbar Kareem Abdul Jabbar Norm Nixon	2.00	1.00	.20
☐ 56	Milwaukee Bucks TL .... Marques Johnson Mickey Johnson Quinn Buckner	.15	.07	.01
☐ 57	New Jersey Nets TL .... Mike Newlin Maurice Lucas Mike Newlin	.15	.07	.01
☐ 58	New York Knicks TL .... Bill Cartwright Bill Cartwright M.R. Richardson	.15	.07	.01
☐ 59	Philadelphia 76ers TL .... Julius Erving Caldwell Jones Maurice Cheeks	2.00	1.00	.20
☐ 60	Phoenix Suns TL .... Truck Robinson Truck Robinson Alvin Adams	.15	.07	.01
☐ 61	Portland Blazers TL .... Jim Paxson Mychal Thompson Kermit Washington Kelvin Ransey	.25	.12	.02
☐ 62	San Antonio Spurs TL .... George Gervin Dave Corzine Johnny Moore	.25	.12	.02
☐ 63	San Diego Clippers TL .... Freeman Williams Swen Nater Brian Taylor	.15	.07	.01
☐ 64	Seattle Sonics TL .... Jack Sikma Jack Sikma Vinnie Johnson	.25	.12	.02
☐ 65	Utah Jazz TL .... Adrian Dantley Ben Poquette Allan Bristow	.25	.12	.02
☐ 66	Washington Bullets TL .... Elvin Hayes Elvin Hayes Kevin Porter	.25	.12	.02
☐ E67	Charlie Criss .... Atlanta Hawks	.15	.07	.01
☐ E68	Eddie Johnson .... Atlanta Hawks	.15	.07	.01
☐ E69	Wes Matthews .... Atlanta Hawks	.15	.07	.01
☐ E70	Tom McMillen .... Atlanta Hawks	.35	.17	.03
☐ E71	Tree Rollins .... Atlanta Hawks	.30	.15	.03
☐ E72	M.L. Carr .... Boston Celtics	.25	.12	.02
☐ E73	Chris Ford .... Boston Celtics	.25	.12	.02
☐ E74	Gerald Henderson .... Boston Celtics	.40	.20	.04
☐ E75	Kevin McHale .... Boston Celtics	15.00	7.50	1.50
☐ E76	Rick Robey .... Boston Celtics	.15	.07	.01
☐ E77	Darwin Cook .... Milwaukee Bucks	.15	.07	.01

☐ E78 Mike Gminski .... Milwaukee Bucks	1.75	.85	.17
☐ E79 Maurice Lucas .... Milwaukee Bucks	.25	.12	.02
☐ E80 Mike Newlin .... New York Knicks	.15	.07	.01
☐ E81 Mike O'Koren .... Milwaukee Bucks	.30	.15	.03
☐ E82 Steve Hawes .... Atlanta Hawks	.15	.07	.01
☐ E83 Foots Walker .... Milwaukee Bucks	.15	.07	.01
☐ E84 Campy Russell .... New York Knicks	.15	.07	.01
☐ E85 DeWayne Scales .... New York Knicks	.15	.07	.01
☐ E86 Randy Smith .... New York Knicks	.15	.07	.01
☐ E87 Marvin Webster .... New York Knicks	.15	.07	.01
☐ E88 Sly Williams .... New York Knicks	.15	.07	.01
☐ E89 Mike Woodson .... Milwaukee Bucks	.50	.25	.05
☐ E90 Maurice Cheeks .... Philadelphia 76ers	1.25	.60	.12
☐ E91 Caldwell Jones .... Philadelphia 76ers	.25	.12	.02
☐ E92 Steve Mix .... Philadelphia 76ers	.15	.07	.01
☐ E93A Checklist 1-110 ERR .... (WEST above card number)	.75	.06	.01
☐ E93B Checklist 1-110 COR	.75	.06	.01
☐ E94 Greg Ballard .... Washington Bullets	.15	.07	.01
☐ E95 Don Collins .... Washington Bullets	.15	.07	.01
☐ E96 Kevin Grevey .... Washington Bullets	.15	.07	.01
☐ E97 Mitch Kupchak .... Washington Bullets	.15	.07	.01
☐ E98 Rick Mahorn .... Washington Bullets	3.00	1.50	.30
☐ E99 Kevin Porter .... Washington Bullets	.15	.07	.01
☐ E100 Nate Archibald SA .... Boston Celtics	.30	.15	.03
☐ E101 Larry Bird SA .... Boston Celtics	7.50	3.75	.75
☐ E102 Bill Cartwright SA .... New York Knicks	.40	.20	.04
☐ E103 Darryl Dawkins SA .... Philadelphia 76ers	.25	.12	.02
☐ E104 Julius Erving SA .... Philadelphia 76ers	4.25	2.10	.42
☐ E105 Kevin Porter SA .... Washington Bullets	.15	.07	.01
☐ E106 Bobby Jones SA .... Philadelphia 76ers	.25	.12	.02
☐ E107 Cedric Maxwell SA .... Boston Celtics	.25	.12	.02
☐ E108 Robert Parish SA .... Boston Celtics	.80	.40	.08
☐ E109 M.R.Richardson SA .... New York Knicks	.25	.12	.02
☐ E110 Dan Roundfield SA .... Atlanta Hawks	.25	.12	.02
☐ MW67 David Greenwood .... Chicago Bulls	.25	.12	.02
☐ MW68 Dwight Jones .... Chicago Bulls	.15	.07	.01
☐ MW69 Reggie Theus .... Chicago Bulls	.25	.12	.02
☐ MW70 Bobby Wilkerson .... Cleveland Cavaliers	.15	.07	.01
☐ MW71 Mike Bratz .... Cleveland Cavaliers	.15	.07	.01
☐ MW72 Kenny Carr .... Cleveland Cavaliers	.15	.07	.01
☐ MW73 Geoff Huston .... Cleveland Cavaliers	.15	.07	.01
☐ MW74 Bill Laimbeer .... Cleveland Cavaliers	6.50	3.25	.65
☐ MW75 Roger Phegley .... Cleveland Cavaliers	.15	.07	.01
☐ MW76 Checklist 1-110	.75	.06	.01
☐ MW77 Abdul Jeelani .... Dallas Mavericks	.15	.07	.01
☐ MW78 Bill Robinzine .... Dallas Mavericks	.15	.07	.01
☐ MW79 Jim Spanarkel .... Dallas Mavericks	.15	.07	.01
☐ MW80 Kent Benson .... Detroit Pistons	.25	.12	.02
☐ MW81 Keith Herron .... Detroit Pistons	.15	.07	.01
☐ MW82 Phil Hubbard .... Detroit Pistons	.25	.12	.02
☐ MW83 John Long .... Detroit Pistons	.15	.07	.01
☐ MW84 Terry Tyler .... Detroit Pistons	.15	.07	.01
☐ MW85 Mike Dunleavy .... Houston Rockets	2.50	1.25	.25
☐ MW86 Tom Henderson .... Houston Rockets	.15	.07	.01
☐ MW87 Billy Paultz .... Houston Rockets	.15	.07	.01
☐ MW88 Robert Reid .... Houston Rockets	.15	.07	.01
☐ MW89 Mike Bantom .... Indiana Pacers	.15	.07	.01
☐ MW90 James Edwards .... Cleveland Cavaliers	.25	.12	.02
☐ MW91 Billy Knight .... Indiana Pacers	.15	.07	.01
☐ MW92 George McGinnis .... Indiana Pacers	.25	.12	.02
☐ MW93 Louis Orr .... Indiana Pacers	.15	.07	.01
☐ MW94 Ernie Grunfeld .... Kansas City Kings	.50	.25	.05
☐ MW95 Reggie King .... Kansas City Kings	.15	.07	.01
☐ MW96 Sam Lacey .... Kansas City Kings	.15	.07	.01
☐ MW97 Junior Bridgeman .... Milwaukee Bucks	.25	.12	.02
☐ MW98 Mickey Johnson .... Milwaukee Bucks	.15	.07	.01
☐ MW99 Sidney Moncrief .... Milwaukee Bucks	1.25	.60	.12
☐ MW100 Brian Winters .... Milwaukee Bucks	.15	.07	.01
☐ MW101 Dave Corzine .... San Antonio Spurs	.35	.17	.03
☐ MW102 Paul Griffin .... San Antonio Spurs	.15	.07	.01
☐ MW103 Johnny Moore .... San Antonio Spurs	.35	.17	.03
☐ MW104 Mark Olberding .... San Antonio Spurs	.15	.07	.01
☐ MW105 James Silas .... Cleveland Cavaliers	.15	.07	.01
☐ MW106 George Gervin SA .... San Antonio Spurs	.35	.17	.03
☐ MW107 Artis Gilmore SA .... Chicago Bulls	.25	.12	.02
☐ MW108 Marq.Johnson SA .... Milwaukee Bucks	.20	.10	.02
☐ MW109 Bob Lanier SA .... Milwaukee Bucks	.25	.12	.02
☐ MW110 Moses Malone SA .... Houston Rockets	1.25	.60	.12
☐ W67 T.R. Dunn .... Denver Nuggets	.25	.12	.02
☐ W68 Alex English .... Denver Nuggets	1.50	.75	.15
☐ W69 Billy McKinney .... Denver Nuggets	.30	.15	.03
☐ W70 Dave Robisch .... Denver Nuggets	.15	.07	.01
☐ W71 Joe Barry Carroll .... Golden State Warriors	1.00	.50	.10
☐ W72 Bernard King .... Golden State Warriors	3.50	1.75	.35
☐ W73 Sonny Parker .... Golden State Warriors	.15	.07	.01
☐ W74 Purvis Short .... Golden State Warriors	.50	.25	.05
☐ W75 Larry Smith .... Golden State Warriors	1.50	.75	.15
☐ W76 Jim Chones .... Los Angeles Lakers	.15	.07	.01
☐ W77 Michael Cooper .... Los Angeles Lakers	1.25	.60	.12
☐ W78 Mark Landsberger .... Los Angeles Lakers	.15	.07	.01
☐ W79 Alvan Adams .... Phoenix Suns	.25	.12	.02
☐ W80 Jeff Cook .... Phoenix Suns	.15	.07	.01
☐ W81 Rich Kelley .... Phoenix Suns	.15	.07	.01
☐ W82 Kyle Macy .... Phoenix Suns	.50	.25	.05
☐ W83 Billy Ray Bates .... Portland Trail Blazers	.35	.17	.03

☐ W84 Bob Gross .... Portland Trail Blazers	.15	.07	.01
☐ W85 Calvin Natt .... Portland Trail Blazers	.25	.12	.02
☐ W86 Lonnie Shelton .... Seattle Supersonics	.15	.07	.01
☐ W87 Jim Paxson .... Portland Trail Blazers	.75	.35	.07
☐ W88 Kelvin Ransey .... Portland Trail Blazers	.15	.07	.01
☐ W89 Kermit Washington .... Portland Trail Blazers	.15	.07	.01
☐ W90 Henry Bibby .... San Diego Clippers	.15	.07	.01
☐ W91 Michael Brooks .... San Diego Clippers	.15	.07	.01
☐ W92 Joe Bryant .... San Diego Clippers	.15	.07	.01
☐ W93 Phil Smith .... San Diego Clippers	.15	.07	.01
☐ W94 Brian Taylor .... San Diego Clippers	.15	.07	.01
☐ W95 Freeman Williams .... San Diego Clippers	.25	.12	.02
☐ W96 James Bailey .... Seattle Supersonics	.15	.07	.01
☐ W97 Checklist 1-110	.75	.06	.01
☐ W98 John Johnson .... Seattle Supersonics	.15	.07	.01
☐ W99 Vinnie Johnson .... Seattle Supersonics	3.75	1.85	.37
☐ W100 Wally Walker .... Seattle Supersonics	.30	.15	.03
☐ W101 Paul Westphal .... Seattle Supersonics	.30	.15	.03
☐ W102 Allan Bristow .... Utah Jazz	.25	.12	.02
☐ W103 Wayne Cooper .... Utah Jazz	.25	.12	.02
☐ W104 Carl Nicks .... Utah Jazz	.15	.07	.01
☐ W105 Ben Poquette .... Utah Jazz	.15	.07	.01
☐ W106 Kar.Abdul Jabbar SA .... Los Angeles Lakers	4.50	2.25	.45
☐ W107 Dan Issel SA .... Denver Nuggets	.25	.12	.02
☐ W108 Dennis Johnson SA .... Phoenix Suns	.20	.10	.02
☐ W109 Magic Johnson SA .... Los Angeles Lakers	7.50	3.75	.75
☐ W110 Jack Sikma SA .... Seattle Supersonics	.35	.17	.03

1977-78 Trail Blazers Police

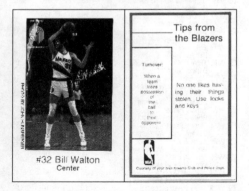

#32 Bill Walton
Center

This set contains 14 cards measuring 2 5/8" by 4 1/8" featuring the Portland Trail Blazers. The cards are unnumbered except for uniform number. Backs contain safety tips ("Tips from the Blazers") and are written in black ink with red accent. The set was sponsored by the Kiwanis and the Police Department.

	NRMT	VG-E	GOOD
COMPLETE SET (14)	50.00	25.00	5.00
COMMON CARD (1-14)	2.50	1.25	.25
☐ 10 Corky Calhoun	2.50	1.25	.25
☐ 13 Dave Twardzik	3.50	1.75	.35
☐ 14 Lionel Hollins	3.50	1.75	.35
☐ 15 Larry Steele	2.50	1.25	.25
☐ 16 Johnny Davis	2.50	1.25	.25
☐ 20 Maurice Lucas	5.00	2.50	.50
☐ 23 T.R. Dunn	3.50	1.75	.35
☐ 25 Tom Owens	2.50	1.25	.25
☐ 30 Bob Gross	2.50	1.25	.25
☐ 32 Bill Walton	10.00	5.00	1.00
☐ 36 Lloyd Neal	2.50	1.25	.25
☐ xx Jack Ramsay CO	3.50	1.75	.35
☐ xx Jack McKinney .... assistant coach	3.50	1.75	.35
☐ xx Ron Culp, trainer	2.50	1.25	.25

1979-80 Trail Blazers Police

This set contains 16 cards measuring 2 5/8" by 4 1/8" featuring the Portland Trail Blazers. Backs contain safety tips and are available with either light red or maroon printing on the backs. The year of issue and a facsimile autograph are printed on the front of the cards. The set was sponsored by 7-Up, Safeway, Kiwanis, KEX-1190AM, and the Police Departments.

	MINT	EXC	G-VG
COMPLETE SET (16)	12.00	6.00	1.20
COMMON PLAYER (1-16)	.60	.30	.06
☐ 4 Jim Paxson	1.00	.50	.10
☐ 9 Lionel Hollins	1.00	.50	.10
☐ 10 Ron Brewer	.75	.35	.07
☐ 11 Abdul Jeelani	.60	.30	.06
☐ 13 Dave Twardzik	.75	.35	.07
☐ 15 Larry Steele	.60	.30	.06
☐ 20 Maurice Lucas	1.25	.60	.12
☐ 23 T.R. Dunn	.60	.30	.06
☐ 25 Tom Owens	.60	.30	.06
☐ 30 Bob Gross	.60	.30	.06
☐ 42 Kermit Washington	.75	.35	.07
☐ 43 Mychal Thompson	1.25	.60	.12
☐ 44 Kevin Kunnert	.60	.30	.06
☐ xx Jack Ramsay CO	.75	.35	.07
☐ xx Morris "Bucky" Buckwalter, Assistant Coach	.60	.30	.06
☐ xx Bill Schonely, ... Voice of the Blazers	.60	.30	.06

1981-82 Trail Blazers Police

This set contains 16 cards measuring 2 5/8" by 4 1/8" featuring the Portland Trail Blazers. Backs contain safety tips and are

written in black ink with red accent. Cards are unnumbered except for uniform number. The year of issue is indicated on the card front. The set was produced courtesy of Kiwanis, the Trail Blazers, the NBA, and the Portland Police Bureau.

	MINT	EXC	G-VG
COMPLETE SET (16)	10.00	5.00	1.00
COMMON PLAYER (1-16)	.50	.25	.05
☐ 3 Jeff Lamp	.50	.25	.05
☐ 4 Jim Paxson	.75	.35	.07
☐ 10 Darnell Valentine	.75	.35	.07
☐ 12 Billy Ray Bates	.75	.35	.07
☐ 14 Kelvin Ransey	.75	.35	.07
☐ 30 Bob Gross	.75	.35	.07
☐ 31 Peter Verhoeven	.50	.25	.05
☐ 32 Mike Harper	.50	.25	.05
☐ 33 Calvin Natt	.75	.35	.07
☐ 40 Peter Gudmundsson	.50	.25	.05
☐ 42 Kermit Washington	.75	.35	.07
☐ 43 Mychal Thompson	1.00	.50	.10
☐ 44 Kevin Kunnert	.50	.25	.05
☐ xx Jack Ramsay CO	.75	.35	.07
☐ xx Morris Buckwalter, Assistant Coach	.50	.25	.05
☐ xx Jimmy Lynam, Assistant Coach	.50	.25	.05

1982-83 Trail Blazers Police

This set contains 16 cards measuring 2 5/8" by 4 1/8" featuring the Portland Trail Blazers. Backs contain safety tips and are written in black ink with red accent. The year of issue and a facsimile autograph are given on the front.

	MINT	EXC	G-VG
COMPLETE SET (16)	8.00	4.00	.80
COMMON PLAYER	.45	.22	.04

		MINT	EXC	G-VG
☐ 2	Linton Townes	.45	.22	.04
☐ 3	Jeff Lamp	.45	.22	.04
☐ 4	Jim Paxson	.65	.30	.06
☐ 12	Lafayette Lever	.90	.45	.09
☐ 14	Darnell Valentine	.45	.22	.04
☐ 22	Jeff Judkins	.45	.22	.04
☐ 24	Audie Norris	.45	.22	.04
☐ 31	Peter Verhoeven	.45	.22	.04
☐ 33	Calvin Natt	.65	.30	.06
☐ 34	Kenny Carr	.65	.30	.06
☐ 42	Wayne Cooper	.65	.30	.06
☐ 43	Mychal Thompson	.90	.45	.09
☐ xx	Jack Ramsay CO	.65	.30	.06
☐ xx	Morris Buckwalter, Assistant Coach	.45	.22	.04
☐ xx	Jim Lynam, Assistant Coach	.45	.22	.04

1983-84 Trail Blazers Police

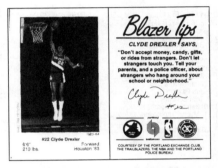

This set contains 16 cards measuring 2 5/8" by 4 1/8" featuring the Portland Trail Blazers. Backs contain safety tips ("Blazer Tips") and are written in black ink with red accent. Drexler and the coaches are the only cards without small inset photo. The year of issue is indicated on the front of the card. A facsimile autograph is printed on the back of the card.

	MINT	EXC	G-VG
COMPLETE SET (16)	7.00	3.50	.70
COMMON PLAYER	.35	.17	.03
☐ 3 Jeff Lamp	.35	.17	.03
☐ 4 Jim Paxson	.50	.25	.05
☐ 12 Lafayette Lever	.65	.30	.06
☐ 14 Darnell Valentine	.50	.25	.05
☐ 22 Clyde Drexler	3.00	1.50	.30
☐ 24 Audie Norris	.35	.17	.03
☐ 31 Peter Verhoeven	.35	.17	.03
☐ 33 Calvin Natt	.50	.25	.05
☐ 34 Kenny Carr	.50	.25	.05
☐ 42 Wayne Cooper	.50	.25	.05
☐ 43 Mychal Thompson	.65	.30	.06
☐ 54 Tom Piotrowski	.35	.17	.03
☐ xx Jack Ramsay CO	.50	.25	.05
☐ xx Morris Buckwalter, Assistant Coach	.35	.17	.03
☐ xx Rick Adelman, Assistant Coach	.50	.25	.05
☐ xx Ron Culp, Trainer	.35	.17	.03
☐ xx Dave Twardzik and Bill Schonely, The Blazer Voices	.35	.17	.03

1984-85 Trail Blazers Franz

This 13-card set was produced for the Franz Bakery in Portland, Oregon by the Star Company. One card was placed in each loaf of Franz Bread as a promotional giveaway. Cards were printed

with FDA approved vegetable ink. Cards measure 2 1/2" by 3 1/2" and have a red border around the fronts of the cards and red printing on the backs. Cards feature the Franz logo on the fronts.

	MINT	EXC	G-VG
COMPLETE SET (13)	60.00	30.00	6.00
COMMON PLAYER (1-13)	1.50	.75	.15
☐ 1 Jack Ramsay CO	2.25	1.10	.22
☐ 2 Sam Bowie	4.50	2.25	.45
☐ 3 Kenny Carr	2.25	1.10	.22
☐ 4 Steve Colter	1.50	.75	.15
☐ 5 Clyde Drexler	35.00	17.50	3.50
☐ 6 Jerome Kersey	15.00	7.50	1.50
☐ 7 Audie Norris	1.50	.75	.15
☐ 8 Jim Paxson	2.25	1.10	.22
☐ 9 Tom Scheffler	1.50	.75	.15
☐ 10 Bernard Thompson	1.50	.75	.15
☐ 11 Mychal Thompson	3.00	1.50	.30
☐ 12 Darnell Valentine	2.25	1.10	.22
☐ 13 Kiki Vandeweghe	4.50	2.25	.45

1984-85 Trail Blazers Police

This set contains 16 cards measuring 2 5/8" by 4 1/8" featuring the Portland Trail Blazers. Backs contain safety tips ("Blazer Tips") and are written in black ink with red accent. The cards are numbered in the upper left corner of the obverse; the year of issue is indicated in the lower right corner.

	MINT	EXC	G-VG
COMPLETE SET (16)	7.00	3.50	.70
COMMON PLAYER (1-16)	.25	.12	.02
☐ 1 Portland Team	.25	.12	.02
☐ 2 Jim Paxson	.50	.25	.05
☐ 3 Bernard Thompson	.35	.17	.03
☐ 4 Darnell Valentine	.25	.12	.02
☐ 5 Jack Ramsay CO	.35	.17	.03
Rick Adelman, Asst.			
and Morris Buckwalter,			
Assistant Coach			

☐ 6 Steve Colter	.25	.12	.02
☐ 7 Clyde Drexler	2.00	1.00	.20
☐ 8 Audie Norris	.25	.12	.02
☐ 9 Jerome Kersey	1.00	.50	.10
☐ 10 Sam Bowie	.60	.30	.06
☐ 11 Kenny Carr	.35	.17	.03
☐ 12 Lloyd Neal	.25	.12	.02
☐ 13 Mychal Thompson	.50	.25	.05
☐ 14 Geoff Petrie	.35	.17	.03
☐ 15 Tom Scheffler	.25	.12	.02
☐ 16 Kiki Vandeweghe	.60	.30	.06

1985-86 Trail Blazers Franz

The 1985-86 Franz Portland Trail Blazers set was produced by The Star Company for Franz Bread. There are 12 player cards and one coach card. The front borders are reddish orange, and the backs feature statistics and biographical information. The cards measure standard size, 2 1/2" by 3 1/2".

	MINT	EXC	G-VG
COMPLETE SET (13)	55.00	27.50	5.50
COMMON PLAYER (1-13)	1.50	.75	.15
☐ 1 Jack Ramsay CO	2.25	1.10	.22
☐ 2 Sam Bowie	3.50	1.75	.35
☐ 3 Kenny Carr	2.25	1.10	.22
☐ 4 Steve Colter	1.50	.75	.15
☐ 5 Clyde Drexler	20.00	10.00	2.00
☐ 6 Ken Johnson	1.50	.75	.15
☐ 7 Caldwell Jones	2.25	1.10	.22
☐ 8 Jerome Kersey	10.00	5.00	1.00
☐ 9 Jim Paxson	2.25	1.10	.22
☐ 10 Terry Porter	20.00	10.00	2.00
☐ 11 Mychal Thompson	3.00	1.50	.30
☐ 12 Darnell Valentine	2.25	1.10	.22
☐ 13 Kiki Vandeweghe	3.50	1.75	.35

1986-87 Trail Blazers Franz

The 1986-87 Franz Portland Trail Blazers set was produced by The Star Company for Franz Bread. There are 12 player cards and one coach card. The front borders are reddish-orange, and the backs feature statistics and biographical information. Card backs are printed in pink and red on white card stock. The cards measure standard size, 2 1/2" by 3 1/2".

	MINT	EXC	G-VG
COMPLETE SET (13)	35.00	17.50	3.50
COMMON PLAYER (1-13)	1.50	.75	.15
☐ 1 Walter Berry	3.00	1.50	.30
☐ 2 Sam Bowie	3.00	1.50	.30
☐ 3 Kenny Carr	2.25	1.10	.22
☐ 4 Clyde Drexler	15.00	7.50	1.50
☐ 5 Michael Holton	2.25	1.10	.22
☐ 6 Steve Johnson	2.25	1.10	.22
☐ 7 Caldwell Jones	2.25	1.10	.22

		MINT	EXC	G-VG
☐ 8	Jerome Kersey	7.50	3.75	.75
☐ 9	Fernando Martin	1.50	.75	.15
☐ 10	Jim Paxson	2.25	1.10	.22
☐ 11	Terry Porter	9.00	4.50	.90
☐ 12	Kiki Vandeweghe	3.00	1.50	.30
☐ 13	Mike Schuler CO	1.50	.75	.15

1987-88 Trail Blazers Franz

This 13-card was produced by Fleer as a promotion for Franz Bread. The cards measure the standard size (2 1/2" by 3 1/2") and were distributed in loaves of Franz Bread. The backs have biographical and statistical information. The cards are numbered on the back.

		MINT	EXC	G-VG
COMPLETE SET (13)		30.00	15.00	3.00
COMMON PLAYER (1-13)		1.00	.50	.10
☐ 1	Clyde Drexler	12.00	6.00	1.20
☐ 2	Kevin Duckworth	5.00	2.50	.50
☐ 3	Michael Holton	1.50	.75	.15
☐ 4	Steve Johnson	1.00	.50	.10
☐ 5	Caldwell Jones	1.50	.75	.15
☐ 6	Jerome Kersey	6.00	3.00	.60
☐ 7	Maurice Lucas	2.50	1.25	.25
☐ 8	Jim Paxson	1.50	.75	.15
☐ 9	Terry Porter	7.00	3.50	.70
☐ 10	Mike Schuler CO	1.00	.50	.10
☐ 11	Kiki Vandeweghe	2.00	1.00	.20
☐ 12	Steve Johnson	1.00	.50	.10
☐ 13	Kiki Vandeweghe	2.50	1.25	.25

1988-89 Trail Blazers Franz

The 1988-89 Franz Portland Trail Blazers set was produced by The Fleer Corporation for Franz Bread. There are 12 player cards

and one coach card. The front borders are white with red bars and the backs feature statistics and biographical information. Card backs are printed in pink and red on white card stock. The cards measure standard size, 2 1/2" by 3 1/2".

		MINT	EXC	G-VG
COMPLETE SET (13)		25.00	12.50	2.50
COMMON PLAYER (1-13)		1.00	.50	.10
☐ 1	Richard Anderson	1.00	.50	.10
☐ 2	Sam Bowie	2.00	1.00	.20
☐ 3	Mark Bryant	1.50	.75	.15
☐ 4	Clyde Drexler	10.00	5.00	1.00
☐ 5	Kevin Duckworth	3.00	1.50	.30
☐ 6	Rolando Ferreira	1.50	.75	.15
☐ 7	Steve Johnson	1.00	.50	.10
☐ 8	Caldwell Jones	1.50	.75	.15
☐ 9	Jerome Kersey	4.00	2.00	.40
☐ 10	Terry Porter	5.00	2.50	.50
☐ 11	Mike Schuler CO	1.00	.50	.10
☐ 12	Jerry Sichting	1.50	.75	.15
☐ 13	Kiki Vandeweghe	2.00	1.00	.20

1989-90 Trail Blazers Franz

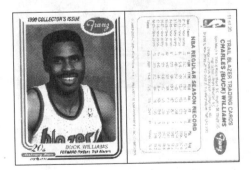

This 20-card set was produced by the Fleer Corporation for Franz Bread. The set commemorates the 20th anniversary season of the Trail Blazers and showcases current players as well as some "Blazer Greats" from past teams. The cards measure the standard size (2 1/2" by 3 1/2"). The front features color action photos on white card stock, with orange border stripes on the left side and black border stripes on the right side and bottom of the picture. The Franz Bread logo appears in the upper right corner. The horizontally oriented back has biographical and statistical information, printed in pink and red on white card stock. The cards are numbered on the back.

		MINT	EXC	G-VG
COMPLETE SET (20)		20.00	10.00	2.00
COMMON PLAYER (1-20)		.65	.30	.06

			MINT	EXC	G-VG
☐	1	Rick Adelman CO	.90	.45	.09
☐	2	Mark Bryant	.90	.45	.09
☐	3	Wayne Cooper	.90	.45	.09
☐	4	Kevin Duckworth	2.00	1.00	.20
☐	5	Clyde Drexler	7.50	3.75	.75
☐	6	Byron Irvin	.90	.45	.09
☐	7	Jerome Kersey	3.00	1.50	.30
☐	8	Drazen Petrovic	.90	.45	.09
☐	9	Terry Porter	3.50	1.75	.35
☐	10	Cliff Robertson	3.00	1.50	.30
☐	11	Buck Williams	2.50	1.25	.25
☐	12	Lionel Hollins	.90	.45	.09
☐	13	Maurice Lucas	1.50	.75	.15
☐	14	Calvin Natt	.90	.45	.09
☐	15	Lloyd Neal	.65	.30	.06
☐	16	Jim Paxson	.65	.30	.06
☐	17	Geoff Petrie	.90	.45	.09
☐	18	Larry Steele	.65	.30	.06
☐	19	Mychal Thompson	.90	.45	.09
☐	20	Bill Walton	2.00	1.00	.20

1990-91 Trail Blazers British Petroleum

Photo by Bryan Drake

Clyde Drexler   BP

These large (approximately 8 1/2" by 11") high-gloss action player photos were taken by Bryan Drake. The photos are printed on thin paper and have white, red, and white borders (in that order), on a black background. The player's name appears below the picture, between the team and the sponsor's logos. The backs are blank. The set features members of the Portland Trail Blazers.

			MINT	EXC	G-VG
	COMPLETE SET (6)		12.00	6.00	1.20
	COMMON PLAYER (1-6)		1.50	.75	.15
☐	1	Danny Ainge	1.50	.75	.15
☐	2	Clyde Drexler	5.00	2.50	.50
☐	3	Kevin Duckworth	1.50	.75	.15
☐	4	Jerome Kersey	2.00	1.00	.20
☐	5	Terry Porter	2.50	1.25	.25
☐	6	Buck Williams	2.00	1.00	.20

1990-91 Trail Blazers Franz

This 20-card set was produced by the Fleer Corporation for Franz Bread for distribution in the Portland area. The cards measure the standard size (2 1/2" by 3 1/2"). The fronts feature color action player photos on a white card face, with black borders on the left side and red borders on the right. The Franz logo appears in a blue oval in the upper left corner, with the words "1991 Collector's Issue" to the right. The player's name, position, and team name appear below the picture. The back has biographical information and player statistics printed in pink and red on white. The cards are numbered on the back. The team card can be found with and without the notation, 1989-90 Western Conference Champions, at the bottom of the (horizontally oriented) obverse.

			MINT	EXC	G-VG
	COMPLETE SET (20)		15.00	7.50	1.50
	COMMON PLAYER (1-20)		.50	.25	.05
☐	1	Team Card	.75	.35	.07
☐	2	'89-90 Playoffs	.50	.25	.05
☐	3	'89-90 Playoffs	.50	.25	.05
☐	4	'89-90 Playoffs	.50	.25	.05
☐	5	'89-90 Playoffs	.50	.25	.05
☐	6	Bill Walton	1.50	.75	.15
☐	7	Rick Adelman CO	.75	.35	.07
☐	8	John Schalow CO and	.50	.25	.05
		John Wetzel CO			
☐	9	Alaa Abdelnaby	1.00	.50	.10
☐	10	Danny Ainge	1.00	.50	.10
☐	11	Mark Bryant	.75	.35	.07
☐	12	Wayne Cooper	.50	.25	.05
☐	13	Clyde Drexler	4.00	2.00	.40
☐	14	Kevin Duckworth	1.25	.60	.12
☐	15	Jerome Kersey	1.50	.75	.15
☐	16	Drazen Petrovic	.75	.35	.07
☐	17	Terry Porter	2.00	1.00	.20
☐	18	Cliff Robinson	1.25	.60	.12
☐	19	Buck Williams	1.50	.75	.15
☐	20	Danny Young	.50	.25	.05

1957-59 Union Oil Booklets *

These booklets were distributed by Union Oil. The front cover of each booklet features a drawing of the subject player. The booklets are numbered and were issued over several years beginning in 1957. These are 12-page pamphlets and are approximately 4" by 5 1/2". The set is subtitled "Family Sports Fun." This was apparently primarily a Southern California promotion.

			NRMT	VG-E	GOOD
	COMPLETE SET (44)		150.00	75.00	15.00
	COMMON PLAYER (1-44)		3.00	1.50	.30
☐	1	Elroy Hirsch	7.50	3.75	.75
		Football 57			
☐	2	Les Richter	5.00	2.50	.50
		Football 57			
☐	3	Frankie Albert	5.00	2.50	.50
		Football 57			
☐	4	Y.A. Tittle	10.00	5.00	1.00
		Football 57			
☐	5	Bill Russell	15.00	7.50	1.50
		Basketball 57			
☐	6	Forrest Twogood	5.00	2.50	.50
		Basketball 57			
☐	7	Bob Richards	5.00	2.50	.50
		Body Conditioning 57			
☐	8	Phil Woolpert	5.00	2.50	.50
		Basketball 58			
☐	9	Bill Sharman	7.50	3.75	.75
		Basketball 58			
☐	10	Alf Engen	3.00	1.50	.30
		Skiing 58			
☐	11	Bob Mathias	5.00	2.50	.50
		Track 58			

☐ 40 Jack Kramer .... Tennis 59	5.00	2.50	.50
☐ 41 Ernie Banks .... Baseball 59	9.00	4.50	.90
☐ 42 Cary Middlecoff .... Golf 59	3.00	1.50	.30
☐ 43 Greta Andersen .... Swimming 59	3.00	1.50	.30
☐ 44 Lon Garrison .... Camping 59	3.00	1.50	.30

1961 Union Oil

The 1961 Union Oil basketball card set contains 10 oversized (3" by 3 15/16"), attractive, brown-tinted cards. The cards are unnumbered and feature players from the Hawaii Chiefs of the American Basketball League. The backs, printed in dark blue ink, feature a short biography of the player, an ad for KGU radio and the Union Oil circle 76 logo. The catalog number for this set is UO-17.

	NRMT	VG-E	GOOD
COMPLETE SET (10)	100.00	50.00	10.00
COMMON PLAYER (1-10)	10.00	5.00	1.00
☐ 1 Frank Burgess	10.00	5.00	1.00
☐ 2 Jeff Cohen	10.00	5.00	1.00
☐ 3 Lee Harman	10.00	5.00	1.00
☐ 4 Rick Herrscher	10.00	5.00	1.00
☐ 5 Lowery Kirk	10.00	5.00	1.00
☐ 6 Dave Mills	10.00	5.00	1.00
☐ 7 Max Perry	10.00	5.00	1.00
☐ 8 George Price	10.00	5.00	1.00
☐ 9 Fred Sawyer	10.00	5.00	1.00
☐ 10 Dale Wise	10.00	5.00	1.00

1988-89 Warriors Smokey

The 1988-89 Smokey Golden State Warriors set contains four 5" by 8" (approximately) cards featuring color action photos. The card backs feature a large fire safety cartoon and minimal player information. The cards are unnumbered and are ordered below alphabetically. The set was sponsored by the California Department of Forestry and Fire Protection and the Bureau of Land Management. The player's name, number, and position are overprinted in the lower right corner of each obverse.

	MINT	EXC	G-VG
COMPLETE SET (4)	20.00	10.00	2.00
COMMON PLAYER (1-4)	3.00	1.50	.30
☐ 1 Winston Garland 12 .... (Guard)	3.50	1.75	.35
☐ 2 Chris Mullin 17 .... (Guard/Forward)	9.00	4.50	.90

☐ 12 Duke Snider .... Baseball 58	10.00	5.00	1.00
☐ 13 Payton Jordan .... Track 58	3.00	1.50	.30
☐ 14 Bob Lemon .... Baseball 58	7.50	3.75	.75
☐ 15 Red Schoendienst .... Baseball 58	7.50	3.75	.75
☐ 16 Johnny Dieckman .... Fishing 58	3.00	1.50	.30
☐ 17 Pancho Gonzalez .... Tennis 58	3.00	1.50	.30
☐ 18 Mal Whitfield .... Track 58	3.00	1.50	.30
☐ 19 Mike Peppe .... Swimming 58	3.00	1.50	.30
☐ 20 Bill Rigney .... Baseball 58	3.00	1.50	.30
☐ 21 Nancy Chaffee Kiner .... Tennis 58	3.00	1.50	.30
☐ 22 Lloyd Mangrum .... Golf 58	3.00	1.50	.30
☐ 23 Pat McCormick .... Diving 58	3.00	1.50	.30
☐ 24 Perry T. Jones .... Tennis 58	3.00	1.50	.30
☐ 25 Howard Hill .... Archery 58	3.00	1.50	.30
☐ 26 Herb Parsons .... Hunting 58	3.00	1.50	.30
☐ 27 Bob Waterfield .... Football 58	9.00	4.50	.90
☐ 28 Pete Elliott .... Football 58	5.00	2.50	.50
☐ 29 Elroy Hirsch .... Football 58	7.50	3.75	.75
☐ 30 Frank Gifford .... Football 58	10.00	5.00	1.00
☐ 31 George Yardley .... Basketball 58	5.00	2.50	.50
☐ 32 John Wooden .... Basketball 58	7.50	3.75	.75
☐ 33 Ralph Borrelli .... Tumbling 58	3.00	1.50	.30
☐ 34 Bob Cousy .... Basketball 58	9.00	4.50	.90
☐ 35 Yves Latreille .... Skiing 58	3.00	1.50	.30
☐ 36 Slats Gill .... Basketball 59	5.00	2.50	.50
☐ 37 Jess Mortensen .... Track 59	3.00	1.50	.30
☐ 38 Jackie Jensen .... Baseball 59	6.00	3.00	.60
☐ 39 Warren Spahn .... Baseball 59	9.00	4.50	.90

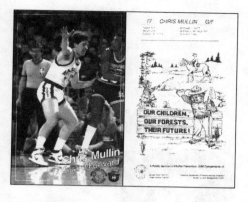

	3	Ralph Sampson 50 (Center)	5.00	2.50	.50
	4	Larry Smith 13 (Forward)	3.50	1.75	.35

1991 Wooden Award Winners

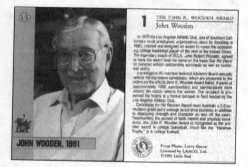

This 21-card set was released by Little Sun of Monrovia, California, to commemorate the John R. Wooden Award. Only 28,000 sets were produced, and the set number is given on the certification card. The set is accompanied by a deluxe card album with two-up plastic sheets to house the cards. The cards chronicle the career of John Wooden and feature all 14 winners (in their college uniforms) of college basketball's most prestigious award. The cards measure the standard size (2 1/2" by 3 1/2"). With the exception of some early black and white Wooden photos, the fronts feature borderless color player photos. Each picture is bordered on the left side by a gray stripe, with the Little Sun logo superimposed at the top. A lavender stripe traverses the bottom of the card face and gives a title for that card. The backs have biographical information and full close-ups of each player printed in a blue Mezzo-tint process. The cards are numbered on the back.

			MINT	EXC	G-VG
		COMPLETE SET (21)	14.00	7.00	1.40
		COMMON PLAYER (1-21)	.50	.25	.05
	1	John Wooden 1991	.75	.35	.07
	2	Wooden Trophy	.50	.25	.05
	3	John Wooden Purdue	.50	.25	.05
	4	John Wooden UCLA	.50	.25	.05
	5	Wooden Summer Camp	.50	.25	.05
	6	Duke Llewellyn	.50	.25	.05
	7	Marques Johnson	.60	.30	.06
	8	Phil Ford	.60	.30	.06
	9	Larry Bird	2.00	1.00	.20

	10	Darrell Griffith	.60	.30	.06
	11	Danny Ainge	.75	.35	.07
	12	Ralph Sampson	.75	.35	.07
	13	Michael Jordan	3.00	1.50	.30
	14	Chris Mullin	1.00	.50	.10
	15	Walter Berry	.60	.30	.06
	16	David Robinson	2.50	1.25	.25
	17	Danny Manning	.75	.35	.07
	18	Sean Elliott	.75	.35	.07
	19	Lionel Simmons	1.00	.50	.10
	20	Larry Johnson	2.00	1.00	.20
	21	Press Conference 1991	.50	.25	.05
	xx	Certification of Limited Edition	.50	.25	.05

1981-82 Arizona Police

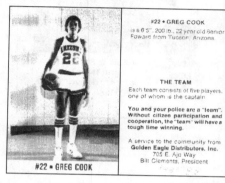

This 20-card set measures 2 5/8" by 3 5/8". It is sponsored by Golden Eagle Distributors. A posed color photo appears on the front of the card, with the name and uniform number underneath the picture. The back of the card provides basic biographical information, a discussion or definition of an aspect of basketball, and a safety message.

			MINT	EXC	G-VG
		COMPLETE SET (20)	20.00	10.00	2.00
		COMMON PLAYER (1-20)	1.00	.50	.10
	1	Ken Atkins CO	1.00	.50	.10
	2	John Belobraydic 55	1.00	.50	.10
	3	Brock Brunkhorst 10	1.00	.50	.10
	4	Jeff Collins 24	1.00	.50	.10
	5	Greg Cook 22	3.00	1.50	.30
	6	Len Gordy CO	1.00	.50	.10
	7	Gary J. Heintz CO	1.00	.50	.10
	8	Keith Jackson 21	1.00	.50	.10
	9	Mark Jung 33	1.00	.50	.10
	10	Jack Magno 41	1.00	.50	.10
	11	Donald Mellow 35	1.00	.50	.10
	12	Charles Miller 52	1.00	.50	.10
	13	Pete Murphy 15	1.00	.50	.10
	14	Kevin Ronndfield 44	1.00	.50	.10
	15	Frank Smith 31	1.00	.50	.10
	16	Fred Snowden CO	1.50	.75	.15
	17	Ernest Taylor-Harris 32	1.00	.50	.10
	18	Harvey Thompson 34	1.00	.50	.10
	19	John Vlahogeorge 14	1.00	.50	.10
	20	Ricky Walker 12	1.50	.75	.15

1984-85 Arizona Police

This 16-card set measures approximately 2 1/4" by 3 3/4". It is jointly sponsored by the Tucson Police Department and Golden Eagle Distributors. The front of the card features a posed color photo of the player on the top portion, and the name and uniform number underneath the picture. The back of the card

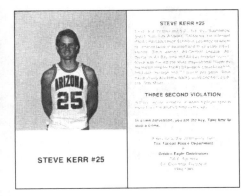

STEVE KERR #25

STEVE KERR #25

THREE SECOND VIOLATION

STEVE KERR #25

gives basic biographical information, a discussion or definition of an aspect of basketball, and a safety message. This set includes future NBA stars Sean Elliott and Steve Kerr.

	MINT	EXC	G-VG
COMPLETE SET (14)	12.00	6.00	1.20
COMMON PLAYER (1-14)	.75	.35	.07
☐ 1 Anthony Cook 00	2.00	1.00	.20
☐ 2 Eric Cooper 21	.75	.35	.07
☐ 3 Brian David 34	.75	.35	.07
☐ 4 John Edgar 50	.75	.35	.07
☐ 5 Sean Elliott 32	4.00	2.00	.40
☐ 6 Bruce Fraser 22	.75	.35	.07
☐ 7 David Haskin 24	.75	.35	.07
☐ 8 Rolf Jacobs 13	.75	.35	.07
☐ 9 Steve Kerr 25	2.00	1.00	.20
☐ 10 Ken Lofton 11	2.00	1.00	.20
☐ 11 Craig McMillan 20	.75	.35	.07
☐ 12 Lute Olson CO	1.25	.60	.12
☐ 13 Joe Turner 33	.75	.35	.07
☐ 14 Bruce Wheatley 45	.75	.35	.07

gives basic biographical information (including the player's nickname where appropriate), a discussion or definition of an aspect of basketball, and a safety message. Among the players in the set is Steve Kerr, who would later go on to a career in the NBA.

	MINT	EXC	G-VG
COMPLETE SET (16)	12.00	6.00	1.20
COMMON PLAYER (1-16)	.75	.35	.07
☐ 1 Brock Brunkhorst 10	.75	.35	.07
☐ 2 Ken Burmeister CO	.75	.35	.07
☐ 3 Ricky Byrdsong CO	.75	.35	.07
☐ 4 John Edgar 50	.75	.35	.07
☐ 5 Bruce Fraser 22	.75	.35	.07
☐ 6 David Haskin 24	.75	.35	.07
☐ 7 Keith Jackson 21	.75	.35	.07
☐ 8 Rolf Jacobs 13	.75	.35	.07
☐ 9 Steve Kerr 25	3.00	1.50	.30
☐ 10 Craig McMillan 20	.75	.35	.07
☐ 11 Lute Olson CO	1.25	.60	.12
☐ 12 Eddie Smith 14	.75	.35	.07
☐ 13 Morgan Taylor 34	.75	.35	.07
☐ 14 Scott Thompson CO	.75	.35	.07
☐ 15 Joe Turner 33	.75	.35	.07
☐ 16 Pete Williams 32	.75	.35	.07

1986-87 Arizona Police

JUD BUECHLER #33

THE TEAM

JUD BUECHLER #33

This 12-card set was cosponsored by The Tucson Police Department and Golden Eagle Distributors. The cards measure 2 1/4" by 3 3/4". The front features a borderless posed photo of the player. The player's name, number, and the Pacific-10 Conference logo appear in the white stripe below the picture. The back has brief biographical information, a definition of an aspect of the game of basketball, and an anti-crime or public service message. The cards are unnumbered and are checklisted below in alphabetical order, with the uniform number after the player's name.

	MINT	EXC	G-VG
COMPLETE SET (12)	10.00	5.00	1.00
COMMON PLAYER (1-12)	.75	.35	.07
☐ 1 Jud Buechler 33	2.00	1.00	.20
☐ 2 Anthony Cook 00	1.50	.75	.15
☐ 3 Brian David 34	.75	.35	.07
☐ 4 Sean Elliott 32	2.50	1.25	.25
☐ 5 Bruce Fraser 22	.75	.35	.07
☐ 6 Steve Kerr 25	1.50	.75	.15
☐ 7 Ken Lofton 11	1.50	.75	.15
☐ 8 Harvey Mason 44	.75	.35	.07
☐ 9 Craig McMillan 20	.75	.35	.07
☐ 10 Lute Olsen CO	1.00	.50	.10
☐ 11 Tom Tolbert 31	1.50	.75	.15
☐ 12 Joe Turner 33	.75	.35	.07

1985-86 Arizona Police

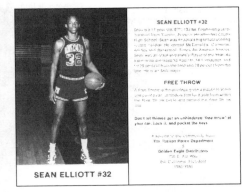

SEAN ELLIOTT #32

FREE THROW

SEAN ELLIOTT #32

This 14-card set measures approximately 2 1/4" by 3 3/4". It is jointly sponsored by the Tucson Police Department and Golden Eagle Distributors. The front of the card features a posed color photo of the player on the top portion, and the name and uniform number underneath the picture. The back of the card

1987-88 Arizona Police

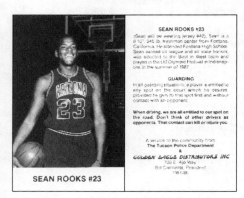

SEAN ROOKS #23

SEAN ROOKS #23
(Sean will be wearing jersey #42). Sean is a 6'10", 245 lb. freshman center from Fontana, California. He attended Fontana High School. Sean earned all league and all state honors, was selected to the Best in West team and played in the US Olympic Festival in Indianapolis in the summer of 1987.

GUARDING
In all guarding situations, a player is entitled to any spot on the court which he desires provided he gets to that spot first and without contact with an opponent.

When driving, we are all entitled to our spot on the road. Don't think of other drivers as opponents. That contact can kill or injure you.

A service to the community from
The Tucson Police Department
&
GOLDEN EAGLE DISTRIBUTORS INC
705 E. Ajo Way
Bill Clements, President
1987-88

This 14-card set measures approximately 2 1/4" by 3 3/4". It is jointly sponsored by the Tucson Police Department and Golden Eagle Distributors. The front of the card features a posed color photo of the player on the top portion, and the name and uniform number underneath the picture. The back of the card gives basic biographical information, a discussion or definition of an aspect of basketball, and a safety message. On three cards the jersey number does not correspond to the number the player actually wears during games (Georgeson wears 45, Muehlebach 24, and Rooks 42). Future NBA players included in this set are Sean Elliott and Steve Kerr.

	MINT	EXC	G-VG
COMPLETE SET (14)	10.00	5.00	1.00
COMMON PLAYER (1-14)	.65	.30	.06
☐ 1 Jud Buechler 35	1.25	.60	.12
☐ 2 Anthony Cook 00	1.25	.60	.12
☐ 3 Brian David 34	.65	.30	.06
☐ 4 Sean Elliott 32	2.00	1.00	.20
☐ 5 Mark Georgeson 34	.65	.30	.06
☐ 6 Steve Kerr 25	1.25	.60	.12
☐ 7 Ken Lofton 11	1.25	.60	.12
☐ 8 Harvey Mason 44	.65	.30	.06
☐ 9 Craig McMillan 20	.65	.30	.06
☐ 10 Matt Muehlebach 44	1.25	.60	.12
☐ 11 Lute Olson CO	1.00	.50	.10
☐ 12 Sean Rooks 23	1.25	.60	.12
☐ 13 Tom Tolbert 23	1.00	.50	.10
☐ 14 Joe Turner 33	.65	.30	.06

1988-89 Arizona Police

This 13-card set measures approximately 2 1/4" by 3 3/4". It is jointly sponsored by the Tucson Police Department and Golden Eagle Distributors. The front of the card features a posed color photo of the player on the top portion, and the name and uniform number underneath the picture. The back of the card gives basic biographical information, a discussion or definition of an aspect of basketball, and a safety message. Future NBA star Sean Elliott (misspelled Elliot) is included in this set.

	MINT	EXC	G-VG
COMPLETE SET (13)	10.00	5.00	1.00
COMMON PLAYER (1-13)	.65	.30	.06
☐ 1 Jud Buechler 35	1.00	.50	.10
☐ 2 Anthony Cook 00	1.00	.50	.10
☐ 3 Ron Curry 33	.65	.30	.06
☐ 4 Brian David 34	.65	.30	.06
☐ 5 Sean Elliott 32	2.00	1.00	.20
(Misspelled Elliot)			
☐ 6 Mark Georgeson 45	.65	.30	.06
☐ 7 Ken Lofton 11	1.25	.60	.12

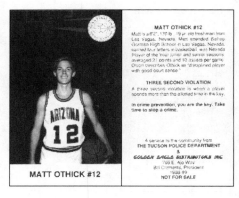

MATT OTHICK #12

MATT OTHICK #12
Matt is a 6'2", 170 lb. 19 yr. old freshman from Las Vegas, Nevada. Matt attended Bishop Gorman High School in Las Vegas, Nevada. earned four letters in basketball, was Nevada Player of the Year junior and senior seasons, averaged 21 points and 10 assists per game. Olson describes Othick as "a disciplined player with good court sense."

THREE SECOND VIOLATION
A three second violation is when a player spends more than the allotted time in the key.

In crime prevention, you are the key. Take time to stop a crime.

A service to the community from
THE TUCSON POLICE DEPARTMENT
&
GOLDEN EAGLE DISTRIBUTORS INC
705 E. Ajo Way
Bill Clements, President
1988-89
NOT FOR SALE

☐ 8 Harvey Mason 44	.65	.30	.06
☐ 9 Matt Muehlebach 24	1.00	.50	.10
☐ 10 Lute Olson CO	1.00	.50	.10
☐ 11 Matt Othick 12	.65	.30	.06
☐ 12 Sean Rooks 42	1.00	.50	.10
☐ 13 Wayne Womack 30	.65	.30	.06

1990-91 Arizona Promos *

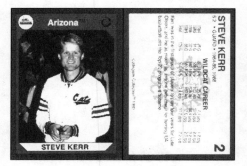

STEVE KERR

This 10-card standard size (2 1/2" by 3 1/2") set was produced by Collegiate Collection and features some of the great players of Arizona over the past few years. This set involves players of different sports and we have added a two-letter abbreviation next to the person's name to indicate what sport is pictured on the card. The back of the card either has statistical or biographical information about the player during their college career.

	MINT	EXC	G-VG
COMPLETE SET (10)	5.00	2.50	.50
COMMON PLAYER (1-10)	.50	.25	.05
☐ 1 Chuck Cecil FB	.50	.25	.05
☐ 2 Steve Kerr BK	.60	.30	.06
☐ 3 Lute Olson CO BK	.50	.25	.05
(Watch Visible)			
☐ 4 Chris Singleton FB	.75	.35	.07
☐ 5 Lute Olson CO BK	.50	.25	.05
☐ 6 Vance Johnson FB	.60	.30	.06
☐ 7 Dick Tomey CO FB	.50	.25	.05
(Waist)			
☐ 8 Robert Lee Thompson FB	.50	.25	.05
☐ 9 Sean Elliott BK	1.00	.50	.10
☐ 10 Dick Tomey CO FB	.50	.25	.05
(Head and Shoulders)			

1990-91 Arizona 125 *

This 125-card set was produced by Collegiate Collection and measures the standard size (2 1/2" by 3 1/2"). The front features a mix of black and white or color player photos, with red and dark blue borders. All four corners of the picture are cut off. In white lettering the school name appears above the picture, with the player's name at the bottom of the card face. In a horizontal format the back presents biographical information and career summary, on a white background with dark blue lettering and borders. The cards are numbered on the back.

	MINT	EXC	G-VG
COMPLETE SET (125)	15.00	7.50	1.50
COMMON PLAYER (1-125)	.10	.05	.01

		MINT	EXC	G-VG
☐ 1	Steve Kerr	.35	.17	.03
☐ 2	Sean Elliott	.75	.35	.07
☐ 3	Vance Johnson	.35	.17	.03
☐ 4	Lute Olson	.20	.10	.02
☐ 5	Chris Singleton	.35	.17	.03
☐ 6	Robert Gamez	.35	.17	.03
☐ 7	Ricky Hunley	.35	.17	.03
☐ 8	Terry Francona	.20	.10	.02
☐ 9	Chuck Cecil	.20	.10	.02
☐ 10	Craig Lefferts	.20	.10	.02
☐ 11	Warren Rustand	.10	.05	.01
☐ 12	Tommy Tunnicliffe	.10	.05	.01
☐ 13	Steve Strong	.10	.05	.01
☐ 14	T. Bell	.20	.10	.02
☐ 15	Jerry Kindall CO	.20	.10	.02
☐ 16	Kevin Long	.10	.05	.01
☐ 17	Fred Snowden CO	.10	.05	.01
☐ 18	Anthony Smith	.20	.10	.02
☐ 19	Laurie Brunet	.10	.05	.01
☐ 20	Wes Clements	.10	.05	.01
☐ 21	Larry Demic	.20	.10	.02
☐ 22	Peter Evans	.10	.05	.01
☐ 23	Gilbert Heredia	.10	.05	.01
☐ 24	Chuck Cecil	.20	.10	.02
☐ 25	Todd Trafton	.20	.10	.02
☐ 26	Alan Durden	.10	.05	.01
☐ 27	Eric Meeks	.10	.05	.01
☐ 28	Steve Kerr	.35	.17	.03
☐ 29	Rosie Wegrich	.10	.05	.01
☐ 30	Danny Lockett	.10	.05	.01
☐ 31	Dana Wells	.10	.05	.01
☐ 32	Katrena Johnson	.10	.05	.01
☐ 33	Anthony Cook	.20	.10	.02
☐ 34	Anita Moss	.10	.05	.01
☐ 35	David Adams	.10	.05	.01
☐ 36	Eddie Leon	.10	.05	.01
☐ 37	Vance Johnson	.35	.17	.03
☐ 38	Sean Elliott	.75	.35	.07
☐ 39	Alan Zinter	.35	.17	.03
☐ 40	Russell Brown	.10	.05	.01
☐ 41	Joe Magrane	.25	.12	.02
☐ 42	Derek Hill	.25	.12	.02
☐ 43	Hubie Oliver	.20	.10	.02
☐ 44	Scott Geyer	.10	.05	.01
☐ 45	Bill Wright	.10	.05	.01
☐ 46	Max Zendejas	.20	.10	.02
☐ 47	Jim Young CO	.20	.10	.02
☐ 48	Mark Arneson	.20	.10	.02
☐ 49	Doug Pfaff	.10	.05	.01
☐ 50	George DiCarlo	.10	.05	.01
☐ 51	Brad Henke	.10	.05	.01
☐ 52	Bruce Hill	.35	.17	.03
☐ 53	Ron Hassey	.25	.12	.02
☐ 54	Jim Gault	.10	.05	.01
☐ 55	Bryon Evans	.35	.17	.03
☐ 56	Hoan Hansen	.10	.05	.01
☐ 57	Pete Williams	.10	.05	.01
☐ 58	Frank Busch	.10	.05	.01
☐ 59	David Wood	.20	.10	.02
☐ 60	Dave Murray	.10	.05	.01
☐ 61	Carla Garrett	.10	.05	.01
☐ 62	Ivan Lesnik	.10	.05	.01
☐ 63	J.T. Snow	.20	.10	.02
☐ 64	Al Fleming	.10	.05	.01
☐ 65	Don Lee	.10	.05	.01
☐ 66	Dave Towne	.10	.05	.01
☐ 67	Brad Anderson	.10	.05	.01
☐ 68	Chuck Cecil	.20	.10	.02
☐ 69	Mike Dawson	.20	.10	.02
☐ 70	Ed Vosberg	.20	.10	.02
☐ 71	Joe Tofflemire	.10	.05	.01
☐ 72	Rick LaRose	.10	.05	.01
☐ 73	Larry Silveria	.10	.05	.01
☐ 74	Lamonte Hunley	.10	.05	.01
☐ 75	June Olkowski	.10	.05	.01
☐ 76	Dave Stegman	.10	.05	.01
☐ 77	Melissa McLinden	.10	.05	.01
☐ 78	Chris Johnson	.10	.05	.01
☐ 79	Ken Lofton	.35	.17	.03
☐ 80	Ken Erickson	.10	.05	.01
☐ 81	Martina Koch	.10	.05	.01
☐ 82	Joel Estes	.10	.05	.01
☐ 83	Diane Johnson	.10	.05	.01
☐ 84	Jon Abbott	.10	.05	.01
☐ 85	Sean Elliott	.75	.35	.07
☐ 86	Thom Hunt	.10	.05	.01
☐ 87	Jeff Kiewel	.10	.05	.01
☐ 88	Morris Udall	.35	.17	.03
☐ 89	Becky Bell	.10	.05	.01
☐ 90	Ruben Rodriguez	.10	.05	.01
☐ 91	Randy Robbins	.10	.05	.01
☐ 92	Eddie Smith	.10	.05	.01
☐ 93	Steve Kerr	.35	.17	.03
☐ 94	Dwight Taylor	.10	.05	.01
☐ 95	Mike Candrea	.10	.05	.01
☐ 96	Vance Johnson	.35	.17	.03
☐ 97	Bob Elliott	.10	.05	.01
☐ 98	Glenn Parker	.10	.05	.01
☐ 99	Joe Nehls	.10	.05	.01
☐ 100	Director Card 1-99	.10	.05	.01
☐ 101	Derek Huff	.10	.05	.01
☐ 102	Mark Roby	.10	.05	.01
☐ 103	Lute Olson CO	.20	.10	.02
☐ 104	Art Luppino	.10	.05	.01
☐ 105	Kevin Long	.10	.05	.01
☐ 106	Bob Elliott	.10	.05	.01
☐ 107	George Young	.10	.05	.01
☐ 108	Don Pooley	.10	.05	.01
☐ 109	Byron Evans	.35	.17	.03
☐ 110	Sean Elliott	.75	.35	.07
☐ 111	Kim Haddow	.10	.05	.01
☐ 112	David Adams	.10	.05	.01
☐ 113	Bobby Thompson	.10	.05	.01
☐ 114	Brad Anderson	.10	.05	.01
☐ 115	Eddie Wilson	.10	.05	.01
☐ 116	Dan Pohl	.20	.10	.02
☐ 117	Joe Hernandez	.10	.05	.01
☐ 118	J.F.(Pop) McKale	.10	.05	.01
☐ 119	Gayle Hopkins	.10	.05	.01
☐ 120	Carl Cooper	.10	.05	.01
☐ 121	Ken Lofton	.35	.17	.03
☐ 122	Robert Lee Thompson	.10	.05	.01
☐ 123	Robert Ruman	.10	.05	.01
☐ 124	Meg Ritchie	.10	.05	.01
☐ 125	John Byrd Salmon	.10	.05	.01

1990 Arizona State Promos *

This ten-card standard size (2 1/2" by 3 1/2") set was issued by Collegiate Collection to honor some of the leading athletes in all sports played at Arizona State. The front features a full-color photo while the back of the card has information or statistical information about the player featured. To help identify the player there is a two-letter abbreviation of the athlete's sport next to the player's name.

	MINT	EXC	G-VG
COMPLETE SET (10)	5.00	2.50	.50
COMMON PLAYER (1-10)	.50	.25	.05

		MINT	EXC	G-VG
☐ 1	Reggie Jackson BB	1.00	.50	.10
☐ 2	Lafayette Lever BK	.60	.30	.06
☐ 3	Linty Ingram BB	.50	.25	.05
☐ 4	Luis Zendejas BB	.50	.25	.05
☐ 5	Byron Scott BK	.75	.35	.07
☐ 6	Sam Williams BK	.50	.25	.05
☐ 7	Lenny Randle BB	.50	.25	.05
☐ 8	Brian Noble FB	.60	.30	.06
☐ 9	Trace Armstrong FB	.60	.30	.06
☐ 10	Sun Devil Stadium	.50	.25	.05

1990 Arizona State 200 *

This 200-card set was produced by Collegiate Collection and measures the standard size (2 1/2" by 3 1/2"). The front features a mix of black and white or color player photos, with crimson and gold borders. All four corners of the picture give the appearance of being cut off in the design of the card. In gold lettering the school name appears above the picture, with the player's name at the bottom of the card face. In a horizontal format the back presents biographical information, career summary, and statistics, on a white background with gold lettering and borders. The cards are numbered on the back.

	MINT	EXC	G-VG
COMPLETE SET (200)	22.00	11.00	2.20
COMMON PLAYER (1-200)	.10	.05	.01

		MINT	EXC	G-VG
☐ 1	Reggie Jackson	.75	.35	.07
☐ 2	Gerald Riggs	.35	.17	.03
☐ 3	John Jefferson	.35	.17	.03
☐ 4	Sam Williams	.20	.10	.02
☐ 5	Charley Taylor	.35	.17	.03
☐ 6	Mike Davies	.10	.05	.01
☐ 7	Barry Bonds	.75	.35	.07
☐ 8	Byron Scott	.35	.17	.03
☐ 9	Lafayette"Fat" Lever	.35	.17	.03
☐ 10	Oddibe McDowell	.20	.10	.02

		MINT	EXC	G-VG
☐ 11	Dan Saleaumua	.20	.10	.02
☐ 12	Lionel Hollins	.20	.10	.02
☐ 13	Donnie Hill	.20	.10	.02
☐ 14	Doug Allen	.10	.05	.01
☐ 15	Kurt Nimphius	.15	.07	.01
☐ 16	Mike Benjamin	.10	.05	.01
☐ 17	Mark Malone	.20	.10	.02
☐ 18	Scott Lloyd	.20	.10	.02
☐ 19	Fair Hooker	.20	.10	.02
☐ 20	Jim Brock	.20	.10	.02
☐ 21	Linty Ingram	.10	.05	.01
☐ 22	Larry Gorden	.10	.05	.01
☐ 23	Chris Beasley	.10	.05	.01
☐ 24	Bruce Hill	.20	.10	.02
☐ 25	Elliot(Bump) Wills	.20	.10	.02
☐ 26	Steve Beck	.10	.05	.01
☐ 27	Scott Stephen	.10	.05	.01
☐ 28	Mike Haynes	.25	.12	.02
☐ 29	Packard Stadium West	.10	.05	.01
☐ 30	Vernon Maxwell	.25	.12	.02
☐ 31	Alton Lister	.25	.12	.02
☐ 32	Eric Allen	.20	.10	.02
☐ 33	Lafayette(Fat) Lever	.35	.17	.03
☐ 34	Al Bannister	.15	.07	.01
☐ 35	Skip McClendon	.15	.07	.01
☐ 36	David Fulcher	.35	.17	.03
☐ 37	Todd Kahs	.10	.05	.01
☐ 38	Larry Gura	.20	.10	.02
☐ 39	Aaron Cox	.35	.17	.03
☐ 40	Bob Kohrs	.20	.10	.02
☐ 41	Mark Landsberger	.20	.10	.02
☐ 42	Mike Richardson	.20	.10	.02
☐ 43	Shawn Patterson	.25	.12	.02
☐ 44	Paul Williams	.10	.05	.01
☐ 45	Danny Villa	.20	.10	.02
☐ 46	Eddie Bane	.20	.10	.02
☐ 47	Mike Pagel	.20	.10	.02
☐ 48	Jim Jeffcoat	.35	.17	.03
☐ 49	John Harris	.20	.10	.02
☐ 50	Lenny Randle	.20	.10	.02
☐ 51	Jeff Van Raaphorst	.20	.10	.02
☐ 52	Alvin Davis	.35	.17	.03
☐ 53	Freddie Williams	.10	.05	.01
☐ 54	Kevin Higgins	.10	.05	.01
☐ 55	Brian Noble	.25	.12	.02
☐ 56	Junior Ah You	.25	.12	.02
☐ 57	Kendall Carter	.10	.05	.01
☐ 58	Tony Novick	.10	.05	.01
☐ 59	Liz Aronshone	.10	.05	.01
☐ 60	Buzz Hayes	.10	.05	.01
☐ 61	Danny White	.25	.12	.02
☐ 62	Mistler	.10	.05	.01
☐ 63	Heather Farr	.25	.12	.02
☐ 64	Byron Scott	.35	.17	.03
☐ 65	Bill Mayfair	.10	.05	.01
☐ 66	Tammy Webb	.10	.05	.01
☐ 67	Curly Culp	.35	.17	.03
☐ 68	Mona Plummer Aquatic	.10	.05	.01
☐ 69	Norris Stevenson	.10	.05	.01
☐ 70	John Henry Johnson	.35	.17	.03
☐ 71	Roger Schmuck	.10	.05	.01
☐ 72	Al Harris	.25	.12	.02
☐ 73	Pearl Sinn	.10	.05	.01
☐ 74	John Finn	.10	.05	.01
☐ 75	Bruce Hardy	.10	.05	.01
☐ 76	Lisa Zeys	.10	.05	.01
☐ 77	Andrew Parker	.10	.05	.01
☐ 78	Ben Malone	.20	.10	.02
☐ 79	Brent McClanahan	.25	.12	.02
☐ 80	Sheri Rhodes	.10	.05	.01
☐ 81	Mike Black	.10	.05	.01
☐ 82	Floyd Bannister	.25	.12	.02
☐ 83	Danielle Ammaccapore	.25	.12	.02
☐ 84	Trace Armstrong	.25	.12	.02
☐ 85	Darryl Clack	.20	.10	.02
☐ 86	Steve Holden	.20	.10	.02
☐ 87	Pam Richmond	.10	.05	.01
☐ 88	Whiteman Tennis	.10	.05	.01
☐ 89	Art Malone	.20	.10	.02
☐ 90	Regina Stahl	.10	.05	.01
☐ 91	Darryl Harris	.10	.05	.01
☐ 92	Activity Center	.10	.05	.01
☐ 93	Randall McDaniel	.35	.17	.03
☐ 94	Sun Devil Stadium	.10	.05	.01
☐ 95	Luis Zendejas	.25	.12	.02
☐ 96	Sun Angel Track	.10	.05	.01
☐ 97	J.D. Hill	.20	.10	.02
☐ 98	Rod Severn	.10	.05	.01
☐ 99	Bobby Douglas	.25	.12	.02
☐ 100	Director Card 1-99	.10	.05	.01
☐ 101	1977 National Champs	.10	.05	.01
☐ 102	Bobby Winkles CO	.15	.07	.01
☐ 103	Zeke Jones	.10	.05	.01
☐ 104	Christy Nore	.10	.05	.01

☐ 105	Dan Devine	.20	.10	.02
☐ 106	Andy Astbury	.10	.05	.01
☐ 107	Lisa Stuck	.10	.05	.01
☐ 108	Dave Severn	.10	.05	.01
☐ 109	JoAnne Carner	.25	.12	.02
☐ 110	Doug Sachs	.10	.05	.01
☐ 111	Horner and Brooks	.25	.12	.02
	(Bob and Hubie)			
☐ 112	Herman Finzier	.10	.05	.01
☐ 113	Team 1957	.10	.05	.01
☐ 114	Lynda Tolbert	.10	.05	.01
☐ 115	Team 1981	.10	.05	.01
☐ 116	Bob Gilder	.10	.05	.01
☐ 117	Ulis Williams	.10	.05	.01
☐ 118	Tracy Cox	.10	.05	.01
☐ 119	"The Catch" Jefferson	.25	.12	.02
☐ 120	Mike Orn	.10	.05	.01
☐ 121	Team 1965	.10	.05	.01
☐ 122	Ron Brown	.25	.12	.02
☐ 123	1986 Team	.10	.05	.01
☐ 124	Jim Gressley	.10	.05	.01
☐ 125	Lucy Casazez	.10	.05	.01
☐ 126	Bwayne Evans	.10	.05	.01
☐ 127	Kathy Escarlega	.10	.05	.01
☐ 128	Ned Wulk	.20	.10	.02
☐ 129	Jim Carter	.20	.10	.02
☐ 130	Frank Covelli	.10	.05	.01
☐ 131	Dan St. John	.10	.05	.01
☐ 132	Jacinta Bartholomew	.10	.05	.01
☐ 133	Team 1967	.10	.05	.01
☐ 134	Jackie Brummer	.10	.05	.01
☐ 135	Danny White	.35	.17	.03
☐ 136	Alan Waldan	.10	.05	.01
☐ 137	Coleen Sommer	.10	.05	.01
☐ 138	1975 Team	.10	.05	.01
☐ 139	Eddie Urabano	.10	.05	.01
☐ 140	Jane Bastanchury	.10	.05	.01
☐ 141	Team 1969	.10	.05	.01
☐ 142	Leon Burton	.10	.05	.01
☐ 143	Mona Plummer	.10	.05	.01
☐ 144	Bob Mulgado	.10	.05	.01
☐ 145	Henry Carr	.20	.10	.02
☐ 146	Dan Severn	.10	.05	.01
☐ 147	Milissa Belose	.10	.05	.01
☐ 148	Ron Freeman	.10	.05	.01
☐ 149	Kim Neal	.10	.05	.01
☐ 150	Howard Twitty	.20	.10	.02
☐ 151	Reggie Jackson	.75	.35	.07
☐ 152	Lynn Nelson	.10	.05	.01
☐ 153	Ken Landacox	.10	.05	.01
☐ 154	Joe Caldwell	.15	.07	.01
☐ 155	Bob Breunig	.35	.17	.03
☐ 156	Larry Lawson	.10	.05	.01
☐ 157	Debbie Ochs	.10	.05	.01
☐ 158	Mike Devereaux	.10	.05	.01
☐ 159	Mike Sodders	.10	.05	.01
☐ 160	Keith Russell	.10	.05	.01
☐ 161	Art Becker	.20	.10	.02
☐ 162	Woody Green	.20	.10	.02
☐ 163	Ken Phelps	.20	.10	.02
☐ 164	Sherry Poole	.10	.05	.01
☐ 165	Rickey Peters	.15	.07	.01
☐ 166	Sherri Norris	.10	.05	.01
☐ 167	Paul Limne	.10	.05	.01
☐ 168	Whizzer White	.35	.17	.03
☐ 169	Maria Turjillo	.10	.05	.01
☐ 170	Karli Urban	.10	.05	.01
☐ 171	Sal Bando	.25	.12	.02
☐ 172	Bob Horner	.35	.17	.03
☐ 173	Hubie Brooks	.35	.17	.03
☐ 174	Mike Haynes	.35	.17	.03
☐ 175	Chris Jogis	.10	.05	.01
☐ 176	Charley Taylor	.35	.17	.03
☐ 177	Bernie Wrightson	.10	.05	.01
☐ 178	Kevin Romine	.20	.10	.02
☐ 179	Cassandra Lander	.10	.05	.01
☐ 180	1970 Football Team	.10	.05	.01
☐ 181	Sterling Slaughter	.15	.07	.01
☐ 182	Jerry Maddox	.10	.05	.01
☐ 183	Rick Monday	.25	.12	.02
☐ 184	Freddie Lewis	.20	.10	.02
☐ 185	Gary Gentry	.10	.05	.01
☐ 186	Tom Purtzer	.25	.12	.02
☐ 187	Jodi Rathburn	.10	.05	.01
☐ 188	Carl Donnelly	.10	.05	.01
☐ 189	Frank KushCO	.15	.07	.01
☐ 190	Glenn McMinn	.10	.05	.01
☐ 191	Kym Hampton	.10	.05	.01
☐ 192	Marty Barrett	.20	.10	.02
☐ 193	Rick McKinney	.10	.05	.01
☐ 194	Michael Berlenheiter	.10	.05	.01
☐ 195	Duffy Dyer	.10	.05	.01
☐ 196	Mary Littlewood	.10	.05	.01
☐ 197	Ben Hawkins	.20	.10	.02

☐ 198	Dan Hayden	.10	.05	.01
☐ 199	Cheryl Gibson	.10	.05	.01
☐ 200	Director Card 101-200	.10	.05	.01

1982-83 Arkansas

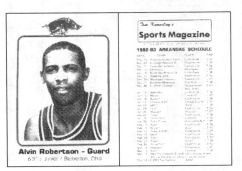

Alvin Robertson - Guard
6'3" / Junior / Barberton, Ohio

This 16-card set measures standard card size, 2 1/2" by 3 1/2". The card set was sponsored by Tom Kamerling's Sports Magazine. The black and white posed photo on the card's front is enclosed by a red border. The Arkansas Razorback logo appears above the photo, and the player's name, position, height, college classification, and hometown below the photo. The back of the card has the 1982-83 game schedule. Future NBA players included in this set are Joe Kleine, Alvin Robertson, and Darrell Walker.

		MINT	EXC	G-VG
COMPLETE SET (16)		50.00	25.00	5.00
COMMON PLAYER (1-16)		1.00	.50	.10
☐ 1	Charles Balentine	2.00	1.00	.20
☐ 2	Darryl Bedford	1.00	.50	.10
☐ 3	Robert Brannon	1.00	.50	.10
☐ 4	Willie Cutts	1.00	.50	.10
☐ 5	Keenan DeBose	1.00	.50	.10
☐ 6	Carey Kelly	1.00	.50	.10
☐ 7	Robert Kitchen	1.00	.50	.10
☐ 8	Joe Kleine	7.50	3.75	.75
☐ 9	Ricky Norton	2.00	1.00	.20
☐ 10	Eric Poerschke	1.00	.50	.10
☐ 11	Mike Ratliff	1.00	.50	.10
☐ 12	Alvin Robertson	20.00	10.00	2.00
☐ 13	John Snively	1.00	.50	.10
☐ 14	Eddie Sutton CO	3.00	1.50	.30
☐ 15	Leroy Sutton	1.00	.50	.10
☐ 16	Darrell Walker	7.50	3.75	.75

1991 Arkansas 100 *

This 100-card multi-sport set was produced by Collegiate Collection for Arkansas Razorback fans and measures the standard size (2 1/2" by 3 1/2"). The fronts features a mix of black and white or color player photos, with the player's name in a stripe below the picture. In a horizontal format the backs present biographical information, career summary, or statistics on a white background. The cards are numbered on the back. The cards were available in foil packs of seven cards per pack.

		MINT	EXC	G-VG
COMPLETE SET (100)		12.00	6.00	1.20
COMMON PLAYER (1-100)		.10	.05	.01
☐ 1	Frank Broyles CO	.20	.10	.02
☐ 2	Lance Alworth	.50	.25	.05
☐ 3	Sidney Moncrief	.50	.25	.05
☐ 4	Kevin McReynolds	.50	.25	.05

☐ 5 John Barnhill	.10	.05	.01
☐ 6 Dan Hampton	.50	.25	.05
☐ 7 Mike Conley	.20	.10	.02
☐ 8 John McDonnell	.10	.05	.01
☐ 9 Miller Barber	.20	.10	.02
☐ 10 Clyde Scott	.10	.05	.01
☐ 11 Kendall Trainor	.10	.05	.01
☐ 12 Les Lancaster	.20	.10	.02
☐ 13 Tom Pagnozzi	.20	.10	.02
☐ 14 Errick Floreal	.10	.05	.01
☐ 15 Tony Brown	.20	.10	.02
☐ 16 Derek Russell	.35	.17	.03
☐ 17 Niall O'Shaughnessy	.25	.12	.02
☐ 18 Jimmy Walker	.20	.10	.02
☐ 19 Ben Cowins	.15	.07	.01
☐ 20 Keith Wilson	.15	.07	.01
☐ 21 Tony Cherio	.10	.05	.01
☐ 22 Chip Hooper	.15	.07	.01
☐ 23 Tim Sherill	.10	.05	.01
☐ 24 Paul Donovan	.10	.05	.01
☐ 25 Billy Ray Smith	.25	.12	.02
☐ 26 Steve Little	.15	.07	.01
☐ 27 Steve Atwater	.25	.12	.02
☐ 28 Roddie Haley	.10	.05	.01
☐ 29 Ron Favrot	.10	.05	.01
☐ 30 Peter Doohan	.10	.05	.01
☐ 31 Darrell Akerfelds	.20	.10	.02
☐ 32 Dickey Morton	.15	.07	.01
☐ 33 Lon Farrell	.10	.05	.01
☐ 34 Jerry Spencer	.10	.05	.01
☐ 35 Scott Hastings	.20	.10	.02
☐ 36 Dick Bumpas	.10	.05	.01
☐ 37 Johnny Ray	.20	.10	.02
☐ 38 Joe Kleine	.25	.12	.02
☐ 39 George Cole	.10	.05	.01
☐ 40 Bruce Lahay	.10	.05	.01
☐ 41 Jim Benton	.10	.05	.01
☐ 42 Stanley Redwine	.10	.05	.01
☐ 43 Jim Kremers	.10	.05	.01
☐ 44 Marvin Delph	.15	.07	.01
☐ 45 Joe Falcon	.15	.07	.01
☐ 46 Bill Montgomery	.15	.07	.01
☐ 47 Lou Holtz CO	.25	.12	.02
☐ 48 John Daley	.10	.05	.01
☐ 49 Bill McClard	.10	.05	.01
☐ 50 Gary Anderson	.35	.17	.03
☐ 51 Alvin Robertson	.50	.25	.05
☐ 52 Glen Rose	.10	.05	.01
☐ 53 Ronnie Caveness	.15	.07	.01
☐ 54 Jeff King	.10	.05	.01
☐ 55 Bobby Joe Edmonds	.25	.12	.02
☐ 56 James Shibest	.10	.05	.01
☐ 57 Reuben Raina	.10	.05	.01
☐ 58 Martin Smith	.10	.05	.01
☐ 59 Wear Schoonover	.10	.05	.01
☐ 60 Bruce James	.10	.05	.01
☐ 61 Billy Moore	.10	.05	.01
☐ 62 Jim Mabay	.10	.05	.01
☐ 63 Ron Calcagni	.15	.07	.01
☐ 64 Wilson Matthews	.10	.05	.01
☐ 65 Martine Bercher	.10	.05	.01
☐ 66 Martin Terry	.10	.05	.01
☐ 67 Andrew Lang	.10	.05	.01
☐ 68 Mike Reppond	.10	.05	.01
☐ 69 Ron Brewer	.25	.12	.02
☐ 70 Ish Ordonez	.10	.05	.01
☐ 71 Steve Korte	.20	.10	.02
☐ 72 Jim Barnes	.20	.10	.02
☐ 73 Steve Cox	.20	.10	.02
☐ 74 Bud Brooks	.10	.05	.01
☐ 75 Roland Sales	.10	.05	.01
☐ 76 Chuck Dicus	.15	.07	.01
☐ 77 Rodney Brand	.10	.05	.01
☐ 78 Wayne Martin	.25	.12	.02
☐ 79 Greg Kolenda	.10	.05	.01
☐ 80 Ron Huery	.20	.10	.02
☐ 81 Brad Taylor	.15	.07	.01
☐ 82 Bill Burnett	.20	.10	.02
☐ 83 Glenn Ray Hines	.20	.10	.02
☐ 84 Leotis Harris	.10	.05	.01
☐ 85 Darrell Walker	.25	.12	.02
☐ 86 Joe Ferguson	.35	.17	.03
☐ 87 Grey Horne	.10	.05	.01
☐ 88 Lloyd Phillips	.20	.10	.02
☐ 89 James Rouse	.20	.10	.02
☐ 90 Ken Hatfield	.20	.10	.02
☐ 91 Bobby Crockett	.20	.10	.02
☐ 92 Quinn Grovey	.20	.10	.02
☐ 93 Wayne Harris	.25	.12	.02
☐ 94 Jim Mooty	.10	.05	.01
☐ 95 Barry Foster	.35	.17	.03
☐ 96 Mel McGaha	.15	.07	.01
☐ 97 Jim Lee Howell	.15	.07	.01
☐ 98 Jack Robbins	.10	.05	.01
☐ 99 Cliff Powell	.10	.05	.01
☐ 100 Director Card	.10	.05	.01

1987-88 Auburn Police *

This 16-card set was issued by Auburn University and includes members from different sports programs. Supposedly only 5,000 sets were made by McDag Productions, and the cards were distributed by the Opelika, Alabama police department. The cards measure the standard size (2 1/2" by 3 1/2") and color player photos on white card stock. The backs present safety tips for children. The last three cards of the set feature "Tiger Greats," former Auburn athletes Bo Jackson, Rowdy Gaines, and Chuck Person. The sports represented in this set are football (1, 3, 5, 11-13, 16), basketball (4, 6, 9-10, 14), baseball (2), and swimming (15).

	MINT	EXC	G-VG
COMPLETE SET (16)	20.00	10.00	2.00
COMMON PLAYER (1-16)	.50	.25	.05
☐ 1 Pat Dye CO	.50	.25	.05
☐ 2 Frank Thomas	9.00	4.50	.90
☐ 3 Jeff Burger	.75	.35	.07
☐ 4 Sonny Smith	.75	.35	.07
☐ 5 Kurt Crain	.50	.25	.05
☐ 6 Joe Ciampi	.50	.25	.05
☐ 7 Aubie (Mascot)	.50	.25	.05
☐ 8 Tiger (Mascot)	.50	.25	.05
☐ 9 Jeff Moore	.75	.35	.07
☐ 10 Vickie Orr	.75	.35	.07
☐ 11 Tracy Rocker	1.00	.50	.10
☐ 12 Brian Shulman	.50	.25	.05
☐ 13 Lawyer Tillman	1.00	.50	.10
☐ 14 Chuck Person	2.00	1.00	.20
☐ 15 Rowdy Gaines	1.00	.50	.10
☐ 16 Bo Jackson	9.00	4.50	.90

1987-88 Baylor Police *

This 17-card set was sponsored by the Hillcrest Baptist Medical Center, the Waco Police Department, and the Baylor University Department of Public Safety. The cards measure (not given in article) and the sports represented are baseball (1-3), basketball (4-6), track (7-10), and football (11-17). The front feature color action shots of the players on white card stock. At the top the words "Baylor Bears 1987-88" are printed between the Hillcrest and Baylor University logos. Player information is given below the picture. The back has more logos, brief career summaries, and "Bear Briefs," which consist of instructional sports information and an anti-drug or crime message.

	MINT	EXC	G-VG
COMPLETE SET (17)	20.00	10.00	2.00
COMMON PLAYER (1-17)	1.00	.50	.10
☐ 1 Nate Jones	1.00	.50	.10
☐ 2 Pat Combs	2.50	1.25	.25
☐ 3 Mickey Sullivan	1.00	.50	.10
☐ 4 Michael Williams	3.00	1.50	.30
☐ 5 Darryl Middleton	1.50	.75	.15
☐ 6 Gene Iba CO	1.50	.75	.15
☐ 7 Victor Valen	1.00	.50	.10
☐ 8 Raymond Pierre	1.00	.50	.10
☐ 9 Darnell Chase	1.00	.50	.10
☐ 10 Clyde Hart CO	1.00	.50	.10
☐ 11 Ray Crockett	1.00	.50	.10
☐ 12 Joel Porter	1.00	.50	.10
☐ 13 James Francis	3.50	1.75	.35
☐ 14 Russell Sheffield	1.00	.50	.10
☐ 15 Matt Clark	1.00	.50	.10
☐ 16 Eugene Hall	1.00	.50	.10
☐ 17 Grant Teaff CO	1.50	.75	.15

1987-88 Brigham Young

This 25-card set was issued by Brigham Young University. Supposedly only 20,000 sets were produced, and each set was numbered from 1 to 20,000 on the back of every card. The cards measure the standard size (2 1/2" by 3 1/2"). The player cards feature color photos, while the team photo card is sepia-toned. The cards have a blue border, with the BYU logo in the lower right corner. Popular players on the team are featured on two cards, one action shot and one portrait. The backs have biographical and statistical information, as well as the card number.

		MINT	EXC	G-VG
COMPLETE SET (25)		15.00	7.50	1.50
COMMON PLAYER (1-25)		.50	.25	.05
□ 1	Michael Smith	2.00	1.00	.20
□ 2	BYU Header card	.75	.35	.07
□ 3	Jim Usevitch	.50	.25	.05
□ 4	Nathan Call	.50	.25	.05
□ 5	Brian Taylor	.60	.30	.06
□ 6	Ladell Anderson	.75	.35	.07
□ 7	Roger Reid	.50	.25	.05
□ 8	Carl Ingersoll	.50	.25	.05
□ 9	Jeff Chatman	.75	.35	.07
□ 10	Team Photo	.75	.35	.07
□ 11	Mike Herring	.50	.25	.05
□ 12	Chris Lynch	.50	.25	.05
□ 13	Steve Schreiner	.50	.25	.05
□ 14	Gary Trost	.50	.25	.05
□ 15	David Lynch	.50	.25	.05
□ 16	Brian Taylor	.75	.35	.07
□ 17	Andy Toolson	.50	.25	.05
□ 18	Jim Usevitch	.50	.25	.05
□ 19	Vince Bryan	.50	.25	.05
□ 20	Mark Clausen	.50	.25	.05
□ 21	Alan Astle	.50	.25	.05
□ 22	Nathan Call	.50	.25	.05
□ 23	Jeff Chatman	.75	.35	.07
□ 24	Marty Haws	.50	.25	.05
□ 25	Michael Smith	1.50	.75	.15

1989-90 Clemson

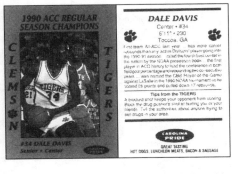

This 16-card set was sponsored by Carolina Pride, and its company logo appears in the lower left corner of the card face as well as on the back. The cards were issued on an unperforated sheet with four rows of four cards; after cutting, the cards measure the standard size (2 1/2" by 3 1/2"). The fronts feature color head and shoulders player photos on a white card face. Blue borders on the bottom and right of the picture form a shadow. The school and team names are printed in orange and blue above the picture, with an orange pawprint in the upper right corner. Player identification is given in the blue border below the picture. The backs have biographical information, player evaluation, and basketball advice in the form of "Tips

from the Tigers." The cards are unnumbered and checklisted below in alphabetical order, with the uniform number after the player's name.

		MINT	EXC	G-VG
COMPLETE SET (16)		12.00	6.00	1.20
COMMON PLAYER (1-16)		.75	.35	.07
□ 1	Colby Brown 44	.75	.35	.07
□ 2	Donnell Bruce 14	.75	.35	.07
□ 3	Wayne Buckingham 42	.75	.35	.07
□ 4	Elden Campbell 41	3.50	1.75	.35
□ 5	Marion Cash 12	.75	.35	.07
□ 6	Dale Davis 34	2.50	1.25	.25
□ 7	Cliff Ellis CO	1.00	.50	.10
□ 8	Derrick Forrest 13	.75	.35	.07
□ 9	Len Gordy CO	.75	.35	.07
□ 10	Eugene Harris CO	.75	.35	.07
□ 11	Kirkland Howling 4	.75	.35	.07
□ 12	Ricky Jones 25	.75	.35	.07
□ 13	Zlatko Josic 32	.75	.35	.07
□ 14	Shawn Lastinger 15	.75	.35	.07
□ 15	Sean Tyson 22	.75	.35	.07
□ 16	David Young 11	.75	.35	.07

1990-91 Clemson

This 16-card set measures standard card size 2 1/2" by 3 1/2", and was issued by Carolina Pride. The orange color front of the card has an action color photo in the middle, with black text on each of its four sides. The back of each card includes basic biographical information and a basketball tip.

		MINT	EXC	G-VG
COMPLETE SET (16)		12.00	6.00	1.20
COMMON PLAYER (1-16)		.60	.30	.06
□ 1	Andre Bovain 31	.60	.30	.06
□ 2	Colby Brown 44	.60	.30	.06
□ 3	Donnell Bruce 14	.60	.30	.06
□ 4	Eric Burks 24	.60	.30	.06
□ 5	Dale Davis 34	3.00	1.50	.30
□ 6	Cliff Ellis CO	.90	.45	.09
□ 7	Len Gordy CO	.60	.30	.06
□ 8	Eugene Harris CO	.60	.30	.06
□ 9	Steve Harris 13	.90	.45	.09
□ 10	Ricky Jones 25	.60	.30	.06
□ 11	Shawn Lastinger 15	.60	.30	.06
□ 12	Jimmy Mason 10	.60	.30	.06
□ 13	Tyrone Paul 32	.60	.30	.06
□ 14	Sean Tyson 22	.60	.30	.06
□ 15	Joey Watts 20	.60	.30	.06
□ 16	David Young 11	.60	.30	.06

1990-91 Clemson Promos *

This ten-card set measures the standard card size of 2 1/2" by 3 1/2" and was issued by Collegiate Collection to honor some

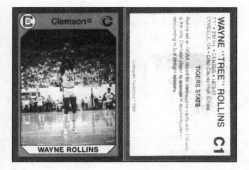

of the great ahtletes who played at Clemson. The front of the card features a full-color photo of the person featured while the back of the card has details about the person pictured. As this set is a multi-sport set we have used a two-letter identification of the sport next to the person's name.

	MINT	EXC	G-VG
COMPLETE SET (10)	5.00	2.50	.50
COMMON PLAYER (1-10)	.50	.25	.05
☐ C1 Wayne Rollins BK	.60	.30	.06
☐ C2 CU-USC Series FB	.50	.25	.05
☐ C3 William Perry FB Bio	.75	.35	.07
☐ C4 Michael Dean Perry FB	.75	.35	.07
☐ C5 Orange Bowl FB	.50	.25	.05
☐ C6 Ken Hatfield CO FB	.50	.25	.05
☐ C7 Tim Teufel BB	.60	.30	.06
☐ C8 Dwight Clark FB	.75	.35	.07
☐ C9 William Perry FB Stat	.75	.35	.07
☐ C10 Frank Howard CO FB	.50	.25	.05

1990-91 Clemson 200 *

This 200-card set was produced by Collegiate Collection and measures the standard size (2 1/2" by 3 1/2"). The front features a mix of black and white or color player photos, with dark blue and orange borders. All four corners of the picture are cut off. In dark blue lettering the school name appears above the picture, with the player's name at the bottom of the card face. In a horizontal format the back presents biographical information, career summary, and statistics, on a white background with dark blue lettering and borders. The cards are numbered on the back.

	MINT	EXC	G-VG
COMPLETE SET (200)	22.00	11.00	2.20
COMMON PLAYER (1-200)	.10	.05	.01
☐ 1 William Perry	.35	.17	.03
☐ 2 Kevin Mack	.25	.12	.02

☐ 3 Wayne(Tree) Rollins	.25	.12	.02
☐ 4 Donald Igwebuike	.15	.07	.01
☐ 5 Michael Dean Perry	.35	.17	.03
☐ 6 Larry Nance	.35	.17	.03
☐ 7 Steve Fuller	.20	.10	.02
☐ 8 Horace Grant	.50	.25	.05
☐ 9 Frank Howard CO	.15	.07	.01
☐ 10 Orange Bowl Champs '82	.10	.05	.01
☐ 11 Brian Barnes	.25	.12	.02
☐ 12 Bobby Joe Conrad	.20	.10	.02
☐ 13 John Phillips	.10	.05	.01
☐ 14 Kevin Johnson	.10	.05	.01
☐ 15 Terry Allen	.25	.12	.02
☐ 16 Chris Morocco	.10	.05	.01
☐ 17 Elden Campbell	.50	.25	.05
☐ 18 Jimmy Key	.35	.17	.03
☐ 19 Tracy Johnson	.10	.05	.01
☐ 20 Bill Spiers	.25	.12	.02
☐ 21 Lawson Duncan	.10	.05	.01
☐ 22 Eric Eichmann	.10	.05	.01
☐ 23 Tim Teufel	.25	.12	.02
☐ 24 Vincent Hamilton	.10	.05	.01
☐ 25 Mike Eppley	.10	.05	.01
☐ 26 Hans Koeleman	.10	.05	.01
☐ 27 Tennis Facilities	.10	.05	.01
☐ 28 Marvin Sim	.10	.05	.01
☐ 29 Tigers Win Classic	.10	.05	.01
☐ 30 Jim Riggs	.15	.07	.01
☐ 31 Adubarie Otorubio	.10	.05	.01
☐ 32 Mike Milchin	.15	.07	.01
☐ 33 Bruce Murray	.10	.05	.01
☐ 34 Banks McFadden	.10	.05	.01
☐ 35 Murray Jarman	.10	.05	.01
☐ 36 The Kick 1986	.10	.05	.01
☐ 37 Gary Conner	.10	.05	.01
☐ 38 Jason Griffith	.10	.05	.01
☐ 39 Terrance Flagler	.25	.12	.02
☐ 40 Grayson Marshall	.10	.05	.01
☐ 41 David Treadwell	.20	.10	.02
☐ 42 Perry Tuttle	.25	.12	.02
☐ 43 Billy Williams	.10	.05	.01
☐ 44 Homer Jordan	.15	.07	.01
☐ 45 Dale Hatcher	.20	.10	.02
☐ 46 Steve Reese	.10	.05	.01
☐ 47 Ray Williams	.20	.10	.02
☐ 48 Obed Ariri	.15	.07	.01
☐ 49 Soccer Team Wins '87	.10	.05	.01
☐ 50 Miquel Nido	.10	.05	.01
☐ 51 Cliff Austin	.20	.10	.02
☐ 52 Chris Sherman	.10	.05	.01
☐ 53 Jeff Nunamacher	.10	.05	.01
☐ 54 Steve Berlin	.10	.05	.01
☐ 55 Jess Neely	.20	.10	.02
☐ 56 Rick Rudeen	.10	.05	.01
☐ 57 Jeff Bryant	.20	.10	.02
☐ 58 Jerry Butler	.20	.10	.02
☐ 59 Randy Mazey	.10	.05	.01
☐ 60 Bob Paulling	.10	.05	.01
☐ 61 Matuszewski and Walters	.10	.05	.01
☐ 62 James Farr	.10	.05	.01
☐ 63 Bob Boettner	.10	.05	.01
☐ 64 Chuck McSwain	.20	.10	.02
☐ 65 Jim Stuckey	.20	.10	.02
☐ 66 Neil Simons	.10	.05	.01
☐ 67 Rodney Williams	.10	.05	.01
☐ 68 Butch Zatezalo	.10	.05	.01
☐ 69 Dr.I.M. Ibrahim	.10	.05	.01
☐ 70 Richard Matuszewski	.10	.05	.01
☐ 71 Dwight Clark	.50	.25	.05
☐ 72 Chuck Baldwin	.10	.05	.01
☐ 73 Kenny Flowers	.20	.10	.02
☐ 74 Michael Tait	.10	.05	.01
☐ 75 John Lee	.10	.05	.01
☐ 76 Horace Wyatt	.10	.05	.01
☐ 77 Terrence Herrington	.10	.05	.01
☐ 78 Gary Cooper	.20	.10	.02
☐ 79 Bert Hefferman	.20	.10	.02
☐ 80 Tigers with ACC Title	.10	.05	.01
☐ 81 Fred Cone	.15	.07	.01
☐ 82 Clarence Rose	.10	.05	.01
☐ 83 Jean Desdunes	.10	.05	.01
☐ 84 Donnell Woodford	.25	.12	.02
☐ 85 Ric Aronberg	.10	.05	.01
☐ 86 Mike Brown	.10	.05	.01
☐ 87 Howard Hall of Fame	.10	.05	.01
☐ 88 Swimming Pool	.10	.05	.01
☐ 89 Terry Kinard	.20	.10	.02
☐ 90 Chris Patton	.20	.10	.02
☐ 91 Baseball Stadium	.10	.05	.01
☐ 92 Cliff Ellis	.10	.05	.01
☐ 93 1989 Senior Football	.10	.05	.01
☐ 94 The Clemson Tiger	.10	.05	.01
☐ 95 Howard's Rock	.10	.05	.01
☐ 96 Jeff Davis	.20	.10	.02

☐ 97	Derrick Forrest	.10	.05	.01
☐ 98	Mack Dickson	.10	.05	.01
☐ 99	Clemson Wins Nebraska	.10	.05	.01
☐ 100	Director Card 1-99	.10	.05	.01
☐ 101	Hill shot from field	.10	.05	.01
☐ 102	Ray Williams	.20	.10	.02
☐ 103	Jim McCollom	.10	.05	.01
☐ 104	Charlie Waters	.25	.12	.02
☐ 105	Soccer and Tennis Area	.10	.05	.01
☐ 106	Bill Wilhelm	.10	.05	.01
☐ 107	Bubba Brown	.10	.05	.01
☐ 108	Ken Hatfield is hired	.10	.05	.01
☐ 109	Lester Brown	.10	.05	.01
☐ 110	James Robinson	.10	.05	.01
☐ 111	Perry and Perry	.25	.12	.02
☐ 112	Nuamoi Nwokocha	.10	.05	.01
☐ 113	Frank Howard CO	.15	.07	.01
☐ 114	Bill Foster CO	.10	.05	.01
☐ 115	Wesley McFadden	.10	.05	.01
☐ 116	Clemson 35, Penn 10	.10	.05	.01
☐ 117	Jay Berger	.10	.05	.01
☐ 118	Andy Headen	.20	.10	.02
☐ 119	Hall of Famers	.10	.05	.01
☐ 120	Hill Shot from Board	.10	.05	.01
☐ 121	Harry Olszewski	.10	.05	.01
☐ 122	CU clinches season	.10	.05	.01
☐ 123	Super Bowl Rings	.10	.05	.01
☐ 124	Otis Moore	.10	.05	.01
☐ 125	Kirk Howling	.10	.05	.01
☐ 126	Defensive Rankings	.10	.05	.01
☐ 127	Bostic Brothers	.20	.10	.02
☐ 128	Bob Pollock	.10	.05	.01
☐ 129	Randy Scott	.10	.05	.01
☐ 130	Noel Loban	.10	.05	.01
☐ 131	Clemson and Stanford	.10	.05	.01
☐ 132	All Americans	.10	.05	.01
☐ 133	Danny Ford record	.10	.05	.01
☐ 134	Larry Penley	.10	.05	.01
☐ 135	Littlejohn Coliseum	.10	.05	.01
☐ 136	Clyde Browne	.10	.05	.01
☐ 137	Clemson 13, Okla. 6	.10	.05	.01
☐ 138	Clemson and West Virginia	.10	.05	.01
☐ 139	Clemson and Notre Dame	.10	.05	.01
☐ 140	Bush in jacket	.35	.17	.03
☐ 141	Fuller and Butler	.25	.12	.02
☐ 142	Safety Celebration	.10	.05	.01
☐ 143	Oswald Drawdy	.10	.05	.01
☐ 144	Phillips	.10	.05	.01
☐ 145	Chuck Kriese	.10	.05	.01
☐ 146	Balloon Launch	.10	.05	.01
☐ 147	Perry with poster	.25	.12	.02
☐ 148	Jim Davis	.10	.05	.01
☐ 149	Jim Brennan	.10	.05	.01
☐ 150	Death Valley	.10	.05	.01
☐ 151	Tina Krebs	.10	.05	.01
☐ 152	Andy Johnston	.10	.05	.01
☐ 153	Wayne Coffman	.10	.05	.01
☐ 154	Andy Tribble	.10	.05	.01
☐ 155	Mitzi Kremer	.10	.05	.01
☐ 156	Rusty Adkins	.10	.05	.01
☐ 157	Choppy Patterson	.10	.05	.01
☐ 158	Jill Bakehorn	.10	.05	.01
☐ 159	Baker vs. Tanner	.10	.05	.01
☐ 160	Jerry Butler	.25	.12	.02
☐ 161	Championship Rings	.10	.05	.01
☐ 162	Shawn Weatherly	.25	.12	.02
☐ 163	Homecoming	.10	.05	.01
☐ 164	Barbara Kennedy	.10	.05	.01
☐ 165	Sports Facilities	.10	.05	.01
☐ 166	Tommy Mahaffey	.10	.05	.01
☐ 167	Dillard Pruitt	.15	.07	.01
☐ 168	Bill Yarborough	.10	.05	.01
☐ 169	Billy O'Dell	.20	.10	.02
☐ 170	Joe Blalock	.10	.05	.01
☐ 171	Ute Jamrozy	.10	.05	.01
☐ 172	Jerry Pryor	.10	.05	.01
☐ 173	Susan Hill	.10	.05	.01
☐ 174	Eddie Griffin	.10	.05	.01
☐ 175	Jane Forman	.10	.05	.01
☐ 176	Obed Ariri	.15	.07	.01
☐ 177	Richie Mahaffey	.10	.05	.01
☐ 178	Bobby Gage	.10	.05	.01
☐ 179	John Heisman	.25	.12	.02
☐ 180	Joe Landrum	.10	.05	.01
☐ 181	Soccer and Tennis	.10	.05	.01
☐ 182	Clemson vs. USC	.10	.05	.01
☐ 183	Linda White	.10	.05	.01
☐ 184	Denise Murphy	.10	.05	.01
☐ 185	Mary Ann Cubelic	.10	.05	.01
☐ 186	Pam Hayden	.10	.05	.01
☐ 187	Coy Cobb	.10	.05	.01
☐ 188	Randy Mahaffey	.15	.07	.01
☐ 189	Lou Cordileone	.10	.05	.01

☐ 190	1949 Gator Bowl	.10	.05	.01
☐ 191	Karen Ann Jenkins	.10	.05	.01
☐ 192	Bobbie Mims	.10	.05	.01
☐ 193	Janet Knight	.10	.05	.01
☐ 194	Ray Matthews	.10	.05	.01
☐ 195	Gigi Fernandez	.20	.10	.02
☐ 196	Joey McKenna	.10	.05	.01
☐ 197	Denny Walling	.10	.05	.01
☐ 198	Janet Ellison	.10	.05	.01
☐ 199	Donnie Mahaffey	.10	.05	.01
☐ 200	Director Card 101-200	.10	.05	.01

1990-91 Connecticut Police

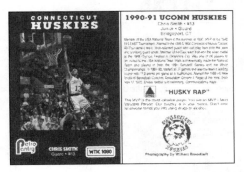

This 16-card set was sponsored by Petro Pantry food stores, WTIC 1080 radio, and Citgo. The cards were issued in four strips of four cards each; after perforation, they measure the standard size (2 1/2" by 3 1/2"). The front features a color action player photo on a dark blue background. In white lettering the team name appears above the picture. Player information is given below the picture, sandwiched between sponsors' logos. The back has biographical information, career summary, and "Husky Rap," which consists of an anti-drug or alcohol message. A Huskie's logo at the bottom completes the card back. The cards are unnumbered and are checklisted below in alphabetical order, with the uniform number after the player's name.

	MINT	EXC	G-VG
COMPLETE SET (16)	12.00	6.00	1.20
COMMON PLAYER (1-16)	.75	.35	.07
☐ 1 Scott Burrell 24	1.50	.75	.15
☐ 2 Jim Calhoun CO	1.00	.50	.10
☐ 3 Dan Cyrulik 55	.75	.35	.07
☐ 4 Lyman DePriest 23	1.00	.50	.10
☐ 5 Shawn Ellison 32	.75	.35	.07
☐ 6 John Gwynn 15	.75	.35	.07
☐ 7 Gilad Katz 10	.75	.35	.07
☐ 8 Oliver Macklin 11	.75	.35	.07
☐ 9 Steve Pikiell 21	.75	.35	.07
☐ 10 Tim Pikiell 31	.75	.35	.07
☐ 11 Rod Sellers 22	.75	.35	.07
☐ 12 Chris Smith 13	1.50	.75	.15
☐ 13 Marc Suhr 30	.75	.35	.07
☐ 14 Torano Walker 42	.75	.35	.07
☐ 15 Murray Williams 20	.75	.35	.07
☐ 16 Jonathan Mascot	.75	.35	.07

1983-84 Dayton Blue Shield

This 20-card set of Dayton Flyers was sponsored by Blue Shield and television Channel 7. The cards measure the standard size (2 1/2" by 3 1/2"). The front features borderless blue-tinted posed player photos, with the player's name above and team name below in red lettering on white card stock. The horizontally-

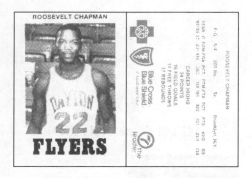

oriented backs are printed in blue and provide biographical information and the sponsors' logos. The cards are unnumbered and are checklisted below in alphabetical order. There was a 21st card in the set which was pulled from the set just prior to mass distribution due to the fact that the player quit the team.

		MINT	EXC	G-VG
	COMPLETE SET (20)	25.00	12.50	2.50
	COMMON PLAYER (1-20)	1.00	.50	.10
☐ 1	Jack Butler and Dan Hipsher (Coaches)	1.50	.75	.15
☐ 2	Roosevelt Chapman	5.00	2.50	.50
☐ 3	Dan Christie	1.00	.50	.10
☐ 4	Dave Colbert	1.00	.50	.10
☐ 5	Rory Dahlinghaus	1.00	.50	.10
☐ 6	Don Donoher CO	2.00	1.00	.20
☐ 7	Damon Goodwin	1.00	.50	.10
☐ 8	Anthony Grant	1.00	.50	.10
☐ 9	Ted Harris	1.00	.50	.10
☐ 10	Mike Hartsock	1.00	.50	.10
☐ 11	Paul Hawkins	1.00	.50	.10
☐ 12	Mick Hubert	1.00	.50	.10
☐ 13	Don Hughes	1.00	.50	.10
☐ 14	Larry Schellenberg	1.00	.50	.10
☐ 15	Jim Shields	1.00	.50	.10
☐ 16	Sedric Toney	1.50	.75	.15
☐ 17	Jeff Tressler	1.00	.50	.10
☐ 18	Ed Young	1.00	.50	.10
☐ 19	Jeff Zern	1.00	.50	.10
☐ 20	Flyer Fan Card	1.00	.50	.10

1986-87 DePaul Playing Cards

This set of playing cards was issued to honor Ray Meyer, who retired fifth on the all-time list of most career victories for Division I coaches. The cards measure the standard size (2 1/2" by 3 1/2"). The fronts feature posed or action black and white photos that span Meyer's career and his teams. The backs are turquoise with a white border and white lettering. At the top is a DePaul Blue

Demons logo in white, then the school name, and in the lower half of the card is a head shot of Ray Meyer in a heart-shaped opening. At the bottom the coach's name is given along with the words "42 Memorable Years." Numerical values have been assigned to all the cards (ace 1; jack 11, etc.). The cards are listed according to suits as follows: hearts (H), clubs (C), diamonds (D), and spades (S). The two jokers are listed at the end.

		MINT	EXC	G-VG
	COMPLETE SET (54)	30.00	15.00	3.00
	COMMON PLAYER	.50	.25	.05
☐ H1	Ray Meyer	1.00	.50	.10
☐ H2	1st Team (1942)	.50	.25	.05
☐ H3	Dick Triptow	.50	.25	.05
☐ H4	1st NIT Championship 1945	.50	.25	.05
☐ H5	George Mikan	1.50	.75	.15
☐ H6	NIT Starting Five 1945	.50	.25	.05
☐ H7	Ed Mikan and Whitey Kachan	.75	.35	.07
☐ H8	Early Great Team	.50	.25	.05
☐ H9	George Mikan and Bill Donato	1.00	.50	.10
☐ H10	Bato Govedarica	.50	.25	.05
☐ H11	1948 Team	.50	.25	.05
☐ H12	Ray, Marge, and Family	.75	.35	.07
☐ H13	Dick Heise	.50	.25	.05
☐ C1	Coach of the Year 1944	.75	.35	.07
☐ C2	Frank Blum and Jim Lamkin	.50	.25	.05
☐ C3	Bill Robinzine and Ron Sobieszcyk	.75	.35	.07
☐ C4	Howie Carl	.50	.25	.05
☐ C5	McKinley Cowsen	.50	.25	.05
☐ C6	M.C. Thompson	.50	.25	.05
☐ C7	Emmette Bryant	.50	.25	.05
☐ C8	NIT Tournament 1963	.50	.25	.05
☐ C9	Tom Meyer	.50	.25	.05
☐ C10	Starting Five 1965-66	.50	.25	.05
☐ C11	Dave Mills	.50	.25	.05
☐ C12	400th Victory Celebration	.50	.25	.05
☐ C13	Joey Meyer	.75	.35	.07
☐ D1	Basketball Hall of Fame	.50	.25	.05
☐ D2	Jim Mitchem	.50	.25	.05
☐ D3	Mark Aguirre	1.00	.50	.10
☐ D4	Gary Garland	.75	.35	.07
☐ D5	Final Four NCAA 1978-79	.50	.25	.05
☐ D6	Curtis Watkins	.50	.25	.05
☐ D7	Joe Ponsetto	.50	.25	.05
☐ D8	Ray and Digger Phelps	.75	.35	.07
☐ D9	Ron Norwood	.50	.25	.05
☐ D10	Dave Corzine	.75	.35	.07
☐ D11	Ray and Al McGuire	.75	.35	.07
☐ D12	Bill Robinzine Jr.	.50	.25	.05
☐ D13	500th Victory	.50	.25	.05
☐ S1	700th Victory	.50	.25	.05
☐ S2	Jerry McMillan	.50	.25	.05
☐ S3	Last Home Game	.50	.25	.05
☐ S4	Rosemont Horizon	.50	.25	.05
☐ S5	Ray and Joey	.75	.35	.07
☐ S6	Terry Cummings turns Pro	1.00	.50	.10
☐ S7	Terry Cummings	1.00	.50	.10
☐ S8	No. 1 Basketball Family	.50	.25	.05
☐ S9	Last Game at Alumni Hall	.50	.25	.05
☐ S10	Mark Aguirre and Clyde Bradshaw	.75	.35	.07
☐ S11	Mark Aguirre and Terry Cummings	1.00	.50	.10
☐ S12	1979-80 Team	.50	.25	.05
☐ S13	1970-80 Team Clowning	.50	.25	.05
☐ xx	Joker Card Year by year record	.50	.25	.05
☐ xx	Joker Card Milestones	.50	.25	.05

1987-88 Duke Police

This 13-card set featuring the Duke Blue Devils basketball team measures the standard card size of 2 1/2" by 3 1/2". This set features members of the semi-finalists of the 1988 NCAA Tournament. The set is sponsored by Adolescent Care Unit and Glaxo and their company names are on the top of the card. Underneath their names is the Blue Devils' identification. The full-color players photo is in the middle of the card and on the bottom of the card is the players name, uniform number, and position. The back has basic biographical information about the players along with both a basketball and a anti-crime or drug message. Some of the key players in the set include future NBA players Danny Ferry and Alaa Abdelnaby. The set was produced by Sports Marketing of Seattle, Washington.

	MINT	EXC	G-VG
COMPLETE SET (13)	25.00	12.50	2.50
COMMON PLAYER	1.00	.50	.10
☐ 13 Joe Cook	1.00	.50	.10
☐ 14 Quin Snyder	1.50	.75	.15
☐ 21 Robert Brickey	2.00	1.00	.20
☐ 22 Greg Koubek	1.50	.75	.15
☐ 30 Alaa Abdelnaby	3.50	1.75	.35
☐ 31 Kevin Strickland	1.50	.75	.15
☐ 33 John Smith	1.00	.50	.10
☐ 35 Danny Ferry	5.00	2.50	.50
☐ 42 George Burgin	1.00	.50	.10
☐ 44 Phil Henderson	2.00	1.00	.20
☐ 45 Clay Buckley	1.00	.50	.10
☐ 55 Billy King	1.50	.75	.15
☐ xx Mike Krzyzewski CO	5.00	2.50	.50

1982-83 Fairfield

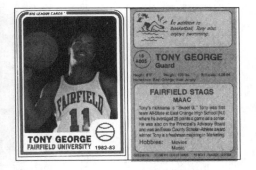

This 18-card set for Fairfield University is numbered on the back and measures the standard, 2 1/2" by 3 1/2". The cards were produced by Big League Cards. The front features a posed color photo enframed by black and red borders, with the player's name, the university, and a basketball logo below the picture. The back gives biographical information.

	MINT	EXC	G-VG
COMPLETE SET (18)	18.00	9.00	1.80
COMMON PLAYER (1-18)	1.00	.50	.10
☐ 1 Jay Byrne	1.00	.50	.10
☐ 2 Vin Cazzetta	1.00	.50	.10
☐ 3 Pete DeBisschop	1.00	.50	.10
☐ 4 Joe DeSantis CO	1.50	.75	.15
☐ 5 Tony George	1.00	.50	.10
☐ 6 Craig Golden	1.00	.50	.10
☐ 7 Bobby Hurt	1.00	.50	.10
☐ 8 Ed Janka CO	1.00	.50	.10
☐ 9 Jerry Johnson	1.00	.50	.10
☐ 10 John Leonard	1.00	.50	.10
☐ 11 Terry O'Connor	1.00	.50	.10
☐ 12 Tim O'Toole	1.00	.50	.10
☐ 13 Brendan Potter	1.00	.50	.10
☐ 14 Ron Ross CO	1.00	.50	.10
☐ 15 Greg Schwartz	1.00	.50	.10
☐ 16 Don Wilson	1.00	.50	.10
☐ 17 Pat Yerina	1.00	.50	.10
☐ 18 Fairfield Stags	1.00	.50	.10

1988-89 Florida Burger King *

This 14-card set was sponsored by University Athletic Association in conjunction with Burger King. The cards measure the standard size (2 1/2" by 3 1/2"). The front features a color action shot of an athlete engaging in the particular sport highlighted on the card. The pictures are outlined by a thin black border on white card stock. The Burger King and the Gators' logo round out the card face. The back provides additional information on the sport as well as an anti-drug or crime message. The cards are numbered on the back.

	MINT	EXC	G-VG
COMPLETE SET (14)	9.00	4.00	.75
COMMON PLAYER (1-14)	.75	.35	.07
☐ 1 Men's Swimming	.75	.35	.07
☐ 2 Baseball	1.00	.50	.10
☐ 3 Men's Basketball	1.50	.75	.15
☐ 4 Women's Tennis	1.00	.50	.10
☐ 5 Women's Track and Field	.75	.35	.07
☐ 6 Gymnastics	.75	.35	.07
☐ 7 Cross Country	.75	.35	.07
☐ 8 Women's Volleyball	.75	.35	.07
☐ 9 Women's Swimming	.75	.35	.07
☐ 10 Women's Basketball	1.00	.50	.10
☐ 11 Men's Track and Field	.75	.35	.07
☐ 12 Men's Tennis	.75	.35	.07
☐ 13 Women's Golf	.75	.35	.07
☐ 14 Men's Golf	.75	.35	.07

1990-91 Florida State 200 *

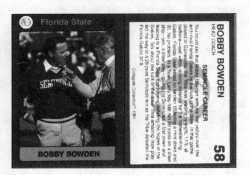

This 200-card set by Collegiate Collection features past and current athletes of Florida State University. The cards measure the standard size 2 1/2" by 3 1/2". The front has an action color photo of the player enclosed by a thin black border against a maroon background. The player's name appears in black print in a yellow box below the picture. The Florida State Seminoles logo is in the upper left hand corner. Biographical information is found on the back, with the card number located in the upper right hand corner.

	MINT	EXC	G-VG
COMPLETE SET (200)	22.00	11.00	2.20
COMMON PLAYER (1-200)	.10	.05	.01

		MINT	EXC	G-VG
☐	1 Dick Howser	.25	.12	.02
☐	2 Edwin Alicea	.15	.07	.01
☐	3 Randy White	.10	.05	.01
☐	4 Steve Gabbard	.10	.05	.01
☐	5 Pat Tomberlin	.20	.10	.02
☐	6 Herb Gainer	.10	.05	.01
☐	7 Bobby Jackson	.15	.07	.01
☐	8 Redus Coggin	.10	.05	.01
☐	9 Pat Carter	.10	.05	.01
☐	10 Kevin Grant	.10	.05	.01
☐	11 Peter Tom Willis	.50	.25	.05
☐	12 Phil Carollo	.10	.05	.01
☐	13 Derek Schmidt	.10	.05	.01
☐	14 Rick Stockstill	.15	.07	.01
☐	15 Mike Martin	.10	.05	.01
☐	16 Terry Anthony	.10	.05	.01
☐	17 Darrin Holloman	.10	.05	.01
☐	18 John McLean	.10	.05	.01
☐	19 Rudy Maloy	.10	.05	.01
☐	20 Gary Huff	.25	.12	.02
☐	21 Jamey Shouppe	.10	.05	.01
☐	22 Isaac Williams	.10	.05	.01
☐	23 Weegie Thompson	.25	.12	.02
☐	24 Jose Marzan	.10	.05	.01
☐	25 Gerald Nichols	.10	.05	.01
☐	26 John Brown	.10	.05	.01
☐	27 Danny McManus	.20	.10	.02
☐	28 Parrish Barwick	.10	.05	.01
☐	29 Paul McGowan	.10	.05	.01
☐	30 Keith Jones	.15	.07	.01
☐	31 Alphonso Williams	.10	.05	.01
☐	32 Luis Alicea	.20	.10	.02
☐	33 Tony Yeomans	.10	.05	.01
☐	34 Michael Tanks	.10	.05	.01
☐	35 Stan Shiver	.10	.05	.01
☐	36 Willie Jones	.10	.05	.01
☐	37 Wally Woodham	.10	.05	.01
☐	38 Chip Ferguson	.10	.05	.01
☐	39 Sam Childers	.10	.05	.01
☐	40 Paul Piurowski	.10	.05	.01
☐	41 Joey Ionata	.10	.05	.01
☐	42 John Hadley	.10	.05	.01
☐	43 Tanner Holloman	.10	.05	.01
☐	44 Fred Jones	.10	.05	.01
☐	45 Terry Warren	.10	.05	.01
☐	46 John Merna	.10	.05	.01
☐	47 Jimmy Jordan	.15	.07	.01
☐	48 Dave Capellen	.10	.05	.01
☐	49 Martin Mayhew	.20	.10	.02
☐	50 Barry Barco	.10	.05	.01
☐	51 Ronald Lewis	.10	.05	.01
☐	52 Tom O'Malley	.10	.05	.01
☐	53 Rick Tuten	.20	.10	.02
☐	54 Ed Fulton	.10	.05	.01
☐	55 Marc Ronan	.10	.05	.01
☐	56 Bobby Bowden	.20	.10	.02
☐	57 Bobby Bowden	.20	.10	.02
☐	58 Bobby Bowden	.20	.10	.02
☐	59 Bobby Bowden	.20	.10	.02
☐	60 Bobby Bowden	.20	.10	.02
☐	61 John Grubb	.20	.10	.02
☐	62 Joe Wessel	.10	.05	.01
☐	63 Alphonso Carreker	.20	.10	.02
☐	64 Shelton Thompson	.10	.05	.01
☐	65 Tracy Sanders	.10	.05	.01
☐	66 Bobby Bowden	.20	.10	.02
☐	67 Bobby Bowden	.20	.10	.02
☐	68 Bobby Bowden	.20	.10	.02
☐	69 Bobby Bowden	.20	.10	.02
☐	70 Bobby Bowden	.20	.10	.02
☐	71 David Palmer	.20	.10	.02
☐	72 Jason Kuipers	.10	.05	.01
☐	73 Dayne Williams	.10	.05	.01
☐	74 Mark Salva	.10	.05	.01
☐	75 Bobby Butler	.10	.05	.01
☐	76 Bobby Bowden	.20	.10	.02
☐	77 Bobby Bowden	.20	.10	.02
☐	78 Bobby Bowden	.20	.10	.02
☐	79 Bobby Bowden	.20	.10	.02
☐	80 Bobby Bowden	.20	.10	.02
☐	81 Mike Loynd	.20	.10	.02
☐	82 Dexter Carter	.50	.25	.05
☐	83 Dedrick Dodge	.10	.05	.01
☐	84 Greg Allen	.15	.07	.01
☐	85 Barry Blackwell	.10	.05	.01
☐	86 Bobby Bowden	.20	.10	.02
☐	87 Bobby Bowden	.20	.10	.02
☐	88 Bobby Bowden	.20	.10	.02
☐	89 Bobby Bowden	.20	.10	.02
☐	90 Bobby Bowden	.20	.10	.02
☐	91 Bill Capece	.15	.07	.01
☐	92 Eric Hayes	.10	.05	.01
☐	93 Garth Jax	.20	.10	.02
☐	94 Odell Haggins	.10	.05	.01
☐	95 Leroy Butler	.10	.05	.01
☐	96 Monk Bonasorte	.10	.05	.01
☐	97 Richie Lewis	.35	.17	.03
☐	98 Terry Kennedy	.20	.10	.02
☐	99 Hubert Green	.20	.10	.02
☐	100 Director Card	.10	.05	.01
☐	101 Doc Hermann	.10	.05	.01
☐	102 Gary Futch	.10	.05	.01
☐	103 Tony Romeo	.10	.05	.01
☐	104 Lee Corso	.20	.10	.02
☐	105 Steve Bratton	.10	.05	.01
☐	106 Barry Rice	.10	.05	.01
☐	107 Jeff Hogan	.10	.05	.01
☐	108 John Wachtel	.10	.05	.01
☐	109 Dick Artmeier	.10	.05	.01
☐	110 Vic Szezepanik	.10	.05	.01
☐	111 Danny Litwhiler	.15	.07	.01
☐	112 Jack Fenwick	.10	.05	.01
☐	113 Nolan Henke	.10	.05	.01
☐	114 Mark Meseroll	.10	.05	.01
☐	115 Jimmy Everett	.10	.05	.01
☐	116 Gary Schull	.10	.05	.01
☐	117 Les Murdock	.10	.05	.01
☐	118 Ron Schomburger	.10	.05	.01
☐	119 Scott Warren	.10	.05	.01
☐	120 Eric Williams	.10	.05	.01
☐	121 Buddy Strauss	.10	.05	.01
☐	122 Juan Bonilla	.10	.05	.01
☐	123 Rowland Garrett	.15	.07	.01
☐	124 Kenny Knox	.15	.07	.01
☐	125 Bill Cappleman	.15	.07	.01
☐	126 Bill Kimber	.10	.05	.01
☐	127 Mike Fuentes	.15	.07	.01
☐	128 Bill Proctor	.10	.05	.01
☐	129 Kurt Unglaub	.10	.05	.01
☐	130 Woody Woodward	.15	.07	.01
☐	131 Dave Cowens	.35	.17	.03
☐	132 Lee Nelson	.10	.05	.01
☐	133 Robert Urich	.50	.25	.05
☐	134 Ron Fraser	.15	.07	.01
☐	135 Randy Coffield	.10	.05	.01
☐	136 Jimmy Lee Taylor	.10	.05	.01
☐	137 Max Wettstein	.10	.05	.01
☐	138 Brian Williams	.10	.05	.01
☐	139 T.K. Wetherell	.10	.05	.01
☐	140 Dale McCullers	.10	.05	.01
☐	141 Peter Tom Willis	.50	.25	.05
☐	142 Doug Little	.10	.05	.01
☐	143 J.T. Thomas	.20	.10	.02
☐	144 Hassan Jones	.25	.12	.02
☐	145 Deion Sanders	.75	.35	.07

☐ 146	Barry Smith	.10	.05	.01
☐ 147	Hugh Durham	.20	.10	.02
☐ 148	Bill Moremen	.10	.05	.01
☐ 149	Gary Henry	.10	.05	.01
☐ 150	John Madden	.35	.17	.03
☐ 151	J.T. Thomas	.20	.10	.02
☐ 152	Tony Avitable	.10	.05	.01
☐ 153	Keith Kinderman	.10	.05	.01
☐ 154	Bill Dawson	.10	.05	.01
☐ 155	Mike Good	.10	.05	.01
☐ 156	Kim Hammond	.10	.05	.01
☐ 157	Buddy Blankenship	.10	.05	.01
☐ 158	Jimmy Black	.10	.05	.01
☐ 159	Vic Prinzi	.10	.05	.01
☐ 160	Bobby Renn	.10	.05	.01
☐ 161	Mark Macek	.20	.10	.02
☐ 162	Wayne McDuffie	.10	.05	.01
☐ 163	Joe Avezzano	.20	.10	.02
☐ 164	Hector Gray	.10	.05	.01
☐ 165	Grant Guthrie	.10	.05	.01
☐ 166	Tom Bailey	.10	.05	.01
☐ 167	Ron Sellers	.20	.10	.02
☐ 168	Dick Hermann	.10	.05	.01
☐ 169	Bob Harbison	.10	.05	.01
☐ 170	Winfred Bailey	.10	.05	.01
☐ 171	James Harris	.10	.05	.01
☐ 172	Jerry Jacobs	.10	.05	.01
☐ 173	Mike Kincaid	.10	.05	.01
☐ 174	Jimmy Heggins	.10	.05	.01
☐ 175	Steve Kalenich	.10	.05	.01
☐ 176	Del Williams	.15	.07	.01
☐ 177	Fred Pickard	.10	.05	.01
☐ 178	Walt Sumner	.15	.07	.01
☐ 179	Bud Whitehead	.10	.05	.01
☐ 180	Bobby Anderson	.15	.07	.01
☐ 181	Paul Azinger	.20	.10	.02
☐ 182	Burt Reynolds	1.00	.50	.10
☐ 183	Ron King	.10	.05	.01
☐ 184	H. Donald Loucks	.10	.05	.01
☐ 185	Jim Lyttle	.15	.07	.01
☐ 186	Richard Amman	.10	.05	.01
☐ 187	Bobby Crenshaw	.10	.05	.01
☐ 188	Bill Dawkins	.10	.05	.01
☐ 189	Ken Burnett	.10	.05	.01
☐ 190	Duane Carrell	.15	.07	.01
☐ 191	Gene McDowell	.15	.07	.01
☐ 192	Paul Wernke	.10	.05	.01
☐ 193	Beryl Rice	.10	.05	.01
☐ 194	Dave Fedor	.10	.05	.01
☐ 195	Brian Schmidt	.10	.05	.01
☐ 196	Rhett Dawson	.10	.05	.01
☐ 197	Greg Futch	.10	.05	.01
☐ 198	Joe Majors	.10	.05	.01
☐ 199	Stan Dobosz	.10	.05	.01
☐ 200	Director Card	.10	.05	.01

1989-90 Fresno State Smokey

This 16-card set was sponsored by the USDA Forest Service, several other federal agencies, and Grandy's restaurants. The cards measure the standard size (2 1/2" by 3 1/2"). The fronts feature either posed or action color player photos with a white card face background. The school name appears in red lettering above the picture, with the team name in the blue stripe just below it. Red and blue stripes appear below the picture,

overlayed by the Smokey and Grandy's logos. The back has brief biographical information and a fire prevention cartoon starring Smokey the Bear. The cards are unnumbered and are checklisted below in alphabetical order, with the uniform number after the player's name.

	MINT	EXC	G-VG
COMPLETE SET (16)	9.00	4.50	.90
COMMON PLAYER (1-16)	.50	.25	.05

☐ 1	Ron Adams CO	.60	.30	.06
☐ 2	Bijou Baly 15	.60	.30	.06
☐ 3	Dave Barnett 12	.60	.30	.06
☐ 4	Tod Bernard 33	.60	.30	.06
☐ 5	Chris Henderson 25	.60	.30	.06
☐ 6	Wilbert Hooker 30	.60	.30	.06
☐ 7	Pasi Lahtinen 3	.60	.30	.06
☐ 8	Dimitri Lambrecht 32	.60	.30	.06
☐ 9	Sammie Lindsey 50	.60	.30	.06
☐ 10	Joey Paglierani 00	.60	.30	.06
☐ 11	Todd Peebles 23	.60	.30	.06
☐ 12	Pat Riddlesprigger 34	.60	.30	.06
☐ 13	Sammy Taylor 22	.60	.30	.06
☐ 14	Carlo Williams 44	.60	.30	.06
☐ 15	Rey Young 54	.60	.30	.06
☐ 16	Greg Zuffelato 24	.60	.30	.06

1990-91 Fresno State Smokey

This 16-card set was sponsored by Grandy's and measures the standard, 2 1/2" by 3 1/2". The front features a color action photo enframed by a blue border on red background, with the player's name, position, and years below the photo, as well as a picture of Smokey the Bear in the left hand corner and a Grandy's logo in the right. The back has biographical information and a public service announcement (with cartoon) concerning wildfire prevention. Ron Anderson of the Philadelphia 76ers is included in this set.

	MINT	EXC	G-VG
COMPLETE SET (16)	8.00	4.00	.80
COMMON PLAYER (1-16)	.50	.25	.05

☐ 1	Ron Anderson	1.50	.75	.15
☐ 2	Dave Barnett 12	.50	.25	.05
☐ 3	Tod Bernard 33	.50	.25	.05
☐ 4	Tyrone Bradley	.50	.25	.05
☐ 5	Gary Colson CO	.50	.25	.05
☐ 6	Carl Ray Harris 11	.50	.25	.05
☐ 7	Doug Harris 20	.50	.25	.05
☐ 8	Wilbert Hooker 30	.50	.25	.05
☐ 9	Dimitri Lambrecht 32	.50	.25	.05
☐ 10	Sammie Lindsey 50	.50	.25	.05
☐ 11	Michael Pearson 3	.50	.25	.05
☐ 12	Pat Riddlesprigger 34	.50	.25	.05
☐ 13	Sammy Taylor 22	.50	.25	.05
☐ 14	Rey Young 54	.50	.25	.05
☐ 15	Fresno State Mascot	.50	.25	.05
☐ 16	Selland Arena	.50	.25	.05

1981-82 Georgetown Police

This set contains 20 cards measuring approximately 2 5/8" by 4 1/8" featuring the Georgetown Hoyas. The fronts of the cards have a blue border. Backs contain safety tips with black print on white card stock. The set was also sponsored by Safeway. The cards are numbered below by "Tip Number" as listed on the card back.

	MINT	EXC	G-VG
COMPLETE SET (20)	125.00	60.00	12.50
COMMON PLAYER (1-20)	1.00	.50	.10
☐ 1 Jack the Bulldog (Mascot)	1.00	.50	.10
☐ 2 Elvado Smith	1.00	.50	.10
☐ 3 Eric Smith	1.00	.50	.10
☐ 4 Pat Ewing	100.00	50.00	10.00
☐ 5 Anthony Jones	4.00	2.00	.40
☐ 6 Bill Martin	3.00	1.50	.30
☐ 7 Bill Stein, Assistant Coach	1.00	.50	.10
☐ 8 Norman Washington, Grad. Asst. Coach	1.00	.50	.10
☐ 9 Ed Spriggs	2.00	1.00	.20
☐ 10 Eric Floyd	9.00	4.50	.90
☐ 11 Gene Smith	2.00	1.00	.20
☐ 12 Fred Brown	2.00	1.00	.20
☐ 13 Mike Hancock	1.00	.50	.10
☐ 14 Kurt Kaull	1.00	.50	.10
☐ 15 Ed Meyers	1.00	.50	.10
☐ 16 Ron Blaylock	1.00	.50	.10
☐ 17 David Blue	1.00	.50	.10
☐ 18 John Thompson CO	5.00	2.50	.50
☐ 19 Ralph Dalton	2.00	1.00	.20
☐ 20 Hoyas Team 1981-1982	2.00	1.00	.20

1982-83 Georgetown Police

This set contains 15 cards measuring approximately 2 5/8" by 4 1/8" featuring the Georgetown Hoyas. The fronts of the cards have a blue border. Backs contain safety tips with black print on white card stock. The cards are numbered below by "Tip Number" as listed on the card back. The set was also sponsored by Games Production, Inc.

	MINT	EXC	G-VG
COMPLETE SET (15)	75.00	37.50	7.50
COMMON PLAYER (1-15)	1.00	.50	.10
☐ 1 John Thompson CO	4.00	2.00	.40
☐ 2 Patrick Ewing	45.00	22.50	4.50
☐ 3 David Dunn	1.00	.50	.10
☐ 4 Ralph Dalton	2.00	1.00	.20
☐ 5 Fred Brown	2.00	1.00	.20
☐ 6 Horace Broadnax	2.00	1.00	.20
☐ 7 David Blue	1.00	.50	.10

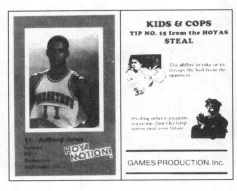

☐ 8 Michael Jackson (listed as Center on card front)	4.00	2.00	.40
☐ 9 David Wingate	5.00	2.50	.50
☐ 10 Vadi Smith	1.00	.50	.10
☐ 11 Gene Smith	2.00	1.00	.20
☐ 12 Victor Morris	2.00	1.00	.20
☐ 13 Bill Martin	3.00	1.50	.30
☐ 14 Kurt Kaull	1.00	.50	.10
☐ 15 Anthony Jones	2.00	1.00	.20

1983-84 Georgetown Police

This set contains 15 cards measuring approximately 2 5/8" by 4 1/8" featuring the Georgetown Hoyas. Backs contain safety tips. The set was also sponsored by Coca Cola.

	MINT	EXC	G-VG
COMPLETE SET (15)	50.00	25.00	5.00
COMMON PLAYER (1-15)	1.00	.50	.10
☐ 1 John Thompson CO	3.00	1.50	.30
☐ 2 Hoya 1983-84 Team	2.00	1.00	.20
☐ 3 Michael Jackson	3.00	1.50	.30
☐ 4 Bill Martin	2.00	1.00	.20
☐ 5 Jack the Bulldog, Hoya Mascot	1.00	.50	.10
☐ 6 Gene Smith	2.00	1.00	.20
☐ 7 Fred Brown	2.00	1.00	.20
☐ 8 Horace Broadnax	2.00	1.00	.20
☐ 9 Victor Morris	1.00	.50	.10
☐ 10 Patrick Ewing	30.00	15.00	3.00
☐ 11 Ralph Dalton	2.00	1.00	.20
☐ 12 Michael Graham	2.00	1.00	.20
☐ 13 Clifton Dairsow	1.00	.50	.10
☐ 14 David Wingate	3.00	1.50	.30
☐ 15 Reggie Williams	4.00	2.00	.40

1984-85 Georgetown Police

This set contains 14 cards each measuring approximately 2 5/8" by 4 1/8" featuring the Georgetown Hoyas. Fronts of the cards make reference to Georgetown's National Championship the year before. This set was also sponsored by Coca Cola. Backs contain safety tips and are written in black ink with a red accent.

		MINT	EXC	G-VG
COMPLETE SET (14)		40.00	20.00	4.00
COMMON PLAYER (1-14)		1.00	.50	.10
☐ 1	John Thompson CO	3.00	1.50	.30
☐ 2	Horace Broadnax	2.00	1.00	.20
☐ 3	Ralph Dalton	2.00	1.00	.20
☐ 4	Patrick Ewing	25.00	12.50	2.50
☐ 5	Kevin Floyd	1.00	.50	.10
☐ 6	Ron Highsmith	1.00	.50	.10
☐ 7	Michael Jackson	3.00	1.50	.30
☐ 8	Bill Martin	2.00	1.00	.20
☐ 9	Grady Mateen	1.00	.50	.10
☐ 10	Perry McDonald	2.00	1.00	.20
☐ 11	Reggie Williams	3.00	1.50	.30
☐ 12	David Wingate	3.00	1.50	.30
☐ 13	NCAA Championship Trophy	1.00	.50	.10
☐ 14	Team Photo	2.00	1.00	.20

1985-86 Georgetown Police

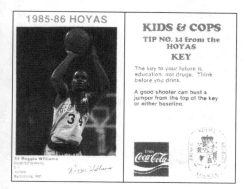

The 1985-86 Police Georgetown Hoyas set contains 16 cards measuring approximately 2 1/2" by 4". There are 13 player cards, plus one coach card, one team picture card, and one mascot card. The card fronts feature color photos and facsimile signatures. Each card back has one basketball tip and one safety tip.

		MINT	EXC	G-VG
COMPLETE SET (16)		10.00	5.00	1.00
COMMON PLAYER (1-16)		.50	.25	.05
☐ 1	1985-86 Hoyas Team Photo	1.00	.50	.10
☐ 2	John Thompson CO	1.50	.75	.15
☐ 3	Horace Broadnax	.75	.35	.07
☐ 4	Ralph Dalton	.75	.35	.07
☐ 5	Johnathan Edwards	.50	.25	.05
☐ 6	Hoyas Mascot	.50	.25	.05
☐ 7	Ronnie Highsmith	.50	.25	.05
☐ 8	Jaren Jackson	.75	.35	.07
☐ 9	Michael Jackson	1.50	.75	.15
☐ 10	Grady Mateen	.50	.25	.05
☐ 11	Perry McDonald	1.00	.50	.10
☐ 12	Victor Morris	.50	.25	.05
☐ 13	Charles Smith	3.00	1.50	.30
☐ 14	Reggie Williams	1.50	.75	.15
☐ 15	David Wingate	1.50	.75	.15
☐ 16	Bobby Winston	.50	.25	.05

1986-87 Georgetown Police

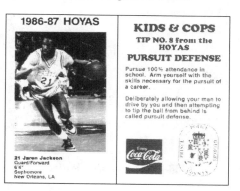

The 1986-87 Police Georgetown Hoyas set contains 14 cards measuring approximately 2 1/2" by 4". There are 12 player cards, plus one coach card and one team picture card. The card fronts have color photos, and each card back has one basketball tip and one safety tip.

		MINT	EXC	G-VG
COMPLETE SET (14)		8.00	4.00	.80
COMMON PLAYER (1-14)		.50	.25	.05
☐ 1	1986-87 Hoyas	.75	.35	.07
☐ 2	John Thompson CO	1.25	.60	.12
☐ 3	Anthony Allen	.50	.25	.05
☐ 4	Dwayne Bryant	.75	.35	.07
☐ 5	Johnathan Edwards	.50	.25	.05
☐ 6	Ben Gillery	.50	.25	.05
☐ 7	Ronnie Highsmith	.50	.25	.05
☐ 8	Jaren Jackson	.75	.35	.07
☐ 9	Sam Jefferson	.75	.35	.07
☐ 10	Perry McDonald	.75	.35	.07
☐ 11	Charles Smith	1.00	.50	.10
☐ 12	Mark Tillmon	.75	.35	.07
☐ 13	Reggie Williams	1.25	.60	.12
☐ 14	Bobby Winston	.50	.25	.05

1987-88 Georgetown Police

The 1987-88 Police Georgetown Hoyas set contains 16 cards measuring approximately 2 1/2" by 4". There are 14 player cards, plus one coach card and one team picture card. The card fronts have color photos, and each card back has one basketball tip and one safety tip.

1987-88 HOYAS

KIDS & COPS
TIP NO. 13 from the HOYAS
PURSUIT DEFENSE

Pursue 100% attendance in school. Arm yourself with the skills necessary for the pursuit of a career.

Pursuit defense is when your man dribbles around you to the basket and you attempt to catch him.

13 Charles Smith
6'1" Junior
Guard Washington, D.C.

	MINT	EXC	G-VG
COMPLETE SET (16)	7.00	3.50	.70
COMMON PLAYER (1-16)	.50	.25	.05
☐ 1 1987-88 Hoyas	.75	.35	.07
☐ 2 John Thompson CO	1.00	.50	.10
☐ 3 Anthony Allen	.50	.25	.05
☐ 4 Dwayne Bryant	.75	.35	.07
☐ 5 Johnathan Edwards	.50	.25	.05
☐ 6 Ben Gillery	.50	.25	.05
☐ 7 Ronnie Highsmith	.50	.25	.05
☐ 8 Jaren Jackson	.75	.35	.07
☐ 9 Sam Jefferson	.50	.25	.05
☐ 10 Johnny Jones	.50	.25	.05
☐ 11 Tom Lang	.50	.25	.05
☐ 12 Perry McDonald	.75	.35	.07
☐ 13 Charles Smith	1.25	.60	.12
☐ 14 Mark Tillmon	1.00	.50	.10
☐ 15 Anthony Tucker	.50	.25	.05
☐ 16 Bobby Winston	.50	.25	.05

1988-89 Georgetown Police

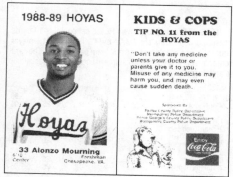

1988-89 HOYAS

KIDS & COPS
TIP NO. 11 from the HOYAS

"Don't take any medicine unless your doctor or parents give it to you. Misuse of any medicine may harm you, and may even cause sudden death.

Sponsored by
Fairfax County Police Department
Metropolitan Police Department
Prince George's County Public Department
Montgomery County Police Departments

33 Alonzo Mourning
6'10" Freshman
Center Chesapeake, VA.

The 1988-89 Police Georgetown Hoyas set contains 17 cards measuring approximately 2 1/2" by 4". There are 14 player cards, plus one coach card, one team picture card and one mascot card. The card fronts have color photos, and each card back has one safety tip.

	MINT	EXC	G-VG
COMPLETE SET (17)	9.00	4.50	.90
COMMON PLAYER (1-17)	.50	.25	.05
☐ 1 1988-89 Hoyas	.75	.35	.07
☐ 2 John Thompson CO	1.00	.50	.10
☐ 3 Anthony Allen	.50	.25	.05
☐ 4 Dwayne Bryant	.50	.25	.05
☐ 5 Johnathan Edwards	.50	.25	.05
☐ 6 Ronnie Thompson	.75	.35	.07

☐ 7 Milton Bell	.50	.25	.05
☐ 8 Jaren Jackson	.75	.35	.07
☐ 9 Sam Jefferson	.50	.25	.05
☐ 10 Johnny Jones	.50	.25	.05
☐ 11 Alonzo Mourning	3.00	1.50	.30
☐ 12 John Turner	1.50	.75	.15
☐ 13 Charles Smith	1.00	.50	.10
☐ 14 Mark Tillmon	.75	.35	.07
☐ 15 Dikembe Mutombo	3.00	1.50	.30
☐ 16 Bobby Winston	.50	.25	.05
☐ 17 McGruff The Crime Dog and Jack The Bulldog	.50	.25	.05

1989-90 Georgetown Police

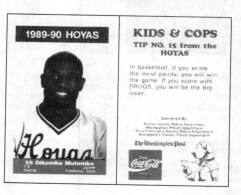

1989-90 HOYAS

KIDS & COPS
TIP NO. 15 from the HOYAS

In basketball, if you score the most points, you will win the game. If you score with DRUGS, you will be the big loser.

Sponsored By
Fairfax County Police Department
Metropolitan Police Department
Prince George's County Police Department
Montgomery County Police Departments

The Washington Post

55 Dikembe Mutombo
7'2" Junior
Center Kinshasa, Zaire

The 1989-90 Police Georgetown Hoyas set contains 17 cards measuring approximately 2 1/2" by 4". The front has a posed color photo of the player, enclosed by a blue border on the top and a gray one below. The back is printed in blue and red ink and has a safety tip from McGruff the Crime Dog. The cards are numbered below by "Tip Number" as listed on the card back.

	MINT	EXC	G-VG
COMPLETE SET (17)	6.00	3.00	.60
COMMON PLAYER (1-17)	.40	.20	.04
☐ 1 1989-90 Hoyas	.60	.30	.06
☐ 2 John Thompson CO	.75	.35	.07
☐ 3 Anthony Allen	.40	.20	.04
☐ 4 Dwayne Bryant	.40	.20	.04
☐ 5 David Edwards	.40	.20	.04
☐ 6 Ronny Thompson	.60	.30	.06
☐ 7 Milton Bell	.40	.20	.04
☐ 8 Kayode Vann	.40	.20	.04
☐ 9 Sam Jefferson	.40	.20	.04
☐ 10 Johnny Jones	.40	.20	.04
☐ 11 Alonzo Mourning	1.50	.75	.15
☐ 12 Mike Sabol	.40	.20	.04
☐ 13 Michael Tate	.60	.30	.06
☐ 14 Mark Tillmon	.60	.30	.06
☐ 15 Dikembe Mutombo	1.50	.75	.15
☐ 16 Antoine Stoudamire	.40	.20	.04
☐ 17 McGruff The Crime Dog and Jack the Bulldog	.40	.20	.04

1990-91 Georgetown Police

The 1990-91 Police Georgetown Hoyas set contains 15 cards measuring approximately 2 1/2" by 4". The front has a posed color photo of the player, enclosed by gray borders above and below. The back is printed in blue and red ink and has a safety tip from McGruff the Crime Dog. The cards are numbered below by "Tip Number" as listed on the card back.

1990-91 HOYAS

KIDS & COPS
TIP NO. 5 from the HOYAS

If your friends tell you drugs are cool, then they aren't your friends.

Sponsored By:
Fairfax County Police Department
Metropolitan Police Department
Prince George's County Police Department
Montgomery County Police Department

33 Alonzo Mourning
6'10"   Junior
Center/Forward   Chesapeake, VA.

	MINT	EXC	G-VG
COMPLETE SET (15)	5.00	2.50	.50
COMMON PLAYER (1-15)	.30	.15	.03
☐ 1 1990-91 Hoyas Team Photo	.50	.25	.05
☐ 2 Kayode Vann	.30	.15	.03
☐ 3 Mike Sabol	.30	.15	.03
☐ 4 Antoine Stoudamire	.30	.15	.03
☐ 5 Alonzo Mourning	1.00	.50	.10
☐ 6 Ronny Thompson	.50	.25	.05
☐ 7 Dikembe Mutombo	1.00	.50	.10
☐ 8 Charles Harrison	.30	.15	.03
☐ 9 Brian Kelly	.30	.15	.03
☐ 10 Robert Churchwell	.30	.15	.03
☐ 11 Joey Brown	.30	.15	.03
☐ 12 Vladimir Bosanac	.30	.15	.03
☐ 13 Lamont Morgan	.30	.15	.03
☐ 14 John Thompson CO	.75	.35	.07
☐ 15 McGruff The Crime Dog and Jack The Bulldog	.30	.15	.03

1991 Georgetown 100

This 100-card set was produced by Collegiate Collection and measures the standard size (2 1/2" by 3 1/2"). The fronts feature color player photos, with dark blue borders and the player's name in the gray stripe below the picture. The horizontally oriented backs present biographical information, career summary, or statistics on a white background with dark blue lettering and borders. The cards are numbered on the back.

	MINT	EXC	G-VG
COMPLETE SET (100)	12.00	6.00	1.20
COMMON PLAYER (1-100)	.10	.05	.01
☐ 1 John Thompson CO	.35	.17	.03
☐ 2 Patrick Ewing	.75	.35	.07
☐ 3 Eric Floyd	.35	.17	.03
☐ 4 Reggie Williams	.25	.12	.02
☐ 5 John Duren	.20	.10	.02

	MINT	EXC	G-VG
☐ 6 Craig Shelton	.20	.10	.02
☐ 7 Charles Smith	.25	.12	.02
☐ 8 Michael Jackson	.20	.10	.02
☐ 9 Jared Jackson	.15	.07	.01
☐ 10 David Wingate	.25	.12	.02
☐ 11 Mark Tillmon	.20	.10	.02
☐ 12 Fred Brown	.15	.07	.01
☐ 13 Kurt Kaull	.10	.05	.01
☐ 14 Ron Highsmith	.10	.05	.01
☐ 15 Dwayne Bryant	.10	.05	.01
☐ 16 Michael Jackson	.20	.10	.02
☐ 17 Al Dutch	.10	.05	.01
☐ 18 Ben Gillery	.10	.05	.01
☐ 19 Ralph Dalton	.10	.05	.01
☐ 20 1984 NCAA Champs	.10	.05	.01
☐ 21 Craig Esherick	.10	.05	.01
☐ 22 Bobby Winston	.10	.05	.01
☐ 23 Bill Martin	.15	.07	.01
☐ 24 Horace Broadnax	.10	.05	.01
☐ 25 John Thompson CO	.35	.17	.03
☐ 26 Dwayne Bryant	.10	.05	.01
☐ 28 Perry McDonald	.10	.05	.01
☐ 29 Reggie Williams	.25	.12	.02
☐ 30 Patrick Ewing	.75	.35	.07
☐ 31 Patrick Ewing	.75	.35	.07
☐ 32 Peter McDonald	.10	.05	.01
☐ 33 Sam Jefferson	.10	.05	.01
☐ 34 Michael Jackson	.20	.10	.02
☐ 35 Anthony Allen	.10	.05	.01
☐ 36 Mike Riley	.10	.05	.01
☐ 37 John Duren	.20	.10	.02
☐ 38 Mark Tillmon	.20	.10	.02
☐ 39 Mike Frazier	.10	.05	.01
☐ 40 Eric Smith	.10	.05	.01
☐ 41 Ed Spriggs	.15	.07	.01
☐ 42 Johnathan Edwards	.10	.05	.01
☐ 43 Derrick Jackson	.10	.05	.01
☐ 44 Mike Hancock	.10	.05	.01
☐ 45 Tom Scates	.10	.05	.01
☐ 46 David Blue	.10	.05	.01
☐ 47 Charles Smith	.25	.12	.02
☐ 48 John Thompson CO	.35	.17	.03
☐ 49 Patrick Ewing	.75	.35	.07
☐ 50 Al Dutch	.10	.05	.01
☐ 51 Eric Floyd	.35	.17	.03
☐ 52 Craig Shelton	.20	.10	.02
☐ 53 Reggie Williams	.25	.12	.02
☐ 53 Tom Lang	.10	.05	.01
☐ 54 Michael Jackson	.20	.10	.02
☐ 55 Patrick Ewing	.75	.35	.07
☐ 56 Bill Thomas	.10	.05	.01
☐ 57 Ed Hopkins	.10	.05	.01
☐ 58 John Thompson	.35	.17	.03
☐ 59 Jon Smith	.10	.05	.01
☐ 60 Merlin Wilson	.10	.05	.01
☐ 61 Gene Smith	.15	.07	.01
☐ 62 Johnny Jones	.10	.05	.01
☐ 63 Senior Night	.10	.05	.01
☐ 64 Eric Floyd	.35	.17	.03
☐ 65 Reggie Williams	.25	.12	.02
☐ 66 Steve Martin	.10	.05	.01
☐ 67 Mark Gallagher	.10	.05	.01
☐ 68 Mike McDermont	.10	.05	.01
☐ 69 Greg Brooks	.10	.05	.01
☐ 70 Larry Long	.10	.05	.01
☐ 71 Felix Yeoman	.10	.05	.01
☐ 72 Lonnie Duren	.10	.05	.01
☐ 73 Terry Fenlon	.10	.05	.01
☐ 74 Steve Martin	.10	.05	.01
☐ 75 Fred Brown	.15	.07	.01
☐ 76 Bill Lynn	.10	.05	.01
☐ 77 Patrick Ewing	.75	.35	.07
☐ 78 Mike Laska	.10	.05	.01
☐ 79 Paul Tagliabue	.75	.35	.07
☐ 80 Don Weber	.10	.05	.01
☐ 81 Jared Jackson	.10	.05	.01
☐ 82 1982 NCAA Finalists	.10	.05	.01
☐ 83 1985 NCAA Finalists	.10	.05	.01
☐ 84 Jim Brown	.10	.05	.01
☐ 85 Jim Christy	.10	.05	.01
☐ 86 Tim Mercier	.10	.05	.01
☐ 87 Joe Missett	.10	.05	.01
☐ 88 Charlie Adrian	.10	.05	.01
☐ 89 John Thompson CO	.35	.17	.03
☐ 90 Craig Esherick	.10	.05	.01
☐ 91 Dennis Cesar	.10	.05	.01
☐ 92 Ken Pichette	.10	.05	.01
☐ 93 Charlie Adrian	.10	.05	.01
☐ 94 Mike Laughna	.10	.05	.01
☐ 95 Tommy O'Keefe	.10	.05	.01
☐ 96 Merlin Wilson	.10	.05	.01
☐ 97 Craig Shelton	.20	.10	.02
☐ 98 Derrick Jackson	.10	.05	.01
☐ 99 Mike Riley	.10	.05	.01
☐ 100 Director Card	.10	.05	.01

1990-91 Georgia Smokey

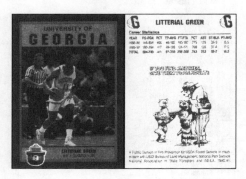

This 16-card set was sponsored by the USDA Forest Service in conjunction with several other federal agencies. The cards measure the standard size (2 1/2" by 3 1/2") and feature on fronts color action photos bordered in red. Inside the border the school name and player identification are given in gray stripes above and below the picture, with the Smokey icon in the lower left corner. The background color outside the red border varies from card to card, ranging from black to gray. The back presents either career statistics or summary, as well as a fire prevention cartoon starring Smokey. The cards are unnumbered and are checklisted below in alphabetical order, with the uniform number after the player's name.

	MINT	EXC	G-VG
COMPLETE SET (16)	10.00	5.00	1.00
COMMON PLAYER (1-16)	.75	.35	.07
□ 1 Arlando Bennett 32	.75	.35	.07
□ 2 Charles Claxton 33	.75	.35	.07
□ 3 Rod Cole 22	.75	.35	.07
□ 4 Bernard Davis 23	.75	.35	.07
□ 5 Hugh Durham CO	1.00	.50	.10
□ 6 Shaun Golden 10	.75	.35	.07
□ 7 Litterial Green 11	2.50	1.25	.25
□ 8 Antonio Harvey 34	.75	.35	.07
□ 9 Neville Austin 35	.75	.35	.07
□ 10 Lem Howard 25	.75	.35	.07
□ 11 Marcel Kon 51	.75	.35	.07
□ 12 Jody Patton 12	.75	.35	.07
□ 13 Kendall Rhine 15	1.00	.50	.10
□ 14 Reggie Tinch 24	.75	.35	.07
□ 15 Marshall Wilson 44	.75	.35	.07
□ 16 1990-91 Bulldogs Team Photo	.75	.35	.07

1988-89 Georgia Tech Nike

This 12-card set was sponsored by Nike, whose company name appears on both sides of the card. The cards measure the standard size, 2 1/2" by 3 1/2". The fronts feature either posed or action color photos, with a gold border on the left and dark blue borders on the bottom and right of the picture. The backs have biographical information and a tip from the Yellow Jackets consisting of an anti-drug message. The key cards are the first appearances of Brian Oliver and Dennis Scott on a basketball card of ant type. Sets were given out to fans attending a certain Georgia Tech home game during the 1988-89 season.

	MINT	EXC	G-VG
COMPLETE SET (12)	25.00	12.50	2.50
COMMON PLAYER (1-12)	1.00	.50	.10
□ 1 Maurice Brittain 52	1.00	.50	.10
□ 2 Karl Brown 5	1.00	.50	.10
□ 3 Bobby Cremins CO	2.50	1.25	.25

	MINT	EXC	G-VG
□ 4 Brian Domalik 12	1.00	.50	.10
□ 5 Tom Hammonds 20	3.50	1.75	.35
□ 6 Johnny McNeil 44	1.00	.50	.10
□ 7 James Munlyn 24	1.00	.50	.10
□ 8 Brian Oliver 13	4.50	2.25	.45
□ 9 Willie Reese 31	1.00	.50	.10
□ 10 Dennis Scott 4	9.00	4.50	.90
□ 11 Anthony Sherrod 42	2.00	1.00	.20
□ 12 David Whitmore 23	1.00	.50	.10

1989-90 Georgia Tech Police/Coke

This 20-card set was sponsored by the Atlanta City Police Department and produced by Coca-Cola. The cards measure the standard size, 2 1/2" by 3 1/2". The cards were distributed in the Atlanta area by the Police Athletic League; reportedly 10,000 sets were distributed. The fronts feature either posed or action color photos on a white card stock. The backs have biographical information and a tip from the Yellow Jackets consisting of an anti-drug message.

	MINT	EXC	G-VG
COMPLETE SET (20)	20.00	10.00	2.00
COMMON PLAYER (1-20)	.50	.25	.05
□ 1 Kenny Anderson 12 (Portrait)	6.00	3.00	.60
□ 2 Kenny Anderson 12 (Free Throw)	4.00	2.00	.40
□ 3 Kenny Anderson 12 (Jump Shot)	4.00	2.00	.40
□ 4 Rod Balanis 34	.50	.25	.05
□ 5 Darryl Barnes 15	.50	.25	.05
□ 6 Brian Black 23	.50	.25	.05
□ 7 Karl Brown 5	.75	.35	.07
□ 8 Bobby Cremins CO	1.00	.50	.10
□ 9 Brian Domalik 3	.50	.25	.05
□ 10 Matt Geiger 52	.75	.35	.07
□ 11 Malcolm Mackey 32	1.50	.75	.15
□ 12 Johnny McNeil 44	.50	.25	.05
□ 13 James Munlyn 24	.50	.25	.05
□ 14 Ivano Newbill 33	.50	.25	.05

		MINT	EXC	G-VG
☐ 15	Brian Oliver 13	1.00	.50	.10
☐ 16	Dennis Scott 4	2.50	1.25	.25
	(Free Throw)			
☐ 17	Dennis Scott 4	2.50	1.25	.25
	(Shooting)			
☐ 18	Greg White 14	.50	.25	.05
☐ 19	Team Photo	.75	.35	.07
☐ 20	Lethal Weapon 3	2.00	1.00	.20
	Brian Oliver,			
	Dennis Scott, and			
	Kenny Anderson			

1990-91 Georgia Tech Police/Coke

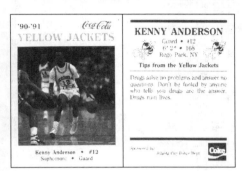

This 20-card set was sponsored by the Atlanta City Police Department and Coca-Cola, and the latter sponsor's logos appear in the upper right corner of the card face as well as at the bottom of the back. It is reported that 10,000 sets were issued in two lots: the first 5,000 went out to the housing projects and kids in the Atlanta Police Athletic Program, and the second lot was offered to the general public. The cards measure the standard size (2 1/2" by 3 1/2"). The front features a borderless color action photo of the player on white card stock. The team name appears in gold lettering above the picture, with player information in black lettering below the picture. The back has brief biographical information and "Tips from the Yellow Jackets," which consist of various public service announcements. The cards are unnumbered and are checklisted below in alphabetical order.

		MINT	EXC	G-VG
	COMPLETE SET (20)	12.00	6.00	1.20
	COMMON PLAYER (1-20)	.40	.20	.04
☐ 1	Kenny Anderson 12	2.50	1.25	.25
	(Shooting lay-up)			
☐ 2	Kenny Anderson 12	2.50	1.25	.25
	(Driving past defender)			
☐ 3	Kenny Anderson 12	2.50	1.25	.25
	(Dribbling)			
☐ 4	Ron Balanis 34	.40	.20	.04
☐ 5	Darryl Barnes 15	.40	.20	.04
☐ 6	Jon Barry 14	1.00	.50	.10
☐ 7	Brian Black 23	.40	.20	.04
☐ 8	Bobby Cremins CO	1.00	.50	.10
☐ 9	Brian Domalik 3	.40	.20	.04
☐ 10	James Gaddy 10	.40	.20	.04
☐ 11	Todd Harlicka 30	.40	.20	.04
☐ 12	Bryan Hill 11	.40	.20	.04
☐ 13	Matt Geiger 52	.60	.30	.06
☐ 14	Brian Gemberling 41	.40	.20	.04
☐ 15	Malcolm Mackey 32	1.00	.50	.10
☐ 16	Malcolm Mackey 32	1.00	.50	.10
☐ 17	James Munlyn 24	.40	.20	.04
☐ 18	Ivano Newbill 33	.40	.20	.04
☐ 19	Greg White 31	.40	.20	.04
☐ 20	Team Photo	.60	.30	.06

1991 Georgia Tech *

This 200 card set was produced by Collegiate Collection and measures the standard size (2 1/2" by 3 1/2"). The fronts feature color photos with blue boarders and the players's name appearing in a gold stripe. The backs present statistics or career summary on a white background with blue lettering.

		MINT	EXC	G-VG
	COMPLETE SET (200)	22.00	11.00	2.20
	COMMON PLAYER (1-200)	.10	.05	.01
☐ 1	John Dewberry	.10	.05	.01
☐ 2	Ida Neal	.10	.05	.01
☐ 3	Lenny Horton	.10	.05	.01
☐ 4	Dennis Scott	.50	.25	.05
☐ 5	Steve Davenport	.10	.05	.01
☐ 6	Dolores Bootz	.10	.05	.01
☐ 7	Dante Jones	.20	.10	.02
☐ 8	Cory Collier	.10	.05	.01
☐ 9	Lee Ann Woodhull	.10	.05	.01
☐ 10	John Ivemeyer	.10	.05	.01
☐ 11	Ronny Cone	.10	.05	.01
☐ 12	George Malone	.10	.05	.01
☐ 13	Darrell Norton	.10	.05	.01
☐ 14	Bud Isom	.10	.05	.01
☐ 15	Tom Hammonds	.25	.12	.02
☐ 16	Bobby Dodd	.15	.07	.01
☐ 17	Cindy Cockran	.10	.05	.01
☐ 18	Andre Thomas	.10	.05	.01
☐ 19	Chuck Easley	.10	.05	.01
☐ 20	Willie Burns	.10	.05	.01
☐ 21	Eric Thomas	.15	.07	.01
☐ 22	Jerry Mays	.15	.07	.01
☐ 23	Sammy Drummer	.10	.05	.01
☐ 24	Tory Ehle	.10	.05	.01
☐ 25	Rob Healy	.10	.05	.01
☐ 26	Brook Steppe	.20	.10	.02
☐ 27	Darrell Gast	.10	.05	.01
☐ 28	David Bell	.10	.05	.01
☐ 29	Keith Glanton	.10	.05	.01
☐ 30	Brian Oliver	.30	.15	.03
☐ 31	Sean Smith	.10	.05	.01
☐ 32	Cedric Stallworth	.10	.05	.01
☐ 33	Craig Neal	.10	.05	.01
☐ 34	Danny Harrison	.10	.05	.01
☐ 35	Duane Ferrell	.20	.10	.02
☐ 36	Eric Bearden	.10	.05	.01
☐ 37	Andy Hearn	.10	.05	.01
☐ 38	Jim Anderson	.10	.05	.01
☐ 39	Anthony Harrison	.10	.05	.01
☐ 40	Marielle Walker	.10	.05	.01
☐ 41	Dean Weaver	.10	.05	.01
☐ 42	Yvon Joseph	.10	.05	.01
☐ 43	Mike Kelley	.10	.05	.01
☐ 44	John Davis	.10	.05	.01
☐ 45	Mark Hogan	.10	.05	.01
☐ 46	Karl Brown	.15	.07	.01
☐ 47	Kyle Ambrose	.10	.05	.01
☐ 48	Steve Mullen	.10	.05	.01
☐ 49	Willis Crockett	.20	.10	.02
☐ 50	Jeff Mathis	.10	.05	.01
☐ 51	Ellis Gardner	.10	.05	.01
☐ 52	Larry Good	.10	.05	.01
☐ 53	Billy Lothridge	.15	.07	.01
☐ 54	Bill Kinard	.15	.07	.01
☐ 55	Brent Cunningham	.10	.05	.01

#	Player	MINT	EXC	G-VG
☐ 56	Teddy Peeples	.10	.05	.01
☐ 57	Pat Swilling	.35	.17	.03
☐ 58	John Salley	.35	.17	.03
☐ 59	Lawrence Lowe	.10	.05	.01
☐ 60	Sheila Wagner	.25	.12	.02
☐ 61	Cam Bonifay	.10	.05	.01
☐ 62	George Brodnax	.10	.05	.01
☐ 63	Fred Braselton	.10	.05	.01
☐ 64	Joe Avel	.10	.05	.01
☐ 65	Franklin Brooks	.10	.05	.01
☐ 66	Rod Stephens	.10	.05	.01
☐ 67	Bill Curry	.20	.10	.02
☐ 68	Tim Manion	.10	.05	.01
☐ 69	Rick Strom	.10	.05	.01
☐ 70	Toby Pearson	.10	.05	.01
☐ 71	Jim Breland	.10	.05	.01
☐ 72	Don Bessillieu	.10	.05	.01
☐ 73	Craig Baynham	.15	.07	.01
☐ 74	Maxie Baughan	.20	.10	.02
☐ 75	Wade Mitchell	.10	.05	.01
☐ 76	Sammy Lilly	.10	.05	.01
☐ 77	Gary Lee	.10	.05	.01
☐ 78	Paul Jurgensen	.10	.05	.01
☐ 79	Robert Lavette	.15	.07	.01
☐ 80	Robert Jaracz	.10	.05	.01
☐ 81	Mike Oven	.10	.05	.01
☐ 82	Paul Menegazz	.10	.05	.01
☐ 83	Billy Martin	.10	.05	.01
☐ 84	Bobby Moorhead	.10	.05	.01
☐ 85	Wade Martin	.10	.05	.01
☐ 86	Buzz	.10	.05	.01
☐ 87	Malcolm King	.10	.05	.01
☐ 88	Bobby Ross	.20	.10	.02
☐ 89	Gary Lanier	.10	.05	.01
☐ 90	Bill Curry	.20	.10	.02
☐ 91	Bonnie Tale	.10	.05	.01
☐ 92	William Alexander	.10	.05	.01
☐ 93	Rick Lantz	.10	.05	.01
☐ 94	Eddie McAshen	.10	.05	.01
☐ 95	Kim King	.10	.05	.01
☐ 96	Cleve Pounds	.10	.05	.01
☐ 97	Rambling Wreck	.10	.05	.01
☐ 98	Bud (Coach) Carson	.15	.07	.01
☐ 99	Bobby Dodd Stadium	.10	.05	.01
☐ 100	Director Card	.10	.05	.01
☐ 101	Willie Burks	.10	.05	.01
☐ 102	Sheldon Fox	.10	.05	.01
☐ 103	Scott Erwin	.10	.05	.01
☐ 104	Danny Harrison	.10	.05	.01
☐ 105	Eric Thomas	.15	.07	.01
☐ 106	Kent Hill	.20	.10	.02
☐ 107	Ray Blemker	.10	.05	.01
☐ 108	Terry Randell	.10	.05	.01
☐ 109	Pete Silas	.10	.05	.01
☐ 110	Bob McDonnell	.10	.05	.01
☐ 111	Kevin Brown	.25	.12	.02
☐ 112	Ralph Malone	.10	.05	.01
☐ 113	Jerry Mays	.15	.07	.01
☐ 114	Mark Bradley	.10	.05	.01
☐ 115	Thomas Palmer	.10	.05	.01
☐ 116	Calvin Tiggle	.10	.05	.01
☐ 117	Roger Kinard	.10	.05	.01
☐ 118	Thomas Balkcom	.10	.05	.01
☐ 119	Steve Newbern	.10	.05	.01
☐ 120	Tripp Isenhour	.10	.05	.01
☐ 121	Rod Stephens	.10	.05	.01
☐ 122	Mark Price	.15	.07	.01
☐ 123	Keith Fleming	.10	.05	.01
☐ 124	Bobby Cremins CO	.20	.10	.02
☐ 125	Eddie Ivery Lee	.15	.07	.01
☐ 126	Darryl Jenkins	.10	.05	.01
☐ 127	Jerimiah McClary	.10	.05	.01
☐ 128	Dirk Morris	.10	.05	.01
☐ 129	Riccardo Ingram	.10	.05	.01
☐ 130	Lisa Neal	.10	.05	.01
☐ 131	Robert Massey	.20	.10	.02
☐ 132	Cedric Stallworth	.10	.05	.01
☐ 133	Ty Griffin	.25	.12	.02
☐ 134	Bruce Dalrymple	.20	.10	.02
☐ 135	Johnny McNeil	.10	.05	.01
☐ 136	Stefen Scotton	.10	.05	.01
☐ 137	Jim Lavin	.10	.05	.01
☐ 138	Joe Siffri	.10	.05	.01
☐ 139	Gary Newson	.10	.05	.01
☐ 140	Cristy Guardao	.10	.05	.01
☐ 141	Scott Petway	.10	.05	.01
☐ 142	Jim Poole	.20	.10	.02
☐ 143	Kenneth Wilson	.10	.05	.01
☐ 144	Bridget Koster	.10	.05	.01
☐ 145	James Purvis	.10	.05	.01
☐ 146	Walt McConnell	.10	.05	.01
☐ 147	Jay Martin	.10	.05	.01
☐ 148	T.J. Edwards	.10	.05	.01
☐ 149	Chris Simmons	.10	.05	.01
☐ 150	Jennifer Beemstebuer	.10	.05	.01
☐ 151	Eric Smith	.10	.05	.01
☐ 152	George Paulson	.10	.05	.01
☐ 153	Nacho Gervas	.10	.05	.01
☐ 154	Mark White	.10	.05	.01
☐ 155	Antonio McKay	.10	.05	.01
☐ 156	Taz Anderson	.15	.07	.01
☐ 157	Sam Bracken	.10	.05	.01
☐ 158	Kate Brandt	.10	.05	.01
☐ 159	Melvin Dole	.10	.05	.01
☐ 160	Tico Brown	.15	.07	.01
☐ 161	Lisa Kofskey	.10	.05	.01
☐ 162	Charlie Rymer	.10	.05	.01
☐ 163	Leigh Roberts	.10	.05	.01
☐ 164	Scott Jordan	.15	.07	.01
☐ 165	Bill McDonald	.10	.05	.01
☐ 166	Harper Brown	.10	.05	.01
☐ 167	Jim Caldwell	.10	.05	.01
☐ 168	Bud Blemker	.10	.05	.01
☐ 169	Bill Flowers	.10	.05	.01
☐ 170	Roger Kasier	.10	.05	.01
☐ 171	Margaret Gales	.10	.05	.01
☐ 172	Kathy Harrison	.10	.05	.01
☐ 173	Kenny Thorne	.10	.05	.01
☐ 174	Kim Lash	.10	.05	.01
☐ 175	Jens Skjoedt	.10	.05	.01
☐ 176	Bobby Kimmel	.10	.05	.01
☐ 177	Phil Wagner	.10	.05	.01
☐ 178	Jim Wood	.10	.05	.01
☐ 179	Rick Yunkus	.15	.07	.01
☐ 180	Unknown	.00	.00	.00
☐ 181	Rick Lockhood	.10	.05	.01
☐ 182	Jay Nichols	.10	.05	.01
☐ 183	Paige Lord	.10	.05	.01
☐ 184	Bryan Shelton	.15	.07	.01
☐ 185	Carrie Ollar	.10	.05	.01
☐ 186	Donnie Chisolm	.10	.05	.01
☐ 187	Floyd Faucette	.10	.05	.01
☐ 188	Jeff Ford	.10	.05	.01
☐ 189	Drew Hill	.35	.17	.03
☐ 190	Leon Hardman	.10	.05	.01
☐ 191	Ricky Gilbert	.10	.05	.01
☐ 192	Roger Kinard	.10	.05	.01
☐ 193	K.G. Whittle	.10	.05	.01
☐ 194	Andre Simm	.10	.05	.01
☐ 195	Franz Sydow	.10	.05	.01
☐ 196	Mackel Harris	.10	.05	.01
☐ 197	Eddie Lee Ivery	.35	.17	.03
☐ 198	Kris Krentra	.10	.05	.01
☐ 199	Lenny Snow	.10	.05	.01
☐ 200	Director Card	.10	.05	.01

1980-81 Illinois Arby's

This 15-card set was sponsored by Arby's Restaurants and features players of the 1980-81 Fighting Illini squad. The cards measure the standard 2 1/2" by 3 1/2". The player's signature and an Arby's advertisement appear below a color posed photo of the player. The horizontally oriented back provides biographical and statistical information.

	MINT	EXC	G-VG
COMPLETE SET (15)	30.00	15.00	3.00
COMMON PLAYER (1-15)	1.00	.50	.10

		MINT	EXC	G-VG
☐ 1	Kevin Bontemps	1.00	.50	.10
☐ 2	James Griffin	1.00	.50	.10
☐ 3	Derek Harper	7.50	3.75	.75
☐ 4	Lou Henson CO	2.00	1.00	.20
☐ 5	Derek Holcomb	1.50	.75	.15
☐ 6	Eddie Johnson	7.50	3.75	.75
☐ 7	Bryan Leonard	1.00	.50	.10
☐ 8	Dick Nagy CO	1.00	.50	.10
☐ 9	Perry Range	1.00	.50	.10
☐ 10	Quinn Richardson	1.00	.50	.10
☐ 11	Mark Smith	1.00	.50	.10
☐ 12	Neale Stoner	1.00	.50	.10
☐ 13	Craig Tucker	1.00	.50	.10
☐ 14	Tony Yates CO	1.50	.75	.15
☐ 15	Team Photo	1.50	.75	.15

1981-82 Illinois Arby's

This 16-card set was sponsored by Arby's Restaurants and features players of the 1981-82 Fighting Illini squad. The cards measure the standard 2 1/2" by 3 1/2". The player's signature and an Arby's advertisement appear below a color posed photo of the player. The horizontally-oriented back provides biographical and statistical information. Lou Henson's last name is misspelled on the back of his card (Hensen).

		MINT	EXC	G-VG
	COMPLETE SET (16)	15.00	7.50	1.50
	COMMON PLAYER (1-16)	.75	.35	.07
☐ 1	Kevin Bontemps	.75	.35	.07
☐ 2	Jay Daniels	.75	.35	.07
☐ 3	James Griffin	.75	.35	.07
☐ 4	Derek Harper	3.50	1.75	.35
☐ 5	Lou Henson CO UER	1.00	.50	.10
	(Misspelled Hensen on card back)			
☐ 6	Dan Klier	.75	.35	.07
☐ 7	Bryan Leonard	.75	.35	.07
☐ 8	Dee Maras	.75	.35	.07
☐ 9	George Montgomery	.75	.35	.07
☐ 10	Dick Nagy CO	.75	.35	.07
☐ 11	Perry Range	.75	.35	.07
☐ 12	Quinn Richardson	.75	.35	.07
☐ 13	Craig Tucker	.75	.35	.07
☐ 14	Anthony Welch	1.00	.50	.10
☐ 15	Tony Yates CO	1.00	.50	.10
☐ 16	Team Photo	1.00	.50	.10

1986-87 Indiana Greats I

This 42-card set is the first series of the All-Time Greats of Indiana University. The cards measure the standard size, 2 1/2" by 3 1/2", and were sponsored by Bank One of Indiana. The fronts present a mixture of black and white or color photos, posed and action. The horizontally-oriented backs have biographical and statistical

information on the player, with the card number in the upper right hand corner.

		MINT	EXC	G-VG
	COMPLETE SET (42)	20.00	10.00	2.00
	COMMON PLAYER (1-42)	.50	.25	.05
☐ 1	Bob Knight CO	1.50	.75	.15
☐ 2	Walt Bellamy	.75	.35	.07
☐ 3	Pete Obremskey	.50	.25	.05
☐ 4	Jim Wisman	.50	.25	.05
☐ 5	Frank Radovich	.50	.25	.05
☐ 6	Ted Kitchel	.50	.25	.05
☐ 7	Don Schlundt	.75	.35	.07
☐ 8	Uwe Blab	.50	.25	.05
☐ 9	Lou Watson	.50	.25	.05
☐ 10	Bobby Masters	.50	.25	.05
☐ 11	Steve Redenbaugh	.50	.25	.05
☐ 12	Bob Wilkinson	.60	.30	.06
☐ 13	Kent Benson	.75	.35	.07
☐ 14	Everett Dean	.60	.30	.06
☐ 15	Rick Ford	.50	.25	.05
☐ 16	Hallie Bryant	.50	.25	.05
☐ 17	Dan Dakich	.50	.25	.05
☐ 18	Sam Gee	.50	.25	.05
☐ 19	George McGinnis	1.00	.50	.10
☐ 20	John Ritter	.50	.25	.05
☐ 21	Jon McGlocklin	.75	.35	.07
☐ 22	Landon Turner	1.00	.50	.10
☐ 23	Gary Long	.50	.25	.05
☐ 24	Jim Crews	.75	.35	.07
☐ 25	Steve Downing	.75	.35	.07
☐ 26	Vern Huffman	.50	.25	.05
☐ 27	Ernie Andres	.50	.25	.05
☐ 28	Charles Hodson	.50	.25	.05
☐ 29	Jerry Thompson	.50	.25	.05
☐ 30	Tom Abernethy	.60	.30	.06
☐ 31	Tom Bolyard	.50	.25	.05
☐ 32	Jimmy Rayl	.75	.35	.07
☐ 33	John Laskowski	.60	.30	.06
☐ 34	Archie Dees	.50	.25	.05
☐ 35	Joby Wright	.75	.35	.07
☐ 36	Gary Greiger	.50	.25	.05
☐ 37	Randy Wittman	.75	.35	.07
☐ 38	Steve Green	.50	.25	.05
☐ 39	Erv Inniger	.50	.25	.05
☐ 40	Steve Risley	.50	.25	.05
☐ 41	Bill DeHeer	.50	.25	.05
☐ 42	Checklist Card	.50	.25	.05

1987-88 Indiana Greats II

This 42-card set is the second series of the All-Time Greats of Indiana University. The cards measure the standard size, 2 1/2" by 3 1/2", and were sponsored by Bank One of Indiana. The fronts present a mixture of black and white or color photos, posed and action. The horizontally oriented backs have biographical and statistical information on the player, with the card number in the upper right hand corner. The back of the checklist card contains an offer to buy either Series I or II for 10.00 from the Big Red Gift Center.

		MINT	EXC	G-VG
	COMPLETE SET (42)	20.00	10.00	2.00
	COMMON PLAYER (1-42)	.50	.25	.05
☐ 1	Steve Alford's Farewell	1.00	.50	.10
☐ 2	Bob Dro	.50	.25	.05
☐ 3	Butch Joyner	.50	.25	.05
☐ 4	Bobby Leonard	.60	.30	.06
☐ 5	Branch McCracken	.60	.30	.06
☐ 6	Roy Tolbert	.75	.35	.07
☐ 7	Wayne Radford	.60	.30	.06
☐ 8	Earl Schneider	.50	.25	.05
☐ 9	Jim Strickland	.50	.25	.05
☐ 10	Al Harden	.50	.25	.05
☐ 11	Bob Menke	.50	.25	.05
☐ 12	Steve Alford	1.00	.50	.10
☐ 13	Mike Woodson	.75	.35	.07
☐ 14	Tom/Dick Van Arsdale	.75	.35	.07
☐ 15	Wally Choice	.50	.25	.05
☐ 16	Charlie Hall	.50	.25	.05
☐ 17	Indiana Coach Legend	.60	.30	.06
☐ 18	Stew Robinson	.60	.30	.06
☐ 19	Dynamic Duo	.50	.25	.05
☐ 20	Steve Alford	1.00	.50	.10
☐ 21	Quinn Buckner	.75	.35	.07
☐ 22	Indiana Coach Legends	.60	.30	.06
☐ 23	Winston Morgan	.50	.25	.05
☐ 24	1975-76 Seniors	.50	.25	.05
☐ 25	Jim Thomas	.60	.30	.06
☐ 26	Vern Payne	.50	.25	.05
☐ 27	Scott May	.75	.35	.07
☐ 28	Dave Porter	.50	.25	.05
☐ 29	Dick Farley	.50	.25	.05
☐ 30	Isiah Thomas	2.50	1.25	.25
☐ 31	Butch Carter	.60	.30	.06
☐ 32	Burke Scott	.50	.25	.05
☐ 33	Jack Johnson	.50	.25	.05
☐ 34	Charley Kraak	.50	.25	.05
☐ 35	Marv Huffman	.50	.25	.05
☐ 36	Steve Bouchie	.60	.30	.06
☐ 37	Bob Knight's Record	1.00	.50	.10
☐ 38	Bill Garrett	.50	.25	.05
☐ 39	Jerry Bass	.50	.25	.05
☐ 40	Jay McCreary	.50	.25	.05
☐ 41	Ken Johnson	.50	.25	.05
☐ 42	Checklist Card	.50	.25	.05
	(Send-in offer on back)			

1987-88 Kansas Nike

This 16-card set was sponsored by Nike and issued on an unperforated sheet with four rows of four cards. After cutting, they measure the standard size (2 1/2" by 3 1/2"). The fronts feature a mix of posed and action color player photos on a white card face. Above the picture appears the team name, year, and the Nike logo. The picture is bordered by red on the left and by dark blue on the right and bottom. The Jayhawk logo appears in the lower left corner, with player identification in the blue border below the picture. The backs have biographical information, player evaluation, and basketball advice in the form of "Tips from the Jayhawks." The cards are unnumbered and checklisted below in alphabetical order, with the uniform number after the player's name.

		MINT	EXC	G-VG
	COMPLETE SET (16)	21.00	10.50	2.10
	COMMON PLAYER (1-16)	1.00	.50	.10
☐ 1	Sean Alvarado 52	1.00	.50	.10
☐ 2	Scooter Barry 10	2.00	1.00	.20
☐ 3	Marvin Branch 54	1.00	.50	.10
☐ 4	Larry Brown CO	1.50	.75	.15
☐ 5	Jeff Gueldner 33	1.50	.75	.15
☐ 6	Keith Harris 45	1.00	.50	.10
☐ 7	Otis Livingston 12	1.00	.50	.10
☐ 8	Mike Maddox 32	1.00	.50	.10
☐ 9	Danny Manning 25	6.00	3.00	.60
☐ 10	Archie Marshall 23	1.00	.50	.10
☐ 11	Mike Masucci 44	1.00	.50	.10
☐ 12	Lincoln Minor 11	1.00	.50	.10
☐ 13	Milt Newton 21	2.00	1.00	.20
☐ 14	Chris Piper 24	1.00	.50	.10
☐ 15	Kevin Pritchard 14	3.00	1.50	.30
☐ 16	Mark Randall 42	3.00	1.50	.30

1989-90 Kansas Leesley

This 16-card set was licensed to Leesley by the University of Kansas. The cards measure the standard size (2 1/2" by 3 1/2") and feature on the fronts color action player shots, with white and black borders on dark blue background. The player's name is given below the picture, with the Jayhawk team logo on an orange basketball in the lower left corner. The backs present biographical information and a player profile. The cards are numbered on the back in continuation of the Kansas Football card set.

		MINT	EXC	G-VG
	COMPLETE SET (16)	8.00	4.00	.80
	COMMON PLAYER (41-56)	.50	.25	.05
☐ 41	Frequent Flyers Poster Poster Card	.50	.25	.05
☐ 42	Jeff Gueldner	.60	.30	.06
☐ 43	Freeman West	.50	.25	.05
☐ 44	Rick Calloway	.75	.35	.07
☐ 45	Mark Randall	1.00	.50	.10
☐ 46	Mike Maddox	.75	.35	.07
☐ 47	Alonzo Jamison	.75	.35	.07
☐ 48	Kevin Pritchard	1.00	.50	.10
☐ 49	Terry Brown	.75	.35	.07
☐ 50	Kirk Wagner	.50	.25	.05
☐ 51	Pekka Markkanen	.50	.25	.05
☐ 52	Sean Tunstall	.60	.30	.06
☐ 53	Macolm Nash	.50	.25	.05
☐ 54	Todd Alexander	.50	.25	.05
☐ 55	Adonis Jordan	.75	.35	.07
☐ 56	Roy Williams CO	.75	.35	.07
☐ xx	Title Card	.50	.25	.05
	(unnumbered)			

1977-78 Kentucky Wildcat News

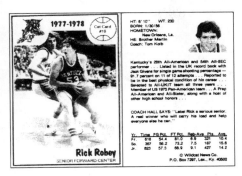

This 22-card set measures 2 1/2" by 3 3/4". The front features a black and white action photo with a royal blue border on white card stock. The player cards have the Wildcat logo, year, and the card number (in a basketball) across the top of the card face. The player's name and position appear below the picture. The back has a black and white head shot of the player in the upper right corner, with biographical and statistical information filling in the remainder of the space. This set features early cards of Kyle Macy and Rick Robey, who later played with different NBA teams.

	NRMT	VG-E	GOOD
COMPLETE SET (22)	40.00	20.00	4.00
COMMON PLAYER (1-22)	1.00	.50	.10
☐ 1 The Fabulous Five	2.50	1.25	.25
☐ 2 Joe Hall's First UK Team	1.50	.75	.15
☐ 3 1975 NCAA Runners-Up	1.00	.50	.10
☐ 4 1977-78 Wildcats	1.00	.50	.10
☐ 5 Leonard Hamilton CO	2.00	1.00	.20
☐ 6 Joe Dean CO	1.00	.50	.10
☐ 7 Joe B. Hall CO	2.00	1.00	.20
☐ 8 Dick Parsons CO	1.00	.50	.10
☐ 9 Scott Courts	1.00	.50	.10
☐ 10 Chuck Aleksinas	1.50	.75	.15
☐ 11 LaVon Williams	1.50	.75	.15
☐ 13 Dwane Casey	3.00	1.50	.30
☐ 14 Fred Cowan	1.50	.75	.15
☐ 15 Kyle Macy	6.00	3.00	.60
☐ 16 Tim Stephens	1.00	.50	.10
☐ 17 James Lee	3.00	1.50	.30
☐ 18 Jay Shidler	2.50	1.25	.25
☐ 19 Rick Robey	6.00	3.00	.60
☐ 20 Truman Claytor	2.00	1.00	.20
☐ 22 Mike Phillips	2.00	1.00	.20

1978-79 Kentucky Foodtown

This 22-card set was sponsored by Foodtown. The cards measure approximately 2 1/2" by 3 3/4". The front features a black and white action photo, with the Wildcat logo, year, and the card number (in a basketball) to the left of the picture. The player's name and position appear below the picture, and a royal blue border outlines the card face. The back has a black and white head shot of the player in the upper right corner, with biographical and statistical information filling in the remainder of the space. This set features an early card of Kyle Macy, who later played in the NBA.

	NRMT	VG-E	GOOD
COMPLETE SET (22)	20.00	10.00	2.00
COMMON PLAYER (1-22)	.75	.35	.07
☐ 1 Homeward Bound (Joe B. Hall and wife)	1.00	.50	.10

☐ 2 Celebratin' Seniors	.75	.35	.07
☐ 3 Moment of Glory (Jack Givens)	1.00	.50	.10
☐ 4 Hagan's Hall of Fame Induction	1.00	.50	.10
☐ 5 1978-79 Wildcats	.75	.35	.07
☐ 6 1978 NCAA Champions	.75	.35	.07
☐ 7 Dwight Anderson	2.00	1.00	.20
☐ 8 Clarence Tillman	.75	.35	.07
☐ 9 Chuck Verderber	1.00	.50	.10
☐ 10 Dwane Casey	2.00	1.00	.20
☐ 11 Truman Claytor	1.50	.75	.15
☐ 12 Tim Stephens	.75	.35	.07
☐ 13 Kyle Macy	2.50	1.25	.25
☐ 14 LaVon Williams	1.00	.50	.10
☐ 15 Jay Shidler	1.50	.75	.15
☐ 16 Freddie Cowan	1.00	.50	.10
☐ 17 Chuck Aleksinas	1.00	.50	.10
☐ 18 Chris Gettelfinger	.75	.35	.07
☐ 19 Joe B. Hall CO	1.00	.50	.10
☐ 20 Dick Parsons CO	.75	.35	.07
☐ 21 Leonard Hamilton CO	1.00	.50	.10
☐ 22 Joe Dean CO	.75	.35	.07

1979-80 Kentucky Foodtown

This 22-card set was sponsored by Foodtown. The cards measure 2 1/2" by 3 3/4". The front features a black and white action photo, with the player's name printed vertically to the right of the picture. The card number (in a basketball), the year, and the Wildcat logo appear at the bottom of the card face. A royal blue border outlines the card face. The back has a black and white head shot of the player in the upper right corner, with biographical information filling in the remainder of the space. This set features cards of Kyle Macy, Sam Bowie, and Dirk Minnifield, who later played with different NBA teams.

	NRMT	VG-E	GOOD
COMPLETE SET (22)	15.00	7.50	1.50
COMMON PLAYER (1-22)	.50	.25	.05
☐ 1 1979-1980 Wildcats	.75	.35	.07

		MINT	EXC	G-VG
☐ 2	Kyle Macy	1.50	.75	.15
☐ 3	Jay Shidler	1.00	.50	.10
☐ 4	LaVon Williams	.75	.35	.07
☐ 5	Chris Gettelfinger	.50	.25	.05
☐ 6	Fred Cowan	.75	.35	.07
☐ 7	Dwight Anderson	1.50	.75	.15
☐ 8	Bo Lanter	.50	.25	.05
☐ 9	Chuck Verderber	.75	.35	.07
☐ 10	Dirk Minniefield	1.50	.75	.15
☐ 11	Sam Bowie	2.00	1.00	.20
☐ 12	Charles Hurt	1.50	.75	.15
☐ 13	Derrick Hord	1.00	.50	.10
☐ 14	Tom Heitz	.50	.25	.05
☐ 15	Joe Dean CO	.50	.25	.05
☐ 16	Leonard Hamilton CO	.75	.35	.07
☐ 17	Dick Parsons CO	.50	.25	.05
☐ 18	Joe B. Hall CO	.75	.35	.07
☐ 19	Rupp Arena	.50	.25	.05
☐ 20	Kyle Macy	1.00	.50	.10
☐ 21	The Freshman Five	.75	.35	.07
☐ 22	The Seniors	.75	.35	.07

1982-83 Kentucky Schedules

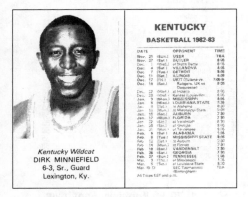

Kentucky Wildcat
DIRK MINNIEFIELD
6-3, Sr., Guard
Lexington, Ky.

This seven-card set features schedule cards each measuring approximately 2 1/4" by 3 1/4". The card fronts feature a borderless black and white player photo with a dark blue tint. Player information is given in the white stripe below the picture. In dark blue lettering the back has the 1982-83 basketball schedule.

		MINT	EXC	G-VG
	COMPLETE SET (7)	15.00	7.50	1.50
	COMMON PLAYER (1-7)	2.00	1.00	.20
☐ 1	Dicky Beal	2.00	1.00	.20
☐ 2	Bret Bearup	2.00	1.00	.20
☐ 3	Derrick Hord	3.00	1.50	.30
☐ 4	Charles Hurt	3.00	1.50	.30
☐ 5	Jim Master	3.00	1.50	.30
☐ 6	Dirk Minniefield	3.00	1.50	.30
☐ 7	Melvin Turpin	3.00	1.50	.30

1987-88 Kentucky Coke/Valvoline *

This 22-card set of standard size (2 1/2" by 3 1/2") cards was co-sponsored by Coca-Cola and Valvoline, and their company logos appear on the bottom of the card face. The card sets were given out by the Kentucky county sheriff's departments and the Kentucky Highway Patrol to kids 17 and under. Supposedly about 350 sets were given to the approximately 120 counties in the state of Kentucky. One card per week was given out from May 25 to October 19, 1987. Once all 22 were collected, they could be turned in to a local sheriff's department for prizes. The front features a color action player photo, on a blue card face with a white outer border. The player's name and the "Champions

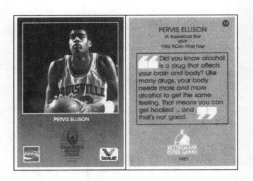

Against Drugs" insignia appear below the picture. The back has a anti-drug or alcohol tip on a gray background, with white border. The cards are numbered on the back. The set was presumably issued in junction with Kentucky's hosting of the 1987 Bluegrass State Games. The set features stars from a variety of sports as well as public figures. The two cards in the set numbered "SC" for special card were produced and distributed several years later; they were in fact produced in much larger quantities than the original 22 cards.

		MINT	EXC	G-VG
	COMPLETE SET (24)	30.00	15.00	3.00
	COMMON PLAYER (1-22)	.60	.30	.06
☐ 1	Martha Layne Collins Governor of Kentucky	.60	.30	.06
☐ 2	Kenny Walker	1.00	.50	.10
☐ 3	Dr. William Devries	.60	.30	.06
☐ 4	Dan Issel	1.00	.50	.10
☐ 5	Doug Flynn	.75	.35	.07
☐ 6	Melinda Cumberledge	.60	.30	.06
☐ 7	Melvin Turpin and Sam Bowie	1.00	.50	.10
☐ 8	Darrell Griffith	1.25	.60	.12
☐ 9	Winston Bennett	1.00	.50	.10
☐ 10	Ricky Skaggs	.60	.30	.06
☐ 11	Wildcat Mascot	.60	.30	.06
☐ 12	Cardinal Mascot	.60	.30	.06
☐ 13	Pee Wee Reese	1.25	.60	.12
☐ 14	Mary T. Meagher	.60	.30	.06
☐ 15	Jim Master	.75	.35	.07
☐ 16	Kyle Macy	1.00	.50	.10
☐ 17	Pervis Ellison	1.50	.75	.15
☐ 18	Dale Baldwin	.60	.30	.06
☐ 19	Frank Minniefield	1.00	.50	.10
☐ 20	Mark Higgs	.75	.35	.07
☐ 21	Rex Chapman	2.50	1.25	.25
☐ 22	A.B.(Happy) Chandler	.75	.35	.07
☐ SC	Billy Packer	1.50	.75	.15
☐ SC	David Robinson	12.50	6.25	1.25

1988 Kentucky Soviets

This 18-card set was issued as an insert in the U.S. AAU All-Stars vs. Soviet Junior Nationals official program for the game played at Memorial Coliseum in Lexington, KY, May 14, 1988. The set is the only one printed during the Russian Junior team's U.S. tour. The cards were issued in two panels; after perforation, the cards measure 2 5/8" by 3 5/8". The front features a mix of posed or action, black and white player photos, with a light blue background and thin black border on white card stock. A 1888-1988 AAU/USA 100th anniversary emblem is superimposed at the left corner of the photo. Player information appears below the picture in the lower left corner. An AAU/Soviet tour emblem in the lower right corner rounds out the card face. The back has a black and white head shot of the player in the upper left corner. Biographical information appears in a light blue-tinted box,

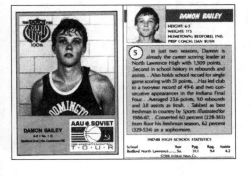

with high school statistics at the bottom. The cards are numbered on the back.

	MINT	EXC	G-VG
COMPLETE SET (18)	30.00	15.00	3.00
COMMON PLAYER (1-18)	.50	.25	.05

		MINT	EXC	G-VG
☐ 1	Checklist	.50	.25	.05
☐ 2	Scott Davenport CO	.50	.25	.05
☐ 3	Keith Adkins	.50	.25	.05
☐ 4	Mike Allen	.50	.25	.05
☐ 5	Damon Bailey	10.00	5.00	1.00
☐ 6	Scott Boley	.50	.25	.05
☐ 7	David DeMarcus	.50	.25	.05
☐ 8	Richie Farmer	2.50	1.25	.25
☐ 9	Travis Ford	1.00	.50	.10
☐ 10	Pat Graham	2.50	1.25	.25
☐ 11	Robbie Graham	.50	.25	.05
☐ 12	Allan Houston	5.00	2.50	.50
☐ 13	Shawn Kemp	5.00	2.50	.50
☐ 14	Don MacLean	5.00	2.50	.50
☐ 15	Kenneth Martin	.50	.25	.05
☐ 16	Chris Mills	1.50	.75	.15
☐ 17	Derek Miller	.50	.25	.05
☐ 18	Sean Woods	1.00	.50	.10

1988-89 Kentucky 269

The 1988-89 University of Kentucky Wildcats set contains 269 standard-sized (2 1/2" by 3 1/2") cards featuring "Kentucky's Finest" basketball players. The fronts have deep blue and white borders. The backs have various statistical and biographical information. This set was issued in eight-card cello packs.

	MINT	EXC	G-VG
COMPLETE SET (269)	30.00	15.00	3.00
COMMON PLAYER (1-269)	.10	.05	.01

		MINT	EXC	G-VG
☐ 1	Adolph Rupp CO	.50	.25	.05
☐ 2	Cliff Hagan	.50	.25	.05
☐ 3	Frank Ramsey	.35	.17	.03
☐ 4	Ralph Beard	.20	.10	.02
☐ 5	Alex Groza	.20	.10	.02
☐ 6	Wallace Jones	.10	.05	.01
☐ 7	Dan Issel	.35	.17	.03
☐ 8	Cotton Nash	.20	.10	.02
☐ 9	Kevin Grevey	.20	.10	.02
☐ 10	Kyle Macy	.25	.12	.02
☐ 11	Kenny Walker	.20	.10	.02
☐ 12	Louie Dampier	.20	.10	.02
☐ 13	Vernon Hatton	.10	.05	.01
☐ 14	Johnny Cox	.10	.05	.01
☐ 15	Jack Givens	.20	.10	.02
☐ 16	Bill Spivey	.10	.05	.01
☐ 17	Pat Riley	.35	.17	.03
☐ 18	Ellis Johnson	.10	.05	.01
☐ 19	Forest Sale	.10	.05	.01
☐ 20	Kenny Rollins	.10	.05	.01
☐ 21	Sam Bowie	.20	.10	.02
☐ 22	John DeMoisey	.10	.05	.01
☐ 23	Leroy Edwards	.10	.05	.01
☐ 24	Lee Huber	.10	.05	.01
☐ 25	Rick Robey	.20	.10	.02
☐ 26	Bob Burrow	.10	.05	.01
☐ 27	Cliff Barker	.10	.05	.01
☐ 28	Bernie Opper	.10	.05	.01
☐ 29	Ralph Carlisle	.10	.05	.01
☐ 30	Joe B. Hall	.15	.07	.01
☐ 31	Bob Brannum	.10	.05	.01
☐ 32	Jack Parkinson	.10	.05	.01
☐ 33	Jack Tingle	.10	.05	.01
☐ 34	Joe Holland	.10	.05	.01
☐ 35	Jim Line	.10	.05	.01
☐ 36	Bobby Watson	.10	.05	.01
☐ 37	Bill Evans	.10	.05	.01
☐ 38	Bill Lickert	.10	.05	.01
☐ 39	Larry Conley	.15	.07	.01
☐ 40	Eddie Sutton	.15	.07	.01
☐ 41	Larry Steele	.20	.10	.02
☐ 42	Tom Parker	.10	.05	.01
☐ 43	Shelby Linville	.10	.05	.01
☐ 44	Lou Tsioropoulos	.10	.05	.01
☐ 45	Gayle Rose	.15	.07	.01
☐ 46	Jim Andrews	.10	.05	.01
☐ 47	Ed Davender	.15	.07	.01
☐ 48	Winston Bennett	.20	.10	.02
☐ 49	Willie Rouse	.10	.05	.01
☐ 50	Mike Pratt	.15	.07	.01
☐ 51	Harry C. Lancaster	.10	.05	.01
☐ 52	Dirk Minniefield	.20	.10	.02
☐ 53	Russell Rice	.10	.05	.01
☐ 54	Carey Spicer	.10	.05	.01
☐ 55	Paul McBrayer	.10	.05	.01
☐ 56	Burgess Carey	.10	.05	.01
☐ 57	Ermal Allen	.20	.10	.02
☐ 58	Dale Barnstable	.10	.05	.01
☐ 59	Kenton Campbell	.10	.05	.01
☐ 60	Guy Strong	.10	.05	.01
☐ 61	Lucian Whitaker	.10	.05	.01
☐ 62	Bennie Coffman	.10	.05	.01
☐ 63	C.M. Newton	.20	.10	.02
☐ 64	Walt Hirsch	.10	.05	.01
☐ 65	John Brewer	.15	.07	.01
☐ 66	Phil Grawemeyer	.10	.05	.01
☐ 67	John Crigler	.10	.05	.01
☐ 68	Gerry Calvert	.10	.05	.01
☐ 69	Ed Beck	.10	.05	.01
☐ 70	Jerry Bird	.10	.05	.01
☐ 71	Harold Ross	.10	.05	.01
☐ 72	Adrian Smith	.20	.10	.02
☐ 73	Don Mills	.10	.05	.01
☐ 74	Ned Jennings	.10	.05	.01
☐ 75	Sid Cohen	.10	.05	.01
☐ 76	Dickie Parsons	.10	.05	.01
☐ 77	Larry Pursiful	.10	.05	.01
☐ 78	Herky Rupp	.15	.07	.01
☐ 79	Charles Ishmael	.10	.05	.01
☐ 80	Jim McDonald	.10	.05	.01
☐ 81	Terry Mobley	.10	.05	.01
☐ 82	Tommy Kron	.10	.05	.01
☐ 83	Randy Embry	.10	.05	.01
☐ 84	Steve Clevenger	.10	.05	.01
☐ 85	Jim LeMaster	.10	.05	.01
☐ 86	Basil Hayden	.10	.05	.01
☐ 87	Cliff Berger	.10	.05	.01
☐ 88	Jim Dinwiddie	.10	.05	.01
☐ 89	Randy Pool	.10	.05	.01
☐ 90	Terry Mills	.15	.07	.01
☐ 91	Bob McCowan	.10	.05	.01
☐ 92	Mike Casey	.10	.05	.01
☐ 93	Kent Hollenbeck	.10	.05	.01
☐ 94	Scotty Baesier	.10	.05	.01
☐ 95	Phil Argento	.10	.05	.01
☐ 96	John R. Adams	.10	.05	.01
☐ 97	Larry Stamper	.10	.05	.01
☐ 98	Ray Edelman	.10	.05	.01

#	Name			
☐ 99	Ronnie Lyons	.10	.05	.01
☐ 100	G.J. Smith	.10	.05	.01
☐ 101	Jerry Hale	.10	.05	.01
☐ 102	Bob Guyette	.10	.05	.01
☐ 103	Mike Flynn	.10	.05	.01
☐ 104	Jimmy Dan Connor	.20	.10	.02
☐ 105	Larry Johnson	.10	.05	.01
☐ 106	Joey Holland	.10	.05	.01
☐ 107	Reggie Warford	.10	.05	.01
☐ 108	Merion Haskins	.10	.05	.01
☐ 109	James Lee	.20	.10	.02
☐ 110	Dwane Casey	.25	.12	.02
☐ 111	Truman Claytor	.20	.10	.02
☐ 112	LaVon Williams	.20	.10	.02
☐ 113	Jay Shidler	.25	.12	.02
☐ 114	Fred Cowan	.15	.07	.01
☐ 115	Dwight Anderson	.25	.12	.02
☐ 116	Chuck Verderber	.15	.07	.01
☐ 117	Bo Lanter	.10	.05	.01
☐ 118	Charles Hurt	.20	.10	.02
☐ 119	Derrick Hord	.20	.10	.02
☐ 120	Tom Heitz	.10	.05	.01
☐ 121	Dicky Beal	.15	.07	.01
☐ 122	Bret Bearup	.15	.07	.01
☐ 123	Melvin Turpin	.20	.10	.02
☐ 124	Jim Master	.15	.07	.01
☐ 125	Troy McKinley	.10	.05	.01
☐ 126	Roger Harden	.15	.07	.01
☐ 127	James Blackmon	.20	.10	.02
☐ 128	Leroy Byrd	.10	.05	.01
☐ 129	Cedric Jenkins	.15	.07	.01
☐ 130	Rob Lock	.15	.07	.01
☐ 131	Richard Madison	.15	.07	.01
☐ 132	Cawood Ledford	.10	.05	.01
☐ 133	'47-'48 Team	.10	.05	.01
☐ 134	'48-'49 Team	.10	.05	.01
☐ 135	'50-'51 Team	.10	.05	.01
☐ 136	'57-'58 Team	.10	.05	.01
☐ 137	'77-'78 Team	.10	.05	.01
☐ 138	Stan Key	.10	.05	.01
☐ 139	Mike Phillips	.15	.07	.01
☐ 140	Joe B. Hall	.15	.07	.01
☐ 141	Mike Flynn	.15	.07	.01
☐ 142	Thad Jaracz	.20	.10	.02
☐ 143	Larry Conley	.20	.10	.02
☐ 144	Rex Chapman	.35	.17	.03
☐ 145	Pat Riley	.35	.17	.03
☐ 146	Melvin Turpin	.20	.10	.02
☐ 147	Kenny Walker	.20	.10	.02
☐ 148	Wallace Jones	.10	.05	.01
☐ 149	Alex Groza	.20	.10	.02
☐ 150	Mike Pratt	.15	.07	.01
☐ 151	Cliff Barker	.10	.05	.01
☐ 152	Jim Andrews	.10	.05	.01
☐ 153	Kenny Walker	.20	.10	.02
☐ 154	Kevin Grevey	.20	.10	.02
☐ 155	Kyle Macy	.25	.12	.02
☐ 156	Jim Line	.10	.05	.01
☐ 157	Pat Riley	.35	.17	.03
☐ 158	Larry Steele	.20	.10	.02
☐ 159	Jack Givens	.20	.10	.02
☐ 160	Ed Davender	.15	.07	.01
☐ 161	Ralph Beard	.15	.07	.01
☐ 162	Vernon Hatton	.10	.05	.01
☐ 163	Frank Ramsey	.25	.12	.02
☐ 164	Bob Burrow	.10	.05	.01
☐ 165	Sam Bowie	.25	.12	.02
☐ 166	Dan Issel	.35	.17	.03
☐ 167	Rick Robey	.25	.12	.02
☐ 168	Winston Bennett	.20	.10	.02
☐ 169	Louie Dampier	.20	.10	.02
☐ 170	Gayle Rose	.20	.10	.02
☐ 171	Cliff Hagan	.35	.17	.03
☐ 172	Cotton Nash	.20	.10	.02
☐ 173	Mike Pratt	.15	.07	.01
☐ 174	Richard Madison	.15	.07	.01
☐ 175	Kyle Macy	.20	.10	.02
☐ 176	Rob Lock	.15	.07	.01
☐ 177	Larry Johnson	.10	.05	.01
☐ 178	Cedric Jenkins	.15	.07	.01
☐ 179	Dan Issel	.35	.17	.03
☐ 180	Charles Hurt	.20	.10	.02
☐ 181	Cliff Hagan	.35	.17	.03
☐ 182	Wallace Jones	.10	.05	.01
☐ 183	Roger Harden	.15	.07	.01
☐ 184	Bob Guyette	.10	.05	.01
☐ 185	Kevin Grevey	.20	.10	.02
☐ 186	Jack Givens	.20	.10	.02
☐ 187	Ed Davender	.15	.07	.01
☐ 188	Jimmy Dan Connor	.15	.07	.01
☐ 189	Fred Cowan	.15	.07	.01
☐ 190	Larry Conley	.20	.10	.02
☐ 191	Leroy Byrd	.10	.05	.01
☐ 192	Sam Bowie	.25	.12	.02
☐ 193	James Blackmon	.20	.10	.02
☐ 194	Winston Bennett	.20	.10	.02
☐ 195	Dicky Beal	.15	.07	.01
☐ 196	Jim Andrews	.10	.05	.01
☐ 197	Kenny Walker	.20	.10	.02
☐ 198	Pat Riley	.35	.17	.03
☐ 199	Frank Ramsey	.20	.10	.02
☐ 200	Truman Claytor	.15	.07	.01
☐ 201	Dwane Casey	.20	.10	.02
☐ 202	Rex Chapman	.35	.17	.03
☐ 203	Jim Master	.15	.07	.01
☐ 204	Mike Phillips	.15	.07	.01
☐ 205	Dirk Minniefield	.20	.10	.02
☐ 206	Jimmy Dan Connor	.15	.07	.01
☐ 207	Bill Lickert	.10	.05	.01
☐ 208	Leroy Byrd	.10	.05	.01
☐ 209	Mike Pratt	.15	.07	.01
☐ 210	Rob Lock	.15	.07	.01
☐ 211	Dickie Parsons	.10	.05	.01
☐ 212	Frank Ramsey	.20	.10	.02
☐ 213	Adolph Rupp CO	.30	.15	.03
☐ 214	G.J. Smith	.10	.05	.01
☐ 215	Rick Robey	.20	.10	.02
☐ 216	James Blackmon	.20	.10	.02
☐ 217	Mike Casey	.15	.07	.01
☐ 218	LaVon Williams	.15	.07	.01
☐ 219	Larry Pursiful	.10	.05	.01
☐ 220	Terry Mobley	.10	.05	.01
☐ 221	Kyle Macy	.25	.12	.02
☐ 222	Larry Conley	.20	.10	.02
☐ 223	Dirk Minniefield	.20	.10	.02
☐ 224	Jim Master	.15	.07	.01
☐ 225	Jerry Bird	.10	.05	.01
☐ 226	Dan Issel	.35	.17	.03
☐ 227	Larry Johnson	.10	.05	.01
☐ 228	Bret Bearup	.15	.07	.01
☐ 229	Ronnie Lyons	.10	.05	.01
☐ 230	James Lee	.20	.10	.02
☐ 231	Don Mills	.10	.05	.01
☐ 232	Truman Claytor	.15	.07	.01
☐ 233	Rex Chapman	.35	.17	.03
☐ 234	Fred Cowan	.15	.07	.01
☐ 235	Truman Claytor	.15	.07	.01
☐ 236	Dicky Beal	.15	.07	.01
☐ 237	Larry Johnson	.10	.05	.01
☐ 238	John R. Adams	.10	.05	.01
☐ 239	Sam Bowie	.20	.10	.02
☐ 240	Thad Jaracz	.15	.07	.01
☐ 241	Phil Argento	.10	.05	.01
☐ 242	Cedric Jenkins	.15	.07	.01
☐ 243	Charles Hurt	.20	.10	.02
☐ 244	Charles Hurt	.20	.10	.02
☐ 245	Cliff Hagan	.30	.15	.03
☐ 246	Kent Hollenbeck	.10	.05	.01
☐ 247	Wallace Jones	.10	.05	.01
☐ 248	Roger Harden	.15	.07	.01
☐ 249	Bob Guyette	.10	.05	.01
☐ 250	Richard Madison	.15	.07	.01
☐ 251	Kevin Grevey	.20	.10	.02
☐ 252	Jack Givens	.20	.10	.02
☐ 253	Tommy Kron	.20	.10	.02
☐ 254	Derrick Hord	.20	.10	.02
☐ 255	Tom Heitz	.15	.07	.01
☐ 256	Cliff Hagan	.30	.15	.03
☐ 257	Louie Dampier	.20	.10	.02
☐ 258	Jimmy Dan Connor	.15	.07	.01
☐ 259	Dwane Casey	.20	.10	.02
☐ 260	Cliff Hagan	.30	.15	.03
☐ 261	Walt Hirsch	.10	.05	.01
☐ 262	Merion Haskins	.10	.05	.01
☐ 263	Roger Harden	.15	.07	.01
☐ 264	Bob Guyette	.10	.05	.01
☐ 265	Phil Grawemeyer	.10	.05	.01
☐ 266	Jay Shidler	.15	.07	.01
☐ 267	Jim Dinwiddie	.10	.05	.01
☐ 268	Fred Cowan	.15	.07	.01
☐ 269	Leroy Byrd	.15	.07	.01

1988-89 Kentucky Awards

This 18-card set was issued as an insert in a basketball program. The cards honor Kentucky players for various outstanding achievements. The cards were issued in two panels; after perforation, the cards measure 2 5/8" by 3 5/8". In a horizontal format, the front features a color action player photo, with blue and black borders on white card stock. The

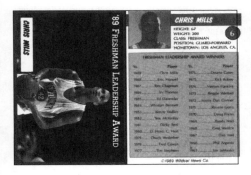

name of the award appears in white lettering in the upper left corner of the photo, with the player's name in a white box in the lower left corner. The back has a black and white head shot of the player in the upper left corner. Biographical information appears in a light blue-tinted box. The cards are numbered on the back, and we have listed the award below after the player's name.

written vertically in an orange bar to the left of the picture, while the player's name appears in a gray bar above the picture. The back has a black and white head shot of the player in the upper left corner. Biographical information appears in a blue-tinted box. The cards are numbered on the back, beginning with 19 in continuation of the numbering of the previous year's issue. The award is listed below after the player's name.

	MINT	EXC	G-VG
COMPLETE SET (18)	20.00	10.00	2.00
COMMON PLAYER (1-18)	.50	.25	.05
☐ 1 Sean Sutton Leadership	1.00	.50	.10
☐ 2 Chris Mills Most Valuable Player	2.00	1.00	.20
☐ 3 Mike Scott Outstanding Senior	.50	.25	.05
☐ 4 Richie Farmer Best Free Throw Percentage	1.50	.75	.15
☐ 5 Derrick Miller Fewest Turnovers	.75	.35	.07
☐ 6 Chris Mills Freshman Leadership	2.00	1.00	.20
☐ 7 Mike Scott Scholastic	.50	.25	.05
☐ 8 Sean Sutton Most Assists	.75	.35	.07
☐ 9 Chris Mills Most Rebounds	2.00	1.00	.20
☐ 10 LeRon Ellis Leading Scorer	2.00	1.00	.20
☐ 11 Reggie Hanson Best Defender	1.50	.75	.15
☐ 12 Deron Feldhaus 110 Percent Award	.75	.35	.07
☐ 13 Sean Sutton and Leron Ellis Sacrifice Award	1.00	.50	.10
☐ 14 LeRon Ellis Best Field Goal Percentage	2.00	1.00	.20
☐ 15 Sean Sutton Best 3-pt. Field Goal Percentage	1.00	.50	.10
☐ 16 Reggie Hanson Most Steals	1.50	.75	.15
☐ 17 Eddie Sutton CO	.75	.35	.07
☐ 18 Checklist Card (Misspelled sacrifice as saracfice)	.50	.25	.05

	MINT	EXC	G-VG
COMPLETE SET (18)	15.00	7.50	1.50
COMMON PLAYER (19-36)	.50	.25	.05
☐ 19 Checklist Card	.50	.25	.05
☐ 20 Richie Farmer Best FT Shooter	1.50	.75	.15
☐ 21 Reggie Hanson Most Rebounds	1.50	.75	.15
☐ 22 Deron Feldhaus Fewest Turnovers	.75	.35	.07
☐ 23 UK Assistants Best Defense	.50	.25	.05
☐ 24 Deron Feldhaus Mr. Hustle Award	.75	.35	.07
☐ 25 Reggie Hanson Leadership	1.50	.75	.15
☐ 26 John Pelphrey Student Athlete	.75	.35	.07
☐ 27 Derrick Miller Outstanding Senior	.50	.25	.05
☐ 28 Deron Feldhaus Most Improved	.75	.35	.07
☐ 29 Happy Chandler Fan of the Year	1.00	.50	.10
☐ 30 John Pelphrey Best Playmaker	.50	.25	.05
☐ 31 Hanson/Pelphrey Mr. Deflection	.75	.35	.07
☐ 32 Reggie Hanson Most Valuable	1.50	.75	.15
☐ 33 Deron Feldhaus Best FG Shooter	.75	.35	.07
☐ 34 Sean Woods Most Assists	.75	.35	.07
☐ 35 Derrick Miller Leading Scorer	1.00	.50	.10
☐ 36 Rick Pitino Coach of the Year	2.00	1.00	.20

1989-90 Kentucky Awards

This 18-card set was issued as an insert in a basketball program. The cards honor Kentucky players for various outstanding achievements. The cards were issued in two panels; after perforation, the cards measure approximately 2 5/8" by 3 5/8". The front features a color action player photo, with dark blue and black borders on white card stock. The name of the award is

1989-90 Kentucky Team of the 80's

This 18-card set was issued as an insert in a basketball program. The cards honor outstanding Kentucky players for the decade of the 1980's. The cards were issued in two panels; after perforation, the cards measure 2 5/8" by 3 5/8". The front features a color action player photo, on a light blue background that washes out as one moves from top to bottom. A thin black border outlines this blue background. The player's name appears in black lettering above the picture. The left lower corner of the photo is cut out, and in the triangular-shaped area appears a basketball icon and the pro team(s) played for. The back is blue

tinted, and it has a black and white head shot of the player on the left side, with biographical information around the picture and career college statistics on the bottom. The cards are numbered on the back, beginning with 37 in continuation of the numbering of the previous year's issue.

		MINT	EXC	G-VG
COMPLETE SET (18)		18.00	9.00	1.80
COMMON PLAYER (37-54)		.50	.25	.05
☐ 37	Checklist Card	.50	.25	.05
☐ 38	Kyle Macy	1.50	.75	.15
☐ 39	Rex Chapman	2.50	1.25	.25
☐ 40	Kenny Walker	1.50	.75	.15
☐ 41	Winston Bennett	1.25	.60	.12
☐ 42	Melvin Turpin	1.25	.60	.12
☐ 43	Sam Bowie	2.00	1.00	.20
☐ 44	Dicky Beal	.75	.35	.07
☐ 45	Dirk Minniefield	1.00	.50	.10
☐ 46	Jim Master	.75	.35	.07
☐ 47	Rob Lock	.50	.25	.05
☐ 48	Chris Mills	1.50	.75	.15
☐ 49	Roger Harden	.50	.25	.05
☐ 50	Jay Shidler	.75	.35	.07
☐ 51	LeRon Ellis	1.00	.50	.10
☐ 52	Fred Cowan	.75	.35	.07
☐ 53	Derrick Hord	1.00	.50	.10
☐ 54	Coaches	1.00	.50	.10
	Joe Hall			
	Eddie Sutton			
	Rick Pitino			

1989-90 Kentucky 300 *

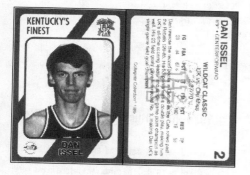

The 1989 University of Kentucky Basketball/Football set contains 300 cards, each measuring standard size (2 1/2" by 3 1/2"). The fronts feature a mix of black and white photos for earlier players and color for later ones, with rounded corners and blue borders. The pictures are superimposed over a blue and white diagonally striped card face, with a blue border. The top reads "Kentucky's

Finest," and the school logo appears in the upper right corner. The horizontally oriented backs are printed in blue on white and present biographical information, career summaries, or statistics. The cards are numbered on the back.

		MINT	EXC	G-VG
COMPLETE SET (300)		27.00	13.50	2.70
COMMON PLAYER (1-300)		.07	.03	.01
☐ 1	C.M. Newton	.10	.05	.01
☐ 2	Dan Issel	.30	.15	.03
☐ 3	Alex Groza	.15	.07	.01
☐ 4	Jack Givens	.15	.07	.01
☐ 5	Kenny Walker	.15	.07	.01
☐ 6	Cliff Hagan	.25	.12	.02
☐ 7	Ralph Beard	.15	.07	.01
☐ 8	Dirk Minniefield	.15	.07	.01
☐ 9	Louie Dampier	.15	.07	.01
☐ 10	Dicky Beal	.10	.05	.01
☐ 11	Larry Pursiful	.07	.03	.01
☐ 12	Rex Chapman	.25	.12	.02
☐ 13	Rick Pitino CO	.20	.10	.02
☐ 14	Marvin Akers	.07	.03	.01
☐ 15	Allen Feldhaus	.10	.05	.01
☐ 16	Carroll Burchett	.07	.03	.01
☐ 17	Sam Potter	.07	.03	.01
☐ 18	Ted Deeken	.07	.03	.01
☐ 19	Dwight Anderson	.15	.07	.01
☐ 20	Charles Schrader	.07	.03	.01
☐ 21	Bill Trott	.07	.03	.01
☐ 22	Henry Besuden	.07	.03	.01
☐ 23	Edwin Knadler	.07	.03	.01
☐ 24	Vince Del Negro	.10	.05	.01
☐ 25	James Durham	.07	.03	.01
☐ 26	Mickey Gibson	.07	.03	.01
☐ 27	John Mauer	.07	.03	.01
☐ 28	John McIntosh	.07	.03	.01
☐ 29	Van Buren Ropke	.07	.03	.01
☐ 30	B.G. Marsh	.07	.03	.01
☐ 31	Tom Zerfoss	.07	.03	.01
☐ 32	George Zerfoss	.07	.03	.01
☐ 33	Harry Denham	.07	.03	.01
☐ 34	Mike Scott	.07	.03	.01
☐ 35	Adolph Rupp CO	.25	.12	.02
☐ 36	Jack Parkinson	.07	.03	.01
☐ 37	1953-54 Team	.07	.03	.01
☐ 38	Pat Riley	.25	.12	.02
☐ 39	Joe B. Hall	.10	.05	.01
☐ 40	Memorial Coliseum	.07	.03	.01
☐ 41	Sam Bowie	.15	.07	.01
☐ 42	Bob Burrow	.07	.03	.01
☐ 43	Melvin Turpin	.15	.07	.01
☐ 44	Frank Ramsey	.20	.10	.02
☐ 45	Pat Riley	.25	.12	.02
☐ 46	Mascot	.07	.03	.01
☐ 47	Charles Hurt	.15	.07	.01
☐ 48	Cliff Barker	.07	.03	.01
☐ 49	Kevin Grevey	.15	.07	.01
☐ 50	Bill Spivey	.07	.03	.01
☐ 51	George C. Buchheit	.07	.03	.01
☐ 52	Ray Mills	.07	.03	.01
☐ 53	Irving Thomas	.10	.05	.01
☐ 54	Chuck Aleksinas	.10	.05	.01
☐ 55	Paul Andrews	.07	.03	.01
☐ 56	Brad Bounds	.07	.03	.01
☐ 57	Clyde Parker	.10	.05	.01
☐ 58	Bill Busey	.07	.03	.01
☐ 59	Billy Ray Cassady	.07	.03	.01
☐ 60	George Critz	.07	.03	.01
☐ 61	Paul Noel	.07	.03	.01
☐ 62	Pat Doyle	.07	.03	.01
☐ 63	Rick Drewitz	.07	.03	.01
☐ 64	Fred Curtis	.07	.03	.01
☐ 65	Darrell Darby	.07	.03	.01
☐ 66	Humzey Yessin	.07	.03	.01
☐ 67	Chris Gettelfinger	.07	.03	.01
☐ 68	Sam Harper	.07	.03	.01
☐ 69	Bill Davis	.07	.03	.01
☐ 70	Lincoln Collinsworth	.07	.03	.01
☐ 71	Keith Farnsley	.07	.03	.01
☐ 72	Foster Helm	.07	.03	.01
☐ 73	Dick Howe	.07	.03	.01
☐ 74	Phil Johnson	.07	.03	.01
☐ 75	Roger Layne	.07	.03	.01
☐ 76	Art Laib	.07	.03	.01
☐ 77	Dave Lawrence	.07	.03	.01
☐ 78	Larry Lentz	.07	.03	.01
☐ 79	Steve Lochmueller	.07	.03	.01
☐ 80	Louis McGinnis	.07	.03	.01
☐ 81	Doug Pendygraft	.07	.03	.01
☐ 82	Tommy Porter	.07	.03	.01
☐ 83	Linville Puckett	.15	.07	.01
☐ 84	Don Rolfes	.07	.03	.01

☐	85	Mark Soderberg	.07	.03	.01	☐	179	Darrell Cox	.07	.03	.01

☐ #	Name				☐ #	Name			
☐ 85 Mark Soderberg	.07	.03	.01		☐ 179 Darrell Cox	.07	.03	.01
☐ 86 Tim Stephens	.07	.03	.01		☐ 180 Jerry Eisaman	.07	.03	.01
☐ 87 Gene Stewart	.07	.03	.01		☐ 181 Ben Zaranka	.07	.03	.01
☐ 88 George Yates	.07	.03	.01		☐ 182 Wash Serini	.07	.03	.01
☐ 89 Randy Noll	.07	.03	.01		☐ 183 Dallas Owens	.07	.03	.01
☐ 90 Earl Adkins	.07	.03	.01		☐ 184 Bernie Scruggs	.07	.03	.01
☐ 91 Truitt Demoisey	.07	.03	.01		☐ 185 Wallace Jones	.07	.03	.01
☐ 92 Todd Ziegler	.07	.03	.01		☐ 186 Walt Yowarsky	.10	.05	.01
☐ 93 Clint Wheeler	.07	.03	.01		☐ 187 Clarkie Mayfield	.07	.03	.01
☐ 94 Patrick Campbell	.07	.03	.01		☐ 188 John Grimsley	.15	.07	.01
☐ 95 Charles Alberts	.07	.03	.01		☐ 189 Jerry Woolum	.07	.03	.01
☐ 96 Brinkley Barnett	.07	.03	.01		☐ 190 John Tatterson	.07	.03	.01
☐ 97 Cecil Bell	.07	.03	.01		☐ 191 Delmar Hughes	.07	.03	.01
☐ 98 Mel Brewer	.07	.03	.01		☐ 192 Lowell Hughes	.07	.03	.01
☐ 99 Jake Bronston	.07	.03	.01		☐ 193 Frank Lemaster	.07	.03	.01
☐ 100 Albert Cummins	.15	.07	.01		☐ 194 Bill Ransdell	.07	.03	.01
☐ 101 Jerry D. Claiborne	.15	.07	.01		☐ 195 Tony Mayes	.07	.03	.01
☐ 102 Bill Leskovar	.07	.03	.01		☐ 196 Dominic Fucci	.07	.03	.01
☐ 103 Sam Ball	.07	.03	.01		☐ 197 David Roller	.07	.03	.01
☐ 104 Sonny Collins	.25	.12	.02		☐ 198 Bernie A. Shively	.07	.03	.01
☐ 105 Bob Hardy	.07	.03	.01		☐ 199 William Tuttle	.10	.05	.01
☐ 106 Mike Siganos	.07	.03	.01		☐ 200 Jerry Claiborne	.15	.07	.01
☐ 107 Al Bruno	.07	.03	.01		☐ 201 Warfield Donohue	.07	.03	.01
☐ 108 Rick Norton	.07	.03	.01		☐ 202 Russell Ellington	.07	.03	.01
☐ 109 Ray Correll	.07	.03	.01		☐ 203 Kenny England	.07	.03	.01
☐ 110 Irvin Goode	.07	.03	.01		☐ 204 J.C. Everett	.07	.03	.01
☐ 111 Bob Gain	.15	.07	.01		☐ 205 Jake Gaiser	.07	.03	.01
☐ 112 Paul Bryant	.30	.15	.03		☐ 206 Elmer Gilb	.07	.03	.01
☐ 113 Rick Kestner	.07	.03	.01		☐ 207 Jim Goforth	.07	.03	.01
☐ 114 Larry Seiple	.10	.05	.01		☐ 208 James Goodman	.07	.03	.01
☐ 115 George Blanda	.35	.17	.03		☐ 209 George Gumbert	.07	.03	.01
☐ 116 Calvin Bird	.07	.03	.01		☐ 210 Joseph Hagan	.07	.03	.01
☐ 117 Don Phelps	.07	.03	.01		☐ 211 W.C. Harrison	.07	.03	.01
☐ 118 Herschel Turner	.07	.03	.01		☐ 212 D.W. Hart	.07	.03	.01
☐ 119 Harry Jones	.07	.03	.01		☐ 213 Elmo Head	.07	.03	.01
☐ 120 Larry Jones	.07	.03	.01		☐ 214 Walter Hodge	.07	.03	.01
☐ 121 Doug Moseley	.07	.03	.01		☐ 215 Charles T. Hughes	.07	.03	.01
☐ 122 Rodger Bird	.07	.03	.01		☐ 216 Lowell Hughes	.07	.03	.01
☐ 123 Howard Schnellenberger	.25	.12	.02		☐ 217 R.Y. Ireland	.07	.03	.01
☐ 124 Vito Parilli	.20	.10	.02		☐ 218 Irvine Jeffries	.07	.03	.01
☐ 125 Jim Kovach	.15	.07	.01		☐ 219 Jim King	.07	.03	.01
☐ 126 Randy Jenkins	.07	.03	.01		☐ 220 Bill Kleiser	.07	.03	.01
☐ 127 Emery Clark	.07	.03	.01		☐ 221 Gary Gamble	.07	.03	.01
☐ 128 David Hardt	.07	.03	.01		☐ 222 Lawrence McGinnis	.07	.03	.01
☐ 129 Andy Molls	.07	.03	.01		☐ 223 Ralph Morgan	.07	.03	.01
☐ 130 Tom Dornbrook	.07	.03	.01		☐ 224 Hays Owens	.07	.03	.01
☐ 131 George Adams	.15	.07	.01		☐ 225 James Park	.07	.03	.01
☐ 132 Lou Michaels	.10	.05	.01		☐ 226 Buddy Parker	.07	.03	.01
☐ 133 Paul Calhoun	.07	.03	.01		☐ 227 Sam Ridgeway	.07	.03	.01
☐ 134 Joey Worley	.07	.03	.01		☐ 228 R.C. Preston	.07	.03	.01
☐ 135 Doug Kotar	.10	.05	.01		☐ 229 Roy Roberts	.07	.03	.01
☐ 136 Dicky Lyons	.10	.05	.01		☐ 230 Wilber Schu	.07	.03	.01
☐ 137 Art Still	.15	.07	.01		☐ 231 Evan Settle	.07	.03	.01
☐ 138 Warren Bryant	.10	.05	.01		☐ 232 Bobby Slusher	.07	.03	.01
☐ 139 Joe Federspiel	.10	.05	.01		☐ 233 Bill Smith	.07	.03	.01
☐ 140 Mark Higgs	.15	.07	.01		☐ 234 Vince Splane	.07	.03	.01
☐ 141 Steve Meilinger	.10	.05	.01		☐ 235 Carl Staker	.07	.03	.01
☐ 142 Wilbur Hackett	.07	.03	.01		☐ 236 John Stough	.07	.03	.01
☐ 143 Marc Logan	.10	.05	.01		☐ 237 Milt Ticco	.07	.03	.01
☐ 144 Rick Nuzum	.07	.03	.01		☐ 238 Homer Thompson	.07	.03	.01
☐ 145 Wilbur Jamerson	.07	.03	.01		☐ 239 Clarence Tillman	.07	.03	.01
☐ 146 Felix Wilson	.07	.03	.01		☐ 240 Garland Townes	.07	.03	.01
☐ 147 Rod Stewart	.07	.03	.01		☐ 241 Charles Worthington	.07	.03	.01
☐ 148 Tom Hutchinson	.07	.03	.01		☐ 242 Rudy Yessin	.07	.03	.01
☐ 149 Greg Long	.07	.03	.01		☐ 243 Kark Zerfoss	.07	.03	.01
☐ 150 Mike Fanuzzi	.07	.03	.01		☐ 244 Bob Lavin	.07	.03	.01
☐ 151 Richard S. Webb Jr.	.07	.03	.01		☐ 245 J.A. Dishman	.07	.03	.01
☐ 152 John S. Kelly	.07	.03	.01		☐ 246 Jim Server	.07	.03	.01
☐ 153 Eger V. Murphree	.07	.03	.01		☐ 247 Fred Fest	.07	.03	.01
☐ 154 Ermal Allen	.10	.05	.01		☐ 248 Ralph Boren	.07	.03	.01
☐ 155 John G. Heber	.07	.03	.01		☐ 249 James McFarland	.07	.03	.01
☐ 156 Howard Kinne	.07	.03	.01		☐ 250 A.T. Rice	.07	.03	.01
☐ 157 Albert D. Kirwan	.07	.03	.01		☐ 251 Walter White	.07	.03	.01
☐ 158 Price McLean	.07	.03	.01		☐ 252 Tom Moseley	.07	.03	.01
☐ 159 Curtis M. Sanders	.07	.03	.01		☐ 253 Paul Jenkins	.07	.03	.01
☐ 160 Bob Davis	.07	.03	.01		☐ 254 Lovell Underwood	.07	.03	.01
☐ 161 Bert Johnson	.07	.03	.01		☐ 255 William Tuttle	.10	.05	.01
☐ 162 Ralph Kercheval	.10	.05	.01		☐ 256 Bob Tallent	.07	.03	.01
☐ 163 Charles Hughes	.07	.03	.01		☐ 257 Jack Tucker	.07	.03	.01
☐ 164 Clyde Johnson	.07	.03	.01		☐ 258 Roger Newman	.07	.03	.01
☐ 165 Blanton Collier	.10	.05	.01		☐ 259 Stanley Milward	.07	.03	.01
☐ 166 Charlie Bradshaw	.10	.05	.01		☐ 260 Bill Sturgill	.07	.03	.01
☐ 167 John Ray	.07	.03	.01		☐ 261 Gayle Mohney	.07	.03	.01
☐ 168 Fran Curci	.10	.05	.01		☐ 262 Will Milward	.07	.03	.01
☐ 169 James Park	.07	.03	.01		☐ 263 Ercel Little	.07	.03	.01
☐ 170 Ivy Joe Hunter	.10	.05	.01		☐ 264 Garland Lewis	.07	.03	.01
☐ 171 Chris Chenault	.07	.03	.01		☐ 265 Ron Kennett	.07	.03	.01
☐ 172 Jeff Van Note	.15	.07	.01		☐ 266 Howard Kreuter	.07	.03	.01
☐ 173 Dick Barbee	.07	.03	.01		☐ 267 William King	.07	.03	.01
☐ 174 Darryl Bishop	.07	.03	.01		☐ 268 Walter Johnson	.10	.05	.01
☐ 175 Jay Rhodemyre	.10	.05	.01		☐ 269 Jim Jordan	.07	.03	.01
☐ 176 William Rodes	.07	.03	.01		☐ 270 Mulford Davis	.07	.03	.01
☐ 177 Noah Mullins	.07	.03	.01		☐ 271 Berkley Davis	.07	.03	.01
☐ 178 Gene Myers	.07	.03	.01		☐ 272 Cecil Combs	.07	.03	.01

		MINT	EXC	G-VG
☐ 273	Carl Combs	.07	.03	.01
☐ 274	Milerd Anderson	.07	.03	.01
☐ 275	George Vulich	.07	.03	.01
☐ 276	Paul Adkins	.07	.03	.01
☐ 277	Hugh Coy	.07	.03	.01
☐ 278	J. Rice Walker	.07	.03	.01
☐ 279	Adrian Back	.07	.03	.01
☐ 280	Charley Combs	.07	.03	.01
☐ 281	Harry Hurd	.07	.03	.01
☐ 282	Tom Harper	.07	.03	.01
☐ 283	Dan Hall	.07	.03	.01
☐ 284	Ed Lander	.07	.03	.01
☐ 285	Bill Barlow	.07	.03	.01
☐ 286	James Sharp	.07	.03	.01
☐ 287	Al Robinson	.07	.03	.01
☐ 288	Frank Phipps	.07	.03	.01
☐ 289	Bob Fowler	.07	.03	.01
☐ 290	George Skinner	.07	.03	.01
☐ 291	Harry Bliss	.07	.03	.01
☐ 292	Bill Bibb	.07	.03	.01
☐ 293	Herschel Scott	.07	.03	.01
☐ 294	Clair Dees	.07	.03	.01
☐ 295	Lawrence Burnham	.07	.03	.01
☐ 296	Lloyd Ramsey	.07	.03	.01
☐ 297	Bruce Davis	.07	.03	.01
☐ 298	Bob Taylor	.07	.03	.01
☐ 299	Alonzo Nelson	.07	.03	.01
☐ 300	Herbert Jerome	.07	.03	.01

1990 Kentucky Class A

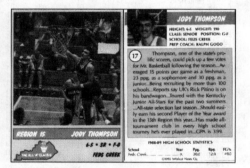

This 18-card set was issued as an insert in the Kentucky All "A" Classic official program for the state tournament played at Memorial Coliseum in Lexington, KY, February 7-10, 1990. The set consists of a checklist card, a special card honoring current Lexington mayor Scotty Baesler as a "Class A Great" player of the past, and 16 cards honoring the coaches' preseason choices for best players in each of the sixteen regions. The cards were issued in two panels; after perforation, the cards measure 2 5/8" by 3 5/8". The front features a mix of posed or action, black and white player photos, with a peach color background and thin blue border on white card stock. Below the picture, the region number and player's name appears in a gray stripe, with player information further below in the right corner. A Kentucky shaped emblem in the lower left corner rounds out the card face. The back has a black and white head shot of the player in the upper left corner. Biographical information appears in a peach-tinted box, with high school statistics on the bottom. The cards are numbered on the back.

	MINT	EXC	G-VG
COMPLETE SET (18)	10.00	5.00	1.00
COMMON PLAYER (1-18)	.50	.25	.05
☐ 1 Checklist Card	.50	.25	.05
☐ 2 Scott Baesler	1.00	.50	.10
☐ 3 Eugene Alexander	.50	.25	.05
☐ 4 Sergio Luyk	.50	.25	.05
☐ 5 Chris Knight	.50	.25	.05
☐ 6 Chris Huffman	1.00	.50	.10
☐ 7 Shannon Phillips	.50	.25	.05

		MINT	EXC	G-VG
☐ 8	Glen Wathen	.50	.25	.05
☐ 9	Jason Hagan	.50	.25	.05
☐ 10	Bryan Milburn	.50	.25	.05
☐ 11	Andre McClendon	.50	.25	.05
☐ 12	Chris Harrison	.50	.25	.05
☐ 13	Daniel Swintosky	.50	.25	.05
☐ 14	Jamie Cromer	.50	.25	.05
☐ 15	Mo Hollingsworth	.50	.25	.05
☐ 16	Jeff Moore	.50	.25	.05
☐ 17	Jody Thompson	.50	.25	.05
☐ 18	Mike Helton	.50	.25	.05

1990 Kentucky Soviets

This 18-card set was issued in two panels inside the AAU/Soviet Tour program for the game played in Memorial Coliseum at Lexington, Kentucky, on May 15, 1990. After perforation, the cards measure approximately 2 5/8" by 3 5/8" and showcase the Kentucky AAU All-Stars. The fronts feature a mix of action or posed, black and white player photos, with red borders on a white and blue diagonally-striped background. The words "Ky. AAU All-Stars" appear in blue lettering in white stripe above the picture; the player's name is presented in the same format below the picture. The backs have black and white head shots of the player in the upper left corners. In a lavender colored box, they present career summaries, with high school statistics appearing at the bottom of the card. The cards are numbered on the back in the upper right corners.

	MINT	EXC	G-VG
COMPLETE SET (18)	12.00	6.00	1.20
COMMON PLAYER (1-18)	.50	.25	.05
☐ 1 Checklist Card	.50	.25	.05
☐ 2 Kentucky/USSR rosters	.50	.25	.05
☐ 3 Jim Lankster	.50	.25	.05
☐ 4 Paul Bingham	.50	.25	.05
☐ 5 James Crutcher	.50	.25	.05
☐ 6 Jason Eitutis	.50	.25	.05
☐ 7 Greg Glass	.50	.25	.05
☐ 8 Arlando Johnson	.50	.25	.05
☐ 9 Gimel Martinez	.50	.25	.05
☐ 10 Jamal Mashburn	3.00	1.50	.30
☐ 11 Jeff Moore	.50	.25	.05
☐ 12 Dwayne Morton	1.50	.75	.15
☐ 13 Keith Peel	.50	.25	.05
☐ 14 Andy Penick	.50	.25	.05
☐ 15 Daniel Swintosky	.50	.25	.05
☐ 16 Jody Thompson	.50	.25	.05
☐ 17 Carlos Toomer	.50	.25	.05
☐ 18 Kelly Wells	.50	.25	.05

1983-84 Louisville 5x7

This 20-card set consists of oversized cards measuring approximately 7" by 5". On the left portion the front features a borderless color action photo, measuring 4" by 5". On the

remaining portion, a head shot of the player, player information (in white lettering), and a Cardinal logo appear on a red background. The back of the cards presents biographical information, career summary, and statistics in a two-column format, along with the player's autograph.

	MINT	EXC	G-VG
COMPLETE SET (20)	55.00	27.50	5.50
COMMON PLAYER	2.00	1.00	.20

		MINT	EXC	G-VG
☐ 00	Robbie Valentine	2.00	1.00	.20
☐ 4	Lancaster Gordon	5.00	2.50	.50
☐ 12	Kent Jones	2.00	1.00	.20
☐ 20	Milt Wagner	5.00	2.50	.50
☐ 23	Chris West	2.00	1.00	.20
☐ 24	Will Olliges	2.00	1.00	.20
☐ 25	James Jeter	2.00	1.00	.20
☐ 30	Manuel Forrest	3.00	1.50	.30
☐ 32	Mark McSwain	3.00	1.50	.30
☐ 33	Charles Jones	3.00	1.50	.30
☐ 35	Darrell Griffith	7.50	3.75	.75
☐ 40	Barry Sumpter	3.00	1.50	.30
☐ 42	Jeff Hall	3.00	1.50	.30
☐ 45	Danny Mitchell	2.00	1.00	.20
☐ 55	Billy Thompson	6.00	3.00	.60
☐ xx	Denny Crum (Head Coach)	5.00	2.50	.50
☐ xx	Assistant Coaches Bobby Dotson Wade Houston Jerry Jones	3.00	1.50	.30
☐ xx	Cheerleaders	3.00	1.50	.30
☐ xx	Pep Band	2.00	1.00	.20
☐ xx	Freedom Hall Home of the Cardinals	2.00	1.00	.20

1988-89 Louisville 194

The 1988-89 University of Louisville Cardinals basketball set contains 194 standard-sized (2 1/2" by 3 1/2") cards featuring "Louisville's Finest" basketball players. The fronts have red and white borders. The backs have various statistical and biographical information. This set was issued in eight-card cello packs.

	MINT	EXC	G-VG
COMPLETE SET (194)	25.00	12.50	2.50
COMMON PLAYER (1-194)	.10	.05	.01

☐ 1	Denny Crum CO	.20	.10	.02
☐ 2	Wesley Unseld	.50	.25	.05
☐ 3	Darrell Griffith	.30	.15	.03
☐ 4	John Dromo	.20	.10	.02
☐ 5	Bernard (Peck) Hickman	.20	.10	.02
☐ 6	Butch Beard	.20	.10	.02
☐ 7	Herbert Crook	.20	.10	.02
☐ 8	Milt Wagner	.20	.10	.02
☐ 9	Lancaster Gordon	.20	.10	.02
☐ 10	Billy Thompson	.25	.12	.02
☐ 11	Rodney McCray	.20	.10	.02
☐ 12	Scooter McCray	.15	.07	.01
☐ 13	Wade Houston	.20	.10	.02
☐ 14	Jerry Jones	.10	.05	.01
☐ 15	Derek Smith	.20	.10	.02
☐ 16	Tony Branch	.15	.07	.01
☐ 17	Wesley Cox	.15	.07	.01
☐ 18	Manuel Forrest	.15	.07	.01
☐ 19	Jerry Eaves	.15	.07	.01
☐ 20	1980 NCAA Champs	.10	.05	.01
☐ 21	Junior Bridgeman	.20	.10	.02
☐ 22	Jeff Hall	.15	.07	.01
☐ 23	Charles Jones	.15	.07	.01
☐ 24	Rick Wilson	.10	.05	.01
☐ 25	The Cardinal Bird	.10	.05	.01
☐ 26	Wiley Brown	.15	.07	.01
☐ 27	Charlie Tyra	.15	.07	.01
☐ 28	Phil Bond	.10	.05	.01
☐ 29	James Jeter	.10	.05	.01
☐ 30	Poncho Wright	.15	.07	.01
☐ 31	Vladmir Gastevich	.10	.05	.01
☐ 32	Terry Howard	.10	.05	.01
☐ 33	Mark McSwain	.15	.07	.01
☐ 34	Ricky Gallon	.15	.07	.01
☐ 35	1975 NCAA Final Four	.10	.05	.01
☐ 36	1972 NCAA Final Four	.10	.05	.01
☐ 37	Mike Lawhon	.10	.05	.01
☐ 38	Bill Bunton	.15	.07	.01
☐ 39	Roger Burkman	.15	.07	.01
☐ 40	Henry Bacon	.10	.05	.01
☐ 41	Larry Williams	.15	.07	.01
☐ 42	Phil Bond	.15	.07	.01
☐ 43	Bobby Brown	.10	.05	.01
☐ 44	Charles Jones	.15	.07	.01
☐ 45	Mike Grosso	.10	.05	.01
☐ 46	Freedom Hall	.10	.05	.01
☐ 47	Fred Holden	.10	.05	.01
☐ 48	1948 NAIB Champs	.10	.05	.01
☐ 49	Glen Combs	.20	.10	.02
☐ 50	Jadie Frazier	.10	.05	.01
☐ 51	Marty Pulliam	.10	.05	.01
☐ 52	Eddie Whitehead	.10	.05	.01
☐ 53	Bobby Turner	.10	.05	.01
☐ 54	Will Olliges	.10	.05	.01
☐ 55	Eddie Creamer	.10	.05	.01
☐ 56	Corky Cox	.10	.05	.01
☐ 57	Bob Lochmueller	.10	.05	.01
☐ 58	Jeff Hall	.15	.07	.01
☐ 59	Al Vilcheck	.10	.05	.01
☐ 60	Jim Morgan	.10	.05	.01
☐ 61	Jim Price	.20	.10	.02
☐ 62	Ron Thomas	.20	.10	.02
☐ 63	Bobby Dotson	.10	.05	.01
☐ 64	Jerry Jones	.15	.07	.01
☐ 65	1956 NIT Champs	.10	.05	.01
☐ 66	John Reuther	.10	.05	.01
☐ 67	Ron Hawley	.10	.05	.01
☐ 68	Kent Jones	.10	.05	.01
☐ 69	1983 NCAA Final Four	.10	.05	.01
☐ 70	1982 NCAA Final Four	.10	.05	.01
☐ 71	1959 Louisville Cardinals	.10	.05	.01
☐ 72	Fred Sawyer	.10	.05	.01
☐ 73	Kenny Reeves	.10	.05	.01
☐ 74	Chris West	.10	.05	.01
☐ 75	Dick Peloff	.10	.05	.01
☐ 76	Allen Murphy	.10	.05	.01
☐ 77	John Prudhoe	.10	.05	.01
☐ 78	Mike Abram	.10	.05	.01
☐ 79	Bud Olsen	.15	.07	.01
☐ 80	Ron Rubenstein	.10	.05	.01
☐ 81	Gerald Moreman	.10	.05	.01
☐ 82	Chuck Noble	.15	.07	.01
☐ 83	Bill Darragh	.15	.07	.01
☐ 84	Jerry Dupont	.10	.05	.01
☐ 85	Danny Mitchell	.10	.05	.01
☐ 86	John Turner	.10	.05	.01
☐ 87	Daryl Cleveland	.10	.05	.01
☐ 88	Greg Deuser	.10	.05	.01
☐ 89	Don Goldstein	.10	.05	.01
☐ 90	Marv Selvy	.10	.05	.01
☐ 91	Dave Gilbert	.10	.05	.01
☐ 92	Tommy Finnegan	.10	.05	.01
☐ 93	Joe Liedtke	.10	.05	.01
☐ 94	Jack Coleman	.10	.05	.01
☐ 95	Dennis Clifford	.10	.05	.01
☐ 96	Robbie Valentine	.10	.05	.01

☐ 97 Ron Rooks	.10	.05	.01
☐ 98 The Coaching Staff	.10	.05	.01
☐ 99 Denny Crum CO	.20	.10	.02
☐ 100 Manuel Forrest	.15	.07	.01
☐ 101 Darrell Griffith	.30	.15	.03
☐ 102 Wesley Cox	.15	.07	.01
☐ 103 Wes Unseld	.35	.17	.03
☐ 104 John Dromo	.20	.10	.02
☐ 105 Peck Hickman	.20	.10	.02
☐ 106 Butch Beard	.20	.10	.02
☐ 107 Herbert Crook	.20	.10	.02
☐ 108 Milt Wagner	.20	.10	.02
☐ 109 Lancaster Gordon	.20	.10	.02
☐ 110 Billy Thompson	.25	.12	.02
☐ 111 Rodney McCray	.20	.10	.02
☐ 112 Scooter McCray	.15	.07	.01
☐ 113 Derek Smith	.15	.07	.01
☐ 114 Tony Branch	.15	.07	.01
☐ 115 Manuel Forrest	.15	.07	.01
☐ 116 Jerry Eaves	.15	.07	.01
☐ 117 Jeff Hall	.15	.07	.01
☐ 118 Charles Jones	.15	.07	.01
☐ 119 Rick Wilson	.10	.05	.01
☐ 120 Wiley Brown	.15	.07	.01
☐ 121 Charlie Tyra	.15	.07	.01
☐ 122 Phil Rollins	.10	.05	.01
☐ 123 Poncho Wright	.15	.07	.01
☐ 124 Terry Howard	.10	.05	.01
☐ 125 Mark McSwain	.15	.07	.01
☐ 126 Ricky Gallon	.10	.05	.01
☐ 127 Mike Lawhon	.10	.05	.01
☐ 128 Roger Burkman	.15	.07	.01
☐ 129 Henry Bacon	.10	.05	.01
☐ 130 Larry Williams	.10	.05	.01
☐ 131 Phil Bond	.15	.07	.01
☐ 132 Stanley Bunton	.10	.05	.01
☐ 133 Fred Holden	.10	.05	.01
☐ 134 Marty Pulliam	.10	.05	.01
☐ 135 Bobby Turner	.10	.05	.01
☐ 136 Will Olliges	.10	.05	.01
☐ 137 Al Vilcheck	.10	.05	.01
☐ 138 Jim Price	.20	.10	.02
☐ 139 Chris West	.10	.05	.01
☐ 140 Allen Murphy	.10	.05	.01
☐ 141 Mike Abram	.10	.05	.01
☐ 142 Danny Mitchell	.10	.05	.01
☐ 143 John Turner	.10	.05	.01
☐ 144 Daryl Cleveland	.10	.05	.01
☐ 145 Don Goldstein	.10	.05	.01
☐ 146 Marv Selvy	.10	.05	.01
☐ 147 Dave Gilbert	.10	.05	.01
☐ 148 Joe Liedtke	.10	.05	.01
☐ 149 Robbie Valentine	.10	.05	.01
☐ 150 Tony Branch	.15	.07	.01
☐ 151 Manuel Forrest	.15	.07	.01
☐ 152 Jerry Eaves	.15	.07	.01
☐ 153 Rick Wilson	.10	.05	.01
☐ 154 Jeff Hall	.15	.07	.01
☐ 155 Charles Jones	.15	.07	.01
☐ 156 Derek Smith	.15	.07	.01
☐ 157 Scooter McCray	.15	.07	.01
☐ 158 Robbie Valentine	.10	.05	.01
☐ 159 Mike Abram	.10	.05	.01
☐ 160 Rodney McCray	.20	.10	.02
☐ 161 Roger Burkman	.15	.07	.01
☐ 162 Henry Bacon	.10	.05	.01
☐ 163 Mike Lawhon	.10	.05	.01
☐ 164 Ricky Gallon	.10	.05	.01
☐ 165 Billy Thompson	.25	.12	.02
☐ 166 Milt Wagner	.20	.10	.02
☐ 167 Lancaster Gordon	.20	.10	.02
☐ 168 Butch Beard	.20	.10	.02
☐ 169 Herbert Crook	.20	.10	.02
☐ 170 Wes Unseld	.35	.17	.03
☐ 171 Wesley Cox	.15	.07	.01
☐ 172 Darrell Griffith	.30	.15	.03
☐ 173 Denny Crum CO	.20	.10	.02
☐ 174 Mark McSwain	.15	.07	.01
☐ 175 Wiley Brown	.15	.07	.01
☐ 176 Will Olliges	.10	.05	.01
☐ 177 Phil Bond	.15	.07	.01
☐ 178 Phil Bond	.15	.07	.01
☐ 179 Wiley Brown	.15	.07	.01
☐ 180 Mark McSwain	.15	.07	.01
☐ 181 Denny Crum CO	.20	.10	.02
☐ 182 Darrell Griffith	.30	.15	.03
☐ 183 Wesley Cox	.15	.07	.01
☐ 184 Peck Hickman	.20	.10	.02
☐ 185 Lancaster Gordon	.20	.10	.02
☐ 186 Billy Thompson	.25	.12	.02
☐ 187 Rodney McCray	.20	.10	.02
☐ 188 Stanley Bunton	.10	.05	.01
☐ 189 Henry Bacon	.10	.05	.01
☐ 190 Scooter McCray	.15	.07	.01

☐ 191 Derek Smith	.15	.07	.01
☐ 192 Jerry King	.10	.05	.01
☐ 193 Van Vance and Jock Sutherland	.10	.05	.01
☐ 194 Bill Olsen	.10	.05	.01

1989-90 Louisville 300 *

This 300-card set was produced by Collegiate Collection and measures the standard size (2 1/2" by 3 1/2"). The fronts feature a mix of black and white photos for earlier players and color for later ones, with rounded corners and red borders. The pictures are superimposed over a red and white diagonally-striped card face, with a red outer border. The top reads "Louisville's Finest," and the school logo appears in the upper right corner. The horizontally oriented backs are printed in red on white and present biographical information, career summaries, or statistics. The cards are numbered on the back.

	MINT	EXC	G-VG
COMPLETE SET (300)	27.00	13.50	2.70
COMMON PLAYER (1-300)	.07	.03	.01

☐ 1 Denny Crum CO	.20	.10	.02
☐ 2 Darrell Griffith	.25	.12	.02
☐ 3 Wes Unseld	.30	.15	.03
☐ 4 Pervis Ellison	.30	.15	.03
☐ 5 Charlie Tyra	.10	.05	.01
☐ 6 Phil Bond	.10	.05	.01
☐ 7 Butch Beard	.15	.07	.01
☐ 8 Jim Price	.15	.07	.01
☐ 9 Jerry Eaves	.10	.05	.01
☐ 10 Manuel Forrest	.10	.05	.01
☐ 11 Butch Beard	.15	.07	.01
☐ 12 Herbert Crook	.15	.07	.01
☐ 13 John Turner	.07	.03	.01
☐ 14 Wes Unseld	.30	.15	.03
☐ 15 Fred Holden	.07	.03	.01
☐ 16 Bill Bunton	.15	.07	.01
☐ 17 Milt Wagner	.15	.07	.01
☐ 18 Ricky Gallon	.10	.05	.01
☐ 19 Jerry King	.07	.03	.01
☐ 20 Don Goldstein	.07	.03	.01
☐ 21 Rick Wilson	.10	.05	.01
☐ 22 John Reuther	.07	.03	.01
☐ 23 Charles Jones	.10	.05	.01
☐ 24 Bobby Turner	.07	.03	.01
☐ 25 Darrell Griffith	.25	.12	.02
☐ 26 Scooter McCray	.10	.05	.01
☐ 27 George Hauptfuhrer	.07	.03	.01
☐ 28 Frank Epley	.07	.03	.01
☐ 29 Ed Kupper	.07	.03	.01
☐ 30 Don Kinker	.07	.03	.01
☐ 31 Roger Burkman	.10	.05	.01
☐ 32 Jerry Eaves	.10	.05	.01
☐ 33 Derek Smith	.10	.05	.01
☐ 34 Jeff Hall	.10	.05	.01
☐ 35 Billy Thompson	.20	.10	.02
☐ 36 Mike Abram	.10	.05	.01
☐ 37 Mark McSwain	.10	.05	.01
☐ 38 Herbert Crook	.15	.07	.01
☐ 39 Kenny Payne	.15	.07	.01
☐ 40 Johnny Knopf	.07	.03	.01
☐ 41 Pervis Ellison	.25	.12	.02

Basketball / 213

☐ 42	Deward Compton	.07	.03	.01	☐ 136	Jeff Morrow	.07	.03	.01

Basketball / 213

#	Name	A	B	C
42	Deward Compton	.07	.03	.01
43	Poncho Wright	.10	.05	.01
44	Scooter McCray	.10	.05	.01
45	Rodney McCray	.15	.07	.01
46	Milt Wagner	.15	.07	.01
47	Lancaster Gordon	.15	.07	.01
48	Manuel Forrest	.15	.07	.01
49	Charles Jones	.15	.07	.01
50	Cal Johnson	.07	.03	.01
51	Forrest Able	.07	.03	.01
52	Bob Peterson	.07	.03	.01
53	Clyde(Ace) Parker	.10	.05	.01
54	Roy Rubin	.07	.03	.01
55	Al Russak	.07	.03	.01
56	Roy Combs	.07	.03	.01
57	Robert Davis	.07	.03	.01
58	Randall Ford	.07	.03	.01
59	Clyde Bryant	.07	.03	.01
60	Frank Lentz	.07	.03	.01
61	Bob Dunbar	.07	.03	.01
62	William Powell	.07	.03	.01
63	Bob Manion	.07	.03	.01
64	Al Glaza	.07	.03	.01
65	Harold Andrews	.07	.03	.01
66	Wade Houston	.10	.05	.01
67	Joe Reuther	.07	.03	.01
68	Judd Rothman	.07	.03	.01
69	Tony Kinnaird	.07	.03	.01
70	Danny Brown	.07	.03	.01
71	Ike Whitfield	.07	.03	.01
72	Billy Harmon	.07	.03	.01
73	Joe Meiman	.07	.03	.01
74	Ed Linonis	.07	.03	.01
75	Larry Carter	.07	.03	.01
76	Ken Bradley	.07	.03	.01
77	Ken Butters	.07	.03	.01
78	John Studer	.07	.03	.01
79	Dennis Deeken	.07	.03	.01
80	Bob Gorius	.07	.03	.01
81	Paul Pry	.07	.03	.01
82	Ron Stallings	.07	.03	.01
83	John Varoscak	.07	.03	.01
84	Bob Naber	.07	.03	.01
85	Howard Stacey	.07	.03	.01
86	Buddy Leathers	.07	.03	.01
87	Joe Kitchen	.07	.03	.01
88	Alex Mantel	.07	.03	.01
89	Rodger Tieman	.07	.03	.01
90	Dick Keffer	.07	.03	.01
91	Dick Robison	.07	.03	.01
92	Barry Sumpter	.10	.05	.01
93	Herb Harah	.07	.03	.01
94	Bill Sullivan	.07	.03	.01
95	Chet Beam	.07	.03	.01
96	Roscoe Shackelford	.07	.03	.01
97	David Smith	.07	.03	.01
98	Jerry Armstrong	.07	.03	.01
99	James"Lum" Edwards	.07	.03	.01
100	Jesse"Oz" Johnson	.07	.03	.01
101	Howard Schnellenberger	.20	.10	.02
102	Johnny Unitas	.75	.35	.07
103	Lenny Lyles	.10	.05	.01
104	Ken Porco	.07	.03	.01
105	Jay Gruden	.07	.03	.01
106	Tom Lucia	.07	.03	.01
107	Ken Kortas	.10	.05	.01
108	Howard Stevens	.15	.07	.01
109	Doug Buffone	.15	.07	.01
110	Lenny Lyles	.10	.05	.01
111	Wilbur Summers	.07	.03	.01
112	Dean May	.07	.03	.01
113	Deon Booker	.07	.03	.01
114	Walter Peacock	.07	.03	.01
115	Ernest Givens	.25	.12	.02
116	Otis Wilson	.15	.07	.01
117	Mark Clayton	.35	.17	.03
118	Dwayne Woodruff	.15	.07	.01
119	Frank Minnifield	.20	.10	.02
120	Ernie Green	.20	.10	.02
121	Wally Oyler	.07	.03	.01
122	Nathan Poole	.07	.03	.01
123	Ron Davenport	.10	.05	.01
124	Tom Laframboise	.07	.03	.01
125	Ed Rubbert	.07	.03	.01
126	Jon Cade	.07	.03	.01
127	Howard Schnellenberger	.20	.10	.02
128	Rick Lantz	.07	.03	.01
129	Brad Bradford	.07	.03	.01
130	Danny Hope	.07	.03	.01
131	Bob Maddox	.07	.03	.01
132	Gary Nord	.07	.03	.01
133	Ty Smith	.07	.03	.01
134	Christ Vagotis	.07	.03	.01
135	Trent Walters	.07	.03	.01
136	Jeff Morrow	.07	.03	.01
137	Vince Gibson	.07	.03	.01
138	Lee Corso	.15	.07	.01
139	Frank Camp	.07	.03	.01
140	Benny Russell	.07	.03	.01
141	Paul Mattingly	.07	.03	.01
142	Joe Jacoby	.15	.07	.01
143	Jay Gruden	.07	.03	.01
144	Chris Thieneman	.07	.03	.01
145	Matt Battaglia	.07	.03	.01
146	Eddie Johnson	.07	.03	.01
147	Stu Stramm	.07	.03	.01
148	Donald Craft	.07	.03	.01
149	Pete Compise	.07	.03	.01
150	Jim Zamberlan	.07	.03	.01
151	Marc Mitchell	.07	.03	.01
152	Tom Abood	.07	.03	.01
153	Lee Calland	.07	.03	.01
154	Larry Ball	.07	.03	.01
155	Phil Ellis	.07	.03	.01
156	Greg Pianko	.07	.03	.01
157	Bruce Armstrong	.10	.05	.01
158	Calvin Prince	.07	.03	.01
159	Marty Smith	.07	.03	.01
160	Joe Trabue	.07	.03	.01
161	Gene Sartini	.07	.03	.01
162	Rodney Knighton	.07	.03	.01
163	George Cain	.07	.03	.01
164	Stu Gibson	.07	.03	.01
165	Larry Compton	.07	.03	.01
166	Charlie Mudd	.07	.03	.01
167	Al MacFarlane	.07	.03	.01
168	Willie Shelby	.07	.03	.01
169	Herbie Phelps	.07	.03	.01
170	Dale Orem	.07	.03	.01
171	Lee Bouggess	.10	.05	.01
172	John Neidert	.07	.03	.01
173	Amos Martin	.10	.05	.01
174	Norman Heard	.07	.03	.01
175	Charlie Johnson	.07	.03	.01
176	Len Depaola	.10	.05	.01
177	Dave Nuss	.07	.03	.01
178	Tom Lucia	.07	.03	.01
179	Bill Gatti	.07	.03	.01
180	Greg Hickman	.07	.03	.01
181	Wayne Patrick	.07	.03	.01
182	Otto Knop Sr.	.07	.03	.01
183	John Giles	.07	.03	.01
184	Doug Hockensmith	.07	.03	.01
185	A.J.Jacobs	.07	.03	.01
186	Pat Patterson	.07	.03	.01
187	David Hatfield	.07	.03	.01
188	Eric Vaughn	.07	.03	.01
189	Brian Miller	.07	.03	.01
190	Leon Williams	.07	.03	.01
191	Kenny Robinson	.07	.03	.01
192	John Madeya	.07	.03	.01
193	Zarko Ellis	.07	.03	.01
194	Cookie Brinkman	.07	.03	.01
195	Kevin Miller	.07	.03	.01
196	Ricky Skiles	.07	.03	.01
197	John Adams	.07	.03	.01
198	Dave Betz	.07	.03	.01
199	Jeff Henry	.07	.03	.01
200	Tom Jackson	.25	.12	.02
201	Louisville Cardinals	.07	.03	.01
202	Louisville Cardinals	.07	.03	.01
203	Louisville Cardinals	.07	.03	.01
204	Louisville Cardinals	.07	.03	.01
205	Louisville Cardinals	.07	.03	.01
206	Pervis Ellison	.25	.12	.02
207	Wes Unseld	.30	.15	.03
208	Charlie Tyra	.10	.05	.01
209	Darrell Griffith	.20	.10	.02
210	Steve Clark	.07	.03	.01
211	Ellis Bryant	.07	.03	.01
212	Gil Waggoner	.07	.03	.01
213	Bob Borah	.07	.03	.01
214	Bill Akridge	.07	.03	.01
215	Cliff York	.07	.03	.01
216	Harry Hinton	.07	.03	.01
217	Ray Potts	.07	.03	.01
218	Bob Wellman	.07	.03	.01
219	Truett Demoisey	.07	.03	.01
220	John Prudhoe	.07	.03	.01
221	Dale Hall	.07	.03	.01
222	Phil Rollins	.07	.03	.01
223	Ron Thomas	.10	.05	.01
224	John Turner	.07	.03	.01
225	Charles Tyra	.10	.05	.01
226	Henry Bacon	.07	.03	.01
227	Butch Beard	.15	.07	.01
228	Phillip Bond	.10	.05	.01
229	Junior Bridgeman	.20	.10	.02

☐ 230	Jim Price	.15	.07	.01
☐ 231	Jack Coleman	.07	.03	.01
☐ 232	Wesley Cox	.15	.07	.01
☐ 233	Jerry Eaves	.10	.05	.01
☐ 234	Lancaster Gordon	.15	.07	.01
☐ 235	Milt Wagner	.15	.07	.01
☐ 236	Mike Grosso	.10	.05	.01
☐ 237	Rick Wilson	.10	.05	.01
☐ 238	Wes Unseld	.30	.15	.03
☐ 239	Scooter McCray	.10	.05	.01
☐ 240	Allen Murphy	.07	.03	.01
☐ 241	Chuck Noble	.10	.05	.01
☐ 242	Bud Olsen	.10	.05	.01
☐ 243	Roger Burkman	.10	.05	.01
☐ 244	Henry Bacon	.07	.03	.01
☐ 245	Jim Price	.15	.07	.01
☐ 246	Al Vilcheck	.07	.03	.01
☐ 247	Ron Thomas	.10	.05	.01
☐ 248	Mike Lawhon	.07	.03	.01
☐ 249	Don Goldstein	.07	.03	.01
☐ 250	John Turner	.07	.03	.01
☐ 251	Fred Sawyer	.07	.03	.01
☐ 252	Wiley Brown	.10	.05	.01
☐ 253	Pervis Ellison	.30	.15	.03
☐ 254	Herbert Crook	.15	.07	.01
☐ 255	Mark McSwain	.10	.05	.01
☐ 256	Jeff Hall	.10	.05	.01
☐ 257	Billy Thompson	.20	.10	.02
☐ 258	Milt Wagner	.15	.07	.01
☐ 259	Charles Jones	.10	.05	.01
☐ 260	Lancaster Gordon	.15	.07	.01
☐ 261	Poncho Wright	.10	.05	.01
☐ 262	Jerry Eaves	.10	.05	.01
☐ 263	Scooter McCray	.10	.05	.01
☐ 264	Rodney McCray	.15	.07	.01
☐ 265	Derek Smith	.15	.07	.01
☐ 266	Darrell Griffith	.20	.10	.02
☐ 267	Roger Burkman	.10	.05	.01
☐ 268	Kevin Walls	.15	.07	.01
☐ 269	Allen Murphy	.07	.03	.01
☐ 270	Junior Bridgeman	.20	.10	.02
☐ 271	Wesley Cox	.15	.07	.01
☐ 272	Bill Bunton	.15	.07	.01
☐ 273	Phillip Bond	.10	.05	.01
☐ 274	Ricky Gallon	.10	.05	.01
☐ 275	Manuel Forrest	.10	.05	.01
☐ 276	Jerry Jones	.07	.03	.01
☐ 277	Scooter McCray	.10	.05	.01
☐ 278	Larry Williams	.10	.05	.01
☐ 279	Peck Hickman	.15	.07	.01
☐ 280	John Dromo	.15	.07	.01
☐ 281	Darrell Griffith	.20	.10	.02
☐ 282	Derek Smith	.15	.07	.01
☐ 283	Paul Pry	.07	.03	.01
☐ 284	Henry Bacon	.07	.03	.01
☐ 285	Charles Jones	.10	.05	.01
☐ 286	Butch Beard	.15	.07	.01
☐ 287	Herbert Crook	.15	.07	.01
☐ 288	Denny Crum CO	.15	.07	.01
☐ 289	Mike Abram	.07	.03	.01
☐ 290	Pervis Ellison	.25	.12	.02
☐ 291	Billy Thompson	.15	.07	.01
☐ 292	Rodney McCray	.15	.07	.01
☐ 293	Terry Howard	.07	.03	.01
☐ 294	Mike Grosso	.10	.05	.01
☐ 295	Kenny Payne	.10	.05	.01
☐ 296	Chris West	.07	.03	.01
☐ 297	Darrell Griffith	.20	.10	.02
☐ 298	Denny Crum CO	.15	.07	.01
☐ 299	Jeff Hall	.10	.05	.01
☐ 300	Billy Thompson	.20	.10	.02

1986 LSU Police *

This 16-card set was sponsored by LSU, Baton Rouge General Medical Center, Chemical Dependency Unit of Baton Rouge, and various law enforcement agencies and produced by McDag Productions. The General and the Chemical Dependency Unit logos adorn the top of the observe and the bottom of the reverse. The cards measure 2 1/2" by 3 1/2". The fronts feature a mix of borderless posed and action color photos of the players on white card stock. Player information appears below the pictures between two Tiger logos. The back has additional player information with two more Tiger logos at the top. The card backs provide "Tips from the Tigers" in the form of an anti-

crime or drug message. The cards are unnumbered and we have checklisted them below in alphabetical order. Since this set includes athletes from two different sports, we have indicated the sport after the player's name (B for baseball; BK for basketball).

	MINT	EXC	G-VG
COMPLETE SET (16)	9.00	4.50	.90
COMMON PLAYER (1-16)	.50	.25	.05

		MINT	EXC	G-VG
☐ 1	Joey Belle B	3.00	1.50	.30
☐ 2	Skip Bertman B CO	.50	.25	.05
☐ 3	Ricky Blanton BK	.75	.35	.07
☐ 4	Dale Brown BK CO	.75	.35	.07
☐ 5	Ollie Brown BK	.50	.25	.05
☐ 6	Mark Guthrie B	.75	.35	.07
☐ 7	Rob Leary B	.50	.25	.05
☐ 8	Stan Loewer B	.50	.25	.05
☐ 9	Greg Patterson B	.50	.25	.05
☐ 10	Jeff Reboulet B	.50	.25	.05
☐ 11	Don Redden BK	.75	.35	.07
☐ 12	Derrick Taylor BK	.75	.35	.07
☐ 13	Jose Vargas BK	.75	.35	.07
☐ 14	John Williams BK	1.00	.50	.10
☐ 15	Nikita Wilson BK	.75	.35	.07
☐ 16	Anthony Wilson BK	.50	.25	.05

1987-88 LSU Police *

This 16-card set was sponsored by LSU, Baton Rouge General Medical Center, Chemical Dependency Unit of Baton Rouge, and various law enforcement agencies and was produced by McDag Productions. The General and the Chemical Dependency Unit logos adorn the bottom of both sides of the card. Six thousand sets were printed, and they were distributed by participating police agencies in the Baton Rouge area. The cards measure 2 1/2" by 3 1/2" and are numbered on the back. The fronts feature borderless action or posed color photos of the players on white card stock. The upper left and right corners give the school name and player information. The backs have additional player information and "Tips from the Tigers", which consist of anti-drug or alcohol messages. This set includes athletes from basketball (1-7, 16) and baseball (8-15). Of special interest is card number 16, issued in memory of the late Pete Maravich, the all-time leading scorer in college basketball history.

	MINT	EXC	G-VG
COMPLETE SET (16)	10.00	5.00	1.00
COMMON PLAYER (1-16)	.50	.25	.05
☐ 1 Dale Brown BK CO	.75	.35	.07
☐ 2 Ricky Blanton BK	.75	.35	.07
☐ 3 Jose Vargas BK	.75	.35	.07
☐ 4 Fess Irvin BK	.50	.25	.05
☐ 5 Darryl Joe BK	.75	.35	.07
☐ 6 Bernard Woodside BK	.50	.25	.05
☐ 7 Neboisha Bukumirovich BK	.50	.25	.05
☐ 8 Parker Griffin B	.50	.25	.05
☐ 9 Skip Bertman B CO	.50	.25	.05
☐ 10 Dan Kite B	.50	.25	.05
☐ 11 Russ Springer B	.75	.35	.07
☐ 12 Ben McDonald B	2.50	1.25	.25
☐ 13 Richie Vasquez B	.50	.25	.05
☐ 14 Andy Galy B	.50	.25	.05
☐ 15 Pete Bush B	.50	.25	.05
☐ 16 Pete Maravich BK	2.50	1.25	.25

1988-89 LSU Police *

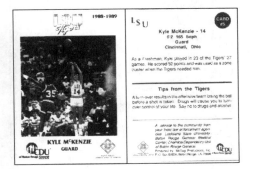

This 16-card set was sponsored by LSU, Baton Rouge General Medical Center, Chemical Dependency Unit of Baton Rouge, and various law enforcement agencies and was produced by McDag Productions. The General Medical Center and Chemical Dependency Unit logos adorn the bottom of both sides of the card. The cards were distributed in the Baton Rouge area by participating law enforcement agencies, the Medical Center, and the Chemical Dependency Unit. The cards measure 2 1/2" by 3 1/2" and are numbered on the back. The fronts feature borderless action or posed color photos of the players on white card stock. The title "LSU Tigers" is centered at the top of the card face, with player information below the picture. The back has additional player information and "Tips from the Tigers", which consist of an anti-drug or alcohol message. This set features athletes from basketball (1-8) and baseball (9-16). This set includes early cards of Chris Jackson, who plays in the NBA, and of Ben McDonald, who pitched for the USA Olympic Baseball Team.

	MINT	EXC	G-VG
COMPLETE SET (16)	10.00	5.00	1.00
COMMON PLAYER (1-16)	.50	.25	.05
☐ 1 Ricky Blanton	.75	.35	.07
☐ 2 Dale Brown CO	.75	.35	.07
☐ 3 Wayne Simms	.50	.25	.05
☐ 4 Chris Jackson	2.00	1.00	.20

	MINT	EXC	G-VG
☐ 5 Kyle McKenzie	.50	.25	.05
☐ 6 Lyle Mouton	.50	.25	.05
☐ 7 Vernel Singleton	.75	.35	.07
☐ 8 Russell Grant	.50	.25	.05
☐ 9 Skip Bertman CO	.50	.25	.05
☐ 10 Ben McDonald	2.00	1.00	.20
☐ 11 Pete Bush	.50	.25	.05
☐ 12 Mike Bianco	.50	.25	.05
☐ 13 Craig Cala	.50	.25	.05
☐ 14 Mat Gruver	.50	.25	.05
☐ 15 Keith Osik	.50	.25	.05
☐ 16 Russell Springer	.75	.35	.07

1990 LSU Promos *

This ten-card standard size (2 1/2" by 3 1/2") set features some of the best athletes of LSU's history. Since this set features athletes from different sports we have placed a two-letter abbreviation of the sport next to the player's name.

	MINT	EXC	G-VG
COMPLETE SET (10)	5.00	2.50	.50
COMMON PLAYER (1-10)	.50	.25	.05
☐ 1 Billy Cannon FB	.75	.35	.07
☐ 2 Chris Jackson BK	1.00	.50	.10
☐ 3 Tiger Stadium	.50	.25	.05
☐ 4 Wendell Harris FB	.50	.25	.05
☐ 5 Bob Pettit BK	.75	.35	.07
☐ 6 Pete Maravich BK	1.00	.50	.10
☐ 7 Pete Maravich Center	.50	.25	.05
☐ 8 Dale Brown CO BK	.50	.25	.05
☐ 9 Mike V Mascot FB	.50	.25	.05
☐ 10 Joe Dean BK	.50	.25	.05

1990 LSU 200 *

This 200-card set was produced by Collegiate Collection and measures the standard size (2 1/2" by 3 1/2"). Although a few color photos are included, the front features mostly black and white player photos, with borders in the team's colors of gold and purple. All four corners of the picture are cut off. In purple lettering the school name appears above the picture, with the player's name at the bottom of the card face. In a horizontal format the back presents biographical information, career summary, and statistics, on a white background with purple lettering and borders. The cards are numbered on the back.

	MINT	EXC	G-VG
COMPLETE SET (200)	22.00	11.00	2.20
COMMON PLAYER (1-200)	.10	.05	.01
☐ 1 Pete Maravich	.50	.25	.05
☐ 2 Chris Jackson	.35	.17	.03
☐ 3 Y.A. Tittle	.50	.25	.05
☐ 4 Ricky Blanton	.20	.10	.02
☐ 5 Charles Alexander	.15	.07	.01

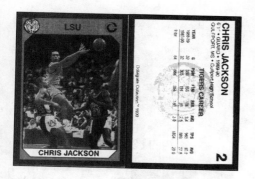

CHRIS JACKSON
6'1" • GUARD • 1989-90
GULFPORT, MS • Gulfport High School

TIGERS CAREER

Collegiate Collection™ 1990

2

☐ 6 Joe Dean	.10	.05	.01
☐ 7 Billy Cannon	.25	.12	.02
☐ 8 Dalton Hilliard	.25	.12	.02
☐ 9 Bert Jones	.25	.12	.02
☐ 10 Tommy Hodson	.30	.15	.03
☐ 11 Dale Brown	.15	.07	.01
☐ 12 Mike Archer	.15	.07	.01
☐ 13 Jimmy Taylor	.30	.15	.03
☐ 14 John Williams	.20	.10	.02
☐ 15 Brian Kinchen	.15	.07	.01
☐ 16 Chris Carrier	.10	.05	.01
☐ 17 Jess Fatheree	.10	.05	.01
☐ 18 Chris Jackson	.35	.17	.03
☐ 19 Orlando McDaniel	.10	.05	.01
☐ 20 Billy Hendrix	.10	.05	.01
☐ 21 Eddie Ray	.15	.07	.01
☐ 22 Glenn Hansen	.10	.05	.01
☐ 23 Bo Strange	.15	.07	.01
☐ 24 Eric Hill	.15	.07	.01
☐ 25 Leonard Mitchell	.15	.07	.01
☐ 26 Larry Shipp	.10	.05	.01
☐ 27 Malcolm Scott	.10	.05	.01
☐ 28 Adam Duhe	.10	.05	.01
☐ 29 George Brancato	.10	.05	.01
☐ 30 Jim Roshso	.10	.05	.01
☐ 31 Karl Wilson	.10	.05	.01
☐ 32 Ethan Martin	.10	.05	.01
☐ 33 Julie Gross	.10	.05	.01
☐ 34 Lyman White	.10	.05	.01
☐ 35 Eddie Palubinskas	.15	.07	.01
☐ 36 Michael Brooks	.15	.07	.01
☐ 37 Frank Brian	.15	.07	.01
☐ 38 Gaynell Tinsley	.15	.07	.01
☐ 39 Mike Anderson	.10	.05	.01
☐ 40 Howard Carter	.15	.07	.01
☐ 41 Jerry Stovall	.20	.10	.02
☐ 42 Nikita Wilson	.15	.07	.01
☐ 43 Bill Fortier	.10	.05	.01
☐ 44 Mike Vincent	.10	.05	.01
☐ 45 Richard Granier	.10	.05	.01
☐ 46 DeWayne Scales	.15	.07	.01
☐ 47 Pinky Rohm	.10	.05	.01
☐ 48 Bernie Moore Stadium	.10	.05	.01
☐ 49 Tob Caston	.10	.05	.01
☐ 50 Durand Macklin	.15	.07	.01
☐ 51 John Ed Bradley	.10	.05	.01
☐ 52 Mark Lumpkin	.10	.05	.01
☐ 53 Joyce Walker	.10	.05	.01
☐ 54 Bobby Lowther	.10	.05	.01
☐ 55 Al Sanders	.10	.05	.01
☐ 56 Curt Gore	.10	.05	.01
☐ 57 Eric Martin	.15	.07	.01
☐ 58 George Nattin	.10	.05	.01
☐ 59 Roland Barray	.10	.05	.01
☐ 60 Craig Duhe	.10	.05	.01
☐ 61 Maree Jackson	.10	.05	.01
☐ 62 Sparky Wade	.10	.05	.01
☐ 63 Karl Dunbar	.10	.05	.01
☐ 64 Mike Williams	.10	.05	.01
☐ 65 Al Green	.10	.05	.01
☐ 66 Lew Sibley	.10	.05	.01
☐ 67 John Sage	.10	.05	.01
☐ 68 Craig Burns	.10	.05	.01
☐ 69 Schwoonda Williams	.10	.05	.01
☐ 70 Wendell Davis	.20	.10	.02
☐ 71 Dick Maile	.10	.05	.01
☐ 72 Kenny Bordelon	.15	.07	.01
☐ 73 Rusty Jackson	.10	.05	.01
☐ 74 Pete Maravich	.50	.25	.05
☐ 75 Garry James	.20	.10	.02
☐ 76 Lance Smith	.10	.05	.01
☐ 77 Willie Teal	.15	.07	.01

☐ 78 John Wood	.10	.05	.01
☐ 79 Mike Robichaux	.15	.07	.01
☐ 80 Earl Leggett	.15	.07	.01
☐ 81 Alex Box Stadium	.10	.05	.01
☐ 82 Steve Cassidy	.10	.05	.01
☐ 83 Kenny Konz	.15	.07	.01
☐ 84 Wendell Harris	.15	.07	.01
☐ 85 Alan Risher	.15	.07	.01
☐ 86 Gerald Keigley	.10	.05	.01
☐ 87 Robert Dugas	.10	.05	.01
☐ 88 Chris Williams	.10	.05	.01
☐ 89 John DeMarie	.15	.07	.01
☐ 90 Eddie Fuller	.15	.07	.01
☐ 91 Chris Jackson	.35	.17	.03
☐ 92 Bo Harris	.15	.07	.01
☐ 93 Mel Lyle	.10	.05	.01
☐ 94 Greg Jackson	.15	.07	.01
☐ 95 Liffort Hubley	.10	.05	.01
☐ 96 Shawn Burks	.10	.05	.01
☐ 97 David Browndyke	.15	.07	.01
☐ 98 Jerry Reynolds	.20	.10	.02
☐ 99 Eric Andolsek	.15	.07	.01
☐ 100 Director Card 1-99	.10	.05	.01
☐ 101 Jon Streete	.10	.05	.01
☐ 102 Barry Wilson	.10	.05	.01
☐ 103 Remi Prudhomme	.15	.07	.01
☐ 104 Abe Mickal	.15	.07	.01
☐ 105 Henry Thomas	.15	.07	.01
☐ 106 George Tarasovic	.15	.07	.01
☐ 107 Tiger Stadium	.10	.05	.01
☐ 108 Benjy Thibodeaux	.10	.05	.01
☐ 109 Jeffery Dale	.15	.07	.01
☐ 110 Sid Fournet	.15	.07	.01
☐ 111 John Adams	.10	.05	.01
☐ 112 Dennis Gaubatz	.15	.07	.01
☐ 113 Ben McDonald	.50	.25	.05
☐ 114 Joe Tuminello	.10	.05	.01
☐ 115 Billy Truax	.15	.07	.01
☐ 116 Warren Rabb	.15	.07	.01
☐ 117 Albert Richardson	.10	.05	.01
☐ 118 Jay Whitey	.10	.05	.01
☐ 119 Clinton Burrell	.15	.07	.01
☐ 120 Mike Miley	.15	.07	.01
☐ 121 Tommy Casanova	.20	.10	.02
☐ 122 George Bevan	.10	.05	.01
☐ 123 Binks Miciotto	.10	.05	.01
☐ 124 Joe Michaelson	.10	.05	.01
☐ 125 Mickey Mangham	.15	.07	.01
☐ 126 Ronnie Estay	.10	.05	.01
☐ 127 John Hazard	.10	.05	.01
☐ 128 Darrell Phillips	.10	.05	.01
☐ 129 Nacho Ablergamo	.10	.05	.01
☐ 130 John Garlington	.15	.07	.01
☐ 131 Arthur Cantrelle	.10	.05	.01
☐ 132 Monk Guillot	.10	.05	.01
☐ 133 Gene Knight	.10	.05	.01
☐ 134 Gerry Kent	.10	.05	.01
☐ 135 Ron Sancho	.15	.07	.01
☐ 136 Kenny Higgs	.20	.10	.02
☐ 137 Rip Collins	.10	.05	.01
☐ 138 Bob Pettit	.25	.12	.02
☐ 139 Mike Vincent	.10	.05	.01
☐ 140 Tyler LaFauci	.10	.05	.01
☐ 141 Richard Broks	.10	.05	.01
☐ 142 Billy Booth	.10	.05	.01
☐ 143 Brad Davis	.10	.05	.01
☐ 144 Roy Winston	.20	.10	.02
☐ 145 Andy Hamilton	.20	.10	.02
☐ 146 Rene Bourgeois	.10	.05	.01
☐ 147 Terry Robiskie	.15	.07	.01
☐ 148 Godfrey Zaunbrecher	.10	.05	.01
☐ 149 George Atiyeh	.10	.05	.01
☐ 150 Billy Hardin	.10	.05	.01
☐ 151 Jeff Wickersham	.20	.10	.02
☐ 152 Charlie McClendon	.15	.07	.01
☐ 153 Hokie Gajan	.20	.10	.02
☐ 154 Pete Maravich Center	.10	.05	.01
☐ 155 Bill Arnsparger	.15	.07	.01
☐ 156 Max Fuglar	.20	.10	.02
☐ 157 Greg Lafleur	.10	.05	.01
☐ 158 George Rice	.10	.05	.01
☐ 159 Dave McCormick	.10	.05	.01
☐ 160 Fred Miller	.10	.05	.01
☐ 161 Steve Van Buren	.25	.12	.02
☐ 162 Sid Bowman	.10	.05	.01
☐ 163 Wes Grisham	.10	.05	.01
☐ 164 Jeff Torrance	.10	.05	.01
☐ 165 Buddy Blair	.10	.05	.01
☐ 166 Doug Moreau	.15	.07	.01
☐ 167 Mike DeMarie	.10	.05	.01
☐ 168 James Britt	.10	.05	.01
☐ 169 Matt DeFrank	.10	.05	.01
☐ 170 Al Moreau	.10	.05	.01
☐ 171 Joe Bill Padcock	.10	.05	.01

☐ 172	Pat Screen	.10	.05	.01
☐ 173	Ralph Norwood	.10	.05	.01
☐ 174	Marcus Quinn	.10	.05	.01
☐ 175	Johnny Robinson	.20	.10	.02
☐ 176	Tony Moss	.10	.05	.01
☐ 177	Dan Alexander	.15	.07	.01
☐ 178	Norman Jefferson	.10	.05	.01
☐ 179	Bert Jones	.25	.12	.02
☐ 180	Joe LaBruzzo	.15	.07	.01
☐ 181	Jimmy Field	.10	.05	.01
☐ 182	David Woodley	.20	.10	.02
☐ 183	Paul Dietzel	.20	.10	.02
☐ 184	Abner Wimbley	.10	.05	.01
☐ 185	Steve Ensminger	.10	.05	.01
☐ 186	Carlos Carson	.20	.10	.02
☐ 187	Ken Kanauna Sr.	.10	.05	.01
☐ 188	Paul Ziegler	.10	.05	.01
☐ 189	Chris Jackson	.35	.17	.03
☐ 190	Chris Jackson	.35	.17	.03
☐ 191	W.T. Robinson Tennis	.10	.05	.01
☐ 192	Donnie Leaycraft	.10	.05	.01
☐ 193	Fernando Perez	.10	.05	.01
☐ 194	Steve Faulk	.10	.05	.01
☐ 195	Warren Capone	.15	.07	.01
☐ 196	Howard Carter	.15	.07	.01
☐ 197	Glenn Hansen	.10	.05	.01
☐ 198	Durand Macklin	.15	.07	.01
☐ 199	Sam Grezaffi	.15	.07	.01
☐ 200	Director Card	.10	.05	.01

1987-88 Maine Police *

1987-1988 MAINE
BLACK BEARS

Basketball

KIDS & KOPS
Tip *No. 13* from the
BLACK BEARS

DUMB FOULS

Going along with the crowd
is dumb. Drug use & van-
dalism are crimes that hurt
you and other people.

Dumb fouls are those caused by playing defense with
the hands instead of the
mind.

Amadou Coco Barry
Basketball - Center
6'6 250 lbs
Junior - Ag. Res. Ec.
Dakar, Senegal

Bangor Daily News Charities

This 14-card set of Maine Black Bears is part of a "Kids and Kops"
promotion, and one card was printed each Saturday in the Bangor
Daily News. The cards measure approximately 2 1/2" by 4". The
fronts feature posed color player photos, outlined by a black
border on white card stock. Player information is given below the
picture in the lower left corner, with a facsimile autograph in
turquoise in the lower right corner. The cards were to be collected
from any participating police officer. Once five cards had been
collected (including card number 1), they could be turned in at a
police station for a University of Maine ID card, which permitted
free admission to selected university activities. When all 14 cards
had been collected, they could be turned in at a police station to
register for the Grand Prize drawing (bicycle) and to pick up a free
"Kids and Kops" tee-shirt. The backs have tips in the form of an
anti-drug or alcohol message and logos of Burger King, University
of Maine, and Pepsi across the bottom. With the exception of the
rules card, the cards are numbered on the back. Sports represented
in this set include hockey (2), basketball (3, 9, 13), tennis (4),
baseball (5), swimming (6), soccer (7), track (8), football (10),
field hockey (11), and softball (12).

	MINT	EXC	G-VG
COMPLETE SET (14)	15.00	7.50	1.50
COMMON PLAYER (1-14)	1.00	.50	.10
☐ 1 Bananas (Mascot) and	3.00	1.50	.30

	K.C. Jones			
☐ 2 Mike McHugh	1.00	.50	.10
☐ 3 Matt Rossignol	1.00	.50	.10
☐ 4 Cindy Sprague	1.00	.50	.10
☐ 5 Gary LaPierre	1.00	.50	.10
☐ 6 Dana Billington	1.00	.50	.10
☐ 7 Scott Atherley	1.00	.50	.10
☐ 8 Elke Brutsaert	1.00	.50	.10
☐ 9 Elizabeth(Liz) Coffin	1.00	.50	.10
☐ 10 David Ingalls	1.00	.50	.10
☐ 11 Wendy J. Nadeau	1.00	.50	.10
☐ 12 Stacy Caron	1.00	.50	.10
☐ 13 Amadou Coco Barry	1.00	.50	.10
☐ xx Kids and Kops Rules	1.00	.50	.10

1982-83 Marquette Lite Beer

This 16-card set measures the standard card size, 2 1/2" by 3
1/2", and was issued in conjunction with Lite Beer. The front of
the card features a black and white action photo inside an
"arrowhead" against a pale yellow background, surrounded by
the player's name, height, and position, with the team name
("Warriors") emblazoned across the bottom. The back has
biographical and statistical information. The set also features
an early card of Glenn "Doc" Rivers.

	MINT	EXC	G-VG
COMPLETE SET (16)	15.00	7.50	1.50
COMMON PLAYER (1-16)	1.00	.50	.10

☐ 1 Ric Cobb CO	1.50	.75	.15
☐ 2 Dwayne"DJ" Johnson	1.00	.50	.10
☐ 3 Mandy Johnson	1.00	.50	.10
☐ 4 Vic Lazzaretti	1.00	.50	.10
☐ 5 Rick Majerus CO	2.00	1.00	.20
☐ 6 Marc Marotta	1.00	.50	.10
☐ 7 Lloyd Moore	1.00	.50	.10
☐ 8 Paul Newman	1.00	.50	.10
☐ 9 Tom Pipines	1.00	.50	.10
☐ 10 Hank Raymonds CO	1.50	.75	.15
☐ 11 Terry Reason	1.00	.50	.10
☐ 12 Glenn"Doc" Rivers	5.00	2.50	.50
☐ 13 Terrell Schlundt	1.50	.75	.15
☐ 14 Don Smolinski	1.00	.50	.10
☐ 15 Kerry Trotter	1.00	.50	.10
☐ xx Title Card	1.00	.50	.10

1988-89 Maryland Police

This set consists of 12 cards, measuring the standard card size
2 1/2" by 3 1/2". The company name of the sponsor, Group
Health Association, appears in the right corner on the front of
the card. The action color photo on the front is bordered on
three sides by Maryland's colors (red and yellow), with the

		MINT	EXC	G-VG
☐	1 Kevin Williams	1.00	.50	.10
☐	2 Terry Griggley	.50	.25	.05
☐	3 Tab Harris	.50	.25	.05
☐	4 Chandra Davis	.50	.25	.05
☐	5 Tom McGrath	.50	.25	.05
☐	6 Angie Perry	.50	.25	.05
☐	7 Christine Lee	.50	.25	.05
☐	8 Lawrence David	.50	.25	.05
☐	9 Michael Cutright	.75	.35	.07
☐	10 Anthony Pullard	1.50	.75	.15
☐	11 Mark Thompson	.50	.25	.05
☐	12 Kim Turner	.50	.25	.05
☐	13 Steve Boulet	.50	.25	.05
☐	14 Charlie Phillips	.50	.25	.05
☐	15 Mark Bowling	.50	.25	.05
☐	16 David J. Drez	.50	.25	.05
	Team Physician			

player's name, uniform number, classification, and position listed below the photo. The Terrapin logo in the lower left hand corner completes the front of the card. The back includes biographical information and a basketball tip.

	MINT	EXC	G-VG
COMPLETE SET (12)	9.00	4.50	.90
COMMON PLAYER (1-12)	.60	.30	.06

		MINT	EXC	G-VG
☐	1 Vincent Broadnax 40	.60	.30	.06
☐	2 Dave Dickerson 23	.60	.30	.06
☐	3 John Johnson 21	.60	.30	.06
☐	4 Matt Kaluzienski 13	.60	.30	.06
☐	5 Mitch Kasoff 5	.60	.30	.06
☐	6 Cedric Lewis 43	.60	.30	.06
☐	7 Jesse Martin 14	.60	.30	.06
☐	8 Todd Massenburg 25	1.25	.60	.12
☐	9 Jerrod Mustaf 32	2.00	1.00	.20
☐	10 Greg Nared 22	.60	.30	.06
☐	11 Bob Wade CO	.75	.35	.07
☐	12 Walt Williams 42	1.25	.60	.12

1989 McNeese State *

This 16-card set was sponsored by the Behavioral Health Unit of Lake Charles Memorial Hospital, and the sponsor's logo appears at the bottom of both sides of the card. The cards measure the standard size (2 1/2" by 3 1/2"); they were produced by McDag Productions. The front features a color posed player photo, with the McNeese logo and player information in the upper corners. The back presents biographical information and "Tips from The Cowboys," which consist of mental health tips. The cards are numbered on the back. Sports represented in this set include basketball (1-6, 9-12), softball (7), golf (8), and baseball (13-15).

	MINT	EXC	G-VG
COMPLETE SET (16)	7.50	3.75	.75
COMMON PLAYER (1-16)	.50	.25	.05

1988-89 Michigan Nike

This 16-card set was sponsored by Nike and distributed at Michigan Wolverine games during the 1988-89 season. The cards measure 2 1/2" by 3 1/2". The front features a color action photo, with a yellow border on the left side and purple borders on the right and below. The sponsor logo appears in the upper right corner, and player information is given in the bottom border. The back has biographical information and an anti-drug tip. The cards are unnumbered and are checklisted below in alphabetical order.

	MINT	EXC	G-VG
COMPLETE SET (16)	45.00	22.50	4.50
COMMON PLAYER (1-16)	2.00	1.00	.20

		MINT	EXC	G-VG
☐	1 Demetrius Calip	3.00	1.50	.30
☐	2 Bill Frieder CO	3.00	1.50	.30
☐	3 Mike Griffin	2.00	1.00	.20
☐	4 Sean Higgins	5.00	2.50	.50
☐	5 Mark Hughes	2.00	1.00	.20
☐	6 Marc Koenig	2.00	1.00	.20
☐	7 Terry Mills	5.00	2.50	.50
☐	8 J.P. Oosterbaan	2.00	1.00	.20
☐	9 Rob Pelinka	2.00	1.00	.20
☐	10 Glen Rice	9.00	4.50	.90
☐	11 Eric Riley	2.00	1.00	.20
☐	12 Rumeal Robinson	6.00	3.00	.60
☐	13 Chris Seter	2.00	1.00	.20
☐	14 Kirk Taylor	2.00	1.00	.20
☐	15 Loy Vaught	6.00	3.00	.60
☐	16 James Voskuil	2.00	1.00	.20

1989 Michigan Wolverines

This 17-card set measures approximately 2 3/8" by 4" and is numbered on the back. The set features members of the 1989 Michigan Wolverines championship basketball team. The front features a color photo, and the school and team name are

Loy Vaught #35
Center, 6-9, 225, Jr
Grand Rapids, MI (East Kentwood)
Outstanding shooter who played a very key role for the Wolverines in the 1988-89 championship season, starting over half of the team's 37 games and being one of the first players off of the bench in the others...third team All-Big Ten selection...was the Big Ten's leading field goal shooter with a 66.1% mark...that mark was good enough for second in the nation...led the team in rebounding, grabbing 8.0 rebounds per contest...was the third leading scorer on the team, netting 12.6 points per contest, led the team in rebounding in 18 games...had nine double-doubles, games in which he had double figures in points and rebounds...saved one of his biggest games for the semi-final victory over Illinois, in which he grabbed a career best 16 rebounds...also led the team in field goal shooting as a sophomore, hitting 62.1% of his shots...has a chance to become the school's all-time leading field goal shooter

UNIVERSITY OF MICHIGAN
Card 11 of 17

LOY VAUGHT

printed in the school's colors (purple and yellow) on the top of the card. Below the photo appears the team logo (lower left hand corner) and the player's name. The back has biographical information (black lettering on white card stock). Future NBA players Glen Rice, Rumeal Robinson, and Sean Higgins are featured in this set.

	MINT	EXC	G-VG
COMPLETE SET (17)	15.00	7.50	1.50
COMMON PLAYER (1-17)	1.00	.50	.10

		MINT	EXC	G-VG
☐	1 Steve Fisher CO	1.00	.50	.10
☐	2 Brian Dutcher	1.00	.50	.10
☐	3 Kirk Taylor	1.00	.50	.10
☐	4 Chris Seter	1.00	.50	.10
☐	5 Glen Rice	3.00	1.50	.30
☐	6 Rob Pelinka	1.00	.50	.10
☐	7 Rumeal Robinson	2.00	1.00	.20
☐	8 Terry Mills	2.00	1.00	.20
☐	9 Demetrius Calip	1.50	.75	.15
☐	10 James Voskuil	1.00	.50	.10
☐	11 Loy Vaught	2.00	1.00	.20
☐	12 J.P. Oosterbaan	1.00	.50	.10
☐	13 Sean Higgins	2.00	1.00	.20
☐	14 Marc Koenig	1.00	.50	.10
☐	15 Mark Hughes	1.00	.50	.10
☐	16 Eric Riley	1.00	.50	.10
☐	17 Mike Griffin	1.00	.50	.10

1991 Michigan 56 *

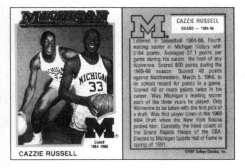

CAZZIE RUSSELL
GUARD — 1964-66

CAZZIE RUSSELL

Lettered in basketball 1964-66. Fourth leading scorer in Michigan history with 2,164 points. Averaged 27.1 points per game during his career, the best of any Wolverine. Scored 800 points during the 1965-66 season. Scored 48 points against Northwestern, March 5, 1966, to tie school record for points in a game. Scored 40 or more points twice in his career. Was Michigan's leading scorer each of the three years he played. Only Wolverine to be taken with the first pick of a draft. Was first player in the 1966 NBA Draft when the New York Knicks picked him. Currently the head coach of the Grand Rapids Hoops of the CBA. Elected to Michigan Sports Hall of Fame in spring of 1991.

©1991 College Classics, Inc.

This 56-card multi-sport set was issued by College Classics and measures the standard size 2 1/2" by 3 1/2". The fronts feature a mix of color or black and white player photos. The yellow borders (on white card stock) and blue lettering reflect the team's colors. In the cut-out corners appear a Michigan Wolverine football helmet (on the football cards) or an "M" (for other sports). The backs have a career summary in a light blue

box with orange borders, with an "M" in the upper left corner. This set features a card of Gerald Ford, center for the Wolverine football squad from 1932-34. Ford autographed 200 of his cards, one of which was to be included in each of the 200 cases of 50 sets. A letter of authenticity on Gerald Ford stationery accompanies each Ford autographed card. All 200 cases were reportedly purchased by American Card Investors. The cards are unnumbered and we have checklisted them below according to alphabetical order.

	MINT	EXC	G-VG
COMPLETE SET (56)	15.00	7.50	1.50
COMMON PLAYER (1-56)	.30	.15	.03

		MINT	EXC	G-VG
☐	1 Jim Abbott	1.00	.50	.10
☐	2 Moby Benedict	.30	.15	.03
☐	3 Red Berenson	.50	.25	.05
☐	4 John Blum	.30	.15	.03
☐	5 Marty Bodnar	.30	.15	.03
☐	6 Dave Brown	.50	.25	.05
☐	7 M.C. Burton	.30	.15	.03
☐	8 Andy Cannavino	.30	.15	.03
☐	9 Anthony Carter	.75	.35	.07
☐	10 Gil Chapman	.30	.15	.03
☐	11 Bob Chappuis	.30	.15	.03
☐	12 Casey Close	.50	.25	.05
☐	13 Evan Cooper	.30	.15	.03
☐	14 Tom Curtis	.30	.15	.03
☐	15 Diane Dietz	.30	.15	.03
☐	16 Dean Dingman	.30	.15	.03
☐	17 Mark Donahue	.30	.15	.03
☐	18 Donald Dufek	.50	.25	.05
☐	19 Bump Elliott	.50	.25	.05
☐	20 Greg Everson	.30	.15	.03
☐	21 Gerald Ford	1.00	.50	.10
☐	22 Wally Grant	.30	.15	.03
☐	23 Curtis Greer	.50	.25	.05
☐	24 Ali Haji-Sheikh	.50	.25	.05
☐	25 Elroy Hirsch	.75	.35	.07
☐	26 Stefan Humphries	.30	.15	.03
☐	27 Phil Hubbard	.50	.25	.05
☐	28 Ron Johnson	.50	.25	.05
☐	29 Brad Jones	.30	.15	.03
☐	30 Eric Kattus	.50	.25	.05
☐	31 Ron Kramer	.50	.25	.05
☐	32 Barry Larkin	1.00	.50	.10
☐	33 Michael Leach	.30	.15	.03
☐	34 Jim Mandich	.50	.25	.05
☐	35 Wilf Martin	.30	.15	.03
☐	36 Tim McCormick	.50	.25	.05
☐	37 Hal Morris	1.00	.50	.10
☐	38 Jeff Norton	.30	.15	.03
☐	39 Frank Nunley	.30	.15	.03
☐	40 Calvin O'Neal	.50	.25	.05
☐	41 Steve Ontiveros	.50	.25	.05
☐	42 Bennie Oosterbaan	.30	.15	.03
☐	43 Richard Rellford	.30	.15	.03
☐	44 Steve Richmond	.30	.15	.03
☐	45 Cazzie Russell	.75	.35	.07
☐	46 Chris Sabo	1.00	.50	.10
☐	47 Alicia Seegert	.30	.15	.03
☐	48 Warren Sharples	.30	.15	.03
☐	49 Ted Sizemore	.50	.25	.05
☐	50 Lary Sorensen	.50	.25	.05
☐	51 Bob Timberlake	.50	.25	.05
☐	52 Rudy Tomjanovich	.50	.25	.05
☐	53 John Wangler	.50	.25	.05
☐	54 Gary Wayne	.30	.15	.03
☐	55 Tripp Welborne	.30	.15	.03
☐	56 Wistert Brothers	.30	.15	.03

1990-91 Michigan State Promos *

This ten-card standard size (2 1/2" by 3 1/2") set features some of the great athletes from Michigan State History. Most of the cards in the set feature an action photograph on the front of the card along with either statistical or biographical information on the back of the card. Since this set involves more than one sport we have put a two-letter abbreviation to indicate the sport played.

	MINT	EXC	G-VG
COMPLETE SET (10)	5.00	2.50	.50
COMMON PLAYER (1-10)	.50	.25	.05

			MINT	EXC	G-VG
☐	1	Ron Scott HK	.50	.25	.05
☐	2	Steve Garvey BB	.75	.35	.07
☐	3	Percy Snow FB	.75	.35	.07
☐	4	Magic Johnson BK	1.00	.50	.10
☐	5	Andre Rison FB	.75	.35	.07
☐	6	Lorenzo White FB	.60	.30	.06
☐	7	Kirk Gibson FB/BB	.75	.35	.07
☐	8	Tony Mandarich FB	.60	.30	.06
☐	9	Gregory Kelser BK	.60	.30	.06
☐	10	Kip Miller HK	.60	.30	.06

1990-91 Michigan State 200 *

This 200-card set was produced by Collegiate Collection and measures the standard size (2 1/2" by 3 1/2"). The fronts feature black and white shots for earlier players or color shots for later players, with borders in the team's colors white and green. The card design gives the impression that all four corners of the pictures are cut off. In green lettering the school name appears above the picture, with the player's name at the bottom of the card face. In a horizontal format the back presents biographical information and career summary, on a white background with green lettering and borders. The cards are numbered on the back.

	MINT	EXC	G-VG
COMPLETE SET (200)	22.00	11.00	2.20
COMMON PLAYER (1-200)	.10	.05	.01

			MINT	EXC	G-VG
☐	1	Ray Stachowicvz	.10	.05	.01
☐	2	Larry Fowler	.10	.05	.01
☐	3	Allen Brenner	.10	.05	.01
☐	4	Greg Montgomery	.10	.05	.01
☐	5	Ron Goovert	.10	.05	.01
☐	6	Ed Bagdon	.10	.05	.01
☐	7	Carl(Buck) Nystrom	.10	.05	.01
☐	8	Earl Lattiner	.10	.05	.01
☐	9	Bob Kula	.10	.05	.01

			MINT	EXC	G-VG
☐	10	James Ellis	.10	.05	.01
☐	11	Brad Van Pelt	.20	.10	.02
☐	12	Andre Rison	.30	.15	.03
☐	13	Sherman Lewis	.20	.10	.02
☐	14	Eric Allen	.20	.10	.02
☐	15	Robert Apisa	.20	.10	.02
☐	16	Earl Morrall	.30	.15	.03
☐	17	Danny Litwhiler	.15	.07	.01
☐	18	Harold Lucas	.10	.05	.01
☐	19	Lorenzo White	.25	.12	.02
☐	20	Dorne Dibble	.15	.07	.01
☐	21	Ronald Saul	.15	.07	.01
☐	22	Ed Budde	.20	.10	.02
☐	23	Eugene Washington	.20	.10	.02
☐	24	John S. Pingel	.10	.05	.01
☐	25	Morten Andersen	.20	.10	.02
☐	26	Lynn Chandnois	.15	.07	.01
☐	27	Don Coleman	.10	.05	.01
☐	28	Dave Behrman	.15	.07	.01
☐	29	Bill Simpson	.15	.07	.01
☐	30	LeRoy Bolden	.10	.05	.01
☐	31	Lorenzo White	.25	.12	.02
☐	32	Sidney P. Wagner	.10	.05	.01
☐	33	Ellis Duckett	.10	.05	.01
☐	34	Dick Tamburo	.15	.07	.01
☐	35	Gerald Planutis	.10	.05	.01
☐	36	Steve Juday	.20	.10	.02
☐	37	Everett Grandelius	.15	.07	.01
☐	38	Spartans All American	.15	.07	.01
☐	39	Ray Stachowicz	.10	.05	.01
☐	40	Mark Brammer	.15	.07	.01
☐	41	James Burroughs	.15	.07	.01
☐	42	Harlon Barnett	.20	.10	.02
☐	43	Charles(Bubba) Smith	.50	.25	.05
☐	44	Percy Snow	.30	.15	.03
☐	45	Norman Masters	.10	.05	.01
☐	46	Jerry West	.10	.05	.01
☐	47	Williams and Daugherty	.15	.07	.01
☐	48	Tom Yewcic	.15	.07	.01
☐	49	Kirk Gibson	.25	.12	.02
☐	50	Clinton Jones	.20	.10	.02
☐	51	Frank E. Pellerin	.10	.05	.01
☐	52	Don(Zippy) Thompson	.10	.05	.01
☐	53	Kirk Gibson	.25	.12	.02
☐	54	Edward Erickson	.10	.05	.01
☐	55	Doug Roberts	.10	.05	.01
☐	56	Percy Snow	.30	.15	.03
☐	57	Dick Idzkowski	.10	.05	.01
☐	58	Robert W.(Bob) Carey	.15	.07	.01
☐	59	Clarence Munn	.15	.07	.01
☐	60	Dan Currie	.15	.07	.01
☐	61	Al Dorow	.15	.07	.01
☐	62	Amo Bessone	.10	.05	.01
☐	63	Joseph DeLamielleure	.20	.10	.02
☐	64	Tom Ross	.10	.05	.01
☐	65	Steve Preston	.10	.05	.01
☐	66	Gibson and Garvey	.25	.12	.02
☐	67	Eric Allen	.15	.07	.01
☐	68	George Smith	.10	.05	.01
☐	69	John Chandik	.10	.05	.01
☐	70	Cordell Ross	.10	.05	.01
☐	71	George Saimes	.20	.10	.02
☐	72	Walt Kowalczyk	.15	.07	.01
☐	73	Billy Joe Dupree	.25	.12	.02
☐	74	Phil Fulton	.10	.05	.01
☐	75	Weldon Olson	.10	.05	.01
☐	76	Kirk Gibson	.25	.12	.02
☐	77	Andre Rison	.25	.12	.02
☐	78	Dean Look	.15	.07	.01
☐	79	Hugh (Duffy) Daugherty	.15	.07	.01
☐	80	Don McAuliffe	.20	.10	.02
☐	81	Ronald Curl	.10	.05	.01
☐	82	Percy Snow	.30	.15	.03
☐	83	Carl Banks	.35	.17	.03
☐	84	Joe Selinger	.10	.05	.01
☐	85	Mel Behney	.15	.07	.01
☐	86	Lorenzo White	.25	.12	.02
☐	87	Ron Pruitt	.20	.10	.02
☐	88	George Webster	.20	.10	.02
☐	89	Tony Mandarich	.25	.12	.02
☐	90	Ray Stachowicz	.10	.05	.01
☐	91	Blake Miller	.10	.05	.01
☐	92	Dupree, Van Pelt, and Daugherty	.20	.10	.02
☐	93	Morten Andersen	.20	.10	.02
☐	94	Kevin Dalson	.10	.05	.01
☐	95	Norm Barnes	.10	.05	.01
☐	96	Andre Rison	.25	.12	.02
☐	97	Craig Simpson	.20	.10	.02
☐	98	Kirk Gibson	.25	.12	.02
☐	99	Ralph Mojsiejenko	.15	.07	.01
☐	100	Director Card 1-99	.10	.05	.01
☐	101	Michael Robinson	.10	.05	.01
☐	102	Jack Quiggle	.10	.05	.01

☐ 103	Robert Anderegg	.10	.05	.01
☐ 104	Rick Miller	.15	.07	.01
☐ 105	Steve Garvey	.30	.15	.03
☐ 106	John Herman Kobs	.10	.05	.01
☐ 107	Steve Garvey	.30	.15	.03
☐ 108	Vernon Carr	.10	.05	.01
☐ 109	Albert R. Ferrari	.10	.05	.01
☐ 110	Lance Olson	.10	.05	.01
☐ 111	Lee Lafayette	.10	.05	.01
☐ 112	Gregory Kelser	.15	.07	.01
☐ 113	Stan Washington	.10	.05	.01
☐ 114	Ron Perranoski	.20	.10	.02
☐ 115	Doug Volmar	.10	.05	.01
☐ 116	Robert Clancy	.10	.05	.01
☐ 117	Bob Boyd	.15	.07	.01
☐ 118	Lindsay Hairston	.15	.07	.01
☐ 119	Kevin Willis	.20	.10	.02
☐ 120	Bill Rapchak	.10	.05	.01
☐ 121	Marcus Sanders	.10	.05	.01
☐ 122	Mike Brkovich	.15	.07	.01
☐ 123	Jay Vincent	.15	.07	.01
☐ 124	Ron Scott	.15	.07	.01
☐ 125	Craig Simpson	.15	.07	.01
☐ 126	Mike Davidson	.10	.05	.01
☐ 127	Jim Watt	.10	.05	.01
☐ 128	Johnny Green	.15	.07	.01
☐ 129	Robert Chapman	.10	.05	.01
☐ 130	Pete Gent	.20	.10	.02
☐ 131	Magic Johnson	.50	.25	.05
☐ 132	Gregory Kelser	.20	.10	.02
☐ 133	Magic Johnson	.50	.25	.05
☐ 134	Bobby Reynolds	.10	.05	.01
☐ 135	Joe Murphy	.30	.15	.03
☐ 136	Mike Donnelly	.10	.05	.01
☐ 137	Bob Essensa	.20	.10	.02
☐ 138	Kevin Smith	.10	.05	.01
☐ 139	Kirk Manns	.10	.05	.01
☐ 140	Scott Skiles	.20	.10	.02
☐ 141	Matthew Aitch	.10	.05	.01
☐ 142	Rudy Benjamin	.10	.05	.01
☐ 143	Michael Robinson	.10	.05	.01
☐ 144	Kip Miller	.25	.12	.02
☐ 145	Kelly Miller	.20	.10	.02
☐ 146	Ron Mason	.15	.07	.01
☐ 147	Dan McFall	.10	.05	.01
☐ 148	Sam Vincent	.15	.07	.01
☐ 149	Carlton Valentine	.10	.05	.01
☐ 150	Ron Charles	.15	.07	.01
☐ 151	John Bennington	.10	.05	.01
☐ 152	Scott Skiles	.20	.10	.02
☐ 153	William Kilgore	.10	.05	.01
☐ 154	Dick Holmes	.10	.05	.01
☐ 155	Steven Colp	.10	.05	.01
☐ 156	Robert Ellis	.10	.05	.01
☐ 157	Brian Wolcott	.10	.05	.01
☐ 158	Ken Redfield	.10	.05	.01
☐ 159	Jud Heathcote	.15	.07	.01
☐ 160	Dave Fahs	.10	.05	.01
☐ 161	Pete Newell	.10	.05	.01
☐ 162	Larry Polec	.10	.05	.01
☐ 163	Kevin Willis	.15	.07	.01
☐ 164	Gaye Cooley	.10	.05	.01
☐ 165	Richard Vary	.10	.05	.01
☐ 166	Al Weston	.10	.05	.01
☐ 167	Scott Makarewicz	.10	.05	.01
☐ 168	Darryl Johnson	.15	.07	.01
☐ 169	Derek Perry	.10	.05	.01
☐ 170	Ralph Simpson	.20	.10	.02
☐ 171	Terry Furlow	.15	.07	.01
☐ 172	Forrest Anderson	.10	.05	.01
☐ 173	Ted Williams	.15	.07	.01
☐ 174	Dan Masteller	.10	.05	.01
☐ 175	Brad Lamont Jr.	.10	.05	.01
☐ 176	Steve Garvey	.30	.15	.03
☐ 177	Mike Eddington	.10	.05	.01
☐ 178	Jud Heathcote	.15	.07	.01
☐ 179	Kevin Willis	.15	.07	.01
☐ 180	Ben Van Alstyne	.10	.05	.01
☐ 181	Chet Aubuchon	.15	.07	.01
☐ 182	Magic Johnson	.50	.25	.05
☐ 183	Larry Hedden	.10	.05	.01
☐ 184	Larry Ike	.10	.05	.01
☐ 185	Frank Kush	.15	.07	.01
☐ 186	Magic Johnson	.50	.25	.05
☐ 187	Mitch Messier	.15	.07	.01
☐ 188	Julius McCoy	.10	.05	.01
☐ 189	Magic Johnson	.50	.25	.05
☐ 190	Forrest Anderson	.15	.07	.01
☐ 191	Gus Ganakas	.15	.07	.01
☐ 192	Jay Vincent	.15	.07	.01
☐ 193	Horace Walker	.10	.05	.01
☐ 194	Magic Johnson	.50	.25	.05
☐ 195	Tom Smith	.10	.05	.01
☐ 196	Don McSween	.10	.05	.01

☐ 197	Rod Brind'Amour	.30	.15	.03
☐ 198	Sam Vincent	.15	.07	.01
☐ 199	Terry Donnelly	.10	.05	.01
☐ 200	Director Card 101-199	.10	.05	.01

1988-89 Missouri

This 16-card set of Missouri Tigers was sponsored by Kodak, KMIZ-17 TV, and Columbia Photo. The cards measure the standard 2 1/2" by 3 1/2". The cards were originally issued in four-card sheets. The front features a color photo, with borders above and below in the school's colors (black and yellow). The player's name, uniform number, classification, and position appear below the picture, with a tiger pawprint in the lower left hand corner. Biographical information and "tips for better sports pictures" are provided on the card backs. The first three panels of cards were given out at games between Missouri and Oklahoma State (January 21), Nebraska (February 19), and Colorado. The final panel was available at Columbia Photo and Video sometime after March 4.

		MINT	EXC	G-VG
	COMPLETE SET (16)	20.00	10.00	2.00
	COMMON PLAYER (1-16)	1.00	.50	.10
☐ 1	Nathan Buntin	1.50	.75	.15
☐ 2	Derrick Chievous PRO	2.00	1.00	.20
☐ 3	Greg Church	1.00	.50	.10
☐ 4	Jamal Coleman	1.00	.50	.10
☐ 5	Jim Horton	1.00	.50	.10
☐ 6	Byron Irvin	2.00	1.00	.20
☐ 7	Gary Leonard	2.00	1.00	.20
☐ 8	John McIntyre	1.00	.50	.10
☐ 9	Anthony Peeler	2.00	1.00	.20
☐ 10	Mike Sandbothe	1.00	.50	.10
☐ 11	Doug Smith	6.00	3.00	.60
☐ 12	Norm Stewart CO	1.50	.75	.15
☐ 13	Steve Stipanovich	2.00	1.00	.20
☐ 14	Jon Sundvold PRO	2.00	1.00	.20
☐ 15	Bradd Sutton	1.00	.50	.10
☐ 16	Mike Wawrzyniak	1.00	.50	.10

1989-90 Missouri

This 16-card set was originally issued on three four-card sheets and sponsored by Kodak, Jiffy Lube, and Columbia Photo and Video. The cards measure the standard 2 1/2" by 3 1/2". The front has an action color photo, with borders in the school's colors (yellow and black). The player's name, classification, and position appear below the card, with a tiger pawprint in the lower left hand corner. The back has biographical information and a tip for better sports pictures.

	MINT	EXC	G-VG
COMPLETE SET (16)	20.00	10.00	2.00
COMMON PLAYER (1-16)	1.00	.50	.10
☐ 1 Nathan Buntin 22	1.50	.75	.15
☐ 2 John Burns 33	1.00	.50	.10
☐ 3 Jamal Coleman 32	1.00	.50	.10
☐ 4 Lee Coward 4	1.50	.75	.15
☐ 5 Larry Drew	2.00	1.00	.20
☐ 6 Travis Ford 5	1.50	.75	.15
☐ 7 Chris Heller 41	1.00	.50	.10
☐ 8 Jim Horton 13	1.00	.50	.10
☐ 9 John McIntyre 23	1.00	.50	.10
☐ 10 Anthony Peeler 44	2.00	1.00	.20
☐ 11 Todd Satalowich 54	1.00	.50	.10
☐ 12 Doug Smith 34	5.00	2.50	.50
☐ 13 Norm Stewart CO	1.50	.75	.15
☐ 14 Steve Stipanovich	2.00	1.00	.20
☐ 15 Bradd Sutton 35	1.00	.50	.10
☐ 16 Jeff Warren 45	1.00	.50	.10

1990-91 Nebraska Police *

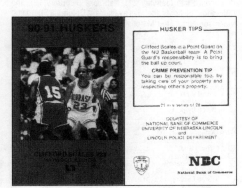

This 28-card set was sponsored by the National Bank of Commerce, the University of Nebraska-Lincoln, and the Lincoln Police Department. The cards measure approximately 2 1/2 by 4" and are printed on thin cardboard stock. The front features color action player photos against a red background. In black lettering the words "90-91 Huskers" appear over the picture, with the player's name and hometown given below. The back has "Husker Tips," which consists of a comment about the player and a crime prevention tip. Sponsors' logos at the bottom round out the back. The cards are numbered on the back. The sports represented in this set are football (2-13), volleyball (14-15), wrestling (16), gymnastics (17-20), basketball (21-24), softball (25, 27), and baseball (26, 28).

	MINT	EXC	G-VG
COMPLETE SET (28)	12.00	6.00	1.20
COMMON PLAYER (1-28)	.40	.20	.04
☐ 1 Bob Devaney ATH DIR	.60	.30	.06
☐ 2 Reggie Cooper	.40	.20	.04
☐ 3 Terry Rodgers	.40	.20	.04
☐ 4 Kenny Walker	1.25	.60	.12
☐ 5 Gregg Barrios	.40	.20	.04
☐ 6 Mike Croel	1.50	.75	.15
☐ 7 Tom Punt	.40	.20	.04
☐ 8 Mike Grant	.40	.20	.04
☐ 9 Joe Sims	.40	.20	.04
☐ 10 Mickey Joseph	.60	.30	.06
☐ 11 Lance Lewis	.40	.20	.04
☐ 12 Bruce Pickens	1.50	.75	.15
☐ 13 Nate Turner	.40	.20	.04
☐ 14 Linda Barsness	.40	.20	.04
☐ 15 Becky Bolli	.40	.20	.04
☐ 16 Jason Kelber	.40	.20	.04
☐ 17 Brad Bryan	.40	.20	.04
☐ 18 Ted Dimas	.40	.20	.04
☐ 19 Nita Lichtenstein	.40	.20	.04
☐ 20 Lisa McCrady	.40	.20	.04
☐ 21 Clifford Scales	.60	.30	.06
☐ 22 Ann Halsne	.40	.20	.04
☐ 23 Carl Hayes	.40	.20	.04
☐ 24 Kelly Hubert	.40	.20	.04
☐ 25 Deanna Mays	.40	.20	.04
☐ 26 Shawn Buchanan	.40	.20	.04
☐ 27 Michelle Cuddeford	.40	.20	.04
☐ 28 Eddie Anderson	.60	.30	.06

1986-87 North Carolina Police

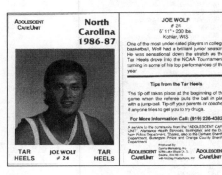

This 13-card set was sponsored by Adolescent CareUnit, Alamance Health Services, and various police departments. The cards measure the standard size (2 1/2" by 3 1/2"). The front features a posed color head-and-shoulders shot of the player on a white card face. In black lettering, the Adolescent Care Unit logo, the school name, and year appear above the picture. The player's name and number are given below, sandwiched between the team name. The back is printed in black on white card stock and presents biographical information and "Tips from the Tar Heels," which consist of anti-drug and alcohol messages. The cards are unnumbered and checklisted below by uniform number.

	MINT	EXC	G-VG
COMPLETE SET (13)	20.00	10.00	2.00
COMMON PLAYER	1.00	.50	.10
☐ 3 Jeff Denny	1.00	.50	.10
☐ 14 Jeff Lebo	2.00	1.00	.20
☐ 20 Steve Bucknall	2.00	1.00	.20
☐ 21 Michael Norwood	1.00	.50	.10
☐ 24 Joe Wolf	2.00	1.00	.20
☐ 30 Kenny Smith	3.00	1.50	.30
☐ 32 Pete Chilcutt	2.00	1.00	.20
☐ 33 Ranzino Smith	1.50	.75	.15
☐ 34 J.R. Reid	3.00	1.50	.30
☐ 35 Dave Popson	2.00	1.00	.20

		MINT	EXC	G-VG
☐ 42	Scott Williams	2.00	1.00	.20
☐ 43	Curtis Hunter	1.50	.75	.15
☐ 45	Marty Hensley	1.00	.50	.10

1987-88 North Carolina Police

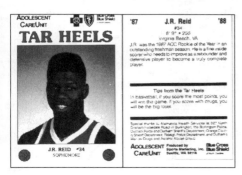

This 12-card set was sponsored by Adolescent CareUnit, Alamance Health Services, and various police departments. The cards measure the standard size (2 1/2" by 3 1/2"). The front features a posed color head-and-shoulders shot of the player on a white card face. In black lettering, the Adolescent CareUnit and Blue Cross/Blue Shield logos appear above the picture. In contrast to the previous year's issue, these cards have "Tar Heels" printed in large blue type above the picture. The player's name and number are given below, sandwiched between two blue basketballs. The back is printed in black on white card stock and presents biographical information and "Tips from the Tar Heels," which consist of anti-drug and alcohol messages. The cards are unnumbered and checklisted below by uniform number.

		MINT	EXC	G-VG
	COMPLETE SET (12)	16.00	8.00	1.60
	COMMON PLAYER	1.00	.50	.10
☐ 3	Jeff Denny	1.00	.50	.10
☐ 11	Rodney Hyatt	1.00	.50	.10
☐ 14	Jeff Lebo	1.50	.75	.15
☐ 20	Steve Bucknall	2.00	1.00	.20
☐ 21	King Rice	2.00	1.00	.20
☐ 22	Kevin Madden	2.00	1.00	.20
☐ 32	Pete Chilcutt	2.00	1.00	.20
☐ 33	Ranzino Smith	1.50	.75	.15
☐ 34	J.R. Reid	2.00	1.00	.20
☐ 42	Scott Williams	2.00	1.00	.20
☐ 44	Rick Fox	3.00	1.50	.30
☐ 45	Marty Hensley	1.00	.50	.10

1988-89 North Carolina Police

This 13-card set was sponsored by Adolescent CareUnit, Alamance Health Services, and local law enforcement agencies. The cards measure the standard size (2 1/2" by 3 1/2"). The front features a color action photo of the player, with black borders on a medium blue card face. In black lettering, the Adolescent CareUnit and Blue Cross/Blue Shield logos appear within the border above the picture. These cards have "Tar Heels" printed in large white type above the picture. The player's name and number are given below, with the letters "NC" superimposed over one another in the lower left corner. The back is printed in black on white card stock and presents biographical information and "Tips from the Tar Heels," which consist of anti-drug and

alcohol messages. The cards are unnumbered and checklisted below by uniform number. The Defense card is mysteriously listed on the back as '87 and '88 in the upper corners.

		MINT	EXC	G-VG
	COMPLETE SET (13)	12.00	6.00	1.20
	COMMON PLAYER	1.00	.50	.10
☐ 3	Jeff Denny	1.00	.50	.10
☐ 14	Jeff Lebo	1.50	.75	.15
☐ 20	Steve Bucknall	1.50	.75	.15
☐ 21	King Rice	1.50	.75	.15
☐ 22	Kevin Madden	1.50	.75	.15
☐ 32	Pete Chilcutt	1.50	.75	.15
☐ 42	Scott Williams	1.50	.75	.15
☐ 44	Rick Fox	2.00	1.00	.20
☐ 45	Marty Hensley	1.00	.50	.10
☐ xx	Dean Smith CO	1.50	.75	.15
☐ xx	Defense (Scott Williams and Jeff Lebo defending)	1.00	.50	.10
☐ xx	The Fast Break (King Rice dribbling)	1.00	.50	.10
☐ xx	A Fun Game (bench scene with Rick Fox and Scott Williams)	1.50	.75	.15

1989-90 North Carolina Coke

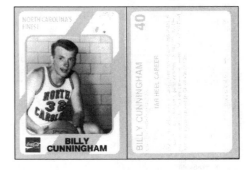

This 200-card set was produced by Collegiate Collection and sponsored by Coca-Cola, and the Coke logo appears in the lower left corner on the card face. The cards measure the standard size (2 1/2" by 3 1/2"). The fronts feature a mix of black and white photos for earlier players and color for later ones, with rounded corners and powder blue borders. The pictures are superimposed over a powder blue and white diagonally striped card face, with a powder blue outer border. The top reads "North Carolina's Finest," and the school logo appears in the upper right corner. The horizontally oriented backs are printed in powder blue on white and present biographical information, career summaries, or statistics. The cards are numbered on the back. The following numbers are found without the trademark notation, 18, 23, 25, 26, 50-54, 59, 66, 67, 74, 75, 111, 142, 174, 177, 187, 188, 192, 194, 195, and 197.

	MINT	EXC	G-VG
COMPLETE SET (200)	20.00	10.00	2.00
COMMON PLAYER (1-200)	.07	.03	.01

		MINT	EXC	G-VG
☐ 1	Dean Smith	.15	.07	.01
☐ 2	Dean Smith	.15	.07	.01
☐ 3	Dean Smith	.15	.07	.01
☐ 4	Dean Smith	.15	.07	.01
☐ 5	Dean Smith	.15	.07	.01
☐ 6	Dean Smith	.15	.07	.01
☐ 7	Phil Ford	.15	.07	.01
☐ 8	Phil Ford	.15	.07	.01
☐ 9	Phil Ford	.15	.07	.01
☐ 10	Phil Ford	.15	.07	.01
☐ 11	Phil Ford	.15	.07	.01
☐ 12	Phil Ford	.15	.07	.01
☐ 13	Michael Jordan	1.00	.50	.10
☐ 14	Michael Jordan	1.00	.50	.10
☐ 15	Michael Jordan	1.00	.50	.10
☐ 16	Michael Jordan	1.00	.50	.10
☐ 17	Michael Jordan	1.00	.50	.10
☐ 18	Michael Jordan	1.00	.50	.10
☐ 19	James Worthy	.25	.12	.02
☐ 20	James Worthy	.25	.12	.02
☐ 21	James Worthy	.25	.12	.02
☐ 22	James Worthy	.25	.12	.02
☐ 23	James Worthy	.25	.12	.02
☐ 24	Larry Miller	.10	.05	.01
☐ 25	Larry Miller	.10	.05	.01
☐ 26	Larry Miller	.10	.05	.01
☐ 27	Larry Miller	.10	.05	.01
☐ 28	Charlie Scott	.15	.07	.01
☐ 29	Charlie Scott	.15	.07	.01
☐ 30	Charlie Scott	.15	.07	.01
☐ 31	Charlie Scott	.15	.07	.01
☐ 32	Sam Perkins	.20	.10	.02
☐ 33	Sam Perkins	.20	.10	.02
☐ 34	Sam Perkins	.20	.10	.02
☐ 35	Sam Perkins	.20	.10	.02
☐ 36	Sam Perkins	.20	.10	.02
☐ 37	Billy Cunningham	.15	.07	.01
☐ 38	Billy Cunningham	.15	.07	.01
☐ 39	Billy Cunningham	.15	.07	.01
☐ 40	Billy Cunningham	.15	.07	.01
☐ 41	Lennie Rosenbluth	.10	.05	.01
☐ 42	Lennie Rosenbluth	.10	.05	.01
☐ 43	Lennie Rosenbluth	.10	.05	.01
☐ 44	Bobby Jones	.15	.07	.01
☐ 45	Bobby Jones	.15	.07	.01
☐ 46	Bobby Jones	.15	.07	.01
☐ 47	Mitch Kupchak	.10	.05	.01
☐ 48	Mitch Kupchak	.10	.05	.01
☐ 49	Mitch Kupchak	.10	.05	.01
☐ 50	1980-81 Tar Heels	.07	.03	.01
☐ 51	Walter Davis	.15	.07	.01
☐ 52	Walter Davis	.15	.07	.01
☐ 53	Walter Davis	.15	.07	.01
☐ 54	Walter Davis	.15	.07	.01
☐ 55	Mike O'Koren	.10	.05	.01
☐ 56	Mike O'Koren	.10	.05	.01
☐ 57	Mike O'Koren	.10	.05	.01
☐ 58	Mike O'Koren	.10	.05	.01
☐ 59	The Huddle	.07	.03	.01
☐ 60	Larry Brown	.10	.05	.01
☐ 61	Billy Cunningham	.15	.07	.01
☐ 62	Matt Doherty	.10	.05	.01
☐ 63	Phil Ford	.15	.07	.01
☐ 64	Doug Moe	.15	.07	.01
☐ 65	Michael Jordan	1.00	.50	.10
☐ 66	Kenny Smith	.15	.07	.01
☐ 67	Kenny Smith	.15	.07	.01
☐ 68	Kenny Smith	.15	.07	.01
☐ 69	Bob Lewis	.07	.03	.01
☐ 70	Bob Lewis	.07	.03	.01
☐ 71	Bob Lewis	.07	.03	.01
☐ 72	Charlie Scott	.15	.07	.01
☐ 73	Sam Perkins	.20	.10	.02
☐ 74	Doug Moe	.15	.07	.01
☐ 75	Doug Moe	.15	.07	.01
☐ 76	Robert McAdoo	.20	.10	.02
☐ 77	Robert McAdoo	.20	.10	.02
☐ 78	Pete Brennan	.07	.03	.01
☐ 79	Pete Brennan	.07	.03	.01
☐ 80	J.R. Reid	.20	.10	.02
☐ 81	J.R. Reid	.20	.10	.02
☐ 82	J.R. Reid	.20	.10	.02
☐ 83	Tommy Kearns	.07	.03	.01
☐ 84	Tommy Kearns	.07	.03	.01
☐ 85	John Dillon	.07	.03	.01
☐ 86	The Smith Center	.07	.03	.01
☐ 87	Dick Grubar	.07	.03	.01
☐ 88	Dick Grubar	.07	.03	.01
☐ 89	Rusty Clark	.10	.05	.01
☐ 90	Rusty Clark	.10	.05	.01
☐ 91	Bill Bunting	.10	.05	.01
☐ 92	Bill Bunting	.10	.05	.01
☐ 93	Jimmy Black	.10	.05	.01
☐ 94	Jimmy Black	.10	.05	.01
☐ 95	5 Tournament Titles	.07	.03	.01
☐ 96	UNC Cheerleaders	.07	.03	.01
☐ 97	Bobby Jones	.15	.07	.01
☐ 98	J.R. Reid	.20	.10	.02
☐ 99	Frank McGuire	.10	.05	.01
☐ 100	1957 NCAA Champions	.07	.03	.01
☐ 101	Bill Guthridge	.07	.03	.01
☐ 102	York Larese	.15	.07	.01
☐ 103	York Larese	.15	.07	.01
☐ 104	Frank McGuire	.15	.07	.01
☐ 105	Bones McKinney	.10	.05	.01
☐ 106	Larry Miller	.10	.05	.01
☐ 107	Kenny Smith	.15	.07	.01
☐ 108	Steve Previs	.07	.03	.01
☐ 109	Steve Previs	.07	.03	.01
☐ 110	Larry Brown	.15	.07	.01
☐ 111	Larry Brown	.15	.07	.01
☐ 112	Eddie Fogler	.15	.07	.01
☐ 113	Eddie Fogler	.15	.07	.01
☐ 114	James Worthy	.25	.12	.02
☐ 115	Robert McAdoo	.20	.10	.02
☐ 116	UNC Basketball	.07	.03	.01
☐ 117	UNC Basketball	.07	.03	.01
☐ 118	Cartwright Carmichael	.07	.03	.01
☐ 119	Steve Hale	.07	.03	.01
☐ 120	Steve Hale	.07	.03	.01
☐ 121	Joe Quigg	.07	.03	.01
☐ 122	Joe Quigg	.07	.03	.01
☐ 123	Bob Cunningham	.07	.03	.01
☐ 124	Bob Cunningham	.07	.03	.01
☐ 125	Jim Delany	.07	.03	.01
☐ 126	Bones McKinney	.10	.05	.01
☐ 127	Jerry Vayda	.07	.03	.01
☐ 128	Matt Doherty	.10	.05	.01
☐ 129	Matt Doherty	.10	.05	.01
☐ 130	Bob Paxton	.10	.05	.01
☐ 131	Dave Chadwick	.07	.03	.01
☐ 132	Dave Hanners	.07	.03	.01
☐ 133	Jim Jordan	.07	.03	.01
☐ 134	Jeff Lebo	.10	.05	.01
☐ 135	Jeff Lebo	.10	.05	.01
☐ 136	Lee Shaffer	.07	.03	.01
☐ 137	Lee Shaffer	.07	.03	.01
☐ 138	Joe Wolf	.10	.05	.01
☐ 139	Joe Wolf	.10	.05	.01
☐ 140	Warren Martin	.07	.03	.01
☐ 141	Warren Martin	.07	.03	.01
☐ 142	Carmichael Aud.	.07	.03	.01
☐ 143	Jim Hudock	.07	.03	.01
☐ 144	Darrell Elston	.07	.03	.01
☐ 145	Brad Hoffman	.07	.03	.01
☐ 146	Harvey Salz	.07	.03	.01
☐ 147	Dave Colescott	.07	.03	.01
☐ 148	Ed Stahl	.07	.03	.01
☐ 149	Joe Brown	.07	.03	.01
☐ 150	Gerald Tuttle	.07	.03	.01
☐ 151	Richard Tuttle	.07	.03	.01
☐ 152	Tony Radovich	.07	.03	.01
☐ 153	Dave Popson	.10	.05	.01
☐ 154	Donnie Walsh	.07	.03	.01
☐ 155	Rich Yonakor	.10	.05	.01
☐ 156	Jeff Wolf	.10	.05	.01
☐ 157	Pete Budko	.10	.05	.01
☐ 158	Randy Wiel	.07	.03	.01
☐ 159	Tom Gauntlett	.07	.03	.01
☐ 160	Mike Pepper	.07	.03	.01
☐ 161	Jim Braddock	.07	.03	.01
☐ 162	Yogi Poteet	.10	.05	.01
☐ 163	Charlie Shaffer	.07	.03	.01
☐ 164	Lee Dedmon	.07	.03	.01
☐ 165	Bob Bennett	.07	.03	.01
☐ 166	Ray Hite	.07	.03	.01
☐ 167	Tom Zaliagiris	.07	.03	.01
☐ 168	Kim Huband	.07	.03	.01
☐ 169	Ranzino Smith	.10	.05	.01
☐ 170	Donn Johnson	.07	.03	.01
☐ 171	Dale Gipple	.07	.03	.01
☐ 172	Curtis Hunter	.10	.05	.01
☐ 173	John Yokley	.07	.03	.01
☐ 174	Bryan McSweeney	.07	.03	.01
☐ 175	John O'Donnell	.07	.03	.01

☐ 176	Hugh Donahue	.07	.03	.01
☐ 177	1968-69 Tar Heels	.07	.03	.01
☐ 178	Bruce Buckley	.07	.03	.01
☐ 179	Ray Respess	.07	.03	.01
☐ 180	Buzz Peterson	.10	.05	.01
☐ 181	Mike Cooke	.07	.03	.01
☐ 182	Mickey Bell	.07	.03	.01
☐ 183	John Virgil	.07	.03	.01
☐ 184	Charles Waddell	.07	.03	.01
☐ 185	Mark Mirken	.07	.03	.01
☐ 186	Ralph Fletcher	.07	.03	.01
☐ 187	1971-72 ACC Champs	.07	.03	.01
☐ 188	Ged Doughton	.07	.03	.01
☐ 189	Bill Chambers	.07	.03	.01
☐ 190	Billy Chambers	.07	.03	.01
☐ 191	James Daye	.07	.03	.01
☐ 192	Jeb Barlow	.07	.03	.01
☐ 193	Chris Brust	.07	.03	.01
☐ 194	Eric Kenny	.07	.03	.01
☐ 195	1970-71 NIT Champs	.07	.03	.01
☐ 196	Don Eggleston	.07	.03	.01
☐ 197	Ricky Webb	.07	.03	.01
☐ 198	Jim Frye	.07	.03	.01
☐ 199	Timo Makkonen	.07	.03	.01
☐ 200	1982 NCAA Champions	.07	.03	.01

1990-91 North Carolina Promos *

This ten-card set features various sports stars of North Carolina from recent years. Since this set features athletes from more than one sport we have put a two letter abbreviation next to the player's name which identifies the sport he plays. This set includes a Michael Jordan card. All the cards in the set feature full-color photos of the athletes on the front along with either a biography or statistics of the players pictured on the card.

	MINT	EXC	G-VG
COMPLETE SET (10)	5.00	2.50	.50
COMMON PLAYER (1-10)	.50	.25	.05

☐ NC1	Michael Jordan BK	1.50	.75	.15
☐ NC2	Ethan Horton FB	.60	.30	.06
☐ NC3	Steve Hale BK	.50	.25	.05
☐ NC4	Mark Maye FB	.50	.25	.05
☐ NC5	Matt Doherty BK	.50	.25	.05
☐ NC6	Tyrone Anthony FB	.50	.25	.05
☐ NC7	Sam Perkins BK	.75	.35	.07
☐ NC8	Kelvin Bryant FB	.75	.35	.07
☐ NC9	Kenny Smith BK	.60	.30	.06
☐ NC10	Kenan Stadium	.50	.25	.05

1990-91 North Carolina 200 *

This 200-card set was produced by Collegiate Collection and measures the standard size (2 1/2" by 3 1/2"). The front features a mix of black and white or color player photos, on a light blue background with a powder blue outer border. All four corners of the picture are cut off. In black lettering the school name

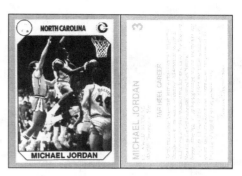

appears above the picture, with the player's name at the bottom of the card face. In a horizontal format the back presents biographical information, career summary, and statistics, on a white background with powder blue borders. The cards are numbered on the back.

	MINT	EXC	G-VG
COMPLETE SET (200)	20.00	10.00	2.00
COMMON PLAYER (1-200)	.07	.03	.01

☐ 1	Dean Smith CO	.15	.07	.01
☐ 2	John Swofford	.07	.03	.01
☐ 3	Michael Jordan	1.00	.50	.10
☐ 4	Lawrence Taylor	.50	.25	.05
☐ 5	James Worthy	.25	.12	.02
☐ 6	Kelvin Bryant	.15	.07	.01
☐ 7	Phil Ford	.15	.07	.01
☐ 8	Chris Hanburger	.15	.07	.01
☐ 9	Walter Davis	.15	.07	.01
☐ 10	Ethan Horton	.15	.07	.01
☐ 11	J.R. Reid	.15	.07	.01
☐ 12	Rod Elkins	.10	.05	.01
☐ 13	Buzz Peterson	.10	.05	.01
☐ 14	Darrell Nicholson	.07	.03	.01
☐ 15	Mark Maye	.10	.05	.01
☐ 16	Kenny Smith	.15	.07	.01
☐ 17	Matt Kupec	.10	.05	.01
☐ 18	Dave Popson	.10	.05	.01
☐ 19	Matt Doherty	.10	.05	.01
☐ 20	Buddy Curry	.07	.03	.01
☐ 21	Donnell Thompson	.10	.05	.01
☐ 22	Sam Perkins	.15	.07	.01
☐ 23	Mack Brown	.15	.07	.01
☐ 24	Ranzino Smith	.10	.05	.01
☐ 25	Curtis Hunter	.10	.05	.01
☐ 26	Doug Paschal	.07	.03	.01
☐ 27	Dean Smith	.15	.07	.01
☐ 28	Steve Streater	.10	.05	.01
☐ 29	David Drechsler	.07	.03	.01
☐ 30	Jimmy Black	.07	.03	.01
☐ 31	Kelvin Bryant	.15	.07	.01
☐ 32	Steve Hale	.07	.03	.01
☐ 33	Kenny Smith	.15	.07	.01
☐ 34	Tim Goad	.07	.03	.01
☐ 35	Harris Barton	.10	.05	.01
☐ 36	Jeff Lebo	.10	.05	.01
☐ 37	Rick Donnalley	.10	.05	.01
☐ 38	Don McCauley	.10	.05	.01
☐ 39	Sam Perkins	.15	.07	.01
☐ 40	Bill Paschall	.07	.03	.01
☐ 41	Scott Stankavage	.10	.05	.01
☐ 42	Joe Wolf	.10	.05	.01
☐ 43	Rueben Davis	.10	.05	.01
☐ 44	Michael Jordan	1.00	.50	.10
☐ 45	Jeff Garnica	.07	.03	.01
☐ 46	Kevin Anthony	.07	.03	.01
☐ 47	Eddie Fogler CO	.10	.05	.01
☐ 48	Warren Martin	.07	.03	.01
☐ 49	Buddy Curry	.07	.03	.01
☐ 50	Jim Braddock	.07	.03	.01
☐ 51	Matt Kupec	.07	.03	.01
☐ 52	Dean Smith CO	.15	.07	.01
☐ 53	Danny Talbott	.07	.03	.01
☐ 54	Sam Perkins	.15	.07	.01
☐ 55	Randy Weil	.07	.03	.01
☐ 56	Mike Chatham	.07	.03	.01
☐ 57	Jimmy Black	.07	.03	.01
☐ 58	Harris Barton	.10	.05	.01
☐ 59	David Popson	.10	.05	.01
☐ 60	Tom Biddle	.07	.03	.01

☐ 61	Michael Jordan	1.00	.50	.10
☐ 62	Ron Wooten	.07	.03	.01
☐ 63	J.R. Reid	.15	.07	.01
☐ 64	Lawrence Taylor	.50	.25	.05
☐ 65	Matt Doherty	.10	.05	.01
☐ 66	Alan Caldwell	.07	.03	.01
☐ 67	Warren Martin	.07	.03	.01
☐ 68	Tyrone Anthony	.07	.03	.01
☐ 69	Brook Barwick	.07	.03	.01
☐ 70	Steve Hale	.07	.03	.01
☐ 71	Mike Salzano	.07	.03	.01
☐ 72	Kelvin Bryant	.15	.07	.01
☐ 73	Ken Willard	.15	.07	.01
☐ 74	Jeff Lebo	.10	.05	.01
☐ 75	Kenny Smith	.15	.07	.01
☐ 76	Ramses	.07	.03	.01
☐ 77	Mike Voight	.07	.03	.01
☐ 78	James Worthy	.20	.10	.02
☐ 79	Joe Wolf	.10	.05	.01
☐ 80	Ethan Horton	.10	.05	.01
☐ 81	Ricky Barden	.10	.05	.01
☐ 82	Steve Hale	.07	.03	.01
☐ 83	Joe Wolf	.10	.05	.01
☐ 84	Bob Loomis	.07	.03	.01
☐ 85	Kenan Stadium	.07	.03	.01
☐ 86	Lawrence Taylor	.50	.25	.05
☐ 87	Sam Perkins	.20	.10	.02
☐ 88	Ron Wooten	.07	.03	.01
☐ 89	Michael Jordan	1.00	.50	.10
☐ 90	Tom Guanlett	.07	.03	.01
☐ 91	Tyrone Anthony	.07	.03	.01
☐ 92	Mark Maye	.07	.03	.01
☐ 93	Michael Jordan	1.00	.50	.10
☐ 94	Kenny Smith	.15	.07	.01
☐ 95	David Drechsler	.07	.03	.01
☐ 96	York Larese	.15	.07	.01
☐ 97	Joe Quigg	.07	.03	.01
☐ 98	Lennie Rosenbluth	.10	.05	.01
☐ 99	Pete Brennan	.07	.03	.01
☐ 100	Director Card 1-99	.07	.03	.01
☐ 101	Chris Kupec	.07	.03	.01
☐ 102	Moyer Smith	.07	.03	.01
☐ 103	Brad Hoffman	.07	.03	.01
☐ 104	James Worthy	.20	.10	.02
☐ 105	Hosea Rodgers	.07	.03	.01
☐ 106	Johnny Swofford	.07	.03	.01
☐ 107	Charlie Justice	.20	.10	.02
☐ 108	Mitch Kupchak	.15	.07	.01
☐ 109	Steve Previs	.07	.03	.01
☐ 110	Jimmy DeRatt	.07	.03	.01
☐ 111	Phil Ford	.15	.07	.01
☐ 112	Chris Kupec	.07	.03	.01
☐ 113	Lou Angelo	.07	.03	.01
☐ 114	John Bunting	.07	.03	.01
☐ 115	Dick Grubar	.07	.03	.01
☐ 116	Gerald Tuttle	.07	.03	.01
☐ 117	Bill Guthridge CO	.07	.03	.01
☐ 118	Junior Edge	.07	.03	.01
☐ 119	Art Weiner	.07	.03	.01
☐ 120	Dave Hanners CO	.07	.03	.01
☐ 121	George Barclay	.07	.03	.01
☐ 122	Joe Brown	.07	.03	.01
☐ 123	Mitch Kupchak	.15	.07	.01
☐ 124	Ken Powell	.07	.03	.01
☐ 125	Larry Miller	.10	.05	.01
☐ 126	Jerry Sain	.07	.03	.01
☐ 127	Don McCauley	.10	.05	.01
☐ 128	Bobby Jones	.15	.07	.01
☐ 129	Jimmy Jerome	.07	.03	.01
☐ 130	Larry Miller	.10	.05	.01
☐ 131	Ronny Johnson	.07	.03	.01
☐ 132	Ron Rusnak	.07	.03	.01
☐ 133	Charlie Scott	.15	.07	.01
☐ 134	Pete Budko	.10	.05	.01
☐ 135	Robert Pratt	.07	.03	.01
☐ 136	Bill Bunting	.10	.05	.01
☐ 137	Al Goldstein	.07	.03	.01
☐ 138	Charlie Carr	.07	.03	.01
☐ 139	Charlie Scott	.15	.07	.01
☐ 140	Ken Huff	.10	.05	.01
☐ 141	Don McCauley	.10	.05	.01
☐ 142	Dave Colescott	.07	.03	.01
☐ 143	Charlie Justice	.20	.10	.02
☐ 144	Ernie Williamson	.07	.03	.01
☐ 145	Dave Chadwick	.07	.03	.01
☐ 146	Rick Yonaker	.10	.05	.01
☐ 147	George Karl	.10	.05	.01
☐ 148	Ken Willard	.15	.07	.01
☐ 149	Phil Blazer	.07	.03	.01
☐ 150	Dean Smith CO	.15	.07	.01
☐ 151	Carl Snavely	.07	.03	.01
☐ 152	James Worthy	.20	.10	.02
☐ 153	Ron Rusnak	.07	.03	.01
☐ 154	Mike O'Koren	.10	.05	.01

☐ 155	Lewis and Miller	.10	.05	.01
☐ 156	Gene Brown	.07	.03	.01
☐ 157	Ed Stahl	.07	.03	.01
☐ 158	Rusty Clark	.10	.05	.01
☐ 159	Joe Robinson	.07	.03	.01
☐ 160	Gayle Bomar	.07	.03	.01
☐ 161	Bob Lewis	.07	.03	.01
☐ 162	Jim Delaney	.07	.03	.01
☐ 163	Paul Hoolahan	.07	.03	.01
☐ 164	Rod Broadway	.07	.03	.01
☐ 165	Darrell Elston	.07	.03	.01
☐ 166	Mickey Bell	.07	.03	.01
☐ 167	Ray Farris	.07	.03	.01
☐ 168	Charlie Justice	.20	.10	.02
☐ 169	Buddy Payne	.07	.03	.01
☐ 170	Lee Shaffer	.07	.03	.01
☐ 171	Mike Voight	.07	.03	.01
☐ 172	Kim Huband	.07	.03	.01
☐ 173	Dean Smith CO	.15	.07	.01
☐ 174	Charlie Justice	.20	.10	.02
☐ 175	George Karl	.10	.05	.01
☐ 176	Ed Sutton	.10	.05	.01
☐ 177	Ken Craven	.07	.03	.01
☐ 178	Jeff Wolf	.07	.03	.01
☐ 179	Tom Zaliagiris	.07	.03	.01
☐ 180	Charles Waddell	.07	.03	.01
☐ 181	Lee Demond	.07	.03	.01
☐ 182	Irv Holdash	.07	.03	.01
☐ 183	Jack Cummings	.07	.03	.01
☐ 184	Bob Lewis	.07	.03	.01
☐ 185	Phil Ford	.15	.07	.01
☐ 186	Bobby Lacey	.07	.03	.01
☐ 187	Larry Brown	.15	.07	.01
☐ 188	Larry Voight	.07	.03	.01
☐ 189	Mike O'Koren	.10	.05	.01
☐ 190	Crowell Little	.07	.03	.01
☐ 191	Paul Miller	.07	.03	.01
☐ 192	Tommy Kearns	.07	.03	.01
☐ 193	Frank McGuire CO	.10	.05	.01
☐ 194	Sammy Johnson	.07	.03	.01
☐ 195	Carmichael Auditorium	.07	.03	.01
☐ 196	Nick Vidnovic	.07	.03	.01
☐ 197	Paul Severin	.07	.03	.01
☐ 198	Don Walsh	.07	.03	.01
☐ 199	Smith Center	.07	.03	.01
☐ 200	Director Card 101-199	.07	.03	.01

1989 North Carolina State Coke

This 200-card set was produced by Collegiate Collection and sponsored by Coca-Cola, and the Coke logo appears in the lower left corner on the card face. The cards measure the standard size (2 1/2" by 3 1/2"). The fronts feature a mix of black and white photos for earlier players and color for later ones, with rounded corners and red borders. The pictures are superimposed over a red and white diagonally-striped card face, with a red outer border. The top reads "N.C. State's Finest," and the school logo appears in the upper right corner. The horizontally oriented backs are printed in red on white and present biographical information, career summaries, or statistics. The cards are numbered on the back.

		MINT	EXC	G-VG
COMPLETE SET (200)		16.00	8.00	1.60
COMMON PLAYER (1-200)		.07	.03	.01
☐ 1	Rick Anheuser	.07	.03	.01
☐ 2	Rick Anheuser	.07	.03	.01
☐ 3	Rick Anheuser	.07	.03	.01
☐ 4	Pete Auksel	.07	.03	.01
☐ 5	Pete Auksel	.07	.03	.01
☐ 6	Pete Auksel	.07	.03	.01
☐ 7	Clyde Austin	.10	.05	.01
☐ 8	Clyde Austin	.10	.05	.01
☐ 9	Clyde Austin	.10	.05	.01
☐ 10	Thurl Bailey	.15	.07	.01
☐ 11	Thurl Bailey	.15	.07	.01
☐ 12	Thurl Bailey	.15	.07	.01
☐ 13	Eddie Bartels	.07	.03	.01
☐ 14	Eddie Bartels	.07	.03	.01
☐ 15	Eddie Bartels	.07	.03	.01
☐ 16	Alvin Battle	.07	.03	.01
☐ 17	Alvin Battle	.07	.03	.01
☐ 18	Alvin Battle	.07	.03	.01
☐ 19	William Bell	.07	.03	.01
☐ 20	William Bell	.07	.03	.01
☐ 21	Eddie Bierderbach	.07	.03	.01
☐ 22	Eddie Bierderbach	.07	.03	.01
☐ 23	Eddie Bierderbach	.07	.03	.01
☐ 24	Dick Braucher	.07	.03	.01
☐ 25	Dick Braucher	.07	.03	.01
☐ 26	Dick Braucher	.07	.03	.01
☐ 27	Chuck Brown	.10	.05	.01
☐ 28	Chuck Brown	.10	.05	.01
☐ 29	Chuck Brown	.10	.05	.01
☐ 30	Vic Bubas	.10	.05	.01
☐ 31	Vic Bubas	.10	.05	.01
☐ 32	Tom Burleson	.15	.07	.01
☐ 33	Tom Burleson	.15	.07	.01
☐ 34	Tom Burleson	.15	.07	.01
☐ 35	Charles Shackleford	.10	.05	.01
☐ 36	Charles Shackleford	.10	.05	.01
☐ 37	Charles Shackleford	.10	.05	.01
☐ 38	Terry Shackleford	.07	.03	.01
☐ 39	Ronnie Shavik	.07	.03	.01
☐ 40	Ronnie Shavik	.07	.03	.01
☐ 41	Ronnie Shavik	.07	.03	.01
☐ 42	Jon Garwood Speaks	.07	.03	.01
☐ 43	Jon Garwood Speaks	.07	.03	.01
☐ 44	Jon Garwood Speaks	.07	.03	.01
☐ 45	Craig Watts	.07	.03	.01
☐ 46	Phil Spence	.07	.03	.01
☐ 47	Phil Spence	.07	.03	.01
☐ 48	Phil Spence	.07	.03	.01
☐ 49	Tim Stoddard	.10	.05	.01
☐ 50	Tim Stoddard	.10	.05	.01
☐ 51	Tim Stoddard	.10	.05	.01
☐ 52	Glenn Joseph Sudhop	.07	.03	.01
☐ 53	Glenn Joseph Sudhop	.07	.03	.01
☐ 54	Glenn Joseph Sudhop	.07	.03	.01
☐ 55	Joe Cafferky	.07	.03	.01
☐ 56	Joe Cafferky	.07	.03	.01
☐ 57	Larry Wosley	.07	.03	.01
☐ 58	Kenny Carr	.10	.05	.01
☐ 59	Kenny Carr	.10	.05	.01
☐ 60	Kenny Carr	.10	.05	.01
☐ 61	Horace McKinney	.10	.05	.01
☐ 62	John Richter	.07	.03	.01
☐ 63	Warren Cartier	.07	.03	.01
☐ 64	Paul Coder	.07	.03	.01
☐ 65	Paul Coder	.07	.03	.01
☐ 66	Paul Coder	.07	.03	.01
☐ 67	Bill Kretzer	.07	.03	.01
☐ 68	Darnell Adell	.07	.03	.01
☐ 69	Gary Stokan	.07	.03	.01
☐ 70	Pete Coker	.07	.03	.01
☐ 71	Dereck Whittenburg	.10	.05	.01
☐ 72	Pete Coker	.07	.03	.01
☐ 73	Craig Davis	.07	.03	.01
☐ 74	Smedes York	.07	.03	.01
☐ 75	Craig Davis	.07	.03	.01
☐ 76	Dick Dickey	.07	.03	.01
☐ 77	Dick Dickey	.07	.03	.01
☐ 78	Dick Dickey	.07	.03	.01
☐ 79	Tommy Dinardo	.07	.03	.01
☐ 80	Tommy Dinardo	.07	.03	.01
☐ 81	Van Williford	.07	.03	.01
☐ 82	Bob Distefano	.07	.03	.01
☐ 83	Dan Englehardt	.07	.03	.01
☐ 84	Dan Englehardt	.07	.03	.01
☐ 85	Gary Stokan	.07	.03	.01
☐ 86	Smedes York	.07	.03	.01
☐ 87	Van Willingford	.07	.03	.01
☐ 88	Vinny Del Negro	.10	.05	.01
☐ 89	Vinny Del Negro	.10	.05	.01
☐ 90	Vinny Del Negro	.10	.05	.01
☐ 91	Larry Larkins	.07	.03	.01
☐ 92	Larry Larkins	.07	.03	.01
☐ 93	Larry Larkins	.07	.03	.01
☐ 94	Larry Larkins	.07	.03	.01
☐ 95	Sidney Lowe	.10	.05	.01
☐ 96	Sidney Lowe	.10	.05	.01
☐ 97	Ernest Myers	.07	.03	.01
☐ 98	Ernest Myers	.07	.03	.01
☐ 99	Ernest Myers	.07	.03	.01
☐ 100	Checklist 1-100	.07	.03	.01
☐ 101	Hal Blondeau	.07	.03	.01
☐ 102	Les Robinson	.10	.05	.01
☐ 103	Nathaniel McMillan	.10	.05	.01
☐ 104	Nathaniel McMillan	.10	.05	.01
☐ 105	Nathaniel McMillan	.10	.05	.01
☐ 106	Charles G. Nevitt	.10	.05	.01
☐ 107	Charles G. Nevitt	.10	.05	.01
☐ 108	Charles G. Nevitt	.10	.05	.01
☐ 109	Quinton Leonard	.07	.03	.01
☐ 110	Bruce Hoadley	.07	.03	.01
☐ 111	Les Robinson	.10	.05	.01
☐ 112	Bruce Hoadley	.07	.03	.01
☐ 113	Emmett Lay	.07	.03	.01
☐ 114	Emmett Lay	.07	.03	.01
☐ 115	Larry Worsley	.07	.03	.01
☐ 116	Harold Thompson	.07	.03	.01
☐ 117	Harold Thompson	.07	.03	.01
☐ 118	Harold Thompson	.07	.03	.01
☐ 119	Howard Turner	.07	.03	.01
☐ 120	Mike O'Neal Warren	.07	.03	.01
☐ 121	Mike O'Neal Warren	.07	.03	.01
☐ 122	Kenny Matthews	.07	.03	.01
☐ 123	Anthony Warren	.07	.03	.01
☐ 124	Anthony Warren	.07	.03	.01
☐ 125	Vann Williford	.07	.03	.01
☐ 126	Raymond Walters	.07	.03	.01
☐ 127	Raymond Walters	.07	.03	.01
☐ 128	Raymond Walters	.07	.03	.01
☐ 129	Craig T. Watts	.07	.03	.01
☐ 130	Larry Worsley	.07	.03	.01
☐ 131	Craig T. Watts	.07	.03	.01
☐ 132	Anthony Webb	.15	.07	.01
☐ 133	Anthony Webb	.15	.07	.01
☐ 134	Anthony Webb	.15	.07	.01
☐ 135	Ray Hodgdon	.07	.03	.01
☐ 136	Herb Applebaum	.07	.03	.01
☐ 137	Bill Kretzer	.07	.03	.01
☐ 138	Charles Whitney	.10	.05	.01
☐ 139	Charles Whitney	.10	.05	.01
☐ 140	Charles Whitney	.10	.05	.01
☐ 141	Dereck Whittenburg	.10	.05	.01
☐ 142	Dereck Whittenburg	.10	.05	.01
☐ 143	Tom Mattocks	.07	.03	.01
☐ 144	Tom Mattocks	.07	.03	.01
☐ 145	Tom Mattocks	.07	.03	.01
☐ 146	Mark Moeller	.07	.03	.01
☐ 147	Mark Moeller	.07	.03	.01
☐ 148	Mark Moeller	.07	.03	.01
☐ 149	Cheerleader/Mascot	.07	.03	.01
☐ 150	Quinton Jackson	.07	.03	.01
☐ 151	Quinton Jackson	.07	.03	.01
☐ 152	Steve Nuce	.07	.03	.01
☐ 153	Steve Nuce	.07	.03	.01
☐ 154	Steve Nuce	.07	.03	.01
☐ 155	Scott Parzych	.07	.03	.01
☐ 156	Scott Parzych	.07	.03	.01
☐ 157	Scott Parzych	.07	.03	.01
☐ 158	Dan Wherry	.07	.03	.01
☐ 159	Hal Blondeau	.07	.03	.01
☐ 160	Dan Wherry	.07	.03	.01
☐ 161	Mascots	.07	.03	.01
☐ 162	Max Perry	.07	.03	.01
☐ 163	Max Perry	.07	.03	.01
☐ 164	David Thompson	.30	.15	.03
☐ 165	David Thompson	.30	.15	.03
☐ 166	David Thompson	.30	.15	.03
☐ 167	Monte Towe	.10	.05	.01
☐ 168	Monte Towe	.10	.05	.01
☐ 169	Monte Towe	.10	.05	.01
☐ 170	Press Maravich	.10	.05	.01
☐ 171	Terry Gannon	.07	.03	.01
☐ 172	Nick Pond	.07	.03	.01
☐ 173	Lou Pucillo	.07	.03	.01
☐ 174	Ray Hodgdon	.07	.03	.01
☐ 175	Darnell Adell	.07	.03	.01
☐ 176	Herb Applebaum	.07	.03	.01
☐ 177	Max Perry	.07	.03	.01
☐ 178	John Richter	.07	.03	.01
☐ 179	Kenny Polston	.07	.03	.01
☐ 180	Terry Gannon	.07	.03	.01
☐ 181	Pete Coker	.07	.03	.01
☐ 182	Quinton Jackson	.07	.03	.01
☐ 183	Jim Rezinger	.07	.03	.01
☐ 184	Kenny Poston	.07	.03	.01

		MINT	EXC	G-VG
☐ 185	Rick Hoot	.07	.03	.01
☐ 186	Everett Case	.10	.05	.01
☐ 187	Everett Case	.10	.05	.01
☐ 188	Everett Case	.10	.05	.01
☐ 189	Kenny Mathews	.07	.03	.01
☐ 190	Reynold Stadium	.07	.03	.01
☐ 191	James T. Valvano	.20	.10	.02
☐ 192	James T. Valvano	.20	.10	.02
☐ 193	James T. Valvano	.20	.10	.02
☐ 194	Cheerleaders	.07	.03	.01
☐ 195	Ray Hodgdon	.07	.03	.01
☐ 196	Lou Pucillo	.07	.03	.01
☐ 197	Kenny Poston	.07	.03	.01
☐ 198	Everett Case	.10	.05	.01
☐ 199	Reynolds Coliseum	.07	.03	.01
☐ 200	Checklist 101-200	.07	.03	.01

AUSTIN CARR

1989-90 North Carolina State Police

This 16-card set of standard size (2 1/2" by 3 1/2") cards was
sponsored by Hardee's WPTF/680 AM radio, and IBM; these
company logos adorn the top of observe and the bottom of the
reverse. The front features a color action player photo, with red
borders on the top, right, and for most of the bottom. The
school name and player identification is given in the top and
bottom borders, with the year "1989-90" in the lower left
corner. The back has biographical information and "Tips from
the Wolfpack," which consist of anti-drug messages. The cards
are unnumbered and are checklisted below in alphabetical
order, with the uniform number after the player's name.

		MINT	EXC	G-VG
COMPLETE SET (16)		12.00	6.00	1.20
COMMON PLAYER (1-16)		.75	.35	.07
☐ 1	Chris Corchiani 13	1.50	.75	.15
☐ 2	Brian D'Amico 54	.75	.35	.07
☐ 3	Bryant Feggins 34	.75	.35	.07
☐ 4	Tom Gugliotta 24	.75	.35	.07
☐ 5	Mickey Hinnant 3	.75	.35	.07
☐ 6	Brian Howard 22	.75	.35	.07
☐ 7	Jamie Knox 23	.75	.35	.07
☐ 8	David Lee 25	.75	.35	.07
☐ 9	Avie Lester 32	1.00	.50	.10
☐ 10	Rodney Monroe 21	2.00	1.00	.20
☐ 11	Andrea Stinson 32	.75	.35	.07
☐ 12	Kevin Thompson 42	.75	.35	.07
☐ 13	Jim Valvano CO	1.25	.60	.12
☐ 14	Roland Whitley 15	.75	.35	.07
☐ 15	"Wuf" Mascot	.75	.35	.07
☐ 16	Kay Yow	.75	.35	.07
	Women's Coach			

1990-91 Notre Dame

This set is a retrospective on famous and outstanding players
at Notre Dame, consisting of 59 cards measuring the standard

size, 2 1/2" by 3 1/2". The cards are numbered up to "58 of 58";
the Anson card is unnumbered and is the only baseball player
in the set. On the front, older players appear in black and white
photos while newer players appear in color. The photos are
enframed by a black line on a white background, with the school
name and the Notre Dame logo (upper right hand corner) above
the photo, and the player's name below. The card backs provide
biographical information, including the player's position and
the team they played on. Past and present NBA players included
are Gary Brokaw, Austin Carr, Adrian Dantley, Bill Hanzlik, Tom
Hawkins, Toby Knight, Bill Laimbeer, John Paxson, David
Rivers, John Shumate, Kelly Tripucka, and Orlando Woolridge.

		MINT	EXC	G-VG
COMPLETE SET (59)		12.50	6.25	1.25
COMMON PLAYER (1-59)		.20	.10	.02
☐ 1	Richard(Digger) Phelps	.30	.15	.03
☐ 2	Collis Jones	.30	.15	.03
☐ 3	Dick Rosenthal	.20	.10	.02
☐ 4	Tim Singleton	.30	.15	.03
☐ 5	Austin Carr	.50	.25	.05
☐ 6	Kevin O'Shea	.20	.10	.02
☐ 7	Keith Tower	.20	.10	.02
☐ 8	Tom Hawkins	.30	.15	.03
☐ 9	Leo Barnhorst	.30	.15	.03
☐ 10	John Shumate	.50	.25	.05
☐ 11	Donald Royal	.30	.15	.03
☐ 12	Edward(Moose) Krause	.30	.15	.03
☐ 13	Bill Laimbeer	1.00	.50	.10
☐ 14	Adrian Dantley	1.00	.50	.10
☐ 15	Keith Robinson	.50	.25	.05
☐ 16	Edward(Monk) Malloy	.30	.15	.03
☐ 17	Leo Klier	.30	.15	.03
☐ 18	Rich Branning	.30	.15	.03
☐ 19	Don(Duck) Williams	.30	.15	.03
☐ 20	Kevin Ellery	.20	.10	.02
☐ 21	Eddie Smith	.20	.10	.02
☐ 22	Ken Barlow	.30	.15	.03
☐ 23	LaPhonso Ellis	.50	.25	.05
☐ 24	John Nyikos	.20	.10	.02
☐ 25	Daimon Sweet	.20	.10	.02
☐ 26	Jack Stephens	.20	.10	.02
☐ 27	Orlando Woolridge	.50	.25	.05
☐ 28	Noble Kizer	.20	.10	.02
☐ 29	John Smyth	.20	.10	.02
☐ 30	John Paxson	1.00	.50	.10
☐ 31	Paul Nowak	.20	.10	.02
☐ 32	Elmer Bennett	.30	.15	.03
☐ 33	Toby Knight	.30	.15	.03
☐ 34	Dave Batton	.30	.15	.03
☐ 35	Bob Whitmore	.20	.10	.02
☐ 36	David Rivers	.50	.25	.05
☐ 37	Gary Brokaw	.50	.25	.05
☐ 38	Gary Novak	.20	.10	.02
☐ 39	Lloyd Aubrey	.20	.10	.02
☐ 40	Robert Faught	.20	.10	.02
☐ 41	Raymond Scanlan	.20	.10	.02
☐ 42	Bill Hanzlik	.30	.15	.03
☐ 43	Vince Boryla	.30	.15	.03
☐ 44	Eddie Riska	.20	.10	.02
☐ 45	Dwight Clay	.20	.10	.02
☐ 46	Bruce Flowers	.20	.10	.02
☐ 47	Ray Meyer	.30	.15	.03
☐ 48	Monty Williams	.20	.10	.02
☐ 49	John Moir	.20	.10	.02
☐ 50	Bill Hassett	.20	.10	.02

☐ 51	Bob Arnzen	.30	.15	.03
☐ 52	Robert Rensberger	.20	.10	.02
☐ 53	Larry Sheffield	.20	.10	.02
☐ 54	Kelly Tripucka	.50	.25	.05
☐ 55	Ron Reed	.30	.15	.03
☐ 56	George Ireland	.30	.15	.03
☐ 57	Tracy Jackson	.50	.25	.05
☐ 58	Walt Sahm	.20	.10	.02
☐ xx	Adrian(Cap) Anson (unnumbered)	.50	.25	.05

1991 Oklahoma State 100 *

This 100-card multi-sport set was produced by Collegiate Collection and measures the standard size (2 1/2" by 3 1/2"). The fronts features a mix of black and white or color player photos, with the player's name in a stripe below the picture. In a horizontal format the backs present biographical information, career summary, or statistics on a white background. The cards are numbered on the back.

	MINT	EXC	G-VG
COMPLETE SET (100)	12.00	6.00	1.20
COMMON PLAYER (1-100)	.10	.05	.01

☐ 1	Henry Iba	.30	.15	.03
☐ 2	Barry Sanders	1.00	.50	.10
☐ 3	Thurman Thomas	.75	.35	.07
☐ 4	Robin Ventura	.75	.35	.07
☐ 5	Bob Kurland	.30	.15	.03
☐ 6	Athletic Tradition	.10	.05	.01
☐ 7	1959 NCAA Baseball Champions	.10	.05	.01
☐ 8	1945 NCAA Basketball Champions	.10	.05	.01
☐ 9	Bob Tway	.20	.10	.02
☐ 10	Allie Reynolds	.20	.10	.02
☐ 11	Rodney Harling	.10	.05	.01
☐ 12	Ed Gallagher	.10	.05	.01
☐ 13	Walt Garrison	.20	.10	.02
☐ 14	Terry Miller	.15	.07	.01
☐ 15	Bob Fenimore	.10	.05	.01
☐ 16	Gerald Hudson	.10	.05	.01
☐ 17	Hart Lee Dykes	.20	.10	.02
☐ 18	1976 Big 8 Conference	.10	.05	.01
☐ 19	Jimmy Johnson	.25	.12	.02
☐ 20	Terry Brown	.15	.07	.01
☐ 21	Derrel Gofourth	.10	.05	.01
☐ 22	Paul Blair	.20	.10	.02
☐ 23	John Little	.10	.05	.01
☐ 24	1983 Bluebonnet Bowl	.10	.05	.01
☐ 25	John Smith	.10	.05	.01
☐ 26	1976 Tangerine Bowl	.10	.05	.01
☐ 27	Gary Cutsinger	.10	.05	.01
☐ 28	Rusty Hilger	.20	.10	.02
☐ 29	Ron Baker	.10	.05	.01
☐ 30	Pat Jones	.15	.07	.01
☐ 31	Phillip Dokes	.10	.05	.01
☐ 32	Neil Armstrong	.15	.07	.01
☐ 33	Joel Horlen	.20	.10	.02
☐ 34	Jon Kolb	.15	.07	.01
☐ 35	1958 NCAA Wrestling Champs	.10	.05	.01
☐ 36	Doug Tewell	.15	.07	.01
☐ 37	1984 Gator Bowl Catch	.10	.05	.01

☐ 38	Scott Verplank	.25	.12	.02
☐ 39	1946 Sugar Bowl	.10	.05	.01
☐ 40	John Starks	.15	.07	.01
☐ 41	Liz Brown	.10	.05	.01
☐ 42	1984 Gator Bowl	.10	.05	.01
☐ 43	Yojiro Uetake	.10	.05	.01
☐ 44	1988 Holiday Bowl	.10	.05	.01
☐ 45	Ernest Anderson	.10	.05	.01
☐ 46	Leslie O'Neal	.20	.10	.02
☐ 47	Ken Monday	.10	.05	.01
☐ 48	Leonard Thompson	.15	.07	.01
☐ 49	Jess(Cob) Rennick	.10	.05	.01
☐ 50	Mike Gundy	.20	.10	.02
☐ 51	Mark Moore	.10	.05	.01
☐ 52	Clinette Jordan	.10	.05	.01
☐ 53	O.A.(Bum) Phillips	.20	.10	.02
☐ 54	John Ward	.10	.05	.01
☐ 55	Larry Roach	.15	.07	.01
☐ 56	Jerry Sherk	.15	.07	.01
☐ 57	Matt Monger	.10	.05	.01
☐ 58	Dick Soergel	.10	.05	.01
☐ 59	Ricky Young	.10	.05	.01
☐ 60	Labron Harris and 1963 NCAA Championship Team	.10	.05	.01
☐ 61	Barry Sanders	1.00	.50	.10
☐ 62	Gary Green	.15	.07	.01
☐ 63	Henry Iba	.25	.12	.02
☐ 64	David Edwards	.20	.10	.02
☐ 65	Tom Chesbro	.10	.05	.01
☐ 66	Chris Rockins	.10	.05	.01
☐ 67	Buddy Ryan	.25	.12	.02
☐ 68	Thurman Thomas	.75	.35	.07
☐ 69	Frank Lewis	.20	.10	.02
☐ 70	Doug Dascenzo	.20	.10	.02
☐ 71	Pete Incaviglia	.35	.17	.03
☐ 72	Willie Wood	.25	.12	.02
☐ 73	James Butler	.10	.05	.01
☐ 74	Lori McNeil	.20	.10	.02
☐ 75	Monty Farris	.25	.12	.02
☐ 76	Barry Sanders	1.00	.50	.10
☐ 77	Mickey Tettleton	.25	.12	.02
☐ 78	Barry and Thurman	.75	.35	.07
☐ 80	Gale McArthur	.10	.05	.01
☐ 81	Thurman Thomas	.75	.35	.07
☐ 82	Danny Edwards	.10	.05	.01
☐ 83	Barry Sanders	1.00	.50	.10
☐ 84	Mike Sheets	.10	.05	.01
☐ 85	Jerry Adair	.15	.07	.01
☐ 86	Thurman Thomas	.75	.35	.07
☐ 87	Garth Brooks	.10	.05	.01
☐ 88	John Farrell	.10	.05	.01
☐ 89	Mike Holder and 1987 NCAA Championship Team	.10	.05	.01
☐ 90	Jim Traber	.20	.10	.02
☐ 91	Lindy Miller	.15	.07	.01
☐ 92	Mike Henneman	.25	.12	.02
☐ 93	Thurman Thomas	.75	.35	.07
☐ 94	John Washington	.10	.05	.01
☐ 95	Michael Daniel	.10	.05	.01
☐ 96	Ralph Higgins	.10	.05	.01
☐ 97	1987 Sun Bowl	.10	.05	.01
☐ 98	Garrett Limbrick	.10	.05	.01
☐ 99	Eddie Sutton	.15	.07	.01
☐ 100	Director Card	.10	.05	.01

1989-90 Oregon State

This 16-card set was printed on thin cardboard stock and issued in one sheet; after perforation, the cards measure approximately 3" by 4 1/16". The set may also have been issued as single unperforated cards. It is reported that some autographed sets were available in limited quantities. The front features a black and white action player photo, with white borders. The player's name appears in an orange and black basketball superimposed in the upper left corner. The player's name and position appear below the picture in a black stripe. In orange lettering, the team name "Beavers" is printed, with an oversized "B". The backs are printed in orange and black, and present a black and white head shot as well as biographical and statistical information. The cards are unnumbered and are checklisted below in alphabetical order, with the uniform number after the player's name. This set includes an early card of Gary

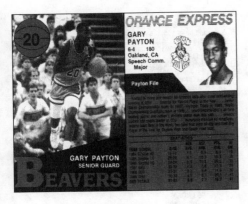

Payton, who was chosen as the second pick by Seattle in the 1990 NBA draft.

	MINT	EXC	G-VG
COMPLETE SET (16)	15.00	7.50	1.50
COMMON PLAYER (1-16)	1.00	.50	.10
☐ 1 Teo Alibegovic 12	1.00	.50	.10
☐ 2 Karl Anderson 22	1.00	.50	.10
☐ 3 Jim Anderson CO	1.50	.75	.15
☐ 4 Will Brantley 25	1.00	.50	.10
☐ 5 Bob Cavell 4	1.00	.50	.10
☐ 6 Allan Celestine 40	1.00	.50	.10
☐ 7 Kevin Grant 11	1.00	.50	.10
☐ 8 Kevin Harris 14	1.00	.50	.10
☐ 9 Scott Haskin 44	1.00	.50	.10
☐ 10 Earl Martin 24	1.00	.50	.10
☐ 11 Lamont McIntosh 33	1.00	.50	.10
☐ 12 Charles McKinney 23	1.00	.50	.10
☐ 13 Gary Payton 20	6.00	3.00	.60
☐ 14 Chris Rueppell 21	1.00	.50	.10
☐ 15 Travis Stel 13	1.00	.50	.10
☐ 16 Jim Anderson CO	1.00	.50	.10

1989-90 Pitt Foodland

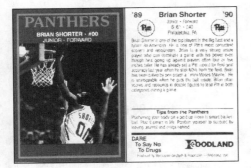

This 12-card set featuring members of the Pittsburgh Panthers basketball team was sponsored by Foodland; each card measures the standard size 2 1/2" by 3 1/2". The front features an action color photo enframed by orange border on blue background. Above the photo appears the school's name "Panthers" (in orange print), player's name, jersey number, classification, and position. The sponsor's name is found below the photo. The back is filled with biographical information, a basketball tip from the Panthers, and an anti-drug message.

	MINT	EXC	G-VG
COMPLETE SET (12)	9.00	4.50	.90
COMMON PLAYER	.60	.30	.06

		MINT	EXC	G-VG
☐	00 Brian Shorter	1.50	.75	.15
☐	3 Sean Miller	1.25	.60	.12
☐	12 Pat Cavanaugh	.60	.30	.06
☐	20 Darelle Porter	.60	.30	.06
☐	21 Rod Brookin	1.00	.50	.10
☐	22 Jason Matthews	1.00	.50	.10
☐	23 Travis Ziegler	.60	.30	.06
☐	33 Darren Morningstar	.75	.35	.07
☐	42 Gilbert Johnson	.60	.30	.06
☐	55 Bobby Martin	1.00	.50	.10
☐	xx Pitt Panther (team mascot)	.60	.30	.06
☐	xx Paul Evans CO	.60	.30	.06

1990-91 Pitt Foodland

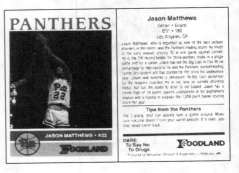

This 12-card was sponsored by Foodland and measures the standard size (2 1/2" by 3 1/2"). The front features a borderless color action photo of the player, with "Panthers" written in blue letter on white above the picture. Two color stripes appear below the picture; in the blue one appears the player's name and number, while in the thicker orange one appears the sponsor's logo. A basketball icon superimposed over these two bars at the left completes the card face. The back has biographical information, a tip from the Pittsburgh Panthers in the form of an anti-drug or alcohol message, and the sponsor's logo. The cards are unnumbered and are checklisted them below in alphabetical order, with uniform number after the player's name.

	MINT	EXC	G-VG
COMPLETE SET (12)	8.00	4.00	.80
COMMON PLAYER (1-12)	.60	.30	.06

		MINT	EXC	G-VG
☐	1 Antoine Jones 21	.60	.30	.06
☐	2 Gandhi Jordan 4	.60	.30	.06
☐	3 Bobby Martin 55	1.00	.50	.10
☐	4 Jason Matthews 22	1.00	.50	.10
☐	5 Chris McNeal 24	.60	.30	.06
☐	6 Jermaine Morgan 42	.60	.30	.06
☐	7 Sean Miller 3	1.00	.50	.10
☐	8 Darren Morningstar 33	.75	.35	.07
☐	9 Omo Moses 44	.60	.30	.06
☐	10 Darelle Porter 20	.60	.30	.06
☐	11 Ahmad Shareef 13	.60	.30	.06
☐	12 Brian Shorter 00	1.25	.60	.12

1979-80 St. Bonaventure

This 18-card set measures the standard size, 2 1/2" by 3 1/2". The front features a sepia-toned photo with the player's name above and jersey number in a basketball logo at upper right hand corner; the team name "Bonnies" appears below the photo. The photo is also enframed by a thin brown border on white card stock. The back is filled with biographical and statistical information.

	NRMT	VG-E	GOOD
COMPLETE SET (18)	35.00	17.50	3.50
COMMON PLAYER (1-18)	2.00	1.00	.20
☐ 1 Earl Belcher 25	3.00	1.50	.30
☐ 2 Dan Burns 41	2.00	1.00	.20
☐ 3 Bruno DeGiglio 24	2.00	1.00	.20
☐ 4 Jim Elenz 10	2.00	1.00	.20
☐ 5 Lacey Fulmer 20	2.00	1.00	.20
☐ 6 Delmar Harrod 52	2.00	1.00	.20
☐ 7 Alfonza Jones 12	2.00	1.00	.20
☐ 8 Mark Jones 11	2.00	1.00	.20
☐ 9 Bill Kalbaugh CO	2.00	1.00	.20
☐ 10 Lloyd Praedel 44	2.00	1.00	.20
☐ 11 Pat Rodgers 35	2.00	1.00	.20
☐ 12 Bob Sassone CO	2.00	1.00	.20
☐ 13 Jim Satalin CO	2.00	1.00	.20
☐ 14 Mark Spencer 15	2.00	1.00	.20
☐ 15 Eric Stover 40	2.00	1.00	.20
☐ 16 Shawn Waterman 33	2.00	1.00	.20
☐ 17 Brian West 30	2.00	1.00	.20
☐ 18 Title Card	2.00	1.00	.20

1990-91 San Jose State Smokey

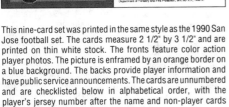

This nine-card set was printed in the same style as the 1990 San Jose football set. The cards measure 2 1/2" by 3 1/2" and are printed on thin white stock. The fronts feature color action player photos. The picture is enframed by an orange border on a blue background. The backs provide player information and have public service announcements. The cards are unnumbered and are checklisted below in alphabetical order, with the player's jersey number after the name and non-player cards listed at the end.

	MINT	EXC	G-VG
COMPLETE SET (9)	7.00	3.50	.70
COMMON PLAYER (1-9)	1.00	.50	.10
☐ 1 Troy Batiste 23	1.00	.50	.10
☐ 2 Terry Cannon 10	1.00	.50	.10
☐ 3 Robert Dunlap 50	1.00	.50	.10
☐ 4 Kevin Logan 31	1.00	.50	.10
☐ 5 Stan Morrison CO	1.00	.50	.10
☐ 6 Daryl Scott 32	1.00	.50	.10
☐ 7 Charles Terrell 4	1.00	.50	.10
☐ 8 Event Center	1.00	.50	.10
☐ 9 Smokey Bear	1.00	.50	.10

1991 South Carolina 200 *

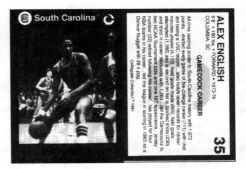

This 200-card multi-sport set was produced by Collegiate Collection and measures the standard size (2 1/2" by 3 1/2"). The fronts features a mix of black and white or color player photos, with black borders and the player's name in the maroon stripe below the picture. In a horizontal format the backs present biographical information, career summary, or statistics on a white background with black lettering and borders. The cards are numbered on the back.

	MINT	EXC	G-VG
COMPLETE SET (200)	22.00	11.00	2.20
COMMON PLAYER (1-200)	.10	.05	.01
☐ 1 Frank McGuire CO	.25	.12	.02
☐ 2 Todd Ellis	.25	.12	.02
☐ 3 Alex English	.30	.15	.03
☐ 4 Cocky ?	.10	.05	.01
☐ 5 Kevin Darmody	.10	.05	.01
☐ 6 Kent Hagood	.10	.05	.01
☐ 7 Duane Kendall	.10	.05	.01
☐ 8 Harold Green	.25	.12	.02
☐ 9 Linwood Moye	.10	.05	.01
☐ 10 George Rogers	.25	.12	.02
☐ 11 Hardin Brown	.10	.05	.01
☐ 12 Kent Demars	.10	.05	.01
☐ 13 Bonnie Kenny	.10	.05	.01
☐ 14 Adrian Adkins	.10	.05	.01
☐ 15 George Felton	.10	.05	.01
☐ 16 Marty Baltzegar	.10	.05	.01
☐ 17 Chris Wade	.10	.05	.01
☐ 18 Nancy Wilson	.10	.05	.01
☐ 19 James Seawright	.10	.05	.01
☐ 20 Lisa Dias	.10	.05	.01
☐ 21 Kevin White	.10	.05	.01
☐ 22 June Raines	.10	.05	.01
☐ 23 Gretchen Koenig	.10	.05	.01
☐ 24 Carton Hilton	.10	.05	.01
☐ 25 Derrick Little	.10	.05	.01
☐ 26 Zam Fredrick	.10	.05	.01
☐ 27 Karen Sanchelli	.10	.05	.01
☐ 28 Ron Rabune	.10	.05	.01
☐ 29 Carolina Culik	.10	.05	.01
☐ 30 Greg Kraft	.10	.05	.01
☐ 31 Warren Lipka	.10	.05	.01
☐ 32 Martha Parker	.10	.05	.01
☐ 33 Vic McConnell	.10	.05	.01
☐ 34 Stephane Simian	.10	.05	.01
☐ 35 Alex English	.30	.15	.03
☐ 36 Doug Allison	.10	.05	.01
☐ 37 Randy Harwell	.10	.05	.01
☐ 38 Jimmy Hawthorne	.10	.05	.01
☐ 39 Fritgerald Davis	.10	.05	.01
☐ 40 Linda Mescan	.10	.05	.01
☐ 41 Rita Winebarger	.10	.05	.01

☐	42	Bill Hency	.10	.05	.01
☐	43	Mark Berson	.10	.05	.01
☐	44	Todd Ellis	.20	.10	.02
☐	45	Joyce Compton	.10	.05	.01
☐	46	Darlene Lowery	.10	.05	.01
☐	47	David Poinsett	.10	.05	.01
☐	48	Shonna Banner	.10	.05	.01
☐	49	Joe Cardwell	.10	.05	.01
☐	50	Arlo Elkins	.10	.05	.01
☐	51	Greg Morhardt	.10	.05	.01
☐	52	Sparky Woods	.10	.05	.01
☐	53	Charles Arndt	.10	.05	.01
☐	54	Joe Morrison	.20	.10	.02
☐	55	Jeff Grantz	.10	.05	.01
☐	56	Fritz Von Kolnitz	.10	.05	.01
☐	57	Mike Caskey	.10	.05	.01
☐	58	John Roche	.20	.10	.02
☐	59	Alex Hawkins	.20	.10	.02
☐	60	Phil Lavole	.10	.05	.01
☐	61	Lee Collins	.10	.05	.01
☐	62	Jack Thompson	.10	.05	.01
☐	63	Andrew Provence	.10	.05	.01
☐	64	Kevin Joyce	.20	.10	.02
☐	65	Brian Winstead	.10	.05	.01
☐	66	J. McIver Riley	.10	.05	.01
☐	67	Bobby Heald	.15	.07	.01
☐	68	Cerrick Hordges	.10	.05	.01
☐	69	Leon Cunningham	.10	.05	.01
☐	70	Randy Martz	.15	.07	.01
☐	71	Rex Enright	.10	.05	.01
☐	72	Chris Boyle	.10	.05	.01
☐	73	Grady Wallace	.10	.05	.01
☐	74	Paul Hollins	.10	.05	.01
☐	75	Norman Rucks	.10	.05	.01
☐	76	Dan Reeves	.35	.17	.03
☐	77	Tim Lewis	.10	.05	.01
☐	78	Tom Riker	.10	.05	.01
☐	79	King Dixon	.15	.07	.01
☐	80	Bobby Cremins	.20	.10	.02
☐	81	Billy Gambrell	.15	.07	.01
☐	82	Bob Rinehart	.10	.05	.01
☐	83	Max Runager	.15	.07	.01
☐	84	Mike Cook	.10	.05	.01
☐	85	Gary Gregor	.15	.07	.01
☐	86	Bill Landrum	.20	.10	.02
☐	87	Mark Van Bever	.10	.05	.01
☐	88	Pat Dufficy	.10	.05	.01
☐	89	Joe Datin	.10	.05	.01
☐	90	Ronnie Collins	.10	.05	.01
☐	91	Del Wilkes	.10	.05	.01
☐	92	Earl Bass	.10	.05	.01
☐	93	Johnny Gregory	.10	.05	.01
☐	94	Lou Sossamon	.10	.05	.01
☐	95	Lindy James	.10	.05	.01
☐	96	Sam Daniel	.10	.05	.01
☐	97	Sharon Gilmore	.10	.05	.01
☐	98	Steve Wadiak	.10	.05	.01
☐	99	Joe Smith	.10	.05	.01
☐	100	Director Card	.10	.05	.01
☐	101	James Sumpter	.15	.07	.01
☐	102	Mark Nelson	.10	.05	.01
☐	103	Terry Dozier	.10	.05	.01
☐	104	Scott Hagler	.10	.05	.01
☐	105	Todd Berry	.10	.05	.01
☐	106	Jack Gillon	.10	.05	.01
☐	107	Carl Hill	.10	.05	.01
☐	108	Steve Liebler	.10	.05	.01
☐	109	Earl Johnson	.10	.05	.01
☐	110	Dominique Blasingame	.10	.05	.01
☐	111	Jim Desmond	.10	.05	.01
☐	112	Keith Bing	.10	.05	.01
☐	113	Garret Carter	.10	.05	.01
☐	114	Ken Diller	.10	.05	.01
☐	115	Chris Corley	.10	.05	.01
☐	116	Jay Sandberry	.10	.05	.01
☐	117	Ron Bass	.10	.05	.01
☐	118	Charlie Gowan	.10	.05	.01
☐	119	Ray Carpenter	.10	.05	.01
☐	120	Glen Thompson	.10	.05	.01
☐	121	Pat Mihn	.10	.05	.01
☐	122	Bryant Gillard	.10	.05	.01
☐	123	Darryl Martin	.10	.05	.01
☐	124	Matt McKernan	.10	.05	.01
☐	125	Mike Doyle	.10	.05	.01
☐	126	Brad Jergenson	.10	.05	.01
☐	127	Mark Fryer	.10	.05	.01
☐	128	Michael Foster	.10	.05	.01
☐	129	Anthony Smith	.10	.05	.01
☐	130	Robert Robinson	.10	.05	.01
☐	131	Mark Fleetwood	.10	.05	.01
☐	132	Skeets Thomas	.10	.05	.01
☐	133	Bobby Richardson CO	.25	.12	.02
☐	134	Rodney Price	.10	.05	.01
☐	135	Willie McIntee	.10	.05	.01
☐	136	Kenny Haynes	.10	.05	.01
☐	137	Arn Thorsson	.10	.05	.01
☐	138	Willie Scott	.10	.05	.01
☐	139	Ricky Daniels	.10	.05	.01
☐	140	Bill Barnhill	.10	.05	.01
☐	141	Gordon Beckham	.10	.05	.01
☐	142	Tim Dyches	.10	.05	.01
☐	143	John Hudson	.10	.05	.01
☐	144	Brian Williams	.10	.05	.01
☐	145	Jim Walsh	.10	.05	.01
☐	146	Keith Switer	.10	.05	.01
☐	147	Thomas Dendy	.10	.05	.01
☐	148	Gerald Peacock	.10	.05	.01
☐	149	Bill Bradshaw	.10	.05	.01
☐	150	Mike Brittain	.10	.05	.01
☐	151	Tim Berra	.20	.10	.02
☐	152	Eric Poole	.10	.05	.01
☐	153	Leonard Burton	.15	.07	.01
☐	154	Danny Smith	.10	.05	.01
☐	155	Scott Windsor	.10	.05	.01
☐	156	Art Whisnant	.10	.05	.01
☐	157	Jim Slaughter	.10	.05	.01
☐	158	Skip Harlicka	.10	.05	.01
☐	159	Bishop Strickland	.15	.07	.01
☐	160	Brian Winters	.20	.10	.02
☐	161	Rod Carroway	.10	.05	.01
☐	162	Allen Mitchell	.10	.05	.01
☐	163	Kenneth Robinson	.10	.05	.01
☐	164	Paul Vogel	.10	.05	.01
☐	165	Norman Floyd	.10	.05	.01
☐	166	Carl Brazell	.10	.05	.01
☐	167	Rod Carroway	.10	.05	.01
☐	168	Fred Ziegler	.10	.05	.01
☐	169	Frank Mincevich	.10	.05	.01
☐	170	Bobby Bryant	.15	.07	.01
☐	171	J.D. Fuller	.10	.05	.01
☐	172	Harry South	.10	.05	.01
☐	173	Tom O'Conner	.10	.05	.01
☐	174	Kevin Hendrix	.10	.05	.01
☐	175	Greg Philpot	.10	.05	.01
☐	176	Warren Muier	.10	.05	.01
☐	177	Chris Mayotte	.10	.05	.01
☐	178	Cookie Pericola	.10	.05	.01
☐	179	Tommy Suggs	.10	.05	.01
☐	180	Don Bailey	.10	.05	.01
☐	181	Zam Fredrick	.10	.05	.01
☐	182	Chris Major	.15	.07	.01
☐	183	Mike Hold	.10	.05	.01
☐	184	Brendan McCormach	.10	.05	.01
☐	185	David Taylor	.10	.05	.01
☐	186	Hank Small	.10	.05	.01
☐	187	Bryant Meeks	.10	.05	.01
☐	188	Brantley Southers	.10	.05	.01
☐	189	John Sullivan	.10	.05	.01
☐	190	Elylen Johnson	.10	.05	.01
☐	191	Harry Skipper	.10	.05	.01
☐	192	Derrick Frazier	.10	.05	.01
☐	193	Raynard Brown	.10	.05	.01
☐	194	Quinton Lewis	.10	.05	.01
☐	195	Tony Gyton	.10	.05	.01
☐	196	John Leheup	.15	.07	.01
☐	197	Dick Harris	.15	.07	.01
☐	198	Shelia Foster	.10	.05	.01
☐	199	Johnny Gramling	.10	.05	.01
☐	200	Director Card	.10	.05	.01

1987-88 Southern Police *

This 16-card set of standard size (2 1/2" by 3 1/2") cards was sponsored by McDonald's, Southern University, and local law enforcement agencies and was produced by McDag Productions. The McDonald's logo appears at the bottom of both sides of the card. The front features a mix of action or posed, black and white player photos. The pictures are bordered in turquoise on the sides, yellow above, and white below. The school name and player information appear in black lettering in the yellow border. A picture of the school mascot in the lower right corner rounds out the card face. The back presents biographical information, Jag Facts, and "Tips from The Jaguars" in the form of an anti-drug message. The cards are numbered on the back. The sports represented in this set are football (1-3, 14-16) and basketball (4-13).

	MINT	EXC	G-VG
COMPLETE SET (16)	9.00	4.50	.90
COMMON PLAYER (1-16)	.60	.30	.06
☐ 1 Marino Casem CO	.60	.30	.06
☐ 2 Gerald Perry	2.00	1.00	.20
☐ 3 Michael Ball and	.60	.30	.06
Toren Robinson			
☐ 4 Ben Jobe CO	.60	.30	.06
☐ 5 Daryl Battles	.60	.30	.06
☐ 6 Patrick Garner	.60	.30	.06
☐ 7 Avery Johnson	1.25	.60	.12
☐ 8 Rodney Washington	.60	.30	.06
☐ 9 Kevin Florent	.60	.30	.06
☐ 10 Dervynn Johnson	.60	.30	.06
☐ 11 Claudene Stovall	.60	.30	.06
☐ 12 Michelle Currie	.60	.30	.06
☐ 13 Gibbie Phillips	.60	.30	.06
☐ 14 Allan Ratliff	.60	.30	.06
☐ 15 Eric Foxworth	.60	.30	.06
☐ 16 Jeff Swain	.60	.30	.06

1987-88 Southern Mississippi

This 14-card set, measuring 2 3/8" by 3 1/2", was co-sponsored by Deposit Guaranty National Bank and Coca-Cola, and their company names appear at the bottom corners on the front. The front has a posed action photo on a yellow background; two cards of the set feature two players. Player's names and team logo surmount the photo. The back presents biographical information and the card number.

	MINT	EXC	G-VG
COMPLETE SET (14)	12.00	6.00	1.20
COMMON PLAYER (1-14)	1.00	.50	.10
☐ 1 The Freshmen	1.00	.50	.10
☐ 2 The Coaches	1.00	.50	.10
☐ 3 Casey Fisher	1.00	.50	.10
☐ 4 Derrek Hamilton	1.00	.50	.10
☐ 5 Randolph Keys	3.00	1.50	.30
☐ 6 John White	1.00	.50	.10

	MINT	EXC	G-VG
☐ 7 D.J. and Allen	1.00	.50	.10
D.J. Bowe and			
Allen Chapman			
☐ 8 The Browns	1.00	.50	.10
John Brown and			
Willie Brown			
☐ 9 Jurado Hinton	1.00	.50	.10
☐ 10 Jay Ladner	1.00	.50	.10
☐ 11 Randy Pettus	1.00	.50	.10
☐ 12 Jimmy Smith	1.00	.50	.10
☐ 13 Roger Boyd	1.00	.50	.10
☐ 14 The Team	1.00	.50	.10

1986-87 Southwestern Lousiana Police *

This 16-card set was sponsored by the Chemical Dependency Unit of Acadiana in Lafayette, the University of Southwest Louisiana, and local law enforcement agencies and was produced by McDag Productions. Only 3,500 sets were produced. The cards were distributed by the CDU adolescent program and by law enforcement officers, and they measure the standard size (2 1/2" by 3 1/2"). The front features borderless color action player photos, on white card stock with black lettering. The CDU logo and the words "USL Ragin' Cajuns" appear on the top of the card, with player information below the picture. The back has biographical information and "Tips from the Ragin' Cajuns" which encourage children to avoid drug use. Sports represented in the set include basketball (1, 4, 9, 11, 15), baseball (2, 5, 8, 16), softball (7, 14), track (3), and tennis (6, 10, 12-13). The cards are unnumbered and we have checklisted them below in alphabetical order.

	MINT	EXC	G-VG
COMPLETE SET (16)	7.00	3.50	.70
COMMON PLAYER (1-16)	.50	.25	.05
☐ 1 Stephen Beene	.50	.25	.05
☐ 2 Eddie Citronnelli	.50	.25	.05
☐ 3 Hollis Conway	1.00	.50	.10
☐ 4 Teena Cooper	.50	.25	.05
☐ 5 Herb Erhardt	.50	.25	.05
☐ 6 Bret Garnett	.50	.25	.05
☐ 7 Allison Gray	.50	.25	.05
☐ 8 Bobby Hobbs	.50	.25	.05
☐ 9 Brian Jolivette	.50	.25	.05
☐ 10 Dianne Lowings	.50	.25	.05
☐ 11 Rodney McNeil	.50	.25	.05
☐ 12 Cathy O'Donovan	.50	.25	.05
☐ 13 Ashley Rhoney	.50	.25	.05
☐ 14 Alisa Smith	.50	.25	.05
☐ 15 Randal Smith	.50	.25	.05
☐ 16 Merv Waukau	.50	.25	.05

1988-89 Syracuse Louis Rich

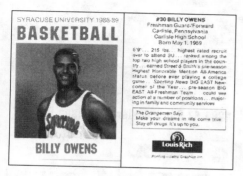

This 12-card set was sponsored by Louis Rich; their company logo appears on the bottom of the reverse. The cards measure the standard size (2 1/2" by 3 1/2"). The front features a posed color photo of the player, shot from waist up on a blue background. The lettering and border on the card face are orange on white card stock. The back has biographical information and career summary, and "The Orangemen Say" feature, which consists of an anti-drug or alcohol message. The cards are unnumbered and are checklisted below in alphabetical order. Future NBA stars showcased in this set are Sherman Douglas, Derrick Coleman, and Billy Owens.

		MINT	EXC	G-VG
	COMPLETE SET (12)	75.00	37.50	7.50
	COMMON PLAYER (1-12)	3.00	1.50	.30
☐ 1	Jim Boeheim CO	5.00	2.50	.50
☐ 2	Derrick Coleman	30.00	15.00	3.00
☐ 3	Sherman Douglas	15.00	7.50	1.50
☐ 4	Herman Harried	3.00	1.50	.30
☐ 5	Dave Johnson	3.00	1.50	.30
☐ 6	Rich Manning	5.00	2.50	.50
☐ 7	Billy Owens	30.00	15.00	3.00
☐ 8	Matt Roe	5.00	2.50	.50
☐ 9	Erik Rogers	3.00	1.50	.30
☐ 10	Anthony Scott	3.00	1.50	.30
☐ 11	Dave Siock	3.00	1.50	.30
☐ 12	Stephen Thompson	9.00	4.50	.90

1989-90 Syracuse Pepsi/Burger King

This 15-card set was sponsored by Pepsi, Y94FM radio, and Burger King. The cards measure approximately 2 5/8" by 3 1/2" and are numbered on the back. The action color photo on the front is outlined by orange border on white background. Below the photo in an orange bar appears the school's name, year, and the player's name in white lettering. The back has biographical information and a brief anti-drug message. Several players have two cards in this set: Derrick Coleman, Stephen Thompson, and Billy Owens.

		MINT	EXC	G-VG
	COMPLETE SET (15)	12.00	6.00	1.20
	COMMON PLAYER (1-15)	.40	.20	.04
☐ 1	Derrick Coleman 44	3.00	1.50	.30
☐ 2	LeRon Ellis 25	.90	.45	.09
☐ 3	Rich Manning 34	.40	.20	.04
☐ 4	Stephen Thompson 32	.90	.45	.09
☐ 5	Michael Edwards 5	.40	.20	.04
☐ 6	David Johnson 23	2.00	1.00	.20
☐ 7	Billy Owens 30	3.00	1.50	.30
☐ 8	Conrad McRae 13	.40	.20	.04
☐ 9	Jim Boeheim CO	.75	.35	.07
☐ 10	Stephen Thompson 32	.90	.45	.09
☐ 11	Mike Hopkins 33	.40	.20	.04
☐ 12	Tony Scott 40	.40	.20	.04
☐ 13	Billy Owens 30	3.00	1.50	.30
☐ 14	Erik Rogers 41	.40	.20	.04
☐ 15	Derrick Coleman 44	3.00	1.50	.30

1988-89 Tennessee Smokey

This 12-card set features members of the Tennessee Volunteers basketball team and measures the standard card size, 2 1/2" by 3 1/2". The front features a color action photo; above and below appear orange and gray lettering and borders. The Smokey the Bear logo in the lower left hand corner completes the front. The back gives brief biographical information and a public service announcement (illustrated with cartoon) concerning wildfire prevention.

		MINT	EXC	G-VG
	COMPLETE SET (12)	15.00	7.50	1.50
	COMMON PLAYER	1.00	.50	.10
☐ 11	Clarence Swearengen	1.50	.75	.15
☐ 23	Greg Bell	1.00	.50	.10
☐ 24	Rickey Clark	1.00	.50	.10
☐ 25	Travis Henry	1.00	.50	.10
☐ 31	Dyron Nix	5.00	2.50	.50
☐ 33	Mark Griffin	1.00	.50	.10
☐ 34	Ronnie Reese	1.00	.50	.10
☐ 50	Doug Roth	1.00	.50	.10
☐ 51	Ian Lockhart	1.00	.50	.10
☐ xx	Don Devoe CO	1.00	.50	.10
☐ xx	Smokey The Hound (mascot)	1.00	.50	.10
☐ xx	Thompson-Boling Arena	1.00	.50	.10

1991 Texas A and M 100 *

This 100-card multi-sport set was produced by Collegiate Collection and measures the standard size (2 1/2" by 3 1/2"). The fronts features a mix of black and white or color player photos, with the player's name in a stripe below the picture. In a horizontal format the backs present biographical information, career summary, or statistics on a white background. The cards are numbered on the back.

		MINT	EXC	G-VG
COMPLETE SET (100)		12.00	6.00	1.20
COMMON PLAYER (1-100)		.10	.05	.01
☐	1 Rod Bernstine	.30	.15	.03
☐	2 Paul(Bear) Bryant	.30	.15	.03
☐	3 Shirley Furlong	.10	.05	.01
☐	4 R.C. Slocum	.20	.10	.02
☐	5 Gary Kubiak	.20	.10	.02
☐	6 Gary Horton	.10	.05	.01
☐	7 Billy Cannon	.20	.10	.02
☐	8 John Beasley	.15	.07	.01
☐	9 Ray Childress	.25	.12	.02
☐	10 John David Crow	.25	.12	.02
☐	11 Bob Ellis	.15	.07	.01
☐	12 Billy Hodge	.10	.05	.01
☐	13 Layne Talbot	.10	.05	.01
☐	14 Larry Stegent	.15	.07	.01
☐	15 Lisa Langston	.10	.05	.01
☐	16 Tom Chandler	.10	.05	.01
☐	17 Scott Livingstone	.25	.12	.02
☐	18 Jimmy Teal	.10	.05	.01
☐	19 Ted Nelson	.10	.05	.01
☐	20 Lance Pavlas	.10	.05	.01
☐	21 James(Hoot) Gibson	.10	.05	.01
☐	22 Mickey Washington	.10	.05	.01
☐	23 Rodney Hodde	.10	.05	.01
☐	24 Rob Swain	.10	.05	.01
☐	25 Thomas Sanders	.15	.07	.01
☐	26 Loyd Taylor	.10	.05	.01
☐	27 Danny Roberts	.10	.05	.01
☐	28 Bob Brock	.10	.05	.01
☐	29 Curtis Dickey	.20	.10	.02
☐	30 John Thornton	.10	.05	.01
☐	31 Matt McCall	.10	.05	.01
☐	32 David Kent	.10	.05	.01
☐	33 Melinda Clark	.10	.05	.01
☐	34 Brad Dusek	.15	.07	.01
☐	35 Mark Ross	.10	.05	.01
☐	36 Gary Oliver	.10	.05	.01
☐	37 Charley Milstead	.10	.05	.01
☐	38 Mark Johnson	.10	.05	.01
☐	39 Ever Magallanes	.10	.05	.01
☐	40 Mark Thurmond	.15	.07	.01
☐	41 Keith Langston	.10	.05	.01
☐	42 Phillip Taylor	.10	.05	.01
☐	43 Jacob Green	.20	.10	.02
☐	44 Randy Matson	.20	.10	.02
☐	45 Shawn Andaya	.10	.05	.01
☐	46 Kevin Monk	.10	.05	.01
☐	47 Larry Kelm	.15	.07	.01
☐	48 Tory Parks	.10	.05	.01
☐	49 Barry Davis	.10	.05	.01
☐	50 Kitty Holley	.10	.05	.01
☐	51 Kent Adams	.10	.05	.01
☐	52 Randy Hall	.10	.05	.01
☐	53 Dave Goff	.10	.05	.01
☐	54 Rolf Krueger	.15	.07	.01
☐	55 Lynn Hickey	.10	.05	.01
☐	56 Sylvester Morgan	.10	.05	.01
☐	57 Bucky Sams	.15	.07	.01
☐	58 Jeff Nelson	.10	.05	.01
☐	59 Gary Jones	.10	.05	.01
☐	60 John Byington	.10	.05	.01
☐	61 Pat Thomas	.15	.07	.01
☐	62 Mark Dennard	.10	.05	.01
☐	63 James(Mike) Heitmann	.10	.05	.01
☐	64 Kyle Field	.10	.05	.01
☐	65 Edd Hargett	.15	.07	.01
☐	66 Robert Slavens	.10	.05	.01
☐	67 Scott Slater	.10	.05	.01
☐	68 Louis Cheek	.10	.05	.01
☐	69 Ken Ford	.10	.05	.01
☐	70 Bill Hobbs	.10	.05	.01
☐	71 Bob Long	.10	.05	.01
☐	72 Jeff Paine	.10	.05	.01
☐	73 Garth Tennaper	.10	.05	.01
☐	74 David Bandy	.10	.05	.01
☐	75 Dennis Swilley	.15	.07	.01
☐	76 Mike Whitewell	.10	.05	.01
☐	77 Jim Cashion	.10	.05	.01
☐	78 Lisa Jordon	.10	.05	.01
☐	79 Yvonne Van Brandt	.10	.05	.01
☐	80 A-M Marching Band	.10	.05	.01
☐	81 Bobby Joe Conrad	.15	.07	.01
☐	82 Mike Mosley	.15	.07	.01
☐	83 Olsen Field	.10	.05	.01
☐	84 Jeff Schow	.10	.05	.01
☐	85 Al Givens	.10	.05	.01
☐	86 Steve Hughes	.10	.05	.01
☐	87 Lisa Herner	.10	.05	.01
☐	88 Traci Thomas	.10	.05	.01
☐	89 Karen Guerrero	.10	.05	.01
☐	90 Billy Pickard	.10	.05	.01
☐	91 David Ogrin	.10	.05	.01
☐	92 Kim Bauer	.10	.05	.01
☐	93 Warren Trahan	.10	.05	.01
☐	94 Bobby Kleinecke	.10	.05	.01
☐	95 Dave Elmendorf	.20	.10	.02
☐	96 Vicki Brown	.10	.05	.01
☐	97 Yvonne Hill	.10	.05	.01
☐	98 David Rollen	.10	.05	.01
☐	99 David Hardy	.10	.05	.01
☐	100 Director Card	.10	.05	.01

1990-91 UCLA

This 40-card set was produced by Collegiate Collection and features the men's and women's basketball teams. The standard size (2 1/2" by 3 1/2") cards feature on the fronts a mix of posed or action color player photos (with rounded corners), with a thin black border on royal blue background. While the school name appears above the picture in yellow lettering, the player's name appears in black lettering in a yellow stripe below the picture. The UCLA and Collegiate Collection logos at the top complete the card face. The horizontally oriented backs provide brief biography, statistics, and the card number, all within a royal blue border. Due to a production error, the Keith Owens card incorrectly depicts Destah Owens. A coupon was included in the set to exchange for a free replacement card. Note that the back of the corrected card differs from the regular issue in format and color. Men's basketball is represented by cards 1-15 and 35-39; women's basketball by cards 16-34.

	MINT	EXC	G-VG
COMPLETE SET (40)	12.50	6.25	1.25
COMMON PLAYER (1-40)	.30	.15	.03
☐ 1 Team Photo	.50	.25	.05
☐ 2 Tracy Murray	1.00	.50	.10
☐ 3 Ed O'Bannon	2.00	1.00	.20
☐ 4 Darrick Martin	1.00	.50	.10
☐ 5 Mitchell Butler	1.00	.50	.10
☐ 6 Mike Lanier	.75	.35	.07
☐ 7 Chris Kenny	.50	.25	.05
☐ 8A Keith Owens ERR	1.50	.75	.15
(Photo actually Destah Owens)			
☐ 8B Keith Owens COR	1.50	.75	.15
☐ 9 Dave Paulsell	.30	.15	.03
☐ 10 Shon Tarver	1.00	.50	.10
☐ 11 Rodney Zimmerman	.30	.15	.03
☐ 12 Zan Mason	.30	.15	.03
☐ 13 Gerald Madkins	1.00	.50	.10
☐ 14 Don MacLean	2.00	1.00	.20
☐ 15 Lou Richie	.30	.15	.03
☐ 16 Billie Moore CO	.30	.15	.03
☐ 17 Rehema Stephens	.30	.15	.03
☐ 18 Nicole Anderson	.30	.15	.03
☐ 19 Amy Jalewalia	.30	.15	.03
☐ 20 Pam Walker CO	.30	.15	.03
☐ 21 Lynn Kamrath	.30	.15	.03
☐ 22 Detra Lockhart	.30	.15	.03
☐ 23 Stacie Gravely	.30	.15	.03
☐ 24 Laura Collins	.30	.15	.03
☐ 25 Genevieve Vanoostveen	.30	.15	.03
☐ 26 Dede Mosman	.30	.15	.03
☐ 27 Nicole Young	.30	.15	.03
☐ 28 Dawn Baker	.30	.15	.03
☐ 29 Melissa Gische	.30	.15	.03
☐ 30 Rachelle Roulier	.30	.15	.03
☐ 31 Marcy Tarabochia	.30	.15	.03
☐ 32 Natalie Williams	.30	.15	.03
☐ 33 Kathy Olivier CO	.30	.15	.03
☐ 34 Mary Hegarty CO	.30	.15	.03
☐ 35 Jim Harrick CO	.50	.25	.05
☐ 36 Brad Holland CO	.50	.25	.05
☐ 37 Tony Fuller CO	.30	.15	.03
☐ 38 Ken Barone CO	.30	.15	.03
☐ 39 Mark Gottfried CO	.30	.15	.03
☐ 40 Checklist Card	.30	.15	.03

1991 UCLA 144

This 144-card set was produced by Collegiate Collection and measures the standard size (2 1/2" by 3 1/2"). The fronts feature a mix of black and white or color player photos, with royal blue borders and the player's name in the yellow stripe below the picture. The horizontally oriented backs present biographical information, career summary, or statistics on a white background with blue lettering and borders. The cards are numbered on the back.

	MINT	EXC	G-VG
COMPLETE SET (144)	15.00	7.50	1.50
COMMON PLAYER (1-144)	.10	.05	.01
☐ 1 John Wooden CO	.30	.15	.03
☐ 2 Kareem Abdul Jabbar	.50	.25	.05
☐ 3 Bill Walton	.35	.17	.03
☐ 4 Larry Farmer	.20	.10	.02
☐ 5 Marques Johnson	.25	.12	.02
☐ 6 Walt Hazzard	.20	.10	.02
☐ 7 Henry Bibby	.15	.07	.01
☐ 8 Gail Goodrich	.20	.10	.02
☐ 9 Jim Harrick	.15	.07	.01
☐ 10 Kareem Abdul Jabbar	.50	.25	.05
☐ 11 Mike Warren	.20	.10	.02
☐ 12 Gary Maloncon	.10	.05	.01
☐ 13 Keith Wilkes	.10	.05	.01
☐ 14 Kiki Vandeweghe	.20	.10	.02
☐ 15 1969 NCAA Champs	.10	.05	.01
☐ 16 Sidney Wicks	.20	.10	.02
☐ 17 Andre McCarter	.15	.07	.01
☐ 18 Michael Holton	.10	.05	.01
☐ 19 Greg Lee	.10	.05	.01
☐ 20 John Wooden CO	.25	.12	.02
☐ 21 Gene Bartow	.10	.05	.01
☐ 22 Richard Washington	.15	.07	.01
☐ 23 Brad Wright	.10	.05	.01
☐ 24 Pooh Richardson	.25	.12	.02
☐ 25 Terry Shofield	.10	.05	.01
☐ 26 Gig Sims	.10	.05	.01
☐ 27 Darren Daye	.15	.07	.01
☐ 28 Dave Immel	.10	.05	.01
☐ 29 Tommy Curtis	.10	.05	.01
☐ 30 Bill Walton	.35	.17	.03
☐ 31 Larry Brown	.15	.07	.01
☐ 32 Kevin Walker	.10	.05	.01
☐ 33 Kareem Abdul Jabbar	.50	.25	.05
☐ 34 Kenny Heitz	.15	.07	.01
☐ 35 Gary Cunningham	.10	.05	.01
☐ 36 Lynn Shackelford	.20	.10	.02
☐ 37 Keith Wilkes	.20	.10	.02
☐ 38 1975 NCAA Champs	.10	.05	.01
☐ 39 Raymond Townsend	.15	.07	.01
☐ 40 Pete Trgovich	.15	.07	.01
☐ 41 Kelvin Butler	.10	.05	.01
☐ 42 Ed Sheldrake	.10	.05	.01
☐ 43 Larry Hollyfield	.20	.10	.02
☐ 44 Montel Hatcher	.15	.07	.01
☐ 45 Denise Curry	.15	.07	.01
☐ 46 Curtis Rowe	.20	.10	.02
☐ 47 David Meyers	.20	.10	.02
☐ 48 Lucius Allen	.20	.10	.02
☐ 49 Kenny Fields	.15	.07	.01
☐ 50 John Vallely	.20	.10	.02
☐ 51 Wooden and Nell	.20	.10	.02
☐ 52 Sidney Wicks	.20	.10	.02
☐ 53 1973 NCAA Champs	.10	.05	.01
☐ 54 Jack Haley	.15	.07	.01
☐ 55 Ralph Drollinger	.15	.07	.01
☐ 56 Don Johnson	.10	.05	.01
☐ 57 Bill Ellis	.10	.05	.01
☐ 58 Willie Naulls	.15	.07	.01
☐ 59 Ron Livingston	.10	.05	.01
☐ 60 Bill Putnam	.10	.05	.01
☐ 61 Rod Foster	.15	.07	.01
☐ 62 Bill Walton	.35	.17	.03
☐ 63 Roy Hamilton	.15	.07	.01
☐ 64 Jim Spillane	.10	.05	.01
☐ 65 Ralph Jackson	.15	.07	.01
☐ 66 Morris Taft	.10	.05	.01
☐ 67 Dick Ridgeway	.10	.05	.01
☐ 68 Dave Minor	.10	.05	.01
☐ 69 1965 Champs	.10	.05	.01
☐ 70 Karl Kraushaar	.10	.05	.01
☐ 71 Craig Jackson	.15	.07	.01
☐ 72 Kenny Washington	.20	.10	.02
☐ 73 Keith Wilkes	.20	.10	.02
☐ 74 Stuart Gray	.20	.10	.02
☐ 75 John Green	.10	.05	.01
☐ 76 Doug McIntosh	.15	.07	.01
☐ 77 Walt Hazzard	.20	.10	.02
☐ 78 Frank Lubin	.10	.05	.01
☐ 79 Don Piper	.10	.05	.01
☐ 80 1967 Champs	.10	.05	.01
☐ 81 Kenny Booker	.15	.07	.01
☐ 82 Marques Johnson	.20	.10	.02
☐ 83 Bill Walton	.35	.17	.03
☐ 84 1972 Champs	.10	.05	.01
☐ 85 Steve Patterson	.15	.07	.01
☐ 86 1964 NCAA Champs	.10	.05	.01
☐ 87 Alan Sawyer	.10	.05	.01
☐ 88 Walt Torrence	.10	.05	.01
☐ 89 Gail Goodrich	.20	.10	.02
☐ 90 Ralph Bunche	.15	.07	.01

☐	91	Swen Nater	.20	.10	.02
☐	92	Larry Farmer	.15	.07	.01
☐	93	Kareem Abdul-Jabbar	.50	.25	.05
☐	94	Mike Sanders	.15	.07	.01
☐	95	Niguel Miguel	.15	.07	.01
☐	96	Jackie Robinson	.30	.15	.03
☐	97	Dick West	.10	.05	.01
☐	98	Rafer Johnson	.25	.12	.02
☐	99	John Berberich	.10	.05	.01
☐	100	Director Card	.10	.05	.01
☐	101	Richard Linthicum	.10	.05	.01
☐	102	Chuck Clustka	.10	.05	.01
☐	103	Wooden, Crum, and Cunningham	.15	.07	.01
☐	104	Jerry Norman	.10	.05	.01
☐	105	John Moore	.10	.05	.01
☐	106	Trevor Wilson	.25	.12	.02
☐	107	David Greenwood	.20	.10	.02
☐	108	Wooden and Morgan	.20	.10	.02
☐	109	Kareem Abdul Jabbar	.50	.25	.05
☐	110	Ann Meyers	.20	.10	.02
☐	111	Denny Crum	.15	.07	.01
☐	112	Pierce Works	.10	.05	.01
☐	113	Carl Cozens	.10	.05	.01
☐	114	George Stanich	.10	.05	.01
☐	115	Don Ashen	.10	.05	.01
☐	116	David Greenwood	.15	.07	.01
☐	117	1971 Team Photo	.10	.05	.01
☐	118	Johns Barksdale	.10	.05	.01
☐	119	1978 Champion	.10	.05	.01
☐	120	John Stanich	.10	.05	.01
☐	121	Don Barksdale	.10	.05	.01
☐	122	1968 Champs	.10	.05	.01
☐	123	Carl Knowles	.10	.05	.01
☐	124	Don Bragg	.15	.07	.01
☐	125	Ducky Drake CO	.15	.07	.01
☐	126	John Ball	.10	.05	.01
☐	127	Pauley Pavilion	.10	.05	.01
☐	128	Sam Balter	.10	.05	.01
☐	129	A Caddy Works Team	.10	.05	.01
☐	130	John Wooden CO	.25	.12	.02
☐	131	Fred Goss	.15	.07	.01
☐	132	Keith Erickson	.20	.10	.02
☐	133	Pete Blackman	.10	.05	.01
☐	134	Gail Goodrich	.20	.10	.02
☐	135	Kent Miller	.10	.05	.01
☐	136	Jack Ketchum	.10	.05	.01
☐	137	1970 Team Photo	.10	.05	.01
☐	138	Jim Milhorn	.10	.05	.01
☐	139	Bill Rankin	.10	.05	.01
☐	140	Kenny Heitz	.15	.07	.01
☐	141	Bob(Ace) Caikins	.10	.05	.01
☐	142	J.D. Morgan	.10	.05	.01
☐	143	Fred Slaughter	.15	.07	.01
☐	144	Director Card	.10	.05	.01

1988-89 UNLV HOF/Police

This 12-card set was produced by Hall of Fame Cards, Inc.; cards measure the standard size (2 1/2" by 3 1/2"). The front features a color action shot of the player, trimmed in red borders on a gray card face. The words "Runnin' Rebels" appears in red lettering above the picture, while the school name, player's name, and his position appear below. The back is printed in red and includes biographical information, career statistics at UNLV, and an anti-drug message titled "Rebel Rap." The cards are numbered on the back and checklisted below accordingly. Supposedly there were only 10,000 sets produced.

		MINT	EXC	G-VG
COMPLETE SET (12)		40.00	20.00	4.00
COMMON PLAYER (1-12)		1.50	.75	.15
☐ 1	Stacey Augmon	10.00	5.00	1.00
☐ 2	Greg Anthony	7.50	3.75	.75
☐ 3	Anderson Hunt	6.00	3.00	.60
☐ 4	George Ackles	4.00	2.00	.40
☐ 5	David Butler	4.00	2.00	.40
☐ 6	Clint Rossum	1.50	.75	.15
☐ 7	Moses Scurry	3.00	1.50	.30
☐ 8	Barry Young	1.50	.75	.15
☐ 9	James Jones	1.50	.75	.15
☐ 10	Stacey Cvijanovich	1.50	.75	.15
☐ 11	Chris Jeter	1.50	.75	.15
☐ 12	Bryan Emerzian	1.50	.75	.15

1989-90 UNLV HOF/Police

This 14-card set was produced by Hall of Fame Cards, Inc. and measures the standard size (2 1/2" by 3 1/2"). The front features a color action player photo outlined by a thin black border. The school name is superimposed at the right upper corner of the picture. The background is red for the top half of the card face and gray for the bottom half. The player's name is printed in red lettering below the picture. In a horizontal format the back has biographical information and the slogan "Say No to Drugs." The cards are numbered on the back. Supposedly less than 6000 sets were produced.

		MINT	EXC	G-VG
COMPLETE SET (14)		30.00	15.00	3.00
COMMON PLAYER (1-14)		1.00	.50	.10
☐ 1	Stacey Augmon	6.00	3.00	.60
☐ 2	Greg Anthony	4.00	2.00	.40
☐ 3	Larry Johnson	10.00	5.00	1.00
☐ 4	George Ackles	3.00	1.50	.30
☐ 5	Moses Scurry	2.00	1.00	.20
☐ 6	Anderson Hunt (Hank Gathers visible in background)	5.00	2.50	.50
☐ 7	Travis Bice	1.00	.50	.10
☐ 8	David Butler	2.00	1.00	.20
☐ 9	Stacey Cvijanovich	1.00	.50	.10
☐ 10	Chris Jeter	1.00	.50	.10
☐ 11	Bryan Emerzian	1.00	.50	.10
☐ 12	James Jones (Hank Gathers visible in background)	3.00	1.50	.30
☐ 13	Barry Young	1.00	.50	.10
☐ 14	Dave Rice	1.00	.50	.10

1989-90 UNLV 7-Eleven

This 13-card set was sponsored by 7-Eleven, 98.5 KLUC-FM radio, and Nationwide Communications Inc. The cards measure the standard size (2 1/2" by 3 1/2") and are printed on very thin card stock. The fronts feature color action player photos, with black borders on red card face. The team and player's names appear in red lettering in gray boxes above and below the picture respectively. The backs are printed in black on white card stock and provide biographical information and player profile. The cards are unnumbered and are checklisted below in alphabetical order, with the uniform number after the player's name.

	MINT	EXC	G-VG
COMPLETE SET (13)	20.00	10.00	2.00
COMMON PLAYER (1-13)	.75	.35	.07
☐ 1 Greg Anthony 50	2.50	1.25	.25
☐ 2 Stacy Augmon 32	3.50	1.75	.35
☐ 3 Travis Bice 13	.75	.35	.07
☐ 4 David Butler 00	1.50	.75	.15
☐ 5 Stacey Cvijanovich 05	.75	.35	.07
☐ 6 Bryan Emerzian 15	.75	.35	.07
☐ 7 Anderson Hunt 12	2.00	1.00	.20
☐ 8 Chris Jeter 53	.75	.35	.07
☐ 9 Larry Johnson 04	9.00	4.50	.90
☐ 10 James Jones 34	.75	.35	.07
☐ 11 Moses Scurry 35	1.50	.75	.15
☐ 12 Barry Young 33	.75	.35	.07
☐ 13 Jerry Tarkanian CO	1.50	.75	.15

1990-91 UNLV HOF/Police

This 15-card set was produced by Hall of Fame Cards, Inc. and features the UNLV Runnin' Rebels, the 1990 NCAA national champions. The cards measure the standard size (2 1/2" by 3 1/2"). The fronts feature color action player photos; cards

numbered 11-13 feature "Future Rebels" and have posed color photos. All cards have red borders on the top and bottom and white borders on the sides. A red diagonal cuts across the lower right corner of the picture, with the words "1990 Nat'l Champions" in white lettering. The player's name and position are given in white lettering in the bottom red border. The backs have statistical information and the slogan "Say No to Drugs" in either horizontal or vertical formats. The cards are numbered on the back. Supposedly only 15,000 sets were produced; each set is individually numbered on card number 4 Anderson Hunt.

	MINT	EXC	G-VG
COMPLETE SET (15)	20.00	10.00	2.00
COMMON PLAYER (1-15)	.75	.35	.07
☐ 1 Larry Johnson	5.00	2.50	.50
☐ 2 Stacey Augmon	3.00	1.50	.30
☐ 3 Greg Anthony	2.00	1.00	.20
☐ 4 Anderson Hunt	1.50	.75	.15
☐ 5 Travis Bice	.75	.35	.07
☐ 6 George Ackles	1.25	.60	.12
☐ 7 Bryan Emerzian	.75	.35	.07
☐ 8 Dave Rice	.75	.35	.07
☐ 9 Chris Jeter	.75	.35	.07
☐ 10 Anderson Hunt	1.50	.75	.15
☐ 11 Evric Gray	.75	.35	.07
☐ 12 Bobby Joyce	.75	.35	.07
☐ 13 H. Waldman	.75	.35	.07
☐ 14 Larry Johnson	5.00	2.50	.50
☐ 15 Runnin' Rebels	.75	.35	.07
(Card lists records broken by UNLV)			

1990-91 UNLV Smokey

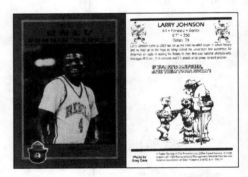

This 15-card set was sponsored by the USDA Forest Service in cooperation with other federal agencies. The standard size (2 1/2" by 3 1/2") cards were issued as a set of single cards or as a sheet consisting of four rows of four cards (the 16th slot is blank). The front features a color action player photo, with gray border on dark red background. In black lettering the words "1990-91 UNLV Runnin' Rebels" are printed above the picture, with the player's name and number below. The Smokey the Bear logo in the lower left corner completes the card face. The back presents biographical information and a fire prevention cartoon starring Smokey. The cards unnumbered and we have checklisted them below in alphabetical order, with the jersey number to the right of the name.

	MINT	EXC	G-VG
COMPLETE SET (15)	20.00	10.00	2.00
COMMON PLAYER (1-15)	.75	.35	.07
☐ 1 George Ackles 44	1.25	.60	.12
☐ 2 Greg Anthony 50	2.00	1.00	.20
☐ 3 Stacey Augmon 32	3.00	1.50	.30
☐ 4 Travis Bice 3	.75	.35	.07
☐ 5 Bryan Emerzian 15	.75	.35	.07
☐ 6 Evric Gray 23	.75	.35	.07
☐ 7 Anderson Hunt 12	1.50	.75	.15
☐ 8 Chris Jeter 53	.75	.35	.07

☐ 9 Larry Johnson 4	6.00	3.00	.60
☐ 10 Bobby Joyce 42	.75	.35	.07
☐ 11 Melvin Love 40	.75	.35	.07
☐ 12 Dave Rice 30	.75	.35	.07
☐ 13 Elmore Spencer 24	2.00	1.00	.20
☐ 14 Jerry Tarkanian CO	1.50	.75	.15
☐ 15 H. Waldman 31	.75	.35	.07

1990-91 UNLV Season to Remember

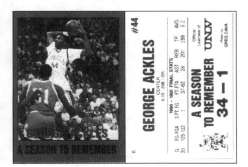

This 15-card set features the UNLV Runnin' Rebels, who were eliminated in the 1991 NCAA Final Four. The cards measure the standard size (2 1/2" by 3 1/2"). The front features a color action photo of the player, with a thin black border on dark red background. The school name is superimposed at the right upper corner of the picture, and the player's name is inscribed across the bottom of the picture. In black lettering the words "A Season to Remember" appear below the photo. The back gives biographical and statistical information in a horizontal format, and repeats the words "A Season to Remember," with the team record "34-1." The cards are numbered on the back.

	MINT	EXC	G-VG
COMPLETE SET (15)	15.00	7.50	1.50
COMMON PLAYER (1-15)	.50	.25	.05

☐ 1 Larry Johnson	4.00	2.00	.40
☐ 2 Stacey Augmon	2.25	1.10	.22
☐ 3 Greg Anthony	1.50	.75	.15
☐ 4 Anderson Hunt	1.00	.50	.10
☐ 5 Travis Bice	.50	.25	.05
☐ 6 George Ackles	1.00	.50	.10
☐ 7 Bryan Emerzian	.50	.25	.05
☐ 8 Dave Rice	.50	.25	.05
☐ 9 Chris Jeter	.50	.25	.05
☐ 10 Elmore Spencer	1.00	.50	.10
☐ 11 Evric Gray	.50	.25	.05
☐ 12 Bobby Joyce	.50	.25	.05
☐ 13 H. Waldman	.50	.25	.05
☐ 14 Melvin Love	.50	.25	.05
☐ 15 Rebel All-Americans	1.25	.60	.12
(Hunt, Anthony, Ackles, Johnson, and Augmon)			

1989-90 UTEP Drug Emporium

This 24-card set was sponsored by 7-Together and Drug Emporium and their names are on the top of the card. The cards measure (the standard) 2 1/2" by 3 1/2". The team name/subtitle ("Star Miners") is given above the photo, and the player's name and position below it, with black and white photos for older players and color for newer players. Biographical information is on the back. Current and past NBA Stars featured in this set are Nate Archibald and Tim Hardaway; also note the presence of a card of Nolan Richardson, who went on to coach the

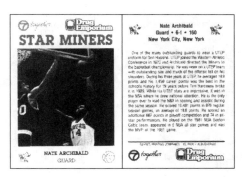

Arkansas Razorbacks. The set is not numbered so the subjects are listed below in alphabetical order by name.

	MINT	EXC	G-VG
COMPLETE SET (24)	10.00	5.00	1.00
COMMON PLAYER (1-24)	.20	.10	.02

☐ 1 Nate Archibald	.75	.35	.07
☐ 2 Jim Barnes	.40	.20	.04
☐ 3 Rus Bradburd	.20	.10	.02
☐ 4 Dallas David	.20	.10	.02
☐ 5 Antonio Davis	.50	.25	.05
☐ 6 Ralph Davis	.30	.15	.03
☐ 7 Norm Ellenberger CO	.30	.15	.03
☐ 8 Francis Ezenwa	.20	.10	.02
☐ 9 Greg Foster	.50	.25	.05
☐ 10 Joe Griffin	.20	.10	.02
☐ 11 Henry Hall	.20	.10	.02
☐ 12 Tim Hardaway	5.00	2.50	.50
☐ 13 Don Haskins CO	.30	.15	.03
☐ 14 Merle Heimer	.20	.10	.02
☐ 15 Bobby Joe Hill	.40	.20	.04
☐ 16 Greg Lackey	.20	.10	.02
☐ 17 David Lattin	.50	.25	.05
☐ 18 Marlon Maxey	.20	.10	.02
☐ 19 Mark McCall	.20	.10	.02
☐ 20 Chris Perez	.20	.10	.02
☐ 21 Nolan Richardson	.50	.25	.05
☐ 22 Arlandis Rush	.20	.10	.02
☐ 23 Alprentice Stewart	.20	.10	.02
☐ 24 David Van Dyke	.20	.10	.02

1988-89 Virginia Hardee's

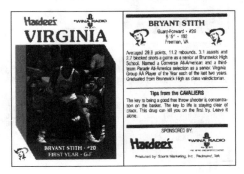

This 16-card set was sponsored by Hardee's Restaurants in conjunction with WINA Radio AM 1070, and their company names appear on the top of the card. The cards measure (the standard) 2 1/2" by 3 1/2". The action color photos are surrounded on their sides and bottom by blue and orange thick borders (the school's colors), with the Cavalier logo in the lower left hand corner. The player's name, jersey number, year, and position appear below the photo. The back gives biographical information

	MINT	EXC	G-VG
COMPLETE SET (16)	40.00	20.00	4.00
COMMON PLAYER (1-16)	2.00	1.00	.20
☐ 1 Brent Bair 42	2.00	1.00	.20
☐ 2 Matt Blundin 30	3.00	1.50	.30
☐ 3 Mark Cooke 31	2.00	1.00	.20
☐ 4 John Crotty 22	6.00	3.00	.60
☐ 5 Brent Dabbs 32	2.00	1.00	.20
☐ 6 Jeff Daniel 44	2.00	1.00	.20
☐ 7 Terry Holland CO	4.00	2.00	.40
☐ 8 Dirk Katstra 24	2.00	1.00	.20
☐ 9 Richard Morgan 11	4.00	2.00	.40
☐ 10 Anthony Oliver 10	2.00	1.00	.20
☐ 11 Bryant Stith 20	6.00	3.00	.60
☐ 12 Kenny Turner 12	2.00	1.00	.20
☐ 13 Curtis Williams 21	2.00	1.00	.20
☐ 14 Cheerleaders	2.00	1.00	.20
☐ 15 Coaching Staff	2.00	1.00	.20
☐ 16 Title Card	2.00	1.00	.20

1989-90 Wisconsin Smokey

This 14-card set was sponsored by the USDA Forest Service in cooperation with the National Association of State Foresters and BD and A, Inc. The cards were issued on an unperforated sheet with four rows of four cards; two of the cards slots are blacked out where the photo should appear and feature a fire cartoon on their backs. After cutting, the cards measure the standard size (2 1/2" by 3 1/2"). The fronts feature a mix of posed and action color player photos on a white card face. Above the picture appears the school name (in red lettering) and a black stripe. Red and black stripes traverse the card below the picture, with the Smokey logo in the lower left corner and player identification to the right. The backs have biographical

information, player evaluation, and a fire prevention cartoon starring Smokey. The cards are unnumbered and checklisted below in alphabetical order, with the uniform number after the player's name.

	MINT	EXC	G-VG
COMPLETE SET (14)	8.00	4.00	.80
COMMON PLAYER (1-14)	.60	.30	.06
☐ 1 Bobby Douglass 10	.60	.30	.06
☐ 2 John Ellenson 40	.60	.30	.06
☐ 3 Brian Good 12	.60	.30	.06
☐ 4 Damon Harrell 41	.60	.30	.06
☐ 5 Larry Hisle Jr. 4	1.00	.50	.10
☐ 6 Danny Jones 50	.60	.30	.06
☐ 7 Jason Johnsen 5	.60	.30	.06
☐ 8 Grant Johnson 52	.60	.30	.06
☐ 9 Tim Locum 44	.60	.30	.06
☐ 10 Carlton McGee 32	.60	.30	.06
☐ 11 Kurt Portmann 53	.60	.30	.06
☐ 12 Willie Simms 23	.60	.30	.06
☐ 13 Patrick Tompkins 43	.60	.30	.06
☐ 14 Steve Yoder CO	.60	.30	.06

Basketball Alphabetical Index

This alphabetical index presents all the cards issued for any particular player (or person) included in the card sets listed in this *Sport Americana Basketball Card Price Guide*. It will prove to be an invaluable tool for the seasoned and novice collector alike. Although this book was carefully compiled and proofread, in the very nature of the task it is inevitable that errors, misspellings, and inconsistencies may occur. Please keep a record of any errors that come to your attention and send them to the author, so that these corrections may be incorporated into future editions of the basketball alphabetical checklist.

How to Use the Alphabetical Checklist

This alphabetical checklist has been designed to be user friendly. The set code abbreviations used throughout are easily memorized. The format adopted for card identification is explained below. However, the large number of card sets contained in this volume require that the reader become familiar first with the abbreviations and format used in card identification. **PLEASE READ THE FOLLOWING SECTION CARE-FULLY BEFORE ATTEMPTING TO USE THE CHECKLIST.**

The player cards are listed alphabetically by the player's current last name. Nicknames (e.g., "Fat" Lever) and former names (e.g., Lew Alcindor) are given in parentheses on the second line of each entry. Different players with otherwise identical names are sometimes distinguished by additional information [e.g., Adams, John Louisville versus Adams, John LSU]. The codes following the players' names are indented and give the card sets and card numbers in the sets

in which the players appeared. The set code abbreviations are designed so that each code is distinctive for a particular card set.

Depending on the particular card set, the set code abbreviations consist of from three to five distinctive elements:

a) Year of issue (listed in ascending chronological order);
b) Maker (producer or manufacturer);
c) Set code suffixes (always after a slash);
d) Number on card (always separated from the maker or set code suffix by a dash);
e) Individual card descriptive suffixes.

When two different makers issued cards for a player in the same year, the cards are listed alphabetically according to the maker's name (e.g., 1991 Courtside precedes 1991 Star Pics).

Many cards can be distinguished by three parameters. For some cards, however, it is necessary to have four parameters for unambiguous identification. For example, there are two 1988-89 Dallas Maverick Bud Light card sets. Note in the following sample entry the use of set code suffixes to distinguish different cards from each of these sets:

Davis, Brad
    88Mavs/BLC-15 =1988-89 Dallas Mavericks Bud Light
                    Big League Cards #15
    88Mavs/CardN-15 =1988-89 Dallas Mavericks Bud Light
                    Card Night #15

The card number typically corresponds to the particular number on the card itself; in some instances, the card number also involves letter prefixes. For example, the 1990-91 North Carolina Promo cards are numbered "NC1-NC10." For the most part, cards in unnumbered sets are usually entered alphabetically according to the player's last name and assigned a number arbitrarily. In a few instances unnumbered cards are simply identified as if their card number were "x" or "xx."

Although individual card suffixes are not necessary for unambiguous card identification, they do provide the reader with additional information about the card. These abbreviations were added by the author and always follow the card number. In rare cases involving numbers with letter prefixes or the "x/xx" designations, the set code suffixes were omitted to avoid a cumbersome designation. Some of the set code suffixes utilized in this book are AS (All-Star card), CO (coach card), LL (League Leader card), M (multi-player or miscellaneous card), and TC (Team Checklist card).

Lastly, the user of this checklist will notice that the cards of players from sports other than basketball (as well as subjects not even from the world of sports) are contained in this checklist. This circumstance arose because of the decision to include multi-sport sets containing basketball cards in this checklist. In the price guide, these multi-sport cards sets are typically indicated by an asterisk (*), which is placed after the set code suffix in the alphabetical checklist.

Basketball Alphabetical Set Codes

Code	Explanation
A1	A1 Premium Beer
ActPh	Action Photos
Alta	Alta-Dena
AR	Arkansas
Arby's	Arby's
AS	All-Star(s)
ASG	All-Star Game
Ash	Ashland Oil
Award	Awards or Award Winners
AZ	Arizona
AZSt	Arizona State
B	Bowman
BASF	BASF
Bell	Bell Brand
Best	Best of the Old/New
Bird	Larry Bird
BK	Burger King
Blaz	Trailblazers
BLC	Big League Cards
Blue	Blue Shield
Book	Bookmarks
BP	British Petroleum

Bread	Bread for Health
Buck	Buckman Discs
Bucks	Milwaukee Bucks
BudL	Bud Light
Bullet	Bullets
Busch	Busch Bavarian
BYU	Brigham Young University
CardN	Card Night
Carl	Carl's Jr.
Carn	Carnation Milk
Carv	Carvel Discs
CBA	Continental Basketball Association
Celt	Celtics
Circ	Circle K
CL	Checklist
Class	Classic Draft Picks
Clem	Clemson
Clip	Clippers
CO	Coach(es)
Cocoa	Cocoa Puffs
Coke	Coke or Coca-Cola
Col	Colonels
CollB	CollectABooks
Conv	Converse
Court	Courtside
CrtKg	Court Kings
Crunch	Crunch'n'Munch
CT	Connecticut
Dell	Dell Flipbooks
Ent	Entemann's
Eq	Equal
Erving	Julius Erving
Essex	Essex Meats
ExhSC	Exhibits Sports Champions
F	Fleer
Fairf	Fairfield
FL	Florida
Flor	Floridians
FLSt	Florida State
Food	Foodland or Foodtown
Foot	Foot Locker Slam Fest
Fourn	Fournier NBA Estrellas
Franz	Franz
Fresno	Fresno State
GA	Georgia
GATech	Georgia Tech
Gator	Gatorade
George	Georgetown
Getty	Getty
Giant	Giant Self Service
Globe	Globetrotters
Great	Greats
Green	Green Border
Gunth	Gunther Beer
Handy	Handyman
Hardee	Hardee's
Hawks	Atlanta Hawks
Hawth	Hawthorne Milk
HOF	Hall of Fame Bookmarks

Hoops .... Hoops
Humpt .... Humpty Dumpty Discs
Icee .... Icee Ber
IL .... Illinoi
IN .... Indiana
Ins .... (Sticker or Poster) Insert
JB .... Jack in the Box
JMS .... JMS
Kareem .... Kareem Abdul Jabbar
Keds .... Keds KedKards
Kell .... Kellogg's
Kings .... Sacramento Kings
KS .... Kansas
KY .... Kentucky
Laker .... Los Angeles Lakers
Lanc .... Lancaster
Life .... Lifebuoy
Linn .... Linnett
Lite .... Lite Beer
LL .... League Leader card
Louville .... Louisville
LSU .... Louisiana State University
M .... Multi-player or miscellaneous card
Magic .... Magic Photos or Orlando Magic
Majik .... Majik Market
Mara .... Marathon Oil
Marine .... MarineMidland
Marq .... Marquette
Mavs .... Mavericks
McDon .... McDonald's
McNees .... McNeese State
MD .... Maryland
ME .... Maine
MI .... Michigan
MISt .... Michigan State
MJ .... Michael Jordan
MO .... Missouri
Nab .... Nabisco
NBAPA .... NBA Players Association
NC .... North Carolina
NCSt .... North Carolina State
ND .... Notre Dame
NE .... Nebraska
Nets .... New Jersey Nets
Nike .... Nike
Nugget .... Denver Nuggets
OKSt .... Oklahoma State
OldH .... Old Home
OpenP .... Open Pantry
ORSt .... Oregon State
Pacer .... Indiana Pacers
Panin .... Panini stickers
PartM .... Partridge Meats
PC .... ProCards
Pep .... Pepsi
PhilM .... Philip Morris
Pitt .... Pittsburgh
Pizza .... Pizza Hut
Pol .... Police

Polar .... Polaroid
Prism .... Prism Stickers
Proto .... Prototypes
ProV .... Pro Visions
Publix .... Publix
Quaker .... Quaker Sports Oddities
RCCola .... Royal Crown Cola
R .... Rookie(s)
Rich .... Louis Rich
Rocket .... San Diego Rockets
Rook .... Rookie Sensations
ROY .... Rookies of the Year
Royal .... Royal Desserts
Safe .... Safeway
SanJ .... San Jose State
SC .... South Carolina
Sch .... Schedules
Schick .... Schick Legends
School .... Schoolyard Stars
Season .... Season to Remember
Seven 7-Eleven
Sixers .... Philadelphia 76ers
Shur .... Shur-Fresh
SlamD .... Slam Dunk
Smok .... Smokey Bear
SoMiss .... Southern Mississippi
Sonic .... Supersonics
South .... Southern University
Sov .... Soviets
Spurs .... San Antonio Spurs
Star .... Star Company
StarP .... Star Pics
StBon .... St. Bonaventure
Stand .... Standups
Sunb .... Sunbeam Bread
Super .... Superstars or Supers
SWLou .... Southwestern Louisiana
Syr .... Syracuse
T .... Topps
TC .... Team Checklist card
TCMA .... TCMA
Test .... Test Issue
TexAM .... Texas A & M
Thirst .... Thirst Break
Tm .... Team
TN .... Tennessee
Trio .... Trio Stickers
TWolv .... Timberwolves
Union .... Union Oil
Up .... Update
VA .... Virginia
Warr .... Warriors
WhHen .... White Hen Pantry
Wildct .... Wildcat News
Wooden ...... Wooden Award

Allen, Anthony
86George/Pol-3
87George/Pol-3
88George/Pol-3
89George/Pol-3
91George/100-35
Allen, Doug
90AZSt/200*-14
Allen, Eric
90AZSt/200*-32
Allen, Eric MSU
90MlSt/200*-14
90MlSt/200*-67
Allen, Ermal
88KY/269-57
89KY/300*-154
Allen, Forrest C.
(Phog)
68HOF-1
Allen, Greg
90FLSt/200*-84
Allen, Lucius
69Sonic/Sunb-1
69T-6
70T-31
71T-27
72T-145
73NBAPA-1
73T-88
74T-19
75T-52
76T-34
77T-87
78T-6
91UCLA/144-48
Allen, Mike
88KY/Sov-4
Allen, Randy
89Kings/Carl-40
90Hoops-254
90SkyBox-243
Allen, Sonny
89PC/CBA-126
Allen, Ted
48ExhSC-1
Allen, Terry
90Clem/200*-15
Allison, Doug
91SC/200*-36
Allyson, June
48T/Magic*-F9
Alworth, Lance
91AR/100*-2
Ambrose, Kyle
91GATech*-47
Ammaccapore, Danielle
90AZSt/200*-83
Amman, Richard
90FLSt/200*-186
Andaya, Shawn
91TexAM-45
Anderegg, Robert
90MlSt/200*-103
Andersen, Greta
57Union-43
Andersen, Morten
90MlSt/200*-25
90MlSt/200*-93
Anderson, Bobby
90FLSt/200*-180
Anderson, Brad
90AZ/125*-114
90AZ/125*-67
Anderson, Dwight
78KY/Food-7
79KY/Food-7
82TCMA/CBA-11
88KY/269-115
89KY/300*-19
Anderson, Eddie
90NE/Pol*-28
Anderson, Ernest

91OKSt*-45
Anderson, Forrest
90MlSt/200*-172
90MlSt/200*-190
Anderson, Gary
91AR/100*-50
Anderson, Greg
88F-101
88Spurs/Pol-1
89F-85
89Hoops-7
89Hoops/II-342
90F/Up-U51
90Hoops-173
90Panin-100
90SkyBox-155
Anderson, Jim OSU
89ORSt-16CO
89ORSt-3CO
Anderson, Jim
91GATech*-38
Anderson, Jorgen
55Ash-62
Anderson, Karl
89ORSt-2
Anderson, Kenny
89GATech/Pol-1
89GATech/Pol-2
89GATech/Pol-20M
89GATech/Pol-3
90GATech/Pol-1
90GATech/Pol-2
90GATech/Pol-3
91Court-3
91StarP-5
91StarP-70
Anderson, Ladell
87BYU-6
Anderson, Mike
90LSU/200*-39
Anderson, Milerd
89KY/300*-274
Anderson, Mitchell
83Star/NBA-134
84Star/NBA-226
85Star/NBA-139
Anderson, Nick
89Magic/Pep-1
90F-132
90F/Rook-7
90Hoops-214
90Hoops/II-373TC
90Panin-123
90SkyBox-199
Anderson, Nicole
90UCLA-18
Anderson, Richard
83Nugget/Pol-35
83Star/NBA-182
88Blaz/Franz-1
89F-126
89Hoops-182
90Hoops-49
90SkyBox-25
Anderson, Ron
84Star/NBA-214
89F-112
89Hoops-32
89Sixers/Kodak-1
90F-138
90Fresno/Smok-1
90Hoops-224
90Panin-128
90SkyBox-210
91F-150
Anderson, Taz
91GATech*-156
Anderson, Tim
90PC/CBA-141
Anderson, Willie
88Spurs/Pol-2
89F-140

89Hoops-235
90F-168
90Hoops-263
90Hoops/Super-86
90Panin-46
90SkyBox-252
91F-182
Anderzunas, Wally
70T-21
Andolsek, Eric
90LSU/200*-99
Andres, Ernie
86IN/GreatI-27
Andrews, Harold
89Louville/300*-65
Andrews, Jim
88KY/269-152
88KY/269-196
88KY/269-46
Andrews, Paul
89KY/300*-55
Angelo, Lou
90NC/200*-113
Anheuser, Rick
89NCSt/Coke-1
89NCSt/Coke-2
89NCSt/Coke-3
Ansley, Michael
89Magic/Pep-2
90F/Up-U66
90Hoops-215
90SkyBox-200
Anson, Adrian
(Cap)
90ND-xx
Anthony, Greg
88UNLV/HOF-2
89UNLV/HOF-2
89UNLV/Seven-1
90UNLV/HOF-3
90UNLV/Season-15M
90UNLV/Season-3
90UNLV/Smok-2
91Class-2
91Court-4
91StarP-15
Anthony, Kevin
90NC/200*-46
Anthony, Terry
90FLSt/200*-16
Anthony, Tyrone
90NC/200*-68
90NC/200*-91
90NC/Promos*-NC6
Apisa, Robert
90MlSt/200*-15
Applebaum, Herb
89NCSt/Coke-136
89NCSt/Coke-176
Archer, Mike
90LSU/200*-12
Archibald, Nate
71T-29
72T-115
72T-169AS
72T-171LL
72T-172LL
72T-176LL
73T-153LL
73T-154LL
73T-158LL
73T-1AS
74T-170
75Carv-1
75T-124M
75T-15AS
75T-5LL
76Buck-1
76T-129AS
76T-20
77T-127
78RCCola-2

78T-26
79T-110
80T-124
80T-172
80T-4
80T-78
81T-3
81T-45M
81T-E100
83Star/NBA-39
84Star/Arena-C1
89UTEP/Drug-1
Ard, Jim
71T-191
Arden, Eve
48T/Magic*-F16
Argento, Phil
88KY/269-241
88KY/269-95
Ariri, Obed
90Clem/200*-176
90Clem/200*-48
Arizin, Paul
57T-10
61F-2
61F-45IA
Armstrong, B.J.
89Bulls/Eq-1
90F-22
90Hoops-60
90SkyBox-37
91F-25
Armstrong, Bruce
89Louville/300*-157
Armstrong, Jerry
89Louville/300*-98
Armstrong, Neill
91OKSt*-32
Armstrong, Paul
48Bowman-13
52Bread-1
Armstrong, Trace
90AZSt/Promos*-9
90AZSt/200*-84
Arndt, Charles
91SC/200*-53
Arneson, Mark
90AZ/125*-48
Arnette, Jay
63Kahn's-1
64Kahn's-4
Arnsparger, Bill
90LSU/200*-155
Arnzen, Bob
71T-94
90ND-51
Aronberg, Ric
90Clem/200*-85
Aronshone, Liz
90AZSt/200*-59
Arthur, Jean
48T/Magic*-F19
Artmeier, Dick
90FLSt/200*-109
Ashen, Don
91UCLA/144-115
Ashley, Robert
55Ash-37
Askew, Vincent
89PC/CBA-103
90PC/CBA-155
Askins, Keith
90Heat/Publix-1
Astbury, Andy
90AZSt/200*-106
Astle, Alan
87BYU-21
Atha, Dick
57T-14
Atherley, Scott
87ME/Pol*-7
Atiyeh, George

90LSU/200*-149
Atkins, Ken
81AZ/Pol-1CO
Atkinson, Kenny
90PC/CBA-123
Attles, Al
61F-1
69T-24
70T-59
Atwater, Steve
91AR/100*-27
Aubrey, Lloyd
90ND-39
Aubuchon, Chet
90MlSt/200*-181
90NC/200*-195
Auerbach, Arnold
(Red)
68HOF-2
84Star/Celt-1M
84Star/Celt-23
Augmon, Stacey
88UNLV/HOF-1
89UNLV/HOF-1
89UNLV/Seven-2
90UNLV/HOF-2
90UNLV/Season-15M
90UNLV/Season-2
90UNLV/Smok-3
91StarP-17
Augustine, Jerry
79Bucks/OpenP-1
Auksel, Pete
89NCSt/Coke-4
89NCSt/Coke-5
89NCSt/Coke-6
Ausbie, Hubert
(Geese)
71Globe-21
71Globe-22
71Globe-23
71Globe-24
71Globe-25
71Globe-26M
71Globe-64M
71Globe-66M
71Globe-69M
71Globe/Cocoa-18
71Globe/Cocoa-19
71Globe/Cocoa-1M
71Globe/Cocoa-4M
71Globe/Cocoa-6M
71Globe/Cocoa-7M
71Globe/Cocoa-9M
Austefjord, Haakon
90PC/CBA-49
Austin, Alex
90PC/CBA-166
Austin, Cliff
90Clem/200*-51
Austin, Clyde
89NCSt/Coke-7
89NCSt/Coke-8
89NCSt/Coke-9
Austin, Isaac
91Class-38
Austin, Neville
90GA/Smok-9
Avent, Anthony
91Class-9
91Court-5
91StarP-24
Aver, Joe
91GATech*-64
Averitt, Bird
74T-231
75T-229
76T-49
77T-8
Avezzano, Joe
90FLSt/200*-163
Avitable, Tony

90FLSt/200*-152
Awrey, Don
75Nab-22
Awtrey, Dennis
71T-124
72Icee-1
72T-139
73T-114
74T-74
75Suns-2
75T-130M
75T-39
76Suns-2
77Suns/Discs-21
79Bulls/Pol-20
Ayers, Randy
91StarP-59CO
Azinger, Paul
90FLSt/200*-181
Bach, John
85Star/CO-1
Back, Adrian
89KY/300*-279
Bacon, Henry
88Louville/194-129
88Louville/194-162
88Louville/194-189
88Louville/194-40
89Louville/300*-226
89Louville/300*-244
89Louville/300*-284
Baer, Buddy
48T/Magic*-A24
Baer, Max
48T/Magic*-A13
Baesler, Scott
88KY/269-94
90KY/ClassA-2
Bagdon, Ed
90MISt/200*-6
Bagley, John
83Star/NBA-229
84Star/NBA-215
85Star/NBA-153
86F-5
87F-5
88F-77
89Hoops-163
90Hoops-38
90SkyBox-13
Bailey, Carl
80TCMA/CBA-18
81TCMA/CBA-31
Bailey, Damon
88KY/Sov-5
Bailey, Don
91SC/200*-180
Bailey, James
79Sonic/Pol-2
80T-157
80T-34
80T-81
80T-91
81T-W96
83Star/NBA-74
84Star/NBA-26
Bailey, Thurl
83Star/NBA-135
84Star/NBA-227
85Star/NBA-140
86F-6
87F-6
88F-111
88Jazz/Smok-1
89F-151
89Hoops-251
89Jazz/OldH-1
89NCSt/Coke-10
89NCSt/Coke-11
89NCSt/Coke-12
90F-182
90Hoops-285

90Hoops/Super-95
90Jazz/Star-5
90Panin-54
90SkyBox-274
91F-197
Bailey, Tom
90FLSt/200*-166
Bailey, Winfred
90FLSt/200*-170
Bair, Brent
88VA/Hardee-1
Bakehorn, Jill
90Clem/200*-158
Baker, Dawn
90UCLA-28
Baker, Ron
91OKSt*-29
Balanis, Rod
89GATech/Pol-4
90GATech/Pol-4
Baldwin, Chuck
90Clem/200*-72
Baldwin, Dale
87KY/Coke-18
Balentine, Charles
82AR-1
Ball, Cedric
90PC/CBA-125
Ball, John
91UCLA/144-126
Ball, Larry
89Louville/300*-154
Ball, Michael
87South/Pol*-3M
Ball, Sam
89KY/300*-103
Ballard, Greg
80T-172
80T-84
81T-E94
83Star/NBA-205
84Star/NBA-186
87F-7
Balter, Sam
91UCLA/144-128
Baltzegar, Marty
91SC/200*-16
Baly, Bijou
89Fresno/Smok-2
Bando, Sal
79Bucks/OpenP-2
90AZSt/200*-171
Bandy, David
91TexAM-74
Bane, Eddie
90AZSt/200*-46
Banks, Carl
88Foot-1
90MISt/200*-83
Banks, Ernie
57Union-41
Banks, Freddie
89PC/CBA-203
90PC/CBA-194
Banks, Gene
83Star/NBA-242
84Star/NBA-65
85Star/NBA-118
87F-8
Banner, Shonna
91SC/200*-48
Bannister, Alan
90AZSt/200*-34
Bannister, Floyd
90AZSt/200*-82
Bannister, Ken
84Star/NBA-27
89Hoops/II-326
90Clip/Star-1
90SkyBox/II-390
Bannister, Roger
81T/Thirst-56

Bantom, Mike
74T-124
75T-97
77T-68
78T-123
79T-9
80T-122
80T-34
81T-MW89
Barbee, Dick
89KY/300*-173
Barber, Miller
91AR/100*-9
Barclay, George
90NC/200*-121
Barco, Barry
90FLSt/200*-50
Barden, Ricky
90NC/200*-81
Bardo, Steve
90PC/CBA-138
90StarP-4
Bari, Lyn
48T/Magic*-F17
Barker, Cliff
88KY/269-151
88KY/269-27
89KY/300*-48
Barkley, Charles
84Star/CrtKg-41
84Star/NBA-202
85JMS-4
85Star/NBA-2
85Star/RTm-3
85Star/TmSuper-PS8
86F-7
86Star/CrtKg-3
87F-9
87F/Ins-6
88F-129AS
88F-85
88Fourn-17
89F-113
89F/AS-4
89Hoops-110
89Hoops-96AS
89Sixers/Kodak-2
90F-139
90F/AS-1
90Hoops-1AS
90Hoops-225
90Hoops/CollB-13
90Hoops/II-374TC
90Hoops/Super-73
90Panin-127
90Panin-JAS
90SkyBox-211
91F-151
91F-213
91F/ProV-3
Barksdale, Don
91UCLA/144-121
Barksdale, Johns
91UCLA/144-118
Barlow, Bill
89KY/300*-285
Barlow, Jeb
89NC/Coke-192
Barlow, Ken
90ND-22
Barnes, Binnie
48T/Magic*-J10
Barnes, Brian
90Clem/200*-11
Barnes, Darryl
89GATech/Pol-5
90GATech/Pol-5
Barnes, Harry
68Rocket/Jack-2
Barnes, Jim
70T-121
89UTEP/Drug-2

91AR/100*-72
Barnes, Marvin
(Bad News)
75T-252AS
75T-225LL
75T-283M
76T-35
82TCMA/CBA-90
Barnes, Norm
90MISt/200*-95
Barnett, Brinkley
89KY/300*-96
Barnett, Dave
89Fresno/Smok-3
90Fresno/Smok-2
Barnett, Dick
69T-18
70T-43
71T-17
72T-52
Barnett, Harlon
90MISt/200*-42
Barnett, Jim
68Rocket/Jack-3
69T-51
70T-142
71T-104
72T-71
73T-108
74T-47
75T-92
Barnhill, Bill
91SC/200*-140
Barnhill, John
71T-222
91AR/100*-5
Barnhorst, Leo
54Bullet/Gunth-1
90ND-9
Barnstable, Dale
88KY/269-58
Barone, Ken
90UCLA-38CO
Barr, Mike
73T-198
Barray, Roland
90LSU/200*-59
Barrett, Marty
90AZSt/200*-192
Barrett, Mike
71T-162
Barrios, Gregg
90NE/Pol*-5
Barros, Dana
90F-175
90Hoops-274
90SkyBox-263
90Sonic/Kayo-14
90Sonic/Smok-1
Barry, Amadou Coco
87ME/Pol*-13
Barry, Jon
90GATech/Pol-6
Barry, Rick
71T-147LL
71T-149LL
71T-170
71T/Ins-13A
72T-242
72T-244
72T-250AS
72T-259LL
72T-262LL
72T-44
73T-156LL
73T-90
74T-147LL
74T-50AS
74T-87M
75T-100AS
75T-122M
75T-1LL

75T-3LL
75T-6M
76Buck-2
76T-132AS
76T-50
77Pep/AS-1
77T-130
78RCCola-3
78T-60
79T-120
80T-116
80T-28
81TCMA-36
85Star/Schick-2
Barry, Scooter
89PC/CBA-198
90PC/CBA-195
Barsness, Linda
90NE/Pol*-14
Bartels, Eddie
89NCSt/Coke-13
89NCSt/Coke-14
89NCSt/Coke-15
Bartholomew, Jacinta
90AZSt/200*-132
Barton, Harris
90NC/200*-35
90NC/200*-58
Bartow, Gene
91UCLA/144-21CO
Barwick, Brook
90NC/200*-69
Barwick, Parrish
90FLSt/200*-28
Basehart, Richard
48T/Magic*-J36
Baskerville, Jerry
80TCMA/CBA-10
Basnight, Jarvis
89PC/CBA-33
Bass, Bob
79Spurs/Pol-x
Bass, Earl
91SC/200*-92
Bass, Jerry
87IN/GreatII-39
Bass, Ron
91SC/200*-117
Bassett, Tim
75T-274
77T-54
78T-96
79T-73
Bastanchury, Jane
90AZSt/200*-140
Bates, Billy Ray
80TCMA/CBA-43
81Blaz/Pol-12
81T-W83
81TCMA/CBA-10
Batiste, Troy
90SanJ/Smok-1
Battaglia, Matt
89Louville/300*-145
Battle, Alvin
89NCSt/Coke-16
89NCSt/Coke-17
89NCSt/Coke-18
Battle, John
87Hawks/Pizza-6
89F-1
89Hoops-154
90F-1
90Hoops-27
90SkyBox-1
91F-1
Battle, Kenny
90F/Up-U74
90Hoops-233
90SkyBox/II-405
Battles, Daryl
87South/Pol*-5

Batton, Dave
90ND-34
Bauer, Kim
91TexAM-92
Baugh, Sammy
48ExhSC-2
Baughan, Maxie
91GATech*-74
Baum, John
72T-191
Baxter, Ron
82TCMA/CBA-31
Baxter, William
55Ash-2
Baylor, Elgin
61F-3
61F-46IA
61Lakers/Bell-1
68T/Test-18
69T-35
70T-113AS
70T-65
71T-10
81TCMA-19
Baynham, Craig
91GATech*-73
Beal, Dicky
82KY/Sch-1
88KY/269-121
88KY/269-195
88KY/269-236
89KY/300*-10
89KY/Tm80-44
Beam, Chet
89Louville/300*-95
Beamon, Bob
81T/Thirst-34
Beard, Butch
72T-142
73T-136
74T-67
75T-2LL
75T-33
76T-6
78T-17
88Louville/194-106
88Louville/194-168
88Louville/194-6
89Louville/300*-11
89Louville/300*-227
89Louville/300*-286
89Louville/300*-7
Beard, Ralph
48T/Magic*-B1
88KY/269-161
88KY/269-4
89KY/300*-7
Bearden, Eric
91GATech*-36
Bearup, Bret
82KY/Sch-2
88KY/269-122
88KY/269-228
Beasley, Chris
90AZSt/200*-23
Beasley, John
71T-211
91TexAM-8
Beaty, Zelmo
68T/Test-17
71T-148LL
71T-165
71T/Ins-17A
72T-220
72T-256AS
73T-225
74T-252
75T-177
85Star/Schick-3
Beck, Byron
71T-210
72T-187

73T-258
74T-222M
74T-264
75T-258
Beck, Ed
88KY/269-69
Beck, Ernie
57T-36
Beck, Steve
90AZSt/200*-26
Becker, Art
72T-178
90AZSt/200*-161
Becker, George
48T/Magic*-D7
Becker, Mark
90PC/CBA-127
Beckham, Gordon
91SC/200*-141
Bedell, Bob
71T-153
Bedford, Darryl
82AR-2
Bedford, William
90F/Up-U28
90Hoops-102
90Piston/Star-2
90SkyBox-83
Bednarik, Charles P.
(Chuck)
48T/Magic*-C7
Bee, Clair F.
54Bullet/Gunth-2CO
68HOF-3
Beene, Stephen
86SWLou/Pol*-1
Behagen, Ron
74T-11
75T-106
76T-138
Behney, Mel
90MISt/200*-85
Behrman, Dave
90MISt/200*-28
Belcher, Earl
79StBon-1
Bell, Alexander Graham
48T/Magic*-N8
Bell, Becky
90AZ/125*-89
Bell, Cecil
89KY/300*-97
Bell, David
91GATech*-28
Bell, Greg
88TN/Smok-23
Bell, Mickey
89NC/Coke-182
90NC/200*-166
Bell, Milton
88George/Pol-7
89George/Pol-7
Bell, T.
90AZ/125*-14
Bell, William
89NCSt/Coke-19
89NCSt/Coke-20
Bellamy, Walt
61F-4
69T-95
69T/Ins-1
70T-18
71T-116
71T/Ins-41
72T-173LL
72T-97
73T-46
74T-65
74T-81M
81TCMA-42
85Star/Schick-4
86IN/Greatl-2

Belle, Joey
86LSU/Pol*-1
Belobraydic, John
81AZ/Pol-2
Belose, Milissa
90AZSt/200*-147
Benbow, Leon
75T-196
Benbrook, Tom
55Ash-74
Bench, Johnny
68PartM-1
71Keds*-2M
Bendix, William
48T/Magic*-J17
Benedict, Billy
48T/Magic*-J28
Benedict, Moby
91MI/56*-2
Benjamin, Benoit
86F-8
87F-10
88F-61
89F-69
89Hoops-114
90F-84
90Hoops-142
90Hoops/Super-43
90Panin-33
90SkyBox-124
90Sonic/Kayo-5
91F-189
Benjamin, Al
90AZSt/200*-16
Benjamin, Rudy
90MISt/200*-142
Bennett, Arlando
90GA/Smok-1
Bennett, Bob
89NC/Coke-165
Bennett, Constance
48T/Magic*-J38
Bennett, Elmer
90ND-32
Bennett, Mel
80TCMA/CBA-40
Bennett, Winston
87KY/Coke-9
88KY/269-168
88KY/269-194
88KY/269-48
89KY/Tm80-41
90Hoops-70
90Panin-104
90SkyBox-48
Bennington, John
90MISt/200*-151
Benson, Kent
77Bucks/ActPh-1
79Bucks/OpenP-6
79Bucks/Pol-54
79T-121
80T-109
80T-21
81T-MW80
83Star/NBA-86
84Star/NBA-262
85Star/NBA-12
86IN/Greatl-13
Bentley, Doug
48ExhSC-3M
Bentley, Max
48ExhSC-3M
Benton, Jim
91AR/100*-41
Berberich, John
91UCLA/144-99
Bercher, Martine
91AR/100*-65
Berenson, Gordon
(Red)
91MI/56*-3

Berger, Cliff
88KY/269-87
Berger, Jay
90Clem/200*-117
Bergines, William
55Ash-85
Bergman, Ingrid
48T/Magic*-F4
Berlenheiter, Michael
90AZSt/200*-194
Berlin, Steve
90Clem/200*-54
Bernard, Tod
89Fresno/Smok-4
90Fresno/Smok-3
Bernstine, Rod
91TexAM-1
Berra, Tim
91SC/200*-151
Berry, Curtis
81TCMA/CBA-41
82TCMA/Lanc-11
82TCMA/Lanc-12IA
Berry, Ricky
88Kings/Carl-34
89F-134
89Hoops-186
Berry, Todd
91SC/200*-105
Berry, Walter
86Blaz/Franz-1
88F-102
89Hoops-44
91Wooden-15
Berson, Mark
91SC/200*-43
Bertman, Skip
86LSU/Pol*-2CO
87LSU/Pol*-9CO
88LSU/Pol*-9CO
Beshore, Delmer
79Bulls/Pol-1
Bessillieu, Don
91GATech*-72
Bessone, Amo
90MISt/200*-62
Besuden, Henry
89KY/300*-22
Betz, Dave
89Louville/300*-198
Bevan, George
90LSU/200*-122
Bianchi, Al
57T-59
75Suns-3
84Suns/Pol-x
Bianco, Mike
88LSU/Pol*-12
Bibb, William
55Ash-14
89KY/300*-292
Bibby, Henry
73T-48
74T-16
75T-146
76T-36
77T-2
78T-65
79T-3
80T-10
80T-150
81T-W90
81TCMA/CBA-5
82TCMA/Lanc-8IA
89PC/CBA-147
90PC/CBA-117
91UCLA/144-7
Bice, Travis
89UNLV/HOF-7
89UNLV/Seven-3
90UNLV/HOF-5
90UNLV/Season-5

90UNLV/Smok-4
Bickerstaff, Bernie
89Hoops-269CO
Bickford, Charles
48T/Magic*-J43
Biddle, Tom
90NC/200*-60
Bierderbach, Eddie
89NCSt/Coke-21
89NCSt/Coke-22
89NCSt/Coke-23
Billington, Dana
87ME/Pol*-6
Bing, Dave
68T/Test-10
69T-55
69T/Ins-16
70T-125
70T/Ins-7
71Keds*-1M
71T-78
71T/Ins-27
72T-35
73NBAPA-2
73T-158LL
73T-170
74T-40AS
74T-86M
75T-121M
75T-160
75T-5LL
76T-76
78T-61
81TCMA-22
85Star/Schick-5
Bing, Keith
91SC/200*-112
Bingham, Paul
90KY/Sov-4
Biondi, Matt
89Foot-6
Bird, Calvin
89KY/300*-116
Bird, Jerry
55Ash-15
88KY/269-225
88KY/269-70
Bird, Larry
80T-165
80T-48
80T-49
80T-6
80T-94
80T-98
81T-45M
81T-E101
83Star/ASG-2
83Star/ASG-29M
83Star/NBA-26
84Star/Arena-A1
84Star/ASG-2
84Star/Award-15LL
84Star/Award-8
84Star/Bird-1
84Star/Bird-10
84Star/Bird-11
84Star/Bird-12
84Star/Bird-13
84Star/Bird-14
84Star/Bird-15
84Star/Bird-16
84Star/Bird-17
84Star/Bird-18
84Star/Bird-2
84Star/Bird-3
84Star/Bird-4
84Star/Bird-5
84Star/Bird-6
84Star/Bird-7
84Star/Bird-8
84Star/Bird-9
84Star/Celt-11M

84Star/Celt-14
84Star/Celt-24
84Star/Celt-4
84Star/Celt-7
84Star/CrtKg-18
84Star/NBA-1
84Star/NBA-12
84Star/PolASG-2
85JMS-14
85Prism-1M
85Star/Crunch-2
85Star/Lakers-2
85Star/Lakers-9
85Star/LiteAS-2
85Star/NBA-95
85Star/ROY-6
85Star/TmSuper-BC1
86F-9
86F/Ins-2
86Star/CrtKg-4
87F-11
87F/Ins-4
88F-124AS
88F-9
88F/Ins-2
88Fourn-1
89Conv-2
89F-8
89F/AS-10
89Hoops-150
90F-8
90F/AS-2
90Hoops-2AS
90Hoops-39
90Hoops/CollB-37
90Hoops/II-356TC
90Hoops/Super-6
90Panin-135
90Panin-HAS
90Panin-L
90SkyBox-14
91F-8
91Wooden-9
81T-4
Bird, Rodger
89KY/300*-122
Birdsong, Otis
79T-87
80T-101
80T-145
80T-28
80T-86
81T-17
81T-54M
83Star/NBA-146
84Nets/Getty-2
84Star/ASG-3
84Star/CrtKg-43
84Star/NBA-89
84Star/PolASG-3
85Star/NBA-59
86F-10
86Star/LifeNets-2
Bishop, Darryl
89KY/300*-174
Bishop, Gale
48Bowman-3
Blab, Uwe
86IN/GreatI-8
88Mavs/BLC-33
88Mavs/CardN-33
89Hoops-104
90Hoops-264
90SkyBox-253
Black, Brian
89GATech/Pol-6
90GATech/Pol-7
Black, Charles
(Hawk)
48Bowman-50
Black, Jimmy
89NC/Coke-93

89NC/Coke-94
90FLSt/200*-158
90NC/200*-30
90NC/200*-57
Black, Mike
90AZSt/200*-81
Black, Norman
81TCMA/CBA-57
Black, Tom
70Sonic/Sunb-1
Blackburn, Bob
83Sonic/Pol-10
Blackman, Pete
91UCLA/144-133
Blackman, Rolando
83Star/NBA-50
84Star/Arena-B2
84Star/CrtKg-27
84Star/NBA-251
85Star/NBA-159
86F-11
86Star/CrtKg-5
87F-12
88F-28
88Mavs/BLC-22
88Mavs/CardN-22
89Conv-3
89F-32
89Hoops-20
90F-38
90Hoops-14AS
90Hoops-82
90Hoops/CollB-38
90Hoops/II-360TC
90Hoops/Super-21
90Panin-55
90SkyBox-60
91F-43
Blackmon, James
88KY/269-127
88KY/269-193
88KY/269-216
Blackwell, Barry
90FLSt/200*-85
Blackwell, Cory
84Star/NBA-114
Blade, Freeman
80TCMA/CBA-32
81TCMA/CBA-42
Blair, Buddy
90LSU/200*-165
Blair, Paul
91OKSt*-22
Blake, Rodney
90PC/CBA-128
Blakley, Anthony
89PC/CBA-191
Blalock, Joe
90Clem/200*-170
Blanda, George
81T/Thirst-40
89KY/300*-115
Blankenship, Buddy
90FLSt/200*-157
Blanks, Lance
90F/Up-U29
90StarP-69
Blanton, Ricky
86LSU/Pol*-3
87LSU/Pol*-2
88LSU/Pol*-1
90LSU/200*-4
90PC/CBA-168
Blasingame, Dominique
91SC/200*-110
Blaylock, Mookie
90F-117
90Hoops-193
90Nets/Kayo-1
90Panin-162
90SkyBox-176
91F-128

Blaylock, Ron
81George/Pol-16
Blazer, Phil
90NC/200*-149
Blears, Lord Jan
48T/Magic*-D21
Blemker, Bud
91GATech*-168
Bliss, Harry
89KY/300*-291
Block, John
68Rocket/Jack-4
69T-9
70T-58
71T-16
72T-41
73T-169
74T-168
75T-64
Blomberg, Ron
81T/Thirst-22
Blondeau, Hal
89NCSt/Coke-101
89NCSt/Coke-159
Blue, David
81George/Pol-17
82George/Pol-7
91George/100-46
Blum, Frank
86DePaul-C2
Blum, John
91MI/56*-4
Blundin, Matt
88VA/Hardee-2
Blunt, Herb
89PC/CBA-99
Bockhorn, Arlen
58Kahn's-1
59Kahn's-1
60Kahn's-1
61F-5
61Kahn's-1
62Kahn's-1
63Kahn's-2
64Kahn's-5
Bodnar, Marty
91MI/56*-5
Boeheim, Jim
88Syr/Rich-1CO
89Syr/Pep-9CO
Boerwinkle, Tom
69T-7
70T-68
71T-15
72Icee-2
72T-65
74T-69
75T-102
76Buck-3
76T-85
77Bulls/WhHen-1
77T-69
90Bulls/Eq-2
Boettner, Bob
90Clem/200*-63
Bogues, Tyrone
(Muggsy)
88F-13
88Fourn-14
89Conv-4
89Hoops-218
90F-16
90Hoops-50
90Hoops/CollB-26
90Hoops/Super-9
90Panin-81
90SkyBox-26
91F-17
Bol, Manute
86F-12
87F-13
89F-52

89Hoops-75
90F-62
90F/Up-U69
90Hoops-112
90Hoops/II-424
90Hoops/Super-33
90Panin-25
90SkyBox-94
90SkyBox/II-403
Bolden, LeRoy
90MISt/200*-30
Bolden, Pat
90PC/CBA-6
Boley, Scott
88KY/Sov-6
Bolger, Bill
54Bullet/Gunth-3
Bolli, Becky
90NE/Pol*-15
Bolyard, Tom
86IN/GreatI-31
Bomar, Buddy
48ExhSC-4
Bomar, Gayle
90NC/200*-160
Bonasorte, Monk
90FLSt/200*-96
Bond, Boot
82TCMA/CBA-2
Bond, Phil
88Louville/194-131
88Louville/194-177
88Louville/194-178
88Louville/194-42
89Louville/300*-228
89Louville/300*-273
89Louville/300*-6
Bonds, Barry
90AZSt/200*-7
Bonifay, Cam
91GATech*-61
Bonilla, Juan
90FLSt/200*-122
Bonner, Anthony
90F/Up-U82
90StarP-12
Bontemps, Kevin
80IL/Arby's-1
81IL/Arby's-1
Bontranger, Steve
89PC/CBA-152
90PC/CBA-28
Booker, Deon
89Louville/300*-113
Booker, Kenny
91UCLA/144-81
Boone, David
89PC/CBA-201
Boone, Ron
71T-178
72T-239
73T-217
73T-237LL
74T-195AS
74T-210LL
75T-221LL
75T-235AS
75T-286M
76T-95
77T-119
78T-49
80T-111
80T-66
Booth, Billy
90LSU/200*-142
Bootz, Dolores
91GATech*-6
Boozer, Bob
60Kahn's-2
61F-6
61Kahn's-2

62Kahn's-2
63Kahn's-3
69Sonic/Sunb-2
69T-89
69T/Ins-23
70T-41
71T-43
90Bulls/Eq-3
Borah, Bob
89Louville/300*-213
Bordelon, Kenny
90LSU/200*-72
Boren, Ralph
89KY/300*-248
Borgmann, Bernhard
68HOF-4
Borrelli, Ralph
57Union-33
Boryla, Vince
52Bread-2
90ND-43
Bosanac, Vladimir
90George/Pol-12
Bostic, Jeff
90Clem/200*-127M
Bostic, Joe
90Clem/200*-127M
Boswell, Tom
77T-19
79T-82
80T-170
80T-82
83Star/NBA-136
Bouchie, Steve
87IN/GreatII-36
Boudreau, Lou
48T/Magic*-K1
48T/Magic*-K5
Bouggess, Lee
89Louville/300*-171
Boulet, Steve
89McNees*-13
Bounds, Brad
89KY/300*-56
Bourgeois, Rene
90LSU/200*-146
Bovain, Andre
90Clem-1
Boven, Donald
52Bread-3
Bowden, Bobby
90FLSt/200*-56
90FLSt/200*-57
90FLSt/200*-58
90FLSt/200*-59
90FLSt/200*-60
90FLSt/200*-66
90FLSt/200*-67
90FLSt/200*-68
90FLSt/200*-69
90FLSt/200*-70
90FLSt/200*-76
90FLSt/200*-77
90FLSt/200*-78
90FLSt/200*-79
90FLSt/200*-80
90FLSt/200*-86
90FLSt/200*-87
90FLSt/200*-88
90FLSt/200*-89
90FLSt/200*-90
Bowe, D.J.
87SoMiss-7M
Bowie, Anthony
90SkyBox-105
90F-69
Bowie, Sam
79KY/Food-11
84Blaz/Franz-2
84Blaz/Pol-10
84Star/CrtKg-44
84Star/NBA-162

85Blaz/Franz-2
85Star/NBA-104
85Star/RTm-4
86Blaz/Franz-2
86F-13
87KY/Coke-7M
88Blaz/Franz-2
88KY/269-165
88KY/269-192
88KY/269-21
88KY/269-239
89Hoops-111
89Hoops/II-337
89KY/300*-41
89KY/Tm80-43
90F-118
90Hoops-194
90Hoops/CollB-1
90Nets/Kayo-2
90Panin-160
90SkyBox-177
91F-129
Bowling, Mark
89McNees*-15
Bowman, Nate
70T-138
Bowman, Sid
90LSU/200*-162
Boyd, Bob
90MISt/200*-117
Boyd, Dwight
89PC/CBA-34
Boyd, Fred
73T-91
74T-154
75T-167
Boyd, Roger
87SoMiss-13
Boyle, Chris
91SC/200*-72
Boynes, Winford
80T-107
80T-71
Bracey, Steve
73T-119
Bracken, Sam
91GATech*-157
Bradburd, Rus
89UTEP/Drug-3
Braddock, James J.
48T/Magic*-A14
Braddock, Jim
89NC/Coke-161
90NC/200*-50
Bradford, Brad
89Louville/300*-129
Bradley, Bill
68T/Test-8
69T-43
70T-7
71T-2
72T-122
73NBAPA-3
73T-82
74T-113
74T-93M
75Carv-2
75T-128M
75T-37
75T-3LL
76Buck-4
76T-43
81TCMA-18
Bradley, Charles
83Sonic/Pol-12
90PC/CBA-112
Bradley, Dudley
80T-123
80T-35
84Star/NBA-187
Bradley, Jim
75T-304

Bradley, John Ed
90LSU/200*-51
Bradley, Ken
89Louville/300*-76
Bradley, Omar
48T/Magic*-08
Bradley, Tyrone
90Fresno/Smok-4
Bradshaw, Bill
91SC/200*-149
Bradshaw, Charlie
89KY/300*-166
Bradshaw, Clyde
86DePaul-10
Bragan, Jimmy
68PartM-2
Bragg, Don
91UCLA/144-124
Braman, Buzz
89Sixers/Kodak-16CO
Brammer, Mark
90MISt/200*-40
Brancato, George
90LSU/200*-29
Branch, Tony
88Louville/194-114
88Louville/194-150
88Louville/194-16
Brand, Rodney
91AR/100*-77
Brandon, Terrell
91Class-6
91Court-6
91StarP-39
Brandt, Kate
91GATech*-158
Branning, Rich
90ND-18
Brannon, Robert
82AR-3
Brannum, Bob
88KY/269-31
Branson, Brad
81TCMA/CBA-65
Brantley, Will
89ORSt-4
Braselton, Fred
91GATech*-63
Bratton, Steve
90FLSt/200*-105
Bratz, Mike
77Suns/Discs-23
80T-139
80T-39
81T-47M
81T-MW71
83Star/NBA-253
84Star/NBA-151
Braucher, Dick
89NCSt/Coke-24
89NCSt/Coke-25
89NCSt/Coke-26
Braun, Carl
48Bowman-72
57T-4
61F-7
81TCMA-23
81TCMA-40M
Braxton, Mel
89PC/CBA-185
Brazell, Carl
91SC/200*-166
Breaker, Bubby
89PC/CBA-153
Breeze, David
55Ash-49
Breland, Jim
91GATech*-71
Brennan, James
55Ash-86
Brennan, Jim
90Clem/200*-149

Brennan, Pete
89NC/Coke-78
89NC/Coke-79
90NC/200*-99
Brenner, Allen
90MISt/200*-3
Breuer, Randy
83Star/NBA-40
84Star/NBA-126
85Star/Bucks-2
86Star/LifeBucks-2
87Bucks/Polar-45
88Bucks/Green-2
88F-73
89Hoops-153
89TWolv/BK-45
90F-111
90Hoops-184
90Panin-77
90SkyBox-167
Breunig, Bob
90AZSt/200*-155
Brewer, Jim
74T-134
75T-46
76T-74
77T-9
Brewer, John
55Ash-16
88KY/269-65
Brewer, Mel
89KY/300*-98
Brewer, Ron
79Blaz/Pol-10
79T-79
80T-1
80T-165
80T-176
80T-49
83Star/NBA-243
84Star/NBA-66
91AR/100*-69
Brian, Frank
52Royal-4
90LSU/200*-37
Brickey, Robert
87Duke/Pol-21
90PC/CBA-167
Brickowski, Frank
84Star/NBA-115
88F-103
88Spurs/Pol-3
89F-141
89Hoops-206
90F-169
90F/Up-U52
90Hoops-265
90Hoops/II-417
90Panin-48
90SkyBox-254
91F-113
90SkyBox/II-394
Bridgeman, Junior
76T-11
77Bucks/ActPh-2
77T-114
78T-56
79Bucks/OpenP-7
79Bucks/Pol-2
79T-91
80T-137
80T-49
81T-MW97
83Star/NBA-41
84Star/Arena-C2
84Star/NBA-14
87Bucks/Polar-2
88Louville/194-21
89Louville/300*-229
89Louville/300*-270
Bridges, Bill
68T/Test-16

69T-86
70T-71
71T-132
72T-17
73T-174
74T-13
Brind'Amour, Rod
90MISt/200*-197
Brinkman, Cookie
89Louville/300*-194
Brisker, John
71T-146LL
71T-147LL
71T-180
71T/Ins-21A
72T-236
73Sonic/Shur-1
73T-7
74T-18
75T-149
Bristow, Allan
75T-74
80T-152
80T-169
80T-35
80T-81
81T-65M
81T-W102
Britt, James
90LSU/200*-168
Brittain, Mike
91SC/200*-150
Brittain, Maurice
88GATech/Nike-1
Britton, Dave
81TCMA/CBA-52
Brkovich, Mike
90MISt/200*-122
Broadnax, Horace
82George/Pol-6
83George/Pol-8
84George/Pol-8
85George/Pol-3
91George/100-24
Broadnax, Vincent
88MD/Pol-1
Broadway, Rod
90NC/200*-164
Brock, Bob
91TexAM-28
Brock, Jeffrey
55Ash-3
Brock, Jim
90AZSt/200*-20CO
Brock, Lou
81T/Thirst-11
Brockington, John
74Nab-8
75Nab-8
Brodnax, George
91GATech*-62
Brogan, Jim
80TCMA/CBA-8
81TCMA/CBA-75
Brokaw, Gary
71Bucks/Linn-2
75T-178
90ND-37
Broks, Richard
90LSU/200*-141
Bronston, Jake
89KY/300*-99
Brookfield, Price
48Bowman-26
Brookin, Rod
89Pitt/Food-21
Brooks, Bud
91AR/100*-74
Brooks, Franklin
91GATech*-65
Brooks, Garth
91OKSt*-87

Brooks, Greg
91George/100-69
Brooks, Hazel
48T/Magic*-F20
Brooks, Hubie
90AZSt/200*-111M
90AZSt/200*-173
Brooks, Kevin
91Class-12
91Court-7
91StarP-8
Brooks, Michael
81T-W91
83Star/NBA-122
90LSU/200*-36
Brooks, Scott
89F-114
89Hoops-34
89Sixers/Kodak-3
90F-140
90Hoops-226
90Hoops/II-419
90SkyBox-212
90SkyBox/II-396
Brown, Bobby
88Louville/194-43
Brown, Boyd
48T/Magic*-E10
Brown, Bubba
90Clem/200*-107
Brown, Carl
90PC/CBA-80
Brown, Chucky
89NCSt/Coke-27
89NCSt/Coke-28
89NCSt/Coke-29
90SkyBox-49
90F/Up-U16
90Hoops-71
Brown, Colby
90Clem-2
Brown, Dale
86LSU/Pol*-4CO
87LSU/Pol*-1CO
88LSU/Pol*-2CO
90LSU/200*-11
90LSU/Promos*-8CO
Brown, Danny
89Louville/300*-70
Brown, Dave
91MI/56*-6
Brown, Dee
90F/Up-U6
90StarP-8
91F-228
91F-9
91F/Rook-6
91StarP-40
Brown, Eric
89PC/CBA-7
Brown, Fred
73Sonic/Shur-2
73T-103
74T-125
74T-97M
75T-41
76T-15
77T-30
78Sonic/Pol-1
78T-59
79Sonic/Pol-13
79T-46
80T-165
80T-77
81George/Pol-12
81T-43
82George/Pol-5
83George/Pol-7
83Sonic/Pol-15
83Star/NBA-194
91George/100-12
91George/100-75

Brown, Gene
90NC/200*-156
Brown, Hardin
91SC/200*-11
Brown, Harper
91GATech*-166
Brown, Herb
87Suns/Circ-2CO
Brown, Hubie
78Hawks/Coke-1CO
79Hawks/Majik-x
85Star/CO-2
Brown, Jim
91George/100-84
Brown, Jimmy
81T/Thirst-38
Brown, Joe
89NC/Coke-149
90NC/200*-122
Brown, Joey
90George/Pol-11
Brown, John
87SoMiss-8M
Brown, John FSU
90FLSt/200*-26
Brown, John MO
74T-139
75T-191
79Hawks/Majik-50
Brown, Johnny Mack
48T/Magic*-J1
Brown, Karl
88GATech/Nike-2
89GATech/Pol-7
91GATech*-46
Brown, Larry
71T-152
72T-264LL
88Spurs/Pol-4CO
89Hoops-102CO
89NC/Coke-110
89NC/Coke-111
89NC/Coke-60
90Hoops-328CO
90NC/200*-187
91F-183CO
90SkyBox/II-324CO
91UCLA/144-31
Brown, Lester
90Clem/200*-109
Brown, Liz
91OKSt*-41
Brown, Mack
90NC/200*-23
Brown, Marc
91Court-8
Brown, Mike
87Bulls/Ent-5
89Hoops/II-336
89Jazz/OldH-2
90Clem/200*-86
90F-183
90Hoops-286
90Jazz/Star-6
90SkyBox-275
Brown, Myron
91Class-24
91Court-9
91StarP-43
Brown, Ollie
86LSU/Pol*-5
Brown, Randy
91Class-21
91Court-10
91StarP-45
Brown, Raymond
89PC/CBA-35
Brown, Raynard
91SC/200*-193
Brown, Rickey
83Star/NBA-264
84Star/NBA-77

Brown, Roger
71Pacer/Mara-1
71T-148LL
71T-225
71T/Ins-5A
72T-210
73T-231
73T-236LL
74T-209LL
74T-240
85Star/Schick-6
Brown, Ron
90AZSt/200*-122
Brown, Russell
90AZ/125*-40
Brown, Terry
89KS/Leesley-49
91OKSt*-20
Brown, Tico
80TCMA/CBA-31
81TCMA/CBA-32
82TCMA/CBA-33
91GATech*-160
Brown, Timmy
81T/Thirst-42
Brown, Tony
82TCMA/CBA-71
84Star/NBA-53
87F-14
89PC/CBA-134
91AR/100*-15
Brown, Vicki
91TexAM-96
Brown, Walter A.
68HOF-5
Brown, Wiley
88Louville/194-120
88Louville/194-175
88Louville/194-179
88Louville/194-26
89Louville/300*-252
89PC/CBA-42
Brown, Willie
87SoMiss-8M
Browndyke, David
90LSU/200*-97
Browne, Clyde
90Clem/200*-136
Browning, Jim
48T/Magic*-D4
Broyles, Frank
91AR/100*-1
Bruce, Donnell
90Clem-3
Brummer, Jackie
90AZSt/200*-134
Brunet, Laurie
90AZ/125*-19
Brunkhorst, Brock
81AZ/Pol-3
84AZ/Pol-1
Bruno, Al
89KY/300*-107
Brust, Chris
89NC/Coke-193
Brutsaert, Elke
87ME/Pol*-8
Bryan, Brad
90NE/Pol*-17
Bryan, Fred
90PC/CBA-42
Bryan, Vince
87BYU-19
Bryant, Bobby
91SC/200*-170
Bryant, Clyde
89Louville/300*-59
Bryant, Dwayne
86George/Pol-4
87George/Pol-4
88George/Pol-4
89George/Pol-4

91George/100-15
91George/100-26
Bryant, Ellis
89Louville/300*-211
Bryant, Emmette
69T-47
70T-116
70T/Ins-11
71T-48
73Sonic/Shur-3
86DePaul-C7
Bryant, Hallie
86IN/GreatI-16
Bryant, Jeff
90Clem/200*-57
Bryant, Joe
80T-162
80T-74
81T-W92
Bryant, Kelvin
90NC/Promos*-NC8
90NC/200*-31
90NC/200*-6
90NC/200*-72
Bryant, Mark
88Blaz/Franz-3
89Blaz/Franz-2
89F-127
89Hoops-36
90Blaz/Franz-11
90F/Up-U80
90Hoops-243
90SkyBox-231
Bryant, Paul
(Bear)
89KY/300*-112
91TexAM-2
Bryant, Wallace
83Star/NBA-170
84Star/NBA-252
Bryant, Warren
89KY/300*-138
Bubas, Vic
89NCSt/Coke-30
89NCSt/Coke-31
Buchanan, Shawn
90NE/Pol*-26
Buchheit, George C.
89KY/300*-51
Buckhalter, Joe
61Kahn's-3
Buckley, Bruce
89NC/Coke-178
Buckley, Clay
87Duke/Pol-45
Bucknall, Steve
86NC/Pol-20
87NC/Pol-20
88NC/Pol-20
Buckner, Quinn
77Bucks/ActPh-3
78T-29
79Bucks/OpenP-8
79Bucks/Pol-21
80T-11
80T-138
80T-144
80T-50
81T-56M
83Star/NBA-28
84Star/NBA-3
85Star/NBA-82
87IN/GreatII-21
Buckwalter, Morris
(Bucky)
79Blaz/Pol-x
81Blaz/Pol-x
82Blaz/Pol-x
83Blaz/Pol-x
84Blaz/Pol-5M
Budde, Ed
90MISt/200*-22

Budge, Donald
48Kell*-11
Budko, Pete
89NC/Coke-157
90NC/200*-134
Budko, Walter
48Bowman-70
52Bread-4
Buechler, Jud
86AZ/Pol-1
87AZ/Pol-1
88AZ/Pol-1
90F/Up-U59
90Nets/Kayo-3
90StarP-36
Buffone, Doug
89Louville/300*-109
Bukumirovich, Neboisha
87LSU/Pol*-7
Bull, Sitting
48T/Magic*-S3
Bullard, Matt
90StarP-51
Bumpas, Dick
91AR/100*-36
Bunche, Ralph
91UCLA/144-90
Bunn, John W.
68HOF-6
Buntin, Nathan
88MO-1
89MO-1
Bunting, Bill
89NC/Coke-91
89NC/Coke-92
90NC/200*-136
Bunting, John
90NC/200*-114
Bunton, Bill
88Louville/194-38
89Louville/300*-16
89Louville/300*-272
Bunton, Stanley
88Louville/194-132
88Louville/194-188
Burchett, Carroll
89KY/300*-16
Burden, Ticky
76T-51
Burger, Jeff
87Auburn/Pol*-3
Burgess, Frank
61Union-1
Burgin, George
87Duke/Pol-42
Burkman, Roger
88Louville/194-128
88Louville/194-161
88Louville/194-39
89Louville/300*-243
89Louville/300*-267
89Louville/300*-31
Burks, Luther
89PC/CBA-116
90PC/CBA-184
Burks, Shawn
90LSU/200*-96
Burks, Steve
82TCMA/CBA-56
Burks, Eric
90Clem-4
Burleson, Tom
75T-24
76T-41
77T-97
80T-131
80T-22
89NCSt/Coke-32
89NCSt/Coke-33
89NCSt/Coke-34
Burmeister, Ken
84AZ/Pol-2CO

Burnett, Bill
91AR/100*-82
Burnett, Ken
90FLSt/200*-189
Burnham, Lawrence
89KY/300*-295
Burns, Craig
90LSU/200*-68
Burns, Dan
79StBon-2
Burns, David
82TCMA/CBA-84
Burns, John
89MO-2
Burns, Lewis
55Ash-38
Burns, Tommy
48T/Magic*-A1
Burns, Willie
91GATech*-20
Burrell, Clinton
90LSU/200*-119
Burrell, Scott
90CT/Pol-1
Burroughs, James
90MISt/200*-41
Burrow, Robert
55Ash-17
57T-64
88KY/269-164
88KY/269-26
89KY/300*-42
Burson, Jay
89PC/CBA-81
Burton, Leon
90AZSt/200*-142
Burton, Leonard
91SC/200*-153
Burton, M.C.
91MI/56*-7
Burton, Willie
90F/Up-U47
90Heat/Publix-2
90Hoops/II-398LS
90StarP-27
91F-105
91F/Rook-9
90SkyBox/II-360LP
Burtt, Steve
84Star/NBA-152
Busch, Frank
90AZ/125*-58
Buse, Don
73T-222
75T-299
77Suns/Discs-10
77T-94
78T-35
79T-114
80T-157
80T-69
83Star/NBA-217
84Star/NBA-271
86Kings/Smok-1CO
Busey, Bill
89KY/300*-58
Bush, George
90Clem/200*-140
Bush, Pete
87LSU/Pol*-15
88LSU/Pol*-11
Buss, Jerry
85Star/Lakers-1M
Butler, Bobby
90FLSt/200*-75
Butler, David
88UNLV/HOF-5
89UNLV/HOF-8
89UNLV/Seven-4
90StarP-64
Butler, Greg
89Knicks/Marine-1

90PC/CBA-202
Butler, Jack
83Dayton/Blue-1M
Butler, James
91OKSt*-73
Butler, Jerry
90Clem/200*-160
90Clem/200*-58
90Clem/200*-141M
Butler, Kelvin
91UCLA/144-41
Butler, Leroy
90FLSt/200*-95
Butler, Lois
48T/Magic*-J20
Butler, Mitchell
90UCLA-5
Butters, Ken
89Louville/300*-77
Button, Richard
48ExhSC-5A
48ExhSC-5B
Byington, John
91TexAM-60
Byrd, Leroy
88KY/269-128
88KY/269-191
88KY/269-208
88KY/269-269
Byrd, Richard E.
48T/Magic*-P2
Byrdsong, Ricky
84AZ/Pol-3CO
Byrne, Jay
82Fairf-1
Byrnes, Tommy
48Bowman-64
Cable, Barney
61Hawks/Essex-1
Cade, Jon
89Louville/300*-126
Cafferky, Joe
89NCSt/Coke-55
89NCSt/Coke-56
Cage, Michael
84Star/NBA-15
85Star/NBA-89
87F-15
88F-62
89F-145
89Hoops-245
90F-176
90Hoops-275
90Hoops/Super-92
90Panin-22
90SkyBox-264
90Sonic/Kayo-4
90Sonic/Smok-2
Caikins, Bob
(Ace)
91UCLA/144-141
Cain, George
89Louville/300*-163
Cala, Craig
88LSU/Pol*-13
Calcagni, Ron
91AR/100*-63
Caldwell, Adrian
90SkyBox-106
Caldwell, Alan
90NC/200*-66
Caldwell, Jim
91GATech*-167
Caldwell, Joe
69T-41
70T-37
70T/Ins-2
71T-155
71T/Ins-10A
72T-206
73T-255
74T-204

74T-221M
90AZSt/200*-154
Calhoun, Corky
73T-166
74T-107
76T-12
77Blaz/Pol-10
Calhoun, Jim
90CT/Pol-2CO
90StarP-40CO
Calhoun, Paul
89KY/300*-133
Calhoun, Rory
48T/Magic*-J12
Calip, Demetrius
88MI/Nike-1
89MI-9
Call, Nathan
87BYU-22
87BYU-4
Calland, Lee
89Louville/300*-153
Callandrillo, Dan
82TCMA/CBA-35
Calloway, Rick
89KS/Leesley-44
Calverley, Ernie
48Bowman-1
Calvert, Gerry
55Ash-18
88KY/269-68
Calvin, Mack
71Flor/McDon-2
71T-151LL
71T-160
71T/Ins-4A
72T-179
72T-262LL
73T-230AS
74T-210LL
74T-221M
74T-245AS
75T-224LL
75T-226LL
75T-227AS
75T-278M
76T-62
77T-96
87Bucks/Polar-xx
88Bucks/Green-16M
Calza, George
48T/Magic*-D16
Campbell, Elden
90Clem/200*-17
90StarP-35
90F/Up-U43
Cameron, Rod
48T/Magic*-J29
Camp, Frank
89Louville/300*-139
Campbell, Kenton
88KY/269-59
Campbell, Lee
90PC/CBA-185
Campbell, Patrick
89KY/300*-94
Campbell, Tony
89Hoops-19
89TWolv/BK-19
90F-112
90Hoops-185
90Panin-73
90SkyBox-168
91F-121
Candrea, Mike
90AZ/125*-95
Cann, Howard G.
68HOF-7
Cannavino, Andy
91MI/56*-8
Cannon, Billy
90LSU/Promos*-1

90LSU/200*-7
91TexAM-7
Cannon, Larry
71T-196
71T/Ins-16A
Cannon, Terry
90SanJ/Smok-2
Cantrelle, Arthur
90LSU/200*-131
Capece, Bill
90FLSt/200*-91
Capellen, Dave
90FLSt/200*-48
Capone, Warren
90LSU/200*-195
Cappleman, Bill
90FLSt/200*-125
Cardwell, Joe
91SC/200*-49
Carey, Burgess
88KY/269-56
Carey, Robert W.
(Bob)
90MISt/200*-58
Carl, Howie
86DePaul-C4
Carlisle, Ralph
88KY/269-29
Carlisle, Rick
84Star/Arena-A3
84Star/NBA-4
Carlson, Don
(Swede)
48Bowman-37
Carlson, H. Clifford
68HOF-8
Carlton, Steve
81T/Thirst-10M
81T/Thirst-9
Carmichael, Brent
89PC/CBA-91
Carmichael, Cartwright
89NC/Coke-118
Carner, JoAnne
90AZSt/200*-109
Carnera, Primo
48T/Magic*-A12
48T/Magic*-D19
Carnevale, Bernard
68HOF-47
Carollo, Phil
90FLSt/200*-12
Caron, Stacy
87ME/Pol*-12
Carpenter, Leonard
55Ash-50
Carpenter, Ray
91SC/200*-119
Carr, Antoine
84Star/NBA-78
87Hawks/Pizza-7
88F-1
89Hoops-278
90F-163
90Hoops-255
90Kings/Safe-2
90Panin-38
90SkyBox-244A
90SkyBox-244B
91F-174
Carr, Austin
72Icee-3
72T-90
73NBAPA-5
73T-115
74T-60
74T-85M
75T-105
76T-53
77T-32
78T-9
79T-76

80T-102
80T-14
90ND-5
Carr, Charlie
90NC/200*-138
Carr, Henry
90AZSt/200*-145
Carr, Kenny
80T-116
80T-47
81T-47M
81T-MW72
82Blaz/Pol-34
83Blaz/Pol-34
83Star/NBA-98
84Blaz/Franz-3
84Blaz/Pol-11
84Star/Blaz-1
84Star/NBA-163
85Blaz/Franz-3
85Star/NBA-105
86Blaz/Franz-3
89NCSt/Coke-58
89NCSt/Coke-59
89NCSt/Coke-60
Carr, M.L.
77T-47
78T-82
79T-107
80T-135
80T-69
81T-E72
83Star/NBA-29
84Star/Celt-13M
84Star/Celt-22
84Star/NBA-5
Carr, Vernon
90MISt/200*-108
Carreker, Alphonso
90FLSt/200*-63
Carrell, Duane
90FLSt/200*-190
Carrier, Chris
90LSU/200*-16
Carrier, Darrell
71Col/Mara-1
71T-149LL
71T-177
72T-207
Carroll, Joe Barry
81T-W71
83Star/NBA-252
85Star/NBA-132
86F-14
87F-16
88F-50
89F-95
89Hoops-198
90Hoops-92
90Panin-66
90SkyBox-72
Carroway, Rod
91SC/200*-161
91SC/200*-167
Carson, Bud
91GATech*-98CO
Carson, Carlos
90LSU/200*-186
Carter, Anthony
91MI/56*-9
Carter, Butch
83Star/NBA-158
84Star/NBA-28
87IN/GreatII-31
Carter, Dexter
90FLSt/200*-82
Carter, Fred
70T-129
71T-14
72T-29
73NBAPA-4
73T-111

74T-75
74T-94M
75Sixers/McDon-1
75T-129M
75T-38
76T-111
89Sixers/Kodak-15CO
Carter, Garret
91SC/200*-113
Carter, Gary
82TCMA/CBA-62
Carter, George
71T-205
71T/Ins-20A
72T-197
73T-191
74T-178
74T-230M
75T-230
75T-281M
Carter, Howard
83Nugget/Pol-32
83Star/NBA-183
90LSU/200*-196
90LSU/200*-40
Carter, James
90PC/CBA-109
Carter, Jim
90AZSt/200*-129
Carter, Kendall
90AZSt/200*-57
Carter, Larry
89Louville/300*-75
Carter, Pat
90FLSt/200*-9
Carter, Perry
91StarP-55
Cartier, Warren
89NCSt/Coke-63
Cartwright, Bill
80T-148
80T-158
80T-166
80T-42
80T-53
80T-60
80T-68
80T-94
81T-26
81T-58M
81T-E102
83Star/NBA-62
84Star/NBA-29
85Star/NBA-167
87F-17
88Bulls/Ent-24
89Bulls/Eq-2
89F-19
89Hoops-255
90Bulls/Eq-4
90F-23A
90F-23B
90Hoops-65
90Hoops/Super-15
90SkyBox-38
91F-26
Casanova, Tommy
90LSU/200*-121
Casazez, Lucy
90AZSt/200*-125
Case, Everett
89NCSt/Coke-186
89NCSt/Coke-187
89NCSt/Coke-188
89NCSt/Coke-198
Casem, Marino
87South/Pol*-1CO
Casey, Dwane
77KY/Wildct-13
78KY/Food-10
88KY/269-110
88KY/269-201

88Louville/194-144
88Louville/194-87
Clevenger, Steve
88KY/269-84
Clifford, Dennis
88Louville/194-95
Clifton, Nat
57T-1
Close, Casey
91MI/56*-12
Clustka, Chuck
91UCLA/144-102
Clutter, Jack
55Ash-63
Clyde, Andy
48T/Magic*-J2
Cobb, Coy
90Clem/200*-187
Cobb, John
48ExhSC-7
Cobb, Ric
82Marq/Lite-1CO
Cobb, Ty
48T/Magic*-K13
Cockran, Cindy
91GATech*-17
Coder, Paul
89NCSt/Coke-64
89NCSt/Coke-65
89NCSt/Coke-66
Cody, Buffalo Bill
48T/Magic*-S2
Coffield, Randy
90FLst/200*-135
Coffin, Elizabeth
(Liz)
87ME/Pol*-9
Coffman, Bennie
88KY/269-62
Coffman, Wayne
90Clem/200*-153
Cofield, Fred
89PC/CBA-92
Coggin, Redus
90FLst/200*-8
Cohen, Jeff
61Union-2
Cohen, Sid
88KY/269-75
Coker, Pete
89NCSt/Coke-181
89NCSt/Coke-70
89NCSt/Coke-72
Colangelo, Jerry
75Suns-4
Colbert, Claudette
48T/Magic*-F15
Colbert, Dave
83Dayton/Blue-4
Cole, George
91AR/100*-39
Cole, Jervis
89PC/CBA-202
90PC/CBA-198
Cole, Lynn
55Ash-76
Cole, Rod
90GA/Smok-3
Coleman, Ben
90SkyBox-156
Coleman, Derrick
88Syr/Rich-2
89Syr/Pep-1
89Syr/Pep-15
90F/Up-U60
90Hoops/II-390LS
90Nets/Kayo-4
90StarP-43
91F-130
91F/Rook-3
90SkyBox/II-362LP
91StarP-2

Coleman, Don
90MlSt/200*-27
Coleman, E.C.
75T-127M
75T-163
77T-123
78T-12
Coleman, Jack
57T-70
88Louville/194-94
89Louville/300*-231
Coleman, Jamal
88MO-4
89MO-3
Coleman, Vince
89Foot-3
Coles, Vernell
(Bimbo)
90F/Up-U48
90Heat/Publix-3
90StarP-25
91F-106
Colescott, Dave
89NC/Coke-147
90NC/Coke*-142
Collier, Blanton
89KY/300*-165
Collier, Cory
91GATech*-8
Collins, Don
81T-E95
83Star/NBA-254
Collins, Doug
74T-129
75Sixers/McDon-3
75T-129M
75T-148
76T-38
77T-65
78RCCola-5
78T-2
79T-64
80T-148
80T-32
87Bulls/Ent-12CO
Collins, Jeff
81AZ/Pol-4
Collins, Jimmy
70T-157
Collins, Laura
90UCLA-24
Collins, Lee
91SC/200*-61
Collins, Martha Layne
87KY/Coke-1
Collins, Paul
55Ash-4
Collins, Rip
90LSU/200*-137
Collins, Ronnie
91SC/200*-90
Collins, Sonny
89KY/300*-104
Collinsworth, Lincoln
89KY/300*-70
Colp, Steven
90MlSt/200*-155
Colson, Gary
90Fresno/Smok-5CO
Colter, Steve
84Blaz/Franz-4
84Blaz/Pol-6
84Star/NBA-164
85Blaz/Franz-4
89Hoops-214
90Kings/Safe-4
90SkyBox-286
90SkyBox/II-408
Combs, Carl
89KY/300*-273
Combs, Cecil
89KY/300*-272

Combs, Charley
89KY/300*-280
Combs, Edwin Leroy
83Star/NBA-159
90PC/CBA-113
Combs, Glen
71T-215
72T-194
72T-261LL
73T-209
73T-236LL
74T-199
88Louville/194-49
Combs, Pat
87Baylor/Pol*-2
Combs, Roy
89Louville/300*-56
Comegys, Dallas
88Spurs/Pol-5
Compise, Pete
89Louville/300*-149
Compton, Deward
89Louville/300*-42
Compton, Joyce
91SC/200*-45
Compton, Larry
89Louville/300*-165
Conacher, Roy
48ExhSC-8
Cone, Fred
90Clem/200*-81
Cone, Ronny
91GATech*-11
Conley, Larry
88KY/269-143
88KY/269-190
88KY/269-222
88KY/269-39
Conley, Mike
88Foot-2
89Foot-1
91AR/100*-7
Conlin, Ed
57T-58
Conlon, Marty
90PC/CBA-53
Conner, Gary
90Clem/200*-37
Conner, Lester
83Star/NBA-255
84Star/NBA-153
85Star/NBA-133
89F-96
89Hoops-222
90F-119
90Hoops-195
90Nets/Kayo-5
90Panin-169
90SkyBox-178
Connor, George
48T/Magic*-C9
Connor, Jimmy Dan
88KY/269-104
88KY/269-188
88KY/269-206
88KY/269-258
Conrad, Bobby Joe
90Clem/200*-12
91TexAM-81
Constantine, Marc
55Ash-87
Conway, Hollis
86SWLou/Pol*-3
Coogan, Jackie
48T/Magic*-J5
Cook, Anthony
85AZ/Pol-1
86AZ/Pol-2
87AZ/Pol-2
88AZ/Pol-2
90AZ/125*-33
90F/Up-U24

Cook, Bob
(Tarmac)
48ExhSC-9
Cook, Darwin
81T-E77
83Star/NBA-147
84Nets/Getty-3
84Star/NBA-90
85Star/NBA-60
86Star/LifeNets-4
Cook, Greg
81AZ/Pol-5
Cook, Jeff
80Suns/Pep-9
81T-W80
83Star/NBA-230
87Suns/Circ-3
Cook, Joe
87Duke/Pol-13
Cook, Mike
91SC/200*-84
Cooke, Joe
71T-62
Cooke, Mark
88VA/Hardee-3
Cooke, Mike
89NC/Coke-181
Cooley, Gaye
90MlSt/200*-164
Cooper, Carl
90AZ/125*-120
Cooper, Cecil
79Bucks/OpenP-3
Cooper, Eric
85AZ/Pol-2
Cooper, Evan
91MI/56*-13
Cooper, Gary
90Clem/200*-78
Cooper, Jackie
48T/Magic*-J7
Cooper, Joe
81TCMA/CBA-16
82TCMA/CBA-70
82TCMA/Lanc-10IA
Cooper, Michael
80T-133
80T-45
81T-W77
82Lakers/BASF-2
83Lakers/BASF-2
83Star/NBA-15
84Lakers/BASF-2
84Star/Arena-D2
84Star/NBA-114
84Star/PolASG-26
84Star/SlamD-2
85JMS-19
85Star/Lakers-11M
85Star/NBA-27
86F-17
87F-21
88F-65
89F-75
89Hoops-187
90F-90
90Hoops-153
90SkyBox-134
Cooper, Reggie
90NE/Pol*-2
Cooper, Teena
86SWLou/Pol*-4
Cooper, Wayne
80T-113
80T-25
81T-W103
82Blaz/Pol-42
83Blaz/Pol-42
83Star/NBA-99
84Star/NBA-138
85Nugget/Pol-6
85Star/NBA-51

86F-18
88Nugget/Pol-42
89Blaz/Franz-3
89Hoops-122
89Hoops/II-335
90Blaz/Franz-12
90Hoops-244
90SkyBox-232
Copeland, Lanard
89Sixers/Kodak-4
90PC/CBA-79
90SkyBox-213
Corbett, James J.
48T/Magic*-A3
Corbin, Tyrone
89Hoops-263
89Hoops/II-319
89TWolv/BK-23
90F-113
90Hoops-186
90Hoops/Super-58
90Panin-75
90SkyBox-169
91F-122
Corchiani, Chris
89NCSt/Pol-1
91Class-26
91Court-13
91StarP-46
Cordileone, Lou
90Clem/200*-189
Corley, Chris
91SC/200*-115
Cornelius, Greg
81TCMA/CBA-47
Correll, Ray
89KY/300*-109
Corrigan, Doug
48T/Magic*-L7
Corso, Lee
89Louville/300*-138
90FLst/200*-104
Corzine, Dave
81T-62
81T-MW101
83Star/NBA-169
84Star/CrtKg-24
84Star/NBA-102
85Star/NBA-119
85Star/TmSuper-CB4
86DePaul-10
87Bulls/Ent-10
87F-22
88Bulls/Ent-40
88F-15
89F-109
89Hoops-93
89Hoops/II-343
89Magic/Pep-4
90Hoops-217
90Hoops/II-436
90SkyBox-202
90Sonic/Kayo-6
90Sonic/Smok-3
90SkyBox/II-417
Costello, Larry
57T-33
61F-9
61F-48IA
Costner, Tony
90PC/CBA-54
Couch, Sean
89PC/CBA-47
Coughran, John
82TCMA/CBA-12
Counts, Mel
69T-49
70Suns/A1-1A
70Suns/A1-1B
70Suns/Carn-1
70T-103
71T-127

72T-67
73T-151
75T-199
Courts, Scott
77KY/Wildct-9
Cousy, Robert J.
(Bob)
57T-17
57Union-34
61F-10
61F-49IA
68HOF-49
81TCMA-41
85Star/Schick-7
Covelli, Frank
90AZSt/200*-130
Cowan, Fred
77KY/Wildct-14
78KY/Food-16
79KY/Food-6
88KY/269-114
88KY/269-189
88KY/269-234
88KY/269-268
89KY/Tm80-52
Coward, Lee
89MO-4
Cowens, Dave
71T-47
71T/Ins-30
72T-7
73NBAPA-6
73T-157LL
73T-40AS
74T-148LL
74T-155
74T-82M
75Carv-4
75T-117M
75T-170
75T-4LL
76Buck-5
76T-131AS
76T-30
77Dell-2
77Pep/AS-2
77T-90
78RCCola-6
78T-40
79T-5
80T-7
80T-95
90FLSt/200*-131
Cowins, Ben
91AR/100*-19
Cowsen, McKinley
86DePaul-C5
Cox, Aaron
90AZSt/200*-39
Cox, Chubby
80TCMA/CBA-1
Cox, Corky
88Louville/194-56
Cox, Darrell
89KY/300*-179
Cox, Johnny
88KY/269-14
Cox, Steve
91AR/100*-73
Cox, Tracy
90AZSt/200*-118
Cox, Wesley
88Louville/194-102
88Louville/194-17
88Louville/194-171
88Louville/194-183
89Louville/300*-232
89Louville/300*-271
Coy, Hugh
89KY/300*-277
Cozens, Carl
91UCLA/144-113

Craft, Donald
89Louville/300*-148
Craig, Steve
81TCMA/CBA-83
Crain, Kurt
87Auburn/Pol*-5
Craven, Ken
90NC/200*-177
Crawford, Fred
70T-162
Crawford, Laurent
89PC/CBA-4
Creamer, Eddie
88Louville/194-55
Cremins, Bobby
88GATech/Nike-3CO
89GATech/Pol-8CO
90GATech/Pol-8CO
91SC/200*-80
Crenshaw, Bobby
90FLSt/200*-187
Crews, Jim
86IN/Greatl-24
Crigler, John
88KY/269-67
Criss, Charlie
78Hawks/Coke-2
78T-87
79Hawks/Majik-14
80T-15
80T-164
81T-E67
Crite, Winston
89PC/CBA-132
Crittenden, Howard
55Ash-64
Critz, George
89KY/300*-60
Crockett, Bobby
91AR/100*-91
Crockett, Ray
87Baylor/Pol*-11
Crockett, Willis
91GATech*-49
Croel, Mike
90NE/Pol*-6
Croft, Bobby
71Col/Mara-2
Cromer, Jamie
90KY/ClassA-14
Crompton, Geoff
80TCMA/CBA-12
83Star/NBA-231
Crook, Herbert
88Louville/194-107
88Louville/194-169
88Louville/194-7
89Louville/300*-12
89Louville/300*-254
89Louville/300*-287
89Louville/300*-38
89PC/CBA-138
Cross, Pete
70Sonic/Sunb-3
71Sonic/Sunb-2
71T-33
72T-49
Crotty, John
88VA/Hardee-4
91Court-14
91StarP-6
Crow, John David
91TexAM-10
Crum, Denny
83Louville-x
88Louville/194-1
88Louville/194-173
88Louville/194-181
88Louville/194-99
89Louville/300*-1
89Louville/300*-288
89Louville/300*-298

91UCLA/144-103M
91UCLA/144-111
Crum, Francis
55Ash-39
Crutcher, James
90KY/Sov-5
Cubelic, Mary Ann
90Clem/200*-185
Cuddeford, Michelle
90NE/Pol*-27
Cueto, Al
71T-223
Culbertson, Richard
55Ash-5
Culik, Carolina
91SC/200*-29
Culp, Curly
90AZSt/200*-67
Culp, Ron
77Blaz/Pol-TR
83Blaz/Pol-TR
Cumberledge, Melinda
87KY/Coke-6
Cummings, Jack
90NC/200*-183
Cummings, Pat
79Bucks/Pol-6
83Star/NBA-51
84Star/NBA-30
85Star/NBA-168
86F-19
89Hoops-158
Cummings, Robert
48T/Magic*-J15
Cummings, Terry
83Star/All-R-1
83Star/NBA-123
84Star/CrtKg-37
84Star/NBA-125
85Star/Bucks-3
85Star/NBA-124
85Star/ROY-3
85Star/TmSuper-MB1
86DePaul-11
86DePaul-S6
86DePaul-S7
86F-20
86Star/CrtKg-8
86Star/LifeBucks-3
87Bucks/Polar-34
87F-23
88Bucks/Green-3
88F-74
89F-142
89Hoops-100
89Hoops-256AS
89Hoops/II-312
90F-170
90Hoops-266
90Hoops/CollB-14
90Hoops/Super-87
90Panin-45
90SkyBox-255
91F-184
Cummins, Albert
89KY/300*-100
Cunningham, Billy
69T-40
69T/Ins-21
70T-108AS
70T-140
70T/Ins-16
71T-79
71T/Ins-40
72T-167AS
72T-215
73T-200AS
74T-221M
74T-235
75Sixers/McDon-4
75T-129M
75T-20

76T-93
81TCMA-43
83Star/Sixers-2
89NC/Coke-37
89NC/Coke-38
89NC/Coke-39
89NC/Coke-40
89NC/Coke-61
Cunningham, Bob
89NC/Coke-123
89NC/Coke-124
Cunningham, Brent
91GATech*-55
Cunningham, Dick
70T-49
72T-62
73T-134
Cunningham, Gary
91UCLA/144-103M
91UCLA/144-35
Cunningham, Leon
91SC/200*-69
Curci, Fran
89KY/300*-168
Cureton, Earl
83Star/NBA-87
84Star/NBA-263
85Star/NBA-13
89Hoops-112
Curl, Ronald
90MISt/200*-81
Currie, Dan
90MISt/200*-60
Currie, Michelle
87South/Pol*-12
Curry, Bill
91GATech*-67
91GATech*-90
Curry, Buddy
90NC/200*-20
90NC/200*-49
Curry, Dell
88F-14
89Hoops-299
90F-18
90Hoops-52
90Hoops/II-387
90Panin-80
90SkyBox-28
91F-19
Curry, Denise
91UCLA/144-45
Curry, Ron
88AZ/Pol-3
Curtis, Ann
48ExhSC-10
Curtis, Fred
89KY/300*-64
Curtis, Tom
91MI/56*-14
Curtis, Tommy
91UCLA/144-29
Custer, General
48T/Magic*-S1
Cutrell, Porter
89PC/CBA-177
Cutright, Michael
89McNees*-9
Cutsinger, Gary
91OKSt*-27
Cutts, Willie
82AR-4
Cuyler, Sylvester
80TCMA/CBA-2
Cvijanovich, Stacey
88UNLV/HOF-10
89UNLV/HOF-8
89UNLV/Seven-5
Cyrulik, Dan
90CT/Pol-3
D'Amico, Brian
89NCSt/Pol-2

D'Antoni, Mike
74T-138
75T-176
Dabbs, Brent
88VA/Hardee-5
Dahlinghaus, Rory
83Dayton/Blue-5
Dailey, Quintin
83Star/All-R-2
83Star/NBA-171
84Star/NBA-103
85Star/NBA-120
85Star/TmSuper-CB3
89Hoops-221
90Hoops-276
90SkyBox-265
90Sonic/Kayo-8
90Sonic/Smok-4
Dairsow, Clifton
83George/Pol-13
Dakich, Dan
86IN/Greatl-17
Dale, Jeffery
90LSU/200*-109
Daley, John
91AR/100*-48
Dallmar, Howard
48Bowman-14
Dalson, Kevin
90MISt/200*-94
Dalton, Ralph
81George/Pol-19
82George/Pol-4
83George/Pol-11
84George/Pol-3
85George/Pol-4
91George/100-19
Daly, Chuck
89Hoops-11
90Hoops-312CO
90Piston/Star-13CO
90Piston/Unocal-2CO
91F-58CO
90SkyBox/II-308CO
Dampier, Louis
71Col/Mara-3
71T-224
71T/Ins-11A
72T-198
72T-261LL
72T-264LL
73T-183
73T-236LL
74T-209LL
74T-212LL
74T-224M
74T-255AS
75T-223LL
75T-270
75T-280M
78T-51
88KY/269-12
88KY/269-169
88KY/269-257
89KY/300*-9
Dandridge, Bobby
70T-63
71Bucks/Linn-3
71T-135M
71T-59
71T/Ins-6
72T-42
73T-33
74T-126
75Carv-5
75T-17
76Buck-6
76T-81
77T-25
78T-92
79T-130AS
80T-173

80T-85
Danforth, Bob
82TCMA/Lanc-7
Daniel, Jeff
88VA/Hardee-6
Daniel, Michael
91OKSt*-95
Daniel, Sam
91SC/200*-96
Daniels, Jay
81IL/Arby's-2
Daniels, Lloyd
89PC/CBA-45
Daniels, Mel
71Pacer/Mara-2
71T-150LL
71T-195
71T/Ins-8A
72T-200
72T-263LL
73T-195AS
73T-238LL
74T-192
75T-292
85Star/Schick-8
Daniels, Ricky
91SC/200*-139
Daniels, Robert
55Ash-77
Dantley, Adrian
77T-56
78RCCola-7
78T-132
79Lakers/Alta-1
79T-54
80T-128
80T-156
80T-157
80T-34
80T-61
80T-9
81T-40
81T-65M
83Star/NBA-133
84Star/ASG-16
84Star/Award-13LL
84Star/Award-4
84Star/CrtKg-36
84Star/NBA-228
84Star/PolASG-16
85Star/Crunch-8
85Star/LiteAS-8
85Star/NBA-138
85Star/ROY-9
86F-21
86F/Ins-3
86Star/CrtKg-9
87F-24
88F-39
88Fourn-8
88Mavs/CardN-4
89F-33
89Hoops-125
90F-39
90Hoops-83
90ND-14
90SkyBox-61
Darby, Darrell
89KY/300*-65
Darmody, Kevin
91SC/200*-9
Darragh, William
55Ash-25
88Louville/194-83
Dascenzo, Doug
91OKSt*-70
Datin, Joe
91SC/200*-89
Daugherty, Brad
87F-25
88F-22
89F-166M

89F-25
89Hoops-48AS
89Hoops-50
90F-31
90Hoops-73
90Hoops/Super-19
90Panin-105
90SkyBox-50
91F-34
Daugherty, Hugh
(Duffy)
90MISt/200*-47M
90MISt/200*-92M
90MISt/200*-79
Davender, Ed
88KY/269-160
88KY/269-187
88KY/269-47
Davenport, Ron
89Louville/300*-123
Davenport, Scott
88KY/Sov-2CO
Davenport, Steve
91GATech*-5
David, Brian
85AZ/Pol-3
86AZ/Pol-3
87AZ/Pol-3
88AZ/Pol-4
David, Dallas
89UTEP/Drug-4
David, Lawrence
89McNees*-8
Davidson, Mike
90MISt/200*-126
Davie, Charlie
73T-8
Davies, Robert E.
(Bob)
48Bowman-10
52Bread-6
68HOF-48
85Star/Schick-9
Davies, Mike
90AZSt/200*-6
Davis, Alvin
90AZSt/200*-52
Davis, Antonio
89UTEP/Drug-5
90StarP-3
Davis, Barry
91TexAM-49
Davis, Berkley
89KY/300*-271
Davis, Bernard
90GA/Smok-4
Davis, Bill
89KY/300*-69
Davis, Bob
82TCMA/CBA-81
89KY/300*-160
Davis, Brad
80TCMA/CBA-36
81T-48M
81TCMA/CBA-15
83Star/NBA-52
84Star/Arena-B3
84Star/NBA-253
85Star/NBA-161
86F-22
88Mavs/BLC-15
88Mavs/CardN-15
89Hoops-296
90F-40
90Hoops-84
90LSU/200*-143
90SkyBox-62
Davis, Bruce
89KY/300*-297
Davis, Chandra
89McNees*-4
Davis, Charles

72T-27
83Star/NBA-206
84Star/NBA-127
85Star/Bucks-4
86Star/LifeBucks-4
88Bulls/Ent-22
89Bulls/Eq-3
89Hoops-13
90Hoops-62
Davis, Craig
89NCSt/Coke-73
89NCSt/Coke-75
Davis, Dale
90Clem-5
91Class-8
91Court-15
91StarP-63
Davis, Dwight
73T-104
74T-158
74T-85M
75T-11
Davis, Fritgerald
91SC/200*-39
Davis, Harry
80TCMA/CBA-3
81TCMA/CBA-84
Davis, Jeff
90Clem/200*-96
Davis, Jim
69T-53
70T-54
71T-97
72T-51
75T-174
90Clem/200*-148
Davis, John
91GATech*-44
Davis, Johnny
77Blaz/Pol-16
78T-22
79T-92
80T-122
80T-145
80T-58
80T-86
81T-16
81T-53M
83Star/NBA-265
84Star/NBA-216
85Star/NBA-154
Davis, Lee
71T-212
73T-253
75T-234
Davis, Melvin
(Mel)
71Globe-18M
71Globe-30M
71Globe-33
71Globe-34
71Globe-35
71Globe-36
71Globe-37M
71Globe-38
71Globe/Cocoa-10M
71Globe/Cocoa-27
71Globe/Cocoa-5M
71Globe/Cocoa-8M
74T-43
75T-179
77T-38
80TCMA/CBA-34
Davis, Mickey
71Bucks/Linn-4
73T-107
74T-73
75T-126M
75T-53
Davis, Mike
70T-29
71T-99

72T-39
82TCMA/CBA-61
90PC/CBA-133
Davis, Mulford
89KY/300*-270
Davis, Percy
81TCMA/CBA-33
Davis, Ralph
89UTEP/Drug-6
Davis, Ralph E.
60Kahn's-3
Davis, Robert
89Louville/300*-57
Davis, Ron
80TCMA/CBA-30
81TCMA/CBA-80
Davis, Rueben
90NC/200*-43
Davis, Terry
89Heat/Publix-1
90F/Up-U49
90Heat/Publix-4
90SkyBox-144
Davis, Walt
57T-49
Davis, Walter
77Suns/Discs-6
78RCCola-8
78T-10
79T-80
80Suns/Pep-1
80T-158
80T-172
80T-70
80T-78
81T-33
82Suns/Giant-1
83Star/NBA-109
84Star/ASG-17
84Star/NBA-39
84Star/PolASG-17
84Suns/Pol-6
85Star/NBA-36
85Star/ROY-8
86F-23
87F-26
87Suns/Circ-4
88Nugget/Pol-6
89F-39
89Hoops-61
89NC/Coke-51
89NC/Coke-52
89NC/Coke-53
89NC/Coke-54
89Nugget/Pol-2
90F-47
90Hoops-93
90NC/200*-9
90Panin-64
90SkyBox-73
Davis, Warren
71T-219
73T-229
Davis, Wendell
90LSU/200*-70
Dawkins, Bill
90FLSt/200*-188
Dawkins, Darryl
77T-132
78T-34
79T-105
80T-160
80T-55
81T-29
81T-E103
83Star/NBA-148
84Nets/Getty-4
84Star/NBA-88
85Star/NBA-61
86F-24
86Star/CrtKg-10
86Star/LifeNets-5

Dawkins, Johnny
87F-27
88F-104
88Spurs/Pol-6
89F-143
89Hoops-78
89Hoops/II-311
89Sixers/Kodak-5
90F-141
90Hoops-227
90Hoops/Super-72
90Panin-131
90SkyBox-214
91F-152
Dawson, Bill
90FLSt/200*-154
Dawson, Mike
90AZ/125*-69
Dawson, Rhett
90FLSt/200*-196
Dawson, Tony
89PC/CBA-56
90PC/CBA-37
Day, Ned
48ExhSC-11
Daye, Darren
83Star/NBA-207
84Star/NBA-188
85Star/NBA-111
91UCLA/144-27
Daye, James
89NC/Coke-191
Dean, Everett S.
54Quaker-24
68HOF-9
86IN/GreatI-14
Dean, Joe
77KY/Wildct-6CO
78KY/Food-22CO
79KY/Food-15CO
90LSU/200*-6
90LSU/Promos*-10
DeBernardi, Forrest S.
68HOF-10
DeBisschop, Pete
82Fairf-3
DeBortoli, Joel
90PC/CBA-140
DeBose, Keenan
82AR-5
DeBusschere, Dave
68T/Test-11
69T-85
70T-135
71T-107
71T/Ins-10
72Icee-6
72T-105
73NBAPA-7
73T-30AS
74T-93M
81TCMA-39
85Star/Schick-10
Dedmon, Lee
89NC/Coke-164
Deeken, Dennis
89Louville/300*-79
Deeken, Ted
89KY/300*-18
Dees, Archie
58Kahn's-2
86IN/GreatI-34
Dees, Clair
89KY/300*-294
DeFrank, Matt
90LSU/200*-169
DeGiglio, Bruno
79StBon-3
DeHavilland, Olivia
48T/Magic*-F7
DeHeer, Bill
86IN/GreatI-41

88Louville/194-4
89Louville/300*-280
Drucker, Jim
81TCMA/CBA-88
Drummer, Sammy
91GATech*-23
Drummond, Kenny
89PC/CBA-189
Drysdale, Don
81T/Thirst-14
Duckett, Ellis
90MISt/200*-33
Duckett, Richard
57Kahn's-1
Duckworth, Kevin
87Blaz/Franz-2
88Blaz/Franz-5
88F-93
89Blaz/Franz-4
89F-129
89Hoops-103
89Hoops-193AS
90Blaz/BP-3
90Blaz/Franz-14
90F-155
90Hoops-246
90Hoops/Super-82
90Panin-10
90SkyBox-234
91F-169
Dude, Little
90PC/CBA-95
Dudley, Charles
75T-194
Dudley, Chris
90Nets/Kayo-6
91F-131
90SkyBox/II-398
Dufek, Donald
91MI/56*-18
Dufficy, Pat
91SC/200*-88
Dugas, Robert
90LSU/200*-87
Duhe, Adam
90LSU/200*-28
Duhe, Craig
90LSU/200*-60
Dukes, Walter
57T-30
61F-11
61F-50IA
Dumars, Joe
86F-27
87F-31
88F-40
89F-45
89Hoops-1
90F-55
90Hoops-103
90Hoops-3AS
90Hoops/CollB-27
90Hoops/II-362TC
90Hoops/Super-28
90Panin-86
90Piston/Star-3
90Piston/Unocal-3
90SkyBox-84
91F-59
Dumas, Richard
91Class-36
91Court-17
91StarP-71
Dunbar, Bob
89Louville/300*-61
Dunbar, Karl
90LSU/200*-63
Duncan, Calvin
90PC/CBA-17
Duncan, Lawson
90Clem/200*-21
Dunlap, Robert

90SanJ/Smok-3
Dunleavy, Mike
81T-MW85
84Star/Arena-C3
84Star/NBA-128
85Star/Bucks-5
85Star/TmSuper-MB4
87Bucks/Polar-x
88Bucks/Green-16M
90Hoops/II-351CO
90Hoops/II-410CO
91F-98CO
90SkyBox/II-313CO
Dunn, David
82George/Pol-3
Dunn, T.R.
77Blaz/Pol-23
79Blaz/Pol-23
81T-W67
82Nugget/Pol-23
83Nugget/Pol-23
83Star/NBA-184
84Star/NBA-139
85Nugget/Pol-10
85Star/NBA-52
89Nugget/Pol-3
90SkyBox/II-378
Dupont, Jerry
88Louville/194-84
Dupree, Billy Joe
90MISt/200*-73
Durden, Alan
90AZ/125*-26
Duren, John
91George/100-37
91George/100-5
Duren, Lonnie
91George/100-72
Durham, Hugh
90FLSt/200*-147CO
90GA/Smok-5CO
Durham, James
89KY/300*-25
Durham, Pat
90PC/CBA-18
Durnan, Bill
48ExhSC-16
Durrant, Devin
84Star/NBA-54
Durrett, Ken
72T-134
Duryea, C.E.
48T/Magic*-N3
Dusek, Brad
91TexAM-34
Dusek, Ernie
48T/Magic*-D8
Dusek, Rudy
48T/Magic*-D9
Dutch, Al
91George/100-17
91George/100-50
Dutcher, Brian
89MI-2
Dwan, Jack
48Bowman-51
Dwyer, Richard
54Quaker-22
Dyches, Tim
91SC/200*-142
Dye, Pat
87Auburn/Pol*-1CO
Dyer, Duffy
90AZSt/200*-195
Dykes, Hart Lee
91OKSt*-17
Eackles, Ledell
89F-158
89Hoops-194
90F-191
90Hoops-296
90Panin-150

90SkyBox-287
91F-204
Eakins, Jim
71T-197
72T-213
73T-178
74T-230M
74T-258
75T-297
Earhart, Amelia
48T/Magic*-L5
Easley, Chuck
91GATech*-19
Eastman, Ben
48T/Magic*-E3
Eaton, Mark
83Star/NBA-138
84Star/Award-19LL
84Star/CrtKg-32
84Star/NBA-225
84Star/NBA-286
85Star/NBA-141
86F-28
86Star/CrtKg-11
87F-32
88F-112
88F-131AS
88Jazz/Smok-2
89F-152
89Hoops-155
89Hoops-174AS
89Jazz/OldH-3
90F-184
90Hoops-287
90Hoops/CollB-39
90Hoops/Super-96
90Jazz/Star-3
90Panin-53
90SkyBox-276
91F-198
Eaves, Jerry
83Star/NBA-139
88Louville/194-116
88Louville/194-152
88Louville/194-19
88Louville/194-64
89Louville/300*-233
89Louville/300*-262
89Louville/300*-32
89Louville/300*-9
Eckwood, Stan
80TCMA/CBA-41
Eddleman, Dwight
52Bread-7
Eddington, Mike
90MISt/200*-177
Edelman, Ray
88KY/269-98
Edgar, John
84AZ/Pol-4
85AZ/Pol-4
Edge, Charlie
75T-269
Edge, Junior
90NC/200*-118
Edison, Thomas A.
48T/Magic*-N2
Edmonds, Bobby Joe
91AR/100*-55
Edmonson, Keith
83Star/NBA-185
Edwards, Danny
910KSt*-82
Edwards, David
89George/Pol-5
910KSt*-64
Edwards, Franklin
83Star/NBA-3
84Star/Arena-E3
85Star/NBA-90
86Kings/Smok-2
Edwards, James

78T-27
79T-113
80T-103
80T-124
80T-36
80T-54
81T-53M
81T-MW90
83Star/NBA-111
84Star/NBA-40
84Suns/Pol-53
85Star/NBA-37
86F-29
87Suns/Circ-5
89F-46
89Hoops-284A
89Hoops-284B
90F-56
90Hoops-104
90Panin-90
90Piston/Star-4
90Piston/Unocal-4
90SkyBox-85
91F-60
Edwards, James
(Lum)
89Louville/300*-99
Edwards, Johnathon
85George/Pol-5
86George/Pol-5
87George/Pol-5
88George/Pol-5
89PC/CBA-57
91George/100-42
Edwards, Kevin
89F-81
89Heat/Publix-3
89Hoops-41
90F-99
90Heat/Publix-6
90Hoops-165
90Hoops/Super-51
90Panin-152
90SkyBox-146
91F-108
Edwards, Leroy
88KY/269-23
Edwards, Michael
89Syr/Pep-5
Edwards, Theodore
(Blue)
90F-185
90Hoops-288
90Jazz/Star-4
90Panin-52
90SkyBox-277
91F-199
91F-227
Egan, Johnny
69T-16
70T-34
81TCMA-33
Eggleston, Don
89NC/Coke-196
Eggleston, Marty
89PC/CBA-48
Ehle, Tory
91GATech*-24
Ehlers, Eddie
48Bowman-19
Ehlo, Craig
84Star/NBA-238
89F-26
89Hoops-106
90F-32
90Hoops-74
90Panin-106
90SkyBox-51
91F-35
Eichmann, Eric
90Clem/200*-22
Eisaman, Jerry

89KY/300*-180
Eisenhower, Dwight
48T/Magic*-O10
Eitutis, Jason
90KY/Sov-6
Ekker, Ron
89PC/CBA-12
Elenz, Jim
79StBon-4
Elie, Mario
89PC/CBA-109
90PC/CBA-151
Elkins, Arlo
91SC/200*-50
Elkins, Rod
90NC/200*-12
Ellenberger, Norm
89UTEP/Drug-7
Ellery, Kevin
90ND-20
Ellington, Russell
89KY/300*-202
Elliott, Bob
48T/Magic*-K3
90AZ/125*-97
90AZ/125*-106
Elliott, Chalmers
(Bump)
48ExhSC-17
91MI/56*-19
Elliott, Pete
48T/Magic*-C2
57Union-28
Elliott, Sean
85AZ/Pol-5
86AZ/Pol-4
87AZ/Pol-4
88AZ/Pol-5
90AZ/125*-110
90AZ/125*-2
90AZ/125*-38
90AZ/125*-85
90AZ/Promos*-9
90F-171
90F/Rook-2
90Hoops-267
90Panin-44
90SkyBox-256
91F-185
91Wooden-18
Ellis, Bill
91UCLA/144-57
Ellis, Bo
81TCMA/CBA-25
Ellis, Bob
91TexAM-11
Ellis, Cliff
90Clem/200*-92
90Clem-6CO
Ellis, Dale
83Star/NBA-53
84Star/Arena-B4
84Star/NBA-254
85Star/NBA-162
87F-33
88F-107
89F-146
89F/AS-8
89Hoops-10
89Hoops-43AS
90F-177
90Hoops-277
90Hoops/Super-89
90Panin-21
90SkyBox-266
90Sonic/Smok-5
91F-114
Ellis, James
90MISt/200*-10
Ellis, Jim
89PC/CBA-195
Ellis, Joe

69T-57
70T-28
71T-51
72T-14
73T-171
Ellis, LaPhonso
90ND-23
Ellis, LeRon
88KY/Award-10
88KY/Award-14
89KY/Tm80-51
89Syr/Pep-2
91Class-14
91Court-18
91StarP-54
Ellis, Leroy
69T-42
70T-35
70T/Ins-9
71T-111
71T/Ins-20
72T-157
72T-18
73T-34
74T-111
74T-94M
75T-104
81TCMA-27
Ellis, Phil
89Louville/300*-155
Ellis, Robert
90MISt/200*-156
Ellis, Todd
91SC/200*-2
91SC/200*-44
Ellis, Zarko
89Louville/300*-193
Ellison, Janet
90Clem/200*-198
Ellison, Pervis
87KY/Coke-17
89Kings/Carl-42
89Louville/300*-206
89Louville/300*-253
89Louville/300*-290
89Louville/300*-4
89Louville/300*-41
90F-164
90F/Up-U97
90Hoops-257
90Hoops/II-438
90SkyBox-246
90StarP-50
91F-205
90SkyBox/II-419
Ellison, Shawn
90CT/Pol-5
Elmendorf, Dave
91TexAM-95
Elmore, Len
75T-259
76T-71
83Star/NBA-63
Elston, Darrell
75T-308
89NC/Coke-144
90NC/200*-165
Embry, Randy
88KY/269-83
Embry, Wayne
59Kahn's-2
60Kahn's-4
61F-12
61Kahn's-4
62Kahn's-3
63Kahn's-4
64Kahn's-6
65Kahn's-1
Emerzian, Bryan
88UNLV/HOF-12
89UNLV/HOF-11
89UNLV/Seven-6

90UNLV/HOF-7
90UNLV/Season-7
90UNLV/Smok-5
Engelland, Chip
89PC/CBA-78
Engen, Alf
57Union-10
England, Kenny
89KY/300*-203
Englehardt, Dan
89NCSt/Coke-83
89NCSt/Coke-84
Engler, Chris
83Star/NBA-256
English, A.J.
90F/Up-U98
90StarP-46
91F-206
English, Alex
77Bucks/ActPh-4
79T-31
80T-107
80T-19
81T-W68
82Nugget/Pol-2
83Nugget/Pol-2
83Star/ASG-15
83Star/ASG-x
83Star/NBA-186
84Star/ASG-18
84Star/CrtKg-22
84Star/NBA-137
84Star/PolASG-18
85Nugget/Pol-1
85Star/NBA-50
86F-30
86F/Ins-4
86Star/CrtKg-12
87F-34
87F/Ins-11
88F-34
88F/Ins-4
88Fourn-19
88Nugget/Pol-2A
88Nugget/Pol-2B
89F-40
89Hoops-120
89Hoops-133AS
89Nugget/Pol-4
90F-48
90F/Up-U19
90Hoops-94
90Hoops/II-407
90Hoops/Super-26
90SkyBox-74
91SC/200*-3
91SC/200*-35
90SkyBox/II-375
English, Claude
71T-46
Enright, Rex
91SC/200*-71
Ensminger, Steve
90LSU/200*-185
Epley, Frank
89Louville/300*-28
Eppley, Mike
90Clem/200*-25
Erhardt, Herb
86SWLou/Pol*-5
Erickson, Edward
90MISt/200*-54
Erickson, Keith
69T-29
70T-38
71T-61
72T-140
73T-117
73T-68M
74T-53
75Suns-5
75T-113

75T-130M
76Suns-3
76T-4
91UCLA/144-132
Erickson, Ken
90AZ/125*-80
Errol, Leon
48T/Magic*-J25
Erving, Julius
72T-195
72T-255AS
72T-263LL
73T-204M
73T-234LL
73T-240AS
74T-200AS
74T-207LL
74T-226M
75T-221LL
75T-282M
75T-300AS
76T-1
76T-127AS
77Dell-3
77Pep/AS-3
77T-100
78RCCola-10
78T-130
79T-20
80T-1
80T-137
80T-142
80T-146
80T-176
80T-23
80T-51
80T-6
81T-30
81T-59M
81T-E104
83Star/ASG-1
83Star/ASG-26
83Star/ASG-4
83Star/NBA-1
83Star/Sixers-10
83Star/Sixers-18
83Star/Sixers-22
83Star/Sixers-24
83Star/Sixers-4
84Star/Arena-E1
84Star/ASG-4
84Star/CrtKg-4
84Star/Erving-1
84Star/Erving-10
84Star/Erving-11
84Star/Erving-12
84Star/Erving-13
84Star/Erving-14
84Star/Erving-15
84Star/Erving-16
84Star/Erving-17
84Star/Erving-18
84Star/Erving-2
84Star/Erving-3
84Star/Erving-4
84Star/Erving-5
84Star/Erving-6
84Star/Erving-7
84Star/Erving-8
84Star/Erving-9
84Star/NBA-204
84Star/NBA-281
84Star/PolASG-28
84Star/PolASG-4
84Star/SlamD-4
85JMS-5
85Star/Crunch-3
85Star/Gator-5
85Star/LiteAS-3
85Star/NBA-3
85Star/SlamD-3
85Star/TmSuper-PS1

86F-31
86F/Ins-5
86Star/Best-6
86Star/CrtKg-13
87F-35
Escarlega, Kathy
90AZSt/200*-127
Esherick, Craig
91George/100-21
91George/100-90
Espeland, Gene
89PC/CBA-113
Esposito, Phil
74Nab-11
75Nab-11
Essensa, Bob
90MISt/200*-137
Estay, Ronnie
90LSU/200*-126
Estes, Joel
90AZ/125*-82
Evans, Bill
88KY/269-37
Evans, Bryon
90AZ/125*-55
90AZ/125*-109
Evans, Dwayne
90AZSt/200*-126
Evans, Mike
79Spurs/Pol-1
82TCMA/CBA-13
83Nugget/Pol-5
83Star/NBA-187
84Star/NBA-140
85Nugget/Pol-2
85Star/NBA-53
87F-36
Evans, Paul
89Pitt/Food-x
Evans, Peter
90AZ/125*-22
Evans, William
55Ash-19
Everett, J.C.
89KY/300*-204
Everett, Jimmy
90FLSt/200*-115
Evers, Johnny
48T/Magic*-K18
Everson, Greg
91MI/56*-20
Ewing, Patrick
81George/Pol-4
82George/Pol-2
83George/Pol-10
84George/Pol-4
85Prism-2
85Star/NBA-166
86F-32
86F/Ins-6
86Star/Best-1
86Star/CrtKg-14
87F-37
88F-130AS
88F-80
88F/Ins-5
88Fourn-15
89F-100
89F-167M
89F/AS-7
89Hoops-159AS
89Hoops-80
89Knicks/Marine-2
90F-125
90F/AS-12
90Hoops-203
90Hoops-4AS
90Hoops/CollB-15
90Hoops/II-372TC
90Hoops/II-388
90Hoops/Super-67
90Panin-140

90Panin-IAS
90SkyBox-187
91F-136
91F-215
91F/ProV-4
91George/100-2
91George/100-30
91George/100-31
91George/100-49
91George/100-55
91George/100-77
Ezenwa, Francis
89UTEP/Drug-8
Faggins, Terry
89PC/CBA-142
Fahs, Dave
90MISt/200*-160
Falcon, Joe
91AR/100*-45
Fannin, Omar
55Ash-51
Fanuzzi, Mike
89KY/300*-150
Farley, Dick
87IN/GreatII-29
Farmer, Jim
89Hoops-227
89Hoops/II-334
89PC/CBA-58
Farmer, Larry
91UCLA/144-4
91UCLA/144-92
Farmer, Mike
60Kahn's-5
Farmer, Richie
88KY/Award-4
88KY/Sov-8
89KY/Award-20
Farmer, Tony
91Class-50
91Court-19
91StarP-36
Farnsley, Keith
89KY/300*-71
Farr, Heather
90AZSt/200*-63
Farr, James
90Clem/200*-62
Farragut, David
48T/Magic*-O5
Farrell, John
91OKSt*-88
Farrell, Lon
91AR/100*-33
Farris, Monty
91OKSt*-75
Farris, Ray
90NC/200*-167
Fatheree, Jess
90LSU/200*-17
Faucette, Floyd
91GATech*-187
Faught, Robert
90ND-40
Faulk, Steve
90LSU/200*-194
Favrot, Ron
91AR/100*-29
Federspiel, Joe
89KY/300*-139
Fedor, Dave
90FLSt/200*-194
Feerick, Bob
48Bowman-6
Feggins, Bryant
89NCSt/Pol-3
Feher, Butch
76Suns-4
Feldhaus, Allen
89KY/300*-15
Feldhaus, Deron
88KY/Award-12

89KY/Award-22
89KY/Award-24
89KY/Award-28
89KY/Award-33
Felix, Ray
54Bullet/Gunth-4
57T-35
61Lakers/Bell-2
81TCMA-12
Fellmuth, Catherine
54Quaker-8
Felton, George
91SC/200*-15
Fenimore, Bob
91OKSt*-15
Fenlon, Terry
91George/100-73
Fenwick, Jack
90FLSt/200*-112
Ferguson, Chip
90FLSt/200*-38
Ferguson, Joe
91AR/100*-86
Fernandez, Gigi
90Clem/200*-195
Fernsten, Eric
83Star/NBA-64
Ferrari, Albert R.
61Hawks/Essex-2
90MISt/200*-109
Ferreira, Rolando
88Blaz/Franz-6
Ferrell, Duane
91GATech*-35
90SkyBox-2
Ferrer, Jim
89PC/CBA-106
Ferrier, James
48Kell*-12
Ferrin, Arnold
52Bread-8
Ferry, Danny
87Duke/Pol-35
90F-33
90Hoops-336
90Hoops/II-406
90SkyBox-300
90StarP-10
91F-36
90SkyBox/II-374
Fest, Fred
89KY/300*-247
Ficke, Bill
82Nugget/Pol-x
83Nugget/Pol-x
Field, Jimmy
90LSU/200*-181
Fields, Kenny
84Star/NBA-129
85Star/Bucks-6
86Star/LifeBucks-5
89PC/CBA-131
91UCLA/144-49
Figaro, Kevin
82TCMA/CBA-68
Finch, Larry
74T-215
74T-225M
75T-281M
Finkel, Henry
68Rocket/Jack-5
69T-34
70T-27
71T-18
73T-66M
73T-94
74T-118
75T-26
Finn, John
90AZSt/200*-74
Finnegan, Tommy
88Louville/194-92

Finzier, Herman
90AZSt/200*-112
Fiorentino, Tony
89Heat/Publix-4CO
90Heat/Publix-16CO
Fischer, Bill
48T/Magic*-C5
Fisher, Casey
87SoMiss-3
Fisher, Roy
91Court-20
91StarP-68
Fisher, Scott
89PC/CBA-200
Fisher, Steve
89MI-1CO
Fitch, Bill
89Hoops/II-327CO
90Nets/Kayo-13CO
91F-132CO
90SkyBox/II-317CO
Fitzsimmons, Bob
48T/Magic*-A4
Fitzsimmons, Cotton
85Star/CO-3
89Hoops-14CO
90Hoops-325CO
91F-159CO
90SkyBox/II-321CO
Flagler, Terrance
90Clem/200*-39
Fleetwood, Mark
91SC/200*-131
Fleisher, Larry
91StarP-30
Fleming, Al
90AZ/125*-64
Fleming, Ed
57T-79
Fleming, Reg
74Nab-13
Fleming, Vern
84Star/NBA-196
84Star/NBA-55
85Star/NBA-83
85Star/RTm-6
86F-33
87F-38
88F-55
89F-64
89Hoops-231
90F-76
90Hoops-133
90Hoops/Super-39
90Panin-114
90SkyBox-114
91F-81
Fletcher, Ralph
89NC/Coke-186
Floreal, Errick
91AR/100*-14
Florent, Kevin
87South/Pol*-9
Flowers, Bill
91GATech*-169
Flowers, Bruce
90ND-46
Flowers, Kenny
90Clem/200*-73
Floyd, Charlie
81TCMA/CBA-46
82TCMA/CBA-45
82TCMA/Lanc-16
82TCMA/Lanc-17
Floyd, Eric
(Sleepy)
81George/Pol-10
83Star/NBA-257
84Star/NBA-154
85Star/NBA-134
86F-34

87F-39
88F-51
89F-59
89Hoops-117
90F-70
90Hoops-124
90Hoops/Super-35
90Panin-71
90SkyBox-107
91F-74
91George/100-3
91George/100-51
91George/100-64
Floyd, James
55Ash-6
Floyd, Kevin
84George/Pol-5
Floyd, Norman
91SC/200*-165
Flynn, Doug
87KY/Coke-5
Flynn, Mike
88KY/269-103
88KY/269-141
Fogle, Larry
80TCMA/CBA-23
81TCMA/CBA-81
Fogler, Eddie
89NC/Coke-112
89NC/Coke-113
90NC/200*-47CO
Fontaine, Joan
48T/Magic*-F8
Fontaine, Levi
71T-92
Fontenet, B.B.
82TCMA/CBA-26
Fonville, Charlie
48T/Magic*-E12
Ford, Chris
73T-79
74T-112
75T-47
76T-29
77T-121
78T-15
79T-124
80T-67
80T-97
81T-E73
90Hoops-306CO
90Hoops/II-347CO
91F-10CO
90SkyBox/II-302CO
Ford, Danny
90Clem/200*-133
Ford, Don
77T-43
79Lakers/Alta-2
79T-77
80T-11
80T-99
89PC/CBA-127
Ford, Gerald
91MI/56*-21
Ford, Jake
70Sonic/Sunb-4
71Sonic/Sunb-3
Ford, Jeff
91GATech*-188
Ford, Ken
91TexAM-69
Ford, Phil
79T-108
80T-128
80T-129
80T-40
80T-41
81T-18
81T-54M
83Star/NBA-75
85Star/ROY-7

89NC/Coke-10
89NC/Coke-11
89NC/Coke-12
89NC/Coke-63
89NC/Coke-7
89NC/Coke-8
89NC/Coke-9
90NC/200*-111
90NC/200*-185CO
90NC/200*-7
91Wooden-8
Ford, Randall
89Louville/300*-58
Ford, Rick
86IN/Greatl-15
Ford, Travis
88KY/Sov-9
89MO-6
Forman, Jane
90Clem/200*-175
Forrest, Bayard
77Suns/Discs-35
Forrest, Derrick
90Clem/200*-97
Forrest, Manuel
83Louville-30
88Louville/194-100
88Louville/194-115
88Louville/194-151
88Louville/194-18
89Louville/300*-10
89Louville/300*-275
89Louville/300*-48
Fortier, Bill
90LSU/200*-43
Foster, Barry
91AR/100*-95
Foster, Bill
90Clem/200*-114
Foster, Fred
70T-53
72T-66
73T-56
75T-29
Foster, Greg
89UTEP/Drug-9
90F/Up-U99
90StarP-57
Foster, Harold E.
68HOF-12
Foster, Michael
91SC/200*-128
Foster, Rod
83Star/NBA-112
84Star/NBA-41
84Suns/Pol-10
91UCLA/144-61
Foster, Shelia
91SC/200*-198
Fournet, Sid
90LSU/200*-110
Foust, Larry
57T-18
61Hawks/Essex-3
81TCMA-2
Fowler, Bob
89KY/300*-289
Fowler, Larry
90MISt/200*-2
Fox, Jim
68Suns/Carn-1
69Suns/Carn-2
69T-88
70T-98
71T-3
72T-34
73Sonic/Shur-4
73T-24
74T-34
75T-164
Fox, Reggie
90PC/CBA-163

Fox, Rick
87NC/Pol-44
88NC/Pol-44
88NC/Pol-x
91Class-16
91Court-21
91StarP-69
Foxworth, Eric
87South/Pol*-15
Fraler, Harold
55Ash-7
Francewar, Kevin
89PC/CBA-118
Francis, Clarence
(Bevo)
81T/Thirst-28
Francis, George Jr.
55Ash-8
Francis, James
87Baylor/Pol*-13
Francona, Terry
90AZ/125*-8
Frank, Tellis
89Heat/Publix-5
90Hoops-166
90Panin-153
90SkyBox-147
Franklin, Benjamin
48T/Magic*-N4
Franz, Ron
71Flor/McDon-3
71T-172
Fraser, Bruce
84AZ/Pol-5
85AZ/Pol-6
86AZ/Pol-5
Fraser, Ron
90FLSt/200*-134
Fratello, Mike
78Hawks/Coke-4CO
79Hawks/Majik-x
87Hawks/Pizza-1CO
89Hoops-179CO
Frawley, William
48T/Magic*-J27
Frazier, Derrick
91SC/200*-192
Frazier, Jadie
88Louville/194-50
Frazier, Mike
91George/100-39
Frazier, Raymond
55Ash-40
Frazier, Walt
69T-98
69T/Ins-17
70T-106AS
70T-120
70T-6LL
70T/Ins-1
71T-65
71T/Ins-25
72Icee-7
72T-165AS
72T-60
73T-10AS
73T-68M
74T-150AS
74T-93M
75Carv-7
75T-128M
75T-55AS
75T-6M
76Buck-7
76T-64
77T-129
78RCCola-11
78T-83
81TCMA-30
85Star/Schick-11
Frederick, Anthony
90PC/CBA-102

86George/Pol-6
87George/Pol-6
88Kings/Carl-50
91George/100-18
Gilliam, Armon
88F-89
89F-120
89Hoops-64
90F-19
90F/Up-U70
90Hoops-54
90Panin-83
90SkyBox-29
91F-153
Gilliam, Herm
69T-87
70T-73
71T-123
72T-113
73T-106
74T-5
75T-43
76T-87
Gilliam, John
74Nab-6
75Nab-6
Gillon, Jack
91SC/200*-106
Gilmore, Artis
72T-180
72T-251AS
72T-260LL
72T-263LL
73T-207M
73T-235LL
73T-238LL
73T-250AS
74T-180AS
74T-211LL
74T-224M
75T-222LL
75T-225LL
75T-250AS
75T-280M
75T-310
76T-25
77Bulls/WhHen-2
77T-115
78RCCola-13
78T-73
79Bulls/Pol-53
79T-25
80T-109
80T-134
80T-17
80T-59
81T-46M
81T-7
81T-MW107
83Star/ASG-17
83Star/ASG-x
83Star/NBA-244
84Star/Award-14LL
84Star/CrtKg-34
84Star/NBA-64
85Star/NBA-145
86F-37
87F-40
90Bulls/Eq-5
Gilmore, Sharon
91SC/200*-97
Gilmur, Charles
48Bowman-31
52Bread-11
Gipple, Dale
89NC/Coke-171
Gipson, Al
89PC/CBA-148
Gische, Melissa
90UCLA-29
Givens, Al
91TexAM-85

Givens, Jack
78Hawks/Coke-5
78KY/Food-3
79Hawks/Majik-21
88KY/269-15
88KY/269-159
88KY/269-186
88KY/269-252
89KY/300*-4
Givins, Ernest
89Louville/300*-115
Gladden, Darryl
81TCMA/CBA-56
82TCMA/CBA-43
82TCMA/Lanc-18
82TCMA/Lanc-19
Glanton, Keith
91GATech*-29
Glanzer, Barry
89PC/CBA-66
Glass, Gerald
90F/Up-U56
90StarP-67
Glass, Greg
90KY/Sov-7
Glass, Willie
89PC/CBA-107
Glaza, Allan
55Ash-27
89Louville/300*-64
Gleason, James
48T/Magic*-J30
Glenn, Mike
83Star/NBA-266
84Star/NBA-79
Gminski, Mike
81T-E78
83Star/NBA-149
84Nets/Getty-5
84Star/NBA-91
85Star/NBA-62
86F-38
86Star/LifeNets-6
87F-41
88F-87
89F-116
89Hoops-33
89Sixers/Kodak-6
90F-142
90Hoops-228
90Hoops/Super-74
90Panin-130
90SkyBox-215
Goad, Tim
90NC/200*-34
Godfread, Dan
90PC/CBA-48
90StarP-42
Goff, Dave
91TexAM-53
Goforth, Jim
89KY/300*-207
Gofourth, Derrel
91OKSt*-21
Gola, Tom
57T-44
61F-14
61F-51IA
Golden, Craig
82Fairf-6
Golden, Shaun
90GA/Smok-6
Goldstein, Al
90NC/200*-137
Goldstein, Don
88Louville/194-145
88Louville/194-89
89Louville/300*-20
89Louville/300*-249
Gomez, Lefty
81T/Thirst-2
Gondrezick, Glen

82Nugget/Pol-22
Gonzalez, Pancho
57Union-17
Good, Larry
91GATech*-52
Good, Mike
90FLSt/200*-155
Goode, Irvin
89KY/300*-110
Goodman, Jim
89KY/300*-208
90PC/CBA-43
Goodrich, Gail
68Suns/Carn-2
69Suns/Carn-3
69T-2
69T/Ins-7
70T-93
71T-121
72T-174LL
72T-50
73NBAPA-9
73T-55
74T-120AS
74T-90M
75Carv-9
75T-110
75T-125M
76Buck-8
76T-125
77T-77
78T-95
79T-32
91UCLA/144-134
91UCLA/144-8
91UCLA/144-89
Goodwin, Damon
83Dayton/Blue-7
Goovert, Ron
90MISt/200*-5
Gorcey, Leo
48T/Magic*-J24
Gorden, Larry
90AZSt/200*-22
Gordon, Lancaster
83Louville-4
84Star/NBA-18
88Louville/194-109
88Louville/194-167
88Louville/194-185
88Louville/194-9
89Louville/300*-234
89Louville/300*-260
89Louville/300*-47
Gordy, Len
81AZ/Pol-6CO
90Clem-7CO
Gore, Curt
90LSU/200*-56
Goring, Butch
79Lakers/Alta-6
Gorius, Bob
89Louville/300*-80
Goss, Fred
91UCLA/144-131
Gotch, Frank
48T/Magic*-D1
Gottfried, Mark
90UCLA-39CO
Goudin, Lucien
48ExhSC-20
Gould, Terry
89PC/CBA-13
Govan, Gerald
71T-176
72T-238
73T-233
74T-218
74T-229M
75T-276
Govedarica, Bato
86DePaul-H10

Gowan, Charlie
91SC/200*-118
Grable, Betty
48T/Magic*-F5
Graboski, Joe
57T-41
Graebner, Clark
71Keds*-1M
Graham, Ernie
81TCMA/CBA-21
Graham, Kevin
81TCMA/CBA-22
Graham, Michael
83George/Pol-12
Graham, Orlando
90PC/CBA-186
Graham, Otto
48ExhSC-21
Graham, Pat
88KY/Sov-10
Graham, Paul
90PC/CBA-156
Graham, Robbie
88KY/Sov-11
Gramling, Johnny
91SC/200*-199
Grandelius, Everett
90MISt/200*-37
Grandison, Ronnie
89Hoops-248
Granger, Stewart
83Star/NBA-233
Granier, Richard
90LSU/200*-45
Grant, Anthony
83Dayton/Blue-8
Grant, Gary
89F-70
89Hoops-274
90Clip/Star-4
90F/Up-U40
90Hoops-145
90Panin-31
90SkyBox-127
91F-89
Grant, Greg
90F/Up-U63
90Hoops-235
90Hoops/II-421
90SkyBox-221
90SkyBox/II-400
Grant, Harvey
89Hoops-67
90F-192A
90F-192B
90Hoops-297
90Panin-149
90SkyBox-288
91F-207
Grant, Horace
87Bulls/Ent-11
88Bulls/Ent-54
88F-16
89Bulls/Eq-4
89F-20
89Hoops-242
90Bulls/Eq-6
90Clem/200*-8
90F-24
90Hoops-63
90Panin-95
90SkyBox-39
91F-27
Grant, Kevin
89ORSt-7
90FLSt/200*-10
Grant, Mike
90NE/Pol*-8
Grant, Russell
88LSU/Pol*-8
Grant, Travis

74T-259
75T-245
75T-285M
Grant, Wally
91MI/56*-22
Grantz, Jeff
91SC/200*-55
Gravely, Stacie
90UCLA-23
Grawemeyer, Phil
55Ash-20
88KY/269-265
88KY/269-66
Gray, Allison
86SWLou/Pol*-7
Gray, Evric
90UNLV/HOF-11
90UNLV/Smok-6
90UNLV/Season-11
Gray, Hector
90FLSt/200*-164
Gray, Herb
81TCMA/CBA-86
Gray, Leonard
75T-78
76T-136
77T-7
Gray, Roland
89PC/CBA-72
Gray, Stuart
84Star/NBA-57
89Hoops-253
89Hoops/II-352
90Hoops-204
90SkyBox-188
91UCLA/144-74
Gray, Sylvester
89Hoops-204
89PC/CBA-36
Grayer, Jeff
88Bucks/Green-4
90F-104
90Hoops-174
90SkyBox-157
Grayer, Steve
89PC/CBA-5
90PC/CBA-19
Green, A.C.
87F-42
88F-66
89F-76
89Hoops-124
90F-92
90Hoops-156
90Hoops-17AS
90Hoops/Super-49
90Panin-6
90Panin-C
90SkyBox-137
91F-99
Green, Al
80TCMA/CBA-6
90LSU/200*-65
Green, Carlton
80TCMA/CBA-45
Green, Ernie
89Louville/300*-120
Green, Gary
91OKSt*-62
Green, Harold
91SC/200*-8
Green, Hubert
90FLSt/200*-99
Green, Jacob
91TexAM-43
Green, John
91UCLA/144-75
Green, Johnny
70T-3LL
70T-81
71T-140LL
71T-86

71T/Ins-14
72T-48
73T-124
81TCMA-40M
90MISt/200*-128
Green, Ken
81TCMA/CBA-53
Green, Lamar
70Suns/A1-2
70Suns/Carn-2
71T-39
72T-119
73T-9
Green, Litterial
90GA/Smok-7
Green, Mike
74T-254
75T-247
75T-278M
77T-99
Green, Rickey
81TCMA/CBA-70
83Star/NBA-140
84Star/ASG-20
84Star/Award-18LL
84Star/CrtKg-11
84Star/NBA-229
84Star/PolASG-20
85Star/NBA-142
86F-39
87F-43
89Hoops-56
90Hoops-134
90Hoops/II-425
90SkyBox-115
90SkyBox/II-404
Green, Sean
91Class-31
91Court-24
91StarP-22
Green, Sidney
83Star/NBA-172
84Star/NBA-104
86F-40
87F-44
88F-81
89Hoops-97
89Hoops/II-305
89Magic/Pep-5
90F-134
90F/Up-U88
90Hoops-218
90Hoops/II-435
90Panin-122
90SkyBox-203
90SkyBox/II-413
Green, Sihugo
58Kahn's-3
61F-15
Green, Steve
86IN/GreatI-38
Green, Woody
90AZSt/200*-162
Greenberg, Fran
81TCMA/CBA-79
Greene, Gerald
89PC/CBA-44
Greenwood, David
79Bulls/Pol-34
80T-25
80T-62
80T-89
80T-92
81T-MW67
83Star/NBA-173
84Star/NBA-105
86F-41
87F-45
90Hoops/II-433
90Piston/Star-5
90SkyBox-86
90SkyBox/II-414

91UCLA/144-107
91UCLA/144-116
Greer, Curtis
91MI/56*-23
Greer, Hal
61F-16
68T/Test-2
69T-84
69T/Ins-13
70T-155
70T/Ins-10
71T-60
71T/Ins-13
72T-56
73NBAPA-10
Gregor, Gary
68Suns/Carn-3
69T-11
70T-89
71T-56
72T-36
91SC/200*-85
Gregory, Johnny
91SC/200*-93
Greiger, Gary
86IN/GreatI-36
Gressley, Jim
90AZSt/200*-124
Grevey, Kevin
77T-23
78T-113
79T-34
80T-12
80T-90
81T-E96
83Star/NBA-43
84Star/Arena-C4
84Star/NBA-130
85Star/Bucks-7
88KY/269-154
88KY/269-185
88KY/269-251
88KY/269-9
89KY/300*-49
Grezaffi, Sam
90LSU/200*-199
Griffin, Andra
81TCMA/CBA-17
Griffin, Eddie
90Clem/200*-174
Griffin, James
80IL/Arby's-2
81IL/Arby's-3
Griffin, Joe
89UTEP/Drug-10
Griffin, Mark
88TN/Smok-33
Griffin, Mike
88MI/Nike-3
89MI-17
Griffin, Paul
79Spurs/Pol-30
81T-MW102
Griffin, Parker
87LSU/Pol*-8
Griffith, Darrell
81T-41
83Louville-35
83Star/NBA-141
84Star/Award-16LL
84Star/CrtKg-45
84Star/NBA-230
84Star/PolASG-29
84Star/SlamD-5
85Star/Gator-6
85Star/NBA-143
85Star/ROY-5
85Star/SlamD-4
86F-42
86Star/CrtKg-16
87F-46
87KY/Coke-8

88Louville/194-101
88Louville/194-172
88Louville/194-182
88Louville/194-3
89F-153
89Hoops-241
89Jazz/OldH-4
89Louville/300*-2
89Louville/300*-209
89Louville/300*-25
89Louville/300*-266
89Louville/300*-281
89Louville/300*-297
90Hoops-289
90Jazz/Star-9
90Panin-50
90SkyBox-278
91Wooden-10
Griffith, Jason
90Clem/200*-38
Griggley, Terry
89McNees*-2
Grimsley, John
89KY/300*-188
Grisham, Wes
90LSU/200*-163
Grissom, Greg
89PC/CBA-100
Gross, Bob
77Blaz/Pol-30
77T-11
78T-98
79Blaz/Pol-30
79T-4
80T-158
80T-53
81Blaz/Pol-30
81T-W84
Gross, Julie
90LSU/200*-33
Grosso, Mike
88Louville/194-45
89Louville/300*-236
89Louville/300*-294
Grove, Orval
48Kell*-2
Grovey, Quinn
91AR/100*-92
Groza, Alex
52Bread-12
88KY/269-149
88KY/269-5
89KY/300*-3
Groza, Lou
48Kell*-6
Grubar, Dick
89NC/Coke-87
89NC/Coke-88
90NC/200*-115
Grubb, John
90FLSt/200*-61
Gruden, Jay
89Louville/300*-105
89Louville/300*-143
Grunfeld, Ernie
77Bucks/ActPh-6
81T-MW94
83Star/NBA-65
84Star/NBA-31
85Star/NBA-169
Gruver, Mat
88LSU/Pol*-14
Guanlett, Tom
90NC/200*-90
Gudmondsson, Peter
81Blaz/Pol-40
Gueldner, Jeff
89KS/Leesley-42
Guerin, Richie
61F-17
61F-52IA
81TCMA-40M

Guerrero, Karen
91TexAM-89
Guest, Darren
89PC/CBA-93
Gugliotta, Tom
89NCSt/Pol-4
Guillot, Monk
90LSU/200*-132
Gumbert, George
89KY/300*-209
Gundy, Mike
91OKSt*-50
Guokas, Matt
70T-124
71T-113
72T-9
73T-155LL
73T-18
74T-117
75T-28
89Hoops/II-321CO
90Hoops-323CO
90Hoops/II-352CO
91F-145CO
90SkyBox/II-319CO
Gura, Larry
90AZSt/200*-38
Guthridge, Bill
89NC/Coke-101
90NC/200*-117CO
Guthrie, Grant
90FLSt/200*-165
Guthrie, Mark
86LSU/Pol*-6
Guy, Tony
82TCMA/CBA-79
Guyette, Bob
88KY/269-102
88KY/269-184
88KY/269-249
88KY/269-264
Gwynn, John
90CT/Pol-6
Gyton, Tony
91SC/200*-195
Habegger, Les
78Sonic/Pol-13CO
79Sonic/Pol-11
Hackenschmidt, George
48T/Magic*-D2
Hackett, Wilbur
89KY/300*-142
Haddix, Harvey
81T/Thirst-8
Haddow, Kim
90AZ/125*-111
Hadley, John
90FLSt/200*-42
Haffner, Scott
89Heat/Publix-6
90SkyBox-148
Hagan, Cliff
56Busch-1
57T-37
61F-18
61F-53
61Hawks/Essex-4
78KY/Food-4
88KY/269-171
88KY/269-181
88KY/269-2
88KY/269-245
88KY/269-256
88KY/269-260
89KY/300*-6
Hagan, Glenn
80TCMA/CBA-22
81TCMA/CBA-20
Hagan, Jason
90KY/ClassA-9
Hagan, Joseph
89KY/300*-210

Hagg, Gunner
48T/Magic*-E7
Haggins, Odell
90FLSt/200*-94
Hagler, Scott
91SC/200*-104
Hagood, Kent
91SC/200*-6
Hairston, Harold
(Happy)
64Kahn's-1
69T-83
70T-77
71T-25
71T/Ins-19
72T-121
73T-137
74T-68
74T-90M
75Carv-10
75T-125M
75T-159
Hairston, Lindsay
90MISt/200*-118
Haji-Sheikh, Ali
91MI/56*-24
Halas, George
54Quaker-19
Halbert, Chuck
48Bowman-43
Hale, Bruce
48Bowman-15
52Bread-13
Hale, Jerry
88KY/269-101
Hale, Steve
89NC/Coke-119
89NC/Coke-120
90NC/200*-32
90NC/200*-70
90NC/200*-82
90NC/Promos*-NC3
Haley, Jack
88Bulls/Ent-15
90Hoops-197
90Nets/Kayo-9
90SkyBox-180
91UCLA/144-54
Haley, Roddie
91AR/100*-28
Halimon, Shaler
70T-127
71T-89
Hall, Bob
(Showboat)
71Globe-63M
71Globe-1
71Globe-2
71Globe-3
Hall, Charlie
87IN/GreatI-16
Hall, Dale
89Louville/300*-221
Hall, Dan
89KY/300*-283
Hall, Eugene
87Baylor/Pol*-16
Hall, Henry
89UTEP/Drug-11
Hall, Jeff
83Louville-42
88Louville/194-117
88Louville/194-154
88Louville/194-22
88Louville/194-58
89Louville/300*-256
89Louville/300*-299
89Louville/300*-34
Hall, Joe B.
77KY/Wildct-2M
77KY/Wildct-7CO
78KY/Food-19CO

57Union-25
Hill, J.D.
90AZSt/200*-97
Hill, Simmie
73T-184
Hill, Susan
90Clem/200*-173
Hill, Tyrone
90F/Up-U31
90Hoops/II-400LS
90StarP-38
91F-67
90SkyBox/II-358LP
Hill, Yvonne
91TexAM-97
Hilliard, Dalton
90LSU/200*-8
Hilliard, Keith
82TCMA/Lanc-27
82TCMA/Lanc-28
Hillman, Darnell
73T-244
74T-182
75T-290
76T-86
77T-5
78T-119
79T-47
Hilton, Carton
91SC/200*-24
Hilton, Fred
72T-23
73T-36
Himes, Doug
71Globe-57
71Globe-58
Hines, Glenn Ray
91AR/100*-83
Hinkle, Paul D.
68HOF-16
Hinnant, Mickey
89NCSt/Pol-5
Hinson, Roy
83Star/NBA-234
84Star/NBA-218
85Star/NBA-155
86F-46
87F-51
88F-78
89F-97
89Hoops-276
90Hoops-198
90Hoops/Super-63
90Panin-157
90SkyBox-181
Hinton, Harry
89Louville/300*-216
Hinton, Jurado
87SoMiss-9
Hinz, Gib
82TCMA/CBA-48
Hipsher, Dan
83Dayton/Blue-1M
Hirsch, Elroy
57Union-1
57Union-29
91MI/56*-25
Hirsch, Walt
88KY/269-261
88KY/269-64
Hisle, Larry
79Bucks/OpenP-4
Hite, Ray
89NC/Coke-166
Hoadley, Bruce
89NCSt/Coke-110
89NCSt/Coke-112
Hobbs, Bill
91TexAM-70
Hobbs, Bobby
86SWLou/Pol*-8
Hobson, Howard A.

68HOF-17
Hockensmith, Doug
89Louville/300*-184
Hodde, Rodney
91TexAM-23
Hodgdon, Ray
89NCSt/Coke-135
89NCSt/Coke-174
89NCSt/Coke-195
Hodge, Billy
91TexAM-12
Hodge, Donald
91Class-23
91Court-26
91StarP-48
Hodge, Jeff
89PC/CBA-23
Hodge, Walter
89KY/300*-214
Hodges, Craig
83Star/NBA-125
84Star/NBA-131
85Star/Bucks-8
85Star/NBA-125
86F-47
86Star/LifeBucks-6
87Bucks/Polar-15
87F-52
88Bulls/Ent-14
89Bulls/Eq-5
89Hoops-113
90F-25
90Hoops-64
90Panin-96
90SkyBox-40
Hodson, Charles
86IN/GreatI-28
Hodson, Tommy
90LSU/200*-10
Hoffman, Brad
89NC/Coke-145
90NC/200*-103
Hoffman, Paul
52Bread-14
54Bullet/Gunth-7
Hogan, Ben
48ExhSC-24
Hogan, Jeff
90FLSt/200*-107
Hogan, Mark
91GATech*-45
Holcomb, Derek
80IL/Arby's-5
Hold, Mike
91SC/200*-183
Holdash, Irv
90NC/200*-182
Holden, Fred
88Louville/194-133
88Louville/194-47
89Louville/300*-15
Holden, Steve
90AZSt/200*-86
Holder, Mike
91OKSt*-89
Holland, Brad
80T-11
80T-144
90UCLA-36CO
Holland, Joe
88KY/269-34
88KY/269-106
Holland, Terry
88VA/Hardee-7
Holland, Wilbur
77Bulls/WhHen-3
77T-53
78T-4
79T-99
Hollenbeck, Kent
88KY/269-246
88KY/269-93

Holley, Kitty
91TexAM-50
Hollingsworth, Mo
90KY/ClassA-15
Hollins, Lionel
76T-119
77Blaz/Pol-14
77T-39
78T-74
79Blaz/Pol-9
79T-129
80T-119
80T-36
81T-31
83Star/NBA-88
84Star/NBA-239
85Star/TmSuper-HR5
89Blaz/Franz-12
90AZSt/200*-12
Hollins, Paul
91SC/200*-74
Hollis, Richard
90PC/CBA-38
Holloman, Darrin
90FLSt/200*-17
Holloman, Tanner
90FLSt/200*-43
Hollyfield, Larry
91UCLA/144-43
Holman, Nat
68HOF-18
Holmes, Dick
90MISt/200*-154
Holmes, Larry
81TCMA/CBA-29
Holt, Michael
55Ash-88
Holton, Michael
84Star/NBA-42
86Blaz/Franz-5
87Blaz/Franz-3
89Hoops-119
90SkyBox-30
91UCLA/144-18
Holtz, Lou
91AR/100*-47
Holup, Joe
57T-76
Holzman, William
(Red)
48Bowman-32
85Star/Schick-15
Hood, Steve
91Class-32
91Court-27
91StarP-44
Hooker, Fair
90AZSt/200*-19
Hooker, Wilbert
89Fresno/Smok-6
90Fresno/Smok-8
Hoolahan, Paul
90NC/200*-163
Hooper, Chip
91AR/100*-22
Hoot, Rick
89NCSt/Coke-185
Hope, Danny
89Louville/300*-130
Hopkins, Bob
57T-53
Hopkins, Ed
91George/100-57
Hopkins, Gayle
90AZ/125*-119
Hopkins, Mike
89Syr/Pep-11
Hoppe, Willie
48ExhSC-25
Hoppen, Dave
89Hoops-99
90Hoops-55

90SkyBox-31
Hopson, Dennis
89Hoops-199
90F-120
90F/Up-U14
90Hoops-199
90Hoops/II-404
90Hoops/Super-61
90SkyBox-182
90SkyBox/II-371
Hord, Derrick
79KY/Food-13
82KY/Sch-3
88KY/269-119
88KY/269-254
89KY/Tm80-53
Hordges, Cerrick
91SC/200*-68
Horford, Tito
88Bucks/Green-6
Horlen, Joel
91OKSt*-33
Hornacek, Jeff
87Suns/Circ-6
89F-121
89Hoops-229
90F-147
90Hoops-236
90Hoops/Super-76
90Panin-17
90SkyBox-222
90Suns/Smok-2
91F-160
Horne, Grey
91AR/100*-87
Horner, Bob
90AZSt/200*-111M
90AZSt/200*-172
Hornsby, Rogers
48T/Magic*-K8
Horton, Ethan
90NC/Promos*-NC2
90NC/200*-10
90NC/200*-80
Horton, Gary
91TexAM-6
Horton, Jim
88MO-5
89MO-8
Horton, Lenny
80TCMA/CBA-17
81TCMA/CBA-66
91GATech*-3
Hosket, Bill
70T-104
Houbregs, Bob
54Bullet/Gunth-8
57T-56
Houston, Allan
88KY/Sov-12
Houston, Wade
83Louville-x
88Louville/194-13
89Louville/300*-66
Houzer, Larry
89PC/CBA-54
90PC/CBA-36
Howard, Brian
89NCSt/Pol-6
90PC/CBA-5
Howard, Frank
90Clem/200*-113
90Clem/200*-9
90Clem/Promos*-C10
Howard, Greg
70Suns/A1-5
70T-117
Howard, Lem
90GA/Smok-10
Howard, Terry
88Louville/194-124
88Louville/194-32

89Louville/300*-293
Howe, Dick
89KY/300*-73
Howell, Bailey
61F-20
61F-55IA
69T-5
69T/Ins-3CO
Howell, Jim Lee
91AR/100*-97
Howling, Kirk
90Clem/200*-125
Howser, Rick
90FLSt/200*-1
Huband, Kim
89NC/Coke-168
90NC/200*-172
Hubbard, Phil
80T-110
80T-22
81T-50M
81T-MW82
83Star/NBA-235
84Star/NBA-219
85Star/NBA-156
86F-48
87F-53
91MI/56*-27
Hubbell, Carl
81T/Thirst-7
Huber, Lee
88KY/269-24
Hubert, Kelly
90NE/Pol*-24
Hubert, Mick
83Dayton/Blue-12
Hubley, Liffort
90LSU/200*-95
Hudock, Jim
89NC/Coke-143
Hudson, Gerald
91OKSt*-16
Hudson, John
91SC/200*-143
Hudson, Lou
69T-65
69T/Ins-14
70T-115AS
70T-30
70T-3LL
70T/Ins-19
71T-110
71T/Ins-1
72T-130
73NBAPA-14
73T-150
74T-130
74T-81M
75Carv-14
75T-116M
75T-25
76Buck-11
76T-96
77T-85
78T-24
79T-119
Huery, Ron
91AR/100*-80
Huff, Derek
90AZ/125*-101
Huff, Gary
90FLSt/200*-20
Huff, Ken
90NC/200*-140
Huffman, Chris
90KY/ClassA-6
Huffman, Marv
87IN/GreatI-35
Huffman, Vern
86IN/GreatI-26
Hughes, Charles T.
89KY/300*-163

Janka, Ed
  82Fairf-8CO
Jaracz, Robert
  91GATech*-80
Jaracz, Thad
  88KY/269-142
  88KY/269-240
Jarman, Murray
  90Clem/200*-35
Jarvinen, M.
  48T/Magic*-E17
Jax, Garth
  90FLSt/200*-93
Jeanette, Harry E.
  (Buddy)
  48Bowman-38CO
  52Bread-15
  52Royal-8
Jeelani, Abdul
  (Gary Cole)
  79Blaz/Pol-11
  80T-142
  80T-51
  81T-MW77
Jeffcoat, Jim
  90AZSt/200*-48
Jefferson, John
  90AZSt/200*-3
  90AZSt/200*-119
Jefferson, Norman
  90LSU/200*-178
Jefferson, Sam
  86George/Pol-9
  87George/Pol-9
  88George/Pol-9
  89George/Pol-9
  91George/100-33
Jeffries, Irvine
  89KY/300*-218
Jeffries, James J.
  48T/Magic*-A5
Jeffries, Royce
  90PC/CBA-103
Jenkins, Ab
  54Quaker-13
Jenkins, Cedric
  88KY/269-129
  88KY/269-178
  88KY/269-242
Jenkins, Karen Ann
  90Clem/200*-191
Jenkins, Paul
  89KY/300*-253
Jenkins, Randy
  89KY/300*-126
Jennings, Keith
  (Mister)
  91Court-30
Jennings, Ned
  88KY/269-74
Jensen, Jackie
  57Union-38
Jepsen, Les
  90F/Up-U32
  90StarP-33
Jergenson, Brad
  91SC/200*-126
Jerome, Herbert
  89KY/300*-300
Jerome, Jimmy
  90NC/200*-129
Jeter, Chris
  88UNLV/HOF-11
  89UNLV/HOF-10
  89UNLV/Seven-8
  90UNLV/HOF-9
  90UNLV/Season-9
Jeter, James
  83Louville-25
  88Louville/194-29
  90UNLV/Smok-8
Jobe, Ben

87South/Pol*-4CO
Joe, Darryl
  87LSU/Pol*-5
  89PC/CBA-108
Jogis, Chris
  90AZSt/200*-175
Johnson, Arlando
  90KY/Sov-8
Johnson, Arnie
  48Bowman-44
Johnson, Avery
  87South/Pol*-7
  90SkyBox/II-380
Johnson, Bert
  89KY/300*-161
Johnson, Bob
  68PartM-9
Johnson, Buck
  89Hoops-237
  90F-71
  90Hoops-125
  90Hoops/Super-37
  90Panin-70
  90SkyBox-108
  91F-75
Johnson, Cal
  89Louville/300*-50
Johnson, Charles
  74T-14
  75T-86
  76T-137
  79T-116
Johnson, Charlie
  89Louville/300*-175
Johnson, Chris
  90AZ/125*-78
Johnson, Clarence
  83Star/NBA-175
Johnson, Clay
  81TCMA/CBA-48
  82Lakers/BASF-3
Johnson, Clemon
  83Star/NBA-5
  83Star/Sixers-15
  84Star/Arena-E5
  84Star/NBA-205
  85JMS-9
  85Star/NBA-4
  85Star/TmSuper-PS4
Johnson, Clyde
  89KY/300*-164
Johnson, Darryl
  89PC/CBA-184
  90MISt/200*-168
Johnson, David
  88Syr/Rich-5
  89Syr/Pep-6
Johnson, Dennis
  78Sonic/Pol-3
  78T-78
  79Sonic/Pol-9
  79T-6
  80Suns/Pep-4
  80T-121
  80T-8
  81T-34
  81T-W108
  83Star/NBA-32
  84Star/Arena-A4
  84Star/Celt-19
  84Star/NBA-6
  85JMS-15
  85Star/Lakers-3
  85Star/NBA-97
  85Star/TmSuper-BC4
  86F-50
  87F-54
  88F-10
  89F-9
  89Hoops-121
  90F-9
  90Hoops-41

90SkyBox-16
Johnson, Dervynn
  87South/Pol*-10
Johnson, Diane
  90AZ/125*-83
Johnson, Don
  91UCLA/144-56
Johnson, Donn
  89NC/Coke-170
Johnson, Dwayne
  (DJ)
  82Marq/Lite-2
Johnson, Earl
  91SC/200*-109
Johnson, Earvin
  (Magic)
  80T-111
  80T-146
  80T-6
  80T-66
  81T-21
  81T-W109
  82Lakers/BASF-4
  83Lakers/BASF-4
  83Star/ASG-18
  83Star/NBA-13
  84Lakers/BASF-3
  84Star/Arena-D3
  84Star/ASG-21
  84Star/Award-17LL
  84Star/Award-6
  84Star/Celt-10
  84Star/Celt-11M
  84Star/Celt-5
  84Star/CrtKg-15
  84Star/NBA-172
  84Star/PolASG-21
  85JMS-24
  85Star/Crunch-10
  85Star/Lakers-14
  85Star/Lakers-7
  85Star/LiteAS-11
  85Star/NBA-28
  85Star/TmSuper-LA2
  86F-53
  86F/Ins-7
  86Star/CrtKg-17
  87F-56
  87F/Ins-1
  88F-123AS
  88F-67
  88F/Ins-6
  88Fourn-4
  89Conv-6
  89F-77
  89F/AS-5
  89Hoops-166AS
  89Hoops-270
  90F-93
  90F/AS-4
  90Hoops-157
  90Hoops-18AS
  90Hoops/CollB-29
  90Hoops/II-367TC
  90Hoops/Super-47
  90MISt/200*-131
  90MISt/200*-133
  90MISt/200*-182
  90MISt/200*-186
  90MISt/200*-189
  90MISt/200*-194
  90MISt/Promos*-4
  90Panin-1
  90Panin-B
  90SkyBox-138
  91F-100
  91F/ProV-6
Johnson, Eddie
  78Hawks/Coke-8
  78T-108
  79Hawks/Majik-3
  79T-24

80IL/Arby's-6
  80T-128
  80T-148
  80T-152
  80T-32
  80T-9
  81T-44M
  81T-E68
  83Star/NBA-219
  83Star/NBA-268
  84Star/NBA-273
  84Star/NBA-81
  85Kings/Smok-8
  85Star/NBA-44
  85Star/NBA-76
  86F-51
  86Kings/Smok-3
  87F-55
  88F-90
  89F-122
  89Hoops-195
  89Louville/300*-146
  90F-148
  90Hoops-237
  90Hoops/Super-78
  90SkyBox-223
  90Sonic/Kayo-10
  90Suns/Smok-3
  91F-190
Johnson, Ellis
  88KY/269-18
Johnson, Elylen
  91SC/200*-190
Johnson, Eric
  90SkyBox-280
Johnson, Frank
  83Star/NBA-209
  84Star/NBA-189
  86F-52
  89Hoops-57
  89Hoops/II-333
Johnson, Gary
  (Cat)
  82TCMA/CBA-39
  82TCMA/Lanc-25
  82TCMA/Lanc-26
Johnson, George
  71T-21
  75T-13
  78T-55
  79T-39
  80T-113
  80T-114
  80T-141
  80T-37
  80T-45
  80T-53
  84Star/NBA-206
Johnson, George E.
  74T-54
Johnson, George L.
  83Star/NBA-160
  84Star/NBA-92
Johnson, George T.
  74T-159
Johnson, Gilbert
  89Pitt/Food-42
Johnson, Gus
  69T-12
  69T/Ins-18
  70Suns/Carn-6
  70T-92
  71T-77
  71T/Ins-44
  72T-6
Johnson, Jack
  48T/Magic*-A6
  87IN/GreatII-3
Johnson, Jerry
  82Fairf-9
Johnson, Jesse
  (Oz)

89Louville/300*-100
Johnson, Jimmy
  91OKSt*-19
Johnson, John
  71T-4
  72T-43
  73T-47
  74T-66
  75T-147
  78Sonic/Pol-4
  79Sonic/Pol-14
  79T-104
  80T-166
  80T-25
  80T-78
  80T-92
  81T-W98
Johnson, John Henry
  90AZSt/200*-70
Johnson, John MD
  88MD/Pol-3
Johnson, Katrena
  90AZ/125*-32
Johnson, Ken
  85Blaz/Franz-6
  87IN/GreatII-41
Johnson, Kevin
  89F-123
  89Hoops-35
  90Clem/200*-14
  90F-149
  90Hoops-19AS
  90Hoops-238A
  90Hoops-238B
  90Hoops/CollB-40
  90Hoops/II-375TC
  90Hoops/Super-75
  90Panin-16
  90SkyBox-224A
  90SkyBox-224B
  90Suns/Smok-4
  91F-161
  91F-210
  91F/School-4
Johnson, Larry
  88KY/269-105
  88KY/269-177
  88KY/269-227
  88KY/269-237
Johnson, Larry UNLV
  89UNLV/HOF-3
  89UNLV/Seven-9
  90UNLV/HOF-1
  90UNLV/HOF-14
  90UNLV/Season-1
  90UNLV/Season-15M
  90UNLV/Smok-9
  91Class-1
  91Class-44
  91Class-45M
  91Court-1
  91Court-31
  91Court-45
  91StarP-18
  91Wooden-20
Johnson, Lynbert
  (Cheese)
  81TCMA/CBA-89
Johnson, Mandy
  82Marq/Lite-3
Johnson, Mark
  91TexAM-38
Johnson, Marques
  77Bucks/ActPh-7
  78RCCola-16
  78T-126
  79Bucks/OpenP-9
  79Bucks/Pol-8
  79T-70AS
  80T-136
  80T-138
  80T-139

Lafleur, Greg
90LSU/200*-157
Laframboise, Tom
89Louville/300*-124
LaGarde, Tom
78Sonic/Pol-5
79Sonic/Pol-4
80T-104
80T-16
81T-10
81T-48M
Lahay, Bruce
91AR/100*-40
Lahtinen, Pasi
89Fresno/Smok-7
Laib, Art
89KY/300*-76
Laimbeer, Bill
81T-MW74
83Star/ASG-6
83Star/NBA-90
84Star/ASG-6
84Star/NBA-265
84Star/PolASG-6
85Star/NBA-10
85Star/TmSuper-DP4
86F-61
87F-61
88F-42
89Conv-8
89F-48
89Hoops-135
90F-58
90Hoops-108
90Hoops/Super-29
90ND-13
90Panin-88
90Piston/Star-9
90Piston/Unocal-7
90SkyBox-90
91F-62
Lake, Arthur
48T/Magic*-J8
Lamar, Dwight
74T-177
74T-228M
75T-256
Lamarr, Hedy
48T/Magic*-J14
Lambert, Ward L.
68HOF-25
Lambrecht, Dimitri
89Fresno/Smok-8
90Fresno/Smok-9
Lamkin, Jim
86DePaul-C2
Lamont, Brad Jr.
90MISt/200*-175
Lamour, Dorothy
48T/Magic*-F10
Lamp, Jeff
81Blaz/Pol-3
82Blaz/Pol-3
83Blaz/Pol-3
83Star/NBA-101
86Star/LifeBucks-7
89Hoops-144
Lampley, Jim
89PC/CBA-6
90PC/CBA-116
Lancaster, Harry C.
88KY/269-51
Lancaster, Les
91AR/100*-12
Landacox, Ken
90AZSt/200*-153
Lander, Cassandra
90AZSt/200*-179
Lander, Ed
89KY/300*-284
Landrum, Bill
91SC/200*-86

Landrum, Joe
90Clem/200*-180
Landry, Greg
74Nab-10
Landsberger, Mark
79Bulls/Pol-54
80T-134
80T-46
81T-W78
82Lakers/BASF-6
83Star/NBA-269
90AZSt/200*-41
Lane, Jerome
88Nugget/Pol-35
89Hoops-201
89Nugget/Pol-8
90Hoops-96
90SkyBox-77
LaNeve, Ronald
55Ash-91
Lang, Andrew
90SkyBox-225
91AR/100*-67
Lang, Tom
87George/Pol-11
91George/100-53
Langston, Keith
91TexAM-41
Langston, Lisa
91TexAM-15
Lanier, Bob
71T-63
71T/Ins-11
72T-80
73NBAPA-16
73T-110
74T-131
74T-86M
75Carv-18
75Nab-19
75T-121M
75T-30
76Buck-14
76T-10
77T-61
78RCCola-18
78T-125
79T-58
80T-104
80T-127
80T-46
80T-82
81T-25
81T-MW109
83Star/NBA-45
Lanier, Gary
91GATech*-89
Lanier, Mike
90UCLA-6
Lanier, Willie
75Nab-10
Lankster, Jim
90KY/Sov-3
Lanter, Bo
79KY/Food-8
88KY/269-117
Lantz, Rick
89Louville/300*-128
91GATech*-93
Lantz, Stu
68Rocket/Jack-9
70T-44
71T-108
72T-16
73T-96
74T-101
74T-86M
75T-127M
75T-88
Lapchick, Joe
68HOF-26

LaPierre, Gary
87ME/Pol*-5
LaReau, Bernie
79Spurs/Pol-x
Larese, York
89NC/Coke-102
89NC/Coke-103
90NC/200*-96
Larkin, Barry
91MI/56*-32
Larkins, Larry
89NCSt/Coke-91
89NCSt/Coke-92
89NCSt/Coke-93
89NCSt/Coke-94
LaRose, Rick
90AZ/125*-72
LaRusso, Rudy
61F-26
61Lakers/Bell-6
61F-57IA
Laska, Mike
91George/100-78
Laskowski, John
86IN/Greatl-33
Lastinger, Shawn
90Clem-11
Latreille, Yves
57Union-35
Lattimer, Earl
90MISt/200*-8
Lattin, Dave
68Suns/Carn-6
89UTEP/Drug-17
Laughlin, Bobby
55Ash-54
Laughna, Mike
91George/100-94
Lavelli, Dante
52Bread-17
Lavette, Robert
91GATech*-79
Lavin, Bob
89KY/300*-244
LaVine, Jackie
54Quaker-15
Lavole, Phil
91SC/200*-60
Lawhon, Mike
88Louville/194-127
88Louville/194-163
88Louville/194-37
89Louville/300*-248
Lawrence, Dave
89KY/300*-77
Lawrence, Larry
81TCMA/CBA-43
Lawson, Larry
90AZSt/200*-156
Lay, Emmett
89NCSt/Coke-113
89NCSt/Coke-114
Layden, Frank
78Hawks/Coke-9CO
84Star/Award-2
88Jazz/Smok-3CO
89Jazz/OldH-7CO
Layne, Roger
89KY/300*-75
Layton, Dennis
(Moe)
72T-106
73T-81
Lazzaretti, Vic
82Marq/Lite-4
Leach, Michael
91MI/56*-33
Leaks, Manny
71T-217
73Bullet/Stand-5
73T-74
74T-48

Leary, Rob
86LSU/Pol*-7
Leathers, Buddy
89Louville/300*-86
Leavell, Allen
80T-117
80T-126
80T-29
80T-79
81T-52M
83Star/NBA-79
84Star/NBA-240
85Star/NBA-19
86F-62
89Hoops-77
Leaycraft, Donnie
90LSU/200*-192
Lebo, Jeff
86NC/Pol-14
87NC/Pol-14
88NC/Pol-14
88NC/Pol-x
89NC/Coke-134
89NC/Coke-135
90NC/200*-36
90NC/200*-74
Leckner, Eric
89F-154
89Hoops-12
89Jazz/OldH-8
90F-187
90F/Up-U85
90Hoops-291
90Hoops/II-429
90Kings/Safe-6
90SkyBox-281
91F-21
90SkyBox/II-410
Ledford, Cawood
88KY/269-132
Lee, Butch
78Hawks/Coke-10
Lee, Christine
89McNees*-7
Lee, Clyde
69T-93
70T-144
71T-12
72T-138
73T-143
74T-32
75T-93
Lee, David
89NCSt/Pol-8
Lee, Don
90AZ/125*-65
Lee, Gary
91GATech*-77
Lee, George
61F-27
Lee, Greg
91UCLA/144-19
Lee, James
77KY/Wildct-17
81TCMA/CBA-11
82TCMA/CBA-19
82TCMA/Lanc-13
82TCMA/Lanc-14
88KY/269-109
88KY/269-230
Lee, John
90Clem/200*-75
Lee, Keith
89Hoops-236
Lee, Kirk
90Nets/Kayo-10
Lee, Ron
76Suns-6
77Suns/Discs-30
77T-117
78T-97
81T-50M

Lee, Theodis Ray
71Globe-54
71Globe-55
Lee, Treg
91Court-32
91StarP-3
Lefferts, Craig
90AZ/125*-10
Leggett, Earl
90LSU/200*-80
Legler, Tim
89PC/CBA-73
90PC/CBA-8
Leheup, John
91SC/200*-196
Lehmann, George
71T-192
72T-211
73T-194
Lemaster, Frank
89KY/300*-193
LeMaster, Jim
88KY/269-85
Lemon, Bob
57Union-14
Lemon, Meadowlark
71Globe-10
71Globe-11
71Globe-12
71Globe-13
71Globe-14
71Globe-15
71Globe-16
71Globe-17
71Globe-18M
71Globe-19M
71Globe-20
71Globe-64M
71Globe-66M
71Globe-67M
71Globe-69M
71Globe-70
71Globe-72M
71Globe-9
71Globe/Cocoa-10M
71Globe/Cocoa-22
71Globe/Cocoa-23
71Globe/Cocoa-26
71Globe/Cocoa-2M
71Globe/Cocoa-3
71Globe/Cocoa-4M
71Globe/Cocoa-6M
71Globe/Cocoa-7M
71Globe/Cocoa-9M
Lentz, Frank
89Louville/300*-60
Lentz, Larry
89KY/300*-78
Leon, Eddie
90AZ/125*-36
Leonard, Bob
57T-74
61F-28
71Pacer/Mara-5
81TCMA-35
85Star/Schick-17
87IN/Greatl-4
Leonard, Bryan
80IL/Arby's-7
81IL/Arby's-7
Leonard, Ed
90PC/CBA-39
Leonard, Gary
88MO-7
Leonard, John
82Fairf-10
82TCMA/CBA-36
Leonard, Quinton
89NCSt/Coke-109
Les, Jim
89Jazz/OldH-9
90PC/CBA-1

90LSU/200*-54
Loynd, Mike
90FLSt/200*-81
Lubin, Frank
91UCLA/144-78
Lucas, Harold
90MISt/200*-18
Lucas, Jerry
63Kahn's-6
64Kahn's-8A
64Kahn's-8B
65Kahn's-2
68T/Test-21
69T-45
69T/Ins-15
70T-46
71T-81
72Icee-12
72T-15
73T-125
81TCMA-38
Lucas, John
77T-58
78T-106
79T-127
80T-115
80T-126
80T-65
80T-79
81T-51M
83Star/NBA-246
84Star/NBA-242
85Star/NBA-21
87Bucks/Polar-10
87F-66
Lucas, Maurice
75T-302
76T-107
77Blaz/Pol-20
77T-80
78RCCola-19
78T-50
79Blaz/Pol-20
79T-26
80T-142
80T-54
81T-57M
81T-E79
82Suns/Giant-2
83Star/ASG-19
83Star/NBA-113
84Star/NBA-45
84Suns/Pol-21
85Star/NBA-30
86F-66
87Blaz/Franz-7
89Blaz/Franz-13
Lucia, Tom
89Louville/300*-106
89Louville/300*-178
Luckman, Sid
48ExhSC-31
Luisetti, Angelo
68HOF-28
Lujack, Johnny
48ExhSC-32
48T/Magic*-C6
Luke, Keye
48T/Magic*-J4
Lumpkin, Mark
90LSU/200*-52
Lumpkin, Phil
75Suns-8
75T-114
Luppino, Art
90AZ/125*-104
Luyk, Sergio
90KY/ClassA-4
Lyle, Mel
90LSU/200*-93
Lyles, Lenny
89Louville/300*-103

89Louville/300*-110
Lynam, Jim
81Blaz/Pol-CO
82Blaz/Pol-x
89Hoops-68CO
89Sixers/Kodak-14CO
90Hoops-324CO
91F-155CO
90SkyBox/II-320CO
Lynch, Chris
87BYU-12
Lynch, David
87BYU-15
Lynch, Kevin
91Class-18
91Court-34
91StarP-47
Lynn, Bill
91George/100-76
Lyons, Dicky
89KY/300*-136
Lyons, Ronnie
88KY/269-229
88KY/269-99
Lysiak, Tom
75Nab-14
Lyttle, Jim
90FLSt/200*-185
Mabay, Jim
91AR/100*-62
MacArthur, Douglas
48T/Magic*-O7
Macauley, Edward C.
(Easy Ed)
48T/Magic*-B3
57T-27
81TCMA-13
68HOF-29
Macek, Mark
90FLSt/200*-161
MacFarlane, Al
89Louville/300*-167
Mack, Connie
48T/Magic*-K9
Mack, Kevin
90Clem/200*-2
Mack, Oliver
82TCMA/CBA-16
Mack, Tony
89PC/CBA-173
Mackey, Malcolm
89GATech/Pol-11
90GATech/Pol-15
90GATech/Pol-16
Macklin, Durand
90LSU/200*-198
90LSU/200*-50
Macklin, Oliver
90CT/Pol-8
MacLane, Barton
48T/Magic*-J45
MacLean, Don
88KY/Sov-14
90UCLA-14
MacLeod, John
75Suns-9CO
80Suns/Pep-12CO
84Suns/Pol-x
85Star/CO-5
88Mavs/BLC-x
88Mavs/CardN-x
89Hoops-171
Macon, Mark
91Class-4
91Court-35
91StarP-26
Macy, Kyle
77KY/Wildct-15
78KY/Food-13
79KY/Food-2
79KY/Food-20
80Suns/Pep-11

81T-W82
83Star/NBA-114
84Star/NBA-46
84Suns/Pol-4
87KY/Coke-16
88KY/269-10
88KY/269-155
88KY/269-175
88KY/269-221
89KY/Tm80-38
Madden, John
90FLSt/200*-150
Madden, Kevin
87NC/Pol-22
88NC/Pol-22
Maddox, Bob
89Louville/300*-131
Maddox, Jerry
90AZSt/200*-182
Maddox, Mike
89KS/Leesley-46
Madeya, John
89Louville/300*-192
Madison, Guy
48T/Magic*-J44
Madison, Richard
88KY/269-131
88KY/269-174
88KY/269-250
Madkins, Gerald
90UCLA-13
Magallanes, Ever
91TexAM-39
Magno, Jack
81AZ/Pol-10
Magrane, Joe
90AZ/125*-41
Mahaffey, Donnie
90Clem/200*-199
Mahaffey, Randy
71T-221
90Clem/200*-188
Mahaffey, Richie
90Clem/200*-177
Mahaffey, Tommy
90Clem/200*-166
Mahnken, John
48Bowman-63
Mahorn, Rick
81T-E98
83Star/NBA-211
84Star/NBA-191
85Star/NBA-16
89F-93
89Hoops-46
89Hoops/II-330
89Sixers/Kodak-8
90F-144
90Hoops-230
90Panin-132
90SkyBox-217
91F-156
Maile, Dick
90LSU/200*-71
Majerle, Dan
89F-124
89Hoops-183
90F-150A
90F-150B
90Hoops-239
90Panin-14
90SkyBox-226
90Suns/Smok-5
91F-163
Majerus, Rick
82Marq/Lite-5CO
Major, Chris
91SC/200*-182
Majors, Joe
90FLSt/200*-198
Makarewicz, Scott
90MISt/200*-167

Makkonen, Timo
89NC/Coke-199
Malloy, Edward
(Monk)
90ND-16
Maloncon, Gary
91UCLA/144-12
Malone, Art
90AZSt/200*-89
Malone, Ben
90AZSt/200*-78
Malone, George
91GATech*-12
Malone, Jeff
83Star/NBA-212
84Star/NBA-192
85Star/NBA-112
86F-67
87F-67
88F-117
88Fourn-21
89F-160
89Hoops-85
90F-195
90F/Up-U94
90Hoops-301
90Hoops/II-437
90Hoops/Super-97
90Jazz/Star-7
90SkyBox-292
91F-200
90SkyBox/II-418
Malone, Karl
86F-68
87F-68
88F-114
88F/Ins-8
88Fourn-16
88Jazz/Smok-4
89Conv-9
89F-155
89F-163M
89F/AS-1
89Hoops-116AS
89Hoops-30
89Jazz/OldH-10
90F-188
90F/AS-7
90Hoops-21AS
90Hoops-292
90Hoops/CollB-5
90Hoops/II-380TC
90Hoops/Super-94
90Jazz/Star-1
90SkyBox-282
91F-201
91F-219
91F/ProV-5
91F/School-5
Malone, Mark
90AZSt/200*-17
Malone, Moses
75T-222LL
75T-254
75T-286M
76T-101
77T-124
78T-38
79T-100AS
80T-107
80T-114
80T-159
80T-2
80T-45
80T-71
80T-74
80T-90
81T-14
81T-52M
81T-MW110
83Star/ASG-27M

83Star/ASG-7
83Star/NBA-7
83Star/Sixers-14
83Star/Sixers-20
83Star/Sixers-25
83Star/Sixers-3M
84Star/Arena-E7
84Star/Award-20LL
84Star/CrtKg-17
84Star/NBA-201
84Star/NBA-285
85JMS-2
85Prism-3
85Prism-4M
85Star/Crunch-5
85Star/LiteAS-5
85Star/NBA-6
85Star/TmSuper-PS6
86F-69
86Star/CrtKg-21
87F-69
88F-118
89F-165M
89F-4
89Hoops-290
89Hoops-84AS
90F-3
90Hoops-31
90Hoops/Super-4
90Panin-115
90SkyBox-6
Maloney, Jim
71Keds*-1M
Maloy, Rudy
90FLSt/200*-19
Mandarich, Tony
90MISt/200*-89
90MISt/Promos*-8
Mandich, Jim
91MI/56*-34
Mangham, Mickey
90LSU/200*-125
Mangrum, Lloyd
48Kell*-15
57Union-22
Manion, Bob
89Louville/300*-63
Manion, Tim
91GATech*-68
Mann, Cyrus
82TCMA/CBA-21
Manning, Danny
88Fourn-30
89F-71
89Hoops-40
90Clip/Star-7
90F-87
90Hoops-147
90Hoops/CollB-17
90Hoops/II-366TC
90Hoops/Super-46
90Panin-32
90SkyBox-129
91F-92
91Wooden-17
Manning, Ed
70T-132
71T-122
Manning, Rich
88Syr/Rich-6
89Syr/Pep-3
Mannion, Pace
83Star/NBA-259
84Star/NBA-232
87Bucks/Polar-3
Manns, Kirk
90MISt/200*-139
Mantel, Alex
89Louville/300*-88
Mantle, Mickey
81T/Thirst-12
Maras, Dee

91SC/200*-33
McCormach, Brendan
91SC/200*-184
McCormick, Dave
90LSU/200*-159
McCormick, Pat
57Union-23
McCormick, Tim
84Star/NBA-118
85Star/NBA-68
85Star/RTm-10
87F-71
89F-60
89Hoops-272
90F/Up-U2
90Hoops/II-401
91MI/56*-36
90SkyBox/II-366
McCowan, Bob
88KY/269-91
McCoy, Julius
90MISt/200*-188
McCracken, Branch
68HOF-30
87IN/GreatII-5
McCrady, Lisa
90NE/Pol*-20
McCray, Rodney
83Star/NBA-81
84Star/NBA-243
85Star/NBA-22
85Star/TmSuper-HR4
86F-71
87F-72
88F-52
88Kings/Carl-22
88Louville/194-11
88Louville/194-111
88Louville/194-160
88Louville/194-187
89F-135
89Hoops-257
89Kings/Carl-22
89Louville/300*-264
89Louville/300*-292
89Louville/300*-45
90F-165
90F/Up-U21
90Hoops-259
90Hoops/II-409
90Hoops/Super-84
90SkyBox-248
91F-46
90SkyBox/II-377
McCray, Scooter
83Sonic/Pol-7
83Star/NBA-199
88Louville/194-112
88Louville/194-12
88Louville/194-157
88Louville/194-190
89Louville/300*-239
89Louville/300*-26
89Louville/300*-263
89Louville/300*-277
89Louville/300*-44
McCreary, Jay
87IN/GreatII-40
McCullers, Dale
90FLSt/200*-140
McCullough, John
82TCMA/CBA-34
McDade, Von
91Class-42
91StarP-28
McDaniel, Lashun
89PC/CBA-10
McDaniel, Orlando
90LSU/200*-19
McDaniel, Randall
90AZSt/200*-93
McDaniel, Shawn

90PC/CBA-22
McDaniel, Xavier
86F-72
87F-73
88F-108
88Fourn-20
89F-148
89Hoops-70
90F-179
90F/Up-U77
90Hoops-280
90Hoops/CollB-42
90Hoops/II-379TC
90Panin-23
90SkyBox-269
90Sonic/Smok-9
91F-164
McDaniels, Jim
72T-137
73Sonic/Shur-8
73T-152
McDermont, Mike
91George/100-68
McDermott, Bob
48ExhSC-35
McDonald, Ben
87LSU/Pol*-12
88LSU/Pol*-10
90LSU/200*-113
90PC/CBA-157
McDonald, Darryl
90PC/CBA-104
McDonald, Glenn
76T-47
McDonald, Jim
88KY/269-80
McDonald, Perry
84George/Pol-10
85George/Pol-11
86George/Pol-10
87George/Pol-12
91George/100-28
McDonald, Peter
91George/100-32
McDonnell, John
91AR/100*-8
McDowall, Roddy
48T/Magic*-J3
McDowell, Eugene
90FLSt/200*-191
90PC/CBA-31
McDowell, Hank
83Star/NBA-127
84Star/NBA-244
McDowell, Oddibe
90AZSt/200*-10
McDuffie, Wayne
90FLSt/200*-162
McDuffie, Willie
90PC/CBA-158
McElroy, James
(Jimmy)
79Hawks/Majik-33
79T-131
80T-170
80T-63
McFadden, Banks
90Clem/200*-34
McFadden, Wesley
90Clem/200*-115
McFall, Dan
90MISt/200*-147
McFarland, James
89KY/300*-249
McGaha, Mel
91AR/100*-96
McGee, Michael
(Mike)
82Lakers/BASF-8
83Lakers/BASF-7
83Star/NBA-19

84Lakers/BASF-7
84Star/Arena-D4
84Star/NBA-179
85JMS-25
89F-98
90SkyBox-227
McGeorge, Rich
79Bucks/OpenP-11
McGinnis, George
72T-183
72T-243
73T-180AS
73T-208
73T-234LL
74T-207LL
74T-211LL
74T-220AS
74T-223M
74T-223M
75Sixers/McDon-5
75T-184
75T-221LL
75T-226LL
75T-279M
76T-128AS
76T-70
77T-50
78RCCola-22
78T-90
79T-125
80T-127
80T-39
81T-MW92
86IN/GreatI-79
McGinnis, Lawrence
89KY/300*-222
McGinnis, Louis
89KY/300*-80
McGlocklin, Jon
69T-14
70T-139
71Bucks/Linn-6
71T-74
72T-54
73T-123
74T-37
75T-35
79Bucks/OpenP-10
86IN/GreatI-21
McGowan, Paul
90FLSt/200*-29
McGrath, Tom
89McNees*-5
McGuire, Al
86DePaul-11
McGuire, Dick
52Royal-2
57T-16
81TCMA-26
McGuire, Frank
89NC/Coke-104
89NC/Coke-99
90NC/200*-193
91SC/200*-1CO
McHale, Kevin
81T-E75
83Star/NBA-34
84Star/Arena-A6
84Star/ASG-7
84Star/Award-5
84Star/Celt-3
84Star/Celt-8M
84Star/CrtKg-42
84Star/NBA-9
84Star/PolASG-7
85JMS-13
85Star/Lakers-6
85Star/NBA-84
85Star/TmSuper-BC3
86F-73
86Star/CrtKg-22
87F-74

87F/Ins-5
88F-11
88F/Ins-9
88Fourn-3
89Conv-10
89F-11
89Hoops-156AS
89Hoops-280
90F-12
90Hoops-44
90Hoops-6AS
90Hoops/CollB-6
90Hoops/Super-7
90Panin-136
90SkyBox-19
91F-13
91F/School-3
McHugh, Mike
87ME/Pol*-2
McIntee, Willie
91SC/200*-135
McIntosh, Doug
91UCLA/144-76
McIntosh, John
89KY/300*-28
McIntosh, Kennedy
73Sonic/Shur-9
73T-164
74T-173
McIntosh, Lamont
89ORSt-11
McIntyre, Jim
48T/Magic*-B5
McIntyre, John
88MO-8
89MO-9
90PC/CBA-180
McKale, J.F.
(Pop)
90AZ/125*-118
McKenna, Joey
90Clem/200*-196
McKenna, Kevin
83Star/NBA-163
90PC/CBA-91
McKenzie, Kyle
88LSU/Pol*-5
McKenzie, Stan
68Suns/Carn-7
69Suns/Carn-5
70T-52
72T-84
73T-32
McKernan, Matt
91SC/200*-124
McKey, Derrick
88F-109
89F-149
89Hoops-233
90F-180
90Hoops-281
90Hoops/Super-90
90Panin-24
90SkyBox-270
90Sonic/Kayo-3
90Sonic/Smok-10
91F-193
McKinley, Troy
88KY/269-125
McKinney, Billy
81T-W69
82Nugget/Pol-7
83Star/NBA-128
McKinney, Charles
89ORSt-12
McKinney, Horace
(Bones)
48Bowman-46
52Bread-19
89NC/Coke-105
89NC/Coke-126
89NCSt/Coke-61

McKinney, Jack
77Blaz/Pol-x
McKinney, Rick
90AZSt/200*-193
McKinnon, Adrian
89PC/CBA-96
McLaughlin, Eric
89PC/CBA-133
McLean, John
90FLSt/200*-18
McLean, Price
89KY/300*-158
McLemore, McCoy
68Suns/Carn-8
70T-19
71T-83
McLinden, Melissa
90AZ/125*-77
McMahon, Jack
57T-66
63Kahn's-7CO
64Kahn's-2CO
McManus, Danny
90FLSt/200*-27
McMillan, Craig
84AZ/Pol-10
85AZ/Pol-11
86AZ/Pol-9
87AZ/Pol-9
McMillan, Jerry
86DePaul-S2
McMillan, Nate
87F-75
88F-110
89F-150
89Hoops-192
89NCSt/Coke-103
89NCSt/Coke-104
89NCSt/Coke-105
90F-181
90Hoops-282
90Panin-19
90SkyBox-271A
90SkyBox-271B
90Sonic/Kayo-11
90Sonic/Smok-11
McMillen, Tom
77T-66
78Hawks/Coke-11
79Hawks/Majik-54
81T-E70
83Star/NBA-213
84Star/NBA-193
85Star/NBA-113
McMillian, Jim
71T-41
72T-89
73NBAPA-19
73T-4
74T-38
75Carv-21
75T-27
76T-9
77T-107
78T-88
McMillon, Shellie
61Hawks/Essex-11
McMinn, Glenn
90AZSt/200*-190
McMullen, Mitch
89PC/CBA-125
McNamara, Mark
83Star/NBA-248
84Star/NBA-70
89Hoops-289
90Hoops-158
90Hoops/II-434
90SkyBox-139
90SkyBox/II-402
McNeal, Chris
90Pitt/Food-5
McNeil, Johnny

91Class-3
Myers, Ernest
89NCSt/Coke-97
89NCSt/Coke-98
89NCSt/Coke-99
Myers, Gene
89KY/300*-178
Myers, Pete
89Knicks/Marine-6
90SkyBox-184
Naber, Bob
89Louville/300*-84
Nadeau, Wendy J.
87ME/Pol*-11
Nagurski, Bronko
54Quaker-26
Nagy, Dick
80IL/Arby's-8CO
81IL/Arby's-10CO
Naismith, James
68HOF-34
Namath, Joe
81PhilM-6
Nance, Larry
82Suns/Giant-3
83Star/NBA-115
84Star/Award-9
84Star/CrtKg-19
84Star/NBA-47
84Star/PolASG-31
84Star/SlamD-11
84Star/SlamD-7
84Suns/Pol-22
85Star/Gator-2
85Star/NBA-34
85Star/SlamD-6
86F-78
86Star/CrtKg-24
87F-78
87Suns/Circ-7
88F-24
89F-28
89Hoops-217AS
89Hoops-25
90Clem/200*-6
90F-35
90Hoops-78
90Hoops/CollB-18
90Hoops/Super-17
90Panin-107
90SkyBox-55
91F-37
Nared, Greg
88MD/Pol-10
Nash, Cotton
88KY/269-172
88KY/269-8
Nash, Macolm
89KS/Leesley-53
Nash, Noreen
48T/Magic*-F22
Nater, Swen
74T-205AS
74T-208LL
74T-227M
75T-225LL
75T-231AS
75T-284M
76T-103
77T-92
78Clipp/Handy-6
78T-23
79T-109
80T-112
80T-16
80T-163
80T-75
81T-38
81T-63M
83Lakers/BASF-8
83Star/NBA-20
84Star/Arena-D5

91UCLA/144-91
Natt, Calvin
80T-14
80T-162
81Blaz/Pol-33
81T-W85
82Blaz/Pol-33
83Blaz/Pol-33
83Star/NBA-103
84Star/NBA-145
85Nugget/Pol-12
85Star/NBA-55
86F-79
89Blaz/Franz-14
Natt, Kenny
81TCMA/CBA-38
82TCMA/CBA-20
Nattin, George
90LSU/200*-58
Naulls, Willie
57T-29
61F-32
91UCLA/144-58
Neal, Craig
90PC/CBA-175
91GATech*-33
Neal, Freddie
(Curly)
71Globe-18M
71Globe-26M
71Globe-27
71Globe-28
71Globe-29
71Globe-30M
71Globe-31
71Globe-32
71Globe-64M
71Globe-65
71Globe-66M
71Globe-67M
71Globe-69M
71Globe-72M
71Globe/Cocoa-10M
71Globe/Cocoa-24
71Globe/Cocoa-25
71Globe/Cocoa-28
71Globe/Cocoa-2M
71Globe/Cocoa-4M
71Globe/Cocoa-6M
71Globe/Cocoa-7M
71Globe/Cocoa-8M
71Globe/Cocoa-9M
Neal, Ida
91GATech*-2
Neal, Kim
90AZSt/200*-149
Neal, Lloyd
73T-129
75T-58
76T-7
77Blaz/Pol-36
84Blaz/Pol-12
89Blaz/Franz-15
Nealy, Ed
83Star/NBA-222
89Bulls/Eq-8
90Hoops/II-426
90SkyBox-43
90SkyBox/II-406
Neely, Jess
90Clem/200*-55
Nehls, Joe
90AZ/125*-99
Neidert, John
89Louville/300*-172
Nelson, Alonzo
89KY/300*-299
Nelson, Byron
81T/Thirst-46
Nelson, Don
69T-82
70T-86

71T-114
72T-92
73T-78
74T-46
75Carv-24
75T-2LL
75T-44
79Bucks/Pol-x
85Star/Bucks-1
85Star/CO-7
86Star/LifeBucks-1CO
89Hoops-273CO
90Hoops-313CO
90Hoops/II-345CO
91F-70CO
90SkyBox/II-309CO
Nelson, Jeff
91TexAM-58
Nelson, Korky
80TCMA/CBA-13
Nelson, Lee
90FLSt/200*-132
Nelson, Louie
73Bullet/Stand-6
75T-18
76T-17
Nelson, Lynn
90AZSt/200*-152
Nelson, Mark
91SC/200*-102
Nelson, Ted
91TexAM-19
Nessley, Martin
89PC/CBA-24
Netolicky, Bob
71Pacer/Mara-8
71T-183
72T-228
73T-256
75T-314
Neumann, Johnny
72T-184
73T-243
74T-238
82TCMA/CBA-60
Nevitt, Charles G.
89NCSt/Coke-106
89NCSt/Coke-107
89NCSt/Coke-108
Newbern, Melvin
90StarP-52
Newbill, Ivano
89GATech/Pol-14
90GATech/Pol-18
Newell, Pete
90MISt/200*-161
Newlin, Mike
72T-128
73T-156LL
73T-44
74T-127
75T-103
75T-123M
76T-139
77T-37
78T-124
79T-15
80T-119
80T-143
80T-36
80T-55
81T-57M
81T-E80
Newman, Don
81TCMA/CBA-71
Newman, Johnny
89F-102
89Hoops-58
89Knicks/Marine-7
90F-127A
90F-127B
90F/Up-U12

90Hoops-206
9^Hoops/II-386
90Hoops/II-403
90SkyBox-190
91F-23
90SkyBox/II-370
Newman, Paul
82Marq/Lite-8
Newman, Roger
89KY/300*-258
Newmark, Dave
70T-156
Newsome, Eric
89PC/CBA-86
Newton, C.M.
88KY/269-63
89KY/300*-1
Newton, Milt
89PC/CBA-136
Nichols, Gerald
90FLSt/200*-25
Nichols, Jack
52Royal-3
57T-9
Nicholson, Darrell
90NC/200*-14
Nicks, Carl
81T-W104
82TCMA/CBA-77
Nido, Miquel
90Clem/200*-50
Niesen, Gertrude
48T/Magic*-J11
Niles, Mike
80Suns/Pep-10
Nillen, John
82TCMA/CBA-55
Nimitz, Chester
48T/Magic*-O2
Nimphius, Kurt
81TCMA/CBA-9
83Star/NBA-56
84Star/Arena-B7
84Star/NBA-256
89Sixers/Kodak-9
90AZSt/200*-15
Nix, Dyron
88TN/Smok-31
90SkyBox-118B
90SkyBox-118A
Nixon, Kevin
89PC/CBA-175
Nixon, Norm
78T-63
79Lakers/Alta-4
79T-97
80T-135
80T-160
80T-47
80T-55
81T-22
81T-55M
82Lakers/BASF-9
83Star/NBA-129
84Star/NBA-20
86F-80
Noble, Brian
90AZSt/200*-55
90AZSt/Promos*-8
Noble, Chuck
57T-11
88Louville/194-82
89Louville/300*-241
Noel, Paul
89KY/300*-61
Nolan, Gary
68PartM-4
Noll, Randy
89KY/300*-89
Nord, Gary
89Louville/300*-132
Nordmann, Bob

61Kahn's-5
Nore, Christy
90AZSt/200*-104
Norlander, John
48Bowman-27
Norman, Jerry
91UCLA/144-104
Norman, Ken
89F-72
89Hoops-162
90Clip/Star-9
90F-88
90Hoops-149
90Panin-35
90SkyBox-131
91F-93
Norris, Audie
82Blaz/Pol-24
83Blaz/Pol-24
83Star/NBA-104
84Blaz/Franz-7
84Blaz/Pol-8
84Star/Blaz-3
84Star/NBA-166
Norris, Sherri
90AZSt/200*-166
Norton, Darrell
91GATech*-13
Norton, Jeff
91MI/56*-38
Norton, Rick
89KY/300*-108
Norton, Ricky
82AR-9
Norwood, Michael
86NC/Pol-21
Norwood, Ralph
90LSU/200*-173
Norwood, Ron
86DePaul-D9
Norwood, Willie
72T-94
73T-39
74T-156
75T-168
Nostrand, George
48Bowman-42
Novak, Gary
90ND-38
Novick, Tony
90AZSt/200*-58
Nowak, Paul
90ND-31
Nuce, Steve
89NCSt/Coke-152
89NCSt/Coke-153
89NCSt/Coke-154
Nunamacher, Jeff
90Clem/200*-53
Nunley, Frank
91MI/56*-39
Nunnally, Doc
89PC/CBA-112
90PC/CBA-161
Nuss, Dave
89Louville/300*-177
Nutt, Dennis
89PC/CBA-8
90PC/CBA-82
Nuxhall, Joe
81T/Thirst-23
Nuzum, Rick
89KY/300*-144
Nwokocha, Nuamoi
90Clem/200*-112
Nyikos, John
90ND-24
Nystrom, Carl
(Buck)
90MISt/200*-7
O'Bannon, Ed
90UCLA-3

Piurowski, Paul
90FLSt/200*-40
Plansky, Mark
89PC/CBA-190
90PC/CBA-111
Planutis, Gerald
90MISt/200*-35
Plummer, Gary
84Star/NBA-156
Plummer, Mona
90AZSt/200*-143
Plunkett, Jim
74Nab-9
75Nab-9
Poerschke, Eric
82AR-10
Pohl, Dan
90AZ/125*-116
Poindexter, Cliff
77T-21
Poinsett, David
91SC/200*-47
Polec, Larry
90MISt/200*-162
Pollard, Jim
48Bowman-66
52Royal-7
Pollock, Bob
90Clem/200*-128
Polston, Kenny
89NCSt/Coke-179
Polynice, Olden
89Hoops-152
90F/Up-U93
90Hoops-283
90SkyBox-272
90Sonic/Smok-15
91F-94
Pond, Nick
89NCSt/Coke-172
Ponsetto, Joe
86DePaul-D7
Pool, Randy
88KY/269-89
Poole, Barney
48T/Magic*-C1
Poole, Eric
91SC/200*-152
Poole, Nathan
89Louville/300*-122
Poole, Sherry
90AZSt/200*-164
Pooley, Don
90AZ/125*-108
Popson, Dave
86NC/Pol-35
89NC/Coke-153
89PC/CBA-110
90F/Up-U7
90NC/200*-18
90NC/200*-59
Poquette, Ben
80T-155
80T-171
80T-18
80T-83
81T-65M
81T-W105
83Star/NBA-237
84Star/NBA-221
85Star/NBA-157
Porche, Maia A.
90Piston/Star-14
Porco, Ken
89Louville/300*-104
Pores, Chas.
48T/Magic*-E8
Porter, Darelle
89Pitt/Food-20
90Pitt/Food-10
Porter, Dave
87IN/GreatII-28

Porter, Howard
72T-127
73T-167
74T-122
75T-138
77T-102
78T-28
Porter, Joel
87Baylor/Pol*-12
Porter, Kevin
73Bullet/Stand-7
73T-53
74T-12
74T-98M
75T-133M
75T-5LL
75T-79
76T-84
77T-16
78T-118
79T-13
80T-130
80T-174
80T-60
80T-86
81T-66M
81T-E105
81T-E99
81T/Thirst-19
Porter, Terry
85Blaz/Franz-10
86Blaz/Franz-11
87Blaz/Franz-9
87F-89
88Blaz/Franz-10
88F-96
88Fourn-12
89Blaz/Franz-9
89F-131
89Hoops-105
90Blaz/BP-5
90Blaz/Franz-17
90F-158
90Hoops-249A
90Hoops-249B
90Hoops/CollB-16
90Hoops/Super-79
90Panin-11
90SkyBox-238
91F-171
Porter, Tommy
89KY/300*-82
Portmann, Kurt
90PC/CBA-129
Post, Wiley
48T/Magic*-L3
Poston, Kenny
89NCSt/Coke-184
89NCSt/Coke-197
Poteet, Yogi
89NC/Coke-108
89NC/Coke-162
Potter, Brendan
82Fairf-13
Potter, Sam
89KY/300*-17
Potts, Bobby
82TCMA/CBA-9
Potts, Ray
89Louville/300*-217
Pounds, Cleve
91GATech*-96
Powell, Cliff
91AR/100*-99
Powell, Cincy
71Col/Mara-7
71T-207
72T-189
73T-186
74T-198
Powell, Ken
90NC/200*-124
Powell, Mike

89Foot-9
Powell, William
48T/Magic*-F11
89Louville/300*-62
Power, Tyrone
48T/Magic*-F6
Powless, John
55Ash-69
Praedel, Lloyd
79StBon-10
Pratt, Mike
71Col/Mara-8
88KY/269-150
88KY/269-173
88KY/269-209
88KY/269-50
Pratt, Robert
90NC/200*-135
Pressey, Paul
83Star/All-R-6
83Star/NBA-48
84Star/Arena-C9
84Star/NBA-136
85Star/Bucks-13
85Star/NBA-130
85Star/TmSuper-MB3
86F-88
86Star/LifeBucks-12
87Bucks/Polar-25
87F-90
88Bucks/Green-12
88F-75
88Fourn-29
89F-89
89Hoops-79
90F-107
90F/Up-U90
90Hoops-180
90Hoops/II-432
90SkyBox-163
91F-186
90SkyBox/II-415
Pressley, Dominic
90PC/CBA-66
Pressley, Harold
86Kings/Smok-7
88Kings/Carl-21
89F-137
89Hoops-24
89Kings/Carl-21
90F-166
90Hoops-260
90Panin-37
90SkyBox-249
Preston, R.C.
89KY/300*-228
Preston, Steve
90MISt/200*-65
Previs, Steve
89NC/Coke-108
89NC/Coke-109
90NC/200*-109
Price, Cebert
55Ash-47
Price, George
61Union-8
Price, Jim
71Bucks/Linn-7
73T-38
74T-137
75Carv-25
75T-107
76T-32
88Louville/194-138
88Louville/194-61
89Louville/300*-230
89Louville/300*-245
89Louville/300*-8
Price, Mark
88F-25
89Conv-11
89F-166M

89F-29
89Hoops-160
89Hoops-28AS
90F-36
90Hoops-79
90Hoops/CollB-8
90Hoops/II-359TC
90Panin-103
90SkyBox-56
91F-38
Price, Mike
73T-51
Price, Rodney
91SC/200*-134
Price, Tim
89PC/CBA-65
Prince, Calvin
89Louville/300*-158
Prinzi, Vic
90FLSt/200*-159
Pritchard, Kevin
89KS/Leesley-48
90F/Up-U34
90StarP-65
Proctor, Bill
90FLSt/200*-128
Proski, Joe
75Suns-11
84Suns/Pol-x
Provence, Andrew
91SC/200*-63
Prudhoe, John
55Ash-33
88Louville/194-77
89Louville/300*-220
Prudhomme, Remi
90LSU/200*-103
Pruitt, Dillard
90Clem/200*-167
Pruitt, Ron
90MISt/200*-87
Pry, Paul
89Louville/300*-283
89Louville/300*-81
Pryor, Jerry
90Clem/200*-172
Pucillo, Lou
89NCSt/Coke-173
89NCSt/Coke-196
Puckett, Linville
55Ash-22
89KY/300*-83
Puddy, Glenn
90PC/CBA-78
Pullard, Anthony
89McNees*-10
90StarP-17
Pulliam, Marty
88Louville/194-134
88Louville/194-51
Punt, Tom
90NE/Pol*-7
Pursiful, Larry
88KY/269-219
88KY/269-77
89KY/300*-11
Purtzer, Tom
90AZSt/200*-186
Putnam, Bill
91UCLA/144-60
Putman, Don
48Bowman-28
Quam, George
54Quaker-3
Queen, Mel
68PartM-6
Queenan, Daren
89PC/CBA-27
Quick, Bob
70T-161
71T-117

Pickard, Fred
90FLSt/200*-177
Pickins, Bruce
90NE/Pol*-12
Pierce, Ricky
83Star/NBA-130
85Star/NBA-129
86F-87
86Star/LifeBucks-11
87F-87
88Bucks/Green-11
89F-88
89Hoops-212
90F-106
90Hoops-179
90Hoops/CollB-21
90Hoops/Super-56
90Panin-99
90SkyBox-162
90Sonic/Kayo-9
91F-195
Pierre, Raymond
87Baylor/Pol*-8
Pierson, Jerry
55Ash-44
Pietkiewicz, Stan
80TCMA/CBA-15
Pikiell, Steve
90CT/Pol-9
Pikiell, Tim
90CT/Pol-10
Pinckney, Ed
87F-88
89F-13
89Hoops-9
90F-15
90Hoops-47
90SkyBox-22
91F-15
Pingel, John S.
90MISt/200*-24
Piontek, Dave
57Kahn's-6
57T-31
58Kahn's-9
59Kahn's-5
Piotrowski, Tom
83Blaz/Pol-54
83Star/NBA-105
Piper, Don
91UCLA/144-79
Pipines, Tom
82Marq/Lite-9
Pippen, Scottie
87Bulls/Ent-8
88Bulls/Ent-33
88F-20
89Bulls/Eq-11
89F-23
89Hoops-244
90Bulls/Eq-12
90F-30
90Hoops-69
90Hoops-9AS
90Hoops/CollB-44
90Hoops/Super-13
90Panin-93
90SkyBox-46
91F-33
Pitino, Rick
89KY/300*-13
89KY/Award-36
89KY/Tm80-54
Pittman, Charles
82TCMA/CBA-4
83Star/NBA-116
84Star/NBA-48
84Suns/Pol-32
85Star/NBA-39
Pittman, Johnny
91StarP-23

90Hoops/CollB-9
90Hoops/Super-31
90Panin-30
90SkyBox-100
91F-71
Richmond, Pam
90AZSt/200*-87
Richmond, Steve
91MI/56*-44
Richter, John
89NCSt/Coke-178
89NCSt/Coke-62
Richter, Les
57Union-2
Rickenbacker, Eddie
48T/Magic*-L4
54Quaker-14
Ricketts, Richard
(Dick)
57Kahn's-8
57T-8
Riddle, Jerry
55Ash-56
Riddlesprigger, Pat
89Fresno/Smok-12
90Fresno/Smok-12
Ridgeway, Dick
91UCLA/144-67
Ridgeway, Sam
89KY/300*-227
Riebe, Mel
48Bowman-8
Rigby, Cathy
76Nab-23M
Riggs, Bobby
48ExhSC-41
Riggs, Gerald
90AZSt/200*-2
Riggs, Jim
90Clem/200*-30
Rigney, Bill
57Union-20
Riker, Tom
91SC/200*-78
Riley, Eric
88MI/Nike-11
89MI-16
Riley, Jackie
54Quaker-16
Riley, J. McIver
91SC/200*-66
Riley, Mike
89PC/CBA-178
91George/100-36
91George/100-99
Riley, Pat
68Rocket/Jack-10
70T-13
72T-144
73T-21
74T-31
75Suns-12
75T-71
84Star/Celt-15
85Star/CO-9
85Star/Lakers-12
85Star/LiteAS-13CO
88KY/269-145
88KY/269-157
88KY/269-17
88KY/269-198
89Hoops-108CO
89KY/300*-38
89KY/300*-45
90Hoops-317CO
91F-139CO
Riley, Ron
73T-141
75T-87
Rinaldi, Rich
73NBAPA-23
73T-149

Rinehart, Bob
91SC/200*-82
Riordan, Mike
70T-26
71T-126
72T-37
73Bullet/Stand-8
73NBAPA-24
73T-35
74T-102
75T-95
76T-56
Risen, Arnie
48Bowman-58
52Bread-24
57T-40
Risher, Alan
90LSU/200*-85
Riska, Eddie
90ND-44
Risley, Steve
86IN/GreatI-40
Rison, Andre
90MISt/200*-12
90MISt/200*-77
90MISt/200*-96
90MISt/Promos*-5
Ritchie, Meg
90AZ/125*-124
Ritter, John
86IN/GreatI-20
Rivers, David
89F-94
89Hoops-203
89Hoops/II-346
90Hoops-150
90ND-36
Rivers, Glenn
(Doc)
82Marq/Lite-12
83Star/NBA-271
84Star/NBA-84
85Star/NBA-47
86F-91
87F-92
87Hawks/Pizza-11
88F-3
89F-5
89Hoops-252
90F/Up-U3
90Hoops-32
90Hoops/CollB-10
90Hoops/Super-1
90Panin-116
90SkyBox-7
Roach, Larry
91OKSt*-55
Robbins, Austin
(Red)
71T-233
72T-212
73T-193
75T-287M
75T-295
Robbins, Jack
91AR/100*-98
Robbins, Lee Roy
48Bowman-56
Robbins, Randy
90AZ/125*-91
Roberson, Rick
70T-23
72T-126
73T-144
74T-57
74T-96M
Roberts, Anthony
78T-62
81TCMA/CBA-59
83Star/NBA-190
Roberts, Danny
91TexAM-27

Roberts, Doug
90MISt/200*-55
Roberts, Fred
83Star/NBA-251
84Star/NBA-234
84Star/NBA-74
88Bucks/Green-13
89Hoops-136
90F-108
90Hoops-181
90SkyBox-164
91F-117
Roberts, Marv
74T-194
75T-238
Roberts, Roy
89KY/300*-229
Roberts, Stanley
91Class-15
Robertson, Alvin
82AR-12
84Star/NBA-198
84Star/NBA-75
85Star/NBA-150
85Star/RTm-11
86F-92
87F-93
88F-105
88F-128AS
88Fourn-27
88Spurs/Pol-7
89F-90
89Hoops-5
89Hoops/II-350
90F-109
90Hoops-182
90Hoops/CollB-33
90Hoops/II-369TC
90Hoops/Super-55
90Panin-101
90SkyBox-165
91AR/100*-51
91F-118
91F-222
91F/School-6
Robertson, Cliff
89Blaz/Franz-10
Robertson, Oscar
60Kahn's-8
61F-36
61F-61
61Kahn's-7
62Kahn's-7
63Kahn's-9
64Kahn's-10A
64Kahn's-10B
65Kahn's-3
68T/Test-22
69T-50
69T/Ins-24
70T-100
70T-114AS
70T/Ins-6
71T-1
71T-136M
71T-141LL
71T-143LL
71T/Ins-34
72Icee-15
72T-25
73T-70
74Nab-17
74T-55
74T-91M
81T/Thirst-26
81TCMA-17
85Star/Schick-21
Robertson, Pablo
(Pabs)
71Globe-4
71Globe-5
71Globe-6

71Globe-63M
71Globe-7
71Globe-8
71Globe/Cocoa-13
71Globe/Cocoa-15
Robey, Rick
77KY/Wildct-19
79T-96
80T-136
80T-24
80T-9
80T-97
81T-E76
83Star/NBA-117
84Star/NBA-49
84Suns/Pol-8
85Star/NBA-40
88KY/269-167
88KY/269-215
88KY/269-25
Robichaux, Mike
90LSU/200*-79
Robinson, Al
89KY/300*-287
Robinson, Betty
54Quaker-11
Robinson, Cliff USC
80T-145
80T-57
83Star/NBA-238
85Star/NBA-114
86F-93
88F-88
Robinson, Cliff UConn
90Blaz/Franz-18
90F-159
90Hoops-250
90Panin-12
90SkyBox-239
91F-172
Robinson, Dave
55Ash-45
Robinson, David
87KY/Coke-SC
88Spurs/Pol-8
89Hoops-138
89Hoops/II-310
90F-172
90F/AS-10
90F/Rook-1
90Hoops-24AS
90Hoops-270
90Hoops-NO
90Hoops/CollB-34
90Hoops/II-378ATC
90Hoops/II-378ATC
90Hoops/Super-88
90Panin-43
90SkyBox-260
90StarP-2
91F-187
91F-225
91F/ProV-1
91Wooden-16
Robinson, Flynn
69T-92
70T-40
70T-4LL
72T-104
74T-197
Robinson, Jackie
91UCLA/144-96
Robinson, James
90Clem/200*-110
Robinson, Joe
90NC/200*-159
Robinson, Johnny
90LSU/200*-175
Robinson, Keith
90ND-15
90StarP-13
Robinson, Kenneth

91SC/200*-163
Robinson, Kenny
89Louville/300*-191
Robinson, Leonard
(Truck)
75T-151
76T-104
77T-74
78T-30
79T-95
80Suns/Pep-7
80T-113
80T-26
80T-37
80T-96
81T-35
81T-60M
83Star/NBA-67
84Star/NBA-33
Robinson, Les
89NCSt/Coke-102
89NCSt/Coke-111
Robinson, Michael
90MISt/200*-101
90MISt/200*-143
Robinson, Paul
68PartM-10
Robinson, Ray
48T/Magic*-A19
Robinson, Robert
91SC/200*-130
Robinson, Ron
74T-251
Robinson, Rumeal
88MI/Nike-12
89MI-7
90F/Up-U4
90Hoops/II-399LS
91F-3
90SkyBox/II-355LP
Robinson, Sam
71Flor/McDon-7
71T-184
Robinson, Stew
87IN/GreatII-18
Robinson, Toren
87South/Pol*-3M
Robinson, Wil
74T-179
Robinson, W.T.
90LSU/200*-191
Robinzine, Bill Jr.
79T-68
80T-13
80T-93
81T-MW78
86DePaul-12
86DePaul-C3
Robisch, Dave
72T-223
73T-199
74T-183
74T-222M
75T-224LL
75T-318
80T-12
80T-136
80T-24
80T-90
81T-W70
82Nugget/Pol-25
83Star/NBA-224
Robiskie, Terry
90LSU/200*-147
Robison, Dick
89Louville/300*-91
Roby, Mark
90AZ/125*-102
Rocha, Red
48Bowman-18
Roche, John
72T-182

910KSt*-2
910KSt*-61
910KSt*-76
910KSt*-83
910KSt*-78
Sanders, Curtis M.
89KY/300*-159
Sanders, Deion
90FLSt/200*-145
Sanders, Frankie
82TCMA/CBA-87
Sanders, Jeff
89Bulls/Eq-12
90SkyBox-47
Sanders, Marcus
90MISt/200*-121
Sanders, Mike
83Star/NBA-118
84Star/NBA-50
84Suns/Pol-7
85Star/NBA-41
87F-96
87Suns/Circ-8
89F-30
89Hoops-226
89Hoops/II-340
90F-80
90Hoops-137
90SkyBox-120
91UCLA/144-94
Sanders, Ricky
88Foot-7
Sanders, Thomas
91TexAM-25
Sanders, Tom
(Satch)
69T-72
70T-163
72T-74
81TCMA-21
Sanders, Tracy
90FLSt/200*-65
Sanderson, Derek
74Nab-15
Saperstein, Abraham M.
68HOF-51
Sappleton, Wayne
84Star/NBA-97
Sartini, Gene
89Louville/300*-161
Sassone, Bob
79StBon-12CO
Satalin, Jim
79StBon-13CO
Satalowich, Todd
89MO-11
Saul, Ronald
90MISt/200*-21
Sauldsberry, Woody
57T-34
Saunders, Flip
89PC/CBA-165
90PC/CBA-70
Savoldi, Joe
48T/Magic*-D22
Sawyer, Alan
91UCLA/144-87
Sawyer, Fred
61Union-9
88Louville/194-72
89Louville/300*-251
Sayers, Gale
81T/Thirst-49
Scales, Clifford
90NE/Pol*-21
Scales, DeWayne
81T-E85
90LSU/200*-46
Scanlan, Raymond
90ND-41
Scates, Tom
91George/100-45

Schabinger, Arthur A.
68HOF-39
Schaefer, Herman
48Bowman-62
Schafer, Tom
89PC/CBA-84
Schalow, John
90Blaz/Franz-8M
Schaus, Fred
52Bread-25
52Royal-1
55Ash-93
61Lakers/Bell-7CO
Schayes, Adolph
(Dolph)
57T-13
61F-39
61F-63
81TCMA-7
Schayes, Dan
(Danny)
83Nugget/Pol-34
83Star/NBA-191
84Star/NBA-146
85Nugget/Pol-5
85Star/NBA-56
86F-98
88F-37
88Nugget/Pol-34
89F-43
89Hoops-82
89Nugget/Pol-12
90F-53
90F/Up-U55
90Hoops-100
90Hoops/II-418
90SkyBox-81
91F-119
90SkyBox/II-395
Scheer, Carl
82Nugget/Pol-x
83Nugget/Pol-x
Scheffler, Steve
90F/Up-U13
90StarP-61
Scheffler, Tom
84Blaz/Franz-9
84Blaz/Pol-15
84Star/NBA-168
Schellenberg, Larry
83Dayton/Blue-14
Schintzius, Dwayne
90F/Up-U91
90StarP-24
Schlueter, Dale
70T-164
71T-76
72T-69
74T-167
75T-154
Schlundt, Don
86IN/Greatl-7
Schlundt, Terrell
82Marq/Lite-13
Schmeling, Max
48T/Magic*-A10
Schmidt, Brian
90FLSt/200*-195
Schmidt, Derek
90FLSt/200*-13
Schmuck, Roger
90AZSt/200*-71
Schneider, Earl
87IN/Greatl-8
Schnellenberger, Howard
89KY/300*-123
89Louville/300*-101
89Louville/300*-127
Schnittker, Dick
57T-80
Schoendienst, Red
57Union-15

Schomburger, Ron
90FLSt/200*-118
Schonely, Bill
79Blaz/Pol-x
83Blaz/Pol-x
Schoonover, Wear
91AR/100*-59
Schow, Jeff
91TexAM-84
Schrader, Charles
89KY/300*-20
Schreiner, Steve
87BYU-13
Schrempf, Detlef
87F-97
88Mavs/BLC-32
89F-67
89Hoops-282
90F-81
90Hoops-138
90Panin-113
90SkyBox-121
91F-85
Schu, Wilber
89KY/300*-230
Schuler, Mike
86Blaz/Franz-13CO
87Blaz/Franz-10CO
88Blaz/Franz-11CO
90Clip/Star-10CO
90Hoops-316CO
91F-95CO
90SkyBox/II-312CO
Schull, Gary
90FLSt/200*-116
Schultz, Dave
81T/Thirst-44
Schultz, Mike
82TCMA/CBA-42
Schwartz, Greg
82Fairf-15
Schweitz, John
82TCMA/CBA-67
84Star/NBA-119
Scolari, Fred
52Bread-26
Scott, Alvin
77Suns/Discs-14
80Suns/Pep-2
83Star/NBA-119
84Star/NBA-51
84Suns/Pol-14
Scott, Anthony
88Syr/Rich-10
Scott, Barbara Ann
48ExhSC-42A
48ExhSC-42A
Scott, Burke
87IN/Greatll-32
Scott, Byron
83Lakers/BASF-10
83Star/NBA-22
84Lakers/BASF-9
84Star/Arena-D7
84Star/NBA-181
85JMS-27
85Star/Lakers-5
85Star/NBA-32
85Star/TmSuper-LA4
86F-99
87F-98
88F-122AS
88F-68
88Fourm-6
89F-78
89Hoops-15
90AZSt/200*-64
90AZSt/200*-8
90AZSt/Promos*-5
90F-94
90Hoops-159
90Hoops/Super-48

Scott, Charlie
71T-146LL
71T-151LL
71T-190
71T/Ins-18A
72T-258AS
72T-259LL
72T-47
73T-140
74T-35
74T-95M
75Carv-27
75T-130M
75T-65
76T-24
77T-125
78T-43
79T-106
80T-149
80T-83
Scott, Clyde
91AR/100*-10
Scott, Daryl
90SanJ/Smok-6
Scott, Dennis
88GATech/Nike-10
89GATech/Pol-16
89GATech/Pol-17
89GATech/Pol-20M
90F/Up-U68
90Hoops/II-393LS
90StarP-9
91F-147
91F/Rook-4
91GATech*-4
90SkyBox/II-363LP
Scott, Herschel
89KY/300*-293
Scott, Malcolm
90LSU/200*-27
Scott, Mike
88KY/Award-3
88KY/Award-7
89KY/300*-34
Scott, Randy
90Clem/200*-129
Scott, Ray
69T-69
70T-48
71T-227
Scott, Ron
90MISt/Promos*-1
90MISt/200*-124
Scott, Tony
89Syr/Pep-12
Scott, Willie
91SC/200*-138
Screen, Pat
90LSU/200*-172
Scruggs, Bernie
89KY/300*-184
Scurry, Carey
89PC/CBA-28
Scurry, Moses
88UNLV/HOF-7
89UNLV/HOF-5
89UNLV/Seven-11
Seals, Bruce
76T-63
77T-113
Seals, Donald
82TCMA/Lanc-29

Sealyham, White
48T/Magic*-G4
Sears, Kenny
57T-7
Seaver, Tom
81T/Thirst-10M
81T/Thirst-13
Seawright, James
91SC/200*-19
Seegert, Alicia
91MI/56*-47
Seikaly, Rony
89F-83
89Heat/Publix-11
89Hoops-243
90F-102
90Heat/Publix-11
90Hoops-169
90Hoops/CollB-11
90Hoops/II-368TC
90Hoops/Super-53
90Panin-154
90SkyBox-151
91F-112
Seiple, Larry
89KY/300*-114
Selinger, Joe
90MISt/200*-84
Sellers, Brad
87Bulls/Ent-4
88Bulls/Ent-2
88F-21
89F-24
89Hoops-139
89Hoops/II-348
90Hoops-192
90SkyBox-175
Sellers, Ron
90FLSt/200*-167
Sellers, Rod
90CT/Pol-11
Selvin, Maurice
89PC/CBA-17
Selvy, Frank
57T-51
61F-40
61Lakers/Bell-8
81TCMA-24
Selvy, Marv
88Louville/194-146
88Louville/194-90
Senesky, George
48Bowman-25
52Bread-27
Serini, Wash
89KY/300*-182
Server, Jim
89KY/300*-246
Seter, Chris
88MI/Nike-13
89MI-4
Settle, Evan
89KY/300*-231
Severin, Paul
90NC/200*-197
Severn, Dan
90AZSt/200*-146
Severn, Dave
90AZSt/200*-108
Severn, Rod
90AZSt/200*-98
Sexton, Frank
48T/Magic*-D15
Seymour, Paul
52Bread-28
57T-72
Shackleford, Charles
89Hoops-169
89NCSt/Coke-35
89NCSt/Coke-36
89NCSt/Coke-37
90F-122

75T-306
82TCMA/CBA-25
Smith, Alisa
  86SWLou/Pol*-14
Smith, Anthony
  90AZ/125*-18
  91SC/200*-129
Smith, Barry
  90FLSt/200*-146
Smith, Bill
  89KY/300*-233
Smith, Billy Ray
  91AR/100*-25
Smith, Bobby
  (Bingo)
  68Rocket/Jack-11
  70T-74
  71T-93
  71T/Ins-36
  72T-149
  73T-49
  74T-78
  75T-120M
  75T-175
  76T-114
  77T-126
Smith, Bubba
  71Keds*-1M
  71Keds*-2M
  90MISt/200*-43
Smith, Charles
  85George/Pol-13
  87George/Pol-13
  88George/Pol-13
  91George/100-47
  91George/100-7
Smith, Charles PITT
  89F-73
  89Hoops-262
  90Clip/Star-11
  90F-89
  90Hoops-151
  90Hoops/CollB-47
  90Hoops/Super-44
  90Panin-36
  90SkyBox-132
  91F-96
Smith, Chris
  90CT/Pol-12
Smith, Clarence
  71Globe-45
  71Globe-46
  71Globe-47
  71Globe-48
  71Globe/Cocoa-16
  71Globe/Cocoa-17
Smith, Clinton
  89PC/CBA-104
  90PC/CBA-154
Smith, Danny
  91SC/200*-154
Smith, David
  89Louville/300*-97
Smith, Dean
  88NC/Pol-x
  89NC/Coke-1
  89NC/Coke-2
  89NC/Coke-3
  89NC/Coke-4
  89NC/Coke-5
  89NC/Coke-6
  90NC/200*-1
  90NC/200*-150
  90NC/200*-173
  90NC/200*-27
  90NC/200*-52
Smith, Derek
  83Star/NBA-131
  84Star/NBA-21
  85Star/NBA-92
  86F-103
  86Kings/Smok-10

88Louville/194-113
88Louville/194-15
88Louville/194-156
88Louville/194-191
89Hoops-83
89Louville/300*-265
89Louville/300*-282
89Louville/300*-33
89Sixers/Kodak-11
90F-145
90Hoops-231
90SkyBox-218
Smith, Doug
  88MO-11
  89MO-12
  91StarP-33
Smith, Eddie
  90ND-21
Smith, Eddie AZ
  84AZ/Pol-12
  90AZ/125*-92
Smith, Elmore
  72T-76
  73NBAPA-27
  73T-19
  74T-49
  75T-16
  76T-65
  77T-106
  78T-57
  79T-117
Smith, Elvado
  81George/Pol-2
Smith, Eric
  81George/Pol-3
  91George/100-40
Smith, Frank
  81AZ/Pol-15
Smith, Gene
  81George/Pol-11
  82George/Pol-11
  83George/Pol-6
  91George/100-61
Smith, George
  90MISt/200*-68
Smith, Greg
  69T-81
  70T-166
  71T-129
  72T-114
  74T-128
Smith, J.
  88KY/269-100
  88KY/269-214
Smith, Jimmy
  87SoMiss-12
Smith, Joe
  91SC/200*-99
Smith, John
  81TCMA/CBA-37
  82TCMA/CBA-69
  87Duke/Pol-33
  91OKSt*-25
Smith, Jon
  91George/100-59
Smith, Keith
  90PC/CBA-150
Smith, Kenny
  86NC/Pol-30
  88F-100
  88Kings/Carl-30
  89F-138
  89Hoops-232
  89Kings/Carl-30
  89NC/Coke-107
  89NC/Coke-66
  89NC/Coke-68
  90F-4
  90F/Up-U36
  90NC/200*-16
  90NC/200*-33

90NC/200*-75
90NC/200*-94
90Panin-120
91F-230
91F-78
90SkyBox/II-385
Smith, Kevin
  82TCMA/CBA-59
  90MISt/200*-138
Smith, LaBradford
  91StarP-49
Smith, Lance
  90LSU/200*-76
Smith, Larry
  81T-51M
  81T-W75
  83Star/NBA-261
  84Star/NBA-157
  85Star/NBA-136
  86F-104
  87F-101
  88Warr/Smok-4
  89Hoops-168
  89Hoops/II-309
  89Hoops-128
  90SkyBox-111
  91F-79
Smith, Mark
  80IL/Arby's-11
Smith, Martin
  91AR/100*-58
Smith, Marty
  89Louville/300*-159
Smith, Michael
  87BYU-1
  87BYU-25
  90F/Up-U10
  90Panin-133
  90SkyBox-24
Smith, Moyer
  90NC/200*-102
Smith, Otis
  89Hoops-86
  89Hoops/II-303
  89Magic/Pep-6
  90F-135
  90Hoops-221
  90Panin-121
  90SkyBox-206
  91F-149
Smith, Phil
  75T-139
  76T-89
  77T-12
  78T-33
  79T-53
  80T-163
  80T-40
  81T-W93
Smith, Randal
  86SWLou/Pol*-15
Smith, Randy
  72T-8
  73T-173
  74T-8
  75Carv-30
  75T-118M
  75T-63
  76T-135AS
  76T-40
  77T-82
  78Clipp/Handy-1
  78T-112
  79T-85
  80T-38
  80T-95
  81T-E86
Smith, Ranzino
  86NC/Pol-33
  87NC/Pol-33
  89NC/Coke-169
  90NC/200*-24

Smith, Riley
  90PC/CBA-191
Smith, Robert
  82TCMA/CBA-30
Smith, Sam
  71Col/Mara-10
  79Bulls/Pol-28
Smith, Sean
  91GATech*-31
Smith, Sonny
  87Auburn/Pol*-4
Smith, Stan
  71Keds*-2M
Smith, Steve
  91StarP-21
Smith, Tom
  90MISt/200*-195
Smith, Tony
  90F/Up-U45
Smith, Ty
  89Louville/300*-133
Smith, Vadi
  82George/Pol-10
Smith, Willie
  82TCMA/CBA-15
  90Hoops/II-414
  90NC/Promos*-NC9
Smits, Rik
  89F-68
  89Hoops-37
  90F-82
  90Hoops-139
  90Hoops/Super-42
  90Panin-109
  90SkyBox-122
  91F-86
Smolinski, Don
  82Marq/Lite-14
Smrek, Mike
  90Hoops-119
  90SkyBox-101
Smyth, John
  90ND-29
Snavely, Carl
  90NC/200*-151
Snead, Samuel J.
  48Kell*-17
Snedeker, Jeff
  87Bucks/Polar-TR
  88Bucks/Green-16TR
Snider, Duke
  57Union-12
Snite, Fred Sr.
  54Quaker-2
Snively, John
  82AR-13
Snow, J.T.
  90AZ/125*-63
Snow, Lenny
  91GATech*-199
Snow, Percy
  90MISt/200*-44
  90MISt/200*-56
  90MISt/200*-82
  90MISt/Promos*-3
Snowden, Fred
  81AZ/Pol-16CO
  90AZ/125*-17
Snyder, Dick
  68Suns/Carn-9
  69Suns/Carn-7
  69T-73
  70Sonic/Sunb-8
  70T-64
  71Sonic/Sunb-9
  72T-136
  73NBAPA-28
  73Sonic/Shur-10
  73T-86
  74T-115
  74T-97M
  75T-120M

75T-83
76T-2
78Sonic/Pol-9
Snyder, Quin
  87Duke/Pol-14
Sobers, Ricky
  75Suns-13
  76Suns-8
  76T-102
  77T-42
  78RCCola-29
  78T-93
  79Bulls/Pol-40
  79T-71
  80T-137
  80T-23
  81T-8
  83Star/NBA-214
  84Star/NBA-121
  85Star/NBA-70
Sobie, Ron
  57T-69
Sobieszcyk, Ron
  86DePaul-C3
Sodders, Mike
  90AZSt/200*-159
Soderberg, Mark
  89KY/300*-85
Soergel, Dick
  91OKSt*-58
Sojourner, Mike
  75T-62
  76T-79
Sojourner, Willie
  72T-232
  75T-312
Sommer, Coleen
  90AZSt/200*-137
Sorensen, Lary
  79Bucks/OpenP-5
  91MI/56*-50
Sorenson, Dave
  71T-71
  72T-12
  73T-14
Sossamon, Lou
  91SC/200*-94
South, Harry
  91SC/200*-172
Southers, Brantley
  91SC/200*-188
Spadafore, Frank
  55Ash-94
Spahn, Warren
  57Union-39
Spanarkel, Jim
  81T-48M
  81T-MW79
  83Star/NBA-57
  84Star/Arena-B8
Sparrow, Guy
  57T-38
Sparrow, Rory
  80TCMA/CBA-20
  83Star/NBA-68
  84Star/NBA-34
  85Star/NBA-170
  86F-105
  87Bulls/Ent-1
  87F-102
  89F-84
  89Heat/Publix-12
  89Hoops-207
  90Hoops-170
  90Hoops/II-430
  90Hoops/Super-52
  90Kings/Safe-10
  90SkyBox-152
  91F-180
  90SkyBox/II-411
Speaker, Tris
  48T/Magic*-K7

Speaks, Jon Garwood
89NCSt/Coke-42
89NCSt/Coke-43
89NCSt/Coke-44
Spector, Arthur
48Bowman-57
Spence, Phil
89NCSt/Coke-46
89NCSt/Coke-47
89NCSt/Coke-48
Spencer, Elmore
90UNLV/Smok-13
90UNLV/Season-10
Spencer, Felton
90F/Up-U57
90Hoops/II-395LS
90StarP-41
91F-127
91F/Rook-10
90SkyBox/II-361LP
Spencer, Jerry
91AR/100*-34
Spencer, Mark
79StBon-14
Spicer, Carey
88KY/269-54
Spiers, Bill
90Clem/200*-20
Spillane, Jim
91UCLA/144-64
Spitz, Mark
81T/Thirst-45
Spivey, Bill
88KY/269-16
89KY/300*-50
Spivey, Ron
89PC/CBA-146
90PC/CBA-176
Splane, Vince
89KY/300*-234
Spoelstra, Art
57T-52
Sprague, Cindy
87ME/Pol*-4
Spriggs, Ed
81George/Pol-9
91George/100-41
Spriggs, Larry
81TCMA/CBA-36
82TCMA/CBA-50
83Lakers/BASF-11
83Star/NBA-23
84Lakers/BASF-10
84Star/NBA-182
89PC/CBA-121
Springer, Russell
87LSU/Pol*-11
88LSU/Pol*-16
Springs, Albert
89PC/CBA-137
90PC/CBA-152
St.John, Dan
90AZSt/200*-131
Stacey, Howard
89Louville/300*-85
Stachowicz, Ray
90MISt/200*-1
90MISt/200*-39
90MISt/200*-90
Stacom, Kevin
75T-117M
75T-99
77T-108
Stagg, Amos Alonzo
54Quaker-7
68HOF-40
Stahl, Ed
89NC/Coke-148
90NC/200*-157
Stahl, Regina
90AZSt/200*-90
Staker, Carl

89KY/300*-235
Stallings, Ron
89Louville/300*-82
Stallworth, Bud
73Sonic/Shur-11
73T-58
75T-108
Stallworth, Cedric
91GATech*-32
Stallworth, Dave
69T-74
70T-78
71T-49
72T-132
73Bullet/Stand-9
73T-133
Stamper, Larry
88KY/269-97
Standlee, Norm
48Kell*-8
Stanich, George
91UCLA/144-114
Stanich, John
91UCLA/144-120
Stankavage, Scott
90NC/200*-41
Stansbury, Terence
84Star/NBA-59
85Star/Gator-3
85Star/NBA-85
85Star/SlamD-7
Stanwick, Barbara
48T/Magic*-F2
Starks, John
89PC/CBA-188
91OKSt*-40
Starr, Bart
81T/Thirst-36
Staubach, Roger
74Nab-1
75Nab-1
Staverman, Larry
59Kahn's-8
60Kahn's-9
Steele, Larry
72T-26
73T-69
74T-21
75T-6M
75T-94
77Blaz/Pol-15
79Blaz/Pol-15
88KY/269-158
88KY/269-41
89Blaz/Franz-18
Steers, Leo
48T/Magic*-E2
Steffy, Joe
48T/Magic*-C8
Stegent, Larry
91TexAM-14
Stegman, Dave
90AZ/125*-76
Stein, Bill
81George/Pol-7
Steinke
48T/Magic*-D25
Stel, Travis
89ORSt-15
Stengel, Casey
81PhilM-1
Stephen, Scott
90AZSt/200*-27
Stephens, Everette
89PC/CBA-192
90PC/CBA-46
Stephens, Frank
71Globe-42M
71Globe-50
71Globe-51
71Globe-52
71Globe-53

Stephens, Jack
90ND-26
Stephens, Rehema
90UCLA-17
Stephens, Rod
91GATech*-66
Stephens, Tim
77KY/Wildct-16
78KY/Food-12
89KY/300*-86
Steppe, Brook
83Star/NBA-165
91GATech*-26
Stevens, Barry
90PC/CBA-174
Stevens, Howard
89Louville/300*-108
Stevenson, Gil
48T/Magic*-R2
Stevenson, Mark
90StarP-29
Stevenson, Norris
90AZSt/200*-69
Stewart, Alprentice
89UTEP/Drug-23
Stewart, Gene
89KY/300*-87
Stewart, Jim
68PartM-8
Stewart, Rod
89KY/300*-147
Stewart, Norm
88MO-12CO
89MO-13CO
Still, Art
89KY/300*-137
Stillwell, Joseph
48T/Magic*-O1
Stinson, Andrea
89NCSt/Pol-11
Stipanovich, Steve
83Star/NBA-157
84Star/NBA-60
85Star/NBA-86
86F-106
87F-103
88F-59
88MO-13
89Hoops-148
89MO-14
Stith, Bryant
88VA/Hardee-11
Stockstill, Rick
90FLSt/200*-14
Stockton, John
84Star/NBA-235
85Star/NBA-144
85Star/RTm-8
88F-115
88F-127AS
88Fourn-32
88Jazz/Smok-6
89F-156
89F-163M
89Hoops-140
89Hoops-297AS
89Jazz/OldH-13
90F-189
90F/AS-9
90Hoops-25AS
90Hoops-294
90Hoops/CollB-22
90Hoops/Super-93
90Jazz/Star-2
90Panin-51
90Panin-AAS
90SkyBox-284
91F-203
91F-217
91F-221
Stoddard, Tim
89NCSt/Coke-49

89NCSt/Coke-50
89NCSt/Coke-51
Stofa, John
68PartM-11
Stokan, Gary
89NCSt/Coke-85
89NCSt/Coke-69
Stokes, Maurice
57Kahn's-9
57T-42
Stokholm, Carol
54Quaker-17
Stone, George
71T-201
Stoner, Neale
80IL/Arby's-12
Stones, Dwight
88Foot-8
Storm, Gale
48T/Magic*-J39
Stotts, Terry
81TCMA/CBA-68
90PC/CBA-160
Stoudamire, Antoine
89George/Pol-16
90George/Pol-4
Stough, John
89KY/300*-236
Stovall, Claudene
87South/Pol*-11
Stovall, Jerry
90LSU/200*-41
Stover, Eric
79StBon-15
Stramm, Stu
89Louville/300*-147
Strange, Bo
90LSU/200*-23
Strauss, Buddy
90FLSt/200*-121
Streater, Steve
90NC/200*-28
Streete, Jon
90LSU/200*-101
Strickland, Bishop
91SC/200*-159
Strickland, Jim
87IN/GreatII-9
Strickland, Kevin
87Duke/Pol-31
Strickland, Rod
89F-104
89Hoops-8
89Knicks/Marine-9
90F-173
90Hoops-271
90Panin-47
90SkyBox-261
91F-188
Stroeder, John
87Bucks/Polar-54
Strom, Rick
91GATech*-69
Strong, Derek
90StarP-63
Strong, Guy
55Ash-12
88KY/269-60
Strong, Steve
90AZ/125*-13
Strothers, Lamont
91Class-33
91StarP-9
Stuck, Lisa
90AZSt/200*-107
Stuckey, Jim
90Clem/200*-65
Stuckey, Kelby
90PC/CBA-197
Studer, John
89Louville/300*-78
Sturgill, Bill

89KY/300*-260
Sudhop, Glenn
89NCSt/Coke-52
89NCSt/Coke-53
89NCSt/Coke-54
Suggs, Tommy
91SC/200*-179
Suhey, Steve
48T/Magic*-C10
Suhr, Brendan
79Hawks/Majik-x
87Hawks/Pizza-2CO
Suhr, Marc
90CT/Pol-13
Sullivan, Barry
48T/Magic*-J35
Sullivan, Bill
89Louville/300*-94
Sullivan, John
91SC/200*-189
Sullivan, John L.
48T/Magic*-A2
Sullivan, Mickey
87Baylor/Pol*-3
Summers, Wilbur
89Louville/300*-111
Sumner, Walt
90FLSt/200*-178
Sumpter, Barry
83Louville-40
89Louville/300*-92
90PC/CBA-143
Sumpter, James
91SC/200*-101
Sundvold, Jon
83Sonic/Pol-14
83Star/NBA-200
84Star/NBA-122
85Star/NBA-151
87F-104
88MO-14
89Heat/Publix-13
89Hoops-175
90Heat/Publix-12
90Hoops-171A
90Hoops-172B
90SkyBox-153
Sutherland, Jock
88Louville/194-193M
Sutton, Bradd
88MO-15
89MO-15
Sutton, Ed
90NC/200*-176
Sutton, Eddie
82AR-14CO
88KY/269-40
88KY/Award-17CO
89KY/Tm80-54
91OKSt*-99
Sutton, Greg
91Class-39
Sutton, Leroy
82AR-15
Sutton, Lorenzo
89PC/CBA-129
Sutton, Sean
88KY/Award-13
88KY/Award-1
88KY/Award-15
88KY/Award-8
Swain, Jeff
87South/Pol*-16
Swain, Rob
91TexAM-24
Swartz, Dan
55Ash-58
Swearengin, Clarence
88TN/Smok-11
Sweet, Daimon
90ND-25
Swenson, Olaf

89George/Pol-2CO
90George/Pol-14CO
91George/100-1CO
91George/100-25
91George/100-48
91George/100-58
91George/100-89
Thompson, Kevin
89NCSt/Pol-12
Thompson, LaSalle
83Star/NBA-226
84Star/NBA-277
85Kings/Smok-13
85Star/NBA-78
86F-110
86Kings/Smok-12
87F-107
88Fourn-31
89Hoops-281
90F-83
90Hoops-140
90Panin-112
90SkyBox-123
91F-87
Thompson, Leonard
910KSt*-48
Thompson, Mark
89McNees*-11
Thompson, M.C.
86DePaul-C6
Thompson, Mychal
79Blaz/Pol-43
79T-63
81Blaz/Pol-43
81T-36
81T-61M
82Blaz/Pol-43
83Blaz/Pol-43
83Star/NBA-106
84Blaz/Franz-11
84Blaz/Pol-13
84Star/Blaz-4
84Star/NBA-170
85Blaz/Franz-11
85Star/NBA-109
86F-111
87F-108
88F-69
89Blaz/Franz-19
89F-79
89Hoops-4
90F-95
90Hoops-160
90Panin-2
90SkyBox-141
Thompson, Paul
83Star/NBA-240
Thompson, Robert Lee
(Bobby)
90AZ/125*-113
90AZ/125*-122
90AZ/Promos*-8
Thompson, Ronnie
88George/Pol-6
89George/Pol-6
90George/Pol-6
Thompson, Scott
84AZ/Pol-14CO
Thompson, Shelton
90FLSt/200*-64
Thompson, Stephen
88Syr/Rich-12
89Syr/Pep-10
89Syr/Pep-4
90PC/CBA-73
90StarP-11
Thompson, Weegie
90FLSt/200*-23
Thorn, Rod
70T-167
Thornton, Bob
89Sixers/Kodak-12

90Hoops-232
90SkyBox-219
Thornton, Dallas
71Globe-84
Thornton, John
91TexAM-30
Thorpe, Otis
84Star/NBA-278
85Kings/Smok-14
85Star/NBA-79
85Star/RTm-7
86Kings/Smok-13
87F-109
88F-99
89F-62
89Hoops-265
90F-74
90Hoops-129
90Hoops/Super-36
90Panin-68
90SkyBox-112A
90SkyBox-112B
91F-80
Thorsson, Arn
91SC/200*-137
Threatt, Sedale
83Star/NBA-10
84Star/NBA-209
85JMS-8
85Star/NBA-7
85Star/TmSuper-PS10
86F-112
87Bulls/Ent-2
87F-110
89Hoops-287
90Hoops-284
90SkyBox-273
90Sonic/Kayo-13
90Sonic/Smok-16
91F-196
Thurmond, Mark
91TexAM-40
Thurmond, Nate
68T/Test-13
69T-10
69T/Ins-12
70T-111AS
70T-90
71T-131
71T/Ins-7
72T-28
73NBAPA-29
73T-157LL
73T-5
74Nab-21
74T-105
74T-87M
75T-119M
75T-85
81TCMA-29
85Star/Schick-22
Ticco, Milt
89KY/300*-237
Tidrick, Hal
48Bowman-36
Tieman, Rodger
89Louville/300*-89
Tillet, Maurice
48T/Magic*-D12
Tillis, Darren
83Star/NBA-262
Tillman, Clarence
78KY/Food-8
89KY/300*-239
Tillman, Lawyer
87Auburn/Pol*-13
Tillmon, Mark
87George/Pol-14
88George/Pol-14
89George/Pol-14
90PC/CBA-201
91George/100-11

91George/100-38
Timberlake, Bob
91MI/56*-51
Timmons, Steve
89Foot-5
Tinch, Reggie
90GA/Smok-14
Tingle, Jack
88KY/269-33
Tinker, Joe
48T/Magic*-K18
Tinsley, Gaynell
90LSU/200*-38
Tinsley, George
71Flor/McDon-8
Tisdale, Wayman
86F-113
87F-111
88F-60
88Kings/Carl-23
89F-139
89Hoops-225
89Kings/Carl-23
90F-167
90Hoops-262
90Hoops/CollB-12
90Hoops/II-377TC
90Hoops/Super-85
90Kings/Safe-11
90Panin-40
90SkyBox-251
91F-181
Tittle, Y.A.
57Union-4
90LSU/200*-3
Tobey, David
68HOF-43
Tofflemire, Joe
90AZ/125*-71
Tolbert, Lynda
90AZSt/200*-114
Tolbert, Ray
83Star/NBA-95
87IN/GreatII-6
Tolbert, Tom
86AZ/Pol-11
87AZ/Pol-13
90Hoops-121
90SkyBox-103
91F-72
Tolle, Harlan
55Ash-59
Tomberlin, Pat
90FLSt/200*-5
Tomey, Dick
90AZ/Promos*-10CO
90AZ/Promos*-7CO
Tomjanovich, Rudy
71T-91
72T-103
73NBAPA-30
73T-145
74T-146LL
74T-28
74T-88M
75T-123M
75T-2LL
75T-70
76T-66
77T-15
78RCCola-31
78T-58
79T-41
80T-120
80T-32
91MI/56*-52
Toney, Andrew
83Star/ASG-12
83Star/NBA-11
83Star/Sixers-11
83Star/Sixers-6
84Star/Arena-E9

84Star/ASG-12
84Star/CrtKg-35
84Star/NBA-210
84Star/PolASG-12
85JMS-7
85Star/NBA-8
85Star/TmSuper-PS7
86F-114
86Star/CrtKg-29
Toney, Sedric
83Dayton/Blue-16
90PC/CBA-165
Toolson, Andy
87BYU-17
90Jazz/Star-8
Toomer, Carlos
90KY/Sov-17
Torrance, Jeff
90LSU/200*-164
Torrence, Walt
91UCLA/144-88
Torres, George
81TCMA/CBA-4
Towe, Monte
89NCSt/Coke-167
89NCSt/Coke-168
89NCSt/Coke-169
Tower, Keith
90ND-7
Tower, Oswald
68HOF-44
Towne, Dave
90AZ/125*-66
Townes, Garland
89KY/300*-240
Townes, Linton
82Blaz/Pol-2
Townsend, Raymond
80TCMA/CBA-16
91UCLA/144-39
Traber, Jim
910KSt*-90
Trabue, Joe
89Louville/300*-160
Trafton, Todd
90AZ/125*-25
Trahan, Warren
91TexAM-93
Trainor, Kendall
91AR/100*-11
Trapp, George
72T-38
73T-22
74T-76
75T-84
Trapp, John Q.
68Rocket/Jack-12
70T-12
71T-68
Travaglini, Bob
82Nugget/Pol-x
Treadwell, David
90Clem/200*-41
Treloar, John
90PC/CBA-131
Tresh, Mike
48Kell*-3
Tressler, Jeff
83Dayton/Blue-17
Tresvant, John
69Sonic/Sunb-9
69T-58
70T-126
71T-37
72T-87
73T-26
Trevor, Claire
48T/Magic*-J37
Trgovich, Pete
91UCLA/144-40
Tribble, Andy
90Clem/200*-154

Triplett, Wally
48T/Magic*-R1
Trippi, Charlie
48Kell*-9B
48Kell*-9A
Triptow, Dick
86DePaul-H3
Tripucka, Kelly
83Star/NBA-85
84Star/ASG-13
84Star/CrtKg-5
84Star/NBA-268
84Star/PolASG-13
85Prism-7
85Star/NBA-17
85Star/TmSuper-DP2
86F-115
86Star/CrtKg-30
87F-112
89F-18
89Hoops-55
90F-21
90Hoops-59
90Hoops/Super-11
90ND-54
90Panin-84
90SkyBox-35
Trost, Gary
87BYU-14
Trott, Bill
89KY/300*-21
Trotter, Kerry
82Marq/Lite-15
Trout, Paul
(Dizzy)
48Kell*-4
Truax, Billy
90LSU/200*-115
Trumpy, Bob
68PartM-12
Tsioropoulos, Lou
57T-57
88KY/269-44
Tucker, Anthony
87George/Pol-15
Tucker, Craig
80IL/Arby's-13
81IL/Arby's-13
82TCMA/CBA-47
Tucker, Jack
89KY/300*-257
Tucker, Trent
83Star/All-R-7
83Star/NBA-69
84Star/NBA-35
85Star/NBA-171
87F-113
89F-105
89Hoops-87
89Knicks/Marine-10
90F-129
90Hoops-208
90SkyBox-193
91F-140
Tuminello, Joe
90LSU/200*-114
Tunney, Gene
48T/Magic*-A9
81T/Thirst-55M
Tunnicliffe, Tommy
90AZ/125*-12
Tunstall, Sean
89KS/Leesley-52
Turjillo, Maria
90AZSt/200*-169
Turner, Bill
70T-158
Turner, Bobby
88Louville/194-135
88Louville/194-53
89Louville/300*-24
Turner, Clyde

(Bulldog)
48ExhSC-44
Turner, Elston
83Star/NBA-58
84Star/Arena-B9
84Star/NBA-147
85Nugget/Pol-8
85Star/NBA-57
88Nugget/Pol-20
89PC/CBA-95
Turner, Herschel
89KY/300*-118
Turner, Howard
89NCSt/Coke-119
Turner, Jeff
84Nets/Getty-10
84Star/NBA-199
84Star/NBA-98
86Star/LifeNets-12
89Hoops/II-322
90SkyBox-208
Turner, Joe
84AZ/Pol-15
85AZ/Pol-13
86AZ/Pol-12
87AZ/Pol-14
Turner, John
88George/Pol-12
91StarP-57
Turner, John Louisville
88Louville/194-143
88Louville/194-86
89Louville/300*-13
89Louville/300*-224
89Louville/300*-250
Turner, Kenny
88VA/Hardee-12
Turner, Kim
89McNees*-12
Turner, Lana
48T/Magic*-F3
Turner, Landon
86IN/Greatl-22
Turner, Nate
90NE/Pol*-13
Turner, Reginald
89PC/CBA-70
Turner, Tony
81TCMA/CBA-27
Turpin, Mel
82KY/Sch-7
84Star/CrtKg-50
84Star/NBA-213
85Star/NBA-158
86F-116
87KY/Coke-7M
88KY/269-123
88KY/269-146
89Hoops/II-316
89KY/300*-43
89KY/Tm80-42
90Hoops-302
Tuten, Rick
90FLSt/200*-53
Tuttle, Gerald
89NC/Coke-150
90NC/200*-116
Tuttle, Perry
90Clem/200*-42
Tuttle, Richard
89NC/Coke-151
Tuttle, William
89KY/300*-199
89KY/300*-255
Twardzik, Dave
74T-243
75T-246
75T-287M
76T-42
77Blaz/Pol-13
77T-62
78T-122

79Blaz/Pol-13
80T-115
80T-117
80T-27
80T-65
83Blaz/Pol-x
Tway, Bob
91OKSt*-9
Twitty, Howard
90AZSt/200*-150
Twogood, Forrest
57Union-6
Twyman, Jack
57Kahn's-10
57T-71
58Kahn's-10
59Kahn's-9
60Kahn's-10
61F-42
61F-65
61Kahn's-9
62Kahn's-9
63Kahn's-12
64Kahn's-12
65Kahn's-4
81TCMA-28
Tyler, Terry
79T-84
80T-102
80T-108
80T-151
80T-20
80T-43
80T-56
81T-MW84
83Star/NBA-96
84Star/NBA-269
85Kings/Smok-15
86Kings/Smok-14
87F-114
88Mavs/BLC-41
88Mavs/CardN-41
Tyra, Charles
55Ash-36
57T-68
81TCMA-40M
88Louville/194-121
88Louville/194-27
89Louville/300*-208
89Louville/300*-225
89Louville/300*-5
Tyson, Sean
90Clem-14
Udall, Morris
90AZ/125*-88
Uetake, Yojiro
91OKSt*-43
Underwood, Lovell
89KY/300*-254
Underwood, Paul
55Ash-46
Unger, Garry
74Nab-14
Unglaub, Kurt
90FLSt/200*-129
Unitas, Johnny
81PhilM-8
81T/Thirst-33
89Louville/300*-102
Unseld, Wes
69T-56
69T/Ins-22
70T-5LL
70T-72
70T/Ins-21
71T-95
71T/Ins-35
72Icee-17
72T-175LL
72T-21
73Bullet/Stand-10
73NBAPA-31

73T-176
74T-121
75T-115
75T-133M
75T-4LL
76T-5
77T-75
78RCCola-32
78T-7
79T-65
80T-143
80T-175
80T-31
80T-87
88Louville/194-103
88Louville/194-170
88Louville/194-2
89Hoops-53
89Louville/300*-14
89Louville/300*-207
89Louville/300*-238
89Louville/300*-3
90Hoops-331CO
90Hoops/II-344CO
91F-209CO
90SkyBox/II-327CO
Uplinger, Harold
54Bullet/Gunth-11
Upshaw, Kelvin
89Hoops-264
90SkyBox-104
Urabano, Eddie
90AZSt/200*-139
Urban, Karli
90AZSt/200*-170
Urich, Robert
90FLSt/200*-133
Usevitch, Jim
87BYU-18
87BYU-3
Vagotis, Christ
89Louville/300*-134
Valen, Victor
87Baylor/Pol*-7
Valentine, Carlton
90MISt/200*-149
Valentine, Darnell
81Blaz/Pol-10
82Blaz/Pol-14
83Blaz/Pol-14
83Star/NBA-107
84Blaz/Franz-12
84Blaz/Pol-4
84Star/Blaz-5
84Star/NBA-171
85Blaz/Franz-12
87F-115
91F-39
Valentine, Robbie
83Louville-00
88Louville/194-149
88Louville/194-158
88Louville/194-96
Valentine, Ron
81TCMA/CBA-45
Vallely, John
91UCLA/144-50
Valvano, James T.
89NCSt/Coke-191
89NCSt/Coke-192
89NCSt/Coke-193
89NCSt/Pol-13CO
Van Alstyne, Ben
90MISt/200*-180
Van Arsdale, Dick
68Suns/Carn-10
69Suns/Carn-8
69T-31
70Suns/A1-8A
70Suns/A1-8B
70Suns/Carn-9
70T-45

71T-85
71T/Ins-26
72Icee-18
72T-95
73NBAPA-32
73T-25
74T-160
74T-95M
75Carv-31
75Suns-14
75T-150
76Suns-10
76T-26
81TCMA-10
85Star/Schick-23
87IN/GreatlI-14M
Van Arsdale, Tom
68PartM-14
69T-79
70T-145
70T/Ins-23
71T-75
71T/Ins-12
72T-79
73NBAPA-33
73T-146
74T-20
74T-94M
75T-7
76Suns-11
76T-99
85Star/Schick-24
87IN/GreatlI-14M
Van Bever, Mark
91SC/200*-87
Van Brandt, Yvonne
91TexAM-79
Van Breda Kolff, Bill
70Suns/Carn-10CO
Van Breda Kolff, Jan
75T-307
77T-109
79T-123
80T-146
80T-58
Van Brocklin, Norm
81T/Thirst-31
Van Buren, Steve
48ExhSC-45
90LSU/200*-161
Van Dyke, David
89UTEP/Drug-24
Van Lier, Norm
70T-97
71T-143LL
71T-19
71T/Ins-45
72T-111
73T-31
74T-140AS
74T-84M
75Carv-32
75T-119M
75T-155
76Buck-19
76T-108
77Bulls/WhHen-7
77T-4
78RCCola-33
78T-102
90Bulls/Eq-15
Van Note, Jeff
89KY/300*-172
Van Pelt, Brad
90MISt/200*-11
90MISt/200*-92M
Van Raaphorst, Jeff
90AZSt/200*-51
Van Soelen, Greg
89PC/CBA-16
Vance, Ellis
(Gene)

48Bowman-20
52Bread-30
Vance, Van
88Louville/194-193M
Vandeweghe, Kiki
82Nugget/Pol-55
83Nugget/Pol-55
83Star/ASG-23
83Star/NBA-181
84Blaz/Franz-13
84Blaz/Pol-16
84Star/ASG-25
84Star/CrtKg-46
84Star/NBA-161
84Star/PolASG-25
85Blaz/Franz-13
85Star/NBA-103
86Blaz/Franz-12
86F-117
86Star/CrtKg-31
87Blaz/Franz-11
87Blaz/Franz-13
87F-116
88Blaz/Franz-13
89F-106
89Hoops-295
89Knicks/Marine-11
90Hoops-209
90SkyBox-194
91F-141
91UCLA/144-14
Vandiver, Shaun
91StarP-62
Vann, Kayode
89George/Pol-8
90George/Pol-2
Vanoostveen, Genevieve
90UCLA-25
Vargas, Jose
86LSU/Pol*-13
87LSU/Pol*-3
Varoscak, John
89Louville/300*-83
Vary, Richard
90MISt/200*-165
Vasquez, Richie
87LSU/Pol*-13
Vaughn, Dave
75T-287M
Vaughn, Eric
89Louville/300*-188
Vaught, Loy
88MI/Nike-15
89MI-11
90Clip/Star-12
90F/Up-U42
90StarP-37
Vayda, Jerry
89NC/Coke-127
Venable, Jerry
71Globe-49
71Globe-56
Ventura, Robin
91OKSt*-4
Verderber, Chuck
78KY/Food-9
79KY/Food-9
88KY/269-116
Verga, Bob
71T-167
71T/Ins-6A
Verhoeven, Peter
81Blaz/Pol-31
82Blaz/Pol-31
83Blaz/Pol-31
83Star/NBA-108
84Star/NBA-279
Veripapa, Andy
48ExhSC-46
Verplank, Scott
91OKSt*-38
Versace, Dick

89Hoops-292CO
90Hoops-315CO
90SkyBox/II-311CO
Vickers, Martha
48T/Magic*-F21
Vidnovic, Nick
90NC/200*-196
Vilcheck, Al
88Louville/194-137
88Louville/194-59
89Louville/300*-246
Villa, Danny
90AZSt/200*-45
Vincent, Jay
83Star/NBA-59
84Star/Arena-B10
84Star/NBA-260
85Star/NBA-165
86F-118
88F-38
89Hoops-191
89Hoops/II-345
90Hoops-161
90MISt/200*-123
90MISt/200*-192
Vincent, Mike
90LSU/200*-139
Vincent, Sam
88Bulls/Ent-11
89Hoops-149
89Hoops/II-328
89Magic/Pep-7
90F-137
90Hoops-223A
90Hoops-223B
90Hoops/Super-69
90MISt/200*-148
90MISt/200*-198
90SkyBox-209
Virgil, John
89NC/Coke-183
Vlahogeorge, John
81AZ/Pol-19
Voce, Gary
90PC/CBA-115
Vogel, Paul
91SC/200*-164
Voight, Larry
90NC/200*-188
Voight, Mike
90NC/200*-171
90NC/200*-77
Volkov, Alexander
90Hoops-34
90SkyBox-9
Volmar, Doug
90MISt/200*-115
Von Kolnitz, Fritz
91SC/200*-56
Vosberg, Ed
90AZ/125*-70
Voskuil, James
88MI/Nike-16
89MI-10
Vranes, Danny
83Sonic/Pol-11
83Star/NBA-201
84Star/NBA-123
85Star/NBA-71
Vroman, Brett
80TCMA/CBA-38
Vulich, George
89KY/300*-275
Wachtel, John
90FLSt/200*-108
Waddell, Charles
89NC/Coke-184
90NC/200*-180
Wade, Bob
88MD/Pol-11CO
Wade, Chris
91SC/200*-17

Wade, Mark
89PC/CBA-53
90PC/CBA-33
Wade, Sparky
90LSU/200*-62
Wadiak, Steve
91SC/200*-98
Wadleslaw
48T/Magic*-D24
Waggoner, Gil
89Louville/300*-212
Wagner, Hans
48T/Magic*-K11
Wagner, Kirk
89KS/Leesley-50
Wagner, Milt
83Louville-20
88Louville/194-108
88Louville/194-166
88Louville/194-8
89Louville/300*-17
89Louville/300*-235
89Louville/300*-258
89Louville/300*-46
90PC/CBA-135
90SkyBox/II-393
Wagner, Phil
91GATech*-177
Wagner, Sheila
91GATech*-60
Wagner, Sidney P.
90MISt/200*-32
Wagner, Steve
79Bucks/OpenP-12
Wainwright, Jonathan
48T/Magic*-O6
Waiters, Granville
83Star/NBA-167
84Star/NBA-62
87Bulls/Ent-7
Waites, Gary
91StarP-52
Wakefield, Andre
80TCMA/CBA-37
Wakefield, Dick
48Kell*-5
Wakely, Jimmy
48T/Magic*-J22
Waldan, Alan
90AZSt/200*-136
Waldman, H.
90UNLV/HOF-13
90UNLV/Season-13
90UNLV/Smok-15
Walk, Neal
69Suns/Carn-9
69T-46
70Suns/A1-9A
70Suns/A1-9B
70Suns/Carn-11
70T-87
71T-9
72T-82
73T-98
74T-17
74T-95M
75T-19
Walker, Brady
52Bread-31
Walker, Chet
68T/Test-3
69T-91
70Bulls/Hawth-3
70T-4LL
70T-60
70T/Ins-14
71T-141LL
71T-66
71T/Ins-33
72T-152
73NBAPA-34
73T-45

74Nab-23
74T-171
74T-84M
75Nab-23
75T-119M
90Bulls/Eq-16
Walker, Clarence
(Foots)
78T-127
79T-42
80T-101
80T-13
80T-161
80T-29
81T-E83
83Star/NBA-155
Walker, Darrell
82AR-16
83Star/NBA-70
84Star/NBA-36
85Star/NBA-172
87F-117
89F-161
89Hoops-134
90F-196
90Hoops-303
90Hoops/Super-98
90Panin-141
90SkyBox-293
91AR/100*-85
Walker, Doak
48T/Magic*-C3
Walker, Earl
89PC/CBA-22
Walker, Horace
90MISt/200*-193
Walker, Jimmy
69T-8
70T-25
71T-90
71T/Ins-16
72T-124
73T-61
74T-45
74T-89M
75T-31
76T-92
91AR/100*-18
Walker, Joyce
90LSU/200*-53
Walker, J. Rice
89KY/300*-278
Walker, Kenny
87KY/Coke-2
88F-83
88KY/269-11
88KY/269-147
88KY/269-153
88KY/269-197
89Hoops-3
89Knicks/Marine-12
89KY/300*-5
89KY/Tm80-40
90F-130
90Hoops-210
90NE/Pol*-4
90Panin-143
90SkyBox-195
Walker, Kevin
91UCLA/144-32
Walker, Marielle
91GATech*-40
Walker, Pam
90UCLA-20CO
Walker, Ricky
81AZ/Pol-20
Walker, Torano
90CT/Pol-14
Walker, Wally
78Sonic/Pol-10
79Sonic/Pol-10
81T-W100
Warren, Jeff
89MO-16

83Star/NBA-84
Wallace, Grady
91SC/200*-73
Wallace, Joe
90PC/CBA-200
Walling, Denny
90Clem/200*-197
Walls, Kevin
89Louville/300*-268
Walsh, David H.
68HOF-45
Walsh, Donnie
89NC/Coke-154
90NC/200*-198
Walsh, Jim
91SC/200*-145
Walters
90Clem/200*-61M
Walters, Raymond
89NCSt/Coke-126
89NCSt/Coke-127
89NCSt/Coke-128
Walters, Trent
89Louville/300*-135
Walton, Bill
74T-39
75T-77
76T-57
77Blaz/Pol-32
77Dell-6
77Pep/AS-8
77T-120
78RCCola-34
78T-1
79T-45
80T-127
80T-46
83Star/NBA-121
84Star/CrtKg-9
84Star/NBA-101
85JMS-10
85Star/NBA-101
86F-119
86Star/Best-8
89Blaz/Franz-20
90Blaz/Franz-6
91UCLA/144-3
91UCLA/144-30
91UCLA/144-62
91UCLA/144-83
Walton, Lloyd
77Bucks/ActPh-9
79Bucks/Pol-11
Wangler, John
91MI/56*-53
Wanzer, Bobby
57Kahn's-11
Ward, Joe
90PC/CBA-76
Ward, John
91OKSt*-54
Warford, Reggie
88KY/269-107
Warlick, Bob
68Suns/Carn-11
Warmerdam, Cornelius
48T/Magic*-E13
Warner, Cornell
71Bucks/Linn-10
72T-59
73T-12
74T-109
75T-72
Warren, Anthony
89NCSt/Coke-123
89NCSt/Coke-124
Warren, Bob
73T-196
73T-237LL
75T-313

Warren, John
70T-91
71T-118
72T-64
Warren, Mike
91UCLA/144-11
Warren, Scott
90FLSt/200*-119
Warren, Terry
90FLSt/200*-45
Warrick, Bryan
83Star/NBA-215
84Star/NBA-23
Washburn, Chris
87Hawks/Pizza-13
Washington, Don
75T-267
Washington, Duane
(Pearl)
88F-71
89Hoops-101
89PC/CBA-31
89PC/CBA-145
90PC/CBA-173
Washington, Eugene
90MISt/200*-23
Washington, Jim
69T-17
70T-14
71T-28
72T-22
73T-87
74T-41
75T-172
Washington, John
91OKSt*-94
Washington, Kenny
91UCLA/144-72
Washington, Kermit
74T-166
78Clipp/Handy-8
78T-16
79Blaz/Pol-42
79T-128
80T-10
80T-150
80T-167
80T-77
81Blaz/Pol-42
81T-61M
81T-W89
Washington, Mickey
91TexAM-22
Washington, Norman
81George/Pol-8
Washington, Richard
77T-78
78T-121
79Bucks/Pol-31
80T-105
80T-75
91UCLA/144-22
Washington, Rodney
87South/Pol*-8
Washington, Stan
90MISt/200*-113
Washington, Tom
72T-240
72T-260LL
73T-182
Waterfield, Bob
48ExhSC-47
48Kell*-10
57Union-27
Waterman, Shawn
79StBon-16
Waters, Charlie
90Clem/200*-104
Wathen, Glen
90KY/ClassA-8
Watkins, Curtis
86DePaul-D6

Watrous, Francis
55Ash-72
Watson, Bobby
88KY/269-36
Watson, Lou
86IN/Greatl-9
Watt, Jim
90MlSt/200*-127
Watts, Craig T.
89NCSt/Coke-129
89NCSt/Coke-131
89NCSt/Coke-45
Watts, Don
(Slick)
74T-142
75T-132M
75T-59
76T-105
77T-51
Watts, Joey
90Clem-15
Waukau, Merv
86SWLou/Pol*-16
Wawrzyniak, Mike
88MO-16
Wayne, Gary
91MI/56*-54
Weakly, Paul
90PC/CBA-4
Weatherly, Shawn
90Clem/200*-162
Weatherspoon, Nick
73Bullet/Stand-11
74T-61
75T-48
78Clipp/Handy-2
79T-61
Weaver, Dean
91GATech*-41
Webb, Anthony
(Spud)
86F-120
87Hawks/Pizza-14
88F-4
88Fourn-10
89F-6
89Hoops-115A
89Hoops-115B
89NCSt/Coke-132
89NCSt/Coke-133
89NCSt/Coke-134
90F-5
90Hoops-35
90Hoops/CollB-24
90Hoops/Super-3
90Panin-118
90SkyBox-10
91F-4
Webb, Ricky
89NC/Coke-197
Webb, Richard S. Jr.
89KY/300*-151
Webb, Tammy
90AZSt/200*-66
Weber, Don
91George/100-80
Weber, Jerry
55Ash-83
Webster, Demone
90PC/CBA-144
90PC/CBA-25
Webster, George
90MlSt/200*-88
Webster, Marvin
77T-71
78RCCola-35
78T-19
79T-88
80T-152
80T-64
81T-E87
83Star/NBA-71

Wedman, Scott
75T-89
76T-142
77T-17
78RCCola-36
78T-79
79T-7
80T-130
80T-42
81T-19
83Star/NBA-36
84Star/Arena-A8
84Star/NBA-11
85JMS-17
85Star/NBA-102
Weems, Kelsey
90PC/CBA-101
Wegrich, Rosie
90AZ/125*-29
Weil, Randy
90NC/200*-55
Weiner, Art
90NC/200*-119
Weir, Murray
48ExhSC-48
48T/Magic*-B2
Weiss, Bob
69T-62
70Bulls/Hawth-4
70Bulls/Hawth-5
70T-16
71T-128
72T-141
73T-132
74T-33
90Hoops-305CO
90Hoops/ll-346CO
91F-5CO
90SkyBox/ll-301CO
Welborne, Tripp
91MI/56*-55
Welch, Anthony
81IL/Arby's-14
Wellman, Bob
89Louville/300*-218
Wells, Dana
90AZ/125*-31
Wells, Kelly
90KY/Sov-18
Wells, Tony
81TCMA/CBA-69
Welp, Christian
89F-118
89Hoops-164
89Hoops/ll-331
90Hoops-122
Wennington, Bill
88Mavs/BLC-23
88Mavs/CardN-23
89Hoops-81
90Hoops-89
90Hoops/ll-431
90Kings/Safe-12
90SkyBox-68
90SkyBox/ll-412
Wernke, Paul
90FLSt/200*-192
Wesenhahn, Bob
61Kahn's-24
Wesley, Walt
69T-22
70T-55
71T-52
71T/Ins-4
72T-109
73Bullet/Stand-12
73T-118
74T-143
Wessel, Joe
90FLSt/200*-62
West, Brian
79StBon-17

West, Chris
83Louville-23
88Louville/194-139
88Louville/194-74
89Louville/300*-296
West, Dick
91UCLA/144-97
West, Doug
90F/Up-U58
90SkyBox/ll-397
West, Freeman
89KS/Leesley-43
West, Jerry
60Kahn's-11
61F-43
61F-66lA
61Kahn's-11
61Lakers/Bell-9
62Kahn's-10
63Kahn's-13
68T/Test-19
69T-90
69T/Ins-2
70T-107AS
70T-160
70T-1LL
70T-2LL
70T/Ins-15
71T-143LL
71T-50
71T/Ins-31
72Icee-19
72T-158
72T-164AS
72T-176LL
72T-75
73T-100AS
74T-176
81TCMA-32
90MlSt/200*-46
West, Mark
83Star/NBA-60
84Star/Arena-B11
84Star/NBA-223
88F-91
89F-125
89Hoops-228
90F-153
90Hoops-242
90Panin-15
90SkyBox-230
91F-165
Westhead, Paul
90Hoops/ll-422CO
91F-53CO
90SkyBox/ll-307CO
Weston, Al
90MlSt/200*-166
Westphal, Paul
73T-126
74T-64
75Carv-33
75Suns-15
75T-186
76Suns-12
76T-55
77Suns/Discs-44
77T-10
78RCCola-37
78T-120
79T-30AS
80T-123
80T-133
80T-149
80T-21
80T-38
80T-7
80T-83
80T-95
81T-W101
83Star/NBA-120
84Suns/Pol-44

Wetherell, T.K.
90FLSt/200*-139
Wettstein, Max
90FLSt/200*-137
Wetzel, John
70Suns/A1-10
73T-72
74T-77
75Suns-16
87Suns/Circ-10CO
90Blaz/Franz-8M
90FLSt/200*-179
Whatley, Ennis
83Star/NBA-178
84Star/NBA-111
90PC/CBA-120
Wheatley, Bruce
85AZ/Pol-14
90PC/CBA-32
Wheeler, Clint
89KY/300*-93
Wherry, Dan
89NCSt/Coke-158
89NCSt/Coke-160
Whisnant, Art
91SC/200*-156
Whitaker, Lucian
88KY/269-61
White, Danny
90AZSt/200*-61
90AZSt/200*-135
White, Devon
88Foot-9
White, Greg
89GATech/Pol-18
90GATech/Pol-19
White, Jo Jo
70T-143
71T-69
71T/Ins-5
72T-45
73NBAPA-35
73T-168
74Nab-19
74T-27
74T-82M
75T-117M
75T-135AS
76Buck-20
76T-115
77T-35
78RCCola-38
78T-85
79T-11
White, John
87SoMiss-6
White, Kevin
91SC/200*-21
White, Linda
90Clem/200*-183
White, Lorenzo
90MlSt/Promos*-6
90MlSt/200*-19
90MlSt/200*-31
90MlSt/200*-86
White, Lyman
90LSU/200*-34
White, Peter
55Ash-95
White, Randy
90F-44
90F/Up-U23
90FLSt/200*-3
90SkyBox-69
91F-47
White, Rory
84Star/NBA-24
85Star/NBA-93
White, Rudy
81TCMA/CBA-18
White, Tony
89PC/CBA-158
White, Vincent

White, Walter
71Globe-61
71Globe-62
89KY/300*-251
White, Whizzer
90AZSt/200*-168
White, Willie
84Star/NBA-148
85Nugget/Pol-11
Whitehead, Bud
90FLSt/200*-179
Whitehead, Eddie
88Louville/194-52
Whitehead, Jerome
78Clipp/Handy-7
80T-105
80T-17
83Star/NBA-132
84Star/NBA-159
85Star/NBA-137
Whitehouse, Donald
55Ash-60
Whitewell, Mike
91TexAM-76
Whitey, Jay
90LSU/200*-118
Whitfield, Ike
89Louville/300*-71
Whitfield, Mal
57Union-18
Whitley, Roland
89NCSt/Pol-14
Whitmore, Bob
90ND-35
Whitmore, David
88GATech/Nike-12
Whitney, Charles
89NCSt/Coke-138
89NCSt/Coke-139
89NCSt/Coke-140
Whitney, Dave
90PC/CBA-132
Whitney, Eli
48T/Magic*-N1
Whitsell, Jerry
55Ash-84
Whittaker, George
89PC/CBA-181
Whittenburg, Dereck
89NCSt/Coke-141
89NCSt/Coke-142
89NCSt/Coke-71
Wickersham, Jeff
90LSU/200*-151
Wicks, Sidney
72Icee-20
72T-20
73T-160
74T-175
74T-96M
75T-131M
75T-40
76T-31
77T-52
78Clipp/Handy-4
78T-109
79T-16
91UCLA/144-16
91UCLA/144-52
Wiel, Randy
89NC/Coke-158
Wiggins, Mitchell
83Star/NBA-179
84Star/NBA-249
85Star/NBA-25
90F-75
90Hoops-130
90Panin-72
90SkyBox-113
Wiley, Morlon
88Mavs/BLC-20
88Mavs/CardN-20

89Hoops-247
89Hoops/II-301
Wilfong, Win
57T-65
59Kahn's-10
60Kahn's-12
Wilhelm, Bill
90Clem/200*-106
Wilhelm, Hoyt
81T/Thirst-4
Wilkens, Len
61F-44
68T/Test-15
69Sonic/Sunb-10
69T-44
70Sonic/Sunb-9
70T-6LL
70T-80
71Sonic/Sunb-10
71T-80
72T-176LL
72T-81
73NBAPA-36
73T-158LL
73T-165
74T-149LL
74T-85M
78Sonic/Pol-12CO
79Sonic/Pol-16CO
81TCMA-11
83Sonic/Pol-16
85Star/CO-10
89Hoops-216CO
90Hoops-309CO
90Hoops/II-349CO
91F-41CO
90SkyBox/II-305CO
Wilkerson, Bobby
78T-41
79T-67
80T-118
80T-57
81T-MW70
86IN/Greatl-12
Wilkes, Del
91SC/200*-91
Wilkes, Keith
(Jamaal)
75T-50
76T-16
77T-33
78T-3
79T-35
80T-123
80T-7
81T-23
82Lakers/BASF-11
83Lakers/BASF-12
83Star/ASG-24
83Star/NBA-24
84Star/NBA-183
85JMS-21
85Star/NBA-94
85Star/ROY-11
91UCLA/144-37
91UCLA/144-73
Wilkes, James
91UCLA/144-13
Wilkins, Dominique
83Star/All-R-8
83Star/NBA-263
84Star/CrtKg-12
84Star/NBA-76
84Star/PolASG-33
84Star/SlamD-9
85Star/Gator-8
85Star/NBA-42
85Star/SlamD-10
85Star/SlamD-8
86F-121
86F/Ins-11
86Star/CrtKg-32

87F-118
87F/Ins-7
87Hawks/Pizza-15
88F-125AS
88F-5
88F/Ins-11
88Fourn-9
89F-165M
89F-7
89Hoops-130
89Hoops-234AS
90F-6
90Hoops-12AS
90Hoops-36
90Hoops/CollB-35
90Hoops/II-355TC
90Hoops/Super-2
90Panin-117
90SkyBox-11
91F-212
91F-6
Wilkins, Eddie Lee
84Star/NBA-37
89Knicks/Marine-14
90F/Up-U65
90Hoops-211
90SkyBox-196
Wilkins, Gerald
86F-122
87F-119
88F-84
89F-107A
89F-107B
89Hoops-63
89Knicks/Marine-13
90F-131
90Hoops-212
90Hoops/Super-65
90Panin-142
90SkyBox-197
91F-142
Wilkins, Jeff
81TCMA/CBA-8
83Star/NBA-144
84Star/NBA-236
Wilkinson, Dale
82TCMA/CBA-38
Willard, Jess
48T/Magic*-A7
Willard, Ken
90NC/200*-148
90NC/200*-73
Williams, Alphonso
90FLSt/200*-31
Williams, Art
68Rocket/Jack-13
69T-96
70T-151
72T-19
73T-147
Williams, Bernie
68Rocket/Jack-14
70T-122
72T-186
73T-257
Williams, Billy BB
81T/Thirst-15
Williams, Billy
90Clem/200*-43
Williams, Brian
90FLSt/200*-138
91Class-5
91SC/200*-144
Williams, Buck
83Star/ASG-13
83Star/NBA-145
84Nets/Getty-11
84Star/CrtKg-6
84Star/NBA-99
85Prism-8
85Star/NBA-58
85Star/ROY-4

86F-123
86Star/LifeNets-13
87F-120
88F-79
88Fourn-25
89Blaz/Franz-11
89F-132
89Hoops-145
89Hoops/II-315
90Blaz/BP-6
90Blaz/Franz-19
90F-160
90Hoops-251
90Hoops/CollB-36
90Panin-9
90SkyBox-240
91F-173
91F-224
Williams, Carlo
89Fresno/Smok-14
Williams, Charlie
71T-158
72T-231
Williams, Chris
90LSU/200*-88
Williams, Chuck
71T-218
73T-232
73T-239LL
74T-212LL
74T-228M
74T-241
75T-226LL
75T-281M
75T-315
78T-89
Williams, Curtis
88VA/Hardee-13
Williams, Dan
89PC/CBA-205
Williams, Dayne
90FLSt/200*-73
Williams, Del
90FLSt/200*-176
Williams, Don
(Duck)
90ND-19
Williams, Earl
75T-109
Williams, Eric
90FLSt/200*-120
Williams, Fly
75T-293
Williams, Freddie
90AZSt/200*-53
Williams, Freeman
78Clipp/Handy-3
80T-161
80T-29
81T-63M
81T-W95
Williams, Gene
69Suns/Carn-10
Williams, Gus
76T-69
77T-89
78Sonic/Pol-11
78T-39
79Sonic/Pol-1
79T-27
80T-163
80T-168
80T-3
80T-40
80T-80
80T-91
83Sonic/Pol-5
83Star/ASG-25
83Star/NBA-202
84Star/CrtKg-40
84Star/NBA-185
85Star/NBA-110

86F-124
Williams, Herb
83Star/NBA-168
84Star/NBA-63
85Star/NBA-87
86F-125
87F-121
88Mavs/CardN-32
89F-37
89Hoops-131
90F-45
90Hoops-90
90Panin-58
90SkyBox-70
91F-48
Williams, Ike
48T/Magic*-A18
Williams, Isaac
90FLSt/200*-22
Williams, Jayson
90F/Up-U73
90StarP-5
Williams, John
(Hot Rod)
87F-123
88F-26
89F-31
89Hoops-118
90F-37
90Hoops-80
90Hoops/Super-18
90Panin-108
90SkyBox-58
91F-40
Williams, John S.
86LSU/Pol*-14
87F-122
88F-119
89F-162
89Hoops-254
90Hoops-304
90Hoops/Super-100
90LSU/200*-14
90Panin-146
90SkyBox-294
Williams, Ken
90F/Up-U38
Williams, Kevin
84Star/NBA-224
88F-72
89McNees*-1
Williams, LaVon
77KY/Wildct-11
78KY/Food-14
79KY/Food-4
88KY/269-112
88KY/269-218
Williams, Larry
88Louville/194-130
88Louville/194-41
89Louville/300*-278
Williams, Leon
89Louville/300*-190
Williams, Michael
87Baylor/Pol*-4
89Hoops-224
89Hoops/II-344
90F/Up-U39
90SkyBox-36
91F-88
90SkyBox/II-388
Williams, Mike
89PC/CBA-155
90LSU/200*-64
90PC/CBA-60
Williams, Monty
90ND-48
Williams, Murray
90CT/Pol-15
Williams, Natalie
90UCLA-32
Williams, Nate

72T-151
73T-54
74T-116
75T-182
76T-88
Williams, Paul
90AZSt/200*-44
Williams, Pete
84AZ/Pol-16
85Nugget/Pol-4
90AZ/125*-57
Williams, Ray
78T-129
79T-48
80T-153
80T-65
81T-28
83Star/NBA-72
85JMS-16
Williams, Ray CLEM
90Clem/200*-102
90Clem/200*-47
Williams, Reggie
83George/Pol-15
84George/Pol-11
85George/Pol-14
86George/Pol-13
89F-74
89Hoops-128
90Hoops-272
91F-54
91George/100-29
91George/100-4
91George/100-53
91George/100-65
90SkyBox/II-416
Williams, Ricky
81TCMA/CBA-19
Williams, Rob
82Nugget/Pol-21
83Nugget/Pol-21
83Star/All-R-9
83Star/NBA-192
Williams, Rodney
90Clem/200*-67
Williams, Ron
(Fritz)
69T-36
70T-8
71T-141LL
71T-38
71T/Ins-29
72T-123
73T-23
75T-198
Williams, Roy
89KS/Leesley-56CO
Williams, Sam
83Star/NBA-12
84Star/Arena-E10
84Star/NBA-211
90AZSt/200*-4
90AZSt/Promos*-6
Williams, Schwoonda
90LSU/200*-69
Williams, Scott
86NC/Pol-42
87NC/Pol-42
88NC/Pol-42
88NC/Pol-x
88NC/Pol-x
90StarP-26
Williams, Sly
81T-E88
83Star/NBA-274
84Star/NBA-87
Williams, Stan
82TCMA/Lanc-22
Williams, Ted
90MISt/200*-173
90MISt/200*-47M
Williams, Ulis

90AZSt/200*-117
Williams, Walt
  88MD/Pol-12
Williamson, Ernie
  90NC/200*-144
Williamson, John
  74T-234
  75T-251
  75T-282M
  76T-113
  77T-44
  78RCCola-39
  78T-11
  79T-55
  80T-129
  80T-84
Williford, Vann
  71T-229
  89NCSt/Coke-125
  89NCSt/Coke-81
  89NCSt/Coke-87
Willis, Kevin
  85Star/NBA-48
  85Star/RTm-9
  86F-126
  87F-124
  87Hawks/Pizza-16
  88F-6
  89Hoops-98
  90F-7
  90Hoops-37
  90MISt/200*-119
  90MISt/200*-163
  90MISt/200*-179
  90Panin-119
  90SkyBox-12
  91F-7
Willis, Peter Tom
  90FLSt/200*-11
  90FLSt/200*-141
Willoughby, Bill
  83Star/NBA-156
Wills, Elliott
  (Bump)
  90AZSt/200*-25
Wilson, Anthony
  86LSU/Pol*-16
Wilson, Barry
  90LSU/200*-102
Wilson, Ben
  89PC/CBA-2
Wilson, Bill
  54Quaker-9
Wilson, Bob
  75T-169
Wilson, Don
  82Fairf-16
Wilson, Eddie
  90AZ/125*-115
Wilson, Felix
  89KY/300*-146
Wilson, George
  (Jif)
  64Kahn's-3
  68Suns/Carn-12
  70T-11
  71T-26
Wilson, Karl
  90LSU/200*-31
Wilson, Keith
  90PC/CBA-108
  91AR/100*-20
Wilson, Marshall
  90GA/Smok-15
Wilson, Merlin
  91George/100-60
  91George/100-96
Wilson, Michael
  82TCMA/CBA-72
  84Star/NBA-100
Wilson, Nancy
  91SC/200*-18

Wilson, Nikita
  86LSU/Pol*-15
  90LSU/200*-42
Wilson, Othell
  84Star/NBA-160
  86Kings/Smok-15
Wilson, Otis
  89Louville/300*-116
Wilson, Rick
  78Hawks/Coke-14
  80TCMA/CBA-7
  88Louville/194-119
  88Louville/194-153
  88Louville/194-24
  89Louville/300*-21
Wilson, Ricky
  89PC/CBA-135
Wilson, Trevor
  90F/Up-U5
  90StarP-7
  91UCLA/144-106
Wilson, Whip
  48T/Magic*-J42
Wiltjer, Greg
  89PC/CBA-67
  90PC/CBA-11
Wimbley, Abner
  90LSU/200*-184
Windsor, Scott
  91SC/200*-155
Winebarger, Rita
  91SC/200*-41
Winfield, Lee
  70Sonic/Sunb-10
  70T-147
  71Sonic/Sunb-11
  71T-103
  72T-33
  73Sonic/Shur-12
  73T-42
  74T-157
  75T-192
Wingate, David
  82George/Pol-9
  83George/Pol-14
  84George/Pol-7
  85George/Pol-15
  87F-125
  89Hoops/II-323
  90F-174
  90Hoops-273
  90SkyBox-262
  91George/100-10
Wingo, Hawthorne
  75Carv-34
  75T-166
Winkles, Bob
  90AZSt/200*-102
Winstead, Brian
  91SC/200*-65
Winston, Bobby
  85George/Pol-16
  86George/Pol-14
  87George/Pol-16
  88George/Pol-16
  91George/100-22
Winston, Roy
  90LSU/200*-144
Winters, Brian
  75T-143
  76T-46
  77Bucks/ActPh-10
  77T-48
  78RCCola-40
  78T-76
  79Bucks/Pol-32
  79T-21
  80T-120
  80T-5
  81T-MW100
  91SC/200*-160
Winters, Roland

48T/Magic*-J18
Wise, Dale
  61Union-10
Wise, Earl
  90StarP-31
Wise, Willie
  71T-194
  71T/Ins-2A
  72T-185
  72T-254AS
  73T-245
  74T-185AS
  74T-229M
  75T-255
  75T-287M
Wisman, Jim
  86IN/GreatI-4
Wistert, Albert
  91MI/56*-56M
Wistert, Alvin
  91MI/56*-56M
Wistert, Francis
  91MI/56*-56M
Witherspoon, Leroy
  89PC/CBA-102
Witting, Paul
  55Ash-96
Wittman, Randy
  83Star/NBA-275
  84Star/NBA-86
  85Star/NBA-49
  86F-127
  86IN/GreatI-37
  87F-126
  87Hawks/Pizza-17
  88F-7
  89Hoops-238
  90Hoops-141
  90SkyBox/II-389
Witts, Garry
  82TCMA/CBA-23
Wohl, Dave
  72T-99
  73T-6
  74T-108
  75T-162
  86Star/LifeNets-1CO
  89Heat/Publix-15CO
  90Heat/Publix-15CO
Wolcott, Brian
  90MISt/200*-157
Wolf, Charley
  61Kahn's-12CO
  62Kahn's-11CO
Wolf, Jeff
  89NC/Coke-156
  90NC/200*-178
Wolf, Joe
  86NC/Pol-24
  89Hoops-173
  89NC/Coke-138
  89NC/Coke-139
  90Hoops-152
  90Hoops/II-412
  90NC/200*-42
  90NC/200*-79
  90NC/200*-83
  90SkyBox-133
  91F-55
  90SkyBox/II-381
Womack, Wayne
  88AZ/Pol-13
Wood, Al
  83Sonic/Pol-9
  83Star/NBA-203
  84Star/NBA-124
  85Star/NBA-72
  86F-128
Wood, David
  90AZ/125*-59
Wood, Jim
  91GATech*-178

Wood, John
  90LSU/200*-78
Wood, Leon
  84Star/NBA-200
  84Star/NBA-212
  85Star/NBA-9
  85Star/TmSuper-PS5
  87F-127
  89PC/CBA-119
Wood, Willie
  91OKSt*-72
Wooden, John R.
  57Union-32
  68HOF-46
  91UCLA/144-1
  91UCLA/144-103M
  91UCLA/144-108
  91UCLA/144-130
  91UCLA/144-20
  91Wooden-1
  91Wooden-3
  91Wooden-4
Wooden, Nell
  91UCLA/144-51M
Woodham, Wally
  90FLSt/200*-37
Woodhull, Lee Ann
  91GATech*-9
Woodley, David
  90LSU/200*-182
Woodruff, Dwayne
  89Louville/300*-118
Woods, James
  80TCMA/CBA-11
Woods, Sean
  88KY/Sov-18
  89KY/Award-34
Woods, Sparky
  91SC/200*-52
Woodside, Bernard
  87LSU/Pol*-6
Woodson, Mike
  81T-E89
  83Star/NBA-227
  84Star/NBA-280
  85Kings/Smok-16
  85Star/NBA-80
  86F-129
  87F-128
  87IN/GreatII-13
  88F-63
  89F-63
  89Hoops-49
  90Hoops-131
  90SkyBox/II-386
Woodward, Woody
  90FLSt/200*-130
Woolford, Donnell
  90Clem/200*-84
Woolpert, Phil
  57Union-8
Woolridge, Orlando
  83Star/NBA-180
  84Star/CrtKg-38
  84Star/NBA-112
  84Star/PolASG-34
  84Star/SlamD-10
  85Star/Gator-9
  85Star/NBA-123
  85Star/SlamD-9
  85Star/TmSuper-CB2
  86F-130
  87F-129
  89Hoops-279A
  89Hoops-279B
  90F-96
  90F/Up-U27
  90Hoops-162
  90Hoops/II-411
  90ND-27
  90SkyBox-142
  91F-56

90SkyBox/II-382
Woolum, Jerry
  89KY/300*-189
Wooten, Ron
  90NC/200*-62
  90NC/200*-88
Workman, Haywoode
  89PC/CBA-176
Workman, Tom
  71T-163
Works, Pierce
  91UCLA/144-112
Worley, Joey
  89KY/300*-134
Worsley, Larry
  89NCSt/Coke-115
  89NCSt/Coke-130
Worthen, Sam
  82TCMA/CBA-37
Worthington, Charles
  89KY/300*-241
Worthy, James
  82Lakers/BASF-12
  83Lakers/BASF-13
  83Star/All-R-10
  83Star/NBA-25
  84Lakers/BASF-11
  84Star/Arena-D8
  84Star/Celt-9
  84Star/CrtKg-49
  84Star/NBA-184
  85JMS-23
  85Prism-1M
  85Star/NBA-33
  85Star/TmSuper-LA3
  86F-131
  86Star/CrtKg-33
  87F-130
  88F-70
  89F-80
  89Hoops-210
  89Hoops-219AS
  89NC/Coke-114
  89NC/Coke-19
  89NC/Coke-20
  89NC/Coke-21
  89NC/Coke-22
  89NC/Coke-23
  90F-97
  90Hoops-163
  90Hoops-26AS
  90Hoops/CollB-48
  90Hoops/Super-50
  90NC/200*-104
  90NC/200*-152
  90NC/200*-5
  90NC/200*-78
  90Panin-5
  90Panin-EAS
  90SkyBox-143
  91F-104
Wosley, Larry
  89NCSt/Coke-57AS
Wright, Bill
  90AZ/125*-45AS
Wright, Brad
  91UCLA/144-23AS
Wright, Gerry
  90PC/CBA-52
Wright, Howard
  71Col/Mara-11
  71Pacer/Mara-9
Wright, Joby
  86IN/GreatI-35
Wright, Joey
  91Class-40
  91Court-43
  91StarP-27
Wright, Larry
  77T-112
Wright, Lonnie
  71Flor/McDon-9

71T-206
Wright, Orville
48T/Magic*-L9
Wright, Poncho
88Louville/194-123
88Louville/194-30
89Louville/300*-261
89Louville/300*-43
Wright, Wilbur
48T/Magic*-L9
Wrightson, Bernie
90AZSt/200*-177
Wulk, Ned
90AZSt/200*-128
Wyatt, Horace
82TCMA/CBA-29
90Clem/200*-76
Wyatt, Jane
48T/Magic*-J41
Wylie, Joe
91Class-28
91Court-44
91StarP-42
Wynder, A.J.
90PC/CBA-139
90PC/CBA-26
Yarborough, Bill
90Clem/200*-168
Yardley, George
57T-2
57Union-31
81TCMA-25
85Star/Schick-25
Yates, George
89KY/300*-88

Yates, Wayne
61Lakers/Bell-10
Yates, Tony
80IL/Arby's-14CO
81IL/Arby's-15CO
Yelverton, Charlie
72T-133
Yeoman, Felix
91George/100-71
Yeomans, Tony
90FLSt/200*-33
Yepremian, Garo
81T/Thirst-29
Yerina, Pat
82Fairf-17
Yessin, Humzey
89KY/300*-66
Yessin, Rudy
89KY/300*-242
Yewcic, Tom
90MISt/200*-48
Yoest, Mike
90PC/CBA-193
Yokley, John
89NC/Coke-173
Yonakor, Rich
81TCMA/CBA-55
89NC/Coke-155
90NC/200*-146
York, Cliff
89Louville/300*-215
York, Smedes
89NCSt/Coke-74
89NCSt/Coke-86

Youmans, Gary
89PC/CBA-76
Young, Barry
81TCMA/CBA-74
82TCMA/CBA-28
88UNLV/HOF-8
89UNLV/HOF-13
89UNLV/Seven-12
Young, Claude
(Buddy)
48ExhSC-49
Young, Cy
48T/Magic*-K16
Young, Danny
85Star/NBA-73
87F-131
89Hoops-71
90Blaz/Franz-20
90F-161
90Hoops-252
90SkyBox-241
Young, David
90Clem-16
Young, Ed
83Dayton/Blue-18
Young, George
90AZ/125*-107
Young, Jim
90AZ/125*-47CO
Young, Nicole
90UCLA-27
Young, Perry
89PC/CBA-41
90PC/CBA-97

Young, Rey
89Fresno/Smok-15
90Fresno/Smok-14
Young, Ricky
91OKSt*-59
Yow, Kay
89NCSt/Pol-16CO
Yowarsky, Walt
89KY/300*-186
Yule, Joe
48T/Magic*-J33
Yunkus, Rick
91GATech*-179
Zale, Tony
48Kell*-18
48T/Magic*-A17
Zaliagiris, Tom
89NC/Coke-167
90NC/200*-179
Zamberlan, Jim
89Louville/300*-150
Zaranka, Ben
89KY/300*-181
Zaslofsky, Max
48Bowman-55
52Bread-32CO
Zatezalo, Butch
90Clem/200*-68
Zaunbrecher, Godfrey
90LSU/200*-148
Zbyszko, Stanuslaus
48T/Magic*-D3
Zeller, Dave
61Kahn's-13

Zendejas, Luis
90AZSt/200*-95
90AZSt/Promos*-4
Zendejas, Max
90AZ/125*-46
Zerfoss, George
89KY/300*-32
Zerfoss, Kark
89KY/300*-243
Zerfoss, Tom
89KY/300*-31
Zern, Jeff
83Dayton/Blue-19
Zeys, Lisa
90AZSt/200*-76
Ziegler, Fred
91SC/200*-168
Ziegler, Paul
90LSU/200*-188
Ziegler, Todd
89KY/300*-92
Ziegler, Travis
89Pitt/Food-23
Zimmerman, Rodney
90UCLA-11
Zinter, Alan
90AZ/125*-39
Zuffelato, Greg
89Fresno/Smok-16
Zworykin, V.K.
48T/Magic*-N5

GARY'S COLLECTABLES
PREMIUM CARDS
Baseball

Football

Basketball

Send Want Lists

GARY ALEXANIAN
P.O. Box 6511
Moraga, CA 94570

★ Sets For Sale ★

1981-82 Topps (198) 90.00
1982-83 Marquette Lite Beer 15.00
1982-83 TCMA Lancaster Lightning 25.00
1984 Star Company Slam Dunk 100.00
1984 Star Company NBA Awards Banquet 65.00
1984-85 Star Company comprehensive NBA set 2,500.00
1985 Star Company NBA Coaches 25.00
1985 NBA Prism-Stickers (8) 50.00
1985-86 Star Company comprehensive NBA set 1,500.00
1985-86 Star Company Best of the Old & New 2,695.00
1986 Star Company Court Kings III (33) 225.00
1986 Star Company Lifebuoy Nets 15.00
1987-88 Fleer Wax Pack 30.00
1987-88 Fleer Wax Box 950.00
1987-88 Fleer set with sticker set 265.00
1988-89 Mavericks Card Night with Tarpley (14) 35.00

George W. Henn
(908) 739-9704 evenings

23 Scholer Drive
Union Beach, NJ 07735

SUPERSTAR TREATMENT